Major Authors and Illustrators for Children and Young Adults

Major Authors and Illustrators for Children and Young Adults

A SELECTION OF SKETCHES FROM
Something about the Author

Laurie Collier and Joyce Nakamura

VOLUME 5: O - S

5

Gale Research Inc. • DETROIT • LONDON

The paper used in this publication meets the minimum requirements of American National Standard for Information Sciences–Permanence Paper for Printed Library Materials, ANSI Z39.48-1984. ™

Library of Congress Catalog Card Number 92-073849
ISBN 0-8103-7702-0 (Set)
ISBN 0-8103-8495-7 (Volume)

Printed in the United States of America
Published simultaneously in the United Kingdom
by Gale Research International Limited
(An affiliated company of Gale Research Inc.)

10 9 8 7 6 5 4 3 2

Contents

Introduction

Major Authors and Illustrators for Children and Young Adults (MAICYA) is a one-stop reference source that provides useful information on the lives and works of significant authors and illustrators, covering all genres and age groups. Specifically developed to meet the needs of smaller public and school libraries, *MAICYA* contains updated and revised sketches on nearly 800 of the most widely read authors and illustrators appearing in Gale's *Something about the Author (SATA)* series, named an "Outstanding Reference Source," the highest honor given by the American Library Association and Adult Services Division.

MAICYA provides more complete coverage than any other similar publication, with the same comprehensiveness as the parent *SATA* series. You'll find the six-volume *MAICYA* set a valuable reference tool whether you are a student, librarian, parent, professional, or simply interested in the field of children's literature.

Advisory Board Reviewed Author Selection

To ensure that *MAICYA* would meet the needs of its users, the editors of *Something about the Author* compiled the initial author list using the responses to a survey that was mailed to 1500 school and public libraries. This list was then submitted for review to an advisory board of librarians who specialize in children's and young adult services, and finalized with their suggestions. We would like to thank our board once again for their efforts and acknowledge them here:

- Barbara M. Barstow, Assistant Children's Services Manager, Cuyahoga County Public Library, Parma, Ohio;
- Barbara Froling Immroth, Graduate School of Library and Information Science, University of Texas at Austin;
- Dolores Jones, Curator, de Grummond Collection, McCain Library and Archives, University of Southern Mississippi;
- Cathi Dunn MacRae, young adult columnist for *Wilson Library Bulletin* and Young Adult Services Librarian at Boulder Public Library, Colorado;
- Philip Marshall, Assistant County Librarian, Education and Children's Services, Nottinghamshire County Council, England;
- Ray Stearn, Children's Services Librarian East Area, Rochdale Libraries, England.

Broad Coverage in a Single Source

The authors and illustrators covered in *MAICYA* encompass the entire spectrum of children's literature. *MAICYA* listees represent primarily English-speaking countries, particularly the United States, Canada, and the United Kingdom. Also included, however, are authors from around the world whose works are available in English translation. Authors and illustrators from both classic and contemporary time periods are represented as well. Following is just a sampling of the hundreds of notable individuals you'll find in *MAICYA*:

PICTURE BOOKS: Janet and Allan Ahlberg · Mitsumasa Anno · Graeme Base · Ludwig Bemelmans · Jan and Stan Berenstain · Margaret Wise Brown · Eric Carle · Demi · Leo and Diane Dillon · Wanda Gag · Tana Hoban · Shirley Hughes · Ann Jonas · Ezra Jack Keats · Robert McCloskey · Jan Pienkowsi · Jerry Pinkney · Maurice Sendak · Peter Spier · John Steptoe · Chris Van Allsburg · Brian Wildsmith · Ed Young · Margot Zemach · Lisbeth Zwerger . . .

FOLK AND FAIRY TALES: Verna Aardema · Hans Christian Andersen · Peter Christian Asbjoernsen · Marcia Brown · Barbara Cooney · Wanda Gag · Paul Galdone · Brothers Grimm · Joel Chandler Harris · Michael Hague · Margaret Hodges · Joseph Jacobs · Charles Perrault · Barbara Leonie Picard · Jane Yolen . . .

ANIMAL STORIES: Sheila Burnford · Walter Farley · Fred Gipson · Marguerite Henry · Eric Knight · Walt Morey · Sterling North · Marjorie Kinnan Rawlings · Albert Payson Terhune . . .

SPORTS STORIES: Nate Aaseng · Matt Christopher · Scott Corbett · Robert Lipsyte · Alfred Slote · John Tunis . . .

MYSTERY AND ADVENTURE: David Adler • Vivien Alcock • Enid Blyton • Frank Bonham • Eleanor Cameron • Jean Craighead George • James Howe • Joan Lowery Nixon • Gary Paulsen • Ellen Raskin • Donald J. Sobol • Mark Twain . . .

SCIENCE FICTION AND FANTASY: Lloyd Alexander • Isaac Asimov • Ben Bova • Susan Cooper • Roald Dahl • Edward Eager • Monica Hughes • Ursula K. Le Guin • Madeleine L'Engle • C. S. Lewis • Astrid Lindgren • Anne McCaffrey • Robin McKinley • A. A. Milne • E. Nesbit • Mary Norton • J. R. R. Tolkien • P. L. Travers • E. B. White • George Selden Thompson • Patricia Wrightson . . .

REALISTIC FICTION: Louisa May Alcott • Judy Blume • Sue Ellen Bridgers • Bruce Brooks • Frances Hodgson Burnett • Alice Childress • Beverly Cleary • Robert Cormier • Paula Danziger • Mary Mapes Dodge • Virginia Hamilton • Norma Klein • Elaine Konigsburg • L. M. Montgomery • Walter Dean Myers • Katherine Paterson • Richard Peck • Mildred D. Taylor • Laura Ingalls Wilder . . .

HISTORICAL FICTION: Joan Aiken • Joan Blos • Hester Burton • Patricia Clapp • Peter Dickinson • Sid Fleischman • Leon Garfield • Peter Haertling • Erik Christian Haugaard • Jill Paton Walsh • Scott O'Dell • Elizabeth George Speare • Rosemary Sutcliff . . .

POETRY AND NONSENSE VERSE: Arnold Adoff • William Blake • William Cole • Eugene Field • Aileen Fisher • Mary Ann Hoberman • Langston Hughes • Edward Lear • Myra Cohn Livingston • David McCord • Clement Clarke Moore • Eve Merriam • Lilian Moore • Jack Prelutsky • Laura E. Richards • Dr. Seuss • Shel Silverstein • Robert Louis Stevenson • Kaye Starbird • James Thurber • Valerie Worth . . .

BIOGRAPHY: Aliki • Ingri and Edgar Parin d'Aulaire • Clyde Robert Bulla • Alice Dalgliesh • James Daugherty • Russell Freedman • Jean Fritz • Clara Ingram Judson • Patricia Miles Martin • F. N. Monjo • Dorothy Sterling • Elizabeth Yates . . .

NONFICTION: Irving Adler • Brent Ashabranner • Franklyn M. Branley • Joanna Cole • Leonard Everett Fisher • Gail Gibbons • Shirley Glubok • Patricia Lauber • David Macaulay • Robert McClung • Milton Meltzer • Dorothy Hinshaw Patent • Millicent E. Selsam • Alvin and Virginia Silverstein • Herbert Zim . . .

Although the individuals listed are known for works produced in these genres, they are by no means restricted to one particular genre or age group. The great diversity of backgrounds for these and other artists is fully explored in *MAICYA.*

Compilation Methods

Every effort was made to obtain new information directly from the authors and illustrators themselves. All living listees in *MAICYA* were mailed copies of their sketches at their last-known addresses, and nearly 60 percent of the listees responded to these requests for verification and updating of data. For deceased listees, or those who failed to respond to mailing, other reliable biographical sources were consulted, such as those indexed in Gale's *Biography and Genealogy Master Index,* as well as bibliographical sources, such as *National Union Catalog, LC Marc,* and *British National Bibliography.* Further details came from published interviews, feature stories, and book reviews.

Easy-to-Use Entry Format

A typical entry in *MAICYA* contains the following clearly labeled information sections:

> *PERSONAL:* date and place of birth and death; parents' names and occupations; name of spouse, date of marriage, and names of children; educational institutions attended and degrees received; religious and political affiliations; hobbies and other interests.

> *ADDRESSES:* complete home, office, and agent's address.

> *CAREER:* name of employer, position, and dates for each career post; military service; exhibitions of artistic work.

> *MEMBER:* memberships and offices held in professional and civic organizations.

> *AWARDS, HONORS:* literary and professional awards received.

> *WRITINGS:* title-by-title chronological bibliography of books written and/or illustrated, listed by genre when known; lists of other notable publications, such as plays, screenplays, and periodical contributions.

> *ADAPTATIONS:* a selected list of notable film, TV, stage, video, audio, and braille versions of the listee's work.

> *WORK IN PROGRESS:* description of projects in progress.

> *SIDELIGHTS:* specifically written for *MAICYA*, with information gathered from published sources, to provide users with a succinct yet comprehensive portrait of the author or illustrator's life and creative development.

> *WORKS CITED:* a full list of all sources quoted in *SIDELIGHTS.*

> *FOR MORE INFORMATION SEE:* references for further reading.

Designed to capture and hold students' interest, *MAICYA* also features an inviting layout of author photos, illustrations, book covers, and movie stills.

Easy Access to Information

Each volume contains a full list of the authors and illustrators included in the set, with cross references and page numbers for quick access to sketch material. In-text cross references also serve as aids. *MAICYA* is also included in Gale's *Contemporary Authors* cumulative index.

In Appreciation

The editors wish to thank: Donna Olendorf, editor of *Something about the Author,* Susan M. Trosky, editor of *Contemporary Authors,* and James G. Lesniak, editor of *Contemporary Authors New Revision Series,* for their cooperation and assistance, and especially for that of their project-team members; Autobiography Series project-team members; Laura Standley Berger for coordinating selection and processing of graphics; Kenneth R. Shepherd for his technical assistance; and Gerard J. Senick, editor of *Children's Literature Review,* for his editorial assistance with the author list.

Comments Are Welcome

MAICYA is intended to serve as a useful reference tool for a wide audience, so your comments about this work are encouraged. Suggestions of authors and illustrators to include in future editions of *MAICYA* are also welcome. Send comments and suggestions to: The Editors, *Major Authors and Illustrators for Children and Young Adults,* Gale Research Inc., 835 Penobscot Bldg., Detroit, MI 48226-4094. You may also call us toll-free at 1-800-347-GALE, or fax to 313-961-6599.

Major Authors and Illustrators for Children and Young Adults

Volume 1

A

B

Volume 2

C

D

E

F

Volume 3

G

H

I

J

Volume 4

K

L

M

N

Volume 5

O

P

Q

R

S

Volume 6

T

U

V

W

Y

Z

Major Authors and Illustrators for Children and Young Adults

O

Graham Oakley

OAKLEY, Graham 1929-

PERSONAL: Born August 27, 1929, in Shrewsbury, England; son of Thomas (a shop manager) and Flora (Madeley) Oakley. *Education:* Attended Warrington Art School, 1950. *Hobbies and other interests:* Music.

ADDRESSES: Home and office—Kellaways Mill, NR Chippenham, Wiltshire, England.

CAREER: Free-lance artist and book illustrator. Scenic artist for English repertory companies, 1950-55; Royal Opera House, designer's assistant, 1955-57; worked at Crawford's Advertising Agency, 1960-62; British Broadcasting Corporation, television set designer for motion pictures and series, including *How Green Was My Valley, Nicholas Nickleby, Treasure Island,* and *Softly, Softly,* 1962-67. *Military service:* Served in the British Army, 1947-49.

AWARDS, HONORS: Kate Greenaway Medal nomination, 1976, and *New York Times* best illustrated children's book of the year citation, 1977, both for *The Church Mice Adrift; Boston Globe-Horn Book* Award illustration special citation, and American Library Association notable book citation, both 1980, both for *Graham Oakley's Magical Changes;* Kate Greenaway Medal nomination, and Kurt Maschler Award runner-up, both 1982, both for *The Church Mice in Action.*

WRITINGS:

SELF-ILLUSTRATED CHILDREN'S BOOKS

Graham Oakley's Magical Changes, Macmillan, 1979, Atheneum, 1980.
Hetty and Harriet, Macmillan, 1981, Atheneum, 1982.
Henry's Quest, Macmillan, 1985, Atheneum, 1986.
Once upon a Time: A Prince's Fantastic Journey, Macmillan, 1990.

SELF-ILLUSTRATED "CHURCH MICE" SERIES

The Church Mouse (also see below), Atheneum, 1972.
The Church Cat Abroad (also see below), Atheneum, 1973.
The Church Mice and the Moon (also see below), Atheneum, 1974.
The Church Mice Spread Their Wings, Macmillan (London), 1975, Atheneum, 1976.
The Church Mice Adrift, Macmillan, 1976, Atheneum, 1977.
The Church Mice at Bay, Macmillan, 1978, Atheneum, 1979.
The Church Mice at Christmas, Atheneum, 1980.
The Church Mice in Action, Macmillan, 1982, Atheneum, 1983.
The Church Mice Chronicles (contains *The Church Mouse, The Church Cat Abroad,* and *The Church Mice and the Moon*), Macmillan, 1986.

From *The Church Mice and the Moon,* written and illustrated by Graham Oakley.

The Diary of a Church Mouse, Macmillan, 1986, Atheneum, 1987.

Also author and illustrator of *The Churchmice and the Ring,* 1992.

ILLUSTRATOR

John Ruskin, *The King of the Golden River,* Hutchinson, 1958.
Hugh Popham, *Monsters and Marlinspikes,* Hart-David, 1958.
Popham, *The Fabulous Voyage of the Pegasus,* Criterion, 1959.
Robert Louis Stevenson, *Kidnapped,* Dent, 1960, with N. C. Wyeth, Crown, 1989.
David Scott Daniell, *Discovering the Bible,* University of London Press, 1961.
Charles Kervern, *White Horizons,* University of London Press, 1962.
Mollie Clarke, adapter, *The Three Feathers: A German Folk Tale Retold,* Hart-Davis, 1963, Follett, 1968.
Richard Garnett, *The White Dragon,* Hart-Davis, 1963, Vanguard, 1964.
Garnett, *Jack of Dover,* Vanguard, 1966.
Patricia Ledward, *Grandmother's Footsteps,* Macmillan, 1966.
Taya Zinkin, *Stories Tole round the World,* Oxford University Press, 1968.
Brian Read, *The Water Wheel,* World's Work, 1970.
Tanith Lee, *Dragon Hoard,* Farrar, Straus, 1971.
Elizabeth MacDonald, *The Two Sisters,* World's Work, 1975.

ADAPTATIONS: The Church Mouse was adapted for videocassette by Live Oak Media, 1988.

SIDELIGHTS: British author and illustrator Graham Oakley is recognized for his strong storytelling abilities and his satirical presentation of modern society. The text and elaborate illustrations in his books work together to convey witty and often hilariously comic stories. In his popular "Church Mice" series, for example, Oakley uses the adventures of a group of lively mice and their protector, Sampson the cat, to ridicule such contemporary figures as scientists, the media, and hippies. And in his other works, Oakley uses a similar combination of understated writing and vastly populated pictures—the pictures supplying the story with more meaning than that found in the words alone. "Oakley's witty stories are books to be *enjoyed*—and how often is this vital ingredient missing from children's picture books," points out Edward Hudson in *Children's Book Review.* And Elaine Edelman, writing in the *New York Times Book Review,* maintains: "Oakley is one of the craftiest picture-book people working today."

Born in Shrewsbury, England, Oakley attended the Warrington Art School before beginning his career as a scenic artist for repertory companies in London. He then moved on to the Royal Opera House in Covent Garden where he worked as a design assistant, later joining the British Broadcasting Corporation (BBC-TV) as a television set designer before choosing to become a free-lance author and illustrator. It was while he was working as an illustrator for Macmillan that Oakley first envisioned the fictitious English country town of Wortlethorpe as the setting for a series of children's books. "I was going to open with a high view on top of the town and a series of stories about each building, starting with the church and moving on to the library and the town hall, but the first book, *The Church Mouse* was so successful I never got to the library," explains Oakley in an interview with Barbara A. Bannon for *Publishers Weekly.*

The Church Mouse, the first book in the "Church Mice" series, introduces the mice who populate the church in Wortlethorpe along with their guardian Sampson the cat. This strange alliance between cat and mice is explained by the setting of the story—Sampson has heard so many sermons on brotherly love and meekness that he thinks of mice as his brothers. Originally, there is only one mouse, Arthur, occupying the church, but he goes to the parson and asks if his town friends can live in the church for free if they perform chores and do odd jobs. All is well until Sampson dreams he is back in his mouse hunting days and wakes up to find himself chasing mice around the church. Before the situation can be dealt with, though, a burglar comes to the church that night and Sampson and the mice save the day. "The story goes with a swing and the slapstick and circumstantial detail are livened with a measure of wit," observes Margery Fisher in *Growing Point. The Church Mouse* is filled with "fascinating activities" asserts a *Times Literary Supplement* contributor, adding: "Oakley shows in this book how effectively words and pictures can be grafted together so that our understanding of the story depends on the combination of the two."

The following books in the "Church Mice" series have the occupants of the Wortlethorpe church taking part in a number of equally amusing adventures. In *The Church Cat Abroad,* Oakley has Sampson travelling to an exotic South Sea island to shoot a commercial for cat food in order to earn some money to fix the church's roof. Hudson comments in his review of *The Church Cat Abroad* that it is "a story full of humorous incidents and superb illustrations. Oakley is a true artist of the highest calibre with an ability to create and exploit humorous situations to the full." *The Church Mice in Action,* published in 1982, also has Sampson doing something he'd rather not in order to earn money to fix up the church. This time he's entered a cat show, but events take an unexpected turn when he is kidnapped by horrible men on a tandem bicycle. The mice, who have been arguing over whether or not it's fair to lure the other cats into fights to give Sampson a better chance, are able to rescue him and all is well in the end. "In *The Church Mice in Action,*" assert Donnarae MacCann and Olga Richard in the *Wilson Library Bulletin,* "Oakley creates a book for all ages by combining satiric cartoons, a tongue-in-cheek literary style, and a cleverly improbable story line."

Oakley departs from the town of Wortlethorpe with his 1979 *Graham Oakley's Magical Changes,* in which he "embarks on a technical experiment in picture-book making that is likely to become a landmark in the history of the genre," describes Elaine Moss in *Signal.* The pages of the book contain no words and are split in half horizontally so that they can be mixed and matched in over five hundred different combinations. The images created revolve around six slender cylinders on the left side pages and four thicker ones on the right, creating such surreal combinations as six city gentlemen holding umbrella handles attached to a full clothesline above their heads, and a four poster bed supporting a railway arch with a thundering train racing over it. "By creating such juxtapositions between the ordinary and the fabulous Oakley emphasizes the strangeness of life," relates Jon C. Stott in *World of Children's Books.* "Most books with half pages for flipping are gimmicks; *Magical Changes* is not—it offers an often humorous, often ironic commentary on life." With *Graham Oakley's Magical Changes,* Leigh Dean concludes in *Children's Book Review Service,* "Oakley has touched the eye, the imagination, and the emotions at a depth where words seem inadequate to describe the genius of this book."

Deviating from the "Church Mice" series again in 1981, Oakley presents two hens in *Hetty and Harriet* who are in search of the perfect place to live. The trip is Harriet's idea, and Hetty goes along partly because she is bullied into it, but also because she really has nothing better to do. During the course of their search, the two hens encounter a number of dangers in both the country and the city. Worst of all is the egg production plant, but they manage to escape such threats and end up finding the ideal home—the farmyard from which they began. Writing in the *School Library Journal,* Kenneth Marantz comments that "details of nature, or tongue-in-cheek signs in town, abound. Both text and illustration exude the joy of fine storytelling." Finding the book a "delight," Linda Yeatman concludes in the *British Book News:* "Oakley has developed his own special blend of lifelike representation and fantasy in children's books and *Hetty and Harriet* is a superb example of his skill."

A more recent work, *Henry's Quest,* is set in the future and centers around a young boy's search for a mythical substance—gasoline. The world that Oakley presents is one in which civilization has returned to an age similar to that of medieval times. The country in which Henry lives is surrounded by a large forest, and because the king once read an old copy of *King Arthur and the Knights of the Round Table,* it is alive with the same kinds of things found in the book, such as knights and chivalry. When the king wants to marry off his daughter, he decides to send the suitors on a quest for the substance known as gasoline. Although Henry is only a shepherd-boy and not a knight, he is allowed to participate. He begins his journey through the forest, passing technological gadgets, such as televisions, that have been thrown aside as junk. On the other side of the forest is an evil civilization in which he finds not only gasoline, but also industrialism and corruption. He brings all of these things home, but none, not even the gas, seems to catch on. "The text is very subtle, as funny as it is serious, and the pictures are the stuff of dreams and nightmares, rich with literary and historical illusion," relates Elizabeth Ward in *Washington Post Book World.* "*Henry's Quest* is definitely not a book to be taken too lightly."

WORKS CITED:

Bannon, Barbara A., "A Conversation with Graham Oakley," *Publishers Weekly,* February 26, 1979, pp. 74-75.

Dean, Leigh, review of *Graham Oakley's Magical Changes, Children's Book Review Service,* June, 1980, p. 103.

Edelman, Elaine, review of *Hetty and Harriet, New York Times Book Review,* May 30, 1982, p. 14.

Fisher, Margery, review of *The Church Mouse, Growing Point,* November, 1972, pp. 2027-28.

Hudson, Edward, review of *The Church Cat Abroad, Children's Book Review,* spring, 1974, p. 12.

Hudson, review of *The Church Mice and the Moon, Children's Book Review,* spring, 1975, p. 14.

"In the Garden of Eden," *Times Literary Supplement,* November 3, 1972, p. 1327.

MacCann, Donnarae, and Olga Richard, review of *The Church Mice in Action, Wilson Library Bulletin,* October, 1983, p. 131.

Marantz, Kenneth, review of *Hetty and Harriet, School Library Journal,* April, 1982, p. 61.

Moss, Elaine, "W(h)ither Picture Books? Some Tricks of the Trade," *Signal,* January, 1980, pp. 3-7.

Stott, Jon C., review of *Magical Changes, World of Children's Books,* Volume 6, 1981, p. 26.

Ward, Elizabeth, "Reading for after School," *Washington Post Book World,* September 14, 1986, p. 11.

Yeatman, Linda, review of *Hetty and Harriet, British Book News,* spring, 1982, p. 3.

FOR MORE INFORMATION SEE:

BOOKS

Chevalier, Tracy, editor, *Twentieth-Century Children's Writers,* 3rd edition, St. James Press, 1989, pp. 732-33.

Children's Literature Review, Volume 7, Gale, 1984, pp. 212-23.

Cullinan, Bernice E., Mary K. Karrer, and Arlene M. Pillar, *Literature and the Child,* Harcourt, 1981, pp. 115-60.

Moss, Elaine, *Children's Books of the Year: 1974,* Hamish Hamilton, 1975, p. 54.

PERIODICALS

Bulletin of the Center for Children's Books, June, 1982; May, 1983; March, 1987.

Growing Point, October, 1973, p. 2245; December, 1974, p. 2541; January, 1979, p. 3450.

Horn Book, June, 1979, p. 294; August, 1983, p. 434.

Junior Bookshelf, April, 1979, pp. 99-100; February, 1982, p. 19.

New York Times Book Review, December 10, 1972, p. 8; May 4, 1975, p. 42; May 2, 1976, p. 46; May 8, 1977, p. 41.

Publishers Weekly, February 15, 1980, p. 110; January 9, 1981, p. 76; February 11, 1983, p. 71; February 13, 1987, p. 91.

School Library Journal, May, 1973, pp. 65, 67; December, 1973, p. 44; April, 1975, p. 46; April, 1976, pp. 62-63; April, 1977, p. 56; March, 1979, p. 143; May, 1980, p. 62; October, 1980, p. 162; December, 1986, p. 107.

Times Educational Supplement, November 21, 1980, pp. 29-30; November 19, 1982, p. 32; March 6, 1987, p. 37.

Times Literary Supplement, November 23, 1973, p. 1440; December 5, 1975, pp. 1452-53; December 10, 1976, p. 1551; November 28, 1986, p. 1345.

* * *

O'BRIEN, E. G.
See CLARKE, Arthur C(harles)

* * *

O'BRIEN, Robert C.
See CONLY, Robert Leslie

* * *

ODAGA, Asenath (Bole) 1938- (Kituomba)

PERSONAL: Born July 5, 1938, in Rarieda, Kenya; daughter of Blasto Akumu Aum (a farmer and catechist) and Patricia Abuya Abok (a farmer); married James Charles Odaga (a manager), January 27, 1957; children:

Asenath Odaga

From *The Diamond Ring,* by Asenath Odaga. Illustrated by Adrienne Moore.

Odhiambo Odongo, Akelo, Adhiambo, Awuor. *Education:* University of Nairobi, B.A. (with honors) and Dip.Ed., both 1974, M.A., 1981. *Religion:* Protestant. *Hobbies and other interests:* Reading, photography, music, cooking, walking, painting, collecting traditional costumes and other artifacts of Kenyan people.

ADDRESSES: Home and office—P.O. Box 1743, Kisumu, Kenya.

CAREER: Church Missionary Society's Teacher Training College, Ngiya, Kenya, teacher, 1957; Kambare School, Kenya, teacher, 1957-58; Butere Girls School, Kakamega, Kenya, 1959-60; Nyakach Girls School, Kisumu district, Kenya, headmistress, 1961-63; Kenya Railways, Nairobi, Kenya, assistant secretary, 1964; Kenya Dairy board, Nairobi, assistant secretary, 1965-66; Kenya Library Services, Nairobi, secretary, 1967; *East African Standard,* Nairobi, advertising assistant, 1968; Kerr Downey and Selby Safaris, Nairobi, office manager, 1969-70; Christian Churches Educational Association, Nairobi, assistant director of curriculum development, 1974-75; University of Nairobi, Institute of African Studies, Nairobi, research fellow, 1976-81; free-lance researcher, writer, and editor, 1982-91. Manager of Thu Tinda Bookshop and Lake Publishers and Enterprises Ltd., both 1982-91; affiliated with Odaga & Associates (consulting firm), 1984-91. Chairperson of the board of governors of Nyakach Girls High School; Museum Management Committee, Kisumu, member and vice-chairperson, 1984-90.

MEMBER: International Board on Books for Young People (member of executive committee, 1990-92), Writers' Association of Kenya (founding member and member of executive committee, 1990-91), Children's Literature Association of Kenya (chairperson, 1988—), Kenya Women's Literature Group (chairperson, 1987-91), Kenya Association of University Women (chairperson of Kisumu chapter, 1983-87), Kenya Business and Professional Women's Club (past chairperson), Rarieda Women's Group, Akala Women's Group (patron).

AWARDS, HONORS: Best Story award, *Voice of Women* magazine, 1967, for short story, "The Suitor," and play, *Three Brides in an Hour.*

WRITINGS:

FOR CHILDREN

The Secret of Monkey the Rock, illustrated by William Agutu, Thomas Nelson, 1966.

Jande's Ambition, illustrated by Adrienne Moore, East African Publishing, 1966.

The Diamond Ring, illustrated by A. Moore, East African Publishing, 1967.

The Hare's Blanket and Other Tales, illustrated by A. Moore, East African Publishing, 1967.

The Angry Flames, illustrated by A. Moore, East African Publishing, 1968.

Sweets and Sugar Cane, illustrated by Beryl Moore, East African Publishing, 1969.

The Villager's Son, illustrated by Shyam Varma, Heinemann Educational (London), 1971.

Kip on the Farm, illustrated by B. Moore, East African Publishing, 1972.

(Editor with David Kirui and David Crippen) *God, Myself, and Others* (Christian religious education), Evangel, 1976.

Kip at the Coast, illustrated by Gay Galsworthy, Evans, 1977.

Kip Goes to the City, illustrated by Galsworthy, Evans, 1977.

Poko Nyar Mugumba (title means "Poko Mugumba's Daughter"), illustrated by Sophia Ojienda, Foundation, 1978.

Thu Tinda: Stories from Kenya, Uzima, 1980.

The Two Friends (folktales), illustrated by Barrack Omondi, Bookwise (Nairobi), 1981.

Kenyan Folk Tales, illustrated by Margaret Humphries, Humphries (Caithness, Scotland), 1981.

(With Kenneth Cripwell) *Look and Write Book One,* Thomas Nelson, 1982.

(With Cripwell) *Look and Learn Book Two,* Thomas Nelson, 1982.

Ange ok Tel (title means "Regret Never Comes First"), illustrated by Joseph Odaga, Lake Publishers & Enterprises (Kisumu), 1982.

My Home Book One, Lake Publishers & Enterprises, 1983.

Ogilo Nungo Piny Kirom (title means "Ogilo, the Arms Can't Embrace the Earth's Waist"), illustrated by Henry Kirui Koske, Heinemann Educational (Nairobi), 1983.

Nyamgondho Whuod Ombare (title means "'Nyamgondho, the Son of Ombare' and Other Stories"), illustrated by J. Odaga, Lake Publishers & Enterprises, 1986.
Munde and His Friends, illustrated by Peter Odaga, Lake Publishers & Enterprises, 1987.
The Rag Ball, illustrated by J. Odaga, Lake Publishers & Enterprises, 1987.
Munde Goes to the Market, illustrated by P. Odaga, Lake Publishers & Enterprises, 1987.
Weche, Sigendi gi Timbe Luo Moko (title means "Stories and Some Customs of the Luo"), Lake Publishers & Enterprises, 1987.
Story Time (folktales), Lake Publishers & Enterprises, 1987.
The Silver Cup, Lake Publishers & Enterprises, 1988.
A Night on a Tree, Lake Publishers & Enterprises, 1991.
Ogilo and the Hippo, Heinemann, 1991.

OTHER

Nyathini Koa e Nyuolne Nyaka Higni Adek (title means "Your Child from Birth to Age Three"), Evangel, 1976.
Miaha (five-act play; title means "The Bride"), first produced in Nairobi, 1981.
(With S. Kichamu Akivaga) *Oral Literature: A School Certificate Course,* Heinemann Educational (Nairobi), 1982.
Simbi Nyaima (four-act play; title means "The Sunken Village"; first produced in Kisumu, 1982), Lake Publishers & Enterprises, 1983.
Nyamgondho (four-act play), first produced in Kisumu, 1983.
Yesterday's Today: The Study of Oral Literature, Lake Publishers & Enterprises, 1984.
The Shade Changes (fiction), Lake Publishers & Enterprises, 1984.
The Storm, Lake Publishers & Enterprises, 1985.
Literature for Children and Young People in Kenya, Kenya Literature Bureau (Nairobi), 1985.
Between the Years (fiction), Lake Publishers & Enterprises, 1987.
A Bridge in Time (fiction), Lake Publishers & Enterprises, 1987.
Riana (fiction), Lake Publishers & Enterprises, 1987.
A Taste of Life, Lake Publishers & Enterprises, 1988.
Love Potion, A Reed on the Roof, Block Ten, with Other Stories, Lake Publishers & Enterprises, 1988.
(Contributor) Woffram Frommlet, editor, *African Radio Plays,* Nomos, 1991.

Contributor, sometimes under the name Kituomba, to periodicals, including *Women's Mirror* and *Viva.* Member of editorial committee of Western Kenya branch of Wildlife Society.

WORK IN PROGRESS: Wat Ng'ue, a book of fiction in Luo; a Luo-English dictionary; an African recipe book; research on women in oral literature, women's groups and their economic role in the advancement of women's powers, Luo oral literature, and Luo sayings.

SIDELIGHTS: Asenath Odaga commented: "I love and enjoy writing for children because, through my writing, I'm able to escape with them into the simple make believe world I create in their books. I also love to share my thoughts and experience with my younger readers, especially when I go out to meet and talk to them.

"'Please tell us something about your childhood which you still remember clearly,' I often get asked. Well, I remember a host of things from my childhood, which was a very happy one. I recall the warm moon-bathed nights when we sat around the fire and listened to our grandmother's stories, or when we sat around the fire after supper, sang, and laughed as we shelled groundnut or maize for our parents. I remember, too, when I became top of my class, and my teacher made my classmates carry me around our classroom two times. That was all the reward I ever received for taking first position all those years! There was also that morning I woke up late and found that a pack of hungry hyenas had broken into Baba's sheep pen and had killed over thirty sheep! And I had slept through it all! I never wanted to fall asleep again!

"When I write for children I always set loose my imagination and allow it to run wild, creating a secret make believe world into which I love to roam with my young readers."

* * *

O'DELL, Scott 1898-1989

PERSONAL: Born May 23, 1898, in Los Angeles, CA; died of prostate cancer, October 15, 1989, in Mount Kisco, NY; son of Bennett Mason (an official of the Union Pacific Railroad) and May Elizabeth (Gabriel) O'Dell. *Education:* Attended Occidental College, 1919, University of Wisconsin, 1920, Stanford University, 1920-21, and University of Rome, 1925.

ADDRESSES: Office—Houghton Mifflin Co., 2 Park St., Boston, MA 02108. *Agent*—McIntosh & Otis, Inc., 310 Madison Ave., New York, NY 10017.

CAREER: Writer, 1934-89. Formerly worked as a technical director for Paramount and as a cameraman for Metro-Goldwyn-Mayer. Also grew citrus fruit and taught a mail-order course in photoplay writing. *Military service:* U.S. Air Force, 1942-43.

MEMBER: Authors Guild.

AWARDS, HONORS: Rupert Hughes Award, 1960, John Newbery Medal, American Library Association (ALA), Lewis Carroll Shelf Award, and Southern California Council on Literature for Children and Young People Notable Book Award, all 1961, Hans Christian Andersen Award of Merit, International Board on Books for Young People, 1962, William Allen White Award, and German Juvenile International Award, both 1963, Nene Award, Hawaii Library Association, 1964, OMAR Award, 1985, and ALA Notable Book Citation, all for *Island of the Blue Dolphins;* Newbery Honor

Scott O'Dell

Book, 1967, German Juvenile International Award, 1968, and *Horn Book* honor citation, all for *The King's Fifth;* Newbery Honor Book, 1968, ALA Notable Book citation, and *Horn Book* honor citation, all for *The Black Pearl;* Newbery Honor Book, 1971, ALA Notable Book citation, and *Horn Book* honor citation, all for *Sing Down the Moon;* Hans Christian Andersen Medal for lifetime achievement, 1972.

"Children's Books of the Year" citations, Child Study Association of America, 1970, for *Sing Down the Moon,* 1972, for *The Treasure of Topo-el-Bampo,* 1974, for *Child of Fire,* 1975, for *The Hawk That Dare Not Hunt by Day,* 1976, for *Zia* and *The 290,* and 1987, for *Streams to the River, River to the Sea: A Novel of Sacagawea;* Freedoms Foundation Award, 1973, for *Sing Down the Moon; New York Times* Outstanding Book citation, 1974, and ALA Notable Book citation, both for *Child of Fire;* University of Southern Mississippi Medallion, 1976; ALA Notable Book citation, for *Zia;* Regina Medal, Catholic Library Association, 1978, for body of work; *Focal* Award, Los Angeles Public Library, 1981, for "excellence in creative work that enriches a child's understanding of California"; Parents Choice Award for Literature, Parents Choice Foundation, 1984, for *Alexandra,* and 1986, for *Streams to the River, River to the Sea;* Scott O'Dell Award for Historical Fiction, 1986, for *Streams to the River, River to the Sea;* School Library Media Specialist of Southeastern New York award for contribution to children's literature, 1989; Northern Westchester Center for the Arts Award, 1989. The Scott O'Dell Award for Historical Fiction was established in 1984 by the *Bulletin of the Center for Children's Books.*

WRITINGS:

FOR YOUNG PEOPLE

Island of the Blue Dolphins, Houghton, 1960.
The King's Fifth, illustrated by Samuel Bryant, Houghton, 1966.
The Black Pearl, illustrated by Milton Johnson, Houghton, 1967.
The Dark Canoe, illustrated by Johnson, Houghton, 1968.
Journey to Jericho, illustrated by Leonard Weisgard, Houghton, 1969.
Sing Down the Moon, Houghton, 1970.
The Treasure of Topo-el-Bampo, illustrated by Lynd Ward, Houghton, 1972.
The Cruise of the Arctic Star, illustrated by S. Bryant, Houghton, 1973.
Child of Fire, Houghton, 1974.
The Hawk That Dare Not Hunt by Day, Houghton, 1975.
Zia, illustrated by Ted Lewin, Houghton, 1976 (British edition illustrated by S. Reynolds, Oxford University Press, 1977).
The 290, Houghton, 1976.
Carlota, Houghton, 1977 (British edition published as *The Daughter of Don Saturnino,* Oxford University Press, 1979).
Kathleen, Please Come Home, Houghton, 1978.
The Captive, Houghton, 1979.
Sarah Bishop, Houghton, 1980.
The Feathered Serpent, Houghton, 1981.
The Spanish Smile, Houghton, 1982.
The Castle in the Sea, Houghton, 1983.
The Amethyst Ring, Houghton, 1983.
Alexandra, Houghton, 1984.
The Road to Damietta, Houghton, 1985.
Streams to the River, River to the Sea: A Novel of Sacagawea, Houghton, 1986.
The Serpent Never Sleeps: A Novel of Jamestown and Pocahontas, illustrated by Lewin, Houghton, 1987.
Black Star, Bright Dawn, Houghton, 1988.
My Name Is Not Angelica, Houghton, 1989.

OTHER

Representative Photoplays Analyzed: Modern Authorship, Palmer Institute of Authorship, 1924.
Woman of Spain: A Story of Old California (novel), Houghton, 1934.
Hill of the Hawk (novel), Bobbs-Merrill, 1947.
(With William Doyle) *Man Alone,* Bobbs-Merrill, 1953 (British edition published as *Lifer,* Longmans, 1954).
Country of the Sun, Southern California: An Informal History and Guide, Crowell, 1957.
The Sea Is Red: A Novel, Holt, 1958.
(With Rhoda Kellogg) *The Psychology of Children's Art,* Communications Research Machines, 1967.

Contributor to periodicals, including *Mirror News* (Los Angeles), *Fortnight, Independent* (San Diego), and *Sat-*

urday Review. Book columnist, *Los Angeles Mirror;* book editor, *Los Angeles Daily News,* 1947-55.

ADAPTATIONS: The films *Island of the Blue Dolphins,* Universal, 1964, and *The Black Pearl,* Diamond Films, 1976, were made from O'Dell's novels. *Island of the Blue Dolphins* was made into a filmstrip/cassette set by Pied Piper Productions and a filmstrip by Teaching Films, 1965; Miller-Brody has made record/cassette/filmstrip sets of *The Black Pearl, Sing Down the Moon, The King's Fifth, Child of Fire,* and *Zia,* 1974-77; Random House has made filmstrip/cassette sets of *Child of Fire,* 1979, and *Zia,* 1982. *Island of the Blue Dolphins, The Black Pearl, The Dark Canoe,* and *The King's Fifth* are available in Braille. *Island of the Blue Dolphins, The King's Fifth, Child of Fire, The Cruise of the Arctic Star, Sing Down the Moon,* and *Zia* are available as talking books.

SIDELIGHTS: "Scott O'Dell is one of two or three major American novelists of the past two decades who has written historical fiction for children," wrote Malcolm Usrey in the *Dictionary of Literary Biography.* "His rank as one of the foremost historical novelists is attested to by the number of prestigious awards he has won, by the thousands and thousands of young readers he has claimed, ... and by the critical acclaim he has received for several of his books." O'Dell, who remains best known for his first young adult novel, *Island of the Blue Dolphins,* was convinced throughout his writing career that the historical format could make readers aware of timeless truths such as the possibility for endurance, resourcefulness, and moral courage in the face of inhumanity.

Washington Post Book World contributor Leon Garfield called O'Dell "a much-honored author, a real general of children's literature who comes with as many medals as a prize-winning Swiss chocolate." Indeed, O'Dell won the Newbery Medal for *Island of the Blue Dolphins* and the coveted Hans Christian Andersen award of merit for lifetime achievement. The author was praised especially for his works on the clash between Native American and colonial cultures, but he ranged freely for themes and settings and produced novels about St. Francis of Assisi, Pocahontas, rival gangs in a large California city, and a teenaged sponge diver in Florida, to name a few.

O'Dell told Peter Roop of *Language Arts Magazine:* "History has a very valid connection with what we are now. Many of my books are set in the past but the problems of isolation, moral decisions, greed, need for love and affection are problems of today as well.... I do want to teach through books. Not heavy handedly but to provide a moral backdrop for readers to make their own decisions. After all, I come from a line of teachers and circuit riders going back two hundred years."

Scott O'Dell was born and raised in California. His father worked for the Union Pacific Railroad, so the family moved often but always stayed within the state. At the time of O'Dell's youth, California was still largely rural, even in areas that are now swarming with people. The author was quoted in a Houghton publicity packet as saying that Los Angeles "was a frontier town when I was born there around the turn of the century. It had more horses than automobiles, more jack rabbits than people. The very first sound I remember was a wildcat scratching on the roof as I lay in bed.... That is why, I suppose, the feel of the frontier and the sound of the sea are in my books."

As a youngster, O'Dell ranged through the California sagebrush country with his friends. His memories from that period would give him great pain later: he sometimes killed the local wildlife for sport. When he became a writer, O'Dell took care to provide his characters with a reverence for wild animals. In a piece for *Psychology Today,* O'Dell wrote that *Island of the Blue Dolphins* "began in anger, anger at the hunters who invade the mountains where I live and who slaughter everything that creeps or walks or flies. This anger also was directed at myself, at the young man of many years ago, who thoughtlessly committed the same crimes against nature."

Prior to 1934 O'Dell held numerous jobs within the moving picture industry. He taught a mail-order course in photoplay writing, worked as a technical director at Paramount Studios, and even served as a Technicolor cameraman for Metro-Goldwyn-Mayer. In 1934 he published his first novel, *Woman of Spain: A Story of Old California,* and thereafter he was engaged primarily in writing. From 1947 until 1955 he was book review editor for the *Los Angeles Daily News,* and he continued to release book-length works for adults. His first novel for teens, *Island of the Blue Dolphins,* appeared in 1960.

In the now-classic story, an Indian girl named Karana is stranded on an island off the California coast. She lives in total isolation after a pack of wild dogs kill her brother. For eighteen years Karana struggles to survive in her lonely home. Gradually she comes to respect and even tame some of the wild animals on the island, especially Rontu, the dog who killed her brother. *Washington Post Book World* reviewer Joyce Milton called the resourceful Karana "a one-in-a-million child protagonist—a loner free to work her destiny totally without interference from adults." The work is not romantic, however. Karana faces difficulties at every turn, including an earthquake and a tidal wave.

"*Island of the Blue Dolphins* has few equals in children's literature," wrote Usrey. "... The novel attests to the skills and talents of O'Dell as a writer of historical fiction. He has woven a suspenseful tale around one of the most appealing of all subjects, survival of a man or woman against the odds of nature in an extremely primitive environment.... But the book is more than one of survival; it is the story of great courage, endurance, perseverance, ingenuity, and, perhaps most important of all, it is a story of a woman's surviving great loneliness and an even greater sense of isolation. It is Karana's loneliness and isolation that give the book one of its most powerful and universal themes, that all people need to be with others, to love and to be loved." The critic concluded, "*Island of the Blue Dolphins* is surely O'Dell's masterpiece and one of a half dozen or so great historical novels for children by an American writer in the past two or three decades."

O'Dell wrote a number of other novels about the clash between Native Americans and Spanish or English conquerors. *The King's Fifth,* also a Newbery Honor Book, tells of a young mapmaker who becomes stricken with a lust for gold in the American Southwest during the 1540s. *Sing Down the Moon* describes the enslavement and forced migration of the Navajo people through the eyes of a young Navajo woman, and *Zia* explores the fate of Karana's tribe as they face exploitation by ruthless Spanish colonists. Usrey noted that O'Dell's works reflect "a fairly recent trend in fiction for children; that is not to slight or bend the truth in favor of the European conquerors."

This theme is explored in depth in O'Dell's trilogy about the Spanish conquistadors. The books, *The Captive, The Feathered Serpent,* and *The Amethyst Ring,* recount Spain's bloody victories over the Aztec and Inca empires through the eyes of a teenaged hero, Julian Escobar. Tempted to his own forms of corruption and exploitation, Escobar eventually spurns the conquistador path and returns to Spain to join a penitent monastery. In a review for the *Bulletin of the Center for Children's Books,* Zena Sutherland called the trilogy "an exciting adventure story ... notable for its structure and characterization as well as for the research that colors but does not clog the narrative."

Most of O'Dell's novels are based on historical events, but a few are set in the present, with present-day themes. *Child of Fire* deals with gang wars between Hispanic teenagers. *Alexandra* tells the story of a young diver who discovers cocaine hidden in the sponges she harvests from the sea. *Kathleen, Please Come Home* offers a diary-form exploration of teenaged drug abuse among runaways. In a review of the latter work for the *World of Children's Books,* Sally Rumbaugh wrote: "*Kathleen, Please Come Home* is the story of change, an honest rendition of the struggle and hardships involved in the growth from innocence to maturity. On this level, the novel is archetypal, deeply moving and profound."

O'Dell wrote novels virtually until the moment of his death in 1989. Three of his best-known later works deal with women from American history. *Sarah Bishop* explores the tragedies of the Revolutionary War through the experiences of one immigrant to Long Island. *Streams to the River, River to the Sea: A Novel of Sacagawea* reveals the Lewis and Clark expedition of 1804-1806 through the eyes of their Indian guide, Sacagawea, and *The Serpent Never Sleeps* highlights the life of Pocahontas in colonial Virginia. *Horn Book* contributor Mary M. Burns maintained that in his writings, O'Dell showed "a particular empathy for and interest in those who are caught between two cultures and who, at times, are torn between conflicting loyalties."

Critics have cited O'Dell's books for their strong moral stand on right and wrong, for their concern for the environment and wildlife, and for their sensitive treatment of the high and low points of human nature. O'Dell once told *Horn Book Magazine:* "For children, who believe that nothing much has happened before they appeared and that little of the past they do perceive has any possible bearing on their lives, the historical novel can be an entertaining corrective, a signpost between the fixed, always relevant, past and the changing present."

According to Sally Anne M. Thompson in *Catholic Library World,* no writer understood better than O'Dell how to weave present-day dilemmas into historical circumstances. "O'Dell, with rare talent, [was] able to accurately depict characters through revealing speech and incident," wrote Thompson. "He [did] not tell his reader how life is, or how people are capable of behaving, he merely [created] the situations that force his characters to be themselves.... O'Dell stories entertain the reader, hold his attention and make him care about the dilemmas of the characters. The reader can vicariously experience the defeats and victories of each character. Perhaps this is because he [wrote] about situations pertinent to the human condition; the constant battle between the good and evil obvious even to the pre-adolescent reader. O'Dell [was] capable of subtly

Cover of *Island of the Blue Dolphins,* by Scott O'Dell.

and skillfully weaving this message between the written lines of his stories, much as the Navajo weaves her rug, thread by thread, to form a complete and beautiful expression of herself."

WORKS CITED:

Burns, Mary M., review of *Streams to the River, River to the Sea, Horn Book Magazine,* September-October, 1986, p. 599.
Garfield, Leon, "Young Man among the Mayans," *Washington Post Book World,* March 9, 1980, p. 7.
Milton, Joyce, "Beyond the Blue Dolphins," *Washington Post Book World,* May 2, 1976, p. L2.
O'Dell, Scott, *Psychology Today,* January, 1968.
O'Dell, Scott, "The Tribulations of a Trilogy," *Horn Book Magazine,* April, 1982, pp. 137-144.
O'Dell, Scott, quote in Houghton publicity packet.
Roop, Peter, "Profile: Scott O'Dell," *Language Arts,* November, 1984, pp. 750-752.
Rumbaugh, Sally, review of *Kathleen, Please Come Home, World of Children's Books,* Volume III, number 2, 1978, pp. 74-75.
Something about the Author, Volume 60, Gale, 1991, pp. 111-121.
Sutherland, Zena, review of *The Amethyst Ring, Bulletin of the Center for Children's Books,* March, 1983, pp. 131-132.
Thompson, Sally Anne M., "Scott O'Dell—Weaver of Stories," *Catholic Library World,* March, 1978, pp. 340-342.
Usrey, Malcolm, "Scott O'Dell," *Dictionary of Literary Biography,* Volume 52: *American Writers for Children since 1960: Fiction,* Gale, 1986, pp. 278-295.

FOR MORE INFORMATION SEE:

BOOKS

Authors and Artists for Young Adults, Volume 3, Gale, 1990.
Children's Literature Review, Gale, Volume 1, 1976, Volume 16, 1989.
Contemporary Literary Criticism, Volume 30, Gale, 1984.

OBITUARIES:

PERIODICALS

New York Times, October 17, 1989.

* * *

OGILVY, Gavin
See BARRIE, J(ames) M(atthew)

* * *

O'HARA, Mary
See ALSOP, Mary O'Hara

OLSEN, Ib Spang 1921- (Padre Detine, a joint pseudonym)

PERSONAL: Born June 11, 1921, in Copenhagen, Denmark; son of Ole Christian (a gardener) and Soffu (Nielsen) Olsen; married Grete Geisler, May 3, 1947 (divorced, 1960); married Nulle Oeigaard (an artist), September 8, 1962; children: (first marriage) Tune, Tine; (second marriage) Martin, Lasse. *Education:* Blaagaards Seminarium, teacher training, 1939-43; Royal Danish Academy of Art, study of graphic art, 1945-49. *Politics:* Democratic Socialist.

ADDRESSES: Home—Slotsparken 64, Bagsvaerd 2880, Denmark. *Agent*—International Children's Book Service, Kildeskovsvej 21, Gentofte 2820, Denmark.

CAREER: Illustrator of Sunday magazine supplements for Danish newspapers, 1942; schoolteacher in Denmark, 1952-60; full-time writer and illustrator, 1960—. Has also designed murals for schools, posters, and ceramic pieces. Began work in Danish television, 1964, with numerous animated programs for young people to his credit.

AWARDS, HONORS: Danish Ministry of Culture Award for best illustrated children's book of the year, 1962, for *The Boy in the Moon,* 1963, for *The Rain* and *The Wind,* 1964, for *Nonsense Rhymes,* and 1966, for *The Marsh Crone's Brew;* Danish Society for Bookcraft's

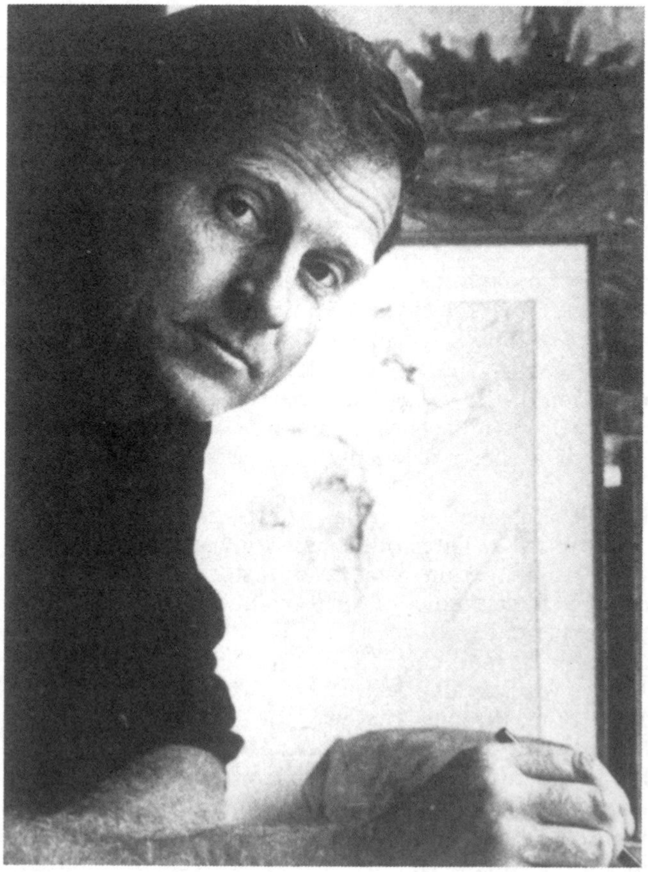

Ib Spang Olsen

honor list of year's outstanding books, 1964, for *The Kiosk on the Square,* 1968, for *Lars Peter's Bicycle,* 1969, for *Hocus Pocus,* 1971, for *Smoke;* Illustrator's Prize, Organization for Friends of Books, 1966; International Board on Books for Young People honors list, 1966, runner-up for Hans Christian Andersen medal, 1968, 1970, Hans Christian Andersen Medal, 1972; Hendrixen Medal for outstanding bookcraft, 1967, for *Halfdans ABC:* diploma, Bratislava Biennial, 1967: honorable mention, Association of Authors of Juvenile Literature in Finland, 1971, for *Lars Peter's Bicycle;* Storm Petersen Legatet, 1971, for body of work; Danish Book Craft Society Prize, 1976.

WRITINGS:

SELF-ILLUSTRATED CHILDRENS BOOKS

Boernene paa vejen, Gjellerups, 1958.
Bedstemors vaegtaeppe, Kunst og Kultur, 1958.
(With Torben Brostroem) *Boern: Det foerste aar i ord og tegninger* (children's verse), Hasselbalch, 1962.
Blaesten, Gyldendal, 1963.
Regnen, Gyldendal, 1963.
Kiosken paa torvet, Gyldendal, 1964.
Marie-hoenen, Gyldendal, 1969.
Hvordan vi fik vores naboer, Gyldendal, 1969.
Pjer Brumme: Historier om en lille bjoern, Gyldendal, 1971.
Folkene paa vejen, Gyldendal, 1972.
(With Martin Hansen) *I Kristoffers spor,* Gyldendal, 1973.
Gamle fru glad, Gyldendal, 1974.
24 breve til nissen, Rhodos, 1975.
Min tjeneste hos bjergmanden, Boernenes Boghandel, 1975.
Thors rejse til Udgaard, Gyldendal, 1975.
Thors rejse til hymer, Gyldendal, 1977.
Thor og hammeren, Gyldendal, 1978.
Lille dreng paa oesterbro, Gyldendal, 1980.
Kanonfotografen: Som man raber i skoven (plays), Schonberg, 1983.
Allan alene, Gyldendal, 1988.

SELF-ILLUSTRATED CHILDREN'S BOOKS; IN ENGLISH TRANSLATION

The Little Locomotive, translated by Virginia Allen Jensen, Coward, 1976, published in England as *The Little Shunting Engine,* World's Work, 1976 (originally published as *Det lille lokomotiv,* G. E. C. Gad, 1956).
The Marsh Crone's Brew, translated by Jensen, Abingdon, 1960 (originally published as *Mosekonens bryg,* Kunst og Kultur, 1957).
The Boy in the Moon, translated by Jensen, Abingdon, 1963, Parents' Magazine, 1971 (originally published as *Drengen i maanen,* Gyldendal, 1962).
Cat Alley, translated by Jensen, Coward, 1971 (originally published as *Kattehuset,* Gylendal, 1968).
Where is Martin?, translated by Jensen, Angus & Robertson, 1969.
Smoke, translated by Jensen, Coward, 1972 (originally published as *Roegen,* Gyldendal, 1970).

From *Old Mother Hubbard and Her Dog,* by Lennart Hellsing. Translated by Virginia Allen Jensen. Illustrated by Ib Spang Olsen.

(Adaptor) Vilhelm Bergsoe, *The Nisse from Timsgaard,* translated by Jensen, Coward, 1974 (originally published as *Nissen fra timsgaard,* Gyldendal, 1973).
(With Lennart Hellsing) *Old Mother Hubbard and Her Dog,* translated by Jensen, Coward, 1976.

ILLUSTRATOR

Prinsessen paa Glasbjerget (folk tales), J. H. Schultz, 1946.
Ester Nagel, compiler, *Danske folkeeventyr,* Kunst og Kultur, 1950.
Frank Jaeger, *Hverdaghistorier,* Wivel, 1951.
Jaeger, *Tune, det foerste aar,* H. Branner, 1951.
Fem smaa troldeboern, Danske, 1952.
Nissen flytter med, Gyldendal, 1955.
Abrikosia, Hoest & Soen, 1958.
Virginia Allen Jensen, *Lars Peter's Birthday,* Abington, 1959.
Jakob Johannes Bech Nygaard, *Tobias, the Magic Mouse,* translated by Edith Joan McCormick, Harcourt, 1968 (originally published as *Tobias tryllemus,* Martins, 1961).
Halfdan Wedel Rasmussen, *Boernerim,* Schoenberg, 1964.
Hans Christian Andersen, *Digte,* edited by Bo Groenbech, Danske Arnkrone, 1966.
Morten poulsens urtehave, Hoest & Soen, 1967.
Rasmussen, *Halfdans abc,* Illustrations-forlaget, 1967.
Molbohistorier, Schoenberg, 1967.

Rasmussen, *Den lille fraekke Frederik og andre boernerim,* Branner & Korch, 1967.
Jensen, *Lars Peter's Bicycle,* Angus & Robertson, 1970 (originally published as *Lars Peters cykel,* Gyldendal, 1968).
Lise Soerensen, *Da lyset gik ud,* Gyldendal, 1968.
Rasmussen, *Hocus Pocus,* Angus & Robertson, 1973 (originally published as *Hokus pokus og andre boernerim,* Schoenberg, 1969).
Ole Restrup, *Odin og Tor,* G. E. C. Gad, 1969.
Kjeld Elfelt, *AEsop: 50 fabler,* Schoenberg, 1970.
Rasmussen, *Otte digte om snaps,* Udgiveren, 1970.
Rasmussen, *Noget om Nanette,* Schoenberg, 1972.
The Thirteen Clocks, Sigvaldi, 1973.
Joergen Lorenzen, *Danske folkeviser: Et hundrede udvalgte danske viser,* G. E. C. Gad, 1974.
Cecil Boedker, *Barnet i sivkurven,* P. Haase og Soens, 1975.
Boedker, *Da jorden forsvandt,* P. Haase og Soens, 1975.
Boedker, *Den udgalgte,* Danske Bibelselskab, 1977.
Ebbe Klovedal Reich, *De forste: 30 fortaellinger om Danmarks fodsel* (first of three volumes of Medieval Danish folksongs), Vindrose, 1981.
Reich, *Ploven og de to svaerd: 30 fortaelinger fra Danmarks unge dage* (second of three volumes of Medieval Danish folksongs), Vindrose, 1982.
Reich, *Den baerende magt; 30 fortaelinger om Danmarks syv-otte yngst slaegtled* (third of three volumes of Medieval Danish folksongs), Vindrose, 1983.

OTHER

(With Erik E. Frederiksen under joint pseudonym Padre Detine) *En Sydamerikaner i Nordsjaelland* (humerous tales), privately printed, 1960.
Om direkte kopl, Grafodan, c. 1971.
(With Gunnar Jakobsen) *Ib Spang Olsens bogarbejder 1944-1981: En bibliografi,* Schonberg, 1982.
Magasinet, Hjemmets sondag og jeg, Fremad, 1984.

Designer of numerous book-jackets; illustrator of Danish language editions of works by Herman Melville, Geoffrey Chaucer, and Mark Twain; animator of films for Danish Television, including *Hvad bliver det naeste?, Taarnuret, Vitaminerne, Den store krage, Nikolai, Stregen der loeb henad,* and *Stregen der loeb opad.* Original illustrations for four books were given by the author to the Kerlan Collection, University of Minnesota.

Ib Spang Olsen's books have been published in his native Denmark, England, the Faroe Islands, Finland, Germany, Greenland, Holland, Japan, Norway, South Africa, Sweden, the United States, and Wales.

SIDELIGHTS: Ib Spang Olsen began his career as an illustrator of books for adults. It was only after his own children were born and he found himself pressed for numerous bedside stories that he turned his efforts towards writing and illustrating literature for a younger audience. "The child seems close, and is, nevertheless, a stranger," he said in his 1972 Hans Christian Andersen Medal acceptance speech given before the International Board on Books for Young People, a copy of which he provided to *Contemporary Authors.* "The child exists in another world. He doesn't tell us about it, and we have forgotten how it was for us when we lived in that world. We can try to put ourselves in his place; we can remember a little, and we try to sense the rest. We employ what we call *fantasy,* but we don't know how much of his fantasy seems like common sense to the child. And when we adults think that a child is being very imaginative, perhaps the child is trying to arrive at a reasonable explanation for something that is puzzling him."

Juxtaposition of the real with the imaginary is a recurrent theme in many of Olsen's works for children, as in his popular book *Where is Martin?.* In this story, Laura follows her small brother Martin from the everyday world of their sterile, modern apartment building into quite another dimension, full of children and magic, where all the rules suddenly change, the uncommon is commonplace, and where strange cats abound. "This is a book of dreams and a dream of a book," writes a reviewer in the *Times pb looking-glass." Olsen composes his prose to reflect the mythic context of his stories, by adopting a more poetic, musical quality than exists in normal speaking or reading language. In accounting for a modern child's unique perception of reality, he attempts to downplay the nostalgic quality resulting from memories of his own childhood. Olsen sees this as a difficulty in writing responsibly for children, because to be truthful, he can only create stories based upon his own recollections and experience.*

The humorous and energetic pictures accompanying the texts of his stories also reflect Olsen's ability to objectively draw upon his own "child within" in recreating that "other world" within the pages of his books. All of the illustrations are created using the "direct-copy" method, which entails drawing directly onto the copy-film. A separate film is created for each of the four colors used in each single illustration, and the films are not combined until the printing process, thereby making the finished book the original artwork. The lithographic quality of the resulting illustration reflects Olsen's interest in classic graphic techniques, and his desire to retain the hand of the artist within an era of large presses and modern printing technology.

WORKS CITED:

Contemporary Authors New Revision Series, Volume 37, Gale, 1992.
Doris de Montreville, *Third Book of Junior Authors,* H. W. Wilson, 1972.
Something about the Author, Volume 6, Gale, 1974.
Times Literary Supplement, October 16, 1969, p. 1200.

FOR MORE INFORMATION SEE:

BOOKS

Lee Kingman and others, compilers, *Illustrators of Children's Books: 1957-1966,* Horn Book, 1968.

PERIODICALS

Bookbird, Volume 19, 1972.

Booklist, November 15, 1972, p. 302: May 15, 1976, p. 1338.
Horn Book, April, 1972, p. 138; August, 1972. p. 364; August, 1976, p. 388; February, 1978, p. 36.
Times Literary Supplement, October 22, 1971, p. 1325; April 28, 1972, p. 488.
Top of the News, January 1973; June, 1973.

* * *

ONEAL, Elizabeth 1934-
(Zibby Oneal)

PERSONAL: Born March 17, 1934, in Omaha, NE; daughter of James D. (a thoracic surgeon) and Mary Elizabeth (Dowling) Bisgard; married Robert Moore Oneal (a plastic surgeon), December 27, 1955; children: Elizabeth, Michael. *Education:* Attended Stanford University, 1952-55; University of Michigan, B.A., 1970. *Politics:* Democrat. *Religion:* Episcopalian.

ADDRESSES: Home and office—501 Onondaga St., Ann Arbor, MI 48104. *Agent*—Marilyn Marlow, Curtis Brown Ltd., 575 Madison Ave., New York, NY 10022.

CAREER: University of Michigan, Ann Arbor, lecturer in English, 1976-85. Member of board of trustees, Greenhills School, Ann Arbor, 1975-79.

MEMBER: PEN, Authors Guild.

AWARDS, HONORS: Friends of American Writers Award, 1972, for *War Work;* "Notable Book" citations and "Best Books for Young Adults" citations, American Library Association, 1980, for *The Language of Goldfish,* 1982, for *A Formal Feeling,* and 1985, for *In Summer Light;* "Best Books of the Year" citation, *New York Times,* 1982, and Christopher Award, 1983, both for *A Formal Feeling; Horn Book* Honor Book, and *Boston Globe/Horn Book* Award, both 1986, both for *In Summer Light.*

Zibby Oneal

WRITINGS:

UNDER NAME ZIBBY ONEAL

War Work (juvenile), illustrated by George Porter, Viking, 1971.
The Improbable Adventures of Marvelous O'Hara Soapstone (juvenile), illustrated by Paul Galdone, Viking, 1972.
Turtle and Snail (juvenile), illustrated by Margot Tomes, Lippincott, 1979.
The Language of Goldfish (young adult novel), Viking, 1980.
A Formal Feeling (young adult novel), Viking, 1982.
Maude and Walter (juvenile), illustrated by Maxie Chambliss, Lippincott, 1985.
In Summer Light (young adult novel), Viking, 1985.
Grandma Moses: Painter of Rural America (biography), Puffin, 1986.
A Long Way to Go (juvenile), illustrated by Michael Dooling, Viking, 1990.

Manuscript collection at Kerlan Collection, University of Minnesota.

WORK IN PROGRESS: Another young adult novel; a novel for younger children.

SIDELIGHTS: Zibby Oneal is best-known as the author of acclaimed young adult novels which, according to Wendy Smith in *Publishers Weekly,* "exhibit a depth and complexity rare in any kind of fiction." Oneal's three young adult novels, *The Language of Goldfish* (1980), *A Formal Feeling* (1982), and *In Summer Light* (1985), have been widely praised for their sensitive and perceptive portrayals of the complex emotions and problems of adolescents. Featuring teenage female protagonists, Oneal's novels deal with a variety of conflict situations—puberty, sexual awareness, self-perception problems, the death of a parent—which her characters resolve on their way towards adulthood and independence. Throughout, Oneal focuses on the inner strength of her characters, which allows them to move forward in their lives. "I feel a responsibility to make children understand that adolescence is a self-absorbed world . . . but it's not a place you can stay forever," she told Smith. "The movement away and out into the world, into concern for other people, has to happen; you aren't an adult until you make that move. Sure, explore your feelings, because if you're hung up on your problems you're never going to be able to move on. So work that out, but then get out into the world."

Oneal was born Elizabeth Bisgard on March 17, 1934, in Omaha, Nebraska, the daughter of James and Mary Elizabeth Bisgard. Her desire to become a writer began with her family, who considered books, as Oneal described in *Sixth Book of Junior Authors and Illustrators,* "as necessary to life as food.... There were toppling stacks of books on every flat surface in the house." Both of her parents regularly read to her, and

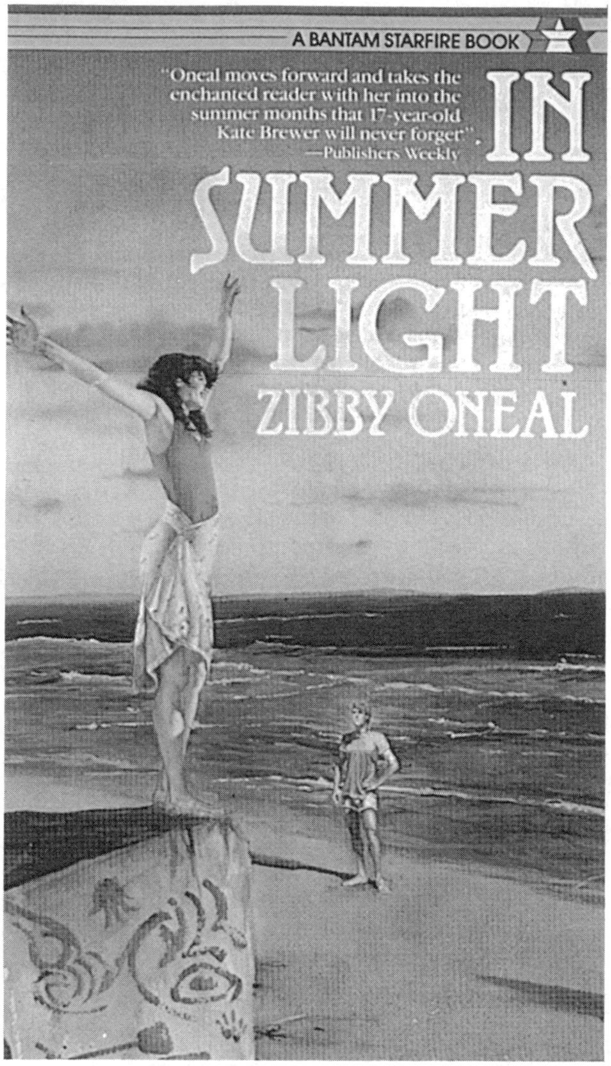

Cover of *In Summer Light,* by Zibby Oneal.

also encouraged her early efforts at storywriting. "I told myself stories all the time," she stated in *Sixth Book of Junior Authors.* "When I was old enough I began to write them down .... I don't believe my parents ever worried. They let me alone to pursue my singleminded path without much comment." Growing up, she was also interested in painting, an activity she partook in with her father, a thoracic surgeon. While she harbored early aspirations to become a painter or even a surgeon, writing and stories remained her primary interest. "I don't recall when I didn't want to be a writer," Oneal was quoted in a 1982 Viking Press promotional release. "It has seemed to me the best and most exciting thing a person can do, for as long as I can remember."

From 1952 to 1955, Oneal attended Stanford University, where she took creative writing classes. On December 27, 1955, she married Robert Moore Oneal, a plastic surgeon. "It was only after I'd married, had two children [Elizabeth and Michael], and had begun to write stories for them that I discovered what I both like and could do," she commented for Viking Press. "The first books came out of these stories created expressly for them." Her first book was published in 1971, *War Work,* a suspense story about three young children on the trail of espionage activities in a Midwestern town during the Second World War. She followed with two picture books for children, *The Improbable Adventures of Marvelous O'Hara Soapstone* (1972) and *Turtle and Snail* (1979). She turned to writing for adolescents after her own children began to grow up. "My characters aged along with them," she described in a publicity release for Delacorte. "Eventually everyone reached adolescence, but my characters remained there, because I found I was deeply interested in exploring this brief time of life, these few years when everything is in the process of becoming what it will be."

Oneal's first young adult novel, *The Language of Goldfish,* was widely acclaimed for its delicate handling of difficult subject matter. The novel deals with the attempted suicide and mental illness of Carrie Stokes, a thirteen-year-old pubescent girl, who is terrified both of herself and of other people. "In a perceptive novel which avoids cliches and exaggeration," notes Christine McDonnell in *Horn Book,* "evocative images create a sense of Carrie's inner experiences: the gaps in her consciousness, her whirling terror, and her longing for a safe place—a place like the island in the goldfish pond, a sanctuary of childhood." The novel was singled out by many critics for its technical merits, including rich characterization and an effective prose style. "The people and events in Carrie's life are a bit flat and a bit hazy around the edges, which is entirely how she perceives them," notes Joyce Milton in the *New York Times Book Review.* "In contrast, [Carrie's] inner turmoil—even during her dizzy spells when reality 'slips sideways'—is conveyed in language that is poetic and precise." Linda R. Silver in *School Library Journal* praised *The Language of Goldfish* for being "a serious but not dismal book, enlivened by flashes of humor, [which] draws out [the] readers' empathetic response and enlarges understanding."

The title of Oneal's second young adult novel, *A Formal Feeling,* is taken from a line of Emily Dickinson's poetry: "After great pain, a formal feeling comes." The novel deals with sixteen-year-old Anne Cameron, on Christmas break from private school, who is struggling with the recent death of her mother, and the marriage of her father to a new wife. The novel charts Anne's deep feelings for her dead mother, and her attempts to reconcile both her mother's strengths and weaknesses—without feeling a sense of betrayal. Again, Oneal was widely praised by critics for her technically accomplished and insightful depiction of the world of adolescents. In *Booklist,* Stephanie Zvirin remarks that "Oneal's pacing is slow and deliberate and her style highly descriptive—characteristics that may make this attractive to more experienced fiction readers—but the novel is filled with scenes of great emotional intensity, and Oneal ... captures Anne's conflicting feelings with subtlety and perception." Calling the novel "clearly one of the best young adult books of the year," *ALAN Review* contributor Robert C. Small describes *A Formal Feeling* as "upper class, literary, cultured, and very intellectual," and praises Oneal's "style, dialogue, descriptions, and action [which] are both natural and beautifully controlled."

In Summer Light, Oneal's third novel, deals with seventeen-year-old Kate Brewer, who struggles with the stifling perceptions she carries both of her parents and of herself. In the shadow of her father, a successful artist, Kate strives to discover her own identity and form a relationship with a young graduate student named Ian. Oneal "uses an elegant dazzle of images to illuminate Kate's Oedipal conflict, while neatly sidestepping the boggy self-pity of so much adolescent fiction," notes *New York Times Book Review* contributor Michele Landsberg. "Through Kate's rapt perceptions of light and color, both the prose and her character gain depth." The novel, which received the *Boston Globe/Horn Book* Award in 1986, arose from Oneal's interest in fairy tales and in William Shakespeare's play *The Tempest.* As Oneal described in *Horn Book:* "I wanted to write about a powerful, arrogant, magical father and about his daughter's involvement with him. I wanted to talk about how a girl begins to move away from this intense childhood involvement; about how it is when, like Miranda in *The Tempest,* she is able to gaze for the first time on a man besides her father."

In addition to her young adult novels and earlier books, Oneal has written a picture-book of stories, *Maude and Walter* (1985), as well as a biography of the American rural painter Grandma Moses. She continues to find major inspiration with writing for young adults. "Adolescents are on the brink of becoming what they will be as adults and their problems and perplexities are a rich source for fiction," she stated in *Twentieth Century Children's Writers.* "How a young person negotiates this brief passage between childhood and the adult world is a subject that I find of continuing interest." Oneal lives in Ann Arbor, Michigan, where she has taught writing at the University of Michigan. She enjoys the mix between her own writing and teaching young people, and is enlightened by her discussions with students where, as she notes in *Sixth Book of Junior Authors,* "we talk and talk about writing books." Oneal adds: "Sometimes in the midst of these discussions I find myself thinking about how almost sinfully lucky it is to be able to spend a life engrossed in the occupation one loves best."

WORKS CITED:

Landsberg, Michele, review of *In Summer Light, New York Times Book Review,* November 24, 1985, p. 21.

McDonnell, Christine, review of *The Language of Goldfish, Horn Book,* August, 1980, p. 416.

Milton, Joyce, review of *The Language of Goldfish, New York Times Book Review,* April 27, 1980, pp. 52, 65.

Oneal, Zibby, promotional piece, Viking Press, 1982.

Oneal, Zibby, "Meet the Author" (publicity release), Delacorte.

Oneal, Zibby, "In Summer Light," *Horn Book,* January-February, 1987, pp. 32-34.

Oneal, Zibby, essay in *Sixth Book of Junior Authors and Illustrators,* edited by Sally Holmes Holtze, H. W. Wilson, 1989, pp. 210-12.

Oneal, Zibby, comments in *Twentieth Century Children's Writers,* 3rd edition, edited by Tracy Chevalier, St. James Press, 1989.

Silver, Linda R., review of *The Language of Goldfish, School Library Journal,* February, 1980, p. 70.

Small, Robert C., review of *A Formal Feeling, ALAN Review,* winter, 1983, p. 23.

Smith, Wendy, "Working Together," *Publishers Weekly,* February 21, 1986, pp. 97-98.

Zvirin, Stephanie, review of *A Formal Feeling, Booklist,* October 1, 1982, p. 199.

FOR MORE INFORMATION SEE:

BOOKS

Children's Literature Review, Volume 13, Gale, 1987.

Contemporary Literary Criticism, Volume 30, Gale, 1984.

PERIODICALS

Best Sellers, April, 1980.

Globe and Mail (Toronto), February 8, 1986.

New Statesman, October 10, 1986.

New York Times Book Review, April 27, 1980; November 14, 1982.

Times Literary Supplement, October 30, 1987.

Washington Post Book World, October 10, 1982.

* * *

ONEAL, Zibby
See ONEAL, Elizabeth

* * *

OPTIC, Oliver
See STRATEMEYER, Edward L.

* * *

ORMEROD, Jan(ette Louise) 1946-

PERSONAL: Born September 23, 1946, in Bunbury, Western Australia; daughter of Jack and Thelma (Harvey) Hendry; married Paul Ormerod (an information scientist), January 21, 1971 (divorced, 1991); children: Sophie, Laura. *Education:* Western Australian Institute of Technology, associateship (graphic design), 1966, (art teaching), 1973; Claremont Teachers College, teacher's certificate, 1967.

ADDRESSES: *Home*—Cambridge, England. *Agent*—Laura Cecil, 17 Alwyne Villas, London N1 2HG, England.

CAREER: Western Australian Education Department, Bunbury, art teacher, 1968-72; Mt. Lawley College of Advance Education, Perth, Western Australia, lecturer in art education, 1973-75; Western Australian Institute of Technology, Perth, part-time lecturer in drawing and

Jan Ormerod

basic design, 1976-79; author and illustrator of children's books.

MEMBER: Society of Authors.

AWARDS, HONORS: Kate Greenaway Medal commendation, 1981, Mother Goose Award and Australian Picture Book of the Year Award from Australian Children's Book Council, both 1982, all for *Sunshine; Sunshine* and *Moonlight* were named American Library Association (ALA) notable books, 1981 and 1982; *Dad's Back, Messy Baby, Sleeping,* and *Reading,* were named ALA notable books, all 1985; Kate Greenaway Medal commendation, 1986, for *Happy Christmas, Gemma; The Story of Chicken Licken* was named an ALA notable book, 1986; *Bend and Stretch, Making Friends, Mom's Home,* and *This Little Nose* were named ALA notable books, all 1987.

WRITINGS:

FOR CHILDREN; SELF-ILLUSTRATED

Sunshine, Lothrop, 1981.
Moonlight, Lothrop, 1982.
Be Brave, Billy, Dent, 1983.
101 Things to Do with a Baby, Lothrop, 1984.
Young Joe, Lothrop, 1985.
(Reteller) *The Story of Chicken Licken,* Walker, 1985, Lothrop, 1986.
Silly Goose, Lothrop, 1986.
Our Ollie, Lothrop, 1986.
Just Like Me, Lothrop, 1986.
The Saucepan Game, Lothrop, 1989.
Kitten Day, Lothrop, 1989.
(Reteller, with David Lloyd) *The Frog Prince,* Lothrop, 1990.
When We Went to the Zoo, Lothrop, 1991.

"JAN ORMEROD BABY BOOK" SERIES; SELF-ILLUSTRATED

Sleeping, Lothrop, 1985.
Reading, Lothrop, 1985.
Dad's Back, Lothrop, 1985.
Messy Baby, Lothrop, 1985.

"JAN ORMEROD NEW BABY BOOK" SERIES; SELF-ILLUSTRATED

Bend and Stretch, Lothrop, 1987.
Making Friends, Lothrop, 1987.
This Little Nose, Lothrop, 1987.
Mom's Home, Lothrop, 1987.

FOR CHILDREN; ILLUSTRATOR

Jan Mark, *Hairs in the Palm of the Hand,* Kestrel, 1981.
Margaret Mahy, *The Chewing-gum Rescue and Other Stories,* Dent, 1982.
Pat Thompson, compiler, *Rhymes around the Day,* Lothrop, 1983.
Karin Lorentzen, *Lanky Longlegs,* translated by Joan Tate, Atheneum, 1983.
Sarah Hayes, *Happy Christmas, Gemma,* Lothrop, 1986.
James M. Barrie, *Peter Pan,* Viking Children's, 1987.
Hayes, *Eat up, Gemma,* Lothrop, 1988.
Vivian French, *One Ballerina Two,* Lothrop, 1991.

WORK IN PROGRESS: Jump, with Michelle Magorian, and *Sunflakes,* edited by Lillian Moore, both for Clarion; *Come Back, Kittens* and *Come Back, Puppies,* both for Lothrop; and *Midnight Pillow Fight,* for Candlewick.

SIDELIGHTS: Australian-born author and illustrator Jan Ormerod has established herself as a sensitive and skillful creator of children's picture books. Often wordless or of minimal text, Ormerod's works are characterized by detailed watercolor illustrations that frequently depict warm domestic scenes. When assessing her work, reviewers have pointed to Ormerod's ability to render everyday events with both insight and gentle humor, a quality that makes her books appealing to both children and their parents. Her work has also been popular with critics; in a 1986 *Washington Post Book World* article Michael Dirda judged Ormerod to be "a contemporary master of the board book."

Ormerod's family life inspired her successful career in children's literature. Her husband, Paul, worked as a children's librarian at the time the couple's first child, Sophie, was born. Sophie's interest in the books her father brought home for her encouraged Ormerod, then an art teacher, to begin creating picture books of her own. Confident of realizing some success in this venture, Ormerod and her husband decided to quit their jobs and move from Australia to London, England, home of a number of publishing companies. Ormerod drew on her training in graphic design to create a portfolio and submitted her illustrations to various London publishing houses. Her efforts resulted in the publication of *Sunshine* in 1981.

In *Sunshine* Ormerod's colorful, naturalistic illustrations depict a little girl's morning routine. Using cartoon-like panels to separate scenes from one another, Ormerod wordlessly presents the little girl (modeled after her daughter Sophie) waking up, prodding her lethargic parents out of bed, getting dressed, eating breakfast, and going to school. Scenes such as the father distractedly allowing the breakfast toast to burn as he reads the newspaper provide comic relief. The companion book to *Sunshine, Moonlight,* uses the same format to describe the end of the little girl's day: she eats dinner, takes a bath, listens to a story, and eventually goes to bed. Despite the absence of words in both books, Michele Landsberg stated in *Reading for the Love of It* that "the drama of nuance and character are fully present." In *Books for Your Children* Margaret Carter described Ormerod's illustrations as "gentle, tolerant, tender, observant and shrewd," and in *Growing Point* Margery Fisher declared, "Domestic truth is achieved by pictures alone in *Moonlight,* and with complete success."

Many of Ormerod's later books also focus on small slices of day-to-day family life. In *Be Brave, Billy,* for instance, a little boy comes to terms with everyday anxieties, and in *101 Things to Do with a Baby* a young girl discovers a variety of activities that can be done with her new sibling. Reviewers praised these titles, assessing that Ormerod sensitively depicts the fears, jealousies, and triumphs of young children. Her illustrations in *101 Things to Do with a Baby* were deemed "magnificent" by Joe McGinniss in the *New York Times Book Review,* who also noted that the pictures evoke "both the tenderness and tumult with which each day in a two-sibling household is filled."

Ormerod's two series of books for very young children also revolve around the home and family ties. The "Jan Ormerod Baby Book" series—highlighting a father and infant's affectionate relationship—includes *Reading, Sleeping, Messy Baby,* and *Dad's Back.* In *Reading* and *Sleeping* the baby attempts to become the center of the father's attention. Father cleans house in *Messy Baby,* while the child follows behind and undoes his handiwork. And in *Dad's Back,* the father's return from an errand gives the child an opportunity to play with his keys, gloves, and scarf. Robert Wool, writing in the *New York Times Book Review,* noted that Ormerod effective-

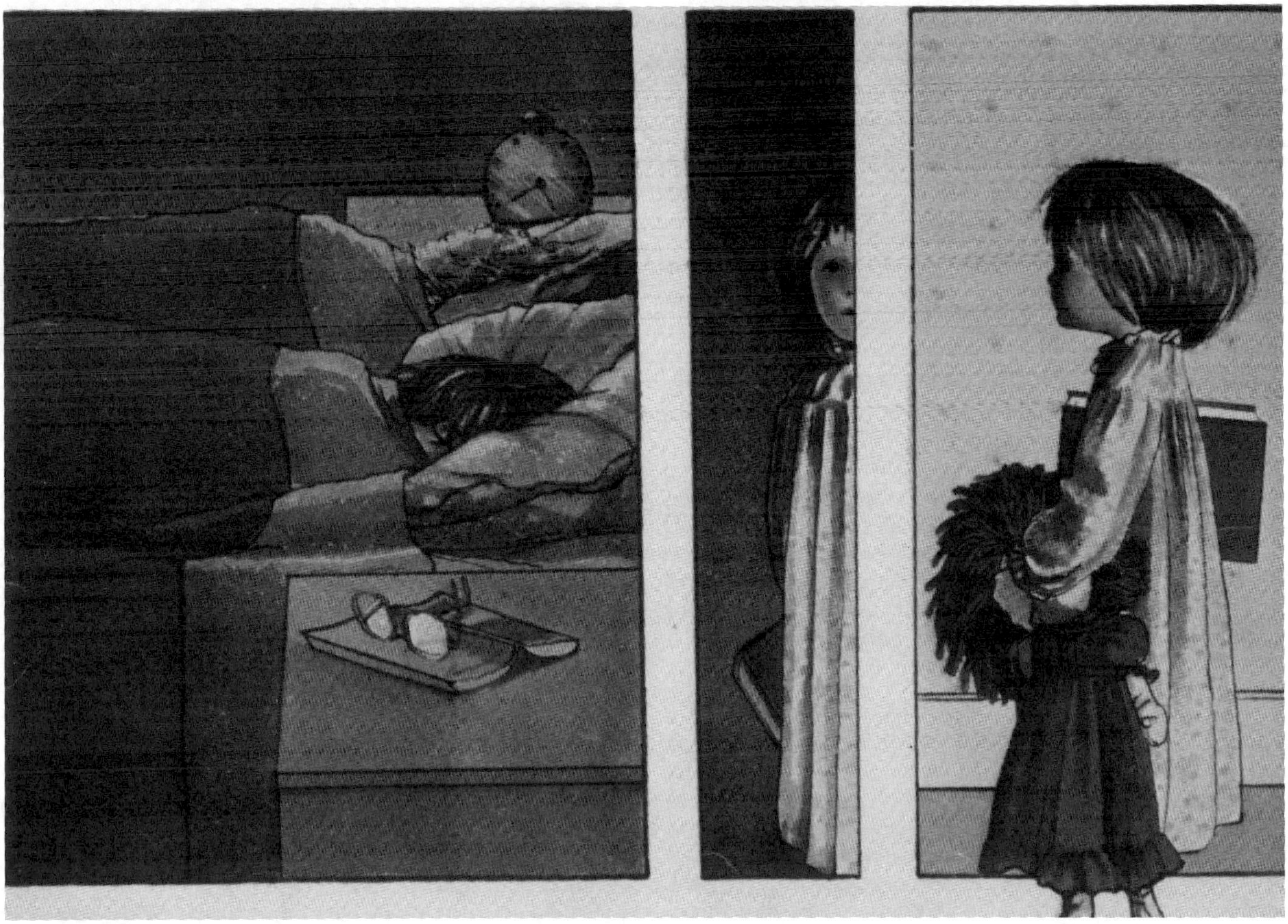

From *Sunshine,* written and illustrated by Jan Ormerod.

ly brought the father and baby's relationship to life "with a novelist's eye for detail and a painter's grasp of nuance." The reviewer added, "Ormerod's marvelous, soft, figurative drawings [make] you smile with recognition."

The 1987 "Jan Ormerod New Baby Book" series also focuses on a family relationship—this time between a pregnant mother and her infant—and includes *Bend and Stretch, Making Friends, Mom's Home,* and *This Little Nose.* In these books Mom exercises with baby underfoot, makes a doll for baby, and brings home a shopping bag full of items for the child to explore. Critics judged that this series reflects Ormerod's familiarity with and understanding of parents and infants. In a *Horn Book* review Karen Jameyson declared that in "Ormerod's hands the most ordinary chunks of everyday life are given vivid shape and substance."

In a departure from her typical home settings, Ormerod uses minimal text and bright illustration panels to describe a family outing in *When We Went to the Zoo.* The reader follows two children and their father as they visit creatures such as gibbons, pelicans, elephants, otters, toucans, and orangutans. Near the zoo's exit the family notices a pair of sparrows building a nest and decides that "in the end we liked that best, spying the sparrows and their nest." Observant readers will have noticed the sparrows earlier, as they are present in the illustrations throughout the family's tour. Critics commented that drawing attention to the sparrows in a zoo of exotic animals reflects Ormerod's ability bring charm to the commonplace.

Ormerod collaborated with David Lloyd in the retelling of the classic fairy tale *The Frog Prince,* which Ormerod illustrated using double-page spreads and decorative borders. In Ormerod's and Lloyd's version, a princess loses her ball in a pond and promises a frog her love if he finds it for her. Once the frog retrieves the ball, however, the princess takes it and runs home, hoping the frog will forget her promise. But the persistent frog follows her, and the princess is forced to keep her promise by letting the frog sit on her lap, eat with her, and sleep on her pillow. After sleeping on her pillow for three nights, the frog transforms into a prince and, "as in all the best deep, dark, and royal stories," the narrator states, "they lived happily ever after."

In addition to her own work, Ormerod has illustrated a number of books by children's authors, including *Hairs in the Palm of the Hand,* by Jan Mark, *Peter Pan,* by James M. Barrie, and *One Ballerina Two,* by Vivian French. According to Michael Patrick Hearn writing in the *New York Times Book Review,* Ormerod "is a keen observer of the intimate details of childhood . . . . she can make the mundane beautiful with her extraordinary figure studies . . . . she can take the simplest subject . . . and weave it into an engrossing picture book."

WORKS CITED:

Carter, Margaret, "Cover Artist—Jan Ormerod," *Books for Your Children,* autumn-winter, 1983, p. 7.

Dirda, Michael, "Books for Beach Bag and Knapsack," *Washington Post Book World,* June 8, 1986, p. 10.

Fisher, Margery, review of *Moonlight, Growing Point,* July, 1982, p. 3917.

Hearn, Michael Patrick, review of *The Frog Prince, New York Times Book Review,* August 19, 1990, p. 29.

Jameyson, Karen, review of *Bend and Stretch* and others, *Horn Book,* March/April, 1988, p. 193.

Landsberg, Michele, "Books to Encourage the Beginning Reader," *Reading for the Love of It: Best Books for Young Readers,* Prentice Hall, 1987, pp. 35-52.

McGinniss, Joe, "How to Survive a Sibling," *New York Times Book Review,* November, 11, 1984, p. 48.

Ormerod, Jan, *When We Went to the Zoo,* Lothrop, 1991.

Ormerod, Jan, and David Lloyd, *The Frog Prince,* Lothrop, 1990.

Wool, Robert, review of *Messy Baby, Reading, Dad's Back,* and *Sleeping, New York Times Book Review,* March 24, 1985, p. 35.

FOR MORE INFORMATION SEE:

BOOKS

Children's Literature Review, Volume 20, Gale, 1990, pp. 174-81.

PERIODICALS

Horn Book, September, 1990, p. 611; May, 1991, p. 319.

School Library Journal, September, 1989, p. 230.

* * *

OSBORNE, David
See SILVERBERG, Robert

* * *

OSBORNE, George
See SILVERBERG, Robert

* * *

OTTLEY, Reginald (Leslie) 1909-1985

PERSONAL: Born in 1909, in London, England; died in 1985 in Brisbane, Queensland, Australia. *Education:* Attended private school in England.

ADDRESSES: *Home*—Tamrookum, via Beaudesert, Queensland 4285, Australia.

CAREER: Writer. Worked as a seaman, cattle worker and horsebreaker in Australian Outback, and manager of a cattle station in Fiji, ca. 1925-39; trained race horses in Sydney, Australia, beginning 1945; cattle ranch manager in New Caledonia. *Military service:* Served in Australian Remount Corps, 1939-45.

MEMBER: Authors Guild Association.

AWARDS, HONORS: Notable book award, American Library Association, 1966, runner-up for Best Book of the Year Award, Australian Children's Book Council, 1966, Children's Spring Book Festival Award, *New York Herald Tribune,* 1966, and National Mass Media Award, Thomas Alva Edison Foundation, 1967, all for *Boy Alone;* notable book award, *School Library Journal,* 1968, for *Rain Comes to Yamboorah;* runner-up for Best Book of the Year Award, Australian Children's Book Council, 1970, for *The Bates Family;* Lewis Carroll Shelf Award, 1971, for *Boy Alone.*

WRITINGS:

Stampede, Laurie, 1961.
By the Sandhills of Yamboorah, Deutsch, 1965, published as *Boy Alone,* Harcourt, 1966.
The Roan Colt of Yamboorah, Deutsch, 1966, published as *The Roan Colt,* Harcourt, 1967.
Rain Comes to Yamboorah, Deutsch, 1967, Harcourt, 1968.
Giselle, Harcourt, 1968.
The Bates Family, Harcourt, 1969.
Brumbie Dust: A Selection of Stories, Harcourt, 1969.
Jim Grey of Moonbah, Harcourt, 1970.
No More Tomorrow, Harcourt, 1971.
The War on Williams Street, Collins, 1971, Thomas Nelson, 1973.
A Word about Horses, Collins, 1973.
Mum's Place, Collins, 1974.

Also author of radio plays, including *The Feather Shoes,* 1964.

SIDELIGHTS: The harsh Australian Outback serves as a setting for many of Reginald Ottley's stories and novels. Ottley, who for many years was considered one of Australia's leading authors for children and young adults, made his reputation on stark and realistic accounts of life in a land where every day brings a new struggle for survival. These daily rounds with cattle and wild horses, brush fires and floods, were presented by a man who had lived through them himself, a rugged adventurer with a storyteller's gift.

"I have heard men telling yarns in ships' foc's'les, and around campfires in the great Outback," Ottley told *Elementary English.* "I have listened to the old men in the Islands—in Fiji, New Caledonia and The Solomons—telling their tales of the past; of their own lore, and of a time when the white man first came to their islands; a time of great full-winged ships heaving at anchor in the bays, or rotting, gutted, on uncharted reefs." The author added: "Stories are part of man's very existence. They are as necessary to him as the food he eats."

Although he spent most of his life in Australia, Ottley was born and raised in England. He and his brothers were sent to a small Church of England school, where he earned the nickname "Dreamy Daniel." In *Fourth Book of Junior Authors and Illustrators,* Ottley remembered: "I had more than my fair share of fights because of my 'dreamy' ways. I was always imagining being lost on desert islands, or galloping horses across wild terrain."

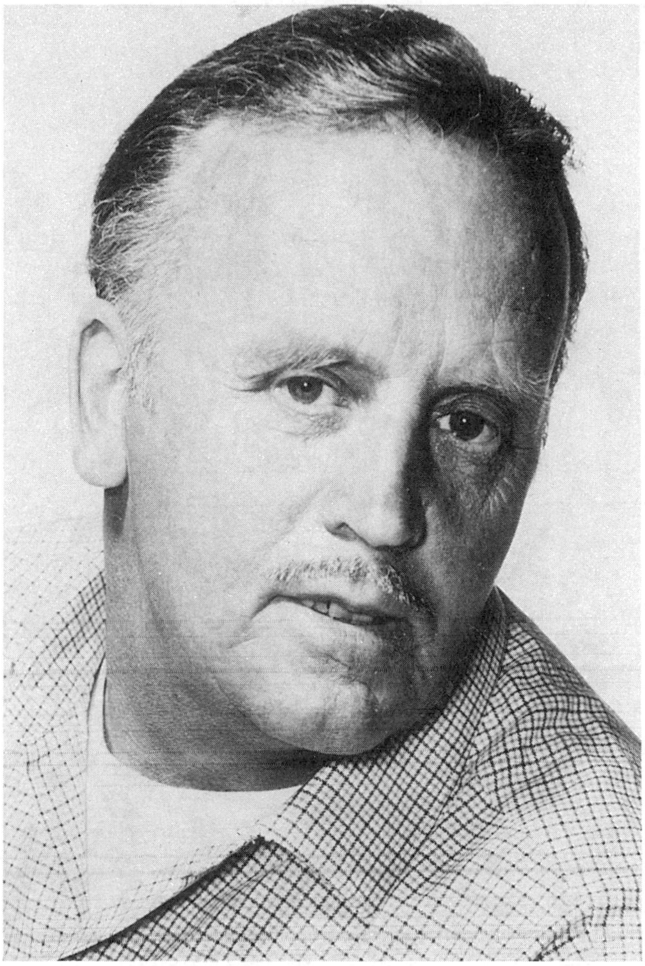

Reginald Ottley

At the tender age of fourteen, Ottley followed his dreams. He left school and ran away to sea. After a year of rough adventures on the world's oceans, he came ashore in Australia. He made his way to the Outback—that large portion of central Australia that is dominated by desert-like conditions—and took a job as a "wood-and-water joey" on a vast grazing ranch. Eventually he became an expert on the ways of the hostile Outback, making a living as a horsebreaker, cattle drover, and property manager.

During the Second World War, Ottley served Australia in the Remount Squadron, taking charge of breaking in new horses. "All told, some five thousand horses passed through my hands," he told the *Fourth Book of Junior Authors and Illustrators.* "The men were incredible characters, drawn from all parts of the Australian Bush." Ottley's post-war travels took him to Fiji and to New Caledonia, where he managed ranches. He also spent some time in Sydney, training racehorses.

All of these experiences began to find their way onto paper in the late 1950s and early 1960s. On a visit to London, Ottley submitted a script about life in the

From *The Roan Colt of Yamboorah,* by Reginald Ottley. Illustrated by David Parry.

Outback to the British Broadcasting Corporation. It was accepted enthusiastically, and he was encouraged to write more. Over a decade-long stretch from the mid-1960s to the mid-1970s, the author produced a number of children's books about Australia and its challenges to human survival. A *Times Literary Supplement* reviewer reported: "No outsider or observer, [Ottley] is writing, one feels, not just from the sort of personal experience a journalist might claim from a few weeks' visit to the Back Country but from a lifetime's involvement with [wild] horses, camels and cattle, and with the hard-drinking, hard riding drovers, horsebreakers and prospectors."

Ottley is best known for his Yamboorah trilogy, published in the United States as *Boy Alone, The Roan Colt,* and *Rain Comes to Yamboorah.* In all three books the hero is an unnamed boy who is coming to age on an isolated cattle ranch in the Outback. *Boy Alone* in particular has drawn praise for its well-drawn portrait of a sensitive child in a world of taciturn cattlemen, where even horses and dogs are bred purely for the work they can perform. "One comes to live fully in this boy's world, and the setting, with its strenuous round of activities, the ever-present dust and heat, ... is powerfully real," wrote Houston L. Maples in *The Washington Post.* Maples concluded that *Boy Alone* is "a book of unflagging vitality, authentic and sometimes grim, yet compassionate and unexpectedly comforting."

The boy's adventures are continued in *The Roan Colt* and *Rain Comes to Yamboorah.* In *The Roan Colt,* the boy saves the life of a horse that is lame and therefore unfit to work; in *Rain Comes to Yamboorah,* he saves the life of a crusty Outback worker named Kanga. *New York Times Book Review* contributor Michele Caraher noted that in these sequels, Ottley "demonstrates the alchemy a skilled writer can work upon a very commonplace theme."

With the exception of *Giselle* (1968) and *The War on Williams Street* (1971), the rest of Ottley's books also portray the tough but rewarding life of Outback ranching. In *The Bates Family,* for instance, a large family must pull together to save cattle and horses during drought *and* flood. Life's drudgery is only made bearable by the compassion members of the close-knit group show one another. A *Times Literary Supplement* reviewer found the work "a moving and convincing story of the interdependence of members of a family," adding: "Children who grumble about making their beds or clearing the table may be shaken into an awareness of what helping can mean."

One of Ottley's favorite subjects was horses, especially the "brumbies," or wild horses of the Outback. Both *Brumbie Dust: A Selection of Stories* (1969) and *A Word about Horses* (1973) were drawn from the author's memories as a wandering stockman and horse trainer. "The desert, the heat, the work, the men and the horses are all fused into a solid Australian essence, which is powerful and without false glamour," wrote a *Times Literary Supplement* correspondent. "... We can envy Mr. Ottley the organic unself-conscious culture of which he is a part and which he portrays so tellingly for children."

Ottley died in Queensland, Australia in 1985. Before his death he told *Elementary English:* "If a writer is honest, he does not write essentially for others. He cannot. He must follow the course of his characters. They may be in his memories, or centered around the life he is living, or has lived, or in a fragment of thought dissected elsewhere. They come vividly, bringing a story which has to be told .... We are all a part of our parents, but a writer is also part of his characters. He has to be. It could be that they create him—not he create them."

WORKS CITED:

"Away from It All," *Times Literary Supplement,* December 4, 1969, p. 1394.

Caraher, Michele, review of *The Roan Colt of Yamboorah, New York Times Book Review,* May 7, 1967, p. 39.

"Faraway Places," *Times Literary Supplement,* June 26, 1969, pp. 692-93.
Maples, Houston L., "Boy Alone," *Washington Post,* May 8, 1966, p. 2.
"Natural Adventures," *Times Literary Supplement,* April 6, 1973, p. 378.
Ottley, Reginald, "On Storytelling," *Elementary English,* February, 1972, pp. 279-80.
Ottley, essay in *Fourth Book of Junior Authors and Illustrators,* H. W. Wilson, 1978, pp. 279-80.

FOR MORE INFORMATION SEE:

BOOKS

Children's Literature Review, Volume 16, Gale, 1989.
Contemporary Authors, Volumes 93-96, Gale, 1980.
Something about the Author, Volume 26, Gale, 1982.

PERIODICALS

Book Week, May 8, 1966.
Growing Point, April, 1966.
Junior Bookshelf, August, 1967; August, 1974.

* * *

OXENBURY, Helen 1938-

PERSONAL: Born June 2, 1938, in Suffolk, England; daughter of Thomas Bernard (an architect) and Muriel (Taylor) Oxenbury; married John Burningham (an author and illustrator), August 15, 1964; children: Lucy, William Benedict, Emily. *Education:* Studied at Ipswich School of Art and Central School of Arts and Crafts, London.

ADDRESSES: Home—5 East Heath Rd., Hampstead, London NW3 1BN, England. *Agent*—Elaine Greene, Ltd., 37 Goldhawk Rd., London W12 8QQ, England.

CAREER: Writer and illustrator of children's books. Stage designer in Colchester, England, 1960, and Tel-Aviv, Israel, 1961; television designer in London, England, 1963.

AWARDS, HONORS: Kate Greenaway Medal, British Library Association for Illustration, 1969, for *The Dragon of an Ordinary Family* and *The Quangle Wangle's Hat;* runner-up, Kurt Maschler Award, 1985, for *The Helen Oxenbury Nursery Story Book.*

WRITINGS:

SELF-ILLUSTRATED

Numbers of Things, F. Watts, 1968, published as *Helen Oxenbury's Numbers of Things,* Delacorte, 1983.
Helen Oxenbury's ABC of Things, Heinemann, 1971, published as *ABC of Things,* F. Watts, 1972.
Pig Tale, Morrow, 1973.
The Queen and Rosie Randall (from an idea by Jill Buttfield-Campbell), Morrow, 1979.
729 Curious Creatures, Harper, 1980, published as *Curious Creatures,* Harper-Collins, 1985.
729 Merry Mix-ups, Harper, 1980, published as *Merry Mix-ups,* Harper-Collins, 1985 (published in England as *729 Animal Allsorts,* Methuen, 1980).
729 Puzzle People, Harper, 1980, published as *Puzzle People,* Harper-Collins, 1985.
Bill and Stanley, Benn, 1981.
Dressing, Simon & Schuster, 1981.
Family, Simon & Schuster, 1981.
Friends, Simon & Schuster, 1981.
Playing, Simon & Schuster, 1981.
Working, Simon & Schuster, 1981.
Tiny Tim: Verses for Children, selected by Jill Bennett, Delacorte, 1982.
Bedtime, Walker, 1982.
Mother's Helper, Dial Books for Young Readers, 1982.
Shopping Trip, Dial Books for Young Readers, 1982.
Good Night, Good Morning, Dial Books for Young Readers, 1982.
Beach Day, Dial Books for Young Readers, 1982.
The Birthday Party, Dial Books for Young Readers, 1983.
The Car Trip, Dial Books for Young Readers, 1983 (published in England as *The Drive,* Walker Books, 1983).
The Checkup, Dial Books for Young Readers, 1983 (published in England as *The First Check-Up,* Walker, 1983).
The Dancing Class, Dial Books for Young Readers, 1983.
Eating Out, Dial Books for Young Readers, 1983.
First Day of School, Dial Books for Young Readers, 1983 (published in England as *Playschool,* Walker Books, 1983).

Helen Oxenbury

Grandma and Grandpa, Dial Books for Young Readers, 1984 (published in England as *Gran and Granpa,* Walker, 1984).
The Important Visitor, Dial Books for Young Readers, 1984 (published in England as *The Visitor,* Walker, 1984).
Our Dog, Dial Books for Young Readers, 1984.
(Reteller) *The Helen Oxenbury Nursery Story Book,* Random House, 1985.
I Can, Random House, 1986.
I Hear, Random House, 1986.
I See, Random House, 1986.
I Touch, Random House, 1986.
Baby's First Book and Doll, Simon & Schuster, 1986.
All Fall Down, Aladdin Books, 1987.
Say Goodnight, Aladdin Books, 1987.
Tickle, Tickle, Aladdin Books, 1987.
Clap Hands, Aladdin Books, 1987.
Monkey See, Monkey Do, Dial Books for Young Readers, 1991.

"TOM AND PIPPO" SERIES; SELF-ILLUSTRATED

Tom and Pippo Go for a Walk, Aladdin Books, 1988.
Tom and Pippo Make a Mess, Aladdin Books, 1988.
Tom and Pippo Read a Story, Aladdin Books, 1988.
Tom and Pippo and the Washing Machine, Aladdin Books, 1988.
Tom and Pippo Go Shopping, Aladdin Books, 1989.
Tom and Pippo See the Moon, Aladdin Books, 1989.
Tom and Pippo's Day, Aladdin Books, 1989.
Tom and Pippo in the Garden, Aladdin Books, 1989.
Tom and Pippo in the Snow, Aladdin Books, 1989.
Tom and Pippo Make a Friend, Aladdin Books, 1989.
Pippo Gets Lost, Aladdin Books, 1989.
Tom and Pippo and the Dog, Aladdin Books, 1989.

ILLUSTRATOR

Alexei Tolstoy, *The Great Big Enormous Turnip,* translated by E. Scimanskaya, F. Watts, 1968.
Edward Lear, *The Quangle-Wangle's Hat,* Heinemann, 1969, F. Watts, 1970.
Manghanita Kempadoo, *Letters of Thanks,* Simon & Schuster, 1969.
Margaret Mahy, *The Dragon of an Ordinary Family,* F. Watts, 1969.
Lewis Carroll, *The Hunting of the Snark,* F. Watts, 1970.
Ivor Cutler, *Meal One,* F. Watts, 1971.
Brian Anderson, compiler, *Cakes and Custard,* Heinemann, 1974, Morrow, 1975, revised abridged version with new illustrations published as *The Helen Oxenbury Nursery Rhyme Book,* Morrow, 1987.
Cutler, *Balooky Klujypop,* Heinemann, 1975.
Cutler, *Elephant Girl,* Morrow, 1976.
Cutler, *The Animal House,* Heinemann, 1976, Morrow, 1977.
Fay Maschler, *A Child's Book of Manners,* J. Cape, 1978, Atheneum, 1979.
Michael Rosen, *We're Going on a Bear Hunt,* Macmillan, 1989.

SIDELIGHTS: "Helen Oxenbury is the book world's foremost authority on the antics (and anatomy) of small people," Tim Wynne-Jones of the Toronto *Globe and Mail* states. Oxenbury was one of the first writers to design "board books," the small, durable, thick-paged creations intended especially for toddlers. In stories such as *Friends, The Car Trip,* and those of the "Tom and Pippo" series, Oxenbury shows babies, toddlers, and preschool-age children discovering new things and learning about life. Her uncomplicated and humorous illustrations have as much to tell her "readers" as her words do. As a result, "there is not a wrinkle of pudgy flesh nor bulge of diaper she has not lovingly portrayed in her bright, watercolor survey of early childhood," Wynne-Jones adds.

Oxenbury didn't plan on becoming an illustrator when she was young. Instead, she found a talent for designing and painting scenery for plays. She began working in local theaters as a teenager, and chose to attend a college where she could study set design. At school she met her future husband, John Burningham, who was interested in illustration and graphic design. She later followed him to Israel, where she worked as a scenery designer. After the couple returned to England, Burningham published his first book, the award-winning children's story *Borka,* and Oxenbury continued working in the theater. Shortly after the couple married in 1965, they had their first two children. Oxenbury left her career as a designer to care for them. "In those days it was jolly difficult to do two things, and we didn't have money for nannies," Oxenbury explained to Michele Field of *Publishers Weekly.* "I wanted something to do at home, and having watched John do children's books, I thought that was possible."

Two of Oxenbury's first projects were illustrations for books by Lewis Carroll, the author of *Alice in Wonderland,* and Edward Lear, known for his fanciful, colorful poems. In choosing to illustrate these works, Oxenbury found the books' humor most appealing. As she revealed in a *Junior Bookshelf* article, it was "the marvellous mixture of weird people in dreamlike situations surprising one by doing and saying quite ordinary and down-to-earth things one minute, and absurd, outrageous things the next" that made up her mind to take the jobs. She captured this contradictory feeling in Edward Lear's *The Quangle Wangle's Hat* with pictures of strange creatures and the magical hat of many ribbons, loops, and bows. As Crispin Fisher notes in *Children and Literature,* "Her landscape is wide and magical, neither inviting nor repelling, but inexplicable—surely right for a Lear setting."

Oxenbury's first solo project was *Numbers of Things,* a picture book which uses familiar objects and animals to introduce young children to counting. Oxenbury covers single numbers from one to ten, then twenty through fifty by tens. The amusing pictures, "with their twenty balloons and fifty ladybirds, will help the child to comprehend the difference in quantity between these numbers," a *Junior Bookshelf* reviewer says. "But a fiddle-dee-dee on its instructional aspect!" a *Publishers Weekly* writes advises. "A hurrah instead for the fun of it all!" With its humorous yet simple approach and "shape, originality and use of colour," Jean Russell writes in *Books for Your Children, Numbers of Things* "immediately established [Oxenbury] as a major children's book artist."

Just like *Numbers of Things,* Oxenbury's follow-up *ABC of Things* has "pictures that are imaginative and humorous as well as handsome," creating "a far better than average ABC book," Zena Sutherland says in the *Bulletin of the Center for Children's Books.* Each letter is joined with several pictures that match it, and can serve to spur the imagination. "The most incongruous associations are made in a perfectly matter-of-fact way," writes a *Times Literary Supplement* reviewer, "setting the mind off in pursuit of the stories that must lie behind them."

Oxenbury began developing sturdy books for toddlers when her youngest child, Emily, was sick. "We were up half the night with her," the author told Field in *Publishers Weekly,* "and we had to think of things to show her to keep her mind off [her illness]." To make a book more appealing to such a young "reader," Oxenbury simplified her drawing style and focused on stories of babies and toddlers. She modified her layout so that a page with words would be paired with a larger, wordless, illustration. Finally, the books were to be made in smaller, square shapes that would be easier for little hands to manage. And the book's thicker pages would stand up to the chewing and abuse that any toddler's toy must survive.

Oxenbury's first series of board books, including *Dressing, Family, Friends, Playing,* and *Working,* are "perfectly in tune with the interests of the teething population, and at the same time executed with wit and the artistic awareness that at this age less is more," Betsy Hearne writes in *Booklist.* "The pictures themselves are simple," Robert Wilson similarly notes in *Washington Post Book World,* ". . . yet everywhere in the drawings there is subtle humor," as well as "a keenness of observation on the artist's part, a familiarity with the ways of the baby." And with their "masterful" portrayals of young children, especially the "delightfully lump-faced baby," Oxenbury's books are "certainly the series most likely to appeal to adults," Lucy Micklethwait concludes in the *Times Literary Supplement.*

Other collections have followed the baby as it grows into new abilities and activities. One series shows a toddler going to the beach, going shopping with mother, and helping out at home. The books are "fun, but more than that," Sutherland says in *Bulletin of the Center for Children's Books;* they are also "geared to the toddler's interests and experiences." Hearne of *Booklist* faults the series because it "sometimes seems to look *at* the child from an adult standpoint rather than look at the world from a child's view." But overall, the critic admits, "youngsters will enjoy the familiar details Oxenbury depicts so humorously without a word."

Later series show children doing many things for the first time, such as going to a birthday party, visiting the doctor, going to school, and eating in a restaurant. Each

From *The Dancing Class,* written and illustrated by Helen Oxenbury.

episode usually involves some sort of mishap; in *The Dancing Class* a little girl trips and causes a pileup of students. "Comedy is always central to Oxenbury's vignettes," as Denise M. Wilms observes in *Booklist,* and both kids and adults are targets in "these affectionate mirror views of their own foibles." In addition, Oxenbury "not only knows how children move but also how they think," Mary M. Burns of *Horn Book* says, for her easy writing style resembles "the matter-of-fact reportorial style used by young children." And as always, her "clever and colorful" illustrations contribute to "the subtle humor" of the story, Amanda J. Williams notes in *School Library Journal* review of *Our Dog.*

Although she is writing and drawing for a very young audience, Oxenbury tries not to underestimate their ability to understand things. "I believe children to be very canny people who immediately sense if adults talk, write, or illustrate down to them, hence the unpopularity of self-conscious, child-like drawings that appear in some children's books," the author wrote in *Junior Bookshelf.* "The illustrator is misguidedly thinking the child will be able to identify more easily with drawings similar to his own, while probably he is disgusted that adults cannot do better." Oxenbury's own drawings are uncluttered rather than simple, and include many humorous details that adults, as well as children, can enjoy.

In *The Helen Oxenbury Nursery Story Book,* for instance, "her drawings really do add another dimension to each tale, and answer some of the questions that spring to a child's mind," Marcus Crouch states in *Junior Bookshelf.* In this collection the author retells, with her own illustrations, favorite stories such as "The Three Pigs," "Little Red Riding Hood," and eight others. "A collection of simple folk tales may not be unique," Ethel L. Heins states in *Horn Book,* "but an extraordinarily attractive one for early independent reading surely is." A major part of the book's charm lies in its pictures, "which give [the stories] a special, strongly personal and essentially youthful feeling," Margery Fisher comments in *Growing Point.* "At every turning of the page an illustration delights the eye," Heins adds. Throughout the book "the artwork exudes vigor, movement," as well as a lively humor "that manages to be both naive and sly."

In the late 1980s Oxenbury introduced the recurring characters of Tom and Pippo in a series of picturebooks. Tom is a young boy with a constant companion in his stuffed monkey, Pippo. Oxenbury's pictures again display her simple yet revealing style; even Pippo's face is "worth watching, whether he is frowning as he is stuffed into the washing machine or reaching down longingly from the clothesline towards Tom's outstretched arm," a *Publishers Weekly* critic writes. The volumes also exhibit the broadly appealing humor that is the author's trademark. "Oxenbury understands her audience; young people as well as adults will find pleasure in repeated readings of these unassuming gems, and no one will be able to resist the facial expressions and postures of the long-suffering Pippo," Ellen Fader says in *Horn Book.*

Although the field of board books is now very popular, "old reliable Helen Oxenbury remains a standard against which to judge new entries," Sandra Martin writes in the Toronto *Globe and Mail.* A reviewer for the *Bulletin of the Center for Children's Books* agrees, stating that Oxenbury is "still one of the best in terms of maintaining simple concepts, lively art, and action generated from object." "All Helen's pictures have a vibrant wit and delicacy which is so vital in stimulating the imaginative child," Russell explains in *Books for Your Children.* "In Oxenbury's case, familiarity breeds not contempt, but admiration," Carolyn Phelan remarks in *Booklist.* "Using everyday concepts, simple drawings, and minimal color, she gives a child's view of ordinary things, creating books that are fresh, original, and appealing to both parents and children."

Despite her success with board books, Oxenbury has been contemplating a move to producing books for a different age group. Not only does she want to gear her work toward children the age of her youngest, but she wants to test her accomplishments in another area. "I don't want to be pigeonholed," the illustrator told Field in *Publishers Weekly.* "It's that which I want to avoid more than anything else." Her main desire, she continued, is to fill the need for quality children's books that stand out among the crowd. "There are millions and millions of mediocre children's books. I hope we're not part of that."

WORKS CITED:

Burns, Mary M., review of *Our Dog, Horn Book,* November/December, 1984, p. 752.

Crouch, Marcus, review of *The Helen Oxenbury Nursery Story Book, Junior Bookshelf,* October, 1985, p. 220.

Fader, Ellen, review of *Tom and Pippo Go Shopping* and others, *Horn Book,* May-June, 1989, pp. 361-362.

Field, Michele, "PW Interviews: John Burningham and Helen Oxenbury," *Publishers Weekly,* July 24, 1987, pp. 168-169.

Fisher, Crispin, "A Load of Old Nonsense, Edward Lear Resurrected by Four Publishers," *Children and Literature: Views and Reviews,* edited by Virginia Haviland, Scott, Foresman, 1973, pp. 198-201.

Fisher, Margery, review of *The Helen Oxenbury Nursery Story Book, Growing Point,* January, 1986, p. 4548.

"Good Enough to Keep," *Times Literary Supplement,* December 3, 1971, pp. 1514-1515.

Hearne, Betsy, review of *Dressing* and others, *Booklist,* May 1, 1981, pp. 1198.

Hearne, Betsy, review of *Beach Day* and others, *Booklist,* May 15, 1983, p. 1258.

Heins, Ethel L., review of *The Helen Oxenbury Nursery Story Book, Horn Book,* January/February, 1986, p. 65.

Review of *I Can* and others, *Bulletin of the Center for Children's Books,* June, 1986, p. 193.

Martin, Sandra, "By the Boards: Words to Chew On," *Globe and Mail* (Toronto), March 16, 1985.

Micklethwait, Lucy, "The Indestructible Word," *Times Literary Supplement,* July 24, 1981, p. 840.

Review of *Numbers of Things, Junior Bookshelf,* April, 1968, p. 97.

Review of *Numbers of Things, Publishers Weekly,* April 8, 1968, p. 51.

Oxenbury, Helen, "Drawing for Children," *Junior Bookshelf,* August, 1970, pp. 199-201.

Phelan, Carolyn, review of *I Can* and others, *Booklist,* June 1, 1986, pp. 1462-1463.

Russell, Jean, "Cover Artist: Helen Oxenbury," *Books for Your Children,* autumn, 1978, p. 3.

Sutherland, Zena, review of *Helen Oxenbury's ABC of Things, Bulletin of the Center for Children's Books,* February, 1973, p. 96.

Sutherland, Zena, review of *Shopping Trip, Bulletin of the Center for Children's Books,* April, 1982, pp. 155-156.

Review of *Tom and Pippo Go for a Walk* and others, *Publishers Weekly,* July 29, 1988, p. 230.

Williams, Amanda J., review of *Our Dog, School Library Journal,* February, 1985, p. 68.

Wilms, Denise M., review of *The Car Trip, The Check-up,* and *First Day of School, Booklist,* September, 1, 1983, p. 89.

Wilson, Robert, "Please Don't Eat the Pages," *Washington Post Book World,* March 8, 1981, pp. 10-11.

Wynne-Jones, Tim, "A Start to the Page-Turning Experience," *Globe and Mail* (Toronto), April 30, 1988.

FOR MORE INFORMATION SEE:

BOOKS

Children's Literature Review, Volume 22, Gale, 1991.

Martin, Douglas, *The Telling Line: Essays on Fifteen Contemporary Book Illustrators,* Julia McRae Books, 1989.

Moss, Elaine, *Children's Books of the Year: 1974,* Hamish Hamilton, 1975.

Sutherland, Zena, and May Hill Arbuthnot, *Children and Books,* 7th edition, Scott, Foresman, 1986.

PERIODICALS

Children's Book Review, April, 1972; December, 1973.

Horn Book, February, 1976.

Kirkus Reviews, January 1, 1989.

New York Times Book Review, November 16, 1975.

School Library Journal, October, 1981; January, 1984; December, 1985; August, 1987; January, 1990.

Times Literary Supplement, November 23, 1973; November 20, 1981.

Washington Post Book World, March 14, 1982.

P

PACKER, Vin
See MEAKER, Marijane (Agnes)

*   *   *

PAD, Peter
See STRATEMEYER, Edward L.

*   *   *

PAGE, Eleanor
See COERR, Eleanor (Beatrice)

*   *   *

PALLADINI, David (Mario) 1946-

PERSONAL: Born April 1, 1946, in Roteglia, Italy; immigrated to United States, 1948; son of Aldo (a landscaper) and Ada Palladini. *Education:* Attended Pratt Institute, 1964-68.

ADDRESSES: Home—Sagaponack, NY

CAREER: Free-lance illustrator. Photographer, Olympic Games, Mexico City, 1968; illustrator, Push Pin Studios, New York City; teacher, School of Visual Arts; lecturer on painting and illustration. *Exhibitions:* American Institute of Graphic Arts, 1969-80; Society of Illustrators, 1969-83; Saks Fifth Avenue Gallery, 1974. Palladini's works are in the collections of the Metropolitan Museum of Art, New York City, and the Museum of Warsaw, Poland.

MEMBER: Society of Illustrators.

AWARDS, HONORS: The Girl Who Cried Flowers and Other Tales was selected for the American Institute of Graphic Arts Children's Books Show, 1973-74, was

From *If You Call My Name,* by Crescent Dragonwagon. Illustrated by David Palladini.

named one of the best illustrated children's books of the year by the *New York Times,* won a Golden Kite Award, 1974, and was a National Book Award nomination, children's book category, 1975; *The Moon Ribbon and Other Tales* was named a Golden Kite honor book, 1976.

ILLUSTRATOR:

JUVENILES

Constance B. Hieatt, *The Sword and the Grail,* Crowell, 1972.
Ruth Goode, *People of the Ice Age,* Crowell, 1973.
Franklyn M. Branley, *The End of the World,* Crowell, 1974.
Jane H. Yolen, *The Girl Who Cried Flowers and Other Tales* (ALA Notable Book) Crowell, 1974.
J. H. Yolen, *The Moon Ribbon and Other Tales,* Crowell, 1976.
J. H. Yolen, *The Hundredth Dove and Other Tales,* Crowell, 1977, reprinted, Schocken, 1987.
Barbara Wersba, *Twenty-Six Starlings Will Fly through Your Mind,* Harper, 1980.
Crescent Dragonwagon, *If You Call My Name,* Harper, 1981.
Stephen King, *The Eyes of the Dragon,* Viking, 1987.
Arthur Yorinks, *Rosalie,* Little, Brown, 1988.
Florence Karpin, *The Prince in the Golden Tower,* Viking, 1989.

Has also done numerous book jackets, including Jane Yolen's *Cards of Grief,* Ace, 1984.

SIDELIGHTS: David Palladini's lush and whimsical illustrations adorn the pages of storybooks by Jane Yolen, Barbara Wersba, and Stephen King, among others. An immigrant who came to America with his family when he was only two, Palladini has received numerous awards for his work in children's books. Some of his art works hang in New York's Metropolitan Museum and at the Museum of Warsaw in Poland. "I think most people who try to become creative writers or actors or artists do so by overcoming the discouraging remarks of other people—all the 'shouldn'ts' and the 'can'ts,'" the artist told *Something about the Author* (*SATA*). "It is characteristic of all the artists I know to continue to create despite the pain."

Palladini was born in 1946 in Roteglia, Italy. He came to America with his parents in 1948. The family settled in Highland Park, a suburb of Chicago. There Palladini attended public schools and drew pictures without any idea of a career as an artist. "Drawing was for me, as it was for many artists I've met since, an escape," Palladini told *SATA.* "I was always drawing or reading and was well known in Highland Park as the kid who had read all the books in the children's library by the time he was twelve. After that, I moved to the adult library."

The books that Palladini found most interesting were those with illustrations and drawings, especially the works of Howard Pyle. Pyle's pictures of Arthurian legends and the medieval period were particularly inspirational to Palladini. "The first drawings that I did as an illustrator were all based on that era, and I still work with the medieval period," Palladini said in *SATA.*

Palladini notes that in high school he exhausted almost every elective course before he entered an art class in his junior year. His art teacher was immediately impressed with his talent and encouraged him to develop it. That very same year, Palladini was offered a four-year scholarship to the Pratt Institute to study art.

At Pratt, Palladini majored in film and photography rather than drawing or painting. In fact, he left college in the middle of his senior year to photograph the 1968 Olympics in Mexico City. "I was a good photographer and when I returned to New York, I had every intention of setting up a studio and becoming a professional," he remembered in *SATA.* "I soon discovered the reality of that world: you need a lot of money to set up and equip a studio. I couldn't afford it so I went to Push Pin Studios, 'the place' for commercial artists in New York. After I showed them my portfolio of drawings from art school they hired me on the spot."

Palladini has never restricted himself merely to children's books. He has also done book jackets for children and adults, movie posters, and paintings. He teaches at the School of Visual Arts and lectures elsewhere on painting and illustration. Still, he finds his work as an illustrator particularly satisfying, because it affords him a great deal of creative freedom. The finished product, he told *SATA,* "looks exactly the way I wanted it to look." He added: "Creating illustrations which are both convincing and fascinating to children is a challenge to me, and that's what I like about it."

Whether done in full color or in black-and-white with a charcoal pencil, Palladini's illustrations convey a fairy-tale world—in all its beauty and its menace—with a touch of realism. "I don't have hobbies; everything I do is related to staying alive and trying to become a better artist ...," Palladini told *SATA.* "One of the things I like about art is that you can sit in a corner with a paper, a pencil and nothing else and create a new reality."

Palladini's advice to young people who are hoping to become artists is to "color outside the lines. The best advice is that you have to believe way beyond believing. You have to believe beyond what your parents try to discourage you from, beyond the fear that everybody's going to laugh. If you believe in your work, you will survive all the obstacles."

WORKS CITED:

Palladini, David, essay in *Something about the Author,* Volume 40, Gale, 1985.

* * *

PALMER, Don
See BENSON, Mildred (Augustine Wirt)

PARISH, Margaret Cecile 1927-1988 (Peggy Parish)

PERSONAL: Born in 1927, in Manning, SC; died November 19, 1988, of a ruptured aneurysm, in Manning, SC; daughter of Herman and Cecil (Rogers) Parish. *Education:* University of South Carolina, B.A., 1948; graduate study at George Peabody College for Teachers (now of Vanderbilt University), 1950.

CAREER: Writer. Also worked as a teacher in Oklahoma, Kentucky, and Texas; worked as an instructor in creative dancing, 1948-52, and in advertising; Dalton School, New York City, elementary school teacher for fifteen years. Children's book reviewer, "Carolina Today" television show, National Broadcasting Corp. (NBC) affiliate, Columbia, SC.

MEMBER: Authors Guild, Authors League of America, Delta Kappa Gamma.

AWARDS, HONORS: School Library Journal named *Dinosaur Time* one of the best books of the year, 1974; Garden State Children's Book Award, State of New Jersey, 1977, for *Dinosaur Time,* 1980, for *Teach Us, Amelia Bedelia,* and 1988; Palmetto State Award, 1977; Milner Award, City of Atlanta, 1984; Keystone State Children's Book Award, State of Pennsylvania, 1986.

Peggy Parish

WRITINGS:

UNDER NAME PEGGY PARISH

My Golden Book of Manners, illustrated by Richard Scarry, Golden Press, 1962.

Good Hunting, Little Indian, illustrated by Leonard Weisgard, Young Scott Books, 1962, revised edition published as *Good Hunting, Blue Sky,* illustrated by James Watts, Harper, 1988.

Let's Be Indians, illustrated by Arnold Lobel, Harper, 1962.

Willy Is My Brother, illustrated by Shirley Hughes, W. R. Scott, 1963.

Amelia Bedelia, illustrated by Fritz Siebel, Harper, 1963.

Thank You, Amelia Bedelia, illustrated by Siebel, Harper, 1964.

The Story of Grains: Wheat, Corn, and Rice, Grosset, 1965.

Amelia Bedelia and the Surprise Shower, illustrated by Siebel, Harper, 1966.

Key to the Treasure, illustrated by Paul Frame, Macmillan, 1966.

Let's Be Early Settlers with Daniel Boone, illustrated by Lobel, Harper, 1967.

Clues in the Woods, illustrated by Frame, Macmillan, 1968.

Little Indian, illustrated by John E. Johnson, Simon & Schuster, 1968.

A Beastly Circus, illustrated by Peter Parnall, Simon & Schuster, 1969.

Jumper Goes to School, illustrated by Cyndy Szekeres, Simon & Schuster, 1969.

Granny and the Indians, illustrated by Brinton Turkle, Macmillan, 1969.

Ootah's Lucky Day, illustrated by Mamoru Funai, Harper, 1970.

Granny and the Desperadoes, illustrated by Steven Kellogg, Macmillan, 1970.

Costumes to Make, illustrated by Lynn Sweat, Macmillan, 1970.

Snapping Turtle's All Wrong Day, illustrated by Johnson, Simon & Schuster, 1970.

Sheet Magic: Games, Toys, and Gifts from Old Sheets, illustrated by Sweat, Macmillan, 1971.

Haunted House, illustrated by Frame, Macmillan, 1971.

Come Back, Amelia Bedelia, illustrated by Wallace Tripp, Harper, 1971.

Granny, the Baby, and the Big Gray Thing, illustrated by Sweat, Macmillan, 1972.

Play Ball, Amelia Bedelia, illustrated by Tripp, Harper, 1972.

Too Many Rabbits, illustrated by Leonard Kessler, Macmillan, 1974.

Dinosaur Time, illustrated by Lobel, Harper, 1974.

December Decorations: A Holiday How-To Book, illustrated by Barbara Wolff, Macmillan, 1975.

Pirate Island Adventure, illustrated by Frame, Macmillan, 1975.

Good Work, Amelia Bedelia, illustrated by Sweat, Morrow, 1976.

Let's Celebrate: Holiday Decorations You Can Make, illustrated by Sweat, Morrow, 1976.

Teach Us, Amelia Bedelia, illustrated by Sweat, Morrow, 1977.

Hermit Dan, illustrated by Frame, Macmillan, 1977.

Mind Your Manners!, illustrated by Hafner, Greenwillow, 1978.

Zed and the Monsters, illustrated by Galdone, Doubleday, 1979.

Beginning Mobiles, illustrated by Sweat, Macmillan, 1979.

Amelia Bedelia Helps Out, illustrated by Sweat, Greenwillow, 1979.

Be Ready at Eight, illustrated by Kessler, Macmillan, 1979.

I Can, Can You?, four volumes, illustrated by Hafner, Greenwillow, 1980 (published in England as *See and Do Book Bag,* four volumes, MacRae, 1980).

Amelia Bedelia and the Baby, illustrated by Sweat, Greenwillow, 1981.

No More Monsters for Me!, illustrated by Simont, Harper, 1981.

Mr. Adams's Mistake, illustrated by Owens, Macmillan, 1982.

The Cats' Burglar, illustrated by Sweat, Greenwillow, 1983.

Hush, Hush, It's Sleepytime, illustrated by Leonid Pinchevsky, Western Publishing, 1984.

Amelia Bedelia Goes Camping, illustrated by Sweat, Greenwillow, 1985.

Merry Christmas, Amelia Bedelia, illustrated by Sweat, Greenwillow, 1986.

The Ghosts of Cougar Island, Dell, 1986.

Amelia Bedelia's Family Album, illustrated by Sweat, Greenwillow, 1988.

Scruffy, illustrated by Kelly Oechsli, Harper, 1988.

OTHER

Contributor of book reviews to newspapers. A collection of Parish's manuscripts is housed at the Kerlan Collection, University of Minnesota, Minneapolis.

ADAPTATIONS: Amelia Bedelia, Thank You, Amelia Bedelia, Come Back, Amelia Bedelia, and *Play Ball, Amelia Bedelia* have been adapted as filmstrips.

SIDELIGHTS: "Children have always been my life," Peggy Parish once commented, "so writing stories for children came naturally." The author of over 40 books for children, Parish wrote mysteries, craft books, and the popular "Amelia Bedelia" series. Parish's books sold over 7 million copies.

Amelia Bedelia, a maid who takes everything she is told literally, appeared in eleven books for young readers. Amelia's literal mindedness comes from reading cookbooks, where you must do exactly what it says. When Amelia is told to make a sponge cake, she uses real sponges in the recipe. When asked to stuff the Christmas stockings, she fills them with turkey dressing. When requested to dust the furniture, Amelia sprinkles dust on everything. ("At my house we undust the furniture," she says. "But each to his own way.")

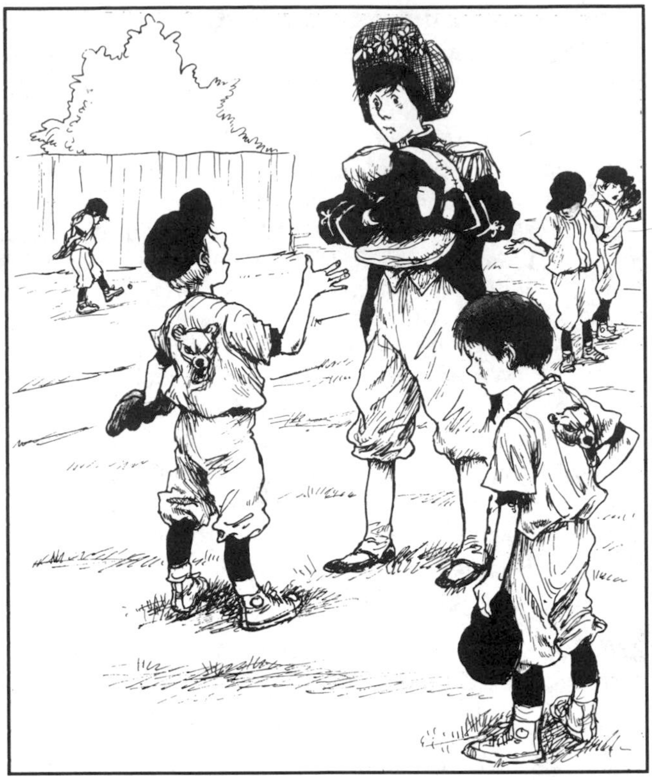

From *Play Ball, Amelia Bedelia,* by Peggy Parish. Illustrated by Wallace Tripp.

According to Nancy Palmer in *School Library Journal,* "Amelia Bedelia is a model of well-intentioned mishap.... [She] has become such an institution and a welcome splash of comedy on the easy-reading shelf that one forgives the slightly patronizing domestic set-up." In the course of her adventures, Amelia goes camping (and "pitches the tent" right into the woods), plays baseball (running home after hitting the ball out of the park), and teaching school (yelling "hey, roll!" when the lesson plan says to call roll).

Enormously popular with beginning readers, the Amelia Bedelia books also teach that words can have several meanings. "Young children struggling to master odd usages will find enormous pleasure in Amelia Bedelia's misinterpretations," Judith Gloyer stated in *School Library Journal.* Writing in the *New York Times Book Review,* Cynthia Samuels noted: "No child can resist Amelia and her literal trips through the minefield of the English language—and no adult can fail to notice that she's usually right when she's wrong. Both parents and children can learn, as well, from Amelia's kind employers. Mr. and Mrs. Rogers always come to understand Amelia's confusion and to admit that the language, not the user, is the culprit."

"The things I have Amelia Bedelia do," Parish explained to Richard I. Ammon in *Teacher,* "must be plausible. When I was writing *Good Work, Amelia Bedelia* I thought of having her make a sponge cake in her own inimitable way. So, I spent one afternoon in the kitchen snipping pieces of a sponge into a cake batter. I didn't know whether it would get gooey, burn up or do what I hoped—stay like a sponge. Fortunately, the sponge stayed like a sponge and that's the way it is in the book."

To celebrate Amelia Bedelia's twenty-fifth "birthday" in 1988, her many readers were encouraged to send birthday greetings to Amelia through special mail boxes installed in bookstores and libraries across the country. Paulette C. Kaufmann, director of children's book marketing for Greenwillow, told Edwin McDowell in the *New York Times* about the celebration: "The contents of those mailboxes have been arriving daily—thousands of letters and drawings from children who have read and loved books about Amelia Bedelia."

WORKS CITED:

Ammon, Richard I., "Amelia Bedelia: Sense, Stuff and Nonsense," *Teacher,* May-June, 1980, pp. 41-43.

Gloyer, Judith, review of *Merry Christmas, Amelia Bedelia, School Library Journal,* October, 1986, p. 111.

McDowell, Edwin, obituary for Peggy Parish, *New York Times,* November 22, 1988.

Palmer, Nancy, review of *Amelia Bedelia Goes Camping, School Library Journal,* May, 1985, p. 107.

Samuels, Cynthia, review of *Amelia Bedelia Goes Camping, New York Times Book Review,* March 10, 1985, p. 29.

FOR MORE INFORMATION SEE:

BOOKS

Norby, Shirley and Gregory Ryan, *Famous Children's Authors,* Dennison, 1988.

"Peggy Parish," *Children's Literature Review,* Volume 22, Gale, 1990, pp. 152-169.

"Peggy Parish," *Something About the Author,* Volume 17, Gale, 1979, pp. 144-146.

PERIODICALS

Bulletin of the Center for Children's Books, July-August, 1985, p. 213.

Kirkus Reviews, July 15, 1986, p. 1123; August 1, 1988, p. 1154.

Publishers Weekly, July 23, 1979, pp. 159-160; December 23, 1988.

School Library Journal, January, 1989.

* * *

PARISH, Peggy
See PARISH, Margaret Cecile

* * *

PARKER, Nancy Winslow 1930-

PERSONAL: Born October 18, 1930, in Maplewood, NJ; daughter of Winslow Aurelius (a textile executive) and Beatrice McCelland (Gaunt) Parker. *Education:* Mills College, B.A., 1952; attended Art Students League, 1956-57, and School of Visual Arts, 1966-67. *Hobbies and other interests:* "Travel, all things French, carpentry, tennis, gardening."

ADDRESSES: Home—51 East 74th St., No. 3R, New York, NY 10021.

CAREER: National Broadcasting Company (NBC), New York City, sales promoter, 1956-60; New York Soccer Club, New York City, sports promoter, 1961-63; Radio Corporation of America (RCA), New York City, sales promoter, 1964-67; Appleton-Century-Crofts (publishers), New York City, art director, 1968-70; Holt, Rinehart & Winston (publishers), New York City, graphic designer, 1970-72; free-lance writer and illustrator, 1972—.

MEMBER: Authors Guild, Mills College Club of New York, Mantoloking Yacht Club.

AWARDS, HONORS: Jane Tinkham Broughton fellowship in writing for children, Bread Loaf Writers Conference, 1975; notable children's book in the field of social studies, 1975, for *Warm as Wool, Cool as Cotton: The Story of Natural Fibers,* and 1976, for *The Goat in the Rug; The Goat in the Rug* was cited as best of the season in children's books, *Saturday Review,* 1976; year's best children's book citation, *Philadelphia Inquirer,* Christopher Award, and exhibited at American Institute of Graphic Arts Children's Book Show, all 1976, all for *Willy Bear; School Library Journal's* best books of spring, named to New York Public Library list of children's books, both 1980, both for *Poofy Loves Company;* Christopher Award, named one of the ten best illustrated books by *New York Times,* and exhibited at American Institute of Graphic Arts Children's Book Show, all 1981, for *My Mom Travels a Lot;* New York Academy of Science honorable mention, 1981, Sequoyah Children's Book Award, Oklahoma Library Association, 1983-84, Alabama Library Association Children's Choice, 1985, all for *The President's Car;* named to New York Public Library list of children's books, 1983, for *The Christmas Camel,* 1985, for *The United Nations from A to Z; Paul Revere's Ride* was included in Library of Congress' Books for Children, No. 2, 1986, *Bugs* was included in Library of Congress' Books for Children, No. 4, 1988; Association of Booksellers for Children Choice, 1988, for *Bugs.*

WRITINGS:

SELF-ILLUSTRATED CHILDREN'S BOOKS

The Man with the Take-Apart Head, Dodd, 1974.

The Party at the Old Farm, Atheneum, 1975.

Mrs. Wilson Wanders Off, Dodd, 1976.

Love from Uncle Clyde (Junior Literary Guild selection), Dodd, 1977.

The Crocodile under Louis Finneberg's Bed, Dodd, 1978.

The President's Cabinet (nonfiction; Junior Literary Guild selection), Parents Magazine Press, 1978, revised as *The President's Cabinet and How It Grew,* introduction by Dean Rusk, HarperCollins, 1991.

The Ordeal of Byron B. Blackbear, Dodd, 1979.

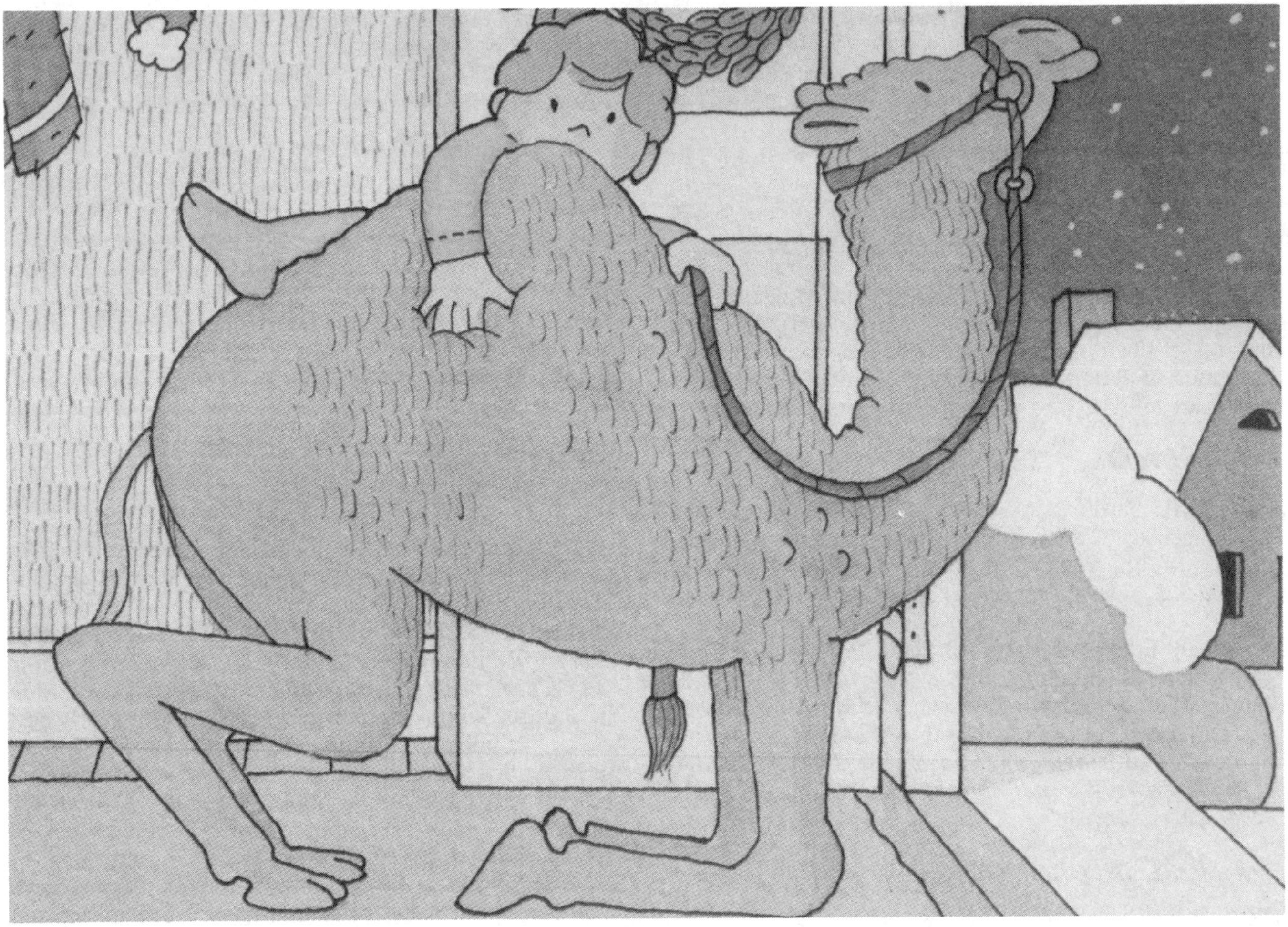

From *The Christmas Camel,* written and illustrated Nancy Winslow Parker.

Puddums, the Cathcarts' Orange Cat, Atheneum, 1980.
Poofy Loves Company (Junior Literary Guild selection; ALA Notable Book), Dodd, 1980.
The Spotted Dog, Dodd, 1980.
The President's Car (nonfiction), introduction by Betty Ford, Crowell, 1981.
Cooper, the McNallys' Big Black Dog, Dodd, 1981.
Love from Aunt Betty, Dodd, 1983.
The Christmas Camel, Dodd, 1983.
The United Nations from A to Z, Dodd, 1985.
(With Joan R. Wright) *Bugs,* Greenwillow, 1987.
(With Wright) *Frogs, Toads, Lizards and Salamanders,* Greenwillow, 1990.

ILLUSTRATOR

John Langstaff, *Oh, A-Hunting We Will Go!* (songbook; Junior Literary Guild selection), Atheneum, 1974.
Carter Hauck, *Warm as Wool, Cool as Cotton: The Story of Natural Fibers,* Seabury, 1975.
Charles L. Blood and Martin Link, *The Goat in the Rug,* Parents Magazine Press, 1976.
Mildred Kantrowitz, *Willy Bear* (Book-of-the-Month Club selection), Parents Magazine Press, 1976.
J. Langstaff, *Sweetly Sings the Donkey* (songbook), Atheneum, 1976.
Ann Lawler, *The Substitute,* Parents Magazine Press, 1977.
John Langstaff, *Hot Cross Buns and Other Old Street Cries* (songbook), Atheneum, 1978.
Jane Yolen, *No Bath Tonight* (Junior Literary Guild selection), Crowell, 1978.
Caroline Feller Bauer, *My Mom Travels a Lot,* Warne, 1981.
Henry Wadsworth Longfellow, *Paul Revere's Ride,* Greenwillow, 1985.
Eve Rice, *Aren't You Coming Too?,* Greenwillow, 1988.
Rachel Field, *General Store,* Greenwillow, 1988.
Eve Rice, *Peter's Pockets,* Greenwillow, 1989.
Nietzel, *The Jacket I Wear in the Snow,* Greenwillow, 1989.
Eve Rice, *At Grammy's House,* Greenwillow, 1990.
Ginger Foglesong Guy, *Black Crow, Black Crow,* Greenwillow, 1990.
Patricia Lillie, *When the Rooster Crowed,* Greenwillow, 1991.
John Greenleaf Whittier, *Barbara Frietchie,* Greenwillow, 1991.

ADAPTATIONS: Bugs was a "Reading Rainbow" selection; *My Mom Travels a Lot* was adapted into a filmstrip by Live Oak; *The Ordeal of Byron B. Blackbear* was made into a film.

SIDELIGHTS: Nancy Winslow Parker is an award-winning children's book author and illustrator. Parker insists that her illustrations and stories have one characteristic in common: they are all done in the spirit of fun. Critiquing a representative group of Parker's works, Dulcy Brainard, writing in *Publishers Weekly,* remarked, "The books are marked by a fresh simplicity and an observant, ironic sense of humor that is particularly apparent in the unexpected ways her pictures expand on the text."

Parker was born in Maplewood, New Jersey, in 1930. Her favorite reading material was *National Geographic,* a magazine of which her family had an extensive collection. Although Parker had dreamed of being an artist since childhood, her family did not think it was a legitimate or profitable career and instead urged her to get a mainstream job. So, after college, Parker moved to New York City, working for a magazine and as a secretary, although she continued her artwork on the side. Eventually, however, she went to the School of Visual Arts and soon found work as an art director and book designer. Parker tried to work as a free-lance illustrator, but realized that she would have to illustrate *and* write stories before being noticed by publishers. After she took this approach, she realized immediate success. In an interview with Brainard in *Publishers Weekly,* Parker commented, "My first story was *The Man with the Take-Apart Head.* It's one of my favorites, and as good as any I've written."

Parker often finds inspiration for her books in real-life situations. Her 1980 work *Poofy Loves Company* was based on an actual incident in which her overly friendly dog ambushed a visiting youngster, messing up her clothes and stealing her cookie. In a *Junior Literary Guild* review of *Poofy Loves Company,* the author recalled that the story "took about fifteen minutes to write, the whole thing coming at once in a delicious outburst of creativity." Praising Parker's re-creation of this event, the critic remarked that the book contained "hilarious four-color pictures."

As shown by *Poofy Loves Company,* animals, especially dogs, are Parker's favorite subjects. Sometimes she includes more exotic animals in her books and is forced to conduct extensive research to ensure the accuracy of her drawings and facts. *Love from Uncle Clyde* is the story of a boy named Charlie who receives an unusual Christmas present—a three-thousand-pound hippopotamus from Africa. These same characters reappear in *The Christmas Camel.* In this book Charlie receives a camel from eccentric Uncle Clyde and labors over the wooly animal's care. However this beast is magical and whisks Charlie to Bethlehem on Christmas Eve for an extraordinary experience.

Parker also illustrates works written by other authors. Two of the books she has illustrated, *Willy Bear,* by Mildred Kantrowitz, and *My Mom Travels a Lot,* by Caroline Feller Bauer, earned the prestigious Christopher Award. Both of these works focus on children handling new, and somewhat scary, situations. In *Willy Bear* a youngster uses his teddy bear to act out his fear of going to school, and in *My Mom Travels a Lot,* a young girl examines the positive and negative aspects of her mother's hectic business career. In each instance, Parker's drawings were credited by reviewers as complementing the text, thus helping to produce superior picture books.

Although Parker has achieved success with fiction for children, she has also delved into the field of nonfiction in her writing and illustrating career. For instance, her 1987 work, *Bugs,* written with Joan R. Wright, examines the physical structure and habitats of several types of insects. Patti Hagan, writing in the *New York Times Book Review* about *Bugs,* remarked that "the color illustrations, with precise anatomical tags, are a fine tool for introducing children" to the creatures portrayed in the book.

WORKS CITED:

Brainard, Dulcy, interview with Nancy Winslow Parker in *Publishers Weekly,* February 22, 1985, pp. 161-162.

Hagan, Patti, review of *Bugs, New York Times Book Review,* February 7, 1988, p. 29.

Review of *Poofy Loves Company, Junior Literary Guild,* March, 1980, p. 8.

* * *

PARNALL, Peter 1936-

PERSONAL: Born May 23, 1936, in Syracuse, NY; married; children: one son, one daughter. *Education:* Attended Cornell University and Pratt Institute School of Art.

ADDRESSES: Home—Rural Route 3, Waldoboro, ME 04572.

CAREER: Illustrator and author. Worked as an art director and free-lance designer, 1958-67.

AWARDS, HONORS: New York Times Best Illustrated Book list, 1967, for *A Dog's Book of Bugs* and *Knee-Deep in Thunder,* and 1968, for *Malachi Mudge;* Dutton Junior Animal Award, 1968, Dorothy Canfield Fisher Award, 1970, and William Allen White Award, 1971, all for *Kavik the Wolf Dog;* Commonwealth Club of California Award, 1971, Woodward Park School Award, 1972, Newbery Honor Award, 1972, Christopher Medal, 1972, and Art Books for Children Award, 1973, all for *Annie and the Old One;* Art Books for Children Award, 1976, for *Everybody Needs a Rock;* Boston Globe Horn Book Award, 1976, Caldecott Honor Medal, 1976, New York Academy of Sciences Award, 1976, Steck-Vaughn Award, 1976, Art Books for Children Award, 1977, 1978, and 1979, all for *The Desert Is Theirs;* Caldecott Honor Medal, 1977, for *Hawk, I'm Your Brother;* Caldecott Honor Medal, 1979, for *The Way to Start a Day;* Parents' Choice Award, 1980, for *Roadrunner;* New York Academy of Sciences Award, 1985, for *The Daywatchers.*

WRITINGS:

SELF-ILLUSTRATED

The Mountain, Doubleday, 1971.
The Great Fish, Doubleday, 1973.
Alfalfa Hill, Doubleday, 1975.
A Dog's Book of Birds, Scribner, 1977.
The Daywatchers, Macmillan, 1984.
Winter Barn, Macmillan, 1986.
Apple Tree, Macmillan, 1987.
Feet, Macmillan, 1988.
Quiet, Morrow, 1989.
Cats from Away, Macmillan, 1989.
The Woodpile, Macmillan, 1990.
The Rock, Macmillan, 1991.
Marsh Cat, Macmillan, 1991.
Stuffer, Macmillan, 1992.

ILLUSTRATOR

Hal Borland, *Beyond Your Doorstep,* Knopf, 1962.
Wayne Short, *The Cheechakoes,* Random House, 1964.
Eunice de Chazneau, *Of Houses and Cats,* Random House, 1965.
Mary Francis Shura, *A Tale of Middle Length,* Atheneum, 1966.
Elizabeth Griffen, *A Dog's Book of Bugs,* Atheneum, 1967.
Sheila Moon, *Knee-Deep in Thunder,* Atheneum, 1967.
William O. Douglas, *A Farewell to Texas,* McGraw, 1967.
Harold E. Burtt, *The Psychology of Birds,* Macmillan, 1967.

Peter Parnall

Edward Cecil (pseudonym of Cecil Maiden), *Malachi Mudge,* McGraw, 1967.
Frank Lee DuMond, *Tall Tales of the Catskills,* Atheneum, 1968.
Jean Craighead George, *The Moon of the Wild Pigs,* Crowell, 1968.
Murray Goodwin, *Underground Hideaway,* Harper, 1968.
Walt Morey, *Kavik the Wolf Dog,* Dutton, 1968.
Patricia Coffin, *The Gruesome Green Witch,* Walker, 1969.
Miska Miles, *Apricot ABC,* Little, Brown, 1969.
Peggy Parish, *A Beastly Circus,* Simon & Schuster, 1969.
Aileen Lucia Fisher, *But Ostriches,* Crowell, 1970.
George Mendoza, *The Inspector,* Doubleday, 1970.
Jan Wahl, *Doctor Rabbit,* Delacorte, 1970.
Cora Annett, *When the Porcupine Moved In,* F. Watts, 1971.
Angus Cameron, *The Nightwatchers,* Four Winds Press, 1971.
Mendoza, *Big Frog, Little Pond,* McCall, 1971.
Mendoza, *Moonfish and Owl Scratchings,* Grosset, 1971.
Miles, *Annie and the Old One,* Little, Brown, 1971.
Wahl, *The Six Voyages of Pleasant Fieldmouse,* Delacorte, 1971.
Margaret Hodges, *The Fire Bringer,* Little, Brown, 1972.
Jane Yolen and Barbara Green, *The Fireside Song Book of Birds and Beasts,* Simon & Schuster, 1972.
Mary Anderson, *Emma's Search for Something,* Atheneum, 1973.
Kent Durden, *Gifts of an Eagle,* Simon & Schuster, 1972.
Mary Ann Hoberman, *A Little Book of Little Beasts,* Simon & Schuster, 1973.
Laurence P. Pringle, *Twist, Wiggle, and Squirm: A Book about Earthworms,* Crowell, 1973.
Miriam Schlein, *The Rabbit's World,* Four Winds Press, 1973.
Josephine Johnson, *Seven Houses,* Simon & Schuster, 1973.
Byrd Baylor, *Everybody Needs a Rock,* Scribner, 1974.
Berniece Freschet, *Year on Muskrat Marsh,* Scribner, 1974.
Keith Robertson, *Tales of Myrtle the Turtle,* Viking, 1974.
Baylor, *The Desert Is Theirs,* Scribner, 1975.
Sally Carrighar, *The Twilight Seas,* Weybright & Talley, 1975.
Millard Lampell, *The Pig with One Nostril,* Doubleday, 1975.
Alice Schick, *The Peregrine Falcons,* Dial Press, 1975.
Baylor, *Hawk, I'm Your Brother,* Scribner, 1976.
Victor B. Scheffer, *A Natural History of Marine Mammals,* Scribner, 1976.
Baylor, *The Way To Start a Day,* Scribner, 1977.
(With Virginia Parnall) Anna Michel, *Little Wild Chimpanzee,* Pantheon, 1978.
William Humphrey, *The Spawning Run,* Delacorte, 1979.
(With V. Parnall) Michel, *Little Wild Elephant,* Pantheon, 1979.
Baylor, *Your Own Best Secret Place,* Scribner, 1979.

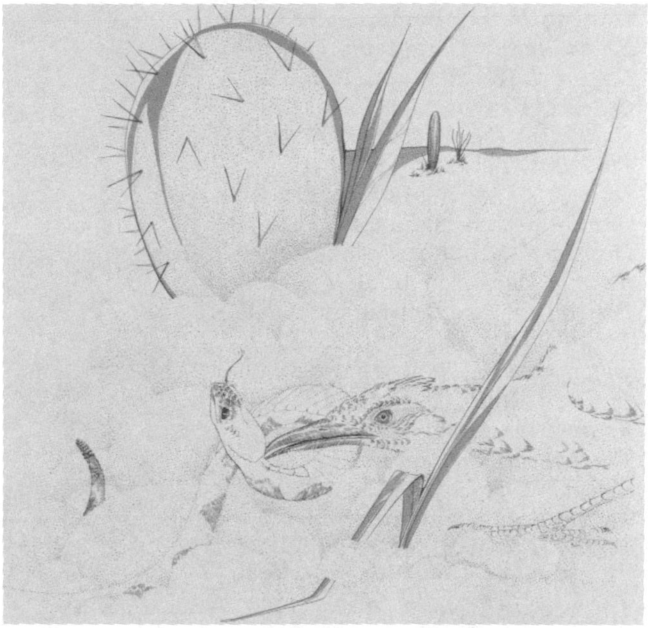

From *Roadrunner,* by Naomi Lewis. Illustrated by Peter Parnall.

Baylor, *The Other Way to Listen,* Scribner, 1980.
Baylor, *If You Are a Hunter of Fossils,* Scribner, 1980.
Naomi John, *Roadrunner,* Dutton, 1980.
Baylor, *Desert Voices,* Scribner, 1981.
(With V. Parnall) Terry Williams, *Between Cattails,* Scribner, 1985.
Baylor, *I'm in Charge of Celebrations,* Scribner, 1986.
Jean Chapman, compiler, *Cat Will Rhyme with Hat: A Book of Poems,* Scribner, 1986.

SIDELIGHTS: Author and illustrator Peter Parnall brings a deep love of wildlife to his work. Although he originally planned on becoming a veterinarian, Parnall changed his mind when he discovered that he preferred drawing animals in their natural habitats to studying them in an office or lab. Parnall always keeps his young audience in mind, working slowly to insure that his depictions are accurately rendered. Musing on his success in the *Third Book of Junior Authors,* Parnall noted that publishing has "been very kind to me and I have been very kind to it by working like a slave trying to improve the fare we publish for our children. Seeing my little neighbors smile at a drawing makes me feel I could make the rain fall up."

Parnall began illustrating books for children in the 1960s. He found inspiration for many of his works by taking long walks in parks and wooded areas. Critics praised the results of these intense periods of observation. "Superbly detailed, elegant in line, bold in composition, Parnall's drawings ... are a striking accompaniment to his series of pieces on the various birds of prey he has observed," wrote a reviewer in the *Bulletin of the Center for Children's Books* about *The Daywatchers.* Another reviewer for the *Bulletin,* commenting on Parnall's *Winter Barn,* remarked that the illustrations "have a still-life quality; their precise drafting and spacious composition underscore the brittle quiet of intense cold. A wintry mood piece."

In recent years, Parnall has worked at home on his farm. He produces about three books a year and admits to enjoying the writing aspect of his work as much as illustrating. "I found I wanted to share some of my love of nature and ecology with children and chose to do it by writing about 'stuff,'" Parnall wrote in an essay for *Something about the Author Autobiography Series.* "Just stuff that is hanging around here and there, like a woodpile, or maybe a stone wall. Things children often ignore. Like a tree."

WORKS CITED:

de Montreville, Doris, and Donna Hill, editors, *Third Book of Junior Authors,* H. W. Wilson, 1972, pp. 220-21.
Review of *The Daywatchers, Bulletin of the Center for Children's Books,* March, 1985.
Something about the Author Autobiography Series, Volume 11, Gale, 1991, pp. 259-73.
Review of *Winter Barn, Bulletin of the Center for Children's Books,* February, 1987.

FOR MORE INFORMATION SEE:

BOOKS

Kingman, Lee, compiler, *Illustrators of Children's Books, 1957-66,* Horn Book, 1968.

PERIODICALS

Booklist, November 15, 1975.
Horn Book, October, 1975.
New York Times Book Review, January 2, 1972.
Saturday Review, September 18, 1971.

* * *

PARSONS, Ellen
See DRAGONWAGON, Crescent

* * *

PASCAL, Francine 1938-

PERSONAL: Born May 13, 1938, in New York, NY; daughter of William and Kate (Dunitz) Rubin; married John Robert Pascal (a journalist and author), August 18, 1965 (died, 1981); children: Laurie, Susan, Jamie (daughter). *Education:* New York University, B.A., 1958. *Hobbies and other interests:* Travel, reading.

ADDRESSES: Home—New York, NY, and France. *Agent*—Amy Berkower, Writers House, 21 West 26th St., New York, NY 10010.

CAREER: Writer and lecturer.

MEMBER: PEN, International Creative Writers League, Dramatist's Guild, National Organization for Women.

AWARDS, HONORS: New York Public Library books for the teenage citation, 1978-1985, for *Hangin' Out with Cici;* American Library Association best book for young adults citation, 1979, for *My First Love and Other Disasters;* Dorothy Canfield Fisher Children's Book Award, Vermont Congress of Parents and Teachers, *Publishers Weekly* Literary Prize list, both 1982, and Bernard Versele Award, Brussels, 1988, all for *The Hand-Me-Down Kid;* Milner Award, Atlanta Public Library, 1988.

WRITINGS:

(With husband, John Pascal) *The Strange Case of Patty Hearst,* New American Library, 1974.
Hangin' Out with Cici, Viking, 1977, paperback edition published as *Hangin' Out with Cici; or, My Mother Was Never a Kid,* Dell, 1985.
My First Love and Other Disasters (also see below), Viking, 1979.
The Hand-Me-Down Kid, Viking, 1980.
Save Johanna! (adult novel), Morrow, 1981.
Love and Betrayal and Hold the Mayo! (sequel to *My First Love and Other Disasters*), Viking, 1985.

"SWEET VALLEY HIGH" SERIES

Double Love, Bantam, 1984.
Secrets, Bantam, 1984.
Playing with Fire, Bantam, 1984.
Power Play, Bantam, 1984.
All Night Long, Bantam, 1984.
Dangerous Love, Bantam, 1984.
Dear Sister, Bantam, 1984.
Heartbreaker, Bantam, 1984.
Racing Hearts, Bantam, 1984.
Wrong Kind of Girl, Bantam, 1984.
Too Good to Be True, Bantam, 1984.
When Love Dies, Bantam, 1984.
Kidnapped!, Bantam, 1984.
Deceptions, Bantam, 1984.
Promises, Bantam, 1985.
Rags to Riches, Bantam, 1985.
Love Letters, Bantam, 1985.
Head over Heels, Bantam, 1985.
Showdown, Bantam, 1985.
Crash Landing!, Bantam, 1985.
Runaway, Bantam, 1985.
Too Much in Love, Bantam, 1986.
Say Goodbye, Bantam, 1986.
Memories, Bantam, 1986.
Nowhere to Run, Bantam, 1986.
Hostage!, Bantam, 1986.
Lovestruck, Bantam, 1986.
Alone in the Crowd, Bantam, 1986.
Bitter Rivals, Bantam, 1986.
Jealous Lies, Bantam, 1986.
Taking Sides, Bantam, 1986.
The New Jessica, Bantam, 1986.
Starting Over, Bantam, 1987.
Forbidden Love, Bantam, 1987.
Out of Control, Bantam, 1987.
Last Chance, Bantam, 1987.
Rumors, Bantam, 1987.
Leaving Home, Bantam, 1987.
Secret Admirer, Bantam, 1987.
On the Edge, Bantam, 1987.
Outcast, Bantam, 1987.
Caught in the Middle, Bantam, 1988.
Pretenses, Bantam, 1988.
Hard Choices, Bantam, 1988.
Family Secrets, Bantam, 1988.
Decisions, Bantam, 1988.
Slam Book Fever, Bantam, 1988.
Playing for Keeps, Bantam, 1988.
Troublemaker, Bantam, 1988.
Out of Reach, Bantam, 1988.
In Love Again, Bantam, 1989.
Against the Odds, Bantam, 1989.
Brokenhearted, Bantam, 1989.
Teacher Crush, Bantam, 1989.
Perfect Shot, Bantam, 1989.
White Lies, Bantam, 1989.
Two-Boy Weekend, Bantam, 1989.
That Fatal Night, Bantam, 1989.
Lost at Sea, Bantam, 1989.
Second Chance, Bantam, 1989.
Ms. Quarterback, Bantam, 1990.
The New Elizabeth, Bantam, 1990.
The Ghost of Tricia Martin, Bantam, 1990.
Friend against Friend, Bantam, 1990.
Trouble at Home, Bantam, 1990.
Who's to Blame, Bantam, 1990.
The Parent Plot, Bantam, 1990.
Boy Trouble, Bantam, 1990.
Who's Who?, Bantam, 1990.
The Love Bet, Bantam, 1990.
Amy's True Love, Bantam, 1991.
Miss Teen Sweet Valley, Bantam, 1991.
The Perfect Girl, Bantam, 1991.
Regina's Legacy, Bantam, 1991.
Rock Star's Girl, Bantam, 1991.

Francine Pascal

Starring Jessica!, Bantam, 1991.
Cheating to Win, Bantam, 1991.
The Dating Game, Bantam, 1991.
The Long-Lost Brother, Bantam, 1991.
The Girl They Both Loved, Bantam, 1991.
Rosa's Lie, Bantam, 1992.
Kidnapped by the Cult, Bantam, 1992.

"SWEET VALLEY HIGH" SUPER EDITIONS

Perfect Summer, Bantam, 1985.
Malibu Summer, Bantam, 1986.
Special Christmas, Bantam, 1986.
Spring Break, Bantam, 1986.
Spring Fever, Bantam, 1987.
Winter Carnival, Bantam, 1987.

"SWEET VALLEY HIGH" SUPER THRILLER SERIES

Double Jeopardy, Bantam, 1987.
On the Run, Bantam, 1988.
No Place to Hide, Bantam, 1988.
Deadly Summer, Bantam, 1989.

"SWEET VALLEY HIGH" SUPER STAR SERIES

Lila's Story, Bantam, 1989.
Bruce's Story, Bantam, 1990.
Enid's Story, Bantam, 1990.
Olivia's Story, Bantam, 1991.

"SWEET VALLEY" MAGNA EDITION

The Wakefields of Sweet Valley, Bantam, 1991.

"SWEET VALLEY TWINS" SERIES

Best Friends, Bantam, 1986.
Teacher's Pet, Bantam, 1986.
The Haunted House, Bantam, 1986.
Choosing Sides, Bantam, 1986.
Sneaking Out, Bantam, 1987.
The New Girl, Bantam, 1987.
Three's a Crowd, Bantam, 1987.
First Place, Bantam, 1987.
Against the Rules, Bantam, 1987.
One of the Gang, Bantam, 1987.
Buried Treasure, Bantam, 1987.
Keeping Secrets, Bantam, 1987.
Stretching the Truth, Bantam, 1987.
Tug of War, Bantam, 1987.
The Bully, Bantam, 1988.
Playing Hooky, Bantam, 1988.
Left Behind, Bantam, 1988.
Claim to Fame, Bantam, 1988.
Center of Attention, Bantam, 1988.
Jumping to Conclusions, Bantam, 1988.
Second Best, Bantam, 1988.
The Older Boy, Bantam, 1988.
Out of Place, Bantam, 1988.
Elizabeth's New Hero, Bantam, 1989.
Standing Out, Bantam, 1989.
Jessica on Stage, Bantam, 1989.
Jessica the Rock Star, Bantam, 1989.
Jessica's Bad Idea, Bantam, 1989.
Taking Charge, Bantam, 1989.
Big Camp Secret, Bantam, 1989.
Jessica and the Brat Attack, Bantam, 1989.
April Fool!, Bantam, 1989.
Princess Elizabeth, Bantam, 1989.
Elizabeth's First Kiss, Bantam, 1990.
War between the Twins, Bantam, 1990.
Summer Fun Book, Bantam, 1990.
The Twins Get Caught, Bantam, 1990.
Lois Strikes Back, Bantam, 1990.
Mary Is Missing, Bantam, 1990.
Jessica's Secret, Bantam, 1990.
Jessica and the Money Mix-Up, Bantam, 1990.
Danny Means Trouble, Bantam, 1990.
Amy's Pen Pal, Bantam, 1990.
Amy Moves In, Bantam, 1991.
Jessica's New Look, Bantam, 1991.
Lucky Takes the Reins, Bantam, 1991.
Mademoiselle Jessica, Bantam, 1991.
Mansy Miller Fights Back, Bantam, 1991.
The Twins' Little Sister, Bantam, 1991.
Booster Boycott, Bantam, 1991.
Elizabeth the Impossible, Bantam, 1991.
Jessica and the Secret Star, Bantam, 1991.
The Slime That Ate Sweet Valley, Bantam, 1991.
The Big Party Weekend, Bantam, 1991.
Brooke and Her Rock-Star Mom, Bantam, 1992.
The Wakefields Strike It Rich, Bantam, 1992.

"SWEET VALLEY TWINS" SUPER SERIES

Class Trip, Bantam, 1988.
Holiday Mischief, Bantam, 1988.

"SWEET VALLEY TWINS" SUPER CHILLER SERIES

Jessica's Christmas Carol, Bantam, 1989.
The Carnival Ghost, Bantam, 1990.
Christmas Ghost, Bantam, 1990.
The Ghost in the Graveyard, Bantam, 1990.

"SWEET VALLEY KIDS" SERIES

Surprise! Surprise!, Bantam, 1989.
Runaway Hamster, Bantam, 1989.
Teamwork, Bantam, 1989.
Lila's Secret, Bantam, 1990.
Elizabeth's Valentine, Bantam, 1990.
Elizabeth's Super-Selling Lemonade, Bantam, 1990.
Jessica's Big Mistake, Bantam, 1990.
Jessica's Cat Trick, Bantam, 1990.
Jessica's Zoo Adventure, Bantam, 1990.
The Twins and the Wild West, Bantam, 1990.
Starring Winston, Bantam, 1990.
The Substitute Teacher, Bantam, 1990.
Sweet Valley Trick or Treat, Bantam, 1990.
Crybaby Lois, Bantam, 1990.
Bossy Steven, Bantam, 1991.
Carolyn's Mystery Dolls, Bantam, 1991.
Fearless Elizabeth, Bantam, 1991.
Jessica and Jumbo, Bantam, 1991.
The Twins Go to the Hospital, Bantam, 1991.
Jessica the Babysitter, Bantam, 1991.
Jessica and the Spelling Bee Surprise, Bantam, 1991.
Lila's Haunted House Party, Bantam, 1991.
Sweet Valley Slumber Party, Bantam, 1991.
Cousin Kelly's Family Secret, Bantam, 1991.
Left-Out Elizabeth, Bantam, 1991.

"SWEET VALLEY KIDS" SUPER SNOOPER SERIES

The Case of the Secret Santa, Bantam, 1990.
The Case of the Magic Christmas Bell, Bantam, 1991.

"CAITLIN" SERIES

"The Love Trilogy," Volume 1: *Loving,* Volume 2: *Love Lost,* Volume 3: *True Love,* Bantam, 1986.
"The Promise Trilogy," Bantam, Volume 1: *Tender Promises,* 1986, Volume 2: *Promises Broken,* 1986, Volume 3: *A New Promise,* 1987.
"The Forever Trilogy," Volume 1: *Dreams of Forever,* Volume 2: *Forever and Always,* Volume 3: *Together Forever,* Bantam, 1987.

OTHER

(With husband, John Pascal and brother, Michael Stewart) *George M!* (musical; also see below), produced on Broadway, 1968.
(With Pascal) *George M!* (television special based on musical of same title), American Broadcasting Companies, Inc. (ABC-TV), 1970.

Creator for television of *The See-through-Kids,* a live-action family series; adapter of television scripts; co-writer with Pascal of television scripts for soap-opera serial *The Young Marrieds,* ABC-TV. Past contributor of humor, nonfiction, and travel articles to *True Confessions, Modern Screen, Ladies' Home Journal,* and *Cosmopolitan.*

ADAPTATIONS: Hangin' Out with Cici was filmed by ABC-TV and broadcast as "My Mother Was Never a Kid," an *ABC Afterschool Special,* 1981; *The Hand-Me-Down Kid* was filmed by ABC-TV and broadcast as an *ABC Afterschool Special,* 1983. Books that have been recorded onto audio cassette and released by Warner Audio include: *Double Love, Secrets,* and *Playing with Fire,* all 1986, *All Night Long, Dangerous Love,* and *Power Play.*

WORK IN PROGRESS: Monthly plot outlines for the "Sweet Valley High," "Sweet Valley Twins," and "Sweet Valley Kids" series; a trilogy of adult novels, centering on three generations of a wealthy Manhattan family; a children's book, centering on an eleven-year-old boy with an extraordinary imagination; a book with one of her daughters; a screenplay.

SIDELIGHTS: Francine Pascal made publishing history in 1985 when *Perfect Summer,* the first "Sweet Valley High" super edition, became the first young adult novel to make the *New York Times* bestseller list. With over sixty-five million books in print, Pascal and the mythical middle-class suburb of Sweet Valley, California are a publishing phenomenon. Although many critics maintain that the various "Sweet Valley" series are simplistic, unbelievable, and sexist, their popularity with young adults is undeniable. The various series revolve around Elizabeth and Jessica Wakefield, beautiful and popular identical twins with completely opposite personalities—while Elizabeth is sweet, sincere, and studious, Jessica is arrogant, superficial, and devious. The events in each story usually focus on relationships with boys or other personal issues, and adults are nearly nonexistent. "Sweet Valley is the essence of high school," asserts Pascal in a *People* interview with Steve Dougherty. "The world outside is just an adult shadow going by. The parents barely exist. Action takes place in bedrooms, cars and school. It's that moment before reality hits, when you really do believe in the romantic values—sacrifice, love, loyalty, friendship—before you get jaded and slip off into adulthood."

Born in New York City, Pascal moved from Manhattan to Jamaica, Queens when she was five. This new neighborhood had houses with yards and children were able to play outside unattended. Movies, adventure comics, and fairy tales were among Pascal's many passions, and because there was no young adult literature at the time, she read the classics. "I have always had a very active imagination—my retreat when things don't go right," explains Pascal in an interview with Marguerite Feitlowitz for *Authors and Artists for Young Adults* (*AAYA*). "I realized early that this set me apart from most people. For example, it wasn't my habit to confide in others very much, particularly my parents. As far back as I can recall, I kept a diary. Important thoughts, imaginings, and events were recounted in my diaries, not to people."

Other forms of writing that Pascal attempted at an early age included poetry and plays. Her brother was a writer, so Pascal wanted to write too, but her parents did not take her writing as seriously as they did his. Her teachers and classmates encouraged her though, and she even performed her plays, casting and directing her friends for neighborhood audiences. Moving from childhood into adolescence, Pascal, unlike her "Sweet Valley" characters, had a less than ideal high school experience. "Going to high school in the fifties, as I did, was not appreciably different from going to high school in the eighties," points out Pascal in her *AAYA* interview. "Both decades are conservative and full of nostalgia. Adolescence is pretty awful no matter when you go through it. And all of us think high school is wonderful for everyone else. The 'Sweet Valley' series come out of what I fantasized high school was like for everyone but me."

College, on the other hand, was something Pascal looked forward to and thoroughly enjoyed. It was a couple days after her last class that she met her future husband, John Pascal, who was then a journalist working for a number of papers. "He was an excellent writer," recalls Pascal in her *AAYA* interview, "and in many ways my mentor. He loved everything I wrote and encouraged me unceasingly." In their early years together, Pascal's husband freelanced while she began her own writing career with articles for such magazines as *True Confessions* and *Modern Screen,* eventually moving up to *Ladies' Home Journal* and *Cosmopolitan.* They began working together as second writers for the soap opera *The Young Marrieds* in 1965, and stayed with the show until it moved to California. The musical *George M!* and the nonfiction work *The Strange Case of Patty Hearst* were among the other writings they collaborated on before Pascal turned her attention to the young adult audience.

The idea for Pascal's first young adult novel, *Hangin' Out with Cici,* came to her early one morning while she was lying in bed. She had never written a novel before, and at the time had no idea what young adult novels were. Upon hearing her idea, Pascal's husband encouraged her to sit down and begin writing immediately, so she did. When the manuscript was finished she mailed it off to three agents, and the book sold within two weeks. *Hangin' Out with Cici* introduces Victoria, a spoiled and selfish young girl who has just been caught smoking a joint during a weekend visit to her aunt. On the train ride home, Victoria somehow wishes herself back in time to 1944, where she makes friends with a girl named Cici. Even wilder than Victoria, Cici shoplifts and sneaks cigarettes before being caught trying to buy a science test with stolen money. Over time, Victoria realizes that Cici is really her mother as a young girl and urges her to confess to her crime. She then wakes up to find herself on the train, where she had been all along—everything was just a dream. From that point on, however, Victoria and her mother have a stronger relationship. "The story contains some funny episodes," comments Ann A. Flowers in *Horn Book,* adding that *Hangin' Out with Cici* is "an amusing fantasy with realistic adolescent characters."

A few other novels followed before Pascal came up with the idea for the "Sweet Valley High" series. *My First Love and Other Disasters,* published in 1979, is the story of Victoria as she takes a summer job as a mother-helper on Fire Island to be close to her first love. Barbara Elleman, writing in *Booklist,* maintains that the novel is "wittily told in the first person vernacular of a 15-year-old" and "captures the kaleidoscopic complexities of living through a first love." *The Hand-Me-Down Kid* offers a younger protagonist. Eleven-year-old Ari Jacobs is the youngest child in her family, and has a distinctly negative view of life until she meets Jane, who is in the same position as herself, yet exudes positiveness. "Narrated in the slightly skewed grammatical style typical of today's adolescent, the story is an amusing contemporary novel with an urban setting, which maintains a perspective on everything from training bras to older brothers and sisters and offers hand-me-down kids a believable example of assertiveness training," remarks Mary M. Burns in *Horn Book.*

Pascal's husband died in 1981, shortly after the 1980 publication of *The Hand-Me-Down Kid.* "It seems unfair that he isn't alive to enjoy the success of my 'Sweet Valley' series," relates Pascal in her interview with Feitlowitz. "He would have gotten a real kick out of it, and could have retired on the money I've made. The house is too quiet now." The idea for this incredibly successful series was not a completely new one. In the late 1970s, Pascal wanted to do something similar, but in the form of a television soap opera for teenagers. No one was interested, but a few years later one of Pascal's editors suggested she try a teenage book series instead, maybe something similar to the television show *Dallas.* When this first attempt failed, Pascal examined the reasons why, coming up with the elements she thought must be present to make a teenage series work. "Each book, I concluded," explains Pascal in her *AAYA* interview, "would have to be a complete story in itself, but with a hook ending to lead you to the sequel. The series would have to have vivid continuing characters. When I came up with the idea for Elizabeth and Jessica, the Jekyll and Hyde twins, I was off and running. I did a proposal over the course of several days, wrote about six pages and that was that." Bantam immediately bought the project and, with successful marketing and packaging, made it a publishing sensation. At the beginning of the series, Pascal presented Sweet Valley as a completely idealized fantasy world. But when she started getting letters from readers telling her how "real" the books were to them, Pascal decided to include some aspects of reality, such as minority characters. "I didn't intend Sweet Valley to be realistic," admits Pascal in her interview with Feitlowitz, "so I'm a little puzzled. It is a soap opera in book form, after all. I guess what these readers mean is that there is emotional reality in the relationship between the characters."

Despite the success of the various "Sweet Valley" series, Pascal has received a great deal of criticism. She argues, however, that her "books encourage young people to read. 'Sweet Valley High' opened a market that simply

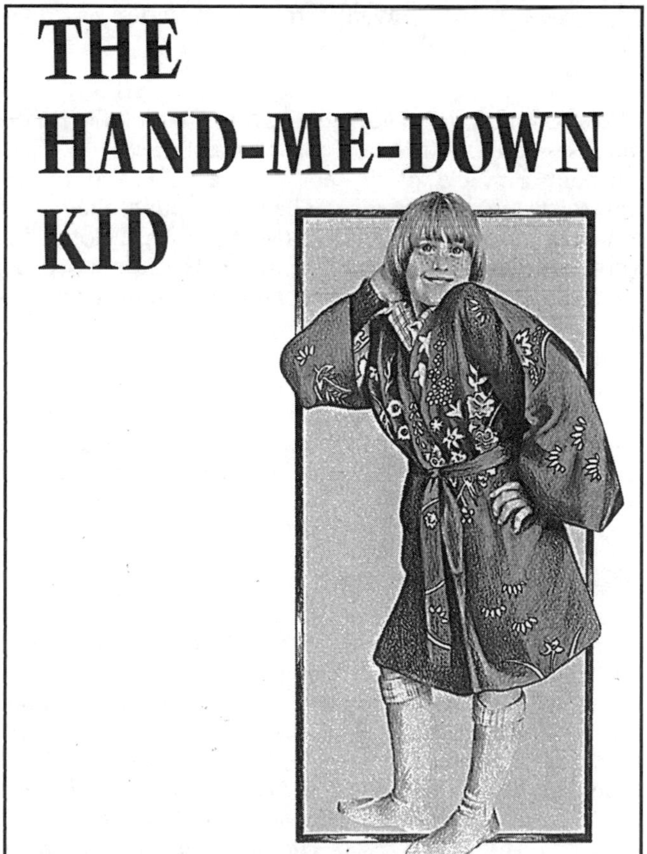

Cover of *The Hand-Me-Down Kid,* by Francine Pascal.

didn't exist before," points out Pascal in her *AAYA* interview. "It is not that those millions of girls were not reading my books, they weren't reading any books. I have gotten many, many letters from kids saying that they never read before 'Sweet Valley High.' If nine out of ten of those girls go on to read Judith Krantz and Danielle Steel, so be it, they are still reading.... The reality is that not everyone is able, or wishes to read great literature. There should be books for all types of readers. Reading time is precious; it's a time for privacy, fantasy, learning, a time to live in our imaginations. No one should be denied that."

The popularity of the "Sweet Valley High" series prompted a number of spin-off series, including "Sweet Valley Twins," which aims at younger readers by placing Elizabeth and Jessica in sixth grade, "Sweet Valley Kids," which presents the twins as six-year-olds, and "Sweet Valley High" super thriller series, which attempts to compete with other young adult mystery and horror writers. In 1991, Pascal brought a new twist to the series with the publication of *The Wakefields of Sweet Valley.* This full-length novel covers one hundred years as it traces five generations of the Wakefield family. It begins in 1860 with the sea voyage of sixteen-year-old Alice Larson of Sweden and eighteen-year-old Theodore Wakefield from England, following the family through wagon trains, earthquakes, the Roaring Twenties, love, courage and heartbreak. In addition to this new saga, there is even a television series based on Sweet Valley in the works.

With so many series going, Pascal is unable to write the books herself. "It would be impossible to do them without a stable of writers," remarks Pascal in her interview with Feitlowitz. "They come out at the rate of one a month plus periodic super editions. I do all the plot outlines, descriptions of characters, time setting, and so forth. I love plot twists and the conflicts between the good and bad twin. Creating Sweet Valley was a real 'high.' I loved making up the history of the place, visualizing it in great detail. We have a stable of authors each of whom generally does one title every three months. I maintain artistic control over every aspect of these novels. I may not write every word, but they are very much mine."

WORKS CITED:

Burns, Mary M., review of *The Hand-Me-Down Kid, Horn Book,* June, 1980, pp. 302-03.

Dougherty, Steve, "Heroines of 40 Million Books, Francine Pascal's 'Sweet Valley' Twins are Perfection in Duplicate," *People,* July 11, 1988, pp. 66-68.

Elleman, Barbara, review of *My First Love and Other Disasters, Booklist,* February 15, 1979, p. 936.

Flowers, Ann A., review of *Hangin' Out with Cici, Horn Book,* October, 1977, p. 541.

Pascal, Francine, in an interview with Marguerite Feitlowitz for *Authors and Artists for Young Adults,* Volume 1, Gale, 1989, pp. 189-202.

FOR MORE INFORMATION SEE:

BOOKS

Children's Literature Review, Volume 25, Gale, 1991, pp. 175-182.

PERIODICALS

Chicago Tribune, June 1, 1987.

Growing Point, September, 1984, pp. 4311-12.

Library Journal, June 15, 1981, pp. 1323-24.

Los Angeles Times, April 20, 1986, section 6, pp. 1, 10-11.

New York Times Book Review, April 29, 1979, p. 38.

People, March 30, 1981.

Publishers Weekly, January 8, 1979, p. 74; July 26, 1985; May 29, 1987, p. 30.

School Library Journal, September, 1977, p. 134; March, 1979, pp. 149-50; September, 1980, p. 76; September, 1984, p. 136; September, 1985, p. 148; March, 1990, pp. 137-40.

Voice of Youth Advocates, October, 1980, p. 27; August, 1984, p. 146; October, 1985, p. 264; December, 1986, p. 231-32; June, 1987, p. 87.

* * *

PATENT, Dorothy Hinshaw 1940-

PERSONAL: Born April 30, 1940, in Rochester, MN; daughter of Horton Corwin (a physician) and Dorothy Kate (Youmans) Hinshaw; married Gregory Joseph Patent (a professor of zoology), March 21, 1964; children: David Gregory, Jason Daniel. *Education:* Stanford University, B.A., 1962; University of California, Berkeley, M.A., 1965, Ph.D., 1968; also studied at Friday Harbor Laboratories, University of Washington, 1965-67. *Hobbies and other interests:* Gardening, cooking, and racquetball.

ADDRESSES: Home—5445 Skyway Dr., Missoula, MT 59801.

CAREER: Writer. Sinai Hospital, Detroit, MI, post-doctoral fellow, 1968-69; Stazione Zoologica, Naples, Italy, post-doctoral researcher, 1970-71; University of Montana, Missoula, faculty affiliate in department of zoology, 1975—, acting assistant professor, 1977.

MEMBER: International Woman's Writing Guild, American Institute of Biological Sciences, Authors Guild, Society of Children's Book Writers.

AWARDS, HONORS: The National Science Teachers Association has cited more than forty of Patent's books as outstanding science trade books; Golden Kite Award in nonfiction, Society of Children's Book Writers, 1977, for *Evolution Goes On Every Day,* and 1980, for *The Lives of Spiders;* "Notable Book" citation, American Library Association, 1982, for *Spider Magic;* "Best Book for Young Adults" citation, American Library Association, 1986, for *The Quest for Artificial Intelligence;* Eva L. Gordon Award, American Nature Study Society, 1987, for the body of her work.

Dorothy Hinshaw Patent

WRITINGS:

FOR CHILDREN

Weasels, Otters, Skunks and Their Family, illustrations by Matthew Kalmenoff, Holiday House, 1973.

Microscopic Animals and Plants, Holiday House, 1974.

Frogs, Toads, Salamanders and How They Reproduce, illustrations by M. Kalmenoff, Holiday House, 1975.

How Insects Communicate, Holiday House, 1975.

Fish and How They Reproduce, illustrations by M. Kalmenoff, Holiday House, 1976.

Plants and Insects Together, illustrations by M. Kalmenoff, Holiday House, 1976.

Evolution Goes On Every Day, illustrations by M. Kalmenoff, Holiday House, 1977.

Reptiles and How They Reproduce, illustrations by M. Kalmenoff, Holiday House, 1977.

The World of Worms, Holiday House, 1978.

Animal and Plant Mimicry, Holiday House, 1978.

(With Paul C. Schroeder) *Beetles and How They Live,* Holiday House, 1978.

Butterflies and Moths: How They Function, Holiday House, 1979.

Sizes and Shapes in Nature: What They Mean, Holiday House, 1979.

Raccoons, Coatimundis and Their Family, Holiday House, 1979.

Bacteria: How They Affect Other Living Things, Holiday House, 1980.

The Lives of Spiders, Holiday House, 1980.

Bears of the World, Holiday House, 1980.

Horses and Their Wild Relatives, Holiday House, 1981.

Horses of America, Holiday House, 1981.

Hunters and the Hunted: Surviving in the Animal World, Holiday House, 1981.

Spider Magic, Holiday House, 1982.

A Picture Book of Cows, photographs by William Munoz, Holiday House, 1982.

Arabian Horses, Holiday House, 1982.

Germs!, Holiday House, 1983.

A Picture Book of Ponies, photographs by W. Munoz, Holiday House, 1983.

Whales: Giants of the Deep, Holiday House, 1984.

Farm Animals, photographs by W. Munoz, Holiday House, 1984.

Where the Bald Eagles Gather, photographs by W. Munoz, Clarion, 1984.

Baby Horses, photographs by W. Munoz, Dodd, 1985.

Quarter Horses, photographs by W. Munoz, Holiday House, 1985.

The Sheep Book, photographs by W. Munoz, Dodd, 1985.

Thoroughbred Horses, Holiday House, 1985.

Draft Horses, photographs by W. Munoz, Holiday House, 1986.

Buffalo: The American Bison Today, photographs by W. Munoz, Clarion, 1986.
Mosquitoes, Holiday House, 1986.
Maggie: A Sheep Dog (Junior Literary Guild selection), photographs by W. Munoz, Dodd, 1986.
The Quest for Artificial Intelligence, Harcourt, 1986.
Christmas Trees (Junior Literary Guild selection), Dodd, 1987.
All about Whales, Holiday House, 1987.
Dolphins and Porpoises, Holiday House, 1987.
The Way of the Grizzly, photographs by W. Munoz, Clarion, 1987.
Wheat: The Golden Harvest, photographs by W. Munoz, Dodd, 1987.
Appaloosa Horses, photographs by W. Munoz, Holiday House, 1988.
Babies!, Holiday House, 1988.
A Horse of a Different Color, photographs by W. Munoz, Dodd, 1988.
The Whooping Crane: A Comeback Story, photographs by W. Munoz, Clarion, 1988.
Humpback Whales, photographs by Mark J. Ferrari and Deborah A. Glockner-Ferrari, Holiday House, 1989.
Grandfather's Nose: Why We Look Alike or Different, illustrations by Diane Palmisciano, F. Watts, 1989.
Singing Birds and Flashing Fireflies: How Animals Talk to Each Other, illustrations by Mary Morgan, F. Watts, 1989.
Where the Wild Horses Roam, photographs by W. Munoz, Clarion, 1989.
Wild Turkey, Tame Turkey, photographs by W. Munoz, Clarion, 1989.
Looking at Dolphins and Porpoises, Holiday House, 1989.
Looking at Ants, Holiday House, 1989.
Seals, Sea Lions and Walruses, Holiday House, 1990.
Yellowstone Fires: Flames and Rebirth, photographs by W. Munoz, Holiday House, 1990.
An Apple a Day: From Orchard to You, photographs by W. Munoz, Cobblehill, 1990.
Flowers for Everyone, photographs by W. Munoz, Cobblehill, 1990.
Gray Wolf, Red Wolf, photographs by W. Munoz, Clarion, 1990.
How Smart Are Animals? (Junior Literary Guild selection), Harcourt, 1990.
A Family Goes Hunting, photographs by W. Munoz, Clarion, 1991.
Miniature Horses, photographs by W. Munoz, Cobblehill, 1991.
The Challenge of Extinction, Enslow, 1991.
Where Food Comes From, photographs by W. Munoz, Holiday House, 1991.
African Elephants: Giants of the Land, photographs by Oria Douglas-Hamilton, Holiday House, 1991.
Feathers, photographs by W. Munoz, Cobblehill, 1992.
Places of Refuge: Our National Wildlife Refuge System, photographs by W. Munoz, Clarion, 1992.
Nutrition: What's in the Food We Eat, photographs by W. Munoz, Holiday, 1992.

FOR ADULTS

(With Diane E. Bilderback) *Garden Secrets,* Rodale Press, 1982, revised and expanded edition published as *The Harrowsmith Country Life Book of Garden Secrets: A Down-to-Earth Guide to the Art and Science of Growing Better Vegetables,* Camden House, 1991.
(With D. E. Bilderback) *Backyard Fruits and Berries,* Rodale Press, 1984.

Contributor to gardening and farming magazines.

WORK IN PROGRESS: Patent is preparing a book on pelicans for Clarion, one on habitat preservation for Enslow, and a three book series comparing the behavior of domesticated animals with their wild relatives for Carolrhoda. Projects scheduled for 1993 publication include books on ospreys and prairie dogs for Clarion, a book on killer whales for Holiday, books on animal tails and a Newfoundland search-and-rescue dog named Hugger for Cobblehill, and one on the loss of diversity in our food sources for Harcourt. Future projects include books on deer, elk, and alligators for Clarion. Patent told *MAICYA* that she has been "trying her hand

From *The Quest for Artificial Intelligence,* by Dorothy Hinshaw Patent.

at fiction for children with the help of a local critique group."

SIDELIGHTS: "The story of my life is a story of love of the earth and of the world of living things," remarks Dorothy Hinshaw Patent in *Something about the Author Autobiography Series* (*SAAS*). Her childhood curiosity about animals and the natural world evolved into educational interests and finally into a lifelong career as a writer. Whether writing about salamanders, eagles, or grizzly bears, Patent transforms hours of research both in the library and in the wild into easily understood books that respect their audience as much as their subject. Her nonfiction books for young people have won over twenty awards from the National Science Teachers Association, and she has been commended by critics for presenting complex scientific information in a clear, spirited style.

"Many writers have known for as long as they can remember that they wanted to write. Not me," says Patent in *SAAS.* "I knew that I loved animals, the woods, and exploring, and I always wanted to learn everything possible about something that interested me. But I never yearned to be a writer." Patent says that she grew up a tomboy, exploring the terrain around her family's homes in Minnesota and later California with her older brother. She was always more interested in catching tadpoles, playing with toads, and collecting insects than in the more conventional interests shared by girls her age. In fact, Patent remembers having trouble making girl friends in school: "To this day I'm not sure why, but maybe it was because I'd never spent much time with girls and didn't know how to act around them."

When she was in elementary school, a gift from her mother turned Patent's general interest in nature into a firm resolve to know all that she could of a specific subject. As a reward for practicing the piano, her mother bought her a pair of golden guppies and she recalls in *SAAS:* "The morning after we bought the fish, I peered into the bowl to check on my new pets. To my surprise, the adult fish weren't alone—three new pairs of eyes stared out at me from among the plants. I couldn't believe this miracle—the female fish had given birth during the night, and now I had five fish instead of two!" Patent's enthusiasm led her to read every book she could about tropical fish and to frequent a special Japanese fish store to learn even more, which came in handy later on, she says, when she wrote *Fish and How They Reproduce.* Another book, *The Challenge of Extinction,* was written partly because of Patent's experience with animals that were abundant in her childhood but are now verging on extinction.

Patent's curiosity helped her to excel in school, as did the encouragement of her family. "Learning was highly valued in my family," she says in *SAAS.* Despite her success academically, she felt like a misfit socially. "I wanted to be like the 'in' crowd . . . ," she recalls. "I admired the girls who became prom queens and cheerleaders. At the time, there was no way I could understand that some of them were living the best part of their lives during high school while the best parts of my life were yet to come and would last much longer." After high school Patent went to nearby Stanford University, one of the few highly-rated schools in the nation that was coeducational at the time and had a strong science program. Patent blossomed in college, where her intelligence and intellectual curiosity were valued. Despite a terrible tragedy during her freshman year—the suicide of her roommate—which put her "into a dark emotional frame of mind that lasted the entire four years," she says in her autobiographical sketch that she became involved with international folk dancing, made good friends, and had interesting, challenging classes. Many of her classes emphasized writing, and "by the end of my freshman year," she recollects, "I could set an internal switch for a paper of a certain length and write it. I'm sure this discipline and training helped me in my writing career." After a trip to Europe with a friend, Patent enrolled in graduate school at the University of California at Berkeley, where she met the man she would marry, Greg Patent, a teaching assistant in her endocrinology class.

Patent and her new husband continued their graduate work and research in Friday Harbor, Washington, Detroit, Michigan, and Naples, Italy, settling for a while in North Carolina before moving to Montana. Searching for a job that would allow her to spend time with her two young boys, Patent recalls in *SAAS:* "When people asked me questions about biology, they often complimented my answers by saying that I explained things well. Maybe I could write about biology. And since I had children, perhaps writing for kids would be a good idea. There was so much exciting information about living things that I could share. I could write for children who were like me, who wanted to learn everything they could about nature."

Though her first two books were not published, one of them piqued the interest of an editor at Holiday House who eventually approached Patent with an idea for a book about the weasel family. Although she knew next to nothing about weasels, Patent agreed to write the book. She spent hours doing research at the University of Montana library in Missoula, and received help from a professor at the university who happened to be one of the world's experts on weasels. She soon developed a pattern of careful research and organization that allowed her to write first one, then two, then three books a year. "Each book was a review," she explains in *SAAS,* "in simple language, of everything known up to that time about the subject. I chose most of the subjects myself, and they were the things that had interested me as a child—frogs, tropical fish, reptiles, butterflies."

In the early 1980s Patent began to work with photographer William Munoz, whose name she found in a Missoula newspaper. The two would travel together to photograph the animals for a book, and became a successful team. The first few books that Patent wrote with the help of Munoz allowed her to stay in Montana, but her desire to write books on grizzly bears, whooping cranes, and wolves soon took them to Alaska, New

Mexico, Texas, and other states. Becoming increasingly concerned with the plight of wildlife, Patent says in her autobiographical sketch that "wild things always seem to lose out in today's world .... We need to realize that we are part of nature, that without nature, we are not whole."

Patent's books, the majority of which explain the history, breeding, growth and habits of various groups of animals, have been widely praised for their clarity, thoroughness, and readability. Whether she is describing worms or whales, Patent's works appeal to students of all ages, from the bright eight-year-old to the curious high school student. She may use difficult vocabulary, but she explains the words used and often supplies a helpful glossary. Also, humorous examples of strange animal behavior and vivid pictures frequently combine to make her books more interesting than the ordinary textbook. In *Children and Books,* Zena Sutherland and May Hill Arbuthnot comment that Patent "communicates a sense of wonder at the complexity and beauty of animal life by her zest for her subject," and Sarah Gagne, who has reviewed many of Patent's works, says that she "could probably make interesting the life and ancestors of even a garden mole."

Patent told *SAAS:* "I hope that my writing can help children get in touch with the world of living things and realize how dependent we are on them, not just on the wild world but on domesticated plants and animals as well. We owe our existence to the earth, and it is the balance of nature that sustains all life; we upset that balance at our peril. I believe that well-informed children can grow up into responsible citizens capable of making the wise but difficult decisions necessary for the survival of a liveable world. I plan to continue to write for those children, helping to provide them with the information they will need in the difficult but exciting times ahead."

WORKS CITED:

Gagne, Sarah, review of *Horses and Their Wild Relatives, Horn Book,* October, 1981, pp. 558-559.

Patent, Dorothy Hinshaw, *Something about the Author Autobiography Series,* Volume 13, Gale, 1991, pp. 137-154.

Sutherland, Zena, and May Hill Arbuthnot, "Informational Books," in *Children and Books,* 7th edition, Scott, Foresman, 1986, pp. 484-548.

FOR MORE INFORMATION SEE:

BOOKS

Children's Literature Review, Volume 19, Gale, 1990, pp. 147-166.

PERIODICALS

Appraisal: Children's Science Books, fall, 1974, p. 33; winter, 1976, p. 33; spring, 1979, pp. 47-48; winter, 1980, pp. 45-46; winter, 1982, p. 52; fall, 1983, p. 52; spring, 1985, p. 32; winter, 1987, pp. 55-56; spring, 1988, p. 28; fall, 1989.

Booklist, June 15, 1987; May 15, 1989; March 15, 1990; June 1, 1991.

Bulletin of the Center for Children's Books, November, 1991.

Horn Book, October, 1973; April, 1978; October, 1979; February, 1980.

Los Angeles Times Book Review, November 14, 1982, p. 8; April 26, 1987, p. 4.

Missoulian, December 19, 1981; May 4, 1984.

New York Times Book Review, May 4, 1975, p. 45.

San Rafael Independent-Journal, January 26, 1974.

School Library Journal, February, 1977, p. 67; March, 1979, p. 150; February, 1980, p. 71; February, 1981, p. 77; November, 1984, p. 127; October, 1985, p. 186; August, 1987, p. 87; August, 1988, p. 91; January, 1989; March, 1990.

* * *

PATERSON, Katherine (Womeldorf) 1932-

PERSONAL: Born October 31, 1932, in Qing Jiang, China; daughter of George Raymond (a clergyman) and Mary (Goetchius) Womeldorf; married John Barstow Paterson (a clergyman), July 14, 1962; children: Elizabeth Po Lin (adopted), John Barstow, Jr., David Lord, Mary Katherine (adopted). *Education:* King College, A.B., 1954; Presbyterian School of Christian Education, M.A., 1957; postgraduate study at Kobe School of

Katherine Paterson

Japanese Language, 1957-60; Union Theological Seminary, New York, NY, M.R.E., 1962. *Politics:* Democrat. *Religion:* Presbyterian Church in the United States. *Hobbies and other interests:* Reading, swimming, tennis, sailing.

ADDRESSES: Home—Norfolk, VA. *Office*—c/o E. P. Dutton, 2 Park Ave., New York, NY 10016.

CAREER: Public school teacher in Lovettsville, VA, 1954-55; Presbyterian Church in the United States, Board of World Missions, Nashville, TN, missionary in Japan, 1957-62; Pennington School for Boys, Pennington, NJ, teacher of sacred studies and English, 1963-65; writer.

MEMBER: Authors Guild, PEN, Children's Book Guild of Washington.

AWARDS, HONORS: American Library Association (ALA) Notable Children's Book award, 1974, for *Of Nightingales That Weep;* ALA Notable Children's Book award, 1976, National Book Award for Children's Literature, 1977, runner-up for Edgar Allan Poe Award (juvenile division) from Mystery Writers of America, 1977, and American Book Award nomination, children's fiction paperback, 1982, all for *The Master Puppeteer;* ALA Notable Children's Book award, 1977, John Newbery Medal, 1978, Lewis Carroll Shelf Award, 1978, and Division II runner-up, Michigan Young Reader's Award, 1980, all for *Bridge to Terabithia;* Lit.D., King College, 1978; ALA Notable Children's Book award, 1978, National Book Award for Children's Literature, 1979, Christopher Award (ages 9-12), 1979, Newbery Honor Book, 1979, CRABbery (Children Raving About Books) Honor Book, 1979, American Book Award nominee, children's paperback, 1980, William Allen White Children's Book Award, 1981, Garden State Children's Book Award, younger division, New Jersey Library Association, 1981, Georgia Children's Book Award, 1981, Iowa Children's Choice Award, 1981, Massachusetts Children's Book Award (elementary), 1981, all for *The Great Gilly Hopkins;* U.S. nominee, Hans Christian Andersen Award, 1980; *New York Times* Outstanding Book List, 1980, Newbery Medal, 1981, CRABbery Honor Book, 1981, American Book Award nominee, children's hardcover, 1981, children's paperback, 1982, and Hans Christian Andersen Award nominee, 1990, all for *Jacob Have I Loved; The Crane Wife* was named to the *New York Times* Outstanding Books and Best Illustrated Books lists, both 1981; Parent's Choice Award, Parent's Choice Foundation, 1983, for *Rebels of the Heavenly Kingdom;* Irvin Kerlan Award, 1983, "in recognition of singular attainments in the creation of children's literature"; University of Southern Mississippi School of Library Service Silver Medallion, 1983, for outstanding contributions to the field of children's literature; *New York Times* notable book citation and "Parent's Choice" citation, both 1985, for *Come Sing, Jimmy Jo;* nominee, Laura Ingalls Wilder Award, 1986; Regina Medal Award, Catholic Library Association, 1988, for demonstrating "the timeless standards and ideals for the writing of good literature for children"; *Boston Globe-Horn Book* Award, 1991, for *The Tale of the Mandarin Ducks.*

WRITINGS:

The Sign of the Chrysanthemum, illustrated by Peter Landa, Crowell Junior Books, 1973.
Of Nightingales That Weep, illustrated by Haru Wells, Crowell Junior Books, 1974.
The Master Puppeteer, illustrated by H. Wells, Crowell Junior Books, 1976.
Bridge to Terabithia, illustrated by Donna Diamond, Crowell Junior Books, 1977.
The Great Gilly Hopkins, Crowell Junior Books, 1978.
Angels and Other Strangers: Family Christmas Stories, Crowell Junior Books, 1979, published in England as *Star of Night: Stories for Christmas,* Gollancz, 1980.
Jacob Have I Loved, Crowell Junior Books, 1980.
Rebels of the Heavenly Kingdom, Lodestar, 1983.
Come Sing, Jimmy Jo, Lodestar, 1985.
Park's Quest, Lodestar, 1988.
The Tale of the Mandarin Ducks, illustrated by Leo and Diane Dillon, Dutton, 1990.
Lyddie, Dutton, 1991.

TRANSLATOR

Sumiko Yagawa, *The Crane Wife,* illustrated by Suekichi Akaba, Morrow, 1981.
Momoko Ishii, *Tongue-Cut Sparrow,* illustrated by S. Akaba, Lodestar, 1987.

Also translator of Hans Christian Andersen's *The Tongue Cut Sparrow,* for Lodestar.

OTHER

Who Am I?, illustrated by David Stone (curriculum unit), CLC Press, 1966.
To Make Men Free (curriculum unit; includes books, records, pamphlets, and filmstrip), John Knox, 1973.
Justice for All People, Friendship, 1973.
Gates of Excellence: On Reading and Writing Books for Children, Lodestar, 1981.
(With husband, John Paterson) *Consider the Lilies: Flowers of the Bible,* illustrated by Anne Ophelia Dowden, Crowell Junior Books, 1986.
The Spying Heart: More Thoughts on Reading and Writing Books for Children, Lodestar, 1989.

Contributor of articles and reviews to periodicals. Reviewer, *Washington Post Book World,* 1975—; member of editorial board, *Writer,* 1987—.

ADAPTATIONS:

"Bridge to Terabithia" (listening record or cassette; filmstrip with cassette), Miller-Brody, 1978, (filmstrip), Random House/Miller-Brody, 1980, (film), PBS-TV, 1985.
The Great Gilly Hopkins (film), Hanna-Barbera, 1980, (listening record or cassette; filmstrip with cassette), Random House.

"Angels and Other Strangers" (cassette), Random House.
"Jacob Have I Loved" (listening cassette; filmstrip with cassette), Random House, 1982, (film) PBS-TV, 1990.
"Getting Hooked on Books: Challenges" (filmstrip with cassette, with teacher's guide, contains "The Great Gilly Hopkins"), Guidance Associates, 1986.

SIDELIGHTS: Katherine Paterson's books about teens who are thrust abruptly into the adult world "have swept every conceivable award for children's literature," to quote *Dictionary of Literary Biography* contributor M. Sarah Smedman. Paterson has won the Newbery Medal twice and the coveted National Book Award twice. Her works have been translated into more than fifteen foreign languages, and they have sold millions of copies worldwide. Smedman calls Paterson "a major artist, skilled, discerning, and compassionate," adding: "What she has written achieves excellence because her artistic vision embraces all that is human and because she is a master craftsman."

All the awards notwithstanding, Paterson is humble about her abilities and her goals. "My gift seems to be that I am one of those fortunate people who can, if she works hard at it, uncover a story that children will enjoy," she wrote in *Theory into Practice.* "My aim is to engage young readers in the life of a story which came out of me but which is not mine, but ours. I don't just want a young reader's time or attention. I want his life. I want his senses, his imagination, his intellect, his emotions, and all the experiences he has known breathing life into the words upon the page. It doesn't matter how high my aim or how polished my craft. I know that without the efforts of my reader, I have accomplished nothing.... I have not written a book for children unless the book is brought to life by the child who reads it."

Paterson often writes about children who are orphaned or estranged from their parents, teens who isolate themselves or who associate only with one or two close friends. These recurring situations reflect the instability of the author's life as she was growing up in a missionary family. Paterson was born in China and spent the first five years of her life there. As a child she could speak Chinese—her parents chose to live among the Chinese people rather than isolate themselves within the tight American community in Shanghai.

World War II forced Paterson's family to return to the United States. They moved more than fifteen times in the next thirteen years. In *Gates of Excellence: On Reading and Writing Books for Children,* Paterson states: "Among the more than twice-told tales in my family is the tragic one about the year we lived in Richmond, Virginia, when I came home from first grade on February 14 without a single valentine. My mother grieved over this event until her death, asking me once why I didn't write a story about the time I didn't get any valentines. 'But, Mother,' I said, *'all* my stories are about the time I didn't get any valentines.'"

In the same source, Paterson describes herself as "a weird little kid" who invented elaborate fantasies to help her cope with her constantly-changing environment. Her family moved throughout the South, staying in Virginia, West Virginia, and North Carolina. She was sometimes the target of bullies, but more often was ignored completely, left to her own resources and to the comfort she could draw from her Christian background. Paterson notes in *Theory into Practice* that she writes for teens because "I have a rejected child, a jealous and jilted adolescent inside who demands, if not revenge, a certain degree of satisfaction. I am sure it is she, or should I say they, who keep demanding that I write for them."

Paterson was an avid reader with a "sensuous love for books as paper, ink, and binding, treasures to be respected and cherished," as she put it in *Gates of Excellence.* Even though she attended thirteen different schools, she managed to earn honor roll grades, and in 1950 she entered King College in Bristol, Tennessee. There she studied English literature. Following her graduation in 1954, she taught elementary school in a small Virginia town for a year, then she sought a master's degree from the Presbyterian School of Christian Education in Richmond.

In 1957 Paterson returned to the Far East, this time as a missionary in Japan. "The only Japanese I had known as a child were enemy soldiers," Paterson told *Something about the Author.* "What made it possible for me to go to Japan at all was a close friend I had in graduate school, a Japanese woman pastor who persuaded me that despite the war, I would find a home in Japan, if I would give the Japanese people a chance. And she was right. In the course of four years I was set fully free from my deep childish hatred. I truly loved Japan, and one of the most heart-warming compliments I ever received came from a Japanese man I worked with who said to me one day that someone had told him I had been born in China. Was that true? I assured him it was. 'I knew it,' he said. 'I've always known there was something Oriental about you.'"

Paterson returned to the United States in 1961. During a fellowship year at Union Theological Seminary in New York she met and married John Barstow Paterson, a Presbyterian minister. Her life took a new direction as the couple settled in Takoma Park, Maryland, and began to raise two sons and two adopted daughters—one born in Hong Kong, the other on an Apache Indian reservation.

Horn Book essayist Virginia Buckley claims that Paterson turned to creative writing "because as a harassed mother she wanted to have something at the end of the day which had not been eaten up or dirtied up or torn apart." Paterson began her professional career formulating curricula for school systems. She turned to fiction and just kept trying. Ten years passed before she felt she had produced a story worthy of publication. In *Gates of Excellence,* she writes that her fame as a novelist "might have happened sooner had I had a room of my own and fewer children, but somehow I doubt it. For as I look back on what I have written, I can see that the very persons who have taken away my time and space are those who have given me something to say."

Paterson's first three novels, *The Sign of the Chrysanthemum* (1973), *Of Nightingales That Weep* (1974), and *The Master Puppeteer* (1976), are all set in Japan during bygone eras. All three concern teens who have lost one or both parents and who must make their own decisions during times of war, famine, and civil strife. In her *Introducing More Books: A Guide for the Middle Grades,* Diana L. Spirt praises the works for the way they blend "a literate mix of adventure and Japanese history with a subtle knowledge of young people." *The Master Puppeteer,* a mystery set in Osaka during the famine of 1783-87, won the author her first National Book Award in 1977.

Other Paterson award-winners are set in America and offer emotionally complex stories with which American teens can readily identify. *Bridge to Terabithia,* the Newbery Medal winner in 1978, tells of a deep friendship between two teenagers that ends with the accidental death of one of them. *The Great Gilly Hopkins* takes a comic view of an alienated foster child and the loving caretaker who eventually wins her affection. That novel won the Christopher Award and the William Allen White Award. *Jacob Have I Loved,* Paterson's other Newbery Medal winner, explores the life of a twin growing up on a Chesapeake island who feels overshadowed by her talented sibling.

Smedman contends that Paterson "writes of Japanese and American youngsters who, despite their cultural differences, are in many ways alike. Entangled in chaotic childhoods, her sensitive but tough young protagonists, each a social or spiritual outsider, set out to achieve self-determined goals. During the course of each story, the child, caught in potentially tragic circumstances, must come to grips with the limitations with which reality circumscribes one's dreams. In each Paterson story, the protagonist turns tragedy to triumph by bravely choosing a way which is not selfishly determined."

After many years in Takoma Park, the Paterson family moved to Norfolk, Virginia, where they now live. Paterson has continued her writing, and she makes frequent tours as a lecturer on children's literature. In *The Writer,* Paterson spoke of the gratification she derives from her work. "I keep learning that if I am willing to go deep into my own heart, I am able, miraculously, to touch other people at the core," she concluded. "But that is because I do have a reader I must try to satisfy—that is the reader I am and the reader I was as a child. I know this reader in a way that I can never know a generic target out there somewhere. This reader demands honesty and emotional depth. She yearns for clear, rhythmically pleasing language. She wants a world she can see, taste, smell, feel, and hear. And above all she wants characters who will make her laugh and cry and bind her to themselves in a fierce

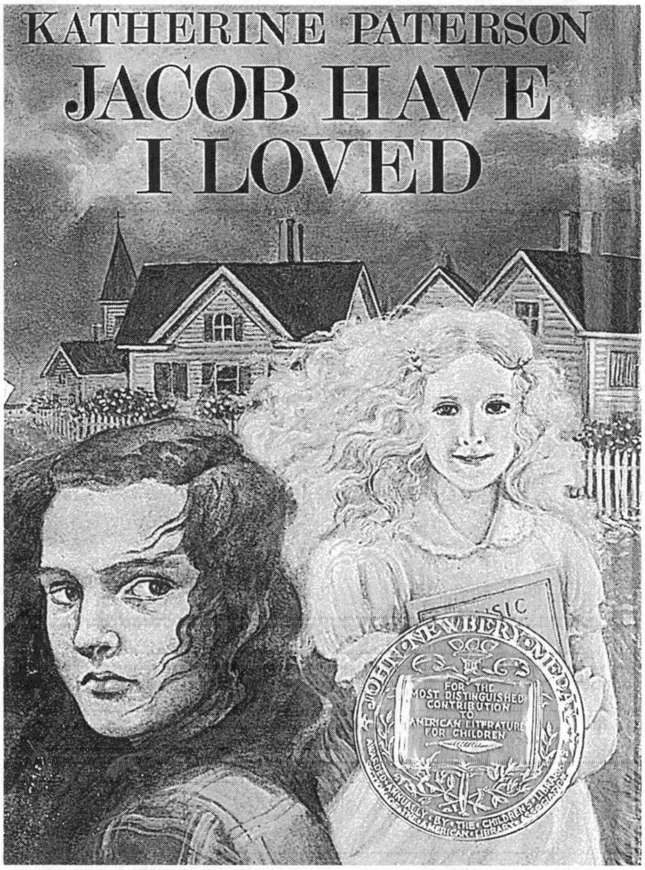

Cover of *Jacob Have I Loved,* by Katherine Paterson.

friendship, as together they move through a story that pulls her powerfully from the first word to the last.

"O.K. So she's a fussy reader. I've never fully satisfied her, but I would love to spend the next twenty-five years trying."

WORKS CITED:

Buckley, Virginia, "Katherine Paterson," *Horn Book,* August, 1978, pp. 368-71.

Dictionary of Literary Biography, Volume 52: *American Writers for Children since 1960: Fiction,* Gale, 1986, pp. 296-314.

Paterson, Katherine, "The Aim of the Writer Who Writes for Children," *Theory into Practice,* autumn, 1982, pp. 325-31.

Paterson, Katherine, *Gates of Excellence: On Reading and Writing Books for Children,* Elsevier/Nelson, 1981.

Paterson, Katherine, "What Writing Has Taught Me: Three Lessons," *The Writer,* August, 1990, pp. 9-10.

Something about the Author, Volume 53, Gale, 1988, pp. 118-28.

Spirt, Diana L., "Forming a View of the World: 'The Master Puppeteer,'" in *Introducing More Books: A Guide for the Middle Grades,* Bowker, 1978, pp. 114-17.

FOR MORE INFORMATION SEE:

BOOKS

Authors and Artists for Young Adults, Volume 1, Gale, 1989.
Children's Literature Review, Volume 7, Gale, 1984.
Contemporary Authors, New Revision Series, Volume 28, Gale, 1990.
Contemporary Literary Criticism, Gale, Volume 12, 1980; Volume 30, 1984.
Fifth Book of Junior Authors and Illustrators, Wilson, 1983.

PERIODICALS

Horn Book, August, 1981.
New York Times Book Review, November 13, 1977; April 30, 1978; December 2, 1979; December 21, 1980; July 17, 1983; May 16, 1985.
Washington Post Book World, November 13, 1977; May 14, 1978; November 9, 1980; November 8, 1981; June 12, 1983; May 12, 1985.

* * *

PATON WALSH, Gillian 1937- (Jill Paton Walsh)

PERSONAL: Born April 29, 1937, in London, England; daughter of John Llewellyn (an engineer) and Patricia (Dubern) Bliss; married Antony Edmund Paton Walsh (a chartered secretary), August 12, 1961; children: Edmund Alexander, Margaret Ann, Helen Clare. *Education:* St. Anne's College, Oxford, Dip. Ed., 1959, M.A. (honours) in English. *Politics:* None. *Religion:* "Skepticism." *Hobbies and other interests:* Photography, gardening, cooking, carpentry, reading.

ADDRESSES: Home—72 Water Lane, Histon, Cambridge CB4 4LR, England.

CAREER: Enfield Girls Grammar School, Middlesex, English teacher, 1959-62; writer, 1962—. Whittall Lecturer, Library of Congress, Washington, DC, 1978. Visiting Faculty Member, Center for the Study of Children's Literature, Simmons College, Boston, 1978-86. Founder, with John Rowe Townsend, of Green Bay Publishers, 1986.

MEMBER: Society of Authors (member of Management Committee), Children's Writers Group.

AWARDS, HONORS: Book World Festival award, 1970, for *Fireweed;* Whitbread Prize (shared with Russell Hoban), 1974, for *The Emperor's Winding Sheet;* Boston *Globe-Horn Book* Award, 1976, for *Unleaving;* Arts Council Creative Writing Fellowship, 1976-77, and 1977-78; Universe Prize, 1984, for *A Parcel of Patterns;* Smarties Prize Grand Prix, 1984, for *Gaffer Samson's Luck.*

Jill Paton Walsh

WRITINGS:

JUVENILE FICTION; UNDER NAME JILL PATON WALSH

Hengest's Tale, illustrated by Janet Margrie, St. Martin's Press, 1966.
The Dolphin Crossing, St. Martin's Press, 1967.
Fireweed, Macmillan, 1969, Farrar Straus, 1970.
Goldengrove, Farrar Straus, 1972.
Toolmaker, illustrated by Jeroo Roy, Heinemann, 1973, Seabury Press, 1974.
The Dawnstone, illustrated by Mary Dinsdale, Hamish Hamilton, 1973.
The Emperor's Winding Sheet, Farrar Straus, 1974.
The Huffler, Farrar Straus, 1975 (published in England as *The Butty Boy,* illustrated by Juliette Palmer, Macmillan, 1975).
Unleaving, Farrar Straus, 1976.
Crossing to Salamis (first novel in trilogy; also see below), illustrated by David Smee, Heinemann, 1977.
The Walls of Athens (second novel in trilogy; also see below), illustrated by David Smee, Heinemann, 1977.
Persian Gold (third novel in trilogy; also see below), illustrated by David Smee, Heinemann, 1978.
Children of the Fox (contains *Crossing to Salamis, The Walls of Athens,* and *Persian Gold*), Farrar Straus, 1978.
A Chance Child, Farrar Straus, 1978.

The Green Book, illustrated by Joanna Stubbs, Macmillan, 1981, illustrated by Lloyd Bloom, Farrar Straus, 1982, published as *Shine,* Macdonald, 1988.
Babylon, illustrated by Jenny Northway, Deutsch, 1982.
A Parcel of Patterns, Farrar Straus, 1983.
Lost and Found, illustrated by Mary Rayner, Deutsch, 1984.
Gaffer Samson's Luck, illustrated by Brock Cole, Farrar Straus, 1984.
Torch, Viking Kestrel, 1987, Farrar Straus, 1988.
Birdy and the Ghosties, illustrated by Alan Marks, Macdonald, 1989.
Grace, Viking, 1991, Farrar, Straus, 1992.
When Grandma Came (picture book), illustrated by Sophie Williams, Viking, 1992.

OTHER; UNDER NAME JILL PATON WALSH

(With Kevin Crossley Holland) *Wordhoard: Anglo-Saxon Stories,* Farrar Straus, 1969.
Farewell, Great King (adult novel), Coward McCann, 1972.
(Editor) *Beowulf* (structural reader), Longman, 1975.
The Island Sunrise: Prehistoric Britain, Deutsch, 1975, published as *The Island Sunrise: Prehistoric Culture in the British Isles,* Seabury Press, 1976.
Five Tides (short stories), Green Bay, 1986.
Lapsing (adult novel), Weidenfeld & Nicolson, 1986, St. Martin's, 1987.
A School for Lovers (adult novel), Weidenfeld & Nicolson, 1989.

Some of Paton Walsh's manuscripts and papers may be found in the Kerlan Collection, University of Minnesota, Minneapolis.

SIDELIGHTS: Jill Paton Walsh is noted for her works which deal realistically with life, death and maturation. "Of [the many] skilled and sensitive writers [for young people]," declares Sheila Egoff in *Thursday's Child,* "[Paton] Walsh is the most formally literary. Her writing is studded with allusions to poetry, art and philosophy that give it an intellectual framework unmatched in children's literature." Paton Walsh's works examine eras and topics such as life, death, and honor in Anglo-Saxon England (*Hengest's Tale* and *Wordhoard*), Victorian child labor in England (*A Chance Child*), growing up in World War II England (*The Dolphin Crossing* and *Fireweed*), life in the Early Stone Age (*Toolmaker*), and loyalty in the midst of destruction in fifteenth-century Byzantium (*The Emperor's Winding Sheet*). She has also written several novels that center on the Cornish coast, where she spent part of her young life.

Jill Paton Walsh was born Jill Bliss, a member of a loving family living in suburban London. Her father was an engineer, one of the earliest experimenters with television, and he and his wife actively stimulated their children to enjoy learning. "For the whole of our childhoods," Paton Walsh writes in her *Something about the Author Autobiography Series* (*SAAS*) entry, "I, and my brothers and sister—I am the eldest of four—were surrounded by love and encouragement on a lavish scale.... And to an unusual degree everyone was without prejudices against, or limited ambitions for, girls. As much was expected of me as of my brothers."

"For five crucial years of my childhood—from the year I was three to the year I was eight—the war dominated and shaped everything around me," Paton Walsh explains in *SAAS,* "and then for many years, until well into my teens, postwar hardships remained." "I do not know if there was a plan of evacuation there when the war began, which my parents did not join in, or if Finchley did not seem a likely target," she continues. Finally her mother's stepfather, upset by a bombing raid, moved the family to his place in Cornwall, in the far west of England. Although Jill's mother soon returned with her younger children to her husband in London, Jill herself remained in Cornwall for the next five years, returning to her family only after her grandmother suffered a fatal heart attack.

"I left St. Ives when I was just eight, and I didn't go back there till I was thirty-six," Paton Walsh explains in *SAAS.* "And it turned out that several people could remember me, and even remember having been in the same class in that little nursery school. A part of me is still rooted on that rocky shore, and it appears again and again in what I write." She stepped out of the comfortable world she had known directly into wartime London. "That first night back," she recalls, "I lay awake listening to the clanging sounds, like dustbins rolling round the night sky, made by German rockets falling somewhere a little distance off."

"The children I talk to nowadays are very interested in the Second World War," Paton Walsh remarks in her *SAAS* essay. "They think it must have been a time of excitement and danger, whereas it was actually dreadfully boring." Wartime restrictions and shortages meant that normal childhood activities—movies, television, radio, and even outdoor play—were severely limited. "I remember, in short, a time of discomfort and gloom, and, above all, upheaval." Part of the upheaval was caused by her mother's relatives, who had been wealthy colonists in Southeast Asia before the war, and who returned to England, newly impoverished, to live with her family. Because they had their own ideas of proper female behavior, Paton Walsh writes, she never knew "whether it was good and clever to give voice to my opinions, or pushy and priggish; not knowing from one day to the next what sort of behaviour would be expected of me." "Yet in the long run," Paton Walsh concludes, "I have benefited greatly from all this. I protected myself. I learned not to care what other people think. I would say what I liked, read what I was interested in, go on my own way, and ignore what the invading hoards of aunts and uncles thought, about me, or about anything else."

Paton Walsh attended a Catholic girl's school in North Finchley, whose environment was quite different from the liberality of her home life. "The nuns who taught me were suspicious of me," she declares in her *SAAS* entry. "They liked girls who worked very hard, not those who found it easy." When Paton Walsh left the school, it was to take a place at Oxford University. "I enjoyed myself vastly at Oxford, made friends, talked late into the night, and even worked sometimes, and work included lectures by both C. S. Lewis and J. R. R. Tolkien. The subject of the lectures and tutorials was always literature or philology—we wouldn't have dared ask those great men about their own work!—but the example they set by being both great and serious scholars, and writers of fantasy and books for children was not lost on me."

By the time Paton Walsh completed her degree, she was engaged to a man she had met at school. She obtained a teaching position, but soon discovered that she disliked being a teacher. "I didn't teach long," she explains in her *SAAS* entry. "I got married in my second year as a teacher, and eighteen months later was expecting a child." The life of a housewife, however, did not suit her either: "I was bored frantic. I went nearly crazy, locked up alone with a howling baby all day and all night . . . . As plants need water and light, as the baby needed milk, I needed something intellectual, cheap, and quiet." So, she says, "I began to write a book. It was a children's book. It never occurred to me to write any other kind."

"Until the moment I began to write I did not know that I was a writer," Paton Walsh explains in *SAAS.* The book she began to work on in those day, she says, "was, unfortunately, a dreadfully bad book. It had twelve chapters of equal length, with a different bit of historical background in each one." Eventually Kevin Crossley Holland, an editor with Macmillan, explained to Paton Walsh that to publish this particular book might be a bad idea. He then offered her an option on her next work. "I set to work joyfully on *Hengest's Tale,*" she recalls, "a gory epic retold out of fragments of *Beowulf,* and I stopped work only for a fortnight—between chapter three and chapter four—when my second child, my daughter Margaret, was born. *Hengest's Tale* was my first published book. And I have never forgotten the difference it made to be able to say, to others, certainly, but above all, to myself, 'I am a writer.'"

"This whole question of where ideas for books come from is very intriguing," Paton Walsh states in her *SAAS* entry. "I suppose, 'Where do you get your ideas?' is the question most often asked by the children I meet. I think they are hoping for useful guidance on how to get ideas for their English homework, and I am a bit ashamed to be so hopeless at helping. But I don't really know where I get ideas from; each one in turn seems like an accident. It's a question of being on the lookout for the kind of accident that makes the idea for a book . . . . But I can say that a large part of it is giving loving attention to places; not necessarily beautiful places, just anywhere. Most of my books really have begun with thinking about the places they are set in." For example, she continues, "I went to Greece to find the landscapes for a classical historical novel, written for adults, called *Farewell, Great King,* but when I got there I found Byzantine things, the marvellous mountaintop deserted city of Mistra above all, and the result of that was *The Emperor's Winding Sheet.* And there are more places singing to me . . . . "

Critics celebrate Paton Walsh's ability to evoke both character and setting, and through them to say something meaningful about growing up. She "has an astonishing ability to create appealing personalities," declares Elizabeth S. Coolidge in the *Washington Post Book World.* In *Unleaving,* the critic continues, "She has written a book about death, and what this means to a philosopher, a teenager, a grandmother and a very small child. Yet *Unleaving* is in no way a gloomy book, but one that leaves the reader with a warm and optimistic view of humankind." "[Paton] Walsh doesn't tidy up the blight for which man was born," states Alice Bach in a *New York Times Book Review* critique of the same book. "She's too wise to attempt answers about growing, living, dying, ethical choices. She exalts the mystery, the unknowing itself." "As time has gone by," Paton Walsh concludes in her *SAAS* entry, "I have won the friendship of many other writers and readers and book-lovers. I feel lucky in this, beyond my deserts . . . . A writer is what I shall be as long as there is a daydream in my head, and I have strength to sit up and type."

WORKS CITED:

Bach, Alice, review of *Unleaving, New York Times Book Review,* August 8, 1976, p. 18.

Coolidge, Elizabeth S., "Two Modern English Morality Tales," *Washington Post Book World,* May 2, 1976, p. L13.

Egoff, Sheila A., "Realistic Fiction," *Thursday's Child: Trends and Patterns in Contemporary Children's Literature,* American Library Association, 1981, pp. 31-65.

Paton Walsh, Jill, "My Life So Far," *Something about the Author Autobiography Series,* Volume 3, Gale, 1987, pp. 189-203.

FOR MORE INFORMATION SEE:

BOOKS

Children's Literature Review, Volume 2, Gale, 1976.

Contemporary Literary Criticism, Volume 35, Gale, 1985.

* * *

PATON WALSH, Jill
See PATON WALSH, Gillian

See PATON WALSH, Gillian

* * *

PAULSEN, Gary 1939-

PERSONAL: Born May 17, 1939, in Minneapolis, MN; son of Oscar (an army officer) and Eunice Paulsen; married second wife, Ruth Ellen Wright (an artist), May 5, 1971; children: (second marriage) James Wright; two children from previous marriage. *Education:* Attended Bemidji College, 1957-58, and University of Colorado, 1976. *Politics:* "As Solzhenitsyn has said, 'If we limit ourselves to political structures we are not artists.'" *Religion:* "I believe in spiritual progress."

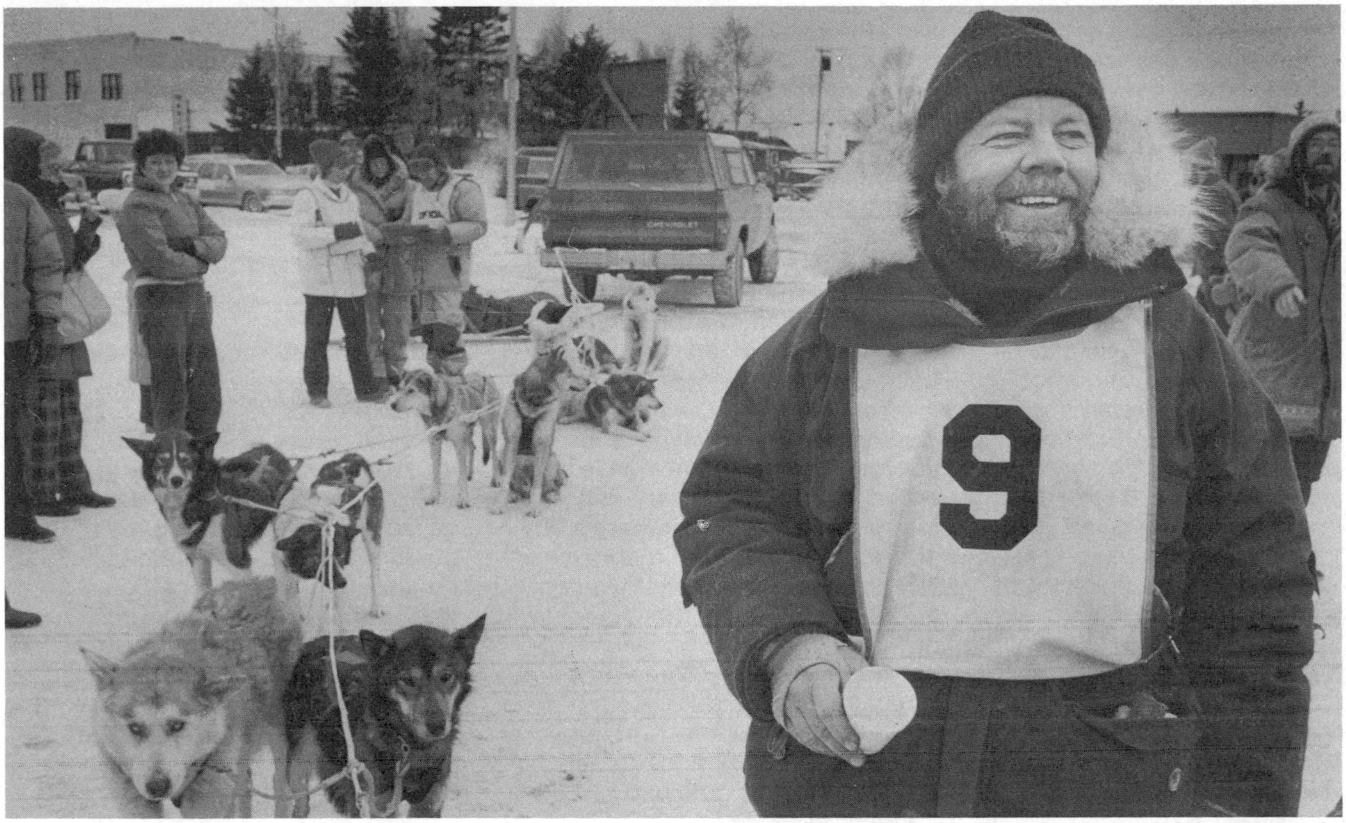

Gary Paulsen

ADDRESSES: Home—Becida, MN. *Agent*—Jonathan Lazear, 430 First Avenue North, Suite 416, Minneapolis, MN 55401.

CAREER: Writer, 1960s—. Has also worked as a teacher, field engineer, editor, soldier, actor, director, farmer, rancher, truck driver, trapper, professional archer, migrant farm worker, singer, and sailor. *Military service:* U.S. Army, 1959-62; became sergeant.

AWARDS, HONORS: Central Missouri Award for Children's Literature, 1976; *The Green Recruit* was chosen one of New York Public Library's Books for the Teen Age, 1980, 1981 and 1982, and *Sailing: From Jibs to Jibing,* 1982; *Dancing Carl* was selected one of American Library Association's Best Young Adult Books, 1983, and *Tracker,* 1984; Society of Midland Authors Award, 1985, for *Tracker;* Parents' Choice Award for Literature, Parents' Choice Foundation, 1985, for *Dogsong;* Newbery Honor Book, 1986, for *Dogsong,* 1988, for *Hatchet,* and 1990, for *The Winter Room; Dogsong* was chosen one of Child Study Association of America's Children's Books of the Year, 1986; award from Minnesota Festival of the Book, 1987-88, for *Hatchet.*

WRITINGS:

JUVENILE FICTION

Mr. Tucket (illustrated by Noel Sickles), Funk & Wagnalls, 1968.
The C.B. Radio Caper (illustrated by John Asquith), Raintree, 1977.
The Curse of the Cobra (illustrated by J. Asquith), Raintree, 1977.
Winterkill, T. Nelson, 1977.
The Foxman, T. Nelson, 1977.
Tiltawhirl John, T. Nelson, 1977.
The Golden Stick (illustrated by Jerry Scott), Raintree, 1977.
The Night the White Deer Died, T. Nelson, 1978.
Hope and a Hatchet, T. Nelson, 1978.
(With Ray Peekner) *The Green Recruit,* Independence Press, 1978.
The Spitball Gang, Elsevier, 1980.
Popcorn Days and Buttermilk Nights, Lodestar Books, 1983.
Dancing Carl, Bradbury, 1983.
Tracker, Bradbury, 1984.
Dogsong, Bradbury, 1985.
Sentries, Bradbury, 1986.
The Crossing, Orchard, 1987.
Hatchet, Bradbury, 1987.
The Island, Orchard, 1988.
The Voyage of the Frog, Orchard, 1989.
The Winter Room, Orchard, 1989.
Hatchet Rack Trim, Puffin, 1989.
The Boy Who Owned the School, Orchard, 1990.
Canyons, Delacorte, 1990.
Woodsong (illustrated by wife, Ruth W. Paulsen), Bradbury, 1990.
The Cookcamp, Orchard, 1991.
River, Doubleday, 1991.

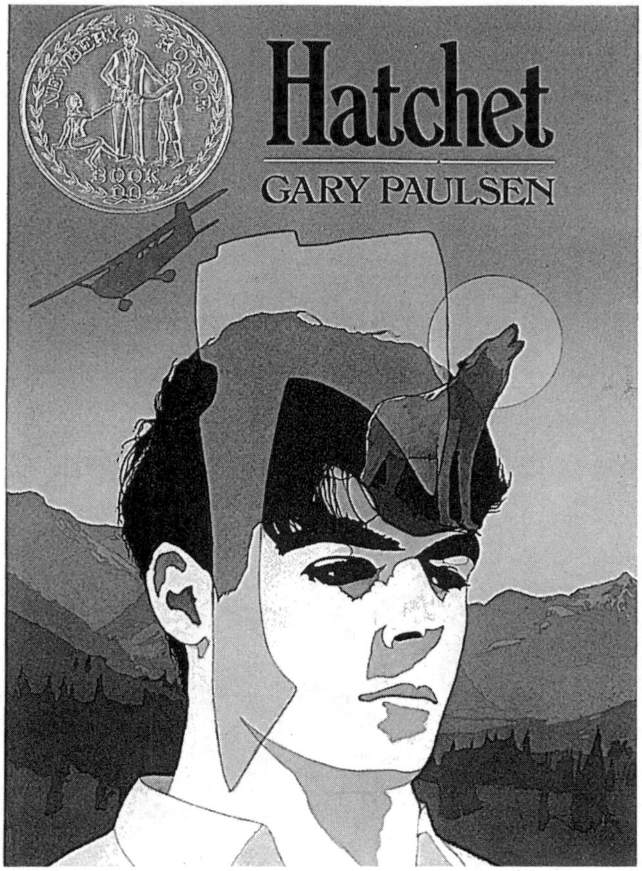

Cover of *Hatchet,* by Gary Paulsen.

JUVENILE NONFICTION

(With Dan Theis) *Martin Luther King: The Man Who Climbed the Mountain,* Raintree, 1976.
The Small Ones (illustrated by K. Goff; photographs by Wilford Miller), Raintree, 1976.
The Grass-Eaters: Real Animals (illustrated by K. Goff; photographs by W. Miller), Raintree, 1976.
Dribbling, Shooting, and Scoring Sometimes (photographs by Heinz Kluetmeier), Raintree, 1976.
Hitting, Pitching, and Running Maybe (photographs by H. Kluetmeier), Raintree, 1976.
Tackling, Running, and Kicking—Now and Again (photographs by H. Kluetmeier), Raintree, 1977.
Riding, Roping, and Bulldogging—Almost (photographs by H. Kluetmeier), Raintree, 1977.
Careers in an Airport (photographs by R. Nye), Raintree, 1977.
Running, Jumping, and Throwing—If You Can (photographs by H. Kluetmeier), Raintree, 1978.
Forehanding and Backhanding—If You're Lucky (photographs by H. Kluetmeier), Raintree, 1978.
(With John Morris) *Hiking and Backpacking* (illustrated by R. W. Paulsen), Simon & Schuster, 1978.
(With J. Morris) *Canoeing, Kayaking, and Rafting* (illustrated by John Peterson and Jack Storholm), Simon & Schuster, 1979.
Downhill, Hotdogging and Cross-Country—If the Snow Isn't Sticky (photographs by H. Kluetmeier and Willis Wood), Raintree, 1979.
Facing Off, Checking and Goaltending—Perhaps (photographs by H. Kluetmeier and Melchior DiGiacomo), Raintree, 1979.
Going Very Fast in a Circle—If You Don't Run Out of Gas (photographs by H. Kluetmeier and Bob D'Olivo), Raintree, 1979.
Launching, Floating High and Landing—If Your Pilot Light Doesn't Go Out (photographs by H. Kluetmeier), Raintree, 1979.
Pummeling, Falling and Getting Up—Sometimes (photographs by H. Kluetmeier and Joe DiMaggio), Raintree, 1979.
Track, Enduro and Motocross—Unless You Fall Over (photographs by H. Kluetmeier), Raintree, 1979.
(With Art Browne, Jr.) *TV and Movie Animals,* Messner, 1980.
Sailing: From Jibs to Jibing (illustrated by R. W. Paulsen), Messner, 1981.

ADULT FICTION

The Implosion Effect, Major Books, 1976.
The Death Specialists, Major Books, 1976.
C.B. Jockey, Major Books, 1977.
The Sweeper, Harlequin, 1981.
Campkill, Pinnacle Books, 1981.
Clutterkill, Harlequin, 1982.
Murphy, Walker, 1987.
Murphy's Gold, Walker, 1988.
The Madonna Stories, Van Bliet, 1988.
Murphy's Herd, Walker, 1989.

PLAYS

Communications (one-act), produced in New Mexico, 1974.
Together-Apart (one-act), produced in Denver, CO, at Changing Scene Theater, 1976.

OTHER

(With Raymond Friday Locke) *The Special War,* Sirkay, 1966.
Some Birds Don't Fly, Rand McNally, 1969.
The Building a New, Buying an Old, Remodeling a Used, Comprehensive Home and Shelter Book, Prentice-Hall, 1976.
Farm: A History and Celebration of the American Farmer, Prentice-Hall, 1977.
Successful Home Repair, Structures, 1978.
Money-Saving Home Repair Guide, Ideals, 1981.
Beat the System: A Survival Guide, Pinnacle Books, 1983.
A Cry in the Wind (screenplay adaptation of *Hatchet*), Concorde-New Horizons, 1990.
Kill Fee, Donald I. Fine, Inc., 1990.
Night Rituals, Bantam, 1991.

Also author of *Meteor,* and of more than 200 short stories and articles.

ADAPTATIONS: Dogsong (filmstrip with cassette), Random House/Miller-Brody, 1986; *Hatchet* (filmstrip with cassette), Random House, 1988; *A Cry in the Wind* (motion picture; based on *Hatchet;* screenplay by Paulsen), released by Concorde-New Horizons, 1990.

SIDELIGHTS: A prolific writer in a number of genres, Gary Paulsen is acclaimed as the author of powerful young adult fiction. Usually set in wilderness areas, Paulsen's young adult books feature teenagers who arrive at self-awareness by way of experiences in nature—often through challenging tests of their own survival instincts. A resident of northern Minnesota, Paulsen often writes from his first-hand knowledge of the outdoors, and from his experiences as a hunter, trapper, and even a dogsledder in the Alaska Iditarod race. His work is widely praised by critics, and he has been awarded Newbery Medal Honor Book citations for three of his books, *Dogsong, Hatchet,* and *The Winter Room.* Paulsen displays an "extraordinary ability to picture for the reader how man's comprehension of life can be transformed with the lessons of nature," writes Evie Wilson in *Voice of Youth Advocates.* "With humor and psychological genius, Paulsen develops strong adolescent characters who lend new power to youth's plea to be allowed to apply individual skills in their risk-taking." In addition to writing young adult fiction, Paulsen has also authored numerous books of children's nonfiction, as well as two plays and many works of adult fiction and nonfiction.

Paulsen was born in Minnesota in 1939, the son of first-generation Danish and Swedish parents. During childhood, he saw little of his father, who served in the military in Europe during World War II, nor his mother, who worked in a Chicago ammunitions factory. "I was reared by my grandmother and several aunts," he said in an interview for *Something about the Author* (*SATA*). "I first saw my father when I was seven in the Philippines where my parents and I lived from 1946 to 1949." When the family returned to the United States, Paulsen suffered from being continually uprooted. "We moved around constantly.... The longest time I spent in one school was for about five months. I was an 'Army brat,' and it was a miserable life. School was a nightmare because I was unbelievably shy, and terrible at sports.... I wound up skipping most of the ninth grade." In addition to problems at school, he faced many ordeals at home. "My father drank a lot, and there would be terrible arguments," he told *SATA*. Eventually Paulsen was sent again to live with relatives, and worked to support himself with jobs as a newspaperboy and as a pin-setter in a bowling alley.

Things began to change for the better during his teen years. He found security and support with his grandmother and aunts, "safety nets" as he described them in his *SATA* interview. A turning point in his life came one sub-zero winter day when, as he was walking past the public library, he decided to stop in to warm himself. "To my absolute astonishment the librarian walked up to me and asked if I wanted a library card," he described in *SATA*. ".... When she handed me the card, she handed me the world. I can't even describe how liberating it was. She recommended westerns and science fiction but every now and then would slip in a classic. I roared through everything she gave me and in the summer read a book a day. It was as though I had been dying of thirst and the librarian had handed me a five-gallon bucket of water. I drank and drank."

From 1957 to 1959, Paulsen attended Bemidji College in Minnesota, paying for his tuition with money he'd earned as a trapper for the state of Minnesota. He served in the U.S. Army from 1959 to 1962, and worked with missiles. After the Army, he took extension courses to become a certified field engineer, and found work in the aerospace departments of the Bendix and Lockheed corporations. There it occurred to him that he might try and become a writer. "I'd finished reading a magazine article on flight-testing ... and thought, *Gad,* what a way to make a living—writing about something you like and getting paid for it!," he told Frank Serdahely in *Writer's Digest.* "I remembered writing some of my past reports, some fictionalized versions I'd included. And I thought: What the hell, I *am* an engineering writer. But, conversely, I also realized I didn't know a thing about writing—*professionally.* After several hours of hard thinking, a way to earn came to me. All I had to do was go to work editing a magazine."

Creating a fictitious resume, Paulsen was able to obtain an associate editor position on a men's magazine in Hollywood, California. Although it soon became apparent to his employers that he had no editorial experience, "they could see I was serious about wanting to learn, and they were willing to teach me," Paulsen told *SATA*. He spent nearly a year with the magazine, finding it "the best of all possible ways to learn about writing. It probably did more to improve my craft and ability than any other single event in my life." Still living in California, Paulsen also found work as a film extra (he once played a drunken Indian in a movie called *Flap*), and took up sculpting as a hobby, once winning first prize in an exhibition. "I worked mostly at wood carving, which I love," he told *SATA*. "But by then I knew I wanted to be writing, and backed off from sculpture. I didn't feel I could do justice to both."

Paulsen's first book, *The Special War,* was published in 1966, and he soon proved himself to be one of the most prolific authors in the United States. In little over a decade, working mainly out of northern Minnesota, he published nearly forty books and close to 200 articles and stories for magazines. Among Paulsen's diverse titles were a number of children's nonfiction books about animals, a biography of Martin Luther King, Jr., several humorous titles under the "Sports on the Light Side" series published by Raintree Press, two plays, adult fiction and nonfiction, as well as some initial ventures into juvenile fiction. On a bet with a friend, he once wrote eleven articles and short stories inside four days and sold all of them. To burn off tension, he took long walks around his Minnesota farm during which, as he was quoted by Serdahely, he would "blow the hell out of a hillside" with a rifle.

His prolific output was interrupted by a libel lawsuit brought against his 1977 young adult novel, *Winterkill.* Paulsen eventually won the case, but, as he told *SATA*, "the whole situation was so nasty and ugly that I stopped writing. I wanted nothing more to do with publishing and burned my bridges, so to speak." Unable to earn any other type of living, he went back to trapping for the state of Minnesota. "The traps we used were snares, which kill the animals right away. It's not pleasant, but it's humane, if death can be humane. I was working a 60-mile line mostly on foot, sometimes on skis, going out in the early morning and heading home at night. Very slow work."

To help Paulsen in his hunting job, a friend gave him a team of sled dogs, a gift which ultimately had a profound influence on Paulsen. "One day about midnight we were crossing Clear Water Lake, which is about three miles long," Paulsen told *SATA*. "There was a full moon shining so brightly on the snow you could read by it. There was no one around, and all I could hear was the rhythm of the dogs' breathing as they pulled the sled." The intensity of the moment prompted an impulsive seven-day trip by Paulsen through northern Minnesota. "I didn't go home—my wife was frantic—I didn't check lines, I just ran the dogs.... For food, we had a few beaver carcasses.... I was initiated into this incredibly ancient and very beautiful bond, and it was as if everything that had happened to me before ceased to exist." Paulsen afterwards made a resolution to permanently give up hunting and trapping, and proceeded to pursue dogsled racing as a hobby. He went so far as to enter the grueling 1200-mile Iditarod race in Alaska, an experience which later provided the basis for his award-winning novel *Dogsong.*

Paulsen's acclaimed young adult fiction—all written since the 1980s—often centers around teenage characters who arrive at an understanding of themselves and their world through pivotal experiences in nature. His writing has been praised for its almost poetic effect, and he is also credited for creating vivid descriptions of his characters' emotional states. His 1984 novel *Tracker* tells about a thirteen-year-old boy who faces his first season of deer hunting season alone as his grandfather lies dying of cancer. Ronald A. Jobe in *Language Arts* praises the novel as "powerfully written," adding that "[Paulsen] explores with the reader the inner-most frustrations, hurts, and fears of the young boy." Of special interest to Paulsen in writing *Tracker* was exploring the almost "mystical relationship that develops between the hunter and the hunted," he stated in his *SATA* interview. "It's a relationship with its own integrity, not to be violated.... At a certain point, the animal senses death coming and accepts it. This acceptance of death is something I was trying to write about in *Tracker."*

Tracker was the first of several of Paulsen's books to receive wide critical and popular recognition. *Dogsong,* a Newbery Medal Honor book, is a rites-of-passage novel about a young Eskimo boy (Russel) who wishes to abandon the increasingly modern ways of his people. Through the guidance of a tribal elder, Russel learns to bow-hunt and dogsled, and eventually leads his own pack of dogs on a trip across Alaska and back. "While the language of [*Dogsong*] is lyrical, Paulsen recognizes the reality of Russel's world—the dirty smoke and the stinking yellow fur of the bear," writes Nel Ward in *Voice of Youth Advocates.* "He also recognizes the reality of killing to save lives, and of dreaming to save sanity, in the communion between present and past, life and death, reality and imagination, in this majestic exploration into the Alaskan wilderness by a master author who knows his subject well." Paulsen's 1987 novel, *Hatchet,* also a Newbery Honor Book, is about a thirteen-year-old thoroughly modern boy (Brian) who is forced to survive alone in the Canadian woods after a plane crash. Like Russel in *Dogsong, Hatchet*'s hero is also transformed by the wilderness. "By the time he is rescued, Brian is permanently changed," notes Suzanne Rahn in *Twentieth-Century Children's Writers;* "he is far more observant and thoughtful, and knows what is really important in his life."

Other books of Paulsen's fiction—*Sentries, The Crossing, The Island, The Voyage of the Frog,* and *The Winter Room*—have furthered his reputation as a leading writer for young adults. Paulsen prefers to write for adolescents because, as he told *SATA*, "[it's] artistically fruitless to write for adults. Adults created the mess which we are struggling to outlive. Adults have their minds set. Art reaches out for newness, and adults aren't new. And adults aren't truthful." His book *Sentries,* a collection of stories, particularly demonstrates his belief that, as he told *SATA*, "young people know the score." *Sentries* juxtaposes the stories of four teenagers on the brink of life-important decisions, with the accounts of three soldiers—from different battles throughout history—whose lives have been devastated by war. *Sentries* particularly speaks to the threat of nuclear war and, as Paulsen commented in his *SATA* interview, contains "mostly a lot of questions, and I'm betting that young people have the answers."

WORKS CITED:

Jobe, Ronald A., review of *Tracker, Language Arts,* September, 1984, p. 527.

Paulsen, Gary, interview with Marguerite Feitlowitz for *Something about the Author,* Volume 54, Gale, 1989, pp. 76-82.

Rahn, Suzanne, entry on Gary Paulsen in *Twentieth-Century Children's Writers,* 3rd edition, edited by Tracy Chevalier, St. James Press, 1989, pp. 763-65.

Serdahely, Franz, "Prolific Paulsen," *Writer's Digest,* January, 1980.

Ward, Nel, review of *Dogsong, Voice of Youth Advocates,* December, 1985, pp. 321-22.

Wilson, Evie, review of *The Island, Voice of Youth Advocates,* June, 1988, pp. 89-90.

FOR MORE INFORMATION SEE:

BOOKS

Authors & Artists for Young Adults, Volume 2, Gale, 1989.

Children's Literature Review, Volume 19, Gale, 1990.

PEARCE, Ann Philippa
See PEARCE, Philippa

* * *

PEARCE, Philippa 1920-
(Ann Philippa Pearce)

Philippa Pearce

PERSONAL: Born 1920 in Great Shelford, Cambridgeshire, England; daughter of Ernest Alexander (a flour miller and corn merchant) and Gertrude Alice (Ramsden) Pearce; married Martin Christie (a fruitgrower), May 9, 1963 (died, 1965); children: Sarah. *Education:* Girton College, Cambridge, B.A., M.A. (with honors), 1942.

ADDRESSES: Home—Cambridge, England. *Office*—c/o Kestrel Books, Penguin Books Ltd., 536 King's Rd., London SW10 0UH, England.

CAREER: Writer, 1967—. Temporary civil servant, 1942-45; British Broadcasting Corp., London, England, script writer and producer in school broadcasting department, 1945-58; Clarendon Press, Oxford, England, editor in educational department, 1959-60; Andre Deutsch Ltd., London, editor of children's books, 1960-67. Part-time radio producer, British Broadcasting Corp., 1960-63.

MEMBER: Society of Authors.

AWARDS, HONORS: Carnegie Commendation, Library Association (England), 1956, for *Minnow on the Say,* 1978, for *The Shadow-Cage and Other Tales of the Supernatural,* and 1979, for *The Battle of Bubble and Squeak;* International Board on Books for Young People honour list selection, 1956, for *Minnow on the Say,* 1960, for *Tom's Midnight Garden,* and 1974, for *What the Neighbours Did and Other Stories;* Lewis Carroll Shelf Award, 1959, for *The Minnow Leads to Treasure,* and 1963, for *Tom's Midnight Garden;* Carnegie Medal, Library Association, 1959, for *Tom's Midnight Garden; New York Herald Tribune* Children's Spring Book Festival Award, 1963, for *A Dog So Small;* Whitbread Award, 1978, for *The Battle of Bubble and Squeak.*

WRITINGS:

UNDER NAME ANN PHILIPPA PEARCE

Minnow on the Say, Oxford University Press, 1954, reprinted under name Philippa Pearce, Puffin, 1979, published as *The Minnow Leads to Treasure,* World Publishing, 1958.

Tom's Midnight Garden, Lippincott, 1958, reprinted under name Philippa Pearce, Dell, 1979.

Still Jim and Silent Jim, Basil Blackwell, 1960.

UNDER NAME PHILIPPA PEARCE

Mrs. Cockle's Cat, Lippincott, 1961.

A Dog So Small, Constable, 1962, Lippincott, 1963.

(With Harold Scott) *From Inside Scotland Yard* (juvenile adaptation of Scott's *Scotland Yard*), Deutsch, 1963, Macmillan, 1965.

The Strange Sunflower, Thomas Nelson (London), 1966.

(With Brian Fairfax-Lucy) *The Children of the House,* Lippincott, 1968.

The Elm Street Lot, British Broadcasting Corp., 1969, enlarged hardcover edition, Kestrel, 1979.

The Squirrel Wife, Longman, 1971, Crowell, 1972.

(Adapter) *Beauty and the Beast,* Crowell, 1972.

(Editor and author of preface) *Stories from Hans Christian Andersen,* Collins, 1972.

What the Neighbours Did and Other Stories, Longman, 1972, published as *What the Neighbors Did and Other Stories,* Crowell, 1973.

Return to Air, Penguin, 1975.

The Shadow-Cage and Other Tales of the Supernatural, Crowell, 1977.

The Battle of Bubble and Squeak, Deutsch, 1978.

(Adapter) *Wings of Courage,* Kestrel, 1982.

A Picnic for Bunnykins, Viking, 1984.

Two Bunnykins Out to Tea, Viking, 1984.

Bunnykins in the Snow, Viking, 1985.

Lion at School and Other Stories, Greenwillow Books, 1985.

The Way to Sattin Shore, Viking, 1985.

Tooth Ball, Deutsch, 1987.

Fresh, Creative Education, 1987.

Who's Afraid?, and Other Strange Stories, Greenwillow Books, 1987.

Emily's Own Elephant, Macrae Books, 1987.

Freddy, Deutsch, 1988.

Old Belle's Summer Holiday, Deutsch, 1989.

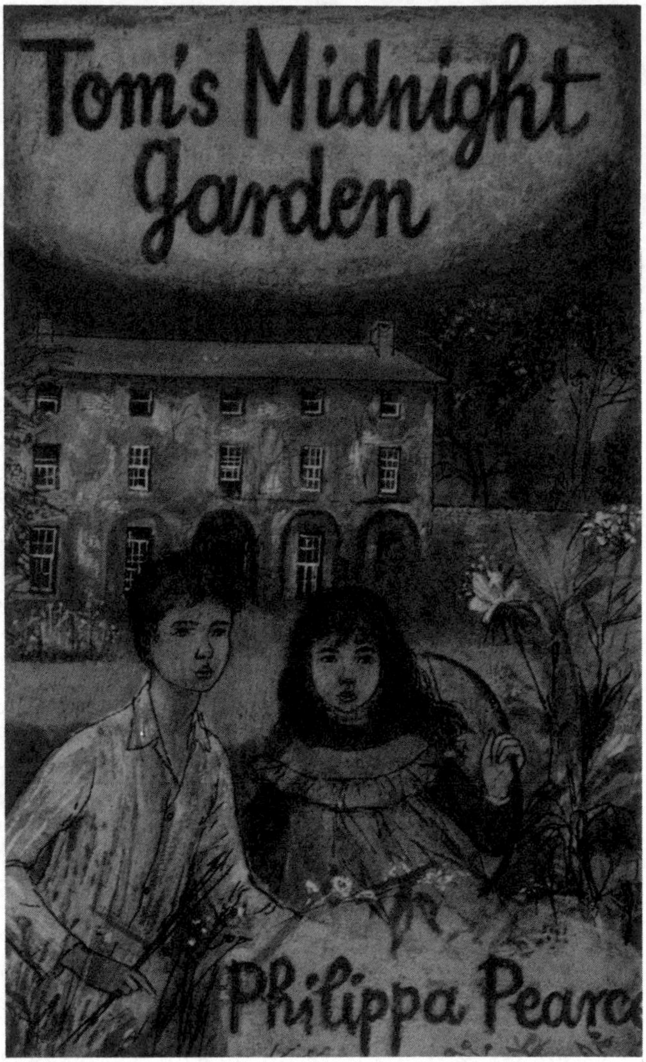

Cover of *Tom's Midnight Garden*, by Philippa Pearce.

Children of Charlecote, Gollancz, 1989.

OTHER

Editor of the first fourteen books in "People of the Past" social history series, 1961-64. Work is represented in anthologies, including *Another Six,* Basil Blackwell, 1959, *The Friday Miracle and Other Stories,* Puffin, 1969, and *Baker's Dozen,* Ward, Lock, 1974. Contributor of short stories to "Listening and Reading" radio series, BBC. Contributor of book reviews to periodicals.

SIDELIGHTS: Philippa Pearce enjoys a reputation as one of England's leading writers for children. Her novel *Tom's Midnight Garden* has been especially praised. John Rowe Townsend, speaking of *Tom's Midnight Garden* in his study *Written for Children: An Outline of English Children's Literature,* claims: "I have no reservations about it. If I were asked to name a single masterpiece of English children's literature since the last war ... it would be this outstandingly beautiful and absorbing book." Similarly, W. L. Webb of the *Manchester Guardian* calls the novel "a rare, moving story, beautifully written, and true in every way that matters.... a modern classic."

Tom's Midnight Garden tells the story of a young boy who must spend the summer with his aunt and uncle in the country. At first bored with his surroundings, he soon learns that at midnight the backyard transforms into the Victorian garden that it was many years before. Every night in his dreams he explores the garden. One night he meets a little girl named Hatty and the two of them begin a series of explorations of the vast garden. Hatty begins to grow older while Tom remains the same age. At story's end, he discovers that the elderly woman who lives in the flat above his aunt and uncle is the girl Hatty he played with in the garden of her childhood.

The garden where Tom and Hatty meet is based on the garden Pearce played in as a girl. Her father was a miller and she lived in a mill house with a walled garden. "It is a beautiful early nineteenth-century house," Pearce tells Roni Natov and Geraldine DeLuca in *The Lion and the Unicorn.* "You see houses like it everywhere in East Anglia, farm houses and mill houses that correspond to a period of great agricultural prosperity, probably during the Napoleonic wars. My father was born in that house because my grandfather was also a miller. We moved in when I was very small; my grandfather died and we took over. This is the house and the garden with its sundial on the wall in *Tom's Midnight Garden.* The garden was absolutely the image of that walled garden in the book." Pearce now lives in a cottage across the street from the mill house.

The idea that characters can meet each other across time came to Pearce from a book by J. W. Dunne, *Experiment in Time.* Dunne theorizes that there are many times co-existing and yet able to blend together. "I never really understood it properly," Pearce admits in *Books for Keeps,* "but it was a sort of theoretical base for the book."

The story was meant to say something about the relationships between the young and the old too. Pearce tells Natov and DeLuca: "*Tom's Midnight Garden* was an attempt to reconcile childhood and old age, to bring them together." Speaking in *Books for Keeps,* she says the real impulse behind the book was "the feeling of time passing, people becoming old. Even though I wasn't old I could see that if you were old you hadn't been old forever."

Eventually Tom is unable to revisit the garden because he has grown too old for it. Hatty, too, cannot return. But when Tom meets his aunt and uncle's neighbor, it is clear to him that she is Hatty grown up. For a brief moment the two friends are reunited. Townsend found "a profound, mysterious sense of time" in the story. Writing in *A Critical History of Children's Literature,* Ruth Hill Viguers claims that in *Tom's Midnight Garden,* "the idea that time has no barriers was embodied in nearly perfect literary form."

Much of Pearce's other fiction is also based on her own childhood. She writes in *Cricket:* "I was the youngest of four children.... We lived in a big, shabby, beautiful mill house by the river. We swam, fished, boated, skated. We always had a dog, and sometimes a cat—the business cat from the mill, who would knock off from catching rats and mice to visit us. When I grew up and went to London to work, I took with me all the places that I had loved. They turned up in the stories I was beginning to write.... I think there is no story I have ever written that didn't start from something in my own life."

Pearce works out the plots of her stories in her head. "I never write things down," she explains to Natov and DeLuca. "I don't keep a folder. I have never in my life kept a note of anything. I let ideas mill around in my head. Things begin to settle out like muddy water. Perhaps if I had kept notes I would have written more, I don't know." She does write down the story as it comes to her, though: "I do believe it is very useful to write down the actual words you think of. When I wake up in the night with just the right words, I write them down so as not to lose them."

WORKS CITED:

Books for Keeps, November, 1983, pp. 14-15.
Cricket, August, 1976, p. 35.
Natov, Roni and Geraldine DeLuca, "An Interview with Philippa Pearce," *The Lion and the Unicorn,* Volume 9, 1985, pp. 75-88.
Townsend, John Rowe, "The New Fantasy," *Written for Children: An Outline of English Children's Literature,* Lothrop, 1967, p. 128.
Viguers, Ruth Hill, "Golden Years and Time of Tumult: 1920-1967," *A Critical History of Children's Literature,* revised edition, Macmillan, 1969, pp. 477.
Webb, W. L., review of *Tom's Midnight Garden, Manchester Guardian,* December 5, 1958, p. 7.

FOR MORE INFORMATION SEE:

BOOKS

Blishen, Edward, editor, *The Thorny Paradise: Writers on Writing for Children,* Kestrel, 1975.
Butts, Dennis, editor, *Good Writers for Young Readers,* Hart-Davis, 1977.
Cameron, Eleanor, *The Green and Burning Tree: On the Writing and Enjoyment of Children's Books,* Little, Brown, 1969.
Children's Literature Review, Volume 9, Gale, 1985.
Crouch, Marcus, *Treasure Seekers and Borrowers: Children's Books in Britain, 1900-1960,* Library Association, 1962.
Crouch, Marcus, *The Nesbit Tradition: The Children's Novel in England, 1945-1970,* Ernest Benn Limited, 1972.
Eyre, Frank, *British Children's Books in the Twentieth Century,* revised edition, Dutton, 1973.
Fisher, Margery, *Intent Upon Reading: A Critical Appraisal of Modern Fiction for Children,* Hodder & Stoughton, 1961.
Rees, David, *The Marble in the Water: Essays on Contemporary Writers of Fiction for Children and Young Adults,* Horn Book, 1980.
Storr, Catherine, editor, *On Children's Literature,* Allen Lane, 1973.
Townsend, John Rowe, *A Sense of Story: Essays on Contemporary Writers for Children,* Lippincott, 1971.

PERIODICALS

Book World, May 7, 1972.
Children's Literature in Education, March, 1971; autumn, 1981.
Commonweal, May 23, 1958.
Growing Point, November, 1983; March, 1986; July, 1987.
Horn Book, April, 1958; April, 1978; June, 1984; May/June, 1987.
Kirkus, July 15, 1959.
New Statesman, November 15, 1958; May 18, 1962.
New York Herald Tribune Book Review, March 9, 1958; November 1, 1959.
New York Herald Tribune Books, May 12, 1963.
New York Times, May 4, 1958.
New York Times Book Review, November 1, 1959; March 12, 1972.
Saturday Review, August 23, 1958; May 11, 1963.
Signal, January, 1973; September, 1984.
Times Educational Supplement, September 30, 1983.
Times Literary Supplement, June 1, 1962; October 22, 1971; December 8, 1972; July 15, 1977; March 14, 1986.
The Use of English, spring, 1970.

* * *

PEASE, Howard 1894-1974

PERSONAL: Born September 6, 1894, in Stockton, CA; died April 14, 1974, in Mill Valley, CA; son of Newton and Stella (Cooley) Pease; married Pauline Nott, November 4, 1927 (deceased); married Rossie Ferrier, September, 1956; children: Philip H. *Education:* Stanford University, A.B., 1924, and later graduate study. *Politics:* Democrat. *Religion:* Unitarian Universalist.

CAREER: Merchant seaman; writer. Taught in California, 1924-25, 1928-34; Vassar College, Poughkeepsie, NY, instructor in English, 1926-27. *Military service:* U.S. Army, World War I; served for two years, one year with an ambulance unit in France.

MEMBER: PEN.

AWARDS, HONORS: Commonwealth Club of California silver medal, 1945, for *Thunderbolt House;* Child Study Association children's book award, 1946, for *Heart of Danger;* Boy's Clubs of America junior book award, 1949, for *Heart of Danger.*

WRITINGS:

TOD MORAN MYSTERIES

The Tattooed Man, Doubleday, 1926.

The Jinx Ship, Doubleday, 1927.
Shanghai Passage, Doubleday, 1929.
The Ship without a Crew, Doubleday, 1934.
Hurricane Weather, Doubleday, 1936.
Foghorns, Doubleday, 1937.
The Black Tanker, Doubleday, 1941.
Night Boat, and Other Tod Moran Mysteries, Doubleday, 1942.
Heart of Danger, Doubleday, 1946.
Captain of the "Araby," Doubleday, 1953.
Mystery on Telegraph Hill, Doubleday, 1961.

OTHER

The Gypsy Caravan, Doubleday, 1930.
Secret Cargo, Doubleday, 1931.
Wind in the Rigging, Doubleday, 1935.
Captain Binnacle (for beginning readers), Dodd, 1938.
Jungle River, Doubleday, 1938.
High Road to Adventure, Doubleday, 1939.
The Long Wharf, Doubleday, 1938.
Thunderbolt House, Doubleday, 1944.
Bound for "Singapore," Doubleday, 1948.
The Dark Adventure, Doubleday, 1950.
Shipwreck, Doubleday, 1957.

Contributor to educational books and journals.

SIDELIGHTS: The late Howard Pease turned a fascination for the sea into a profitable writing career. A former merchant seaman who gathered first-hand research for his novels in exotic ports of call, Pease wrote more than a dozen seafaring adventures for teens, including the popular "Tod Moran" series. Pease offered boys in particular heroes that act independently in order to right wrongs. His plots often hinged upon lost treasure or unsolved murders in settings as close as New Orleans and as far removed as New Guinea.

Howard Pease

"Even as a small child the sea always attracted me," Pease told the *Junior Book of Authors.* "Probably because I lived on inland soil, out of sight of the fogs of the coast yet on a river that flowed into San Francisco Bay." Pease's grandparents had crossed the Great Plains in a covered wagon and settled in Northern California. He grew up there and called the state home for most of his life.

Pease remembered his introduction to creative writing in the second edition of the *Junior Book of Authors:* "One day my sixth grade teacher said, 'This is Friday afternoon, our free period. How would you like to write short stories? All those in favor?'

"Hands swung aloft. One girl pupil remarked, 'That might be fun, Mrs. Gaines; but how in the world would you do it?'

"Our teacher had come prepared; she had forty pictures clipped from magazines, many of them advertisements. She held up a picture of a camel caravan crossing the desert. 'Who would like to write a story about this?' she asked. A boy held up his hand and received the picture. My hand did not go up until I saw a picture of a steamer heading into a storm at sea .... At the end of the term we printed a little magazine filled with our work, and that is how I still happen to have a copy of my first short story—'Turn Back, Never!'" Little did Pease know at the time that he would one day ride into such tempests on the open seas in merchant vessels.

Pease was a freshman at Stanford University when he was sent to fight in the First World War. Upon his return from two years' military service—some of which was spent with a French ambulance corps—he returned to Stanford, determined to become a writer. He chose teaching as a profession at first and wrote in his spare time. His first sale was an adventure story, published in *American Boy* magazine.

That success spurred Pease to action. In order to find material for his fiction, he shipped out of San Francisco as a wiper on a freighter bound for Panama. Pease commented in the first edition of the *Junior Book of Authors:* "I remember standing on the forecastle head with the wind singing past, and thinking: 'This is life—this is living. By thunder, I'm a sailor!'"

The romance never quite wore off, even though Pease found the work aboard ship difficult and routine. He gathered impressions of landscapes, seascapes, and the people who pilot big ships, and all of these experiences found their way into his novels for boys. "Tod Moran, my younger protagonist, is pretty much every youth who goes to sea," Pease told the *Junior Book of Authors.*

Pease did not limit himself to seafaring adventures. He also drove through Mexico on the Pan-American Highway and took walking tours of Europe. With the success of his first two books, *The Tattooed Man* and *The Jinx Ship,* he was able to quit teaching and devote all his time to writing and travel. He and his wife spent months in the Caribbean and Tahiti, and during 1946 they toured the United States, dragging a house trailer behind their car.

Pease eventually settled in Palo Alto, California, where he turned out numerous adventure tales. A dozen of his best-known works feature Tod Moran, a third mate on trading vessels that criss-cross the Pacific. Only a teen himself, Moran is able to solve mysteries and endure deadly typhoons without losing his cool. Moran and the other heroes of Pease's stories face danger and deception in faraway places but always manage to uncover the truth—about themselves as well as the mysteries at hand.

Pease once commented that he wrote stories with many different kinds of youngsters in mind—serious works for scholarly students and escapist fiction for those with learning difficulties. "I've written [some] escape fiction . . . ," he said. "*Jungle River* and *Hurricane Weather* are just stories. In state industrial schools where most of the delinquent boys are so ill-adjusted they cannot face the world, such books are eagerly read. So we need, you see, all kinds of books for all kinds of readers. Still, if you are to become a reader of our better novels instead of a reader only of popular magazines with their romantic serials and murder tales, you must learn while young *how* to read."

WORKS CITED:

Junior Book of Authors, H. W. Wilson, 1934, pp. 292-293.

Junior Book of Authors, 2nd edition, H. W. Wilson, 1951, pp. 239-240.

FOR MORE INFORMATION SEE:

BOOKS

Carlsen, G. Robert, *Books and the Teen-Age Reader,* Harper, 1967.

Twentieth-Century Children's Writers, 3rd edition, St. James Press, 1989.

* * *

PECK, Richard (Wayne) 1934-

PERSONAL: Born April 5, 1934, in Decatur, IL; son of Wayne Morris (a merchant) and Virginia (a dietician; maiden name, Gray) Peck. *Education:* Attended University of Exeter, 1955-56; DePauw University, B.A., 1956; Southern Illinois University, M.A., 1959; further graduate study at Washington University, 1960-61. *Politics:* Republican. *Religion:* Methodist.

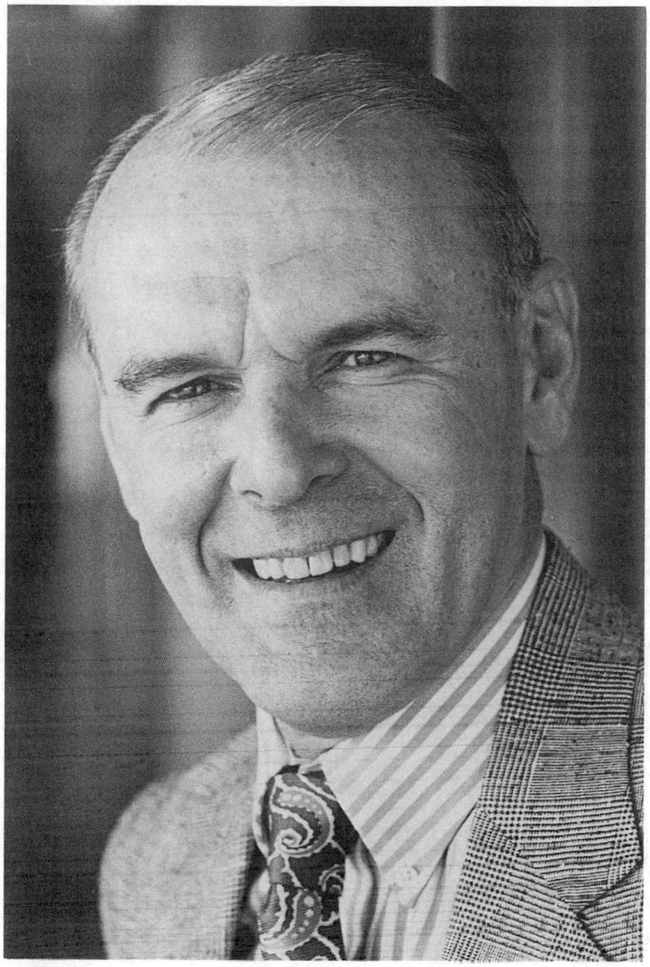

Richard Peck

ADDRESSES: Home—155 East 72nd St., New York, NY 10021. *Office*—c/o Delacorte Press, 1 Dag Hammerskjold Plaza, New York, NY 10017. *Agent*—Sheldon Fogelman, 155 East 72nd St., New York, NY 10021.

CAREER: Southern Illinois University at Carbondale, instructor in English, 1958-60; Glenbrook North High School, Northbrook, IL, teacher of English, 1961-63; Scott, Foresman Co., Chicago, IL, textbook editor, 1963-65; Hunter College of the City University of New York and Hunter College High School, New York City, instructor in English and education, 1965-71; writer, 1971—. Assistant director of the Council for Basic Education, Washington, DC, 1969-70; English-Speaking Union fellow, Jesus College, Oxford University, England, 1973; lecturer. *Military service:* U.S. Army, 1956-58; served in Stuttgart, Germany.

MEMBER: Authors Guild, Authors League of America, Delta Chi.

AWARDS, HONORS: Child Study Association of America's Children's Book of the Year citations, 1970, for *Sounds and Silences,* 1971, for *Mindscapes,* and 1986, for *Blossom Culp and the Sleep of Death;* Writing Award, National Council for the Advancement of Education, 1971; Edgar Allan Poe Award runner-up, Mystery Writers of America, 1974, for *Dreamland Lake;*

"You've probably heard about me already.
I've seen several ghosts and been one myself...."
Ghosts I Have Been
Richard Peck
DELL • 92839 • U.S. $2.75
CAN. $3.75
Rowena
An Outstanding Book of the Year
—THE NEW YORK TIMES

Cover of *Ghosts I Have Been,* by Richard Peck.

Best Books of the Year citations, American Library Association (ALA), 1974, for *Representing Super Doll,* 1976, for *Are You in the House Alone?,* and 1977, for *Ghosts I Have Been;* ALA Notable Book citations, 1975, for *The Ghost Belonged to Me,* and 1985, for *Remembering the Good Times;* Friends of American Writers Award (older category), 1976, for *The Ghost Belonged to Me;* Edgar Allan Poe Award for best juvenile mystery novel, 1976, and Author's Award, New Jersey Institute of Technology, 1978, both for *Are You in the House Alone?; School Library Journal*'s Best Books of the Year citations, 1976, for *Are You in the House Alone?,* 1977, for *Ghosts I Have Been,* and 1985, for *Remembering the Good Times; New York Times* Outstanding Book of the Year citation, 1977, for *Ghosts I Have Been;* Illinois Writer of the Year citation, Illinois Association of Teachers of English, 1977; *School Library Journal*'s Best of the Best 1966-1978 citations, for *Dreamland Lake,* and *Father Figure.*

New York Public Library Books for the Teen Age citations, 1980, for *Pictures That Storm inside My Head,* 1981, for *Ghosts I Have Been,* and 1982, for *Are You in the House Alone?* and *Close Enough to Touch;* ALA Best Books for Young Adults citations, 1981, for *Close Enough to Touch,* 1985, for *Remembering the Good Times,* and 1987, for *Princess Ashley; School Library Journal*'s Best Books for Young Adults citations, 1981, for *Close Enough to Touch,* 1983, for *This Family of Women,* and 1985, for *Remembering the Good Times;* ALA's Young Adult Services Division's Best of the Best Books 1970-1983 citations, for *Are You in the House Alone?* and *Ghosts I Have Been;* ALA's Margaret Edwards Young Adult Author Achievement Award, 1990.

WRITINGS:

YOUNG ADULT NOVELS

Don't Look and It Won't Hurt, Holt, 1972.
Dreamland Lake, Holt, 1973, Dell, 1990.
Through a Brief Darkness, Viking, 1973.
Representing Super Doll, Viking, 1974.
The Ghost Belonged to Me, Viking, 1975.
Are You in the House Alone? (with teacher's guide), Viking, 1976.
Ghosts I Have Been (sequel to *The Ghost Belonged to Me*), Viking, 1977.
Father Figure, Viking, 1978.
Secrets of the Shopping Mall, Delacorte, 1979.
Close Enough to Touch, Delacorte, 1981.
The Dreadful Future of Blossom Culp (sequel to *Ghosts I Have Been*), Delacorte, 1983.
Remembering the Good Times, Delacorte, 1985.
Blossom Culp and the Sleep of Death, Delacorte, 1986.
Princess Ashley, Delacorte, 1987.
Those Summer Girls I Never Met, Delacorte, 1988.
Unfinished Portrait of Jessica, Delacorte, 1991.

JUVENILE

Monster Night at Grandma's House, illustrations by Don Freeman, Viking, 1977.

ADULT NOVELS

Amanda/Miranda (Literary Guild selection; Reader's Digest Condensed Book Club selection), Viking, 1980.
New York Time, Delacorte, 1981.
This Family of Women (Literary Guild alternate selection), Delacorte, 1983.
Voices after Midnight, Dell, 1990.

EDITOR

(With Ned E. Hoopes) *Edge of Awareness: Twenty-five Contemporary Essays,* Dell, 1966.
Sounds and Silences: Poetry for Now, Delacorte, 1970.
Mindscapes: Poems for the Real World, Delacorte, 1971.
Leap into Reality: Essays for Now, Dell, 1972.
Urban Studies: A Research Paper Casebook, Random House, 1973.
Transitions: A Literary Paper Casebook, Random House, 1974.
Pictures That Storm inside My Head (poetry anthology), Avon, 1976.

OTHER

(With Norman Strasma) *Old Town, A Complete Guide: Strolling, Shopping, Supping, Sipping,* 2nd edition, [Chicago], 1965.

(With Mortimer Smith and George Weber) *A Consumer's Guide to Educational Innovations,* Council for Basic Education, 1972.
(With Stephen N. Judy) *The Creative Word 2,* (Peck was not associated with other volumes), Random House, 1974.
(Contributor) Kenneth L. Donelson and Alleen Pace Nilsen, *Literature for Today's Young Adults,* Scott, Foresman, 1980.
(Contributor) Donald R. Gallo, editor, *Sixteen: Short Stories by Outstanding Young Adult Writers,* Delacorte, 1984.
(Contributor) D. R. Gallo, editor, *Visions: Nineteen Short Stories by Outstanding Writers for Young Adults,* Delacorte, 1987.
Write a Tale of Terror, Book Lures, 1987.
(Contributor) Gallo, editor, *Connections: Short Stories by Outstanding Writers for Young Adults,* Delacorte, 1989.
Anonymously Yours (autobiography), Silver Burdette, 1991.

Author of column on the architecture of historic neighborhoods for the *New York Times.* Contributor of poetry to several anthologies. Contributor of poems to *Saturday Review* and *Chicago Tribune Magazine.* Contributor of articles to periodicals, including *American Libraries, PTA Magazine* and *Parents' Magazine.*

ADAPTATIONS: Audio cassette versions of Peck's books include *The Ghost Belonged to Me,* Live Oak Media, 1976, *Don't Look and It Won't Hurt* (filmstrip with cassette), Random House, and *Remembering the Good Times* (cassette), Listening Library, 1987. Television movies based on his books include *Are You in the House Alone?,* CBS, 1977, *Child of Glass* (based on *The Ghost Belonged to Me*), Walt Disney Productions, 1979, and *Father Figure,* Time-Life Productions, 1980. Cineville Production Company bought the film rights to *Don't Look and It Won't Hurt* in 1991.

WORK IN PROGRESS: Bel-Air Bambi and the Mall Rats, a novel, 1992.

SIDELIGHTS: Richard Peck's books on such important teen-age problems as suicide, unwanted pregnancy, death of a loved one, and rape have won critical praise for their realism and emotional power. Peck has written over a dozen very popular books for young adults, books that help young readers to develop self-confidence. He has also written adult novels that show men and women who are not confined to roles that traditionally belong to their gender. When writing for young adults, Peck told Roger Sutton in a *School Library Journal* interview, he thinks about potential readers: "As I'm typing I'm trying to look out over the typewriter and see faces. I don't certainly want to 'write for myself' because I'm trying to write across a generation gap." In books for both age groups, Peck told Jean F. Mercier in *Publishers Weekly,* he tries to "give readers leading characters they can look up to and reasons to believe that problems can be solved." The excellence of his work has been recognized by numerous awards, including the American Library Association's Young Adult Author Achievement Award in 1990.

Peck became familiar with contemporary adolescent problems while teaching high school. He liked his students, but after several years became discouraged and quit. He once said that teaching "had begun to turn into something that looked weirdly like psychiatric social work." Peck decided instead to write books for teenagers that featured the problems he had seen. "Ironically, it was my students who taught me to be a writer, though I had been hired to teach *them,*" he said in a speech published in *Arkansas Libraries.* "They taught me that a novel must entertain first before it can be anything else." He observed that young adults are most concerned with winning approval from their peers and seeking reassurance from their reading material. With these needs in mind, Peck writes about the passage from childhood to adulthood. He believes that in a young adult novel, typically "the reader meets a worthy young character who takes one step nearer maturity, and he or she takes that step independently."

His first novel, *Don't Look and It Won't Hurt,* is about a teenage pregnancy. Knowing that teens don't identify with main characters they view as losers, he told the story of alienation and healing from the viewpoint of the young mother's younger sister. The fifteen-year-old manages to keep her troubled family together, "parenting" her parents in a role reversal that appeals to readers of this age group. She is also helpful in the sister's recovery after deciding to give her baby up for adoption. The novel received much critical praise and became a popular success, and continues to sell in both paperback and hardcover editions.

Peck's controversial novel about a teenage girl who is raped, *Are You in the House Alone?,* received the Edgar Allan Poe Award in 1976. Zena Sutherland, writing in the *Bulletin of the Center for Children's Books,* is impressed by the novel's scope, saying that the author "sees clearly both society's problem and the victim's: the range of attitudes, the awful indignity," the fear and shame that is part of this kind of crime. Peck explained in his speech, "I did not write the novel to tell the young about rape. They already know what that is." He said he wrote it to warn the young that criminals are regrettably sometimes treated with more respect than victims even though victims of crime live in the shadow of that experience for the rest of their lives. Alix Nelson in the *New York Times Book Review* thinks that Peck should be commended for reaching his audience and for teaching them about a topic that many other people in their lives avoid.

Peck's female heroes are known for making their own decisions and exercising their freedom from the demands of peer pressure. He feels that these qualities are especially important for characters in teenage fiction. Writing in *Literature for Today's Young Adults,* Peck explains that young people need to see that the confining codes of behavior they live with as adolescents will not be imposed on them for the rest of their lives. He believes they need to see characters rewarded for making the kinds of free choices that young readers will soon have to make on their way to adulthood. He concludes that the future of young adult fiction is in "books that invite the young to think for themselves instead of for each other." "After twelve novels," he said in the speech, "I find I have only one theme .... It is simply that you will never grow up until you begin to think and act independently of your peers.

"My message is not, you will notice, to think and act independently of your *parents,*" he continued. "The young do not need that message. In the 1980's they have already won all their battles with their parents and their teachers, with all the adult world, and they have turned upon each other." Children raised in permissive homes tend not to look up to anyone because they see their parents and teachers as their servants, Peck told Sutton. They tend to look down on others while viewing themselves as heroes. Peck said in his speech that teens read books "mainly to find friends—friends they can look up to—better friends than they have or are."

Peck does not ignore social issues related to gender. In his books, he realistically portrays women in a period of social change in a variety of social roles. The self-reliant wives and businesswomen of his books "are contrasted with ineffectual girls and sometimes snobby mothers seemingly locked behind wide, curving drives and imposing front doors," Hilary Crew observes in *Top of the News.*

Close Enough to Touch, a love story written in response to a young man's request that Peck should write a book about dating, is "*told by a boy,*" the author said in his speech. "It might please some boys to be given this voice. It might surprise some girls that boys have emotions too. Mother never told them. Mothers are still telling daughters that boys only want one thing. How wrong they are. Boys want a great deal." When the boy's first love dies, he suddenly has to cope with the fact that just as no one had prepared him for intimacy with the opposite sex, no one has prepared him to face grief. "There is no sexual content in this book," Peck continued. "This is a novel about the emotions, not the senses."

Peck believes that American attitudes about public education have resulted in a system that has discouraged young people instead of equipping them for survival in the real world. He said in his speech that, fortunately, "There is another America, of course, beyond this somber landscape. An America revealed chiefly in books—by novels: of the past, on this year's list, of novels yet to be written. This America is one of self-reliance and coming from behind; of characters who learn to accept the consequences of their actions; of happy endings worked for and almost achieved; of being young in an old world and finding your way in it; of a nation of people hasty and forgetful but full still of hope; of limitless distances and new beginnings and starting over; of dreams like mountaintops, and rivers that run to the sea. We owe our young this record of our dreams."

When asked about what he hopes to accomplish with his writing for young adults, Peck told Sutton, "I don't know what books can do, except one point is that I wish every kid knew that fiction can be truer than fact, that it isn't a frivolous pastime unless your reading taste is for the frivolous. I wish they knew that being literate is a way of being successful in any field. I wish they all wanted to pit their own experience against the experiences they see in books. And I wish they had to do a little more of that in order to pass the class in school. But in books you reach an awful lot of promising kids who write back good literate letters and give you hope. So that's the hope I have."

WORKS CITED:

Crew, Hilary, "Blossom Culp and Her Ilk: The Independent Female in Richard Peck's YA Fiction," *Top of the News,* spring, 1987, pp. 297-301.

Mercier, Jean F., "Publishers Weekly: Interview with Richard Peck," *Publishers Weekly,* March 14, 1980.

Nelson, Alix, "Ah, Not to Be Sixteen Again," *New York Times Book Review,* November 14, 1976, p. 29.

Peck, Richard, in *Literature for Today's Young Adults,* edited by Kenneth L. Donelson and Alleen Pace Nilsen, Scott, Foresman, 1980, pp. 34-76, 136-171.

Peck, Richard, "People of the Word," *Arkansas Libraries,* December, 1981, pp. 13-16.

Sutherland, Zena, review of *Are You in the House Alone?, Bulletin of the Center for Children's Books,* March, 1977, pp. 111-112.

Sutton, Roger, "A Conversation with Richard Peck," *School Library Journal,* June, 1990, pp. 36-40.

FOR MORE INFORMATION SEE:

BOOKS

Children's Literature Review, Volume 15, Gale, 1988, pp. 146-166.

Konigsburg, E. L., editor, *In My Own Words Series,* Silver Burdette Press, 1991.

Something about the Author Autobiography Series, Volume 2, Gale, 1986, pp. 175-186.

Twentieth Century Children's Writers, St. Martin's Press, 1989, pp. 768-769.

PERIODICALS

American Libraries, April, 1973.

Arkansas Libraries, December, 1981, pp. 13-16.

Bulletin of the Center for Children's Books, March, 1977.

English Journal, February, 1976, pp. 97-99.

Los Angeles Times, April 3, 1981.

New York Times Book Review, June 27, 1971; November 12, 1972; July 27, 1975, p. 8; November 14, 1976, p. 29; December 2, 1979.

Psychology Today, September, 1975, pp. 11, 75.

Publishers Weekly, March 14, 1980.

School Library Journal, May, 1986, pp. 37-39; June, 1960, pp. 36-40.

Times Literary Supplement, August 21, 1981.

Top of the News, winter, 1978, pp. 173-177.

Washington Post Book World, November 10, 1974, p. 8; May 1, 1983.
Young Adult Cooperative Book Review, February, 1977.

* * *

PECK, Robert Newton 1928-

PERSONAL: Born February 17, 1928, in Vermont; son of F. Haven (a farmer) and Lucile (Dornburgh) Peck; married Dorothy Anne Houston (a librarian and painter), 1958; children: Christopher Haven, Anne Houston. *Education:* Rollins College, A.B., 1953; Cornell University, law student. *Religion:* Protestant. *Hobbies and other interests:* Playing ragtime piano, sports.

ADDRESSES: Home—500 Sweetwater Club Circle, Longwood, FL 32779.

CAREER: Writer and farmer. Worked variously as a lumberjack, in a papermill, as a hog butcher, and as a New York City advertising executive. Director of Rollins College Writers Conference, 1978—. Owner of publishing company, Peck Press. Teacher, and speaker at conferences. *Military service:* U.S. Army, Infantry, 1945-47; served with 88th Division in Italy, Germany, and France; received commendation.

AWARDS, HONORS: American Library Association best book for young adults citation, Spring Book Festival Award older honor, *Book World,* both 1973, Media & Methods Maxi Award (paperback), *Media & Methods,* 1975, and Colorado Children's Book Award, 1977, all for *A Day No Pigs Would Die; New York Times* outstanding book citation, 1973, for *Millie's Boy;* Child Study Association of America children's book of the year citations, 1973, for *Millie's Boy,* 1975, for *Bee Tree and Other Stuff,* 1976, for *Hamilton,* and 1987, for *Soup on Ice;* New York Public Library's books for the teen age citations, 1980 and 1981, for *A Day No Pigs Would Die,* 1980, 1981, and 1982, for *Hang for Treason,* and 1980 and 1982, for *Clunie;* Mark Twain Award, Missouri Association of School Librarians, 1981, for *Soup for President;* Notable Children's Trade Book in the Field of Social Studies citations, National Council for Social Studies and the Children's Book Council, 1982, for *Justice Lion,* and 1986, for *Spanish Hoof;* Michigan Young Reader's Award, Michigan Council of Teachers, 1984, for *Soup;* Bologna International Children's Book Fair, 1985, for *Spanish Hoof.*

Robert Newton Peck

WRITINGS:

YOUNG ADULT FICTION

A Day No Pigs Would Die, Knopf, 1972.
Millie's Boy, Knopf, 1973.
Soup, illustrated by Charles Gehm, Knopf, 1974.
Bee Tree and Other Stuff (poems), illustrated by Laura Lydecker, Walker & Co., 1975.
Fawn, Little, Brown, 1975.
Wild Cat, illustrated by Hal Frenck, Holiday House, 1975.
Soup and Me, illustrated by Charles Lilly, Knopf, 1975.
Hamilton, illustrated by Lydecker, Little, Brown, 1976.
Hang for Treason, Doubleday, 1976.
King of Kazoo (musical), illustrated by William Bryan Park, Knopf, 1976.
Rabbits and Redcoats, illustrated by Lydecker, Walker & Co., 1976.
Trig, illustrated by Pamela Johnson, Little, Brown, 1977.
Last Sunday, illustrated by Ben Stahl, Doubleday, 1977.
The King's Iron, Little, Brown, 1977.
Patooie, illustrated by Ted Lewin, Knopf, 1977.
Soup for President, illustrated by Lewin, Knopf, 1978.
Eagle Fur, Knopf, 1978.
Trig Sees Red, illustrated by Johnson, Little, Brown, 1978.
Mr. Little, illustrated by Stahl, Doubleday, 1979.
Basket Case, Doubleday, 1979.
Hub, illustrated by Lewin, Knopf, 1979.
Clunie, Knopf, 1979.
Soup's Drum, illustrated by Charles Robinson, Knopf, 1980.
Trig Goes Ape, illustrated by Johnson, Little, Brown, 1980.
Soup on Wheels, illustrated by Robinson, Knopf, 1981.
Justice Lion, Little, Brown, 1981.
Kirk's Law, Doubleday, 1981.
Trig or Treat, illustrated by Johnson, Little, Brown, 1982.
Banjo, illustrated by Andrew Glass, Knopf, 1982.
Soup in the Saddle, illustrated by Robinson, Knopf, 1983.
The Seminole Seed, Pineapple Press, 1983.
Soup's Goat, illustrated by Robinson, Knopf, 1984.
Dukes, Pineapple Press, 1984.
Soup on Ice, illustrated by Robinson, Knopf, 1985.
Jo Silver, Pineapple Press, 1985.
Spanish Hoof, Knopf, 1985.
Soup on Fire, illustrated by Robinson, Delacorte, 1987.
Soup's Uncle, illustrated by Robinson, Delacorte, 1988.

Hallapoosa, Walker & Co., 1988.
The Horse Hunters, Random House, 1988.
Arly, Walker & Co., 1989.
Soup's Hoop, illustrated by Robinson, Delacorte, 1990.
Higbee's Halloween, Walker & Co., 1990.
Little Soup's Hayride, Dell, 1991.
Little Soup's Birthday, Dell, 1991.
Arly's Run, Walker & Co., 1991.
Soup in Love, Delacorte, 1992.
FortDog July, Walker & Co., 1992.
Little Soup's Turkey, Dell, 1992.
Soup Ahoy, Delacorte, in press.
Little Soup's Bunny, Dell, in press.

ADULT FICTION

The Happy Sadist, Doubleday, 1962.

NONFICTION

Path of Hunters: Animal Struggle in a Meadow, illustrated by Betty Fraser, Knopf, 1973.
Secrets of Successful Fiction, Writer's Digest Books, 1980.
Fiction Is Folks: How to Create Unforgettable Characters, Writer's Digest Books, 1983.
My Vermont, Peck Press, 1985.
My Vermont II, Peck Press, 1988.

Cover of *A Day No Pigs Would Die,* by Robert Newton Peck.

OTHER

Also author of songs, television commercials, and jingles. Adapter of novels *Soup and Me, Soup for President,* and *Mr. Little* for television's *Afterschool Specials,* American Broadcasting Companies, Inc. (ABC-TV).

ADAPTATIONS: Soup was adapted for television and broadcast by ABC-TV, 1978; *A Day No Pigs Would Die* was adapted for cassette and released by Listening Library.

SIDELIGHTS: The strength of Robert Newton Peck's works stems from their striking depictions of the past. Many of his books bring to life the rural Vermont of his childhood, describing the adventures and encounters with nature that helped shape his life. The six-foot-four-inch tall Peck once described himself as follows: "I wear mule-ear boots, a ten-gallon hat, Western shirts and weigh not quite 200 pounds." Peck went on to observe, "Socially, I'm about as sophisticated as a turnip.... I'm an expert skier, a dismal dancer, and I love horses." Sophisticated or not, the author has penned a long list of books for children, many of which reflect his boyhood struggle with the competitiveness of nature and its impending threat of death. Peck, who lives on a five-hundred-acre ranch in Florida, has also written poetry, adult novels, and how-to books for would-be writers.

Educators figure prominently in Peck's fiction, thanks to the influence of his first, much-admired teacher—he still respectfully refers to her as "Miss Kelly." "A lot of my characters are teachers—all of whom are strong, fair, and respected," Peck once explained. Although reading was a skill revered by the Peck's family and neighbors when he was a boy, not everyone was privileged enough to learn how to do it. In Peck's own family no one had ever attended school before him, although he was the youngest of seven children. Luckily, he was able to convince his parents to let him join the other students. Miss Kelly kindled the minds of the first through sixth grades in what Peck described in an essay for *Something about the Author Autobiography Series* (*SAAS*) as a "tumble-down, one-room, dirt-road school in rural Vermont." There she taught the children to wash up before handling any of the few, but treasured, books. *Ivanhoe, The Wind in the Willows,* and *Tom Sawyer* were some of the classics Miss Kelly read to her classes, along with biographies of outstanding personalities such as Booker T. Washington, Mark Twain, and Charles Lindbergh.

Peck not only grew up to write many books of his own, he also married a librarian, Dorrie, in 1958. The best man at their wedding was none other than Fred Rogers, the star of the popular *Mister Rogers' Neighborhood* television show for children; Peck had met him in college. Writing about his own children, Christopher Haven and Anne Houston, Peck once stated: "I hope they both grow up to have a tough gut and a gentle heart. Because I don't want to sire a world of macho men or feminist women, but rather a less strident society of ladies and gentlemen."

Peck's writing career began with *A Day No Pigs Would Die.* The book was based on memories of his father, "an illiterate farmer and pig-slaughterer whose earthy wisdom continues to contribute to my understanding of the natural order and old Shaker beliefs deeply rooted in the land and its harvest," Peck once observed. In the story, a young boy comes of age when he must summon the will to kill his pet pig on the family farm in Vermont. "The hard facts of farm life are realistically described in terse, vivid prose that has no room for sentimentality," noted a writer in the *Fifth Book of Junior Authors and Illustrators.* The book was met with mixed reviews because of the graphic account of the butchering, but for the most part "Peck has been praised for his down-to-earth, life-is-tough attitude," continued the *Fifth Book of Junior Authors and Illustrators* writer.

A boy named "Soup" is featured in Peck's 1974 book by the same name, and in a number of his following works. "Rob and Soup, though abrim with rascality, respect their beloved Miss Kelly, her Vermont virtue—and her ruler," Peck once remarked. Like Miss Kelly, the character Soup is based on a real person in Peck's life: his closest friend in childhood. Describing the real Soup in his autobiographical essay, Peck expressed his view that "When a boy has a best friend, he's the richest kid on Earth." He went on to note that Soup's "real and righteous name was Luther Wesley Vinson, and he grew up too, to become a minister." Also among Peck's many works are three historical novels which arose from his interest in the Colonial and Revolutionary periods in American history. The children in *Hang for Treason, Fawn,* and *Rabbits and Redcoats* are believable because of Peck's view that children are the same regardless of the time period in which they are born.

Although many of his works have been well-received by children and young adults, Peck once commented that he "didn't start out to write for any particular age group. If my books turn out to be right for teenagers, as well as adults and/or kids, it just happens that way. I can only write about what I know and I've never been shy about telling people what I know. As a matter of fact, when I told my mother ... that three of my books were about to be published by a very important publishing house, she thought for a minute, looked up at me and said, 'Son, you always did have a lot to say.'" No matter who reads his books, though, "motivating the young to read is a task of paramount importance to Peck," noted the *Fifth Book of Junior Authors and Illustrators* writer. One motivator is to read a chapter out loud to children, suggested Peck, so they will be eager to find out what happens next. "My richest talent is making a kid smile. And getting him to read and write," Peck pointed out in his autobiographical essay. He even takes the time to answer up to one hundred weekly letters from fans in the United States and abroad.

When asked why he includes so much of himself in his writing, Peck related in his *Fiction Is Folks* that it's "because I've got so much of *me* to give. Like you, I am abrim with likes, dislikes, talents, cumbersome inabilities, joys, triumphs, and failures ... so why should I even consider wasting such a storehouse?" He went on to say in *SAAS* that "compared to the worth of so many talented authors, my novels aren't really so doggone great. Yet secretly, I truly believe that I am the best teacher of creative writing in the entire galaxy." And most importantly, he concluded, "Life is fun. It's a hoot and a holler. If you can't revel in America and enjoy all the wonderful Americans you meet, you wouldn't be happy in Heaven or even in Florida."

WORKS CITED:

Holtze, Sally Holmes, editor, *Fifth Book of Junior Authors and Illustrators,* H.W. Wilson, 1983, pp. 240-241.

Peck, Robert Newton, *Fiction Is Folks,* Writer's Digest Books, 1983.

Peck, in an essay for *Something about the Author Autobiography Series,* Volume 1, Gale, 1986, pp. 235-247.

FOR MORE INFORMATION SEE:

BOOKS

Chevalier, Tracy, editor, *Twentieth Century Children's Writers,* 3rd edition, St. James Press, 1989.

Contemporary Literary Criticism, Volume 17, Gale, 1981.

PERIODICALS

Horn Book, August, 1973; October, 1973; April, 1976; December, 1976.

New York Times, January 4, 1973.

New York Times Book Review, May 13, 1973.

* * *

PEET, Bill
See PEET, William Bartlett

* * *

PEET, William Bartlett 1915-
(Bill Peet)

PERSONAL: Surname altered to Peet about 1947, though not legally changed; born January 29, 1915, in Grandview, IN; son of Orion Hopkins (a salesman) and Emma (a teacher; maiden name, Thorpe) Peed; married Margaret Brunst, November 30, 1937; children: Bill, Jr., Stephen. *Education:* Attended John Herron Art Institute, 1933-36.

CAREER: Worked briefly as an artist for a greeting card company in the Midwest, 1936-37; Walt Disney Studios, Hollywood, CA, sketch artist and continuity illustrator for motion picture industry, then screenwriter, 1937-64; author and illustrator of children's books.

AWARDS, HONORS: Prizes for paintings at exhibits in Indianapolis and Chicago, 1934-37; John Herron Art Institute citation, 1958, as one of the outstanding students in the history of the school; *Box Office* Blue Ribbon award, 1961, 1964, for best screenplay; Indiana

Author's Day Award for most distinguished Hoosier book of the year for children, 1967, for *Capyboppy;* Southern California Council on Literature for Children and Young People Award for illustration, 1967, for *Farewell to Shady Glade;* named outstanding Hoosier author of children's literature, 1967; Colorado Children's Book Award and California Reading Association Young Reader Medal, both 1976, both for *How Droofus the Dragon Lost His Head;* Little Archer Award from the University of Wisconsin-Oshkosh, 1977, for *Cyrus the Unsinkable Sea Serpent;* Georgia Picture Book Award, 1979, and California Reading Association Young Reader Medal, 1980, both for *Big Bad Bruce;* International Reading Association "Children's Choice" award, 1982, for *Encore for Eleanor;* California Reading Association's Significant Author Award, 1983; George G. Stone Center Recognition of Merit Award for body of work, 1985; Caldecott honor book, 1989, for *Bill Peet: An Autobiography,* which also won the Southern California Children's Book Writer's Medal; Annie Award for distinguished contribution to the art of animation.

WRITINGS:

FOR CHILDREN; SELF-ILLUSTRATED; UNDER NAME BILL PEET

Goliath II, Golden Press, 1959.
Chester the Worldly Pig, Houghton, 1965.
Farewell to Shady Glade, Houghton, 1966.
Capyboppy, Houghton, 1966.
Buford, the Little Bighorn, Houghton, 1967.
Jennifer and Josephine, Houghton, 1967.
Fly, Homer, Fly, Houghton, 1969.

Bill Peet

The Whingdingdilly, Houghton, 1970.
The Wump World, Houghton, 1970.
How Droofus the Dragon Lost His Head, Houghton, 1971.
The Ant and the Elephant, Houghton, 1972.
The Spooky Tail of Prewitt Peacock, Houghton, 1972.
Merle the High Flying Squirrel, Houghton, 1974.
Cyrus the Unsinkable Sea Serpent, Houghton, 1975.
The Gnats of Knotty Pine, Houghton, 1975.
Big Bad Bruce, Houghton, 1977.
Eli, Houghton, 1978.
Cowardly Clyde, Houghton, 1979.
Encore for Eleanor, Houghton, 1981.
Pamela Camel, Houghton, 1984.
Jethro and Joel Were a Troll, Houghton, 1987.
Cock-a-Doodle Dudley, Houghton, 1990.

CHILDREN'S VERSE; SELF-ILLUSTRATED; UNDER NAME BILL PEET

Hubert's Hair-Raising Adventure, Houghton, 1959.
Huge Harold, Houghton, 1961.
Smokey, Houghton, 1962.
The Pinkish, Purplish, Bluish Egg, Houghton, 1963.
Randy's Dandy Lions, Houghton, 1964.
Ella, Houghton, 1964.
Kermit the Hermit, Houghton, 1965.
The Caboose Who Got Loose, Houghton, 1971.
Countdown to Christmas, Golden Gate, 1972.
The Luckiest One of All, Houghton, 1982.
No Such Things, Houghton, 1983.
The Kweeks of Kookatumdee, Houghton, 1985.
Zella, Zack, and Zodiac, Houghton, 1986.

OTHER; UNDER NAME BILL PEET

Bill Peet: An Autobiography, Houghton, 1989.

Author and illustrator of Walt Disney films *One Hundred and One Dalmatians,* 1961, and *The Sword in the Stone,* 1963, and, with others, of *Pinocchio,* 1940, *Dumbo,* 1941, *Fantasia,* 1941, *Song of the South,* 1946, *Cinderella,* 1950, *Alice in Wonderland,* 1951, *Peter Pan,* 1953, *Sleeping Beauty,* 1959, and short subjects.

Peet's books have been translated into many languages, including French, German, Japanese, and Swedish, and many have been issued in Braille.

SIDELIGHTS: William Bartlett Peet's lively drawings were familiar to moviegoers long before he began publishing books for children. As an illustrator for Walt Disney Studios, Peet contributed drawings to such animated classics as *Pinocchio, Fantasia, Cinderella,* and *Peter Pan,* and was the screenwriter for *One Hundred and One Dalmatians* and *The Sword in the Stone.* He left Disney in 1964 and since that time has been populating his books with warm animal characters such as Pamela Camel, Buford the Little Bighorn, and Merle the High Flying Squirrel. His children's books, which are all still in print, have won numerous awards and, according to Jim Trelease in the *New York Times Book Review,* "Children in four states have chosen him as their 'favorite author' in annual state polls."

From *How Droofus the Dragon Lost His Head,* written and illustrated by Bill Peet.

Peet was born in 1915 near Indianapolis, Indiana. Before he was three years old, his father was drafted into the army to serve during World War I. His father had just finished training camp when the war ended, but he never rejoined his family, preferring the life of an itinerant salesman. Peet recalls in *Bill Peet: An Autobiography* that since he had never known his father, he didn't miss him, and he remembers fondly the years he spent living with his grandmother, mother, and brothers. In the attic of his grandmother's home, Peet discovered his love for drawing, a love that would remain with him his entire life.

But drawing sometimes caused Peet trouble. He was not very interested in traditional schoolwork, and constantly drew in the margins of his textbooks, on his desk, and on his ever-present pad of paper. Although the habit irritated many of his teachers, Peet says that "when it came time for the used book sales my illustrated books were best sellers." Peet told *Christian Science Monitor* interviewer Marshall Ingwerson about a teacher who once pleasantly surprised him: "This particular teacher snatched my tablet away just as the others had done and marched to the front of the room with it. Then turning to the class she said, 'I want you to see what William has been doing!' Then with an amused smile the teacher turned the pages for all to see. After returning the tablet she encouraged me with, 'I hope you will do something with your drawing someday.'"

The summer before Peet started high school, his father returned home. It was an unhappy reunion and his beloved grandmother died soon afterward as Peet looked on, helpless. His newly poor family was forced to move frequently, and Peet had to attend one of the country's largest high schools. By the end of his first year he had failed every class except physical education, and his parents' constant quarrelling drove him and his brothers apart. At the suggestion of a childhood friend that he take more art classes, however, Peet dropped some of his academic courses and excelled in each of the art classes he took. His success gave him the momentum to pass his other classes, and in his senior year he received a scholarship to the John Herron Art Institute in Indianapolis. Peet was in his element at the art institute, and comments in his autobiography: "It was all peaches and cream, with no devilish academic problems to boggle my mind."

After leaving school in 1937, "a poor year to start a career as a painter, or a career of any kind for that matter," he remembers, he sold some of his paintings, and filled in the colors on greeting cards for a company in Dayton, Ohio, but still could not make enough money to support a family. However, when Walt Disney Studios responded to a letter he had written, and invited him to report to their California offices for a tryout, Peet shared the roads going west during the Great Depression with many other poor Americans hoping to find jobs in California. He arrived just two days before he was to try out for his new job. All the potential illustrators were placed in a large room where they practiced drawing versions of Mickey Mouse, Donald Duck, and Goofy over and over again, trying to master Disney's roundish drawing style. Peet made the cut, and worked for months as an "in-betweener," the person responsible for filling in all the motion sequences of the characters. His steady job allowed him to marry Margaret, his art-school sweetheart. But the repetitious work soon wore on him. "After drawing [Donald Duck] a few thousand times I had begun to despise [him]...," recalls Peet in his autobiography. "It was too much! I went berserk and shouted at the top of my voice, 'NO MORE DUCKS!!!' much to the horror of my fellow in-betweeners." He stormed off the job, swearing not to return.

When Peet returned the next day to retrieve his jacket, he found an envelope on his desk, which he expected to be his dismissal notice. But when he opened it, he found that he was being assigned instead to work on the new Disney movie, *Pinocchio.* This move signalled the beginning of Peet's gradual climb in the Disney organization, for he progressed from creating small background characters to designing progressively larger and more important scenes, and finally to writing the entire screenplay and drawing the story boards for *One Hundred and One Dalmatians* and *The Sword in the Stone.* Although Peet certainly had a great deal of success in his twenty-seven-year career with Disney, all was not idyllic. Peet, who says in his autobiography that he designed the character of Captain Hook in *Peter Pan* to resemble Walt Disney in looks and in temperament, began to realize in the late 1950s that he needed to escape the stifling demands of adapting someone else's ideas, of continually having his own work changed, and of getting little credit for the work he did. Peet told *Los Angeles Times* writer Myrna Oliver that "Walt was very sensitive about credit. He would say 'Dammit, we are all in this together. But what he meant was 'the credit is all *mine.*' I knew that *we* stood for Walter Elias. Everything came out 'Walt Disney presents' and the rest of our names might as well have been in the phone book."

As Peet's dissatisfaction with Disney grew, he began to devote his free time to developing drawings, characters, and stories of his own. He had no problem with the illustrations, but writing the stories proved difficult. "It finally occurred to me that as long as it was Walt Disney's [story], I could write it," Peet recalls in his autobiography. "But when it came to doing a book for myself, I could never complete one." Peet managed to publish a few books by the time he began designing the animals for the new Disney film, *Jungle Book;* but he and Disney were soon at odds over the voice for a character, and after the short-tempered Disney belittled him, he decided to quit. On his birthday in 1964, Peet became a full-time author of children's books.

Out from under the Disney shadow, Peet was able to develop more inventive stories; his first upon leaving was *Randy's Dandy Lions,* a tale of five timid circus lions too nervous to perform. Although Peet has said that the trainer represents Walt Disney, and he the lions, he is glad that he never worked up the gumption to roar back at the trainer as his lions finally do. However, Peet's favorite book is *Chester the Worldly Pig,* a book that he says in his autobiography "is the one book of mine that reflects my past more than any others." The story traces the adventures of Chester as he leaves the farm to join a circus, only to leave the circus to become a big star on his own.

The author enjoys visiting elementary schools to talk with and draw for children, and once received an idea for a book from them. Peet would often ask the excited students to guess what he was drawing on their blackboard, and they usually knew the answer before he was halfway through. One day, however, Peet outsmarted them by changing the animal as he drew, and soon he had come up with a combination of giraffe, elephant, camel, zebra, reindeer, rhino, and dog that became the basis for *Whingdingdilly,* his story of a dog who wishes to be different, and finds a witch to help him make his dream come true. Children return Peet's attention by writing him thousands of letters. Peet told Oliver: "My favorite compliment from the kids is 'We think your books are funny and make us laugh.' If you are trying to get kids to read, a book should be entertaining. If it isn't fun, it becomes a chore."

Peet's books have attracted much critical attention and have earned him numerous awards. His long experience as an animator shows in his cartoonish drawings; an illustrated page by Peet is always filled with detail and action, and characters come to life before the reader's eyes. Rachel Fordyce notes in *Twentieth-Century Children's Writers* that Peet's books "have an exotic patina of fantasy and realistic detail," and that "the pictures are strong enough to stand on their own." While his characters make the reader laugh, they also draw sympathy. In *American Picture Books from Noah's Ark to The Beast Within,* Barbara Bader calls Peet "the most humane of cartoonists," and Trelease comments that "his characters are less eccentric and have a dollop more warmth than Dr. Seuss' and like Dr. Seuss, Mr. Peet often writes with a message in mind, using animal characters in a fable-like but not didactic fashion." Peet's animal characters are often misfits, but through their resourcefulness and compassion they are able to succeed. Not every critic likes Peet's work, however; Derwent May, writing in *Listener,* insists that the grotesque drawings in *The Whingdingdilly* make it a "coarse and upsetting fantasy," while other critics have complained that Peet's verse is trite and filled with cliches. A *Bulletin of the Center for Children's Books* reviewer contends that children will not be bothered by these elements of Peet's work, for they are having too much fun laughing at Peet's ridiculous drawings.

Peet enjoys the turn that his career has taken, telling Ingwerson: "So my early ambition to illustrate animal stories was finally realized, and a little bit more, since I had never considered writing one. This way I can write about things I like to draw, which makes it more fun than work. And I still carry a tablet around with me and sneak a drawing into it now and then. Sometimes I feel like I'm basically doing the same thing as when I was six years old: drawing lions and tigers in books."

WORKS CITED:

Bader, Barbara, "The Storytellers," in *American Picture Books from Noah's Ark to The Beast Within,* Macmillan, 1976, pp. 199-210.

Bulletin of the Center for Children's Books, June, 1986, p. 194.

Fordyce, Rachel, entry on Peet, *Twentieth-Century Children's Writers,* 3rd edition, St. James Press, 1989.

Ingwerson, Marshall, "It's Just as if I Was Still Six—Drawing Lions in Books," *Christian Science Monitor,* November 9, 1981.

May, Derwent, "Nun's Tale," *Listener,* November 11, 1971, p. 665.

Oliver, Myrna, "For Bill Peet, Work Is a Flight of Fancy," *Los Angeles Times,* December 23, 1990, pp. E1, E14.

Peet, Bill, *Bill Peet: An Autobiography,* Houghton, 1989.

Something about the Author, Volume 41, Gale, 1985, pp. 158-164.

Trelease, Jim, "Disney Animator to Durable Author," *New York Times Book Review,* March 11, 1984, p. 23.

FOR MORE INFORMATION SEE:

BOOKS

Books for Children, 1960-1965, American Library Association, 1966.

Kingman, Lee, and others, compilers, *Illustrators of Children's Books: 1957-1966,* Horn Book, 1968.

Kingman, L., and others, compilers, *Illustrators of Children's Books: 1967-1976,* Horn Book, 1978.

Larrick, Nancy, *A Parent's Guide to Children's Reading,* 3rd edition, Doubleday, 1969.

PERIODICALS

Horn Book, June, 1971.

Library Journal, September, 1970.

New York Times Book Review, May 21, 1989, pp. 31, 46.

PENE du BOIS, William (Sherman) 1916-

PERSONAL: Surname is pronounced "*pen*-due-*bwah*"; born May 9, 1916, in Nutley, NJ; son of Guy (a painter and art critic) and Florence (a children's clothes designer; maiden name, Sherman) Pene du Bois; married Jane Bouche, 1943 (marriage ended); married Willa Kim (a theatrical designer), March 26, 1955. *Education:* Attended Miss Barstow's School, NY, 1921-24, Lycee Hoche, Versailles, France, 1924-28, Lycee de Nice, Nice, France, 1928-29, and Morristown School, NJ, 1930-34. *Politics:* Democrat. *Religion:* Protestant. *Hobbies and other interests:* Tennis, raising dogs.

ADDRESSES: Home—60 boulevard Franck Pilatte, 06300 Nice, France. *Agent*—Watkins/Loomis Agency, 150 East Thirty-fifth St., New York, NY 10016.

CAREER: Author and illustrator of children's books. *Paris Review,* art editor and designer, 1956-66. *Military service:* U.S. Army, 1941-45, served in coast artillery in Bermuda; correspondent for *Yank.*

AWARDS, HONORS: Spring Book Festival Younger Honor Award, *New York Herald Tribune,* 1940, for *The Great Geppy;* Spring Book Festival Middle Honor Award, *New York Herald Tribune,* 1946, for *Harriet,* and 1954, for *My Brother Bird;* Spring Book Festival Older Award, *New York Herald Tribune,* 1947, and Newbery Medal, American Library Association, 1948, both for *The Twenty-one Balloons;* Spring Book Festival Picture Book Honor Award, *New York Herald Tribune,* 1951, for *The Mousewife;* Caldecott Honor Award,

William Pene du Bois

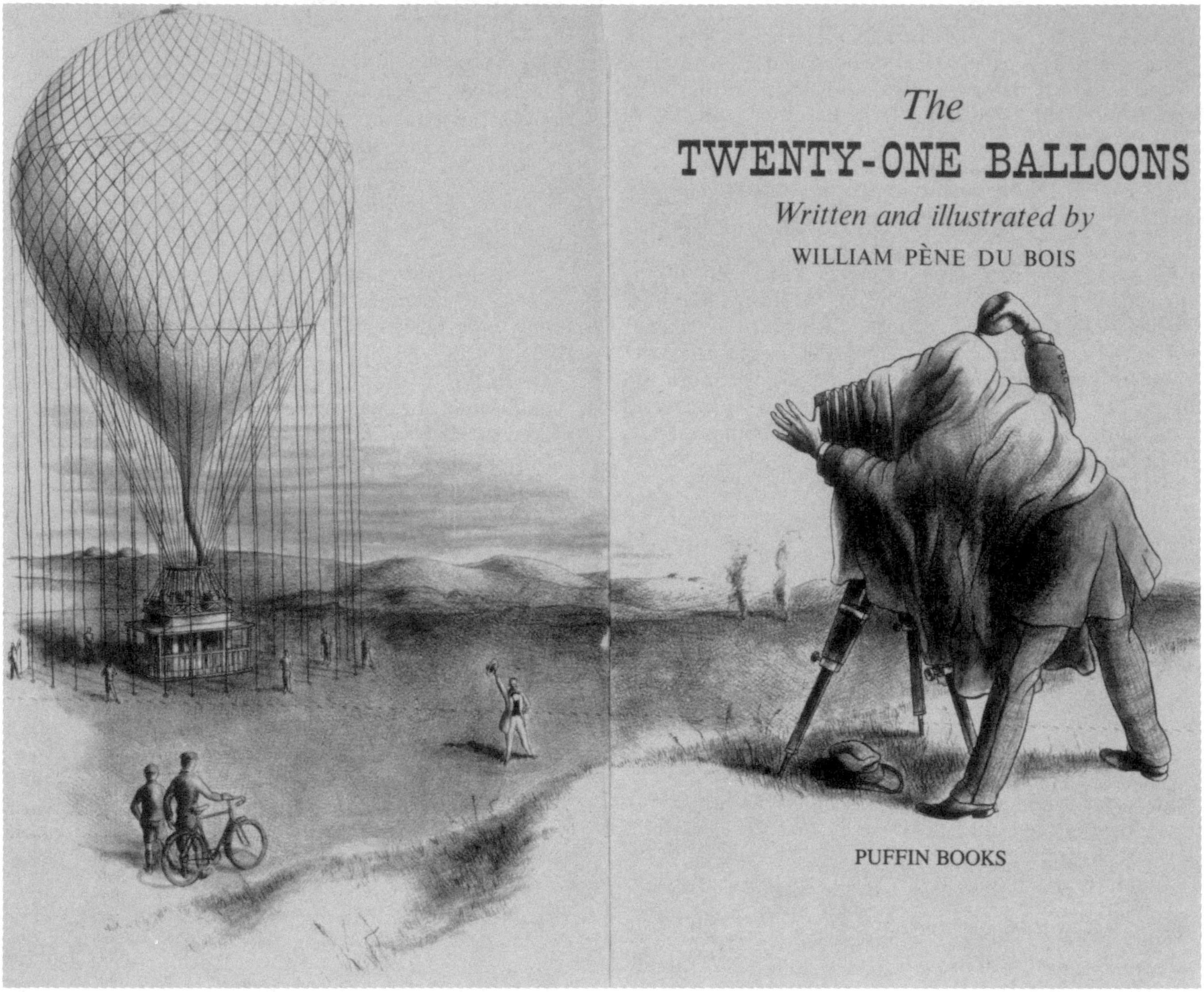

From *The Twenty-one Balloons,* written and illustrated by William Pene du Bois.

American Library Association, 1952, for *Bear Party;* Child Study Award, 1952, for *Twenty and Ten;* Spring Book Festival Prize, *New York Herald Tribune,* 1956, and Caldecott Honor Award, American Library Association, 1957, both for *Lion;* awards from New Jersey Institute of Technology, 1961, for *Otto in Africa* and *The Three Policemen,* 1965, for *The Alligator Case,* 1967, for *The Horse in the Camel Suit,* and 1969, for *Porko von Popbutton;* Clara Ingram Judson Award, 1966, for *A Certain Small Shepherd; New York Times* Best Illustrated Book citation, 1971, Children's Book Showcase Title, 1972, and Lewis Carroll Shelf Award, 1972, all for *Bear Circus;* Art Books for Children Award, 1974, for *The Hare and the Tortoise and the Tortoise and the Hare;* Christopher Award, 1975, for *My Grandson Lew;* Children's Book Showcase Award, 1975, for *Where's Gomer?; New York Times* Best Illustrated Book citation, 1978, for *The Forbidden Forest;* award from *Redbook,* 1985, for *William's Doll.*

WRITINGS:

FOR CHILDREN; SELF-ILLUSTRATED

Elizabeth, the Cow Ghost, Nelson, 1936, published with new illustrations, Viking, 1964.
Giant Otto, Viking, 1936, revised edition with new illustrations published as *Otto in Africa,* 1961.
Otto at Sea, Viking, 1936, published with new illustrations, 1958.
The Three Policemen; Or, Young Bottsford of Farbe Island, Viking, 1938, published with new illustrations, 1960.
The Great Geppy, Viking, 1940.
The Flying Locomotive, Viking, 1941.
The Twenty-one Balloons, Viking, 1947.
Peter Graves, Viking, 1950.
Bear Party, Viking, 1951.
Squirrel Hotel, Viking, 1952, revised edition, G. K. Hall, 1979.
The Giant, Viking, 1954.
Lion, Viking, 1956.

Otto in Texas, Viking, 1959.
The Alligator Case, Harper, 1965.
Lazy Tommy Pumpkinhead, Harper, 1966.
The Horse in the Camel Suit, Harper, 1967.
Pretty Pretty Peggy Moffitt, Harper, 1968.
Porko von Popbutton, Harper, 1969.
Call Me Bandicoot, Harper, 1970.
Otto and the Magic Potatoes, Viking, 1970.
Bear Circus, Viking, 1971.
(With Lee Po) *The Hare and the Tortoise and the Tortoise and the Hare: La Liebre y la tortuga & la tortuga y la liebre* (text in Spanish and English), Doubleday, 1972.
Mother Goose for Christmas, Viking, 1973.
The Forbidden Forest, Harper, 1978.
Gentleman Bear, Farrar, Straus, 1985.

FOR CHILDREN; ILLUSTRATOR

Richard Plant and Oskar Seidlin, *S. O. S. Geneva,* Viking, 1939.
Charles McKinley, *Harriet,* Viking, 1946.
Patricia Gordon, *The Witch of Scrapfaggot Green,* Viking, 1948.
Daisy Ashford, *The Young Visiters; Or Mr. Salteena's Plan,* Doubleday, 1951.
Rumer Godden, *The Mousewife,* Viking, 1951.
Leslie Greener, *Moon Ahead,* Viking, 1951.
Claire Huchet Bishop, *Twenty and Ten,* Viking, 1952.
Evelyn Ames, *My Brother Bird,* Dodd, 1954.
Richard Wilbur, *Digging for China: A Poem,* Doubleday, 1956.
George Plimpton, *The Rabbit's Umbrella,* Viking, 1956.
Marguerite Clement, *In France,* Viking, 1956.
John Steinbeck, *The Short Reign of Pippin IV,* Viking, 1957.
Madeleine Grattan, *Jexium Island,* translated by Peter Grattan, Viking, 1957.
Edward Fenton, *Fierce John, a Story,* Holt, 1959.
The Contents of the Basket and Other Papers on Children's Books and Reading, edited by Frances Lander Spain, New York Public Library, 1960.
Edward Lear, *The Owl and the Pussycat,* Doubleday, 1961.
Dorothy Kunhardt, *Billy the Barber,* Harper, 1961.
George MacDonald, *The Light Princess,* Crowell, 1962.
The Three Little Pigs in Verse; Author Unknown, Viking, 1962.
Jules Verne, *Dr. Ox's Experiment,* Macmillan, 1963.
Rebecca Caudill, *A Certain Small Shepherd,* Holt, 1965.
Roald Dahl, *The Magic Finger,* Harper, 1966.
Betty Yurdin, *The Tiger in the Teapot,* Holt, 1968.
Isaac Bashevis Singer, *The Topsy-Turvy Emperor of China,* Harper, 1971.
Peter Matthiessen, *Seal Pool,* Doubleday, 1972.
Charlotte Shapiro Zolotow, *William's Doll,* Harper, 1972.
Norma Farber, *Where's Gomer?,* Dutton, 1974.
Zolotow, *My Grandson Lew,* Harper, 1974.
Zolotow, *The Unfriendly Book,* Harper, 1975.
Zolotow, *It's Not Fair,* Harper, 1976.
Paul-Jacques Bonzon, *The Runaway Flying Horse,* Parents' Magazine Press, 1976.
Tobi Tobias, *Moving Day,* Random House, 1976.
Mildred Hobzek, *We Came A-Marching ... One, Two, Three,* Parents' Magazine Press, 1978.
Patricia MacLachlan, *The Sick Day,* Pantheon, 1979.
Mark Strand, *The Planet of Lost Things,* C. N. Potter, 1982.
Madeleine Edmondson, *Anna Witch,* Doubleday, 1982.
Strand, *The Night Book,* Crown, 1985.
Bobbye Goldstein, *Bear in Mind: A Book of Bear Poems,* Viking, 1989.
May Garelick, *Just My Size,* HarperCollins, 1990.

Also illustrator of *Castles and Dragons,* edited by Child Study Association, 1958, and *The Poison Belt,* by Arthur Conan Doyle, 1964.

Pene du Bois's manuscripts are housed in the May Massee Collection at Emporia State University, Kansas.

WORK IN PROGRESS: "A book with just one word, which is also the title, *Surprise.* It will be profusely illustrated."

SIDELIGHTS: William Pene du Bois is a widely recognized author and illustrator of children's books. Throughout a prolific career that has spanned five decades, he has illustrated more than fifty books—half of those his own—and garnered several distinguished awards, including the Newbery Medal and two Caldecott Honor Awards. As evidenced by such popular works as *The Twenty-one Balloons* and his "Otto" books, he is best known for artfully combining adventure, fantasy, and humor. His characters are essentially good, though frequently eccentric and absurd, and even his villains are more foolish than evil. His illustrations, too, are acclaimed for their detail, inventiveness, and technical skill.

Pene du Bois was born in New Jersey in 1916 to a family already well established in the art world. His father, Guy Pene du Bois, was a distinguished American painter and art critic, and his mother, Florence, was a children's clothes designer. Even as early as the 1700s, his family was filled with painters, stage designers, and architects, many of whom were known throughout the United States and Europe.

As a child, Pene du Bois developed a strong interest in the circus. After he moved to France with his family at the age of eight, he spent so much time at one French circus that he could name each performer and act by heart. Much of his time, too, was spent poring over the books of Jules Verne, who wrote colorful science-fiction and adventure novels. However, Pene du Bois admits that he was fascinated more by the illustrations in Verne's books—especially those depicting mechanical devices—than by the actual texts. "As a child I hardly read at all, although I loved to look at books," he later said in his Newbery Award acceptance speech, as quoted in *Something about the Author* (*SATA*). "I was the sort of fellow who just looks at the pictures. I try to keep such impatient children in mind in making my books."

During his childhood, Pene du Bois learned much about drawing from his father. Yet he also credits the strict discipline of the Lycee Hoche, one of two French schools he attended, for instilling neatness, clarity, and order in his work habits and artistic style. At the school, for example, whistles and bells signaled every activity, from dressing, to washing, to eating. And meticulousness was of paramount importance to Pene du Bois's arithmetic teacher, who refused any work that failed to meet his strict standards for neatness. "I remember doing a magnificent page of arithmetic," Pene du Bois recalled in *SATA,* "in which I neglected to rule one short line under a subtraction of two one-digit figures.... 'What have we here,' [my teacher] said, 'an artist? Monsieur [Pene] du Bois is drawing free hand.' He neatly tore my work in four pieces." Later, Pene du Bois employed a similar strategy in his own work—if he feels any of his drawings is not his best, he tears it up.

At age fourteen, Pene du Bois moved with his family back to the United States, and two years later, in 1933, he announced his decision to enter Carnegie Technical School of Architecture. "I was awarded a scholarship to that institution," he told *SATA,* "but to my amazement, I sold a children's book I wrote and illustrated as a divertissement during vacation. It was *The Great Geppy.*" So instead of attending Carnegie, Pene du Bois embarked on a new career: writing and illustrating books for children. By age nineteen, he completed and saw the publication of his first book, and by the time he entered the armed forces at age twenty-five, he had written and illustrated five more books for children.

Since then Pene du Bois has continued to write and illustrate children's books at a steady, though unhurried, pace. He likes to prepare himself before working by sharpening his pencils and aligning his drawing instruments neatly on his worktable—reminiscent of his days at the lycee. Then, through a meticulous process, he carefully pencils each line of the illustration before tracing it in ink. He works on only one drawing per day, and he often writes the text for his books only after the illustrations are complete. In this way, his story ideas are almost fully developed by the time he actually composes on paper.

Among Pene du Bois's earliest self-illustrated works is *Giant Otto,* the first in a comical series that features a gigantic hound and his owner, Duke. In *Giant,* Otto joins the French Foreign Legion and successfully wards off an Arab invasion by wagging his tail to create a huge sandstorm. In *Otto at Sea* he bravely saves all the passengers of a sinking ship. Other "Otto" books include *Otto in Texas,* where Otto unmasks oil thieves, and *Otto and the Magic Potatoes,* where Otto and Duke discover that an evil baron is actually a humanitarian who wants to feed the hungry. The "Otto" stories were well received by reviewers, who especially praised Pene du Bois's imaginative and vivid illustrations.

Pene du Bois drew upon his love of the circus for his 1940 book, *Great Geppy.* The title character is a horse that is hired to solve a robbery at a circus. To investigate the crime, Geppy poses as a variety of circus entertainers, including a freak, a tightrope walker, and a lion tamer. In the end he discovers that there never was a theft; the culprit broke into the safe to *donate* money to the struggling circus, not steal any. For his success Geppy is honored as a hero and is even appointed the circus's newest star—he gives an extraordinary performance when shot from a cannon.

During World War II, Pene du Bois served in the U.S. Army, but he didn't stop writing and illustrating. In addition to working as a correspondent for *Yank,* he also edited the camp newspaper, painted portraits, and illustrated strategic maps. And, according to Susan Garness in the *Dictionary of Literary Biography* (*DLB*), he also may have been working on his next children's book, for two years after his discharge, he completed what is perhaps his best known work, *The Twenty-one Balloons.*

Winner of the 1948 Newbery Medal, *The Twenty-one Balloons* relates the fantastic adventures of Professor William Waterman Sherman, a retired mathematics teacher who embarks on a cross-Pacific journey in a hot-air balloon. Unfortunately his balloon is punctured, and he crashes on the island of Krakatoa, whose inhabitants live in luxury atop a volcano filled with diamonds. One day, though, the volcano erupts, and everyone escapes on a platform held aloft by twenty-one balloons. Equipped with parachutes, the Krakatoans later jump to safety, but the professor is left to crash-land in the ocean. Eventually, he is rescued by a freighter and welcomed home as a hero.

In *The Twenty-one Balloons,* some reviewers noted, Pene du Bois pokes fun at the greedy people of society. Once the professor is rescued, for example, many characters are so eager to capture his attention—and some of his glory—that they appear ridiculous and insincere. The Krakatoans, too, are so fearful of losing their diamonds that they foolishly choose to live on an active volcano. However, many reviewers pointed out that these characters are more ludicrous than wicked and that the story itself, although told in a serious tone, is genuinely funny. In addition, they applauded Pene du Bois's detailed illustrations, which augment the narrative. As a reviewer for the *Junior Bookshelf* wrote, "the numerous illustrations are not only most beautiful in themselves but also exact and illuminating interpretations of the story."

During the 1950s Pene du Bois won the Caldecott Honor Award for each of two self-illustrated books, *Bear Party* and *Lion.* The former relates the simple tale of a masquerade party given by "real" teddy bears. Told with little text, the story relies on Pene du Bois's colorful and elaborate drawings, which depict bears dressed in costumes ranging from clowns, to angels, to bullfighters, to knights. The latter story is an original fable that reveals how the Artist Foreman created the Lion at the beginning of the universe. With detailed illustrations, Pene du Bois fills the factory—where angels invent the animals—with charts of ears, tails, and tongues. He also depicts the angels' drawing instruments, which include white paper and gold brushes. The book is "graceful and charming," judged Nancy Ekholm Burkert in *Horn Book,* adding that "the delight of *Lion* in both art and text lies in its celebration of the creation of uniqueness and in the uniqueness of creation."

Pene du Bois next turned his humor on the seven deadly sins, which include gluttony, laziness, and self-adoration. In a series of books, he features characters whose individual weaknesses are magnified to comical proportions. In *Lazy Tommy Pumpkinhead,* for example, a machine performs every daily task for Tommy; however, when it malfunctions, he is dumped into an ice-cold bath and dressed upside down. In another book, *Pretty Pretty Peggy Moffitt,* Peggy constantly trips and falls because she is forever gazing at herself in mirrors. With bruises covering her body, her hopes for a movie audition are destroyed. And in *Call Me Bandicoot,* a wealthy young boy hoards every cigarette butt he can find, in hopes of reusing the tobacco. Ultimately, he's left with a cigarette the size of a football field.

Throughout Pene du Bois's career, he has also illustrated numerous works of other notable children's authors, including Verne, Isaac Bashevis Singer, and Charlotte Shapiro Zolotow. He especially enjoys the challenge of illustrating books entirely different from his own, such as Patricia Gordon's *Witch of Scrapfaggot Green,* which features an evil sorceress. Undoubtedly, though, many of the books he illustrates contain characters and elements familiar to him. In Charles McKinley's *Harriet,* for example, he draws the title character, a horse, much like his own *Geppy.* And in Leslie Greener's *Moon Ahead,* a science fiction story, he indulges his love for precisely drawn illustrations of machinery—a love first inspired by Verne's books. Moreover, fussy characters greatly resembling those in his *Twenty-one Balloons* appear in Daisy Ashford's *Young Visiters.*

Pene du Bois continues to add to his already lengthy list of children's books. And he also continues to attract widespread recognition for his humorous fantasies, amusing characters, and detailed drawings. But he wishes to dispel the myth that creating books for children is a simple task. In a lecture at the New York Public Library, as quoted in *DLB,* he addressed the point: "I have the feeling that when I'm asked 'How did you ever think of such a crazy idea?' the person who asked the question felt that the book was thought of in a moment, illustrated in a week, and printed in a day. There is a widespread feeling that doing children's books is a divertissement or a hobby, never a full-time job, and that it's quick and easy. I don't want to discourage people who want to dash off a children's book, but I would like to slow them down a bit."

WORKS CITED:

Burkert, Nancy Ekholm, "A Second Look: *Lion,*" *Horn Book,* December, 1980, pp. 671-676.

Garness, Susan, "William Pene du Bois," *Dictionary of Literary Biography,* Volume 61: *American Writers for Children since 1960: Poets, Illustrators, and Nonfiction Authors,* Gale, 1987, pp. 27-37.

Something about the Author, Volume 4, Gale, 1973, pp. 69-71.

Review of *The Twenty-one Balloons, Junior Bookshelf,* October, 1950, pp. 130-131.

FOR MORE INFORMATION SEE:

BOOKS

Children's Literature Review, Volume 1, Gale, 1976.

PERIODICALS

Horn Book, July, 1948.

* * *

PEPPE, Rodney (Darrell) 1934-

PERSONAL: Surname is pronounced "*Pep*-py"; born June 24, 1934, in Eastbourne, Sussex, England; son of Lionel Hill (a lieutenant commander in the Royal Navy) and Winifred Vivienne (Parry) Peppe; married Tordis Tatjana Tekkel, July 16, 1960; children: Christen Rodney, Jonathan Noel. *Education:* Attended Eastbourne School of Art, National Diploma in Design, 1958; London County Council Central School of Art and Crafts, Diploma in Illustration, 1959. *Religion:* Church of England. *Hobbies and other interests:* Collecting antique clocks, Japanese *netsuke,* and old children's books; making new characters from wind-up toys; swimming.

Rodney Peppe

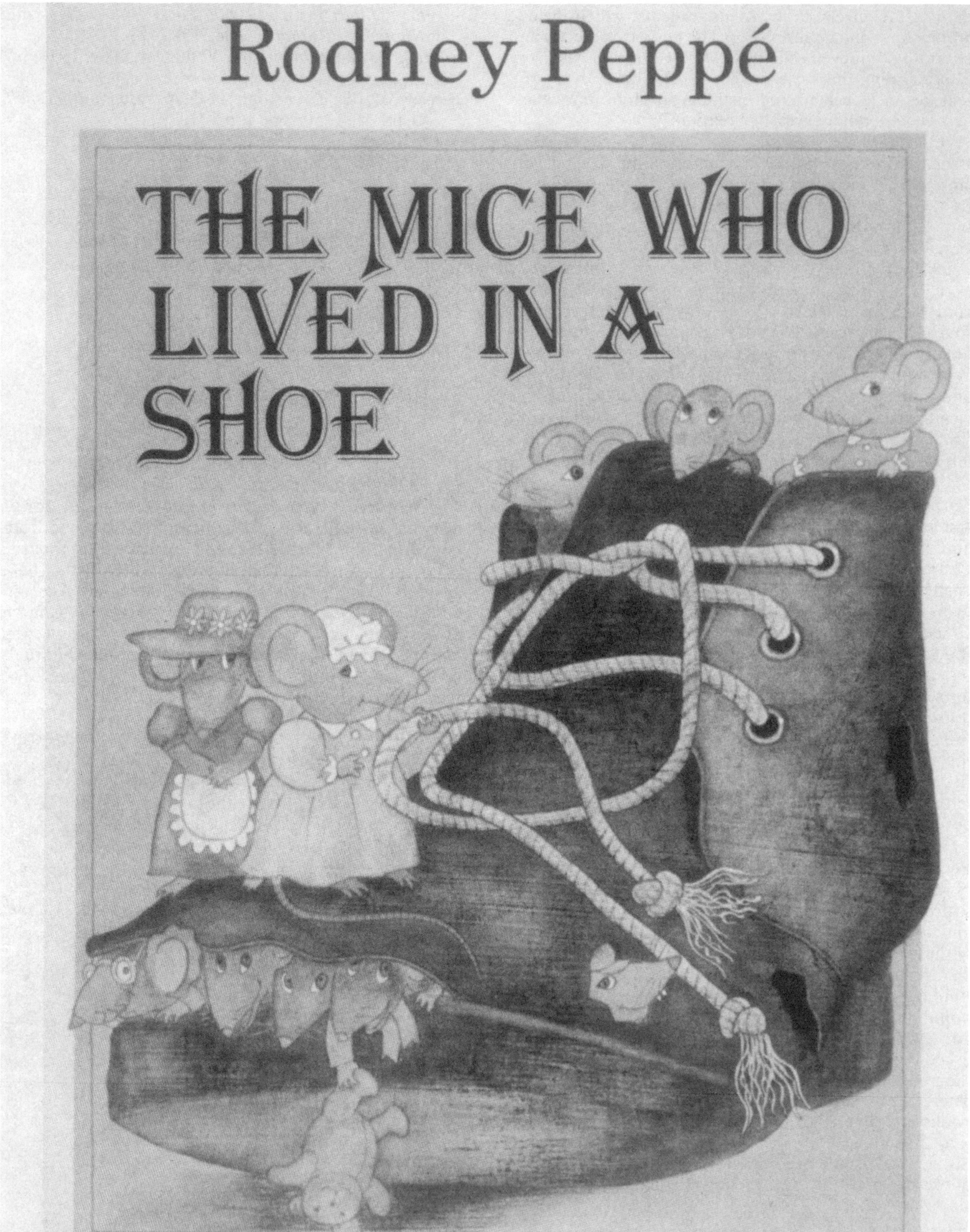

From *The Mice Who Lived in a Shoe,* written and illustrated by Rodney Peppe.

ADDRESSES: Home and studio—Barnwood House, Whiteway, Stroud, Gloucester GL6 7ER, England.

CAREER: S. H. Benson Ltd. (advertising agency), London, England, art director, 1960-64; J. Walter Thompson Co. Ltd. (advertising agency), London, art director for television accounts, 1964-65; Ross Foods Ltd., design consultant, London, 1965-72, Syon Park, Brentford, Middlesex, 1972-73; design consultant to other firms and groups. *Military service:* British Army, Intelligence Corps, 1953-55; served in Malaya.

WRITINGS:

SELF-ILLUSTRATED

The Alphabet Book, Viking (UK), 1968, Four Winds, 1968.
Circus Numbers: A Counting Book, Viking (UK), 1969, Delacorte, 1969.
The House That Jack Built, Viking (UK), 1970, Delacorte, 1970.
Hey Riddle Diddle! A Book of Traditional Riddles, Viking (UK), 1971, Holt, 1971.
Simple Simon, Viking (UK), 1972, Holt, 1973.
Cat and Mouse: A Book of Rhymes, Viking (UK), 1973, Holt, 1973.
Humpty Dumpty, Viking/Puffin Books, 1974, Viking, 1986.
Odd One Out, Viking (UK), 1974, Viking, 1974.
Picture Stories, Viking, 1976.
Rodney Peppe's Puzzle Book, Viking (UK), 1977, Viking, 1977.
Humphrey the Number Horse, Methuen, 1978, Viking, 1979.
Ten Little Bad Boys, Viking (UK), 1978, Viking, 1978.
Three Little Pigs, Viking (UK), 1979, Lothrop, 1979.
My Surprise Pull-Out Word Book: Indoors, Methuen, 1980, F. Watts, 1980.
My Surprise Pull-Out Word Book: Outdoors, Methuen, 1980, F. Watts, 1980.
Run Rabbit, Run!: A Pop-Up Book, Methuen, 1982, Delacorte, 1982.
Make Your Own Paper Toys, Patrick Hardy, 1984.
Press-Out Circus Book, Methuen, 1986.
Press-Out Train Book, Methuen, 1986.
Tell the Time with Mortimer, Methuen, 1986.
Open House, Methuen, 1987, Oxford University Press, 1987.
First Nursery Rhymes, Methuen, 1988, Oxford University Press, 1988.
Thumbprint Circus, Viking (UK), 1988, Delacorte, 1989.
The Animal Directory, Blackie, 1989.
Rodney Peppe's Noah's Ark Frieze, Campbell, 1989.
Alphabet Frieze, Campbell, 1990.
Summer Days, Campbell, 1991.
Winter Days, Campbell, 1991.
ABC Index, Blackie, 1990, Bedrick Blackie, 1991.
The Shapes Finder, Blackie, 1991.

"HENRY" SERIES; SELF-ILLUSTRATED

Henry's Exercises, Methuen, 1975, enlarged edition, 1978.
Henry's Garden, Methuen, 1975, enlarged edition, 1978.
Henry's Present, Methuen, 1975.
Henry's Sunbathe, Methuen, 1975, enlarged edition, 1978.
Henry's Aeroplane, Methuen, 1978.
Henry Eats Out, Methuen, 1978.
Henry's Toy Cupboard, Methuen, 1978.
Hello Henry, Methuen, 1984.
Hurrah for Henry!, Methuen, 1984.

"MICE" SERIES; SELF-ILLUSTRATED

The Mice Who Lived in a Shoe, Viking (UK), 1981, Lothrop, 1981.
The Kettleship Pirates, Viking (UK), 1983, Lothrop, 1983.
The Mice and the Flying Basket, Viking (UK), 1985, Lothrop, 1985.
The Mice and the Clockwork Bus, Viking (UK), 1986, Lothrop, 1987.

"LITTLE TOY BOARD BOOKS" SERIES; SELF-ILLUSTRATED

Little Circus, Methuen, 1983, Viking, 1983.
Little Dolls, Methuen, 1983, Viking, 1983.
Little Games, Methuen, 1983, Viking, 1983.
Little Numbers, Methuen, 1983, Viking, 1983.
Little Wheels, Methuen, 1983, Viking, 1983.

"RODNEY PEPPE'S BLOCK BOOKS" SERIES; SELF-ILLUSTRATED

Animals, Methuen, 1985.
Colours, Methuen, 1985.
Numbers, Methuen, 1985.
People, Methuen, 1985.

"HUXLEY PIG" SERIES; SELF-ILLUSTRATED

Here Comes Huxley Pig, Warne, 1989, Delacorte, 1989.
Huxley Pig at the Circus, Fantail, 1989.
Huxley Pig in the Haunted House, Fantail, 1989.
Huxley Pig the Clown, Warne, 1989, Delacorte, 1989.
Huxley Pig's Airplane, Warne, 1990, Delacorte, 1990.
Huxley Pig at the Beach, Fantail, 1990.
Huxley Pig at the Restaurant, Fantail, 1990.
Huxley Pig's Dressing-up Book, Warne, 1991.
Huxley Pig's Model Car, Warne, 1991, Delacorte, 1991.

OTHER

(Illustrator) Marchant, Jill, and Ralph Marchant, *The Little Painter,* Nelson, 1971, Carolrhoda Books, 1971.
Rodney Peppe's Moving Toys (adult nonfiction), Evans Bros., 1980, Sterling, 1980.

ADAPTATIONS: Peppe's "Huxley Pig" books have been adapted as a television series in Great Britain.

SIDELIGHTS: Since publishing his first book in 1968, Rodney Peppe has been the prolific author-illustrator of over sixty picture books for young children. He is best-known for lively character drawings based on his original wooden model toy-figures, including those for his books in the "Henry," "Mice," and "Huxley Pig" series. Although Peppe began his career as a designer in advertising during the late 1950s, he ventured into children's picture books nearly a decade later, finding them a particularly rewarding endeavor. As he commented in *Contemporary Authors:* "Picture book artists find themselves in rather a privileged position. They are the first communicators of still images to the very young, who as yet cannot read. Their pictures convey ideas which can stimulate the child's visual imagination and prepare him for the wonders to come."

Born in Eastbourne, England, in 1934, Peppe spent his early years near the Himalaya Mountains in India, where his father managed the Peppe family estates and also served in the British and Indian Royal navies. Lionel Peppe's naval duties kept him away from his family for long periods of time, and eventually Peppe's mother Vivienne—wanting her sons to have a standard British education—returned with Rodney and his twin brother, Mark, to Eastbourne. The year was 1942, during the height of the Second World War and the German bombing of England. "From the peacefulness of India, through the excitement of being at sea, we came now to bombs and boarding school," Peppe recounted in *Something about the Author Autobiography Series* (*SAAS*).

Peppe and his brother were enrolled in St. Bede's School, which during the war was relocated to St. Edward's School in Oxford. As a youth, Peppe became interested in model construction, influenced by one of his instructors who had built a model cathedral. Another early interest was the cinema, and at a young age he began drawing cowboys and pirates from films he had seen, as well as caricatures of his favorite cinema stars. Later, when he was a student at the strict St. Edward's School, Peppe was often disciplined for stealing away to view films at Oxford's movie houses. "Much of my free time was spent ... in going with fellow transgressors to see films which I thought then, and think now, were an important part of my education," he recounted in *SAAS.* Although St. Edward's was a restrictive school, the students found various creative ways to express their individuality. "You could see colourful personalities emerging from this insular society with its petty rules, for they eschewed conformity for its own sake, thereby making a statement to the tiny world we lived in, that they were different—special. Of course they paid for it with the rod!"

Peppe had aspirations to one day become an actor, yet eventually decided to pursue art studies. "I can't remember how I decided to train to be an artist rather than an actor, but there certainly wasn't much soul-searching," he wrote in *SAAS.* His parents were persuaded to allow Peppe and his brother to leave St. Edward's early and enroll at the Eastbourne School of Art, where Peppe went on to pursue painting as his major and wood-engraving as a craft. He continued with his studies until 1953 when he began two years of mandatory military service. Peppe was assigned to British Foreign Intelligence and sent to the Asian country of Malaya. There, as he noted in *SAAS,* he "made friends with the country and its people," and also became fascinated by the country's exotic bazaars and lively cabarets. "I haunted the dance halls with my sketchbook" and made "notes and sketches wherever I went and worked on them later to make finished drawings and paintings."

When his military service concluded, Peppe resumed his art studies at Eastbourne. He then attended London's Central School of Art and Crafts, choosing illustration as his major, graduating with a diploma in 1959. He studied under a famous illustrator and designer named Laurence Scarfe, as well as continuing with wood-engraving under noted craftswoman Gertrude Hermes. "At the time I was a film extra during the holidays, which was a pleasant way to eke out my father's allowance," he added in *SAAS.* Peppe completed a three-year illustration study course in two years, eager "to get *on,*" as he wrote in *SAAS.* "Armed with my diploma and a portfolio I walked the streets of London visiting publishers."

Peppe began searching for free-lance illustration work, but instead obtained a job with an advertising agency. "My work at the Central School had been illustrating poems by Keats with detailed wood engravings, or designing programme covers for ballets," he noted in *SAAS.* ".... Now I had to contend with press advertisements extolling the virtues of smoking cigarettes, drinking beer, or buying oil-fired central heating. There was no point of contact." Although the work was initially frustrating, Peppe came to be proficient at it, and still found room for his own creative endeavors. One of his hobbies became cartoon-making, and during his spare time he began filming self-made cartoon figures in the one-room apartment he shared with his wife Tatjana and newly-born son. "My method was to use translucent coloured celluloid cutouts, which I made into jointed characters," he related in *SAAS.* "I photographed these flat puppets on a light box, with single shots, moving them frame by frame."

The demands of his new family prompted Peppe to focus on his advertising career, however, and eventually he landed a job as a designer with a frozen-foods company in London. "It was for three days a week, working at home two days and visiting their offices every Tuesday—and for the same money I was getting for five days a week.... This was the break I had been waiting for." Undaunted by an earlier, unsuccessful try at producing a children's picture book, Peppe began working on what would become *The Alphabet Book,* published in 1968. "Because words play little or no part in alphabet and counting books, these are often the type of books to which graphic designers turn," he observed in *SAAS.* "I was no exception and appreciated especially the self-working themes of these visual primers, which would give me artistic freedom, unfettered by text and yet supported by the solid structure of the alphabet." In a similar manner, Peppe's second book, *Circus Numbers,* was a children's counting primer featuring images of the circus. "I used the ring graphically to contain the circus acts," Peppe noted in *SAAS,* " ... while outside the ring I place large black cardinal numbers, with captions for each act."

Finding success with his illustration work, Peppe went on to produce pictorial renditions of such children's standards as *The House That Jack Built, Hey Riddle Diddle!,* and *Simple Simon.* "I was ducking the issue of writing my own stories," he said in *SAAS.* "I was an artist, not a writer, and I usefully employed what was in the public domain: Nursery Rhymes." This changed with his 1974 book *Odd One Out,* which tells the story of a day in the life of a small boy. "In each picture the young reader can find an 'odd one out,' one deliberate mistake that turns the simple story into an exciting and colourful game," Peppe noted in *SAAS.* "The book was very successful for me and gave me the confidence to invent my own stories and not rely upon traditional rhymes." Peppe soon discovered that his earlier love of making models could also serve his picture books. He constructed a wooden model elephant named Henry and "would position him in various poses and use him as a lay figure from which to draw." Peppe's elephant became the basis for a series of nine "Henry" books. "Apart from finding a new method of producing picture books, Henry started me off on writing simple stories for the very young," he commented in *SAAS.* "I developed his character as a rather incompetent young elephant whose adventures had a habit of going wrong."

One of Peppe's best-received books has been *The Mice Who Lived in a Shoe* which, along with its three sequels, recounts the adventures of a mouse family who live in a weathered, lace-up boot. In addition to garnering favorable reviews from critics, Peppe received requests from children "for instructions on how to build the shoe-house and letters and drawings showing me ingenious examples, using my book as a springboard for ideas," as he noted in *SAAS.* Another successful series for Peppe is his "Huxley Pig" books, featuring another character drawn from a wooden figure designed by Peppe. The Huxley books also led to a television series which aired in Great Britain in 1989. "To see my words turn into model animation, my drawn characters brought to life, with voices, was a particular joy to me," Peppe wrote in *SAAS.* ".... There are three animators and three Huxleys, jointed, so that they can move by stop-frame animation."

In addition to his picture books, Peppe has produced a number of "pop-up" books, including *Run Rabbit, Run!,* published in 1982. He has also written an adult manual for toy-making, entitled *Rodney Peppe's Moving Toys.* "The results of working on this book," Peppe noted in *SAAS,* "with instructions, diagrams, and photographs for making twenty-two moving toys, many based on Victorian mechanism (though my own designs), has been one the greatest influences on my work." Peppe hopes that his own interest in toy-making, illustrations, and model construction not only sparks his readers' interest, but also provides an incentive. He told *Contemporary Authors:* "As a picture book artist I like to think of my books being treated like favourite toys.... It's important too that an adult reading aloud to the child should not be bored or irritated by text and pictures. If, while satisfying these requirements I can foster aesthetic appreciation and encourage the child to make his own pictures, so much the better."

WORKS CITED:

Peppe, Rodney, essay in *Fifth Book of Junior Authors,* edited by Sally Holmes Holtze, H. W. Wilson, 1983, pp. 243-5.

Peppe, comments in *Contemporary Authors,* Volumes 33-36, First Revision, Gale, 1978, p. 632.

Peppe, essay in *Something about the Author Autobiography Series,* Volume 10, Gale, 1990, pp. 201-17.

* * *

PERCY, Charles Henry
See SMITH, Dorothy Gladys

* * *

PERKINS, Lucy Fitch 1865-1937

PERSONAL: Born July 12, 1865, in Maples, IN; died March 18, 1937, in Flintridge, CA; daughter of Appleton Howe (an educator and manufacturer) and Elizabeth (Bennett) Fitch; married Dwight Heald Perkins (an architect), August 18, 1891; children: Eleanor Ellis, Lawrence Bradford. *Education:* Museum of Fine Arts School, Boston, MA, 1883-86.

From *The Filipino Twins,* written and illustrated by Lucy Fitch Perkins.

ADDRESSES: Home—Evanston, IL.

CAREER: Writer of children's books and editor. Prang Educational Company, illustrator in Boston, MA, 1886, and Chicago, IL, 1893-1903; Pratt Institute, School of Fine Arts, Brooklyn, NY, teacher, 1887-91.

MEMBER: Chicago Society of Artists, Midland Authors, Woman's Club, Lyceum Club (London).

WRITINGS:

FICTION FOR CHILDREN; AND ILLUSTRATOR; PUBLISHED BY HOUGHTON

The Dutch Twins, 1911.
The Japanese Twins, 1912.
The Irish Twins, 1913.
The Eskimo Twins, 1914.
The Mexican Twins, 1915.
The Cave Twins, 1916.
The Belgian Twins, 1917.
The French Twins, 1918.
The Spartan Twins, 1918.
Cornelia: The Story of a Benevolent Despot, 1919.
The Scotch Twins, 1919.
The Italian Twins, 1920.
The Puritan Twins, 1921.
The Swiss Twins, 1922.
The Filipino Twins, 1923.
The Colonial Twins of Virginia, 1924.
The American Twins of 1812, 1925.
The American Twins of the Revolution, 1926.
Mr. Chick, His Travels and Adventures, 1926.
The Pioneer Twins, 1927.
The Farm Twins, 1928.
Kit and Kat: More Adventures of the Dutch Twins, 1929.
The Indian Twins, 1930.
The Pickaninny Twins, 1931.
The Norwegian Twins, 1933.
The Spanish Twins, 1934.
The Chinese Twins, 1935.
(With daughter, Eleanor Ellis Perkins) *The Dutch Twins and Little Brother,* 1938.

VERSE FOR CHILDREN; AND ILLUSTRATOR

The Goose Girl, A Mother's Lap-Book of Rhymes and Pictures, McClurg, 1906.

ILLUSTRATOR

Nathaniel Hawthorne, *A Wonder Book,* Stokes, 1908.
Margaret Blanche Pumphrey, *Stories of the Pilgrims,* Rand McNally, 1910.
Maude Warren, *Little Pioneers,* Rand McNally, 1916.
E. E. Perkins, *News from Notown,* Houghton, 1919.
Maude Summers, editor, *The Children's Year Book,* Stoll & Edwards, 1923.
Julia Brown, *The Enchanted Peacock and Other Stories,* Rand McNally, 1925.
Edgar Dubs Shimer, *The Fairyland Reader,* Noble & Noble, 1935.
Verra Xenophontovna, *Folk Tales from the Russian,* Core Collection Books, 1979.

Also illustrator of *Mother Goose Book.*

OTHER

(Editor and illustrator) *Robin Hood: His Deeds and Adventures as Recounted in the Old English Ballads,* Stokes, 1906.
(Editor and illustrator) *The Twenty Best Fairy Tales by Hans Andersen, Grimm, and Miss Mulock,* Stokes, 1907. (Editor and illustrator) *A Midsummer-Night's Dream for Young People* (based on the play by William Shakespeare), Stokes, 1907.
A Book of Joys: The Story of a New England Summer (for adults), McClurg, 1907.
(And illustrator) *Aesop's Fables,* Stokes, 1908.

SIDELIGHTS: Lucy Fitch Perkins was trained in art and began her career as a book illustrator, but she is remembered for her "Twins of the World" series, twenty-six books in which she wrote of the lives of children from more than twenty different countries and cultures.

Perkins was born in rural Indiana, where her family had moved when her father left his job as a school principal in Chicago to enter the lumber business. Perkins and her sister were educated by their parents until the family moved back to their ancestral home in Massachusetts. After graduating from high school, Perkins studied for three years at the Museum of Fine Arts in Boston, worked for a year as an illustrator for the Prang Educational Company, and then went to Brooklyn's Pratt Institute to teach art. Four years later she married Dwight Heald Perkins, a Chicago architect. The couple lived in Evanston, Illinois, and had two children.

Perkins continued to do illustrations for other people's books for several years after her marriage, and she had two books published for which she wrote text to go with the pictures she had done. But the "real beginning" of her writing, she said in *The Junior Book of Authors,* came when a friend who was also a publisher persuaded her to try writing her own books. She soon presented him with a set of sketches for *The Dutch Twins,* which he accepted and published, thus launching the "Twins of the World" series.

Perkins explained that the series grew out of two ideas: "the necessity for mutual respect and understanding between people of different nationalities if we are ever to live in peace" and the belief that "a really big theme can be comprehended by children if it is presented in a way that holds their interest and engages their sympathies."

She drew her inspiration from two experiences, she related: a visit to Ellis Island, where she saw "the oppressed and depressed of all nations" entering the United States to begin life here; and a visit to a Chicago school in which children from twenty-seven different nationalities were being successfully taught. "It seemed to me," Perkins said, "it might help in the fusing process if these children could be interested in the best qualities they bring to our shores."

In her series, Perkins not only depicted the life of children in the countries and times in which the books are set but also treated social issues that had caused immigration to this country and attempted to show what people from different cultures had contributed to the culture of the United States. In this way she was able to engage her young readers' sympathies and to foster understanding among them.

Bertha E. Mahoney and Elinor Whitney, the compilers of *Realms of Gold,* an annotated list of children's books over five hundred years, commented that several of the Twins books are "notable for the careful study of environment and national traits which characterize them all, combined with an interesting story," and they praised Perkins for having "been able to maintain freshness and life in so long a series." According to the *National Cyclopaedia of American Biography,* in October, 1935, Perkins was honored by her publishers at a ceremony at the Chicago Public Library, during which she was given the two millionth copy of a book from the Twins series.

Throughout her writing career, Perkins worked from a studio at her Evanston home. In addition to writing and illustrating books for children, she enjoyed decorative arts, such as making hand-colored prints and painting murals for public buildings and private homes. When she died on March 18, 1937, the twenty-fifth Twins book had just been published, and she was working on another. With the coauthorship of Perkins's daughter, Eleanor Ellis Perkins, the last book of the series, *The Dutch Twins and Little Brother,* was published in 1938.

WORKS CITED:

The National Cyclopaedia of American Biography, Volume 33, University Microfilms, 1967.

Perkins, Lucy Fitch, autobiographical essay in *The Junior Book of Authors,* 2nd edition, edited by Stanley J. Kunitz and Howard Haycraft, H. W. Wilson, 1951, pp. 241-243.

Mahoney, Bertha E., and Whitney, Elinor, compilers, *Realms of Gold,* Doubleday, 1937, pp. 141-142, 628.

FOR MORE INFORMATION SEE:

BOOKS

Twentieth-Century Children's Writers, 3rd edition, St. James Press, 1989.

* * *

PERRAULT, Charles 1628-1703

PERSONAL: Born January 12, 1628, in Paris, France; died May 16, 1703, in Paris, France; son of Pierre Perrault (a lawyer in Parliament); married Marie Guichon, May 1, 1672 (died October, 1678); children: three sons, one daughter. *Education:* Attended college in Beauvais, France.

Charles Perrault

CAREER: Poet, critic, and writer of fairy tales. Called to the bar, Paris, France, 1651, and practiced law until 1654; served as secretary to his brother Claude; was appointed Controller of the Royal Buildings by Jean Baptiste Colbert, Minister of Finance under Louis XIV.

MEMBER: French Academy (served as chancellor, then director).

WRITINGS:

FOR CHILDREN

Histories; or, Tales of Times Past, (originally published as *Histoires; ou, Contes du temps passe avec des moralitez,* [Paris], 1697; also published as *Contes* with introduction by Gilbert Rouger, Editions Garnier Freres, 1967; includes *The Sleeping Beauty, Little Red Riding Hood, Blue-Beard, Puss in Boots, The Fairies, Cinderella, Riquet of the Tuft, Hop-'o My-Thumb*), translation by Robert Samber, J. Pote & R. Montagu, 1729, translation edited by Allison Lurie and Justin G. Schiller with a preface by Michael P. Hearn, Garland Publishing, 1977, numerous other translations have been published under various titles.

FAIRY TALES IN ENGLISH TRANSLATION PUBLISHED SEPARATELY OR AS TITLE STORIES OF COLLECTIONS

The Story of Blue Beard ("La Barbe Bleue" ; also see below), illustrations by Joseph E. Southall, Stone &

From *Cinderella,* by Charles Perrault. Adapted by John Fowles. Illustrated by Sheilah Beckett.

Kimball, 1895, translation by Arthur Quiller-Couch published as *The Whimsical History of Bluebeard,* illustrations by Hans Bendix, Limited Editions, 1952.

The Story of Little Red Riding Hood ("Le Petit Chaperin Rouge"), illustrations by Primrose (pseudonym for Primrose McPherson Robertson), Wilcox & Follett, 1946.

The Sleeping Beauty in the Wood ("La Belle au bois dormant" ; also see below), Limited Editions, 1949, translation by Fabio Coen published as *Sleeping Beauty,* illustrations by Graham Percy, Knopf, 1980.

Puss in Boots ("La Maitre chat; ou, Le Chat botte" ; also see below), translation and illustrations by Marcia Brown, Scribner, 1952, translation by Coen, illustrations by Benvenuti, Knopf, 1979.

Cinderella; or, The Little Glass Slipper ("Cendrillon; ou, a petite pantoufle de verre" ; also see below), translation and illustrations by Brown, Scribner, 1954, translation by Coen published as *Cinderella,* illustrations by Serge Dutfoy, Knopf, 1980.

Cinderella, and Other Stories, translation by Marie Ponsot, illustrations by J. L. Huens, Grosset, 1957.

King Carlo of Capri ("Riquet a la Houppe"), retold by Warren Miller, illustrations by Edward Sorel, Harcourt, 1958.

Puss in Boots [and] *The Sleeping Beauty,* retold by Kathleen N. Daly, illustrations by Paul Durand, Golden Press, 1964.

Bluebeard and Other Fairy Tales, translation by Richard Howard, illustrations by Saul Lambert, Macmillan, 1964.

Little Red Riding Hood, retold by Muriel W. Rothberg, illustrations by Pable Ramirez, World Publishing, 1965, retold by Jane Carruth, illustrations by Elisabeth and Garry Embleton, Hamlyn, 1973.

Tom Thumb ("Petit Poucet"), retold by D. R. Miller, illustrations by Jose Correas, World Publishing, 1965.

Beauty and the Beast, translation by Coen, illustrations by Serge Dutfoy, Knopf, 1980.

Numerous other translations and editions of Perrault's fairy tales have been published.

POEMS

Dialogue de l'amour et de l'amitie, P. Bienfait, 1661.

Saint Paulin, J. B. Coignard, 1686.

Le Siecle de Louis le Grand, J. B. Coignard, 1687.

La Chasse, [Paris], 1692.

La Creation du monde, J. B. Coignard, 1692, published as *Adam; ou, La Creation de l'homme, sa chute, et sa reparation,* 1697.

Ode au Roy, J. B. Coignard, 1693.

(With brothers, Nicolas and Pierre Perrault) *Les Murs de Troie; ou, L'Origine du burlesque,* [Paris], 1953.

OTHER

Paralelle des anciens et des modernes, J. B. Coignard, 1688.

The Vindication of Wives (originally published as *L'Apologie des femmes,* J. B. Coignard, 1694), translation by Roland Grant, Rodale Press, 1954.

Characters Historical and Panegyrical of the Greatest Men That Have Appeared in France during the Last Century (originally published as *Les Hommes illustres qui ont paru en France pendant ce siecle,* A. Dezallier, 1696-1700), translation by J. Ozell, B. Lintott, 1704-05.

Memoires de Charles Perrault, Librarie des Bibliophiles (Paris), 1878.

Oeuvres Completes, three volumes, edited by J. J. Pauvert and M. Soriano, [Paris], 1968-69.

ADAPTATIONS: Short films have been produced of *Little Red Riding Hood* by Thomas A. Edison, Inc., 1917, and National Film Board of Canada, 1968; filmstrips of *Little Red Riding Hood* have also been made by Brunswick Productions (available in both Spanish and French teaching films), 1967, and Cooper Films and Records, 1969. Short films of *Puss in Boots* have been produced by Thomas A. Edison, Inc., 1917, and Encyclopaedia Britannica Films, 1958; the filmstrip *The Story of Puss in Boots* was produced by Encyclopaedia Britannica Films, 1965, and produced as *Puss in Boots,* by Spoken Arts, 1968, H. M. Stone Productions, 1972, Educational Projections Corp., 1973, and Urban Media Materials, 1973. Filmstrips entitled *Le Petit Poucet* were made by Editions Nouvelles, 1948, and Gessler Publishing, 1950. An animated film version of *Cinderella* was produced by Walt Disney Productions, 1949; feature-length adaptations were filmed under different titles, including *The Glass Slipper,* starring Leslie Caron and Michael Wilding, Metro-Goldwyn-Mayer, 1955, and *The Slipper and the Rose,* starring Richard Chamberlain, Universal, 1976; other film versions of *Cinderella* were made by Miniature Opera Co., 1956, and William Gernert, 1958; the filmstrip *Cinderella; or, The Little Glass Slipper* was produced in 1974. Short film versions of *Sleeping Beauty* were produced by World Television Corp., 1952, and Time, Inc., 1952, and animated versions have been produced by Walter Lantz Productions, 1958, and Walt Disney Productions, 1958. The film *Little Tom Thumb* was produced by Importadora, 1958. A filmstrip of *The Fairies* was produced in 1967. *Beauty and the Beast* was produced as an animated film by Walt Disney Productions, 1991.

SIDELIGHTS: Though the stories of *Cinderella, Little Red Riding Hood, Puss in Boots,* and *Sleeping Beauty* are among the best known and most popular works of literature in the world, few people recognize the name of Charles Perrault, the man who is generally believed to be their author. Because his collection of stories, *Histories; or, Tales of Times Past,* was published under the name of Perrault's son, Pierre d'Armancour, there has always been some debate even about the authorship. Glenn S. Burne noted in *Writers for Children* that, according to the best evidence, "the stories were the work of Perrault in probable collaboration with the talented teenage boy, with whom he had a close relationship." Burne went on to say that Perrault published these tales near the end of his career, when his interests were elsewhere, and he probably had no idea that they would become so important.

Born on January 12, 1628, in Paris, France, Perrault was the youngest son of an eminent Parisian lawyer. Both his parents took an active part in educating their children and, when Perrault was sent to a private school at the age of eight, he was one of the top students in his class. Several years later his brilliance led him to argue with a teacher and leave school to study independently with a friend named Beaurain. In his autobiography, *Memoires de Charles Perrault,* Perrault described how the two boys got together mornings and afternoons for three or four years, reading in the course of that time most of the Bible and the classic authors. Perrault first tried his hand at writing when he, his older brother Claude (a medical student who became both a physician and an architect), and Beaurain adapted the sixth book of the *Aeneid* into comic verse, a popular literary practice of the time. Later the brothers collaborated on the first volume of *Les Murs de troie* ("The Walls of Troy").

In 1651 Perrault took the bar exam and was admitted to the practice of law. He soon became disillusioned with it, however, and left in 1654 to serve as a clerk to Claude, who had bought the post of Receiver General of Finances for the city of Paris—buying positions in the government and army was a common practice at the time. During this period Perrault was also continuing his studies and writing poetry, some of which was published and translated into Italian. In the mid-1660s he was appointed by Jean Baptiste Colbert, then Minister of Finance under King Louis XIV, to an advisory council that supervised the making of monuments, medals, and other works glorifying the king. Perrault became secretary to the council, which later became the French Academy, created "for the advancement and perfection of all sciences." When Colbert was appointed Superintendent of the Royal Buildings, he made Perrault his chief clerk. In this capacity Perrault had the pleasure of helping get his brother Claude's design chosen for the forefront of the Louvre Museum. In 1671 Perrault was formally admitted to the French Academy; in 1672 he became its chancellor and, in 1681, its director.

Perrault married Marie Guichon in 1672, and the couple had three sons and a daughter. Several years after his wife's death in 1678, Perrault decided to devote all of his time to writing and educating his children. As he stated in his autobiography, "With this in mind I went to live in the St. Jacques district [of Paris], which being near to the schools, gave me the great facility to send my children there, having always thought that it was best for children to come home to sleep in their father's house when it was possible rather than sending them to board in the school.... I gave them a tutor and I myself took great care to watch over their studies." Burne pointed out in *Writers for Children* that his wife's death may have been a factor in Perrault's writing the fairy tales, "since he maintained that such literature was an effective means of instilling values."

Though it is the fairy tales that are generally remembered, Perrault gained prominence as a literary figure with his poem "Le Siecle de Louis XIV," which he read to the Academy. In this poem he praised the superiority of modern letters as opposed to the classics, thus raising an argument that lasted for many years and brought his name into prominence.

Perrault died on May 16, 1703, at the age of seventy-five. Many critics believe that his now-familiar stories were half-forgotten folk tales that the author merely set down in a simple, readable form. In *Contes* Perrault said of them, "These sorts of tales have the gift of pleasing ... great minds as well as lesser folk, the old as well as young folk; these idle fancies amuse and lull reason, although contrary to the same reason, and can charm reason better than all imaginable probability."

WORKS CITED:

Burne, Glenn S., essay in *Writers for Children*, edited by Jane M. Bingham, Scribner, 1988, pp. 431-37.

Perrault, Charles, *Memoires de Charles Perrault*, Librarie des Bibliophiles, 1878.

Perrault, Charles, *Contes,* introduction by Gilbert Rouger, Editions Garnier Freres, 1967.

FOR MORE INFORMATION SEE:

BOOKS

Barchilon, Jacques, E. E. Flinders, Jr., and J. Anne Foreman, editors, *A Concordance to Charles Perrault's Tales,* Norwood Editions, 1977.
Montgomery, Elizabeth R., *Story Behind Great Stories,* McBride, 1947.

PERIODICALS

Elementary English, October, 1969.
Horn Book, June, 1979.

* * *

PETER
See STRATEMEYER, Edward L.

* * *

PETERS, Linda
See CATHERALL, Arthur

* * *

PETERSEN, P(eter) J(ames) 1941-

PERSONAL: Born October 23, 1941, in Santa Rosa, CA; son of Carl Eric (a farmer) and Alice (a farmer; maiden name, Winters) Petersen; married Marian Braun (a nurse), July 6, 1963; children: Karen, Carla. *Education:* Stanford University, A.B., 1962; San Francisco State College (now University), M.A., 1964; University of New Mexico, Ph.D., 1972.

ADDRESSES: Home—1243 Pueblo Court, Redding, CA 96001. *Office*—Department of English, Shasta College, Box 6006, Redding, CA 96099. *Agent*—Ellen Levine Literary Agency, Inc., 432 Park Ave. S., Suite 1205, New York, NY 10016.

P. J. Petersen

CAREER: Writer. Shasta College, Redding, CA, instructor in English, 1964—.

MEMBER: Society of Children's Book Writers.

AWARDS, HONORS: National Endowment for the Humanities fellowship, 1976-77; *Would You Settle for Improbable?* and *Nobody Else Can Walk It for You* were named to the American Library Association's list of best books for young adults for 1982 and 1983, respectively.

WRITINGS:

Would You Settle for Improbable? Delacorte, 1981.
Nobody Else Can Walk It for You, Delacorte, 1982.
The Boll Weevil Express, Delacorte, 1983.
Here's to the Sophomores, Delacorte, 1984.
Corky and the Brothers Cool, Delacorte, 1985.
Going for the Big One, Delacorte, 1986.
Good-bye to Good Ol' Charlie, Delacorte, 1987.
The Freshman Detective Blues, Delacorte, 1987.
How Can You Hijack a Cave? Delacorte, 1988.
The Fireplug Is First Base, Dutton, 1990.
I Hate Camping, Dutton, 1991.
Liars, Simon & Schuster, 1992.

SIDELIGHTS: After giving up his writing ambitions for almost twenty years and instead enjoying a successful career as an English professor, P. J. Petersen published his first young adult novel, *Would You Settle for Improbable,* in 1981. Then, for the rest of the decade, he published at least a title per year. Petersen's books—which range from ordinary school settings, to mountain adventures, to mysteries—have won him praise from critics and have twice made the American Library Association's list of best books for young adults.

Petersen was born October 23, 1941, in Santa Rosa, California. He enjoyed reading from an early age, and, as he recalled in *Something About the Author* (*SATA*): "I read everyone from Zane Grey (famed for his westerns) to Carolyn Keene (author of the Nancy Drew mysteries). My favorite book was *Tom Sawyer.*" He would often retell the stories he read to his younger brothers, sometimes changing the endings, and took satisfaction in the fact that his siblings frequently couldn't distinguish between his versions and the real ones. Petersen further noted in *SATA:* "I can't remember when I didn't want to be a writer, although I had occasional fleeting desires to perform brain surgery or play center field for the Giants."

Petersen's ambitions lasted throughout and past his adolescence. He declared in *SATA:* "I began writing seriously when I was still in high school and earned my first rejection slips at sixteen. In my early twenties I finished my first novel and sent it off with great hopes. It was rejected by five publishers before I gave up and stuffed it into a drawer. After that painful experience, I avoided similar disappointments by never finishing anything. I spent years writing the first halves of novels." In the meantime, Petersen obtained an A.B. in creative writing from Stanford University in 1962, married a nurse named Marian Braun in 1963, and received a master's degree in English literature from San Francisco State College in 1964. In the same year, he began teaching English at Shasta College in Redding, California. Eventually, he went back to school and obtained a Ph.D. from the University of New Mexico.

Petersen had more or less given up his writing ambitions by the late 1970s. He explained in *SATA:* "I gradually wrote less and less, although I could never quite give up the habit." But, he added, "in the summer of 1978, after returning from my twenty-year high school reunion, I decided to make one final effort at writing." While Petersen was trying to decide on a topic for a novel, his daughter Karen, who was in junior high, began sharing her favorite books with him. He recalled for *SATA:* "Seeing how excited she was about reading, I decided to write a book for her. If I couldn't interest a publisher (and I was understandably pessimistic), I intended to give her the manuscript—a present from a loving father."

The result, *Would You Settle for Improbable?,* became Petersen's first published novel in 1981. He told *SATA:* "My novels deal with the difficult ethical problems that young people face. *Would You Settle for Improbable?* involves the difficulty of changing destructive behavior patterns." One of the book's main characters, Arnold Norberry, is a juvenile delinquent in high school attempting to reform. Petersen wrote a sequel to his first novel, entitled *Here's to the Sophomores,* in 1984. That book focused more on a character named Warren, whose nonconformist ways wreak havoc on his high school peer group.

Petersen has also won acclaim for his novels with more rugged settings. *Nobody Else Can Walk It for You,* the author told *SATA,* "concerns responses to violence." In that story, a group of campers from the YMCA must deal with the antagonism of a hostile motorcycle gang while surviving in the mountains. Similarly, *Going for the Big One* concerns a family hiding out in the wilderness after being abandoned by their stepmother who made the mistake of sharing their refuge with a drug abuser. Another of Petersen's more popular works for young adults is *The Freshman Detective Blues,* which deals poignantly with the protagonist's first love while also telling a mystery story about a skeleton found in a lake bed.

Despite his prolific production and popular success, Petersen proclaimed in *SATA:* "I am not a 'natural' writer. For every hour I spend writing, I probably spend ten hours rewriting. Before beginning a novel, I usually have a story in my head, complete with characters and scenes. However, it takes me many, many drafts to transfer the vision from my mind onto paper. I find description especially difficult. It is far easier to imagine a face or a tree than it is to conjure up the words that will allow a reader to share those pictures. And, regardless of how many revisions I make, the story in my head is always more powerful than what I manage to get on paper." The author further noted that "I have learned to lock up the English teacher in me before approaching the typewriter. Critical editing is necessary, of course, especially with writing like mine that tends to repeat words and sentence patterns, but self editing has to be separate from the act of creation."

WORKS CITED:

Petersen, P. J., in *Something About the Author,* Volume 48, Gale, 1987, pp. 179-181.

FOR MORE INFORMATION SEE:

PERIODICALS

Bulletin of the Center for Children's Books, June, 1982, July/August, 1984, July/August, 1985, September, 1986, February, 1988.
Horn Book, February, 1982.
Wilson Library Bulletin, March, 1982, May, 1984, February, 1988.

* * *

PETERSHAM, Maud (Fuller) 1890-1971

PERSONAL: Born August 5, 1890, in Kingston, NY; died November 29, 1971; daughter of a Baptist minister; married Miska Petersham, 1917; children: Miki (son). *Education:* Graduated from Vassar College; studied art at the New York School of Fine and Applied Art. *Hobbies and other interests:* Ceramics and gardening.

Maud and Miska Petersham

ADDRESSES: Home—Woodstock, NY.

CAREER: Author and illustrator of books for children.

AWARDS, HONORS: Caldecott Medal runner-up, with husband, Miska Petersham, 1942, for *An American ABC;* Caldecott Medal, with Miska Petersham, 1946, for *The Rooster Crows.*

WRITINGS:

FOR CHILDREN; WITH HUSBAND, MISKA PETERSHAM

Miki, Doubleday, Doran, 1929.
The Ark of Father Noah and Mother Noah, Doubleday, Doran, 1930.
The Christ Child, as Told by Matthew and Luke, Doubleday, Doran, 1931.
Auntie and Celia Jane and Miki, Doubleday, Doran, 1932.
The Story Book of Things We Use, J. C. Winston, 1933.
The Story Book of Houses, J. C. Winston, 1933.
The Story Book of Transportation, J. C. Winston, 1933.
The Story Book of Food, J. C. Winston, 1933.
The Story Book of Clothes, J. C. Winston, 1933.
Get-a-Way and Hary Janos, Viking, 1933.
Miki and Mary: Their Search for Treasures, Viking, 1934.
The Story Book of Wheels, Ships, Trains, Aircraft (each story also published separately), J. C. Winston, 1935.
The Story Book of Earth's Treasures: Gold, Coal, Oil, Iron and Steel (each story also published separately), J. C. Winston, 1935.
The Story Book of Foods from the Field: Wheat, Corn, Rice, Sugar (each story also published separately), J. C. Winston, 1936.
Stories from the Old Testament: Joseph, Moses, Ruth, David (each story also published separately), J. C. Winston, 1938.
The Story Book of Things We Wear (each story published separately in 1939 as *The Story Book of Cotton, The Story Book of Wool, The Story Book of Rayon,* and *The Story Book of Silk;* also see below), J. C. Winston, 1939.
(And illustrators) *An American ABC,* Macmillan, 1941.
America's Stamps: The Story of One Hundred Years of U.S. Postage Stamps, Macmillan, 1947.
The Box with Red Wheels, Macmillan, 1949.
The Circus Baby, Macmillan, 1950.
Story of the Presidents of the United States of America, Macmillan, 1953.
Off to Bed: Seven Stories for Wide-Awakes, Macmillan, 1954.
The Boy Who Had No Heart, Macmillan, 1955.
The Silver Mace: A Story of Williamsburg, Macmillan, 1956.
The Peppernuts, Macmillan, 1958.
Shepherd Psalm, Macmillan, 1962.
Let's Learn about Silk, (originally published as *The Story Book of Silk*), illustrated by James E. Barry, Harvey House, 1967.
Let's Learn about Sugar (originally published as *The Story Book of Sugar,* c. 1936), illustrated by Barry, Harvey House, 1969.

ILLUSTRATOR; WITH HUSBAND, MISKA PETERSHAM

William Bowen, *Enchanted Forest,* Macmillan, 1920.
Carl Sandburg, *Rootabaga Stories,* Harcourt, 1922.
Charles Lamb, *Tales from Shakespeare,* Macmillan, 1923.
Sandburg, *Rootabaga Pigeons,* Harcourt, 1923.
Sisters of Mercy (St. Xavier College, Chicago), *Marquette Readers,* Macmillan, 1924.
Mabel Guinnip La Rue, *In Animal Land,* Macmillan, 1924.
Margery Clark, *Poppy Seed Cakes,* Doubleday, 1924.
Inez M. Howard, Alice Hawthorne, and Mae Howard, *Language Garden: A Primary Language Book,* Macmillan, 1924.
Harriott Fansler and Isidoro Panlasigui, *Philippine National Literature,* Macmillan, 1925.
Bessie B. Coleman, W. L. Uhl, and J. F. Hosic, *Pathway to Reading,* Silver, Burdette, 1925.
Florence C. Coolidge, *Little Ugly Face, and Other Indian Tales,* Macmillan, 1925.
John W. Wayland, *History Stories for Primary Grades,* Macmillan, 1925.
Elizabeth C. Miller, *Children of the Mountain Eagle,* Doubleday, 1927.
Everyday Canadian Primer, Macmillan, 1928.
Marguerite Clement, *Where Was Bobby?,* Doubleday, Doran, 1928.
Wilhelmina Harper and A. J. Hamilton, compilers, *Pleasant Pathways,* Macmillan, 1928.
Harper and Hamilton, compilers, *Winding Roads,* Macmillan, 1928-29.
Harper and Hamilton, compilers, *Heights and Highways,* Macmillan, 1929.
Harper and Hamilton, compilers, *Far Away Hills,* Macmillan, 1929.
Miller, *Pran of Albania,* Doubleday, Doran, 1929.
Miller, *Young Trajan,* Doubleday, 1931.
Sydney V. Rowland, W. D. Lewis, and E. J. Marshall, compilers, *Beckoning Road,* J. C. Winston, 1931.
Rowland, Lewis, and Marshall, compilers, *Rich Cargoes,* J. C. Winston, 1931.
Rowland, Lewis, and Marshall, compilers, *Wings of Adventure,* J. C. Winston, 1931.
Rowland, Lewis, and Marshall, compilers, *Treasure Trove,* J. C. Winston, 1931.
Carlo Collodi (pseudonym of Carlo Lorenzini), *Adventures of Pinocchio,* Garden City Publishing, 1932.
Johanna Spyri, *Heidi,* Garden City Publishing, 1932.
Jean Young Ayer, *Picnic Book,* Macmillan, 1934.
Post Wheeler, *Albanian Wonder Tales,* Doubleday, 1936.
Marie Barringer, *The Four and Lena,* Doubleday, 1938.
Miriam Evangeline Mason, *Susannah, the Pioneer Cow,* Macmillan, 1941.
Emilie F. Johnson, *Little Book of Prayers,* Viking, 1941.
Story of Jesus: A Little New Testament, Macmillan, 1942.
Ethan A. Cross and Elizabeth Carney, editors, *Literature,* 1943-46.

Mother Goose, *The Rooster Crows: A Book of American Rhymes and Jingles,* Macmillan, 1945.
Association for Childhood Education, Literature Committee, *Told under the Christmas Tree,* Macmillan, 1948.
Elsie S. Eells, *Tales of Enchantment from Spain,* Dodd, 1950.
Washington Irving, *Rip Van Winkle* [and] *The Legend of Sleepy Hollow,* Macmillan, 1951.
Benjamin Franklin, *Bird in the Hand,* Macmillan, 1951.
Eric P. Kelly, *In Clean Hay,* Macmillan, 1953.
Mason, *Miss Posy Longlegs,* Macmillan, 1955.

The Petershams' work also appeared in children's magazines, including *St. Nicholas, Child Life, Story Parade,* and *Jack and Jill.*

ADAPTATIONS: The Box with Red Wheels was adapted as a filmstrip by Threshold Filmstrips, 1974.

SIDELIGHTS: Maud and Miska Petersham were authors and illustrators of numerous children's books that are loved by young readers throughout the United States. In 1946 when they accepted the Caldecott Medal for outstanding illustration of children's literature, Maud said in an acceptance paper—quoted in *Caldecott Medal Books:* "[We] have put our hearts and all our efforts into the pictures and books we have made." In addition to illustrating the stories of other authors, they wrote and illustrated many books of their own. These include tales of animals, Biblical stories, books of facts, and tales of places around the world. Maud once told *SATA,* "In the books that we make, I am happy when we can picture some of those wonderful things which American children can claim as their heritage."

Maud Petersham, born in Kingston, New York, in 1890, was the third of four daughters of a Baptist minister. She was fascinated by the tales told by visiting missionaries, enjoyed summers spent with her Quaker grandfather, and was excited by new places when the family first moved to Sioux Falls, South Dakota, then to Newburg, New York, and later to Scranton, Pennsylvania. "I loved picture books as a child and was always happy with paper and pencil in my hands." After graduating from Vassar, Maud spent a year at the New York School of Fine and Applied Arts, before taking a position in the art department of International Art Service.

Miska Petersham, the son of a blacksmith and city official, was born near Budapest, Hungary, in 1888. When he was seven years old, he decided he would be an artist instead of a sea captain and saved his money to buy a box of paints. By age twelve he was self-supporting and walked miles each day to attend art school in Budapest. When he graduated his professors awarded him higher honors than any student had won in many years.

If he had stayed in Hungary, however, he would have had to serve in the army, so in 1911 he left to go to England and study art there, planning to live on what he could earn with his art work. Because no one in England could pronounce his Hungarian name, he changed it from Petrezselyem Mikaly to Miska Petersham.

Finding that he could not make a living with art in England and remembering his youthful love of stories of American Indians and the wild West, Miska joined with three friends and sailed to the New World. Upon their arrival the travellers found that they must have money to enter the country, so they pooled all their bills, rolled them up, and secretly slipped the cash from one to another as each had his turn passing through the "golden door" that led to the United States. Miska worked at various commercial art jobs in the United States, but whenever he had saved a hundred dollars he would leave work to paint or travel around the country. He found Americans friendly, but was disappointed to find the Indians not at all like those he had read about in stories.

While working for International Art Service in New York he met Maud Fuller. He offered her professional criticism and tutored her in art. In 1917 they were married and moved into an apartment in Greenwich Village. Maud claimed that, although she had had some formal art training, she learned more from working with her husband. When one of Miska's friends was too busy to illustrate a children's book he was writing, he asked the Petershams to do it. Their work on the book was so successful that other jobs followed, and their art was soon in demand.

In 1923 a son, Miki, was born to the Petershams, and the family built a home in the famous art colony at Woodstock, New York. They felt that after doing pictures for so many books for others they could write and illustrate some books of their own. Their first book, *Miki* (named for their son), is the story of a boy who wants to go to Hungary and is introduced to the life and customs of that country. It was followed by stories from the Bible, inspired by the Broadway play, *Green Pastures. The Ark of Father Noah and Mother Noah* tells how animals got some of their characteristics and even explains the disappearance of the dinosaurs.

In the 1930s the Petershams created a story book series with facts and anecdotes, including such topics as Earth's treasures, clothing, and foods. Their ideas for all these books, according to the authors, "came out of the blue and were connected with life around us, places we visited and what was foremost in our thoughts."

Miska attributed the success of their drawings to the fact that Maud was ambidextrous, using both hands but preferring to draw with her left hand, while he used his right. *Dictionary of Literary Biography* contributor Sharyl Smith quoted Maud as saying that "it seemed easier to think with pictures than with words," so they would start with the drawings. She worked out a rough "dummy" and wrote the text, while Miska laid out the pages. Usually Miska finished the pictures.

The Petershams always tried to be authentic with their drawings. In preparation for the Bible stories they

From *The Rooster Crows: A Book of American Rhymes and Jingles,* compiled and illustrated by Maud and Miska Petersham.

wandered in Palestine for three months to get ideas for illustrations. In 1957, *Caldecott Medal Books* writer Irene Green commented, "When they need to see a thing they must draw they go in search of it, whether into the next county, to Mexico or farther."

In 1960 Miska died. Maud moved to a smaller home in Woodstock, where she lived until her death on November 29, 1971. Her son, his wife, and their two children live in Ohio, where Miki works with a college art department.

WORKS CITED:

Dictionary of Literary Biography, Volume 22: *American Writers for Children, 1900-1960,* Gale, 1983.

Miller, Bertha, and Elinor Whitney Field, editors, *Caldecott Medal Books,* Horn Book, 1957.

FOR MORE INFORMATION SEE:

BOOKS

Twentieth Century Children's Writers, 3rd edition, St. James Press, 1989.

OBITUARIES:

PERIODICALS

New York Times, November 30, 1971.
Publishers Weekly, December 13, 1971.
Washington Post, December 3, 1971.

* * *

PETERSHAM, Miska 1888-1960

PERSONAL: Given name Petrezselyem Mikaly; born September 20, 1888, in Toeroekszentmiklos, near Budapest, Hungary; immigrated to the United States, 1912; became naturalized U.S. citizen; died May, 15, 1960; married Maud Fuller (an author and illustrator), 1917; children: Miki (son). *Education:* Attended art school in Budapest and in London. *Hobbies and other interests:* Stamp collecting.

ADDRESSES: Home—Woodstock, NY.

CAREER: Author and illustrator of books for children.

AWARDS, HONORS: Caldecott Medal runner-up, with wife, Maude Petersham, 1942, for *An American ABC;* Caldecott Medal, with Maude Petersham, 1946, for *The Rooster Crows.*

WRITINGS:

FOR CHILDREN; WITH WIFE, MAUD PETERSHAM

Miki, Doubleday, Doran, 1929.

The Ark of Father Noah and Mother Noah, Doubleday, Doran, 1930.

The Christ Child, as Told by Matthew and Luke, Doubleday, Doran, 1931.

Auntie and Celia Jane and Miki, Doubleday, Doran, 1932.

The Story Book of Things We Use, J. C. Winston, 1933.

The Story Book of Houses, J. C. Winston, 1933.

The Story Book of Transportation, J. C. Winston, 1933.

The Story Book of Food, J. C. Winston, 1933.

The Story Book of Clothes, J. C. Winston, 1933.

Get-a-Way and Hary Janos, Viking, 1933.

Miki and Mary: Their Search for Treasures, Viking, 1934.

The Story Book of Wheels, Ships, Trains, Aircraft (each story also published separately), J. C. Winston, 1935.

The Story Book of Earth's Treasures: Gold, Coal, Oil, Iron and Steel (each story also published separately), J. C. Winston, 1935.

The Story Book of Foods from the Field: Wheat, Corn, Rice, Sugar (each story also published separately), J. C. Winston, 1936.

Stories from the Old Testament: Joseph, Moses, Ruth, David (each story also published separately), J. C. Winston, 1938.

The Story Book of Things We Wear (each story published separately in 1939 as *The Story Book of Cotton, The Story Book of Wool, The Story Book of Rayon,* and *The Story Book of Silk;* also see below), J. C. Winston, 1939.

(And illustrators) *An American ABC,* Macmillan, 1941.

America's Stamps: The Story of One Hundred Years of U.S. Postage Stamps, Macmillan, 1947.

The Box with Red Wheels, Macmillan, 1949.

The Circus Baby, Macmillan, 1950.

Story of the Presidents of the United States of America, Macmillan, 1953.

Off to Bed: Seven Stories for Wide-Awakes, Macmillan, 1954.

The Boy Who Had No Heart, Macmillan, 1955.

The Silver Mace: A Story of Williamsburg, Macmillan, 1956.

The Peppernuts, Macmillan, 1958.

Shepherd Psalm, Macmillan, 1962.

Let's Learn about Silk, (originally published as *The Story Book of Silk*), illustrated by James E. Barry, Harvey House, 1967.

Let's Learn about Sugar (originally published as *The Story Book of Sugar*), illustrated by Barry, Harvey House, 1969.

ILLUSTRATOR; WITH WIFE, MAUD PETERSHAM

William Bowen, *Enchanted Forest,* Macmillan, 1920.

Carl Sandburg, *Rootabaga Stories,* Harcourt, 1922.

Charles Lamb, *Tales from Shakespeare,* Macmillan, 1923.

Sandburg, *Rootabaga Pigeons,* Harcourt, 1923.

Sisters of Mercy (St. Xavier College, Chicago), *Marquette Readers,* Macmillan, 1924.

Mabel Guinnip La Rue, *In Animal Land,* Macmillan, 1924.

Margery Clark, *Poppy Seed Cakes,* Doubleday, 1924.

Inez M. Howard, Alice Hawthorne, and Mae Howard, *Language Garden: A Primary Language Book,* Macmillan, 1924.

Harriott Fansler and Isidoro Panlasigui, *Philippine National Literature,* Macmillan, 1925.

Bessie B. Coleman, W. L. Uhl, and J. F. Hosic, *Pathway to Reading,* Silver, Burdette, 1925.

Florence C. Coolidge, *Little Ugly Face, and Other Indian Tales,* Macmillan, 1925.
John W. Wayland, *History Stories for Primary Grades,* Macmillan, 1925.
Elizabeth C. Miller, *Children of the Mountain Eagle,* Doubleday, 1927.
Everyday Canadian Primer, Macmillan, 1928.
Marguerite Clement, *Where Was Bobby?,* Doubleday, Doran, 1928.
Wilhelmina Harper and A. J. Hamilton, compilers, *Pleasant Pathways,* Macmillan, 1928.
Harper and Hamilton, compilers, *Winding Roads,* Macmillan, 1928-29.
Harper and Hamilton, compilers, *Heights and Highways,* Macmillan, 1929.
Harper and Hamilton, compilers, *Far Away Hills,* Macmillan, 1929.
Miller, *Pran of Albania,* Doubleday, Doran, 1929.
Miller, *Young Trajan,* Doubleday, 1931.
Sydney V. Rowland, W. D. Lewis, and E. J. Marshall, compilers, *Beckoning Road,* J. C. Winston, 1931.
Rowland, Lewis, and Marshall, compilers, *Rich Cargoes,* J. C. Winston, 1931.
Rowland, Lewis, and Marshall, compilers, *Wings of Adventure,* J. C. Winston, 1931.
Rowland, Lewis, and Marshall, compilers, *Treasure Trove,* J. C. Winston, 1931.
Carlo Collodi (pseudonym of Carlo Lorenzini), *Adventures of Pinocchio,* Garden City Publishing, 1932.
Johanna Spyri, *Heidi,* Garden City Publishing, 1932.
Jean Young Ayer, *Picnic Book,* Macmillan, 1934.
Post Wheeler, *Albanian Wonder Tales,* Doubleday, 1936.
Marie Barringer, *The Four and Lena,* Doubleday, 1938.
Miriam Evangeline Mason, *Susannah, the Pioneer Cow,* Macmillan, 1941.
Emilie F. Johnson, *Little Book of Prayers,* Viking, 1941.
Story of Jesus: A Little New Testament, Macmillan, 1942.
Ethan A. Cross and Elizabeth Carney, editors, *Literature,* 1943-46.
Mother Goose, *The Rooster Crows: A Book of American Rhymes and Jingles,* Macmillan, 1945.
Association for Childhood Education, Literature Committee, *Told under the Christmas Tree,* Macmillan, 1948.
Elsie S. Eells, *Tales of Enchantment from Spain,* Dodd, 1950.
Washington Irving, *Rip Van Winkle* [and] *The Legend of Sleepy Hollow,* Macmillan, 1951.
Benjamin Franklin, *Bird in the Hand,* Macmillan, 1951.
Eric P. Kelly, *In Clean Hay,* Macmillan, 1953.
Mason, *Miss Posy Longlegs,* Macmillan, 1955.

The Petershams' work also appeared in children's magazines, including *St. Nicholas, Child Life, Story Parade,* and *Jack and Jill.*

ADAPTATIONS: The Box with Red Wheels was adapted as a filmstrip by Threshold Filmstrips, 1974.

SIDELIGHTS: See entry on wife, Maud Petersham, for joint sidelights entry.

OBITUARIES:

PERIODICALS

New York Times, May 16, 1960.
Publishers Weekly, May 23, 1960.

* * *

PETRY, Ann (Lane) 1908-

PERSONAL: Born October 12, 1908, in Old Saybrook, CT; daughter of Peter Clarke (a pharmacist) and Bertha (James) Lane; married George D. Petry, February 28, 1938; children: Elisabeth Ann. *Education:* University of Connecticut, Ph.D., 1931; attended Columbia University, 1943-44.

ADDRESSES: Home—Old Saybrook, CT. *Agent*—Russell & Volkening, Inc., 551 Fifth Ave., New York, NY 10017.

CAREER: James' Pharmacy, Old Saybrook and Old Lyme, CT, pharmacist, 1931-38; *Amsterdam News,* New York City, writer and advertising saleswoman, 1938-41; *People's Voice,* New York City, reporter and editor of women's page, 1941-44; writer. Also served as a teacher, an advertising copywriter, and as an actress with the American Negro Theatre, all in New York City.

MEMBER: PEN, Authors Guild, Authors League of America (secretary, 1960).

AWARDS, HONORS: Houghton Mifflin literary fellowship, 1946; Litt.D., Suffolk University, 1983; special citation from the City of Philadelphia, 1985; Doctor of Letters, University of Connecticut, 1988; Doctor of Humane Letters, Mount Holyoke College, 1989.

Ann Petry

WRITINGS:

JUVENILE BOOKS

The Drugstore Cat, Crowell, 1949.
Harriet Tubman: Conductor on the Underground Railroad, Harper, 1955 (published in England as *A Girl Called Moses: The Story of Harriet Tubman,* Methuen, 1960).
The Common Ground, Crowell, 1964.
Tituba of Salem Village, Crowell, 1964.
Legends of the Saints, Crowell, 1970.

ADULT FICTION

The Street, Houghton, 1946.
Country Place, Houghton, 1947.
The Narrows, Houghton, 1953.
Miss Muriel and Other Stories, Houghton, 1971.

OTHER

Contributor to *The Writer's Book,* 1950, *A View from the Top of the Mountain: Poems after Sixty,* 1981, and *Rediscoveries II,* 1988; contributor of short stories to anthologies. Contributor to periodicals, including *New Yorker, Holiday,* and *Horn Book.*

SIDELIGHTS: Ann Petry remarked in *Contemporary Authors Autobiography Series* (*CAAS*): "I write about the relationship between black people and white people in the United States: novels, short stories, poetry, books for children and young people. When I write for children I write about survivors: Tituba of Salem Village, indicted for witchcraft in the seventeenth century, Harriet Tubman who helped runaway slaves escape from the South before the Civil War." Petry is herself a survivor, the granddaughter of a runaway slave, a witness to the evils of life in Harlem, and a highly educated woman who turned from her planned career in pharmacy to become a writer.

The decision to leave the certain employment of pharmacy for the less predictable work of writing was not an easy one for Petry, but as she noted in *CAAS,* she decided to take the chance with her talents. "I regard myself as a gambler because each one of [my] books was written against odds that it would ever be finished, enormous odds that only a gambler would have accepted." Today a resident of Old Saybrook, Connecticut, Petry is indeed one gambler who finished with a winning hand. Even her earliest works—adult novels written in the 1940s and early 1950s—are still in print. As a children's writer, she is acclaimed for her realistic accounts of the lives of Harriet Tubman, Tituba of Salem, Massachusetts, and several Catholic saints.

Petry was born Ann Lane in Old Saybrook. Her father was a pharmacist who had established himself in the all-white Connecticut town despite some initial bigotry from the residents. In her early youth, Ann lived with her family in an apartment above the store. "Old Saybrook was a very small town when I was growing up," she remembered in her *CAAS* entry. "A relatively quiet place filled with the salt smell of the sea and with the yammering sound of gulls. At certain seasons of the year the sky over the town is enlivened by the comings and goings of water birds, for the coves and inlets and creeks offer a perfect resting-place for migratory birds. I was familiar with the smell of the marshes at low tide. I knew the difference in the smell of the air when the tide was going out, and I knew how it freshened when the tide was coming in."

As a youngster Petry learned many interesting stories from her extended family of uncles and aunts who had travelled widely. She also heard about her grandfather's escape from a plantation in Virginia by way of the Underground Railroad. "These stories transmitted knowledge, knowledge on how to survive in a hostile environment," Petry stated in *CAAS.* "They were a part of my education."

Her formal instruction began at the age of four, in the public school in Old Saybrook. The experience brought Petry face to face yet again with prejudice, as she and her sister tried to leave the school after their first day. "On our way home . . . ten- and twelve-year-old boys threw stones at us and called us names, using the kind of profanity that their parents used when angry." She continued in *CAAS:* "We ran and ran and ran. They followed us, pausing now and then to arm themselves with more small stones, stones they picked up from the side of the road." The following day, two of Petry's grown uncles provided her with an escort home, and the harassment stopped.

Still, the author was aware that although she was born in New England, she was not in fact a New Englander. She always felt different from the other townspeople, but her parents helped her to develop self-esteem by creating "a warm, rich, life-sustaining environment," as she recalled in *CAAS.* Petry was encouraged to exercise her talents, which included sewing, baking, writing, and reading. By her teen years she was making most of her own clothes and selling cakes for pocket money.

When Petry was still in high school, she was paid five dollars for a slogan she created for a perfume company. The brush with the world of writing was exciting, but she followed a practical course and enrolled in pharmacy classes at the Connecticut College of Pharmacy (now a branch of the University of Connecticut). After receiving her degree in pharmacy in 1931 she returned home and worked in two family-owned businesses, one in Old Saybrook and another in Old Lyme.

Her life changed when she married George Petry on February 28, 1938. The couple moved to New York City, where she determined to find work as a writer. The aspiring author took a job at Harlem's *Amsterdam News,* selling advertising space. In 1941 she moved to the *People's Voice,* another Harlem weekly published by Adam Clayton Powell, Jr. There she covered general news and edited the women's pages. Her days as a reporter brought her into the more dismal sections of Harlem, where then as now life held little opportunity for the black citizens. Slowly, with many rejections but some encouragement, Petry began to write fiction about

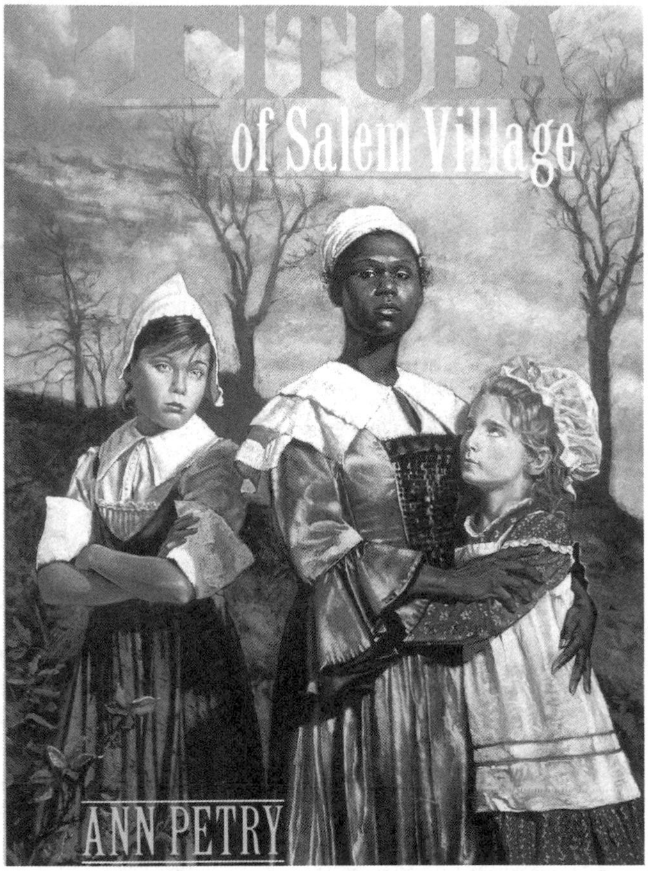

Cover of *Tituba of Salem Village,* by Ann Petry.

incidents in Harlem and in her small New England town. A five-chapter draft and synopsis of her first novel, *The Street,* won her a prestigious Houghton Mifflin literary fellowship in 1946.

With the publication of *The Street* in 1946, Petry became known as the first black female author to address the problems black women face in the slums. Critics have praised her novel as a form of social commentary on the spirit-sapping nature of black American life in the big cities. *Dictionary of Literary Biography* contributor Sandra Carlton Alexander, for instance, writes: "Petry's early work is strongly naturalistic. Its focus is on racism as an environmental force adversely affecting human lives so that its victims can neither understand nor control the devastating effects upon them and those they love." Petry also published a number of short stories that dealt with essentially the same issues.

Petry's work for children has taken a different vein, however. While she has not shied away from the discussion of prejudice or the difficulties blacks face in our race-conscious society, she has chosen to write about women who showed strength of spirit in times of trial. One of her subjects is Harriet Tubman, the Maryland woman who helped several hundred runaway slaves escape through the Underground Railroad. In a *Christian Science Monitor* review of *Harriet Tubman: Conductor on the Underground Railroad,* Elizabeth Yates writes: "Ann Petry, writing with sympathy and fidelity, has made Harriet Tubman live for present-day readers of any age, who pick up this biography and come under its power." Likewise, in their *For Reading Out Loud! A Guide to Sharing Books with Children,* Margaret Mary Kimmel and Elizabeth Segel note: "Ann Petry has written a first-rate biography.... Petry's eloquent prose creates a vivid picture of a slaveholding society, of the operation of the Underground Railroad, and of this remarkable woman."

Equally well-received was Petry's *Tituba of Salem Village,* an account of a slave woman who was falsely accused of witchcraft during the hysteria of the 1690s. *Horn Book* reviewer Jane Manthorne calls the work "a masterful construction of innocence betrayed by mounting malevolence" and claims that the story "promises gripping enthrallment." *Saturday Review* contributor Alice Dalgliesh maintains that *Tituba of Salem Village* is "one of the strongest books of the year, and the best one about witchcraft that has yet been written for young people."

Petry told *Horn Book* magazine that she wants to reveal the evils of slavery in her books for young people, but she has other aims as well. "Over and over again, I have said: These are people. Look at them, listen to them.... Remember them. Remember for what a long, long time black people have been in this country, have been a part of America: a sturdy, indestructible, wonderful part of America, woven into its heart and into its soul.... I tried to make history speak across the centuries in the voices of people—young, old, good, evil, beautiful, ugly."

WORKS CITED:

Alexander, Sandra Carlton, "Ann Petry," *Dictionary of Literary Biography,* Volume 76: *Afro-American Writers, 1940-1955,* Gale, 1988, p. 140-147.

Dalgliesh, Alice, review of *Tituba of Salem Village, Saturday Review,* November 7, 1964, p. 55.

Kimmel, Margaret Mary and Elizabeth Segel, *For Reading Out Loud! A Guide to Sharing Books with Children,* Dell, 1983, p. 101-102.

Manthorne, Jane, review of *Tituba of Salem Village, Horn Book,* February, 1965, p. 65.

Petry, Ann, "The Common Ground," *Horn Book,* April, 1965, pp. 147-151.

Petry, Ann, *Contemporary Authors Autobiography Series,* Volume 6, Gale, 1988, pp. 253-269.

Yates, Elizabeth, "To Freedom by the Underground," *Christian Science Monitor,* August 25, 1955, p. 13.

FOR MORE INFORMATION SEE:

BOOKS

Black American Writers: Past and Present, Scarecrow Press, 1975.

Children's Literature Review, Volume 12, Gale, 1987.

Contemporary Literary Criticism, Gale, Volume 1, 1973; Volume 7, 1977; Volume 18, 1981.

Twentieth-Century Children's Writers, 3rd edition, St. James Press, 1989.

PERIODICALS

New Yorker, February 9, 1946; October 11, 1947; August 29, 1953.

New York Times, February 10, 1946; September 28, 1947; August 16, 1953.

Times Literary Supplement, May 2, 1986.

* * *

PEYTON, K. M.
See PEYTON, Kathleen (Wendy)

* * *

PEYTON, Kathleen (Wendy) 1929-
(Kathleen Herald; K. M. Peyton, a pseudonym)

PERSONAL: Born August 2, 1929, in Birmingham, England; daughter of William Joseph (an engineer) and Ivy Kathleen Herald; married Michael Peyton (a commercial artist and cartoonist), 1950; children: Hilary, Veronica. *Education:* Attended Kingston School of Art, 1947; Manchester Art School, Art Teacher's Diploma, 1952. *Hobbies and other interests:* Sailing, horses, walking, gardening.

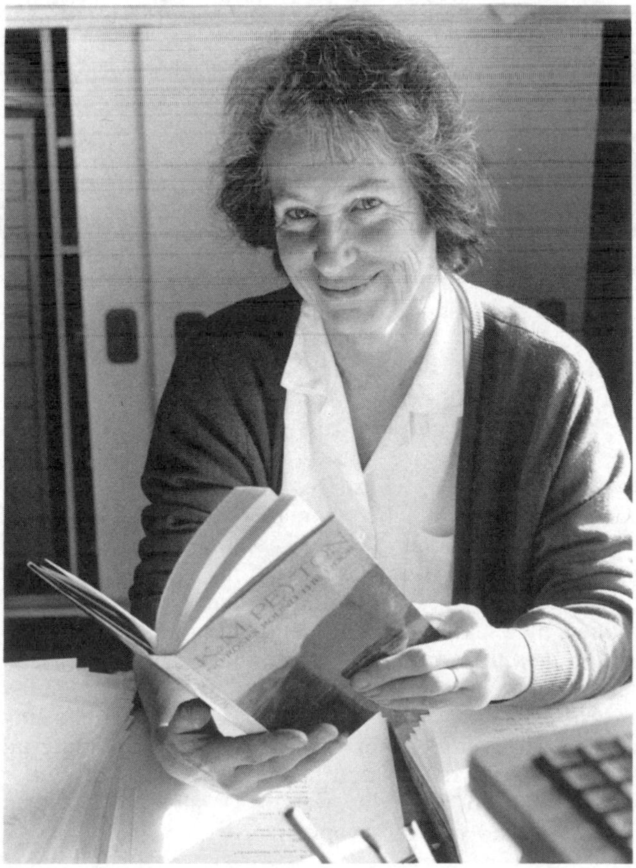

Kathleen Peyton

ADDRESSES: Home—Rookery Cottage, North Fambridge, Essex, England.

CAREER: Northampton High School, Northampton, England, art teacher, 1952-56; writer, 1956—.

MEMBER: Society of Authors.

AWARDS, HONORS: Carnegie Medal Commendation from the British Library Association, 1962, for *Windfall,* 1964, for *The Maplin Bird,* 1965, for *The Plan for Birdsmarsh,* 1966, for *Thunder in the Sky,* 1967, for *Flambards,* 1969, for *Flambards in Summer,* and 1977, for *The Team; New York Herald Tribune* Spring Book Festival Award Honor Book, 1965, for *The Maplin Bird;* Carnegie Medal, 1969, for *The Edge of the Cloud; Boston Globe-Horn Book* Award Honor Book, 1969, for *Flambards; Guardian* Award, 1970, for the "Flambards" trilogy; Child Study Association of America's Children's Books of the Year, 1969, for *Fly-by-Night,* 1971, for *Pennington's Last Term,* 1974, for *Pennington's Heir,* and 1976, for *The Team;* American Library Association's Best Books for Young Adults, 1979, for *Prove Yourself a Hero; School Library Journal*'s Best Books of Spring, 1979, for *A Midsummer Night's Death.* Seven of Peyton's books have been named American Library Association Notable Books, and six have been named to the *Horn Book* honor list.

WRITINGS:

FOR YOUNG ADULTS; UNDER NAME KATHLEEN HERALD

Sabre, the Horse from the Sea, illustrated by Lionel Edwards, A. & C. Black, 1947, Macmillan, 1963.

The Mandrake, illustrated by Edwards, A. & C. Black, 1949.

Crab the Roan, illustrated by Peter Biegel, A. & C. Black, 1953.

FOR YOUNG ADULTS, EXCEPT AS NOTED; UNDER PSEUDONYM K. M. PEYTON

North to Adventure, Collins, 1959, Platt & Munk, 1965.

Stormcock Meets Trouble, Collins, 1961.

The Hard Way Home, illustrated by R. A. Branton, Collins, 1962, published as *Sing a Song of Ambush,* Platt, 1964.

Sea Fever, illustrated by Victor G. Ambrus, World Publishing, 1963.

Brownsea Silver, Collins, 1964.

The Maplin Bird, illustrated by Ambrus, Oxford University Press, 1964, World Publishing, 1965.

The Plan for Birdsmarsh, illustrated by Ambrus, Oxford University Press, 1965, World Publishing, 1966.

Thunder in the Sky, illustrated by Ambrus, Oxford University Press, 1966, World Publishing, 1967.

Flambards (first book in the "Flambards" trilogy; also see below), illustrated by Ambrus, Oxford University Press, 1967, World Publishing, 1968.

(And illustrator) *Fly-by-Night,* Oxford University Press, 1968, World Publishing, 1969.

The Edge of the Cloud (second book in the "Flambards" trilogy; also see below), illustrated by Ambrus, World Publishing, 1969.
Flambards in Summer (third book in the "Flambards" trilogy; also see below), illustrated by Ambrus, Oxford University Press, 1969, World Publishing, 1970.
(And illustrator) *Pennington's Seventeenth Summer* (first book in a trilogy; also see below), Oxford University Press, 1969, published as *Pennington's Last Term,* Crowell, 1971.
(And illustrator) *The Beethoven Medal* (second book in a trilogy; also see below), Oxford University Press, 1971, Crowell, 1972.
(And illustrator) *A Pattern of Roses,* Oxford University Press, 1972, Crowell, 1973.
(And illustrator) *Pennington's Heir* (third book in a trilogy; also see below), Oxford University Press, 1973, Crowell, 1974.
(And illustrator) *The Team,* Oxford University Press, 1975, Crowell, 1976.
The Right-Hand Man, illustrated by Ambrus, Oxford University Press, 1977.
Prove Yourself a Hero, Oxford University Press, 1977, Philomel Books, 1978.
A Midsummer Night's Death: With an Afterword by the Author, Oxford University Press, 1978, Philomel Books, 1979.
Marion's Angels, illustrated by Robert Micklewright, Oxford University Press, 1979.
The Flambards Trilogy (contains *Flambards, The Edge of the Cloud,* and *Flambards in Summer*), Puffin Books, 1980.
Flambards Divided, Oxford University Press, 1981, Philomel Books, 1982.
Dear Fred, Bodley Head, 1981.
Going Home (for children), illustrated by Chris Molan, Oxford University Press, 1982, illustrated by Huck Scarry, Philomel Books, 1982.
Who, Sir? Me, Sir?, Oxford University Press, 1983.
Free Rein, Philomel Books, 1983.
The Last Ditch, Oxford University Press, 1983.
Pennington: A Trilogy (contains *Pennington's Seventeenth Summer, The Beethoven Medal,* and *Pennington's Heir*), Oxford University Press, 1984.
Froggett's Revenge (for children), illustrated by Leslie Smith, Oxford University Press, 1985, illustrated by Maureen Bradley, Puffin Books, 1987.
Downhill All the Way, Oxford University Press, 1988.
(And illustrator) *Plain Jack* (for children), Hamish Hamilton, 1988.
Skylark (for children), illustrated by Liz Roberts, Oxford University Press, 1989.
Darkling, Delacorte, 1989.
Poor Badger (for children), Doubleday, 1990.
(And illustrator) *Apple Won't Jump* (for children), Hamish Hamilton, 1992.
The Boy Who Wasn't There, Delacorte, 1992.

FOR ADULTS

The Sound of Distant Cheering, Bodley Head, 1986.
No Roses Round the Door, Methuen, 1990.
Late to Smile, Methuen, 1992.

ADAPTATIONS: Flambards (television series), ITV (Yorkshire, England), 1976; *A Pattern of Roses* (adapted for television), c. 1985; *Going Home* (cassette), G.K. Hall, 1986.

SIDELIGHTS: Kathleen Peyton is best known for the realistic portrayal of adolescents in her fiction. In addition, Peyton uses her extensive knowledge of horses, sailing, and music to add realistic details to her narratives. But despite this attention to detail, the author's focus has always been on her characters and the creation of entertaining story lines. Peyton's books have won numerous awards and her famous "Flambards" trilogy was adapted into a successful television series.

As a child, Peyton longed to have a pony like those owned by the other children she knew. However, living in the suburbs of London made this virtually impossible. Partly out of frustration, Peyton began to write about the objects of her obsession. "I think I was nine when I started my first story which was long enough to call a book. It was all written in longhand, of course, and was called, I remember, 'Gray Star, the Story of a Race Horse,'" Peyton recalled in *British Children's Authors: Interviews at Home.*

Peyton kept on writing book after book; she also showed promise as an artist. Once, one of her teachers asked her if she would like to illustrate a book. Only if it was one she had written, she replied. The teacher asked to read one of Peyton's works and was so impressed that she encouraged Peyton to send the manuscript to a publisher. She did, and it was accepted for publication. At the time, Peyton was just fifteen years old. The book was, of course, about a horse.

Instead of studying writing, Peyton decided to pursue her artistic talents by going to art school, yet she also continued her writing. "I don't myself even subscribe to the idea that one sets out to be a writer; one writes, and if the work sells and eventually enables one to make a living from it, one presumably is a writer," she commented in *The Thorny Paradise: Writers on Writing for Children.* "I set out to be a painter, and became a teacher, which I liked very much; but I was a writer all the time, and eventually this became my profession."

In school, Peyton fell in love with Michael Peyton, another art student. The two married and went on a long honeymoon—canoeing the Thames, walking across Switzerland, and living in a cave in France. Later they traveled through the United States and Canada, earning money by picking up odd jobs along the way. They settled down on the Essex coast, where sailing began to satisfy their mutual wanderlust. "This led to many adventures, through inexperience in difficult sailing waters, which were later to provide plenty of material for books," Peyton related in the *Third Book of Junior Authors.* The pony-loving writer was also able to keep several horses on her property.

After the birth of her first child, Peyton returned to writing with a different agenda: to make money. She and her husband began to collaborate on adventure novels for teenage boys—he would think up the plots while she wrote the narrative. "I didn't know what was going on half the time," she commented in *The Pied Pipers: Interviews with the Influential Creators of Children's Literature.* This early collaboration accounted for the initials in Peyton's pen name—K. M.—which are a combination of her and her husband's first initials.

In 1963 Peyton published *Sea Fever,* a book about sailing that is based on the Essex coast in the last century. From then on, she moved away from writing strictly adventure stories and began to experiment with novels that looked deeply into the growth and development of the characters. *The Plan for Birdsmarsh,* published in 1965, focuses on a young boy who is brokenhearted when his family farm is sold to make a marina, so he resolves to fight against the development plan. Peyton returned to another interest, flying, to write *Thunder in the Sky.* This book is set during World War I and explores the world of spying.

Published in 1967, *Flambards* became the first book in a trilogy that looks into life in Edwardian England. In this novel, the orphaned Christina goes to live at the decaying mansion Flambards with her uncle Russell. Russell's son, Will, is struggling to find himself and feels caught between his own world and his father's. He likes horses and hunting, but does not wish them to be more important than other human beings. Christina falls in love with him and they marry after they find they have similar beliefs. The next two books in the trilogy, *The Edge of the Cloud* and *Flambards in Summer,* tell how Will becomes a pilot during World War I and is killed, as well as how Christina subsequently marries a former stable hand. Through these events, Peyton deftly shows the changing social class of England during that time period.

Peyton's trilogy about the character Pennington is also well known. Pennington is a rebellious teenager who happens to be extremely talented in music. Based on a real character, Pennington goes through many changes in the course of the novels, eventually winning a coveted award in *The Beethoven Medal* and getting married in *Pennington's Heir.* Peyton enjoyed doing the research for this piece, writing in *The Thorny Paradise* that "I shall be eternally grateful to that particular hero for driving me to play the piano."

While her work is often cited for its excellent character development and plots that are meaningful and socially aware, Peyton admits that she writes primarily to entertain. "When a writer knows he has a juvenile audience, a certain responsibility is inevitably felt, but to think that he can 'con' his audience into what might be called correct attitudes must be doomed to failure," she related in *The Thorny Paradise.*

From *Flambards in Summer,* by K. M. Peyton. Illustrated by Victor G. Ambrus.

WORKS CITED:

de Montreville, Doris, and Donna Hill, editors, *Third Book of Junior Authors,* H. W. Wilson, 1972, pp. 224-25.

Jones, Cornelia, and Olivia R. Way, *British Children's Authors: Interviews at Home,* American Library Association, 1976.

Peyton, K. M. (pseudonym for Kathleen Peyton), "On Not Writing a Proper Book," *The Thorny Paradise: Writers on Writing for Children,* edited by Edward Blishen, Kestrel Books, 1975.

Wintle, Justin, and Emma Fisher, *The Pied Pipers: Interviews with the Influential Creators of Children's Literature,* Paddington Press, 1974.

FOR MORE INFORMATION SEE:

BOOKS

Chevalier, Tracy, editor, *Twentieth-Century Children's Writers,* 3rd edition, St. Martin's, 1989.

Children's Literature Review, Volume 3, Gale, 1978.

Crouch, Marcus S., *The Nesbit Tradition: The Children's Novel in England, 1945-70,* Benn, 1972.
Townsend, John Rowe, *A Sense of Story: Essays on Contemporary Writing for Children,* Longmans, 1971.
Townsend, John Rowe, *A Sounding of Storytellers,* Lippincott, 1979.

PERIODICALS

New Statesman, November 3, 1967.

* * *

PHILLIPS, Jack
See SANDBURG, Carl (August)

* * *

PHIPSON, Joan
See FITZHARDINGE, Joan Margaret

* * *

PICARD, Barbara Leonie 1917-

PERSONAL: Surname rhymes with "hard," accent is on first syllable; born December 4, 1917, in Richmond, Surrey, England; daughter of Eugene Hippolyte and Elsa Martha (Fischer) Picard. *Politics:* Extreme liberalism. *Religion:* Atheist.

ADDRESSES: Office—c/o Oxford University Press, Walton St., Oxford, England.

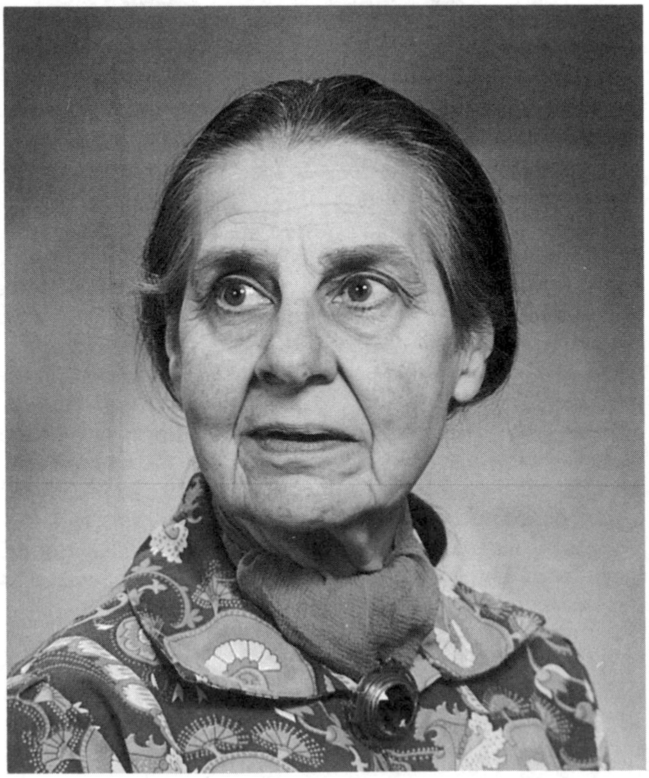

Barbara Leonie Picard

CAREER: Worked in various lending libraries prior to and throughout World War II; writer, 1949—.

AWARDS, HONORS: Several books nominated for the Carnegie Medal, including *Lady of the Linden Tree, One Is One,* and *Ransom for a Knight.*

WRITINGS:

JUVENILE FICTION

The Mermaid and the Simpleton, illustrated by Philip Gough, Oxford University Press, 1949, reprinted, Criterion, 1970.
The Faun and the Woodcutter's Daugher, illustrated by Charles Stewart, Oxford University Press, 1951.
The Lady of the Linden Tree, illustrated by Stewart, Oxford University Press, 1954, revised edition published as *Twice Seven Tales,* Kaye & Ward, 1968.
Ransom for a Knight, illustrated by C. Walter Hodges, Oxford University Press, 1956.
Lost John, illustrated by Charles Keeping, Oxford University Press, 1962, Criterion, 1965.
The Goldfinch Garden, illustrated by Anne Linton, Harrap, 1963, Criterion, 1965.
One Is One, illustrated by Victor Ambrus, Oxford University Press, 1965, Holt, 1966.
The Young Pretenders, illustrated by Ambrus, Edmund Ward, 1966.

RETELLINGS

The Odyssey of Homer, illustrated by Joan Kiddell-Monroe, Oxford University Press, 1952, reprinted, 1991.
Tales of the Norse Gods and Heroes, illustrated by Kiddell-Monroe, Oxford University Press, 1953, reprinted, 1970.
French Legends, Tales, and Fairy Stories, illustrated by Kiddell-Monroe, Oxford University Press, 1955, reprinted, 1992.
Stories of King Arthur and His Knights, wood engravings by Roy Morgan, Oxford University Press, 1955.
German Hero-Sagas and Folk Tales, illustrated by Kiddell-Monroe, Oxford University Press, 1958.
The Iliad of Homer, illustrated by Kiddell-Monroe, Oxford University Press, 1960, reprinted, 1991.
The Story of Rama and Sita, illustrated by Stewart, Harrap, 1960.
Tales of the British People, illustrated by Eric Fraser, Edmund Ward, 1961.
The Tower and the Traitors, Batsford, 1961.
Hero Tales From the British Isles, illustrated by John G. Galsworthy, Edmund Ward, 1963.
Celtic Tales, illustrated by Galsworthy, Edmund Ward, 1964.
The Story of the Pandavas, illustrated by Stewart, Dobson, 1968.
William Tell and His Son, illustrated by Paul Nussbaumer, Sadler, 1969.
Three Ancient Kings: Gilgamesh, Hrolf Kraki, Conary, illustrated by Gough, Warne, 1972.

Tales of Ancient Persia Retold from the Shah-Nama of Firdausi, illustrated by Ambrus, Oxford University Press, 1972, Walck, 1973.

The Iliad and Odyssey of Homer, illustrated by Kiddell-Monroe, Chancellor Press, 1986.

OTHER

(Editor) *Encyclopaedia of Myths and Legends of All Nations,* Edmund Ward, 1962.

SIDELIGHTS: British author Barbara Leonie Picard has garnered praise for her original children's fairy tales, collected in volumes such as *The Mermaid and the Simpleton* and *The Faun and the Woodcutter's Daughter.* These tales have been compared favorably with the works of Hans Christian Andersen and Oscar Wilde. Picard has also expressed her talent in writing historical novels for older children, including *Lost John* and *One Is One;* she has won further acclaim for her retellings of myths and legends, such as *The Iliad* and *The Odyssey,* and *Stories of King Arthur and His Knights.*

Picard was born December 4, 1917, in Richmond, Surrey, England. Though her parents never divorced, they separated when she was a young child, and her father returned to his native France. An influential aunt and uncle separated as well, and Picard noted in an essay for *Something About the Author Autobiography Series* (*SAAS*): "Psychologists would no doubt say that my early decision never to marry resulted from having seen the failure of the two marriages closest to me in my childhood; and who am I to disagree with the professionals? . . . But what I early came to dread was a future of domestic drudgery, such as marriage without affluence would inevitably have brought; and I have never wanted children of my own. For me, these two facts count far more than all the theories of psychologists."

Despite the separations, Picard had a happy, if somewhat solitary, childhood. Her mother employed a governess to teach her to read at the age of four; from then on, she recalled for *SAAS,* she could not get enough of books: "I read everything I could find in the house and all [the books] that were given me . . . . before I was eight I was steeped in the mysteries of Edgar Wallace, the Martian and underearth stories of Edgar Rice Burroughs (I never cared much for Tarzan), and above all, the African adventures of Henry Rider Haggard . . . . My first meeting with Shakespeare was in the pages of *As You Like It,* and I was his for life." Picard later became an admirer also of the modern fairy tales of Oscar Wilde and Hans Christian Andersen.

When she was nine years old, Picard was sent to school at Queen's Park House. After spending one term as a daygirl, she became a weekly boarder, returning home only on weekends. As she remembered in her autobiographical essay, "I had no difficulties in adapting to the society of other children and even made a schoolfriend." But she did not fare so well when, at the age of twelve, she was sent to board at Saint Katharine's School. Picard was made miserable by the emphasis the school placed on sports, which she was not very good at.

From *Tales of the British People,* retold by Barbara Leonie Picard. Illustrated by Eric Fraser.

She did, however, enjoy her Latin lessons, and sketching, though she did not make any friends among the other girls at Saint Katharine's.

At the age of sixteen, Picard decided to opt for working instead of attending college. She had been trying her hand at writing for much of her young life, and her plan was to write for publication during her off-hours. Before she found work, however, she wrote a few short pieces; she recalled for *SAAS:* "I wrote articles and short stories and collected a few rejection slips: but not many of these, as my standards were high and I considered little that I wrote worthy of being offered to any magazine; and even fewer—far fewer—cheques." When Picard did find her first job, working in a Mudie lending library in Eastbourne, it proved so exhausting that for the first few years she was not able to write anything. Finally, in 1937, she and her mother moved closer to the library.

When World War II began, the Mudie library closed; Picard busied herself helping her community until she was offered a place at the Eastbourne Public Library, replacing a man who had volunteered for active duty in England's armed forces. She was grateful, because librarians were exempt from conscription, as she explained in *SAAS:* "I was lucky, because young, childless women were liable to be recruited to help in the war effort, perhaps in the armed services or in a munitions factory; and a pacifist who was also an atheist could hardly have pleaded the Sixth Commandment." Nevertheless, she did not remain uninvolved in the war. Picard recalled in her autobiographical essay that "one of the requirements of the war effort was paper salvage to be pulped for reuse. Sack after sack of donated books was dumped at the town hall. The librarian was insistent that all these should be checked before destruction. I spent hours ... at the heartbreaking task of condemning books to death. I saved all I could: anything rare or valuable, anything which could be useful for the library, and light reading for the Red Cross. But it was still terrible having to play god with books which other people had written, especially when it was books like those that I wanted to write myself."

In spite of this ambition, Picard admitted in *SAAS* that "since the beginning of the war, I had stopped trying to write; I simply had not felt able to." But towards the end of the conflict, while on firewatching duty—she explained in her autobiographical essay that firewatching "meant that every few days one joined a party ... armed with so-called stirrup-pumps and buckets of water (and) spent the night in one or another of the principal buildings in the town"—she "felt as though I wanted to try again." It was then that Picard began working on her fairy stories, which, as she explained for *SAAS,* she "decided to write, purely for my own amusement." But eventually, Picard realized that others might enjoy the tales she created, and she submitted them to Oxford University Press. There were delays in publication because of postwar paper shortages, but by 1949 her first collection of fairy tales, *The Mermaid and the Simpleton,* was printed.

Picard had never particularly intended to write for children, but her first two books of fairy tales were so well-received that Oxford University Press urged her to tackle some retellings of myths and legends for children. The first such effort, *The Odyssey of Homer,* met with as much acclaim as her original tales, and led to Picard's penning such titles as *German Hero-Sagas and Folk Tales* and *Celtic Tales.* She even tackled Hindu mythology and adapted it for children in the works *The Story of Rama and Sita* and *The Story of the Pandavas.* In 1956 Picard wrote her first juvenile historical novel, *Ransom for a Knight.* Though longer than most novels for young readers, Oxford University Press did not hesitate to publish it. Perhaps one of her best-known works in that genre is *One Is One,* the story of a medieval boy named Stephen who eventually settles in a monastery.

WORKS CITED:

Picard, Barbara, essay in *Something about the Author Autobiography Series,* Volume 10, Gale, 1990, pp. 219-241.

FOR MORE INFORMATION SEE:

PERIODICALS

Junior Literary Guild, September, 1964.

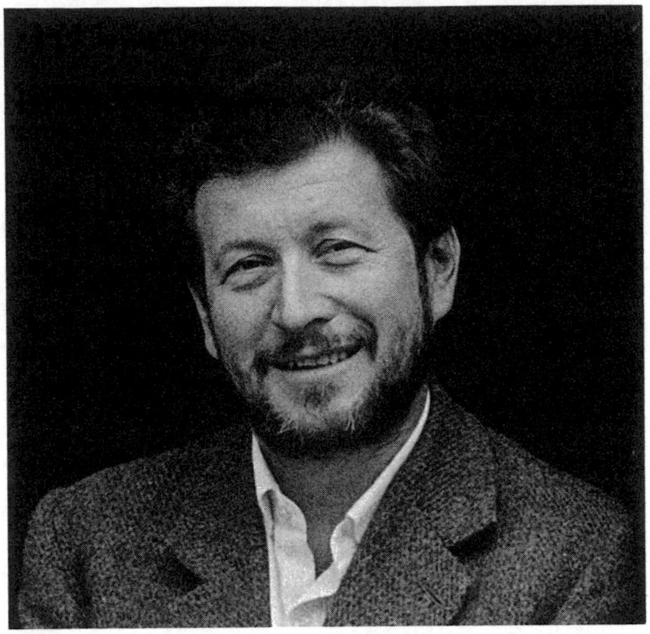

Jan Pienkowski

PIENKOWSKI, Jan (Michal) 1936-

PERSONAL: Born August 8, 1936, in Warsaw, Poland; immigrated to England, 1946; son of Jerzy Dominik and Wanda Maria (a chemist; maiden name, Garlicka) Pienkowski. *Education:* King's College, Cambridge, B.A. (with second class honors), 1957, M.A., 1961. *Religion:* Catholic. *Avocational interests:* Movies, gardening, painting.

ADDRESSES: *Home*—Oakgates, 45 Lonsdale Rd., Barnes SW13 9JR, England. *Office*—Gallery Five Ltd., 121 King St., London W6 9JG, England. *Agent*—Angela Holder, Gallery Five Ltd., 121 King St., London W6 9JG, England.

CAREER: J. Walter Thompson (advertising agency), London, England, art director, 1957-59; William Collins Sons & Co. (publisher), London, art director in publicity, 1959-60; *Time and Tide,* London, art editor, 1960-61; Gallery Five Ltd. (publisher), London, co-founder and art director, 1961-78, consultant art director, 1978—; McCann Erickson (advertising agency), London, television producer, 1962-63; author and illustrator of children's books, 1967—. Graphic illustrator for *Watch!,* BBC-TV, 1969-71. Designed sets for stage productions of the *Meg and Mow Show,* 1981-88, and *Beauty and the Beast,* 1986.

MEMBER: Society of Authors, Polish Hearth.

AWARDS, HONORS: Kate Greenaway Medal, British Library Association, 1971, for *The Golden Bird,* 1972, for *The Kingdom under the Sea and Other Stories,* and 1980, for *Haunted House;* Kurt Maschler Award (runnerup), Book Trust, 1984, for *Christmas: The King James Version.*

WRITINGS:

JUVENILE; SELF-ILLUSTRATED

Numbers, Heinemann, 1973, Harvey House, 1975.
Colours, Heinemann, 1973, published in America as *Colors,* Harvey House, 1975.
Shapes, Heinemann, 1973, Harvey House, 1975.
Sizes, Heinemann, 1973, Harvey House, 1975.
Homes, Heinemann, 1979, Messner, 1983.
Weather, Heinemann, 1979, Messner, 1983.
Haunted House, Dutton, 1979.
ABC, Heinemann, 1980, Simon & Schuster, 1981.
Time, Heinemann, 1980, Messner, 1983.
(With Anne Carter) *Dinner Time,* Gallery Five, 1980, published in America as *Dinnertime,* Price Stern, 1981.
(With Helen Nicoll) *The Quest for the Gloop,* Heinemann, 1980.
Robot, Delacorte, 1981.
Gossip, Price Stern, 1983.
(With H. Nicoll) *Owl at School,* Heinemann, 1984.
Christmas: The King James Version, Knopf, 1984.
Farm, Heinemann, 1985.
Zoo, Heinemann, 1985.
Little Monsters, Price Stern, 1986.
I'm Cat, Simon & Schuster, 1986.
I'm Frog, Simon & Schuster, 1986.
I'm Mouse, Simon & Schuster, 1986.
I'm Panda, Simon & Schuster, 1986.
Faces, Heinemann, 1986.
Food, Heinemann, 1986.
Small Talk, Orchard Books, 1987.
Easter: The King James Version, Random House, 1989.
Oh My! A Fly!, Price Stern Sloan, 1989.
Eggs for Tea, Doubleday, 1989.
Pet Food, Doubleday, 1990.

ILLUSTRATOR

Jessie Gertrude Townsend, *Annie, Bridget and Charlie: An ABC for Children of Rhymes,* Pantheon, 1967.
Joan Aiken, *A Necklace of Raindrops and Other Stories,* J. Cape, 1968, Doubleday, 1969, revised edition, 1972.
Nancy Langstaff and John Langstaff, compilers, *Jim Along, Josie: A Collection of Folk Songs and Singing Games for Young Children,* Harcourt, 1970, new edition published as *Sally Go round the Moon,* Revels, 1986.
Edith Brill, *The Golden Bird,* F. Watts, 1970.
J. Aiken, *The Kingdom under the Sea and Other Stories,* J. Cape, 1971, revised edition, Penguin, 1986.
Agnes Szudek, *The Amber Mountain and Other Folk Stories,* Hutchinson, 1976.
Dinah Starkey, *Ghosts and Bogles,* Hutchinson, 1976.
J. Aiken, *Tale of a One-Way Street and Other Stories,* J. Cape, 1978, Doubleday, 1980.
J. Aiken, *Past Eight O'Clock* (stories), J. Cape, 1986, Viking Kestrel, 1987.

ILLUSTRATOR; "MEG AND MOG" SERIES BY HELEN NICOLL

Meg and Mog, Heinemann, 1972, Atheneum, 1973, revised edition, Heinemann, 1977.
Meg's Eggs, Heinemann, 1972, Atheneum, 1973, revised edition, Heinemann, 1977.
Meg on the Moon, Heinemann, 1973, Penguin, 1978.
Meg at Sea, Heinemann, 1973, Penguin, 1978, revised edition, Heinemann, 1979.
Meg's Car, Heinemann, 1975, David & Charles, 1983.
Meg's Castle, Heinemann, 1975, David & Charles, 1983.
Mog's Mumps, Heinemann, 1976, David & Charles, 1983.
Meg's Veg, Heinemann, 1976, David & Charles, 1983.
Meg and Mog Birthday Book, Heinemann, 1979, David & Charles, 1984.
Mog at the Zoo, Heinemann, 1982, David & Charles, 1983.
Mog in the Fog, Heinemann, 1984.
Mog's Box, Heinemann, 1987.

EDITOR AND ILLUSTRATOR; "JAN PIENKOWSKI'S FAIRY TALE LIBRARY" SERIES

Jacob Grimm and Wilhelm Grimm, *Jack and the Beanstalk,* Heinemann, 1977.
J. Grimm and W. Grimm, *Snow White,* Heinemann, 1977.
J. Grimm and W. Grimm, *Sleeping Beauty,* Heinemann, 1977.
Charles Perrault, *Puss in Boots,* Heinemann, 1977.
C. Perrault, *Cinderella,* Heinemann, 1977.
J. Grimm and W. Grimm, *Hansel and Gretel,* Heinemann, 1977.

OTHER

Meg and Mog (play; first produced in London, England at the Unicorn Theatre, 1981), Samuel French, 1984.

Meg and Mog, Meg's Eggs, Meg at Sea, and *Meg on the Moon* have been recorded on audio cassette and released by Cover to Cover, 1985.

SIDELIGHTS: Jan Pienkowski is well-known to young readers for his colorful picture books. Often citing both his Central European background and comic book art as inspirations, Pienkowski specializes in illustrations that feature heavy lines and flat hues. He is also credited with revitalizing the pop-up book with titles such as *Haunted House* and *Dinnertime.* Despite his success, Pienkowski still sees room for improvement in his work. "Sometimes, I think I'm a total failure," he commented in *Books for Keeps.* "When you show what you've done, every single thing you've got is there. And if you've had a little success it gets worse because there's more at stake.... I am driven from within by an energy that makes me try harder."

Although he had no formal art training, Pienkowski began designing plays, posters, and greeting cards while attending Cambridge University. After graduation, he held a number of jobs in advertising and publishing. Eventually disillusioned by the business world, Pienkowski started a Christmas card company in 1958. Over time, Pienkowski's card designs became very fashionable. In an interview with Cathy Courtney for *Something about the Author (SATA),* Pienkowski noted: "My designs were right for the moment: I did very bright paper bags, paper clothes were all the rage, and stickers."

Pienkowski became heavily involved in book design when he met Helen Nicoll, a director of children's programming for the British Broadcasting Company (BBC). At Nicoll's request, Pienkowski created the opening and closing credits for the television show *Watch!.* When Nicoll left the BBC to raise a family, she and Pienkowski began the "Meg and Mog" book series. Meg (a witch) and Mog (Meg's pet cat) were based on two very popular characters that Pienkowski had originally drawn as part of the opening and closing credits for *Watch!.* "What appealed to me enormously ... [in the] 'Meg and Mog' books is the idea that there is no essential difference between the drawing and the writing," Pienkowski told Courtney. "They both convey information and fight for supremacy. Sometimes the writing is important, sometimes the drawing."

Pienkowski produced his first pop-up books in 1979. One of the most popular of these works is *Haunted House,* in which the reader comes face to face with scary creatures and spooky scenes that shift and change. Because of their complex nature, the board books require a great deal of planning and effort. Pienkowski

From *The Kingdom under the Sea and Other Stories,* by Joan Aiken. Illustrated by Jan Pienkowski.

told Tony Bradman of *Publishing News* that "these mechanical books, although they may have my name in big, bold type or lettering on the cover, they're really a team effort, and they're the work of a ... lot of people."

When not working on new titles, Pienkowski likes to visit schools. Rather than giving prepared speeches, however, he tries to encourage student participation through group art projects. "I like working with other people," Pienkowski related in his *SATA* interview. "I get much better ideas when I do. I don't think I'm as good on my own as when I'm part of a group." Ultimately, Pienkowski is interested in doing one thing for his young audience: entertaining them. He noted for Courtney: "I never discuss my books with children and I don't believe in market research. The most important thing is that it must entertain me, then it's got a chance of entertaining someone else."

WORKS CITED:

Bradman, Tony, "How Girls with Nimble Fingers Have Helped a Publishing Success," *Publishing News,* October 16, 1981.

Pienkowski, Jan, interview in *Books for Keeps,* November 1981.

Pienkowski, Jan, interview with Cathy Courtney for *Something about the Author,* Volume 58, Gale, 1990.

FOR MORE INFORMATION SEE:

BOOKS

Fourth Book of Junior Authors and Illustrators, edited by Doris de Montreville and Elizabeth D. Crawford, Wilson, 1978, pp. 286-88.

PERIODICALS

Arts Review, January 29, 1988, p. 50.

New York Times Book Review, November 11, 1984; March 19, 1989, p. 24.

School Library Journal, September, 1983; September, 1987; October, 1987.

* * *

PIERCE, Meredith Ann 1958-

PERSONAL: Born July 5, 1958, in Seattle, WA; daughter of Frank N. (a professor of advertising) and Jo Ann (an editor and professor of agriculture; maiden name, Bell) Pierce. *Education:* University of Florida, B.A., 1978, M.A., 1980. *Hobbies and other interests:* Music (composition, harp, and voice), picturebook collecting, film and theater, anthropology, archaeology, languages, folklore and mythology, cats, science fiction, fantasy, and children's literature.

ADDRESSES: Home—424-H Northeast Sixth St., Gainesville, FL 32601.

CAREER: Writer. Bookland, Gainesville, FL, clerk, 1981; Waldenbooks, Gainesville, clerk, 1981-87; Alachua County (FL) Library District, library assistant, 1987—. Treasurer, Children's Literature Association

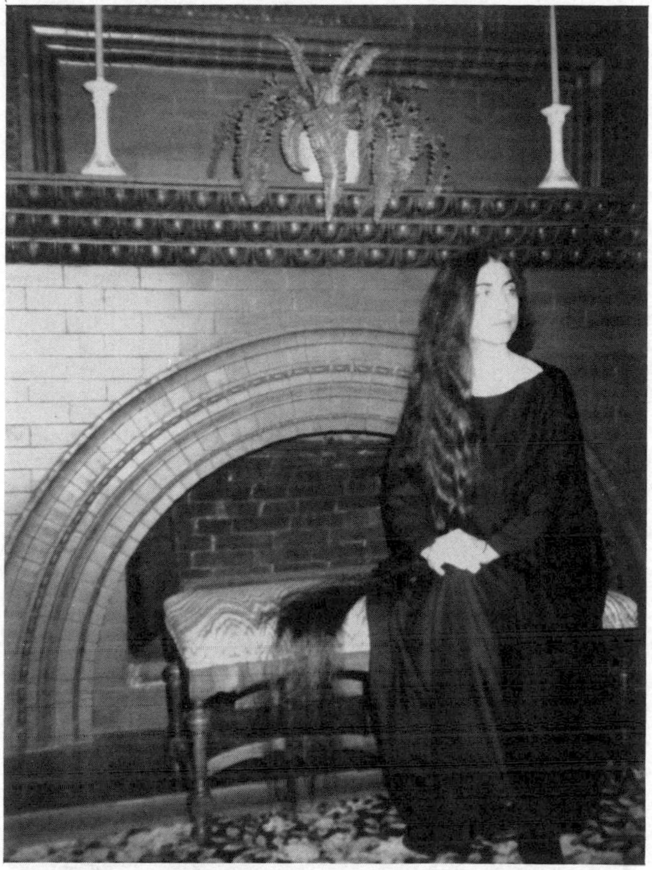

Meredith Ann Pierce

Conference, Gainesville, 1982; University of Florida, instructor of creative writing, graduate teaching assistant, 1978-80, instructor of creative writing, 1984.

MEMBER: Phi Beta Kappa.

AWARDS, HONORS: First prize in junior division, *Scholastic*/Hallmark Cards creative writing contest, 1973, for short story "The Snail"; Best Books for Young Adults citation, American Library Association (ALA), Best of the Best Books 1970-1982 citation, ALA, *New York Times* Notable Children's Book citation, and Parents' Choice Award Superbook citation, all 1982, Children's Book Award, International Reading Association, 1983, California Young Reader Medal, 1986, and *Booklist* Best Books of the Decade (1980-89) list, all for *The Darkangel;* Jane Tinkham Broughton Fellow in writing for children, Bread Loaf Writers' Conference, 1984; Best Books for Young Adults semifinalist, ALA, 1985, for *A Gathering of Gargoyles;* Best Books for Young Adults citation, ALA, 1985, Parents' Choice Award for Literature citation, 1985, and New York Public Library Books for the Teen Age exhibit citation, 1986, all for *The Woman Who Loved Reindeer;* Individual Artist Fellowship Special Award for Children's Literature, Florida Department of State, Division of Cultural Affairs, 1987; Best Books for Young Adults citation, 1991, for *The Pearl of the Soul of the World.*

WRITINGS:

YOUNG ADULT FANTASY NOVELS

The Darkangel (first novel in the "Darkangel" trilogy), Little, Brown, 1982.

A Gathering of Gargoyles (second novel in the "Darkangel" trilogy), Little, Brown, 1984.

Birth of the Firebringer (first novel in the "Firebringer" trilogy), Macmillan, 1985.

The Woman Who Loved Reindeer, Little, Brown, 1985.

The Pearl of the Soul of the World (third novel in the "Darkangel" trilogy), Little, Brown, 1990.

OTHER

Where the Wild Geese Go (picturebook), illustrated by Jamichael Henterly, Dutton, 1988.

(Contributor) *Four from the Witch World* (contains novella "Rampion"), edited by Andre Norton, Tor Books, 1989.

Contributor to anthologies and to periodicals, including *Mythlore, Horn Book, ALAN Review, Voice of Youth Advocates (VOYA),* and *New Advocate.*

WORK IN PROGRESS: Dark Moon, the second novel in the "Firebringer" trilogy.

SIDELIGHTS: Meredith Ann Pierce's novels are highlighted by their imaginative plots and settings, poetic language, and determined, independent characters. Her most noted work, the "Darkangel" fantasy trilogy, relates a young girl's struggle to free herself, her friends, and her world from an evil witch's power. Pierce's work "combines a mythic inventiveness with such elemental themes as love, conflict and quest," Joan Nist observes in the *ALAN Review,* and adds that Pierce "is one of the foremost young authors of fantasy today." As a *Publishers Weekly* reviewer writes, "The author's imagination seems boundless and she writes with such assurance that readers believe in every magic being and occurrence."

Pierce used considerable imagination to entertain herself when she was young, she related in an interview with *Something about the Author* (*SATA*): "I was a great collector of stuffed animals and had several entire imaginary lives." She would spend hours talking and playing with her unseen companions, and often joined her brothers and sister in their own make-believe games.

Pierce also indulged her imagination with books. She made trips to the library with her parents, who frequently read aloud to her. With their encouragement, she began to read by herself around age three. "I was extremely self-contained," she said. "Since I could read real young, I could get my hands on all this information—a book. A lot of kids need an adult or somebody older around to feed them information, because they don't have access to it themselves. But I could read so young that I could feed myself information."

One book that Pierce remembers fondly is Lewis Carroll's classic *Alice in Wonderland.* Her version included records to read along with, and reading it over and over made a great impression on her. "*Alice in Wonderland* is like my religion," Pierce remarked in her interview. "It was introduced into my system before my immune system was complete, so it's wired into my psyche. I can't distinguish between my own mythology and early influences like *Alice in Wonderland* or the movie *The Wizard of Oz.* Some of the stuff that I saw really impressed me when I was very little and just went straight into my neurons—it's inseparable from my way of thinking."

Pierce constantly wrote down ideas and stories when she was a student, but she didn't realize that people could actually make a living writing novels, she said in her interview. "My parents always treated my writing as another one of those obsessive little hobbies; 'Why would you rather be writing a novel than doing something else normal?' Since they were the authority figure I had to pretend that this wasn't the most important thing in my life and find some other career." But at the University of Florida Pierce met professor and children's writer Joy Anderson, who showed her that writing could be a potential career. "Through her I got a much better idea of what writing is all about. She taught not just the craft of writing, but also the marketing aspect."

Anderson was instrumental in helping develop Pierce's talent. As part of her class assignments, students would prepare a manuscript to be submitted to a publisher. In addition, Pierce noted, "Joy was very good about shoring up my confidence and giving me real specific criticism. If someone says 'Oh that's good, oh what a good writer you are, oh that's nice,' that's emotional stroking and I just hate that. But if someone will say, 'I like the opening, the opening was strong, but in the second paragraph when we get to this sentence my mind wandered. What are you going to do to fix it?,' that's something very narrow and focused and precise. Joy would give me very precise suggestions and comments that would leave the solution up to me."

Pierce developed her first novel, *The Darkangel,* in this fashion. The story takes place on the moon and follows the journey of Aeriel, a servant girl who sets out to rescue her mistress from a vampire who is evil but strangely attractive. Finding a publisher for the novel wasn't daunting for Pierce because of her experience in college. "I was very confident by the time I sent off *Darkangel* that Joy had given me not only positive feedback but accurate feedback and that the manuscript was good and that it would be accepted," the author said in her interview. Pierce's intuition was correct, for *The Darkangel* was soon accepted by Little, Brown and was published in 1982 to much critical praise.

One outstanding feature of *The Darkangel* is Aeriel's determination to stand her ground in the face of danger. Although she is threatened by the vampire Irrylath, she frees his gargoyles and returns to his castle to confront him. Aeriel's courage and persistence grew out of one of the author's childhood experiences. As a young child Pierce was forced to deal with an alcoholic and abusive relative who was much older and stronger than she. "One day I found myself in the absurd position of facing someone twice my size who, for no cause, had made up his mind to do me violence," Pierce related in a *Horn Book* article. Tired of living with her fear of this person, Pierce continued, "I found myself being filled by the most supernal fury. How dare this person believe I was just going to stand there and take this?" At that point Pierce determined not to give in, whatever the consequences, and the relative left her alone. This showdown was "a little bit of a revelation—that a lot of human relationships are bluff, and that's an important thing to know," the author stated in her *SATA* interview. "Just because somebody tells you a thing is so, that 'This is the situation and I have great power over you,' doesn't mean it's true."

Although *The Darkangel* concludes with Aeriel marrying Irrylath and making him human by exchanging her heart for his, she is left his bride in name only. In the second volume of Pierce's trilogy, *A Gathering of Gargoyles,* Aeriel discovers Irrylath is still bound to the evil White Witch and cannot love another. To release him, Aeriel searches the moon to find their world's lost lons, ancient animal guardians who will help lead the battle against the Witch's forces.

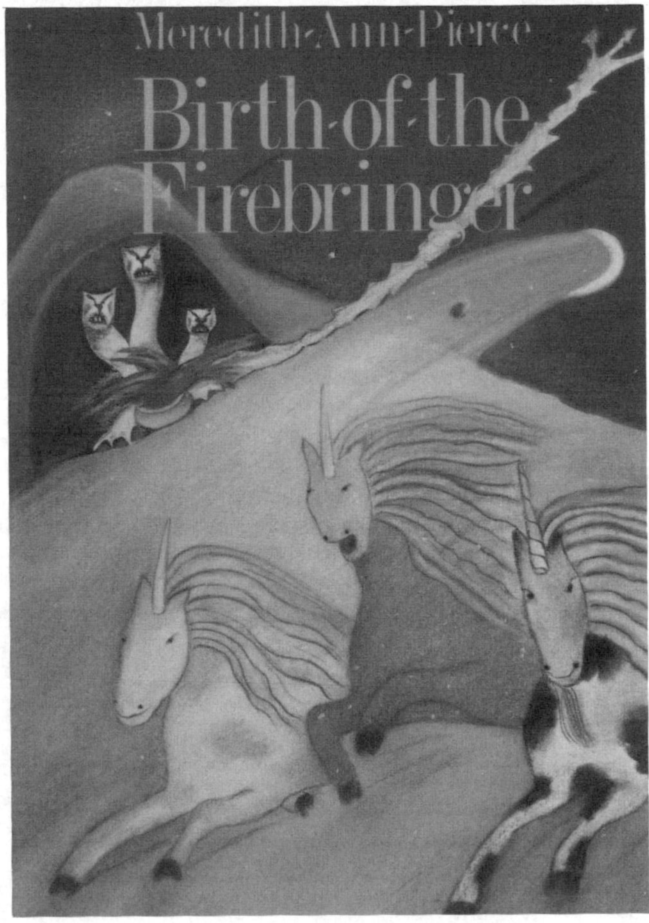

Cover of *Birth of the Firebringer,* by Meredith Ann Pierce.

Critics have responded favorably to this sequel as well. "Pierce is intensely visual, even poetic, in her descriptions and imaginative in her surprising plot turns," Eleanor Cameron reports in the *New York Times Book Review. Fantasy Review* contributor Walter Albert calls *A Gathering of Gargoyles* "perhaps an even finer work" than *The Darkangel,* and praises Pierce for her "stylistic growth." The critic concludes: "If Pierce does no more than equal her achievement in *A Gathering of Gargoyles* in the third volume, the three novels will surely be ranked with the small number of enduring fantasy classics."

In the last novel of the series, *The Pearl of the Soul of the World,* Aeriel takes on yet another urgent task: to bring the White Witch a gift and persuade her to renounce evil. This results in a showdown between good and evil, something that has fascinated Pierce for many years—ever since she discovered the comic *Prince Valiant.* "I just love the whole medieval ethos," the author said in her *SATA* interview. "I know they were all starving to death and had all these diseases and their teeth were falling out and all that. But in a lot of the medieval legends, people were intensely religious and everything was important, everything was a struggle between heaven and hell. Good and evil has influenced my writing even though I'm not a Christian and don't belong to an organized religion. This sort of spirituality pervades the books whether I want it to or not."

Pierce recognizes that her work, like most fantasy and science fiction, has special appeal for young people. "Adolescents are just getting ready to turn into adults," she explained to *SATA* in her interview. "Lots of fantasy and science fiction stories are about metamorphosis or about transporting you from one environment, a familiar environment, into an unknown environment. So what I write lends itself naturally to young adults—but it's also enjoyed by younger kids. I get fan mail from as young as fourth grade gifted all the way up to adults."

In addition, Pierce remarked, she would like to serve as an example for aspiring writers. "Anybody who's out there who's interested in writing I hope they'll read my stuff and say 'Gee, I'd like to write books like that,'" she told *SATA* in her interview. "That is what I used to do when I would read one of my favorite authors when I was little." Pierce is also able to help children who are interested in writing through her work as a librarian. "I see myself in them; I see them as not having the information that they need to decide whether or not they want to be a writer. So I try to supply any child who mentions that they're interested in writing with as much information as they ask for on publishing."

Although Pierce works full-time at the library in addition to writing, she doesn't find either job a burden. "Because writing is so fun and so relaxing to me, it's like going to sleep and dreaming a wonderful dream," she said in her interview. "I'm at work all day and have a reasonably good time telling little children to quit running on the stairs and helping them look for the shark books. Then when I come home, writing is not 'work' in the sense of a struggle; it's not taxing and draining, it's very renewing. In fact, I get very annoyed when I have to stop writing and do something else like shop or take a bath or any of those terribly unimportant things that don't need to be done. So to say that I have two jobs is really very misleading," the author concluded. "I do have two jobs but they're both highly enjoyable; and writing is the most enjoyable thing there is."

WORKS CITED:

Albert, Walter, "One of a Small Number of Fantasy Classics," *Fantasy Review,* May, 1985, p. 20.

Cameron, Eleanor, review of *A Gathering of Gargoyles, New York Times Book Review,* December 30, 1984, p. 19.

Review of *A Gathering of Gargoyles, Publishers Weekly,* November 30, 1984, p. 92.

Nist, Joan, review of *The Woman Who Loved Reindeer, ALAN Review,* winter, 1985, p. 31.

Pierce, Meredith Ann, "A Lion in the Room," *Horn Book,* January-February, 1988, pp. 35-41.

Pierce, Meredith Ann, telephone interview for *Something about the Author* conducted by Diane Telgen, June 4, 1991.

FOR MORE INFORMATION SEE:

BOOKS

Children's Literature Review, Volume 20, Gale, 1990.

PERIODICALS

Bulletin for the Center of Children's Books, July-August, 1982; December, 1985.

English Journal, April, 1985.

Horn Book, May-June, 1988.

New York Times, November 30, 1982.

School Library Journal, June-July, 1988.

* * *

PIG, Edward
See GOREY, Edward (St. John)

* * *

PILGRIM, Anne
See ALLAN, Mabel Esther

* * *

PINKNEY, Jerry 1939-

PERSONAL: Born December 22, 1939, in Philadelphia, PA; son of James H. (a carpenter) and Williemae (a housewife) Pinkney; married wife, Gloria Maultsby, 1960; children: Troy Bernadette, Jerry Brian, Scott Cannon, Myles Carter. *Education:* Attended Philadelphia Museum College of Art (now University of the Arts), 1957-59. *Hobbies and other interests:* "I am a lover of music, with a large music collection. I enjoy all kinds of music: jazz, classical, rock and pop."

Jerry Pinkney

ADDRESSES: Home—41 Furnace Rock Rd., Croton-on-Hudson, NY 10520. *Office*—Department of Art, University of Delaware, Newark, DE 19716.

CAREER: Worked as a designer/illustrator for Rustcraft Greeting Card Co., Dedham, MA, and Barker-Black Studio, Boston, MA, and helped found the Kaleidoscope Studio before opening his own studio, Jerry Pinkney, Inc., Croton-on-Hudson, NY, in 1971. Rhode Island School of Design, visiting critic, 1969-70, member of visiting committee, 1991; Pratt Institute, Brooklyn, NY, associate professor of illustration, 1986-87; University of Delaware, distinguished visiting professor, 1986-88, associate professor of art, 1988—; University of Buffalo, NY, visiting artist, 1989; Syracuse University, NY, guest faculty, 1989; Fashion Institute of Technology, NY, art mentor, 1989; State University of New York at Buffalo, visiting professor, 1991; guest lecturer at numerous schools and universities; served on judging committees for numerous art and illustration shows. United States Postal Service, Stamp Advisory Committee, 1982—, Quality Assurance Committee, 1986—; served on the NASA Artist Team for the space shuttle Columbia. Designer of commemorative stamps for the United States Postal Service "Black Heritage" series and the "Honey Bee" commemorative envelope. *Exhibitions:* Pinkney has exhibited his works at numerous group and one-man shows throughout the U.S. and in Japan and Italy, including shows at the Brooklyn Museum, the National Center of Afro-American Artists, Boston, the Air and Space Museum, Washington, D.C., and the Boston Museum of Fine Arts.

MEMBER: Society of Illustrators, Graphic Artists Guild, Society of Children's Book Writers.

AWARDS, HONORS: Numerous awards for illustration from the Society of Illustrators; New Jersey Institute of Technology award, 1969, for *Babushka and the Pig;* Council on Interracial Books for Children Award, 1973, Children's Book Showcase selection, 1976, and Jane Addams Book Group Award, 1976, all for *Song of the Trees;* Newbery Medal, *Boston Globe-Horn Book* Honor Book, Jane Addams Book Group Award, and National Book Award finalist, all 1977, and Young Readers Choice award, 1979, all for *Roll of Thunder, Hear My Cry; Childtimes: A Three-Generation Memoir* and *Tonweya and the Eagles, and Other Lakota Indian Tales* were both American Institute of Graphic Arts Book Show selections, 1980; *Boston Globe/Horn Book* Award, and Carter G. Woodson Award, both 1980, both for *Childtimes: A Three-Generation Memoir;* Outstanding Science Book Award, National Association of Science Teachers, 1980, Carter G. Woodson Award, and Coretta Scott King Award runner-up, both for *Count on Your Fingers African Style;* Christopher Award and Coretta Scott King Award, both 1986, both for *The Patchwork Quilt; Redbook* Award, 1987, for *Strange Animals of the Sea;* Coretta Scott King Award, 1987, for *Half a Moon and One Whole Star;* Coretta Scott King Award, 1988, and Caldecott Honor Book, 1989, both for *Mirandy and Brother Wind;* Caldecott Honor Book, 1989, for *The Talking Eggs;* Golden Kite Award, 1990, for *Home Place;* citation for children's literature from Drexel University, 1992; Philadelphia College of Art and Design Alumni Award, 1992; David McCord Children's Literature Citation from Framingham State College, 1992.

ILLUSTRATOR:

Joyce Cooper Arkhurst, reteller, *The Adventures of Spider: West African Folk Tales,* Little, Brown, 1964.

Adeline McCall, *This Is Music,* Allyn & Bacon, 1965.

V. Mikhailovich Garshin, *The Traveling Frog,* McGraw, 1966.

Lila Green, compiler, *Folktales and Fairytales of Africa,* Silver Burdett, 1967.

Ken Sobol, *The Clock Museum,* McGraw, 1967.

Harold J. Saleh, *Even Tiny Ants Must Sleep,* McGraw, 1967.

John W. Spellman, editor, *The Beautiful Blue Jay, and Other Tales of India,* Little, Brown, 1967.

Ralph Dale, *Shoes, Pennies, and Rockets,* L. W. Singer, 1968.

Traudl (pseudonym of Traudl Flaxman), *Kostas the Rooster,* Lothrop, 1968.

Cora Annett, *Homerhenry,* Addison-Wesley, 1969.

Irv Phillips, *The Twin Witches of Fingle Fu,* L. W. Singer, 1969.

Fern Powell, *The Porcupine and the Tiger,* Lothrop, 1969.

Ann Trofimuk, *Babushka and the Pig,* Houghton, 1969.

Thelma Shaw, *Juano and the Wonderful Fresh Fish,* Addison-Wesley, 1969.

K. Sobol, *Sizes and Shapes,* McGraw, 1969.

Francine Jacobs, adapter, *The King's Ditch: A Hawaiian Tale,* Coward, 1971.

(Cover illustration) Virginia Hamilton, *The Planet of Junior Brown,* Macmillan, 1971.

J. C. Arkhurst, *More Adventures of Spider,* Scholastic Book Services, 1972.
Adjai Robinson, *Femi and Old Grandaddie,* Coward, 1972.
Mari Evans, *JD,* Doubleday, 1973.
A. Robinson, *Kasho and the Twin Flutes,* Coward, 1973.
Berniece Freschet, *Prince Littlefoot,* Cheshire, 1974.
Beth P. Wilson, *The Great Minu,* Follett, 1974.
Mildred D. Taylor, *Song of the Trees,* Dial, 1975.
Cruz Martel, *Yagua Days,* Dial, 1976.
M. D. Taylor, *Roll of Thunder, Hear My Cry,* Dial, 1976.
Phyllis Green, *Mildred Murphy, How Does Your Garden Grow?,* Addison-Wesley, 1977.
Eloise Greenfield, *Mary McLeod Bethune* (biography), Crowell, 1977.
Verna Aardema, *Ji-Nongo-Nongo Means Riddles,* Four Winds Press, 1978.
L. Green, reteller, *Tales from Africa,* Silver Burdett, 1979.
Rosebud Yellow Robe, reteller, *Tonweya and the Eagles, and Other Lakota Indian Tales,* Dial, 1979.
E. Greenfield and Lessie Jones Little, *Childtimes: A Three-Generation Memoir,* Crowell, 1979.
V. Hamilton, *Jahdu,* Greenwillow, 1980.
Claudia Zaslavsky, *Count on Your Fingers African Style,* Crowell, 1980.
William Wise, *Monster Myths of Ancient Greece,* Putnam, 1981.
Barbara Michels and Bettye White, editors, *Apples on a Stick: The Folklore of Black Children,* Coward, 1983.
Valerie Flournoy, *The Patchwork Quilt,* Dial, 1985.
Crescent Dragonwagon, *Half a Moon and One Whole Star,* Macmillan, 1986.
Barbara Gibson, *Creatures of the Desert World and Strange Animals of the Sea,* edited by Donald J. Crump, National Geographic Society, 1987.
Julius Lester, *The Tales of Uncle Remus,* Dial, 1988.
Nancy White Carlstrom, *Wild, Wild Sunflower Child Anna,* Macmillan, 1987.
J. Lester, *More Tales of Uncle Remus: Further Adventures of Brer Rabbit, His Friends, Enemies and Others,* Dial, 1988.
Julia Fields, *The Green Lion of Zion Street,* Macmillan, 1988.
Pat McKissack, *Mirandy and Brother Wind,* Knopf, 1988.
V. Aardema, *Rabbit Makes a Monkey of Lion,* Dial, 1989.
Robert D. San Souci, *The Talking Eggs,* Dial, 1989.
Marilyn Singer, *Turtle in July,* Macmillan, 1989.
C. Dragonwagon, *Home Place,* Macmillan, 1990.
Jean Marzollo, *Pretend You're a Cat,* Dial, 1990.
J. Lester, *Further Tales of Uncle Remus: The Misadventures of Brer Rabbit, Brer Fox, Brer Wolf, the Doodang, and All the Other Creatures,* Dial, 1990.
Arnold Adoff, *In for Winter, Out for Spring,* Harcourt, 1991.
Zora Neale Hurston, *Their Eyes Were Watching God,* University of Illinois Press, 1991.

Also illustrator of *The Man with His Heart in a Bucket,* Dial, 1991. Contributor of illustrations to textbooks and magazines, including *Boys' Life, Contact, Essence, Post,* and *Seventeen.* Also illustrator of Helen Fletcher's *The Year Around Book,* and of a series of limited edition books for adults published by Franklin Library that includes *Wuthering Heights, The Winthrop Covenant, Early Autumn, Rabbit Run, Gulliver's Travels, Selected Plays, Tom Jones, The Flowering of New England, These Thirteen, The Covenant, Lolita, Rabbit Redux,* and *The Education of Henry Adams.*

ADAPTATIONS: The Patchwork Quilt, Half a Moon and One Whole Star and *Yagua Days* were presented on *Reading Rainbow,* PBS-TV.

SIDELIGHTS: From the day he began copying drawings from comic books and photo magazines, illustrator Jerry Pinkney pushed himself to be the best artist he could be. Pinkney's drive has made him, some four decades later, a nationally-recognized illustrator of children's books, as well as a gifted designer and illustrator of stamps, posters, calendars, and books for adults. Much of his work pays tribute to his African-American heritage, but the artist has illustrated books about Hispanic-Americans and Native Americans as well. Expressing his commitment to multi-cultural works in his autobiographical essay in *Something about the Author Autobiography Series* (*SAAS*), Pinkney says "these books are needed and are my contribution in terms of my concern for this country and the issue of racism."

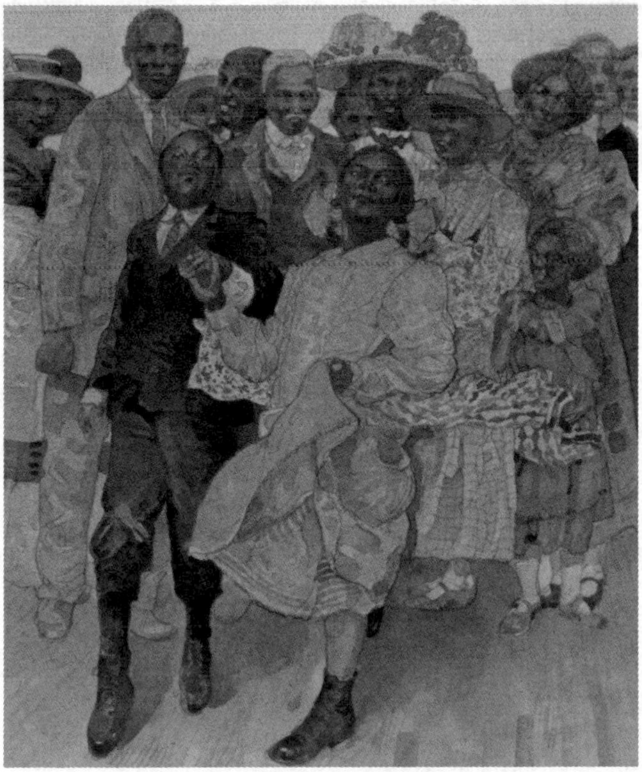

From *Mirandy and Brother Wind,* by Patricia C. McKissack. Illustrated by Jerry Pinkney.

Pinkney was born in 1939 to a large family living on an all-black block in the Germantown section of Philadelphia, Pennsylvania. His neighborhood and extended family provided the young Pinkney with all the entertainment he needed, for the children were always involved in the many family projects, ranging from all-day barbecues to summer-long house raising ventures. He discovered drawing at an early age, however, and remembers in *SAAS* that "I was always caught in the middle between the thing that I wanted to do, which would be to sit and draw, and the other side of me that really wanted to be more social; and yet, being social was more work for me." Pinkney's artistic urges were rewarded in school, where his teachers and fellow students admired and encouraged his work, but he also remembers that "somehow I hooked into that competitive mode so that it became very important that I succeed." This "competitive mode" drove his performance throughout the rest of his schooling, and though Pinkney received consistently high marks in his classes, he was plagued by doubts about his abilities and his intelligence. He says in *SAAS* that he was "unable to make a connection between what I thought about myself and how others felt about my achievements."

Pinkney's mother actively encouraged his study of art, and his father, though skeptical, supported his decision to continue pursuing art studies into high school as well. Dobbins Vocational High School had an excellent program in commercial art, and Pinkney received encouragement and guidance from his teachers and peers. Upon graduation, he applied for and received a four-year scholarship to the Philadelphia Museum College of Art, becoming the first in his family to go to college. There he met and married his wife, Gloria, and established a network of contacts that would support him throughout his artistic career, as well as land him his first job with a greeting card company near Boston. In Boston, Pinkney was involved in the expanding civil rights movement, and as a result of the wide variety of people he met through these activities, Pinkney says in *SAAS* that "I worked toward being a well-rounded artist and I chose not to focus on one style or put all my energies into one visual discipline."

Pinkney's commitment to expanding his artistic range left him frustrated with his job, so with some friends he founded the Kaleidoscope Studio, where he worked for a little over two years before starting a studio of his own—the Jerry Pinkney Studio. Though he kept busy doing advertising and textbook illustration, Pinkney most loved doing illustrations for books and tried to do at least one or two a year. "The marriage of typography and illustration was always very important to me and the picture-book area provided me with the opportunity to illustrate and design," he comments in his autobiographical sketch. Fredrick Woodard, interviewed by Donnarae MacCann and Olga Richard in *Wilson Library Bulletin,* notes that in *Mirandy and Brother Wind* the "stunning color and movement [of Pinkney's illustrations] are in perfect harmony with the beauty of the book's folk language." The book, which won the the Coretta Scott King Award and was named a Caldecott Honor Book, tells the story of a young girl convinced that she will dance with the wind at an upcoming dance. Patricia C. McKissack, reviewing the book in the *New York Times Book Review,* says that the combination of text and pictures "captures the texture of rural life and culture 40 years after the end of slavery."

Soon Pinkney had even more book illustration offers because, he explains in *SAAS,* "the late sixties and early seventies brought an awareness of black writers. Publishers sought out black artists to illustrate black subject matter and the work of black writers. And there I was—it was almost like a setup." Pinkney was soon creating illustrations for a wide variety of projects, including African-American historical calendars, a number of limited-edition books for Franklin Library and, in 1983, a set of stamps for the U.S. Postal Service's Black Heritage series that would include Harriet Tubman, Martin Luther King, Jr., Scott Joplin, and Jackie Robinson. Pinkney comments in *SAAS:* "I was trying to use these projects as vehicles to address the issues of being an African-American and the importance of African-American contributions to society.... I wanted to show that an African-American artist could certainly make it in this country on a national level in the visual graphic arts. And I wanted to show my children the possibilities that lay ahead for them. That was very important. I wanted to be a strong role model for my family and for other African-Americans."

During this period, Pinkney got involved with a number of book projects that brought him a great deal of critical attention. *The Patchwork Quilt,* written by Valerie Flournoy, tells of a wonderful relationship between a grandmother and a granddaughter and celebrates the strength of the black family. Pinkney found people to model the relationships described in the book, and he created his drawings from these modeling sessions. The book won a number of awards, including two that were very important to the illustrator: the Christopher Award and the Coretta Scott King Award. Pinkney carried his live model concept further in crafting the illustrations for Julius Lester's retelling of *The Tales of Uncle Remus.* "After a number of preliminary drawings, I realized that the answer was for me to model and pose as the animals," he says in *SAAS.* "And that's what I did. I got dressed up in vests and baggy pants and I took on the posture and attitude of whatever that animal might be." June Jordan, reviewing the book in *New York Times Book Review,* comments that "every single illustration ... is fastidious, inspired and a marvel of delightful imagination."

Although Pinkney is now an accomplished artist and teaches art to others at numerous universities, he has not lost the drive to improve that launched his career. He tells *SAAS* that his future goals are "to have my work continually grow and to have something artistic to put back into the pot. Another goal is to continue acting as a role model, sharing my time with young artists and children. As for the work itself, my interest is in doing more multi-cultural projects."

Daniel Manus Pinkwater

WORKS CITED:

Jordan, June, "A Truly Bad Rabbit," *New York Times Book Review,* May 17, 1987, p. 32.
McCann, Donnarae and Olga Richard, interview with Fredrick Woodard, "Picture Books for Children," *Wilson Library Bulletin,* April, 1989, pp. 92-93.
Pinkney, Jerry, essay in *Something about the Author Autobiography Series,* Volume 12, Gale, 1991, pp. 249-266.

FOR MORE INFORMATION SEE:

BOOKS

Cederholm, Theresa Dickason, compiler and editor, *Afro-American Artists: A Bibliographical Directory,* Boston Public Library, 1973.
Kingman, Lee and others, compilers, *Illustrators of Children's Books: 1957-1966,* Horn Book, 1968.
Rollock, Barbara, *Black Authors and Illustrators of Children's Books,* Garland, 1988.
Twelve Black Artists from Boston, Brandeis University, 1969.

PERIODICALS

American Artist, May/June, 1982.
Communication Art, May/June, 1975.
Horn Book, March/April, 1988.
New York Times, February 26, 1978; December 13, 1988.

PINKWATER, Daniel Manus 1941- (Manus Pinkwater)

PERSONAL: Born November 15, 1941, in Memphis, TN; son of Philip (a ragman) and Fay (Hoffman) Pinkwater (a chorus girl); married Jill Miriam Schutz (a writer and illustrator), October 12, 1969. *Education:* B.A., 1964. *Politics:* Taoist. *Religion:* Republican. *Hobbies and other interests:* "Various."

ADDRESSES: *Home*—111 Crum Elbow Rd., Hyde Park, NY 12538. *Agent*—Dorothy Markinko, McIntosh and Otis.

CAREER: Writer and illustrator of children's books. Art instructor at various settlement houses around New York City. *All Things Considered,* National Public Radio, regular commentator, 1987—. *Exhibitions:* Various small galleries and university shows.

MEMBER: American Federation of Theater and Radio Artists.

AWARDS, HONORS: New Jersey Institute of Technology award, 1975, for *Fat Elliot and the Gorilla;* American Library Association Notable Book award, 1976, for *Lizard Music;* Junior Literary Guild selection, 1977, for *Fat Men from Space; New York Times* Outstanding Book, 1978, for *The Last Guru;* Children's Choice book award from the International Reading Association and the Children's Book Council, 1981, for *The Wuggie*

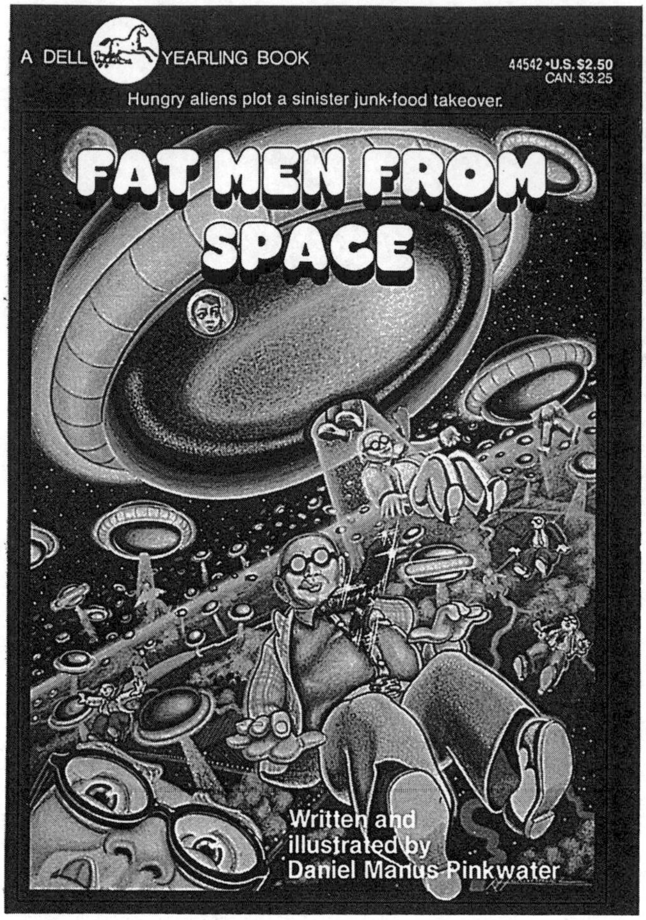
A DELL YEARLING BOOK
44542 • U.S. $2.50 CAN. $3.25
Hungry aliens plot a sinister junk-food takeover.
FAT MEN FROM SPACE
Written and illustrated by Daniel Manus Pinkwater

From *Fat Men from Space*, written and illustrated by Daniel Manus Pinkwater.

Norple Story; Parents' Choice award (literature), 1982, for *Roger's Umbrella;*

WRITINGS:

FOR CHILDREN

Alan Mendelsohn, the Boy from Mars, Dutton, 1979.
Yobgorgle: Mystery Monster of Lake Ontario, Clarion Books, 1979, revised edition, Bantam, 1981.
The Wuggie Norple Story, illustrated by Tomie de Paola, Four Winds, 1980.
The Worms of Kukumlima, Dutton, 1981.
Slaves of Spiegel: A Magic Moscow Story, Four Winds, 1982.
Young Adult Novel (also see below), Crowell, 1982.
Roger's Umbrella, illustrated by James Marshall, Dutton, 1982.
The Snarkout Boys and the Avocado of Death, Lothrop, 1982.
The Snarkout Boys and the Baconburg Horror, Lothrop, 1984.
Jolly Roger, a Dog of Hoboken, Lothrop, 1985.
Borgel, Macmillan, 1990.

Contributor to *Cricket.*

FOR CHILDREN; SELF-ILLUSTRATED

Wizard Crystal, Dodd, 1973.
Magic Camera, Dodd, 1974.
Lizard Music, Dodd, 1976.
The Blue Thing, Prentice-Hall, 1977.
The Big Orange Splot, Hastings House, 1977.
Fat Men from Space (Junior Literary Guild selection), Dodd, 1977.
The Hoboken Chicken Emergency, Prentice-Hall, 1977.
The Last Guru, Dodd, 1978.
Return of the Moose, Dodd, 1979.
Pickle Creature, Four Winds, 1979.
The Magic Moscow, Four Winds, 1980.
Tooth-Gnasher Super Flash, Four Winds, 1981.
Attila the Pun: A Magic Moscow Book, Four Winds, 1981.
I Was a Second Grade Werewolf, Dutton, 1983.
Ducks!, Little, Brown, 1984.
Devil in the Drain, Dutton, 1984.
The Moosepire, Little, Brown, 1986.
The Muffin Fiend, Lothrop, 1986.
The Frankenbagel Monster, Dutton, 1986.
Aunt Lulu, Macmillan, 1988.
Guys from Space, Macmillan, 1989.
Uncle Melvin, Macmillan, 1989.
Doodle Flute, Macmillan, 1991.

FOR CHILDREN; UNDER NAME, MANUS PINKWATER

The Terrible Roar, Knopf, 1970.
(And illustrator) *Bear's Picture,* Holt, 1972.
Fat Elliot and the Gorilla, Four Winds, 1974.
Three Big Hogs, Seabury, 1975.
(And illustrator) *Blue Moose,* Dodd, 1975.
(And illustrator) *Wingman,* Dodd, 1975.

FOR ADULTS

(With wife, Jill Pinkwater) *Superpuppy: How to Choose, Raise, and Train the Best Possible Dog for You,* illustrated by J. Pinkwater, Seabury, 1977.
Young Adults (three parts; first part based on *Young Adult Novel*), Tor, 1985.
Fish Whistle, Commentaries, Uncommentaries, and Vulgar Excesses, Addison-Wesley, 1990.
Chicago Days, Hoboken Nights, Addison-Wesley, 1991.

ADAPTATIONS:

Wingman (cassette), Listening Library, 1981.
Blue Moose (video cassette), Positive Images, 1982.
The Hoboken Chicken Emergency (television movie), Public Broadcasting System (PBS), 1984.
I Was a Second Grade Werewolf (cassette recording), Live Oak Media, 1986.

WORK IN PROGRESS: "Much."

SIDELIGHTS: Were a blue moose to come striding into Daniel Manus Pinkwater's living room one day and ask for a cup of coffee, Pinkwater should not be at all surprised, for that is exactly the kind of situation he has been describing in his years of writing books for children. From his home in upstate New York, Pinkwater writes and illustrates books about the lives of such characters as Aunt Lulu, the Muffin Fiend, and the Frankenbagel Monster. Though Pinkwater's characters are absurd, his intent in writing is not, and he says in an interview for *Something about the Author* (*SATA*): "I want my readers to feel encouraged and *snarky,* because basically they are kids taking on a hostile and/or indifferent world. My books are about finding favoring signs in the world, about discovering riches—things which are not dead. My stories are about people prevailing."

Pinkwater was born in Memphis, Tennessee in 1941, but grew up in Chicago. He remembers the kids in his neighborhood acting out the stories that they had read in adventure books like *20,000 Leagues under the Sea* and *Three Musketeers,* and he told *SATA:* "We heard about books by word of mouth—the kid next door had an older brother who told me about the *Three Musketeers.* I got to read good books, although mainly adventure stories." Pinkwater was a self-described oddball as a child, much like the characters in his stories, but was lucky enough to find a group of boys who shared his interests, keeping him from feeling alienated.

During his time at Bard College in Annandale-on-Hudson, New York, Pinkwater decided to become a sculptor in order to become a good writer. By the time he finished college and a three-year apprenticeship with a sculptor, however, he had changed his mind. "I don't want to be a writer," he remembered thinking in *SATA.* "Writer's lives are disgusting, and writing is a horrible unhealthy activity. You get coffee nerves and a bad back, and eye strain. You smoke, and you sit . . . it's terrible." When four years later he returned to writing, he realized he was a better writer for his sculpting experience. Pinkwater advises anyone who wants to write to first learn to do something other than writing.

Pinkwater told *SATA* that he "didn't decide to start doing children's books, [he] floated into it." He had produced a set of illustrations for the book that was to become *The Terrible Roar,* and didn't want to deal with someone else writing the text for the book. So he wrote it himself. Though his first few books were "just a giggle" for him, he soon found them more and more interesting and soon committed himself to writing full-time. "I thought after two or three books I would have saturated my audience, whom I imagined as fat, bespectacled, intellectual boys," he commented to *SATA.* "I often receive photographs from my readers, including good-looking blonde-haired kids, who are captains of their soccer teams. It's not just the sweaty, spotty, stinky, pimply kids who do college physics in middle school who read my work, although, of course those are my favorites."

Pinkwater enjoys writing for children because he thinks they are more honest and more receptive to art than adults. "They are very matter of fact," he explained in *SATA.* "They like something, or they don't, they can use something or they can't. Adults feel an obligation to consider what reflection their artistic preferences will make upon them as people of cultural breeding and intelligence."

Pinkwater's books have been classified as fantasy and science fiction, but Janice Alberghene argues in *Twentieth-Century Children's Writers* that he "is less interested in the creation of a separate secondary world or alternate universe (as in *Alan Mendelsohn: The Boy from Mars,* or *The Worms of Kukumlima*) than he is in the eruption of the fantastic into everyday reality." Pinkwater often introduces extraordinary events into rather ordinary situations, which has the effect of making the ordinary situations stand out. In *Blue Moose,* the title character walks into a restaurant and is hired as a waiter, and later the kitchen floor turns into a spring meadow. In *The Moosepire,* a railroad boxcar operates as a time machine. Both books bring the mundane to life, showing that imagination can make any situation an exciting adventure.

Pinkwater's books are an adventure at least in part because they seem to go off in so many directions at once. Alberghene finds it "par for the course to find James Dean, *The Sorrows of Young Werewolf,* and a giant avocado capable of being modified into a thought-wave producing 'Alligatron' all within the covers of the same book," as in *The Snarkout Boys and the Avocado of Death.* Pinkwater admitted to *SATA* that he actually looks for a book to get out of hand: "The work is like a skateboard that suddenly gets away from me, and the anticipation is that somehow, miraculously, I will finish with the skateboard." It is this sense of play and absurdity that makes children laugh out loud when they read his books.

Some critics, however, think that the absurdity is overdone. Peter Andrews writes in the *New York Times Book Review:* "[Pinkwater] seems to fancy himself as the master surrealist of children's literature, but he sometimes falls into the trap of thinking that if you are writing nonsense you don't have to be logical." John Cech, reviewing *Yobgorgle: Mystery Monster of Lake Ontario* for *Children's Book Review Service,* finds that the continual "weirdness" drains the patience of even the youngest readers, and suggests that the story is "without substance." Alberghene puts these comments in perspective by noting that children have different standards for judging books than adults, and they find Pinkwater's books quite delightful.

Though Pinkwater's stories are not serious, he is very serious about his work. "I think children's books are the most important thing you can do," Pinkwater told Joann Davis in *Publishers Weekly,* "because these are people who are learning about reading." He says that one of his goals as a writer is to celebrate dying cultural treasures such as beer gardens, used bookstores, old railroad cars, and other aspects of urban life. In addition, Pinkwater doesn't hesitate to mention the names of authors and artists in his works, hoping to encourage young readers to learn more about those people. Though teaching isn't the main focus of his books, Pinkwater says that "it *is* an intention of my books to present the sheer pleasure of the phenomena of civilized life."

Pinkwater told *SATA:* "I also believe it is impossible to make sense of life in this world except through art. That's always been so, but it's more true now than ever before. The only way we can deal with the proliferation of ideas and impetus is to make a story or a picture out of it. At present, there are things happening that I like, as well as things I don't like; by participating I'm able to put some weight on the side of the things I like."

WORKS CITED:

Alberghene, Janice M., essay in *Twentieth-Century Children's Writers,* 3rd edition, St. James Press, 1989, pp. 781-782.
Andrews, Peter, review of *Slaves of Spiegel, The Snarkout Boys and the Avocado of Death,* and *Young Adult Novel, New York Times Book Review,* April 25, 1982, p. 51.
Cech, John, review of *Yobgorgle: Mystery Monster of Lake Ontario, Children's Book Review Service,* winter, 1980, pp. 68-69.
Davis, Joann, "Spring Is a Season of Plenty for Children's Author Daniel Pinkwater," *Publishers Weekly,* May 7, 1982, pp. 53-54.
Pinkwater, Daniel M., interview in *Something about the Author,* Volume 46, Gale, 1987, pp. 178-191.

FOR MORE INFORMATION SEE:

BOOKS

Children's Literature Review, Volume 4, Gale, 1982.
Landsberg, Michele, *Reading for the Love of It,* Prentice-Hall, 1987.
Marquardt, Dorothy A., and Martha E. Ward, *Authors of Books for Young People,* supplement to the 2nd edition, Scarecrow, 1975.
Something about the Author Autobiography Series, volume 3, Gale, 1987.

PERIODICALS

Booklist, April 1, 1974; June 1, 1979; April 1, 1982.
Christian Science Monitor, May 1, 1974; May 4, 1977.
Graphis 155, Volume 27, 1971-72.
Horn Book, April, 1977; August, 1977; April, 1983; September-October, 1984; May-June, 1986.
New York Times Book Review, April 29, 1979; February 24, 1980.
People, December 21, 1981.
Publishers Weekly, June 9, 1975; July 18, 1977; August 1, 1977; September 12, 1977; February 27, 1978; October 17, 1980; April 3, 1981; May 7, 1982; June 27, 1986.
Science Books and Films, September, 1978.
Science Fiction and Fantasy Book Review, July-August, 1982.
Voice of Youth Advocates, June, 1982; August, 1982; August, 1984.
Washington Post Book World, November 5, 1972; June 10, 1984.
Wilson Library Bulletin, March, 1982.

PINKWATER, Manus
See PINKWATER, Daniel Manus

* * *

PIPER, Watty
[Collective pseudonym]

AWARDS, HONORS: Lewis Carroll Shelf Award for *The Little Engine That Could.*

WRITINGS:

Children's Hour with the Birds, Platt & Munk, 1922.
The Rooster, the Mouse, and the Little Red Hen, illustrated by Eulalie (pseudonym for Eulalie M. Banks), Platt & Munk, 1928.
Little Folks of Other Lands, illustrated by Lucille W. Holling and H. C. Holling, Platt & Munk, 1929.
Children of Other Lands, illustrated by L. W. Holling and H. C. Holling, Platt & Munk, 1933.
Farm Friends, Platt & Munk, 1938.
All about Story Book, illustrated by Symeon Shimin, Platt & Munk, 1970.
Watty Piper's Trucks, illustrated by Ann Cummings, Platt & Munk, 1978.

EDITOR

The Gateway to Storyland, illustrated by Eulalie, Platt & Munk, 1925.
Fairy Tales That Never Grow Old, Platt & Munk, 1927.
The Ginger Bread Boy and Other Stories, illustrated by Eulalie, Platt & Munk, 1927.
Mother Goose Rhymes and Nursery Tales, Platt & Munk, 1927.
Stories Children Love, Platt & Munk, 1927.
Animal Friends Story Book, illustrated by P. J. Bayzand, Clara M. Burd, and Hugh Spencer, Platt & Munk, 1928.
Famous Fairy Tales, Platt & Munk, 1928.
Farm Friends Story Book, Platt & Munk, 1928.
The Brimful Book: A Collection of Mother Goose Rhymes, Animal Stories, A.B.C., illustrated by Eulalie, Burd, and W. Gurney, Platt & Munk, 1929.
Mabel Caroline Bragg, *The Little Engine That Could,* illustrated by Lois L. Lenski, Platt & Munk, 1930.
Tick-tock Tales, illustrated by Eulalie and Lenski, Platt & Munk, 1931.
Fairy Tales Children Love, illustrated by Eulalie and Lenski, Platt & Munk, 1932.
Jolly Rhymes of Mother Goose, illustrated by Lenski, Platt & Munk, 1932.
Mother Goose Rhymes, Platt & Munk, 1932.
The Road in Storyland, illustrated by L. W. Holling and H. C. Holling, Platt & Munk, 1932.
Famous Rhymes: Mother Goose, Platt & Munk, 1933.
Little Reader's Library, Platt & Munk, 1933.
Nursery Tales Children Love, illustrated by Eulalie, Platt & Munk, 1933.
Stories Children Love, Platt & Munk, 1933.
Children's Heart Delight Stories, Platt & Munk, 1934.
Favorite Nursery Tales, illustrated by Eulalie, Platt & Munk, 1934.

From *The Little Engine That Could,* by Watty Piper. Illustrated by George and Doris Hauman.

Folk Tales Children Love, Platt & Munk, 1934.

My Indian Library, Platt & Munk, 1935.

Kate Cox Goddard, *Eight Fairy Tales,* Platt & Munk, 1938.

Goddard, *Eight Nursery Tales,* Platt & Munk, 1938.

Stories That Never Grow Old, illustrated by George Hauman and Doris Hauman, Platt & Munk, 1938.

Tales from Storyland, illustrated by G. Hauman and D. Hauman, Platt & Munk, 1938.

Carlo Collodi (pseudonym for Carlo Lorenzini), *Pinocchio,* illustrated by Tony Sarg, Platt & Munk, 1940.

My Picture Story Book: A Collection of Objects, Mother Goose Rhymes, Animal Stories, illustrated by Eulalie, Victor G. Becker, and Arthur O. Scott, Platt & Munk, 1941.

Tales from Storyland, illustrated by G. Hauman and D. Hauman, Platt & Munk, 1941.

The Three Little Pigs, illustrated by Eulalie, Platt & Munk, 1945.

The Bumper Book: A Collection of Stories and Verses for Children, illustrated by Eulalie, Platt & Munk, 1946.

Animal Story Book, illustrated by Wesley Dennis, Platt & Munk, 1954.

Mother Goose: A Treasury of Best Loved Rhymes, illustrated by Tim Hildebrandt and Greg Hildebrandt, Platt & Munk, 1972.

Helen Bannerman, *Little Black Sambo,* Platt & Munk, 1972.

ADAPTATIONS: *The Little Engine That Could* was made into a filmstrip by Society for Visual Education, 1953, with a revised version, including seven-minute recording, produced in 1966; a motion picture of *The Little Engine That Could* was produced by Coronet Instructional Films, 1966; a book and audio cassette version entitled *The Easy-to-Read Little Engine That Could* was adapted by Walter Retan, Putnam, 1986.

SIDELIGHTS: Watty Piper is a house pseudonym used for children's books published by the Platt & Munk company of New York City. Some of the books are original works, but most are retellings of traditional folktales and nursery rhymes, with Piper listed as the "editor." None of the real names of the people who wrote the Piper books are known today because in 1978, when Platt & Munk became a division of the Grosset & Dunlap publishing house and moved from the Bronx to Manhattan, the records of the children's division were lost or thrown away. The books were probably written by the editors of the children's book division or by authors hired for the purpose.

The best-known Piper book is *The Little Engine That Could,* first published in 1930 and reprinted many times since. The story of the heroic little blue switch engine who, when the big red engine breaks down, pulls a trainload of toys and food over a mountain for children on the other side—puffing "I think I can, I think I can, I think I can" on the way up and "I thought I could, I thought I could, I thought I could" on the way down—was adapted from a story called "The Pony Engine" by Mabel Caroline Bragg. "The Pony Engine" was originally published in the September, 1910, issue of *Kindergarten Review,* but it may have been based on a folktale. "Some . . . remember having heard the story as early as the 1880s, suggesting the possibility that its origins lie in oral folk tradition," according to *Dictionary of Literary Biography* contributor Priscilla A. Ord.

The first edition of *The Little Engine That Could* was illustrated by Lois L. Lenski, who also drew the pictures for several other Piper books. The 1954 edition was illustrated by George and Doris Hauman, who were also frequent illustrators of Piper books. In 1959 that edition was one of sixteen books that received the first Lewis Carroll Shelf Award, for books that are "worthy to sit on a shelf with *Alice in Wonderland.*"

The message of *The Little Engine That Could* is that one can accomplish great tasks with perseverance and self-confidence. Some reviewers, such as *Children's Literature* critic Ruth B. Moynahan, have pointed out that, when explaining its popularity, one should consider that the book was published during the Great Depression. *The Little Engine That Could,* Ord quoted Moynahan, "reflects the official optimism with which most of the nation entered the depression . . . . As [President] Hoover told the nation at that time, it was the willingness of all the little people to make temporary sacrifices and work a little harder which would soon solve the problems of the depression." President Franklin Delano Roosevelt also tried to convince the public of this philosophy, which was—history has proven—completely wrong. The depression did not end until the United States entered World War II.

Other stories retold by Piper are Carlo Collodi's *Pinocchio* and Helen Bannerman's *Little Black Sambo.* Most of the Piper books are anthologies instead of single stories; they contain fairy tales by the Brothers Grimm and Hans Christian Andersen, Mother Goose rhymes, Aesop's fables, English folktales such as "Jack and the Beanstalk," and similar works. There are also retellings of such stories as James M. Barrie's *Peter Pan,* Beatrix Potter's *The Tale of Peter Rabbit,* and Robert Browning's *The Pied Piper of Hamelin,* all rewritten to appeal to young children. Authors whose poems have been included in the Piper books include Robert Louis Stevenson, Edward Lear, and A. A. Milne. Most of the books for which Piper is listed as the author, rather than the editor or "reteller," are nonfictional works designed to give children information about such subjects as animals, children in foreign lands, and, in the case of *Watty Piper's Trucks,* various kinds of trucks and what they are used for.

"Scrutiny discloses that books with the same or similar titles include many, but not all, of the same rhymes, verses, tales, or stories, and many of the same works, most in the public domain, have been used and reused in successive volumes since the early 1920s," observed Ord. Furthermore, the Piper books also often reuse illustrations published in earlier books. While this might seem to be a less-than-honest practice by the publisher, Ord argued that there are benefits to this approach in that it has allowed Platt & Munk to provide "attractive, well-illustrated, popular books at modest to moderate cost, well within the economic reach of most adults with 'read-me-a-story' audiences."

WORKS CITED:

Ord, Priscilla A., "Watty Piper," *Dictionary of Literary Biography,* Volume 22: *American Writers for Children, 1900-1960,* Gale, 1983, pp. 276-281.

FOR MORE INFORMATION SEE:

BOOKS

Shaw, John Mackay, *Childhood in Poetry,* Gale, 1967.
Shaw, John Mackay, *Childhood in Poetry: Second Supplement,* Gale, 1976.

* * *

POLDER, Markus
See KRUESS, James

* * *

POLITI, Leo 1908-

PERSONAL: Born November 21, 1908, in Fresno, CA; married Helen Fontes; children; Paul, Suzanne. *Education:* Studied at National Art Institute, Monza, Italy, for six years.

ADDRESSES: Home—Los Angeles, CA *Office*—c/o Macmillan Publishing Co., Inc., 866 Third Ave., New York, NY 10022.

CAREER: Artist; author and illustrator of children's books. Worked as an artist for *Script,* Los Angeles, CA.

AWARDS, HONORS: Caldecott Honor Book, 1947, for *Pedro, the Angel of Olvera Street,* and 1949, for *Juanita;* New York *Herald Tribune* Spring Book Festival Honor Award, 1948, for *Juanita,* and 1949, for *At the Palace Gates;* Caldecott Medal from American Library Association for best illustrated book of the year, 1950, for *Song of the Swallows; New York Herald Tribune* Spring Book Festival Award for picture books, 1952, for *Looking-for-Something;* Southern California Council on Literature for Children and Young People Award for significant contribution to children's literature in the field of illustration, 1961, for *Moy Moy;* Regina Medal of Catholic Library Association for "continued distinguished contribution to children's literature," 1966; Friends of Children and Literature Award, 1980, for "excellence in children's literature with a California theme."

WRITINGS:

SELF-ILLUSTRATED; FOR CHILDREN

Little Pancho, Viking, 1938.
Pedro, the Angel of Olvera Street (ALA Notable Book), Scribner, 1946.
Young Giotto, Horn, 1947.
Juanita, Scribner, 1948.
Song of the Swallows (Junior Literary Guild Selection), Scribner, 1949, new edition, Atheneum, 1981.
Little Leo (Junior Literary Guild selection), Scribner, 1951.
The Mission Bell (ALA Notable Book), Scribner, 1953.
The Butterflies Come, Scribner, 1957.
Saint Francis and the Animals, Scribner, 1959.
A Boat for Peppe, Scribner, 1960.
Moy Moy, Scribner, 1960.
All Things Bright and Beautiful, Scribner, 1962.
Lito and the Clown, Scribner, 1962.
Rosa, Scribner, 1963.

Leo Politi

Piccolo's Prank, Scribner, 1965.
Mieko, Golden Gate, 1969.
Emmet, Scribner, 1971.
The Nicest Gift, Scribner, 1973.
Three Stalks of Corn, Scribner, 1976.
Mr. Fong's Toy Shop, Scribner, 1978.

Contributor to *Expectations 1980* (braille anthology), published by Braille Institute Press.

SELF-ILLUSTRATED; FOR ADULTS

Bunker Hill, Los Angeles: Reminiscences of Bygone Days (adult), Desert-Southwest, 1964.
Tales of the Los Angeles Parks (adult), Best-West, 1966.
The Poinsettia (adult), Best-West, 1967.

ILLUSTRATOR

Ruth Sawyer, *The Least One,* Viking, 1941.
Margarita Lopez, *Aqui se Habla Espanol,* Heath, 1942.
Helen Garrett, *Angelo, the Naughty One,* Viking, 1944.
Frank Henius, editor, *Stories from the Americas,* Scribner, 1944.
Catherine Blanton, *The Three Miracles,* Day, 1946.
Louis Perez, *El Coyote, the Rebel,* Holt, 1947.
Helen Rand Parish, *At the Palace Gates,* Viking, 1949.
M. Lopez de Mestos and Esther Brown, *Vamos a Habla Espanol,* Heath, 1949.
Ann Nolan Clark, *Magic Money* (ALA Notable Book), Viking, 1950.
A. N. Clark, *Looking-for-Something: The Story of a Stray Burro in Ecuador* (Junior Literary Guild selection), Viking, 1952.
Alice Dalgliesh, *The Columbus Story* (ALA Notable Book), Scribner, 1955.
Elizabeth Coatsworth, *The Noble Doll,* Viking, 1961.
Edith Parker-Hinckley, *Two Girls and a Kite,* Moore Historical Foundation, 1984.
Dolores S. Lisica, editor, *Around the World, Around Our Town: Recipes From San Pedro,* R. & E. Miles, 1986.

Also contributor of numerous illustrations to children's magazines.

ADAPTATIONS: Song of the Swallows (filmstrip with record or cassette; cassette with book and teacher's guide), Miller-Brody.

SIDELIGHTS: Leo Politi has been an author and illustrator of children's books since the late 1930s. He is best known for his works that depict life in the historic old Spanish section of Los Angeles surrounding Olvera Street; he is credited with preserving the area's culture for children of all backgrounds to enjoy. Politi has also written and illustrated books about the same area for adults, as well as illustrating children's picture books by other authors, such as Helen Garrett and A. N. Clark. He has garnered several awards for his work, including the prestigious Caldecott Medal in 1950 for *Song of the Swallows.*

Politi was born November 21, 1908, in Fresno, California. When he was a young child, his father bought and

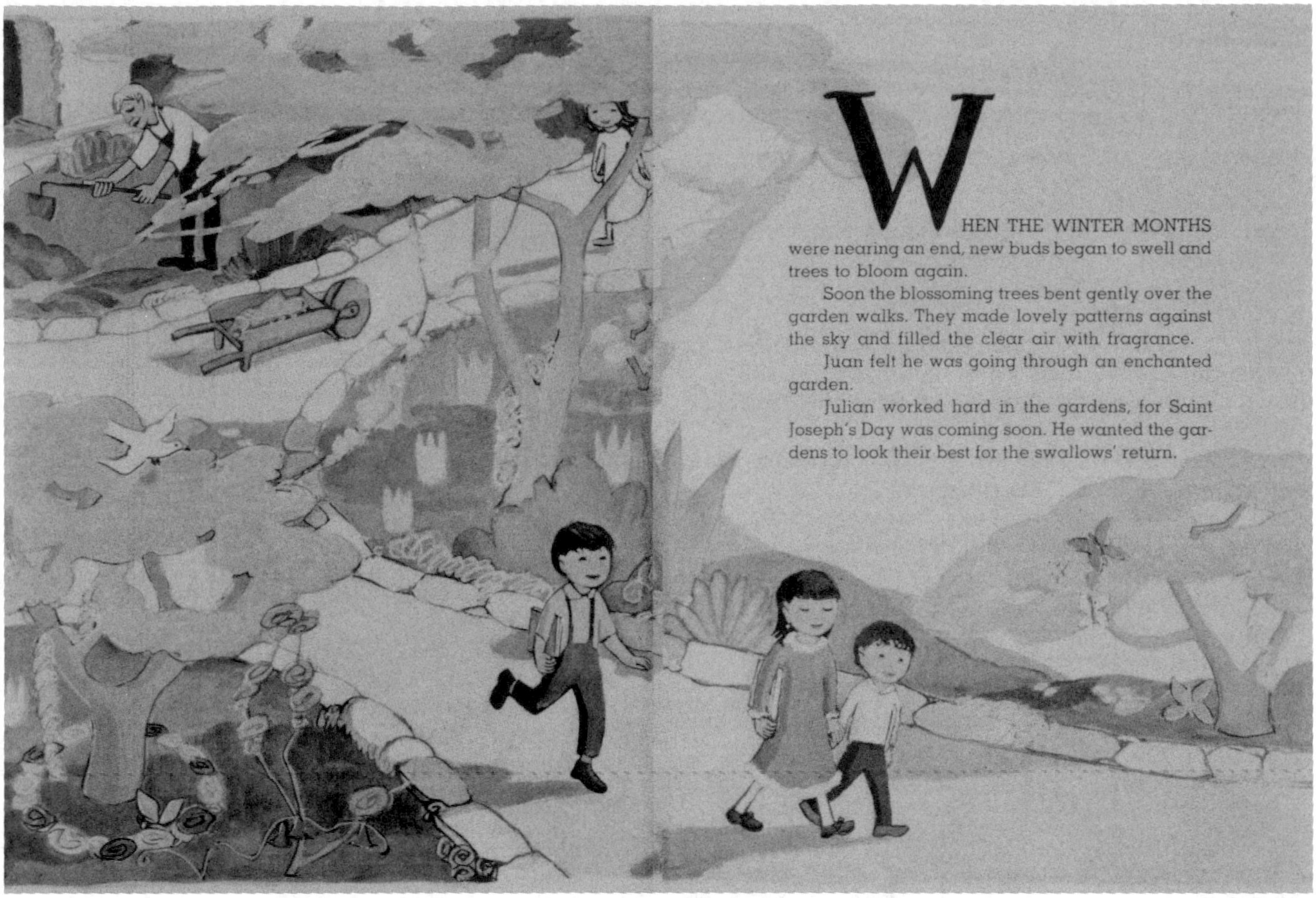

From *Song of the Swallows,* written and illustrated by Leo Politi.

sold horses for a living, and he and his sister often got to ride the ponies before they were purchased. But when Politi was seven years old, his family returned to his mother's hometown in Italy, where, for the most part, he spent the rest of his youth and adolesence. He liked to draw from an early age, and as Rosemary Livsey reported in her article for *Horn Book,* in Italy "he spent happy days playing, studying and drawing everything that he saw, on scraps of paper, in his books, wherever he could find space." Politi and his family also spent a year in London, England, where, as Livsey revealed, he "went often to St. Martin's Lane to watch the artists draw on the sidewalks." Politi told Livsey that he was deeply impressed by "the deftness of their lines and the speed with which the colored chalk pictures appeared on the pavements."

After the Politi family returned to Italy, Politi's mother, convinced of her son's talent, encouraged him to enter a scholarship competition. He won a place at the National Art Institute at Monza, near Milan, Italy. He studied there for six years, at a place Livsey described as "a beautiful old building set in a great park with gardens, trees and even a zoo." She further reported that "much of the students' time was spent out of doors sketching animals, flowers and the countryside." In addition to sketching, Politi also studied architecture, design, and sculpture.

When Politi left the National Art Institute at the age of twenty-one, he was qualified to be an art teacher, but he chose instead to begin creating on his own. With a friend he experimented with textile and tapestry design; he also did his first book illustrations. Politi told Livsey: "It was not my job, but my friend was too busy, so, instead of him, I did the pictures for a textbook to be used in schools for deaf and dumb children. It was a government book. It did not bear my name, nor did I ever see it in print."

Politi eventually returned to California by ship. His path took him through the Panama Canal, and he fell in love with the Latin American countries he visited along the way. As Livsey put it, "the gentleness and beauty of the Latin Americans filled him with a desire to learn more of these people for whom he felt great admiration and kinship." Thus, after Politi married his wife, Helen Fontes, they settled in the Hispanic section of Los Angeles, on Olvera Street. There, he was captivated by the lifestyle of the Mexican immigrants who surrounded him. He attempted to make a living through his artwork; Politi recalled in his book for adults, *Bunker Hill, Los Angeles: Reminiscences of Bygone Days:* "It was during the depression, and many a night my wife sat patiently at my side as I did water colors in front of the El Paseo Cafe. I might sketch the woman making tortillas in the puesto across from us, or the three Mexican musicians singing near us, or the little urchins running up and down the street. Sometimes, with just a knife, I carved on discarded blocks of wood I found. And many a cold night we waited for customers who never came."

Times got better when Politi began doing illustrations for the magazine *Script.* He also published his first children's book, *Little Pancho,* in 1938. He recalled for Livsey: "That Pancho, he was very bad. I had always drawn him for fun, and one night I started to draw him running and he ran all over the page and right into his own story. In one night I had completed the idea." Eventually Politi's work came to the attention of editor Alice Dalgliesh at Scribner's, and he began first illustrating the works of other children's authors, then creating his famous California stories for children.

The first of these was *Pedro, the Angel of Olvera Street.* In this book, Politi told the story of a little boy who sang like an angel and was chosen to lead the neighborhood's customary holiday procession, *la Posada*—a reenactment of Joseph and Mary's search for shelter in Bethlehem on the night of Christ's birth. Politi also chronicled another Olvera Street custom, the pre-Easter blessing of the animals, in his children's book *Juanita.* He explored the annual return of the swallows to the mission at San Juan Capistrano in *Song of the Swallows.* Though Politi most often chronicled the adventures of Mexican-American children, he also wrote about children of other ethnic groups, perhaps most notably in his 1960 book set in Los Angeles' Chinatown, *Moy Moy.*

Politi also met with success writing and illustrating books for adults during the 1960s, including *Bunker Hill, Los Angeles* and *Tales of the Los Angeles Parks.* His later work includes illustrating children's author Edith Parker-Hinckley's *Two Girls and a Kite,* and providing pictures for an adult cookbook edited by Dolores S. Lisica, *Around the World, Around Our Town.*

WORKS CITED:

Livsey, Rosemary, "Leo Politi, Friend of All," *Horn Book,* March/April, 1949, pp. 97-108.

Politi, Leo, *Bunker Hill, Los Angeles: Reminiscences of Bygone Days,* Desert-Southwest, 1964.

FOR MORE INFORMATION SEE:

PERIODICALS

Horn Book, July/August, 1950; April, 1966.

* * *

POLLAND, Madeleine A(ngela Cahill) 1918- (Frances Adrian)

PERSONAL: Born May 31, 1918, in Kinsale, County Cork, Ireland; daughter of Patrick Richard (a civil servant) and Christina (Culkin) Cahill; married Arthur Joseph Polland (an accountant), June 10, 1946 (died, October, 1987); children: Charlotte Frances, Fergus Adrian. *Politics:* Conservative. *Religion:* Roman Catholic. *Hobbies and other interests:* Lawn bowls, travel, museums, art.

ADDRESSES: Home—Edificio Hercules 406, Avenida Gamonal, Arroyo de la Miel, Malaga, Spain.

CAREER: Letchworth Public Library, Letchworth, England, assistant librarian, 1938-42; writer, 1958—. Guest speaker, New York Public Library Children's Book Fair, 1968. *Military service:* Women's Auxiliary Air Force, ground-controlled interception division of radar, 1942-45.

AWARDS, HONORS: New York Herald Tribune Honor Book, 1961, for *Children of the Red King,* and 1962, for *Beorn the Proud.*

WRITINGS:

JUVENILE NOVELS

Children of the Red King, Constable, 1960, Holt, 1961.
The Town across the Water, Constable, 1961, Holt, 1963.
Beorn the Proud, Constable, 1961, Holt, 1962.
Fingal's Quest, Doubleday, 1961.
The White Twilight, Constable, 1962, Holt, 1965.
Chuiraquimba and the Black Robes, Doubleday, 1962.
The City of the Golden House, Doubleday, 1963.
The Queen's Blessing, Constable, 1963, Holt, 1964.
Flame Over Tara, Doubleday, 1964.

Madeleine A. Polland

From *The Queen's Blessing,* by Madeleine Polland. Illustrated by Betty Fraser.

Mission to Cathay, Doubleday, 1965.
Queen without Crown, Constable, 1965, Holt, 1966.
Deirdre, Doubleday, 1967.
To Tell My People, Hutchinson, 1968.
Stranger in the Hills, Doubleday, 1968.
Alhambra, Doubleday, 1970.
To Kill a King, Holt, 1971.
A Family Affair, Hutchinson, 1971.
Daughter of the Sea, Doubleday, 1972, published in England as *Daughter to Poseidon,* Hutchinson, 1972.
Prince of the Double Axe, Abelard-Schuman, 1976.

ADULT NOVELS

Thicker Than Water, Holt, 1966.
Minutes of a Murder, Holt, 1967, published in England as *The Little Spot of Bother,* Hutchinson, 1967.
Random Army, Hutchinson, 1969, published as *Shattered Summer,* Doubleday, 1970.
Package to Spain, Walker, 1971.
(Under pseudonym Frances Adrian) *Double Shadow,* Fawcett, 1978.
All Their Kingdoms, Delacorte, 1981.
The Heart Speaks Many Ways, Delacorte, 1982.
No Price Too High, Delacorte, 1984.
As It Was in the Beginning, Piatkus, 1987.

SIDELIGHTS: Madeleine A. Polland writes novels based on events and people in European, especially Irish, history. "My sense of history," she explains in her article for the *Something About the Author Autobiography Series* (*SAAS*), "has always been an important aspect of my writing: my consciousness of the feet that have walked before mine, and the fact that no matter how early the period, all those concerned were still *people.* Like ourselves."

To make her historical novels as realistic as possible, Polland has often visited the actual places she writes about, and walked the paths the historical people of her stories walked. Except for two stories set in China and Paraguay, she writes in her *SAAS* article, "I had the pleasure of walking through the settings for myself, in Ireland, Scotland, Denmark, England, and Spain, always in the company of some, if not all, of my family."

Polland has claimed that on several occasions she has felt odd sensations when visiting an historical site, sensations which gave her a brief vision of earlier times. Writing in *Horn Book,* she tells of visiting St. Albans in southern England and suddenly feeling afraid: "I was shivering with a dreadful terror that was certainly not my own, nor could I gain any peace until I left the spot and gone away." Only later did she discover that the early Roman invaders had passed through that part of England and the fear she felt was akin to the fear that the early natives must have felt on confronting the Roman soldiers. In *To Tell My People* Polland writes of that time, and she has her character Lumna feel "the onslaught of terror at the first manifestations of a civilization she had never dreamed of. The same terror that I myself knew in the same spot."

Sometimes Polland draws on her own experience to create her fiction. As a little girl, she remembers the Irish civil war and the turmoil of that period, especially the time when her home town was burned to the ground. In *City of the Golden House,* a story set in ancient Rome, Polland drew on her memories to write of the burning of Rome. She explains in *Horn Book:* "I needed to recreate all the horror and terror of the fire of Rome during the reign of Emperor Nero.... I knew quite clearly that although I was writing of the fire of Rome, it was the burning of [my home town of] Kinsale which I recounted: a haunting from my childhood."

Polland's insistence that people of times long past are essentially the same as the people of today has allowed her to create realistic characters in all of her historical fiction. The realism of her characters adds to the realism of her settings as well. A reviewer for *Horn Book* finds that in *The White Twilight* Polland "has told an absorbing story with an unusual historical setting and individual, well-realized characters. The beautiful writing and the strong feeling of place make the story rich and rewarding." A reviewer for *Junior Bookshelf* praises the realistic emotions of *Prince of the Double Axe:* "Death is shown as a kindly end to old age and suffering, fear as natural as loyalty and courage. Altogether, a sensitive and well-told story."

Since the late 1960s, Polland has lived on the Mediterranean coast of Spain, where she and her late husband retired. Speaking of her adopted country in her *SAAS* article, Polland writes: "They say of this coast that if you want to, on Christmas Day you can swim in the morning in the sea, ski through the afternoon in the mountains, and still be home for your Christmas dinner. A lovely life."

WORKS CITED:

Polland, Madeleine A., "On the Writing of Ghost Stories," *Horn Book,* April, 1968, pp. 147-150.

Review of *Prince of the Double Axe, Junior Bookshelf,* February, 1977.

Polland, Madeleine A., Autobiographical essay, *Something About the Author Autobiography Series,* Volume 8, Gale, 1989, pp. 227-242.

Review of *The White Twilight, Horn Book,* June, 1965.

FOR MORE INFORMATION SEE:

BOOKS

de Montreville, Dorris, and Donna Hill, editors, *Third Book of Junior Authors,* H. W. Wilson, 1972.

PERIODICALS

Best Sellers, March 15, 1971; April, 1979; October, 1982.

Books and Bookmen, January, 1973.

British Book News, April, 1987; May, 1987.

Bulletin of the Center for Children's Books, October, 1973.

Christian Science Monitor, November 12, 1970.

Commonweal, May 21, 1971.

Horn Book, June, 1966; August, 1967; October, 1968; October, 1970; December, 1970; June, 1971.

Library Journal, October 15, 1970.

New York Times Book Review, May 9, 1965; July 18, 1965; July 9, 1967; October 27, 1968; February 6, 1972.

Publishers Weekly, February, 1973.

Punch, April 12, 1967.

Saturday Review, July 17, 1965; July 24, 1965.

Spectator, December 5, 1970.

Times Literary Supplement, May 25, 1967; July 27, 1967; November 30, 1967; October 3, 1968; June 26, 1969; October 30, 1970; April 2, 1971; May 14, 1971; December 8, 1972.

* * *

POLLOCK, Mary
See BLYTON, Enid (Mary)

Beatrix Potter

POTTER, (Helen) Beatrix 1866-1943

PERSONAL: Born July 28 (some sources say July 6), 1866, in Bolton Gardens, Kensington, England; died December 22, 1943, in Sawrey, England; daughter of Rupert (a non-practicing barrister and an amateur photographer) and Helen Leech Potter; married William Heelis (a lawyer), 1913. *Education:* Tutored at home by governesses; primarily a self-taught artist except for a brief period of private lessons.

ADDRESSES: Home—Castle Farm, Sawrey, England. (Now a public memorial.)

CAREER: Author and illustrator of books for children. Also worked as a farmer of Herdwick sheep in the Lake District following her marriage; became first woman president of the Herdwick Sheepbreeder's Association, 1930. Was an active conservationist (willed her land to the National Trust for preservation following her death).

WRITINGS:

SELF-ILLUSTRATED CHILDREN'S BOOKS

The Tale of Peter Rabbit, privately printed, 1901, Warne, 1902.

The Tailor of Gloucester, privately printed, 1902, Warne, 1903.

The Tale of Squirrel Nutkin, Warne, 1903.

The Tale of Benjamin Bunny, Warne, 1904.

The Tale of Two Bad Mice, Warne, 1904.

The Tale of Mrs. Tiggy-Winkle, Warne, 1905.

The Pie and the Patty-Pan, Warne, 1905, reprinted as *The Tale of the Pie and the Patty-Pan,* Warne, 1964.
The Tale of Mr. Jeremy Fisher, Warne, 1906.
The Story of a Fierce Bad Rabbit, Warne, 1906.
The Story of Miss Moppet, Warne, 1906.
The Tale of Tom Kitten, Warne, 1907.
The Tale of Jemima Puddle-Duck, Warne, 1908.
The Roly-Poly Pudding, Warne, 1908, reprinted as *The Tale of Samuel Whiskers; or, The Roly-Poly Pudding,* Warne, 1926.
The Tale of the Flopsy Bunnies, Warne, 1909.
Ginger and Pickles, Warne, 1909.
The Tale of Mrs. Tittlemouse, Warne, 1910.
Peter Rabbit's Painting Book, Warne, 1911.
The Tale of Timmy Tiptoes, Warne, 1911.
The Tale of Mr. Tod, Warne, 1912.
The Tale of Pigling Bland, Warne, 1913.
Tom Kitten's Painting Book, Warne, 1917.
The Tale of Johnny Town-Mouse, Warne, 1918.
Jemima Puddle-Duck's Painting Book, Warne, 1925.
Peter Rabbit's Almanac for 1929, Warne, 1928.
The Fairy Caravan, privately printed, 1929, McKay, 1929.
The Tale of Little Pig Robinson, McKay, 1930.
Wag-by-Wall, Horn Book, 1944.
The Sly Old Cat, Warne, 1971.
Yours Affectionately, Peter Rabbit: Miniature Letters by Beatrix Potter, edited by Anne Emerson, Warne, 1983.

VERSE

Appley Dapply's Nursery Rhymes, Warne, 1917.
Cecily Parsley's Nursery Rhymes, Warne, 1922.
Beatrix Potter's Nursery Rhyme Book, Warne, 1984.

ADULT BOOKS

The Art of Beatrix Potter: Direct Reproductions of Beatrix Potter's Preliminary Studies and Finished Drawings, Also Examples of Her Original Manuscript, edited by Leslie Linder and W. A. Herring, Warne, 1955, revised edition, 1972.
The Journal of Beatrix Potter from 1881 to 1897, transcribed from her code writing by Leslie Linder, Warne, 1966.
Letters to Children, Harvard College Library Department of Printing and Graphic Arts, 1967.
Beatrix Potter's Birthday Book, edited by Enid Linder, Warne, 1974.
Dear Ivy, Dear June: Letters from Beatrix Potter, edited by Margaret Crawford Maloney, Other Press, 1977.
Beatrix Potter's Americans: Selected Letters, edited by Jane Crowell Morse, Horn Book, 1981.

ILLUSTRATOR

Illustrator of F. E. Weatherley's *A Happy Pair,* c. 1893; *Comical Customers,* c. 1894; W. P. K. Findlay's *Wayside and Woodland Fungi,* 1967; Joel Chandler Harris's *Tales of Uncle Remus;* and Lewis Carroll's *Alice in Wonderland.*

OTHER

Sister Anne, illustrated by Katharine Sturges, McKay, 1932.
The Tale of the Faithful Dove, illustrated by Marie Angel, Warne (London), 1955, Warne (New York), 1956.
The Tale of Tuppenny, illustrated by Angel, Warne, 1973.

Collections of Potter's works are housed in the Leslie Linder Bequest at the National Book League, London, and at the Free Library, Philadelphia.

ADAPTATIONS:

FILMSTRIPS

Peter Rabbit, Curriculum Films, 1946, revised version, Curriculum Materials Corp., 1957, other filmstrips by Stillfilm, 1949, Museum Extension Service, 1965, and Educational Projections Corp., 1968.
The Tale of Benjamin Bunny, Weston Woods, 1967.
The Tale of Mr. Jeremy Fisher, Weston Woods, 1967.
The Tale of Peter Rabbit, Weston Woods, 1967.
The Tale of Tom Kitten, Weston Woods, 1967.
The Tale of Two Bad Mice, Weston Woods, 1967.

Other filmstrip adaptations include: *Four Tales of Beatrix Potter* (four filmstrips with cassettes and teacher's guide), United Learning; and *Treasury of Animal Stories, Parts I and II,* (four filmstrips, four records or cassettes), read by Frances Sternhagen, Miller-Brody Productions.

MOVIES

Peter Rabbit and the Tales of Beatrix Potter, Metro-Goldwyn-Mayer, 1971.

VIDEOTAPES

Tales of Beatrix Potter (six stories and eight nursery rhymes), Children's Video Library, 1986.
The Tale of Mr. Jeremy Fisher and The Tale of Peter Rabbit (winner of the Performing Arts Home Video Category in the 1988 American Film and Video Festival), Sony Video Software Company, 1988.

RECORDINGS

The Tale of Peter Rabbit and Other Stories (record), Caedmon, 1970.
The Tale of the Flopsy Bunnies and Five Other Beatrix Potter Stories (record or cassette), read by Claire Bloom, Caedmon, 1973.
The Peter Rabbit Books or The Tales of Beatrix Potter, read by Eleanor Quirk, Warne, c. 1973.
Beatrix Potter Nursery Rhymes and Tales (record or cassette), read by Bloom, Caedmon, 1974.
The Pie and the Patty-Pan, Caedmon, 1974.
The Tailor of Gloucester and Other Stories (record or cassette), read by Bloom, Caedmon, 1974.
The Tale of Little Pig Robinson (record or cassette), read by Bloom, Caedmon, 1974.
The Tale of Squirrel Nutkin and Other Tales (record or cassette), read by Bloom, Caedmon, 1974.
The Sly Old Cat and Other Stories, Caedmon, 1976.
The Tale of the Faithful Dove, Caedmon, 1976.
The Tale of Tuppenny from The Fairy Caravan and Other Stories, Caedmon, 1976.

The World of Animal Stories by Beatrix Potter (four cassettes, forty books; or one cassette, ten books), Spoken Arts, 1976.
Peter Rabbit (cassette and paperback text), Spoken Arts, 1986.
The Tale of Benjamin Bunny (cassette with paperback book), Warner Juvenile Books, 1988.
The Tale of Jemima Puddle-Duck (cassette with paperback book), Warner Juvenile Books, 1988.
The Tale of Mr. Tod and The Tale of Timmy Tiptoes (one cassette), Caedmon, 1988.
The Tale of Peter Rabbit (cassette with paperback book), Warner Juvenile Books, 1988.
The Tale of Tom Kitten (cassette with paperback book), Warner Juvenile Books, 1988.

Other works adapted into recordings include: *Peter Rabbit and His Friends—The Favorite Tales of Beatrix Potter* (record or cassette), read by Elinor Basescu, Miller-Brody Productions; *Peter Rabbit & Tales of Beatrix Potter,* Angel Records; *The Tale of Peter Rabbit* (cassette only), Scholastic; *The Tale of Peter Rabbit and Other Stories* (six cassettes with teacher's guide), read by Bloom, Caedmon; *Treasury of Animal Stories, Volume I,* read by Frances Sternhagen, Spoken Arts; and *Treasury of Animal Stories, Volume II,* read by Sternhagen, Spoken Arts.

TELEVISION

Beatrix Potter: A Private World.

SIDELIGHTS: English author and illustrator Beatrix Potter was a beloved children's storyteller and artist. Her classic, enduring series featuring woodland animals that began with the publication of *The Tale of Peter Rabbit* in 1901 and continued over the next ten years as she produced some twenty self-illustrated "tales" have entertained young and old readers for nearly a century. Her menagerie of little animals, including rabbits, squirrels, hedgehogs, and mice were unique in that the author depicted them as animals possessing animal qualities rather than animals possessing human qualities. Indeed, humans played a small role in Potter's works, primarily because she was unable to draw them as accurately as she drew the animals with which she was so familiar. The series was also significant because Potter used adult language to convey her ideas and because she was not afraid to portray realistic events in her stories. "P[otter]'s stories have a simplicity that is complemented by a sense of realism and of humor," wrote Alan Rauch in the *Encyclopedia of British Women's Writers.* "Her characters, who live in a world that can be both comforting and threatening, learn to appreciate the former by experiencing the latter. The impact of her stories is consistently emphasized by the deft accuracy and subtle playfulness of her artwork." Potter wrote and illustrated a handful of books for children later in life, but the creative burst that dominated her work during the first decade of the twentieth century was not to be equalled.

Potter was born on July 28, 1866, and was raised in Victorian England. The first child of wealthy parents (both Rupert and Helen Potter had inherited fortunes earned in the cotton trade), young Potter wanted for nothing except companionship. Her father was a non-practicing lawyer who was extremely knowledgeable about art; he would later help develop his daughter's interest in the subject by exposing her early and often to gardens and museums. Except for these outings, the Potters kept their daughter secluded in the third-floor nursery of the family home in Bolton Gardens, London, leaving her care and education to nurses and governesses. They allowed Potter to keep small pets including tame rabbits, mice, and a family of snails. From the time she was very small Potter displayed a natural curiosity, innate intelligence, and strong sense of independence that would serve her all her life.

When she was six years old, Potter's younger brother Bertram was born. He provided the friendship she desperately needed and shared her interests in drawing and studying nature and wildlife. The two were scientific in their approach, often bringing home dead creatures to skin in order to reveal the bone structure, once even boiling and dissecting the remains of a fox. The family traditionally summered in the Scottish highlands and in the Lake District of northern England, which allowed Potter and Bertram months of roaming the countryside, carefully observing nature, and honing their skills as budding artists. When he was old enough, Bertram was sent away to boarding school, thus leaving Potter alone again. Because of the prolonged periods of isolation, she grew up very shy and uncomfortable around adults, but always had a natural affinity for children.

From *The Complete Adventures of Peter Rabbit,* written and illustrated by Beatrix Potter.

Between the ages of twelve and seventeen Potter took private art instruction from two different teachers, earning an art student's certificate from the Science and Art Department of the Committee of Council on Education—the only certificate of education she ever received. Other than these brief lessons, she was self-taught. Writing in her journal about her first instructor, a Miss Cameron, Potter observed, "I have great reason to be grateful to her, though we were not on particularly good terms for the last good while. I have learnt from her freehand, model, geometry, perspective and a little water-colour flower painting. Painting is an awkward thing to teach except the details of the medium. If you and your master are determined to look at nature and art in two different directions you are sure to stick."

Potter's journal, kept between the ages of fifteen and thirty, revealed another aspect of her personality; it was written in a secret code or "cypher" writing that took years to break and translate following her death. Written in a script so small that it could not be read without a magnifying glass, Potter religiously recorded her thoughts about everything from politics to family history, thus supplying scholars with information about a period in her life that was otherwise unaccounted for. The fact that Potter felt the need to hide these often bland comments as well as the very existence of the journal is an example of her in-bred solitude. In 1966, on the centenary of Potter's birth, *The Journal of Beatrix Potter* was published.

About the time she was twenty, Potter began drawing hundreds of microscopically-detailed pictures of fungi that she hoped would be used in a textbook. Though encouraged by her uncle, Sir Henry Roscoe, a chemist who was interested in botany, Potter's drawings were not considered publishable because she was an untrained scientist. However, her paper, "The Germination of the Spores of Agaricineae," was presented to the distinguished Linnean Society of London in 1897. Interestingly, her drawings were published posthumously in 1967 in *Wayside and Woodland Fungi.* Potter's first published illustrations were of rabbits and other animals for F. E. Weatherley's *A Happy Pair,* a book of children's verse published around 1893.

It was in an 1893 letter to Noel Moore, the son of one of Potter's former governesses, that *The Tale of Peter Rabbit* was born. She had corresponded with the child—sick with scarlet fever—all summer and began the now famous missive, complete with black-and-white drawings, "I don't know what to write you, so I shall tell you the story about four little rabbits, whose names were Flopsy, Mopsy, Cottontail, and Peter . . . . " Seven years later Potter decided the story would make a good children's book, and, after enlarging it, submitted it to several local publishers, including Frederick Warne & Co., all of whom rejected it. Not easily discouraged, she used her savings to have it privately printed and was pleased that the 250 copies sold swiftly. In 1902 Warne reconsidered and agreed to publish the little book (5 3/4" x 4 1/4" to fit small hands, with facing pages of text and illustration) if Potter would provide colored illustrations, which she did. At age thirty-six, still living with her parents, Potter became a successful children's writer.

During the next ten years Potter wrote and illustrated twenty more books—several of which also had their beginnings in letters to children—at a rate of two per year, including *The Tailor of Gloucester* (also initially privately printed and generally considered her best book), *The Tale of Squirrel Nutkin, The Tale of Mrs. Tiggy-Winkle, The Tale of Jemima Puddle-Duck,* and *The Tale of Mr. Tod.* Potter revised her work endlessly, often making minute changes in the text or drawings of a particular book in between editions. Her signature watercolor illustrations were painted in subtle, muted shades of green, grey, brown, and pastels that perfectly complemented the stories. Potter continued to produce books in this format—though at a slower pace—until 1918, including such favorites as *Appley Dapply's Nursery Rhymes* and *The Tale of Johnny Town-Mouse.* Writing in *Horn Book* in 1941, Bertha Mahony Miller summarized Potter's contribution to children's literature thusly: "These books are genuine classics because they have been written out of an environment known and loved, and to which they are true. They live for children because they are of those things which have given their author and illustrator infinite joy . . . . For nearly forty years Beatrix Potter's little books have been providing youngest children with volumes charming on three counts—story, drawings and style of book."

The proceeds from the sales of her books brought Potter financial independence, enabling her to buy Hill Top Farm and Castle Cottage in Sawrey, England, and, ultimately, several thousand acres of surrounding woodland and farmland. Potter continued to live with her parents (renting her property at very generous terms to caretakers) until the age of forty-seven when she disregarded their wishes and married William Heelis, a solicitor who had been instrumental in acquiring the Hill Top land. Earlier, Potter had been engaged to marry Norman Warne of the Warne publishing family—also against her parents' wishes—but his sudden and tragic death from leukemia prevented the union.

By the time Potter became Mrs. Heelis the focus of her life had changed from writing to farming; she devoted herself to breeding Herdwick sheep and in 1930 became the first woman president of the Herdwick Sheepbreeder's Association—an honor she prized. The few books published in her later years were primarily based on ideas conceived in the early part of her life and were not considered critical successes. *The Fairy Caravan* (1929) is notable in that it is more autobiographical than her previous works, but, wrote Marcus Crouch in *Three Bodley Head Monographs,* "It is nevertheless a sad book, as every work of fading genius must be sad." Indeed, Potter herself recognized its weaknesses and only allowed a limited printing in the United States and England. The last book Potter wrote and illustrated was *The Tale of Little Pig Robinson,* published in 1930. Her *Wag-by-Wall* (1944) was written to satisfy requests for a new book from American friends with whom she regularly corresponded at *Horn Book.* Potter's last published work was *The Tale of the Faithful Dove,* written in 1907, but not published until 1956; it contained illustrations by Marie Angel.

Potter died in 1943 in her home in Sawrey at the age of 77, "... as she had lived, as simply as possible, conscious of what she was doing, without fuss or regret," wrote her biographer, Margaret Lane, in *The Tale of Beatrix Potter.* Her home and property were willed to the National Trust for preservation. The modest little woman spawned a vast marketing empire whose diversity and breadth even she could not have imagined. Many of her books have never been out of print and have been translated into a dozen languages, selling hundreds of thousands of copies worldwide. And a thriving business of related products is still going strong, ranging from cassettes and videotapes to calendars and candies based on her endearing creations. Potter will be remembered for the complex person she was: conservationist, naturalist, scientist, artist. In an article for *Illustrators of Children's Books: 1957-1966,* Rumer Godden wrote of her: "Simplicity, modesty, truth, balance: these are the qualities to be found in Beatrix Potter and, overriding all of them, love."

WORKS CITED:

Crouch, Marcus, "Beatrix Potter," *Three Bodley Head Monographs,* Walck, 1961, revised edition, Bodley Head, 1969, pp. 162-224.

Godden, Rumer, "Beatrix Potter: Centenary of an Artist-Writer," *Illustrators of Children's Books, 1957-1966,* compiled by Lee Kingman, Joanna Foster, and Ruth Giles Lontoft, Horn Book, 1968, pp. 54-64.

Lane, Margaret, *The Tale of Beatrix Potter: A Biography,* Warne, 1946, revised edition, 1968.

Miller, Bertha Mahony, "Beatrix Potter and Her Nursery Classics," *Horn Book,* May-June, 1941, pp. 230-38.

Potter, Beatrix, *The Journal of Beatrix Potter from 1881-1897,* transcribed from her code writing by Leslie Linder, Warne, 1966.

Rauch, Alan, *An Encyclopedia of British Women Writers,* Garland, 1988, pp. 370-71.

FOR MORE INFORMATION SEE:

BOOKS

Aldis, Dorothy, *Nothing Is Impossible: The Story of Beatrix Potter,* Atheneum, 1969.

Bingham, Jane M., editor, *Writers for Children,* Scribner, 1988.

Children's Literature Review, Volume 19, Gale, 1990.

Kunitz, Stanley J., and Howard Haycraft, editors, *Junior Book of Authors,* 2nd edition, H. W. Wilson, 1951.

Linder, Leslie, *A History of the Writings of Beatrix Potter,* Warne, 1971.

Smaridge, Norah, *Famous Author-Illustrators for Young People,* Dodd, 1973.

PERIODICALS

Elementary English, March, 1968.

Horn Book, December, 1946.

Publishers Weekly, July 11, 1966.

* * *

PRELUTSKY, Jack 1940-

PERSONAL: Born September 8, 1940, in Brooklyn, NY; son of Charles (an electrician) and Dorothea (a housewife; maiden name, Weiss) Prelutsky; married wife, Carolynn, 1979. *Education:* Attended Hunter College (now of the City University of New York); has studied voice at several music schools. *Hobbies and other interests:* Making plastic and metal sculptures, bicycling, inventing word games, collecting books and model frogs.

ADDRESSES: Home—Olympia, WA; and c/o Greenwillow Books, 1350 Avenue of the Americas, New York, NY 10019.

CAREER: Poet and singer. Has worked as a cab driver, busboy, actor, photographer, furniture mover, potter, sculptor, day laborer, waiter, carpenter, clerk, bookseller, and door-to-door salesman.

AWARDS, HONORS: Nightmares: Poems to Trouble Your Sleep was selected for the Children's Book Show-

Jack Prelutsky

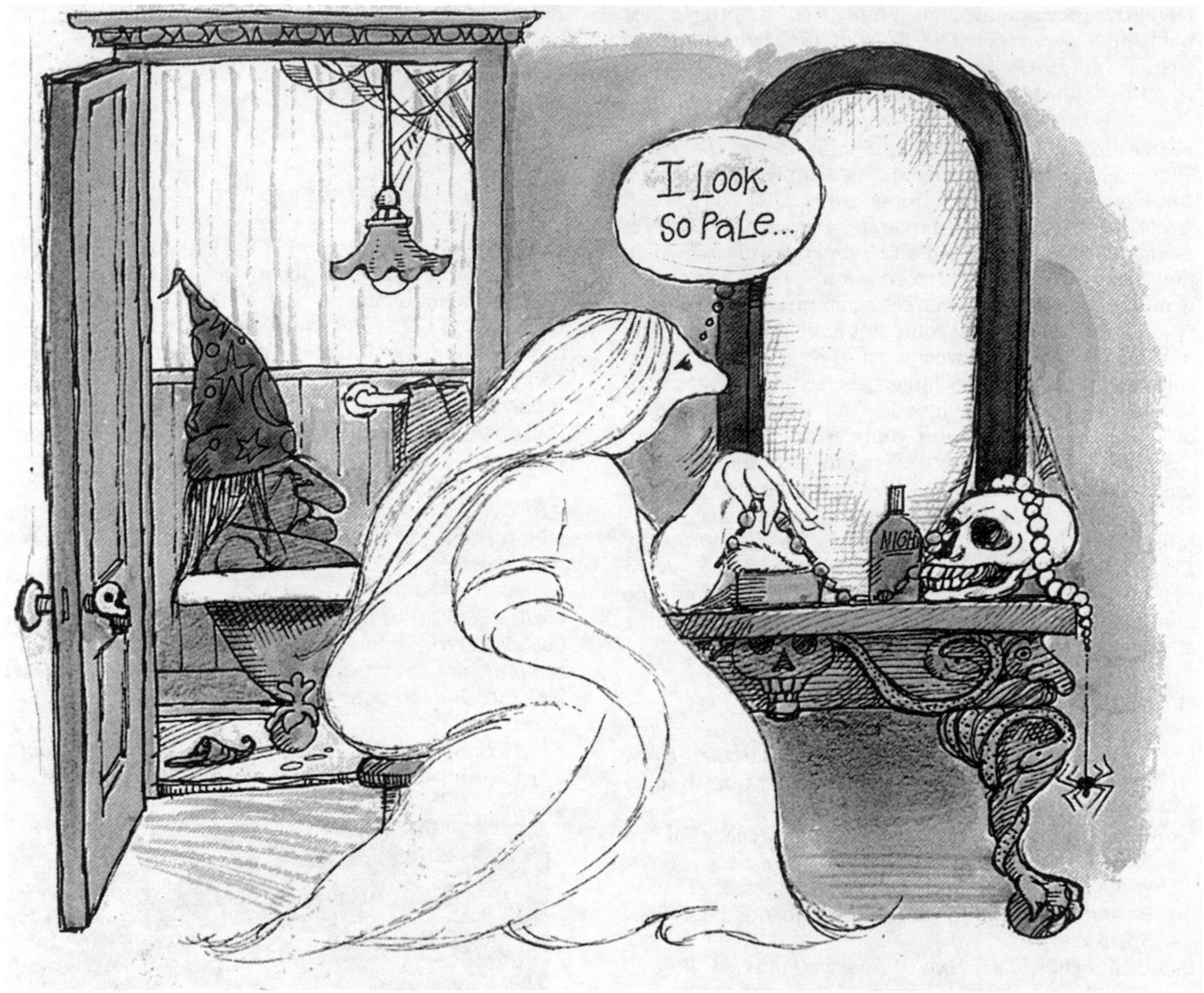

From *It's Halloween,* by Jack Prelutsky. Illustrated by Marylin Hafner.

case of the Children's Book Council, and was included in the American Institute of Graphic Arts Book Show, both 1977, and one of *School Library Journal*'s Best of the Best Books, 1979; Children's Choice, International Reading Association/Children's Book Council, 1978, for *The Mean Old Mean Hyena; The Headless Horseman Rides Tonight: More Poems to Trouble Your Sleep* was selected one of the *New York Times*'s Outstanding Books of the Year and one of the Best Illustrated Books of the Year, both 1980; *School Library Journal*'s Best Books selections, 1980, for *The Headless Horseman Rides Tonight,* 1981, for *The Wild Baby,* 1983, for *The Random House Book of Poetry for Children* and *The Wild Baby Goes to Sea,* and 1986, for *Read-Aloud Rhymes for the Very Young; Booklist* Children's Reviewers' Choice, 1980, for *The Headless Horseman Rides Tonight; The Random House Book of Poetry for Children* was a Child Study Association Children's Book of the Year and Library of Congress Book of the Year, 1983; Parents' Choice Award, Parents' Choice Foundation, and Garden State Children's Book Award, New Jersey Library Association, both 1986, both for *The New Kid on the Block;* Notable Children's Recording, American Library Association, 1987, for "The New Kid on the Block"; *Something Big Has Been Here* was an Association for Library Services to Children Notable Book and *Booklist* Editor's Choice, both 1990.

WRITINGS:

(Translator) Rudolf Neumann, *The Bad Bear,* illustrated by Eva Johanna Rubin, Macmillan, 1967.
(Translator) Heinrich Hoffman, *The Mountain Bounder,* Macmillan, 1967.
A Gopher in the Garden and Other Animal Poems (also see below), illustrated by Robert Leydenfrost, Macmillan, 1967.
(Translator) *No End of Nonsense: Humorous Verses,* illustrated by Wilfried Blecher, Macmillan, 1968.
Lazy Blackbird and Other Verses, illustrated by Janosch, Macmillan, 1969.
(Translator) *Three Saxon Nobles and Other Verses,* illustrated by Eva Johanna Rubin, Macmillan, 1969.

(Translator) James Kruess, *The Proud Wooden Drummer,* illustrated by Rubin, Doubleday, 1969.

The Terrible Tiger, illustrated by Arnold Lobel, Macmillan, 1970.

Toucans Two and Other Poems (also see below), illustrated by Jose Aruego, Macmillan, 1970 (published in England as *Zoo Doings and Other Poems,* Hamish Hamilton, 1971).

Circus!, illustrated by Lobel, Macmillan, 1974.

The Pack Rat's Day and Other Poems (also see below), illustrated by Margaret Bloy Graham, Macmillan, 1974.

Nightmares: Poems to Trouble Your Sleep (American Library Association [ALA] Notable Book), illustrated by Lobel, Greenwillow, 1976.

It's Halloween, illustrated by Marylin Hafner, Greenwillow, 1977.

The Snopp on the Sidewalk and Other Poems (ALA Notable Book; also see below), illustrated by Byron Barton, Greenwillow, 1977.

The Mean Old Mean Hyena, illustrated by Lobel, Greenwillow, 1978.

The Queen of Eene (ALA Notable Book; also see below), illustrated by Victoria Chess, Greenwillow, 1978.

Rolling Harvey down the Hill (also see below), illustrated by Chess, Greenwillow, 1980.

The Headless Horseman Rides Tonight: More Poems to Trouble Your Sleep, illustrated by Lobel, Greenwillow, 1980.

Rainy, Rainy Saturday, illustrated by Hafner, Greenwillow, 1980.

(Adapter) Barbro Lindgren, *The Wild Baby,* illustrated by Eva Eriksson, Greenwillow, 1981.

It's Christmas, illustrated by Hafner, Greenwillow, 1981.

The Sheriff of Rottenshot: Poems by Jack Prelutsky, illustrated by Chess, Greenwillow, 1982.

Kermit's Garden of Verses, illustrated by Bruce McNally, Random House, 1982.

It's Thanksgiving, illustrated by Hafner, Greenwillow, 1982.

The Baby Uggs Are Hatching, illustrated by James Stevenson, Greenwillow, 1982.

Zoo Doings: Animal Poems (includes *A Gopher in the Garden and Other Animal Poems, Toucans Two and Other Poems,* and *The Pack Rat's Day and Other Poems*), illustrated by Paul O. Zelinsky, Greenwillow, 1983.

It's Valentine's Day, illustrated by Yossi Abolafia, Greenwillow, 1983.

(Adapter) Lindgren, *The Wild Baby Goes to Sea,* illustrated by Eriksson, Greenwillow, 1983.

(Compiler and editor) *The Random House Book of Poetry for Children* (ALA Notable Book), illustrated by Lobel, Random House, 1983.

It's Snowing! It's Snowing!, illustrated by Jeanne Titherington, Greenwillow, 1984.

What I Did Last Summer, illustrated by Abolafia, Greenwillow, 1984.

The New Kid on the Block (ALA Notable Book), illustrated by Stevenson, Greenwillow, 1984.

My Parents Think I'm Sleeping, illustrated by Abolafia, Greenwillow, 1985.

(Adapter) Lindgren, *The Wild Baby Gets a Puppy,* illustrated by Eriksson, Greenwillow, 1985.

Ride a Purple Pelican, illustrated by Garth Williams, Greenwillow, 1986.

(Adapter) Rose Lagercrantz and Samuel Lagercrantz, *Brave Little Pete of Geranium Street,* illustrated by Eriksson, Greenwillow, 1986.

(Compiler and editor) *Read-Aloud Rhymes for the Very Young,* illustrated by Marc Brown, Knopf, 1986.

Tyrannosaurus Was a Beast: Dinosaur Poems, illustrated by Lobel, Greenwillow, 1988.

(Collector and editor) *Poems of A. Nonny Mouse,* illustrated by Henrik Drescher, Knopf, 1989.

Beneath a Blue Umbrella, illustrated by Williams, Greenwillow, 1990.

Something Big Has Been Here (ALA Notable Book), illustrated by Stevenson, Greenwillow, 1990.

(Compiler and editor) *For Laughing Out Loud,* illustrated by Marjorie Priceman, Knopf, 1991.

Twickham Tweer (from *The Sheriff of Rottenshot*), illustrated by Eldon Doty, DLM, 1991.

There'll Be A Slight Delay: And Other Poems for Grown-Ups, William Morrow & Co., 1991.

Archives of Prelutsky's work are kept in the University of Southern Mississippi's De Grummond Collection and the University of Minnesota's Kerlan Collection.

ADAPTATIONS:

Nightmares and Other Poems to Trouble Your Sleep (record; cassette), Children's Books and Music, 1985.

It's Thanksgiving (cassette), Listening Library, 1985.

The New Kid on the Block (cassette), Listening Library, 1986.

It's Halloween (cassette), Scholastic, 1987.

It's Christmas (cassette), Scholastic, 1987.

Ride a Purple Pelican (cassette), Listening Library, 1988.

Read-Aloud Rhymes for the Very Young (cassette), Knopf, 1988.

It's Valentine's Day (cassette), Scholastic, 1988.

Something Big Has Been Here (cassette), Listening Library, 1991.

An audio recording has also been produced for *Rainy, Rainy Saturday* (cassette), Random House. Prelutsky's poems have been included in *Graveyard Tales* (record), NAPPS; and *People, Animals and Other Monsters* (record; cassette; includes poems from *The Snopp on the Sidewalk, The Queen of Eene, Rolling Harvey Down the Hill, The Pack-Rat's Day, A Gopher in the Garden,* and *Toucans Two and Other Poems*), Caedmon.

SIDELIGHTS: Born in Brooklyn, New York, Jack Prelutsky was a gifted and restless child whose intelligence made it difficult for him to conform to the undemanding expectations of public school. His overactive mind also made it hard for his mother and teachers to manage him. "In those days," Prelutsky recalls in *Early Years,* "... schools and parents didn't have the knowledge, the machinery or the experience to handle kids like me." However, it soon became clear that this boy with behavior problems also had a rare talent: a magnificent singing voice.

At the age of ten, Prelutsky's abilities were already recognized by many people. Some considered him a prodigy and paid the boy to sing at weddings and other special occasions. The Choir Master of New York's Metropolitan Opera considered the boy so gifted that he willingly gave Prelutsky free singing lessons. As a teenager, the promising opera student attended the High School of Music and Art in New York City, where he also studied piano. He graduated from the school in 1958.

It seemed like Prelutsky was on his way to an operatic career. But then one day his determination was shattered when he heard the world renowned Luciano Pavarotti perform. After that, Prelutsky abandoned the idea of becoming a famous opera singer. "I knew I could never compete with him .... I didn't have the fire in the belly," he comments in *Early Years.* Prelutsky experimented with numerous other professions. He became an excellent photographer, good enough to earn a living and even exhibit some of his work, but not—in his opinion—the best. He undertook a number of manual labor jobs, such as carpentry and furniture moving, as well as other occupations like cab driver, bookseller, and clerk. During the late 1950s and early 1960s, Prelutsky tried the life of the beatnik, bumming around the country and earning a living by playing his guitar and singing. He also made pottery and tried his hand at sculpting and collage. One day, while working in a coffeehouse in Greenwich Village, New York, Prelutsky met and became friends with musician Bob Dylan. They shared a common love of folk music and admired each other's performing abilities. According to Allen Raymond in *Early Years,* Dylan once observed that Prelutsky's voice sounded "like a cross between Woody Guthrie and Enrico Caruso."

Prelutsky had always felt that he was meant to be an artist, but he was not sure if being a folk singer was what he wanted to be for the rest of his life. One day he decided to try drawing. Using ink and watercolors, he labored for six months to create two dozen imaginary animals. The animals were fanciful creations that he made up himself, and had no basis in mythology or literature whatsoever. On an impulse, Prelutsky composed short poems to go with each of the drawings and then put his finished work away and forgot about it. One of his friends, who happened to be an author of children's books, saw the drawings and poems on Prelutsky's desk and persuaded him to get them published.

The first publisher Prelutsky went to turned him down, but the second, Macmillan, was very enthusiastic about his poetry. Susan Hirschman, the children's editor there, did not like the new poet's drawings very much, but Raymond writes that Hirschman believed the new author had "the talent to be one of the best poets in the world for children." Prelutsky credits Hirschman for inspiring him to become the successful poet he is today: "She saw something in my poems. I can't imagine what. I found those original ones recently and if I'd been an editor I'd have suggested to me that I go learn a trade—the poems were a little above average for a 12-year-old."

After his first meeting with Hirschman, Prelutsky was convinced he had found a career in which he could be the best because he resolved to approach his verse in a way that would excite children. He remembered that when he was a boy poetry seemed like terribly dull reading that had no relevance to the real world. His childhood friends, Raymond reports, "used to think poets had to be either boring, ... siss[ies,] or dead." But in his introduction to *The Random House Book of Poetry for Children* the author asserts that children don't have a natural aversion to verse. "For very young children, responding to poetry is as natural as breathing. Even before they can speak, most babies delight in the playful cadences of nursery rhymes and the soothing rhythms of lullabies.... Poetry is as delightful and surprising as being tickled or catching a snowflake on a mitten.... But then something happens to this early love affair with poetry. At some point during their school careers, many children seem to lose their interest and enthusiasm for poetry and their easygoing pleasure in its sounds and images. They begin to find poetry boring and irrelevant, too difficult or too dull to bother with."

Prelutsky was determined never to talk down to children, nor turn them off by creating lifeless, uninvolving poetry. The key, he discovered, was to write verses that children could relate to while also presenting them in an interesting manner. Regarding the content of his verses, *Dictionary of Literary Biography* contributor Anita Trout comments, "Prelutsky's poetry features animals and fantastic beasts which behave in inventive ways. He also writes of people and problems familiar to youngsters: dealing with the neighborhood bully, going to school, and being afraid of the dark. Writing in traditional poetic forms, he employs puns, alliteration, and word play in ways which have caused him to be ranked among the masters of contemporary verse for children." His "primary fascination for children, however," Trout later notes, "seems to be his macabre delight in the darker side of fantasy and human nature." Of his more than thirty poetry collections, many are about monsters and other frightening creatures that often turn out to be friendly, or are presented with such exaggeration that they become humorous. But Prelutsky also recognizes that an occasional fright can be fun and exciting. In books like *Nightmares: Poems to Trouble Your Sleep* and *The Headless Horseman Rides Tonight: More Poems to Trouble Your Sleep* the poems are designed to cause a "shivery delight for the young reader," says Trout.

As for presentation, Prelutsky improved his approach by taking a lesson from his childhood. In *Through the Eyes of a Child: An Introduction to Children's Literature,* he recites a parable about two teachers who display the right and wrong ways to nurture the natural love that children have for poetry. The first teacher would take out a book of poems, read one of the verses to her students, put the book away, and proceed to teach another subject like history or geography. The poems she selected were about bees, flowers, hills, and other topics that failed to capture the student's imaginations. But the second teacher turned poetry into a game. She proclaimed a "silly monster week," and started the celebration by reciting a poem about a silly monster. "She shared a number of other poems during 'silly monster week,'" writes Prelutsky, "always showing her honest enthusiasm and finding imaginative methods of presentation. She used masks, musical instruments, dance, sound effects recordings, and clay sculpture. The children grew so involved that she soon was able to recite poems with no props at all."

In his own poetry, Prelutsky has sought to engage and entertain his audience the same way that this second teacher did. "I realized poetry was a means of communication," he says in *Early Years,* "that it could be as exciting or as boring as that person or that experience." The author does not try to write moralistic poetry, or poetry that contains some deep, inner truth. Instead, he indulges in nonsense verses that aim to delight the audience with their wordplay. The poems in *The Sheriff of Rottenshot* and *Ride a Purple Pelican* offer good examples of verse in which the poet uses repetition, alliteration, rhythm and other devices to entertain children.

Because of Prelutsky's emphasis on the sounds words make, his verses are often most effective when read aloud, or, as he does, performed with guitar accompaniment. Every year, Prelutsky spends a few weeks travelling and visiting schools, where he tells stories, performs songs, and recites poetry. He remarks in *Children's Literature in Education:* "Until I started visiting schools, I tended to work in a sort of vacuum, never really knowing how my books were received by the only really important audience—the children. Book reviews are, of course, important.... [But] it's the children that really matter."

It was during one of his yearly excursions that Prelutsky met his wife, Carolynn. She was a children's librarian in Albuquerque, New Mexico. On the first day they met, Carolynn was assigned to give Prelutsky a tour of the city. The poet realized almost immediately that they made a perfect pair and proposed marriage to her. The next day, Carolynn accepted and they were soon married. Prelutsky settled down in Albuquerque, where he and his wife remained until their move to Washington state in 1990.

Today, Prelutsky continues to entertain children in schools and to lecture and give seminars to educators throughout the country. In addition to his many books of poetry, he has adapted German and Swedish verses and edited several other collections. The combination of writing and performing has made Prelutsky one of the most popular entertainers for young audiences in the United States. "Contemporary poets such as Jack Prelutsky," Trout concludes, "restore the fun and fascination in the study of the English language and its rhythmic patterns."

WORKS CITED:

Allen, Raymond, "Jack Prelutsky ... Man of Many Talents," *Early Years,* November-December, 1986, pp. 38, 40-42.

Dictionary of Literary Biography, Volume 61: *American Writers for Children since 1960: Poets, Illustrators, and Nonfiction Authors,* Gale, 1987, pp. 242-247.

Miles, Betty, editor, "When Writers Visit Schools: A Symposium," *Children's Literature in Education,* Volume 11, number 3, 1980, pp. 133, 135-136.

Prelutsky, Jack, "Introduction," *The Random House Book of Poetry for Children,* Random House, 1983, pp. 18-19.

Prelutsky, Jack, "Through the Eyes of a Poet: Poetry Doesn't Have to Be Boring," *Through the Eyes of a Child: An Introduction to Children's Literature,* by Donna E. Norton, Merrill, 1983, pp. 322-323.

FOR MORE INFORMATION SEE:

BOOKS

Children's Literature Review, Volume 13, Gale, 1987.

Holtze, Sally Holmes, editor, *Fifth Book of Junior Authors and Illustrators,* H. W. Wilson, 1983.

Kirkpatrick, D. L., editor, *Twentieth-Century Children's Writers,* 2nd edition, St. Martin's, 1983.

Shaw, John Mackay, *Childhood in Poetry,* Gale, 1967.

PERIODICALS

Horn Book, December, 1967; August, 1970; April, 1971; August, 1974; December, 1974; October, 1976; October, 1977; April, 1978; June, 1978, October, 1980; October, 1982; September-October, 1984; January-February, 1986; January-February, 1987; September-October, 1988; January-February, 1990.

Juvenile Miscellany, summer, 1985.

Lion and the Unicorn, winter, 1980-81.

Publishers Weekly, July 29, 1988.

Wilson Library Bulletin, May, 1987; May, 1988; June, 1989.

* * *

PRINGLE, Laurence

See PRINGLE, Laurence P(atrick)

* * *

PRINGLE, Laurence P(atrick) 1935- (Laurence Pringle; Sean Edmund, a pseudonym)

PERSONAL: Born November 26, 1935, in Rochester, NY; son of Laurence Erin (a realtor) and Marleah (Rosehill) Pringle; married Judith Malanowicz (a librarian), June 23, 1962 (divorced, 1970); married Alison Newhouse (a free-lance editor), July 14, 1971 (divorced, c. 1974); married Susan Klein (a teacher), March 13, 1983; children: (first marriage) Heidi Elizabeth, Jeffrey Laurence, Sean Edmund; (third marriage) Jesse Erin

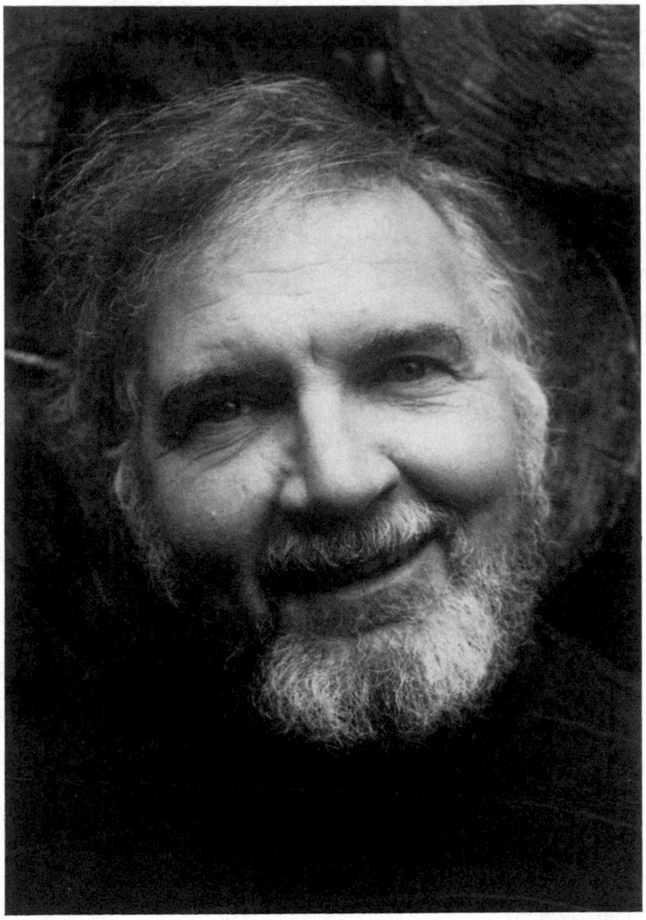

Laurence P. Pringle

(son), Rebecca Anne. *Education:* Cornell University, B.S., 1958; University of Massachusetts, M.S., 1960; attended Syracuse University, 1960-62. *Hobbies and other interests:* Photography, films, sports, surf fishing.

ADDRESSES: Home—11 Castle Hill Lane, West Nyack, NY 10994.

CAREER: Free-lance writer, editor, and photographer. Lima Central School, Lima, NY, science teacher, 1961-62; American Museum of Natural History, *Nature and Science* (children's magazine), New York City, associate editor, 1963-65, senior editor, 1965-67, executive editor, 1967-70; New School for Social Research, New York City, faculty member, 1976-78; Kean College of New Jersey, Union, writer in residence, 1985-86; *Highlights for Children* Writers Workshop, faculty member, 1987-92.

AWARDS, HONORS: Special Conservation Award, National Wildlife Federation, 1978; Eva L. Gordon Award, American Nature Society, 1983; several Notable Book citations, American Library Association.

WRITINGS:

NONFICTION FOR CHILDREN; UNDER NAME LAURENCE PRINGLE, EXCEPT AS NOTED

Dinosaurs and Their World, Harcourt, 1968.

The Only Earth We Have, Macmillan, 1969.

(Editor under name Laurence P. Pringle) *Discovering the Outdoors: A Nature and Science Guide to Investigating Life in Fields, Forests, and Ponds,* Natural History Press, 1969.

(Editor) *Discovering Nature Indoors: A Nature and Science Guide to Investigations with Small Animals,* Natural History Press, 1970.

From Field to Forest: How Plants and Animals Change the Land, with own photographs, World Publishing, 1970.

In a Beaver Valley: How Beavers Change the Land, with own photographs, World Publishing, 1970.

One Earth, Many People: The Challenge of Human Population Growth, Macmillan, 1971.

Ecology: Science of Survival, Macmillan, 1971.

Cockroaches: Here, There, and Everywhere, illustrations by James McCrea and Ruth McCrea, Crowell, 1971.

This Is a River: Exploring an Ecosystem, Macmillan, 1971.

From Pond to Prairie: The Changing World of a Pond and Its Life, illustrations by Karl W. Stuecklen, Macmillan, 1972.

Pests and People: The Search for Sensible Pest Control, Macmillan, 1972.

Estuaries: Where Rivers Meet the Sea, Macmillan, 1973.

Into the Woods: Exploring the Forest Ecosystem, Macmillan, 1973.

Follow a Fisher, illustrations by Tony Chen, Crowell, 1973.

Twist, Wiggle, and Squirm: A Book about Earthworms, illustrations by Peter Parnall, Crowell, 1973.

Recycling Resources, Macmillan, 1974.

Energy: Power for People, Macmillan, 1975.

City and Suburb: Exploring an Ecosystem, Macmillan, 1975.

Chains, Webs, and Pyramids: The Flow of Energy in Nature, illustrations by Jan Adkins, Crowell, 1975.

Water Plants, illustrations by Kazue Mizumura, Crowell, 1975.

The Minnow Family: Chubs, Dace, Minnows, and Shiners, illustrations by Dot Barlowe and Sy Barlowe, Morrow, 1976.

Listen to the Crows, illustrations by Ted Lewin, Crowell, 1976.

Our Hungry Earth: The World Food Crisis, Macmillan, 1976.

Death Is Natural, Four Winds, 1977.

The Hidden World: Life under a Rock, illustrations by Erick Ingraham, Macmillan, 1977.

The Controversial Coyote: Predation, Politics, and Ecology, Harcourt, 1977.

The Gentle Desert: Exploring an Ecosystem, Macmillan, 1977.

Animals and Their Niches: How Species Share Resources, illustrations by Leslie Morrill, Morrow, 1977.

The Economic Growth Debate: Are There Limits to Growth?, F. Watts, 1978.

Dinosaurs and People: Fossils, Facts, and Fantasies, Harcourt, 1978.

Wild Foods: A Beginner's Guide to Identifying, Harvesting, and Cooking Safe and Tasty Plants from the

Outdoors, with own photographs, illustrations by Paul Breeden, Four Winds Press, 1978.
Nuclear Power: From Physics to Politics, Macmillan, 1979.
Natural Fire: Its Ecology in Forests, Morrow, 1979.
Lives at Stake: The Science and Politics of Environmental Health, Macmillan, 1980.
What Shall We Do with the Land? Choices for America, Crowell, 1981.
Frost Hollows and Other Microclimates, Morrow, 1981.
Vampire Bats, Morrow, 1982.
Water: The Next Great Resource Battle, Macmillan, 1982.
Radiation: Waves and Particles, Benefits and Risks, Enslow, 1983.
Wolfman: Exploring the World of Wolves, Scribner, 1983.
Feral: Tame Animals Gone Wild, Macmillan, 1983.
The Earth Is Flat, and Other Great Mistakes, illustrations by Steve Miller, Morrow, 1983.
Being a Plant, Crowell, 1983.
Animals at Play, Harcourt, 1985.
Nuclear War: From Hiroshima to Nuclear Winter, Enslow, 1985.
Here Come the Killer Bees, Morrow, 1986, revised edition published as *Killer Bees,* 1990.
Throwing Things Away: From Middens to Resource Recovery, Crowell, 1986.
Home: How Animals Find Comfort and Safety, Scribner, 1987.
Restoring Our Earth, Enslow, 1987.
Rain of Troubles: The Science and Politics of Acid Rain, Macmillan, 1988.
The Animal Rights Controversy, Harcourt, 1989.
Bearman: Exploring the World of Black Bears, photographs by Lynn Rogers, Scribner, 1989.
Nuclear Energy: Troubled Past, Uncertain Future, Macmillan, 1989.
Living in a Risky World, Morrow, 1989.
The Golden Book of Insects and Spiders, illustrations by James Spence, Golden Book, 1990.
Global Warming: Assessing the Greenhouse Threat, Arcade, 1990.
Saving Our Wildlife, Enslow, 1990.
Batman: Exploring the World of Bats, photographs by Merlin D. Tuttle, Scribner, 1991.
Living Treasure: Saving Earth's Threatened Biodiversity, illustrations by Irene Brady, Morrow, 1991.

OTHER

Wild River (nonfiction for adults), with own photographs, Lippincott, 1972.
(With the editors of Time-Life Books) *Rivers and Lakes* (nonfiction for adults), Time-Life Books, 1985.
Jesse Builds a Road (fiction for children), illustrations by Leslie Morrill, Macmillan, 1989.

Contributor to periodicals, including *Audubon, Highlights for Children, Open Road, Ranger Rick's Nature Magazine,* and *Smithsonian,* sometimes under the pseudonym Sean Edmund.

SIDELIGHTS: Laurence P. Pringle has written dozens of nature books for children, unfolding the mysteries of creatures from cockroaches to dinosaurs, exploring the natural sciences, and examining the environment itself. He also loves to photograph wildlife and natural settings, a hobby he first pursued as a boy. Since becoming a professional writer he has illustrated a number of his books with his own photographs. Several of Pringle's works have won the distinction of being named Notable Books by the American Library Association, and many are considered good general introductions to scientific and ecological subjects—the kind of books that can ignite a young reader's interest and inspire further reading. They also reveal Pringle's commitment to preserving nature, as he explains how humans harm the natural world upon which all life depends. His conservation-oriented work earned him a special award from the National Wildlife Federation in 1978. Another of Pringle's commitments is to children and children's literature. In an essay for *Something about the Author Autobiography Series* (*SAAS*) he shared part of a speech he had given that talked about children's writers: "Perhaps in each of our personal histories there are experiences that have left us with a special regard for children. Perhaps we believe, more strongly than most, that what happens to kids is awfully important. Perhaps we feel that it is too late to influence most adults, but that everything that touches a child's life, including magazine articles and books, can make a difference in the future of that child, and in the future of the world."

Pringle's childhood certainly influenced his future and shaped his interests. Raised in a rural area in western New York, he grew up in the outdoors, learning to hunt, fish, and trap as well as observe and photograph the wild animals around him. The sight of a group of particularly colorful birds one spring sent him looking for his family's book on birds, and he quickly became an avid bird-watcher. "My curiosity became focused on birds," he wrote in his *SAAS* essay, "on identifying them, finding their nests, attracting them. Eventually, as a teenager, I built birdhouses that were occupied by eastern bluebirds and house wrens. For a time I subscribed to *Audubon* magazine, and that may have triggered my interest in wildlife photography."

For Christmas in 1947 Pringle asked for and received a Kodak Baby Brownie camera and immediately set out to begin photographing wildlife. "Great wildlife photos didn't come as easily as I had imagined," he admitted, "nor were many taken with a Baby Brownie or a Kodak Hawkeye, my second camera. I did the best I could, photographing bird nests and wildflowers."

Around the time he got the camera Pringle also acquired his first rifle and began to hunt, "a routine step in that place and time, when virtually all boys (and a good many girls) were encouraged to become hunters," he explained in *SAAS.* His first kill was a gray squirrel. "I recall mixed feelings, including regret as I watched life fade from its eyes," Pringle wrote. "Then and now, taking a life—even an insect's life—stirs in me a mixture of feelings, but hunting success earned respect

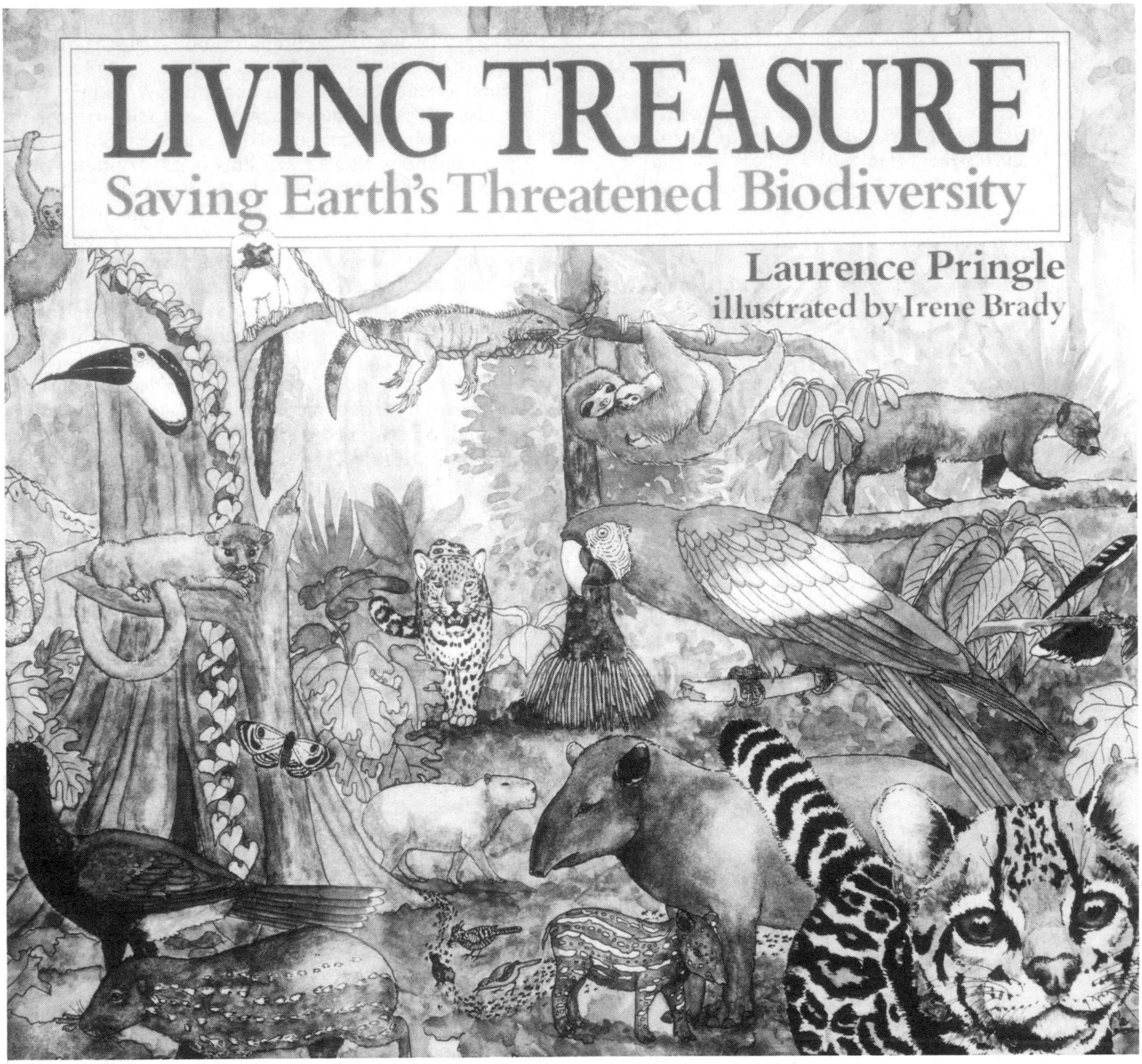

From *Living Treasure: Saving Earth's Threatened Biodiversity*, by Laurence P. Pringle. Illustrated by Irene Brady.

in my environment and I was hungry to succeed at something.... I recall the excitement of being awakened well before dawn and tagging along on deer-hunting trips. Later, as a teenager and in my early twenties, I shot a few deer myself.

"Is that the sound of stereotypes shattering? I am a naturalist, an environmentalist, so I must abhor hunting, right? Wrong. I am not a hunter now, and haven't had a hunting license for at least two decades, but don't rule it forever out of my life.... Since I live in a major metropolitan area, most of my friends are not only nonhunters but also oppose hunting. Their attitudes are understandable, given their experiences, or lack of experiences. Some seem to believe that their food comes from stores. All are content to let others kill the animals they eat, although they've been known to drop live lobsters into boiling water. In the midst of all these paradoxes, I give my greatest respect to those animal-rights advocates who refuse to eat meat and fish, and to those hunters who admit they do it for the meat and the challenge, not because they are helping wildlife populations. (This benefit may sometimes occur but that's not why people hunt.)"

Pringle continued his hunting, muskrat trapping, bird-watching, and photography through high school and beyond. He also sold a short article on crows to the magazine *Open Road* when he was sixteen, but writing had not yet fully captured his attention. When he first seriously considered attending college, a year after graduating from high school, he decided to study wildlife conservation. Not until he had gained both a bachelor's and a master's degree in wildlife biology and had begun a doctorate did Pringle switch to journalism—"a choice I have never regretted," he declared in his essay. Eventually he became an editor for the magazine *Nature and Science* and began writing books. One of the benefits of his writing career, he observed, is "being paid to pursue my curiosity, as I explore a subject that interests me."

A lifetime of studying and writing about nature has enriched Pringle in other ways, too. "As my knowledge of ecology has grown, so has my appreciation of diversity, complexity, and the interdependence of living and nonliving things," he explained. That understanding, as well as his science background, informs his writings. "My books tend to encourage readers to feel a kinship with other living things, and a sense of membership in the earth ecosystem. I have also become an advocate of scientific thinking, or perhaps I should say just clear thinking.

"Challenging authority and accepted truths is a basic part of the scientific process. It has influenced my choice of book subjects, as I have questioned popular but incorrect notions about forest fires, dinosaurs, vampire bats, wolves, coyotes, and killer bees. These books give readers the truth, to the extent we know it, and also demonstrate that the explorations of science aim at a better understanding of the world. As long as we keep exploring, that understanding can change.

"I also encourage a skeptical attitude toward the fruits of technology and various vested interests that come into play with such issues as nuclear power, environmental health, biocides, or acid rain. My books on such subjects are never neutral; sometimes I am tempted to lean heavily toward one side of an issue. The temptation to do so is strong when one side mainly represents short-term economic interest and the other mainly represents concern about public health, maintenance of natural diversity and beauty, and the quality of life for both present and future generations. Temptation is also fueled by the knowledge that students are often subjected to the biased publications and films (free to schools), and advertisements of powerful economic interests, and are ill-prepared to detect the distortions and omissions of these materials.

"My books about controversial issues are not balanced—in the sense of equal space and weight applied to all sides—but are balanced by presenting arguments from the opposing interests, and a reading list that includes a diversity of views for those who want to explore the subject further."

Pringle frequently earns praise for the clarity, accuracy, and broad perspective he brings to his books. Noting that he often openly states his biases, reviewers also commend him for discussing even touchy subjects objectively. One critic, writing for *Kirkus Reviews,* characterized Pringle's books as "straight-talking, clear-thinking overviews," an opinion echoed by many others. His skill at presenting complex subjects in an understandable, noncondescending manner and the thought-provoking aspect of his work impress critics as well. In a *School Library Journal* review, Margaret Bush applauded Pringle's "ability to deduce principles, examine meanings, raise questions and encourage observation—all in a well-woven narrative." All together, his writings represent a "list of sound environmentally oriented titles," according to Diane P. Tuccillo in *School Library Journal.*

WORKS CITED:

Bush, Margaret, review of *Animals at Play* in *School Library Journal,* February, 1986, p. 99.

Pringle, Laurence, autobiographical essay in *Something about the Author Autobiography Series,* Volume 6, Gale, 1988, pp. 219-36.

Review of *What Shall We Do with the Land?* in *Kirkus Reviews,* November 1, 1981, p. 1350.

Tuccillo, Diane P., review of *Restoring Our Earth* in *School Library Journal,* January, 1988, p. 94.

FOR MORE INFORMATION SEE:

BOOKS

Children's Literature Review, Volume 4, Gale, 1984, pp. 172-86.

Hearne, Betsy, and Marilyn Kaye, editors, *Celebrating Children's Books: Essays on Children's Literature in Honor of Zena Sutherland,* Lothrop, 1981.

PERIODICALS

New York Times Book Review, November 9, 1969, p. 44; May 24, 1970, p. 3; December 10, 1978, p. 78.

Scientific American, December, 1975, p. 133.

Times Literary Supplement, March 28, 1980, p. 363.

Washington Post Book World, November 13, 1977, p. E3; May 13, 1984, p. 16.

* * *

PROVENSEN, Alice 1918-

PERSONAL: Surname is pronounced "*Proh*-ven-sen"; born August 14, 1918, in Chicago, IL; daughter of Jay Horace (a broker) and Kathryn (an interior decorator; maiden name, Zelanis) Twitchell; married Martin Elias Provensen (a writer and illustrator of children's books), April 17, 1944 (died March 27, 1987); children: Karen Anna. *Education:* Studied at Art Institute of Chicago, University of California, Los Angeles, and Art Students League, New York.

ADDRESSES: Home—Rural Delivery, Staatsburg, NY 12580.

CAREER: Walter Lantz Studios, Hollywood, CA, employed in animation, 1942-43; Office of Strategic Services, Washington, D.C., graphics, 1943-45; writer and illustrator of children's books, 1946—. *Exhibitions:* With husband, Martin Provensen, at the Baltimore Museum, 1954, American Institute of Graphic Arts in New York City, 1959, and Botolph Group in Boston, 1964.

Alice and Martin Provensen

AWARDS, HONORS: Books represented in Fifty Books of the Year Selections, American Institute of Graphic Arts, 1947, 1948, and 1952; *New York Times* Best Illustrated citation, 1952, for *The Animal Fair; New York Times* Best Illustrated citation, 1953, for *The Golden Bible for Children: The New Testament; New York Times* Best Illustrated citation, 1959, for *The First Noel: The Birth of Christ from the Gospel According to St. Luke; New York Times* Best Illustrated citation, 1963, for *Karen's Curiosity;* Gold Medal, Society of Illustrators, 1960; *New York Herald Tribune* Children's Spring Book Festival honor, 1963, for *Karen's Opposites;* Best Illustrated citation, 1964, for *The Charge of the Light Brigade; New York Times* Best Illustrated and Outstanding Book citations, both 1976, and Art Books for Children listing, 1978 and 1979, all for *The Mother Goose Book;* Art Books for Children listing, 1975, for *My Little Hen; New York Times* Best Illustrated and Outstanding Book citations, both 1978, and Art Books for Children listing, 1979, all for *A Peaceable Kingdom: The Shaker Abecedarius;* Golden Kite honor, 1981, Newbery award, 1982, Caldecott honor citation, 1982, and *Boston Globe*/Horn Book citation, 1982, all for *A Visit to William Blake's Inn: Poems for Innocent and Experienced Travelers; New York Times* Outstanding Books citation and Parents' Choice citation, both 1983, and Caldecott Medal, 1984, all for *The Glorious Flight: Across the Channel with Louis Bleriot, July 25, 1909;* named School Library Media Specialist of South Eastern New York, 1986.

WRITINGS:

(And illustrator) *The Buck Stops Here: The Presidents of the United States,* Harper, 1990.

SELF-ILLUSTRATED FOR CHILDREN; WITH HUSBAND, MARTIN PROVENSEN

The Animal Fair, Simon & Schuster, 1952.
Karen's Curiosity, Golden Press, 1963.
Karen's Opposites, Golden Press, 1963.
What Is a Color?, Golden Press, 1967.
Who's in the Egg?, Golden Press, 1968.
(Editors) *Provensen Book of Fairy Tales,* Random House, 1971.
Play on Words, Random House, 1972.
My Little Hen, Random House, 1973.
Roses Are Red, Random House, 1973.
Our Animal Friends, Random House, 1974, reprinted with new cover art as *Our Animal Friends at Maple Hill Farm,* 1984.
The Mother Goose Book, Random House, 1976.
A Book of Seasons, Random House, 1976.

The Year at Maple Hill Farm, Atheneum, 1978.
A Horse and a Hound, a Goat and a Gander, Atheneum, 1980.
An Owl and Three Pussycats, Atheneum, 1981.
The Glorious Flight: Across the Channel with Louis Bleriot, July 25, 1909, Viking, 1983.
Leonardo da Vinci: The Artist, Inventor, Scientist in Three-Dimensional, Movable Pictures, paper engineering by John Strejan, Viking, 1984.
Town and Country, Crown, 1984.
Shaker Lane, Viking, 1987.

ILLUSTRATOR; WITH HUSBAND, MARTIN PROVENSEN

Margaret Bradford Boni, editor, *Fireside Book of Folksongs,* Simon & Schuster, 1947.
Dorothy Bennett, editor, *The Golden Mother Goose,* Golden Press, 1948.
James A. Beard, *Fireside Cook Book,* Simon & Schuster, 1949.
Robert Louis Stevenson, *A Child's Garden of Verses,* Golden Press, 1951.
Elsa Jane Werner, adapter, *The New Testament,* Golden Press, 1953.
M. B. Boni, editor, *Fireside Book of Lovesongs,* Simon & Schuster, 1954.
Jan Werner Watson, adapter, *Iliad and Odyssey,* Golden Press, 1956.
Anne Terry White, adapter, *Treasury of Myths and Legends,* Golden Press, 1959.
The First Noel: The Birth of Christ from the Gospel According to St. Luke, Golden Press, 1959.
George Wolfson, editor, *Shakespeare: Ten Great Plays,* Golden Press, 1962.
Alfred, Lord Tennyson, *The Charge of the Light Brigade,* Golden Press, 1964.
Louis Untermeyer, adapter, *Aesop's Fables,* Golden Press, 1965.
L. Untermeyer, editor, *Fun and Nonsense,* Golden Press, 1967.
L. Untermeyer, adapter, *Tales from the Ballet,* Golden Press, 1968.
A Peaceable Kingdom: The Shaker Abecedarius, Viking, 1978.
The Golden Serpent, Viking, 1980.
A Visit to William Blake's Inn: Poems for Innocent and Experienced Travelers, Harcourt, 1981.
Old Mother Hubbard, Random House, 1982.
D. H. Lawrence, *Birds, Beasts, and the Third Thing: Poems,* Viking, 1982.
Nancy Willard, *The Voyage of Ludgate Hill: Travels with Robert Louis Stevenson,* Harcourt, 1987.
Old Mother Goose and Other Nursery Rhymes, Western, 1988.

SIDELIGHTS: Award-winning Alice and Martin Provensen are highly regarded for the originality and excellence of their illustrations for children's books. Although Martin's death in 1987 ended a long and successful collaboration, their art has graced the work of numerous others in addition to their own books. Realistic and charming in detail, their illustrations invite visual exploration and encourage a child's imagination. Recipients of the 1984 Caldecott Medal for *The Glorious Flight: Across the Channel with Louis Bleriot, July 25, 1909,* the Provensens have also received numerous awards from the American Institute of Graphic Arts and the Society of Illustrators and their work has frequently been cited for excellence by the *New York Times.*

Coincidentally, the lives of Alice and Martin Provensen followed similar paths prior to their meeting. Both were born in Chicago and grew up appreciating the art of book illustration; both won scholarships to the Art Institute of Chicago, transferring later to the University of California; and both developed training in motion pictures. Martin began working for Walt Disney Studios and after studying for a while in New York City at the Art Students League, Alice returned to California where she worked for Walter Lantz Studios. They met on a movie lot while working for a film for the U.S. Navy, and married in Washington, D.C., in 1944. During the late 1940s, the Provensens moved to New York City and began to jointly illustrate children's books. They travelled throughout Europe in the early 1950s and collected much material for future illustrations.

Upon returning to the United States, they purchased a farm near Staatsburg, New York, where they converted a barn into the studio in which they worked for more than thirty years. Maple Hill Farm has supplied the Provensens with many subjects, especially the animal illustrations for such books as *The Year at Maple Hill Farm* and *Our Animal Friends at Maple Hill Farm.* Calling *Our Animal Friends at Maple Hill Farm* "very satisfying, like a weekend at the farm," George A Woods

From *A Visit to William Blake's Inn,* by Nancy Willard. Illustrated by Alice and Martin Provensen.

indicates in the *New York Times Book Review* that "the Provensens haven't scrubbed everything clean for young visitors either." According to Lois K. Nichols in *Children's Book Review Service,* "The animal inhabitants of Maple Hill Farm are humorously described and illustrated in a way that subtly gives the reader a lot of information about their characteristics, habits, and personalities as well as their relationships with other animals and people." Nancy Willard visited the Provensen's farm in 1983 for an interview in *Lion and the Unicorn,* and Martin stated, "I would hate to think that we are overly sentimental in our relationships with animals. We do recognize that animals are animals, and we find their presence rewarding. We also recognize that some people don't.... But I do think animals have a great deal to teach people."

Discussing the influence upon their work by a shared background in film, Martin indicated to Willard that "it was ideal training for book illustrating. Year after year, we would sit together in a sort of assembly line to do story boards, which were really walls of drawings.... It was great training because we'd be given a sequence, the barest outline, just a thread of narrative, and then it was up to us to improvise on this theme." In response to Willard's observation that some of the pages of the Maple Hill Farm books are organized as a film might be sequenced in a series of frames, Martin agreed that the concepts of sequence and time are vital in illustrating a children's book: "There's no way to beat that way of telling a story, short of going into film."

In their acceptance speech upon winning the Caldecott Medal in 1984 for *The Glorious Flight: Across the Channel with Louis Bleriot, July 25, 1909,* the Provensens indicated that while each children's book has presented a special challenge, *The Glorious Flight* was "not just another book." Building upon their own fascination with airplanes, the Provensens decided to tell the story of Louis Bleriot, who flew the English Channel in 1909. "He was a lovable, wonderful man as well as one of the great pioneers of aviation," declared the Provensens. "Unskilled as a pilot, untutored as a designer (there were no teachers), he had to learn in the air. He was incredibly brave and enormously ingenious. His contraptions flapped, skipped, and sailed ponderously into that new element—the sky." Calling it "a quiet, modest book this, but a perfect example of how a picture-book should be made, in attention to detail and in subordination to an overall design," M. Crouch comments in the *Junior Bookshelf* that "it could not be bettered." Pointing out that the Provensens have taken simple, factual information and personalized it, a *Booklist* reviewer points out that they have "added magnificent illustrations, and thus transformed the facts into a vibrant piece of history.... Cheers for Bleriot, cheers for the Provensens." Or as, Zena Sutherland comments in *Bulletin of the Center for Children's Books,* "What more can one ask of a book than it be visually stunning, entertainingly written, and informative, and true?"

Their work has been an authentic collaboration of effort, with one's work virtually indistinguishable from the other's. Regarding the book itself as "basically a vehicle for the text," Martin recalled, for instance, that for their Newbery Award and Caldecott Honor book, *A Visit to William Blake's Inn: Poems for Innocent and Experienced Travelers,* they immersed themselves in Blake's poetry and biographies. They also wandered through what was left of eighteenth-century London while they were there. "We know how many people love England and especially London, even if they haven't been there." Martin told Willard that working together was "a matter of having confidence in your mutual understanding of what the goal is and how you want the book to look."

WORKS CITED:

Crouch, M., review of *The Glorious Flight: Across the Channel with Louis Bleriot, July 25, 1909, Junior Bookshelf,* June, 1984, p. 120.

Review of *The Glorious Flight: Across the Channel with Louis Bleriot, July 25, 1909, Booklist,* November 1, 1983, pp. 418-19.

Nichols, Lois K., review of *Our Animal Friends at Maple Hill Farm, Children's Book Review Service,* October, 1974, p. 10.

Sutherland, Zena, review of *The Glorious Flight: Across the Channel with Louis Bleriot, July 25, 1909, Bulletin of the Center for Children's Books,* January, 1984, p. 96.

Willard, Nancy, "The Birds and the Beasts Were There: An Interview with Martin Provensen," *Lion and the Unicorn,* Volume 7/8, 1983-84, pp. 171-83.

Woods, George A., review of *Our Animal Friends at Maple Hill Farm, New York Times Book Review,* September 8, 1974, p. 8.

FOR MORE INFORMATION SEE:

BOOKS

Children's Literature Review, Volume 4, Gale, 1982.

Illustrators of Children's Books, 1946-1956, Horn Book, 1958.

Illustrators of Children's Books, 1957-1966, Horn Book, 1968.

Third Book of Junior Authors, edited by de Montreville and Hill, Wilson, 1972.

PERIODICALS

Horn Book, August, 1984, pp. 449-52.

McCall's, November, 1974.

* * *

PROVENSEN, Martin (Elias) 1916-1987

PERSONAL: Surname is pronounced "*Proh*-ven-sen"; born July 10, 1916, in Chicago, IL; died of a heart attack, March 27, 1987, in Clinton Corners, NY; son of Marthin (a musician) and Berendina (a teacher; maiden name, Kruger) Provensen; married Alice Twitchell (a writer and illustrator of children's books), April 17, 1944; children: Karen Anna. *Education:* Studied at Art Institute of Chicago, and University of California, Berkeley.

Cover of *Town & Country,* written and illustrated by Alice and Martin Provensen.

ADDRESSES: Home—Rural Delivery, Staatsburg, NY 12580.

CAREER: Walt Disney Studios, Hollywood, CA, member of story board, 1938-42; writer and illustrator of children's books, 1946-87. *Military service:* U.S. Navy, 1942-45. *Exhibitions:* With wife, Alice Provensen, at the Baltimore Museum, 1954, American Institute of Graphic Arts in New York City, 1959, and Botolph Group in Boston, 1964.

AWARDS, HONORS: Books represented in Fifty Books of the Year Selections, American Institute of Graphic Arts, 1947, 1948, and 1952; *New York Times* Best Illustrated citation, 1952, for *The Animal Fair; New York Times* Best Illustrated citation, 1953, for *The Golden Bible for Children: The New Testament; New York Times* Best Illustrated citation, 1959, for *The First Noel: The Birth of Christ from the Gospel According to St. Luke; New York Times* Best Illustrated citation, 1963, for *Karen's Curiosity;* Gold Medal, Society of Illustrators, 1960; *New York Herald Tribune* Children's Spring Book Festival honor, 1963, for *Karen's Opposites;* Best Illustrated citation, 1964, for *The Charge of the Light Brigade; New York Times* Best Illustrated and Outstanding Book citations, both 1976, and Art Books for Children listing, 1978 and 1979, all for *The Mother Goose Book;* Art Books for Children listing, 1975, for *My Little Hen; New York Times* Best Illustrated and Outstanding Book citations, both 1978, and Art Books for Children listing, 1979, all for *A Peaceable Kingdom: The Shaker Abecedarius;* Golden Kite honor, 1981, Newbery award, 1982, Caldecott honor citation, 1982, and *Boston Globe*/Horn Book citation, 1982, all for *A Visit to William Blake's Inn: Poems for Innocent and Experienced Travelers; New York Times* Outstanding Books citation and Parents' Choice citation, both 1983, and Caldecott Medal, 1984, all for *The Glorious Flight: Across the Channel with Louis Bleriot, July 25, 1909;* named School Library Media Specialist of South Eastern New York, 1986.

WRITINGS:

SELF-ILLUSTRATED FOR CHILDREN; WITH WIFE, ALICE PROVENSEN

The Animal Fair, Simon & Schuster, 1952.
Karen's Curiosity, Golden Press, 1963.
Karen's Opposites, Golden Press, 1963.
What Is a Color?, Golden Press, 1967.
Who's in the Egg?, Golden Press, 1968.
(Editors) *Provensen Book of Fairy Tales,* Random House, 1971.
Play on Words, Random House, 1972.
My Little Hen, Random House, 1973.
Roses Are Red, Random House, 1973.
Our Animal Friends, Random House, 1974, reprinted with new cover art as *Our Animal Friends at Maple Hill Farm,* 1984.
The Mother Goose Book, Random House, 1976.
A Book of Seasons, Random House, 1976.
The Year at Maple Hill Farm, Atheneum, 1978.
A Horse and a Hound, a Goat and a Gander, Atheneum, 1980.
An Owl and Three Pussycats, Atheneum, 1981.
The Glorious Flight: Across the Channel with Louis Bleriot, July 25, 1909, Viking, 1983.
Leonardo da Vinci: The Artist, Inventor, Scientist in Three-Dimensional, Movable Pictures, paper engineering by John Strejan, Viking, 1984.
Town and Country, Crown, 1984.
Shaker Lane, Viking, 1987.

ILLUSTRATOR; WITH WIFE, ALICE PROVENSEN

Margaret Bradford Boni, editor, *Fireside Book of Folksongs,* Simon & Schuster, 1947.
Dorothy Bennett, editor, *The Golden Mother Goose,* Golden Press, 1948.
James A. Beard, *Fireside Cook Book,* Simon & Schuster, 1949.
Robert Louis Stevenson, *A Child's Garden of Verses,* Golden Press, 1951.
Elsa Jane Werner, adapter, *The New Testament,* Golden Press, 1953.
M. B. Boni, editor, *Fireside Book of Lovesongs,* Simon & Schuster, 1954.
Jan Werner Watson, adapter, *Iliad and Odyssey,* Golden Press, 1956.
Anne Terry White, adapter, *Treasury of Myths and Legends,* Golden Press, 1959.
The First Noel: The Birth of Christ from the Gospel According to St. Luke, Golden Press, 1959.

George Wolfson, editor, *Shakespeare: Ten Great Plays,* Golden Press, 1962.

Alfred, Lord Tennyson, *The Charge of the Light Brigade,* Golden Press, 1964.

Louis Untermeyer, adapter, *Aesop's Fables,* Golden Press, 1965.

L. Untermeyer, editor, *Fun and Nonsense,* Golden Press, 1967.

L. Untermeyer, adapter, *Tales from the Ballet,* Golden Press, 1968.

A Peaceable Kingdom: The Shaker Abecedarius, Viking, 1978.

The Golden Serpent, Viking, 1980.

A Visit to William Blake's Inn: Poems for Innocent and Experienced Travelers, Harcourt, 1981.

Old Mother Hubbard, Random House, 1982.

D. H. Lawrence, *Birds, Beasts, and the Third Thing: Poems,* Viking, 1982.

Nancy Willard, *The Voyage of Ludgate Hill: Travels with Robert Louis Stevenson,* Harcourt, 1987.

Old Mother Goose and Other Nursery Rhymes, Western, 1988.

SIDELIGHTS: See entry on wife, Alice Provensen, for joint "Sidelights" on Alice and Martin Provensen.

FOR MORE INFORMATION SEE:

BOOKS

Children's Literature Review, Volume 4, Gale, 1982.

Illustrators of Children's Books, 1946-1956, Horn Book, 1958.

Illustrators of Children's Books, 1957-1966, Horn Book, 1968.

Third Book of Junior Authors, edited by de Montreville and Hill, Wilson, 1972.

PERIODICALS

Horn Book, August, 1984, pp. 449-52.

McCall's, November, 1974.

New York Times, March 30, 1987.

* * *

PULLMAN, Philip (N.) 1946-

Philip Pullman

PERSONAL: Born October 19, 1946, in Norwich, England; son of Alfred Outram (an airman) and Audrey (a housewife; maiden name, Merrifield) Pullman; married Judith Speller (a therapist), August 15, 1970; children: James, Thomas. *Education:* Oxford University, B.A., 1968. *Politics:* Socialist. *Religion:* None. *Hobbies and other interests:* Drawing, music.

ADDRESSES: Home and office—24 Templar Rd., Oxford OX2 8LT, England. *Agent*—Ellen Levine, 432 Park Ave. S., Suite 1205, New York, NY 10016; A. P. Watt, 20 John St., London WC1N 2DL, England.

CAREER: Teacher at Ivanhoe, Bishop Kirk, and Marston middle schools, Oxford, England, 1973-86; writer, 1986—. Lecturer at Westminster College, North Hinksey, Oxford.

AWARDS, HONORS: The Ruby in the Smoke received a Lancashire County Libraries/National and Provincial Children's Book Award and a Best Books for Young Adults listing from *School Library Journal,* both 1987, a Children's Book Award from the International Reading Association and a Best Books for Young Adults listing from the American Library Association, both 1988, and a Preis der Leseratten from ZDF Television (Germany); *Shadow in the North* received a Best Books for Young Adults listing from the American Library Association, 1988, and was nominated for an Edgar Allan Poe Award by the Mystery Writers of America, Inc., 1989.

WRITINGS:

Ancient Civilizations (juvenile), illustrated by G. Long, Wheaton, 1978.

Galatea (novel), Gollancz, 1978, Dutton, 1979.

Count Karlstein (juvenile), Chatto & Windus, 1982, edition with pictures by Patrice Aggs, Doubleday (England), 1991.

The Ruby in the Smoke (young adult; first novel in trilogy), Oxford University Press, 1985, Knopf, 1987.

How to Be Cool (juvenile), Heinemann, 1987, adaptation for television first broadcast by Granada, 1988.

The Shadow in the Plate (young adult; second novel in trilogy), Oxford University Press, 1987, published as *The Shadow in the North,* Knopf, 1988.

Penny Dreadful (picture book), Corgi, 1989.

Spring-Heeled Jack, pictures by David Mostyn, Doubleday (England), 1989.

Frankenstein (play; adapted from Mary Shelley's novel of the same title), Oxford University Press, 1990.
The Tiger in the Well (young adult; third novel in trilogy), Knopf, 1990.
The Broken Bridge (young adult), Macmillan (England), 1990, Knopf, 1991.

Also author of additional plays, including *The Adventure of the Sumatian Devil* and an adaptation of Alexandre Dumas's *The Three Musketeers.*

WORK IN PROGRESS: A fourth and final novel for young adults to follow the trilogy begun with *The Ruby in the Smoke; The White Mercedes,* a novel for young adults; *Torn Jasmine,* an adventure story for adults.

SIDELIGHTS: Philip Pullman's historical novels for young adults are recognized for their fast-paced suspenseful plots, their concern with the issues of the day, and their unconventional protagonists. Best known for the first three works—*The Ruby in the Smoke, The Shadow in the North,* and *The Tiger in the Well*—of a projected series of four books set in nineteenth-century London, Pullman packs his complex stories with humor and high drama. Besides his popular trilogy, he has also written nonfiction on ancient civilizations, a mock-gothic tale, a picture book, several plays, and an adventure story for adults.

Pullman once commented: "I am first and foremost a storyteller. In whatever form I write—whether it's the novel, or the screenplay, or the stage play, or even if I tell stories (as I sometimes do)—I am always the servant of the story that has chosen me to tell it and I have to discover the best way of doing that. I believe there's a pure line that goes through every story and the more closely the telling approaches that pure line, the better the story will be.

"I have other values as well as those of a storyteller. I believe passionately in social justice and in the right of every citizen to live a decent life, to be well educated, to be part of a society that does not regard money as the most important thing in life. I believe in a society that has a proper human regard for the well-being of all its members, not just the strongest. I find that as I grow older I get more angry, not less, and no doubt this is reflected in the things I'm writing about; my stories are becoming less fantastic and more realistic. Real things spark stories: an incident in a shopping mall, a friend's difficulty in getting hospital treatment, or a vagrant in a local park. And although I've been writing historical fiction, which might seem faraway from the present day, I've begun to see similarities between such things as the condition of the poor in the East End of London in the 1880s and the growing contrast between rich and poor today.

"But I don't write stories to a plan or to make a political point. I've tried, and it doesn't work. The story must tell me. If a story isn't there, no amount of research, study, or passion will make it come. If, when it does come, it's quite different from the story I thought I ought to tell, so be it. I rely on my wife to be my best critic.

"In recent years I've been very pleased to see comics becoming accepted by critics as an art form in their own right. All my life I've loved comics: Batman and Superman were two of my earliest heroes. I notice when I go into schools and talk to pupils that they are often very knowledgeable about how comics work—about how to tell a story and read the pictures—things which adults who only read books, and look down on comics, don't even notice. For some time I've been secretly wanting to write and draw a comic myself. I go to life drawing classes; I'm getting better at drawing people... Maybe one day soon I'll begin."

Critics have acclaimed Pullman's spunky heroine, sixteen-year-old Sally Lockhart, who triumphs over ominous events in England's opium war days in *The Ruby in the Smoke.* Knowledgeable about guns and finances rather than the customary domestic or artistic pursuits of the day, Sally is a courageous, resourceful young woman. In a *Junior Bookshelf* review, Marcus Crouch

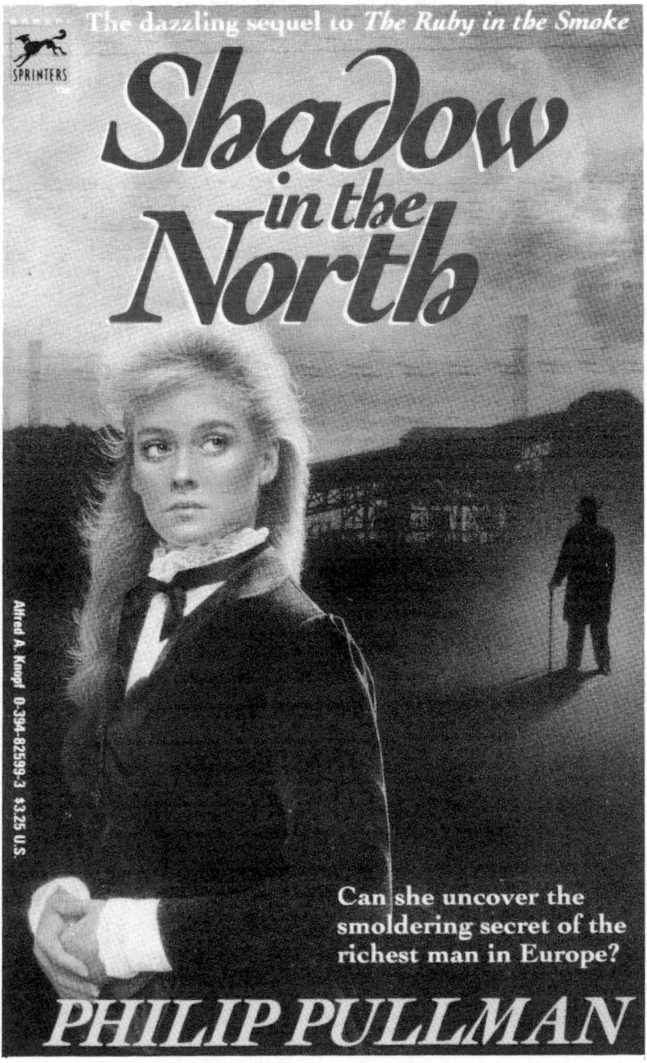

Cover of *Shadow in the North,* by Philip Pullman.

noted that Sally "has an appeal that grows on the reader and before the end I was as much her devoted slave as are the young men in the story." Pullman has also been lauded for his meticulous historical research. "The incident with the opium smoking is acceptable within the context of the novel, and the discussion of the British government's opium trade makes the novel appropriate as Social Studies supplementary reading," Brooke L. Dillon commented in *Voice of Youth Advocates. School Librarian* reviewer David Churchill observed that "The atmosphere and background, although richly detailed and authentic in feel, are never laboured because they are so varied." In Pullman's sequel, *The Shadow in the Plate,* Sally is a successful financial consultant working with photographer-sleuth Frederick Garland in increasingly violent Dickensonian surroundings. Dennis Hamley noted in *School Librarian* that the "atmosphere tingles with authenticity," and Crouch praised the book as "well researched, told with gusto, and with a string of colourful, larger-than-life characters."

The third book about Sally Lockhart, *The Tiger in the Well,* finds twenty-four-year-old Sally living with her two-year-old daughter, Harriet, born out of wedlock in Victorian England. Challenged by new threats from sinister sources who pursue her through the London ghetto, she is ultimately befriended by Jewish immigrants and a compassionate social worker, overcoming her enemies once again with courage and wit. "The story, carried by Sally's independent, resolute character and an exceedingly clever, complex plot, works its way through scenes of ever-increasing crisis and excitement to a stunning conclusion," Ann A. Flowers reported in *Horn Book.* "The saga of Sally Lockhart, Victorian, unmarried mother and business tycoon, ends on a high note," determined Crouch. "Here violent action and strong emotion are held together with social significance ... Exploitation, racial violence, police corruption, all these are shown as the product of the spirit of the age, not its causes," the critic continued. Ilene Cooper praised Pullman's use of detail in *Booklist,* noting that "nineteenth-century London comes alive here.... Remarkable, too, is the way Pullman interweaves a subplot about Jewish immigration and the conditions of the lower classes."

With his ability to select significant social events of various times and interpret them for contemporary readers, in addition to his storytelling strengths and memorable characters, Pullman's historical fiction appeals to a wide range of readers. Despite his focus on early England, his intriguing plots and lively pace make his work captivating to young adults not only in Great Britain but around the world.

WORKS CITED:

Churchill, David, review of *The Ruby in the Smoke, School Librarian,* June, 1986, p. 174.
Cooper, Ilene, review of *The Tiger in the Well, Booklist,* October 15, 1990, p. 439.
Crouch, Marcus, review of *The Ruby in the Smoke, Junior Bookshelf,* April, 1986, pp. 80-1.
Crouch, review of *The Tiger in the Well, Junior Bookshelf,* June, 1991, p. 127.
Dillon, Brooke L., review of *The Ruby in the Smoke, Voice of Youth Advocates,* October, 1987, p. 206.
Flowers, Ann A., review of *The Tiger in the Well, Horn Book,* p. 207.
Hamley, Dennis, review of *The Shadow in the Plate, School Librarian,* December, 1986, p. 368.

FOR MORE INFORMATION SEE:

BOOKS

Children's Literature Review, Volume 20, Gale, 1990.

PERIODICALS

Bulletin of the Center for Children's Books, May, 1987.
Five Owls, January/February, 1991.
School Library Journal, September, 1990.
Times Literary Supplement, December 1, 1978.
Voice of Youth Advocates, December, 1990.

* * *

PYLE, Howard 1853-1911

PERSONAL: Born March 5, 1853, in Wilmington, DE; died November 9, 1911, in Florence, Italy; son of William (an owner of a leather business) and Margaret Churchman (Painter) Pyle; married Anne Poole (a singer), April 12, 1881; children: seven. *Education:* Attended private schools, art school in Philadelphia for

Howard Pyle

three years, and Art Student's League in New York. *Religion:* Society of Friends (Quaker).

ADDRESSES: Home—Wilmington, DE.

CAREER: Author, artist, painter, teacher of illustration, and writer of children's stories; employed as an illustrator for *Scribner's Monthly;* taught illustration at Drexel Institute of Arts and Sciences in Philadelphia, 1894-1900, later establishing his own art school in Wilmington.

MEMBER: National Institute of Arts and Letters, Associate National Academy, National Academy, Century Club (New York), Franklin Inn Club (Philadelphia).

WRITINGS:

SELF-ILLUSTRATED, EXCEPT AS NOTED

The Merry Adventures of Robin Hood of Great Renown in Nottinghamshire, Scribner, 1883.
Pepper and Salt; or, Seasoning for Young Folk, Harper, 1885.
Otto of the Silver Hand, Scribner, 1888.
The Wonder Clock; or, Four and Twenty Marvellous Tales, Being One for Each Hour of the Day (with verses by sister, Katherine Pyle), Harper, 1888.
The Rose of Paradise, Harper, 1888.
Book of Pirates, Harper, 1891, published as *Howard Pyle's Book of Pirates,* edited by Merle Johnson, Harper, 1921.
Men of Iron, Harper, 1892.
A Modern Aladdin; or, The Wonderful Adventures of Oliver Munier, Harper, 1892.
The Story of Jack Ballister's Fortunes, Century, 1895.
Twilight Land, Harper, 1895.
The Garden behind the Moon: A Real Story of the Moon Angel, Scribner, 1895.
The Price of Blood: An Extravaganza of New York Life in 1807, R. G. Badger, 1899.
The Story of King Arthur and His Knights, Scribner, 1903, published as *The Book of King Arthur,* Children's Press, 1969.
The Story of the Champions of the Round Table, Scribner, 1905.
Stolen Treasure (stories), Harper, 1907.
(With Winthrop Packard, Molly Elliot Seawell, and others) *Strange Stories of the Revolution,* Harper, 1907.
The Story of Sir Launcelot and His Companions, Scribner, 1907.
(With J. H. Upshur, Paul Hull, Reginald Gourlay, and others) *Adventures of Pirates and Sea-Rovers,* Harper, 1908.
The Ruby of Kishmoor, Harper, 1908.
The Story of the Grail and the Passing of Arthur, Scribner, 1910.

ILLUSTRATOR

Yankee Doodle: An Old Friend in a New Dress, Dodd, 1881.
Alfred Lord Tennyson, *Lady of Shalott,* Dodd, 1881.
Charles Carleton Coffin, *Old Times in the Colonies,* Harper, 1881.
Rossiter Johnson, *Phaeton Rogers,* Scribner, 1881.
William Makepeace Thackeray, *The Chronicle of the Drum,* Scribner, 1882.
Helen Campbell, *Under Green Apple Boughs,* Fords, Howard, 1882.
Will Carlton, *Farm Ballads,* Harper, 1882.
James Baldwin, *Story of Siegfried,* 1882.
C. C. Coffin, *Building the Nation: Events in the History of the United States from the Revolution to the Beginning of the War between the States,* Harper, 1883.
Horace E. Scudder, *A History of the United States of America Preceded by a Narrative of the Discovery and Settlement of North America and of the Events Which Led to the Independence of the Thirteen English Colonies for the Use of Schools and Academies,* Sheldon, 1884.
Oliver Wendell Holmes, *Illustrated Poems,* Houghton, 1885.
Francis S. Drake, *Indian History for Young Folks,* Harper, 1885.
Driedrich Knickerbocker (pseudonym of Washington Irving), *A History of New York,* two volumes, Grolier Club, 1886.
Thomas Wentworth Higginson, *A Larger History of the United States of America,* Harper, 1886.
Carlton, *City Ballads,* Harper, 1886.
Baldwin, *Story of the Golden Age* (also see below), Scribner, 1887.
Thomas Buchanan Read, *The Closing Scene,* Lippincott, 1887.
Elbridge S. Brooks, *Storied Holidays: A Cycle of Historic Red-Letter Days,* D. Lothrop, 1887.
Edmund Clarence Stedman, *The Star Bearer,* D. Lothrop, 1888.
Wallace Bruce, *Old Homestead Poems,* Harper, 1888.
Lafcadio Hearn, *Youma: The Story of a West Indian Slave,* Harper, 1890.
Harold Frederic, *In the Valley,* Scribner, 1890.
John Greenleaf Whittier, *The Captain's Well,* New York Ledger, 1890.
James Lane Allen, *Flute and Violin, and Other Kentucky Tales and Romances,* Harper, 1891.
O. W. Holmes, *One Hoss Shay, with its Companion Poems,* Houghton, 1892.
O. W. Holmes, *Poetical Works of Oliver Wendell Holmes,* two volumes, Houghton, 1892.
Dorothy Q. Holmes, *Together with A Ballad of the Boston Tea Party and Grandmother's Story of the Bunker Hill Battle,* Houghton, 1893.
O. W. Holmes, *Autocrat of the Breakfast Table,* two volumes, Houghton, 1893.
John Flavel Mines, *A Tour around New York* [and] *My Summer Acre,* Harper, 1893.
Coffin, *Abraham Lincoln,* Harper, 1893.
Mary E. Wilkens, *Giles Corey,* Harper, 1893.
Thomas A. Janvier, *In Old New York,* Harper, 1894.
William Dean Howells, *Stops of Various Quills,* Harper, 1895.
E. S. Brooks, *Great Men's Shoes,* Putnam, 1895.

Brooks, *The True Story of George Washington,* D. Lothrop, 1895.
Arthur Conan Doyle, *The Parasite: A Story,* Harper, 1895.
Robert Louis Stevenson, *The Novels and Tales of Robert Louis Stevenson,* three volumes, Scribner, 1895.
Harriet Beecher Stowe, *Writings of Harriet Beecher Stowe,* two volumes, Riverside Press, 1896.
Silas Weir Mitchell, *Hugh Wynne, Free Quaker,* Century, 1896.
T. N. Page, *In Ole Virginia,* Scribner, 1896.
Henry Van Dyke, *First Christmas Tree,* Scribner, 1897.
Woodrow Wilson, *George Washington,* Harper, 1897.
Francis Parkman, *Works of Francis Parkman,* three volumes, Little, Brown, 1897-98.
Mary E. Burt, *Odysseus, the Hero of Ithaca* (includes illustrations previously published in *Story of the Golden Age*), Scribner, 1898.
Henry Cabot Lodge, *Story of the Revolution,* Scribner, 1898.
Ernest Ingersoll, *The Book of Oceans,* Century, 1898.
Wilkens, *Silence, and Other Stories,* Harper, 1898.
Margaret Deland, *Old Chester Tales,* Harper, 1899.
Paul Leicester Ford and Janice Meredith, *A Story of the American Revolution,* two volumes, Dodd, 1899.
Mary Johnston, *To Have and to Hold,* Houghton, 1900.
Edwin Markham, *The Man with the Hoe, and Other Poems* (also see below), Doubleday, 1900.
Charles Holmes, editor, *Modern Pen Drawings European and American* (includes illustrations previously published in *The Man with the Hoe*), The Studio, 1901.
John Lothrop Motley, *Works of John Lothrop Motley,* Harper, 1900.
Nathaniel Hawthorne, *Complete Writings of Nathaniel Hawthorne,* Houghton, 1900.
Maud Wilder Goodwin, *Sir Christopher: A Romance of a Maryland Manor in 1644,* Little, Brown, 1901.
Robert Neilson, *Captain Renshaw; or, The Maid of Cheapside: A Romance of Elizabethan London* (also see below), L. C. Page, 1901.
Hartman, Sadakichi, *A History of American Art* (includes illustrations previously published in *Captain Renshaw*), L. C. Page, 1901.
Wilson, *A History of the American People,* five volumes, Harper, 1902, published with additional illustrations, Harper, 1918.
Harper's Encyclopedia of United States History, ten volumes, Harper, 1902.
James Russell Lowell, *The Poetical Works of James Russell Lowell,* five volumes, Riverside Press, 1904.
Wilbur F. Gordy, *A History of the United States,* Scribner, 1904.
Justus Miles Forman, *The Island of Enchantment,* Harper, 1905.
J. B. Cabell, *The Line of Love,* Harper, 1905.
Whittier, *Snow Bound: A Winter Idyl,* Houghton, 1906.
Cabell, *Gallantry: An Eighteenth Century Dizain,* Harper, 1907.
Henry Peterson, *Dulcibel: A Tale of Old Salem,* Winston, 1907.
Cabell, *Chivalry,* Harper, 1909.
L. E. Chittenden, *Lincoln and the Sleeping Sentinel,* Harper, 1909.
Margaret Sutton Briscoe, John Kendrick Bangs, and others, *Harper's Book of Little Plays,* Harper, 1910.
Thackeray, *The Works of William Makepeace Thackeray,* edited by Lady Ritchie, Harper, 1910.
William Gilmore Beymer, *On Hazardous Service: Scouts and Spies of the North and South,* Harper, 1912.
Don Seitz, *The Buccaneers,* Harper, 1912.
Fanny E. Coe, *Founders of Our Country,* American Book Co., 1912.
Cabell, *The Soul of Melicent,* F. Stokes, 1913.
W. H. W. Bicknell, *Etchings,* Bibliophile Society, 1913.
Deland, *Around Old Chester,* Harper, 1915.
W. F. Gordy, *Stories of Later American History,* Scribner, 1915.
Mark Twain (pseudonym of Samuel Langhorne Clemens), *Saint Joan Of Arc,* Harper, 1919.
Francis J. Dowd, editor, *Book of the American Spirit,* Harper, 1923.
Henry Gilbert, *Robin Hood,* Magazine Press, 1964.

Contributor of illustrations and writings to various periodicals and newspapers, including *Chicago Tribune, Collier's Weekly, Cosmopolitan, Harper's Monthly, Harper's Young People, Ladies' Home Journal, St. Nicholas,* and *Scribner's.*

OTHER

Within the Capes, Scribner, 1885.
(With others) *School and Playground* (stories), D. Lothrop, 1891.
(Editor) Alexandre Olivier Exquemelin, *The Buccaneers and Marooners of America,* Macmillan, 1891.
The Divinity of Labor (address), J. Rogers, 1898.
Rejected of Men: A Story of To-day, Harper, 1903.
(Contributor) Howells, editor, *Shapes that Haunt the Dusk,* Harper, 1907.
(Contributor) Katherine N. Birdsall and George Haven Putnam, editors, *The Book of Laughter,* Putnam, 1911.
King Stork, illustrated by Trina Schart Hyman, Little, Brown, 1973.

ADAPTATIONS:

MOVIE

The Black Shield of Falworth (adaptation of *Men of Iron*), starring Tony Curtis and Janet Leigh, Universal Pictures, 1954.

PLAYS

Sophie L. Goldsmith, *Wonder Clock Plays,* Harper, 1925.
Mary T. Pyle, *Robin Hood Plays Matchmaker* (one-act), Dramatists Play Service, 1939.
Pyle, *The Apple of Contentment* (one-act), Dramatists Play Service, 1939.
Pyle, *Three Strangers Come to Sherwood* (one-act), Dramatists Play Service, 1942.

RECORDINGS

Tales of King Arthur and his Knights, read by Ian Richardson, Caedmon, 1975.

SIDELIGHTS: Howard Pyle was a prolific author, editor, and illustrator, remembered for his adaptations of the Robin Hood story and Arthurian legends. He was also influential as a teacher of illustration; former students such as N. C. Wyeth and Maxfield Parrish recalled him as a demanding yet generous and devoted master. Through his skill and his tutelage Pyle was largely responsible for establishing a new standard of excellence in turn-of-the-century American graphic art.

Pyle was born in Wilmington, Delaware, on March 5, 1853, to William Pyle, the owner of a leather business, and Margaret Painter Pyle. He recalled in the April 1912 *Women's Home Companion* that his childhood was a "bright and happy" one during which his mother instilled in him a love of books and illustrations, reading to him from adventure stories such as *Robinson Crusoe* and other classics like *Pilgrim's Progress, Grimm's Fairy Tales,* and *The Arabian Nights.* The lush gardens in which he played stimulated his imagination, and he aspired to become a storyteller before he could even read or write.

By his own recollection an indifferent student, Pyle attended the Friend's School in Wilmington and later the small private school of T. Clarkson Taylor. He resisted his parents' desire that he attend university, set instead on a career as an artist, and subsequently he studied painting in Philadelphia with F. A. Van der Wielan. After three years under Van der Wielan, Pyle returned home to Wilmington and his father's leather business.

Pyle's first break as an artist came in 1876, when he wrote and illustrated a story about his visit to the Chincoteague Islands off the Maryland-Virginia coast. The piece, "Chincoteague: The Island of Ponies," was accepted by *Scribner's Monthly* magazine for its April, 1877, issue. Encouraged by this success and by the urging of Roswell Smith, one of the owners of *Scribner's,* Pyle decided to move to New York.

Pyle spent an impoverished eighteen months in New York before his first important piece, *A Wreck in the Offing,* was accepted by *Harper's Weekly.* This effort, for which he was paid seventy-five dollars, confirmed in Pyle's mind not only his life's career, but the future importance of illustration to the art world. Soon he left New York to return again to Wilmington, finding, as he wrote in a 1909 issue of *Harper's Weekly,* "the diversions in New York too many and attractive for sustained and serious effort." Back in Wilmington he settled into the work routine—shut in his studio from morning until nightfall—that made possible his prodigious output.

In 1883 Pyle saw published one of his best-known works, *The Merry Adventures of Robin Hood of Great Renown in Nottinghamshire.* He had first conceived of the project while in New York, hoping to sell stories and illustrations based on the famous outlaw to the juvenile magazine *St. Nicholas.* He approached the project with his customary care, extensively researching costumes, architectural styles, and settings; his main literary source was Joseph Ritson's 1795 collection of Robin Hood ballads. As was the case throughout his career, he created not just the stories, but the whole book: text, illustrations, and even a form of calligraphy featured in headings and captions. Pyle had been raised in a Quaker family, but he loved high adventure, and his Robin Hood stories are filled with excitement. Many of the episodes of the Robin Hood tales most vividly remembered by readers—Robin's contest on the log with Little John, for example, and his wooing of Friar Tuck—were popularized by Pyle's version.

In April, 1881, Pyle married Anne Poole, a singer. The couple eventually had seven children; but tragedy struck the Pyle family in 1889. While he and his wife vacationed in Jamaica, their seven-year-old son, Sellers, died unexpectedly. The boy was buried before the Pyles could return home. In his grief Pyle wrote *The Garden Behind the Moon,* a fairy-tale that is also a meditation on the necessity of accepting death.

From *The Story of King Arthur and His Knights,* retold and illustrated by Howard Pyle.

Adding to the demands on his time posed by work and family, Pyle began teaching illustration in 1894. He taught first at Drexel Institute in Philadelphia, but by the turn of the century had set up his own school in Wilmington. Pyle's students came away from their studies with vivid, fond memories of their teacher, whose course of study included enjoying the activities rural Delaware had to offer: hunting, bicycle riding, and evening walks. Pyle in his teaching stressed the dramatic—he required that his pupils write stories as well as illustrate them, and that they imaginatively insert themselves into any scene they were attempting to depict.

In 1903 Pyle suggested to Scribners publishers that he adapt a series of adventure tales from the King Arthur legends. Already in his career Pyle had written and illustrated two chivalric novels; *Otto of the Silver Hand* is a grim tale of life in the Middle Ages bearing little resemblance to the rousing adventures of Robin Hood; *Men of Iron* is a more straightforward adventure yarn set in the year 1400. Neither work was particularly successful. For his Arthur books Pyle drew background material from a variety of sources; his chief problem in retelling the legends was condensing the wealth of information into four volumes.

The series, beginning with *The Story of King Arthur and His Knights* and extending through *The Story of the Grail and the Passing of Arthur,* is still enjoyed today, despite the difficult style Pyle used to emulate medieval speech. The author downplayed some of the legend's sexual themes, concentrating instead on adventure and the nobility of his chivalric heroes. He turns many episodes of his Arthur stories into homilies, stressing the higher virtues of a knight over his more violent qualities.

Pyle traveled to Europe the year the last Arthur book was published. The trip was an opportunity to see firsthand the many famous paintings he had previously studied only in books. The works of the masters made a great impression on him, but his enjoyment was tragically cut short. He suffered an attack of renal colic in Italy and never fully recovered. He died in Florence in November 1911.

Howard Pyle greatly influenced children's literature and the course of American graphic art. His vivid and exciting retellings of Anglo-Saxon myths have popularized them for American audiences for nearly a century. As an artist he approached his craft with skill and integrity, setting a high standard of quality for illustrations that audiences have admired for generations after his death.

WORKS CITED:

Pyle, Howard, "When I Was a Little Boy," *Women's Home Companion,* April 1912.

Pyle, Howard, *Harper's Weekly,* June 12, 1909.

FOR MORE INFORMATION SEE:

BOOKS

Abbot, Charles, *Howard Pyle: A Chronicle,* Harper, 1923.

Bingham, Jane M., editor, *Writers for Children,* Scribner, 1988.

May, Jill P., "Howard Pyle," *Dictionary of Literary Biography,* Volume 42: *American Writers for Children before 1900,* Gale, 1985.

Nesbitt, Elizabeth, *Howard Pyle,* Walek, 1966.

Pitz, Henry C., *Howard Pyle: Writer, Illustrator, Founder of the Brandywine School,* Clarkson N. Potter, 1975.

PERIODICALS

Mentor, June 1927.

Outlook, February 23, 1907.

Q

Robert M. Quackenbush

QUACKENBUSH, Robert M(ead) 1929-

PERSONAL: Born July 23, 1929, in Hollywood, CA; son of Roy Maynard (an engineer) and Virginia (Arbogast) Quackenbush; married Margery Clouser, July 3, 1971; children: Piet Robert. *Education:* Art Center College of Design, B.A., 1956; Center for Modern Psychoanalytic Studies, graduate, 1991.

ADDRESSES: *Home*—460 East 79th St., New York, NY 10021. *Office*—223 East 78th St., New York, NY 10021.

CAREER: Scandinavian Airlines System, advertising art director in the United States and Stockholm, Sweden, 1956-61; free-lance illustrator, painter, and writer, 1961—; Robert Quackenbush Gallery, New York, NY, owner and teacher of art classes, 1968—; certified psychoanalyst, 1991—. *Military service:* U.S. Army, 1951-53.

MEMBER: Authors Guild, Authors League of America, Mystery Writers Club of America, Society of Children's Book Writers, Holland Society, National Association for the Advancement of Psychoanalysis, Society for Modern Psychoanalysis.

AWARDS, HONORS: American Institute of Graphic Arts Fifty Best Books award, 1963, for *Poems for Galloping;* Society of Illustrators citations, 1965, for *The Selfish Giant,* 1967, for *If I Drove a Truck,* 1969, for *Little Hans, the Devoted Friend* and *The Pilot,* and 1985, for *The Scarlet Letter;* Golden Kite honor book, 1973, for *Red Rock over the River;* American Flag Institute Award for outstanding contribution in the field of children's literature, 1976, 1977, and 1984; Edgar Allan Poe Special Award, 1981, for *Detective Mole and the Halloween Mystery.*

WRITINGS:

SELF-ILLUSTRATED CHILDREN'S BOOKS

Old MacDonald Had a Farm, Lippincott, 1972.
Go Tell Aunt Rhody, Lippincott, 1973.
She'll Be Comin' 'Round the Mountain, Lippincott, 1973.
Clementine, Lippincott, 1975.
There'll Be a Hot Time in the Old Town Tonight: The Great Chicago Fire of 1871 Told with Song and Pictures, Lippincott, 1974.
The Man on the Flying Trapeze, Lippincott, 1975.
Too Many Lollipops, Parents' Magazine Press, 1975.
Animal Cracks, Lothrop, 1975.
Skip to My Lou, Lippincott, 1975.
Pop! Goes the Weasel and Yankee Doodle, Lippincott, 1976.
Pete Pack Rat, Lothrop, 1976.
Take Me Out to the Airfield!: How the Wright Brothers Invented the Airplane, Parents' Magazine Press, 1976, new edition, Houghton, 1991.
Sheriff Sally Gopher and the Haunted Dance Hall, Lothrop, 1977.

The Holiday Song Book, Lothrop, 1977.
Pete Pack Rat and the Gila Monster Gang, Lothrop, 1978.
Mr. Snow Bunting's Secret (Junior Literary Guild selection), Lothrop, 1978.
Calling Doctor Quack, Lothrop, 1978.
Along Came the Model T!: How Henry Ford Put the World on Wheels, Parents' Magazine Press, 1978.
The Most Welcome Visitor, Windmill, 1978.
The Boy Who Dreamed of Rockets: How Robert Goddard Became the Father of Space Travel, Parents' Magazine Press, 1979.
Who Threw That Pie?: The Birth of Movie Comedy, A. Whitman, 1979.
Moose's Store, Lothrop, 1979.
Movie Monsters and Their Masters, A. Whitman, 1980.
Henry's Awful Mistake, Parents' Magazine Press, 1980.
Pete Pack Rat and the Christmas Eve Surprise, Lothrop, 1981.
Henry's Important Date, Parents' Magazine Press, 1981.
The Boy Who Waited for Santa Claus, F. Watts, 1981.
No Mouse for Me, F. Watts, 1981.
City Trucks, A. Whitman, 1981.
Sheriff Sally Gopher and the Thanksgiving Caper, Lothrop, 1982.
Henry Goes West, Parents' Magazine Press, 1982.
First Grade Jitters, Lippincott, 1982.
I Don't Want to Go, I Don't Know How to Act, Lippincott, 1983.
Henry Babysits, Parents' Magazine Press, 1983.
Investigator Ketchem's Crime Book, Avon, 1984.
Funny Bunnies, Clarion, 1984.
Chuck Lends a Paw, Clarion, 1986.
Too Many Ducklings, Western Publishing, 1987.
Mouse Feathers, Clarion, 1988.
Funny Bunnies on the Run, Clarion, 1989.
Robert Quackenbush's Treasury of Humor, Doubleday, 1990.
Benjamin Franklin and His Friends, Pippin Press, 1991.
Henry's World Tour, Doubleday, 1992.

SELF-ILLUSTRATED CHILDREN'S BOOKS; "DETECTIVE MOLE" SERIES

Detective Mole, Lothrop, 1976.
Detective Mole and the Secret Clues, Lothrop, 1977.
Detective Mole and the Tip-Top Mystery, Lothrop, 1978.
Detective Mole and the Seashore Mystery, Lothrop, 1979.
Detective Mole and the Circus Mystery, Lothrop, 1980.
Detective Mole and the Halloween Mystery, Lothrop, 1981.
Detective Mole and the Haunted Castle Mystery, Lothrop, 1985.

SELF-ILLUSTRATED CHILDREN'S BOOKS; "PIET POTTER" SERIES

Piet Potter's First Case, McGraw, 1980.
Piet Potter Returns, McGraw, 1980.
Piet Potter Strikes Again, McGraw, 1981.
Piet Potter to the Rescue, McGraw, 1981.
Piet Potter on the Run, McGraw, 1982.
Piet Potter's Hot Clue, McGraw, 1982.

SELF-ILLUSTRATED CHILDREN'S BOOKS; "MISS MALLARD MYSTERY" SERIES

Express Train to Trouble, Prentice-Hall, 1981.
Cable Car to Catastrophe, Prentice-Hall, 1982.
Dig to Disaster, Prentice-Hall, 1982.
Gondola to Danger, Prentice-Hall, 1983.
Stairway to Doom, Prentice-Hall, 1983.
Rickshaw to Horror, Prentice-Hall, 1984.
Taxi to Intrigue, Prentice-Hall, 1984.
Stage Door to Terror, Prentice-Hall, 1985.
Bicycle to Treachery, Prentice-Hall, 1985.
Surfboard to Peril, Prentice-Hall, 1986.
Texas Trail to Calamity, Prentice-Hall, 1986.
Dog Sled to Dread, Prentice-Hall, 1987.
Danger in Tibet, Pippin Press, 1989.
Lost in the Amazon, Pippin Press, 1990.
Evil Under the Sea, Pippin Press, 1992.

SELF-ILLUSTRATED CHILDREN'S BOOKS; "SHERLOCK CHICK" SERIES

Sherlock Chick's First Case, Parents' Magazine Press, 1986.
Sherlock Chick and the Peekaboo Mystery, Parents' Magazine Press, 1987.
Sherlock Chick and the Giant Egg Mystery, Parents' Magazine Press, 1988.
Sherlock Chick and the Noisy Shed Mystery, Parents' Magazine Press, 1990.

SELF-ILLUSTRATED HUMOROUS BIOGRAPHIES FOR CHILDREN

Oh, What an Awful Mess!: A Story of Charles Goodyear, Prentice-Hall, 1980.
What Has Wild Tom Done Now?!!!, Prentice-Hall, 1981.
Ahoy! Ahoy! Are You There?: A Story of Alexander Graham Bell, Prentice-Hall, 1981.
Here a Plant, There a Plant, Everywhere a Plant, Plant!: A Story of Luther Burbank, Prentice-Hall, 1982.
What Got You Started, Mr. Fulton?: A Story of James Watt and Robert Fulton, Prentice-Hall, 1982.
The Beagle and Mr. Flycatcher: A Story of Charles Darwin, Prentice-Hall, 1983.
Quick, Annie, Give Me a Catchy Line!: A Story of Samuel F. B. Morse, Prentice-Hall, 1983.
Mark Twain? What Kind of Name Is That?: A Story of Samuel Clemens, Prentice-Hall, 1984.
Don't You Dare Shoot That Bear!: A Story of Theodore Roosevelt, Prentice-Hall, 1984.
Who Said There's No Man on the Moon?: A Story of Jules Verne, Prentice-Hall, 1985.
Once Upon a Time!: A Story of the Brothers Grimm, Prentice-Hall, 1985.
Old Silver Leg Takes Over!: A Story of Peter Stuyvesant, Prentice-Hall, 1986.
Who Let Muddy Boots into the White House?: A Story of Andrew Jackson, Prentice-Hall, 1986.
Quit Pulling My Leg!: A Story of Davy Crockett, Prentice-Hall, 1987.
Who's That Girl with the Gun?: A Story of Annie Oakley, Prentice-Hall, 1988.
I Did It with My Hatchet: A Story of George Washington, Pippin Press, 1989.

Clear the Cow Pasture, I'm Coming in for a Landing!: A Story of Amelia Earhart, Prentice-Hall, 1990.
Pass the Quill, I'll Write a Draft: A Story of Thomas Jefferson, Pippin Press, 1990.
Stop the Presses, Nellie's Got a Scoop!: A Story of Nellie Bly, Simon & Schuster, 1992.

ILLUSTRATOR; CHILDREN'S BOOKS

Derrick, Schramm, and Spiegler, editors, *Adventures for Americans,* Harcourt, 1962.
Inez Rice, *A Long, Long Time,* Lothrop, 1964.
Hans Christian Andersen, *The Steadfast Tin Soldier,* Holt, 1964.
Oscar Wilde, *The Selfish Giant,* Holt, 1965.
My City, Macmillan, 1965.
Marie Halun Bloch, *The Two Worlds of Damyan,* Atheneum, 1966.
Robin McKown, *Rakoto and the Drongo Bird,* Lothrop, 1966.
R. McKown, *The Boy Who Woke Up in Madagascar,* Putnam, 1966.
Guy de Maupassant, *The Diamond Necklace,* F. Watts, 1967.
Mary K. Phelan, *Election Day,* Crowell, 1967.
Anthony Rowley, *A Sunday in Autumn,* Singer, 1967.
Margaretha Shemin, *Mrs. Herring,* Lothrop, 1967.
Miriam B. Young, *If I Drove a Truck,* Lothrop, 1967.
Lilian L. Moore, *I Feel the Same Way* (Junior Literary Guild selection), Atheneum, 1967.
M. B. Young, *Billy and Milly,* Lothrop, 1968.
Irma S. Black, *Busy Winds,* Holiday House, 1968.
Eleanor L. Clymer, *Horatio* (Junior Literary Guild selection), Atheneum, 1968.
Stephen Crane, *The Open Boat and Three Other Stories,* F. Watts, 1968.
Herman Melville, *Billy Budd, Foretopsman,* F. Watts, 1968.
Mariana Prieto, *When the Monkeys Wore Sombreros,* Harvey House, 1969.
Natalie S. Carlson, *Befana's Gift,* Harper, 1969.
Era K. Evans, *The Dirt Book: An Introduction to Earth Science,* Little, Brown, 1969.
Wilde, *Little Hans, the Devoted Friend,* Bobbs-Merrill, 1969.
Luther L. Terry and Daniel Horn, *To Smoke or Not to Smoke,* Lothrop, 1969.
Georgess McHargue, *The Baker and the Basilisk* (Junior Literary Guild selection), Bobbs-Merrill, 1970.
M. B. Young, *If I Flew a Plane,* Lothrop, 1970.
Leonore Klein, *D is for Rover,* Harvey House, 1970.
I. S. Black, *Busy Seeds,* Holiday House, 1970.
Charlotte Zolotow, *You and Me,* Macmillan, 1970.
John Stewart, *The Key to the Kitchen,* Lothrop, 1970.
M. B. Young, *Beware the Polar Bear,* Lothrop, 1970.
Guy Daniels, translator, *The Peasant's Pea Patch,* Delacorte, 1971.
Lini R. Grol, *The Bellfounder's Sons,* Bobbs-Merrill, 1971.
Rosemary Pendery, *A Home for Hopper,* Morrow, 1971.
Harry S. George, *Demo of 70th Street,* Walck, 1971.
Jeanette S. Lowrey, *Six Silver Spoons,* Harper, 1971.
Julian May, *Blue River,* Holiday House, 1971.
M. B. Young, *If I Drove a Car,* Lothrop, 1971.
M. B. Young, *If I Sailed a Boat,* Lothrop, 1971.
George Mendoza, *The Scribbler,* Holt, 1971.
M. B. Young, *If I Drove a Train,* Lothrop, 1972.
Ann Cooke, *Giraffes at Home,* Crowell, 1972.
Mindel Sitomer and Harry Sitomer, *Lines, Segments and Polygons,* Crowell, 1972.
M. B. Young, *If I Drove a Tractor,* Lothrop, 1973.
M. B. Young, *If I Rode a Horse,* Lothrop, 1973.
Berniece Freschet, *Prong-Horn on the Powder River,* Crowell, 1973.
Jane Yolen, *Wizard Islands,* Crowell, 1973.
John F. Waters, *Steal Harbor,* Warne, 1973.
M. B. Young, *If I Drove a Bus,* Lothrop, 1973.
Eve Bunting, *A Gift for Lonny,* Ginn, 1973.
M. B. Young, *If I Rode an Elephant,* Lothrop, 1974.
E. Clymer, *Leave Horatio Alone,* Atheneum, 1974.
M. B. Young, *If I Rode a Dinosaur,* Lothrop, 1974.
E. Clymer, *Engine Number Seven,* Holt, 1975.
Natalie Donna, *The Peanut Cookbook,* Lothrop, 1976.
E. Clymer, *Horatio's Birthday,* Atheneum, 1976.
F. N. Mongo, *House on Stink Alley,* Holt, 1977.
E. Clymer, *Horatio Goes to the Country,* Atheneum, 1978.
Walter D. Meyers, *The Pearl and the Ghost or One Mystery after Another,* Viking, 1980.
E. Clymer, *Horatio Solves a Mystery,* Atheneum, 1980.
Charles Keller, compiler, *It's Raining Cats and Dogs: Cat and Dog Jokes,* Pippin Press, 1988.

Also contributor of illustrations to *The Bird Book,* edited by Richard Shaw.

ILLUSTRATOR; ADULT BOOKS

James Fenimore Cooper, *The Pilot,* Limited Editions Club, 1968.
Ann Cornelisen, *Torregreca,* Reader's Digest Condensed Books, 1969.
Mason Weems, *Life of Washington,* Limited Editions Club, 1974.
Pierre Loti, *An Iceland Fisherman,* Reader's Digest Condensed Books, 1978.
Stephen Crane, *Stories,* Franklin Library, 1982.
Norah Lofts, *The Possession of Sister Jeanne,* Reader's Digest Condensed Books, 1983.
Nathaniel Hawthorne, *The Scarlet Letter,* Reader's Digest Association, 1984.

OTHER

(Compiler) *Poems for Counting,* Holt, 1963.
(Compiler) *Poems for Galloping,* Holt, 1963.
The America Songfest (motion picture), Weston Woods, 1976, released as a video cassette, 1990.
Robert Quackenbush School Program Excerpts Plus His Reading of His Book 'Stairway to Doom' (audio tape), Robert Quackenbush Studios, 1985.
On Tour with Robert Quackenbush (video cassette), Robert Quackenbush Studios, 1985.
Dear Mr. Quackenbush: Writing and Illustrating a Mystery, Program 1, (video cassette), Robert Quackenbush Studios, 1989.
The Great American Storybook: The Story of George Washington, Program 1 (video cassette), Robert Quackenbush Studios, 1989.

"Reunion 1988," an original drawing by Robert Quackenbush of some of his characters.

Too Many Lollipops (coloring book), Robert Quackenbush Studios, 1990.

Also contributor to *Daisy Days,* Scott, Foresman, 1978, *The New York Kid's Book,* Doubleday, 1979, *On Parade,* Scott, Foresman, 1987, *Promises to Keep,* Open Court, 1989, and *Silver Secrets,* Silver Burdett, 1990.

ADAPTATIONS: She'll Be Comin' 'Round the Mountain and *Clementine* were adapted as film strips by Weston Woods, 1975; *The Boy Who Waited for Santa Claus* was adapted as a film strip by Westport Communications Group, 1982.

SIDELIGHTS: Robert Quackenbush is known for his many mystery books for young readers. His detective characters include Miss Mallard, a duck character based on Agatha Christie's famous Miss Marple, and such other sleuths as Detective Mole, Sherlock Chick, and Piet Potter (based on Quackenbush's son). Popular with children, Quackenbush's mysteries have also won awards. In 1981, *Detective Mole and the Halloween Mystery* received an Edgar Allan Poe Special Award as the best juvenile mystery of the year. In addition to his mysteries, Quackenbush has also written and illustrated many other children's books, including a series of humorous biographies of famous people.

Quackenbush told *Something About the Author Autobiography Series (SAAS):* "I am involved in a book for a long time. As I work on a book, many things are going on in my life at the same time. Very often the things that are happening around me find their way into the story and/or illustrations. The characters may take on the personalities and characters of people I've met and am involved with at the moment. Or an idea for a story may be sparked by the recollection of something or someone from my past which also becomes integrated into the book.

"Writers and artists are like that, I am told. They repeat moments in their lives—either consciously or unconsciously—in their creation. I have also heard that writers and artists master their conflicts with their talents and that they replicate themselves, at their deepest and most significant level, in whatever they create. True or not, I am sure of one thing: I enjoy being a writer and illustrator of books for young readers." Quackenbush added: "My training and experience as a psychoanalyst has been a valuable tool in the creation of my books."

Speaking to *Contemporary Authors (CA),* Quackenbush revealed that many of his books were written with his son, Piet, in mind. "From the day he was born, he put me in contact with a wealth of material—my own childhood experiences—that had been masked and nearly forgotten by time. These early memories and the people involved in them became the basis for such books as *Animal Cracks* and *Detective Mole* [that I] dedicated to Piet. The books seemed to take on a life of their own and the characters in them went on to individual series books that focused on humor."

His son also inspired a series of easy-to-read mysteries. Quackenbush explains in his *SAAS* article: "A series about Piet was created when children wrote and wanted to know about Piet and what he did in New York. Piet became a detective called Piet Potter and our apartment building and the places the real Piet went for amusement became the focus of the action for each mystery."

Quackenbush clarifies in *CA* that other children have also inspired stories: "While it is true that Piet has been a major source of inspiration for my books for young readers, many other children have given me ideas for books. That is why I am in frequent contact with children of all ages. One way is through after school art classes that I offer at my studio. Another is through school visits across the country. [Children's] thoughts, language, and interests change from month to month. So it is very important to be in touch with them. I like listening to them, hearing their ideas, and using their language in my books."

Quackenbush's mother inspired him to write *Henry's Awful Mistake,* the story of how Henry the duck rid his kitchen of an ant but almost destroyed his house in the process. "I got the idea for *Henry's Awful Mistake,*" he explains in *SAAS,* "when I called my mother out in Arizona one Saturday afternoon. I commented that she sounded depressed. She said she was 'feeling low' because she had planned to have friends over for dinner that evening and discovered a roach in her kitchen. She called the exterminator and he literally demolished her kitchen going after that roach, and she had to cancel her dinner party. 'I'm very sorry to hear about that, Mother,' I said, 'but thank you for the story.'" *Henry's Awful Mistake* has sold over 3,500,000 copies.

Another successful Quackenbush project has been his series of humorous biographies of famous people. Each of these books presents the highlights of a prominent person's life, focusing particularly on humorous events, and illustrates them with large, colorful drawings. The series includes such people as Henry Ford, Annie Oakley, the Brothers Grimm, Jules Verne, and Andrew Jackson. Many of these books are the only biographies on these figures available for young readers.

Quackenbush's artwork is as much appreciated as are his writings. He has illustrated his own books and some sixty other books as well, with artwork ranging from water colors to oil painting, and from pen-and-ink drawings to woodcuts. Richard Calhoun, writing in *Contemporary Graphic Artists,* believes that Quackenbush's woodcuts are his finest work. "Here," Calhoun states, "are lively, detailed creations worthy to stand beside those of such nineteenth- and turn-of-the-twentieth century masters as Howard Pyle and Joseph Pennell, composed with thought and executed by hand and with exceptional quality. Given the impact of technology on graphic art and the current fashionability of minimalism, Quackenbush's work is a comforting reminder of the essential humanity of art."

Over the years, Quackenbush has traveled the world speaking at schools about his books. He has visited schools in Brazil, Thailand, and Germany, as well as throughout the United States. Two days a week he also teaches art classes to adults and children, and he teaches others how to write for children. Quackenbush has a simple rule when he teaches writing. He tells *Something About the Author:* "My basic teaching premise stems from my belief that everyone has a unique story to present and to share with children ... whether it is told with pictures or with words or both. To awaken these stories within my students, I begin by having them draw or write about the rooms they slept in as children. It is truly exciting to watch people discover their childhood worlds again."

WORKS CITED:

Article by Richard Calhoun, *Contemporary Graphic Artists,* Volume 3, Gale, 1988, pp. 167-172.

Contemporary Authors New Revisions Series, Volume 17, Gale, 1986, pp. 376-378.

Quackenbush, Robert M., article in *Something About the Author Autobiography Series,* Volume 7, Gale, 1989, pp. 249-265.

Something About the Author, Volume 7, Gale, 1975, pp. 177-179.

FOR MORE INFORMATION SEE:

BOOKS

Fourth Book of Junior Authors, H. W. Wilson, 1978.

PERIODICALS

American Artist, April, 1965.

Appraisal, winter, 1977; fall, 1978.

Bulletin of the Center for Children's Books, July-August, 1974; March, 1978; May, 1978; March, 1979; June, 1980; May, 1982; October, 1982; January, 1985; May, 1985; July-August, 1985; February, 1986; September, 1986; February, 1987; March, 1988.

Follett Library Newsletter, September, 1987.

Junior Literary Guild, March, 1978.

New York Times Book Review, April 23, 1989.

R

Arthur Rackham

RACKHAM, Arthur 1867-1939

PERSONAL: Born September 19, 1867, in London, England; died September 6, 1939; son of Alfred Thomas (a civil servant; Marshal of the Admiralty Court) and Anne (Stevenson) Rackham; married Edyth Starkie (an artist), July 16, 1903 (died March, 1941); children: Barbara Rackham Edwards. *Education:* Attended Lambeth School of Art.

ADDRESSES: *Home*—Stilegate, Limpsfield, Surrey, England.

CAREER: Artist and illustrator. While studying art in night school, worked in an insurance office, 1885-92; staff artist for the *Westminster Budget* (newspaper); free-lance illustrator, 1893—. *Exhibitions:* Rackham's drawings are exhibited in public collections in Barcelona, Melbourne, Paris, Vienna, and London.

MEMBER: Royal Water-Colour Society, Societe Nationale des Beaux Arts (associate).

AWARDS, HONORS: Gold medal winner at exhibitions in Milan, Italy, 1906, in Barcelona, Spain, 1911, and in Paris, France; master of the Art Workers' Guild, 1919.

ILLUSTRATOR:

Anthony Hope (pseudonym of Anthony Hope Hawkins), *The Dolly Dialogues,* Westminster Gazette, 1894.

S. J. Adair-Fitzgerald, *The Zankiwank and the Bletherwitch,* Dutton, 1896.

Henry Seton Merriman (pseudonym of Hugh Stowell Scott) and S. G. Tallantyre, *The Money-Spinner and Other Character Notes,* Smith, Elder, 1896.

H. S. Merriman, *The Grey Lady,* Smith, Elder, 1897.

Charles Lever, *Charles O'Malley, the Irish Dragoon,* Putnam, 1897.

Maggie Browne (pseudonym of Margaret Hamer Andrewes), *Two Old Ladies, Two Foolish Fairies and a Tom Cat: The Surprising Adventures of Tuppy and Tue,* Cassell, 1897, published as *The Surprising Adventures of Tuppy and Tue,* 1904.

Frances Burney, *Evalina; or, The History of a Young Lady's Entrance into the World,* Newnes, 1898.

R. H. Barham, *The Ingoldsby Legends; or, Mirth and Marvels,* Dent, 1898.

Harriet Martineau, *Feats on the Fjord: A Tale,* Dent, 1899.

Charles and Mary Lamb, *Tales from Shakespeare,* Dent, 1899.

Jonathan Swift, *Gulliver's Travels into Several Remote Nations of the World,* Dent, 1900.

Jacob and Wilhelm Grimm, *Fairy Tales,* translated by Mrs. Edgar Lucas, Freemantle, 1900, twenty-five

tales from a 1909 edition reprinted as *Snowdrop and Other Tales,* Dutton, 1920, revised edition published as *Grimm's Fairy Tales: Twenty Stories,* Viking, 1973.
Agnes Grozier Herbertson, *The Bee-Blowaways,* Cassell, 1900.
C. R. Kenyon, *The Argonauts of the Amazon,* Dutton, 1901.
B. G. Niebuhr, *The Greek Heroes,* Cassell, 1903.
Greene, *The Grey House on the Hill,* Thomas Nelson, 1903.
Mary Cholmondeley, *Red Pottage,* Newnes, 1904.
W. P. Drury, *The Peradventures of Private Paget,* Chapman & Hall, 1904.
Henry Harbour, *Where Flies the Flag,* Collins, 1904.
Richard Henry Dana, *Two Years before the Mast,* Winston, 1904.
Washington Irving, *Rip Van Winkle,* Doubleday, Page, 1905.
A. L. Haydon, *Stories of King Arthur,* Cassell, 1905.
(With H. R. Millars and others) Myra Hamilton, *Kingdoms Curious,* Heinemann, 1905.
James M. Barrie, *Peter Pan in Kensington Gardens,* Scribner, 1906, published in an edition retold by May C. Gillington Byron, Scribner, 1930.
Rudyard Kipling, *Puck of Pook's Hill,* Doubleday, Page, 1906.
Lewis Carroll (pseudonym of Charles L. Dodgson), *Alice's Adventures in Wonderland,* Doubleday, Page, 1907.
A. E. Bonser, B. Sidney Woolf, and E. S. Buchleim, *The Land of Enchantment,* Cassell, 1907.
Eleanor Gates, *Good Night,* Crowell, 1907.
William Shakespeare, *A Midsummer-Night's Dream,* Doubleday, Page, 1908, published with new illustrations, Limited Editions Club, 1939.
De La Motte Fouque, *Undine,* adapted from the German by W. L. Courteney, Doubleday, Page, 1909.
Maggie Browne, *The Book of Betty Barber,* Duckworth, 1910.
Richard Wagner, *The Rhine-gold and the Valkyrie,* Doubleday, Page, 1910.
Wagner, *Siegfried* [and] *The Twilight of the Gods,* Doubleday, Page, 1911.
Aesop, *Aesop's Fables,* translated by V. S. Vernon Jones, Doubleday, Page, 1912.
Mother Goose, *The Old Nursery Rhymes,* Heinemann, 1913, published as *Mother Goose Nursery Rhymes,* Viking, 1975.
Arthur Rackham's Book of Pictures, Century, 1913.
Charles Dickens, *A Christmas Carol,* Lippincott, 1915.
The Allies' Fairy Book, Lippincott, 1916, published as *A Fairy Book,* Doubleday, Page, 1923, published as *Fairy Tales from Many Lands,* Viking, 1974.
J. and W. Grimm, *Little Brother and Little Sister,* Dodd, 1917.
Thomas Malory, *The Romance of King Arthur and His Knights of the Round Table* (abridged from Malory's *Morte d'Arthur* by Alfred Pollard), Macmillan, 1917.
Flora A. Steel, *English Fairy Tales Retold,* Macmillan, 1918.
Algernon C. Swinburne, *The Springtide of Life: Poems of Childhood,* Lippincott, 1918.
Charles Seddon Evans, reteller, *Cinderella,* Lippincott, 1919.
Julia Ellsworth Ford, *Snickety Nick: Rhymes of Witter Bynner,* Moffat, Yard, 1919.
Some British Ballads, Dodd, 1919.
Evans, reteller, *The Sleeping Beauty,* Lippincott, 1920.
Irish Fairy Tales, Macmillan, 1920.
Eden Phillpotts, *A Dish of Apples,* Hodder & Stoughton, 1921.
John Milton, *Comus,* Doubleday, Page, 1921.
Nathaniel Hawthorne, *A Wonder Book,* G. H. Doran, 1922.
Christopher Morley, *Where the Blue Begins,* Doubleday, Page, 1925.
Margery Williams Bianco, *Poor Cecco,* G. H. Doran, 1925.
Shakespeare, *The Tempest,* Doubleday, Page, 1926.
Abbie Farwell Brown, *The Lonesomest Doll,* new edition, Houghton, 1928.
Irving, *The Legend of Sleepy Hollow,* McKay, 1928.
Oliver Goldsmith, *The Vicar of Wakefield,* McKay, 1929.
Izaak Walton, *The Compleat Angler,* McKay, 1931.
Clement C. Moore, *The Night Before Christmas,* Lippincott, 1931.
Dickens, *The Chimes,* Limited Editions Club, 1931.
John Ruskin, *The King of the Golden River,* Lippincott, 1932.
Hans Christian Andersen, *Fairy Tales,* McKay, 1932.
Christina Rossetti, *Goblin Market,* Lippincott, 1933.
The Arthur Rackham Fairy Book, Lippincott, 1933.
Robert Browning, *The Pied Piper of Hamelin,* Lippincott, 1934.
Edgar Allen Poe, *Tales of Mystery and Imagination,* Lippincott, 1935.
Henrik Ibsen, *Peer Gynt,* Lippincott, 1936.
Kenneth Grahame, *The Wind in the Willows,* Limited Editions Club, 1940.

Contributor of drawings to numerous periodicals, including the *Westminster Gazette, Scraps, Illustrated Bits, Daily Graphic, Pall Mall Budget, The Ladies' Field, Cassell's Magazine, Little Folks, Punch,* and *St. Nicholas.*

SIDELIGHTS: Though his father planned a business career for him, Arthur Rackham worked in an insurance office for seven years while he attended art school at night and began to get established in the profession he had leaned toward since childhood. His best-known legacy is a long list of books, many classics among them—including *Gulliver's Travels, Rip Van Winkle,* and *Peter Pan*—graced with the imaginative illustrations that earned him critical acclaim from readers of all ages and a wide following in his lifetime. After his death, his early works became collectors' treasures.

Rackham was born on September 19, 1867, in London, to Alfred Thomas Rackham, a civil servant, and Anne Stevenson Rackham. There were twelve children in the family; Rackham told *The Junior Book of Authors* that his boyhood "was spent in a noisy, merry, busy little community of work and play almost large enough to be independent of outside engagements."

After his years in the insurance office, Rackham joined the staff of the newspaper, *Westminster Budget,* where he worked from 1892 to 1896 and became known for his feature, "Sketches from the Life." At the same time, he was doing free-lance work. The year 1899 was a difficult period for him—the "worst time in my life," as he described it in *Bookman*—because of changing values in art and the growing popularity of photography. But his unique talent began to gain recognition from other artists, and soon he was sought by art societies, dealers, and publishers. His work in *Fairy Tales of the Brothers Grimm,* published in 1900, marked the beginning of his fame as an illustrator.

By 1910 Rackham was regarded as a leading illustrator. He had been "elected an associate member of the Royal Society of Painters in Water Colours in 1902 and was promoted to full membership six years later," according to *Fantastic Illustration and Design in Britain, 1850-1930.* He had become a member of the Art Workers' Guild in 1909 and was very active in that organization during the years from 1917 to 1919; in 1919 he held the master's chair. He spoke publicly about art and illustration, and in the 1920s he visited the United States more than once to meet some of his following here. In 1923 he addressed a high school class in New Jersey, and during his 1929 trip he was discomfited by the noise of New York but pleased by the warm reception he was given.

Rackham's immediate family was involved in art, too. He married the portrait painter Edyth Starkie in 1903, and their daughter, Barbara, born in 1908, was sometimes a model for her father. Much later, in 1931, she traveled to Denmark with him on his search for illustrations for Hans Christian Andersen's *Fairy Tales.* After the Rackhams built a house at Limpsfield, Surrey, their garden provided inspiration for Rackham's work, especially a favorite old beech tree that served as a model for some of the many trees with gnarled branches and human-like faces that were hallmarks of his work.

Early in Rackham's career, according to a *Horn Book* article by George Macy, Kenneth Grahame asked Rackham to illustrate his book, *The Wind in the Willows.* Rackham had been too busy to accept the invitation and had regretted it for nearly thirty years. In 1936, Macy visited Rackham to persuade him to illustrate another book, but the outcome of the visit was an agreement that Rackham would illustrate *The Wind in the Willows* first.

It was the last book Rackham illustrated. He had agreed to deliver the watercolors to the publisher in the spring of 1938, but at that time he had to undergo surgery for cancer. He continued the job nevertheless, able toward the end to work only half an hour a day, and finished in the late summer of 1939, just before England declared war on Germany. On September 7, he died.

Robert Lawson paid this tribute to the artist in *Horn Book* in 1940: "The appreciation of Rackham's genius has suffered, I think, by its complete perfection. All his drawings appear so polished, so finished, so graceful, that many fail to realize the great strength and firm knowledge that underlie this seeming ease." And in October, 1967, Ellen Shaffer also said in *Horn Book,* "It has been nearly thirty years since the death of Arthur Rackham; a whole new generation has reached maturity in that period and been charmed by his work, as were their parents and their grandparents before them. Their children, too, are delighting in the books he illustrated, and their appreciation of his art will grow with the years."

WORKS CITED:

Johnson, Diana L., *Fantastic Illustration and Design in Britain, 1850-1930,* Museum of Art, Rhode Island School of Design, 1979, pp. 82-85.

Kunitz, Stanley J., and Howard Haycraft, editors, *The Junior Book of Authors,* 2nd edition, H. W. Wilson, 1951, pp. 252-253.

Lawson, Robert, "The Genius of Arthur Rackham," *Horn Book,* May-June, 1940, pp. 147-151.

Macy, George, "Arthur Rackham and 'The Wind in the Willows,'" *Horn Book,* May-June, 1940, pp. 153-158.

From *Aesop's Fables,* translated by V. S. Vernon Jones. Illustrated by Arthur Rackham.

Rackham, Arthur, "The Worst Time in My Life," *Bookman,* October, 1925.
Shaffer, Ellen, "Arthur Rackham, 1867-1939," *Horn Book,* October, 1967, pp. 617-621.

FOR MORE INFORMATION SEE:

BOOKS

Hudson, Derek, *Arthur Rackham, His Life and Work,* Scribners, 1960.

PERIODICALS

Horn Book, May-June, 1940; February, 1972.

* * *

RAMAL, Walter
See de la MARE, Walter (John)

* * *

RANDALL, Robert
See SILVERBERG, Robert

* * *

RANSOME, Arthur (Michell) 1884-1967

PERSONAL: Born January 18, 1884, in Leeds, Yorkshire, England; died June 3, 1967, in England; son of Cyril Ransome (a college history professor); married Ivy Constance Walker, 1909 (marriage dissolved); married Evgenia Shelepin, 1924; children: (first marriage) Tabitha. *Education:* Educated at Rugby School, 1897-1901; attended Yorkshire College (now Leeds University), 1901.

CAREER: Writer, critic, and journalist. Freelance writer, ghost writer, and publishers reader, beginning 1903; assistant editor, *Temple Bar* magazine; traveled to Russia to learn the language and study their folklore, 1913; correspondent in Russia for *Daily News,* 1915-19, and *Observer,* 1917-19; sailed his own boat in the Baltic, beginning 1921, and later visited China, Egypt, and the Sudan; correspondent and columnist, *Manchester Guardian,* 1921-29; writer of fiction for children, beginning 1929.

Arthur Ransome

AWARDS, HONORS: Awarded the first Carnegie Medal, 1936, for *Pigeon Post;* Litt.D., University of Leeds, 1952; Commander of the Order of the British Empire, 1953; M.A., University of Durham; ALA Notable Book citation and *Horn Book* honor list citation, both for *The Fool of the World and the Flying Ship.*

WRITINGS:

FOR CHILDREN

The Child's Book of the Seasons, Anthony Treherne, 1906.
The Things in Our Garden, Anthony Treherne, 1906.
Pond and Stream, Anthony Treherne, 1906.
Highways and Byways in Fairyland, Alston Rivers, 1906, McBride, 1909.
The Imp and the Elf and the Ogre, Nisbet, 1910.
Old Peter's Russian Tales (also see below), illustrated by Dmitri Mitrokhin, F. A. Stokes, 1917, new edition, Puffin, 1974.
Aladdin and His Wonderful Lamp in Rhyme, illustrated by Mackenzie, Nisbet, 1920.
The Soldier and Death: A Russian Folk Tale in English, Wilson, 1920, Huebsch, 1922.
Swallows and Amazons, J. Cape, 1930, 2nd edition illustrated by Clifford Webb, 1931, illustrated by Helene Carter, Lippincott, 1931, new edition illustrated by the author, Penguin, 1968.
Swallowdale, illustrated by Webb, J. Cape, 1931, illustrated by Carter, Lippincott, 1932, new edition, Penguin, 1968.
(Self-illustrated) *Peter Duck,* J. Cape, 1932, additional illustrations by Carter, Lippincott, 1933.
(Self-illustrated) *Winter Holiday,* J. Cape, 1933, illustrated by Carter, Lippincott, 1934, new edition, J. Cape, 1961.
Coot Club, illustrated by the author and Carter, J. Cape, 1934, Lippincott, 1935.
(Self-illustrated) *Pigeon Post,* J. Cape, 1936, illustrated by Mary E. Shepard, Lippincott, 1937.
(Self-illustrated) *We Didn't Mean to Go to Sea,* J. Cape, 1937, Macmillan, 1938.
(Self-illustrated) *Secret Water,* J. Cape, 1939, Macmillan, 1940.
(Self-illustrated) *The Big Six,* J. Cape, 1940, Macmillan, 1941.
(Self-illustrated) *Missee Lee,* J. Cape, 1941, Macmillan, 1942.
(Self-illustrated) *The Picts and the Martyrs; or, Not Welcome at All,* Macmillan, 1943.
Great Northern?, J. Cape, 1947, Macmillan, 1948.
The Fool of the World and the Flying Ship (excerpt from *Old Peter's Russian Tales*), Farrar, Straus, 1968.

The War of the Birds and the Beasts and Other Russian Tales, edited by Hugh Brogan, illustrated by Faith Jacques, J. Cape, 1984.
Coots in the North and Other Stories, edited by Brogan, J. Cape, 1988.

NONFICTION

Bohemia in London, illustrated by Fred Taylor, Dodd, 1907.
A History of Story-Telling: Studies in the Development of Narrative, illustrated by J. Gavin, T. C. & E. C. Jack, 1909, Stokes, 1910.
Edgar Allan Poe: A Critical Study, Kennerly, 1910.
Oscar Wilde: A Critical Study, Secker, 1912, Kennerly, 1913.
Portraits and Speculations, Macmillan, 1913.
Russia in 1919, Huebsch, 1919 (published in England as *Six Weeks in Russia in 1919,* Allen & Unwin, 1919).
The Crisis in Russia, Huebsch, 1921.
"Racundra's" First Cruise, Huebsch, 1923.
The Chinese Puzzle, Allen & Unwin, 1927.
Rod and Line: With Aksakov on Fishing, J. Cape, 1929.
Fishing, University Press, 1955.
Mainly about Fishing, Black, 1959.
The Autobiography of Arthur Ransome, edited by Rupert Hart-Davis, J. Cape, 1976.

EDITOR

The World's Story Tellers, T. C. & E. C. Jack, 1908.
The Book of Friendship, T. C. & E. C. Jack, 1909.
The Book of Love, T. C. & E. C. Jack, 1910.
John MacGregor, *The Voyage Alone in the Yawl Rob Roy,* Hart-Davis, 1954.

OTHER

The Souls of the Streets, and Other Little Papers, Brown, Langham, 1904.
The Stone Lady: Ten Little Papers and Two Mad Stories, Brown, Langham, 1905.
The Hoofmarks of the Faun, Secker, 1911.
(Translator) Remy de Gourmont, *A Night in the Luxembourg,* Swift, 1912.
The Elixir of Life, Methuen, 1915.
(Translator) Yury N. Libedinsky, *A Week,* Allen & Unwin, 1923.

ADAPTATIONS: The Fool of the World and the Flying Ship was produced by Weston Woods Films, 1979.

SIDELIGHTS: Arthur Ransome has written some of the most enduring books for children. His "Swallows and Amazons" series had a distinct influence on the development of English children's literature in the 1930s. He wrote about the real lives of real children, often based on happy holiday vacations he himself had in his youth. His stories were founded upon a solid foundation of technical expertise in outdoor activities such as camping, sailing, and fishing. In addition, as a translator and reteller of Russian folktales he produced two outstanding collections: *Old Peter's Russian Tales* and *The War of the Birds and the Beasts.*

Born in 1884 in Leeds, England, Ransome was the son of a history professor who loved fishing and sailing and a mother who loved reading and had a gift for watercolor painting. Both parents encouraged reading, and for his fourth birthday Ransome received his own copy of Daniel Defoe's *Robinson Crusoe* as a reward for already having read it. An interest in the outdoors came through his father and his paternal grandfather, whom he called "a first-rate naturalist, as interesting a companion on a country walk as any small boy could wish for, and a very good, ingenious fisherman." "My maternal grandfather, Edward Baker Boulton, was just as ... interesting to small boys.... Though he had spent most of his life in Australia, his heart had never been in his sheep-farming. He was a good water-colour painter and cared for nothing else.... My mother inherited this gift," Ransome wrote in *The Autobiography of Arthur Ransome.*

But his father worried about Ransome's future because he did not seem able to stick to anything for long. "I was for ever after some new thing," he admitted in his autobiography, "and, much worse, for ever planning that it should be the occupation of a lifetime." Ransome's father died, however, when the author was just twelve years old and still in the lower grades. After some unhappy years at a school in Windermere and at Rugby School, Ransome entered Leeds University, where his father had taught, and for a few months studied chemistry. But he wanted to be a writer, to write wonderful stories like those he had enjoyed so much in his youth. His relatives did everything they could to persuade him to forget such a precarious way of making a living, but he persisted in his dream and soon left the university to make a life for himself in London.

At age seventeen he found a job as an office boy in a publishing firm, and little by little, by hard work, he managed to place some of his stories and essays in the newspapers. He enjoyed acquaintance with literary people such as G. K. Chesterton, E. Nesbit (also a writer for children), and Edward Thomas, a young poet.

Whenever he could afford it, Ransome spent a vacation in his favorite Lake district resort, Coniston, near his boyhood vacation home. There he became acquainted with the Collingwood family, whose head was W. G. Collingwood, biographer of the local art critic John Ruskin. Collingwood was the author of several books, including *Thorstein of the Mere,* "about the coming of the Horsemen to Coniston ... and the valley of the Crake, where I had spent the happiest days of my childhood," Ransome recalled, "a book that had delighted my father as well as his children." With the Collingwoods Ransome enjoyed picnics, explorations, and sailing days that would some twenty-five years later be revived in his "Swallows and Amazons" books. The boat they sailed that first summer was the *Swallow.*

Encouraged by these friends, Ransome decided to quit his job and begin to write full-time. He wrote a few easy books for children that showed his interest in nature and also ventured into serious literary criticism with a book about Edgar Allan Poe and another on Oscar Wilde.

In 1909 Ransome married Ivy Walker, who brought him little happiness and many complications as well as a daughter, Tabitha. At the same time the publisher to whom Ransome had entrusted several valuable manuscripts fled abroad under suspicion of embezzlement, and publication of Ransome's book on Oscar Wilde brought on an unexpected lawsuit. It was a low point in Ransome's life. "I had put all my eggs in one basket," he declared, "[and] the bottom of that basket had fallen out." It became more difficult for him to concentrate on writing. With the help of many friends, however, he resolved to pursue his interest in translating the Russian tales he had seen in the London Library, and he set out for Russia to study the language and the folktales at first hand. He went by way of Copenhagen, Denmark, "with the pious memory of Hans Christian Andersen," wondering would he "yet learn to write tales that English children might overhear with pleasure?" In St. Petersburg he dedicated himself to learning Russian, pressing everyone he met into the role of teacher, making friends with Russian children and studying their first readers—an ingenious method, especially for one who wished to retell the tales for children. Thus he came to understand the background of the tales from the most simple to the more complex, and soon was filling notebooks with his translations. He would read as many versions of a story as possible and then set them aside to write the tale for himself.

Gradually his affairs straightened out; his marriage was dissolved, and he began to take an interest in Russian life as the country entered World War I, with strikes, marching soldiers, and talk of revolution. After a month's visit to England, Ransome found himself back in Russia with an assignment as foreign correspondent for London's *Daily News.* News from the Russian front was in great demand. Later he served as reporter for the *Manchester Guardian.* His cables about the war and the Russian revolution were based on frequent contacts with the leaders Lenin and Trotsky. He was also sent to Bucharest, Romania, and later to the Middle and Far East. In 1924 Ransome married Evgenia Shelepin, Trotsky's secretary, who was a supportive wife and companion to him until his death.

Despite the excitements of being a war correspondent, Ransome realized in 1929 that he was not fulfilling his longtime goal of being a writer of successful children's books. He gave notice to his employers that he would be returning to England to resume a literary career. He finally settled down in an old farmhouse in the Lake district. His mind immediately went back to the happy memories of his summer adventures with the Collingwoods, and he sketched out the plan for *Swallows and Amazons:* two groups of children, boys and girls, from two different families are on holiday where a tiny, deserted lake island beckons them to explore. "The whole book was clear in my head, I had only to write it," Ransome wrote. But it was not to be so easy. Halfway through the first draft he had to write a series of articles for the *Guardian* to make ends meet financially; he found, however, that he could not write both imaginative stories and serious essays at the same time. On another assignment overseas he became miserably ill and had to return to England where he worked on *Swallows and Amazons* while recuperating.

The book's publication in 1930 in England, and a year later in the United States, brought thoughtful, appreciative reviews in distinguished journals. *New York Times Book Review* contributor Anne T. Eaton, for instance, noted that "this is a book for almost any age. Boys and girls from 9 to 12 are absorbed in the story, while for adults it is like watching, from another room and unobserved, delightful and natural children at play." After such a kind reception Ransome was encouraged to go on to the next adventure of the Swallows and Amazons, *Swallowdale,* and to continue his efforts. By 1936 five books about these child adventurers had been published and their author had received the first-ever Carnegie Medal. Gillian Avery pointed out in *Twentieth-Century Children's Writers* that Ransome "succeeds in conveying the intense importance and excitement of day-to-day details.... Ransome has given to his child characters a dignity and a stature that real children would dearly like to possess; it is one of the elements of his eternal appeal." Ransome indeed went to great pains to be sure that what he wrote for children was as accurate as possible in every detail. His camping and sailing and fishing instructions can be followed with good results today, though of course they contain few of the technical shortcuts made possible by modern equipment.

We Didn't Mean to Go to Sea (1937), the fifth book in the "Swallows and Amazons" series, is favored by some critics as "the most exciting, the 'biggest' in theme, and the most unified in action," as John Rowe Townsend claimed in *Written for Children.* Drifting out onto the North Sea in a fog, the characters are forced to sail a large boat across to Holland. It is realistic in its details because Ransome and his wife practiced the trip in his own boat, a fairly dangerous piece of research. Eaton called this "excellent reading.... This author's fine power of characterization is one of the reasons why an adult can read Mr. Ransome's books with genuine pleasure."

Great Northern? (1947) has been praised as one of the earliest books for children to raise the issue of protection of wildlife from wanton destruction or greed. In this story the children join forces against a human enemy who is despoiling the nest of a rarely seen waterfowl, the Great Diver (known in the United States as the loon). Correctly identifying the bird, photographing it, determining its range and nesting habits, and securing its preservation, are scientific interests, now aided by the many bird and waterfowl guides available to all ages. This book broke new ground in children's literature, and it is not the only one of Ransome's works that makes the environment a concern.

Great Northern? shows another strength of Ransome's writing: his ability to write about a land or countryside vividly. In *Great Northern?* it is the rocky coasts, the purple-heathered hills and valleys of the Hebrides. In

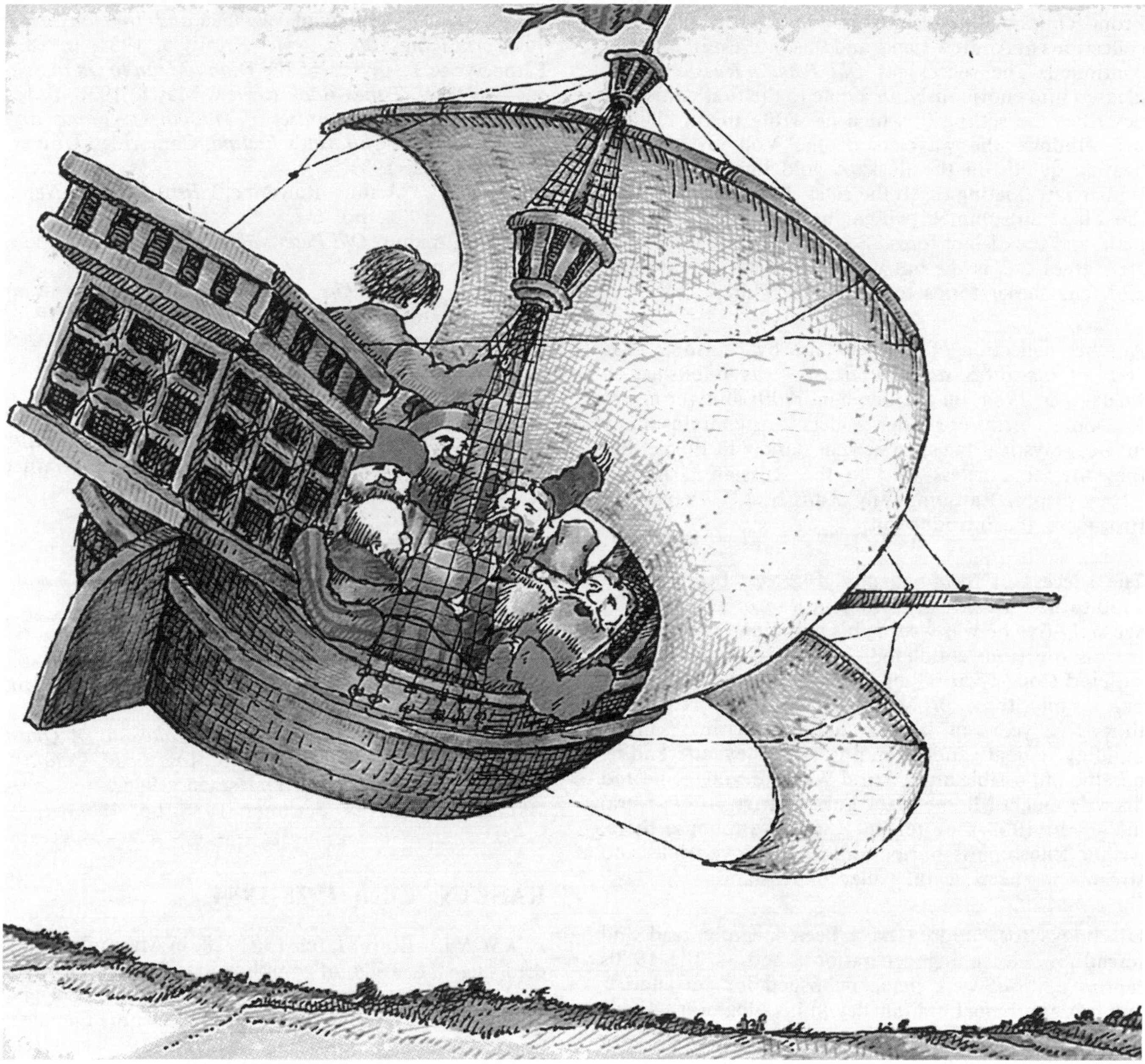

From *The Fool of the World and the Flying Ship,* retold by Arthur Ransome. Illustrated by Uri Shulevitz.

We Didn't Mean to Go to Sea it is the wild shores and the choppy gray and white seas along the Suffolk coast.

Ransome generously illustrated the "Swallows and Amazons" books with sketches of various sizes, maps, and drawings of birds, boats, the kinds of knots and needles used in netting and fishing, and natural settings. Although he was not a trained artist, Ransome chose to illustrate these books himself because, he reasoned, the stories came out of the mouths of children, so to be fully convincing they should look as if the children sketched them. "The pictures are not, in the true sense, illustrations; they are really part of the text," Hugh Shelley explained in *Arthur Ransome.* Ransome's illustrations "are intentionally amateurish and so aim to help the reader to trust in the reality of the story. They were, therefore, an extremely interesting innovation in the technique of illustrating—one must still use the word—children's books."

Ransome took a keen interest in what contemporary artists were doing, and himself selected Fred Taylor to illustrate his adult book, *Bohemia in London* (1907). Taylor introduced him to a sketch club in London and encouraged him to draw. Even while working hard on translations of *Old Peter's Russian Tales* he kept in friendly touch with both English and Russian artists, notably Dmitri Mitrokhin, who illustrated that collection. Ransome was working in the war-torn city of St. Petersburg at the time, and in order to meet a deadline, the British ambassador allowed him to send all of Mitrokhin's pictures and his own final corrections for *Old Peter* safely home in the Embassy bag.

From childhood Ransome had read the fairy tale collections of Andrew Lang, and this interest in folktales continued. The success of *Old Peter's Russian Tales* pleased him enormously. In a note to the first edition he describes the setting in which he wrote them: "Under my windows the wavelets of the Volkhov ... are beating quietly in the dusk. A gold light burns on a timber raft floating down the river. Beyond the river in the blue midsummer twilight are the broad Russian plain and the distant forest. Somewhere in that forest of great trees ... is the hut where old Peter sits at night and tells these stories to his grandchildren."

Another collection of Russian tales by Ransome, *The War of the Birds and the Beasts,* was published in England in 1984, on the one-hundredth anniversary of Ransome's birth. For older readers, this contains many magical-mystical tales, somewhat darker in theme, but they are nonetheless true to the Russian character. "They display Ransome only at his best," wrote Hugh Brogan in the introduction.

The success of *Swallows and Amazons* beginning in 1930 turned the tide of fortune in Ransome's favor. By age sixty-five he was writing his autobiography—recalling his life from childhood to the year 1932. He had suffered from a variety of illnesses and farsightedness, but despite these problems he spent the remaining thirty-five years of his life happily writing, sailing, building a boat, and attending sports events. Sailing became impossible after World War II began, so he and his wife sought a home in the Lake district. After several moves, in 1963 they rented a small farmhouse there. Arthur Ransome is buried amid his beloved hills and streams in the peaceful valley of Rusland.

His books for children have been steadily read and reread by succeeding generations, and in the 1980s reprint editions were being published for yet another and more turbulent era. Shelley in his biography *Arthur Ransome* predicted that the popularity of Ransome's books would continue "because his basic stories are universal and even on the surface they do not date," for Ransome is "a very great craftsman who only cares about what he makes—and who makes only what he truly cares about." Other writers also emphasize the sound values that pervade Ransome's works. In *We Didn't Mean to Go to Sea,* for example, "events from outside force right conduct on those with the knowledge to perform it," Fred Inglis wrote in *The Promise of Happiness.* "Right conduct brings right feeling—fulfillment and happiness." As Neil Philip concluded in *British Book News,* children are "drawn in, too, by Ransome's lucid, direct prose, by his lively dialogue, and by the skill with which he sews his imagined fictions on to a real and intimately known and loved landscape."

WORKS CITED:

Avery, Gillian, "Arthur Ransome," *Twentieth Century Children's Writers,* 3rd edition, St. Martin's Press, 1989, p. 807.

Eaton, Anne T., review of *Swallows and Amazons, New York Times Book Review,* April 5, 1931, p. 18.

Eaton, Anne T., review of *We Didn't Mean to Go to Sea, New York Times Book Review,* May 8, 1938, p. 12.

Inglis, Fred, *The Promise of Happiness: Value and Meaning in Children's Fiction,* Cambridge University Press, 1981.

Philip, Neil, "Arthur Ransome," *British Book News,* spring, 1984, pp. 6-7.

Ransome, Arthur, *Old Peter's Russian Tales,* T. Nelson, 1958, pp. v-vi.

Ransome, Arthur, *The Autobiography of Arthur Ransome,* edited by Rupert Hart-Davis, J. Cape, 1976.

Ransome, Arthur, *The War of the Birds and the Beasts and Other Russian Tales,* edited and introduced by Hugh Brogan, J. Cape, 1984, p. 11.

Shelley, Hugh, *Arthur Ransome,* Walck, 1964.

Townsend, John Rowe, *Written for Children: An Outline of English-Language Children's Literature,* Garnet Miller, 1965, p. 108.

FOR MORE INFORMATION SEE:

BOOKS

Brogan, Hugh, *The Life of Arthur Ransome,* J. Cape, 1984.

Children's Literature Review, Volume 8, Gale, 1985.

Hardyment, Christina, *Arthur Ransome and Captain Flint's Trunk,* J. Cape, 1984.

Wardale, Roger, *Arthur Ransome's Lakeland: A Quest for the Real "Swallows and Amazons" Country,* Claphism, Yorkshire, Dalesman, 1986.

Writers for Children, Scribner, 1988, pp. 455-461.

* * *

RASKIN, Ellen 1928-1984

PERSONAL: Born March 13, 1928, in Milwaukee, WI; died August 8, 1984, of complications from connective-tissue disease, in New York, NY; daughter of Sol and Margaret (Goldfisch) Raskin; married Dennis Flanagan (editor of *Scientific American*), August 1, 1960; children: (first marriage) Susan Metcalf. *Education:* Attended University of Wisconsin, 1945-49. *Hobbies and other interests:* Book collecting, gardening.

CAREER: Commercial illustrator and designer, New York City, beginning 1950; author and illustrator of children's books, 1966-1984. Instructor in illustration at Pratt Institute, 1963, Syracuse University, 1976; guest lecturer at University of Berkeley, 1969, 1972, and 1977. *Exhibitions*—Group shows: American Institute of Graphic Arts, 50 Years of Graphic Arts in American show, 1966; Biennale of Illustrations, Bratislava, Czechoslovakia, 1969; Biennale of Applied Graphic Art, Brno, Czechoslovakia, 1972; Contemporary American Illustrators of Children's Books, 1974-75.

MEMBER: American Institute of Graphic Arts, Asia Society, Authors Guild, Authors League of America.

AWARDS, HONORS: Distinctive Merit Award, 1958, Silver Medal, 1959, both from Art Directors Clubs; *New*

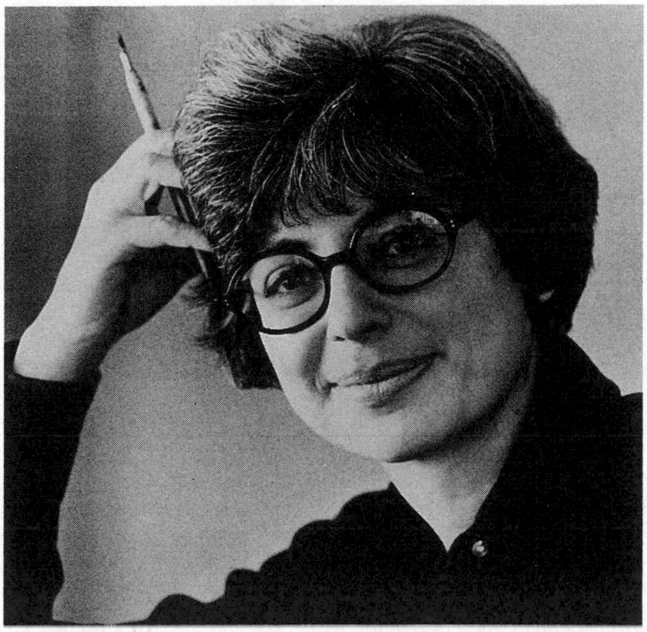

Ellen Raskin

York Herald Tribune Spring Book Festival Award (best picture book), 1966, for *Nothing Ever Happens on My Block; Songs of Innocence* was included in American Institute of Graphic Arts exhibit of 50 best books of the year, 1966; *Spectacles* was named one of the best illustrated children's books by *New York Times Book Review,* 1968; Children's Book Council chose *The Mysterious Disappearance of Leon (I Mean Noel),* 1972, *Who, Said Sue, Said Whoo?,* 1974, and *Figgs & Phantoms,* 1975, for the Children's Book Showcase; *Boston Globe-Horn Book* Honor, 1973, for *Who, Said Sue, Said Whoo?; Figgs & Phantoms* was chosen for the American Institute of Graphic Arts Children's Book Show, 1973-74, and as a Newbery honor book, 1975; Edgar Allan Poe Special Award, Mystery Writers of America, 1975, for *The Tattooed Potato and Other Clues; Boston Globe-Horn Book* Best Fiction Award, 1978, Newbery Medal, 1979, and American Book Award nomination, all for *The Westing Game;* an Ellen Raskin Lecture Symposium has been established in Milwaukee.

WRITINGS:

ALL SELF-ILLUSTRATED

Nothing Ever Happens on My Block (ALA Notable Book), Atheneum, 1966.

(Composer of music and illustrator) William Blake, *Songs of Innocence,* two volumes, Doubleday, 1966.

Silly Songs and Sad (poetry), Crowell, 1967.

Spectacles (ALA Notable Book), Atheneum, 1968.

Ghost in a Four-Room Apartment (Junior Literary Guild selection), Atheneum, 1969.

And It Rained (ALA Notable Book), Atheneum, 1969.

(Adapter) Christina Rosetti, *Goblin Market,* Dutton, 1970.

A & THE; or, William T. C. Baumgarten Comes to Town, Atheneum, 1970.

The World's Greatest Freak Show, Atheneum, 1971.

The Mysterious Disappearance of Leon (I Mean Noel) (Junior Literary Guild selection; ALA Notable Book), Dutton, 1972.

Franklin Stein (ALA Notable Book), Atheneum, 1972.

Moe Q. McGlutch, He Smokes Too Much, Parents Magazine Press, 1973.

Who, Said Sue, Said Whoo? (poetry; ALA Notable Book), Atheneum, 1973.

Moose, Goose and Little Nobody (ALA Notable Book), Parents Magazine Press, 1974.

Figgs & Phantoms (ALA Notable Book), Dutton, 1974.

The Tattooed Potato and Other Clues (ALA Notable Book), Dutton, 1975.

Twenty-two, Twenty-three, Atheneum, 1976.

The Westing Game, Dutton, 1978.

ILLUSTRATOR

Claire H. Bishop, editor, *Happy Christmas: Tales for Boys and Girls,* Frederick Ungar, 1956.

Dylan Thomas, *A Child's Christmas in Wales,* New Directions, 1959.

Ruth Krauss, *Mama I Wish I Was Snow, Child You'd Be Very Cold,* Atheneum, 1962.

Edgar Allan Poe, *Poems of Edgar Allan Poe,* edited by Dwight Macdonald, Crowell, 1965.

Aileen Fisher and Olive Rabe, *We Dickensons,* Atheneum, 1965.

Louis Untermeyer, editor, *Paths of Poetry: Twenty-five Poets and Their Poems,* Delacorte, 1966.

Molly Cone, *The Jewish Sabbath,* Crowell, 1966.

Arthur G. Razzell and K. G. Watts, *Probability,* Doubleday, 1967.

Robert Herrick, *Poems of Robert Herrick,* edited by Winfield T. Scott, Crowell, 1967.

D. H. Lawrence, *D. H. Lawrence: Poems Selected for Young People,* edited by William Cole, Viking, 1967.

Vera Cleaver and Bill Cleaver, *Ellen Grae,* Lippincott, 1967.

A. G. Razzell and K. G. Watts, *This Is Four: The Idea of a Number,* Doubleday, 1967.

V. Cleaver and B. Cleaver, *Lady Ellen Grae,* Lippincott, 1968.

Nancy Larrick, editor, *Piping Down the Valleys Wild: Poetry for the Young of All Ages,* Delacorte, 1968.

A. Fisher and O. Rabe, *We Alcotts,* Atheneum, 1968.

A. G. Razzell and K. G. Watts, *Symmetry,* Doubleday, 1968.

Susan Bartlett, *Books: A Book to Begin On,* Holt, 1968.

Suzanne Stark Morrow, *Inatuk's Friend* (Junior Literary Guild selection), Atlantic-Little, Brown, 1968.

Renee K. Weiss, editor, *A Paper Zoo: A Collection of Animal Poems by Modern American Poets,* Macmillan, 1968.

Rebecca Caudill, *Come Along!,* Holt, 1969.

A. G. Razzell and K. G. Watts, *Circles and Curves,* Doubleday, 1969.

Sara Brewton and John E. Brewton, editors, *Shrieks at Midnight: Macabre Poems, Eerie and Humorous,* Crowell, 1969.

A. G. Razzell and K. G. Watts, *Three and the Shape of Three,* Doubleday, 1969.

Alan Gardner, *Elidor,* Walck, 1970.

OTHER

Also designer of over one thousand book jackets.

Collections of Raskin's papers are housed at the Milwaukee Public Library, at the Kerlan Collection, University of Minnesota, and at the Children's Cooperative Book Center, University of Wisconsin, Madison.

SIDELIGHTS: Ellen Raskin was known as an illustrator of children's picture books and as a writer of mystery novels for older children. In both roles, she won critical and popular acclaim. In her picture books, according to Marilyn H. Karrenbrock in the *Dictionary of Literary Biography,* Raskin was "an inveterate puzzlemaker, a trickster, a razzle-dazzle-sleight-of-hand artist." This talent for puzzle-making served Raskin well in her novels, as well, in which she combined wildly preposterous plots with solid mysteries.

Speaking to Jim Roginski in *Behind the Covers: Interviews with Authors and Illustrators of Books for Children and Young Adults,* Raskin explained how she wrote a book: "I always write five times as much as I have to and then cut and cut, and make everything readable. The most important thing for me are the first few words, the first line to catch the reader. You can always start over again. I do. I write too much as it is. And, before you ask, I never know the ending. If I do know the ending by the second draft, I don't want to write the book. The ending is my reward for doing that book. So maybe on the fourth draft when I type out the ending I love it! I always have happy endings, too, because I write children's books and I do them specifically for children. And I never make fun of people. I'm very sensitive to that. Perhaps because I was made fun of as a child by other children; or perhaps because I love my characters too much."

Figgs & Phantoms is one of Raskin's most popular mysteries and an example of her creative approach. Focusing on a family of onetime vaudeville performers, the book features characters with names like Mona Lisa Newton, Florence Italy Figg, and Sissie Figg Newton. Truman the Human Pretzel can bend himself into any shape; the brothers Romulus the Walking Encyclopedia and Remus the Talking Adding Machine can answer any question; and Newt Newton is the town's worst used car salesman, trading plain-colored Cadillacs for shiny Edsels. Word play, eccentric twists of plot, and typographical jokes abound. Many of the jokes concern the rare book business (Florence Italy Newton is a bookdealer) and allusions are made to a score of books and authors. As Alice Bach noted in the *New York Times Book Review:* "Underneath the swagger and intricacies of a mystery salted with book-lined clues the author has written an elegant romance, extended a Victorian bouquet to all bibliophiles."

More importantly, *Figgs & Phantoms* tells a serious story of a young girl coming to grips with the death of a beloved relative. Young Mona Figg follows her deceased Uncle Flo into the afterworld and in so doing, learns of her own need to live life to the fullest capacity. "Readers may find the book a mystery, or an allegory, or a philosophical story—or possibly a spoof on all three," Ethel L. Heins wrote in *Horn Book.* A critic for *Kirkus Reviews* found some flaws in the story: "The zaniness here seems more often forced than inspired.... Still a juvenile novel—however unstrung—that takes such farcical liberties with death, grief and readers' expectations is rare enough to rate a hearing, and the Figgs—all mask and gesture though they are—do come up with a few show-stopping lines."

The Newbery Medal-winning *The Westing Game* "brought a glowing close to a fine career," as Karrenbrock noted. Telling the story of a quirky will left by wealthy industrialist Samuel Westing (who lived in "Westing House"), the book gathers together a group of oddly-assorted characters who must, to inherit a fortune, play "the Westing game"—a game with apparently different rules for each player. The game may also uncover the identity of Samuel Westing's killer. Disguises, shifting identities, and the confusing nature of the puzzle game provide Turtle Wexler, the book's 13-year-old protagonist, with plenty to investigate. "Raskin," wrote Denise M. Wilms in *Booklist,* "is an arch storyteller here, cagily dropping clues and embellishing

From *Figgs and Phantoms,* written and illustrated by Ellen Raskin.

her intricate plot with the seriocomic foibles of an eminently eccentric cast."

Raskin explained in *Horn Book* how she wrote *The Westing Game:* "I sat down at the typewriter with no wish of an idea, just the urge to write another children's book.... It is 1976, the Bicentennial year. My story will have a historical background; its locale, the place I know best: Milwaukee.... Recalling that Amy Kellman's daughter asked for a puzzle-mystery, I decide that the format of my historical treatise will be a puzzle-mystery (whatever that is). I type out the words of 'America the Beautiful' and cut them apart. Meanwhile on television ... come reports of the death of an infamous millionaire. Anyone who can spell *Howard Hughes* is forging a will.... Now I have Lake Michigan, a jumbled 'America the Beautiful,' the first draft of a very strange will, and a dead millionaire—a fine beginning for a puzzle-mystery."

Critics enjoyed the book's puzzle-mystery. Georgess McHargue in the *New York Times Book Review* found the book to be trickier than the ordinary mystery novel. "This is not a book for the easily confused, the unsophisticated, or the purist mystery fan," McHague wrote, "but it's great fun for those who enjoy illusion, word play or sleight of hand and don't mind a small rustle of paper in the background." Similarly, Sid Fleischman wrote in the *Washington Post Book World* that "here the terrain is lush with puns and other word play, with comic shribbery and broadleafed notions.... [Raskin] piles mystery upon mystery.... Her literary choreography is bouncy, complex and full of surprises."

In her Newbery Medal acceptance speech, Raskin clarified that *The Westing Game* had won the award, not her. "It is the book that is the important thing, not who I am or how I did it, but the book. Not me, the book. I fear for the book in this age of inflated personalities, in which the public's appetite for an insight into the lives of the famous has been whetted by publicity-puffers and profit-pushers into an insatiable hunger for gossip. I worry that who-the-writer-is has become of more interest than what-the-writer-writes. I am concerned that this dangerous distortion may twist its way into children's literature.

"I do understand the attempt to introduce books to children through their authors, and in my travels I have seen it done effectively and well. I salute all efforts to encourage reading. But an author is not a performer; meeting an author is not a substitute for reading a book. It is the book that lives, not the author."

WORKS CITED:

Bach, Alice, review of *The Tattooed Potato and Other Clues, New York Times Book Review,* May 4, 1975, pp. 34-35.

Fleischman, Sid, "A Raskin Riddle," *Washington Post Book World,* June 11, 1978, p. E4.

Heins, Ethel L., review of *Figgs & Phantoms, Horn Book,* October, 1974, pp. 138-139.

Karrenbrock, Marilyn H., "Ellen Raskin," *Dictionary of Literary Biography,* Volume 52: *American Writers for Children since 1960: Fiction,* Gale, 1986, pp. 314-325.

Kirkus Reviews, April 15, 1974, pp. 425-426.

McHargue, Georgess, review of *The Westing Game, New York Times Book Review,* June 25, 1978, pp. 36-37.

Raskin, Ellen, "Newbery Medal Acceptance," *Horn Book,* August, 1979, pp. 385-391.

Roginski, Jim, *Behind the Covers: Interviews with Authors and Illustrators of Books for Children and Young Adults,* Libraries Unlimited, 1985, pp. 167-176.

Wilms, Denise M., review of *The Westing Game, Booklist,* June 1, 1978.

FOR MORE INFORMATION SEE:

BOOKS

Bader, Barbara, *American Picture Books from Noah's Ark to the Beast Within,* Macmillan, 1976.

Children's Literature Review, Gale, Volume 1, 1976, Volume 12, 1987.

OBITUARIES:

PERIODICALS

New York Times, August 10, 1984.

Publishers Weekly, August 31, 1984.

School Library Journal, September, 1984.

* * *

RAWLINGS, Marjorie Kinnan 1896-1953

PERSONAL: Born August 8, 1896, in Washington, DC; died of a cerebral hemorrhage, December 14, 1953, in St. Augustine, FL; buried in Antioch Cemetery, Island Grove, FL; daughter of Frank R. (a patent attorney) and Ida May (Traphagen) Kinnan; married Charles A. Rawlings (a writer), May, 1919 (divorced, 1933); married Norton Sanford Baskin (a hotel owner), October, 1941. *Education:* University of Wisconsin, A.B., 1918.

CAREER: Young Women's Christian Association (Y.W.C.A.) National Headquarters, New York City, publicist, 1918-19; assistant service editor, *Home Sector* magazine, 1919; newspaper writer with the *Louisville Courier-Journal,* Louisville, KY, and the *Rochester Journal,* Rochester, NY, 1919-23; verse writer for United Features Syndicate, 1925-27; author, 1931-53. Also owner and manager of a 72-acre orange grove in Florida.

MEMBER: National Academy of Arts and Letters (elected, 1938), Phi Beta Kappa, Kappa Alpha Theta.

AWARDS, HONORS: Second place, *McCall's* Child Authorship Contest, 1912, for short story; second place, Scribner Prize Contest, 1931, for novella "Jacob's Ladder"; O. Henry Memorial Awards, 1933, for short story "Gal Young Un," and 1946, for short story "Black Secret"; Pulitzer Prize for fiction, 1939, for *The Year-*

Marjorie Kinnan Rawlings

ling; LL.D., Rollins College, 1939; L.H.D., University of Florida, 1941; Newbery Medal Honor Book, 1956, for *The Secret River;* Lewis Carroll Shelf Award, 1963, for *The Yearling;* honorary degree, University of Tampa.

WRITINGS:

South Moon Under (novel), Scribner, 1933.
Golden Apples (novel), Scribner, 1935.
The Yearling (novel), illustrated by Edward Shenton, Scribner, 1938, illustrated by N. C. Wyeth, 1939, reissued with a study guide by Mary Louise Fagg and Edith Cowles, 1966.
When the Whippoorwill—(short stories; includes "Gal Young Un"), Scribner, 1940.
Cross Creek (autobiographical sketches), illustrated by Shenton, Scribner, 1942, new edition with introduction by Shirley Ann Grau, Time, 1966.
Cross Creek Cookery, illustrated by Robert Camp, Scribner, 1942 (published in England as *The Marjorie Kinnan Rawlings Cookbook: Cross Creek Cookery,* Hammond, 1960).
Jacob's Ladder (novella), illustrated by Jessie Ayers, University of Miami Press, 1950.
The Sojourner (novel), Scribner, 1953.
The Secret River (novel), illustrated by Leonard Weisgard, Scribner, 1955.
The Marjorie Kinnan Rawlings Reader, edited with an introduction by Julia Scribner Bigham, Scribner, 1956.
Selected Letters of Marjorie Kinnan Rawlings, edited by Gordon E. Bigelow and Laura V. Monti, University Presses of Florida, 1983.

Author of syndicated column, "Songs of the Housewife," *Rochester Times-Union,* beginning 1926; contributor of short stories and articles to periodicals, including *New Yorker, Scribner's, Harper's, Atlantic, Collier's,* and *Saturday Evening Post.*

ADAPTATIONS: The Yearling was made into a film starring Gregory Peck and Jane Wyman by Metro-Goldwyn-Mayer (MGM), 1946; the 1948 MGM movie *The Sun Comes Up* was based on several of Rawlings's stories; "Gal Young Un" was adapted for film in 1980; *Cross Creek* was made into a film by Universal in 1983. A reading of *The Yearling* by David Wayne, Eileen Heckart and Luke Yankee is available on record and cassette from Caedmon; a musical play version of *The Yearling* was written by Herbert E. Martin, Lore Noto, and Michael Leonard in 1973.

SIDELIGHTS: When Marjorie Kinnan Rawlings began writing *The Yearling* from her home in Florida, she did not consider her story of a young boy and his pet deer a work for children. Indeed, upon its publication in 1938, *The Yearling* became a critically acclaimed and best-selling "adult" novel, winning the Pulitzer Prize for fiction and later inspiring a popular film. Since then, however, the novel has developed into a children's favorite, according to Agnes Regan Perkins in *Writers for Children,* "not only because of its touching story ... but also because of its strong characterization of the independent Florida [people known as] 'Crackers' and its vivid evocation of the wild beauty of the Florida scrub country."

Rawlings was born and raised in Washington, D.C., where her father worked as a patent attorney. Even as a young girl, Rawlings enjoyed writing; with the encouragement of her mother, she frequently contributed to the children's pages of local newspapers and won her first writing contest at age eleven. The countryside also held a special fascination for the author; she spent many summers on family farms, visits which she would later recall as some of her happiest moments. "I had known my maternal grandfather's Michigan farm," Rawlings wrote in *Cross Creek,* "but there I was both guest and child, and the only duties were to gather the eggs from the sweet-smelling hayloft. I had known my father's Maryland farm," she continued, "but ... we lived there only in the too few summers. There was only delight; the flowering locust grove; the gentle cows in pasture; Rock Creek, which ran, ten miles away from its Washington park, at the foot of the hill of the locusts, where my brother and I learned to swim and to fish for tiny and almost untakable fishes."

Rawlings's happy childhood ended with the death of her father in 1914; she then moved with her mother and brother to Madison, Wisconsin, where she entered college. She graduated in 1918, and the following year she married another would-be writer, Charles Rawlings, and moved with him to his hometown in New York. There the couple wrote for newspapers and tried to publish their fiction and poetry. Rawlings was unhappy with life in New York, however; in an attempt to save their marriage, she and her husband purchased an orange grove in Cross Creek, Florida, and moved there in 1928. The move failed to keep the couple together, but the Florida scrubland gave Rawlings an inner peace and a new inspiration for her writing. "We need above all, I think, a certain remoteness from urban confusion," the author explained in *Cross Creek,* "and while this can be found in other places, Cross Creek offers it with such beauty and grace that once entangled with it, no other place seems possible to us, just as when truly in love none other offers the comfort of the beloved. For myself, the Creek satisfies a thing that had gone hungry and unfed since childhood days. I am often lonely. Who is not? But I should be lonelier in the heart of a city."

Rawlings remained in Cross Creek and managed the citrus grove herself after her husband left and her marriage ended. There she began writing a series of stories based on her new home and neighbors; her "Cracker Chidlings" were published in *Scribner's* magazine and brought her to the attention of Maxwell Perkins, an editor with Scribner's publishing house. These first pieces reflected "the point of view of an outsider who finds the locals quaint and amusing," Agnes Regan Perkins stated, but by the time Rawlings published her first novel, *South Moon Under,* her "almost condescending attitude had changed to one of understanding and admiration for the enduring spirit and simple life of the Florida natives."

South Moon Under tells the story of a family of moonshiners and their struggle to survive; the novel includes family conflicts, escapes from government agents, and a murder. In bringing her Florida home to life, Rawlings "has drawn in terms as lush and slow as the scrub grows a country and a people fresh in literature and rich in reality," Jonathan Daniels commented in the *Saturday Review of Literature.* It is not the book's "freshness," however, that gives it "great distinction," the critic concluded. "What makes it one of the really fine books of the year is that the scene and the characters are drawn with a richness and vigor which makes them wholly alive."

Shortly after *South Moon Under* was published, Maxwell Perkins suggested that Rawlings attempt a novel in the same vein as Mark Twain's *Adventures of Huckleberry Finn.* Rawlings found the idea daunting, and wrote another, less well-received novel, *Golden Apples,* before she could be convinced. By 1936 Rawlings had begun the story of a poor, lonely boy who is forced to kill his pet deer after it destroys the crops his family needs to survive. Although *The Yearling* is told entirely from the point of view of young Jody, "I think it will only incidentally be a book *for* boys," the author indicated in a letter to her editor, as quoted by Agnes Regan Perkins. "I hope there will be nostalgic implications for mature people for we never *feel* more sensitively than in extreme youth, and the color and drama of the scrub can be well conveyed through the eyes and mind of a boy."

Taking place in northern Florida shortly after the Civil War, *The Yearling* presents several episodes in the life of the Baxter family "as they farm and fish and hunt for their living, as they visit their neighbors or go to 'the Christmas doin's' in the riverport village," Reese Danley Kilgo summarized in the *Dictionary of Literary Biography.* During the course of a year, Jody Baxter participates in a bear hunt, survives a terrible flood, sees a close friend die, and helps nurse his father back from a life-threatening rattlesnake bite. He also experiences the beauty of his surroundings, witnesses the dance of the whooping cranes, and befriends an orphaned fawn, which he names Flag. By the time Jody must sacrifice his pet, he has learned to accept the pain and responsibility that accompany adulthood. As a result, William Soskin noted in the *New York Herald Tribune Book Review, The Yearling* "is an education in life that is far removed from our dreary urban formulas.... [This] story of a boy and an animal becomes one of the most exquisite I have ever read."

While Jody's adventures and his friendship with the fawn make the novel attractive to children, Rawlings's story contains deeper elements which appeal equally to adults. Christine McDonnell, for instance, remembered *The Yearling* from her childhood reading as "a tear-jerker, with lots of action: hunting, fighting, natural

From *The Yearling,* by Marjorie Kinnan Rawlings. Illustrated by N. C. Wyeth.

disasters," the critic commented in *Horn Book.* "But as an adult reader, these are not the ingredients that interest me. Instead, I was fascinated, shocked actually, by the view of life that Marjorie Kinnan Rawlings reveals in this story, a view so strong, bleak, but reassuring, that I am surprised to find it in a book that has deeply affected so many children." Lloyd Morris elaborated in the *North American Review:* Rawlings "plunges us deeply into the hearts and the perceptions of a child, a wise man, and a brave woman. It recreates for us those fundamental attitudes of the human spirit which make life endurable, and those inalienable experiences of love and beauty which enable us to live it without shame. With *The Yearling,*" the critic concluded, "Mrs. Rawlings rightfully takes her place among our most accomplished writers of fiction."

Rawlings was also skilled in nonfiction, however; in her autobiographical work *Cross Creek,* Gordon E. Bigelow summarized in *Frontier Eden,* Rawlings "pours out anecdote after anecdote in a deceptively easy flow, story mixed with lyric nature description, character sketch with serious meditation, and the whole permeated by her own humanity and a bright glint of humor." Through her tales the author "reveals herself ... her philosophy of life and her mystical feeling for the land and nature," Kilgo related. In particular, Rawlings's "descriptions of persons and places in *Cross Creek* are exceptionally good," the critic added; "with *The Yearling, Cross Creek* has helped make for Rawlings a secure and lasting place in American literature."

"In a time when it was fashionable to be negative and despairing, [Rawlings's] books were affirmative," Bigelow stated. "In a time of great social and economic distress, of moral confusion and uncertainty, her stories quietly reasserted a familiar American ethic." And while the author's "legacy to children's literature essentially consists of just one book," Agnes Regan Perkins concluded, *The Yearling* is a work "that even after fifty years still lives through its strong characters, its telling metaphor, and its vivid scenes." "*The Yearling* has a kind of mythical quality which repays each successive reading," Samuel I. Bellman similarly asserted in *Marjorie Kinnan Rawlings.* "This novel elevates the writer to the rank of those special authors who at least once in their lives are capable of giving us dreams to dream by and words to shape those dreams." And dreams and their fulfillment played a significant part in Rawlings's life, as she disclosed in *Cross Creek:* "It is more important to live the life one wishes to live, and to go down with it if necessary, quite contentedly, than to live more profitably but less happily."

WORKS CITED:

Bellman, Samuel I., *Marjorie Kinnan Rawlings,* Twayne, 1974.

Bigelow, Gordon E., *Frontier Eden: The Literary Career of Marjorie Kinnan Rawlings,* University of Florida Press, 1966.

Daniels, Jonathan, "Scrub Folk," *Saturday Review of Literature,* March 4, 1933, p. 465.

Kilgo, Reese Danley, "Marjorie Kinnan Rawlings," *Dictionary of Literary Biography,* Volume 22: *American Writers for Children, 1900-1960,* Gale, 1931, pp. 282-285.

McDonnell, Christine, "A Second Look: *The Yearling,*" *Horn Book,* June, 1977.

Morris, Lloyd, "New Classicist," *North American Review,* autumn, 1938, pp. 179-184.

Perkins, Agnes Regan, "Marjorie Kinnan Rawlings," *Writers for Children,* edited by Jane M. Bingham, Scribner, 1988, pp. 463-467.

Rawlings, Marjorie Kinnan, *Cross Creek,* Scribner, 1942.

Soskin, William, "A Tom Sawyer of the Florida Scrub Lands," *New York Herald Tribune Book Review,* April 3, 1938, pp. 1-2.

FOR MORE INFORMATION SEE:

BOOKS

Dictionary of Literary Biography, Gale, Volume 9: *American Novelists, 1910-1945,* 1981, Volume 102: *American Short-Story Writers 1910-1945, Second Series,* 1991.

Twentieth-Century Literary Criticism, Volume 4, Gale, 1981.

PERIODICALS

New York Times, January 27, 1980.

New York Times Book Review, October 6, 1935, p. 3; November 30, 1941, p. 2.

Saturday Evening Post, January 30, 1943, pp. 26-26, 58-59.

Southern Literary Journal, spring, 1977, pp. 91-107.

Wilson Library Bulletin, December, 1983, pp. 296-297.

OBITUARIES:

PERIODICALS

Newsweek, December 28, 1953.

New York Times, December 16, 1953.

Saturday Review, January 16, 1954.

Time, December 28, 1953.

* * *

REES, David (Bartlett) 1936-

PERSONAL: Born May 18, 1936, in London, England; son of Gerald (a civil servant) and Margaret (Healy) Rees; married Jenny Lee Watkins (a teacher), July 23, 1966 (divorced, 1974); children: Stephen, Adam. *Education:* Queens' College, Cambridge, B.A., 1958. *Hobbies and other interests:* Travel, classical music, attending concerts.

ADDRESSES: Home—69 Regent Street, Exeter, Devon EX2 9EG, England.

CAREER: Wilson's Grammar School, London, England, schoolmaster, 1960-65; Vyners School, Ickenham, England, schoolmaster, 1965-68; St. Luke's College, Exeter, England, lecturer, 1968-73, senior lecturer in English, 1973-78; University of Exeter, lecturer in

David Rees

English, 1978-84; free-lance writer, 1984—. California State University, San Jose, visiting professor, 1982-83, 1985, and 1987.

AWARDS, HONORS: Guardian Award commendation, 1976, for *Storm Surge;* Carnegie Medal from British Library Association, 1978, for *The Exeter Blitz;* Other Award from Children's Rights Workshop, 1980, for *The Green Bough of Liberty.*

WRITINGS:

FOR YOUNG CHILDREN

The House That Moved, illustrated by Lazlo Acs, Hamish Hamilton, 1978.
The Night before Christmas Eve, illustrated by Peter Kesteven, Wheaton, 1980, Pergamon, 1982.
A Beacon for the Romans, illustrated by Kesteven, Wheaton, 1981.
The Mysterious Rattle, illustrated by Maureen Bradley, Hamish Hamilton, 1982.
The Burglar, illustrated by Ursula Sieger, Arnold/Wheaton, 1986.
Friends and Neighbours, illustrated by Clare Herroneau, Arnold/Wheaton, 1986.

FOR CHILDREN

Landslip, illustrated by Gavin Rowe, Hamish Hamilton, 1977.
The Exeter Blitz, Hamish Hamilton, 1978, Elsevier/Nelson, 1980.
Holly, Mud and Whisky, illustrated by David Grosvenor, Dobson, 1981.
The Flying Island, Third House, 1988.

FOR YOUNG ADULTS

Storm Surge, illustrated by Trevor Stubley, Lutterworth, 1975.
Quintin's Man, Dobson, 1976, Elsevier/Nelson, 1979.
The Missing German, Dobson, 1976.
The Spectrum, Dobson, 1977.
The Ferryman, illustrated with old maps and prints, Dobson, 1977.
Risks, Heinemann, 1977.
In the Tent, Dobson, 1979, Alyson, 1985.
Silence, Dobson, 1979, Elsevier/Nelson, 1981.
The Green Bough of Liberty, illustrated with old maps and prints, Dobson, 1979.
The Lighthouse, Dobson, 1980.
Miss Duffy Is Still with Us, Dobson, 1980.
The Milkman's On His Way, GMP, 1982.
Waves, Longman, 1983.

FOR ADULTS

The Marble in the Water: Essays on Contemporary Writers of Fiction for Children and Young People, Horn Book, 1980.
The Estuary, GMP, 1983.
Out of the Winter Gardens, Olive Press, 1984.
Painted Desert, Green Shade: Essays on Contemporary Writers for Children and Young Adults, Horn Book, 1984.
A Better Class of Blond: A California Diary, Olive Press, 1985.
Islands (short stories), Knights Press, 1985.
Watershed, Knights Press, 1986.
The Hunger, GMP, 1986.
(Editor and contributor, with Peter Robins) *Oranges and Lemons: Stories by Gay Men,* Third House, 1987.
Twos and Threes, Third House, 1987.
Flux (short stories), Third House, 1988.
Quince, Third House, 1988.
The Wrong Apple, Knights Press, 1988.
The Colour of His Hair, Third House, 1989.
Letters to Dorothy (essays and stories), Third House, 1990.
What Do Draculas Do?: Essays on Contemporary Writers for Children and Young Adults, Third House, 1990.
(With Robins) *Fabulous Tricks,* Inbook, 1991.
Dog Days, White Nights (essays), Third House, 1992.
Not for Your Hands (autobiography), Third House, 1992.
Packing It In (travel guide), Millivres Books, 1992.

OTHER

Rees's work is represented in anthologies, including *Remember Last Summer?,* edited by John Foster, Heinemann, 1980; *Cracks in the Image,* GMP, 1981; *School's O.K.,* edited by Josie Karavasil, Evans, 1982; *Messer Rondo and Other Stories,* GMP, 1983; *Knockout Short Stories,* Longman, 1988; *The Freezer Counter,* Third House, 1989. Author of column in *Gay Times;* regular contributor of book reviews to *Children's Literature in Education, Horn Book, Journal of the Royal Society of the Arts, School Librarian,* and *Times Literary Supplement;* contributor to various literature and library journals. Author's manuscripts are included in collection at University of Exeter, England.

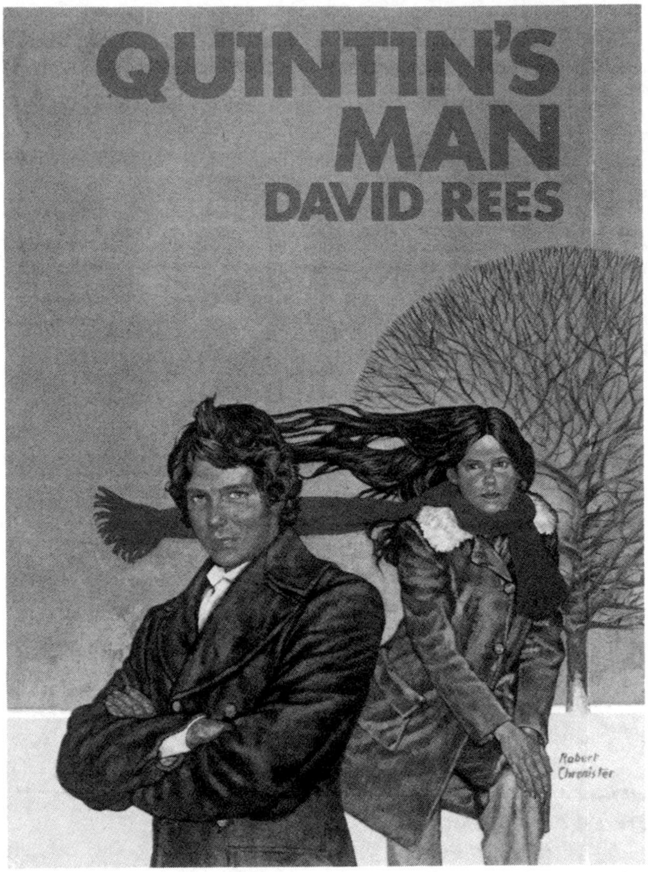

Cover of *Quintin's Man,* by David Rees.

WORK IN PROGRESS: Critical essays on contemporary novelists and composers.

SIDELIGHTS: David Rees has always seen writing as a way to reevaluate his past by letting fictional characters resolve the conflicts he experienced in his early life. In the many books he has written for young adults, the author's characters have experienced situations similar to those from his own adolescence, regardless of their sex or whether the story had a historical or modern setting. "My teenagers do things I never did, but which I perhaps would have enjoyed doing," Rees commented in an autobiographical essay for *Something about the Author Autobiographical Series* (*SAAS*). "I give them more chances and opportunities than I had, and I like to put them in situations where they grow up a bit, where they take a step towards maturity." Unlike many books of the genre, the author's young adult novels are noted for dealing openly with controversial subjects such as homosexuality. As difficult as the subject matter may be for some to deal with, Rees's books are critically respected for their honest, sensitive portrayal of the adolescent passage from youth to adulthood.

Rees was a boy of three when World War II began, and he lived with his family in a suburb of London during the blitz of 1940-41 when Germany was bombing the city almost daily. Even as an adult, he continued to have vivid memories of being awakened by the whine of air-raid sirens, or crouching in the dark listening for the "thump" of anti-aircraft guns repelling an enemy attack. "I don't think I have ever forgiven the Nazis for what they did to my childhood," Rees recalled. "When I was twenty I visited Germany for the first time; I drove across the frontier from Denmark, thinking—it's ridiculous, of course—that I'd put my head in a noose: S.S. storm-troopers would jump out of the bushes and kill me. It was a very unpleasant, creepy feeling. And that was eleven years after it was all over!" The intense childhood memories of this period of his life eventually caused Rees to write *The Exeter Blitz,* his most well-known book, for which he received the Carnegie Medal in 1978.

Rees and his family left London for the safety of a less-populated area, but found that air raids over the seaside resorts along England's southern coast occurred just as frequently. "Bournemouth had proved no safer than London," he recounted, "so we set off again, this time to a farm by the sea in an utterly remote area of Devon, in southwest England. The village—so tiny and scattered it scarcely deserves the name of 'village'—was called Welcombe. And welcome it was for sure. Here, you didn't know the war existed. I learned to swim and surf at Welcombe." It was at this point in his life, at the age of eight, that Rees began to write. "I realized one day that I was turning, in my head, everything I was doing into the third person, as if I wasn't me but someone else, and that I had been doing this, without knowing it, for weeks. It was a short step from thinking in the third person to writing in it."

At the end of World War II, Rees and his family returned to their home in Surbiton, but the memories of those few years in Welcombe provided the fabric for several of his later novels, such as *The Missing German, The Milkman's on His Way,* and *Waves.* Meanwhile, he was enrolled at King's College School, Wimbledon, where he continued his education until the age of eighteen. This period of his life was not as happy as those months in Welcombe, and would never find a place in his books. The school headmaster criticized the young Rees as being "too much of an individual" because of his disavowal of the school emphasis upon sports and the compulsory participation in activities such as the Cadet Corps, both of which the boy felt encouraged conformity. The young Rees felt himself marked as an outsider for other things as well, such as his Roman Catholicism, the Irish heritage with which he strongly identified, his physical immaturity, and the fact that he came from a less affluent background than many of the other students. Although his years at school were socially unhappy ones, Rees excelled in his academics and was able to win a scholarship to Cambridge where he graduated with a degree in English in 1958. At the age of twenty-two, after spending two years in travel throughout parts of Europe, Rees started on the teaching career which he pursued until 1984.

Rees's profession as a fiction writer began in earnest several years later when he began to research his family history. He had always had a fascination with his ancestors, most likely as a result of the close relationship he had with his grandparents as a young child. As he delved further and further back in time, some fascinating stories began to emerge which demanded a retelling. *The Green Bough of Liberty* was the result of his curiosity, as well as a culmination of both an increasing involvement in the teaching of children's literature and his enthusiasm for the works of several writers for young adults. The novel recounts the Irish uprising of 1798, which Rees's ancestors had taken part in, as seen through the eyes of the young protagonist, Ned Byrne. Although the plot revolves around a political rebellion which resulted in war and death, on a deeper level the story is an examination of one young man's ability to come to terms with the emotional aspects of the situation: the false heroics, unmet romantic expectations, the death of a brother, and the true cost of the rebellion to both his family and himself. In many of his later books Rees opted not to put his characters in such a remotely historical setting. For example, *The Exeter Blitz* takes place during its author's own lifetime, giving readers a vivid account of everyday life amidst the German bombing of Exeter, England, during World War II.

With books such as *In the Tent, The Lighthouse,* and *The Milkman's on His Way* Rees began to directly confront the central concerns of his own adolescence: the emotional experiences he underwent while coming to terms with his homosexuality. In *The Milkman's on His Way,* within a setting that recalls summers spent at Welcombe during the war, Rees tells the story of Ewan, who is beginning to suspect that he is gay. The young man experiences a great deal of emotional turmoil, guilt, and uncertainty due to the growing awareness that he feels a sexual attraction for his best friend, Leslie, who is heterosexual. Through the course of the novel, Ewan gradually learns to deal with his feelings, finally being put into a situation where he must openly confront his parents with his homosexuality. By the novel's end, Ewan has come to terms with his own identity and makes the decision to leave home and live in a gay community in London as a symbolic transition to independent adulthood. Although the book was rejected by Rees's usual publisher, Dobson, due to its sometimes graphic portrayals of sexual activity, David Keyes wrote in *Voice of Youth Advocates* that "the frankness seems essential and does not linger." The critic added, "This novel is an important addition to others focusing on this theme." It also proved to be a best-seller.

Rees has been an instructor of English for most of his adult life and enjoys teaching his craft to enthusiastic young writers. "I believe anyone can write, provided he or she can spell, punctuate, and string a sentence together," he said in *SAAS*. "It isn't some extraordinary, special gift of the gods. The chief thing is to want to do it enough. It helps, too, to be able to enjoy reading a lot, to be happy in one's own company, to like being housebound for much of the time, and to refuse to give up because of rejections, or the naggings that come from within. I've taught children who are potentially much better writers than I will ever be, but who, as adults, have written nothing; the only difference between us is this—they have no real urge to do it. Nobody can teach you how; you learn [writing] by doing it. Believe in yourself, and just get on with it!"

WORK CITED:

Something about the Author Autobiographical Series, Volume 5, Gale, 1988.

Voice of Youth Advocates, February, 1984, p. 340.

FOR MORE INFORMATION SEE:

BOOKS

Holmes Holze, Sally, editor, *Fifth Book of Junior Authors,* H. W. Wilson, 1983.
Kingman, Lee, and others, compilers, *Illustrators of Children's Books: 1967-1976,* Horn Book, 1978.
Twentieth Century Children's Writers, St. Martins Press, 1989.
Burton, Peter, *Talking To...*, Third House, 1991.

PERIODICALS

Booklist, December 15, 1978, p. 680; September 1, 1980, p. 40; April 15, 1984, p. 1145.
School Librarian, September, 1984, pp. 210-211; August, 1989, pp. 88-90.
Times Literary Supplement, December 10, 1976, p. 1548; March 28, 1980, p. 362; November 21, 1980, p. 1322.

* * *

REID BANKS, Lynne 1929-

PERSONAL: Listed in some sources under Banks; born July 31, 1929, in London, England; daughter of James Reid Banks (a doctor) and Muriel Alexander (an actress; maiden name, Marsh); married Chaim Stephenson (a sculptor), 1965; children: Adiel, Gillon, Omri (sons).

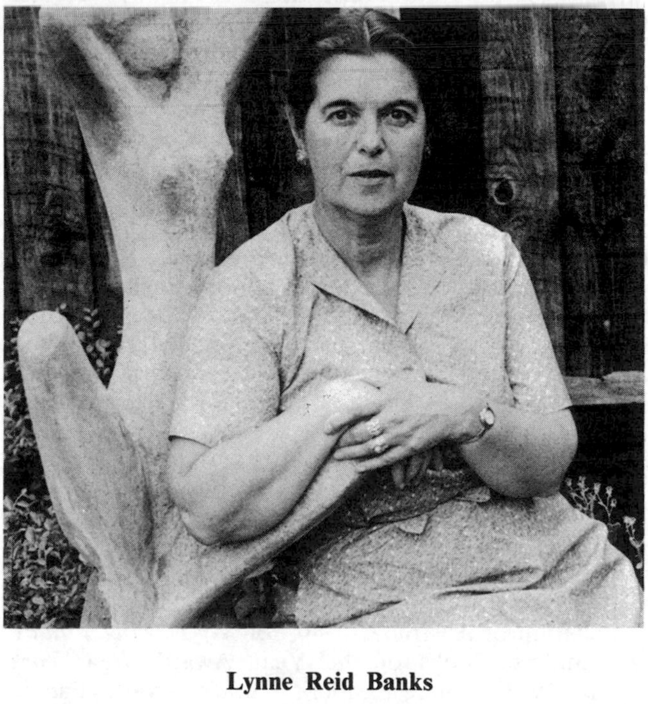

Lynne Reid Banks

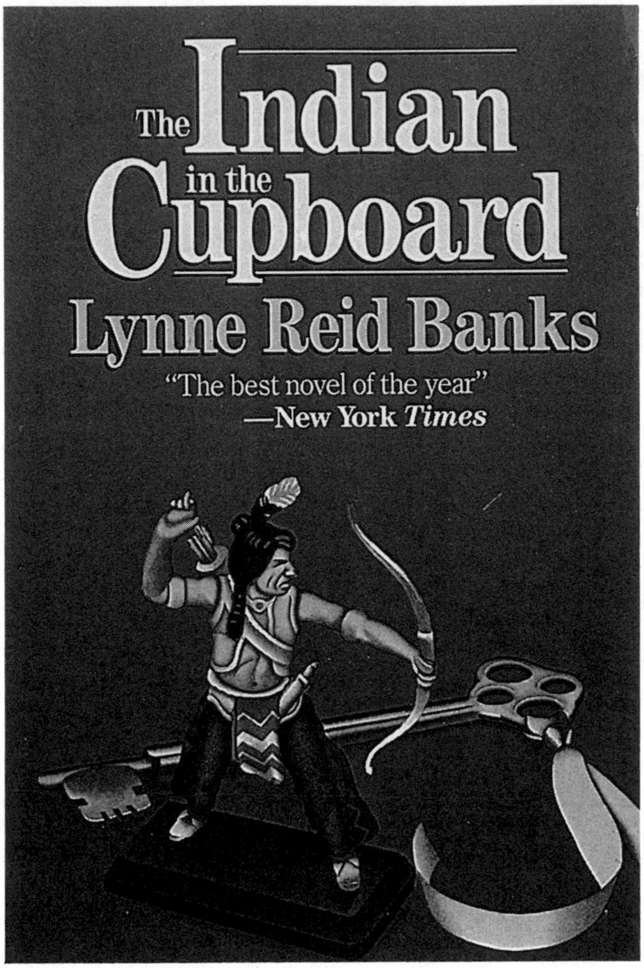

Cover of *The Indian in the Cupboard,* by Lynne Reid Banks. Illustrated by Brock Cole.

Education: Attended Queen's Secretarial College, London, 1945-46, Italia Conte Stage School, 1946, and Royal Academy of Dramatic Art, 1947-49. *Religion:* "Practising Atheist." *Hobbies and other interests:* Theater, gardening, teaching ESL abroad.

ADDRESSES: Home—Dorset, England. *Agent*—Sheila Watson, Watson, Little Ltd., 12 Egbert St., London NW1 8LJ, England.

CAREER: Actress in English repertory companies, 1949-54; free-lance journalist, London, England, 1954-55; Independent Television News, London, television news reporter, 1955-57, television news scriptwriter, 1958-62; taught English as a foreign language in Israel, 1963-71; writer, 1971—.

MEMBER: Society of Authors (London).

AWARDS, HONORS: Yorkshire Arts Literary Award, 1976, and Best Books for Young Adults Award, American Library Association, 1977, both for *Dark Quartet;* West Australian Young Readers' Book Award, Library Association of Australia, 1980, for *My Darling Villain;* Outstanding Books of the Year Award, *New York Times,* 1981, Young Reader's Choice Award, Pacific Northwest Library Association, 1984, California Young Readers Medal, California Reading Association, 1985, Children's Books of the Year Award, Child Study Association, 1986, Young Readers of Virginia Award, 1988, Arizona Young Readers' Award, 1988, all for *The Indian in the Cupboard;* Parents' Choice Award for Literature, Parents' Choice Foundation, 1986, Notable Books Award, *New York Times,* 1986, Children's Books of the Year Award, 1987, Rebecca Caudill Young Reader's Books Award, Illinois Association for Media in Education, 1988, and Indian Paintbrush Award, Wyoming Library Association, 1989, all for *The Return of the Indian;* Gt. Stone Face (New Hampshire librarians) Award, 1991, for *Secret of the Indian.*

WRITINGS:

JUVENILE

One More River, Simon & Schuster, 1973.

The Adventures of King Midas, illustrated by George Him, Dent, 1976.

The Farthest-Away Mountain, illustrated by Victor Ambrus, Abelard Schuman, 1976.

I, Houdini: The Autobiography of a Self-Educated Hamster, illustrated by Terry Riley, Dent, 1978, Doubleday, 1988.

My Darling Villain, Harper, 1977.

Letters to My Israeli Sons: The Story of Jewish Survival, H. W. Allen, 1979, F. Watts, 1980.

The Indian in the Cupboard, illustrated by Robin Jacques, Dent, 1980, illustrated by Brock Cole, Doubleday, 1981.

The Writing on the Wall, Chatto & Windus, 1981, Harper, 1982.

Maura's Angel, illustrated by Robin Jacques, Dent, 1984.

The Fairy Rebel, illustrated by William Geldart, Dent, 1985, Doubleday, 1988.

The Return of the Indian, illustrated by W. Geldart, Doubleday, 1986.

Melusine: A Mystery, Hamish Hamilton, 1988, Harper, 1989.

The Secret of the Indian, Collins, 1988, Doubleday, 1989.

The Magic Hare, illustrated by Hilda Offen, HarperCollins, 1992, illustrated by Barry Moser, Morrow, 1993.

PLAYS

It Never Rains (produced by BBC, 1954), Deane, 1954.

All in a Row, Deane, 1956.

The Killer Dies Twice (three-act), Deane, 1956.

Already It's Tomorrow (produced by BBC, 1962), Samuel French, 1962.

The Unborn, produced in London, England, 1962.

The Wednesday Caller, produced by BBC, 1963.

The Last Word on Julie, produced by ATV, 1964.

The Gift (three-act), produced in London, 1965.

The Stowaway (radio play), produced by BBC, 1967.

The Eye of the Beholder, produced by ITV, 1977.

Lame Duck (radio play), produced by BBC, 1978.

Purely from Principal (radio play), produced by BBC, 1985.

The Travels of Yoshi and the Tea-Kettle, produced in London, 1991.

OTHER

The L-Shaped Room, Chatto & Windus, 1960, revised edition, Longman, 1977.
House of Hope, Simon & Schuster, 1962, published in England as *An End to Running,* Chatto & Windus, 1962.
Children at the Gate, Simon & Schuster, 1968.
The Backward Shadow, Simon & Schuster, 1970.
The Kibbutz: Some Personal Reflections, Anglo-Israel Association, 1972.
Two Is Lonely, Simon & Schuster, 1974.
Sarah and After: The Matriarchs, Bodley Head, 1975, published as *Sarah and After: Five Women Who Founded a Nation,* Doubleday, 1977.
Dark Quartet: The Story of the Brontes, Weidenfeld & Nicholson, 1976, Delacorte, 1977.
Path to the Silent Country: Charlotte Bronte's Years of Fame, Weidenfeld & Nicholson, 1977.
Defy the Wilderness, Chatto & Windus, 1981.
Torn Country: An Oral History of the Israeli War of Independence, F. Watts, 1982.
The Warning Bell, Hamish Hamilton, 1984.
Casualties, Hamish Hamilton, 1986.

Contributor to numerous periodicals, including *Ladies' Home Journal, Observer, Guardian, Sunday Telegraph, Independent,* and *Marie-Claire.*

ADAPTATIONS: The L-Shaped Room, starring Leslie Caron, was released by Davis-Royal Films, 1962.

WORK IN PROGRESS: The Mystery of the Cupboard, publication expected by Morrow, Spring 1993; an adult novel, / *The Crossover.*

SIDELIGHTS: Lynne Reid Banks has written about a number of complex subjects—single parenthood, the Middle East, Zionism—but she is best known to young audiences for her imaginative stories like *The Indian in the Cupboard, The Adventures of King Midas,* and *The Fairy Rebel.* Many of Reid Banks's titles for younger readers, such as the "Indian" books, feature magic as a central theme. Teen readers are attracted to works such as *The Writing on the Wall,* in which Reid Banks deals with typical teenage problems, such as dating and family relationships. In many of her works, though not all, Reid Banks tries to draw on personal experience. "I had learned a fundamental lesson," she wrote in an essay for the *Sixth Book of Junior Authors.* "Nothing is ever wasted. And for a writer, there's something more: nothing one ever experiences or feels is wasted. Even the bad things, the negative emotions.... While one is suffering them, I mean at the time, a little voice is saying 'Hold on to it. Remember.' Because one day you may need it."

Reid Banks originally planned on being an actress like her mother. In order to prepare for this career, she attended drama school and worked at various theater-related jobs. "I adored every minute of it.... I was going to take the theater world by storm! Little did any of us know the heartbreak and hardships ahead. Very few of us made it. The vast majority left the profession—we simply couldn't make a living," she noted in her essay. While she did not become an actress, Reid Banks later made use of her threatrical training when she taught English to Hebrew-speaking children in Israel. "Every lesson was a performance—how else could I make them understand me?," she remarked. "And it worked. I was more successful at teaching than I ever was on the stage."

Reid Banks's first literary success was the novel *The L-Shaped Room.* The book chronicles the life of unmarried, twenty-seven-year-old Jane Graham who goes to live in a run-down boardinghouse when she becomes pregnant. Janice Elliott of the *New Statesman* called the novel "touching and competent," as well as "ambitious and mature." "Love is the book's theme, developed in bright, warm prose, through diverse and interesting characters," commented Otis Kidwell Burger in the *New York Times Book Review.* Reid Banks eventually wrote two more novels featuring Jane Graham, *The Backward Shadow* and *Two Is Lonely.*

Reid Banks published her first children's book in 1973. Since that time, she has delighted scores of young fans with tales of magical kings, brave fairies, toys that come to life, and intrepid hamsters. Two of her most popular works are *The Indian in the Cupboard* and its sequel, *The Return of the Indian.* In both volumes, a boy's plastic Indian comes to life every time it is locked in a cupboard. Young Omri soon discovers that his toy, Little Bear, has a taste for adventure—sometimes with near-disastrous results. A reviewer for the *Times Literary Supplement* found *The Indian in the Cupboard* to be "original, lively, compulsive writing" that "will well stand through repeated readings."

While Reid Banks enjoys writing for audiences of all ages, she is especially fond of writing tales for the younger reader. "Writing for young people is a much pleasanter, and easier, thing than writing for adults," she once commented. "I especially enjoy writing wish-fulfillment stories .... But in the end, one has to write what one wants to write, or what one is commissioned to write, and hope for the best. You can't win 'em all."

WORKS CITED:

Burger, Otis Kidwell, "Someone to Love," *New York Times Book Review,* April 6, 1961, p. 38.
Elliott, Janice, "Old Hat," *New Statesman,* July 26, 1968, p. 116.
Review of *The Indian in the Cupboard, Times Literary Supplement,* November 21, 1980.
Reid Banks, Lynne, essay in *Sixth Book of Junior Authors,* edited by Sally Holmes Holtze, Wilson, 1989, pp. 22-24.

FOR MORE INFORMATION SEE:

BOOKS

Contemporary Literary Criticism, Volume 23, Gale, 1983, pp. 40-43.
Twentieth Century Children's Writers, edited by Tracy Chevalier, St. James, 1989, pp. 56-58.

PERIODICALS

Los Angeles Times Book Review, April 23, 1989, p. 10.
New York Times Book Review, April 16, 1989, p. 26.
Times Literary Supplement, December 1, 1988.

* * *

REY, H(ans) A(ugusto) 1898-1977 (Uncle Gus)

PERSONAL: Original surname, Reyersbach; legally changed to Rey; born September 16, 1898, in Hamburg, Germany; immigrated to United States, 1940, naturalized U.S. citizen, 1946; died August 26, 1977, in Boston, MA; son of Alexander and Martha (Windmuller) Reyersbach; married Margret Elizabeth Waldstein (an author and illustrator), 1935. *Education:* Attended University of Munich, 1919-20, and University of Hamburg, 1920-23. *Hobbies and other interests:* Watching nature, reading, making gadgets, swimming and snorkeling, and stargazing.

ADDRESSES: Home—14 Hilliard St., Cambridge, MA 02138; (summer) Waterville Valley, Campton P.O., NH.

CAREER: Executive in import/export business, Rio de Janeiro, Brazil, 1924-36; writer and illustrator of children's books, Paris, France, 1937-40; writer and illustrator of books, mainly juvenile, New York City, 1940-63, Cambridge, MA, 1963-77. Taught astronomy at Cambridge Center for Adult Education. *Military service:* German Army, 1916-19; served with Infantry and Medical Corps in France and Russia.

MEMBER: American Association for the Advancement of Science, Federation of American Scientists, Amateur Astronomers Association, Astronomical League, Water-

Margret and H. A. Rey

ville Valley (NH) Athletic and Improvement Association.

AWARDS, HONORS: Lewis Carroll Shelf Award, 1960, for *Curious George Takes a Job;* Children's book award, Child Study Association of America, 1966, for *Curious George Goes to the Hospital; Curious George* was named best picture book in the 1987 Children's Choice Awards held by *School Library Journal* and a notable book by the American Library Association.

WRITINGS:

JUVENILE BOOKS, EXCEPT WHERE INDICATED; ALL SELF-ILLUSTRATED

Zebrology (drawings), Chatto & Windus, 1937.
Aerodome for Scissors and Paint, Chatto & Windus, 1939.
Raffy and the Nine Monkeys, Chatto & Windus, 1939, published in U.S. as *Cecily G. and the Nine Monkeys,* Houghton, 1942.
Au Clair de la lune and Other French Nursery Songs, Greystone, 1941.
(Under pseudonym Uncle Gus) *Christmas Manger* (with text from the Bible), Houghton, 1942.
(Under pseudonym Uncle Gus) *Uncle Gus's Circus,* Houghton, 1942.
(Under pseudonym Uncle Gus) *Uncle Gus's Farm,* Houghton, 1942.
Elizabite: The Adventures of a Carnivorous Plant, Harper, 1942.
(Compiler) *Humpty Dumpty and Other Mother Goose Songs,* Harper, 1943.
(Compiler) *We Three Kings and Other Christmas Carols* (music arranged by Henry F. Waldstein), Harper, 1944.
Look for the Letters: A Hide-and-Seek Alphabet, Harper, 1945.
The Stars: A New Way to See Them (for adults), Houghton, 1952, published in England as *A New Way to See the Stars,* Hamlyn, 1966, enlarged edition, Houghton, 1967.
Find the Constellations, Houghton, 1954, revised edition, 1976.

WITH WIFE, MARGRET REY; ALL SELF-ILLUSTRATED

How the Flying Fishes Came into Being, Chatto & Windus, 1938.
Anybody at Home? (verse; puzzle book), Chatto & Windus, 1939, Houghton, 1942.
How Do You Get There? (puzzle book), Houghton, 1941.
Tit for Tat (verse), Harper, 1942.
Tommy Helps, Too, Houghton, 1943.
Where's My Baby (verse; puzzle book), Houghton, 1943.
Feed the Animals (verse; puzzle book), Houghton, 1944.
Billy's Picture, Harper, 1948.
See the Circus (verse; puzzle book), Houghton, 1956.

"CURIOUS GEORGE" SERIES (PUBLISHED IN ENGLAND AS "ZOZO" SERIES BY CHATTO & WINDUS, 1942-67)

Curious George (also see below), Houghton, 1941.
(With M. Rey) *Curious George Takes a Job* (also see below), Houghton, 1947.
(With M. Rey) *Curious George Rides a Bike* (also see below), Houghton, 1952, new edition, 1973.
Curious George Gets a Medal (also see below), Houghton, 1957.
(With M. Rey) *Curious George Flies a Kite* (also see below), Houghton, 1958.
Curious George Learns the Alphabet (also see below), Houghton, 1963.
(With M. Rey) *Curious George Goes to the Hospital* (also see below), Houghton, 1966.

ILLUSTRATOR

Mararet Wise Brown, *The Polite Penguin,* Harper, 1941.
Brown, *Don't Frighten the Lion!,* Harper, 1942.
Emmy Payne, *Katy No-Pocket,* Houghton, 1944.
Charlotte Zolotow, *The Park Book,* Harper, 1944.
M. Rey, *Pretzel,* Harper, 1944.
M. Rey, *Spotty,* Harper, 1945.
M. Rey, *Pretzel and the Puppies,* Harper, 1946.
Mary Had a Little Lamb, Penguin, 1951, published in England as *Mary Had a Little Lamb and Other Nursery Songs,* Puffin, 1951.
Christian Morgenstern, *The Daynight Lamp and Other Poems,* translation from German by Max Knight, Houghton, 1973.

Contributor, with wife, Margret Rey, to the "Zozo Page for Children," *Good Housekeeping,* 1951.

ADAPTATIONS:

MOVIES AND FILMSTRIPS

Curious George Rides a Bike (animated film; with teaching guide; also see below), Weston Woods Studios, 1958, released as filmstrip, 1960.
Curious George (filmstrip; with record and teaching guide; also see below), Teaching Resources Films, 1971, released as animated film, Churchill Films, 1986.
Curious George Flies a Kite (filmstrip; with record and teaching guide), Teaching Resources Films, 1971.
Curious George Gets a Medal (filmstrip; with record and teaching guide; also see below), Teaching Resources Films, 1971.
Curious George Goes to the Hospital (filmstrip; with record and teaching guide), Teaching Resources Films, 1971.
Curious George Takes a Job (filmstrip; with record and teaching guide; also see below), Teaching Resources Films, 1971, released as slides with recorded narration and music, Knowledge Systems, 1982.
Curious George Learns the Alphabet (filmstrip; with cassette; also see below), Teaching Resources Films, 1977.
Pretzel and Other Stories (filmstrip; with cassette), Educational Enrichment Materials, 1978.

"Curious George" was also the subject of eighteen animated shorts, produced in 1972, and compiled on videotape in three volumes by Sony.

RECORDINGS

Curious George and Other Stories about Curious George (includes *Curious George Takes a Job, Curious George Rides a Bike,* and *Curious George Gets a Medal*), read by Julie Harris, Caedmon Records, 1972.

Curious George Learns the Alphabet and Other Stories about Curious George, read by Harris, Caedmon Records, 1973.

BOOKS; ALL TITLES ALSO KNOWN AS MARGRET AND H. A. REY'S ...

(Edited by Margret Rey and Alan J. Shalleck) *Curious George Goes Fishing,* adapted from Curious George animated film series, Houghton, 1987.

(Edited by M. Rey and Shalleck) *Curious George Visits a Police Station,* adapted from animated film series, Houghton, 1987.

(Edited by M. Rey and Shalleck) *Curious George Goes to an Ice Cream Shop,* adapted from the animated film series, Houghton, 1987.

Rey's character was also adapted to the books *Curious George Bakes a Cake, Curious George Goes Camping, Curious George Goes to a Toy Store,* and *Curious George Goes to an Air Show.*

SIDELIGHTS: H. A. Rey was the creator of the widely popular Curious George stories, for which he won awards from both the Child Study Association of America and *School Library Journal.* In addition to writing and illustrating seven Curious George books, Rey lent his talents to numerous other books. He was an accomplished astronomer and created two books on stargazing, illustrated stories by other authors, and created puzzle and "pop-up" books. His books have been translated into nine languages and have a combined sales of more than twenty million copies.

Rey was born in Hamburg, Germany. By the age of two he was displaying a talent for drawing. He developed his artistic skill during his school years, often drawing in his sketchbook during other lessons. When World War II broke out he was drafted into the army, but as he stated in *Junior Book of Authors:* "I did better with my pencil than with my rifle." When he got out of the army, Rey wanted to go to an art school, but he could not afford the tuition. Instead he attended two German universities and performed free-lance art work in his spare time. Before Rey formally finished school, family members offered him a job at their import/export firm in Rio de Janeiro, Brazil—Rey accepted. While in Brazil, he met Margret Waldstein, a young woman who had also grown up in Hamburg. The two shared an interest in art and a distaste for the Nazi government of Germany; they were soon married. They moved to Paris where Rey began to write and draw children's books. In 1940 they were forced to flee Paris on bicycles when Nazi Germany invaded France. They took with them only a small amount of food and some of Rey's manuscripts. Escaping France, they travelled to America.

Rey completed several books before moving to the U.S., often collaborating on them with Margret. Most of the books involve animals as the main characters. When he was growing up, Rey lived near a zoo. Visiting the zoo often, he developed a fondness for a variety of exotic animals. "I ... was more familiar with elephants and kangaroos than with cows or sheep," he stated in *The Junior Book of Authors.* The first book that Rey wrote and illustrated, *Cecily G. and the Nine Monkeys,* displayed his love of animals. In the story, Cecily G. is a lonely giraffe (the 'G' in her name stands for giraffe) who has been separated from her family. The nine monkeys are a family who have been driven out of their home by woodcutters and are traveling in search of a new place to live. Cecily and the monkeys meet and instantly become friends. The family stays in Cecily's home with her, sleep in her long giraffe's bed, and play inventive games with her. In addition to using her long body as a bridge, they ski down her neck, use her as a see-saw, parachute off her head with their umbrellas, and even use her as a makeshift harp during a concert. *Cecily G. and the Nine Monkeys* introduced readers to an important character. In listing each of the monkeys, Rey used two words to describe the monkey named George, clever and *curious.* Rey found George so entertaining that he devoted an entire book to the little monkey's adventures. He titled it simply *Curious George.*

Curious George begins with George playing in his African jungle home. Rey introduces his character with this description: "He was a good little monkey and always very curious." While playing, George notices a man, dressed in yellow and wearing a large yellow hat, watching him. Naturally, George is very curious about this man. When the man places his hat on the ground, George cannot resist the urge to investigate. Before George knows what has happened, the man with the yellow hat—the only name he is given in the books—has snatched the little monkey up and taken him back to his ship. The man explains to George that he is taking him to the city to live in a zoo. He tells George that he may look around the boat, but to be careful and stay out of trouble. George does just the opposite and ends up falling into the ocean while trying to fly like a sea gull. Once in the city George finds himself in more trouble. He plays with a phone and accidently dials the fire department. The fire department arrives, finds there is no fire, and puts George in jail for playing pranks. He escapes from the jail, grabs a bunch of balloons, and sails off over the city. In the end George is found by the man with the yellow hat and is taken to his happy new home in the zoo.

The universal appeal of *Curious George* is illustrated by an incident that occurred shortly after H. A. finished the book. Just prior to fleeing France the Reys, suspected of spying, were arrested by the French police. During the Rey's interrogation, an officer came across H. A.'s *Curious George* manuscript. Attempting to find evidence in the book that would confirm the Reys as spies, the man instead found himself amused and enchanted by the story of the little monkey. Reasoning that the

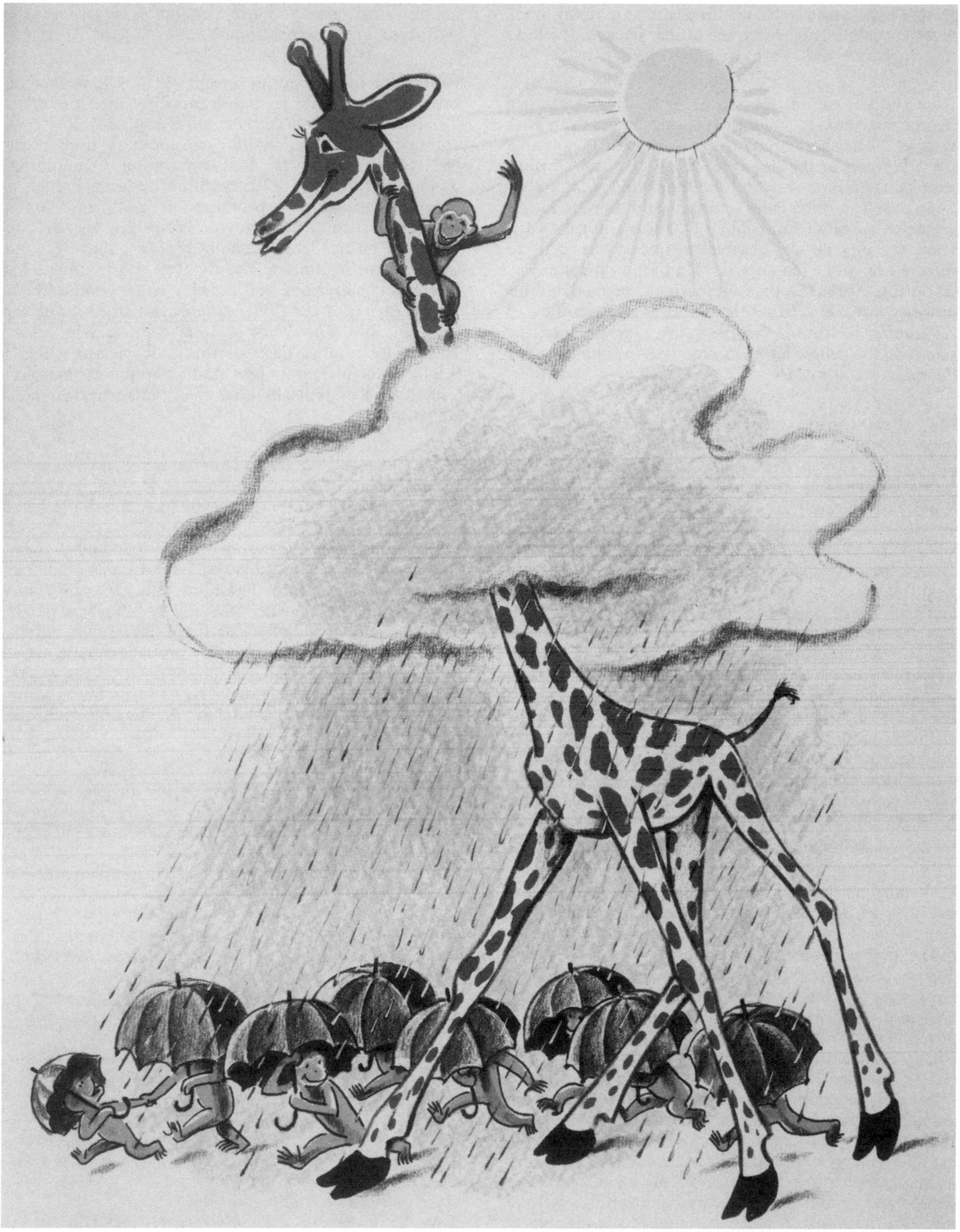

From *Cecily G. and the Nine Monkeys,* written and illustrated by H. A. and Margret Rey.

person who wrote such an innocent and funny book could not possibly be a spy, the officer released the Reys and they were able to escape the Nazi invasion.

Over the course of six more books Rey continued George's adventures, often collaborating on them with Margret. "The share of my wife's work varies," Rey told *Something about the Author* (*SATA*). "Basically I illustrate and Margret writes." In the books that follow George gets a job, rides a bike, and flies a kite—managing to cause something of a ruckus in each case. Along the way he also receives a medal, gets to fly in outer space, and even appears in a motion picture. Rey makes it clear that George's intentions are good, but his curiosity just seems to get the best of him. Regardless of the amount of trouble George manages to get into, the man with the yellow hat always arrives in time to rescue George from disaster.

The last two Curious George stories that Rey worked on before his death, *Curious George Learns the Alphabet* and *Curious George Goes to the Hospital,* differed from the previous books in their attempt to be both educational and entertaining. In *Curious George Learns the Alphabet,* the man with the yellow hat teaches George his ABCs. In *Curious George Goes to the Hospital,* George comes down with mysterious stomach pains and must be taken to the hospital. He is taken to the children's ward where he meets young boys and girls who also need medical attention. George does not feel well at first, but after the doctors help him he is back to his old, curious self. He decides to explore the hospital and, as usual, causes a commotion due to his curiosity. The Reys collaborated with the Children's Hospital Medical Center in Boston, Massachusetts, to familiarize children with hospitals, their procedures, and the people who work in them. By presenting the hospital in a story with a comforting and familiar character like George, the Reys hoped to ease some of the anxiety a child entering a hospital might have.

Readers of all ages are fascinated by George. Children love George because his appearance and behavior are very similar to that of a child: He has wild adventures and is never punished for his antics. While his escapades always cause trouble, they usually result in some good and George is rewarded or praised. "Good intentions, even motivated by curiosity," opined Louisa Smith in *Dictionary of Literary Biography* (*DLB*), "lead to poetic justice." Discussing the reasons for George's popularity, Margot Dukler commented in *Elementary English:* "The most important is the ease with which the children can identify with him. He is an animal who is doing the things that they would like to do but don't dare." Adults also like George. Their children can identify with him yet, because he is a monkey, can distinguish between George's world and reality. George is drawn in a cartoon style, one that illustrates his good nature and innocence. If Rey presented George as a more devilish character, parents may not find him so attractive. "You see a very likable monkey, with a very sweet, simple face," described Dukler in *Elementary English.* "He can look happy or sad, or maybe surprised, but he never loses the sweetness in his expression."

In addition to the Curious George series, Rey worked on several other books. He wrote and illustrated *Elizabite: The Adventures of a Carnivorous Plant,* the story of a plant with a large appetite for just about anything it can get its leaves on. *Pretzel* tells the story of a dachshund, named Pretzel, who is extraordinarily long. Pretzel is unhappy because his appearance does not please Greta, the female dog that he loves. When Greta gets into trouble, Pretzel's length enables him to rescue her, and she sees his true, unique, beauty. Rey also combined his interests in stargazing and drawing in two books about astronomy: *Find the Constellations,* which he wrote for children, and *The Stars: A New Way to See Them,* written for adults. Each of the books features Rey's bright, colorful illustrations and a unique system—invented by Rey himself—that easily identifies the constellations.

"Making picture books for children is the most wonderful profession I can think of," stated Rey in *The Junior Book of Authors.* "Not only do you have fun doing it but your fellow men even pay you for it." Rey's career as an author and illustrator spanned more than thirty years. In that time he created some of the most beloved books in children's literature. The humor in his books, borrowed from the slapstick comedy of Charlie Chaplin and the simple logic of comic strips, make them all the more appealing to children. Rey brought a basic sensibility to all of his books. He summarized his work ethic in *SATA:* "I believe I know what children like. I know what *I* liked as a child, and I don't do any book that I, as a child, *wouldn't* have liked."

WORKS CITED:

Dukler, Margot, *Elementary English,* January, 1958, pp. 3-11.

Junior Book of Authors, H. W. Wilson Company, second edition, revised, 1951.

Rey, H. A., *Curious George,* Houghton, 1941.

Smith, Louisa, *Dictionary of Literary Biography,* Volume 22: *American Writers for Children, 1900-1960,* Gale, 1983, pp. 286-89.

Something about the Author, Volume 26, Gale, 1982, p. 165.

FOR MORE INFORMATION SEE:

BOOKS

Children's Literature Review, Volume 5, Gale, 1983

Contemporary Authors, New Revision Series, Volume 6, Gale, 1982.

Cricket, Volume 1, number 2, 1973.

Twentieth-Century Children's Writers, 2nd edition, St. Martin's, 1983.

PERIODICALS

People, June 1, 1987, p. 98.

From *Curious George Goes to the Hospital,* written and illustrated by H. A. and Margret Rey.

OBITUARIES:

PERIODICALS

AB Bookman's Weekly, October 17, 1977.
New York Times, August 28, 1977.
Publishers Weekly, October 3, 1977.

* * *

REY, Margret (Elisabeth) 1906-

PERSONAL: Born in May, 1906, in Hamburg, Germany; came to the United States in 1940, naturalized citizen, 1946; married H(ans) A(ugusto) Rey (a writer and illustrator), 1935 (died, 1977). *Education:* Attended Bauhaus, 1927, Dusseldorf Academy of Art, 1928-29, and University of Munich, 1930-31.

ADDRESSES: Home and Office—14 Hilliard St., Cambridge, MA 02138. *Agent*—A. P. Watt & Son, 26-28 Bedford Row, London WC1R 4HL, England.

CAREER: Reporter and advertising copywriter in Berlin, Germany, 1928-29; held one-woman shows of watercolors in Berlin, 1929-34; photographer in London, England, Hamburg, Germany, and Rio de Janeiro, Brazil, 1930-35; free-lance writer in Paris, France, 1936-40, in New York City, 1940-63, and in Cambridge, MA, 1963—; writer of children's books, 1937—; Brandeis University, Waltham, MA, instructor in creative writing, 1978—.

AWARDS, HONORS: Children's Book Award from Child Study Association of America, 1966, for *Curious George Goes to the Hospital.*

WRITINGS:

ALL ILLUSTRATED BY HUSBAND, H. A. REY

Pretzel, Harper, 1944.
Spotty, Harper, 1945.
Pretzel and the Puppies, Harper, 1946.
Billy's Picture, Harper, 1948.

WITH H. A. REY; ILLUSTRATED BY H. A. REY

How the Flying Fishes Came Into Being, Chatto & Windus, 1938.
Raffy and the Nine Monkeys, Chatto & Windus, 1939, published as *Cecily G. and the Nine Monkeys,* Houghton, 1942.
Anybody at Home? (verse), Chatto & Windus, 1939, Houghton, 1943.
How Do You Get There?, Houghton, 1941.
Elizabite: The Adventures of a Carnivorous Plant, Harper, 1942.
Tit for Tat (verse), Harper, 1942.
Where's My Baby? (verse), Houghton, 1943.
Feed the Animals (verse), Houghton, 1944.
Mary Had a Little Lamb, Penguin, 1951.
See the Circus (verse), Houghton, 1956.

"CURIOUS GEORGE" SERIES (ALL TITLES PUBLISHED IN ENGLAND AS "ZOZO" SERIES); ILLUSTRATED BY H. A. REY

Curious George, Houghton, 1941.
Curious George Takes a Job, Houghton, 1947.
Curious George Rides a Bike, Houghton, 1952.
Curious George Gets a Medal, Houghton, 1957.
Curious George Flies a Kite, Houghton, 1958.
Curious George Learns the Alphabet, Houghton, 1963.
Curious George Goes to the Hospital, Houghton, 1966.

EDITOR, WITH ALLAN J. SHALLECK; BASED ON "CURIOUS GEORGE" FILM SERIES

Curious George and the Dump Truck, Houghton, 1984.
Curious George Goes to the Circus, Houghton, 1984.
Curious George Goes to the Aquarium, Houghton, 1984.
Curious George Goes Sledding, Houghton, 1984.
Curious George Goes Hiking, Houghton, 1985.
Curious George Walks the Pets, Houghton, 1986.
Curious George Plays Baseball, Houghton, 1986.
Curious George Goes to a Costume Party, Houghton, 1986.
Curious George at the Ballet, Houghton, 1986.
Curious George Visits the Police Station, Houghton, 1987.
Curious George Goes Fishing, Houghton, 1987.
Curious George at the Laundromat, Houghton, 1987.
Curious George Visits the Zoo, Houghton, 1988.
Curious George at the Fire Station, Houghton, 1988.
Curious George at the Airport, Houghton, 1988.
Curious George & the Pizza, Houghton, 1988.
Curious George at the Beach, Houghton, 1988.
Curious George at the Railroad Station, Houghton, 1988.
Curious George Goes to a Restaurant, Houghton, 1988.
Curious George Visits an Amusement Park, Houghton, 1988.
Curious George and the Dinosaur, Houghton, 1989.
Curious George Goes to an Ice Cream Shop, Houghton, 1989.
Curious George Goes to School, Houghton, 1989.
Curious George Goes to the Dentist, Houghton, 1989.
Curious George Bakes a Cake, Houghton, 1990.
Curious George Goes Camping, Houghton, 1990.
Curious George Goes to an Air Show, Houghton, 1990.
Curious George Goes to a Toy Store, Houghton, 1990.

OTHER

Contributor, with H. A. Rey, of the "Zozo Page for Children," *Good Housekeeping,* 1951. The Reys' works have been translated into numerous languages.

ADAPTATIONS:

MOVIES AND FILMSTRIPS

Curious George Rides a Bike (motion picture with teaching guide), Weston Woods Studios, 1958.
Curious George Rides a Bike (filmstrip with text), Weston Woods Studios, 1960.
Curious George (filmstrip with record and teaching guide), Teaching Resources Films, 1971.
Curious George Flies a Kite (filmstrip with record and teaching guide), Teaching Resources Films, 1971.
Curious George Gets a Medal (filmstrip with record and teaching guide), Teaching Resources Films, 1971.
Curious George Goes to the Hospital (filmstrip with record and teaching guide), Teaching Resources Films, 1971.
Curious George Takes a Job (filmstrip with record and teaching guide), Teaching Resources Films, 1971.

RECORDINGS

Curious George and Other Stories about Curious George, read by Julie Harris, Caedmon Records, 1972.
Curious George Learns the Alphabet and Other Stories about Curious George, ready by Julie Harris, Caedmon Records, 1973.

WORK IN PROGRESS: Curious George films for television.

SIDELIGHTS: Born and educated in Germany, Margret Rey studied art at various German schools before moving to Brazil in 1935. While working as a photographer there, she met H. A. Rey, with whom she founded Rio de Janeiro's first advertising agency. The couple subsequently married and moved to Paris, where Margret worked as a free-lance writer while H. A. sold sketches to numerous French publications.

In Paris the Reys began collaborating on children's books, with Margret providing the text for H. A.'s illustrations. Their book *Raffy and the Nine Monkeys* inspired their popular "Curious George" series, written in the United States after the Reys fled the Nazi conquest of Paris during World War II.

The Reys commented in *Authors and Illustrators of Children's Books: Writings on Their Lives and Works:* "Among children we seem to be known best as the parents of *Curious George,* the little monkey hero of some of our books. 'I thought you were monkeys too,' said a little boy who had been eager to meet us, disappointment written all over his face." "*Curious George* consistently heads the popularity list of what children themselves call 'funny books,' noted *Twentieth-Century Children's Writers* contributor James E. Higgins.

Margret Rey once told *Contemporary Authors:* "I now am involved in supervising the production of Curious George films for television and am teaching a course on the craft of writing. I enjoy teaching enormously."

WORKS CITED:

Contemporary Authors, Volume 105, Gale, 1982, pp. 407-408.

Rey, Margret, and H. A. Rey, "Margret and H. A. Rey," in *Authors and Illustrators of Children's Books: Writings on Their Lives and Works,* edited by Miriam Hoffman and Samuel Evans, Bowker, 1972.

Twentieth-Century Children's Writers, 3rd edition, St. James Press, 1989, pp. 820-821.

FOR MORE INFORMATION SEE:

BOOKS

Children's Literature Review, Volume 5, Gale, pp. 188-200.

PERIODICALS

Elementary English, January, 1958, pp. 3-11.

* * *

RHINE, RICHARD
See SILVERSTEIN, Alvin and SILVERSTEIN, Virginia B(arbara Opshelor)

* * *

RHUE, Morton
See STRASSER, Todd

* * *

RICHARDS, Laura E(lizabeth Howe) 1850-1943

PERSONAL: Born February 27, 1850, in Boston, MA; died January 14, 1943; daughter of Samuel Gridley Howe (an author, teacher, and philanthropist) and Julia Ward Howe (author of "The Battle Hymn of the Republic"); married Henry Richards (an architect and illustrator), June 17, 1871; children: Alice Maude, Rosalind, Henry Howe, Julia Ward, Maud, John, Laura Elizabeth. *Education:* Tutored at home by private teachers; later attended Massachusetts schools including Miss Caroline Wilby's School, Boston.

ADDRESSES: Home—Gardiner, ME.

CAREER: Author of books for children, poet, and biographer. Founder and president of Woman's Philanthropic Union, 1895-1921; Camp Merryweather (boy's camp), Lake Cobbosseecontee, ME, founder and director with husband, Henry Richards, 1900-30; president of Maine Consumers League, 1905-11; affiliated with the District Nurse Association and the National Child Labor Committee.

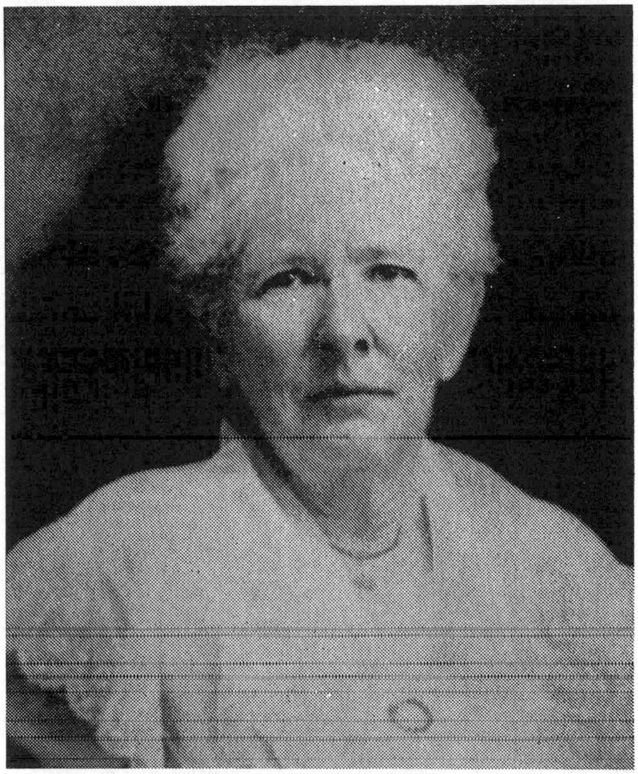

Laura E. Richards

AWARDS, HONORS: Pulitzer Prize for biography, with sister, Maude Howe Elliot, 1917, for *Julia Ward Howe; Tirra Lirra: Rhymes Old and New* was a Junior Literary Guild Selection, 1932; D.H.L., University of Maine, Orono, 1936.

WRITINGS:

FICTION

Little Tyrant, Estes & Lauriat, 1880.

Our Baby's Favorite, Estes & Lauriat, 1881.

Sketches and Scraps, illustrations by husband, Henry Richards, Estes & Lauriat, 1881.

The Joyous Story of Toto, illustrations by E. H. Garrett, Roberts Brothers, 1885.

(With Henry Baldwin) *Kaspar Kroak's Kaleidoscope,* illustrations by A. Hochstein, Nims & Knight, 1886.

Tell-Tale from Hill and Dale, illustrations by Hochstein, Nims & Knight, 1886.

Toto's Merry Winter, Roberts Brothers, 1887.

Queen Hildegarde: A Story for Girls, Estes & Lauriat, 1889.

Captain January, Estes & Lauriat, 1891.

Hildegarde's Holiday: A Sequel to Queen Hildegarde, Estes & Lauriat, 1891.

Hildegarde's Home, Estes & Lauriat, 1892.

Melody: The Story of a Child, Estes & Lauriat, 1893.

Marie, Estes & Lauriat, 1894.

Narcissa; or, The Road to Rome. In Verona, Estes & Lauriat, 1894.

Five Minute Stories, illustrations by A. R. Wheelan, Etheldred B. Barry, and others, Estes & Lauriat, 1895.

From *For Tommy and Other Stories,* by Laura E. Richards. Illustrated by F. T. Merrill.

Hildegarde's Neighbors, Estes & Lauriat, 1895.
Jim of Hellas; or, In Durance Vile [and] *Bethesda Pool,* Estes & Lauriat, 1895.
Nautilus, Estes & Lauriat, 1895.
Isla Herron, illustrations by Frank T. Merrill, Estes & Lauriat, 1896.
"Some Say" [and] *Neighbors in Cyprus,* Estes & Lauriat, 1896.
Hildegarde's Harvest, Estes & Lauriat, 1897.
Three Margarets, illustrations by Barry, Estes & Lauriat, 1897.
Love and Rocks, Estes & Lauriat, 1898.
Margaret Montfort, illustrations by Barry, Estes & Lauriat, 1898.
Rosin the Beau: A Sequel to "Melody" and "Marie," Estes & Lauriat, 1898.
Chop-Chin and the Golden Dragon, Little, Brown, 1899.
The Golden Breasted Kootoo, Little, Brown, 1899.
Peggy, illustrations by Barry, Estes, 1899.
Quicksilver Sue, illustrations by W. D. Stevens, Century, 1899.
Rita, illustrations by Barry, Estes, 1900.
Snow-White; or, The House in the Wood, Estes, 1900.
Fernley House, illustrations by Barry, Estes, 1901.
Geoffrey Strong, Estes, 1901.
The Hurdy-Gurdy, Estes, 1902.
Mrs. Tree, Estes, 1902.
The Golden Windows: A Book of Fables for Young and Old, Little, Brown, 1903.
The Green Satin Gown, illustrations by Barry, Estes, 1903.
More Five Minute Stories, illustrations by Wallace Goldsmith, Estes, 1903.
The Merryweathers, illustrations by daughter, Julia Ward Richards, Estes, 1904.
The Armstrongs, illustrations by J. W. Richards, Estes, 1905.
Mrs. Tree's Will, Estes, 1905.
The Silver Crown: Another Book of Fables, Little, Brown, 1906.
Grandmother: The Story of a Life That Never Was Lived, Estes, 1907.
The Pig Brother and Other Fables and Stories, Little, Brown, 1908.
The Wooing of Calvin Parks, Estes, 1908.
A Happy Little Time: A Partly-True Story for Children of Betty's Age, Estes, 1910.
"Up to Calvin's," Estes, 1910.
The Naughty Comet and Other Fables and Stories, Allenson, 1910, revised edition, 1925.
On Board the Mary Sands, Estes, 1911.
The Little Master, Estes, 1913, published as *Our Little Feudal Cousin of Long Ago, Being the Story of the Little Master, Alan of Morven, a Boy of Scotland, in the Time of Robert the Second,* Page, 1922.
Miss Jimmy, Estes, 1913.
Three Minute Stories, illustrations by Josephine H. Bruce, Page, 1914.
Pippin: A Wandering Flame, Appleton, 1917.
A Daughter of Jeru, Appleton, 1918.
Honor Bright: A Story for Girls, illustrations by Merrill, Page, 1920.
In Blessed Cyrus, Appleton, 1921.
The Squire, Appleton, 1923.
Honor Bright's New Adventure, illustrations by Elizabeth Withington, Page, 1925.
Star Bright: A Sequel to "Captain January," illustrations by Merrill, Page, 1927.
Harry in England, Being the Partly-True Adventures of H. R. in the Year 1857, illustrations by Reginald Birch, Appleton, 1937.

SHORT STORIES

For Tommy and Other Stories, Estes, 1900.

RETELLER

Beauty and the Beast, illustrations by Gordon Browne, Roberts Brothers, 1886.
Hop o' My Thumb, illustrations by Browne, Roberts Brothers, 1886.
The Old Fairy Tales, two volumes, illustrations by Browne, Roberts Brothers, 1886.

PLAYS

The Pig Brother Play-Book, Little, Brown, 1915.

Fairy Operettas, illustrations by Mary Robertson Bassett, Little, Brown, 1916.
Acting Charades, W. H. Baker, 1924.
Seven Original Operettas, W. H. Baker, 1924.

VERSE

Five Mice in a Mouse-Trap, by the Man in the Moon, Done in Vernacular, from the Lunacular, illustrations by Kate Greenaway, Addie Ladyard, and others, Estes, 1880.
In My Nursery, Roberts Brothers, 1890.
Sundown Songs, Little, Brown, 1899.
The Piccolo, Estes, 1906.
Jolly Jingles, Estes, 1912.
To Arms! Songs of the Great War, Page, 1918.
Tirra Lirra: Rhymes Old and New, illustrations by Marguerite Davis, Little, Brown, 1932.
Merry-Go-Round: New Rhymes and Old, illustrations by Winifred E. Lefferts, Appleton, 1935.
I Have a Song to Sing You: Still More Rhymes, illustrations by Birch, Appleton Century, 1938.
The Hottentot and Other Ditties, music by Twining Lynes, Schirmer, 1939.

OTHER

(Editor) *Baby's Rhyme Book,* two volumes, Estes, 1878-79.
(Editor) *Four Feet, Two Feet, and No Feet; or, Furry and Feathery Pets, and How They Live,* Estes & Lauriat, 1886.
Glimpses of the French Court: Sketches from French History, Estes & Lauriat, 1893.
When I Was Your Age, Estes & Lauriat, 1894.
(Editor) *The Letters and Journals of Samuel Gridley Howe,* two volumes, Estes, 1906-09.
Florence Nightengale, Angel of the Crimea: A Story for Young People, Appleton, 1909.
Two Noble Lives: Samuel Gridley Howe, Julia Ward Howe, Estes, 1911.
(With Maude Howe Elliot) *Julia Ward Howe, 1819-1910,* two volumes, Houghton, 1915.
Elizabeth Fry: The Angel of the Prisons, Appleton, 1916.
Abigail Adams and Her Times, Appleton, 1917.
Joan of Arc, Appleton, 1919.
(Editor) Julia Ward Howe, *The Walk with God,* Dutton, 1919.
Laura Bridgman: The Story of an Opened Door, Appleton, 1928.
Stepping Westward, Appleton, 1931.
Samuel Gridley Howe, Appleton, 1935.
E. A. R., Harvard University Press, 1936.
Please, privately printed, 1936.
What Shall the Children Read?, illustrations by C. B. Falls, Appleton, 1939.
(Editor) *Laura E. Richards and Gardiner,* Gannett, 1940.

Also a contributor of stories and verse to various periodicals, including *St. Nicholas, Atlantic Monthly,* and *Century.*

ADAPTATIONS: *Captain January* was produced as a film by Principal, starring "Baby Peggy," 1924, and also by Twentieth Century-Fox, starring Shirley Temple, 1936.

SIDELIGHTS: Laura E. Richards published more than ninety books for children and adults during a career that spanned forty years, from the American "Gilded Age" to the start of World War II. But while the world changed around her, Richards maintained the same easygoing writing style that won her a large readership for the nonsense verse she wrote initially for own children. Richards branched out from verse to publish a series of "girls' stories" and other fictional works for children and young adults, and ultimately she began to publish fiction and nonfiction books for adults in the same easy style that characterized her children's work. Although modern critics and readers of children's literature often find Richards's prose overly sentimental, for a generation or more children and adults alike found comfort in her assured fictional world.

Richards was born in Boston, Massachusetts, in 1850, the fourth of six children born to Samuel Gridley Howe and Julia Ward Howe. Her father was an educator who for many years was director of the Perkins Institute and Massachusetts School for the Blind; he was the first person to teach a blind and deaf person, Laura Bridgman, to communicate. Richards published a biography of that remarkable woman, after whom she was named, as well as biographies of both her father and her mother, author of the "Battle Hymn of the Republic" and a prolific poet, essayist, student of philosophy and literature, and Victorian social activist. For the biography of Julia Ward Howe, Richards and her collaborator, sister Maude Howe Elliot, won the 1917 Pulitzer Prize.

In the *Junior Book of Authors,* Richards remembered passing much of her early childhood in "a delightful old house set in a lovely garden in a suburb of Boston" that her mother named Green Peace. Summers were spent on the coast near Newport. She and her closest brother, Henry, avid readers and "constant playmates," spent much of their time "hunting elephants and rhinoceroses (which other persons did not see) in the garden" and having "wonderful adventures under the dining room table." As Anne Scott MacLeod put it in her essay on Richards published in *Writer's for Children,* it was a childhood "very like the ideal, and [Richards's] long, productive life as a woman and as a writer bore its imprimatur to the end." Richards wrote extensively about her ideal upbringing, especially in an autobiography for children, *When I Was Your Age,* and in a life story written for adults, *Stepping Westward.*

The family eventually moved from Green Peace. As Richards remembered in *Stepping Westward,* "My father had a passion for change, and we were whisked about from place to place, often from motives that we never knew." In 1867 Laura and sister Julia accompanied their parents on a tour of Europe. In Crete, where civil war was raging, Samuel Gridley Howe helped oversee the distribution of relief supplies. In 1869 Laura became engaged to Henry Richards, a childhood friend who became an architect. As Richards put it, "We were young; we had no special prospects, financially speaking.... We waited two years before thinking of marriage.... We came to know each other very well."

After taking a honeymoon tour of Europe, the Richards settled at Green Peace, Laura's childhood home. Henry started his own architectural firm. Laura had never seriously thought of writing until after her marriage and the arrival of children. She wrote, "And when the pleasant pilgrimage was over, what next? My first housekeeping; my first loaf of bread; my first quince marmalade; my first Baby.... I had always rhymed easily; now, with the coming of the babies, and the consequent weeks and months of quiet, came a prodigious welling up of rhymes, mostly bringing their tunes (or what passed for tunes; the baby, bless it, knew no better!) with them. I wrote, and sang, and wrote, and could not stop. The first baby was plump and placid, with a broad, smooth back which made an excellent writing desk." Richards would often lay the baby down upon her lap and place a pad of paper on the child's back for writing. The author first published some of her nonsense verse in *St. Nicholas* magazine, which started publication in 1873.

A lull in business forced the family to move to Gardiner, Maine, in 1876. Richards continued to write. Her first published volume, *Five Mice in a Mouse-Trap,* a collection of anecdotes told by the Man in the Moon, appeared in 1880. Her second, *Sketches and Scraps,* published in 1881, was the only one of her books illustrated by her husband. MacLeod calls it "the first book of nonsense ever written by an American and published in the United States." After the death of infant daughter Maud in 1885 came *The Joyous Story of Toto,* which she wrote, according to MacLeod, "as an antidote to her grief following the death." A second Toto volume, *Toto's Merry Winter,* appeared in 1887.

In 1889 the first of Richards's "girls' stories" appeared, establishing her literary reputation during her lifetime. The sentimental *Queen Hildegarde,* according to MacLeod "typical in most ways of all of Richards's girls' stories," is the story of Hildegarde, a precocious fifteen-year-old daughter of affluent parents who is sent to live on a farm for the summer in lieu of accompanying her family to California. Initially shocked by the simplicity of farm life, Hildegarde quickly learns to befriend some of the local boys and girls and by the end of the story has an operation for a disabled local girl and an education for an ambitious local boy. The Hildegarde character served as a basis for four sequels published from 1891 to 1897; another series of stories featuring a girl named Margaret comprised five volumes published from 1897 to 1901.

Captain January, published in 1891, was the most popular of Richards's books during her life. It is the story of a retired seaman who ten years earlier had rescued an infant child, Star Bright, from a storm. At the time of the story, Star is ten; her aunt, on excursion to the island where Star and the seaman live, recognizes her and wants her daughter to leave with her. Star refuses and remains with her "Daddy Captain" until he dies. *Captain January* was twice adapted for the screen, in 1924 as a silent movie and in 1936 with Shirley Temple as Star.

Richards's verse for children commands more respect from recent critics than her fiction. *Tirra Lirra,* her best collection, consisting of previously published and unpublished material, appeared in 1932. In addition to her many works for children and her biographies of her mother, father, and Laura Bridgman, Richards published an assortment of fictional, poetic, and dramatic works for adults and a group of biographical and historical volumes. She also edited an edition of her father's papers and several volumes of baby's verse. In the *Junior Book of Authors* Richards reminisced, "No one can possibly imagine how I have enjoyed my writing. It was work, but it was also the most delightful play. I am still writing. I have had a very long and very happy life. I hope you will all live as long and be as happy." Continuing to write, Richards published her last volume of verse for adults, entitled *The Hottentot and Other Ditties,* in 1939. Richards died in Gardiner in 1941.

WORKS CITED:

MacLeod, Anne Scott, "Laura E. Richards," in *Writers for Children,* edited Jane M. Bingham, Scribner, 1988.

Richards, Laura E., in *Junior Book of Authors,* edited by Stanley Kunitz and Howard Haycraft, H. W. Wilson, 1934.

Richards, Laura E., *Stepping Westward,* Appleton, 1931.

FOR MORE INFORMATION SEE:

BOOKS

Andrews, Siri, editor, *The Hewins Lectures: 1947-62,* Horn Book, 1963.

Benet, Laura, *Famous Poets for Young People,* Dodd, 1964.

Chevalier, Tracy, editor, *Twentieth-Century Children's Writers,* 3rd edition, St. James Press, 1989.

Dictionary of Literary Biography, Volume 42: *American Writers for Children before 1900,* Gale, 1985.

National Cyclopaedia of American Biography, Volume 39, James T. White, 1954.

Yesterday's Authors of Books for Children, Volume 1, Gale, 1977.

PERIODICALS

Horn Book, Volume 17, number 4, 1941, pp. 247-255.

* * *

RICHLER, Mordecai 1931-

PERSONAL: Born January 27, 1931, in Montreal, Quebec, Canada; son of Moses Isaac and Lily (Rosenberg) Richler; married first wife, Catherine Boudreau (divorced); married Florence Wood, July 27, 1960; children: (second marriage) Daniel, Noah, Emma, Mar-

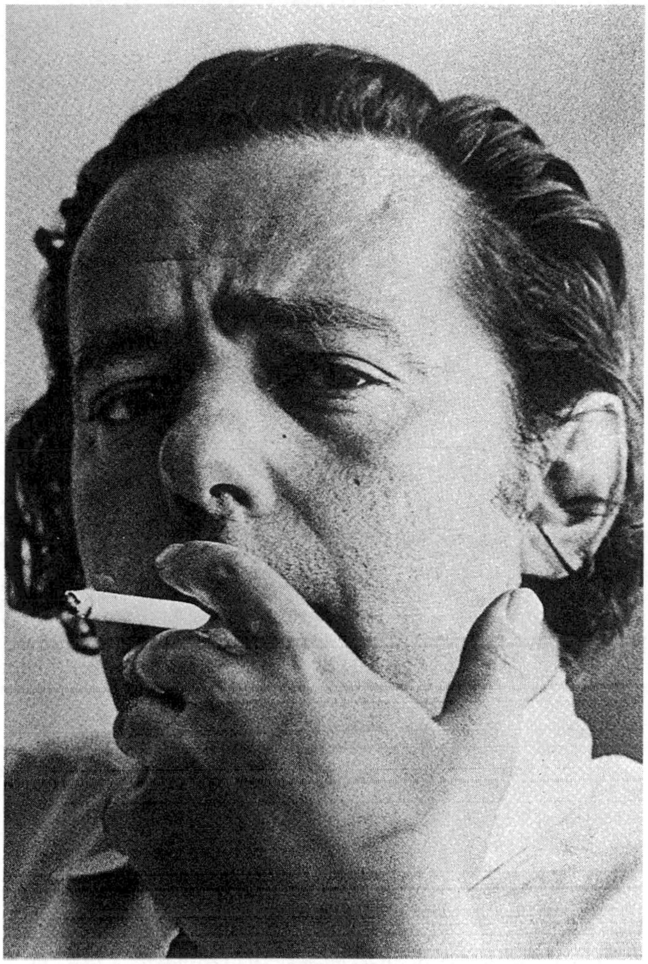

Mordecai Richler

tha, Jacob. *Education:* Attended Sir George Williams University, 1949-51. *Religion:* Jewish.

ADDRESSES: Home and office—1321 Sherbrooke St. W., Apt. 80C, Montreal, Quebec, Canada H3G 1J4. *Agent*—(literary and film) Janklow and Nesbit Associates, 598 Madison Ave., New York, NY 10022.

CAREER: Author and screenwriter. Left Canada in 1951 to become free-lance writer in Paris, France, 1952-53, and London, England, 1954-72; returned to Canada, 1972. Writer in residence, Sir George Williams University, 1968-69; visiting professor, Carleton University, 1972-74.

AWARDS, HONORS: President's medal for nonfiction, University of Western Ontario, 1959; Canadian Council junior art fellowships, 1959 and 1960, senior arts fellowship, 1967; Guggenheim Foundation creative writing fellowship, 1961; *Paris Review* humor prize, 1967, for section from *Cocksure;* Canadian Governor-General's award for literature and London Jewish Chronicle literature award, both 1972, both for *St. Urbain's Horseman;* Berlin Film Festival Golden Bear, Academy Award nomination, and Screenwriters Guild of America award, all 1974, all for screenplay, *The Apprenticeship of Duddy Kravitz; New York Times* Outstanding Book, 1975, Ruth Schwartz award, Canadian Bookseller's award for best children's book, and Canadian Librarian's medal, all 1976, all for *Jacob Two-Two Meets the Hooded Fang;* London *Jewish Chronicle*/H. H. Wingate award for fiction, 1981, for *Joshua Then and Now;* Commonwealth Writers Award, 1990, for *Solomon Gursky Was Here.*

WRITINGS:

NOVELS

The Acrobats (also see below), Putnam, 1954.
Son of a Smaller Hero, Collins (Toronto), 1955, Paperback Library, 1965.
A Choice of Enemies, Collins, 1957.
The Apprenticeship of Duddy Kravitz (also see below), Little, Brown, 1959.
The Incomparable Atuk, McClelland & Stewart, 1963, published as *Stick Your Neck Out,* Simon & Schuster, 1963.
Cocksure, Simon & Schuster, 1968.
St. Urbain's Horseman, Knopf, 1971.
Joshua Then and Now (also see below), Knopf, 1980.
Solomon Gursky Was Here, Viking, 1989.

FOR YOUNG ADULTS

Jacob Two-Two Meets the Hooded Fang, Knopf, 1975.
Jacob Two-Two and the Dinosaur, Knopf, 1987.

SCREENPLAYS

(With Nicholas Phipps) *No Love for Johnnie,* Embassy, 1962.
(With Geoffrey Cotterell and Ivan Foxwell) *Tiara Tahiti,* Rank, 1962.
(With Phipps) *The Wild and the Willing,* Rank, 1962, released as *Young and Willing,* Universal, 1965.
Life at the Top, Royal International, 1965.
The Apprenticeship of Duddy Kravitz (adapted from Richler's novel; also see below), Paramount, 1974.
(With David Giler and Jerry Belson) *Fun with Dick and Jane,* Bart/Palevsky, 1977.
Joshua Then and Now (adapted from Richler's novel), Twentieth Century-Fox, 1985.

TELEVISION SCRIPTS

The Acrobats (based on Richler's novel; also see below), Canadian Broadcasting Corp. (CBC-TV), 1957.
Friend of the People, CBC-TV, 1957.
Paid in Full, ATV (England), 1958.
The Trouble with Benny (based on Richler's short story), ABC (England), 1959.
The Apprenticeship of Duddy Kravitz (based on Richler's novel), CBC-TV, 1960.
The Fall of Mendel Krick, British Broadcasting Corp. (BBC-TV), 1963.

RADIO SCRIPTS

The Acrobats (based on Richler's novel), CBC-Radio, 1957.
Benny, the War in Europe, and Myerson's Daughter Bella, CBC-Radio, 1958.
The Spare Room, CBC-Radio, 1961.

Q for Quest (excerpts from Richler's fiction), CBC-Radio, 1963.
It's Harder to Be Anybody, CBC-Radio, 1965.
Such Was St. Urbain Street, CBC-Radio, 1966.
The Wordsmith (based on Richler's short story), CBC-Radio, 1979.

OTHER

Hunting Tigers under Glass: Essays and Reports, McClelland & Stewart, 1969.
The Street: Stories, McClelland & Stewart, 1969, New Republic, 1975.
(Editor) *Canadian Writing Today* (anthology), Peter Smith, 1970.
Shoveling Trouble (essays), McClelland & Stewart, 1973.
Notes on an Endangered Species and Others (essays), Knopf, 1974.
The Suit (animated filmstrip), National Film Board of Canada, 1976.
Images of Spain, photographs by Peter Christopher, Norton, 1977.
The Great Comic Book Heroes and Other Essays, McClelland & Stewart, 1978.
(Editor) *The Best of Modern Humor,* Knopf, 1983.
Home Sweet Home: My Canadian Album, (nonfiction), Knopf, 1984, published in paperback as *Home Sweet Home,* Penguin, 1985.
(Author of book) *Duddy* (play; based on Richler's novel *The Apprenticeship of Duddy Kravitz*), first produced in Edmonton, Alberta, at the Citadel Theatre, April, 1984.
(Editor) *Writers on World War II,* Knopf, 1991.
Oh Canada! Oh Quebec! Requiem for a Divided Country, Knopf, 1992.

Book columnist for *GQ*. Contributor to Canadian, U.S., and British periodicals, including *New Statesman, Spectator, Observer, Punch, Holiday, New York Review of Books, Commentary, Encounter,* and *London Magazine.* Member of editorial board, Book-of-the-Month Club, 1972-89. Richler's papers are collected at the University of Calgary Library in Alberta.

ADAPTATIONS: Paramount produced *The Apprenticeship of Duddy Kravitz,* starring Richard Dreyfuss, 1974; *Jacob Two-Two Meets the Hooded Fang* was adapted by Cinema Shares International (Canada) as a film starring Alex Karras, 1977, and a recording narrated by Christopher Plummer was made by Caedmon, 1977; Twentieth Century-Fox produced *Joshua Then and Now,* 1985; Plummer also narrated a recording of *Jacob Two-Two and the Dinosaur* for Caedmon, 1988.

SIDELIGHTS: Mordecai Richler, a celebrated adult novelist from Canada, is also well known for several of his books for a younger audience. *The Apprenticeship of Duddy Kravitz,* published in 1959, became required reading in many high schools and was made into a popular movie. Richler also wrote *Jacob Two-Two Meets the Hooded Fang* and *Jacob Two-Two and the Dinosaur,* two successful children's books, after his own young children tired of being told that they were not old enough to read their father's other novels. Richler received several awards for these books that had started out originally as bedtime stories for his youngest son.

From *Jacob Two-Two Meets the Hooded Fang,* by Mordecai Richler. Illustrated by Fritz Wegner.

Richer grew up on St. Urbain Street in Montreal, Canada, an area that at the time was populated almost exclusively by poor Jewish immigrants. "In my day, St. Urbain Street was the lowest rung on a ladder we were all hot to climb," Richler related in his book *Home Sweet Home: My Canadian Album.* The landscape of Richler's youth has become the setting of many of his famous novels, including *The Apprenticeship of Duddy Kravitz.* As an Orthodox Jew, Richler conformed to many traditions of the religion in his youth. He had a change of heart as he got older, however, and rebelled.

After graduation from a religious high school, Richler attended Sir George Williams University in Montreal for two years, as well as working part-time for the *Montreal Herald.* Thirsting for a wider view of the world and disenchanted with higher education, Richler cashed in an insurance policy his mother had taken out on him and used the money to go to Europe when he was nineteen. Living a bohemian life-style, he made friends with expatriate American authors and wrote a novel while living in Paris. A year later he had run out of money, but finished the novel. He returned to Canada, and *The Acrobats* was published in 1954.

That same year, Richler moved to London, where he got married and divorced within a few years. In 1959 he published *The Apprenticeship of Duddy Kravitz.* A coming-of-age novel, the story is comparable in its own way to James Joyce's *Portrait of an Artist as a Young Man* and D. H. Lawrence's *Sons and Lovers.* It concerns a Jewish-Canadian teenager who misinterprets his grandfather's warning that "a man without land is nobody" and goes about lying and manipulating his friends and family in order to purchase property. In the end, Duddy succeeds in his quest, only to find himself criticized and spurned by the very people he wished to impress.

The Apprenticeship of Duddy Kravitz is "the first of Richler's novels to exhibit fully his considerable comic talents, a strain that includes much black humor and a racy, colloquial, ironic idiom that becomes a characteristic feature of Richler's subsequent style," R. H. Ramsey wrote in the *Dictionary of Literary Biography. Duddy* was not an instant popular success, however, taking years before its sales were steady. In the following years, partly out of financial necessity, Richler got involved in television and film, while continuing to write novels. About the same time, he married the Canadian model Florence Wood, with whom he eventually had five children.

Richler wrote the screenplay for the movie version of *Duddy* in 1974. The popular movie, which starred Richard Dreyfuss, was nominated for an Academy Award for best screenplay. Release of the movie regenerated interest in Richler's original book, which by this time was being used as a textbook in high school classrooms in Canada.

After another string of successful adult books, Richler decided to write a novel for younger readers. It was prompted by one of his children, who protested because he was not able to read Richler's other work. "Well then ... isn't there anything of yours we are not too young to read?," the author reported his children as saying in *Canadian Literature.* The novel he wrote to meet the challenge was *Jacob Two-Two Meets the Hooded Fang.* "The book was meant to be family fun, with certain built-in family jokes," he continued. "It began, innocently enough, as a bedtime tale told to amuse our youngest child, Jacob, and as it made him (and even the others) giggle I started to write it down." The other characters in the book are also named after Richler's children.

In the story, Jacob, the youngest of five children, is upset because he has to repeat everything twice in order to be heard. Frustrated also by constant teasings, Jacob dreams of being put on trial in an adult world for the crime of being a child. In his dream, he is imprisoned by the evil Hooded Fang, but ultimately frees himself and the other children from their captor. The book was extremely successful, translated into several languages as well as recorded on cassette and made into a film starring Alex Karras. "I wrote it, first of all, for my own pleasure (and in fulfillment of a rash promise)," Richler confessed. "Of course, I hoped, as I always do, that it would appeal to a large audience." He continued that "the success of *Jacob Two-Two* has surprised, even embarrassed me." A few years later, Richler completed a sequel to this novel, *Jacob Two-Two and the Dinosaur.* In this book, Jacob is given a small reptile as a gift. To his surprise, it grows into a huge dinosaur. Jacob finds it an adventure trying to keep the narrow-minded adults from destroying his playful pet.

"Ironically, I suppose, *Jacob Two-Two,* in hard cover, has already outsold even my most successful adult novel.... Maybe I missed my true vocation," Richler mused. The author has displayed a wide range of skills by chronicling stories for both children and adults throughout his long career. As to which audience the author likes best, he is reluctant to say, but admits that "most delightful of all, hardly a week goes by when I don't get a batch of letters from children in Canada or the United States."

WORKS CITED:

Ramsey, R. H., "Mordecai Richler," *Dictionary of Literary Biography,* Volume 53: *Canadian Writers since 1960,* Gale, 1986, pp. 328-337.

Richler, Mordecai, "Writing Jacob Two-Two," *Canadian Literature,* autumn, 1978, pp. 6-8.

Richler, *Home Sweet Home: My Canadian Album,* Knopf, 1984.

FOR MORE INFORMATION SEE:

BOOKS

Children's Literature Review, Volume 17, Gale, 1989, pp. 63-81.

Klinck, Carl F., and others, editors, *Literary History of Canada: Canadian Literature in English,* University of Toronto Press, 1965.

Ramraj, Victor J., *Mordecai Richler,* Twayne, 1983.

Sheps, G. David, editor, *Mordecai Richler,* McGraw-Hill/Ryerson, 1971.

Woodcock, George, *Mordecai Richler,* McClelland & Stewart, 1970.

PERIODICALS

Esquire, August, 1982.

Maclean's, May 7, 1984.

* * *

RICHTER, Hans Peter 1925-

PERSONAL: Born April 28, 1925, in Cologne, Germany; son of Peter and Anna (Eckert) Richter; married Elfriede Feldmann, May 10, 1952, (died October 14, 1989); children: Ulrike, Claudia, Leonore, Gereon. *Education:* Attended Universities of Cologne, Bonn, Mainz, and Tuebingen; Technical University Hanover, Dr. rer pol., 1968.

ADDRESSES: Home—58 Franz-Werfel-Strasse, D-65 Mainz, Germany.

Hans Peter Richter

CAREER: Independent social psychologist and writer, 1954—; radio and television broadcaster. Professor of scientific methods and sociology, Darmstadt, Germany, 1973. *Military service:* German Army, 1942-45; became lieutenant; wounded in action; received Iron Cross and other decorations.

AWARDS, HONORS: Jugendbuchpreis Sebaldus-Verlag, 1961, for *Damals war es Friedrich;* Cite Internationale des Arts (Paris) stipendiate, 1965-66; Woodward School Book Award, 1971, and American Library Association Mildred L. Batchelder Award, 1972, Japanese book award, 1981, all for *Friedrich.*

WRITINGS:

FOR CHILDREN; FICTION; IN ENGLISH TRANSLATION

Uncle and His Merry-Go-Round, Bancroft & Co., 1959 (originally published as *Karussell und Luftballon,* Obpacher, 1958).

Hengist the Horse, Bancroft & Co., 1960 (originally published as *Das Pferd Max,* Obpacher, 1959).

Friedrich, translation by Edite Kroll, Holt, 1970 (originally published as *Damals war es Friedrich,* Sebaldus, 1961, abridged edition in German edited by Ray Milne published under same title, Oliver & Boyd, 1968).

I Was There, translation by Kroll, Holt, 1972 (originally published as *Wir waren dabei,* Herder (Freiburg), 1962, revised edition, 1964).

The Time of the Young Soldiers, Kestrel, 1975 (originally published as *Die Zeit der jungen Soldaten,* Alsatia, 1967).

FOR CHILDREN; FICTION; UNTRANSLATED WORKS

Der Heilige Martin, Gruenewald, 1959.

Nikolaus der Gute (legends about St. Nicholas), Gruenewald, 1960.

Wie Heinz und Inge sich verlaufen haben, Dessart, 1960.

Hans Kauft ein, Scholz, 1961.

Immer ist etwas los!, Loewe, 1961.

Das war eine Reise!, Sebaldus, 1962.

Birgitta, Gruenewald, 1963.

Peter, Gruenewald, 1963.

Ein Reise um die Erde, Ueberreuter, 1963.

Eine wahre Baerengeschichte, Ueberreuter, 1964.

Nikolaus, Gruenewald, 1965.

Ich war kein braves Kind, Alsatia, 1967.

Der Hundemord, Alsatia, 1968.

Kunibert im Schlafanzug, Engelbert, 1972.

Katzen haben Vorfahrt, Engelbert, 1972.

Einschreiben vom Anwalt, Schaffstein, 1974.

FOR CHILDREN; EDITOR; UNTRANSLATED WORKS

Schriftsteller antworten jungen Menschen auf die Frage: Wozu leben wir?, Alsatia, 1968.

Schriftsteller erzaehlen von ihrer Mutter, Alsatia, 1968.

Schriftsteller erzaehlen von der Gewalt, Alsatia, 1970.

Harte Jugend, Steyler, 1970.

Schriftsteller erzaehlen aus aller Welt, Engelbert, 1973.

Schriftsteller erzaehlen von der Gerechtigkeit, Engelbert, 1977.

FOR ADULTS; NONFICTION; UNTRANSLATED WORKS

Hoerermeinungsforschung auf einem Dorf, Archiv des Suedwestfunk, 1952.

Hausen vor der Hoehe: Eine Rundfunkuntersuchung, two volumes, Archiv des Nordwestdeutschen Rundfunks, 1954.

Informationsbriefe fuer Fuehrungskraefte, Industrie-Verlag, 1955.

Geschichte und Quellensammlung zur Geschichte der Hoererforschung im deutschsprachigen Raum, two volumes, Archiv der Historischen Kommission des deutschen Rundfunks, 1957.

Die Freizeit deines Kindes, Oeffentliches Leben, 1957.

Zwoelf Vorlesungen ueber Marktforschung und Werbung im Aussenhandel, Akademie fuer Welthandel, 1957.

(With Fritz W. Adam) *Beitrag zu einer Phaenomenologie der Berufsunfaehigkeit,* Thieme, 1964.

(Editor) *Der jungen Leser wegen,* Schwann, 1965.

Jagd auf Gereon, Styria, 1967.

Einfuehrungen zu Fernsehspielen und Spielfilmen, Archiv des Zweiten Deutschen Fernsehens, 1970.

Mohammed, Engelbert, 1974.

Saint-Just, Engelbert, 1975.

Gott—Was ist das?, Thienemann, 1980.

Gut und boese, Thienemann, 1980.

Wissenschaft von der Wissenschaft, Thienemann, 1981.

Also author of more than a hundred radio and television scripts and of several book-length publications in journals, including "Einfuehrung in die Philosophie" in *Aufstieg,* 1955, and "Lehrgang der Philosophie," in *Geistesschulung,* 1956. Contributor of more than a hundred essays to books and periodicals.

SIDELIGHTS: Hans Peter Richter is a socio-psychologist, professor, and author of numerous fiction and nonfiction works. In the United States, he is best known for his acclaimed trilogy of autobiographical novels which recall the experiences of young people in Germany during World War II: *Friedrich, I Was There,* and *The Time of the Young Soldiers.* In an essay for *Something about the Author Autobiography Series* (*SAAS*), Richter says he intended "to show how human beings, because of being different, were persecuted, disadvantaged, or even killed ... I have chosen the persecution of Jews during the time of national socialism because I was an eye- and ear-witness, because it is just easier to describe that which one has lived through." Analyzing the impact of Richter's works in *Best Sellers,* Mrs. John G. Gray writes, "The reader is uneasy as thoughts rise from the obvious parallels between Germany and other countries, our own included. Signs are read differently, depending on where a person stands."

Richter was born in Cologne, Germany, on April 28, 1925. He describes himself in *SAAS* as "a real big-city boy, a street brat with many naughty habits." For example, Richter admits that he did not always obey and sometimes refused to study. He recalls his mother as "a born storyteller," and claims that his inclination to tell others about his experiences began with her. Richter credits his interest in literature to Phillip Neumann, his teacher when he was about fourteen. Neumann was very special to Richter and his classmates, and in fact inspired such dedication that this class "regularly met with him twice a year" for fifty years. "Whatever I am, I owe in large part to this teacher," Richter proclaims in *SAAS.* "I am a Neumann through and through, and to this day I bow down in reverence to my former teacher."

Richter was a member of the Hitler Youth and trained to serve in the Germany Army, which he entered in 1942. Richter lost an arm before he could see action, but he remained in the army and was made an officer. When he returned from the war, Richter "did not even have anything to wear; because we were no longer allowed to wear the uniform," he writes in *SAAS.* "At that time I stole from the British occupation troops a bed sheet.... From that bed sheet a woman of my acquaintance tailored a summer suit for me." During these years of deprivation he worked as manager of a theatre, personnel manager of a large repair shop, and cost accountant at a marmalade factory—a position he took because of the availability of food.

When he finally found an opportunity, Richter returned to school. He studied psychology and sociology at the Universities of Cologne, Bonn, Mainz, and Tubingen and attained the status of university professor. Of the subjects he studied, Richter laments in *SAAS* that "unfortunately, because of the times and the political developments, they have been dragged down from the realm of science to the lowlands of everyday interests." Upon graduating, Richter began to produce scholarly writing which outweighs his popular works to this day.

In 1952 Richter married Elfriede Feldmann. He began telling stories to their four children, and eventually a friend suggested that he write the stories down for publication. Richter has since written more than forty works of fiction, many for younger readers.

The first volume of Richter's acclaimed autobiographical war trilogy, *Friedrich,* won the Mildred Batchelder Book Award in 1972. Eric A. Kimmel writes in *Horn Book* that "Richter, more than any other writer of juvenile fiction about the Holocaust, gives a menacing sense of the elaborately planned, systematic, and merciless unfolding of the Nazi persecution. Step by step the Jews, represented by Friedrich and his parents, are deprived of ordinary human dignity, a means of earning a living, property, police protection, and—when nothing is left—life. Friedrich, who was once a normal boy with many friends, dies alone in a bombing raid—a homeless, terrified creature, denied even the right to cringe in a corner of an air raid shelter."

I Was There, the second book in Richter's trilogy, focuses on a character named Heinz who is the son of a Nazi and a willing member of the Hitler Youth. At the same time, he is a decent and kind person. A *Times Literary Supplement* reviewer says, "Beneath the surface the author's restrained emotion gives the book immense and sinister force. Naturally enough, it is easy to convey the compulsion to join in, to conform, that a society such as Nazi Germany brought to bear on the young. It

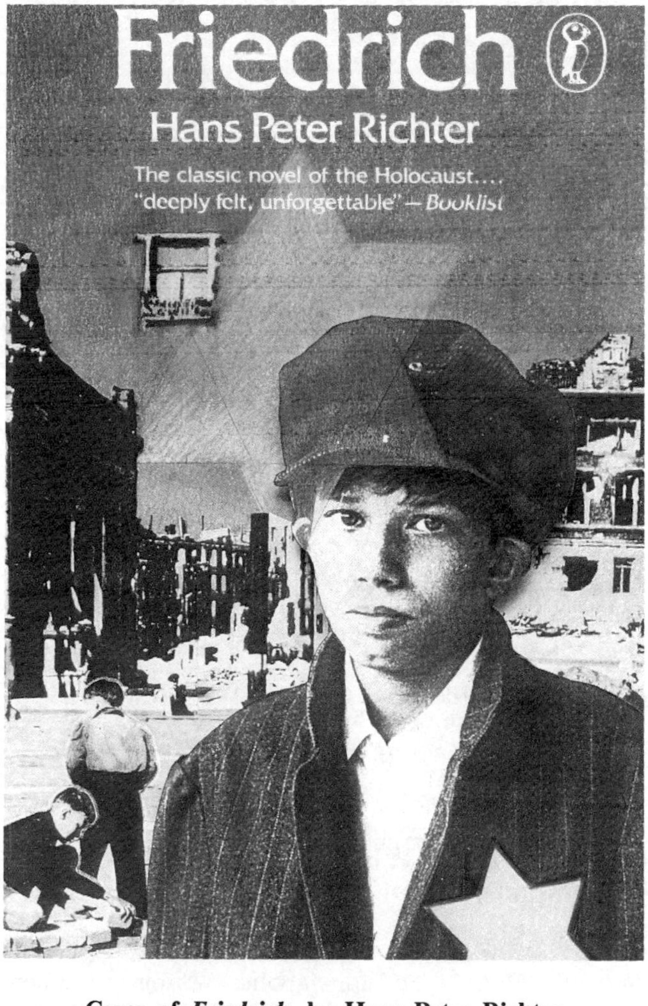

Cover of *Friedrich,* by Hans Peter Richter.

is natural to feel more sympathy than revulsion for the reluctant member of the Hitler Youth."

In the third book of the trilogy, *The Time of the Young Soldiers,* the narrator is a young man who relates his impressions of the Second World War as well as his perceptions of German soldiers. Writing in *Junior Bookshelf,* M. Crouch calls Richter's work "a very remarkable book." "In this quiet story one sees a nation passing from pride to despair, a boy losing his arm, his innocence and any objective in life but survival," Crouch continues. "It is the more moving because it avoids heroics or any overstatement."

Like many Germans, Richter still struggles with some aspects of his nation's history. Although he presents a starkly realistic picture of his experiences in his novels, Richter says in *SAAS* that many people choose to repress this history: "At the end of the Second World War, the German armed forces were defeated, to be sure, but national socialism had not yet outlived itself. In order to eradicate it completely, people tried to suppress it. This attempt has degenerated into a witch hunt that has not ceased to this day. Today, one can exhibit publicly, without hesitation, portraits of Stalin or the Ayatollah Khomeini and praise them. But as soon as a person merely suggests a swastika or mentions Hitler, he has to fear bad consequences."

WORKS CITED:

Crouch, M., review of *The Time of the Young Soldiers, Junior Bookshelf,* June, 1976, p. 171.

Gray, Mrs. John G., review of *I Was There, Best Sellers,* December 15, 1972, pp. 446-447.

Kimmel, Eric A., "Confronting the Ovens: The Holocaust and Juvenile Fiction," *Horn Book,* February, 1977, pp. 87-88.

"Pawns of War," *Times Literary Supplement,* April 6, 1973, p. 380.

Richter, Hans Peter, essay in *Something about the Author Autobiography Series,* Volume 11, Gale, 1991, pp. 275-287.

FOR MORE INFORMATION SEE:

BOOKS

Children's Literature Review, Volume 21, Gale Research, 1980, pp. 186-190.

PERIODICALS

Horn Book, April, 1971; October, 1971; August, 1972; December 1972.

Top of the News, June, 1972.

* * *

RILEY, James Whitcomb 1849-1916 (Benjamin F. Johnson, of Boone)

PERSONAL: Born October 7, 1849, in Greenfield, IN; died July 22, 1916, in Indianapolis, IN; son of Reuben A. (a lawyer) and Elizabeth (Marine) Riley.

James Whitcomb Riley

CAREER: Poet, journalist, and lecturer. Early positions included Bible salesman, housepainter, and sign painter and traveling musician for a patent-medicine company; *Greenfield News,* Greenfield, IN, associate editor, 1874; *Anderson Democrat,* Anderson, IN, assistant editor, 1877; *Indianapolis Journal,* Indianapolis, IN, journalist, reviewer, and poet, 1879-85.

MEMBER: American Academy of Arts and Letters.

AWARDS, HONORS: M.A., Yale University, 1902; Litt.D., Wabash College, 1903, and University of Pennsylvania, 1904; LL.D., Indiana University, 1907; Riley's birthday was declared an official holiday in Indiana, 1915; his home on Lockerbie St. in Indianapolis and his birthplace have been made into public memorials.

WRITINGS:

POETRY AND PROSE; ILLUSTRATED BY WILL VAWTER, EXCEPT AS INDICATED

Riley Child-Rhymes (includes "Little Orphant Annie" [also see below]), Bowen-Merrill, 1899.

Riley Love-Lyrics, illustrated by William B. Dyer, Bowen-Merrill, 1899, illustrated by Vawter, Bobbs-Merrill, 1920.

Riley Farm-Rhymes, Bowen-Merrill, 1901.

The Book of Joyous Children, Scribner, 1902.

His Pa's Romance, Bobbs-Merrill, 1903.

A Defective Santa Claus, illustrated by Vawter and C. M. Relyea, Bobbs-Merrill, 1904.

Riley Songs O'Cheer, Bobbs-Merrill, 1905.

Riley Songs of Summer, Bobbs-Merrill, 1908.

Riley Songs of Home, Bobbs-Merrill, 1910.
When the Frost Is on the Pumpkin, and Other Poems, Bobbs-Merrill, 1911.
A Summer's Day, and Other Poems, Bobbs-Merrill, 1911.
Down around the River, Bobbs-Merrill, 1911.
The Prayer Perfect, and Other Poems, Bobbs-Merrill, 1912.
Knee-Deep in June, and Other Poems, Bobbs-Merrill, 1912.
Away, Bobbs-Merrill, 1913.
Riley Songs of Friendship, Bobbs-Merrill, 1915.
Riley Hoosier Stories, Bobbs-Merrill, 1917.
Riley Fairy Tales, Bobbs-Merrill, 1923.

POETRY AND PROSE; ILLUSTRATED BY HOWARD C. CHRISTY

Home Again with Me, Bobbs-Merrill, 1908.
Riley Roses, Bobbs-Merrill, 1909.
The Girl I Loved, Bobbs-Merrill, 1910.
When She Was about Sixteen, Bobbs-Merrill, 1911.
Good-bye, Jim, Bobbs-Merrill, 1913.
A Discouraging Model, Bobbs-Merrill, 1914.

POETRY AND PROSE; ILLUSTRATED BY ETHEL F. BETTS

The Runaway Boy, Bobbs-Merrill, 1906.
The Raggedy Man, Bobbs-Merrill, 1907.
Riley Child Verse, Bobbs-Merrill, 1908.
A Host of Children, Bobbs-Merrill, 1920.

OTHER POETRY AND PROSE

(Under pseudonym Benjamin F. Johnson, of Boone) *"The Old Swimmin'-Hole," and 'Leven More Poems,* Merrill, Meigs, 1883.
The Boss Girl: A Christmas Story, and Other Sketches, Bowen-Merrill, 1886.
Afterwhiles, Bowen-Merrill, 1887.
Old-fashioned Roses, Bowen-Merrill, 1888.
Pipes O'Pan at Zekesbury, Bowen-Merrill, 1889.
(With Edgar Wilson Nye) *Fun, Wit, and Humor,* Bowen-Merrill, 1890.
Sketches in Prose, and Occasional Verses, Bowen-Merrill, 1891.
An Old Sweetheart, Bowen-Merrill, 1891, reprinted as *An Old Sweetheart of Mine* (also see below), 1902.
Neighborly Poems, Bowen-Merrill, 1891.
Rhymes of Childhood, [Indianapolis], 1891.
The Flying Islands of Night, Bowen-Merrill, 1892, illustrated by Franklin Booth, Bobbs-Merrill, 1913.
Green Fields and Running Brooks, Bowen-Merrill, 1893.
(With Nye) *Poems and Yarns,* Neely, 1893.
Poems Here at Home, illustrated by E. W. Kemble, Century, 1893.
Armanzindy, Bowen-Merrill, 1894.
The Days Gone By, and Other Poems, E. A. Weeks, 1895.
A Tinkle of Bells, and Other Poems, E. A. Weeks, 1895.
A Child-World, Bowen-Merrill, 1897.
Rubaiyat of Doc Sifers, illustrated by C. M. Relyea, Century, 1897.
Home-Folks, Bowen-Merrill, 1900.
Out to Old Aunt Mary's, Bobbs-Merrill, 1903.
Gems from Riley, De Wolfe, Fiske, 1904.
Morning, Bobbs-Merrill, 1907.
The Boys of the Old Glee Club, Bobbs-Merrill, 1907.
The Orphant Annie Book, [Indianapolis], 1908.
Old School Day Romances, illustrated by E. Stetson Crawford, Bobbs-Merrill, 1909.
A Hoosier Romance, 1868, illustrated by John W. Adams, Century, 1910.
The Lockerbie Book, edited by Hewitt H. Howland, Bobbs-Merrill, 1911.
Mrs. Miller, Bobbs-Merrill, 1912.
All the Year Round, illustrated by Gustave Baumann, Bobbs-Merrill, 1912.
A Song of Long Ago, Bobbs-Merrill, 1913.
Her Beautiful Eyes, Bobbs-Merrill, 1913.
He and I, Bobbs-Merrill, 1913.
Do They Miss Me, Bobbs-Merrill, 1913.
When My Dreams Come True, Bobbs-Merrill, 1913.
The Riley Baby Book, illustrated by William Cotton, Bobbs-Merrill, 1913.
The Rose, Bobbs-Merrill, 1913.
When She Comes Home, Bobbs-Merrill, 1914.

From *Out to Old Aunt Mary's,* by James Whitcomb Riley. Illustrated by Howard Chandler Christy.

To My Friend, Bobbs-Merrill, 1914.
Just Be Glad, Bobbs-Merrill, 1914.
The Glad Sweet Face of Her, Bobbs-Merrill, 1914.
Contentment, Bobbs-Merrill, 1914.
The Old Times, Bobbs-Merrill, 1915.
The Old Soldier's Story, Bobbs-Merrill, 1915.
The Hoosier Book, edited by Howland, Bobbs-Merrill, 1916.
The Name of Old Glory, Bobbs-Merrill, 1917.
Little Orphant Annie, illustrated by Diane Stanley, Putnam, 1983.

COLLECTIONS

The Poems and Prose Sketches of James Whitcomb Riley, sixteen volumes, Scribner, 1897-1914.
The Complete Works of James Whitcomb Riley, six volumes, Bobbs-Merrill, 1913.
The Best of James Whitcomb Riley, Indiana University Press, 1982.

Riley's works have also been collected in numerous other volumes.

OTHER

(With Edgar Wilson Nye) *Nye and Riley's Railway Guide,* [Chicago], 1888.
Letters of James Whitcomb Riley, edited by William L. Phelps, Bobbs-Merrill, 1930.

Contributor to periodicals, including *Hearth and Home, Kokomo Tribune, Indianapolis Saturday Herald,* and *Indianapolis Journal.*

ADAPTATIONS: Film adaptations of Riley's works include *The Old Swimmin' Hole,* Charles Ray Film Co., 1921, and Arnold Blumberg, 1967; *The Girl I Loved,* United Artists, 1923; and *An Old Sweetheart of Mine,* Metro Pictures, 1923.

SIDELIGHTS: Author of numerous beloved poetry volumes, James Whitcomb Riley was widely known at the turn of the century for books such as *"The Old Swimmin'-Hole," and 'Leven More Poems, Riley Child-Rhymes, Out to Old Aunt Mary's,* and *An Old Sweetheart.* Riley's poetry, read by both adults and children, is uncomplicated, sentimental, and humorous and often centers on children and Riley's own childhood in rural Indiana. His works were quite popular in his time, and Riley himself became well known on the lecture circuit, where he performed his writings with author Edgar Wilson (Bill) Nye. He charmed audiences with his oratorical skills, and his imitation of rural Indiana dialects earned him the nickname "Hoosier Poet." His poetry is especially prized for its sometimes whimsical reflection of small-town America.

Born in Indiana in 1849, Riley was drawn to poetry even before he was able to read. As a young boy, he once saved money that he would normally have used to buy candy to purchase a book. "The slender little volume must have cost all of twenty-five cents," Marcus Dickey quoted Riley in *The Maturity of James Whitcomb Riley.* "It was Francis Quarles' *Divine Emblems* (first printed in England in 1635)—a neat little affair about the size of a pocket Testament. I carried it around with me all day long. It gave me delight to touch it.... When asked if I could read poetry, I shook my head and turned away embarrassed—but I held on to my Poetry-book."

Riley's interest in books and poetry did not translate into an interest in his schoolwork. Neglectful of his studies, Riley preferred to take walks in the countryside, read books of his own choosing, and create rhymes, the first of which he sent to his young friends on homemade valentines. He remembered fondly, however, the teacher who introduced him to literature. Dickey quoted the poet in *The Youth of James Whitcomb Riley:* "To [my teacher] I owe possibly the first gratitude of my heart and soul, since, after a brief warfare, upon our first acquaintance as teacher and pupil, he informed me gently but firmly that since I was so persistent in secretly reading novels during school hours he would insist upon his right to choose the novel I should read, whereupon the ... dime novels were discarded for masterpieces of fiction."

Riley's dislike of school and his low grades caused tension at home. His father, a lawyer, "had little use for a boy who could not learn arithmetic," revealed Riley in *The Youth of James Whitcomb Riley.* "There were others of the same opinion. My schoolmates had an aptitude for figures and stood well in their classes. The result was half the town pitied me. Again and again I was told I would have to be supported by the family."

Discouraged from pursuing further education, Riley quit school at age twenty and went on to work at various odd jobs, such as selling Bibles and painting houses. He then became a sign painter, and "while waiting for the turn of fortune, I covered all the barns and fences with advertisements," Dickey quoted Riley in *The Youth of James Whitcomb Riley.* "All the while I was nibbling at the rhyme-maker's trade, and this was a source of irritation to my father.... He thought I should devote my time exclusively to painting." Nonetheless, Riley joined a traveling patent-medicine show, where he worked as a sign painter, advertising jingle writer, and minstrel. This gave Riley an opportunity to perform his rhymes and to become an observer of rural life, which would figure prominently in his poetry.

In 1874 Riley began working as an associate editor at the *Greenfield News,* and a year later he published a poem in *Hearth and Home* magazine. Riley was not able to become a regular contributor to the magazine, however, because shortly after his poem appeared the publication folded. After a stint at his father's law office, Riley returned to the newspaper business in 1877, when he became an assistant editor at the *Anderson Democrat.* Two years later he landed a position with the *Indianapolis Journal,* where he wrote book reviews, humorous editorials, and poetry. "The world with its excellence and follies flows through the reportorial rooms," Riley remarked in *The Maturity of James Whitcomb Riley.* "Thus, I was brought into contact with all phases of life.

My journalistic work gave me an insight into human nature, which I could have acquired in no other way."

Many of Riley's poems that were published in the *Indianapolis Journal* were later collected in his first book, *"The Old Swimmin'-Hole," and 'Leven More Poems,* which appeared in 1883. These poems recalled his youth: he wrote about how his mother told him stories, about his excitement when his grandmother or the circus came to town, and about the pond where he used to swim. In poems written expressly for children, Riley playfully misspelled words to reflect the way children often mispronounced them. Riley's fun-loving approach is evident in this excerpt of one of his most popular poems, "Little Orphant Annie," which appeared in *Riley Child-Rhymes:* "Little Orphant Annie's come to our house to stay, / An' wash the cups an' saucers up, an' brush the crumbs away, / An' shoo the chickens off the porch, an' dust the hearth, an' sweep, / An' make the fire, an' bake the bread, an' earn her board-an'-keep; / An' all us other childern, when the supper things is done, / We set around the kitchen fire an' has the mostest fun / A-list'nin' to the witch-tales 'at Annie tells about, / An' the Gobble-uns 'at gits you / Ef you / Don't / Watch / Out!"

A prolific writer and important contributor to children's literature, Riley published more than fifty volumes during his lifetime, many of which were popular successes. He is remembered for his insight and humor by children and adults alike. As was noted in *Indiana Authors and Their Books, 1816-1916,* "No American poet—those patriarchs of New England included—has thus far caught the popular fancy, has thus far enjoyed the voluntary following, that was and is his."

WORKS CITED:

Banta, R. E., compiler, *Indiana Authors and Their Books, 1816-1916,* Wabash College, 1949, pp. 270-72.

Dickey, Marcus, *The Youth of James Whitcomb Riley,* Bobbs-Merrill, 1919.

Dickey, Marcus, *The Maturity of James Whitcomb Riley,* Bobbs-Merrill, 1922.

Riley, James Whitcomb, *Riley Child-Rhymes,* Bobbs-Merrill, 1899.

FOR MORE INFORMATION SEE:

BOOKS

Something about the Author, Volume 17, Gale, 1979, pp. 159-71.

* * *

RIQ
See ATWATER, Richard (Tupper)

* * *

RIVERSIDE, John
See HEINLEIN, Robert A(nson)

Willo Davis Roberts

ROBERTS, Willo Davis 1928-

PERSONAL: Born May 28, 1928, in Grand Rapids, MI; daughter of Clayton R. and Lealah (Gleason) Davis; married David W. Roberts (a building supply company manager, photographer, and writer), May 20, 1949; children: Kathleen, David M., Larrilyn (Roberts) Lindquist, Christopher. *Education:* Graduated from high school in Pontiac, MI. *Religion:* Christian.

ADDRESSES: Home—12020 West Engebretsen Rd., Granite Falls, WA 98252. *Agent*—Curtis Brown, 10 Astor Place, New York, NY 10019.

CAREER: Writer. Has worked in hospitals and doctors' offices; co-owner of dairy farm. Lecturer and workshop leader at writers' conferences and schools; consultant to executive board of Pacific Northwest Writers' Conference.

MEMBER: Mystery Writers of America, Society of Children's Book Writers, Authors Guild of Authors League of America, Seattle Freelancers, Eastside Writers.

AWARDS, HONORS: Don't Hurt Laurie! was named a Notable Children's Trade Book by the National Council for the Social Studies and the Children's Book Council, 1977; Young Hoosier Book Award, Association for Indiana Media Educators, 1980, West Australian Young Readers Award, 1981, Georgia Children's Book Award, University of Georgia, 1982, all for *Don't Hurt Laurie!;* Mark Twain Award, Missouri Library Association and Missouri Association of School Librarians, 1983, and California Young Reader Medal, California Reading Association, 1986, all for *The Girl with the Silver Eyes; Eddie and the Fairy Godpuppy* was named a West Virginia Children's Book Award honor book, 1987;

Pacific Northwest Writers Conference Achievement Award, 1986, for body of work; *Baby Sitting Is a Dangerous Job* received the Mark Twain Award, the Young Hoosier Award, the South Carolina Children's Book Award, and the Nevada Young Reader's Award; *Sugar Isn't Everything* was named an outstanding science trade book for children by the National Science Teachers Association and the Children's Book Council; Edgar Allen Poe Award, 1989, for *Megan's Island;* Governor's Award for contribution to the field of children's literature, Washington State, 1990, for body of work.

WRITINGS:

FOR ADULTS

Murder at Grand Bay, Arcadia House, 1955.
The Girl Who Wasn't There, Arcadia House, 1957.
Murder Is So Easy, Vega Books, 1961.
The Suspected Four, Vega Books, 1962.
Nurse Kay's Conquest, Ace Books, 1966.
Once a Nurse, Ace Books, 1966.
Nurse at Mystery Villa, Ace Books, 1967.
Return to Darkness, Lancer Books, 1969.
Devil Boy, New American Library, 1970.
Shroud of Fog, Ace Books, 1970.
The Waiting Darkness, Lancer Books, 1970.
Shadow of a Past Love, Lancer Books, 1970.
The Tarot Spell, Lancer Books, 1970.
The House at Fern Canyon, Lancer Books, 1970.
Invitation to Evil, Lancer Books, 1970.
The Terror Trap, Lancer Books, 1971.
King's Pawn, Lancer Books, 1971.
The Gates of Montrain, Lancer Books, 1971.
The Watchers, Lancer Books, 1971.
The Ghosts of Harrel, Lancer Books, 1971.
The Secret Lives of the Nurses, Pan, 1971, published in the United States as *The Nurses,* Ace Books, 1972.
Inherit the Darkness, Lancer Books, 1972.
Nurse in Danger, Ace Books, 1972.
Becca's Child, Lancer Books, 1972.
Sing a Dark Song, Lancer Books, 1972.
The Face of Danger, Lancer Books, 1972.
Dangerous Legacy, Lancer Books, 1972.
Sinister Gardens, Lancer Books, 1972.
The M.D., Lancer Books, 1972.
Evil Children, Lancer Books, 1973.
The Gods in Green, Lancer Books, 1973.
Nurse Robin, Lennox Hill, 1973.
Didn't Anybody Know My Wife?, Putnam, 1974.
White Jade, Doubleday, 1975.
Key Witness, Putnam, 1975.
Expendable, Doubleday, 1976.
The Jaubert Ring, Doubleday, 1976.
Act of Fear, Doubleday, 1977.
Cape of Black Sands, Popular Library, 1977.
The House of Imposters, Popular Library, 1977.
Destiny's Women, Popular Library, 1980.
The Search for Willie, Popular Library, 1980.
The Face at the Window, Raven Press, 1981.
A Long Time to Hate, Avon, 1982.
The Gallant Spirit, Popular Library, 1982.
Days of Valor, Warner, 1983.
The Sniper, Doubleday, 1984.
Keating's Landing, Warner, 1984.
The Annalise Experiment, Doubleday, 1985.
Different Dream, Different Lands, Worldwide, 1985.
My Rebel, My Love, Pocket Books, 1986.
To Share a Dream, Worldwide, 1986.
Madawaska, Worldwide, 1988.

THE "BLACK PEARL" SERIES; ALL PUBLISHED BY POPULAR LIBRARY

The Dark Dowry, 1978.
The Stuart Strain, 1978.
The Cade Curse, 1978.
The Devil's Double, 1979.
The Radkin Revenge, 1979.
The Hellfire Heritage, 1979.
The Macomber Menace, 1980.
The Gresham Ghost, 1980.

FOR CHILDREN

The View from the Cherry Tree, Atheneum, 1975.
Don't Hurt Laurie!, illustrated by Ruth Sanderson, Atheneum, 1977.
The Minden Curse, illustrated by Sherry Streeter, Atheneum, 1978.
More Minden Curses, illustrated by Streeter, Atheneum, 1980.
The Girl with the Silver Eyes (Junior Literary Guild selection), Atheneum, 1980.
House of Fear, Scholastic, 1983.
The Pet-Sitting Peril (Junior Literary Guild selection), Atheneum, 1983.
No Monsters in the Closet, Atheneum, 1983.
Eddie and the Fairy Godpuppy, illustrated by Leslie Morrill, Atheneum, 1984.
Elizabeth, Scholastic, 1984.
Caroline, Scholastic, 1984.
Baby Sitting Is a Dangerous Job (Junior Literary Guild selection), Atheneum, 1985.
Victoria, Scholastic, 1985.
The Magic Book, Atheneum, 1986.
Sugar Isn't Everything, Atheneum, 1987.
Megan's Island, Atheneum, 1988.
What Could Go Wrong?, Atheneum, 1989.
Nightmare, Atheneum, 1989.
To Grandmother's House We Go, Atheneum, 1990.
Scared Stiff, Atheneum, 1991.
Dark Secrets, Fawcett/Juniper, 1991.
Jo and the Bandit, Atheneum, March, 1992.
What Are We Going to Do about David?, Atheneum, in press.

SIDELIGHTS: Willo Davis Roberts, a prolific and versatile writer of mystery, historical, gothic, and nurses' novels, is probably best known for her award-winning children's books. Originally a writer for adults, Roberts hesitated when her agent and an editor both suggested that she rewrite her novel, *The View from the Cherry Tree,* as a children's book. "I was outraged," Roberts wrote in an autobiographical essay for *Something about the Author Autobiography Series* (*SAAS*). "I wanted grown-ups to read it! Which shows how much I knew.... I hadn't anticipated the non-monetary rewards of writing for kids." Once past her initial reluctance, Roberts's transition to children's literature came easily. "I never had any trouble switching from adult to kids' books," she continued in *SAAS*. "I think in essence I've remained about eleven myself. I remember very clearly what I thought and felt at that age, how painfully shy I was, how I was intimidated by people and circumstances."

Roberts spent her childhood moving with her family from town to town in Michigan. Her father, she says, could do any job that came his way but he was never motivated to stay for long in one place. Although he provided his family with food and warm places to live, he was not very interested in material things. Roberts recalls that when she was in the fourth grade she was enrolled in six different schools because the family moved so often; she consequently never fully learned her multiplication tables. Embarrassment at the kinds of houses her family lived in and shyness made it difficult for Roberts to make friends. Her insecurity in the social world nudged her early in her life into the solitary pursuit of writing.

After graduating from high school, Roberts met and later married her husband David. The couple bought a dairy farm in California, where they began raising their four children. The farm, despite the Robertses' hard work, led the family deep into debt. Roberts, who has never written about the ranch because, she says, she still cannot recall it with a sense of humor, described the long hours of hard work and constant financial stress of dairy farming as the time in her life "when I really learned about poverty." For several years, Roberts had little time for her writing, but sent a few of her manuscripts to publishers. She sold her first novel in 1955, and described the experience in *SAAS:* "The thing that did the most to keep me going was that I finally sold a book, an adult mystery called *Murder at Grand Bay,* for the munificent sum of $150.00, which was a lot of money to us then; it gave me hope that after all those years of submitting stories that were rejected I might be able to earn money for the family on a regular basis. I went out on the back forty and cried my eyes out when I realized that I had to go to work and help bring in money faster than the writing could yet do."

Roberts went to work at a hospital. While working full-time as well as tending a large family and keeping house, she managed to write and sell mystery novels. While she worked at the hospital she became familiar with a popular genre called "nurse novels," and tried her hand at writing one. She sold it for one thousand dollars. Roberts then tranformed the heroines of already written mystery novels into nurses and quickly sold these books as nurse novels. When this genre went out of fashion, Roberts changed the title of the last nurse novel she had written—for which she had not been able to find a publisher—and sold *Return to Darkness* immediately, without changing the text, as a suspense novel.

In the 1970s Roberts submitted her manuscript for *The View from the Cherry Tree* to her editor, who liked it, but suggested that it was not at an adult level. When Roberts revised the novel and sold it as a children's book, it became one of her most successful works. In this mystery, Rob, a boy seeking escape from his family's preparations for his sister's wedding, witnesses a murder from his perch in a cherry tree. He tries to tell various members of his family what he saw, but they are too busy to listen. They are still too busy to be bothered when Rob tells them that someone is trying to get him. He therefore must fend for himself against a murderer in the suspenseful story that follows. "Although written in a direct and unpretentious style," a *Bulletin of the Center for Children's Books* contributor observed, "this is essentially a sophisticated story, solidly constructed, imbued with suspense, evenly paced, and effective in conveying the atmosphere of a household coping with the last-minute problems and pressures of a family wedding."

Don't Hurt Laurie!, Roberts's acclaimed 1977 novel, is the story of eleven-year-old Laurie, the victim of a physically abusive mother. Presented in third person but always from Laurie's perspective, the book conveys the powerlessness of the young girl's situation as long as she is unable to communicate her mother's violent behavior to other adults. Eventually, after her stepbrother witnesses a beating, Laurie's stepfather intervenes. Although *New York Times Book Review* contributor

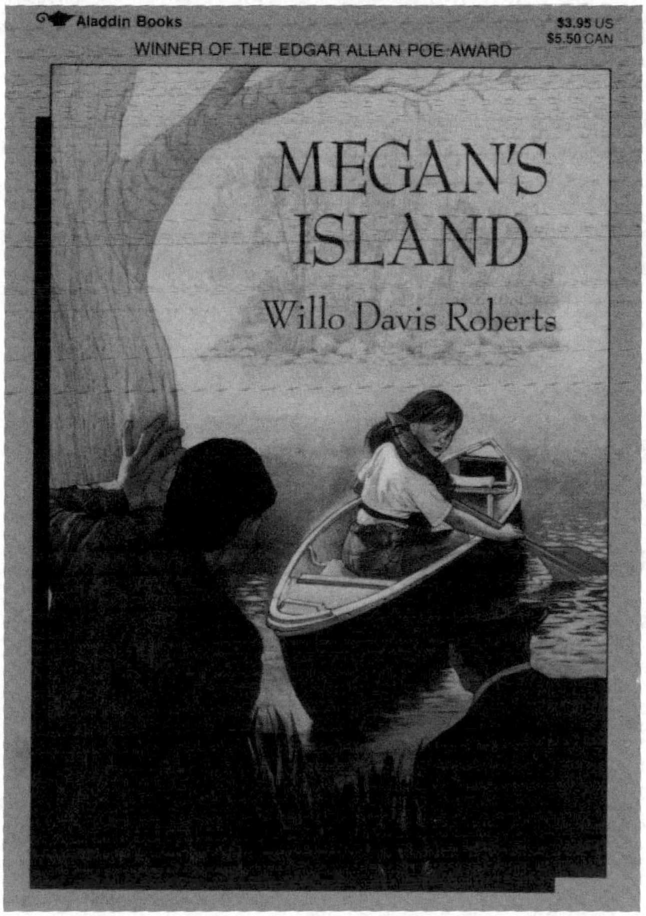

Cover of *Megan's Island,* by Willo Davis Roberts.

Judith Viorst judged that this "persuasive and blood chilling story" is, because of its subject matter, "inevitably lurid, sadistic and violent" reading for a thirteen-year-old, other critics praised its straightforward treatment of a difficult subject. A reviewer for the *Bulletin of the Center for Children's Books* remarked that while "the events are inherently dramatic in a shocking sense," *Don't Hurt Laurie!,* with its "excellent characterization and an easy narrative flow—is both realistic about the problem and realistically encouraging about its alleviation." The book is still popular many years after its publication. It has often been useful to educators and child counselors who work with abused children, Roberts wrote in a letter to *SATA.* The author further noted: "Librarians have told me it is among the most stolen book in their libraries, presumably by battered kids who can't afford to own it but want to read and re-read it."

Roberts's 1985 award-winning novel, *The Girl with the Silver Eyes,* was conceived as an adult novel, but Roberts once again decided to write it as a children's book. In this story, a group of mothers who were exposed to a certain drug during pregnancy have given birth to mutant children with telekinetic powers. The social world, suspicious of difference, has not been kind to these children. Silver-eyed Katie must decide whether to hide her powers in order to fit into her mother's "normal" world, or risk exposure to public hostility so that she can find others like herself. The book received praise for its suspense and style, as well as its treatment of family interactions and social responses to difference.

Megan's Island, Roberts's 1988 mystery, is the story of a sister and brother who discover that their mother is on the run from something or someone unknown to them. After being taken to their grandfather's cottage in the middle of the night, they notice that they are being spied on by strangers. Their mother leaves them with their grandfather, who is then injured, and they turn to Ben, the boy next door, for help. In the novel's eventful conclusion, the children thwart a kidnapping plot. Ruth Sadasivan wrote in the *School Library Journal* that despite its "occasional plot lapses into predictability and implausibility, *Megan's Island* succeeds both as an entertaining mystery and as a novel about human relationships."

In the late 1970s Roberts's husband retired and the couple began a life of writing and travelling around the country in a motor home equipped with office and computer. Many of their trips are research oriented. Roberts has written several historical novels, including her best-seller *Destiny's Women,* and likes to gather information on location. She also travels to schools to speak with her readers. Roberts spends a good deal of time helping aspiring writers. Having survived many hard times before her dream of professional writing was realized, Roberts believes that a writer must accept hard knocks and persist in his or her pursuit, no matter how unattainable the goal may seem. "I know now that it's possible to overcome adverse circumstances, that it's important to a writer to know the sorrows as well as the joys of life, the downs as well as the ups," she said in *SAAS.* "Children often ask how long I'm going to keep on writing. My reply is that I hope to write until the day I die—hopefully many, many more books. I've already done so much that I never realistically believed I could do, way back when I started."

WORKS CITED:

Review of *The View from the Cherry Tree, Bulletin of the Center for Children's Books,* January, 1976, p. 85.

Review of *Don't Hurt Laurie!, Bulletin of the Center for Children's Books,* June, 1977.

Roberts, Willo Davis, *Something about the Author Autobiography Series,* Volume 8, Gale, 1989, pp. 243-261.

Sadasivan, Ruth, review of *Megan's Island, School Library Journal,* April, 1988, p. 104.

Viorst, Judith, review of *Don't Hurt Laurie!, New York Times Book Review,* April 17, 1977, p. 51.

FOR MORE INFORMATION SEE:

PERIODICALS

Bulletin of the Center for Children's Books, November, 1978; October, 1980; March, 1983; April, 1983; September, 1984; April, 1987; April, 1988; March, 1989; September, 1989; June, 1990, February, 1991.

Horn Book, August, 1977; November, 1989; May/June, 1990.

Junior Literary Guild, September, 1980; April, 1988.

New York Times Book Review, October 20, 1974; June 8, 1975.

School Library Journal, May, 1980; October, 1984; May, 1985; May, 1986; March, 1989.

Writer's Digest, August, 1981.

* * *

ROBERTSON, Ellis
See SILVERBERG, Robert

* * *

ROBERTSON, Keith (Carlton) 1914-1991
(Keith Carlton)

PERSONAL: Born May 9, 1914, in Dows, IA; died September 23, 1991, in Hopewell, NJ; son of Myron Clifford (a merchant) and Harriet (Hughes) Robertson; married Elisabeth Hexter (a bookseller), November 2, 1946; children: Christina Harriet, Hope Elisabeth, Jeffry Keith. *Education:* U.S. Naval Academy, B.S., 1937. *Politics:* Republican. *Religion:* Protestant.

ADDRESSES: Home—P.O. Box 398, Booknoll Farm, Hopewell, NJ 08525. *Agent*—c/o Viking Press, 40 West 23rd St., New York, NY 10010.

CAREER: Refrigeration engineer, 1937-41; employee of publishing firm, 1945-47; free-lance writer, 1947-58; Bay Ridge Specialty Co., Inc. (ceramics manufacturer), Trenton, NJ, president, 1958-69; writer, 1969—.

Trustee, Hopewell Museum. *Military service:* U.S. Navy, radioman on battleship, 1931-33; officer, on destroyers, 1941-45; now Captain, U.S. Naval Reserve.

AWARDS, HONORS: Spring Book Festival award, 1956, for *The Pilgrim Goose;* William Allen White Award, 1961, for *Henry Reed, Inc.;* William Allen White award, 1969, Pacific Northwest Library Association's "Young Reader's Choice" award, 1969, and Nene award, 1970, all for *Henry Reed's Baby Sitting Service;* New Jersey Institute of Technology awards, both 1969, for *New Jersey* and *The Money Machine.*

WRITINGS:

FOR CHILDREN; FICTION

Ticktock and Jim, illustrated by Wesley Dennis, Winston, 1948, published as *Watch for a Pony,* Heinemann, 1949.
Ticktock and Jim, Deputy Sheriffs, illustrated by Everett Stahl, Winston, 1949.
The Dog Next Door, illustrated by Morgan Dennis, Viking, 1950.
The Missing Brother, illustrated by Rafaello Busoni, Viking, 1950.
The Lonesome Sorrel, illustrated by Taylor Oughton, Winston, 1952.

Keith Robertson

The Mystery of Burnt Hill, illustrated by Busoni, Viking, 1952.
Mascot of the Melroy, illustrated by Jack Weaver, Viking, 1953.
Outlaws of the Sourland, illustrated by Isami Kashiwagi, Viking, 1953.
Three Stuffed Owls, illustrated by Weaver, Viking, 1954.
Ice to India, illustrated by Weaver, Viking, 1955.
The Phantom Rider, illustrated by Weaver, Viking, 1955.
The Pilgrim Goose, illustrated by Erick Berry, Viking, 1956.
The Pinto Deer, illustrated by Kashiwagi, Viking, 1956.
The Crow and the Castle, illustrated by Robert Grenier, Viking, 1957.
Henry Reed, Inc., illustrated by Robert McCloskey, Viking, 1958.
If Wishes Were Horses, illustrated by Paul Kennedy, Harper, 1958.
Henry Reed's Journey, illustrated by McCloskey, Viking, 1963.
Henry Reed's Baby-Sitting Service, illustrated by McCloskey, Viking, 1966.
The Year of the Jeep, illustrated by W. T. Mars, Viking, 1968.
The Money Machine, illustrated by George Porter, Viking, 1969.
Henry Reed's Big Show, illustrated by McCloskey, Viking, 1970.
In Search of a Sandhill Crane, illustrated by Richard Cuffari, Viking, 1973.
Tales of Myrtle the Turtle, illustrated by Peter Parnall, Viking, 1974.
Henry Reed's Think Tank, Viking Kestrel, 1986.

FOR ADULTS; UNDER PSEUDONYM CARLTON KEITH

The Diamond-Studded Typewriter, Macmillan, 1958, published as *A Gem of a Murder,* Dell, 1959.
Missing, Presumed Dead, Doubleday, 1961.
Rich Uncle, Doubleday, 1963.
The Hiding Place, Doubleday, 1965.
The Crayfish Dinner, Doubleday, 1966, published as *The Elusive Epicure,* Hale, 1966.
A Taste of Sangria, Doubleday, 1968, published as *The Missing Book-Keeper,* Hale, 1969.

OTHER

The Wreck of the Saginaw, illustrated by Jack Weaver, Viking, 1954.
The Navy: From Civilian to Sailor, illustrated by Charles Geer, Viking, 1958.
New Jersey, McCann, 1969.

Robertson's manuscripts are included in the May Massee Collection, Emporia State University, Kansas.

WORK IN PROGRESS: A mystery story for adults and a book for children.

SIDELIGHTS: Keith Robertson's children's books describe "the mythical middle-America upon which nostalgia for a golden past is built," says Joan McGrath in *Twentieth-Century Children's Writers.* In such books as

From *Henry Reed, Inc.*, by Keith Robertson. Illustrated by Robert McCloskey.

the award-winning *Henry Reed, Inc.* and *Henry Reed's Baby-Sitting Service,* Robertson relates the adventures of Henry Reed, an all-American boy who somehow manages to get himself into—and out of—some of the stickiest jams since Tom Sawyer floated down the Mississippi. Similarly, his other children's books share with the Henry Reed stories a focus on intelligent, mischievous boys who get involved in complicated situations. In all of these books, which are aimed at a ten- to fifteen-year-old audience, the main characters are portrayed as wholesome, harmless boys who have great fun exploring the world around them. Robertson also writes mystery novels for adults that employ the same kind of fast-paced, action-packed plots as his children's books.

Robertson was born in Dows, Iowa, in 1914, but his father's wanderlust led the family all over the Midwest; they eventually lived in Minnesota, Kansas, Wisconsin, Oklahoma, Missouri, and Iowa. Robertson's first book, *Ticktock and Jim,* described his life growing up on a farm in Missouri. Robertson told *Something about the Author* (*SATA*): "I started writing when I was a boy in school. Oddly, people will encourage a boy if he says he wants to be a doctor, engineer, or scientist but will tell him he is being impractical if he says he wants to write books. For this and various other reasons, I abandoned my ambition to become a writer for some years."

Upon graduating from high school, Robertson was unsure of what he wanted to do with his life, so he joined the U.S. Navy and spent two years at sea as a radioman. Robertson went straight from sea to school, getting a degree from the U.S. Naval Academy. But four years after graduation, with World War II heating up, he was called back to service. Even though he was an officer, Robertson remembers long stretches of boredom at sea punctuated by brief periods of excitement, according to an autobiographical sketch in *More Junior Authors.* Looking out over the calm sea from the deck of his ship, he made up his mind to become a writer, and two years after the war ended he was able to make that dream come true.

"My first book for young people was largely an accident," Robertson says in *SATA.* After returning from the war, "I was selling books for a firm which specialized in children's books," he continues. "Naturally I read a number and decided to try one myself. Once I had one in print I was hooked." He quit his job, and soon he and his wife, Elisabeth, moved to a small farm in New Jersey. Elisabeth decided to open a used book store, and books soon filled all areas of the house. His three children loved animals, so the barns were filled with horses, sheep, goats, rabbits, geese, chickens, dogs and cats. Amidst this chaos Robertson wrote many of his books for children, which were often set in the semi-rural area in which he lived. Robertson notes in *SATA* that his children "provided [him] with many of the incidents and ideas for [his] books. They have never been in any sense characters in any of them, however."

Robertson told *SATA* that he has developed an interesting technique for writing his books: "For some time I have been dictating my books on tape. I find this works well if one can dictate uninterruptedly. It is particularly good for conversation. However, one tends to be too verbose and the first version needs to be cut considerably." Robertson has vowed that he will continue to write for children, because "the letters an author gets from young readers are enough to make his labors eminently worthwhile and enjoyable."

WORKS CITED:

Fuller, Muriel, editor, *More Junior Authors,* H. W. Wilson, 1963, pp. 171-172.

McGrath, Joan, essay on Keith Robertson, *Twentieth-Century Children's Writers,* St. James Press, 1989, pp. 832-833.

Something about the Author, Volume 1, Gale, 1971, pp. 184-185.

FOR MORE INFORMATION SEE:

PERIODICALS

Horn Book, April, 1971.

Library Journal, June 15, 1968; January 15, 1970; January 15, 1971.

New York Times Book Review, July 28, 1968.

School Library Journal, February, 1978.

* * *

ROBINSON, Lloyd
See SILVERBERG, Robert

* * *

ROCKWELL, Anne F. 1934-

PERSONAL: Born February 8, 1934, in Memphis, TN; daughter of Emerson (an advertising executive) and Sabina (Fromhold) Foote; married Harlow Rockwell (a writer and artist), March 16, 1955 (died April 7, 1988); children: Hannah, Elizabeth (Lizzy), Oliver Penn. *Education:* Attended Sculpture Center and Pratt Graphic Arts Center. *Politics:* "Liberal Democrat." *Religion:* Episcopalian.

ADDRESSES: Home—4 Raymond St., Old Greenwich, CT 06870.

CAREER: Author and illustrator. Silver Burdett Publishers, Morristown, NJ, member of production department, 1952; Young and Rubicam (advertising agency), art-buying secretary, 1953; Goldwater Memorial Hospital, New York City, assistant recreation leader, 1954-56.

MEMBER: Authors Guild.

AWARDS, HONORS: Boys Club Junior Book Award certificate, 1968, for *The Minstrel and the Mountain: A Tale of Peace;* American Institute of Graphic Arts selection for children's book show, 1971-72, for *The Toolbox,* 1973-74, for *Head to Toe, Games (and How to Play Them), The Awful Mess,* and *Paul and Arthur and the Little Explorer;* Children's Book Showcase selection, 1973, for *Toad,* and 1975, for *Befana: A Christmas Story; No More Work* and *Poor Goose: A French Folktale* were selected as children's books of the year by the Child Study Association, 1976; *In Our House* was named a *Redbook* top ten children's picture book of 1985.

Anne Rockwell

WRITINGS:

SELF-ILLUSTRATED, EXCEPT WHERE INDICATED

Paul and Arthur Search for the Egg, Doubleday, 1964.
Gypsy Girl's Best Shoes, Parents Magazine Press, 1966.
Sally's Caterpillar, illustrated by husband, Harlow Rockwell, Parents Magazine Press, 1966.
Filippo's Dome: Brunelleschi and the Cathedral of Florence (Junior Literary Guild selection), Atheneum, 1967.
The Stolen Necklace: A Picture Story from India, World, 1968.
Glass, Stones and Crown: The Abbe Suger and the Building of St. Denis (Junior Literary Guild selection), Atheneum, 1968.
The Good Llama: A Picture Story from Peru, World, 1968.
Temple on the Hill: The Building of the Parthenon (Junior Literary Guild selection), Atheneum, 1969.
The Wonderful Eggs of Furicchia: A Picture Story from Italy (Junior Literary Guild selection), World, 1969.
(Compiler) *Savez-vous planter les choux? and Other French Songs,* World, 1969.
When the Drum Sang: An African Folktale, Parents Magazine Press, 1970.
(Adapter) *The Monkey's Whiskers: A Brazilian Folktale,* Parents Magazine Press, 1971.
El toro pinto and Other Songs in Spanish, Macmillan, 1971.
Paintbrush and Peacepipe: The Story of George Catlin (Junior Literary Guild selection), Atheneum, 1971.
Tuhurahura and the Whale, Parents Magazine Press, 1971.
What Bobolino Knew (Junior Literary Guild selection), McCall Publishing, 1971.
The Dancing Stars: An Iroquois Legend, Crowell, 1972.
Paul and Arthur and the Little Explorer, Parents Magazine Press, 1972.
The Awful Mess, Parents Magazine Press, 1973, reprinted, Scholastic Book Services, 1980.
The Boy Who Drew Sheep, Atheneum, 1973.
Games (and How to Play Them), Crowell, 1973.
(Reteller) *The Wolf Who Had a Wonderful Dream: A French Folktale,* Crowell, 1973.
Befana: A Christmas Story, Atheneum, 1974.
Gift for a Gift, Parents Magazine Press, 1974.
The Gollywhopper Egg, Macmillan, 1974.
The Story Snail, Macmillan, 1974.
(Reteller) *The Three Bears and Fifteen Other Stories,* Crowell, 1975.
Big Boss, Macmillan, 1975.
(Reteller) *Poor Goose: A French Folktale,* Crowell, 1976.
No More Work, Greenwillow, 1976.
I Like the Library, Dutton, 1977.
A Bear, a Bobcat, and Three Ghosts, Macmillan, 1977.
Albert B. Cub and Zebra: An Alphabet Storybook, Crowell, 1977.

Willy Runs Away, Dutton, 1978.
Timothy Todd's Good Things Are Gone, Macmillan, 1978.
Gogo's Pay Day, Doubleday, 1978.
Gogo's Car Breaks Down, illustrated by H. Rockwell, Doubleday, 1978.
Buster and the Bogeyman, Four Winds, 1978.
(Reteller) *The Old Woman and Her Pig and Ten Other Stories,* Crowell, 1979.
The Girl with a Donkey Tail, Dutton, 1979.
The Bump in the Night, Greenwillow, 1979.
Walking Shoes, Doubleday, 1980.
Honk Honk!, Dutton, 1980.
Henry the Cat and the Big Sneeze, Greenwillow, 1980.
Gray Goose and Gander and Other Mother Goose Rhymes, Crowell, 1980.
When We Grow Up, Dutton, 1981.
Up a Tall Tree, illustrated by Jim Arnosky, Doubleday, 1981.
Thump Thump Thump!, Dutton, 1981.
Boats, Dutton, 1982.
(Reteller) Hans Christian Andersen, *The Emperor's New Clothes,* Crowell, 1982.
Big Bad Goat, Dutton, 1982.
The Mother Goose Cookie-Candy Book, Random House, 1983.
Cars, Dutton, 1984.
Trucks, Dutton, 1984.
In Our House, Crowell, 1985.
Planes, Dutton, 1985.
First Comes Spring, Crowell, 1985.
The Three Sillies and Ten Other Stories to Read Aloud, Harper, 1986.
Big Wheels, Dutton, 1986.
Fire Engines, Dutton, 1986.
Things That Go, Dutton, 1986.
At Night, Crowell, 1986.
At the Playground, Crowell, 1986.
In the Morning, Crowell, 1986.
In the Rain, Crowell, 1986.
Come to Town, Crowell, 1987.
Bear Child's Book of Hours, Crowell, 1987.
Bikes, Dutton, 1987.
Handy Hank Will Fix It, Holt Rinehart, 1988.
Hugo at the Window, Macmillan, 1988.
Things to Play With, Macmillan, 1988.
Puss in Boots and Other Stories, Macmillan, 1988.
Trains, Dutton, 1988.
My Spring Robin, illustrated by H. Rockwell and Lizzy Rockwell, Macmillan, 1989.
On Our Vacation, Dutton, 1989.
Apples and Pumpkins, illustrated by L. Rockwell, Macmillan, 1989.
Bear Child's Book of Special Days, Dutton, 1989.
Willy Can Count, Arcade Publishing, 1989.
Root-a-Toot-Toot, Macmillan, 1991.

WITH HUSBAND, HARLOW ROCKWELL; SELF-ILLUSTRATED

Olly's Polliwogs, Doubleday, 1970.
Molly's Woodland Garden, Doubleday, 1971.
The Toolbox, Macmillan, 1971.
Machines, Macmillan, 1972.

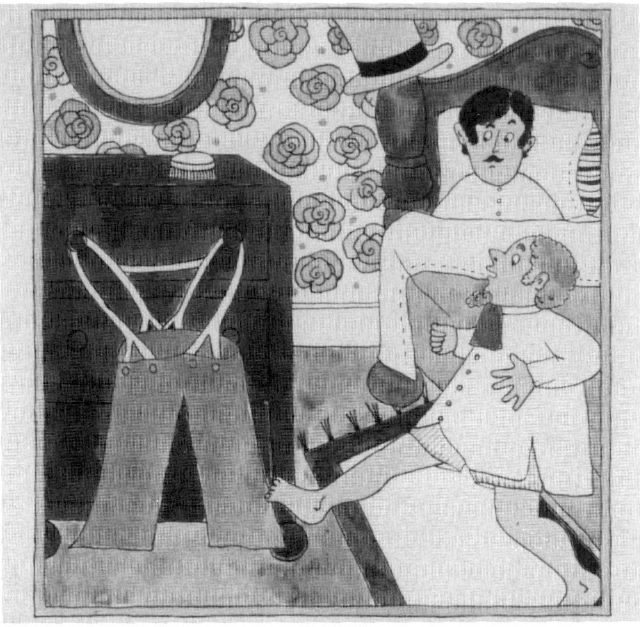

From *The Old Woman and Her Pig and Ten Other Stories,* retold and illustrated by Anne Rockwell.

Thruway, Macmillan, 1972.
Toad, Doubleday, 1972.
Head to Toe, Doubleday, 1973.
Blackout, Macmillan, 1979.
The Supermarket, Macmillan, 1979.
Out to Sea, Macmillan, 1980.
My Barber, Macmillan, 1981.
Happy Birthday to Me, Macmillan, 1981.
I Play in My Room, Macmillan, 1981.
Can I Help?, Macmillan, 1982.
How My Garden Grew, Macmillan, 1982.
I Love My Pets, Macmillan, 1982.
Sick in Bed, Macmillan, 1982.
The Night We Slept Outside, Macmillan, 1983.
My Back Yard, Macmillan, 1984.
Our Garage Sale, Greenwillow, 1984.
When I Go Visiting, Macmillan, 1984.
Nice and Clean, Macmillan, 1984.
My Baby-Sitter, Collier Books, 1985.
The Emergency Room, Collier Books, 1985, published in England as *Going to Casualty,* Hamish Hamilton, 1987.
At the Beach, Macmillan, 1987.
The First Snowfall, Macmillan, 1987.

ILLUSTRATOR

Majorie Hopkins, *The Three Visitors,* Parents Magazine Press, 1967.
Jane Yolen, *The Minstrel and the Mountain: A Tale of Peace,* World, 1967.
Lillian Bason, *Eric and the Little Canal Boat,* Parents Magazine Press, 1967.
M. Hopkins, *The Glass Valentine,* Parents Magazine Press, 1968.
Paul Showers, *What Happens to a Hamburger,* Crowell, 1970.

Kathryn Hitte, *Mexacali Soup,* Parents Magazine Press, 1970.
Joseph Jacobs, *Munacher and Manacher: An Irish Story,* Crowell, 1970.
Anne Petry, *Legends of the Saints,* Crowell, 1970.
J. Jacobs, *Master of All Masters,* Grosset, 1972.
M. Hopkins, *A Gift for Tolum,* Parents Magazine Press, 1972.
Walter Dean Myers, *The Dancers,* Parents Magazine Press, 1972.
Barbara Brenner, *Cunningham's Rooster,* Parents Magazine Press, 1975.
Barbara Williams, *Never Hit a Porcupine,* Dutton, 1977.
Gerda Mantinband, *Bing Bong Band and Fiddle Dee Dee,* Doubleday, 1979.
Clyde Robert Bulla, *The Stubborn Old Woman,* Crowell, 1980.
Patricia Plante and David Bergman, retellers, *The Turtle and the Two Ducks and Ten Other Animal Fables Freely Retold from La Fontaine,* Methuen, 1980.
Steven Kroll, *Toot! Toot!,* Holiday House, 1983.

ADAPTATIONS: The Stolen Necklace: A Picture Story from India was adapted by Paramount/Oxford, 1971; *The Toolbox* and *Machines* were adapted as filmstrips, Threshold Filmstrips, 1974.

SIDELIGHTS: Anne Rockwell is a prolific author and illustrator of children's books with more than eighty titles of her own, close to thirty collaborative efforts with her husband, Harlow Rockwell, and artwork credits for nearly twenty works by other authors. During a career which has spanned several decades, Rockwell has gradually decreased the age of her target audience. Initially producing works for middle-graders, she has turned to books for preschool and beginning readers.

Rockwell was born in Memphis, Tennessee, but also spent time in the Midwest and Southwest while growing up. Although she attended both the Sculpture Center and Pratt Graphic Arts Center, the artist relied mainly on self-teaching to learn her trade. She worked at an advertising agency before marrying another artist, Harlow Rockwell. After the couple had their first child, Rockwell realized that she wanted to produce children's books to share the joy of reading she had first experienced as a youngster.

Rockwell believes that for very young readers pictures can communicate better than words. Her drawings feature animated subjects and backgrounds with numerous details. Rockwell attributes her success as an author and illustrator of children's books to the fact that she can remember what it is like to be a child and is able look at the world from that viewpoint. Having children, Rockwell added, strengthened this ability.

Some of Rockwell's early self-illustrated publications, including *The Dancing Stars: An Iroquois Legend, The Good Llama: A Picture Story from Peru,* and *The Stolen Necklace: A Picture Story from India,* introduce readers to folktales from different cultures. In the late 1970s, however, she changed her focus to informative works for children just learning to read. With works such as *I Like the Library, Walking Shoes,* and *When We Grow Up,* Rockwell provides simple text and detailed and attention-grabbing pictures.

Books such as these earned praise as straightforward presentations of everyday objects and occurrences. Kimberly Olson Fakih, writing in *Publishers Weekly,* highlighted editor Ann Durrell's comment that Rockwell shows genius in her nonfiction works. "In [Rockwell's] books, kids can see what's meaningful to them and what's around them," Durrell stated. An example of her nonfiction work is Rockwell's series of picture books explaining various types of transportation. These books, including *Boats, Cars, Planes, Trucks, Trains,* and *Bikes,* feature lively watercolor illustrations—with animals operating the machinery—and easy-to-understand prose.

Rockwell has also written and illustrated numerous books with her husband, Harlow Rockwell. *Out to Sea* tells of the unintended maritime adventure involving a brother and sister. Another work, *The Emergency Room,* describes a protagonist's trip to the hospital after spraining his ankle. P. Susan Gerrity, writing in *New York Times Book Review,* remarked that the book "provides excellent background information" and will reassure children afraid of visiting the emergency room.

Nearly thirty years after publishing her first story, Rockwell has continued her string of successful, eye-pleasing, and educational works. In her 1990 book *Willy Can Count,* the author presents a counting game played by mother and son during a walk. In her illustrations, Rockwell provides plenty of objects to count, prompting Joanna G. Jones of *School Library Journal* to remark that *Willy Can Count* is "bound to become a favorite."

While grateful for the recognition her works receive, Rockwell prefers not to comment about them. In *Illustrators of Children's Books: 1967-76,* Rockwell mentioned that she believes her "books are a more eloquent statement" about her art than any remarks she could add.

WORKS CITED:

Fakih, Kimberly Olson, "The News is Nonfiction," *Publishers Weekly,* February 26, 1988, pp. 108-111.
Gerrity, P. Susan, review of *The Emergency Room, New York Times Book Review,* April 21, 1985, p. 18.
Illustrators of Children's Books: 1967-76, Horn Book, 1978, p. 392.
Jones, Joanna G., review of *Willy Can Count, School Library Journal,* January 1990, p. 89.

FOR MORE INFORMATION SEE:

PERIODICALS

Books for Keeps, May 1990, p. 12.
Horn Book, November, 1987, p. 731; November, 1989, p. 764.

School Library Journal, August, 1989, p. 131; January, 1991, p. 37.
Times Literary Supplement, October 9, 1987, p. 1120.

* * *

ROCKWELL, Thomas 1933-

PERSONAL: Born March 13, 1933, in New Rochelle, NY; son of Norman (an artist) and Mary (Barstow) Rockwell; married Gail Sudler (an artist), July 16, 1955; children: Barnaby, Abigail. *Education:* Bard College, B.A., 1956.

ADDRESSES: Home—R.D. 3, Lauer Rd., Poughkeepsie, NY 12603. *Agent*—Joan Raines, Raines & Raines Agency, 71 Park Ave., Suite 4A, New York, NY 10016.

CAREER: Writer. Has worked previously in book sales, as a teacher, and in television and advertising.

AWARDS, HONORS: Mark Twain Award, California Young Readers' Medal, and Golden Archer Award, all 1975, for *How to Eat Fried Worms;* South Carolina Children's Book Award, Massachusetts Children's Book Award, Sequoyah Award, and Nene Award, all 1976, Young Hoosier Book Award, 1977, Arizona Young Readers' Award and Tennessee Children's Choice, both 1979, and Iowa Children's Choice, 1980, all for *How to Eat Fried Worms.*

WRITINGS:

Rackety-Bang and Other Verses, illustrated by wife, Gail Rockwell, Pantheon, 1969.
Norman Rockwell's Hometown, illustrated by father, Norman Rockwell, Windmill Books, 1970.
Humpf!, illustrated by Muriel Batherman, Pantheon, 1971.
Squawwwk!, illustrated by G. Rockwell, Little, Brown, 1972.
The Neon Motorcycle, illustrated by Michael Horen, F. Watts, 1973.
How to Eat Fried Worms, illustrated by Emily McCully, F. Watts, 1973.
Hiding Out, illustrated by Charles Molina, Bradbury, 1974.
The Portmanteau Book, illustrated by G. Rockwell, Little, Brown, 1974.
Tin Cans, illustrated by Saul Lambert, Bradbury, 1975.
The Thief, illustrated by G. Rockwell, Delacorte, 1977.
(With father, Norman Rockwell) *Norman Rockwell: My Adventures as an Illustrator; an Autobiography,* Curtis Publishing, 1979.
How to Eat Fried Worms and Other Plays, illustrated by Joel Schick, Delacorte, 1980.
Hey, Lover Boy, Delacorte, 1981.
Oatmeal Is Not for Mustaches, illustrated by Eileen Christelow, Holt, 1984.
How to Fight a Girl, illustrated by Gioia Fiammenghi, Watts, 1987.
(Editor) *The Best of Norman Rockwell,* Courage Books, 1988.

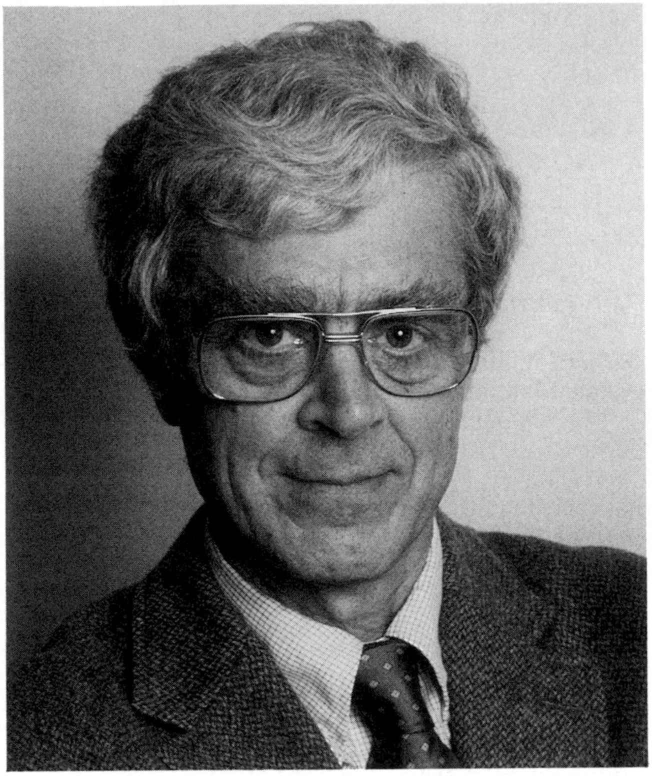

Thomas Rockwell

How to Get Fabulously Rich, illustrated by Anne Canevari Green, F. Watts, 1990.

SIDELIGHTS: Thomas Rockwell, best known for his works for young readers, fashions stories containing outlandish elements as well as universal and serious issues. The author's books are also distinguished by their irreverent tone and sometimes crude humor, which is hilarious to young readers, but often repelling to adults. Despite the penchant for fun exhibited in his publications, Rockwell takes his young audience seriously. He denies the commonly held precept that the field of children's literature somehow restricts an author, in terms of possible subjects or tone. In an *Oklahoma Librarian* printing of his Sequoyah Award acceptance speech, Rockwell mused, "I suppose one of the reasons I write books for children is because I feel I can be more outrageous than if I were writing for adults." In a review of *The Portmanteau Book,* a *Kirkus Reviews* contributor noted that the author "doesn't intend to please grownups" and "his readiness to offend them is the basis of his appeal."

Rockwell grew up in rural Vermont, the second of three sons of renowned painter and illustrator Norman Rockwell whose distinctly American reflections of small-town life often graced the cover of *Saturday Evening Post.* Creativity seemed to run in the family. His siblings were drawn to art, but the young Rockwell was more intrigued by the written word. While he admits to reading almost anything as a child (cereal boxes included), Rockwell's interest in children's literature dimmed as he grew older. When reading to his young son, however, the author once again experienced the satisfaction from such books. With his creative energies kindled, Rockwell began producing his own stories and picture books.

Rockwell's first literary venture was *Rackety-Bang and Other Verses,* published in 1969. A *Publishers Weekly* reviewer called the volume "unconventional" and "stimulating." And Barbara Gibson, writing in *Library Journal,* credited Rockwell with a "fertile imagination" and praised *Rackety-Bang and Other Verses* as an "extraordinary, varied collection."

During the next few years, Rockwell published books such as *Humpf!, Squawwwk!,* and *The Neon Motorcycle.* It was with his next book however, 1973's *How to Eat Fried Worms,* that Rockwell achieved considerable acclaim and secured his position as an important children's writer. *How to Eat Fried Worms* details a fifty-dollar bet in which one boy, Billy Forrester, must eat fifteen worms in fifteen days. A budding culinary genius, Billy dreams up various worm-based menus: fried with ketchup, mustard, and horseradish; baked with onions and sour cream. As Billy methodically executes his side of the bargain, his friends become worried by his unexpected success, scrambling to produce the expected cash.

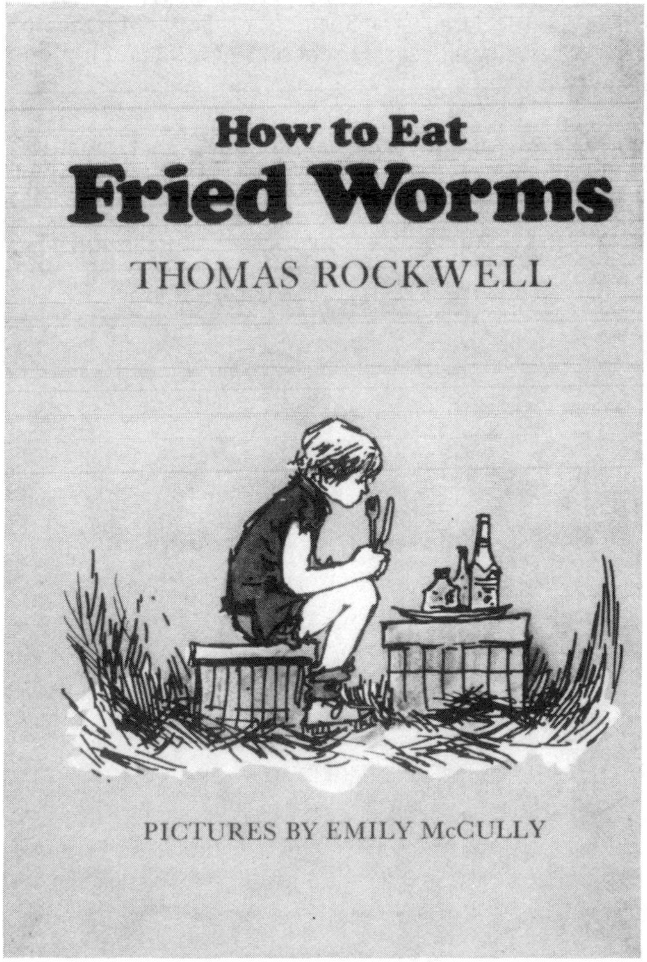

Cover of *How to Eat Fried Worms,* by Thomas Rockwell. Pictures by Emily McCully.

Because of its original plot and vivid description of Billy's feasts, *How to Eat Fried Worms* earned positive critical response and numerous awards. *Childhood Education* contributor Patricia Tonkin categorized the book as "fun," but warned "nervous parents" of the possibility of copycat readers willing to take the same dare as Billy. A *Booklist* reviewer branded the work "a hilarious story that will revolt and delight" and singled out the author's "colorful, original writing" for special praise. Rockwell, however, denies that *How to Eat Fried Worms* is a funny book: "Eating a worm is no joke," he clarified in *Oklahoma Librarian.* "If you don't believe that.... Stop by the side of the road, dig up a worm, lay it out on a paper plate, and then think about eating it. You'll begin to feel serious."

After the success of *How to Eat Fried Worms,* Rockwell continued to produce distinctive books for young readers. The author offers a mixed bag of activities in his 1974 publication *The Portmanteau Book.* Rockwell's use of the word *portmanteau*—defined as something combining more than one use—conveys the nature of the book which offers a hodgepodge of stories, poems, and quizzes. Even the index doles out zany bits of information. A reviewer for *Booklist* explained that the book's "diversity of content and levels of meaning defy pigeonholing."

While maintaining a sense of humor, Rockwell also incorporates social issues into his works. The author's 1975 contribution to children's literature, *Tin Cans,* functions as both a fantasy and a moral story about the methods used to obtain wanted goods. The story concerns David who, while visiting his aunt, meets Jane, a foster child forced to scrounge at garbage dumps. The duo finds a magic Campbell's soup can that, when pointed at an object, will retrieve it. A conflict ensues, however, when the pair debates—from starkly different socio-economic vantage points—the ethicality of keeping the device. Carolyn Johnson, writing in *School Library Journal,* assessed *Tin Cans* as a "smooth fantasy [that] moves to a credible conclusion."

Rockwell returned to a light-hearted subject and again offers a view of the adolescent world in his 1981 book *Hey, Lover Boy.* The protagonist in this work is Paul, a seventh-grader with a penchant for playing pranks on his classmates. The situation is reversed, however, when one of his victims, Margaret, decides to seek revenge. This plot, coupled with Paul's education on the finer points of sex, produces what reviewers pronounced an accurate portrayal of junior-high life. A *Kirkus Reviews* contributor deemed *Hey, Lover Boy* "a funny story, told with ... a real awareness of the intensities and overwhelming uncertainties of adolescence."

In 1987 Rockwell revived the Billy Forrester character from *How to Eat Fried Worms* for the book *How to Fight a Girl.* In the latter tale, Billy buys a trail bike with the money he won from the earlier worm bet. But when Billy becomes an intolerable braggart with his new prize possession, his friends conspire with some neighborhood girls and devise a plan that will get Billy in trouble and force his mother to take away the bike. While judging the dialogue as sometimes disjointed, a *Bulletin of the Center for Children's Books* reviewer remarked that the author has "a knack for capturing the feelings of kids. . . . " Cynthia Samuels, writing in *Washington Post Book World,* deemed *How to Fight a Girl* a "sweet and decent tale."

Rockwell continued his success in children's literature with his 1990 contribution, *How to Get Fabulously Rich.* The work again involves Billy Forrester; this time he schemes to win the lottery. Someone else must buy the ticket for him because he is too young, and his baby sister offers a combination of numbers. With this help, Billy wins, but he and his parents have entirely different ideas about what to buy with the money. A reviewer for *Bulletin of the Center for Children's Books* praised the author's "unsentimental, uncondescending vision" of a boy's life.

WORKS CITED:

Gibson, Barbara, review of *Rackety-Bang and Other Verses, Library Journal,* October, 1969, p. 143.
Review of *Hey, Lover Boy, Kirkus Reviews,* September 1, 1981, p. 1087.
Review of *How to Eat Fried Worms, Booklist,* November 15, 1973, p. 342.
Review of *How to Fight a Girl, Bulletin of the Center for Children's Books,* December, 1987, p. 74.
Review of *How to Get Fabulously Rich, Bulletin of the Center for Children's Books,* December, 1990, p. 99.
Johnson, Carolyn, review of *Tin Cans, School Library Journal,* October, 1975, p. 101.
Review of *Rackety-Bang and Other Verses, Publishers Weekly,* May 26, 1969, p. 55.
Review of *The Portmanteau Book, Booklist,* November 1, 1974, p. 294.
Review of *The Portmanteau Book, Kirkus Reviews,* November 15, 1974, p. 1205.
Rockwell, Thomas, "Sequoyah Award Acceptance Speech 1976," *Oklahoma Librarian,* July 1976, pp. 4-6, 15.
Samuels, Cynthia, "Doing the Real Right Thing," *Washington Post Book World,* November 8, 1987, p. 18.
Tonkin, Patricia, review of *How to Eat Fried Worms, Childhood Education,* March, 1974, p. 294.

FOR MORE INFORMATION SEE:

BOOKS

Children's Literature Review, Volume 6, Gale, 1984, pp. 234-240.

PERIODICALS

School Library Journal, August, 1980, p. 70; January, 1988, p. 76.
Voice of Youth Advocates, October, 1990, p. 220.

ROCKWOOD, Roy
See McFARLANE, Leslie (Charles) and STRATEMEYER, Edward L.

* * *

RODGERS, Mary 1931-

PERSONAL: Born January 11, 1931, in New York, NY; daughter of Richard (a composer) and Dorothy (Feiner) Rodgers; married Julian B. Beaty, Jr., December 7, 1951 (divorced, 1957); married Henry Guettel (a vice-president of a motion picture company), October 14, 1961; children: (first marriage) Richard R., Linda M., Constance P.; (second marriage) Adam, Alexander. *Education:* Attended Wellesley College, 1948-51. *Politics:* Liberal. *Religion:* Jewish.

ADDRESSES: Home—91 Central Park West, New York, NY 10023. *Agent*—Shirley Bernstein, Paramuse Artists, Inc., 1414 Avenue of the Americas, New York, NY 10019.

CAREER: Novelist, screenwriter, composer, and lyricist. Assistant producer of New York Philharmonic's Young People's Concerts, 1957-71; scriptwriter, Hunter College Little Orchestra Society, 1958-59. Member of board of trustees, Brearley School, 1973-76, and Phillips Exeter Academy, 1977—.

MEMBER: Authors League of America, Dramatists Guild (member of council), American Federation of

Mary Rodgers

Television and Radio Artists (AFTRA), Screen Actors Guild, Cosmopolitan Club.

AWARDS, HONORS: Book World Spring Book Festival Award, 1972, Christopher Award, 1973, Sequoyah Award, 1976, South Carolina Children's Award, 1976, California Young Reader Medal (intermediate), 1977, Nene Award, 1977, Surrey School Award, 1977, Georgia Children's Award, 1978, and American Library Association Notable Book, all for *Freaky Friday;* Christopher Award, 1975, for *A Billion for Boris.*

WRITINGS:

FICTION

The Rotten Book, illustrated by Steven Kellogg, Harper, 1969.
Freaky Friday, Harper, 1973.
A Billion for Boris, Harper, 1974.
Summer Switch (sequel to *Freaky Friday*), Harper, 1982.

MUSICAL PLAYS

(Composer) *Davy Jones' Locker* (for marionettes; music and lyrics only), book by Arthur Birnkrant and Waldo Salt, first produced in New York, 1959.
(Author of book and lyrics) *Three to Make Music,* music by sister, Linda Rodgers Melnick, first produced in New York, 1959.
(Composer) *Once Upon a Mattress,* first produced on Broadway at Phoenix Theatre, 1959.
(Composer) *Hot Spot,* first produced on Broadway at Majestic Theatre, 1963.
(Composer) *Mad Show,* first produced Off-Broadway at New Theatre, 1966.
(Composer) *Pinocchio* (for marionettes), lyrics by Sheldon Harnick, first produced in New York, 1973.

Also composer for *Young Mark Twain,* 1964.

SCREENPLAYS

Freaky Friday, Walt Disney Productions, 1977.
(With Jimmy Sangster) *The Devil and Max Devlin,* Walt Disney Productions, 1981.

Also author of television screenplays, *Mary Martin Spectacular,* 1959, and *Feathertop,* 1961; author of several screenplays for Warner Bros.

OTHER

(With mother, Dorothy Rodgers) *A Word to the Wives,* Knopf, 1970.

Coauthor with D. Rodgers of monthly column, "Of Two Minds," for *McCall's,* 1971-78; contributing editor to record and book *Free to Be ... You and Me.*

SIDELIGHTS: A woman of many talents, Mary Rodgers is a composer and lyricist as well as a writer of novels and plays for children. Rodgers is best known in the realm of children's literature for creating humorous fiction for grade school and middle grade readers. Her *Freaky Friday* has won numerous awards and was adapted by the author for a popular Walt Disney movie.

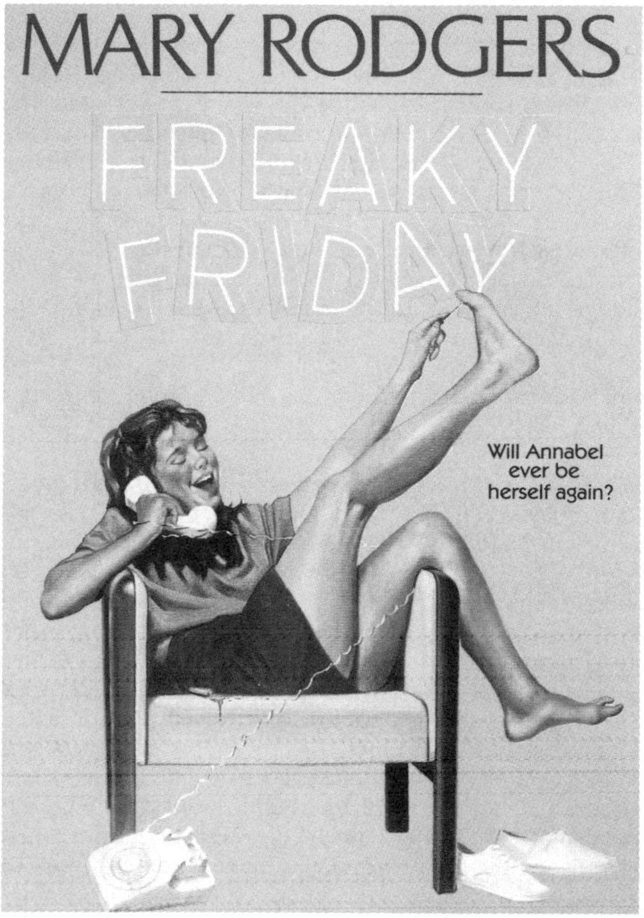

Cover of *Freaky Friday,* by Mary Rodgers.

Rodgers was born into a gifted family on January 11, 1931. Her father, Richard Rodgers, is the creator—with Oscar Hammerstein—of Broadway musicals, including such hits as *The Sound of Music, The King and I, Oklahoma,* and *South Pacific.* Her mother, Dorothy Feiner, is an interior decorator and author. Rodgers grew up in New York City, but she was isolated from the glamour of her parents' professions. In an interview for *Teacher,* she told Lee Bennett Hopkins, "I had a rather boring childhood. I had a regimented life, raised in a regimented house. The only way I could escape the regimentation was to read and read and read."

Rodgers's first accomplishments were in the musical arena. She took piano lessons for eight years and at age sixteen studied music theory and counterpoint privately. While in her teens, she composed a series of pieces for two pianos, which she called "Clean Sheets." Then, as she related in an interview with Jean W. Ross, "I wrote some very bad popular songs for awhile." Rodgers attended Wellesley College, where she majored in music. While there she composed her first published song, "Christmas Is Coming," to lyrics by a fellow student. Rodgers left her senior year to marry her first husband, Henry Beaty, Jr., whom she would divorce in 1957.

In the 1950s and 1960s, Rodgers focused on musical activities. She worked for a number of years as a composer at Golden Records. During this time she collaborated with well-known lyricists like Sammy Kahn, with whom she wrote the lyrics for "Ali Baba," which was recorded by Bing Crosby. She also wrote the scripts for the Little Orchestra Concerts, including *Three to Make Music.* In 1961 Rodgers married Henry Guettel, the vice-president of a motion picture company. From 1957 to 1971, as an assistant to the producer of the New York Philharmonic's Young People's Concerts, Rodgers acted as an editor for famed conductor Leonard Bernstein. In the 1960s she gained celebrity for composing the scores of the Broadway musicals *Once Upon a Mattress, Hot Spot, Mad Show,* and several musicals for children, including *Young Mark Twain* and *Pinocchio.*

Despite her domestic responsibilities, musical career, and managerial activities, Rodgers began a literary career in 1969 with the picture book *The Rotten Book,* about a boy who imagines what it would be like to be very naughty. She once commented, "Since I had nothing to do but take care of five children, a nine-room apartment, an eleven-room house in the country, and show up once a month at the Professional Children's School Board of Trustees meeting, once a month at the Dramatist Guild Council meeting, and eight times a month at the A & P, I thought I'd be delighted to write a children's book, because I had all this extra time on my hands. (Between the hours of two and five a.m., I just loll around the house wondering how to amuse myself.)" When her children were young, Rodgers would sometimes leave home for several weeks at a time to write, leaving her husband and the housekeeper in charge. Finally, with only two children still living at home, she set a new schedule of morning work—amid numerous interruptions.

Rodgers's first book for middle-grade readers was *Freaky Friday,* a fantasy set in Manhattan about thirteen-year-old Annabel Andrews, who wakes up one morning to discover that she is her thirty-five-year-old mother. It was the winner of many awards, which prompted Walt Disney Studios to ask Rodgers to write the screenplay for *Freaky Friday.* The film became a hit when it was released in 1977, earning twenty million dollars. In addition to *Freaky Friday,* Rodgers wrote other screenplays, including *The Devil and Max Devlin* for Disney and several for Warner Brothers, but she generally has found the process frustrating. "I absolutely hated that work," she told Ross. "It was terrible, because I've been brought up in the East, where you're spoiled by editors and publishers and the theater, where nobody's allowed to change anything of yours.... I was in the middle of my fifth screenplay for Warner Brothers, an original, and I found myself really almost unable to work and on the verge of having a nervous breakdown. I called my agent and said, 'Get me out of this.... I'm not doing this ever again.' And I'm very happy I did it."

Humor is a common element of Rodgers's books for young people. *A Billion for Boris,* for example, depicts what happens when Annabel's friend Boris gets a television that broadcasts the next day's news. In *Summer Switch,* a companion book to *Freaky Friday,* Annabel's younger brother Ben turns into his father and vice versa. When the change takes place, Ben is about to be shipped off to summer camp and his father is beginning a business trip. With this combination of fantasy and realism, Rodgers's characters get to see the adult world from a new perspective, maturing as a result.

Rodgers has also teamed up with her mother on a book intended for adults. In *A Word to the Wives* the two discuss the pros and cons of living and raising a family in New York City. The mother-daughter team later answered life-style questions for the column "Of Two Minds," which appeared monthly in *McCall's* from 1971 to 1978.

Rodgers is recognized for providing witty and original insights about the relationship between parents and children. Her works have been praised for their imaginative plots and believable characters, but most of all for their humor. As Karen Nelson Hoyle noted in *Twentieth Century Children's Writers,* "Humor is a scarce but precious commodity in contemporary technological society. Mary Rodgers breathes laughter into the situations, the characters, the language of her books."

WORKS CITED:

Hopkins, Lee Bennett, "'Freaky Friday' from Book to Film," *Teacher,* October, 1977, pp. 80-82.
Hoyle, Karen Nelson, "Mary Rodgers," *Twentieth Century Children's Writers,* St. James, 1989, p. 836.
Rodgers, Mary, in an interview with Jean W. Ross, *Contemporary Authors New Revision Series,* Volume 8, Gale, 1983, pp. 418-421.

FOR MORE INFORMATION SEE:

BOOKS

Children's Literature Review, Volume 20, Gale, 1990, pp. 189-192.

PERIODICALS

Chicago Tribune, May 7, 1972.
Chicago Tribune Book World, May 4, 1972.
Christian Science Monitor, May 1, 1972; November 6, 1974.
Cosmopolitan, June, 1960.
New York Times, March 6, 1981.
New York Times Book Review, November 16, 1969; November 24, 1974; November 14, 1982.
Newsweek, February 28, 1977.

* * *

RODMAN, Eric
See SILVERBERG, Robert

RODMAN, Maia
See WOJCIECHOWSKA, Maia (Teresa)

* * *

ROSS, Tony 1938-

PERSONAL: Born August 10, 1938, in London, England; son of Eric Turle Lee (a magician) and Effie Ross; married Carole Jean D'Arcy (divorced); married second wife, Joan (divorced); married third wife, Zoe, 1979; children: (first marriage) Philippa (adopted); (second marriage) George (stepson), Alexandra; (third marriage) Katherine. *Education:* Liverpool College of Art, diplomas, 1960, 1961. *Politics:* None. *Religion:* Methodist. *Hobbies and other interests:* Sailing small boats, cats, the monarchy, collecting toy soldiers, lamb cutlets.

ADDRESSES: Home—Whisket Cottage, 5 Pexhill Rd., Broken Cross, Macclesfield, Cheshire, England.

CAREER: Smith Kline & French Laboratories, graphic designer, 1962-64; Brunnings Advertising, art director, 1964-65; Manchester Polytechnic, Manchester, England, lecturer, 1965-72, senior lecturer in illustration, 1972-85; full-time writer and illustrator, 1985—. Consultant in graphic design.

MEMBER: Society of Industrial Artists and Designers.

AWARDS, HONORS: I'm Coming to Get You! was named a Children's Choice by the International Reading Association/CBC, and a Best Children's Picture Book of the Year by *Redbook,* both 1985; Greenaway commended book, 1986, for *I Want My Potty;* and 1991, for *Earth Tigerlets, As Explained by Professor Xargle.*

WRITINGS:

JUVENILES; SELF-ILLUSTRATED

Tales from Mr. Toffy's Circus, six volumes, W. J. Thurman, 1973.
(Reteller) *Goldilocks and the Three Bears,* Andersen, 1976.
Hugo and the Wicked Winter, Sidgwick & Jackson, 1977.
Hugo and the Man Who Stole Colors, Follett, 1977.
(Reteller) *The Pied Piper of Hamelin,* Andersen, 1977.
Norman and Flop Meet the Toy Bandit, W. J. Thurman, 1977.
(Reteller) *Little Red Riding Hood,* Andersen, 1978.
Hugo and Oddsock, Andersen, 1978.
(Reteller) *The True Story of Mother Goose and Her Son Jack,* Andersen, 1979.
The Greedy Little Cobbler, Andersen, 1979.
Hugo and the Ministry of Holidays, Andersen, 1980, David & Charles, 1987.
Jack and the Beanstalk, Andersen, 1980, Delacorte, 1981.
Puss in Boots: The Story of a Sneaky Cat, Delacorte, 1981.

From *A Fairy Tale,* written and illustrated by Tony Ross.

Naughty Nigel, Andersen, 1982.
(Reteller) *The Enchanted Pig: An Old Rumanian Tale,* Andersen, 1982.
The Three Pigs, Pantheon, 1983.
(Reteller) *Jack the Giantkiller,* Andersen, 1983, Dial Books for the Young, 1987.
I'm Coming to Get You!, Dial Books for the Young, 1984.
Towser and Sadie's Birthday, Pantheon, 1984.
Towser and the Terrible Thing, Pantheon, 1984.
Towser and the Water Rats, Pantheon, 1984.
Towser and the Haunted House, Andersen, 1985, David & Charles, 1987.
The Boy Who Cried Wolf, Dial Books for the Young, 1985.
Lazy Jack, Andersen, 1985, Dial Books for the Young, 1986.
(Reteller) *Foxy Fables,* Dial Books for the Young, 1986.
I Want My Potty, Kane/Miller, 1986.
Towser and the Funny Face, David & Charles, 1987.
Towser and the Magic Apple, David & Charles, 1987.
(Reteller) *Stone Soup,* Dial Books for the Young, 1987.
Oscar Got the Blame, Andersen, 1987, Dial Books for the Young, 1988.
Super Dooper Jezebel, Farrar, Straus, 1988.
I Want a Cat, Farrar, Straus, 1989.
Treasure of Cozy Cove, Andersen, 1989, Farrar, Straus, 1990.
Mrs. Goat and Her Seven Little Kids, Atheneum, 1990.
Hansel and Gretel, David & Charles, 1990.
This Old Man, Aladdin Books, 1990.
Don't Do That!, Crown, 1991.
A Fairy Tale, Little, Brown, 1991.

ILLUSTRATOR

Iris Grender, *Did I Ever Tell You . . . ?,* Hutchinson, 1977.

Grender, *The Second Did I Ever Tell You . . . ? Book,* Hutchinson, 1978.
Patricia Gray and David Mackay, *Two Monkey Tales,* Longman, 1979.
Bernard Stone, *The Charge of the Mouse Brigade,* Andersen, 1979.
Jean Russell, editor, *The Magnet Book of Strange Tales,* Methuen Children's, 1980.
Philip Curtis, *Mr. Browser Meets the Burrowers,* Andersen, 1980.
Curtis, *Invasion from below the Earth,* Knopf, 1981.
Curtis, *Mr. Browser and the Comet Crisis,* Andersen, 1981.
Stone, *The Tale of Admiral Mouse,* Andersen, 1981.
Grender, *Did I Ever Tell You about My Irish Great Grandmother?,* Hutchinson, 1981.
Naomi Lewis, *Hare and Badger Go to Town,* Andersen, 1981.
Grender, *But That's Another Story,* Knight, 1982.
Eric Morecambe, *The Reluctant Vampire,* Methuen Children's, 1982.
Curtis, *The Revenge of the Brain Sharpeners,* Andersen, 1982.
J. K. Hooper, *Kaspar and the Iron Poodle,* Andersen, 1982.
Russell, editor, *The Magnet Book of Sinister Stories,* Methuen Children's, 1982.
Curtis, *Mr. Browser and the Mini-Meteorites,* Andersen, 1983.
Curtis, *Invasion of the Comet People,* Knopf, 1983.
Curtis, *Mr. Browser and the Brain Sharpeners,* Andersen, 1983.
Grender, *Did I Ever Tell You about My Birthday Party?,* Andersen, 1983.
Hazel Townson, *The Shrieking Face,* Andersen, 1984.
Alan Sillitoe, *Marmalade Jim and the Fox,* Robson, 1984.
Roger Collinson, *Paper Flags and Penny Ices,* Andersen, 1984.
W. J. Corbett, *The End of the Tale,* Methuen, 1985.
Curtis, *Mr. Browser in the Space Museum,* Andersen, 1985.
Curtis, *The Quest of the Quidnuncs,* Andersen, 1986.
Hiawyn Oram, *Jenna and the Troublemaker,* Holt, 1986.
Townson, *Terrible Tuesday,* Morrow, 1986.
Grender, *The Third Did I Ever Tell You . . . ?,* David & Charles, 1987.
Grender, *Did I Ever Tell You . . . What the Children Told Me?,* David & Charles, 1987.
Pat Thomson, *The Treasure Sock,* Delacorte, 1987.
Trinka H. Noble, *Meanwhile Back at the Ranch,* Dial Books for the Young, 1987.
Heather Eyles, *Well I Never!,* Stoddart, 1988.
Jeanne Willis, *Earthlets, As Explained by Professor Xargle,* Dutton, 1989.
Oram, *Anyone Seen Harry Lately?,* David & Charles, 1989.
Barbara S. Hazen, *The Knight Who Was Afraid of the Dark,* Dial Books for the Young, 1989.
The Pop-up Book of Nonsense Verse, Random House, 1989.
Willis, *Earth Tigerlets, As Explained by Professor Xargle,* Dutton, 1991.
Tony Bradman, *Michael,* Macmillan, 1991.
Willis, *Earth Mobiles, As Explained by Professor Xargle,* Dutton, 1992.

OTHER

Author of several animated television films. Contributor of cartoons to magazines, including *Punch* and *Town.*

ADAPTATIONS: I'm Coming to Get You! has been made into a filmstrip; some of Ross's books have been adapted for television.

WORK IN PROGRESS: Writing and illustrating *Dear Mole,* and other children's books; illustrating Jon Talbot's *The Most Unusual Computer,* to be published by Kaye & Ward.

SIDELIGHTS: "My training as an etcher, and my liking of graphic, rather than fine, artists, gave me a love of black line on white paper," Tony Ross once told *Something about the Author* (*SATA*). "My colours tend to be transparent inks and watercolours, laid lightly, not obscuring the line. To me, a children's illustrator is a creator of worlds for kids, and so I prefer to write my own texts. I like telling stories, I like to see children laugh, I like to draw." In books such as *I'm Coming to Get You!, Lazy Jack,* and *Super Dooper Jezebel,* Ross brings a humorous writing and drawing style to both original and traditional stories. This unique approach has quickly boosted Ross's reputation as a author and illustrator of books for children.

Ross was born in 1938, just before the onset of World War II, in Streatham, a suburb of London, England. To escape the war, his family moved to a small town in the north of England near Liverpool when Ross was about three years old. Ross had fun during his school years but never excelled in his studies, as he recalled in an interview for *SATA:* "I wasn't a good student. I was bad at nearly everything. I could draw quite well and I was all right once I got out into the playground or into the sports hall but everything else I was pretty resistant to."

Ross enjoyed drawing as a child and was always interested in art, and at age eighteen he began studying art in Liverpool. While there, he also experienced the exciting social scene and began publishing cartoons. "It was great, the late fifties, early sixties, and the whole Liverpool beat thing was on," the artist told *SATA.* "I was a cartoonist then, I drew some drawings for *Punch* and things like that. We [art students] used to talk about our heroes, who were Saul Steinberg and Andre Francois, the graphic artists rather than painters. So I was always interested in people who worked in black line." Ross added, "I think the main influences I had all started when I was in this silly period at art school, when I was just starting cartooning."

Ross taught high school for a short time while he was an art student, and later he worked as a typographer and became art director for an advertising agency. Eventually he began teaching art and advertising at Manchester Polytechnic, a small college. In his *SATA* interview, Ross recalled how this position led to his career in illustration: "In a time of crisis the Poly decided that there was nobody to look after the illustration group, there were illustration students and no member of staff. So they said, 'Well, you've drawn cartoons, you do it.' I said, 'I can't. I'm a designer, not an illustrator.' They said, 'You're the only one who's drawn things, so you'd better look after them.' So I took over the illustration group and thought 'Well, if I'm doing illustration I'd better do some. I'd better find out what all this nonsense is about.' So I illustrated some books that I wrote, called *Tales from Mr. Toffy's Circus,* simply because I felt I'd better become an illustrator."

As he progressed in his career, Ross developed a distinctive drawing style that involves the black lines and bold colors of the graphic artists he admires. In *I'm Coming to Get You!,* for instance, "the illustrations are in colors as loud as a yell, rendered in a scratchy fashion that intensifies the speedy effects," a *Publishers Weekly* reviewer comments. "There is a dynamic quality to Tony Ross's illustrations, a quality created with raw hues of blue, green, and red and with strong contrasts between light and dark areas," a *Wilson Library Bulletin* critic similarly observes of *Hugo and Oddsock.* "But more important are the slashing, diagonal shapes and lines." The result of these "strong contrasts of light and dark and big and little," according to Donnarae MacCann and Olga Richard of *Wilson Library Bulletin,* is a sly, lively humor.

Ross applies his unique sense of humor to both original stories and retellings of traditional tales. *Super Dooper Jezebel,* for instance, "is typical Ross from the zany cartoon-style watercolors to the ironic biting humor," Heide Pilcher says in *School Library Journal.* Jezebel is perfect in every way: she is tidy, polite, clever in school, and does what she's told. But she is only too ready to tell other people how to behave properly, and so she is not very likable. When she is too busy instructing others to avoid being eaten by a crocodile, Ross makes us "cheer the crocodile for ridding the world of that prim, supercilious, rigid, prudish, gloating Jezebel," MacCann and Richard note in *Wilson Library Bulletin.* Ross manages this feeling with his superb drawings of Jezebel, the critics add.

Lazy Jack, like many of Ross's other books, adds amusing details to the old story of a lazy fellow who wins a sad princess by making her laugh. "Ross' spacious watercolors add narrative twists of their own to this traditional tale," a critic for the *Bulletin of the Center for Children's Books* says. *Lazy Jack* "is tongue-in-cheek, the art absurd, the overall effect a super-silly read aloud," the critic adds. Christina L. Olson also enjoys what she calls "some very Monty Pythonish touches," and adds in her *School Library Journal* review that Ross's "strong color sense creates enormously light-spirited fun."

Ross's willingness to go beyond what's accepted gives his work a uniquely funny viewpoint. But it is the combination of pictures and words that makes his books so enjoyable, says the *Horn Book* reviewer. The artist's illustrations "add much to the humor, interacting with the text in a lively interchange that enriches and extends both." Ross's work is distinguished by his "comic imagination and a superb sense of theater," MacCann and Richard likewise state. As a result, they conclude, "it is hard to think of many cartoonists in recent years who have developed as rapidly as Ross with both a comic touch and a serious design interest."

WORKS CITED:

"Children's Books," *Publishers Weekly,* October 26, 1984, p. 104.

Horn Book, September/October, 1986, p. 604.

Review of *Hugo and Oddsock, Wilson Library Bulletin,* January, 1979, p. 378.

Review of *Lazy Jack, Bulletin of the Center for Children's Books,* July-August, 1986, p. 217.

MacCann, Donnarae and Olga Richard, "Picture Books for Children," *Wilson Library Bulletin,* March, 1985, pp. 482-3.

MacCann, Donnarae and Olga Richard, "Picture Books for Children," *Wilson Library Bulletin,* November, 1986, pp. 47-8.

MacCann, Donnarae and Olga Richard, "Picture Books for Children," *Wilson Library Bulletin,* June, 1989, pp. 96-7.

Olson, Christina L., review of *Lazy Jack, School Library Journal,* September, 1986, p. 127.

Pilcher, Heide, review of *Super Dooper Jezebel, School Library Journal,* December, 1988, p. 92.

Ross, Tony, interview with Cathy Courtney for *Something about the Author,* Volume 65, Gale, 1991, pp. 173-181.

Something about the Author, Volume 17, Gale, 1979, pp. 203-4.

FOR MORE INFORMATION SEE:

PERIODICALS

New York Times Book Review, November 13, 1983.

School Library Journal, July, 1989.

* * *

ROSSETTI, Christina (Georgina) 1830-1894 (Ellen Alleyn)

PERSONAL: Born December 5, 1830, in London, England; died December 29, 1894, in London; buried in Highgate Cemetery, London; daughter of Gabriele (an Italian political refugee and a professor of Italian) and Frances Polidori Rosetti. *Education:* Educated at home by her mother. *Religion:* Anglican.

CAREER: Poet and essayist. Associated with the Pre-Raphaelite group of artists and writers through her brother, Dante Gabriel Rossetti, who was one of the four original leaders of that group. Led an active literary and devoutly religious life; assisted her mother in schoolteaching, 1853-54, and in establishing day schools in London and Somersetshire.

WRITINGS:

JUVENILE POETRY

Verses by Christina G. Rossetti, Dedicated to her Mother, privately printed, 1847.
Goblin Market and Other Poems, illustrated by D. G. Rossetti, Macmillan, 1862.
Sing-Song: A Nursery Rhyme Book, illustrated by Arthur Hughes, Routledge, 1872, Roberts Brothers, 1872.
A Pageant and Other Poems, Roberts Brothers, 1881.
What Is Pink? (from *Sing-Song*), illustrated by Margaret A. Soucheck, Holt, 1963.

JUVENILE STORIES

Speaking Likenesses, illustrated by Arthur Hughes, Macmillan, 1874.
Maude: A Story for Girls, London, Bowden, 1897.

ADULT POETRY

The Prince's Progress and Other Poems, illustrated by Dante Gabriel Rossetti, Macmillan, 1866, 1875.
Poems, Roberts Brothers, 1866.
New Poems, edited by William Rossetti, Macmillan, 1896.
Monna Innominata: Sonnets and Songs, T. B. Mosher, 1899.

Christina Rossetti

ADULT PROSE

Commonplace: A Tale of Today, and Other Stories, Ellis, 1870, Roberts Brothers, 1870.
Annus Domini: A Prayer for Each Day of the Year, Parker, 1874.
Seek and Find: A Double Series of Short Studies on the Benedicite, Society for Promoting Christian Knowledge, 1879.
Called to be Saints: The Minor Festivals Devotionally Studied, Society for Promoting Christian Knowledge, 1881, Young, 1881.
A Strange Journey; or, Pictures from Egypt and the Soudan, Harper, 1882.
Letter and Spirit: Notes on the Commandments, Society for Promoting Christian Knowledge, 1883, Young, 1883.
Time Flies: A Reading Diary, Society for Promoting Christian Knowledge, 1885, Roberts Brothers, 1886.
The Face of the Deep: A Devotional Commentary on the Apocalypse, Society for Promoting Christian Knowledge, 1892, Young, 1892.
Reflected Lights from The Face of the Deep, Dutton, 1899.
Redeeming the Time: Daily Musings for Lent, Young, 1903.

POETRY COLLECTIONS AND SELECTIONS

Goblin Market, The Prince's Progress, and Other Poems, illustrated by D. G. Rossetti, Macmillan, 1888.
Poems, Macmillan, 1891.
Verses, Young, 1895.
The Poetical Works of Christina G. Rossetti, Little, Brown, 1902.
Poems for Children, selected by Melvin Hix, Educational Publishing, 1907.
Poems, illustrated by Florence Harrison, Blackie, 1910.
Selected Poems of Christina G. Rossetti, edited by Charles B. Burke, Macmillan, 1913.
Poems, edited by Kathleen Jarvis, Mowbray, 1955, Philosophical Library 1956.
Poems, edited by Naomi Lewis, E. Hulton, 1959.
Doves and Pomegranates: Poems for Young Readers, selected by David Powell, edited by Naomi Lewis, illustrated by Margery Gill, Bodley Head, 1969, Macmillan, 1971.
A Choice of Christina Rossetti's Verse, edited by Elizabeth Jennings, Faber, 1970.
Selected Poems of Christina Rossetti, edited by Marya Zaturenska, Macmillan, 1970.
Poems: Selections, C. N. Potter, 1986.
Complete Poems of Christina Rossetti, edited with notes and introductions by R. W. Crump, Louisiana State University Press, 3 volumes, 1979, 1986, 1990.

OTHER

The Family Letters of Christina Georgina Rossetti, edited by William Michael Rossetti, Scribner, 1908, Folcroft, 1973.
Three Rossettis, Unpublished Letters to and from Dante Gabriel, Christina, William, edited by J. C. Troxell, Harvard University Press, 1937.

SIDELIGHTS: Nineteenth-century English author Christina Rossetti is best remembered for her collection of children's verse *Goblin Market and Other Poems,* though some of her stories, essays, and religious poetry have also found readers throughout the twentieth century. Most of Rossetti's work was influenced by her devout religious convictions and the pressures placed upon women during Victorian times. "Undeniably, her strong lyric gifts are often held in check by her moral and theological scruples," H. B. de Groot explains in *Dictionary of Literary Biography,* "but at times it is that very tension which gives her best poems their distinctive quality."

Rossetti was born into an artistic family on December 5, 1830, in London, England. Her two older brothers, William Michael and Dante Gabriel, were active in literary circles of the time, and her older sister, Maria, was also a published author. Their mother, a well-read and experienced teacher, educated them at home. She encouraged all the children to read widely and to study several languages. Although Rossetti remained in London most of her life, as a child she loved to roam the grounds of her grandparents' home at Holmer Green, thirty miles from London. These experiences helped her develop a deep appreciation for nature, and perhaps inspired some of the creatures mentioned in her fantasy poem "Goblin Market." She also enjoyed sketching exotic animals at the London Zoological Gardens.

When illness forced their father to resign from his teaching post at King's College, the Rossetti children helped where they could: Maria worked as a governess; William, at age fifteen, left school and found a job as a clerk in the Excise Office, setting aside his interest in writing and publishing; Christina, the youngest and most delicate in health, devoted herself to writing, even prose and encyclopedia articles, to add to their income; Dante Gabriel, finding his way as an artist and poet, became a leader of the Pre-Raphaelite Brotherhood, a group of artists who worked to develop their individual talents based upon no "school" of art, but on their own abilities and a close study of nature.

With her brothers' help, Rossetti's poems began to be published, privately at first and then in the magazine *Athenaeum.* In 1850 seven of her poems were published in *The Germ,* a short-lived magazine sponsored by the Brotherhood. Macmillan finally accepted her *Goblin Market and Other Poems* for book publication in 1862. The long poem "Goblin Market," called a "moral allegory," depicts the temptation of two sisters by sneering, teasing goblins who beguile them with forbidden, luscious fruits. Upon its publication Rossetti was recognized as a poet of promise and distinction. The theme of sisterhood and the relationships between sisters occurs in a number of Rossetti's poems. Other themes include unhappy love, renunciation, death, and devotion to spiritual ideals. Rossetti's next poems for children, her *Sing-Song* verses, were published in 1872. *Sing-Song*'s illustrations, by pre-Raphaelite artist Arthur Hughes, particularly pleased the Rossettis. Hughes's drawings capture not just the carefree air of childhood, as in the scene of wind-blown violets for "Oh wind, where have you been," but also the small animals that Rossetti loved to watch.

From *Speaking Likenesses,* by Christina Rossetti. Illustrated by Arthur Hughes.

Rossetti had two marriage proposals during her lifetime, but declined both due to her strong religious convictions. Nevertheless, this gave to her love poems the sense of sadness and regret that was characteristic of the Victorian woman's plight. Rossetti's love poetry represents a break with the past, because in previous centuries it was most often men who wrote on this subject. Rossetti's "Monna Innominata" (Unnamed Lady) sonnets appeared in *A Pageant and Other Poems,* published in 1881, and were warmly praised. The title poem, "Pageant," was staged several times—once in London's Albert Hall—but it did not achieve the popularity of her earlier poems.

Rossetti worked from 1860 to 1870 at the House of Charity at Highgate, serving the "fallen women" of London—the prostitutes, unmarried mothers, homeless, or down on their luck. Some of her poems reflect her deep sympathy for them. Rossetti's later years were devoted to fighting off her own illnesses while caring for those of her aged mother and aunts. She continued to pray daily and to attend services at Christ Church, where she had gone since childhood. She also kept on writing her religious commentaries; the last published was *The Face of the Deep* in 1892, which was an immediate success. Late in December, 1894, Rossetti died at the Torrington Square house in London.

Considered one of the finest religious poets of her century, Rossetti's conflicting emotions bring about a powerful tension in many of her poems. Yet her verses for children reveal a warmth and gaiety that is unexpected in someone so deeply immersed in the demands of religious and personal scruples. Author Virginia Woolf, writing to Rossetti in *The Second Common Reader* on the one hundredth anniversary of Rossetti's birth, notes her influence: "You carefully ignored any book that could shake your faith or any human being who could trouble your instincts. You were wise perhaps. Your instinct was so sure, so direct, so intense that it produced poems that sing like music in one's ears ... Like all instinctives you had a keen sense of the visual beauty of the world." Jean Pearson sums up Rossetti's work in *British Women Writers* by saying that Rossetti produced "memorable poems whose acute musicality, technical mastery, and expressive tenderness assure her of literary immortality."

WORKS CITED:

de Groot, H. B., essay in *Dictionary of Literary Biography,* Volume 35: *Victorian Poets after 1850,* Gale, 1985, pp. 203-18.

Pearson, Jean, essay in *British Women Writers,* Garland, 1988, p. 394.

Woolf, Virginia, *The Second Common Reader,* Harcourt, Brace & World, 1960, p. 219.

FOR MORE INFORMATION SEE:

BOOKS

Battiscombe, Georgina, *Christina Rossetti: A Divided Life,* Holt, Rinehart and Winston, 1981.

Demers, Patricia, *A Garland from the Golden Age,* Oxford University Press, 1983.

Something about the Author, Volume 20, Gale, 1980.

Zaturenska, Marya, *Christina Rossetti,* Macmillan, 1949.

* * *

ROUNDS, Glen (Harold) 1906-

PERSONAL: Born April 4, 1906, near Wall, SD; son of William E. (a rancher) and Janet I. (Barber) Rounds; married Mary Lucas, December, 1928 (divorced December, 1937); married Margaret Olmsted, January, 1938 (died December, 1968); married Elizabeth Anne High, 1989; children: William E. II. *Education:* Attended Kansas City Art Institute, 1926-27, and Art Student's League, 1930-31.

ADDRESSES: Home—Box 763, Southern Pines, NC 28387.

CAREER: Author and illustrator of adult and children's books, 1936—. Worked previously as mule skinner, cowboy, sign painter, railroad section hand, baker, carnival medicine man, and textile designer. *Military service:* U.S. Army, 1941-45, served in coast artillery and infantry; became staff sergeant.

MEMBER: Authors Guild.

AWARDS, HONORS: Picture book honor, Spring Book Festival, 1942, for *Whitey's First Roundup;* Lewis Carroll Shelf Award, 1958, for *Ol' Paul, the Mighty Logger,* 1960, for *Blind Colt,* 1969, for *Wild Horses of the Red Desert,* 1971, for *Farmer Hoo and the Baboons,* 1973, for *The Stolen Pony,* 1976, for *The Day the Circus Came to Lone Tree,* 1978, for *Mr. Yowder and the Giant Bull Snake;* juvenile award, American Association of University Women, 1961, for *Beaver Business: An Almanac,* 1967, for *The Snake Tree,* 1976, for *Mr. Yowder and the Lion Roar Capsules,* and 1983, for *Wild Appaloosa;* New Jersey Institute of Technology Award, 1963, for *Firefly,* 1972, for *A Twister of Twists, a Tangler of Tongues,* 1977, for *Kickle Snifters and Other Fearsome Critters;* Boys Club Junior Book Award, 1965, for *Rain in the Woods and Other Small Matters;* Aurianne Award, 1966, for *Big Blue Island; Tomfoolery: Trickery and Foolery with Words* was named a *New York Times* outstanding book, 1973; Friends of American Writers Award, 1977, for *Toby, Granny and George;* Kerlan Award from University of Minnesota, 1980; North Carolina Award for Literature, 1981; *Parents' Choice* award, 1984, for *The Morning the Sun Refused to Shine,* and 1985, for *Washday on Noah's Ark.*

WRITINGS:

SELF-ILLUSTRATED

Ol' Paul, the Mighty Logger, Holiday House, 1936, revised edition, 1949, reissued, 1976.

Lumbercamp, Holiday House, 1937, published as *The Whistle Punk of Camp 15,* Holiday House, 1959.

Paydirt, Holiday House, 1938.

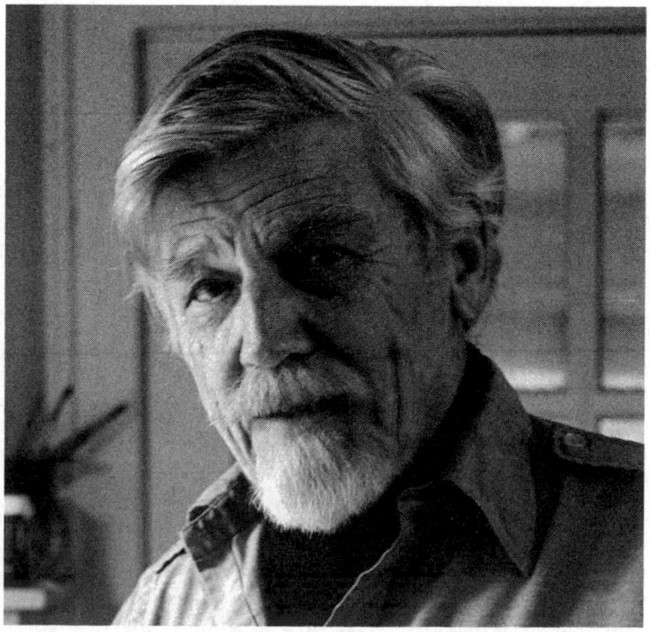

Glen Rounds

The Blind Colt (excerpts contained in *Whitey's Sunday Horse;* Junior Literary Guild selection), Holiday House, 1941.
Whitney's First Roundup (Junior Literary Guild selection), Grosset, 1942.
Whitney's Sunday Horse (also see below), Grosset, 1943.
Whitey Looks for a Job, Grosset, 1944.
Whitey and Jinglebob, Grosset, 1946.
Stolen Pony (sequel to *The Blind Colt*), Holiday House, 1948, revised edition, 1969.
Rodeo: Bulls, Broncos, and Buckaroos, Holiday House, 1949.
Whitey and the Rustlers (also see below), Holiday House, 1951.
Hunted Horses, Holiday House, 1951.
Whitey and the Blizzard (also see below), Holiday House, 1952.
Buffalo Harvest, Holiday House, 1952.
Lone Muskrat, Holiday House, 1953.
Whitney Takes a Trip, Holiday House, 1954.
Whitney Ropes and Rides, Holiday House, 1956.
Swamp Life: An Almanac, Prentice-Hall, 1957.
Wildlife at Your Doorstep: An Illustrated Almanac, Prentice-Hall, 1958, reissued, Holiday House, 1974.
Whitney and the Wild Horse, Holiday House, 1958.
Beaver Business: An Almanac, Prentice-Hall, 1960.
Wild Orphan, Holiday House, 1961.
Whitney and the Colt Killer, Holiday House, 1962.
Whitney's New Saddle (contains *Whitey and the Rustlers* and *Whitney and the Blizzard*), Holiday House, 1963.
Rain in the Woods and Other Small Matters, World, 1964.
The Snake Tree, World, 1966.
The Treeless Plains, Holiday House, 1967.
The Prairie Schooners, Holiday House, 1968.
Wild Horses of the Red Desert, Holiday House, 1969.
Once We Had a Horse, Holiday House, 1971.
The Cowboy Trade Holiday House, 1972.
The Day the Circus Came to Lonetree Holiday House, 1973.
Mr. Yowder and the Lion Roar Capsules, Holiday House, 1976.
The Beaver: How He Works, Holiday House, 1976.
Mr. Yowder and the Steamboat, Holiday House, 1977.
Mr. Yowder and the Giant Bullsnake, Holiday House, 1978.
Mr. Yowder, the Peripatetic Sign Painter: Three Tall Tales, Holiday House, 1980.
Blind Outlaw, Holiday House, 1980.
Mr. Yowder and the Train Robbers, Holiday House, 1981.
Wild Appaloosa, Holiday House, 1983.
Mr. Yowder and the Windwagon, Holiday House, 1983.
The Morning the Sun Refused to Rise: An Original Paul Bunyan Tale, Holiday House, 1984.
Washday on Noah's Ark: A Story of Noah's Ark, Holiday House, 1985.
Old MacDonald Had a Farm, Holiday House, 1989.
I Know an Old Lady Who Swallowed a Fly, Holiday House, 1990.
Cowboys, Holiday House, 1991.
(Reteller) *Three Little Pigs and the Big Bad Wolf,* Holiday House, 1992.

Rounds's works have been translated into Spanish, Dutch, and German.

ILLUSTRATOR

Irma S. Black, *Flipper, a Sea Lion,* Holiday House, 1940.
Walter Blair, *Tall Tale America,* Coward, 1944.
Frank O'Rourke, *"E" Company,* Simon & Schuster, 1945.
Martha Hardy, *Tatoosh,* Macmillan, 1947.
Wheaton P. Webb, *Uncle Swithin's Inventions,* Holiday House, 1947.
Aesop's Fables, Lippincott, 1949.
Vance Randolph, *We Always Lie to Strangers,* Columbia University Press, 1951.
V. Randolph, *Who Blowed up the Church House?,* Columbia University Press, 1952.
Sarah R. Riedman, *Grass, Our Greatest Crop,* Thomas Nelson, 1952.
Jim Kjelgaard, *Haunt Fox,* Holiday House, 1954.
Paul Hyde Bonner, *Those Glorious Mornings,* Scribner, 1954.
V. Randolph, *The Devil's Pretty Daughter,* Columbia University Press, 1955.
Paul M. Sears, *Firefly,* Holiday House, 1956.
V. Randolph, *The Talking Turtle,* Columbia University Press, 1957.
V. Randolph, *Sticks in the Knapsack,* Columbia University Press, 1958.
Elizabeth Seeman, *In the Arms of the Mountain,* Crown, 1961.
Wilson Gage, *A Wild Goose Tale,* World, 1961.
W. Gage, *Dan and the Miranda,* World, 1962.
W. Gage, *Big Blue Island,* World, 1964.
Adrien Stoutenburg, *The Crocodile's Mouth,* Viking, 1966.
Richard Chase, editor, *Billy Boy,* Golden Gate, 1966.
Maria Leach, *How the People Sang the Mountains Up,* Viking, 1967.
Gladys Conklin, *Lucky Ladybugs,* Holiday House, 1968.
A. Stoutenburg, *American Tall Tale Animals,* Viking, 1968.
John Greenway, *Folklore of the Great West,* American West, 1969.
Rebecca Caudill and James Ayars, *Contrary Jenkins,* Holt 1969.
Austin Fife and Alta Fife, *Ballads of the Great West,* American West, 1970.
W. Gage, *Mike's Toads,* World, 1970.
Alexander L. Crosby, *Go Find Hanka!,* Golden Gate, 1970.
Ida Chittum, *Farmer Hoo and the Baboons,* Delacorte, 1971.
Alvin Schwartz, editor, *A Twister of Twists, a Tangler of Tongues,* Lippincott, 1972.
G. Conklin, *Tarantula, the Giant Spider,* Holiday House, 1972.
Sandra S. Sivulich, *I'm Going on a Bear Hunt,* Dutton, 1973.

A. Schwartz, *Tomfoolery: Trickery and Foolery with Words,* Lippincott, 1973.
A. Schwartz, editor, *Witcracks,* Lippincott, 1973.
A. Schwartz, editor, *Cross Your Fingers, Spit in Your Hat: Superstitions and Other Beliefs,* Lippincott, 1974.
A. Schwartz, *Whoppers, Tall Tales and Other Lies,* Lippincott, 1975.
Mark Taylor, *Jennie Jenkins,* Little, Brown, 1975.
Betty Baker, *Three Fools and a Horse,* Macmillan, 1975.
Berniece Freschet, *Lizard in the Sun,* Scribner, 1975.
W. Gage, *Squash Pie,* Morrow, 1976.
A. Schwartz, editor, *Kickle Snifters and Other Fearsome Critters,* Lippincott, 1976.
Robbie Branscum, *Toby, Granny and George,* Doubleday, 1976.
R. Branscum, *The Saving of P.S.,* Doubleday, 1976.
B. Freschet, *The Happy Dromedary,* Scribner, 1977.
B. Freschet, *Little Black Bear Goes for a Walk,* Scribner, 1977.
W. Gage, *Down in the Boondocks,* Morrow, 1977.
G. Conklin, *Praying Mantis,* Holiday House, 1978.
Theo Gilchrest, *Halfway up the Mountain,* Lippincott, 1978.
B. Freschet, *Elephant and Friends,* Scribner, 1978.
Mary Blount Christian, *The Lucky Man,* Macmillan, 1979.
Judith St. George, *The Amazing Voyage of the New Orleans,* Putnam, 1979.
Jim Aylesworth, *Hush Up!,* Holt, 1980.
Jane Yolen, *Uncle Lemon's Spring,* Dutton, 1981.
J. Aylesworth, *Shenandoah Noah,* Holt, 1985.
Jill Wright, *The Old Woman and the Willy Nilly Man,* Putnam, 1987.
J. Aylesworth, *Hanna's Hog,* Atheneum, 1988.
David Adler, *Wild Bill Hickok and Other Old West Riddles,* Holiday House, 1988.
Eric A. Kimmel, *Charlie Drives the Stage,* Holiday House, 1989.
J. Wright, *The Old Woman and the Jar of Umms,* Putnam, 1989.
E. A. Kimmel, *Four Dollars and Fifty Cents,* Holiday House, 1990.

EDITOR AND ILLUSTRATOR

Andy Adams, *Trail Drive* (based on Adams's *Log of a Cowboy*), Holiday House, 1965.
George F. Ruxton, *Mountain Men,* Holiday House, 1966.
Boll Weevil, Golden Gate, 1967.
Casey Jones, Golden Gate, 1968.
The Strawberry Roan, Golden Gate, 1970.
Sweet Betsy from Pike, Golden Gate, 1973.

Author of radio scripts for "School of the Air," Columbia Broadcasting System (CBS), 1938-39. Contributor to *Treasury of American Folklore,* edited by Benjamin Botkin, Crown, 1944, and *Subtreasury of American Humor,* edited by E. B. White and Katherine S. White, Modern Library, 1948. Contributor to *Story Parade.*

ADAPTATIONS: First Roundup was adapted for broadcast by the British Broadcasting Corporation (BBC), 1960; several of Rounds's books have been recorded.

SIDELIGHTS: Glen Rounds is the author and illustrator of nearly fifty books and has provided the artwork for more than sixty publications. His own works often provide adventure-filled stories of the West or expand upon popular American tall tales. Rounds has been classified as a juvenile author because of his direct writing style and clear, often humorous, brush-line drawings. He insists, however, that his works are meant for all age groups.

Rounds was born in South Dakota in 1906, and grew up on ranches in the state and in Montana, learning to draw the animals and workers that shared his environment. As an adult, he wandered the western United States, taking on odd jobs to support himself. His travels, although filled with adventure and storytelling material, did not satisfy Rounds. He was determined to make his living as an artist.

Eventually, Rounds traveled to New York, hoping to sell his pictures. Because he was broke, Rounds would visit editors near lunch time, using his storytelling ability to pique their interest and hopefully wrangle a lunch invitation to continue the tale. Vernon Ives, a founding member of Holiday House, the company which published Rounds's first book, shared his initial impression of Rounds in a *Horn Book* article: "He was a young, footloose westerner with a discerning eye, a quick, sketchy style of drawing that had enormous vitality, and a tongue even more facile than his brush."

Although Rounds considered himself an artist and believed that stories should be told instead of written, editors convinced him that the best way to get his drawings published would be to write text to accompany them. Heeding this advice, Rounds wrote and illustrated *Ol' Paul, the Mighty Logger* in 1936, using unorthodox compilation methods. The author explained in *Horn Book* that instead of researching Paul Bunyan tales, "I made them up as I went along."

In following years, Rounds produced a slew of western adventures. He recounts the various escapades of a cowboy in his "Whitey" series and earned commendation from a *Saturday Review* contributor for his "economy of words and distinctive black-and-white drawings." His picture of prairie life in *The Treeless Plains* was deemed "authentic to the last detail and salted with wry but realistic humor," by Hal Borland in the *New York Times Book Review.* For more than fifty years, Rounds has upheld his streak of successful books. In his 1991 publication, *Cowboys,* Rounds describes an average workday for a ranch hand, augmenting the text with "lively, rough-hewn sketches," according to Diane Roback of *Publishers Weekly.*

Rounds, as both an author and illustrator, is also fond of tall tales. When illustrating books by other authors, the author gravitates toward stories that display tongue-in-cheek humor, such as John Greenway's *Folklore of the Great West,* A. Schwartz's *Whoppers, Tall Tales and Other Lies,* and Jill Wright's *The Old Woman and the Willy Nilly Man.* Rounds adds to these works by

From *Cowboys,* written and illustrated by Glen Rounds.

supplying his trademark brush-line drawings and providing the realistic, animated artwork that has earned him recognition for decades.

WORKS CITED:

Borland, Hal, review of *The Treeless Plains, New York Times Book Review,* May 14, 1967, p. 30.
Freedman, Russell, "Glen Rounds and Holiday House," *Horn Book,* March/April, 1985, pp. 222-225.
Roback, Diane, review of *Cowboys, Publishers Weekly,* May 3, 1991, p. 71.
Review of *Whitey and the Wild Horse, Saturday Review,* May 10, 1958, p. 41.

FOR MORE INFORMATION SEE:

PERIODICALS

Bulletin of the Center for Children's Books, April, 1991, p. 204.
Los Angeles Times Book Review, June 9, 1985, p. 10.
Publishers Weekly, July 15, 1974, pp. 58-59.
School Library Journal, August, 1986, p. 37.

* * *

RUDOMIN, Esther

See HAUTZIG, Esther Rudomin

RUFFINS, Reynold 1930-

PERSONAL: Born August 5, 1930, in New York, NY; son of John (a salesman) and Juanita (Dash) Ruffins; married Joan Young (an artist), May 29, 1954; children: Todd, Lynn, Ben, Seth. *Education:* Graduated from Cooper Union, 1951. *Hobbies and other interests:* Sailing, listening to classical and jazz music.

ADDRESSES: Home—112-38 178th Place, St. Albans, New York, NY 11434. *Office*—38 East 21st St., New York, NY 10010.

CAREER: Push Pin Studios, New York City, designer and illustrator, beginning in 1950s; assistant art director of advertising agency, c. 1954; graphic designer for IBM, Time-Life, Pfizer, Children's Book Council, MacDonald's, CBS-TV, *New York Times,* and *Family Circle* (magazine); illustrator and author of children's books, 1970s—. Instructor, School of Visual Arts, 1967-70; visiting adjunct professor, Syracuse University, College of Visual and Performing Arts, Department of Visual Communications, 1973; instructor, Parsons School of Design. *Exhibitions:* Bologna Children's Book Fair, 1976; New York Historical Society, "Two Hundred Years of American Illustration."

AWARDS, HONORS: Professional Achievement Award, Cooper Union, 1972; *The Chess Book* was selected for the American Institute of Graphic Arts Children's Books Show, 1973-74; "Children's Choice" Award from Children's Book Council and the International Reading Association, 1976, for *The Code and Cipher Book,* 1978, for *The Monster Riddle Book,* 1980, for *My Brother Never Feeds the Cat,* and 1983, for *Words?! A Book about the Origins of Everyday Words and Phrases;* American Library Association Notable Book citation, for *Words?! A Book about the Origins of Everyday Words and Phrases;* Silver Medal, Society of Illustrators, for "Dragon."

WRITINGS:

(And illustrator) *My Brother Never Feeds the Cat* (for children), Scribner, 1979.

ILLUSTRATOR

(With Simms Taback) Harry Hartwick, *The Amazing Maze,* Dutton, 1970.
John F. Waters, *Camels: Ships of the Desert,* Crowell, 1974.
Franklyn M. Branley, *Light and Darkness,* Crowell, 1975.

ILLUSTRATOR; WRITTEN BY JANE SARNOFF; ALL FOR CHILDREN

A Great Bicycle Book, Scribner, 1973.
The Chess Book, Scribner, 1973.
What? A Riddle Book, Scribner, 1974.
A Riddle Calendar: 1975, Scribner, 1974.
The Code and Cipher Book, Scribner, 1975.
The Monster Riddle Book, Scribner, 1975.
I Know! A Riddle Book, Scribner, 1976.
The 1977 Beastly Riddle Calendar, Scribner, 1976.
A Great Aquarium Book: The Putting-It-Together Guide for Beginners, Scribner, 1977.
Giants! A Riddle Book and Mr. Bigperson's Side: A Story Book, Scribner, 1977.
Take Warning! A Book of Superstitions, Scribner, 1978.
Space: A Fact and Riddle Book, Scribner, 1978.
The 1979 Out-of-This-World Riddle Calendar, Scribner, 1979.
Riddle Calendar, 1980, Scribner, 1979.
Light the Candles! Beat the Drums! A Book of Holidays, Occasions, Celebrations, Remembrances, Occurrences, Special Days, Weeks, and Months, Scribner, 1979.
If You Were Really Superstitious, Scribner, 1980.
That's Not Fair, Scribner, 1980.
Words?! A Book about the Origins of Everyday Words and Phrases, Scribner, 1981.

ADAPTATIONS: The Monster Riddle Book (filmstrip with cassette), Random House, 1981.

SIDELIGHTS: A successful designer and commercial artist in New York City, Reynold Ruffins has also produced illustrations for several children's books, as well as a solo picture book, *My Brother Never Feeds the Cat.* As a book illustrator, Ruffins is best-known for his successful collaborations with author Jane Sarnoff, with whom he worked from the early 1970s through the early 1980s. Ruffins and Sarnoff have produced over fifteen books together on such subjects as games and riddles, word origins, and superstitions. Ruffins branched out into children's book illustrating after an established career as a commercial artist which began in the 1950s.

Reynold Ruffins

From *My Brother Never Feeds the Cat,* written and illustrated by Reynold Ruffins.

Along with several other artists, he co-founded Push Pin Studios in New York City in the early 1950s, which became respected as an innovative and trend-setting design firm. Throughout his career, Ruffins has received numerous professional honors, both for his children's book illustrations and commercial art, including several "Children's Choice" citations from the Children's Book Council and a silver medal from the Society of Illustrators for his commercial illustration, "Dragon."

Ruffins was born in 1930 in New York City, and grew up in the borough of Queens. From a young age onward, as he told *Something about the Author* (*SATA*), "I always felt I could draw, and that it was something special." His father, the first black ever hired by the utility company Con Edison, would bring him drawing materials home from work, and also made sure to give him art supplies on special occasions like his birthday. Although his mother's side of the family included many musicians, Ruffins was most interested in drawing, and in grade school was known for sketches. "I was often challenged in school by kids who wanted to see if I could draw Superman or Captain Marvel," he told *SATA*. "I didn't particularly like to do it; I hated the idea of copying, preferring instead to draw from my imagination. But there was the class bully who constantly challenged me, so I did it."

Ruffins went on to attend the High School of Music and Art in New York City. During his senior year, an exhibition of his work gained him much attention, and produced his first art sale: fifty dollars for one of his paintings. "It was a wonderful feeling," he told *SATA,* for "fifty dollars was a lot of money in 1948. I can remember getting off the train at Grand Central with the check in my pocket. I strutted up Park and Fifth Avenue, feeling that the city was *mine.*" After high school, Ruffins continued his art studies at tuition-free Cooper Union in New York. There, he took classes in drawing, painting, illustration and advertising—and contemplated art as a career. "I knew that people made a living at art, but at that time I didn't exactly know how it was done," he told *SATA.* "At Cooper Union, we thought of ourselves as fine artists and easel painters. We came to understand the buying and selling of art, and what we had to do to make money in commercial art, but the thought of leaving a place like Cooper Union and going door to door with our portfolios under our arms scared all of us to death. Of course we all had naive hopes of impressing people, and making a million dollars."

Together with fellow art students from Cooper, Ruffins founded Push Pin Studios in New York. Working out of a loft after school and on weekends, he began to do commercial art while still in high school. Push Pin Studios gained a reputation for producing innovative design work, and showcased its work in a periodical entitled the *Monthly Graphic* (later called the *Push Pin Almanac*). Ruffins told *SATA:* "At any one time there were four or five artists [at Push Pin], Milton Glaser, Seymour Chwast, Paul Davis, John Alcorn, Isadore Seltzer, and myself, to name a few. In the 50s and 60s the studio was on the first floor of a brownstone.... We worked long hours—usually nine in the morning till nine at night. We worked on book jackets, pharmaceutical advertising, projects for CBS- and NBC-TV, and the *Push Pin Almanac.* In the fifties as well as today, Push Pin Studios is a trend setter. We did interesting work for a sophisticated audience." During the late 1960s, Ruffins also worked as an instructor at the School for Visual Arts in New York, followed in 1973 by a visiting professorship at Syracuse University. He first branched out into book illustration in 1970, working with Simms Taback on Harry Hartwick's *The Amazing Maze.*

Shortly thereafter, Ruffins began collaborating on picture books with Jane Sarnoff, a pharmaceutical writer whom he met at a civil rights protest march. Their first children's book, *A Great Bicycle Book,* was published in 1973 and over the years they have produced over fifteen picture books and children's calendars; among the subjects they have covered are riddles, games, holidays, superstitions, and word origins. Ruffins's favorite illustrations are those of monsters and fantasy characters, as in such books as *The Monster Riddle Book* and *Giants! A Riddle Book and Mr. Bigperson's Side.* He told *SATA:* "What I like best about creating monsters is that they can't be drawn right or wrong. They just are what they are." Ruffins published a solo picture book in 1979, *My Brother Never Feeds the Cat,* yet his preference is to solely provide illustrations. Describing his collaborations with Sarnoff, he told *SATA:* "She would write a draft, we'd meet and discuss it, we'd fight a bit, we'd talk things out—it was a very good arrangement. If I thought something would make a great visual, she would write around it. My only collaboration in the writing was in terms of discussion. Pen to paper to typewriter is *not* my thing."

Although Ruffins has had success as a book illustrator, he has maintained a flexibility throughout his career in order to keep himself working as an artist. Much of his illustration work has been in advertising, and he has provided illustrations and design work for a number of corporations. Ruffins commented in *SATA* on the diversity of his work: "My advertising illustration ranges from having to make a black and white drawing of a family about to board an airplane to cooking instructions to a full color painting of a horse and rider in London. The demands of my growing children, and of the market made it necessary for me to develop an ability to work in different ways. An extension of that is learning how to apply these acquired skills to book illustration. Whether it's an advantage or a disadvantage, I've never been locked into one way of working. It sounds immodest, but I have versatility."

Ruffins married Joan Young—an artist who also attended Cooper Union—in 1954. They have four children together, who have provided a special impetus for Ruffins's art career. "My children have influenced me in the sense that they've kept me at it—working. It's so expensive to raise them! I would have worked a lot less if I didn't have children. They've helped me sustain a certain sense of humor." Ruffins lives and works in New York City, where he teaches at Parsons School of Design. He has the following words of advice for young people interested in art: "Draw all the time. Develop a keen sense of observation. In everything there is something to be learned and remembered. For example, if you study a brick, the brick will change as the sun moves across the sky, it will cast a shadow on one side or another. If you are really interested in art, you should keep your eyes and your mind open."

WORKS CITED:

Ruffins, Reynold, in *Something about the Author,* Volume 41, Gale, 1985, pp. 189-196.

FOR MORE INFORMATION SEE:

PERIODICALS

Graphis, Number 177, 1975.

* * *

RUTHIN, Margaret
See CATHERALL, Arthur

* * *

RYDER, Joanne (Rose) 1946-

PERSONAL: Born September 16, 1946, in Lake Hiawatha, NJ; daughter of Raymond and Dorothy (McGaffney) Ryder; married Lawrence Yep (an author). *Education:* Received degree in journalism from Marquette University, 1968; graduate study at University of Chicago, 1968-69. *Hobbies and other interests:* "Traveling whenever I can, spending time walking or hiking outdoors to enjoy nature, gardening and flower arranging, reading and listening to poetry, working and playing with puppets, sharing my interest in animals with children."

ADDRESSES: Home—San Francisco, CA.

CAREER: Harper & Row Publishers, Inc., New York City, editor of children's books, 1970-80; full-time writer, 1980—. Docent (tour guide) at the San Francisco Zoo; lecturer at schools and conferences.

MEMBER: Society of Children's Book Writers, California Academy of Sciences, San Francisco Zoological Society.

AWARDS, HONORS: Simon Underground was selected for the Children's Book Showcase, 1977; New Jersey Author's Award from the New Jersey Institute of Technology, for *Fireflies,* 1978, *Fog in the Meadow,* 1980, and *Snail in the Woods,* 1980; *Fog in the Meadow* was named Outstanding Science Trade Book of the Year for Children by the National Science Teachers Association, 1979, and a Children's Choice Book by the Children's Book Council and the International Reading Association, 1980; *The Snail's Spell* was named a Parents Choice Book by *Parents Magazine* and received the New York Academy of Sciences Children's Science Book Award, younger category, 1982; *Inside Turtle's Shell, and Other Poems of the Field* was named Outstanding Book of the Year for Children by the National Council of Teachers of English, 1985, Outstanding Science Trade Book of the Year for Children by the National Science Teachers Association, 1985, and was included on the Bluebonnet Award list and the Bank Street Outstanding Book of the Year list; *Step into the Night* was named Outstanding Science Trade Book of the Year for Children by the National Science Teachers Association and received the Commonwealth Club of Northern California Children's Book Medal, 1988; *Where Butterflies Grow* was named Outstanding Science Trade Book of the Year for Children by the National Science Teachers Association, 1989.

Joanne Ryder

WRITINGS:

FOR CHILDREN

Simon Underground, illustrated by John Schoenherr, Harper, 1976.
A Wet and Sandy Day, illustrated by Donald Carrick, Harper, 1977.
Fireflies, illustrated by Don Bolognese, Harper, 1977.
Fog in the Meadow, illustrated by Gail Owens, Harper, 1979.
(With Harold S. Feinberg) *Snail in the Woods,* illustrated by Jo Polseno, Harper, 1979.
The Spiders Dance, illustrated by Robert Blake, Harper, 1981.
Beach Party, illustrated by Diane Stanley, F. Warne, 1982.
The Snail's Spell, illustrated by Lynne Cherry, F. Warne, 1982.
The Incredible Space Machines, illustrated by Gerry Daly, Random House, 1982.
C-3PO's Book about Robots, illustrated by John Gampert, Random House, 1983.
Inside Turtle's Shell, and Other Poems of the Field, illustrated by Susan Bonners, Macmillan, 1985.
The Night Flight, illustrated by Amy Schwartz, Four Winds Press, 1985.
The Evening Walk, illustrated by Julie Durrell, Western Publishing, 1985.
Old Friends, New Friends, illustrated by Jane Chambless-Rigie, Western Publishing, 1986.
Chipmunk Song, illustrated by Cherry, Lodestar, 1987.
Animals in the Woods, illustrated by Lisa Bonforte, Western Publishing, 1987, published as *Animals in the Wild,* 1989.
Step into the Night, illustrated by Dennis Nolan, Four Winds Press, 1988.
My Little Golden Book about Cats, illustrated by Dora Leder, Western Publishing, 1988.
Puppies Are Special Friends, illustrated by James Spence, Western Publishing, 1988.
(Adapter) *Hardie Gramatky's Little Toot,* illustrated by Larry Ross, Platt, 1988.
(Adapter) Charles Dickens, *A Christmas Carol,* illustrated by John O'Brien, Platt, 1989.
White Bear, Ice Bear (A "Just for a Day" Book), illustrated by Michael Rothman, Morrow, 1989.
Catching the Wind (A "Just for a Day" Book), illustrated by Rothman, Morrow, 1989.
Mockingbird Morning, illustrated by Nolan, Four Winds Press, 1989.
Where Butterflies Grow, illustrated by Cherry, Lodestar, 1989.
Under the Moon, illustrated by Cheryl Harness, Random House, 1989.
Lizard in the Sun (A "Just for a Day" Book), illustrated by Rothman, Morrow, 1990.
Under Your Feet, illustrated by Nolan, Four Winds Press, 1990.
When the Woods Hum, illustrated by Catherine Stock, Morrow, 1991.
Hello, Tree!, illustrated by Michael Hays, Lodestar, 1991.
The Bear on the Moon, illustrated by Carol Lacey, Morrow, 1991.
Winter Whale, illustrated by Rothman, Morrow, 1991.

Contributor to periodicals.

SIDELIGHTS: Joanne Ryder is an award-winning children's writer who specializes in books about nature. Her works are a unique blend of scientific fact and fantasy. Through simple, poetic prose, Ryder provides her readers with knowledge of the different life forms that exist all around us. Her books describe the growth and life cycles of small creatures, like fireflies, snails, and spiders. Ryder's works also expand young readers' imaginations by challenging them to view the world as an insect or an animal would. In books like *Chipmunk Song, Where Butterflies Grow, Catching the Wind,* or *White Bear, Ice Bear,* Ryder takes children on dreamlike, imaginary travels that change them into chipmunks, butterflies, geese, or bears. With more than thirty popular books to her credit, Ryder ranks among the leading writers of children's nature books.

Ryder was born in the small New Jersey town of Lake Hiawatha. Her parents moved there from New York City during World War II when her father, a rubber chemist, found a job nearby. In an interview for *Something about the Author* (*SATA*), Ryder said that for her parents, "Lake Hiawatha was the 'country'—very different from the crowded city they knew. For me, it was a wonderful place to explore, full of treasures to discover.... I loved living there and playing outdoors. There were always animals around to observe and encounter. We had moles who would burrow under our lawn at night and leave their mounds for me to find in the morning. Chipmunks and lizards darted this way and that across our backyard. Striped garter snakes made their home in the stone wall around ours. I'd see them on sunny days warming themselves on top of the rocky wall. One of my earliest memories is trying to follow a butterfly darting across the road and being scolded by a neighbor for running into the street.

"My parents, probably because they had spent all of their lives in the city, were also fascinated with the country. They both shared with me their different loves. My mother taught me to watch sunsets and to take time to stop and enjoy special moments in nature. I remember her stopping her chores—which she didn't often do—to sit for hours just so she could enjoy observing a hundred tiny birds, migrating spring warblers, who had paused to rest in our tree. 'When Mother Nature puts on a show,' she would say, 'I don't want to miss it. My work can wait till tomorrow.'

"My father liked to pick things up and examine them. He was the one who introduced me to nature up close and made the discoveries we shared very personal ones. He loved to work in his garden. Whenever he would find something interesting, he would call me to come and see. If he could catch it, he would cup the tiny creature in his hands and wait until I ran to him. Then he would open his fingers and show me whatever it was he had found—a beetle, a snail, a fuzzy caterpillar. Then gently he would let me hold it, and I could feel it move, wiggle, or crawl—even breathe—as I held it in my hand."

Ryder's family moved to Brooklyn when she was about five years old, in the same apartment building where her mother had grown up. "It was a bit of a shock for me to live where there were so many people all around," she remembered in *SATA,* "but the city seemed also a magical land, full of special places for me. I loved going to the park and to the museums where there were gigantic dinosaur bones and mysterious mummies and sparkling gems. There were wonders in my own neighborhood too. Every day on my way to school, I passed an old stone lion. I believed he could understand my thoughts, and I would tell him secrets. He was one of my first friends in the city. I also began to have lovely dreams at night in which I could fly over the tall trees outside my home.

"I tell children if they would like to imagine what I was like when I was six, they might read my book *The Night Flight.* I was very much like Anna, the girl in my story. She also gets to do some extraordinary things I wished I could—talk to the fish in the park and have her stone lion become real to take her for a ride through the jungle. But the dream she has of flying easily over the city was very much like my favorite dream. Every now and then, I still dream I can fly, and I always wake up feeling delighted."

"By the time I was ten, I suspected I might want to be a writer," she continued in *SATA.* "I also thought I might like to be a ballet dancer or a veterinarian, too. But I kept on writing, and the writing won out." At this time her family was living in the town of New Hyde Park on Long Island, where Ryder grew up and her parents still live today. In high school, she edited the school newspaper, then studied journalism and edited the college literary magazine at Marquette University. She took graduate courses at the University of Chicago in 1968 in library science and then worked for a number of years as an editor of children's books at Harper and Row, Publishers, in New York City. Ryder told *SATA,* "During the day I worked on other people's books. Then at night I worked on my own stories. After writing several books this way, I decided I wanted to take a leap. I quit my editing job to become a full-time writer. It was the right choice for me, and I have been writing ever since."

Ryder's first book, *Simon Underground,* is about how a mole spends his winter. Her inspiration for the book came from one of the exhibits at New York's American Museum of Natural History: it "was a cutaway of a field showing the animals in winter and spring," she described in *SATA,* "some were sleeping, some were active. A tiny mole dug deep tunnels all winter long and then dug up near the surface in springtime." She imagined the life of the mole, and related it to her own feelings about life in winter and spring. About Ryder's *Chipmunk Song,* a reviewer in *Language Arts* wrote that "one way to understand the world of small animals is to imagine yourself one of them, a tactic that comes naturally to children" and a successful method for Ryder in creating children's books.

"Many of my books ask you to imagine with me what it would be like to live a very different life as another creature," explained Ryder in *SATA.* "I ask you to be a shapechanger—to imagine shrinking small or growing large, to imagine being covered in fur or being a tiny creeper clinging to a leaf. To write these stories, I have to learn about an animal and imagine what it would feel like to live as an animal in its world. This is like a puzzle and a game for me, and I enjoy thinking it out." In *Where Butterflies Grow,* Ryder guides readers through the life cycle of a butterfly. Reviewer Virginia E. Jeschelnig wrote in *School Library Journal:* "For young children, there's no better way to introduce the world of science than through one of nature's miracles, and it is difficult to find a better example than in this wondrous story of birth and transformation.... Through the personalized adventure and Ryder's strong sensory imagery, readers become the tiny creature, growing and changing."

"If you read my books, you will probably discover the things that are special to me, things I like very much," said Ryder in *SATA.* "You can tell because I write about them again and again. I love night—walking at dusk, looking at the sky and stars. I enjoy imagining what hidden animals are doing in the ground under my feet. There are a lot of moles and chipmunks and even worms

On the top of your head
you have two long feelers.
You can stretch and stretch
these feelers
till they look like
long, long horns.

From *The Snail's Spell,* by Joanne Ryder. Illustrated by Lynne Cherry.

in my stories. I like watching dragonflies and butterflies on a sunny day and fireflies flickering at night. In my books there are many creatures who fly, just as I wish I could. I may not be able to fly myself, but I can write about being someone who can.... Children sometimes ask me if I could be any animal which one I would be. That's a tough question, but I think it would be fun to be an otter—either a river otter or a sea otter. They are curious and playful, and they seem to have fun. I also would like to be an animal that flies. It must be exciting to be able to fly, to soar high, and to go wherever you wish."

Ryder now lives in San Francisco with her husband, and she told *SATA* she enjoys living near the water, going to the beach, and walking in the sand. "Looking at the ocean gives me the kind of quiet I need to sort out my thoughts and to imagine new things.... Ideas are like butterflies; you have to catch them quickly and carefully or they will escape and you may lose them forever. They dart off when the phone rings or someone calls you. Sometimes I lose my ideas, but I have learned to try to catch them and put them down right away so I can remember them.

"For a person who enjoys thinking in images and writing poems," Ryder concluded, "writing picture books is a good life and a joyful way to make a living. It's a life I like *very* much. I do believe that the books you read when you are young leave a lasting impression. I am surprised when I reread books I loved as a child to discover the ways they have changed me and become part of me. They are my treasures. When I read them again, they make me smile fondly as if I were meeting old friends. It's nice for me to think that children might have fun reading my books and using their own imaginations to enjoy the natural world. I would wish that my books would turn into old and good friends for them too."

WORKS CITED:

Jeschelnig, Virginia E., *School Library Journal,* September, 1989, p. 233.
Language Arts, December 1987, p. 902.
Ryder, Joanne, interview with Chris Hunter for *Something about the Author,* conducted in Golden Gate Park, San Francisco, CA, August, 1990, published in Volume 65, Gale, 1991.

FOR MORE INFORMATION SEE:

BOOKS

Contemporary Authors, Volume 112, Gale, 1985, p. 426.
Sixth Book of Junior Authors & Illustrators, H. W. Wilson, 1989, pp. 253-255.
Something about the Author, Volume 34, Gale, 1984, p. 181.

* * *

RYE, Anthony
See YOUD, (Christopher) Samuel

* * *

RYLANT, Cynthia 1954-

PERSONAL: Surname is pronounced "rye-*lunt*"; born June 6, 1954, in Hopewell, VA; daughter of John Tune (an army sergeant) and Leatrel (a nurse; maiden name, Rylant) Smith; married and divorced; children: Nathaniel. *Education:* Morris Harvey College (now University of Charleston), B.A., 1975; Marshall University, M.A., 1976; Kent State University, M.L.S., 1982. *Politics:* Democrat. *Religion:* "Christian, no denomination."

CAREER: Writer. Marshall University, Huntington, WV, part-time English instructor, 1979-80; Akron Public Library, Akron, OH, children's librarian, 1983;

University of Akron, Akron, part-time English lecturer, 1983-84; Northeast Ohio Universities College of Medicine, Rootstown, OH, part-time lecturer, 1991—.

AWARDS, HONORS: When I Was Young in the Mountains was named a *Booklist* reviewer's choice, 1982, Caldecott Honor Book, American Library Association (ALA) notable book, and Reading Rainbow selection, all 1983; American Book Award nomination, 1983, and English Speaking Union Book-across-the-Sea Ambassador of Honor Award, 1984, both for *When I Was Young in the Mountains; Waiting to Waltz ... a Childhood* was named an ALA notable book, a *School Library Journal* best book of 1984, a National Council for Social Studies best book, 1984, and a Society of Midland Authors best children's book, 1985; *The Relatives Came* was named a *New York Times* best illustrated, a *Horn Book* honor book, a Child Study Association of America's children's book of the year, all 1985, and a Caldecott Honor Book, 1986; *A Blue-eyed Daisy* was named a Child Study Association of America's children's book of the year, 1985; *Every Living Thing* was named a *School Library Journal* best book, 1985; *A Fine White Dust* was named a *Parents' Choice* selection, 1986, and a Newbery Honor Book, 1987; *Appalachia: The Voices of Sleeping Birds* was named a *Boston Globe/Horn Book* honor book for nonfiction, 1991.

WRITINGS:

PICTURE BOOKS

When I Was Young in the Mountains, illustrated by Diane Goode, Dutton, 1982.
Miss Maggie, illustrated by Thomas DiGrazia, Dutton, 1983.
This Year's Garden, illustrated by Mary Szilagyi, Bradbury, 1984.
The Relatives Came, illustrated by Stephen Gammell, Bradbury, 1985.
Night in the Country, illustrated by Szilagyi, Bradbury, 1986.
Birthday Presents, illustrated by Sucie Stevenson, Orchard Books, 1987.
All I See, illustrated by Peter Catalanotto, Orchard Books, 1988.
Mr. Griggs' Work, illustrated by Julie Downing, Orchard Books, 1989.
An Angel for Solomon Singer, illustrated by Catalanotto, Orchard Books, 1992.

"HENRY AND MUDGE" SERIES; ILLUSTRATED BY SUCIE STEVENSON; PUBLISHED BY BRADBURY

Henry and Mudge: The First Book of Their Adventures, 1987.
Henry and Mudge in Puddle Trouble: The Second Book of Their Adventures, 1987.
Henry and Mudge in the Green Time: The Third Book of Their Adventures, 1987.
Henry and Mudge under the Yellow Moon: The Fourth Book of Their Adventures, 1987.
Henry and Mudge in the Sparkle Days: The Fifth Book of Their Adventures, 1988.

Cynthia Rylant

Henry and Mudge and the Forever Sea: The Sixth Book of Their Adventures, 1989.
Henry and Mudge Get the Cold Shivers: The Seventh Book of Their Adventures, 1989.
Henry and Mudge and the Happy Cat, 1990.
Henry and Mudge and the Bedtime Thumps, 1991.
Henry and Mudge Take the Big Test, 1991.
Henry and Mudge and the Long Weekend, 1992.
Henry and Mudge and the Wild Wind, 1992.

OTHER

Waiting to Waltz ... a Childhood (poetry), illustrated by Stephen Gammell, Bradbury, 1984.
A Blue-eyed Daisy (novel), Bradbury, 1985, published in England as *Some Year For Ellie,* illustrated by Kate Rogers, Viking Kestrel, 1986.
Every Living Thing (stories), Bradbury, 1985.
A Fine White Dust (novel), Bradbury, 1986.
Children of Christmas: Stories for the Season, illustrated by S. D. Schindler, Orchard Books, 1987, published in England as *Silver Packages and Other Stories,* 1987.
A Kindness (novel), Orchard Books, 1989.
But I'll Be Back Again: An Album (autobiography), Orchard Books, 1989.
A Couple of Kooks: And Other Stories about Love, Orchard Books, 1990.

Soda Jerk (poetry), illustrated by Peter Catalanotto, Orchard Books, 1990.
Appalachia: The Voices of Sleeping Birds, illustrated by Barry Moser, Harcourt, 1991.
Missing May, Orchard Books, 1992.

ADAPTATIONS: When I Was Young in the Mountains, 1983, *This Year's Garden,* 1983, and *The Relatives Came,* 1986, were adapted as filmstrips by Random House.

WORK IN PROGRESS: "Mr. Putter and Tabby," a series for beginning readers; "Blue Hill Meadows," a picture book series.

SIDELIGHTS: Cynthia Rylant is an award-winning children's and young adult author whose work includes picture books, poetry, short stories, and novels. With a writing style that has been described as unadorned, clear, and lyrical, the author presents young people's experiences with sensitivity and perceptiveness, branding her protagonists' concerns as legitimate and equally important as those of adults. Rylant's characters tend to be contemplative and set apart from their peers by their situations. Explaining her leaning toward such subjects, the author remarked in *Horn Book,* "I get a lot of personal gratification thinking of those people who don't get any attention in the world and making them really valuable in my fiction—making them absolutely shine with their beauty." She continued, "... I don't ever quite write really happy novels; I don't want to deal with the people who have what they want. I want to deal with people who don't have what they want, to show their lives too."

Critics suggest that Rylant appears sympathetic to her characters' plights because she also faced uncommon hardships as a child. In her autobiography *But I'll Be Back Again: An Album,* the author stated, "They say that to be a writer you must first have an unhappy childhood. I don't know if unhappiness is necessary, but I think maybe some children who have suffered a loss too great for words grow up into writers who are always trying to find those words, trying to find a meaning for the way they have lived."

Rylant's parents had a stormy marriage and separated when the author was four years old; she admits that she naively blamed herself for their troubles. The author and her mother moved to West Virginia where Rylant was left in her grandparents' care while her mother earned a nursing degree. Her father wrote occasionally when she first moved, but the letters eventually stopped. Because none of her relatives spoke about her father, she was afraid to ask questions about him. After years of silence, however, he contacted Rylant. The author dreamed of their reunion, but before it could take place her father, a Korean War veteran who suffered from hepatitis and alcoholism, succumbed to these diseases. He died when she was thirteen. In *But I'll Be Back Again,* the author stated, "I did not have a chance to know him or to say goodbye to him, and that is all the loss I needed to become a writer."

Unhappiness, however, did not dominate the author's childhood. Rylant enjoyed the rustic West Virginia environment while living with her grandparents in a mountain town where many houses had neither electricity nor running water. The lack of amenities did not bother young Rylant; she felt secure surrounded by equally poor yet friendly, church-going neighbors. When the author was eight years old, she and her mother moved to another West Virginia town named Beaver. Judging in retrospect for *Contemporary Authors* (*CA*), she called this new location "without a doubt a small, sparkling universe that gave me a lifetime's worth of material for my writing."

As an adolescent in this rural setting, though, Rylant began to recognize and become envious of the fact that other people had more material possessions than she and her mother did. In addition, Beaver—which had at first offered adventure—now appeared backward and dull compared to larger cities. Reflecting in her autobiography, *But I'll Be Back Again,* Rylant remarked, "As long as I stayed in Beaver, I felt I was somebody important.... But as soon as I left town to go anywhere else, my sense of being somebody special evaporated into nothing and I became dull and ugly and poor." She continued, "I wanted to be someone else, and that turned out to be the worst curse and the best gift of my life. I would finish out my childhood forgetting who I really was and what I really thought, and I would listen to other people and repeat their ideas instead of finding my own. That was the curse. The gift was that I would be willing to try to write books when I grew up."

The first book Rylant produced was *When I Was Young in the Mountains,* a picture book reminiscing about life in West Virginia's Appalachian Mountains which was praised for its simple, yet evocative text and was named a Caldecott honor book. With subsequent picture books, including *The Relatives Came, This Year's Garden,* and her "Henry and Mudge" series, Rylant has received considerable recognition and awards. The author told *CA:* "I like writing picture books because that medium gives me a chance to capture in a brief space what I consider life's profound experiences—grandmother crying at a swimming hole baptism, a family planting a garden together, relatives coming for a visit. There is a poignancy and beauty in these events, and I don't want to write adult poetry about them because then I'll have to layer it with some adult disillusionment."

Rylant continued her use of poetry in books for older readers. In *Waiting to Waltz ... A Childhood,* the author offers an autobiographical collection of thirty free-verse poems which record her coming-of-age. These events include embarrassment because her mother was too busy to join school committees and reckoning with the deaths of both an absent father and a beloved pet. One passage documents the surprising transformation from child to young adult: "Forgetting when /I was last time/ a child./ Never knowing/ when it/ ended." *Waiting to Waltz* also weaves in events and symbols of the 1960s to produce what critics deemed a vivid re-creation of the era.

Another book of verse, *Soda Jerk,* combines illustrations by Peter Catalanotto with twenty-eight related poems by Rylant to present the thoughts of a nameless protagonist who works as an attendant at a soda fountain. The title of this work is the slang term for the job. The jerk, as the narrator calls himself, offers commentary on issues ranging from his customers' lives to his fears about the future. Valerie Sayers, writing in *New York Times Book Review,* remarked that with her short poems, "Rylant manages to shape enough action to fill several short stories and to create a protagonist who is not only likable but charming and engaging." *Soda Jerk,* the critic concluded, "is full of respect for a boy's powers of observation, and its images, both written and painted, are striking."

In 1985 Rylant published her first novel, *A Blue-eyed Daisy.* Set in Appalachia, the episodic work is told by eleven-year-old Ellie Farley during the course of a year. The youngest of five daughters, Ellie contends with her apprehensions and conflicting emotions about growing up. For example, she overcomes her fear of contracting epilepsy after witnessing a classmate's seizure; copes with her unemployed, alcoholic father's imperfections and the possibility of his death after an accident; and battles the nervous anticipation of her first co-ed party. A reviewer for *Publishers Weekly* proclaimed *A Blue-eyed Daisy* an "exquisite novel, written with love."

Rylant's 1986 novel, *A Fine White Dust,* was named a Newbery Honor Book. In this work, a deeply religious seventh-grader named Pete believes he has found a human incarnation of God in a roving preacher named Carson. When attending a revival meeting, Pete is mesmerized by Carson's charismatic presence and, after being "saved," agrees to become his disciple. Despite his hesitance to leave his family and friends, Pete reasons that such a sacrifice is needed to fully embrace the holy life. Pete's mission is never fulfilled, however, because the preacher unexpectedly runs off with a young woman. Although he initially feels betrayed, Pete develops a more mature understanding of love and faith. *Wilson Library Bulletin* contributor Frances Bradburn proclaimed, "The careful crafting of delicate subjects is ... beautifully illustrated" in *A Fine White Dust.*

Another of Rylant's 1990 works, *A Couple of Kooks: And Other Stories about Love,* offers various examples of the emotion. In "A Crush," a mentally handicapped man secretly leaves flowers for a female hardware store worker. An older woman finds love with a man ten years her junior in "Clematis." And in the title story, two teenagers use the nine months of the girl's pregnancy to try to instill their hopes, love, and food preferences on the baby that they will be forced to give up for adoption. Critics commended Rylant for her honest, compassionate portrayal of her subjects' feelings.

With her works for children and young adults, Rylant has earned a loyal readership as well as positive critical response. Yet, when facing the future of her career, Rylant admits to insecurities. In *Horn Book* she explained, "I get afraid of what I am going to do for the next fifty years. Surely, I think to myself, I can't keep this up. I am just going to run dry—or worse, get boring and predictable." Nonetheless, the author does feel a sense of accomplishment beyond the recognition and awards her works have received. In *Horn Book* Rylant confided that writing "has given me a sense of self-worth that I didn't have my whole childhood. I am really proud of that. The [books] have carried me through some troubled times and have made me feel that I am worthy of having a place on this earth."

WORKS CITED:

Bradburn, Frances, review of *A Fine White Dust, Wilson Library Bulletin,* April, 1987, p. 49.

Review of *A Blue-eyed Daisy, Publishers Weekly,* March 8, 1985, p. 91.

Rylant, Cynthia, *But I'll Be Back Again: An Album,* Orchard Books, 1989, pp. 7 and 32-34.

Rylant, Cynthia, *Waiting to Waltz ... a Childhood,* Bradbury, 1984.

Sayers, Valerie, review of *Soda Jerk, New York Times Book Review,* June 3, 1990, p. 24.

Silvey, Anita, "An Interview with Cynthia Rylant," *Horn Book,* November/December, 1987, pp. 695-703.

FOR MORE INFORMATION SEE:

BOOKS

Children's Literature Review, Volume 15, Gale, 1988, pp. 167-174.

From *When I Was Young in the Mountains,* by Cynthia Rylant. Illustrated by Diane Goode.

Something about the Author Autobiography Series, Volume 13, Gale, 1991, pp. 155-163.

PERIODICALS

New York Times Book Review, November 10, 1985, p. 37; June 30, 1990, p. 24.

Washington Post, December 24, 1990.

S

S. L. C.
See CLEMENS, Samuel Langhorne

* * *

SACHS, Marilyn (Stickle) 1927-

PERSONAL: Born December 18, 1927, in New York, NY; daughter of Samuel (in insurance sales) and Anna (Smith) Stickle; married Morris Sachs (a sculptor), January 26, 1947; children: Anne, Paul. *Education:* Hunter College (now Hunter College of the City University of New York), B.A., 1949; Columbia University, M.S., 1953. *Politics:* "I'm for whatever and whoever will help bring about a more human, peaceful society."

Marilyn Sachs

Religion: Jewish. *Hobbies and other interests:* Walking, reading, good company.

ADDRESSES: 733 31st Ave., San Francisco, CA 94121.

CAREER: Brooklyn Public Library, Brooklyn, NY, children's librarian, 1949-60; San Francisco Public Library, San Francisco, CA, part-time children's librarian, 1961-67; writer.

Member: PEN, Authors Guild, Society of Childrens' Book Writers, American Jane Austen Society, English Jane Austen Society, American Civil Liberties Union, SANE (National Committee for a Sane Nuclear Policy), Freeze.

AWARDS, HONORS: Veronica Ganz was named a notable book of 1968 by the American Library Association; outstanding book of the year awards, *New York Times,* 1971, for *The Bears' House,* and 1973, for *A Pocket Full of Seeds;* best book of the year award, *School Library Journal,* 1971, for *The Bears' House,* and 1973, for *The Truth about Mary Rose;* National Book Award finalist, 1972, for *The Bears' House;* Jane Addams Children's Book Honor Award, 1974, for *A Pocket Full of Seeds;* Silver Pencil Award, Collective Propaganda van het Bederlandse Boek (Netherlands), 1974, for *The Truth about Mary Rose,* and 1977, for *Dorrie's Book;* Austrian Children's Book Prize, 1977, for *The Bears' House;* Garden State Children's Book Award, 1978, for *Dorrie's Book; A Summer's Lease* was chosen one of *School Library Journal*'s best books for spring, 1979; *Fleet-Footed Florence* was selected as a children's choice by the International Reading Association, 1982; Association of Jewish Libraries Award, 1983, for *Call Me Ruth; The Fat Girl* was chosen one of American Library Association's best books for young adults, 1984; Christopher Award, 1986, for *Underdog; Fran Ellen's House* was named a notable book of 1987 by the American Library Association; Bay Area Book Reviewers Association Award, 1988, for *Fran Ellen's House;* recognition of merit, George C. Stone Center for Children's Books, 1989, for *The Bear's House* and *Fran Ellen's House;* Jane Addams Children's Book Award, 1990, for *The Big*

Book for Peace; The Big Book for Peace was named a notable book for 1991 by the American Library Association.

WRITINGS:

Amy Moves In, illustrated by Judith Gwyn Brown, Doubleday, 1964.
Laura's Luck, illustrated by Ib Ohlsson, Doubleday, 1965.
Amy and Laura, illustrated by Tracy Sugarman, Doubleday, 1966.
Veronica Ganz, illustrated by Louis Glanzman, Doubleday, 1968.
Peter and Veronica (Junior Literary Guild selection), illustrated by Glanzman, Doubleday, 1969.
Marv (Junior Literary Guild selection), illustrated by Glanzman, Doubleday, 1970.
Reading Between the Lines (play) Children's Book Council, 1971.
The Bears' House, illustrated by Glanzman, Doubleday, 1971.
The Truth about Mary Rose, illustrated by Glanzman, Doubleday, 1973.
A Pocket Full of Seeds (ALA Notable Book), illustrated by Ben Stahl, Doubleday, 1973.
Matt's Mitt, illustrated by Hilary Knight, Doubleday, 1975.
Dorrie's Book, illustrated by Anne Sachs, Doubleday, 1975.
A December Tale, Doubleday, 1976.
A Secret Friend (Junior Literary Guild selection), Doubleday, 1978.
A Summer's Lease Dutton, 1979.
Bus Ride, illustrated by Amy Rowen, Dutton, 1980.
Class Pictures, Dutton, 1980.
Fleet-Footed Florence, illustrated by Charles Robinson, Doubleday, 1981.
Hello . . . Wrong Number, illustrated by Pamela Johnson, Dutton, 1981.
Beach Towels, illustrated by Jim Spence, Dutton, 1982.
Call Me Ruth (Junior Literary Guild selection), Doubleday, 1982.
Fourteen (Junior Literary Guild selection), Dutton, 1983.
The Fat Girl, Dutton, 1983.
Thunderbird, illustrated by Spence, Dutton, 1985.
Underdog (Junior Literary Guild selection), Doubleday, 1985.
Baby Sister, Dutton, 1986.
Almost Fifteen, Dutton, 1987.
Fran Ellen's House, Dutton, 1987.
Just Like a Friend, Dutton, 1989.
At the Sound of the Beep, Dutton, 1990.
(Editor with Ann Durell) *The Big Book for Peace,* illustrated by Thomas B. Allen, Dutton, 1990.
Circles, Dutton, 1991.
What My Sister Remembered, Dutton, 1992.

Contributor to *New York Times* and *San Francisco Chronicle.*

ADAPTATIONS: Veronica Ganz was adapted as a filmstrip and released by Insight Media Programs, 1975.

WORK IN PROGRESS: "A short, funny (I hope) book."

SIDELIGHTS: Marilyn Sachs, the author of more than thirty books for children and young adults, helped launch the trend of realistic fiction for young readers with her first publication in 1964, and she has retained this focus with each successive work. In her books, the protagonists work out problems by telling their stories. Often her characters don't fit into mainstream teenaged life; distanced from their peers by circumstance or choice, they struggle with dilemmas in search of plausible solutions which will still allow them to be true to themselves. The author has been praised by critics for her knack of realistically portraying relationships and has also been commended for incorporating relevant social issues in her works. In addition reviewers have lauded the author's identification with and sympathy for her characters.

Sachs's own childhood provides the framework for many of her stories. A native New Yorker, the author lived in an apartment on Jennings Street in the east Bronx for ten years, beginning when she was four years old. Sachs recalled in an essay for *Something about the Author Autobiography Series* (*SAAS*) that the street had no trees, flowers, or birds, but plenty of children. Because there was not much traffic on the street, the neighborhood children would gather to play games. Although most families who lived on Jennings Street—including her own—were poor, the author remembers this time of her life fondly and has documented it in her works. She told *SAAS:* "*Amy Moves In,* my first book, probably comes closer to describing my life on Jennings Street than any of my other books."

Describing herself as a child, Sachs recalled in *SAAS:* "I was a little, skinny, cowardly kid." Because of this, the author was often the target of neighborhood bullies. She continued, "My older sister, who always seemed to me a glorious figure of righteousness and revenge, frequently had to fight my battles for me. My father gave me boxing lessons but to no avail." To avoid bullies—and because it was one of her favorite pastimes—the author often spent her afternoons at the local library. The young Sachs primarily focused her literary attention on works from previous centuries, reading fairy tales, classics, and historical fiction. However, as she wrote in her *SAAS* essay, "I read other things as well—comic books, magazines, The Bobbsey Twin series, and any books my sister recommended. She was one of the strongest influences in my life when I was a child."

Sachs offered more details of her childhood in *SAAS.* "I was also a liar and a crybaby," she admitted. "I couldn't help the lying. My own rearrangement of reality always seemed much more appealing than what everybody else considered the truth." Yet when she speaks to groups of children about being an author, Sachs points to this childhood habit as a positive qualification for writing fiction. "Basically, the child who lies and the writer who weaves stories out of her own experiences, are each doing the same thing," she remarked in *SAAS.* "They are rearranging the bare, boring facts into a more harmonious, meaningful pattern. The child, of course, gets scolded for lying while the writer is praised for her imagination."

The young Sachs's penchant for telling tales and sometimes rearranging the truth seems to have been inherited. Sachs told *SAAS:* "Everybody told stories in my family, and everybody's stories were different.... My father's stories tended to deal with the epic and heroic.... Like myself, my father often embroidered reality and was the one member of my family not disturbed about my lack of truthfulness." The author remarked that "some of the best stories came from my mother's mother who had come to this country from Russia around 1900 with my mother and oldest uncle. She was the inspiration for the mother in my book *Call Me Ruth,*" in which a young immigrant girl learns to adapt to life in America and is embarrassed by her parents who cling to the traditions of their home country.

Sachs's generally happy childhood was saddened in 1940 when her mother died. The author recalled in *SAAS* that "it wasn't easy for our family to do without her. She brought order and stability to our lives that we never regained after her death." The author's father remarried and the family moved to a new neighborhood, but Sachs liked her old school and decided to finish her high school education there. The author remembers high school fondly. She had many friends, belonged to clubs, and was the editor of the school newspaper.

Sachs planned to go to college even though her father objected because he thought she should work full-time and contribute financially to the household. To achieve her goal, the author moved out of her father's house when she was seventeen and continued her education. She wrote in *SAAS* that "it wasn't easy. I had to support myself and overcome my natural laziness. It was hard juggling all the various part-time jobs I worked at and buckling down to the kind of scholarship Hunter College demanded of its students." Her move to Brooklyn from the Bronx allowed her to meet her future husband, Morris Sachs, when they both belonged to a left-wing youth organization.

The couple got married while they were still in college. After graduating Sachs responded to an ad and got a job as a library trainee with the Brooklyn Public Library. Remembering the bossy librarians of her own youth, her approach to her job was "never to interfere with children who wanted to pick out books for themselves." She stayed at the Brooklyn library for ten years and even went back to school to get her master's degree in library science. In *SAAS* Sachs explained, "I loved my job, most of the kids, and the books. I read and read and read and somewhere along the line I realized what kind of books I wanted to write and who I wanted to write for."

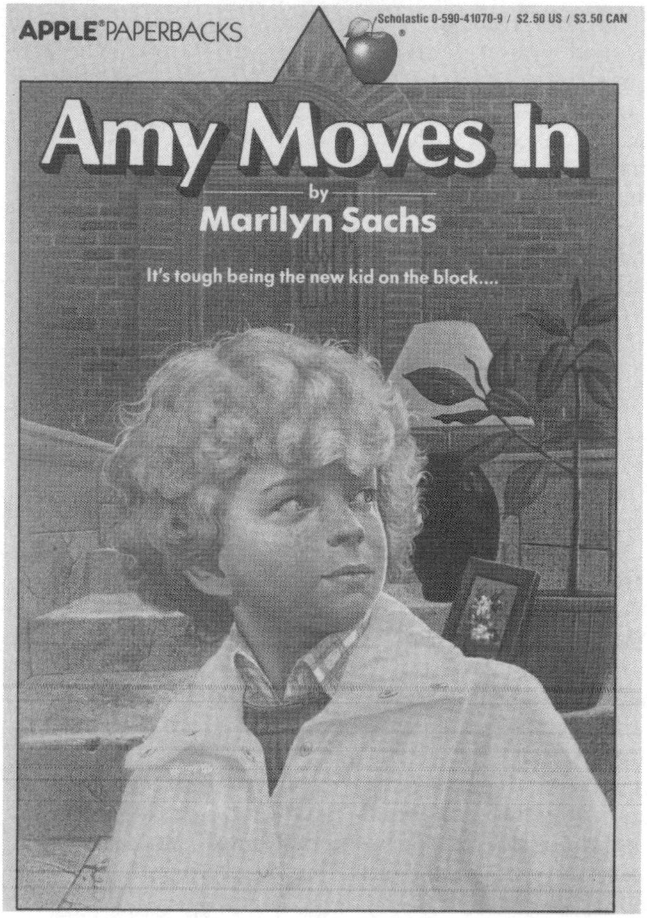

Cover of *Amy Moves In,* by Marilyn Sachs. Illustrated by Judith Gwyn Brown.

After making this decision, Sachs took a six-month leave of absence in 1954 to write her first book, *Amy Moves In.* Sachs disclosed in *SAAS* that this work was "based on my own childhood, [and] had as its main character a girl named Amy who told lies. Her family was poor, Jewish, lived in the city, and didn't celebrate any Jewish holidays in the course of the story. The father had trouble keeping a job and the mother, hurt in an accident, was still in the hospital by the end of the book." The author thought *Amy Moves In* was a "masterpiece," but editors at publishing companies rejected it because Sachs's realistic portrayal of an imperfect family's life during the troubled economic period of the Depression seemed too negative and depressing for young readers. Most children's books published at the time had happy endings, and editors wanted Sachs to change her book to fit this formula. However, the author refused and had to wait ten years to get *Amy Moves In* published.

During that time, Sachs moved to San Francisco, California, with her husband and their two young children, Anne and Paul. The author was able to continue her work as a librarian at the San Francisco Public Library. Sachs admitted that at the time she was so busy caring for her children and working part-time that she didn't think she could be a writer. However, in

1963, she received a letter from a person she had worked with at the Brooklyn Public Library—who had since taken a job as an editor at a book publishing company—asking for the manuscript of *Amy Moves In.* Sachs looked over the work she had once considered a masterpiece and realized that it could be improved, but she sent it anyway, assuming it would be rejected again. Two weeks later she was pleasantly surprised when she received another letter saying the book was going to be published. Sachs's first literary enterprise was received favorably by critics. A *Virginia Kirkus' Service* reviewer called the work a "very funny book that still offers readers valid insights into people and their behavior.... it is true to its time and true to the unchanging conditions of childhood."

The publishing of *Amy Moves In* marked a new phase of Sachs's life—that of a busy author. In her essay for *SAAS* she described her family's existence as "often a circus in those days. We never had much money—artists usually don't—and I never had a room of my own then, as [British author] Virginia Woolf prescribes for serious artists. But I wrote—in between childhood sicknesses, peace marches, flooded toilets, and all the other demands life made on my time. It was hectic and it was good." Sachs continued, "I wrote about a book a year. First, there were the Amy/Laura books which came out of my own childhood. Then *Veronica Ganz* which I always considered one of my best books. Veronica was a composite of all the bullies who terrorized me as a child."

Sachs achieved success, and a loyal readership, with each new work she published. In preparing to write each new book, Sachs's first stage is conducting research on her subject, which can take a month. Next, she drafts a general outline of the book. After this, the actual writing begins which, according to Sachs, usually consists of a half of a chapter per day. While still following this regiment, the author has changed certain aspects of her writing over the years. When she started Sachs wrote in the third person, later switched to a first-person voice, and now uses both. Although Sachs initially incorporated certain events from her childhood into her books, she never repeats an actual incident from start to finish. "One thing you learn as a writer," she disclosed in *SAAS,* "is that you must distance yourself from your own life or nobody will want to read what you write. It's necessary to start off with something that matters to you, but you must learn how to open it up for your readers as well."

The author insists that her childhood love of books—which led to jobs as a librarian—was indispensable for her emergence as a popular children's author. In her essay for *SAAS,* Sachs offered advice to young people wishing to become writers. "Read! As much and as widely as you can. Read for pleasure and without realizing it, you will learn the craft of writing." She also insists that daydreaming "is indispensable for writers. Daydream! And if people ... criticize you for wasting your time ... tell them you are gathering material for your next book."

Explaining her satisfaction with her chosen career path as an author, Sachs remarked in *SAAS* that "one of the pleasures of writing is that what you couldn't do in your own life, you can do in your books. You have a second chance." This vocation has been rewarding for Sachs, and she concluded: "I feel very lucky in my life and my work.... Each book I write is a new territory for me, new research, new thoughts, new daydreams."

WORKS CITED:

Review of *Amy Moves In, Virginia Kirkus' Service,* May 1, 1964, p. 453.

Sachs, Marilyn, *Something about the Author Autobiography Series,* Volume 2, Gale, 1986, pp. 198-204 and 206-211.

FOR MORE INFORMATION SEE:

BOOKS

Children's Literature Review, Volume 2, Gale, 1976.

Contemporary Literary Criticism, Volume 35, Gale, 1985.

PERIODICALS

New York Times Book Review, November 7, 1971; March 11, 1973; March 21, 1976; April 1, 1984.

Times Literary Supplement, October 1, 1976; May 29, 1987.

* * *

SAGE, Juniper
See BROWN, Margaret Wise and HURD, Edith (Thacher)

* * *

SAINT-EXUPERY, Antoine (Jean Baptiste Marie Roger) de 1900-1944

PERSONAL: Born June 29, 1900, in Lyons, France; reported "missing in action," July 31, 1944, in Southern France; son of Cesar de Saint-Exupery; married wife, Consuelo, the former Countess Manuelo. *Education:* Attended the College de Fribourg, Switzerland, Ecole Bossuet and Lycee Saint-Louis (naval preparatory schools), 1917-19, and a school for air cadets at Avord, France, 1922.

CAREER: Aviator and writer. Tile manufacturer, flight instructor, and truck salesperson, 1920s; Latecoere Co. (now Air France), Toulouse, France, commercial air pilot flying between France and western Africa, 1926-27; commander of airport at Cape Juby, Morocco, 1927-28; directed Argentinean subsidiary of company and established airmail route in South America from Brazil to Patagonia, 1929-31; test pilot of hydroplanes over Mediterranean Sea, Perpignan, France, 1933; publicity agent and magazine writer for Air France, 1934; foreign correspondent for newspapers, including *Paris Soir* and *Intransigeant,* covering such events as the Spanish Civil War, beginning in 1935; pilot for Air France, late 1930s; lecturer and free-lance writer in the United States, 1940-

Antoine de Saint-Exupery

43. *Military service:* Served in the French Army Air Force, 1921-26, and during World War II; became captain in Air Corps Reserve, 1939; instructor for flying squadron in northern Africa, 1943; reconnaissance pilot between Algeria, Italy, and southern France, 1944; began final reconnaissance mission, July 29, 1944; received French Legion of Honor Award, 1929, for peaceful negotiations with Spaniards and Moors in Morocco; received a citation and the Croix de Guerre for courage on reconnaissance flights during the Battle of France, May 1940.

AWARDS, HONORS: Prix Femina-Vie Heureuse (France), 1931, for *Night Flight;* Grand Prize of the French Academy, 1939, for *Wind, Sand, and Stars* and previous writings; Prix des Ambassadeurs (France), 1948, for *The Wisdom of the Sands.*

WRITINGS:

IN ENGLISH TRANSLATION

Southern Mail, translated by Stuart Gilbert, illustrated by Lynd Ward, H. S. Smith & R. Haas, 1933, translated by Curtis Cate, Harcourt, 1972 (originally published as *Courrier sud* [also see below], Gallimard, 1929).

Night Flight, preface by Andre Gide, translated by Gilbert, Century, 1932 (originally published as *Vol de nuit,* Gallimard, 1931).

Wind, Sand, and Stars, translated by Lewis Galantiere, Reynal & Hitchcock, 1939 (originally published as *Terre des hommes,* Gallimard, 1939).

Flight to Arras, translated by Galantiere, illustrated by Bernard Lamotte, Reynal & Hitchcock, 1942 (originally published as *Pilote de guerre,* Gallimard, 1942).

Letter to a Hostage, translated by Jacqueline Gerst, Heinemann, 1950 (originally published as *Letter a un otage,* Brentano's, 1943).

Airman's Odyssey (selections), Reynal & Hitchcock, 1943.

The Wisdom of the Sands, translated by Gilbert, Harcourt, 1950 (originally published as *Citadelle,* Gallimard, 1948).

A Sense of Life, translated by Adrienne Foulke, Funk & Wagnalls, 1965 (originally published as *Un Sens a la vie,* Gallimard, 1956).

FOR CHILDREN

(And illustrator) *The Little Prince,* translated by Katherine Woods, Harcourt, 1943 (originally published as *Le Petit Prince,* Reynal & Hitchcock, 1943).

IN FRENCH

Courrier sud (film), [France], 1937.

Oeuvres Completes, Gallimard, 1950.

Carnets, Gallimard, 1953.

Lettres de jeunesse, 1923-1931, Gallimard, 1953, published as *Lettres a l'amie inventee,* Plon, 1953.

Lettres a sa mere, Gallimard, 1955.

Lettres, Club du Meilleur Livre, 1960.

OTHER

Contributor to periodicals, including *Harper's, New York Times Magazine, Senior Scholastic,* and *Navire d'Argent.*

ADAPTATIONS: Night Flight was filmed by Metro-Goldwyn-Mayer, 1933; *The Little Prince* was narrated by Peter Ustinov in a recording for Argo, 1972, and was also read in French as *Le Petit Prince* by Gerard Phillipe and Georges Poujouly for Everest, 1973; Paramount produced *The Little Prince* in 1974, with screenplay and lyrics by Alan Jay Lerner and music by Frederick Loewe.

SIDELIGHTS: An aviator and author, Antoine de Saint-Exupery combined his vocations to produce novels and essays that capture the excitement of the early days of air flight and probe the philosophical concerns of the early twentieth century. While in France he is known for the body of his work, in the English-speaking world he is best known for his fairy tale *The Little Prince.*

The third child of five in the aristocratic Saint-Exupery family, Antoine was born in Lyons, France. When Cesar de Saint-Exupery died in 1904, leaving the family impoverished, young Antoine and his sisters lived in the Var region at the Chateau de la Mole, which belonged to their maternal grandmother. Antoine was schooled at home until the family moved to Le Mans in 1909. There Saint-Exupery attended Notre-Dame de Sainte-Croix, a Jesuit school. He spent many vacations at Amberieu near Bugey, where at the air field he longed to become an aviator. This desire was strengthened when in the summer of 1912 he was given his first airplane ride by the then popular aviator Jules Vedrines.

In 1914 Saint-Exupery was sent to the College de Fribourg in Switzerland, and later he attended two Parisian naval preparatory schools for a short time. When he failed the entrance examinations for the naval academy, some biographers say purposefully, Saint-Exupery began his required military service. Assigned to an aviation regiment in Strasbourg, the young man was able to take flying lessons privately and earned a civilian license. Curtis Cate quoted Saint-Exupery in his biography of the aviator, *Antoine de Saint-Exupery:* "I adore this profession. You can't imagine the calm, the solitude one finds at twelve thousand feet in a *tete a tete* with one's motor. And then the charming camaraderie down below, on the field. You cat-nap on the grass, waiting your turn. You follow your friend's gyrations with your eyes, waiting for your turn to go up in the same plane, and you swap stories. They're all marvelous. Stories of engine failures in mid-country ... fairy tale adventures."

Soon Saint-Exupery was certified as a military pilot and in 1922 he studied at the school for air cadets at Avord.

From *The Little Prince,* written and illustrated by Antoine de Saint-Exupery.

After he finished his required military service, the young pilot, then engaged to Louise de Vilmorin, whose family disapproved of his profession, worked for a tile manufacturer. After Vilmorin broke off their engagement in 1923, Saint-Exupery became a flying instructor and worked as a traveling salesman before finding a position with the Latecoere aviation company. In 1926 he transported mail from Toulouse to Dakar, Senegal, and the following year he managed the airport at Juby in Morocco.

In his first novel, *Southern Mail,* Saint-Ex, as his friends called him, drew on his experiences to describe the romantic adventures of a pilot. As quoted in Rumbold and Stewart's *The Winged Life: A Portrait of Antoine de Saint-Exupery, Poet and Airman,* Saint-Exupery confided: "I have begun a novel. You are going to be amused. I've already done a hundred pages, but am doubtful about them. I'm always running up against the abstract in myself. I have an appalling tendency toward the abstract. It comes perhaps from my eternal loneliness." While establishing an air-mail route in South America from Brazil to Patagonia in 1929, Saint-Exupery met and married Consuelo Gomez Carrillo. In his second novel, *Night Flight,* he contrasted the rigors of night flying with the safety of marriage. Though he was ostracized by some of his friends because of his descriptions of them, it brought him fame when it won the Prix Femina.

While on leave in France in 1931, Saint-Exupery found himself unemployed when the South American airline for which he worked dissolved. He did some piloting of hydroplanes on the Mediterranean Sea for the Latecoere firm until he nearly drowned in a serious crash. By 1934 the author was working as a publicity agent for the newly formed Air France. The following year he became a foreign correspondent and during his short career as a journalist reported on many memorable events. Toward the end of 1935, Saint-Exupery and his mechanic attempted to break the time record for a flight from Paris to Saigon. The duo crashed in the Libyan desert and barely managed to survive until they were rescued by Bedouins. This event and many others formed part of *Wind, Sand and Stars,* a collection of anecdotes, reminiscences, and meditations on flying and politics that was a critical success in both the United States and Europe.

When World War II broke out, Saint-Exupery insisted on serving though he was past the normal age and was assigned to a reconnaissance unit. He took part in several dangerous but futile missions, which became the basis for *Flight to Arras.* With the fall of France to the German forces, the pilot escaped to New York City, where he was joined by his wife. The two years spent there were unhappy yet productive. He wrote free-lance articles for several magazines, completed *Letter to a Hostage,* an inspirational piece for the French under German domination, wrote and illustrated *The Little Prince,* and drafted much of *The Wisdom of the Sands.*

A fairy tale addressed to children, *The Little Prince* is the story of a pilot who crashes in the desert and encounters a child, the Little Prince, who has traveled to earth from his own small planet. The prince asks the pilot to draw a sheep—and a muzzle—for him to take home to keep the baobab trees under control. But the prince cannot let the sheep eat his beloved rose. The Little Prince describes his travels in search of sheep to the pilot before he returns to his home by asking a poisonous desert snake to bite him.

The Little Prince came about accidentally. According to Cate, at a luncheon with his publisher, Curtice Hitchcock, Saint-Exupery began doodling on his napkin. Hitchcock saw the drawing of what Saint-Exupery called "just a little fellow I carry around in my heart" and suggested that the author write a children's book. Though surprised, Saint-Exupery took up the task with enthusiasm.

When asked about his work habits, Saint-Exupery told his English tutor, Adele Breaux, in *Saint-Exupery in America, 1942-1943: A Memoir,* "Mostly at night. I prefer to write then.... I usually begin around eleven o'clock, or even later, with a tray full of tall glasses of strong black coffee within reach. It is quiet at this time of day. No visits, no phone calls, no interruptions. I can concentrate. I write through the night without being aware of fatigue or sleepiness. I never have the slightest ideas as to just when sleep overpowers me. Evidently I put my head down on my arm to think out a situation, and in the late morning I wake up in that position." Although the author had not drawn since childhood, he produced many illustrations in watercolor to bring his prince to life.

The story of *The Little Prince* is geared toward children, yet it contains philosophical overtones that are only understandable to adults. It focusses on themes of love and friendship, exploring what is most important in life, which is made clear in the words of the fox: "It is only with the heart that one can see rightly; what is essential is invisible to the eye." Reviewers have compared *The Little Prince* to works by such authors as Lewis Carroll, Jonathan Swift, and Charles Perrault. The English critic and author P. L. Travers, best known as the creator of *Mary Poppins,* wrote in a review for the *New York Herald Tribune* that *The Little Prince* "will shine upon children with a sidewise gleam. It will strike them in some place that is not the mind and glow there until the time comes for them to comprehend it." Thus, forty years after its publication, *The Little Prince* had sold nearly four million copies and continued to sell two hundred thousand copies annually.

In the spring of 1943 Saint-Exupery joined resistance military forces in North Africa, flying reconnaissance missions despite his age. He never returned from his July 29, 1944, mission, apparently shot down by the enemy over southern France. Four years later *The Wisdom of the Sands,* over one thousand pages, was published. Set in the desert, it is narrated by a Berber chieftain, who recounts his youth, assumption of leadership, and deeds. It has been likened to a series of variations on the themes that Saint-Exupery treated in his earlier works.

Saint-Exupery's writings have been praised for their lyricism, particularly his descriptions of flight, evocations of childhood, and visions of peace, both personal and global. He expresses a common theme, that is, the individual's happiness lies in his acceptance of a duty. With *The Little Prince,* Saint-Exupery both repeated his theme and created a classic of children's literature.

WORKS CITED:

Breaux, Adele, *Saint-Exupery in America, 1942-1943: A Memoir,* Fairleigh Dickinson University Press, 1971.

Cate, Curtis, *Antoine de Saint-Exupery,* Putnam, 1970.

Rumbold, Richard, and Lady Margaret Stewart, *The Winged Life: A Portrait of Antoine de Saint-Exupery, Poet and Airman,* Weidenfeld & Nicolson, 1953.

Travers, P. L., "Across the Sand Dunes to the Prince's Star," *New York Herald Tribune Weekly Book Review,* April 11, 1943, p. 5.

FOR MORE INFORMATION SEE

BOOKS

Children's Literature Review, Volume 10, Gale, 1986.

Dictionary of Literary Biography, Volume 72; *French Novelists, 1930-1960,* Gale, 1988.

Migeo, Marcel, *Saint-Exupery,* translated by Herma Briffault, McGraw-Hill, 1960.

Robinson, Joy D. Marie, *Antoine de Saint-Exupery,* Twayne, 1984.

Smith, Maxwell A., *Knight of the Air: The Life and Works of Antoine de Saint-Exupery,* Pageant Press, 1956.

Twentieth-Century Literary Criticism, Volume 2, Gale, 1979.

PERIODICALS

French Review, April, 1960.

Modern Language Quarterly, March, 1951.

Modern Language Review, April, 1974.

New York Times Book Review, August 31, 1986.

Time, August 4, 1986.

Washington Post Book World, July 27, 1986.

* * *

St. MEYER, Ned
See STRATEMEYER, Edward L.

* * *

SALINGER, J(erome) D(avid) 1919-

PERSONAL: Born January 1, 1919, in New York, NY; son of Sol (an importer) and Miriam (Jillich) Salinger; allegedly married Sylvia (a French physician; maiden name unknown), September, 1945, (divorced, 1947); married Claire Douglas, February 17, 1955 (divorced,

J. D. Salinger

October, 1967); children: (second marriage) Margaret Ann, Matthew. *Education:* Graduated from Valley Forge Military Academy, 1936; attended New York University, Ursinus College, and Columbia University (where he studied with Whit Burnett).

ADDRESSES: Home and office—Cornish, NH. *Agent*—Harold Ober Associates, Inc., 425 Madison Ave., New York, NY 10017.

CAREER: Writer. Worked as an entertainer on the Swedish liner *M.S. Kungsholm* in the Caribbean, 1941. *Military service:* U.S. Army, 1942-46; served in Europe; became staff sergeant; received five battle stars.

WRITINGS:

The Catcher in the Rye, Little, Brown, 1951.

Nine Stories, Little, Brown, 1953, published in England as *For Esme—With Love and Squalor, and Other Stories,* Hamish Hamilton, 1953.

Franny and Zooey (two stories; "Franny" first published in *New Yorker,* January 29, 1955, "Zooey," *New Yorker,* May 4, 1957), Little, Brown, 1961.

Raise High the Roof Beam, Carpenters; and, Seymour: An Introduction (two stories; "Raise High the Roof Beam, Carpenters" first published in *New Yorker,* November 19, 1955, "Seymour," *New Yorker,* June 6, 1959), Little, Brown, 1963.

The Complete Uncollected Short Stories of J. D. Salinger, two volumes, unauthorized edition, [California], 1974.

Contributor to *Collier's, Cosmopolitan, Esquire, Harper's, Saturday Evening Post,* and *Story.*

ADAPTATIONS: "Uncle Wiggily in Connecticut" (published in *Nine Stories*) was made into the motion picture *My Foolish Heart,* 1950.

SIDELIGHTS: With the publication of *The Catcher in the Rye* in 1951, J. D. Salinger not only defined a generation, but also gave young adults a character in whom they could see themselves—Holden Caulfield, "the innocent child in the evil and hostile universe, the child who can never grow up," writes Maxwell Geismar in his *American Moderns: From Rebellion to Conformity.* Its more than ten million copies have been translated into many languages; both a classic and an object of debate, the book made Salinger a literary phenomenon. Although his reputation and readership were unmatched by any other living writer of the time, he retreated to a primitive country house in Cornish, New Hampshire, only a few years after the appearance of his novel; he signed no autographs and refused to give lectures or interviews. "No one else has ever been known in quite the way that Salinger has—first as the creator of a voice and a consciousness in which a vast number of very different readers have recognized themselves, second as an elusive figure uneasy with his audience and distrustful of his public, and finally as a kind of living ghost, fiercely protective of his isolation," asserts Philip Stevick in the *Dictionary of Literary Biography.* A fence was eventually built around Salinger's house, and a *Newsweek* contributor explains that the only way to reach the residence is by way of a dog-patrolled fifty-foot cement tunnel from the garage. In his *J. D. Salinger,* Warren French quotes Salinger as having said: "I feel tremendously relieved that the season for success for *The Catcher in the Rye* is nearly over. I enjoyed a small part of it, but most of it I found hectic and professionally and personally demoralizing." Since 1965 Salinger has published nothing, but his voice continues to speak to countless readers of all ages.

Very little is known about Salinger's childhood. His father was a Jewish importer of hams and cheeses, his mother a Scotch-Irish gentile. Stevick maintains that the family's address indicates they led a prosperous life. Salinger attended several New York public schools before being enrolled in his first private school. In 1934, Salinger entered Valley Forge Military Academy in Pennsylvania, graduating two years later. Soon after, he briefly attended New York University and traveled in Europe. During this time, adds Stevick, Salinger was constantly writing and sending his stories to numerous magazines, and was first published in *Story* in 1940. Twenty-three stories appeared in "middle-range" magazines such as the *Saturday Evening Post, Mademoiselle, Good Housekeeping,* and *Collier's,* and were pirated for an unauthorized collection in 1974. "Salinger has disavowed those early stories and, on one occasion," observes Stevick, "took legal steps to enjoin their unauthorized publication."

Salinger's work first appeared in the *New Yorker* in 1946, and by 1948 he was publishing almost exclusively for this magazine. "He soon became 'a *New Yorker* writer' and a friend of its major editorial figures," observes Stevick, adding that Salinger "was honored by his presence in its elegant pages and by its high standards for fiction." The stories included in *Franny and Zooey* and *Raise High the Roof Beam, Carpenters; and, Seymour: An Introduction* first appeared in the *New Yorker,* and all exhibit a similarity of character. "Salinger discovered a focus that was to continue through a large portion of his fiction, namely the use of childhood, adolescence, or youth as both an object of interest in itself and as a thematic lever by means of which the nature of the wider world could be pried open," maintains Stevick, adding: "Sensitive and perceptive, Salinger's younger characters are unable to prevail against the hypocrisy around them. Or, authentic and bright on the one hand, fatally naive on the other, they conspire in their own failures."

The Catcher in the Rye continues this focus through the character of Holden Caulfield. The novel opens with Holden in a psychiatric hospital, recovering from some sort of breakdown. It is written in the first person, and describes the two days Holden spent in New York after being expelled from his third prep school. Holden's age dictates the type of language used in the novel, so all the slang and four-letter words used by adolescents are included. The novel has experienced a controversial history, focusing primarily on this raw language. French points out that the book was temporarily banned in both South Africa and Australia because it was thought to be immoral. And in 1956, adds French, the National Organization for Decent Literature in Nevada found the novel to be "objectional." It was also banned from an eleventh-grade English class in Oklahoma in 1961, and, in 1970, it was prohibited in one Carolina county for its obscenity. Many small-town libraries even kept their copy of *The Catcher in the Rye* on a restricted shelf after

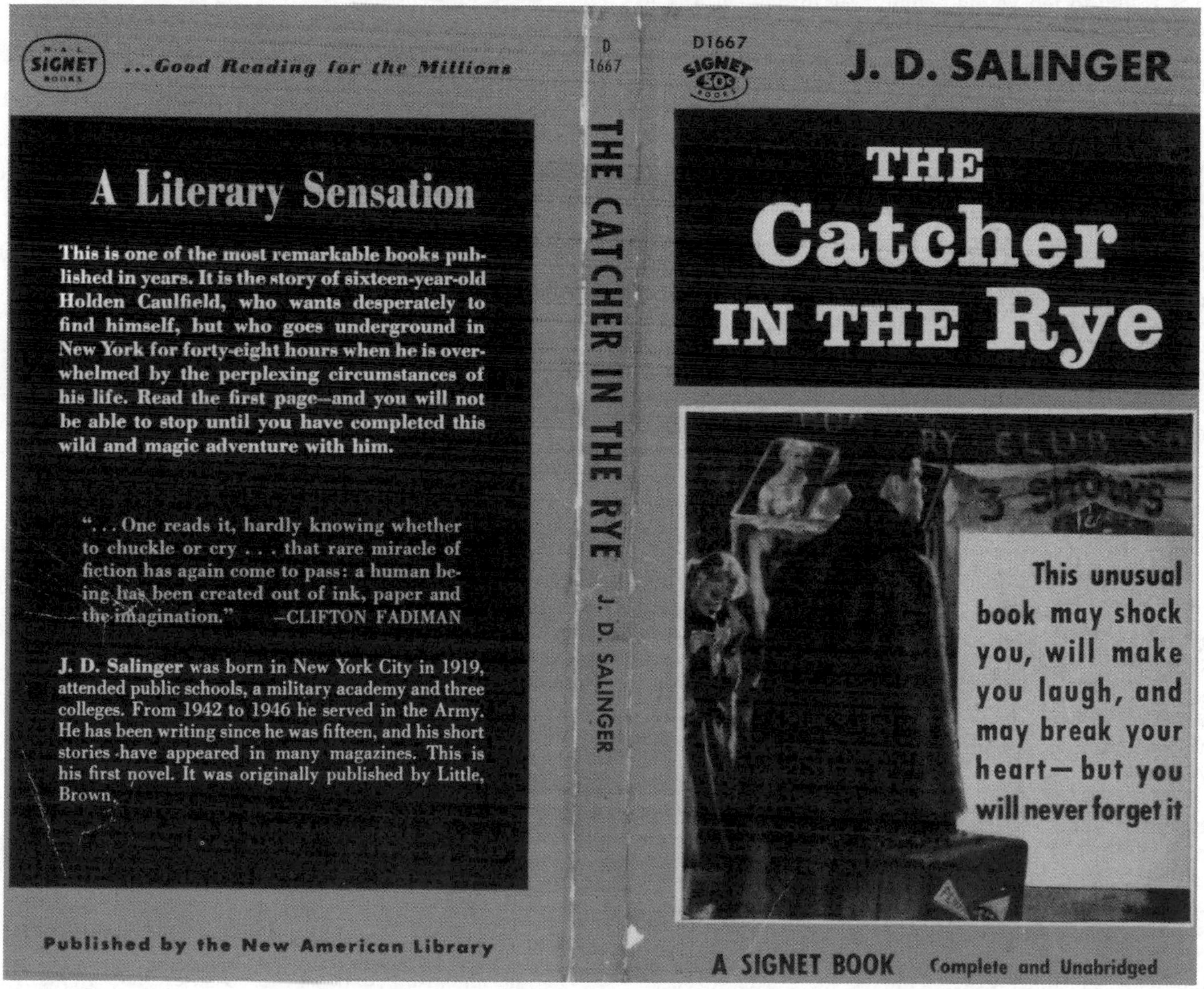

Cover of *The Catcher in the Rye,* by J. D. Salinger.

it had become a part of many high school and college courses. "There is probably not one phrase in the whole book that Holden Caulfield would not have used upon occasion, but when they are piled upon each other in cumulative monotony, the ear refuses to believe," explains Virgilia Peterson in the *New York Herald-Tribune Book Review.* Edward P. J. Corbett, though, argues in *America* that "Holden's swearing is so habitual, so unintentional, so ritualistic that it takes on a quality of innocence." Corbett also contends that "all of the scenes about sexual matters are tastefully, even beautifully, treated." Holden has fundamentally sound values, concludes Corbett, adding that "future controversy will probably center on just what age an adolescent must be before he is ready for this book."

J. D. Salinger is reported to have said he regretted that *The Catcher in the Rye* "might be kept out of the reach of children," states Peter J. Seng in *College English.* "It is hard to guess at the motives behind his remark," continues Seng, "but one of them may have been that he was trying to tell young people how difficult it was to move from their world into the world of adults. He may have been trying to warn them against the pitfalls of the transition." Throughout the novel, Holden is trying to deal with just such a transition and is presented as "the fumbling adolescent nauseated by the grossness of the world's body," asserts James E. Miller, Jr. in his *J. D. Salinger.* "Phoniness" is the word that Holden uses to describe almost everything in the world around him, says Seng, and he wants to protect children from all of these evils. But, as his sister Phoebe points out, Holden doesn't "like" anything—he is unwilling to compromise and this is why he is telling his story from a psychiatric hospital. "Holden will survive," continues Seng, "but first he must learn to love other human beings as well as he loves children. He must acquire a sense of proportion, a sense of humor. He must learn compassion for the human, the pompous, the phoney, the perverse; such people are the fellow inhabitants of his world, and behind their pitiful masks are the faces of the children in the rye."

The problems presented in *The Catcher in the Rye* seem to have a universal relevance. "For many young adults it is the most honest and human story they know about someone they recognize—even in themselves—a young man caught between childhood and maturity and unsure which way to go," point out Kenneth L. Donelson and Alleen Pace Nilsen in *Literature for Today's Young Adults.* "There is no question that Salinger's book captured—and continues to capture—the hearts and minds of countless young adults as no other book has," conclude Donelson and Nilsen. "I have no idea why Salinger has not in recent years graced us with more stories," states *New Republic* contributor Robert Coles. "It is no one's business, really. He has already given us enough," continues Coles, "maybe too much: we so far have not shown ourselves able to absorb and use the wisdom he has offered us."

WORKS CITED:

Coles, Robert, "J. D. Salinger," *New Republic,* April 28, 1973, pp. 30-32.

Corbett, Edward P. J., "Raise High the Barriers Censors," *America,* January 7, 1961, pp. 441-443.

Dictionary of Literary Biography, Volume 102: *American Short-Story Writers, 1910-1945,* Gale, 1991, pp. 258-265.

Donelson, Kenneth L., and Alleen Pace Nilsen, *Literature for Today's Young Adults,* Scott, Foresman, 1980, pp. 163-165.

French, Warren, *J. D. Salinger,* Twayne, 1963.

Geismar, Maxwell, "J. D. Salinger: The Wise Child and the 'New Yorker' School of Fiction," *American Moderns: From Rebellion to Conformity,* Hill and Wang, 1958, pp. 195-209.

Miller, James E., Jr., *J. D. Salinger,* University of Minnesota Press, 1965, p. 48.

Newsweek, July 30, 1979.

Peterson, Virgilia, "Three Days in the Bewildering World of an Adolescent," *New York Herald-Tribune Book Review,* July 15, 1951, p. 3.

Seng, Peter J., "The Fallen Idol: The Immature World of Holden Caulfield," *College English,* December, 1961, pp. 203-209.

FOR MORE INFORMATION SEE:

BOOKS

Alsen, Everhard, *Salinger's Glass Stories as a Composite Novel,* Whitston, 1983.

Authors and Artists for Young Adults, Volume 2, Gale, 1989.

Bloom, Harold, editor, *J. D. Salinger: Modern Critical Views,* Chelsea, 1987.

Carpenter, Humphrey, *Secret Gardens: A Study of the Golden Age of Children's Literature Review,* Volume 18, Gale, 1989.

Concise Dictionary of American Literary Biography: The New Consciousness, 1941-1968, Gale, 1987.

Contemporary Literary Criticism, Gale, Volume 1, 1973, Volume 3, 1975, Volume 8, 1978, Volume 12, 1980, Volume 56, 1989.

Dictionary of Literary Biography, Volume 2: *American Novelists since World War II,* Gale, 1978.

Filler, Louis, editor, *Seasoned "Authors" for a New Season: The Search for Standards in Popular Writing,* Bowling Green University Popular Press, 1980.

French, Warren, *J. D. Salinger, Revisited,* Twayne, 1988.

Grunwald, Henry Anatole, editor, *Salinger: A Critical and Personal Portrait,* Harper, 1962.

Gwynn, F. L., and J. L. Blotner, *The Fiction of J. D. Salinger,* University of Pittsburgh Press, 1958.

Hamilton, Ian, *In Search of J. D. Salinger,* Random House, 1988.

Hamilton, Kenneth, *Jerome David Salinger: A Critical Essay,* Eerdmans, 1967.

Hasson, Ihab, *Radical Innocence: Studies in the Contemporary American Novel,* Princeton University Press, 1961.

Laser, Marvin, and Norman Fruman, editors, *Studies in J. D. Salinger,* Odyssey, 1963.
Lundquist, James, *J. D. Salinger,* Ungar, 1979.
Marsden, Malcolm M., editor, *If You Really Want to Know: A Catcher Casebook,* Scott, 1963.
Rosen, Gerald, *Zen in the Art of J. D. Salinger,* Creative Arts, 1977.
Sadker, Myra Pollack, and David Miller Sadker, *Now Upon a Time: A Contemporary View of Children's Literature,* Harper, 1977.
Short Story Criticism, Volume 2, Gale, 1989.
Sublette, Jack R., *J. D. Salinger: An Annotated Bibliography, 1938-1981,* Garland, 1984.

PERIODICALS

American Book Collector, May-June, 1981.
Atlantic, August, 1961.
Book Week, September 26, 1965.
Commentary, September, 1987.
Criticism, summer, 1967.
English Journal, March, 1964; April, 1983.
Harper's, February, 1959; October, 1962; December, 1962.
Horizon, May, 1962.
Life, November 3, 1961.
Mademoiselle, August, 1961.
Minnesota Review, May-July, 1965.
Modern Fiction Studies, autumn, 1966.
Newsweek, May 30, 1960; January 28, 1963.
New York Post Weekend Magazine, April 30, 1961.
New York Times, November 3, 1974.
People, October 31, 1983.
Saturday Review, September 16, 1961; November 4, 1961.
Studies in Short Fiction, spring, 1967; spring, 1970; winter, 1973; summer, 1981; winter, 1981.
Time, September 15, 1961.
Village Voice, August 22, 1974.

* * *

SALTEN, Felix
See SALZMANN, Siegmund

* * *

SALZMANN, Siegmund 1869-1945 (Martin Finder, Felix Salten)

PERSONAL: Born September 6, 1869, in Budapest, Hungary; died October 8, 1945, in Zurich, Switzerland; son of Philipp and Marie (Singer) Salzmann; married Ottilie Metzl (an actress), April 13, 1902; children: one son, one daughter. *Education:* Attended schools in Vienna, Austria; mostly self-taught. *Religion:* Jewish.

CAREER: Novelist, journalist, playwright, and theatre critic. Worked in insurance office; had long-standing association with Viennese newspaper *Neue Freie Presse.*

MEMBER: Vienna P.E.N. Club (honorary president until 1933).

WRITINGS:

JUVENILE; ALL UNDER PSEUDONYM FELIX SALTEN

Der Hund von Florenz (also see below), Herz-verlag (Wien-Leipzig), 1923, translation by Huntley Paterson published as *The Hound of Florence: A Novel,* illustrated by Kurt Wiese, Simon & Schuster, 1930.

Bambi: Eine Lebensgeschichte aus dem Walde (also see below), P. Zsolnay, 1926, translation by Whittaker Chambers published as *Bambi: A Life in the Woods,* foreword by John Galsworthy, illustrated by Wiese, Simon & Schuster, 1928, new edition, illustrated by Girard Goodenow, Junior Deluxe Editions, 1956, new edition, illustrated by Barbara Cooney, Simon & Schuster, 1970.

Simson: Das Schicksal eines Erwahlten, P. Zsolnay, 1928, translation by Chambers published as *Sampson and Delilah: A Novel,* Simon & Schuster, 1931.

Funfzehn Hasen: Schicksale in Wald und Feld, P. Zsolnay, 1929, translation by Chambers published as *Fifteen Rabbits: A Celebration of Life,* illustrated by John Freas, Simon & Schuster, 1930.

Gute Gesellschaft: Erlebnisse mit Tieren, P. Zsolnay, 1930, translation by Paul R. Milton published as *Good Comrades,* illustrated by Bob Kuhn, Bobbs-Merrill, 1942.

Freunde aus Aller Welt: Roman eines Zoologischen Gartens, P. Zsolnay, 1931, translation by Chambers published as *The City Jungle,* illustrated by Wiese, Simon & Schuster, 1932.

Florian: Das Pferd des Kaisers (also see below), P. Zsolnay, 1933, translation by Erich Posselt and Michael Kraike published as *Florian: The Emperor's Stallion,* Bobbs-Merrill, 1934, new edition with translation by Norman Gullick published as *Florian: The Lippizzaner,* J. A. Allen, 1963.

Die Jugend des Eichornchens Perri (also see below), illustrated by Ludwig Heinrich Jungnickel, P. Zsolnay, 1938, translation by Barrows Mussey published as *Perri: The Youth of a Squirrel,* Bobbs-Merrill, 1938.

Bambis Kinder: Eine Familie im Walde, 1939, translation by Barthold Fles published as *Bambi's Children: The Story of a Forest Family,* edited by R. Sugden Tilley, illustrated by Erna Pinner, Bobbs-Merrill, 1939, new edition, edited by Allen Chaffee, illustrated by Phoebe Erickson, Random House, 1950, new edition, illustrated by William Bartlett, Grossett, 1969.

Renni der Retter: Das Leben eines Kriegshundes, A. Mueller, 1941, translation by Kenneth C. Kaufman published as *Renni the Rescuer: A Dog of the Battlefield,* illustrated by Diana Thorne, Bobbs-Merrill, 1940.

A Forest World, translated from the German by Milton and Sanford J. Greenburger, illustrated by Kuhn, Bobbs-Merrill, 1942.

Djibi: Das Kaetzchen, illustrated by Walter Linsenmaier, A. Mueller, 1945, translation by Raya Levin published as *Jibby the Cat,* Pilot Press, 1946.

(Editor) *Fairy Tales from Near and Far,* translated from the German by Clara Stillman, illustrated by Elice Johnson, Philosophical Library, 1945.

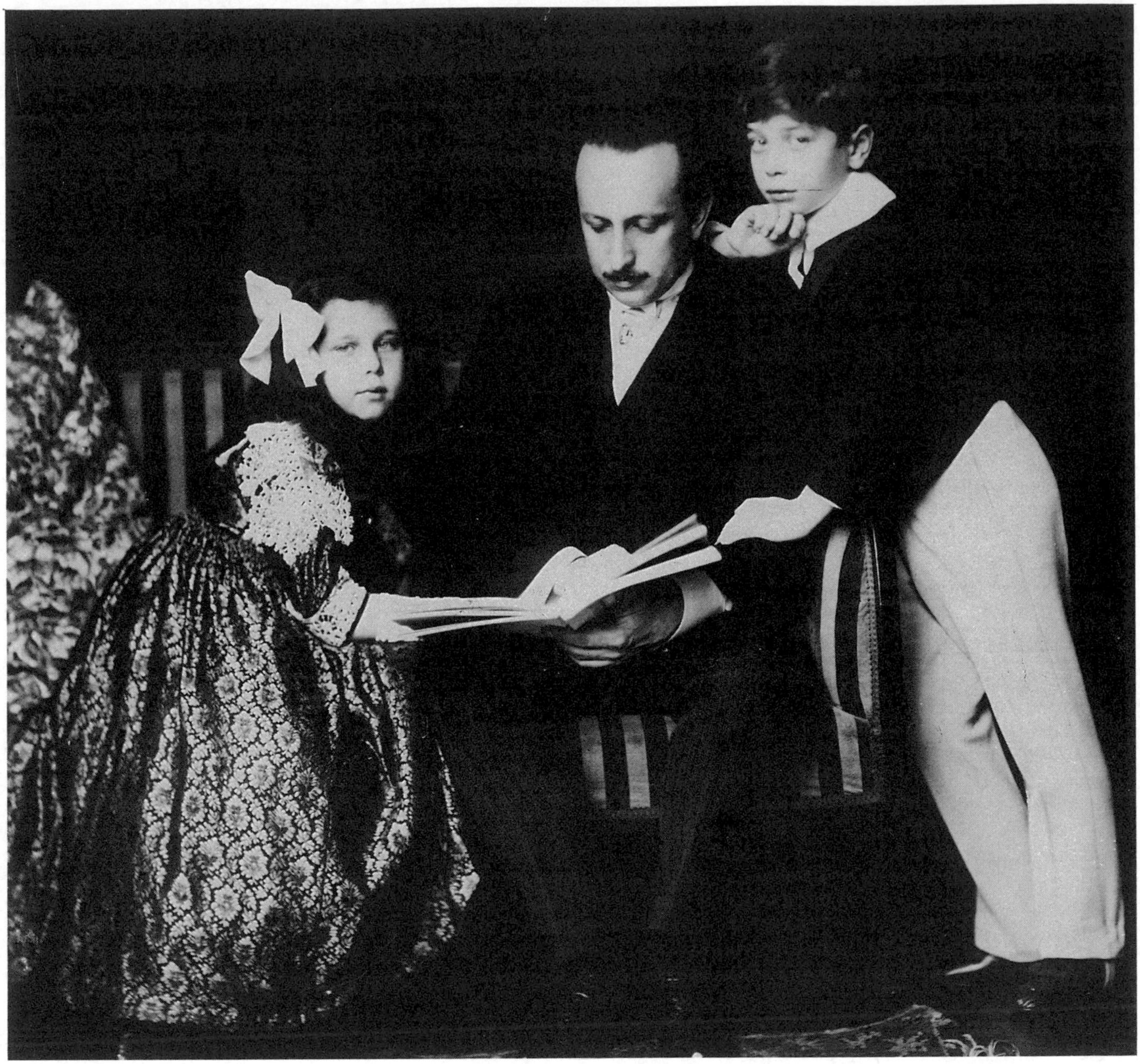

Siegmund Salzmann with his children

Kleine Welt, illustrated by Otto Betschmann, A. Mueller, 1944, translation published as *A Little World Apart,* Pilot Press, 1947.

(Editor) *Felix Salten's Favorite Animal Stories,* illustrated by Fritz Eichenberg, Messner, 1948.

OTHER

Author of the nonfiction works *Neue Menschen auf alter Erde* (title means "New Men of the Old Earth") and *Funf Minuten Amerika* (title means "Five Minutes of America"). Author of numerous plays produced in Europe. Contributor, under the pseudonym Martin Finder, to the magazine *The Beautiful Blue Danube* and other literary journals.

ADAPTATIONS:

MOVIES

Florian, Metro-Goldwyn-Mayer, 1940.

Bambi (animated; also see below), Walt Disney Productions, 1942.

Perri (also see below), Walt Disney Productions, 1957.

The Shaggy Dog, adaptation of *The Hound of Florence,* Walt Disney Productions, 1959.

Bambi Falls in Love (excerpts from the 1942 Disney movie), Walt Disney Home Movies, 1968.

FILMSTRIPS

Bambi (also see below), Encyclopedia Britannica Films, 1957, new version with teacher's guide, Eye Gate House, 1958, new version with captioned and sound versions with teacher's guide, Walt Disney Productions, 1970, new version, Universal Education and Visual Arts, 1971.

"Perri" series (includes *A Time of Adventure, A Time of Danger, A Time of Hunting, A Time of Learning, A Time of Preparing,* and *A Time of Together*), Encyclopedia Britannica, 1957.

RECORDINGS

Bambi (also see below), adapted by Marianne Mantell, read by Glynis Johns, Caedmon Records, 1973.

BOOKS

Grant, Bob, *Walt Disney's Bambi,* edited by Ida Purnell, Heath, 1944.

Bambi's Fragrant Forest (adapted by Disney Productions), Golden Press, 1975.

Bedford, Annie North (a pseudonym of Jane Watson), *Walt Disney's Perri and Her Friends,* edited by Bedford, Simon & Schuster, 1956, new edition, edited by Emily Broun, illustrated by Dick Kelsey, Simon & Schuster, 1957.

Razzi, Jim, *Bambi's Woodland Adventure,* Bantam, c. 1987.

Walt Disney's Bambi Comic Album, Gladstone, 1988.

SIDELIGHTS: Siegmund Salzmann was the creator of the immensely popular children's novel *Bambi: A Life in the Woods.* Although he was a respected author of nonfiction books, articles, and plays, Salzmann was best known for his work under the pseudonym Felix Salten. As Salten, his work in the field of children's literature yielded some of the most beloved twentieth-century novels, including *The Hound of Florence, Fifteen Rabbits,* and *Renni the Rescuer.* However, Salzmann achieved most of his fame by writing the book that introduced readers to the deer who would become internationally known through the Disney movie *Bambi.*

Salzmann was born in Budapest, Hungary, in 1869. When he was three weeks old he was moved to Vienna, Austria, where he spent most of his life. As a child Salzmann faced many hardships. His family was poor, and he was unable to gain a formal education; as a result his literary skills were largely self-taught. He was small for his age, frequently sick, and bullied by other children. Salzmann's poverty as a young man necessitated his acceptance of charity from a cousin. Out of guilt and pride, Salzmann insisted on working in his cousin's insurance office to earn his keep. Much of the work that he was given was drudgery—boring, time-consuming tasks. To provide his mind with more substantial exercise, Salzmann began to write stories. Fortunately, his talent was noticed by a group of influential writers who helped Salzmann establish himself as a journalist.

Emile Zola, the French novelist who founded the Naturalist movement in literature, was an idol of Salzmann's. When Zola died, Salzmann poured his talent, and his passion for Zola's work, into an obituary of the writer. Many readers found the obituary brilliant, and Salzmann gained considerable recognition for his work. In Vienna, his reputation as a journalist and author increased with subsequent writings. He began composing novels of both historical and contemporary natures, as well as plays, short stories, and essays. For a time he held the post of honorary president of the Vienna P.E.N. Club.

In 1923 Salzmann wrote, as Felix Salten, his first children's novel, *The Hound of Florence,* which would later be adapted into the popular Disney film *The Shaggy Dog.* The popularity of this book and subsequent titles spread not just across Austria, but the rest of Europe as well. Salzmann (and Salten) became well known throughout the continent. However, by the end of the thirties things began to go sour. The increasing political influence of Adolf Hitler's Nazi regime in Germany was extending itself into Austria. One of Hitler's primary obsessions was the persecution of Jews, particularly those in prominent positions. As a successful Jew, Salzmann was a target of Nazi harassment. When Germany launched a full scale invasion and occupation of Austria, Salzmann managed to flee the country and escape to Switzerland. He continued his writing in that country until his death in 1945.

Among the works that Salzmann undertook prior to leaving Austria, *Bambi: A Life in the Woods* would prove to be the book with which he was most closely identified. The novel tells the story of a young deer named Bambi growing up in the harsh environment of a German forest. As a youngster living under the protection and love of his mother, Bambi knows little of life's hardships. However, as he grows, he learns that nature can be cruel as well as beautiful. He also learns of a foreign presence, a danger, that often enters his forest home. The presence is man, and Bambi discovers that

From *Bambi,* by Felix Salten. Illustrated by Barbara Cooney.

both his life and the lives of his family and friends are threatened by "Him."

Bambi reflects Salzmann's love of animals and natural beauty, but the book also depicts danger, fear, and sorrow—less attractive aspects of life. Salzmann also used the novel to voice his opinions on humanity's role in nature. Margery Fisher interpreted Salzmann's message as one that called on humankind to appreciate nature without interference. As Fisher wrote in *Who's Who in Children's Books:* "Man's mercy, as we see through Bambi's reactions, is not to possess and tame but to succour and set free."

Although written and well received in 1926, *Bambi* did not reach America until 1928 and did not achieve large-scale success until 1942. In that year Walt Disney Studios released its full-length animated motion picture, titled *Bambi,* to worldwide acclaim. Salzmann worked on the book adaptation for the film while living in exile in Switzerland. When the movie became popular, attention returned to Salzmann's original work. Fisher, however, contends that there is a vast discrepancy between Disney's film version and Salzmann's novel. The reviewer found the film unnaturally whimsical and the novel realistic, often dark. "A child who came to the book after seeing Disney's cartoon," Fisher wrote, "would find it hard to believe that [Salzmann's] young deer was the same character."

In addition to the sequel *Bambi's Children: The Story of a Forest Family,* Salzmann returned to the character of Bambi for a brief appearance in his 1929 novel, translated a year later as *Fifteen Rabbits: A Celebration of Life.* Like the original *Bambi, Fifteen Rabbits* is a story about the trials and rewards of forest life. Salzmann follows the central characters of Hops and Plana, two rabbits, through the summer of their youth, their first harsh winter, and the rewards of their first spring. Along the way they encounter many hardships, losing many of their friends to the predators of the forest, including human hunters.

As he did in *Bambi,* Salzmann narrates *Fifteen Rabbits* from the perspective of wild animals. He details how the rabbits interact with one another, how they perceive other animals, and the chaos that ensues whenever humans enter the forest. In one sequence, Salzmann illustrates the ill effects of human intervention on an animal's life. A friend of Hops and Plana, a little rabbit named Epi, is captured by a young girl and taken to her home. Epi is placed in a box in a room with a small bird, a linnet. His heartsickness overwhelms him, and he is unable to eat or sleep. As Salzmann described the scene in his novel: "Toward evening Epi lay exhausted in his box. The linnet was singing. In his song the forest took form, with all its wild enchantment; passionate yearning for freedom was in his song, burning desire for the tree-tops, for the sun, for the cool green shadows. In his bittersweet trance Epi lay spellbound. He began to see his beloved thicket .... Many rabbits came running up together to greet him. On the meadow of his childhood the games of tag began anew. Epi raised his ears erect, he bounded more wildly than any of the others. Actually he merely gave a feeble twitch. While the linnet sang, Epi rolled over quietly on his side, stretched out and did not ever stir again."

Those familiar with Salzmann's life opine that much of this harsh realism in his fiction can be attributed to the events of his life. He was able to sympathize with animals driven from their homes because he himself was driven from his home by the Nazis. Salzmann knew of life's injustices firsthand—that sorrow and loss are a part of existence—and he sought to include that in his stories. In addition to depicting the love, humor, and beauty of an animal's life, Salzmann also showed its pain and suffering. By bluntly stating that even the most adorable and innocent creatures may meet an unjust end, he sought to inform his readers that nothing is guaranteed, and nothing should be taken for granted. Salzmann stressed that because life's beauty could be snatched away at any moment, it should be viewed as the most valuable and precious of gifts.

WORKS CITED:

Fisher, Margery, *Who's Who in Children's Books: A Treasury of the Familiar Characters of Childhood,* Holt, 1975, pp. 35-36.

Salten, Felix, *Fifteen Rabbits,* Delacorte, 1976, p. 143.

FOR MORE INFORMATION SEE:

BOOKS

Malten, Leonard, *Of Mice and Magic,* McGraw, 1980, p. 66.

* * *

SANCHEZ, Sonia 1934-

PERSONAL: Born September 9, 1934, in Birmingham, AL; daughter of Wilson L. and Lena (Jones) Driver; married Etheridge Knight (divorced); children: Rita, Morani Neusi, Mungu Neusi. *Education:* Hunter College (now Hunter College of the City University of New York), B.A., 1955; post graduate study, New York University. *Politics:* "Peace, freedom, and justice."

ADDRESSES: Home—407 W. Chelten Ave., Philadelphia, PA 19144. *Office*—Department of English/Women's Studies, Temple University, Broad and Montgomery, Philadelphia, PA 19122.

CAREER: Staff member, Downtown Community School, San Francisco, CA, 1965-67, and Mission Rebels in Action, 1968-69; San Francisco State College (now University), San Francisco, instructor, 1966-68; University of Pittsburgh, Pittsburg, PA, assistant professor, 1969-70; Rutgers University, New Brunswick, NJ, assistant professor, 1970-71; Manhattan Community College of the City University of New York, New York City, assistant professor of literature and creative writing, 1971-73; City College of the City University of New York, teacher of creative writing, 1972; Amherst College, Amherst, MA, associate professor, 1972-75; Uni-

Sonia Sanchez

versity of Pennsylvania, Philadelphia, PA, 1976-77; Temple University, Philadelphia, associate professor, 1977, professor, 1979—, faculty fellow in provost's office, 1986-87, presidential fellow, 1987-88.

MEMBER: Literature Panel of the Pennsylvania Council on the Arts.

AWARDS, HONORS: PEN Writing Award, 1969; National Institute of Arts and Letters grant, 1970; Ph.D., Wilberforce University, 1972; National Endowment for the Arts Award, 1978-79; Honorary Citizen of Atlanta, 1982; Tribute to Black Women Award, Black Students of Smith College, 1982; Lucretia Mott Award, 1984; American Book Award, Before Columbus Foundation, 1985, for *homegirls & handgrenades*; Pennsylvania Governor's Award in the humanities, 1989, for bringing great distinction to herself and her discipline through remarkable accomplishment.

WRITINGS:

JUVENILE

It's a New Day: Poems for Young Brothas and Sistuhs, Broadside Press, 1971.

The Adventures of Fat Head, Small Head, and Square Head, Third Press, 1973.

A Sound Investment and Other Stories, Third World Press, 1979.

ADULT

Homecoming (poetry), Broadside Press, 1969.

We a BaddDDD People (poetry), with foreword by Dudley Randall, Broadside Press, 1970.

(Editor) *Three Hundred and Sixty Degrees of Blackness Comin' at You* (poetry), 5X Publishing Co., 1971.

Ima Talken Bout the Nation of Islam, TruthDel, 1972.

Love Poems, Third Press, 1973.

A Blues Book for Blue Black Magical Women (poetry), Broadside Press, 1973.

(Editor and contributor) *We Be Word Sorcerers: 25 Stories by Black Americans,* Bantam, 1973.

I've Been a Woman: New and Selected Poems, Black Scholar Press, 1978.

Crisis in Culture—Two Speeches by Sonia Sanchez, Black Liberation Press, 1983.

homegirls and handgrenades (poetry), Thunder's Mouth Press, 1984.

(Contributor) Mari Evans, editor, *Black Women Writers (1950-1980): A Critical Evaluation,* introduced by Stephen Henderson, Doubleday-Anchor, 1984.

Under a Soprano Sky, Africa World, 1987.

PLAYS

The Bronx Is Next, first produced in New York at Theatre Black, October 3, 1970 (included in *Cavalcade: Negro American Writing From 1760 to the Present,* edited by Arthur Davis and Saunders Redding, Houghton, 1971).

Sister Son/ji, first produced with *Cop and Blow* and *Players Inn* by Neil Harris and *Gettin' It Together* by Richard Wesley as *Black Visions,* Off-Broadway at New York Shakespeare Festival Public Theatre, 1972 (included in *New Plays From the Black Theatre,* edited by Ed Bullins, Bantam, 1969).

Uh Huh; But How Do It Free Us?, first produced in Chicago, at Northwestern University Theater, 1975 (included in *The New Lafayette Theatre Presents: Plays With Aesthetic Comments by Six Black Playwrights, Ed Bullins, J. E. Gaines, Clay Gross, Oyamo, Sonia Sanchez, Richard Wesley,* edited by Bullins, Anchor Press, 1974).

Malcolm Man/Don't Live Here No More, first produced in Philadelphia at ASCOM Community Center, 1979.

I'm Black When I'm Singing, I'm Blue When I Ain't, first produced in Atlanta, Georgia at OIC Theatre, April 23, 1982.

Also author of *Dirty Hearts,* 1972.

CONTRIBUTOR TO ANTHOLOGIES

Giammanco, Robert, editor, *Poetro Negro* (title means "Black Power"), Giu, Laterza & Figli, 1968.

Jones, Le Roi, and Ray Neal, editors, *Black Fire: An Anthology of Afro-American Writing,* Morrow, 1968.

Randall, Dudley, and Margaret G. Burroughs, editors, *For Malcolm: Poems on the Life and Death of Malcolm X,* Broadside Press, 1968.

Lowenfels, Walter, editor, *The Writing on the Wall: One Hundred Eight American Poems of Protest,* Doubleday, 1969.

Adoff, Arnold, editor, *Black Out Loud: An Anthology of Modern Poems by Black Americans,* Macmillan, 1970.

Lowenfels, editor, *In a Time of Revolution: Poems From Our Third World,* Random House, 1970.

Jordan, June M., editor, *Soulscript,* Doubleday, 1970.

Brooks, Gwendolyn, editor, *A Broadside Treasury,* Broadside Press, 1971.

Randall, editor, *Black Poets,* Bantam, 1971.

Coombs, Orde, editor, *We Speak as Liberators: Young Black Poets,* Dodd, 1971.

Bell, Bernard W., editor, *Modern and Contemporary Afro-American Poetry,* Allyn & Bacon, 1972.

Adoff, editor, *The Poetry of Black America: An Anthology of the 20th Century,* Harper, 1973.

Chace, J., and W. Chace, *Making It New,* Canfield Press, 1973.

Gibson, Donald B., editor, *Modern Black Poets,* Prentice-Hall, 1973.

Henderson, Stephen, editor, *Understanding the New Black Poetry: Black Speech and Black Music as Poetic References,* Morrow, 1973.

Hunter, J. Paul, editor, *Norton Introduction to Literature: Poetry,* Norton, 1973.

Schevill, James, editor, *Breakout: In Search of New Theatrical Environments,* Swallow Press, 1973.

Iverson, Lucille, and Kathryn Ruby, editors, *We Become New: Poems by Contemporary Women,* Bantam, 1975.

Troupe, Quincy, and Rainer Schulte, editors, *Giant Talk: An Anthology of Third World Writings,* Random House, 1975.

Chapin, Henry B., editor, *Sports in Literature,* McKay, 1976.

Brooks and Warren, editors, *Understanding Poetry,* Holt, 1976.

Reit, Ann, editor, *Alone Amid All the Noise,* Four Winds/Scholastic, 1976.

Stetson, Erlene, editor, *Black Sister: Poetry by Black American Women, 1746-1980,* Indiana University Press, 1981.

Baraka, Amiri, and Amina Baraka, editors, *Confirmation: An Anthology of African-American Women,* Morrow, 1983.

Hollis, Burney, editor, *Swords Upon This Hill,* Morgan State University Press, 1984.

Rothenberg, Jerome, editor, *Technicians of the Sacred: A Range of Poetries From Africa, America, Asia, Europe and Oceania,* University of California Press, 1985.

Piercy, Marge, editor, *Early Ripening: American Women's Poetry Now,* Pandora, 1987.

Poems also included in *Night Comes Softly, Black Arts, To Gwen With Love, New Black Voices, Blackspirits, The New Black Poetry, A Rock Against the Wind, America: A Prophecy, Nommo, Black Culture,* and *Natural Process.*

OTHER

Author of column for *American Poetry Review,* 1977-78, and for *Philadelphia Daily News,* 1982-83. Contributor of poems to *Minnesota Review, Black World,* and other periodicals. Contributor of plays to *Scripts, Black Theatre, Drama Review,* and other theater journals. Contributor of articles to several journals, including *Journal of African Civilizations.*

SIDELIGHTS: In addition to being an important activist, poet, playwright, professor, and a leader of the black studies movement, Sonia Sanchez has also written books for children. She introduced young people to the poetry of black English in her 1971 work *It's a New Day: Poems for Young Brothas and Sistuhs,* created a moral fable for younger children in 1973's *The Adventures of Fat Head, Small Head, and Square Head,* and produced a collection of short tales for them in 1979's *A Sound Investment and Other Stories.* As William Pitt Root noted in *Poetry* magazine: "One concern [Sanchez] always comes back to is the real education of Black children."

Sanchez was born Wilsonia Driver on September 9, 1934, in Birmingham, Alabama. Her mother died when she was very young, and she had several stepmothers. Her father was a schoolteacher, and as a result she and her siblings spoke standard English instead of a southern or black dialect. It was not until her family moved to Harlem, New York, when she was nine years old that Sanchez learned the speech of the streets that would become so important to her poetry. Sanchez also stuttered as a child; this led her to writing, which she has done since she was very young.

Sanchez also learned about racism at a very young age. She recalled in an interview with Claudia Tate for Tate's *Black Women Writers at Work:* "I also remember an aunt who spat in a bus driver's face—that was the subject of one of my first poems—because he wanted her to get off as the bus was filling up with white people.... Well, my aunt would not get off the bus, so she spat, and was arrested. That was the first visual instance I can remember of encountering racism." She did not leave racism behind when her family moved north, however. She told Tate that "coming north to Harlem for 'freedom' when I was nine presented me with a whole new racial landscape. Here was the realization of the cornerstore, where I watched white men pinch black women on their behinds. And I made a vow that nobody would ever do that to me unless I wanted him to. I continued to live in the neighborhood, went to that store as a nine-year-old child, and continued to go there as a student at Hunter College. When I was sixteen to eighteen they attempted to pinch my behind. I turned around and said, 'Oh no you don't.' They knew I was serious." She has been fighting racism and sexism ever since.

After graduating from Hunter College in 1955, Sanchez did postgraduate study at New York University. During the early 1960s she was an integrationist, supporting the ideas of the Congress of Racial Equality. But after listening to the ideas of Black Muslim leader Malcolm X, who believed blacks would never be truly accepted by whites in the United States, she focused more on her black heritage as something separate from white Americans. She began teaching in the San Francisco area in 1965, first on the staff of the Downtown Community School and later at San Francisco State College (now University). There she was a pioneer in developing black studies courses, including a class in black English.

In 1969, Sanchez published her first book of poetry for adults, *Homecoming.* She followed that up with 1970's *We a BaddDDD People,* which especially focused on black dialect as a poetic medium. At about the same time her first plays, *Sister Son/ji* and *The Bronx Is Next,* were being produced or published. In 1971, she published her first work for children, *It's A New Day: Poems for Young Brothas and Sistuhs.* Shortly afterwards, she joined the Nation of Islam, or the Black Muslims. Sanchez enjoyed the spirituality and discipline of the religion, but she always had problems with its repression of women. She explained to Tate: "It was not easy being in the Nation. I was/am a writer. I was also speaking on campuses. In the Nation at that time women were supposed to be in the background. My contribution to the Nation has been that I refused to let them tell me where my place was. I would be reading my poetry some place, and men would get up to leave, and I'd say, 'Look, my words are equally important.' So I got into trouble.... One dude said to me once that the solution for Sonia Sanchez was for her to have some babies.... I already had two children.... I fought against the stereotype of me as a black woman in the movement relegated to three steps behind. It especially was important for the women in the Nation to see that. I told them that in order to pull this 'mother' out from what it's under we gonna need men, women, children, but most important, we need minds. I had to fight. I had to fight a lot of people in and outside of the Nation due to so-called sexism. I spoke up. I think it was important that there were women there to do that. I left the Nation during the 1975-76 academic year." While she was a Black Muslim, however, Sanchez produced her second children's book, *The Adventures of Fathead, Smallhead, and Squarehead.* A moral fable about a pilgrimage to Mecca, the tale began as a story for her own children. Much of her work for young readers is inspired by her children's requests for stories.

Because of the political nature of most of her writings and her involvement in black power causes, Sanchez feels that her academic career has suffered from persecution by government authorities. She told Tate: "While I helped to organize the black studies program at San Francisco State, the FBI came to my landlord and said put her out. She's one of those radicals.... Then I taught at Manhattan Community College in New York City, and I stayed there until my record was picked up. You know how you have your record on file, and you can go down and look at it. Well, I went down to look at it, because we had had a strike there, and I had been arrested with my students. I went to the dean to ask for my record, and he told me that I could not have my record because it was sent downtown. That's when I began to realize just how much the government was involved with teachers in the university. I then tried to get another job in New York City—no job. I had been white-balled. The word was out, I was too political.... That's how I ended up at Amherst College, because I couldn't get a job in my home state. That's what they do to you. If they can't control what you write, they make alternatives for you and send you to places where you have no constituency."

After leaving Amherst, Sanchez eventually became a professor at Temple University in Philadelphia, Pennsylvania, where she has taught for several years. She has also edited several books, and contributed poetry and articles on black culture to anthologies and periodicals. Summing up the importance of Sanchez's work, Kalamu ya Salaam concluded in *Dictionary of Literary Biography:* "Sanchez is one of the few creative artists who have significantly influenced the course of black American literature and culture."

WORKS CITED:

Root, William Pitt, *Poetry,* October, 1973, pp. 44-48.
Tate, Claudia, editor, *Black Women Writers at Work,* Continuum, 1983, pp. 132-148.
ya Salaam, Kalamu, "Sonia Sanchez," *Dictionary of Literary Biography,* Volume 41: *Afro-American Poets since 1955,* Gale, 1985, pp. 295-306.

FOR MORE INFORMATION SEE:

BOOKS

Children's Literature Review, Volume 18, Gale, 1989.

* * *

SANCHEZ-SILVA, Jose Maria 1911-

PERSONAL: Born November 11, 1911, in Madrid, Spain; son of Lorenzo (a journalist) and Adoracion Garcia-Morales Sanchez-Silva; married Maria del Carmen Delgado, 1933; children: six. *Education:* Attended El Dabate, Madrid.

CAREER: Author. Worked previously as a reporter, editor-in-chief, and assistant director for *Arriba,* Madrid, Spain, during the late 1930s and early 1940s, and as editor of the *Revista de las Artes los Oficios,* beginning in 1946.

MEMBER: General Society of Spanish Authors (appointed to council, 1963).

AWARDS, HONORS: Francisco de Sales Prize, 1942; National Prize for Literature (Spain), 1944, 1957; National Prize for Journalism (Spain), 1945; Mariano de Cavia Prize, 1947; Rodriguez Santamaria Prize, 1948; Grand Cross of the Order of Cisneros (Spain), 1959; Virgen del Carmen Prize, 1960; award for special services from the government of Peru, 1964; Hans Christian Andersen highly commended author, 1966;

Jose Maria Sanchez-Silva

Hans Christian Andersen Award, 1968; Grand Cross of the Order of Alphonso X (Spain), 1968.

WRITINGS:

IN ENGLISH TRANSLATION

Marcelino: A Story from Parents to Children, translated by Angela Britton, Newman Press, 1955 (originally published as *Marcelino Pan y Vino: Cuento de Padres a Hijos,* illustrated by Lorenzo Goni [Madrid], 1953).

The Miracle of Marcelino, translated by John Paul Debicki, Scepter, 1963 (originally published as *Marcelino Pan y Vino: Cuento de Padres a Hijos,* illustrated by Goni, [Madrid], 1953).

The Boy and the Whale translated by Michael Herron, illustrated by Margery Gill, McGraw-Hill, 1964 (originally published as *Adios, Josefina!,* illustrated by Goni, Alameda [Madrid], 1962).

Ladis and the Ant translated by Herron, illustrated by David Knight, McGraw-Hill, 1969 (originally published as *Un Gran Pequeno,* Editorial Marfil [Alcoy], 1967).

Second Summer with Ladis translated by Isabel Quigly, illustrated by Knight, Bodley Head, 1969 (originally published as *El Segundo Verano de Ladis,* Editorial Marfil [Alcoy], 1968).

UNTRANSLATED WORKS

Un Palato en Londres: La Vuelta al Mundo y Otros Viajes (title means "A Country Boy in London: The Return to Earth and Other Journeys"), Editoria Nacional (Madrid), 1952.

Adelaida y Otros Asuntos Personales (title means "Adelaida and Other Personal Affairs"), illustrated by Goni, Editoria Nacional, 1953.

Historias de Mi Calle (title means "Stories of My Street"), [Madrid], 1954.

Quince o Veinte Sombras (title means "Fifteen or Twenty Shadows"), Ediciones CID (Madrid), 1955.

Fabula de la Burrita Non (title means "Fable of the Little Donkey Odd"), illustrated by Goni, Ediciones CID, 1956.

El Hereje: Cuento para Mayores (title means "The Heretic: Tales to Elders"), illustrated by Alvaro Delgado, A. Aguado (Madrid), 1956.

Tres Novelas y Pico (title means "Three Odd Stories"), A. Aguado, 1958.

Cuentos de Navidad (title means "Christmas Stories"), illustrated by Jose Francisco Aguirre, Editorial Magisterio Espanol (Madrid), 1960.

San Martin de Porres (title means "Saint Martin of Porres"), Secretariado Martin de Porres (Palencia), 1962.

Colasin, Colason, Editoria Nacional, 1963.

Pesinoe y Gente de Tierra, [Madrid], 1964.

Cartas a un Nino Sobre Francisco Franco, [Madrid], 1966.

Tres Animales Son (title means "Three Animal Sounds"), Doncel (Madrid), 1967.

Adan y el Senor Dios (title means "Adam and the Lord"), illustrated by Goni, Escelicer (Madrid), 1969.

(With Luis de Diego) *Luiso,* illustrated by Goni, Doncel, 1969.

OTHER

Also author of *El Hombre y la Bufanda* (title means "The Man and the Neckcloth"), 1934; *Aventura en Cielo* (title means "Adventures in Heaven"); *El Espejo Habitado* (title means "The Lived-in Mirror"); and *Historias Menores* (title means "Little Stories"). Scriptwriter for motion picture *Ronda Espanola,* 1952.

SIDELIGHTS: One of the most renowned Spanish children's writers whose works have been translated into English, Jose Maria Sanchez-Silva is known in the United States as the author of *Marcelino, The Boy and the Whale, Ladis and the Ant,* and *Second Summer with Ladis,* all books which were first published in his native language. Sanchez-Silva's children's books have won praise for their poetic fusion of the magical and the real in themes centering on family, religion, and death through portrayals of relationships between children and animals. The Spanish version of *Marcelino,* likened to Antoine de Saint-Exupery's *The Little Prince,* has often been used as a textbook to introduce students to Spanish. "Sanchez-Silva is the greatest Spanish contemporary writer for children both as regards the quality and the quantity of his work," maintains a *Bookbird* contributor.

Sanchez-Silva was born in Madrid to literary parents: his father, Lorenzo, was a journalist, and his mother, Adoracion, wrote poetry. By the time Sanchez-Silva reached ten years of age he fell on hard times: his mother died and his father vanished, leaving him to provide for himself. He went to live with his godmother and worked in a series of odd jobs, including a drugstore errand boy, a hotel kitchen worker, and a tailor's helper. Sanchez-Silva was then placed in an orphanage when his godmother immigrated to Mexico, and in 1926 he began attending school in Madrid. Training in stenography and typing landed him a job in Madrid's city hall after he left school. In 1932 he won a scholarship to El Dabate, a school of journalism, after distinguishing himself in a class he attended there, and soon thereafter he began to work as a journalist. The following year, 1933, Sanchez-Silva married Maria del Carmen Delgado, the daughter of a judge, and over the course of their marriage the couple has had six children.

Sanchez-Silva's first book, *El Hombre y la Bufanda,* ("The Man and the Neckcloth"), a collection of short stories for adults, appeared in 1934, shortly after he and his wife returned from a trip to France, Cuba, Mexico, and the United States. He then settled into newspaper work, except for a short period when he worked as a salesman for the French automobile firm Renault. In 1939 he joined the staff of the Madrid newspaper *Arriba,* eventually becoming editor-in-chief, and then assistant director. In 1946 he was appointed editor of the *Revista de las Artes los Oficios.*

Sanchez-Silva began to travel widely after World War II, journeying to Italy on assignment for *Arriba* in 1946, and to England in 1948 to cover the winter Olympic games. In 1949 he went on what was termed in the *Third Book of Junior Authors* as a "round-the-world pilgrimage (commemorating the four hundredth anniversary of St. Francis Xavier's arrival in Japan)." The next year he covered the World Cup soccer tournament in Brazil, and he went to France, Holland, Belgium, and Sweden as a sports reporter in 1951.

Sanchez-Silva began producing more children's books in the mid-1950s, when he left the world of journalism for a short time. *Marcelino,* published in English in 1955, was among these works; it imaginatively and gently examines the serious topic that German critic Bettina Huerlimann describes in *Three Centuries of Children's Books in Europe* as "the glad acceptance of death." The story features a nine-year-old orphan boy, Marcelino, raised by monks, who enjoys killing his pets through elaborate means (characterized by Huerlimann as "an expression of the juvenile preliminaries to a passion for bull-fighting"). In an attic which the monks forbid him to enter is a figure of Christ carved out of wood. Marcelino persistently steals food to offer to the Christ figure, which comes to life in the boy's presence and finally persuades him to accept death—what Huerlimann terms as actually being "the door to true life."

The Boy and the Whale, published in English in 1964, concerns an imaginary whale who is named Josefina by her keeper, Santiago. The boy keeps Josefina in a glass of water when he goes to bed at night and sends her off to visit relatives when he goes on holiday. At the end of the story, as Santiago stands at the school gates ready to begin his first day in class, Josefina volunteers to die. Laurence Adkins, writing in the *School Librarian and School Library Review,* explains that "at the end [Santiago] can say good-bye with ease because he is grown up."

In *Ladis and the Ant,* published in English in 1969, Sanchez-Silva tells the story of a poor boy, Ladis, who is sent to live in the country with a forester. In the forest Ladis can speak with the ants and learns to love the insect world. The queen ant, Mufra, reduces Ladis in size so he can visit her subjects. Frances M. Postell relates in the *School Library Journal* that Sanchez-Silva imparts interesting information about the living habits of ants, "but the purpose of the contrived fantastical episodes is to provide a bridge for the chasm between the initially lonely, frightened, self-centered boy who returns home stronger, happier, and wiser." In *Second Summer with Ladis,* the sequel to *Ladis and the Ant,* Ladis's ant-friends engage in war with more powerful rivals. Under oath not to disturb the course of nature, Ladis must witness the defeat of his friends. At the end, however, Ladis takes Mufra and a few of her friends home in a matchbox, where they begin the colony anew.

Sanchez-Silva consistently manages to reveal something divine or magical about the everyday struggles of his child subjects. He claims in *Bookbird* to have found "no more dignified task than the occupation of education, upbringing and poetic development of children. I be-

From *Marcelino Pan y Vino,* by Jose Maria Sanchez-Silva. Illustrated by Lorenzo Goni.

lieve that the famous concept of 'Cherchez la femme' [look for the woman] is no longer a possible road for understanding the human predicament. From now on it must be 'Cherchez l'enfant' [look for the child]."

WORKS CITED:

Adkins, Laurence, review of *The Boy and the Whale, School Librarian and School Library Review,* July, 1964, p. 214.

De Montreville, Doris, and Donna Hill, editors, *Third Book of Junior Authors,* H. W. Wilson, 1972.

Hurlimann, Bettina, *Three Centuries of Children's Books in Europe,* edited and translated by Brian W. Alderson, Oxford University Press, 1967, pp. 76-92.

"Jose Maria Sanchez-Silva," *Bookbird,* December 15, 1968, pp. 18-19.

Postell, Frances M., review of *Ladis and the Ant, School Library Journal,* May 1969, pp. 93-94.

FOR MORE INFORMATION SEE:

BOOKS

Chevalier, Tracy, editor, *Twentieth-Century Children's Writers,* 3rd edition, St. James Press, 1989.

Contemporary Literary Criticism, Volume 12, Gale, 1980.

PERIODICALS

Kirkus Reviews, April 15, 1969, p. 442.

Library Journal, May 15, 1969, p. 1207.

New York Times Book Review, July 13, 1969, p. 26.

* * *

SANDBURG, Carl (August) 1878-1967 (Charles Sandburg, Charles A. Sandburg; Jack Phillips, a pseudonym)

PERSONAL: Born January 6, 1878, in Galesburg, IL; died July 22, 1967, in Flat Rock, NC; buried at Remembrance Rock, Carl Sandburg Birthplace, Galesburg, IL; son of August (a railroad blacksmith; original surname Johnson) and Clara (Anderson) Sandburg; married Lillian ("Paula") Steichen, June 15, 1908; children: Margaret, Janet, Helga (originally named Mary Ellen). *Education:* Attended Lombard College, 1898-1902. *Politics:* Initially a Social-Democrat, later Democrat. *Hobbies and other interests:* Walking.

ADDRESSES: Home and office—Connemara Farm, Flat Rock, NC.

CAREER: Held various jobs during his early career, including milk-delivery boy, barber shop porter, fireman, truck operator, apprentice house painter, film salesman for Underwood and Underwood, staff member with the *Milwaukee Sentinel* and *Milwaukee Daily News,* and city hall reporter for the *Milwaukee Journal;* secretary to Milwaukee Mayor Emil Seidel, 1910-12; worked for *Milwaukee Leader* and *Chicago World,* 1912; worked for *Day Book* (daily), Chicago, IL, 1912-13, 1913-17; *System: The Magazine of Business,* Chicago, associate editor, 1913; worked for *Chicago Evening*

Carl Sandburg

American for three weeks in 1917; Newspaper Enterprise Association, Stockholm correspondent, 1918, ran Chicago office, 1919; *Chicago Daily News,* 1917-30, served as reporter (covered Chicago race riots), editorial writer, and motion picture editor, and later continued as columnist until 1932; wrote weekly column syndicated by *Chicago Daily Times,* beginning 1941. Helped to organize Wisconsin Socialist Democratic Party. Presidential Medal of Freedom lecturer, University of Hawaii, 1934; Walgreen Foundation lecturer, University of Chicago, 1940; lectured and sang folk songs to his own guitar accompaniment. *Military service:* Sixth Illinois Volunteers, 1898; served in Puerto Rico during Spanish-American War.

MEMBER: American Academy of Arts and Letters, National Institute of Arts and Letters, Phi Beta Kappa (honorary), Chicago's Tavern Club (honorary), Swedish Club (Chicago; honorary).

AWARDS, HONORS: Levinson Prize, *Poetry* magazine, 1914; Poetry Society of America prize, co-recipient, 1919 and 1921; Phi Beta Kappa poet, Harvard University, 1928, William & Mary College, 1943; Friends of Literature award, 1934, for *Lincoln: The Prairie Years;* Theodore Roosevelt distinguished service medal, 1939; Pulitzer Prize in history, 1939, for *Abraham Lincoln: The War Years;* Pulitzer Prize for poetry, 1951; American Academy of Arts and Letters gold medal for history, 1952 and 1953; Poetry Society of America gold medal for poetry, 1953; Taminent Institution award, 1953, for *Always the Young Strangers;* honored by Sweden's Commander Order of the North Star on his seventy-fifth birthday, 1953; New York Civil War Round Table silver medal, 1954; University of Louisville award of merit, 1955; Albert Einstein award, Yeshiva College, 1956; Roanoke-Chowan Poetry Cup, 1960, for *Harvest Poems, 1910-1960,* and 1961, for *Wind Song;* International Poet's Award, 1963; Presidential Medal of Freedom, 1964; National Association for the Advancement of Colored People award, 1965, acclaiming Sandburg as "a major prophet of civil rights in our time"; Friend of American Writers award. Litt.D., Lombard College, 1928, Knox College, 1929, Northwestern University, 1931, Harvard University, 1940, Yale University, 1940, New York University, 1940, Wesleyan University, 1940, Lafayette College, 1940, Syracuse University, 1941, Dartmouth College, 1941, and University of North Carolina, 1955; LL.D., Rollins College, 1941, Augustana College, 1948, and University of Illinois, 1953; Ph.D., Uppsala University, 1948.

WRITINGS:

(Under name Charles A. Sandburg) *In Reckless Ecstasy,* Asgard Press, 1904.
(Under name Charles A. Sandburg) *The Plaint of a Rose,* Asgard Press, 1905.
(Under name Charles A. Sandburg) *Incidentals,* Asgard Press, 1905.
(Under name Charles A. Sandburg) *You and Your Job,* [Chicago], c. 1906.
(Under name Charles Sandburg) *Joseffy* (promotional biography; commissioned by a wandering magician), Asgard Press, 1910.
Chicago Poems, Holt, 1916.
Cornhuskers, Holt, 1918.
The Chicago Race Riots, July, 1919, Harcourt, Brace & Howe, 1919, reprinted with new introduction, 1969.
Smoke and Steel (also see below), Harcourt, Brace & Howe, 1920.
Slabs of the Sunburnt West (also see below), Harcourt, Brace, 1922.
Selected Poems of Carl Sandburg, edited by Rebecca West, Harcourt, Brace, 1926.
Songs of America, Harcourt, Brace, 1926.
(Editor) *The American Songbag,* Harcourt, Brace, 1927.
Abraham Lincoln: The Prairie Years, two volumes, Harcourt, Brace, 1927.
Good Morning, America (also see below), Harcourt, Brace, 1928.
Steichen, the Photographer, Harcourt, Brace, 1929.
M'Liss and Louie, J. Zeitlin (Los Angeles, CA), 1929.
Potato Face, Harcourt, Brace, 1930.
(With Paul M. Angle) *Mary Lincoln, Wife and Widow,* Harcourt, Brace, 1932.
The People, Yes, Harcourt, Brace, 1936.
Smoke and Steel [and] *Slabs of the Sunburnt West,* Harcourt, Brace, 1938.
A Lincoln and Whitman Miscellany, Holiday Press, 1938.
Abraham Lincoln: The War Years, four volumes, Harcourt, Brace, 1939.
Abraham Lincoln: The Sangamon Edition, six volumes, Scribner, 1940.
Bronze Wood, Grabhorn Press, 1941.
Storm over the Land, Harcourt, Brace, 1942.
Smoke and Steel, Slabs of the Sunburnt West [and] *Good Morning, America,* Harcourt, Brace, 1942.
Home Front Memo, Harcourt, Brace, 1943.
(With Frederick Hill Meserve) *Photographs of Abraham Lincoln,* Harcourt, Brace, 1944.
Poems of the Midwest, two volumes, World Publishing, 1946.
The Lincoln Reader: An Appreciation, privately printed, 1947.
Remembrance Rock (novel), Harcourt, Brace, 1948.
Lincoln Collector: The Story of Oliver R. Barrett's Great Private Collection, Harcourt, Brace, 1949.
(Editor) *Carl Sandburg's New American Songbag,* Broadcast Music, Inc., 1950.
Complete Poems, Harcourt, Brace, 1950, revised and enlarged edition published as *The Complete Poems of Carl Sandburg,* 1970.
A Lincoln Preface, Harcourt, Brace, 1953.
Abraham Lincoln: The Prairie Years and the War Years, Harcourt, Brace, 1954.
The Sandburg Range, Harcourt, Brace, 1957.
Chicago Dynamic, Harcourt, Brace, 1957.
The Fiery Trial, Dell, 1959.
Address before a Joint Session of Congress, February 12, 1959, Harcourt, Brace, 1959, published as *Carl Sandburg on Abraham Lincoln,* [Cedar Rapids], 1959, published as *Abraham Lincoln, 1809-1959,* J. St. Onge, 1959.
Abraham Lincoln (condensation of earlier work), three volumes, Dell, 1959.
Harvest Poems, 1910-1960, Harcourt, Brace, 1960.
Six New Poems and a Parable, privately printed, 1960.
Address upon the Occasion of Abraham Lincoln's One Hundredth Inaugural Anniversary, Black Cat Books, 1961.
Honey and Salt, Harcourt, Brace & World, 1963.
The Letters of Carl Sandburg, edited by Herbert Mitgang, Harcourt, 1968.
Seven Poems, illustrated with seven original etchings by Gregory Masurovsky, Associated American Artists, 1970.
Breathing Tokens, edited by daughter, Margaret Sandburg, Harcourt, 1978.
Ever the Winds of Chance, edited by M. Sandburg and George Hendrick, University of Illinois Press, 1983.
Fables, Foibles and Foobles, edited by Hendrick, University of Illinois Press, 1988.

FOR CHILDREN

Rootabaga Stories (also see below), Harcourt, Brace, 1922.
Rootabaga Pigeons (also see below), Harcourt, Brace, 1923.
Abe Lincoln Grows Up (nonfiction), illustrated by James Daugherty, Harcourt, Brace, 1928.
Rootabaga Country: Selections from Rootabaga Stories and Rootabaga Pigeons, Harcourt, Brace, 1929.
Early Moon (poems), Harcourt, Brace, 1930.
Always the Young Strangers (autobiography), Harcourt, Brace, 1952.

Prairie-Town Boy (autobiography), Harcourt, Brace, 1955.
Wind Song (poems), Harcourt, Brace, 1960.
The Wedding Procession of the Rag Doll and the Broom Handle and Who Was in It (chapter from the "Rootabaga" stories), illustrated by Harriet Pincus, Harcourt, Brace & World, 1967.
A Sandburg Treasury: Prose and Poetry for Young People, Harcourt, 1970.
Rainbows Are Made (poems), edited by Lee Bennett Hopkins, illustrated by Fritz Eichenberg, Harcourt, 1982.

OTHER

Also author of commentary for U.S. Government film, "Bomber"; collaborator on screenplay for the film "King of Kings," 1960. Author of captions for "Road to Victory" mural photograph show, 1942. Contributor of newspaper columns to Chicago Times Syndicate and radio broadcasts such as "Cavalcade of America" and foreign broadcasts for the Office of War Information during World War II. Contributor to *International Socialist Review, Tomorrow, Poetry, Saturday Evening Post, Masses, Little Review, New Leader, Nation,* and *Playboy.* Sandburg made numerous audio recordings of readings from his works, including excerpts from *Always the Young Strangers* and *The People, Yes* for Caedmon; other recordings for Caedmon are *Poems for Children, A Lincoln Album, Carl Sandburg Sings His American Songbag,* and *The Poetry of Carl Sandburg.*

ADAPTATIONS: The World of Carl Sandburg, a stage presentation by Norman Corwin, was published by Harcourt in 1961.

SIDELIGHTS: Carl Sandburg was "the one American writer who distinguished himself in five fields—poetry, history, biography, fiction and music," according to one of his friends, Harry Golden. Also known as the "Singing Bard," Sandburg once earned money by playing the guitar and singing folk songs all around the United States. Although today he is best known for his biographies of Abraham Lincoln and his poetry, the author also published several books for children. Only the three "Rootabaga" stories, however, were originally intended for young people; the other children's books were adaptations from his writings for adults.

Sandburg came from a large family of children born to two Swedish immigrants. He was raised in Galesburg, Illinois, in a small cottage near the railroad roundhouse and yards where his father worked as a blacksmith for fourteen cents an hour. The early years were tough for the young Sandburg. In order to fit into American society better, he called himself Charles in school, and he went by this name while writing his first books, too. When he was only eleven Sandburg had to work before and after school, sweeping floors in a law office and delivering newspapers. After he finished the eighth grade, he left school for a full-time job driving a milk wagon—sometimes even through blizzards. He also carried water for a road crew, sold refreshments at a resort, harvested ice on a frozen lake, and shifted scenery in a theater.

In June, 1897, Sandburg rode a freight train to Kansas to work in the wheat fields. A few months later he was back in Illinois, working for a house painter. When the Spanish-American war broke out he joined the army and served for eight months in Puerto Rico, but he never saw any combat. His first journalistic contributions were letters sent home from the war zone to the Galesburg *Daily Mail.*

When he returned to the United States, Sandburg was eligible for college tuition because of his war service, so he entered Lombard College in Galesburg. At the end of his first year there he was nominated for an appointment to the U.S. Military Academy at West Point, but he failed the entrance tests in arithmetic and grammar. He returned to Lombard College where his activities included playing on the basketball team, singing in the glee club, editing college publications, and delivering a prize-winning oration, all the while working at various odd jobs to support himself. He dropped out of college without getting his diploma, although in his later years he was to receive many honorary degrees.

One of the Lombard professors, Philip Green Wright, encouraged Sandburg to write and reawakened his interest in Abraham Lincoln, which had begun in

From *Wind Song,* by Carl Sandburg. Illustrated by William A. Smith.

childhood with the stories he had heard of the Lincoln-Douglas debate in Galesburg and the parades of Civil War soldiers that he had seen. Wright himself later had Sandburg's first two volumes of poetry published in 1905. In 1907 Sandburg moved to Milwaukee, where the *Daily News* published his first article on Lincoln. The next year he married Lillian Steichen—whom he called Paula—the sister of photographer Edward Steichen, who pioneered the use of photography as an art form.

Sandburg spent two years as a private secretary to the mayor of Milwaukee. During this time he contributed articles to the *International Socialist Review* under the name Jack Phillips. In 1912 the Sandburgs moved to Chicago, where the young journalist wrote for several newspapers and received his first literary recognition when some of his verses were published in *Poetry: A Magazine of Verse.* In March, 1914, his famous poem, "Chicago," won the two hundred dollar Levinson prize. In 1919 and 1921 his poems shared the Poetry Society of America prize, and in the years that followed he received many other awards and honorary college degrees.

Sandburg's first venture into children's literature was *Rootabaga Stories,* a work in the tradition of the American fairy tale that he wrote for his daughters. Sandburg's favorite topic, however, remained the life of Abraham Lincoln, so after his successful "Rootabaga" stories he decided to write a children's biography of the sixteenth president. He continued to satisfy his curiosity about Lincoln during the 1920s by travelling around the country in search of material concerning the president, a trip he financed by giving public performances in which he recited his poems and sang folk songs while accompanying himself on the guitar. He collected and classified Lincolniana for over thirty-five years, gathering such a wealth of documentation that he finally had to rent a barn in which to store it all. Concerning Sandburg's extensive work on Lincoln, Mark E. Neeley, Jr., wrote in the *Dictionary of Literary Biography* that the "historical writings of Carl Sandburg were the most important twentieth century factor in Abraham Lincoln's continuing popularity." In 1927 *Abraham Lincoln: The Prairie Years,* which covered Lincoln's life to 1861 and contained anecdotes and details of frontier days, was published.

Sandburg spent the next eleven years gathering material for his four volumes of *Abraham Lincoln: The War Years,* which were finished in 1939. During this time he interrupted his work on Lincoln to go on some money-making tours and to publish *American Songbag,* a collection of folk music which became a standard source for music and ballads. As a result of his works on Abraham Lincoln, Sandburg was later the first private citizen to deliver an address before a joint session of Congress. It took place on February 12, 1959, the 150th anniversary of Lincoln's birth.

During the Depression years of the 1930s, Sandburg developed an enthusiasm for President Franklin Delano Roosevelt and his New Deal, seeing in him a resemblance to Lincoln. From 1941 to 1945 Sandburg wrote articles for the *Chicago Times* in support of the Allied war effort. At the age of sixty-five he wrote his only novel, *Remembrance Rock,* at the request of the Metro-Goldwyn-Mayer movie studio, which wanted material for a movie that could help the war effort. However, the novel never reached the screen. After the war, the Sandburgs moved from the Midwest to the more favorable climate of Flat Rock, North Carolina. They called their new home there "Connemara." In 1952 Sandburg wrote the autobiography, *Always the Young Strangers,* which covers the first twenty years of his life. *New York Times* critic Robert E. Sherwood called the book "the best biography ever written by an American."

Sandburg won the Pulitzer Prize twice: in 1939 he won the prize in the category of history for *Abraham Lincoln: The War Years* when the committee classified the book as history in order to override a rule forbidding the acceptance of biographies of Washington or Lincoln; and in 1951 he was given the award for poetry. Sandburg died at Connamara on July 22, 1967. On September 17 of that year a national memorial service was held at the Lincoln Memorial to honor Sandburg; several of his fellow poets paid homage to the "Singing Bard" by reading his verses aloud at the ceremony.

WORKS CITED:

Neely, Mark E., Jr., "Carl Sandburg," *Dictionary of Literary Biography,* Volume 17: *Twentieth Century American Historians,* Gale, 1983, pp. 378-382.

Sherwood, Robert E., review of *Always the Young Strangers, New York Times,* January 4, 1954.

FOR MORE INFORMATION SEE:

BOOKS

Biographical Dictionary of American Journalism, Greenwood Press, 1989.

Concise Dictionary of American Literary Biography: Realism, Naturalism, and Local Color, 1865-1917, Gale, 1988.

Contemporary Literary Criticism, Gale, Volume 1, 1973, Volume 4, 1975, Volume 10, 1979, Volume 15, 1980, Volume 35, 1985.

Dictionary of Literary Biography, Volume 54: *American Poets, 1880-1945, Third Series,* Gale, 1987.

Writers for Children, Scribners, 1988.

OBITUARIES:

PERIODICALS

New York Times, July 23, 1967.

Time, July 28, 1967; July 31, 1967.

* * *

SANDBURG, Charles

See SANDBURG, Carl (August)

SANDBURG, Charles A.
See SANDBURG, Carl (August)

* * *

SAUNDERS, Caleb
See HEINLEIN, Robert A(nson)

* * *

SAVITZ, Harriet May 1933-

PERSONAL: Born May 19, 1933, in Newark, NJ; daughter of Samuel and Susan (Trulick) Blatstein; married Ephraim Savitz (a pharmacist); children: Beth, Steven. *Education:* Attended evening classes at Upsala College, one year, and Rutgers University, one year. *Religion:* Jewish.

ADDRESSES: Home—412 Park Place Ave., Bradley Beach, NJ 07720. *Agent*—Curtis Brown Ltd., 10 Astor Place, New York, NY 10003.

CAREER: Writer. Teacher of writing, Philadelphia Writer's Conference; guest lecturer in English literature, University of Pennsylvania. Holds workshops in novel-writing; helped organize workshop at Philadelphia's Free Library for the Blind to sensitize the media to the needs of the disabled.

MEMBER: National League of American Pen Women, National Wheelchair Athletic Association, Disabled in Action, VEEP (Very Exciting Education Program), Pennsylvania Wheelchair Athletic Association, Children's Reading Round Table, Philadelphia (co-founder, 1965; member of steering committee, 1966—).

AWARDS, HONORS: Dorothy Canfield Fisher Memorial Children's Book Award nomination, 1971, for *Fly, Wheels, Fly!; The Lionhearted* was listed in University of Iowa's Books for Young Adults, 1975-76, among the most popular books read by teenagers; Outstanding Author Award, Pennsylvania School Library Association, 1981; received recognition for *Wheelchair Champions,* 1981, from the President's Committee for the Handicapped in celebration of the International Year of Disabled Persons; California Young Reader Medal nomination, high school category, 1983-84, for *Run, Don't Walk.*

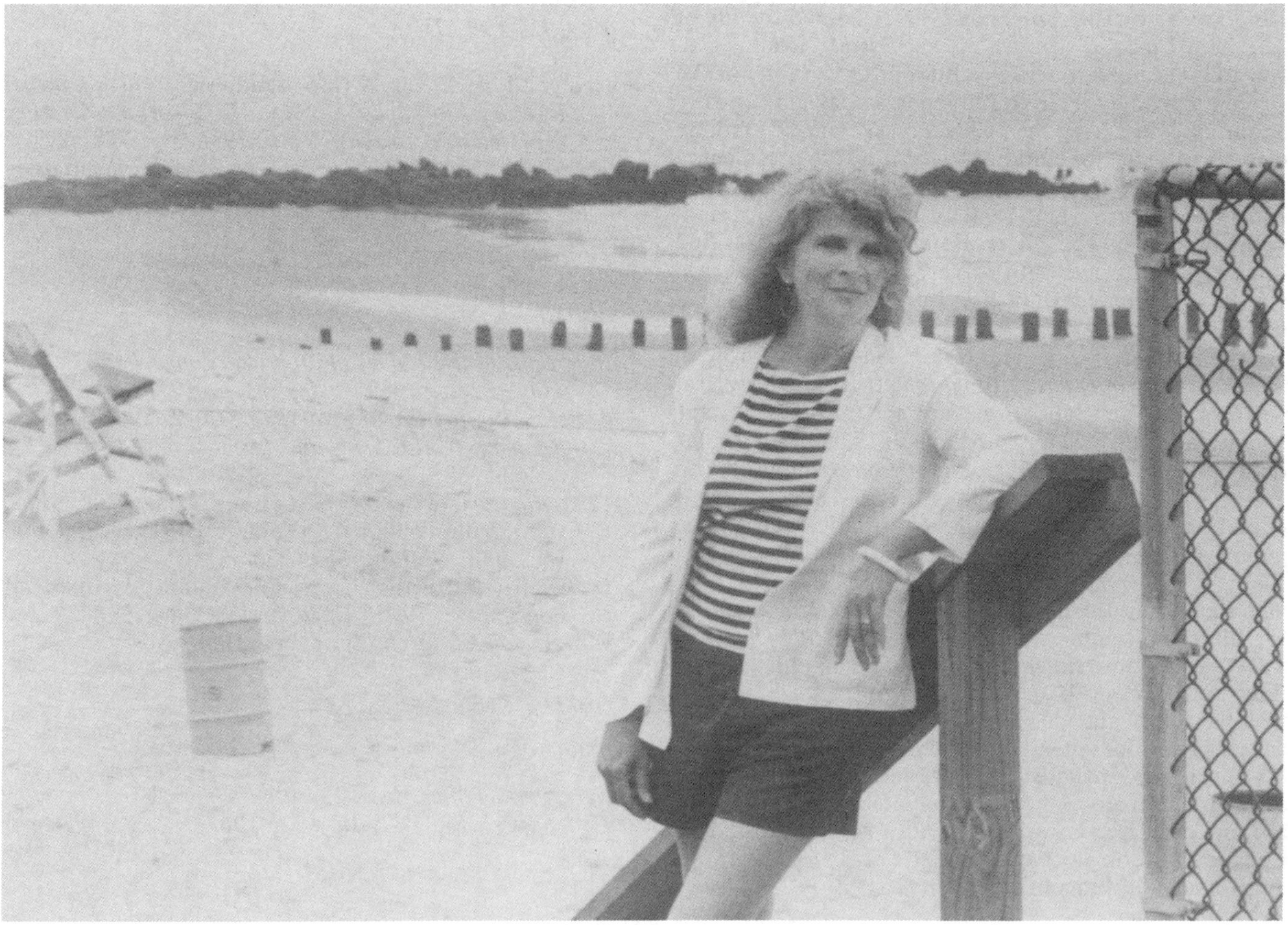

Harriet May Savitz

WRITINGS:

JUVENILE FICTION

(With Maria Caporale Shecktor) *The Moon Is Mine* (short stories), illustrated by Charles Robinson, John Day, 1968.

(With Shecktor) *Peter and Other Stories,* John Day, 1969.

Fly, Wheels, Fly!, John Day, 1970.

On the Move, John Day, 1973.

The Lionhearted, John Day, 1975.

Run, Don't Walk, Watts, 1979.

Wait Until Tomorrow, New American Library, 1981.

If You Can't Be the Sun, Be a Star, New American Library, 1982.

Come Back, Mr. Magic, New American Library, 1983.

Summer's End, New American Library, 1984.

Swimmer, Scholastic Inc., 1986.

The Cats Nobody Wanted, Scholastic Inc., 1989.

(With K. Michael Syring) *The Pail of Nails,* illustrated by Charles Shaw, Abingdon, 1990.

The Bullies & Me, Scholastic Inc., 1991.

NONFICTION

Consider—Understanding Disability as a Way of Life, Sister Kenny Institute, 1975.

Wheelchair Champions: A History of Wheelchair Sports, Crowell, 1978.

The Sweat and the Gold, illustrated by David C. Page, VEEP, 1984.

OTHER

Contributor of short stories to collections, including *Short Story Scene;* contributor to *Encyclopaedia Britannica.* Contributor to magazines and newspapers, including *Philadelphia Inquirer, Denver Post, Scholastic, Boys' Life, Children's Friend,* and *Ranger Rick.*

ADAPTATIONS: Run, Don't Walk was adapted and produced as an American Broadcasting Company "Afterschool Special" by Henry Winkler's production company.

SIDELIGHTS: Caring for others—for the handicapped, the lonely, or the disadvantaged—is a theme that runs through most of Harriet May Savitz's books for young adults. Her motivation may be an unfair law or lack of protection for a significant part of the population. From childhood, she was especially sensitive to the needs of others, as she explained in an essay for *Something about the Author Autobiography Series (SAAS):* "I was always looking at life with a third eye, an eye that I sometimes wished were closed. Why did I have to see the unhappiness in someone's face, or hear the pain in his voice?" But eventually this empathy helped Savitz create believable characters in her fiction: "I learned to use this third eye ... Dialogue became more than just words. It became words mixed with movement and expression and atmosphere. Characters had to be molded like pieces of clay, only instead of being objects that were set on a bureau, or shelf, they were meant to move about and come to life and I had the ability to make them do so."

Cover of *Fly, Wheels, Fly!,* by Harriet May Savitz.

Savitz was born in Newark, New Jersey, in 1933. Her father lost all of his savings during the Depression, so she spent much of her childhood living in a third-floor walk-up apartment in Hackensack where the trains on the railroad below made her bed shake. During these years, she found a sense of security in books and in her imagination. She began writing poems at age nine, and discovered at this early age—when the neighborhood bully took her scrapbook and was so impressed by her poetry that she never bothered Savitz again—that she could touch people with her words.

The family's finances would not allow Savitz to attend a four-year college, so she tried many types of work, but "I lost just about every job I acquired after graduating high school," she explained in *SAAS.* "I always wrote short stories, poems, and articles on the job." Still not willing to give up the idea of college, two nights a week after work she studied poetry, philosophy, and logic at Rutgers University, but without earning credits. Even after she married and became a mother, she continued to write. "I wrote a newsletter for the community where I lived, a short children's story for a religious organization, and many, many long letters, almost short stories in themselves, to friends, to politicians, to editors in the newspaper, to whomever would listen. The words were fighting their way out," she related in *SAAS.*

After her mother's death Savitz discovered that her mother had treasured every bit of writing she had done from the age of nine. About that same time she received in the mail an advertisement for a creative writing class. "Always one for believing that fate should not be denied, I felt it was a sign of what I was to do. I enrolled in the course and sold the first interview that we were assigned," she recalled in *SAAS.* "After ten years of floundering, I had my foot on the first rung of the ladder. All those years I had felt like a writer. Now I was being treated like one." She went on to complete numerous interviews, meeting all kinds of interesting people, learning her craft, and getting paid for it. Soon she began collaborating with Maria Caporale Shecktor, the teacher of her fiction course, on short stories and poetry for children. Together they published *The Moon Is Mine* in 1968 and *Peter, and Other Stories* in 1969.

At an autograph party for *Peter, and Other Stories,* Savitz's editor, Mary Walsh, introduced her to a person who became very important to the direction of her writing career: Charles L. Blockson, a black-history scholar and a promoter of wheelchair sports for the disabled. Through their interest in wheelchair sports, and with the input of quadriplegic Edward A. Davenport, Savitz became deeply involved in making the public more aware of the disabled—a dynamic but almost ignored segment of the population. She began by publishing several fiction books based on the lives of handicapped teenagers, including *Fly, Wheels, Fly!, On the Move,* and *The Lionhearted.* After researching the subject intensively, attending wheelchair sporting events and traveling with the teams, Savitz wrote her landmark nonfiction book *Wheelchair Champions,* published in 1978. Besides the compelling stories of champions, the book also contains a list of goals for the future and a list of questions for readers to consider under the heading "If You Were Suddenly Disabled."

One memorable event that served to inspire all who participated in or witnessed it was Savitz's "incredible journey," when she accompanied Davenport on a 110-mile trip at three miles an hour from Norristown to the capitol in Harrisburg, Pennsylvania—he in his motorized wheelchair and she following in a car. Davenport organized the journey to call public attention to the need for Transbus, a low-floored, ramped bus that handicapped and senior citizens could easily board. On the way they learned how treacherous the route really was—especially for Davenport, who braved weather, insects, traffic, railroad tracks, exhaust fumes, and dust. In her account for *SAAS,* Savitz noted, "We [also] learned about love, the love of the people waiting for us at the next stop, with food, with lodging, with hope. The disabled followed our route and often would be there on the side of the road, waiting to join Ed for a while." By traveling eleven hours a day they made it to Harrisburg on September 6, 1978. The newspaper headline the next day read "Wheelchair Odyssey Ends With Invitation to Speak," and Davenport concluded his mission by speaking before the State Transportation Commission.

In 1979 Savitz published *Run, Don't Walk,* the story of two teenagers who use wheelchairs, one with a golden retriever as a guide dog. Savitz was pleased when the book was made into an American Broadcasting Company "Afterschool Special" produced by Henry Winkler. A 1990 *Reader's Guide for Parents of Children with Mental, Physical, or Emotional Disabilities* cited the book as "a gripping, contemporary story" about the personal, social, and political barriers that the handicapped must overcome.

Recently Savitz moved to the New Jersey shore, which has been a healing and restoring influence since her family vacationed there during her childhood. But at the time, "I didn't know the ocean would become my next story. I didn't know that the waves would begin vomiting medical waste upon the beaches—syringes, bottles of blood instead of starfish and sea glass. I didn't know there would be oil slicks and garbage, all kinds of garbage left upon the beaches," she admitted in *SAAS.* "My poor friend was ill and suffering and the human population was responsible and I could not sit silently by while my friend suffered." Savitz addressed this problem by writing a young adult novel about ocean dumping.

Savitz once commented, "I find that the books walk into my life ... Sometimes I just stand somewhere, sit somewhere, walk somewhere, and I feel it. The book. It's around me, and if I look carefully, listen intently, and let myself feel its presence, the book introduces itself. 'How do you do,' I say. 'Let's get on with it,' it answers. From that moment on there is no other world."

WORKS CITED:

Moore, Cory, *A Reader's Guide for Parents of Children with Mental, Physical, or Emotional Disabilities,* Woodbine House, 1990.

Savitz, Harriet May, *Something about the Author Autobiography Series,* Volume 9, Gale, 1990.

FOR MORE INFORMATION SEE:

BOOKS

Fifth Book of Junior Authors and Illustrators, pp. 272-74, H. W. Wilson Co., 1983.

Something about the Author, Volume 5, Gale, 1973.

PERIODICALS

Bulletin of the Center for Children's Books, November, 1973; November, 1978.

* * *

SAWYER, Ruth 1880-1970

PERSONAL: Born August 5, 1880, in Boston, MA; died June 3, 1970; daughter of Francis Milton (an importer) and Ethelinda J. (Smith) Sawyer; married Albert C. Durand (a doctor), June 4, 1911; children: David, Margaret (Mrs. Robert McCloskey). *Education:* Columbia University, B.S., 1904. *Religion:* Unitarian.

CAREER: Short story writer and author of books for children. New York *Sun,* New York City, feature writer in Ireland, 1905, and 1907. Storyteller for the New York Lecture Bureau, beginning 1908, and started the first

Ruth Sawyer

storytelling program for children at the New York Public Library.

AWARDS, HONORS: Newbery Medal, American Library Association, 1937, and Lewis Carroll Shelf Award, 1964, both for *Roller Skates;* Caldecott Medal, 1945, for *The Christmas Anna Angel* (illustrated by Kate Seredy), and 1954, for *Journey Cake, Ho!* (illustrated by Robert McCloskey); Regina Medal, Catholic Library Association, 1965; Laura Ingalls Wilder Medal, American Library Association, 1965, for her "substantial and lasting contribution to literature for children."

WRITINGS:

JUVENILES

A Child's Year-Book (illustrated by the author), Harper, 1917.
The Tale of the Enchanted Bunnies, Harper, 1923.
Tono Antonio (illustrated by F. Luis Mora), Viking Press, 1934.
Picture Tales from Spain (illustrated by Carlos Sanchez), F. A. Stokes, 1936.
Roller Skates (illustrated by Valenti Angelo), Viking Press, 1936, reprinted, Peter Smith, 1988.
The Year of Jubilo (illustrated by Edward Shenton), Viking Press, 1940, reprinted, 1970, (published in England as *Lucinda's Year of Jubilo,* Bodley Head, 1965).
The Least One (illustrated by Leo Politi), Viking Press, 1941.
Old Con and Patrick (illustrated by Cathal O'Toole), Viking Press, 1946.
The Little Red Horse (illustrated by Jay Hyde Barnum), Viking Press, 1950.
The Gold of Bernardino, privately printed, 1952.
Journey Cake, Ho! (illustrated by Robert McCloskey), Viking Press, 1953, reprinted, Puffin Books, 1978.
A Cottage for Betsy (illustrated by Vera Bock), Harper, 1954.
The Enchanted Schoolhouse (illustrated by Hugh Tory), Viking Press, 1956.
(With Emmy Molles) *Dietrich of Berne and the Dwarf-King Laurin: Hero Tales of the Austrian Tirol,* (illustrated by Frederick Chapman), Viking Press, 1963.
Daddles: The Story of a Plain Hound-Dog (illustrated by Robert Frankenberg), Little, Brown, 1964.
My Spain: A Story-Teller's Year of Collecting, Viking Press, 1967.

CHRISTMAS STORIES

This Way to Christmas, Harper, 1916, revised edition, 1970, new edition illustrated by Maginal Wright Barney, Harper, 1924.
The Long Christmas (illustrated by V. Angelo), Viking Press, 1941, reprinted, 1966.
The Christmas Anna Angel (illustrated by Kate Seredy), Viking Press, 1944.
This Is the Christmas: A Serbian Folk Tale, Horn Book, 1945.
Maggie Rose: Her Birthday Christmas (illustrated by Maurice Sendak), Harper, 1952.
The Year of the Christmas Dragon (illustrated by Hugh Tory), Viking Press, 1960.
Joy to the World: Christmas Legends (illustrated by Trina S. Hyman), Little, Brown, 1966.

ADULT BOOKS

The Primrose Ring, Harper, 1915.
Seven Miles to Arden, Harper, 1916.
Herself, Himself, and Myself, Harper, 1917.
Doctor Danny (stories; illustrated by J. Scott Williams), Harper, 1918.
Leerie (illustrated by Clinton Balmer), Harper, 1920.
The Silver Sixpence (illustrated by James H. Crank), Harper, 1921.
Gladiola Murphy, Harper, 1923.
Four Ducks on a Pond, Harper, 1928.
Folkhouse: The Autobiography of a Home (illustrated by Allan McNab), D. Appleton, 1932.
The Luck of the Road, Appleton-Century, 1934.
Gallant: The Story of Storm Veblen (published serially as *Hillmen's Gold*), Appleton-Century, 1936.

RECORDINGS

Ruth Sawyer: Storyteller, 1965.

OTHER

The Sidhe of Ben-Mor: An Irish Folk Play, Badger, 1910.

From *Roller Skates,* by Ruth Sawyer. Illustrated by Valenti Angelo.

The Awakening (play), first produced in New York City, 1918.
The Way of the Storyteller, Macmillan, 1942, revised edition, Viking Press, 1977.
How to Tell a Story, F. E. Compton, 1962.

Contributor of over 200 articles, stories, poems, and serials to periodicals, including *Atlantic Monthly, Horn Book,* and *Outlook.* The College of Sainte Catherine Library, St. Paul, MN, owns a collection of Sawyer's manuscripts.

ADAPTATIONS: The Primrose Ring was filmed by Lasky Feature Play Co., 1917; the story "Christmas Apple," published in *This Way to Christmas,* was adapted for the stage as a two-scene play by Margaret D. Williams and published by Samuel French, 1939; *Journey Cake, Ho!* was adapted as a filmstrip, with sound and picture-cued text booklet, by Weston Woods Studios, 1967.

SIDELIGHTS: Ruth Sawyer was known as a teller of folktales, which she collected from around the world, and as a writer of stories about children from other cultures. Among her most popular books are the Caldecott Medal-winning *The Christmas Anna Angel,* about a Hungarian girl who yearns for a traditional Christmas celebration, and the Newbery Medal-winning *Roller Skates,* the story of a young girl who explores New York City.

As a child, Sawyer developed a love for stories from her Irish nurse, Johanna, who told her stories at bedtime. The nurse also gave Ruth a love for Irish folklore, an interest which later led her to study and collect folklore from around the world. At Columbia University, Sawyer majored in folklore and storytelling and after graduation, she worked for the New York Public Lecture Bureau, telling stories twice a week at different locations around the city. She also worked as a correspondent in Ireland for the *New York Sun* newspaper.

Many of Sawyer's books were inspired by folktales, especially those from Spain. Her *Picture Tales from Spain* was based on a trip she made to that country and on the stories she was told by the people she met. Another story from Spain was *Tono Antonio,* based on a young boy Sawyer met on this journey. The Spanish stories of Washington Irving had enthralled Sawyer when she was a girl, giving her a desire to visit Spain. "It may seem a far cry," she explained in *Horn Book,* "from a Maine farmhouse in midsummer fog to Granada in winter splendor. In years it spans half a lifetime. But for the child lying stomach down beside the hearth, lost in *The Tales of the Alhambra* and *The Conquest of Granada,* Washington Irving laid a starry trail across the ocean and those years."

One of Sawyer's most popular books was *Roller Skates,* the story of one year in the life of Lucinda, a young girl who is permitted to roller-skate wherever she pleases in New York City. In the course of her travels throughout the city, she meets and befriends people from all sorts of backgrounds, in the process learning something about the importance of individual freedom. In her Newbery Award acceptance speech, Sawyer explained: "If this book has any point at all it lies in that fact of freedom for every child, in his own way, that he, too, may catch the music of the spheres.... A free child is a happy child; and there is nothing more lovely; even a disagreeable child ceases to be disagreeable and is liked."

Roller Skates stirred a controversy when it first appeared because it dealt frankly with death. As Elizabeth Segel noted in *Horn Book,* "By confronting a sordid murder and the death of a tiny child, rather than the more easily accepted deaths of a pet or an aged grandparent, and by integrating these experiences with other aspects of Lucinda's year of discovery and growth, the book, in fact, deals more fully and frankly with the child's experience of death than do many of the books turned out these days."

Yet, most critics focus on the book's primary message of freedom. "Yes, Lucinda lives," Segel wrote, "and her vitality makes *Roller Skates* still readable and engaging. Depicted as neither a typical child nor an object-lesson heroine, Lucinda embodies a freedom as liberating to children's books as her year of roller-skating was to her own life."

Sawyer won a Caldecott Medal for the book *Journey Cake, Ho!,* a story derived from folktales of the American South. When a young boy must go on a search for a new home, he is given a "journey cake" to eat along the way. But the cake falls out of his pack and rolls away, and the boy's frantic efforts to retrieve the cake form the story. "Where did *Journey Cake, Ho!* have its start?," Sawyer asked in an article for *Young Wings.* "It began a hundred years ago in the mountains of Kentucky, North

Carolina, and Tennessee. The people told the story. They sang it. They laughed over it. But the story I have written is different from any versions I have heard, but the bare bones are the same. And I like it."

A large part of Sawyer's work are Christmas stories, many of them based on traditional or folk tales from around the world. *This Way to Christmas* features Sawyer's son David as the main character. When his parents are away, David's Irish caretakers tell Christmas stories to entertain him. These ten stories make up *This Way to Christmas.* Included is one of Sawyer's personal favorites, "The Voyage of the Wee Red Cap," a story she heard from an elderly tinker while visiting Ireland. When she returned to New York, Anne Carroll Moore invited her to tell the story to a group of children at the New York Public Library. "I shall always remember the faces of the American-born Irish boys who came over from a nearby parochial school," Sawyer recalled in *Horn Book.* "I shall always remember Miss Moore's lighting of candles; and the Christmas wishes that came out of that first library story hour. Those candles have never gone out for me; they still burn and always will."

The Long Christmas, dedicated to Sawyer's daughter, is a collection of thirteen holiday stories, one for each day from St. Thomas's Day to Candlemas. It contains, according to Jacqueline Overton in *Horn Book,* "Legends from many countries, ancient and modern, gentle and serious, joyous and gay, and she prefaced them with some of the traditional things that have gone into the keeping of Christmas: The good food, 'gay and of infinite variety,' the lighting, the bedecking, the festivity." Writing of *The Long Christmas* in *Horn Book,* Beryl Robinson remarked: "I return to this book yearly in anticipation of the Christmas season, rereading every tale, choosing those that will be a part of the year's festival."

Sawyer's *The Christmas Anna Angel* was inspired by a real-life experience of her Hungarian friend, Anna Kester. Anna recalled one Christmas in Hungary when she was a little girl and there was a food shortage. Despite the lack of flour and other baking essentials, Anna wanted to have a traditional Christmas cake to hang on the tree. Her desire becomes reality when she dreams of a Christmas angel and an angel appears. "Anna Kester's faithful memory, Ruth Sawyer's warm telling of the story of *The Christmas Anna Angel* and Kate Seredy's lovely pictures have worked their magic," Jacqueline Overton wrote in *Horn Book.* The book won Sawyer a Caldecott Medal in 1954.

Speaking in *Horn Book,* Sawyer once stated: "So often I have heard a sharp criticism from a parent when she has found a shabby, dog-eared book on the library shelf. How shortsighted is such a parent! I rejoice over every one I find. It speaks more eloquently than all the good reviews how much beloved that book has been."

WORKS CITED:

Overton, Jacqueline, "This Way to Christmas with Ruth Sawyer," *Horn Book,* November-December, 1944, pp. 447-460.

Robinson, Beryl, "To Ruth Sawyer," *Horn Book,* October, 1965, pp. 478-480.

Sawyer, Ruth, "Newbery Medal Award, Ruth Sawyer's Acceptance," *Horn Book,* July 1937, pp. 251-256.

Sawyer, Ruth, "I Hope You Like It," *Young Wings,* December, 1953.

Sawyer, Ruth, "Acceptance," *Horn Book,* October, 1965, pp. 474-476.

Segel, Elizabeth, "A Second Look: *Roller Skates,*" *Horn Book,* August, 1979, pp. 454-458.

FOR MORE INFORMATION SEE:

BOOKS

Dictionary of Literary Biography, Volume 22: *American Writers for Children, 1900-1960,* Gale, 1983.

Haviland, Virginia, *Ruth Sawyer,* Walck, 1965.

PERIODICALS

Bulletin of the New York Public Library, November-December, 1956, pp. 593-598.

Horn Book, January, 1936, pp. 34-38.

* * *

SAY, Allen 1937-

PERSONAL: Born August 28, 1937, in Yokohama, Japan; came to the United States c. 1953; son of Masako Moriwaki; children: Yuriko (daughter). *Education:*

Allen Say

Studied at Aoyama Gakuin, Tokyo, Japan, three years, Chouinard Art Institute, one year, Los Angeles Art Center School, one year, University of California, Berkeley, two years, and San Francisco Art Institute, one year. *Hobbies and other interests:* Fly fishing.

ADDRESSES: Home—San Francisco, CA.

CAREER: EIZO Press, Berkeley, CA, publisher, 1968; commercial photographer and illustrator, 1969—; writer and illustrator.

AWARDS, HONORS: American Library Association Notable Book and Best Book for Young Adults, both 1979, both for *The Inn-Keeper's Apprentice; New York Times* Best Illustrated award, 1980, for *The Lucky Yak; Horn Book* honor list, 1984, and Christopher Award, 1985, both for *How My Parents Learned to Eat; New York Times* Ten Best Illustrated Children's Books, 1988, for *A River Dream; Boston Globe/Horn Book* Award, 1988, American Library Association Notable Children's Book, 1988, and Caldecott Honor Book, 1989, all for *The Boy of the Three Year Nap.*

WRITINGS:

SELF-ILLUSTRATED

Dr. Smith's Safari, Harper, 1972.
Once under the Cherry Blossom Tree: An Old Japanese Tale, Harper, 1974.
The Feast of Lanterns, Harper, 1976.
The Innkeeper's Apprentice (young adult), Harper, 1979.
The Bicycle Man, Houghton, 1982.
A River Dream, Houghton, 1988.
The Lost Lake, Houghton, 1989.
El Chino, Houghton, 1990.
Tree of Cranes, Houghton, 1991.

ILLUSTRATOR

Brother Antoninus, *A Canticle to the Waterbirds,* EIZO Press, 1968.
Wilson Pinney, editor, *Two Ways of Seeing,* Little, Brown, 1971.
Eve Bunting, *Magic and Night River,* Harper, 1978.
Annetta Lawson, *The Lucky Yak,* Parnassus Press, 1980.
Thea Brow, *The Secret Cross of Lorraine,* Houghton, 1981.
Ina R. Friedman, *How My Parents Learned to Eat,* Houghton, 1984.
Dianne Snyder, *The Boy of the Three Year Nap,* Houghton, 1988.

WORK IN PROGRESS: Grandfather's Journey.

SIDELIGHTS: Allen Say is a gifted author and illustrator whose books describe the richness of his native culture but also explore the complexities of being both Japanese and American. His tales often narrate the tenuous ways that young boys find guidance and strength from older men. In *A River Dream* and *The Lost Lake,* outdoor experiences provide the setting for youths to understand the natural world and to bond with an important male. Critics praise Say's messages of nonviolence and coexistence with nature but, more than anything, they applaud his consistently vivid, imaginative illustrations. Liz Rosenberg, writing in the *New York Times Book Review,* calls Say "an extraordinarily thoughtful illustrator whose work invariably connects to and comments on the text."

From *El Chino,* written and illustrated by Allen Say.

Say was born in Yokohama, Japan in 1937, and told Leonard S. Marcus, in a *Horn Book* interview, that he began drawing before he could walk, and drew on everything, even the walls. As he grew older, however, his parents discouraged his talent: "At home, drawing really wasn't acceptable. My father, particularly, wanted a successful businessman for a son. To have an artist in the family was a disaster. So I drew, not in a closet, but always with a sense of guilt."

Say received encouragement in his artistic endeavors, however, from two teachers. The first, Mrs. Morita, was an elementary school teacher who treated her students as family, for her husband had been killed in World War II. She taught Say that it was acceptable to draw, and helped him surmount some of his childhood fears. The second teacher was Noro Shinpei, a well-known Japanese cartoonist. Say told Marcus: "Cartoonists were cultural heroes. But it was very unusual in post-war Japan to actually apprentice yourself to a master cartoonist, as I did when I was twelve." Shinpei taught Say all that he knew of Western and Japanese drawing styles, and from him Say inherited the habit of mixing ancient and modern themes in his work. He also found in Shinpei a "spiritual father," telling Marcus that "I didn't know it at the time I first went to see him, but I was trying to replace my father. I was looking for a mentor, and this is what I found." In the award-winning *The Inn-Keeper's Apprentice,* Say recreates the relationship that he developed with Shinpei.

Say moved to the United States when he was sixteen, but recalled that he had virtually stopped drawing and painting by the time he was twenty-five. Hoping to avoid the draft, Say enrolled in architecture school in Berkeley, California, but was drafted anyway. "I was sent to Germany," he told Marcus, "and became the firing-panel operator of a missile system which carried a nuclear warhead—the same A-bomb they dropped on Hiroshima. I was very near to that one as an eight-year-old child. I had a camera, and in order to keep my sanity I started taking pictures." His photos soon appeared in military magazines, and he began a career as a commercial photographer.

Though he had published a few books, Say's first critical success as an author/illustrator came with the 1982 publication of *The Bicycle Man.* The book depicted an encounter between a group of Japanese schoolchildren and two American soldiers in post-World War II Japan. The pen-and-ink and watercolor illustrations capture the tentative understanding that develops between the two groups as the black soldier performs tricks on the principal's bicycle. The Christopher Medal-winning *How My Parents Learned to Eat,* written by Ina Friedman and illustrated by Say, also explores the crossing of cultures as a young Oriental boy's parents learn a new way of approaching food.

By the mid-1980s, Say had decided to give up working on children's books and devote himself entirely to photography. However, an editor cajoled him into doing the illustrations for one last book: *The Boy of the Three-Year Nap.* Say resisted at first, but told Marcus that as he worked on the book, he "started having a very intense experience, and suddenly I decided, at age fifty, that this, more than anything else, was what I wanted to do. I reverted to my childhood, to my happiest days when I used to go to my master's studio, warm my hands in front of one of the charcoal braziers, loosen my fingers, and start working on his beautiful drawings." Say has continued to work as an author/illustrator since then, producing in *El Chino* some of his most intense and dramatic illustrations. The first part of the book describes the life of Bong Way Wong in sepia half-tones, but when Wong becomes "El Chino," the first Chinese bullfighter, the illustrations explode in brilliant watercolors. The message, that people truly flower when they discover their calling, is among Say's most moving and most autobiographical.

When Marcus asked Say whether his early apprenticeship had proven useful to him as a picture-book artist, Say responded: "I learned that action is of the essence. Everything has to be moving. Everything has to be dramatized.... Years ago, I read in the *New Yorker* a remark that had a profound effect on me. Enzo Ferrari [an Italian car designer] wrote that it excited him to take nuts and bolts and breathe life into them. That is what an artist tries to do. Or at least what I try to do."

WORKS CITED:

Marcus, Leonard S., "Rearrangement of Memory: An Interview with Allen Say," *Horn Book,* May/June, 1991, pp. 295-303.

Rozenberg, Liz, "Ole, Billy Wong!," *New York Times Book Review,* November 11, 1990, p. 51.

FOR MORE INFORMATION SEE:

BOOKS

Children's Literature Review, Volume 22, Gale, 1991, pp. 208-212.

PERIODICALS

Horn Book, March/April, 1989, pp. 174-175.

Library Journal, September 15, 1972, p. 2941; May 15, 1974, p. 1469.

New York Times Book Review, May 5, 1974, p. 47; October 24, 1982, p. 41; November 6, 1988, p. 37.

School Library Journal, January, 1977, p. 85; March, 1979, p. 150; January, 1983, p. 66; December, 1988, pp. 101-102; December, 1989, p. 88.

Washington Post Book World, May 19, 1974; May 4, 1975.

* * *

SCARLETT, Susan
See STREATFEILD, (Mary) Noel

* * *

SCARRY, Richard (McClure) 1919-

PERSONAL: Surname rhymes with "carry"; born June 5, 1919, in Boston, MA; son of John James (proprietor of department stores) and Barbara (McClure) Scarry; married Patricia Murphy (a writer of children's books), September 7, 1949; children: Richard McClure II (Huck). *Education:* Boston Museum School of Fine Arts, student, 1938-41. *Hobbies and other interests:* Skiing, sailing, traveling.

ADDRESSES: Home—Schwyzerhus, 3780 Gstaad, Switzerland.

CAREER: Magazine and children's book illustrator, 1946—; writer. *Military service:* U.S. Army, 1941-46; served as art director, editor, writer, and illustrator, Morale Services Section, Allied Forces Headquarters, North African and Mediterranean theaters; became captain.

WRITINGS:

SELF-ILLUSTRATED

The Great Big Car and Truck Book, Simon & Schuster, 1951.

Rabbit and His Friends, Simon & Schuster, 1953.

Nursery Tales, Simon & Schuster, 1958.

Tinker and Tanker (also see below), Garden City Books, 1960.

The Hickory Dickory Clock Book, Doubleday, 1961.

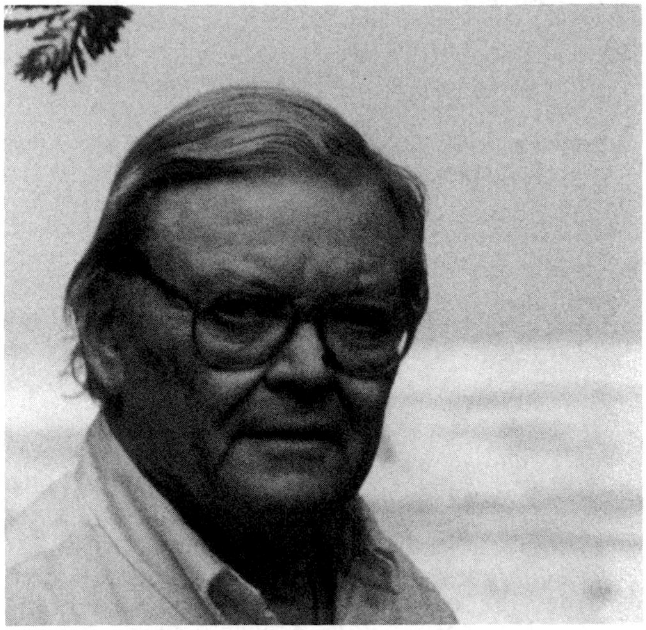

Richard Scarry

Tinker and Tanker Out West (also see below), Doubleday, 1961.
Tinker and Tanker and Their Space Ship (also see below), Doubleday, 1961.
Tinker and Tanker and the Pirates (also see below), Doubleday, 1961.
Tinker and Tanker, Knights of the Round Table (also see below), Doubleday, 1963.
Tinker and Tanker in Africa (also see below), Doubleday, 1963.
Best Word Book Ever, Golden Press, 1963.
The Rooster Struts, Golden Press, 1963, published as *The Golden Happy Book of Animals,* 1964 (published in England as *Animals,* Hamlyn, 1963).
Polite Elephant, Golden Press, 1964.
Feed the Hippo His ABC's, Golden Press, 1964.
Busy, Busy World, Golden Press, 1965.
Richard Scarry's Teeny Tiny Tales, Golden Press, 1965.
The Santa Claus Book, Golden Press, 1965.
The Bunny Book, Golden Press, 1965.
Is This the House of Mistress Mouse?, Golden Press, 1966.
Storybook Dictionary, Golden Press, 1966.
Planes, Golden Press, 1967.
Trains, Golden Press, 1967.
Boats, Golden Press, 1967.
Cars, Golden Press, 1967.
Richard Scarry's Egg in the Hole Book, Golden Press, 1967.
What Animals Do, Golden Press, 1968.
Best Storybook Ever, Golden Press, 1968.
The Early Bird, Random House, 1968.
What Do People Do All Day?, Random House, 1968.
The Adventures of Tinker and Tanker (contains *Tinker and Tanker, Tinker and Tanker Out West,* and *Tinker and Tanker and Their Space Ship*), Doubleday, 1968.
The Great Pie Robbery (also see below), Random House, 1969.
The Supermarket Mystery (also see below), Random House, 1969.
Richard Scarry's Great Big Schoolhouse, Random House, 1969.
More Adventures of Tinker and Tanker (contains *Tinker and Tanker and the Pirates, Tinker and Tanker, Knights of the Round Table,* and *Tinker and Tanker in Africa*), Doubleday, 1971.
ABC Word Book, Random House, 1971.
Richard Scarry's Best Stories Ever, Golden Press, 1971.
Richard Scarry's Fun with Words, Golden Press, 1971.
Richard Scarry's Going Places, Golden Press, 1971.
Richard Scarry's Great Big Air Book, Random House, 1971.
Richard Scarry's Things to Know, Golden Press, 1971.
Funniest Storybook Ever, Random House, 1972.
Nicky Goes to the Doctor, Golden Press, 1972.
Richard Scarry's Great Big Mystery Book (contains *The Great Pie Robbery* and *The Supermarket Mystery*), Random House, 1972.
Hop Aboard, Here We Go, Golden Press, 1972.
Babykins and His Family, Golden Press, 1973.
Silly Stories, Golden Press, 1973.
Richard Scarry's Find Your ABC's, Random House, 1973.
Richard Scarry's Please and Thank You Book, Random House, 1973.
Richard Scarry's Best Rainy Day Book Ever, Random House, 1974.
Cars and Trucks and Things That Go, Golden Press, 1974.
Richard Scarry's Great Steamboat Mystery, Random House, 1975.
Richard Scarry's Best Counting Book Ever, Random House, 1975.
Richard Scarry's Animal Nursery Tales, Golden Press, 1975.
Richard Scarry's Early Words, Random House, 1976.
Richard Scarry's Color Book, Random House, 1976.
Richard Scarry's Busiest People Ever, Random House, 1976.
Richard Scarry's Collins Cubs, Collins, 1976.
Richard Scarry's Picture Dictionary, Collins, 1976.
Richard Scarry's Random Laugh and Learn Library, four books, Random House, 1976.
Learn to Count, Golden Press, 1976.
All Year Long, Golden Press, 1976.
At Work, Golden Press, 1976.
Short and Tall, Golden Press, 1976.
My House, Golden Press, 1976.
On Vacation, Golden Press, 1976.
About Animals, Golden Press, 1976.
On the Farm, Golden Press, 1976.
Six Golden Look-Look Books, six volumes, Golden Press, 1977.
Richard Scarry's Lowly Worm Storybook, Random House, 1977.
Richard Scarry's Best Make-It Book Ever, Random House, 1977.
Tinker and Tanker Journey to Tootletown and Build a Space Ship, Golden Press, 1978.

Richard Scarry's Bedtime Stories, Random House, 1978.
Richard Scarry's Punch-Out Toy Book, Random House, 1978.
Richard Scarry's Postman Pig and His Busy Neighbors, Random House, 1978.
Richard Scarry's Lowly Worm Sniffy Book, Random House, 1978.
Richard Scarry's Stories to Color: With Lowly Worm and Mr. Paint Pig, Random House, 1978.
Storytime, Random House, 1978.
Little Bedtime Story, Random House, 1978.
Things to Learn, Golden Press, 1978.
Mr. Fixit and Other Stories, Random House, 1978.
Busy Town, Busy People, Random House, 1978.
Little ABC, Random House, 1978.
Richard Scarry's Mix or Match Storybook, Random House, 1979.
Richard Scarry's Best First Book Ever, Random House, 1979.
Richard Scarry's Busytown Pop-Up Book, Random House, 1979.
Richard Scarry Huckle's Book, Random House, 1979.
Richard Scarry's Tinker and Tanker Tales of Pirates and Knights, Golden Press, 1979.
Richard Scarry's to Market, to Market, Golden Press, 1979.
Richard Scarry's Peasant Pig and the Terrible Dragon, Random House, 1980.
Richard Scarry's Lowly Worm Word Book, Random House, 1981.
Richard Scarry's Best Christmas Book Ever, Random House, 1981.
Richard Scarry's Busy Houses, Random House, 1981.
Richard Scarry's Funniest Storybook Ever, Random House, 1982.
Richard Scarry's Four Busy Word Books, four volumes, Random House, 1982.
Christmas Mice, Golden Press, 1982.
Lowly Worm Coloring Book, Random House, 1983.
Lowly Worm Cars and Trucks Book, Random House, 1983.
The Best Mistake Ever!, Random House, 1984.
Richard Scarry's Lowly Worm Bath Book, Random House, 1984.
Richard Scarry's Busy Fun and Learn Book, Western Publishing, 1984.
Richard Scarry's Pig Will and Pig Won't: A Book of Manners, Random House, 1984.
Richard Scarry's Biggest Word Book Ever!, Random House, 1985.
My First Word Book, Random House, 1986.
Fun with Letters, Random House, 1986.
Fun with Numbers, three volumes, Random House, 1986.
Norwegian Dictionary: Min Forste Ordbok (subtitle means "My First 'Word Book'"), Arthur Vanous Co., 1986.
Fun with Words, Random House, 1986.
Fun with Reading, Random House, 1986.
Richard Scarry's Splish-Splash Sounds, Western Publishing, 1986.
Big and Little, Western Publishing, 1986.
Things to Love, Western Publishing, 1987.
Richard Scarry's Things That Go, Western Publishing, 1987.
Richard Scarry's Lowly Worm's Schoolbag, Random House, 1987.
Getting Ready for Numbers, Random House, 1987.
Getting Ready for School, Random House, 1987.
Getting Ready for Writing, Random House, 1987.
Busy Workers, Western Publishing, 1987.
Smokey the Fireman, Western Publishing, 1988.
Sniff the Detective, Western Publishing, 1988.
Play Day, Western Publishing, 1988.
Dr. Doctor, Western Publishing, 1988.
Farmer Patrick Pig, Western Publishing, 1988.
Frances Fix-It, Western Publishing, 1988.
Harry and Larry the Fishermen, Western Publishing, 1988.
Richard Scarry's Best Times Ever: A Book about Seasons and Holidays, Western Publishing, 1988.
Scarry's Best Ever, Random House, 1989.
Richard Scarry's Best Ride Ever, Western Publishing, 1989.
Richard Scarry's Best Friend Ever, Western Publishing, 1989.
Richard Scarry's Mother Goose Scratch and Sniff Book, Western Publishing, 1989.
Richard Scarry's Naughty Bunny, Western Publishing, 1989.
Richard Scarry's All about Cars, Western Publishing, 1989.
Richard Scarry's Best Two-Minute Stories Ever!, Western Publishing, 1989.
Richard Scarry's Counting Book, Western Publishing, 1990.
Richard Scarry's Just Right Word Book, David McKay Co., 1990.
Be Careful, Mr. Frumble, Random House, 1990.
Best Read It Yourself Book Ever, Western Publishing, 1990.
Watch Your Step, Mr. Rabbit!, Random House, 1991.
Richard Scarry's ABC's, Western Publishing, 1991.
Richard Scarry's Best Year Ever, Western Publishing, 1991.

Also author of *Richard Scarry's Busy Busy World,* Western Publishing.

ILLUSTRATOR

Kathryn Jackson, *Let's Go Fishing,* Simon & Schuster, 1949.
Jackson, *Mouse's House,* Simon & Schuster, 1949.
Jackson, *Duck and His Friends,* Simon & Schuster, 1949.
Jackson, *Brave Cowboy Bill,* Simon & Schuster, 1950.
Jackson, *The Animals' Merry Christmas,* Simon & Schuster, 1950.
Oliver O'Connor Barrett, *Little Benny Wanted a Pony,* Simon & Schuster, 1950.
Patricia Scarry, *Danny Beaver's Secret,* Simon & Schuster, 1953.
Leah Gale, *The Animals of Farmer Jones,* Simon & Schuster, 1953.
Margaret Wise Brown, *Little Indian,* Simon & Schuster, 1954.

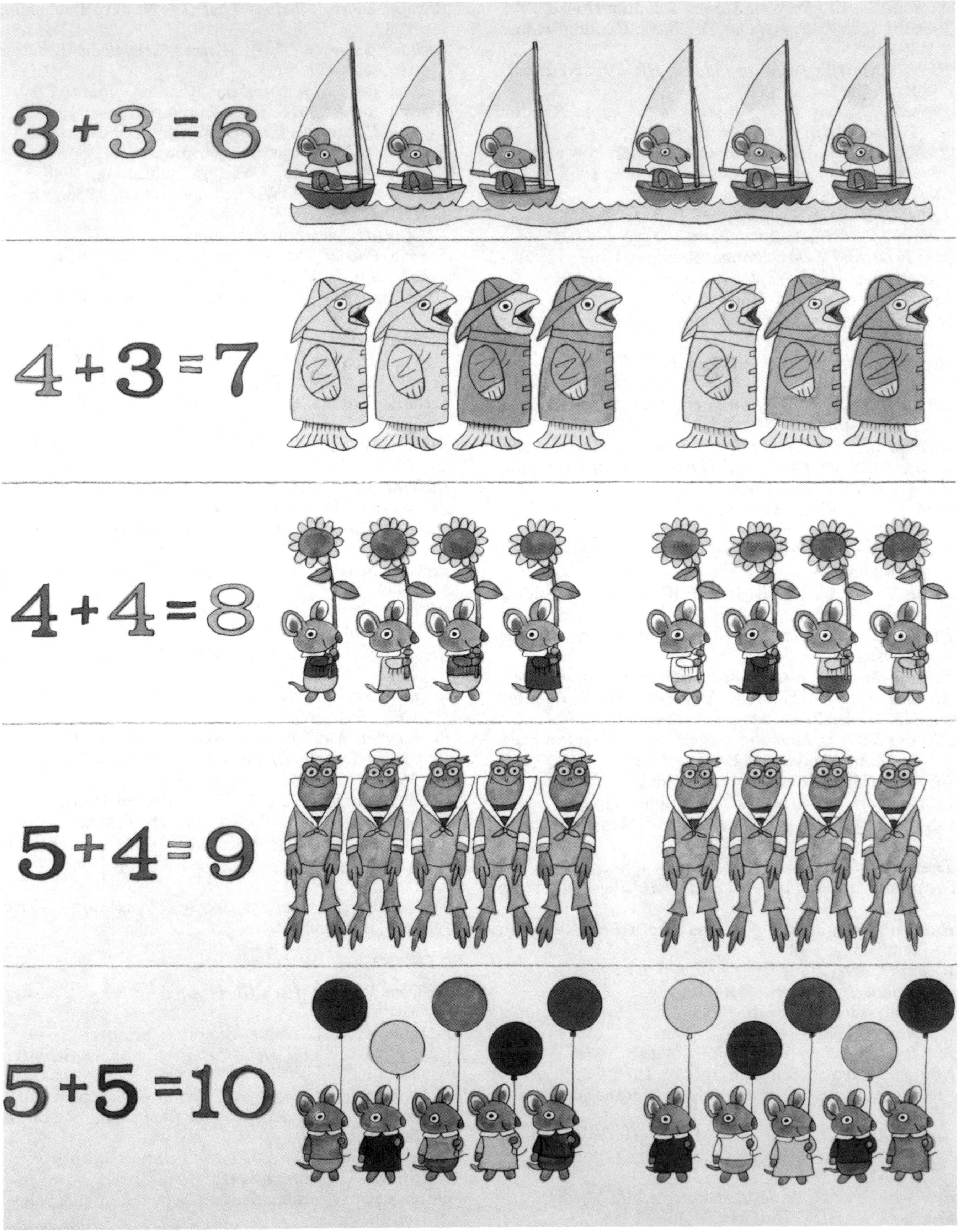

From *Richard Scarry's Best Counting Book Ever,* written and illustrated by Richard Scarry.

P. Scarry, *Pierre Bear,* Golden Press, 1954.
Jane Werner, *Smokey the Bear,* Simon & Schuster, 1955.
Jackson, *Golden Bedtime Book,* Simon & Schuster, 1955.
Mary Maud Reed, *Mon petit dictionnaire geant,* Editions des deux coqs d'or, 1958.
P. Scarry, *Just for Fun,* Golden Press, 1960.
My Nursery Tale Book, Golden Press, 1961.
Selligmann and Levine Milton, *Tommy Visits the Doctor,* Western Publishing, 1962.
Edward Lear, *Nonsense Alphabet,* Doubleday, 1962.
Peggy Parish, *My Golden Book of Manners,* Golden Press, 1962.
M. Reed and E. Oswald, *My First Golden Dictionary Book,* Western Publishing, 1963.
(And editor and translator) Jean de la Fontaine, *Fables,* Doubleday, 1963.
Richard Scarry's Animal Mother Goose, Golden Press, 1964.
Barbara Shook Hazen, *Rudolph the Red-nosed Reindeer,* Golden Press, 1964.
Jackson and others, *My Nursery Tale Book,* Western Publishing, 1964.
Jackson, *The Golden Book of 365 Stories,* Golden Press, 1966.
Ole Risom, *I Am a Bunny,* Golden Press, 1966.
Richard Scarry's Best Mother Goose Ever, Golden Press, 1970.
Richard Scarry's Mother Goose, Golden Press, 1972.
Roberta Miller, *Chipmunk's ABC,* Golden Press, 1976.
The Gingerbread Man, Golden Press, 1981.
My First Golden Dictionary, Western Publishing, 1983.
The Golden Treasury of Fairy Tales,, Western Publishing, 1985.
Richard Scarry's Simple Simon and Other Rhymes, Western Publishing, 1988.
Richard Scarry's Little Miss Muffet and Other Rhymes, Western Publishing, 1988.
Jackson, *Richard Scarry's Best House Ever,* Western Publishing, 1989.
Richard Scarry's Cars and Trucks from A to Z, Random House, 1990.

Also illustrator of coloring activity books and children's foreign language dictionaries. Scarry's works are included in the Kerlan Collection at the University of Minnesota.

ADAPTATIONS:

RECORDINGS

What Do People Do All Day and Other Stories, read by Carol Channing, Caedmon, 1978.
What Do People Do All Day and Great Big Schoolhouse, read by C. Channing, Caedmon, 1979.

OTHER

Richard Scarry's Best Electronic Word Book Ever! (computer software for Commodore 64/128 or Apple computers), CBS Interactive Learning, 1985.

SIDELIGHTS: Richard Scarry is "one of the world's best-selling super-stars of children's literature," according to Barbara Karlan in the *West Coast Review of Books.* The skillful blend of education and entertainment found in Scarry's books makes them appealing both to children and their parents. Each book, be it a dictionary, an alphabet, or a fairy tale, features the author's bright, lively illustrations of such anthropomorphic animal characters as Huckle Cat, Lowly Worm, and Mr. Paint Pig. Publishing statistics testify to the popularity of Scarry's works. His books have been translated into twenty-eight languages and sold over one hundred million copies. Elaine Moss summarizes the books' appeal in *Signal:* "Totally unpretentious, bubbling with humour, alive with activity, peppered with words of wisdom and corny jokes .... Scarry books are a marvellous combination of entertainment, always on a child's level, and incidental instruction. They occupy a unique place in the learning-to-read process."

Scarry was born and raised in Boston, Massachusetts, where his father was the owner of a small chain of department stores. He was not an enthusiastic student; he spent five years struggling through high school. "I couldn't even get into college because I didn't have enough credits," he recalls in *Parents* magazine. Scarry did try a short stint at a Boston business school, but soon dropped out. Since he had always liked drawing and had spent every Saturday morning as a child studying art at the Boston Museum of Fine Arts, he was finally accepted at the Boston Museum School for Fine Arts.

World War II interrupted Scarry's art studies, however. He spent five years in the United States Army. "I had a bit of a problem getting in," he explains in the *Third Book of Junior Authors.* "Because I wore glasses they wouldn't accept me as a volunteer but preferred to draft me instead." Although Scarry was originally scheduled to become a radio repairman, he soon secured a place at an Officer Candidate school. After graduation, he went on to serve as art director for the troops in North Africa and Italy, where he drew maps and designed graphics.

After the war Scarry moved to New York City, originally intending to pursue a career as a commercial artist. However, in 1946 he completed illustrations for a children's book called *The Boss of the Barnyard,* published by Golden Press, and he was ensured a steady flow of work. He illustrated other authors' books for several years before beginning to write and illustrate original stories of his own. "During his free-lance period," writes Bobbie Burch Lemontt in the *Dictionary of Literary Biography,* "he met Patsy Murphy, from Vancouver, British Columbia, who, he says, writes kids' books, 'but can't draw.' After being married in 1949, the couple lived on a farm in Ridgefield, Connecticut, and collaborated on several books."

Scarry's first big commercial success came in 1963 with the publication of *Richard Scarry's Best Word Book Ever.* The book was filled with colorful illustrations and pages of information—it "contains more than 1,400 defined and illustrated objects which can engage a preschooler's interest by the infectious vitality and purposefulness of the selections," states Lemontt—and established Scarry's popularity with children. It "seems," writes *New York Times* contributor Richard Flaste, "to identify everything children meet in their world, and some things in more exotic worlds."

Scarry's work, however, is not without its critics. Some librarians feel that Scarry's use of slapstick humor in his books, with its overtones of violence, could be dangerous for young children. But "it's not true violence, it's fun," he told Rudi Chelminski in *People.* "I have cars pile up and people get into trouble. It's the old banana peel or custard pie in the face. The only thing that really suffers is dignity. Kids love that— and they're right." "A typical 'violent' encounter," explains Edwin McDowell in the *New York Times,* "... is likely to show, for example, canine cop Sergeant Murphy on collision course with a birthday cake. Even then the moment of impact is left to the imagination."

Other critics object to what they see as sexual stereotyping in Scarry's work. But the author told Arthur Bell in *Publisher's Weekly* that one reason he uses animals as subjects is to eliminate the problem of sexual and racial stereotypes: "Children can identify more closely with pictures of animals than they can with pictures of another child. They see an illustration of a blond girl or a dark-haired boy who they know is somebody other than themselves, and competition creeps in. With imagination—and children all have marvelous imagination—they can easily identify with an anteater who is a painter or a goat who is an Indian or a honey-bear schoolteacher."

In 1969 Scarry, his wife, and their son, Huck (an author-illustrator) moved to a mountain chalet in Gstaad, Switzerland. The decision was made after a skiing trip. "It was the usual 21-day excursion," he told Bell. "But coming home, we had to pass through Lausanne in order to catch our plane from Geneva. From the train window I caught a glimpse of a child throwing a snowball—just that, nothing more—and I thought, 'Now is the time to move to Switzerland.'" "The move was not a political one—we had always hoped at sometime to live in Europe," Scarry continues, "but couldn't make plans because of Huck's being in school. But Huck was 15, and Switzerland was magnificent, and suddenly the time seemed right.... We settled our affairs and leased our house, and ... with little more than the clothes on our backs, we moved to Lausanne."

From his European residence Scarry continues to produce highly popular children's books which enchant young people. "One of the greatest compliments any author can receive from a preschool audience," declares Lemontt, "is to have his or her books held together with more tape than there is paper in the book itself. Tearing is an accidental toddler pastime that often suggests a book is good enough to be reread. Richard Scarry's books usually display an abundance of such mending."

WORKS CITED:

Chelminski, Rudi, "This Is the House the Menagerie of Richard Scarry Built," *People,* October 15, 1979, pp. 105-10.

Bell, Arthur, "Richard Scarry's Best Switzerland Ever," *Publishers Weekly,* October 20, 1969, pp. 41-42.

De Montreville, Doris, and Donna Hill, editors, *Third Book of Junior Authors,* H. W. Wilson, 1972.

Flaste, Richard, "Richard Scarry and His People," *New York Times,* March 16, 1976.

Karlan, Barbara, *West Coast Review of Books,* December, 1975.

Lemontt, Bobbie Burch, "Richard Scarry," *Dictionary of Literary Biography,* Volume 61: *American Writers for Children since 1960: Poets, Illustrators, and Nonfiction Authors,* Gale, 1987, pp. 248-57.

McDowell, Edwin, "Behind the Best Sellers: Richard Scarry," *New York Times,* April 27, 1980.

Moss, Elaine, *Signal,* January, 1974.

FOR MORE INFORMATION SEE:

BOOKS

Children's Literature Review, Volume 3, Gale, 1978.

Kingman, Lee, and others, editors, *Illustrators of Children's Books: 1957-1966,* Horn Book, 1968.

Lanes, Selma G., *Down the Rabbit Hole: Adventures and Misadventures in the Realm of Children's Literature,* Atheneum, 1972.

Ward, Martha E., and Dorothy A. Marquardt, *Authors of Books for Young People,* Scarecrow, 1971.

Wintle, Justin, and Emma Fisher, *The Pied Pipers: Interviews with the Influential Creators of Children's Literature,* Paddington Press, 1974.

PERIODICALS

New Yorker, December 14, 1968.

New York Times Book Review, November 6, 1966; December 14, 1968; April 5, 1968; October 1, 1972; May 6, 1973; November 14, 1976; May 27, 1980.

Parents, August, 1980.

Times Literary Supplement, December 3, 1971.

Young Readers Review, September, 1968.

* * *

SCHOENHERR, John (Carl) 1935-

PERSONAL: Born July 5, 1935, in New York, NY; son of John F. and Frances (Braun) Schoenherr; married Judith Gray, September 17, 1960; children: Jennifer Lauren, Ian Gray. *Education:* Studied under Will Barnett and Frank Reilly at Art Students League; Pratt Institute, B.F.A., 1956.

ADDRESSES: Home—135 Upper Creek Rd., Stockton, NJ 08559.

CAREER: Free-lance illustrator and painter. South Hunterdon Juvenile Conference Committee, member, 1968. *Exhibitions:* Paintings exhibited at various locations, including Bronx Zoo, New York, 1968, Carson Gallery of Western American Art, Denver, 1983, Kent

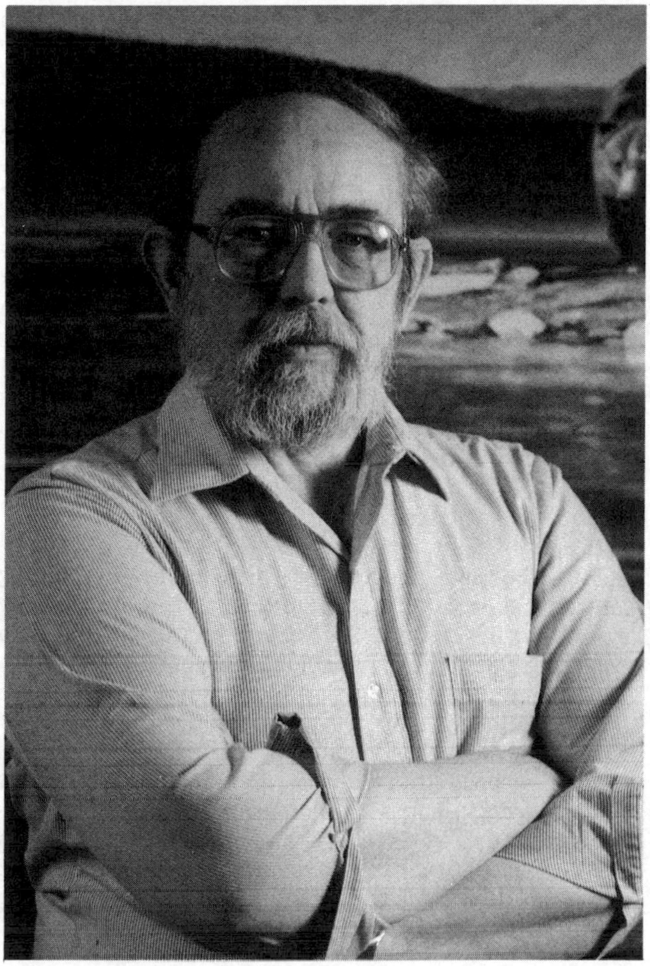

John Schoenherr

State University, 1983, Colorado Historical Society, 1984-87, 1990, and most recently in a number of private collections.

MEMBER: Society of Illustrators, Society of Animal Artists, American Society of Mammalogists, Graphic Artists Guild.

AWARDS, HONORS: First prize, National Speleological Society Salon, 1963; recipient of citations, Society of Illustrators, 1964, 1966, 1967, 1968, 1969, 1970, 1972, 1973, 1974, 1976, 1979, 1980, 1981; Science Fiction Achievement Award (Hugo) for best artist, World Science Fiction Society, 1965; author award, New Jersey Council of Teachers of English, 1969, for *The Barn;* Society of Animal Artists Medal, 1979, 1984; Silver Medal, Philadelphia Academy of Natural Science, 1984; Caldecott Award, American Library Association, 1988, for *Owl Moon.*

ILLUSTRATOR:

Sterling North, *Rascal: A Memoir of a Better Era* (Newbery honor book), Dutton, 1963.
G. W. Moore and G. Nicholas, *Speleology: The Study of Caves,* Heath, 1964.
Walter Morey, *Gentle Ben,* Dutton, 1965.
Robert William Murphy, *The Golden Eagle,* Dutton, 1965.
R. W. Murphy, *The Phantom Setter,* Dutton, 1966.
Bernice Freschet, *Kangaroo Red,* Scribner, 1966.
Daniel P. Mannix, *The Fox and the Hound,* Dutton, 1967.
Era Zistel, *The Dangerous Year,* Random House, 1967.
Adrien Stoutenburg, *A Vanishing Thunder: Extinct and Threatened American Birds,* Natural History Press, 1967.
Arthur Catherall, *A Zebra Came to Drink,* Dutton, 1967.
A. Stoutenburg, *Animals at Bay: Rare and Rescued American Wildlife,* Doubleday, 1968.
(And author) *The Barn* (ALA Notable Book), Little, Brown, 1968.
Jean Craighead George, *The Moon of the Chickarees,* Crowell, 1968.
Julian May, *The Big Island,* Follett, 1968.
S. North, *The Wolfling: A Documentary Novel of the 1870s,* Dutton, 1969.
Allan W. Eckert, *Incident at Hawk's Hill* (Newbery honor book), Little, Brown, 1971.
Ferdinand N. Monjo, *The Jezebel Wolf,* Simon & Schuster, 1971.
J. C. George, *Julie of the Wolves* (Newbery Medal winner), Harper, 1971.
Charles G. D. Roberts, *Red Fox,* Houghton, 1972.
Theodore Clymer, *Travels of Atunga,* Little, Brown, 1973.
Harold Keith, *Susie's Scoundrel,* Crowell, 1974.
(And author) *Art of Painting Wild Animals,* Grumbacher, 1974.
Allison Morgan, *River Song,* Harper, 1975.
Vincent Abraitys, *The Backyard Wilderness,* Columbia Publishing, 1975.
John A. Giegling, *Black Lightning: Three Years in the Life of a Fisher,* Coward, 1975.
Faith McNulty, *Whales: Their Life in the Sea,* Harper, 1975.
Joanne Ryder, *Simon Underground* (Children's Book Showcase selection), Harper, 1976.
Jane Annixter and Paul Annixter, *Wapootin,* Coward, 1976.
Nathaniel Benchley, *Kilroy and the Gull,* Harper, 1977.
Randall Jarrell, *A Bat Is Born* (poetry; excerpted from Jarrell's *The Bat-Poet*), Doubleday, 1977.
J. C. George, *The Wounded Wolf,* Harper, 1978.
Colin Thiel, *Storm Boy,* Harper, 1978.
Robert F. Leslie, *Miracle on Squaretop Mountain,* Dutton, 1979.
(With son, Ian Schoenherr) Lee Harding, *The Fallen Spaceman,* Harper, 1980.
Jane Yolen, *Owl Moon,* Philomel, 1987.
Drew Nelson, *Wild Voices,* Putnam, 1991.
(And author) *Bear,* Philomel, 1991.

BY MISKA MYLES

Mississippi Possum, Little, Brown, 1965.
The Fox and the Fire (*Horn Book* honor book; ALA Notable Book), Little, Brown, 1966.
Rabbit Garden, Little, Brown, 1967.
Nobody's Cat (ALA Notable Book), Little, Brown, 1969.

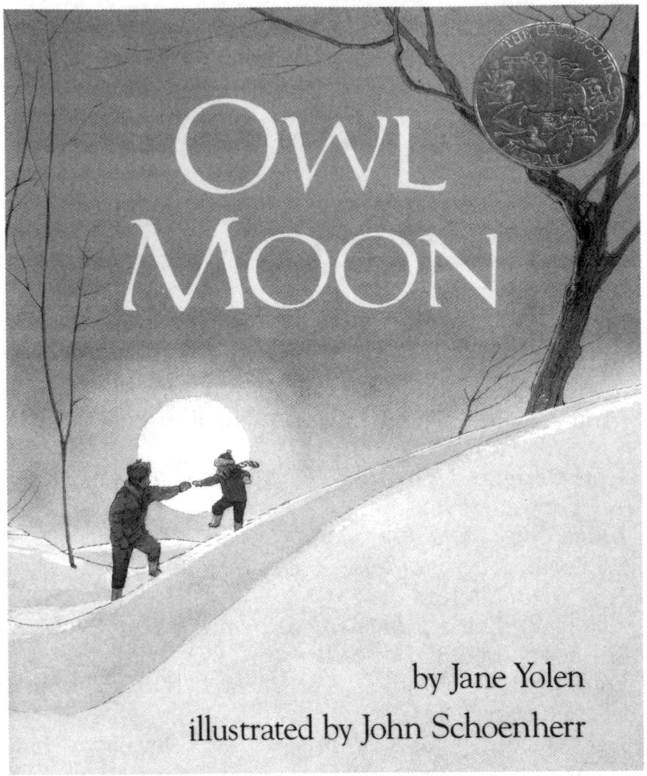

Cover of *Owl Moon,* by Jane Yolen. Illustrated by John Schoenherr.

Eddie's Bear, Little, Brown, 1970.
Hoagie's Rifle-Gun (Junior Literary Guild selection), Little, Brown, 1970.
Wharf Rat, Little, Brown, 1972.
Somebody's Dog, Little, Brown, 1973.
Otter in the Cove, Little, Brown, 1974.
Beaver Moon, Little, Brown, 1978.

SCIENCE FICTION

Frank Herbert, *Dune,* Berkeley, 1977.

Also illustrator of more than three hundred science fiction book covers; contributor of illustrations to *Astounding Science Fiction* magazine.

WORK IN PROGRESS: Paintings and graphics.

SIDELIGHTS: In addition to producing a substantial body of paintings that has been exhibited nationwide, John Schoenherr has illustrated more than forty children's books and hundreds of science fiction book covers. His illustrations for children's books—which are often sentimental depictions of wild animals and their surroundings—have earned the prolific artist a measure of recognition. His watercolor drawings for Jane Yolen's book *Owl Moon,* for example, won the 1988 Caldecott Medal. "I think I identify with wild animals, sometimes even more than with people," Schoenherr remarked in a *U.S. Art* article. "A friend of mine likes to say that I'm a bear disguised as a human being."

For a wildlife artist, Schoenherr certainly had an unlikely childhood—he was born and raised in New York City. "When I was four years old . . . I made the unsettling discovery that nobody out in the street where we lived in Queens could understand a word I said," he told Frances Traher in an interview for *Artists of the Rockies and the Golden West.* "My parents had come into the country in 1914—my mother from Hungary and my father from Germany—and German was what they'd taught me. A couple of houses down from us lived a little boy my own age who chattered away in Chinese, and around the corner Italian prevailed. I was a virtual mute in that polyglot precinct until the day I got so desperate to communicate that I grabbed up a pencil and *drew.* Later I learned English from the comic strips, but I still kept drawing all the time."

Schoenherr's interest in illustration developed steadily. At the age of eight, he was given his first set of oil paints; and by the time he reached thirteen, he was taking Saturday classes at the Art Students League in New York City. Besides art, Schoenherr was fascinated with stone as a young boy, exploring caves and climbing the Long Island rock formations. "Climbing made me aware of the tactility of stone," he told Traher. "You almost climb with the feel of each hold to your fingers. Of late years, I've become aware again of the influence that Edward Weston had as a photographer, with his monumental stones and simplicity and elegance and strength of composition, the way he would reduce things to the minimum that would work and thereby produce a significant image that would move some people."

While he was in high school, Schoenherr developed a competing interest in biology, but his love for art prevailed when he was asked to dissect a frog in biology class. He chose to study at Pratt Institute in Brooklyn after high school. During the summers, Schoenherr would return to the Art Students League to study under Frank Reilly, an illustrator closely devoted to the old French Academy style. "I appreciated certain skills that style engendered," Schoenherr said in *Artists of the Rockies and the Golden West,* "and the perception it produced for seeing values and colors and changes in your subject—but I learned that I had to work out my organization on the painting itself. A too-rigid method wasn't for me. Organization itself, though, I liked; and early on, strong shapes and strong colors—those qualities, and going for the overall look instead of the detailed thing."

At the age of twenty-one, Schoenherr was becoming recognized as a successful science fiction illustrator. He worked extensively for *Astounding Science Fiction* (since renamed *Analog*). Schoenherr credits the publisher of that magazine, John Campbell, for providing the young artist with the opportunities to develop his personal brand of realism. "I'll always be proud of the 'genuine aliens' I designed for the stories Campbell published," Schoenherr told Traher. "Never were they humans with insect antennae. For beings from a heavy planet, I always managed to work out the structural support that logically their existence would have required."

While working as a magazine illustrator, Schoenherr had moved his family onto a farm in rural New Jersey. The woods and meadows surrounding the 1865 farmhouse gave Schoenherr an interest in animals and nature that gradually led him almost exclusively into wildlife illustration. To pursue his interest in the out-of-doors and in larger and more exotic animals, Schoenherr began travelling throughout the United States and abroad. He told Traher: "It was my travels back and forth through northern Arizona and around Albuquerque, and exploring caves in the non-developed areas of the Black Hills, Yellowstone and Montana, that taught me what my great love really is: It's structure. Back East, everything is covered with trees, whereas it's stone and dirt that I love. Deep down, I probably want to be a desert dweller. And yet, our New Jersey place is a tree farm—not for growing them, but for enjoying them. And I have made so much preparation for painting animals. I like raccoons with their robber or carnival masks. I never can decide which it is they wear. And bears! I tend to be more sympathetic with the larger monochromatic animals that I can use a big brush on. Bears, as I say, have a nice form. It's solid. And moose, I like. They look so awkward in an artificial situation; but I've seen a moose go through a cedar swamp over fallen, twisted tree trunks and matted growth without wrestling anything. A moose can be a dynamic, controlled, solid mass in movement."

Schoenherr has illustrated more than forty children's books, many of which have been acclaimed for their knowledgeable handling of animals and nature themes. His greatest achievement in that medium came in 1987, after a five-year pause from book illustration to concentrate on painting. In that year, Schoenherr returned to the children's book scene to illustrate Jane Yolen's *Owl Moon.* His watercolor pictures for the book earned him the American Library Association's Caldecott Award, presented yearly to the best-illustrated children's book. In a reprint of his acceptance speech in *Horn Book Magazine,* Schoenherr describes the satisfaction he receives from drawing animals: "I know the feeling of meeting a wild animal on its own ground. I've been face to face with field mice and Kodiak bears, bull moose and wild geese, wild boar and mountain goats, and, of course, owls. Large or small, I feel awe and wonder and respect. They are all presences and personalities, alien and largely unfathomable, but worth acceptance and contemplation for what they are. This is what I've found worth trying to express in my work. I was glad to discover I was not alone."

WORKS CITED:

Roberts, Nancy, "John Schoenherr: Bearable Endeavors," *U.S. Art,* December, 1988.
Schoenherr, John, "Caldecott Medal Acceptance," *Horn Book Magazine,* July/August, 1988.
Traher, Frances, "John Schoenherr," *Artists of the Rockies and the Golden West,* summer, 1983.

FOR MORE INFORMATION SEE:

BOOKS

Contemporary American Illustrators of Children's Books, Rutgers University Art Gallery, 1974.
De Montreville, Doris, and Elizabeth D. Crawford, editors, *Fourth Book of Junior Authors and Illustrators,* H. W. Wilson, 1978.
Kingman, Lee, and others, compilers, *Illustrators of Children's Books,* Horn Book, *1957-1966,* 1968, *1967-1976,* 1978.
Klemin, Diana, *The Illustrated Book,* Clarkson Potter, 1970.

* * *

SCHWARTZ, Alvin 1927-1992

PERSONAL: Born April 25, 1927, in Brooklyn, NY; died of lymphoma, March 14, 1992, in Princeton, NJ; son of Harry (a taxi driver) and Gussie (Younger) Schwartz; married Barbara Carmer (a learning disabilities specialist), August 7, 1954; children: John, Peter, Nancy, Elizabeth. *Education:* Attended City College (now of the City University of New York), 1944-45; Colby College, A.B., 1949; Northwestern University, M.S. in Journalism, 1951. *Politics:* Independent.

Alvin Schwartz

From *A Twister of Twists, a Tangler of Tongues,* compiled by Alvin Schwartz. Illustrated by Glen Rounds.

ADDRESSES: Agent—Marilyn Marlow, Curtis Brown Ltd., 10 Astor Pl., New York, NY 10003.

CAREER: Newspaper reporter, 1951-55; writer for nonprofit and commercial organizations, 1955-59; Opinion Research Corp., Princeton, NJ, director of communications, 1959-64; Rutgers University, New Brunswick, NJ, adjunct professor of English, 1962-78; free-lance writer and author of books for adults and children, 1963—. Trustee, Joint Free Library of Princeton, 1972-74. Member of National Council, Boy Scouts of America, 1972-74. *Military service:* U.S. Navy, 1945-46.

MEMBER: Authors League of America, Authors Guild, American Folklore Society.

AWARDS, HONORS: New Jersey Institute of Technology Awards, 1966, for *The Night Workers,* 1968, for *The Rainy Day Book,* 1969, for *University,* 1972, for *A Twister of Twists, A Tangler of Tongues,* 1977, for *Kickle Snifters and Other Fearsome Critters,* 1980, for *When I Grew Up Long Ago,* 1981, for *Chin Music* and *Ten Copycats in a Boat and Other Riddles,* and 1987, for *Tales of Trickery from the Land of Spoof.*

American Library Association (ALA) Notable Book citations, 1967, for *Museum,* 1983, for *Unriddling,* and 1984, for *In a Dark, Dark Room, and Other Scary Stories; New York Times* Outstanding Book citations, 1972, for *A Twister of Twists, A Tangler of Tongues,* and 1973, for *Tomfoolery, Trickery and Foolery with Words;* National Council of Teachers of English Citations, 1972, for *A Twister of Twists, A Tangler of Tongues,* and 1975, for *Whoppers;* ALA and the National Endowment for the Humanities Bicentennial Book citations, 1972, for *The Unions,* and 1973, for *Central City/Spread City;* "Notable Children's Trade Book in the Field of Social Studies" citations, National Council for Social Studies and the Children's Book Council, 1973, for *Central City/Spread City,* 1974, for *Cross Your Fingers, Spit in Your Hat,* 1975, for *Whoppers,* 1979, for *Chin Music,* and 1980, for *Flapdoodle;* "Book of the year" citations, Child Study Association of America, 1973, for *Wit-*

cracks, 1974, for *Central City/Spread City* and *Cross Your Fingers, Spit in Your Hat,* 1975, for *Whoppers,* and 1987, for *Tales of Trickery from the Land of Spoof, There Is a Carrot in My Ear and Other Noodle Tales, In a Dark, Dark Room,* and *Ten Copycats in a Boat and Other Riddles;* "Children's Choice" citations, International Reading Association and Children's Book Council, 1975, for *Cross Your Fingers, Spit in Your Hat,* 1976, for *Whoppers,* 1977, for *Kickle Snifters and Other Fearsome Critters,* and 1981, for *Ten Copycats in a Boat; Kickle Snifters and Other Fearsome Critters* was named one of *School Library Journal's* Best Books of the Year, 1976.

New York Public Library's Books for the Teen Age citations, 1980, for *Witcracks,* and 1980, 1981, and 1982, for *Cross Your Fingers, Spit in Your Hat;* Notable Children's Book citation, Association for Library Service to Children (ALA), 1984, Buckeye Children's Book Award, State Library of Ohio, Washington Children's Choice Picture Book Award, Washington Library Media Association, Virginia Children's Book Award, and Garden State Children's Book Award, New Jersey Library Association, all 1986, all for *In a Dark, Dark Room, and Other Scary Stories;* Buckeye Children's Book Award, and Colorado Children's Book Award, both 1986, and Arizona Young Readers Award, Arizona State University, 1987, all for *Scary Stories to Tell in the Dark;* honored for body of work by Rutgers University School of Communications, Information and Library Studies, 1986.

WRITINGS:

JUVENILE

The Night Workers, illustrated with photographs by Ulli Steltzer, Dutton, 1966.

What Do You Think? An Introduction to Public Opinion: How It Forms, Functions, and Affects Our Lives, Dutton, 1966.

The City and Its People: The Story of One City's Government, Dutton, 1967.

Museum: The Story of America's Treasure Houses, Dutton, 1967.

The People's Choice: The Story of Candidates, Campaigns, and Elections, Dutton, 1967.

Old Cities and New Towns: The Changing Face of the Nation, Dutton, 1968.

The Rainy Day Book, Simon & Schuster, 1969.

University: The Students, Faculty, and Campus Life at One University, Viking, 1969.

(Compiler) *A Twister of Twists, A Tangler of Tongues: Tongue Twisters,* illustrated by Glen Rounds, Lippincott, 1972.

Hobbies: An Introduction to Crafts, Collections, Nature Study and Other Life-Long Pursuits, illustrated by Barbara Carmer Schwartz, Simon & Schuster, 1972.

The Unions: What They Are, How They Came to Be, How They Affect Each of Us, Viking, 1972.

(Compiler and reteller) *Witcracks: Jokes and Jests from American Folklore,* illustrated by Rounds, Lippincott, 1973.

(Compiler and reteller) *Tomfoolery: Trickery and Foolery with Words, Collected from American Folklore,* illustrated by Rounds, Lippincott, 1973.

Central City/Spread City: The Metropolitan Regions Where More and More of Us Spend Our Lives, Macmillan, 1973.

(Compiler and reteller) *Cross Your Fingers, Spit in Your Hat: Superstitions and Other Beliefs,* illustrated by Rounds, Lippincott, 1974.

(Reteller) *Whoppers: Tall Tales and Other Lies Collected from American Folklore,* illustrated by Rounds, Lippincott, 1975.

Stores, illustrated with photographs by Samuel Nocella, Jr., Macmillan, 1976.

Kickle Snifters and Other Fearsome Critters, Collected from American Folklore, illustrated by Rounds, Lippincott, 1976.

(Editor and compiler) *When I Grew Up Long Ago: Family Living, Going to School, Games and Parties, Cures and Deaths, a Comet, a War, Falling in Love and Other Things I Remember; Older People Talk about the Days When They Were Young,* illustrated by Harold Berson, Lippincott, 1978.

Chin Music: Tall Talk and Other Talk, illustrated by John O'Brien, Lippincott, 1979.

Flapdoodle: Pure Nonsense from American Folklore, illustrated by O'Brien, Lippincott, 1980.

(Compiler) *Ten Copycats in a Boat and Other Riddles,* illustrated by Marc Simont, Harper, 1980.

(Reteller) *Scary Stories to Tell in the Dark: Collected from American Folklore,* illustrated by Stephen Gammell, Lippincott, 1981.

(Compiler) *The Cat's Elbow and Other Secret Languages,* illustrated by Margot Zemach, Farrar, Straus, 1981.

(Reteller) *There Is a Carrot in My Ear and Other Noodle Tales,* illustrated by Karen Ann Weinhaus, Harper, 1982.

Busy Buzzing Bumblebees and Other Tongue Twisters, illustrated by Kathie Abrams, Harper, 1982.

(Compiler) *Unriddling: All Sorts of Riddles to Puzzle Your Guessery Collected from American Folklore,* illustrated by Susan Truesdell, Lippincott, 1983.

(Reteller) *In a Dark, Dark Room, and Other Scary Stories,* illustrated by Dirk Zimmer, Harper, 1984.

More Scary Stories to Tell in the Dark: Collected and Retold from Folklore, illustrated by Gammell, Lippincott, 1984.

(Reteller) *Fat Man in a Fur Coat and Other Bear Stories,* illustrated by David Christiana, Farrar, Straus, 1984.

(Reteller) *All of Our Noses Are Here and Other Noodle Tales,* illustrated by Weinhaus, Harper, 1985.

(Reteller) *Tales of Trickery from the Land of Spoof,* illustrated by Christiana, Farrar, Straus, 1985.

Telling Fortunes: Love Magic, Dream Signs and Other Ways to Learn the Future, illustrated by Tracey Cameron, Lippincott, 1987.

(Reteller) *Gold and Silver, Silver and Gold: Tales of Hidden Treasure,* illustrated by Christiana, Farrar, Straus, 1988.

I Saw You in the Bathtub and Other Folk Rhymes, illustrated by Syd Hoff, Harper, 1989.

Ghosts!: Ghostly Tales from Folklore, illustrated by Victoria Chess, Harper, 1991.

Scary Stories, No. 3: More Tales To Chill Your Bones, illustrated by Gammell, Harper, 1991.

OTHER

A Parent's Guide to Children's Play and Recreation, Collier, 1963.

How to Fly a Kite, Catch a Fish, Grow a Flower and Other Activities for You and Your Child, illustrated by Mary Weissfeld, Macmillan, 1965.

America's Exciting Cities: A Guide for Parents and Children, Crowell, 1966.

To Be a Father: Stories, Letters, Essays, Poems, Comments, and Proverbs on the Delights and Despairs of Fatherhood, Crown, 1968.

Going Camping: A Complete Guide for the Uncertain Beginner in Family Camping, Macmillan, 1969, 2nd revised edition published as *Going Camping: A Complete Guide for the Family Camper,* 1975.

Contributor to numerous periodicals, including *Redbook, Coronet, Parade, Parents', Public Opinion Quarterly, Journal of Marketing, New York Times,* and *New York Herald Tribune.*

ADAPTATIONS: The following works have been recorded: *Tongue Twisters,* Caedmon, 1974; *Scary Stories to Tell in the Dark,* Caedmon, 1986; *More Scary Stories to Tell in the Dark* (with teacher's guide), Listening Library, 1986; *In a Dark, Dark Room,* Harper, 1986.

WORK IN PROGRESS: Various books for young people dealing with folklore and other subjects.

SIDELIGHTS: Alvin Schwartz has dedicated himself to preserving a treasury of folklore for today's young readers. Schwartz's carefully-documented and meticulously researched books cover every sort of folk tradition from the tall tale to the tongue-twister. He has collected scary stories, superstitions, riddles, and rhymes, principally but not exclusively from American sources. A *Horn Book* writer, reviewing *Unriddling,* notes: "If the current generation grows up with a knowledge of traditional humor, it may well be because of Alvin Schwartz's many volumes of ... American folklore."

Schwartz commented in *Horn Book:* "I first became interested in folklore when most of us do, in childhood. But at that time I had no idea that the games, sayings, songs, rhymes, taunts, and jokes I knew; the things I wrote on walls; the superstitions I relied on; the tales I heard and learned; the customs we practiced at home; or the ways we had of doing things were all folklore. I also did not realize that much of this lore gave my life structure and continuity, that these games, songs, jokes, tales, and customs were often very old, that ordinary people like me had created them, and that all this had survived simply and remarkably because one person had told another."

Schwartz grew up in Brooklyn, New York, part of a large extended family. In the *Fifth Book of Junior Authors and Illustrators,* Schwartz stated: "The elders in my family had immigrated from Hungary and Russia around the turn of the century, and they clung tenaciously to their old ways. As a result, I was affected by two cultures when I was growing up: the traditional beliefs and practices of my family and an American culture that had far less of an effect." As a youngster, Schwartz had two passions—archaeology and journalism. He was quoted in Farrar, Straus publicity material as saying that both fields "involved digging out and understanding the unknown. But journalism also involved writing, and at some point when I was in high school, it was in that direction that I moved."

After wartime service with the United States Navy, Schwartz earned bachelor's and master's degrees in journalism and went to work at a newspaper in Binghamton, New York. By 1960 he had become a communications director for a research organization in Princeton, New Jersey. The urge to write books was strong, however, and in 1963 he quit his full-time job to become a free-lance author. He converted a tool shed in his backyard into an office and made use of libraries in Princeton and Philadelphia for his research.

Schwartz's early children's books are concerned with social issues not often found in a juvenile format—the decay of inner cities, the political process and how candidates get elected, public opinion and how it is formed, and a history of the labor movement in America. He turned to collecting folklore after his 1972 book *A Twister of Twists, A Tangler of Tongues* became a national bestseller. Like many of the author's folklore compilations, *A Twister of Twists* is a humorous look at language suitable for children and adults.

Schwartz is well known today for his work on American folklore. He ranges far and wide for material, digging into dusty library volumes one day and singing rhymes with children the next. His best known works include *Tomfoolery: Trickery and Foolery with Words, Flapdoodle: Pure Nonsense from American Folklore, In a Dark, Dark Room and Other Scary Stories,* and *Tales of Trickery from the Land of Spoof.* As the titles suggest, the subject matter comes from the common human penchant for humor and exaggeration, especially in novel or frightening situations.

The author remarked in his publicity material that he grew up "with ethnic roots but not much knowledge of American traditions," so "exploring my national folklore has been a great and satisfying adventure." What he has learned, he noted in *Horn Book,* is that "the folklore we create, pass on, and change says a good deal about us, about the times in which we live, and about the needs we have. Our jests provide pleasure, but they also provide emotional release. When they deal with racial and ethnic groups and with parents and siblings, they provide weaponry. The tall tales which so amuse us spring from the vastness of a frontier wilderness where life was brutal and the people diminished and fearful.

They created incredible lies in which individuals were larger and taller than life and could not fail, no matter what. Our superstitions provide answers to things we do not understand and cannot explain."

Schwartz encourages young readers to "understand that you are part of a living tradition to which you contribute and from which you draw. You are deeply rooted in the experience of the human race and are part of something remarkable and continuous—the folk. At a time when everyone and everything seem in transit, it is good to know this."

WORKS CITED:

Fifth Book of Junior Authors and Illustrators, H. W. Wilson, 1986, pp. 276-277.

Schwartz, Alvin, "Children, Humor, and Folklore," *Horn Book,* August, 1977, pp. 471-476.

Schwartz, Alvin, in a Farrar, Straus publicity letter.

Review of *Unriddling, Horn Book,* February, 1984, p. 77.

FOR MORE INFORMATION SEE:

BOOKS

Children's Literature Review, Volume 3, Gale, 1978.

Ward, Martha E., and Dorothy A. Marquardt, *Authors of Books for Young People,* supplement to the second edition, Scarecrow, 1979.

PERIODICALS

Horn Book, June, 1977.

Language Arts, April, 1987.

New York Times Book Review, May 6, 1973; January 17, 1982.

* * *

SCHWEITZER, Byrd Baylor
See BAYLOR, Byrd

* * *

SCOTT, Jack Denton 1915-

PERSONAL: Born in 1915, in Elkins, WV; married Maria Luisa Limoncelli, in Elmira, NY, June 22, 1942. *Education:* attended night classes at Columbia University; attended Oxford University.

ADDRESSES: Home—11 Skyline Drive, Corning, NY 14830.

Jack Denton Scott

CAREER: Writer for *Fort Bragg News;* reporter for American and European editions and editor of Middle East edition, *Yank* army weekly, 1942-45; syndicated newspaper columnist of "Adventure Unlimited," *New York Herald-Tribune,* 1957-59; monthly columnist of "World's Largest Outdoor Column," *American Legion Magazine;* restaurant columnist, *Connecticut.* Editor, *Field and Stream;* outdoor editor, *Esquire* and *Sport;* roving editor, *Sports Afield, National Wildlife,* and *International Wildlife.* Writer of children's nonfiction, travel biographies, natural history, cookbooks, and contributor to magazines and anthologies.

MEMBER: Cordon Bleu de France.

AWARDS, HONORS: Loggerhead Turtle: Survivor from the Sea named a *Kirkus* Choice Book, a *School Library Journal* Best Book of the Year and Best of the Best Book, and Outstanding Science Trade Book for Children, 1974; *That Wonderful Pelican* named a *Kirkus* Choice Book, a *School Library Journal* Best Book of the Year and Best of the Best Book, and Outstanding Science Trade Book for Children, 1975; *Canada Geese* named a Junior Literary Guild Selection, Library of Congress Children's Book of the Year, *School Library Journal* Best Book of the Year, 1976; American Institute of Graphic Arts Book Show Award, 1976, for *Discovering the American Stork; Return of the Buffalo* named a *Kirkus* Choice Book and Outstanding Science Trade Book for Children, 1976; *The Gulls of Smuttynose Island* named a Junior Literary Guild Selection, Library of Congress Children's Book of the Year, *School Library Journal* Best Book of the Year, Child Study Children's Book Committee Book of the Year, 1977; *Little Dogs of the Prairie* named American Library Association Notable Children's Book, Outstanding Science Trade Book for Children, 1977; *Island of Wild Horses* named a Junior Literary Guild Selection and Outstanding Science Trade Book for Children, 1978; *City of Birds and Beasts* named a *School Library Journal* Best Book of the Year, 1978; *The Book of the Goat* named a Junior Literary Guild Selection and Child Study Children's Book Committee Book of the Year, 1979; *The Submarine Bird* named a Junior Literary Guild Selection, 1979; *The Book of the Pig* named Outstanding Science Trade Book for Children and American Library Association Children's Book, 1981; *Moose* named American Library Association Notable Children's Book and Outstanding Science Trade Book for Children, 1981; *Orphans from the Sea* named Outstanding Science Trade Book for Children, 1982; *The Fur Seals of Pribilof* named Outstanding Science Trade Book for Children, 1982; *Alligator* named Outstanding Science Trade Book for Children, 1984; *Swans* named a Junior Literary Guild Selection, 1987.

WRITINGS:

NONFICTION; PHOTOGRAPHS BY OZZIE SWEET

Loggerhead Turtle: Survivor from the Sea, Putnam, 1974.
That Wonderful Pelican, Putnam, 1975.
Canada Geese (Junior Literary Guild selection), Putnam, 1976.
Discovering the American Stork, Harcourt, 1976.
Return of the Buffalo, Putnam, 1976.
The Gulls of Smuttynose Island (Junior Literary Guild selection), Putnam, 1977.
Little Dogs of the Prairie, Putnam, 1977.
Island of Wild Horses (Junior Literary Guild selection), Putnam, 1978.
The Book of the Goat (Junior Literary Guild selection), Putnam, 1979.
The Submarine Bird (Junior Literary Guild selection), Putnam, 1979.
The Book of the Pig, Putnam, 1981.
Moose, Putnam, 1981.
Orphans from the Sea, Putnam, 1982.
The Fur Seals of Pribilof, Putnam, 1983.
Alligator, Putnam, 1984.
Swans (Junior Literary Guild selection), Putnam, 1987.

FOR ADULTS

(With Anne Damer) *Too Lively to Live* (detective novel), Doubleday, 1943.
The Weimaraner, Fawcett-Dearing Printing, 1953.
All Outdoors: Hunting and Fishing with the Author of America's Largest Outdoor Column, essays, Stackpole, 1956.
(Editor) *Your Dog's Health Book,* Macmillan, 1956.
Forests of the Night, photographs of India jungles by wife, Maria Luisa Scott, Rinehart, 1959.
How to Write and Sell for the Out-of-Doors, Macmillan, 1962.
Marvels and Mysteries of Our Animal World, Reader's Digest Association, 1964.
Passport to Adventure, photographs by M. L. Scott, Random House, 1966.
Speaking Wildly, essays, illustrated by Lydia Rosier, Morrow, 1966.
Elephant Grass, novel, Harcourt, 1969.
Spargo: A Novel of Espionage, World Publishing, 1971.
The Survivors: Enduring Animals of North America (essays), illustrated by Daphne Gillen, Harcourt, 1975.
Journey into Silence, Reader's Digest Press, 1976.
City of Birds and Beasts: Behind the Scenes at the Bronx Zoo, photographs by Ozzie Sweet, Putnam, 1978.
Window on the Wild (essays), illustrated by Geri Greinke, Putnam, 1980.
Curious Creatures, Reader's Digest Books, 1981.
The Sea File (novel), McGraw, 1981.

COOKBOOKS

The Complete Book of Pasta: An Italian Cookbook, illustrated by Melvin Klapholz, photographs by Samuel Chamberlain, Morrow, 1968, revised edition, Bantam, 1983, published as *The New Complete Book of Pasta: A Classic Revisited,* Morrow, 1985.
(With Antoine Gilly) *Antoine Gilly's Feast of France: A Cookbook of Masterpieces in French Cuisine,* illustrated by William Teodecki, Crowell, 1971.

(With M. L. Scott) *Informal Dinners for Easy Entertaining: Over 150 Easy But Elegant Meals You Can Eat with a Fork,* Simon & Schuster, 1975.
(With M. L. Scott) *Cook Like a Peasant, Eat Like a King,* Follett, 1976.
(With M. L. Scott) *Mastering Microwave Cooking,* Bantam, 1976, revised edition, Consumer Reports Books, 1988.
Best of Pacific Cookbook, Bantam, 1977.
(With M. L. Scott) *A World of Pasta: Unique Pasta Recipes from Around the World,* McGraw, 1978.
(With M. L. Scott) *The Great Potato Cookbook,* Bantam, 1980.
(With M. L. Scott) *The Chicken and Egg Cookbook,* Bantam, 1981.
(With M. L. Scott) *The Complete Convection Oven Cookbook,* Bantam, 1981.
(With M. L. Scott) *The Complete Book of Pies,* Bantam, 1985.
(With M. L. Scott) *Rice: More Than 250 Unexpected Ways to Cook the Perfect Food,* Times Books, 1985.
(With M. L. Scott) *The Great American Family Cookbook,* Bantam, 1986.
(With M. L. Scott) *Meat and Potatoes Cookbook,* Farrar, 1988.
(With M. L. Scott) *Rice: A Cookbook,* Consumer Reports Books, 1989.
(With M. L. Scott and the editors of Consumer Reports Books) *The Bean, Pea, and Lentil Cookbook,* Consumer Reports Books, 1991.

OTHER

(With Donald Ewin Cooke) *Pug Invades the Fifth Column,* D. McKay Co. 1943.
The Duluth Mongoose, illustrated by Lydia Fruhauf, Morrow, 1965.
Discovering the Mysterious Egret, illustrated by Pamela S. Distler, Harcourt, 1978.

Collaborator with playwright Sir Basil Bartlett and novelist Hilary St. George Saunders on the history of the Battle of Britain. Contributor to anthologies, including "My Favorite War Story" in *Thirty-four True Tales by Famous American War Reporters,* compiled by the editors of *Look* magazine, Whittlesey House/McGraw-Hill, 1945; "Nahnook: The Great White Hunter," in *The American Sportsman,* Ridge Press, 1968.

Contributor of articles and essays to educational textbooks, including *Spectrum I: Literature, Language, and Composition,* Ginn & Co., 1969; *Isn't That What Friends Are For?,* Houghton, 1972; *Young America Basic Reading Program,* Lyons and Carnahan, 1972; *Accents,* Houghton, 1978; *Reading Commitment,* Harcourt, 1978; *New Voices I: Literature, Language, and Composition,* Ginn & Co., 1978; *All of Us Together,* Bank Street College of Education, 1979; *Awards,* Houghton, 1981; *Through the Eyes of a Child: An Introduction to Children's Literature,* Merrill, 1983; *Houghton Mifflin Reading Triumphs,* Houghton, 1986. Contributor of over 1,500 articles to numerous periodicals, including *American Heritage, Argosy, Audubon, Bon Appetit, Collier's, Coronet, Cosmopolitan, Family Circle, Holiday, Liberty,* *Outdoor Life, Prism, Reader's Digest, Redbook, Saturday Evening Post, Scouting Magazine,* and *Smithsonian.*

From *Discovering the Mysterious Egret,* by Jack Denton Scott. Illustrated with photographs by Ozzie Sweet.

SIDELIGHTS: Jack Denton Scott is an award-winning author of nonfiction books for children and writer of numerous articles and books for adults, including cookbooks, travel, and fiction. In the realm of children's literature he specializes in life histories of animals. Most of the author's detailed and carefully crafted texts for children are enhanced by the black-and-white photographs of Ozzie Sweet. Critics have indicated that Scott's explorations of the animal kingdom both entertain and educate middle grade and high school readers, often clarifying misconceptions carelessly handled in other books.

Scott grew up in Elmira, New York. At age ten he knew that he wanted to become a writer, and by age sixteen he had published his first article. Three years later he sold his second magazine article, and since then he has written prolifically for many periodicals as a columnist on outdoor life, world travels, and cultures. During World War II he was a war correspondent in Europe, Egypt, and Africa, and wrote numerous articles for *Yank* army weekly. He traveled with soldiers and fliers and once was shot down over England, luckily landing unharmed.

After the war, Scott returned to New York and sold three articles, one of which led to an editorial position at *Field and Stream.* In 1957 he became a syndicated columnist of "Adventure Unlimited" for the *New York Herald Tribune,* beginning what would become a series of extensive journeys throughout the world for Scott and his wife, Maria Luisa—from 1959 to 1964 alone they logged over 600,000 miles. Their experiences in India, which included exploring jungles from the backs of elephants and visiting the royal family of the Maharaja of Bharaptur, resulted in a book offer from Random House. They returned to India and Scott recorded his observations in the travel biography *Passport to Adventure* in collaboration with his wife who provided the photographs. The Scotts' arctic voyage in search of a lost lake and their attempt to reach the North Pole provided the material for *Journey into Silence,* and dangerous encounters with a polar bear and glacial formations inspired numerous stories about the arctic region.

With his wife, Scott has also co-authored seventeen cookbooks, of which *The Complete Book of Pasta* and *Mastering Microwave Cooking* have been reprinted repeatedly, each undergoing twenty-four printings. "Cooking, and especially writing cookbooks," wrote the author in *Something about the Author Autobiography Series* (*SAAS*), "is excellent training ground for the writer. Cooking, first, is a creative art, probably one of the most important acts of a civilized man or woman. It is important to note that people who read cookbooks physically act upon the words that they read. Thus, the words and instructions must be clear and concise, always the mark of good writing."

For his children's books Scott frequently concentrates on a certain species of mammal, bird, or reptile, to entertain and inform. Usually he describes the evolutionary history, physical characteristics, habitat, diet, mating, and reproduction of his subject. Among the animals to receive such attention are the swan, cormorant, egret, Canada goose, buffalo, moose, turtle, alligator, horse, pig, and goat. Scott has teamed up with photographer Ozzie Sweet to produce books with what he described in an essay for *Through the Eyes of a Child* as "action, constant movement, words flowing into photographs, photographs flowing into words, no labored captions, no slowing of pace. Almost a cinematic technique." Scott is a careful researcher and works closely with Sweet to meld text and photographs. "It is teamwork of the highest order, as is our friendship, which goes back many years," Scott told *Something about the Author (SATA.)*

In his books on the cormorant (*The Submarine Bird*) and the loggerhead turtle, for example, Scott introduces the reader to little known animals. A critic in *Publishers Weekly* noted about *Loggerhead Turtle* that "Scott's visual account of the loggerhead's fight for survival sparkles with wit and admiration for a creature which has remained unaffected by evolution. And [Ozzie] Sweet's photos make the most of the text." In other books the author debunks the stereotypes about such common animals as pigs and goats. In *The Book of the Goat,* "The author first tries to undo some negative stereotypes about goats and challenges the dog's position as human's best and oldest friend. He does this by tracing the goat through history where it obviously held a very popular place, even achieving divinity among the Egyptians, Greeks, and Romans," wrote Marilyn R. Singer in *School Library Journal.*

In *SAAS* Scott shared how his ideas became books: "Once, watching the astounding sight of one raccoon dragging another, that had been struck by a car, from the road, and apparently trying to revive it, resulted in ... *The Survivors: Enduring Animals of North America.* Taking a young nephew to the famous Bronx Zoo resulted in a book for young adults, sparked by the youngster's animated questions—*City of Birds and Beasts.*"

In *Through the Eyes of a Child,* Scott explained the demands of writing for children: "Be accurate. Be relaxed; write fluently; never write down to your readers; never try to write up either. Know your audience; also know your subject; but even if you do know it, research it so that you will know perhaps more than you or anyone else will want to know. Put these all together and they may be an axiom for writing nonfiction for your readers. But there is more: There can be no cloudy language; writing must be simple, crisp, clear. This ... should be a primer for all writing. Children demand the best from a writer. If young readers become bored, confused, puzzled by style, or showered with a writer's self-important, complicated words, you've lost readers. Young readers instinctively shy away from the pretentious and the phony."

Scott is a renowned naturalist and has gained the reputation of a creator of high-quality instructional nature books for children in which he expresses his respect for animals and concern for endangered species. "Scott has both a profound knowledge of the animal world and a writing style that is both spontaneous and fluent," wrote Zena Sutherland in a review of *The Survivors* for *Bulletin of the Center for Children's Books,* "The admiration he feels for wild creatures is never excessive; his views on conservation or respect for animals never become didactic." His books have earned numerous awards, but most telling is the approval of his readership. In *Through the Eyes of a Child,* Scott recalled: "One ten-year-old boy wrote me that while he was reading our book, *Canada Geese,* he actually flew south with the geese. I bet he did. I *hope* he did."

WORKS CITED:

Publishers Weekly, February 18, 1974, p. 74.

Something about the Author, Volume 31, Gale, 1983, pp. 149-152.

Scott, Jack Denton, essay in *Something about the Author Autobiography Series,* Volume 14, Gale, 1992, pp. 195-263.

Scott, Jack Denton, "Through the Eyes of an Author: Writing Natural History for Young Readers," *Through the Eyes of a Child: An Introduction to Children's Literature,* by Donna E. Norton, 2nd edition, Merrill, 1987, pp. 590-591.

Singer, Marilyn R., *School Library Journal,* October, 1979, p. 162.
Sutherland, Zena, *Bulletin of the Center for Children's Books,* April, 1976, p. 133.

FOR MORE INFORMATION SEE:

BOOKS

Children's Literature Review, Volume 20, Gale, 1990.

* * *

SEARLE, Ronald (William Fordham) 1920-

PERSONAL: Born March 3, 1920, in Cambridge, England; son of William James and Nellie (Hunt) Searle; married Kaye Webb, 1946 (divorced, 1967); married Monica Koenig (a theater designer), 1967; children: (first marriage) Kate, John. *Education:* Cambridge School of Art, diploma, 1939.

ADDRESSES: *Agent*—Tessa Sayle, 11 Jubilee Place, London SW3 3TE, England; and John Locke Studio, 15 East 76th St., New York, NY 10021.

CAREER: Graphic artist, cartoonist, designer, and animator, 1935—. One man shows at galleries in many cities, including London, New York, San Francisco, Paris, Vienna, Berlin, Dahlem, Munich, Philadelphia, Zurich, Bremen, West Germany, Tolentino, Italy, Linz,

Ronald Searle

Austria, Soedertaelje, Sweden, Lausanne, Switzerland, and Hannover, West Germany. Film designer, 1957—; films designed include *John Gilpin,* 1951, *On the Twelfth Day,* 1954, *Energetically Yours,* 1957, *Germany,* 1960, *The King's Breakfast,* 1963, and *Dick Deadeye,* 1975; designer of animated sequences for the films *Those Magnificent Men in Their Flying Machines,* 1964, *Monte Carlo or Bust,* 1968, and *Scrooge,* 1970. Designer of commemorative medals for the French Mint, 1974—, and British Art Medal Society, 1983—. Editorial director, Perpetua Books, 1951-62. *Military service:* British Army, Royal Engineers, 1939-46; Japanese prisoner of war, 1942-45; Allied Force Headquarters, Department of Psychological Warfare, Port Said Operations, 1956.

MEMBER: Alliance Graphique Internationale, Garrick Club (London).

AWARDS, HONORS: Eleven awards, including Stratford (Ontario) Festival award, International Film Festival award, and Art Directors Club of Los Angeles medal, for animated film *Energetically Yours,* 1958-59; Art Directors Club of Philadelphia award, 1959; Reuben Award, National Cartoonists of America, 1960; gold medal, III Biennale, Tolentino, 1965; Prix de la Critique Belge, 1968; Prix d'Humour, Festival d'Avignon, 1971; Medaille de Ia ville d'Avignon, 1971; Grand Prix de l'Humour Noir "Grandville," 1971; Prix Internationale Charles Huard de dessin de presse, 1972; La Monnaie de Paris Medal, 1974; Royal Designer for Industry, 1988.

WRITINGS:

Forty Drawings, foreword by Frank Kendon, Cambridge University Press, 1946, Macmillan, 1947.
Le Nouveau Ballet anglais (picture album), Editions Montbrun, 1946.
Hurrah for St. Trinian's! and Other Lapses (also see below), foreword by D. B. Wyndham Lewis, Macdonald & Co., 1948.
The Female Approach, with Masculine Sidelights (also see below), foreword by Max Beerbohm, Macdonald & Co., 1949.
Back to the Slaughterhouse and Other Ugly Moments (also see below), Macdonald & Co., 1951.
Weil noch das Laempchen glueht (contains selections from *Hurrah for St. Trinian's, The Female Approach,* and *Back to the Slaughterhouse*), Diogenes, 1952.
Souls in Torment, preface and short dirge by C. Day Lewis, Perpetua, 1953.
Medisances, Editions Neuf, 1953.
The Female Approach: Cartoons, introduction by Malcolm Muggeridge, Knopf, 1954.
The Rake's Progress, Perpetua, 1955, new edition published as *The Rake's Progress: Some Immoral Tales,* Dobson, 1968.
Merry England, Etc., Perpetua, 1956, Knopf, 1957.
(Editor and author of introduction) *The Biting Eye of Andre Francois,* Perpetua, 1960.
The Penguin Ronald Searle, Penguin, 1960.

(Editor) Henri Perruchot, *Toulouse-Lautrec: A Definitive Biography,* translated by Humphrey Hare, Perpetua, 1960, World Publishing, 1961.

(Editor) Perruchot, *Cezanne: A Definitive Biography,* translated by Hare, Perpetua, 1961, World Publishing, 1962.

Which Way Did He Go?, Perpetua, 1961, World Publishing, 1962.

Toulouse-Lautrec (television script), British Broadcasting Corporation, 1961.

From Frozen North to Filthy Lucre: With Remarks by Groucho Marx and Commentaries by Jane Clapperton, Viking, 1964.

Searle in the Sixties, Penguin, 1964.

Pardong, M'sieur: Paris et autres, Denoel, 1965.

Searle's Cats, Dobson, 1967, Greene, 1968, revised and redrawn edition, Souvenir Press, 1987.

The Square Egg, Greene, 1968.

Take One Toad: A Book of Ancient Remedies, Dobson, 1968.

Hell—Where Did All the People Go?, Weidenfeld & Nicolson, 1969, Greene, 1970.

Hommage a Toulouse-Lautrec, introduction by Roland Topor, Editions Empreinte, 1969 (published in England as *The Second Coming of Toulouse-Lautrec,* Weidenfeld & Nicolson, 1970).

Filles de Hambourg, J.-J. Pauvert, 1969 (published in England as *Secret Sketchbook: The Back Streets of Hamburg,* Weidenfeld & Nicolson, 1970).

The Addict: A Terrible Tale, Greene, 1971.

I Disegni di Ronald Searle, Garzante Editore, 1973.

Gilbert & Sullivan: A Selection from Ronald Searle's Original Drawings for the Animated Feature Film "Dick Deadeye" (picture album), Entercom Productions, 1975.

Dick Deadeye; or, Duty Done, Harcourt, 1975.

More Cats, Dobson, 1975, Greene, 1976.

Searle's Zoodiac, Dobson, 1977, published as *Zoodiac,* Pantheon, 1978.

Ronald Searle (monograph), Deutsch, 1978, Mayflower Books, 1979.

The King of Beasts and Other Creatures, Allen Lane, 1980, published as *The Situation Is Hopeless,* Viking, 1981.

Ronald Searle's Big Fat Cat Book, Little, Brown, 1982.

The Illustrated Winespeak: Ronald Searle's Wicked World of Winetasting, Souvenir Press, 1983, Harper, 1984.

Ronald Searle in Perspective, New English Library, 1984, Atlantic Monthly Press, 1985.

Ronald Searle's Golden Oldies, 1941-1961, Pavilion, 1985.

To the Kwai—and Back: War Drawings, 1939-1945, Atlantic Monthly Press, 1986.

Something in the Cellar: Ronald Searle's Wonderful World of Wine, Souvenir Press, 1986, Ten Speed Press, 1988.

Ah Yes, I Remember It Well. . . : Paris 1961-1975, Pavilion, 1987, Salem House, 1988.

Ronald Searle's Non-Sexist Dictionary, Souvenir Press, 1988, Ten Speed Press. 1989.

Slightly Foxed—But Still Desirable: Ronald Searle's Wicked World of Book Collecting, Souvenir Press, 1989.

CO-AUTHOR

(With Kaye Webb) *Paris Sketchbook,* Saturn Press, 1950, Braziller, 1958, revised edition, Perpetua, 1957.

(With Timothy Shy, pseudonym of D. B. Wyndham Lewis) *The Terror of St. Trinian's; or, Angela's Prince Charming,* Parrish, 1952, reprinted, Ian Henry Publications, 1976.

(With Geoffrey Willans) *Down with Skool!: A Guide to School Life for Tiny Pupils and Their Parents* (also see below), Parrish, 1953, Vanguard, 1954.

(With Webb) *Looking at London and People Worth Meeting,* News Chronicle (London), 1953.

(With Willans) *How to be Topp: A Guide to Sukcess for Tiny Pupils, Including All Is to Kno About Space* (also see below), Vanguard, 1954.

(With Willans) *Whizz for Atomms: A Guide to Survival in the 20th Century for Fellow Pupils, Their Doting Maters, Pompous Paters and Any Others Who Are Interested* (also see below), Parrish, 1956, published as *Molesworth's Guide to the Atomic Age,* Vanguard, 1957.

(With Willans) *The Dog's Ear Book: With Four Lugubrious Verses,* Crowell, 1958.

(With Alex Atkinson) *The Big City; or, The New Mayhew,* Perpetua, 1958, Braziller, 1959.

(With Willans) *The Compleet Molesworth* (includes *Down with Skool!, How to Be Topp, Whizz for Atomms,* and *Back in the Jug Agane;* also see below), Parrish, 1958, reprinted, Pavilion, 1984.

(With Willans) *Back in the Jug Agane,* Parrish, 1959, published as *Molesworth Back in the Jug Agane,* Vanguard, 1960.

(With Atkinson) *USA for Beginners,* Perpetua, 1959, published as *By Rocking Chair across America,* Funk, 1959.

(With Atkinson) *Russia for Beginners: By Rocking Chair across Russia,* Perpetua, 1960, published as *By Rocking Chair across Russia,* World Publishing, 1960.

(With Webb) *Refugees 1960,* Penguin, 1960.

(With Atkinson) *Escape from the Amazon!,* Perpetua, 1964.

(With Heinz Huber) *Anatomie eines Adlers: Ein Deutschlandbuch,* Desch, 1966, translation by Constantine Fitz Gibboti published as *Haven't We Met Before Somewhere? Germany from the Inside and Out,* Viking, 1966.

(With Kildare Dobbs) *The Great Fur Opera: Annals of the Hudson's Bay Company, 1670-1970,* Greene, 1970.

(With Irwin Shaw) *Paris! Paris!,* Harcourt, 1977.

ILLUSTRATOR

W. Henry Brown, *Co-operation in a University Town,* Cooperative Printing Society, 1939.

Ronald Hastain, *White Coolie,* Hodder & Stoughton, 1947.

Douglas Goldring, *Life Interests,* Macdonald & Co., 1948.

W. E. Stanton Hope, *Tanker Fleet,* Anglo-Saxon Petroleum Co., 1948.

Frank Whitbourn, *Mr. Lock of St. James's Street: His Continuing Life and Changing Times,* Lock, 1948.

Gillian Olivier, *Turn But a Stone,* Hodder & Stoughton, 1949.

Audrey Hilton, *This England 1946-1949,* Turnstile Press, 1949.

Meet Yourself on Sunday, Naldrett Press, 1949.

Meet Yourself at the Doctor's, Naldrett Press, 1949.

Patrick Campbell, *A Long Drink of Cold Water,* Falcon Press, 1949.

Noel Langley, *The Inconstant Moon,* Arthur Barker, 1949.

Campbell, *A Short Trot with a Cultured Mind,* Falcon Press, 1950.

Oliver Philpott, *Stolen Journey,* Hodder & Stoughton, 1950.

Russell Braddon, *The Piddingtons,* Laurie, 1950.

Bernard Darwin and others, contributors, *The British Inn,* Naldrett Press, 1950.

Campbell, *Life in Thin Slices,* Falcon Press, 1951.

Harry Hearson and John Courtenay Trewin, *An Evening at the Larches,* Elek, 1951.

Braddon, *The Naked Island* (includes drawings made in Changi prison camps by Searle), Laurie, 1952.

Winifred Ellis, *London—So Help Me!,* Macdonald & Co., 1952.

William Cowper, *The Diverting History of John Gilpin,* Chiswick Press, 1952.

Christopher Fry, *An Experience of Cities,* Perpetua, 1952, Oxford University Press, 1953.

Frank Carpenter, *Six Animal Plays,* Methuen, 1953.

Denys Parsons, *It Must Be True,* Macdonald & Co., 1953.

Richard Haydn, *The Journal of Edwin Carp,* Hamish Hamilton, 1954.

Campbell, *Patrick Campbell's Omnibus,* Hulton Press, 1954.

Geoffrey Gorer, *Modern Types,* Cresset Press, 1955.

Reuben Ship, *The Investigator: A Narrative in Dialogue,* Sidgwick & Jackson, 1956.

Mr. Rothman's New Guide to London: Together with a Guide to Some Londoners of the Eighteen-Nineties, Rothmans of Pall Mall, 1958.

Kaye Webb, compiler, *The St. Trinian's Story: The Whole Ghastly Dossier,* Perpetua, 1959.

Fry, *Phoenix Too Frequent: A Comedy,* Oxford University Press, 1959.

Anger of Achilles: Homer's Iliad, translated by Robert Graves, Doubleday, 1959.

Ted Patrick and Silas Spitzer, *Great Restaurants of America,* Lippincott, 1960.

Charles Dickens, *A Christmas Carol,* Perpetua, 1961, World Publishing, 1961.

C. Dickens, *Great Expectations,* abridged edition, edited by D. Dickens, Norton, 1962.

C. Dickens, *Oliver Twist,* abridged edition, edited by D. Dickens, Norton, 1962.

James Thurber, *The Thirteen Clocks and The Wonderful O,* Penguin, 1962.

Allen Andrews and William Richardson, *Those Magnificent Men in Their Flying Machines; or, How I Flew from London to Paris in 25 Hours, 11 Minutes,* Norton, 1965.

Rudolf Eric Raspe and others, *The Adventures of Baron Munchausen,* introduction by S. J. Perelman, Pantheon, 1969.

Jack Davies, Ken Annakin, and Andrews, *Those Daring Young Men in Their Jaunty Jalopies: Monte Carlo or Bust!,* Putnam, 1969 (published in England as *Monte Carlo or Bust!: Those Daring Young Men in Their Jaunty Jalopies,* Dobson, 1969).

E. W. Hildick, *Monte Carlo or Bust!* (novelization of the screenplay *Those Daring Young Men in Their Jaunty Jalopies*), Sphere Books, 1969.

Leslie Bricusse, *Scrooge* (juvenile), Aurora Publications, 1970.

George Rainbird, *The Subtle Alchemist,* revised edition, Michael Joseph, 1973.

Tom Lehrer, *Too Many Songs by Tom Lehrer: With Not Enough Drawings by Ronald Searle,* Pantheon, 1981.

Kingsley Amis and James Cochrane, *The Great British Songbook,* Pavilion Books, 1986.

Russell Davies, *Ronald Searle* (biography), Sinclair-Stevenson, 1990.

OTHER

Contributor to *Encyclopedia Britannica.* Contributor of illustrations to *Lilliput, Holiday, Life, Fortune, TV Guide, New Yorker,* and numerous other periodicals. Member of *Punch* table, 1956-61.

ADAPTATIONS:

A series of cartoons on a fictitious girls' school became the "St. Trinian's" film series. All were produced by Frank Launder and Sidney Gilliat.

The Belles of St. Trinian's, starring Alastair Sim, British Lion Film Production, 1954.

Blue Murder at St. Trinian's, starring Joyce Grenfell, Terry Thomas, and Sim, John Harvel Productions, 1957.

The Pure Hell of St. Trinian's, starring Cecil Parker and Grenfell, Vale Film Productions, 1960.

The Great St. Trinian's Train Robbery, starring Frankie Howerd and Dora Bryan, Braywild Films, 1965.

The Wildcats of St. Trinian's, starting Sheila Hancock and Michael Hordern, Wildcat Film Productions, 1980.

SIDELIGHTS: Ronald Searle is an artist who "can do anything," claims Malcolm Muggeridge in the introduction to *The Female Approach: Cartoons,* "—illustrate, expound or embellish an idea, convey a scene or person." Famous in England and America for his blackly humorous drawings of animals in books such as *The Situation Is Hopeless,* and people, especially the wicked little girls of his "St. Trinian's" series, Searle's highly individual style "created a new approach to caricature by combining the highly conventionalized, two-dimensional drawing that came out of French modernism with a peculiarly British attention to details

From *The Female Approach,* written and illustrated by Ronald Searle.

of costume, furniture, architecture, ornament, facial expression, gesture and the bric-a-brac of social life," says Tom Wolfe in the *New York Times Book Review.* The artist's widespread popularity, beginning in the 1950s, "spawned a massive school of admirers and imitators," states Bill Mauldin in the *New York Times Book Review,* making him a source of inspiration for three generations of political cartoonists and satirists. Searle's comic artwork has influenced graphic artists such as Jeff MacNelly and Pat Oliphant in America, and Gerald Scarfe and Ralph Steadman in England.

Ronald Searle was born and bred in Cambridge, England. "My childhood," Searle reminiscences in an article for *Cartoonist Profiles,* "was unremarkable apart from the fact that I was born and brought up in one of the most beautiful and ancient university towns in England." He began drawing at an early age, but, he adds, "my great love was books. I devoured everything in our town library, beginning with the infant shelves and graduating at the age of twelve to the adult library. My thirst was insatiable." "By the time I was thirteen," he continues, "I wanted my own library, and I began to haunt the secondhand bookstalls.... I earned, begged, and scraped together every penny I could and within five years I had accumulated some five hundred volumes." Among these books were some volumes on caricature and a history of the British humour magazine *Punch* which helped spark Searle's interest in drawing and cartooning.

In the fall of 1933, Searle enrolled in art classes at the Cambridge Art School. "This had caused some argument between my mother and father," he recalls, "for the fee was 7s.6d. a term (about $1.50 then), and we couldn't afford it. But the money was scraped together somehow." He learned to draw classic figures, but, he adds, "side by side with my art-school work I scribbled comic drawings." In 1935, when the cartoonist for the local paper left his job, Searle took his place, submitting drawings for about $2.00 a week. "This represented all the drawing materials I needed, a bit for the family and something over for me. I continued with those weekly cartoons ... until the war, almost without a break. They were dreadful, but they taught me how to draw for reproduction." In 1938, Searle received an art scholarship, and the next year he earned his diploma from the Cambridge Art School.

Shortly after graduation Searle enlisted in the army, serving with the Royal Engineers in a camouflage unit before being sent to the South Pacific. In 1942, he became a prisoner of war and spent the next four years in prison camps in southeast Asia. He told Robert Osborn in *Saturday Review,* "That was the turning point for me.... I was captured when Singapore fell, and for four years I stayed a prisoner, drawing like mad. You learn how to feel things in a prison camp, and I was lucky enough to learn how to draw what I feel." "At art school," Searle told Henry C. Pitz in *American Artist,* "I had learned the academic structure of things and in the army I was able—or rather forced—to adapt and apply it. I wanted to draw things I saw about me and to register the impact of a new life." This work—some of it done with burnt matches and other improvised material—would have cost Searle his life had it been discovered, says Mauldin. Sometimes his pictures were concealed by fellow prisoners suffering from cholera, who depended on Japanese dread of the disease to prevent discovery. "Such an experience," states Muggeridge, "was bound to have a profound effect on someone as sensitive and imaginative as Searle. It might easily have destroyed him. Actually, he survived, not only in body (itself a considerable achievement) but, what was even more important, in spirit. The drawings he made during his confinement are haunting in their tenderness, and ... miraculous in the sureness and soundness of their line."

Searle's wartime sketches formed the basis of an exhibition at the Cambridge School of Art in 1946—a show which, says Wolfe, made the artist famous. His first book, *Forty Drawings,* consisted of a selection of these drawings. Many years later, Searle added reminiscences to his artwork and published the full three hundred sketches with text as *To the Kwai—and Back: War Drawings, 1939-1945.* Mauldin, himself a famous war artist, sums up his feeling about Searle's work, saying, "For me one of the greatest things about this book is its demonstration that the only chance for survival in truly impossible circumstances is to have a sense of humor so ingrained that it can't be kicked out of you.... Most of war seems to be a double image, harrowing and often tragic on one face, ennobling and sometimes whimsical on the flip side."

Searle's sense of humour stood him in good stead when he had to find a way to make a living in post-war Britain. "It seemed to me," Searle explains, "that the only fast and easy way of keeping myself fed was to sell cartoons. So I sold cartoons. This I rapidly discovered needed no particular ability apart from being able to communicate a personal way of looking at things.... Coming as I did from an atmosphere of stinking cells, wasted bodies and grim humour, my humour was 'black.' But so was the post-war climate of rationed England, and my work found a ready market there."

One of Searle's best known examples of black humour are the series of cartoons about St. Trinian's, "an appalling girls' school," writes Muggeridge, "in which gym-frocked monstrosities engage in murderous and criminal pursuits." Searle drew the first cartoon in the early 1940s to amuse the daughters of a friend who were attending St. Trinian's School for Girls in Edinburgh. The artist continued the series after the war; his depictions became enormously popular, and several films were produced which were based on the situations he created.

During the late 1940s and 1950s, Searle worked in many different genres. Besides becoming a regular cartoonist for *Punch,* he illustrated many books, worked on animated films, designed animated sequences and entire films for others, gathered material on refugees for the United Nations, and covered the 1960 election as a caricaturist for *Life* magazine. In 1961 he settled in France, where he lives and works today. "If satisfaction with one's work creeps in," he writes, "the time has come to give up.... A sure sign that there is still hope is when one is miserable at not having met one's own demands." "The hand is feeble," Searle concludes, "and the artist has still to express with exactitude what his brain conjures up. Some day it may be possible."

WORKS CITED:

Mauldin, Bill, "Sketches from Life and Death" (review of *To The Kwai—and Back*), *New York Times Book Review,* August 10, 1991, pp. 9-10.
Osborn, Robert, and Ronald Searle, "The Emasculation of American Humor," *Saturday Review,* November 23, 1957, pp. 16-17.
Pitz, Henry C., "Ronald Searle—British Graphic Artist," *American Artist,* September, 1955.
"Ronald Searle Writes from France," *Cartoonist Profiles,* fall, 1969.
Wolfe, Tom, "Simplicity of Line and a British Clutter" (review of *The Situation Is Hopeless*), *New York Times Book Review,* March 8, 1981, pp. 1-18.

FOR MORE INFORMATION SEE:

BOOKS

Feaver, William, *Masters of Caricature,* Knopf, 1981.
Heller, Steven, *Man Bites Man: Two Decades of Satiric Art,* A & W, 1981.
Miller, Bertha, and others, compilers, *Illustrators of Children's Books: 1946-1956,* Horn Book, 1958.
Searle, Ronald, *The Female Approach: Cartoons,* introduction by Malcolm Muggeridge, Knopf, 1954.
Searle, Ronald, *Ronald Searle* (monograph), Deutsch, 1978, Mayflower Press, 1979.
Searle, Ronald, *Ronald Searle in Perspective,* New English Library, 1984.

PERIODICALS

Bulletin C.E.M. of La Monnaie de Paris, June, 1974.
Chicago Tribune Book World, November 1, 1981; December 5, 1982.
Connaissance des Arts, June, 1979.
Das Schoenste, July, 1962.
Elseviers Weekblad, May 18, 1957.
Gebrauschgraphic, December, 1961.
Graphis, number 23, 1948; number 80, 1958; number 100, 1963.
Graphis 36, 1980/81.
Idea, number 78, 1966.
International Herald Tribune, February 17, 1973.
La Quinzaine Litteraire, December, 1967.
Le Monde, January 3, 1970; February 2, 1973.
Les Lettres Francaises, December 22, 1966; November 15, 1967.
Les Nouvelles Litteraires, December, 1966.
Library Journal, June 1, 1969.
Life, October 31, 1960.
L'oeil, November, 1974.
Los Angeles Times Book Review, April 19, 1981.
Natural History, June, 1971.
New Statesman, November 17, 1978.
New York Times Book Review, November 1, 1981.
Opus, January, 1972.
Paris Match, February 3, 1973.
P. N. Review, number 50, 1986.
Publimondial, number 76, 1955; number 82, 1956.
Quest, March, 1981.
Studio, March, 1963.
Texas Quarterly, number 4, 1960.
Times (London), February 12, 1973; May 8, 1973; November 24, 1978.
Times Literary Supplement, April 6, 1973; June 15, 1973.
Vogue, November 1, 1957.
Washington Post Book World, December 12, 1981.

* * *

SEBASTIAN, Lee
See SILVERBERG, Robert

* * *

SEBESTYEN, Igen
See SEBESTYEN, Ouida

SEBESTYEN, Ouida 1924-
(Igen Sebestyen)

PERSONAL: Name is pronounced "WEE-da See-best-yen"; born February 13, 1924, in Vernon, TX; daughter of James E. (a teacher) and Byrd (a teacher; maiden name, Lantrip) Dockery; married Adam Sebestyen, December 22, 1960 (divorced, 1966); children: Corbin. *Education:* Attended University of Colorado. *Hobbies and other interests:* Sewing, gardening, travel, carpentry.

ADDRESSES: Home—115 South 36th St., Boulder, CO 80303.

CAREER: Writer. Worked previously at a hamburger stand, repairing PT-19s during World War II, cleaning houses, and running a day-care center.

AWARDS, HONORS: New York Times outstanding book citation, *School Library Journal* best book citation, and American Library Association (ALA) best book for young adults and notable book citations, all 1979, International Reading Association Children's Book Award, 1980, and American Book Award, 1982, all for *Words by Heart;* ALA best book for young adults citation, and *School Library Journal* best books of the year citation, both 1980, American Book Award nomination, and Child Study Association recommended titles citation, both 1981, William Allen White Master List, 1982-83, and Zilveren Griffel (Silver Pencil) Award, 1984, all for *Far from Home;* ALA best book for young adults citation, Library of Congress Children's Books, and National Council of Teachers of English Teacher's Choice-*Parents' Choice* remarkable book citation, all 1982, Child Study Children's Book Committee list, and Texas Institute of Letters Children's Book Award, both 1983, and Mark Twain Award list nominee, 1985, all for *IOU's; The Girl in the Box* was nominated for the Colorado Blue Spruce Young Adult Award.

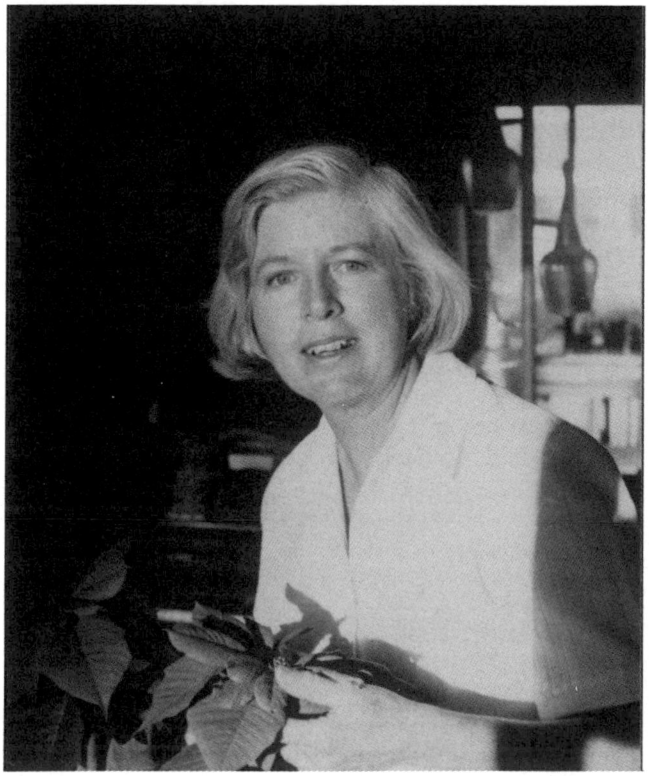

Ouida Sebestyen

WRITINGS:

YOUNG ADULT NOVELS

Words by Heart, Little, Brown, 1979.
Far from Home, Little, Brown, 1980.
IOU's, Little, Brown, 1982.
On Fire, Atlantic, 1985.
The Girl in the Box, Little, Brown, 1988.

OTHER

Also author of short stories under pseudonym Igen Sebestyen. Contributor to anthologies, including *Sixteen,* edited by Donald R. Gallo, Delacorte, 1984.

ADAPTATIONS: Words by Heart was adapted for television and broadcast by PBS-Wonderworks, 1985.

SIDELIGHTS: Ouida Sebestyen's writing career began later than most—her first novel was not published until she was fifty-five. But the book, a moving portrait of a young black girl titled *Words by Heart,* received numerous awards and was hailed by critics for its excellent dialogue and skillful development of character, plot, and relationships. This was not surprising since Sebestyen had set out to be a writer at a young age, refusing to be deterred by numerous rejection letters and near poverty. Since her first book, she has gone on to write several more novels for the young adult audience, all with a trademark style of strong technical skills coupled with a poetic, optimistic look at life.

Sebestyen was raised in the small town of Vernon, Texas, where her father was a schoolteacher. The young girl was an only child, and she led a rather protected life. She loved books so much that she sometimes looked forward to illness as an opportunity to read. "It was almost worth the discomfort of catching every known childhood disease, including a nearly fatal bout of pneumonia, to be able to lie in bed and read, or be read to," Sebestyen confessed in *Something about the Author Autobiography Series* (*SAAS*).

The author was also fascinated by plays, and was given the leading role in many of her school productions. Sebestyen was a dreamy child, one to whom time and worldly events held little meaning. About this tendency, the author wrote in *SAAS* that "everyone of appropriate age, I'm told, remembers what he or she was doing when Pearl Harbor was bombed or Kennedy was shot. Not me." Certain things, however, would imprint on her mind and be stored away for later use in her fiction.

Sebestyen was not particularly fond of school, and found socializing difficult. High school was painful for her, but she made one important choice there that was to affect her life—she decided to be a writer. She wasn't certain whether she could make it in this profession, feeling that spinning tales was not her forte. "But I had always loved words and taken notes and absorbed the world around me with little feelers that seemed to lie in wait on the surface of my skin. If sensitivity counted, I was destined for success," Sebestyen related in *SAAS.* The young adult years of her life were spent writing, traipsing across the West in her parent's station wagon, and working on planes that were used to train World War II pilots. She completed her first novel when she was nineteen and sent it off hopefully to a publisher, but it was rejected. She also tried starting up a theater in her hometown.

Growing discouraged with writing, Sebestyen's spirits were uplifted when she had a story accepted for publication in 1950. With this encouragement, she kept going and had two more published in the following years. One of her stories was almost turned into a television play. Although this never happened, she made a connection through it that helped her get a ticket to go to Iceland. After her visit she travelled home through Ireland, and when she got home she wrote a letter to a Dublin paper thanking the Irish for their hospitality. "It was published, this I know for sure," Sebestyen confided in *SAAS,* "because a visiting Hungarian student . . . read it and sent me a charming letter saying we had the same feelings about the beautiful Irish land and people. We began to correspond. He was coming to the United States. Perhaps we would meet someday! Could it sound any more like a soap opera?" The two eventually met, married, and moved to California. Sebestyen's parents soon joined her there, and for a time it seemed like they would live as one big, happy family. Unfortunately, her father died of cancer within a short time. After her son Corbin was born, Sebestyen began experiencing marital difficulties, and she and her husband eventually got a divorce. Sebestyen decided to relocate to Colorado with her mother and son for a fresh start. Once again, Sebestyen was determined to try to make it as a writer.

Times got tough as rejection letters continued to come in. But just as Sebestyen was going to throw in the towel and get a "real" job, she received notice that one of her short stories—about a black girl who won a contest for memorizing Bible verses—had sold. That got the author to thinking that since the protagonist of her story was a child, maybe children's fiction was a good genre for her to pursue. She then wrote a full-length novel based on the earlier short story. In three months, the manuscript was complete. Shortly afterward, *Words by Heart* was published in almost the same form as it was written.

Words by Heart touches on many topics—enduring family ties, overcoming racism, and keeping a loving attitude. It was translated into many languages and made into a television program that received two Emmy nominations. After this, Sebestyen's career was on a roll. She became an "overnight success"—even though it had taken her about thirty years of hard work to reach this stage. *Far from Home,* published in 1980, is set in her native Texas, and looks at a thirteen-year-old's attempt

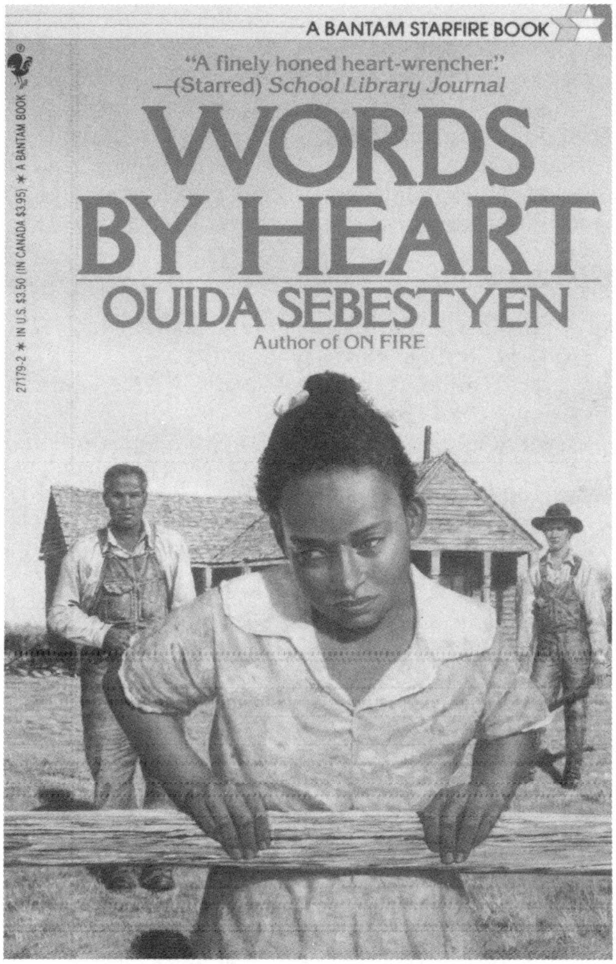

Cover of *Words by Heart,* by Ouida Sebestyen.

to take care of his family after his mother passes away. *IOU's* is loosely based on Sebestyen's relationship with her son. *On Fire* continues the story of one of the characters in *Words by Heart.* Sebestyen's most recent novel, *The Girl in the Box,* is a powerful story of a young girl who has been kidnapped and imprisoned. "Sebestyen's protagonists are spirited, independent teenagers bent on being better than they are now and better than others," Beverly Haley observed in *ALAN Review.* "They are human beings trembling on the edge of adulthood who grow up through the events in their lives. They grow stronger as a result of adversity and the fact that they are misfits in society becuase of age, social class, race, or sex."

Success in writing has brought Sebestyen some financial security that she missed in her days of pursuing her dream. She now owns her small house in Boulder instead of renting it. "My publishers have made it possible for me to discover I can run with the best through a crowded airport, check into a very large hotel alone, and talk with fading shyness to warm and responsive audiences all over the country," she related in *SAAS.*

Sebestyen has often been asked about her stories, which almost always involve the interrelationships of a close family. She commented in *ALAN Review* that "Motherhood was the turning point of both my life and my career. I couldn't have written my ... books before my son was born." She goes on to comment that it is this familial relationship that has given her the impetus and the themes for her writing—"in my mind love, and the miracles of acceptance and connection it generates, are the ultimate things to write about."

WORKS CITED:

Haley, Beverly, "Words by Ouida Sebestyen," *ALAN Review,* spring, 1983, p. 3.

Sebestyen, Ouida, "Family Matters," *ALAN Review,* spring, 1984, pp. 1-3.

Sebestyen, Ouida, essay in *Something about the Author Autobiography Series,* Volume 10, Gale, 1990, pp. 289-303.

FOR MORE INFORMATION SEE:

BOOKS

Children's Literature Review, Volume 17, Gale, 1989.

Contemporary Literary Criticism, Volume 30, Gale, 1984.

Harrison, Barbara, editor, *Innocence and Experience: Essays and Conversations on Children's Literature,* Lothrop, 1987.

Twentieth-Century Children's Writers, 3rd edition, St. James, 1989.

PERIODICALS

Publishers Weekly, May 28, 1979.

* * *

SELDEN, George
See THOMPSON, George Selden

* * *

SELSAM, Millicent E(llis) 1912-

PERSONAL: Born May 30, 1912, in Brooklyn, NY; daughter of Israel and Ida (Abrams) Ellis; married Howard B. Selsam (a writer; died September 7, 1970), September 1, 1936; children: Robert. *Education:* Brooklyn College (now part of the City University of New York), B.A., 1932, Columbia University, M.A., 1934. *Hobbies and other interests:* collecting specimens of marine life for aquarium on Fire Island, swimming, dancing, painting, plants.

ADDRESSES: Home—100 West 94th Street, New York, NY 10025.

CAREER: Author of books for young people. New York City Public Schools, high school teacher, 1935-45. Walker & Company Publishers, New York City, juvenile science editor, 1972—.

MEMBER: American Association for the Advancement of Science (fellow), American Nature Study Society, Authors Guild, Authors League of America, National Audubon Society.

Millicent Ellis Selsam

AWARDS, HONORS: Gold Medal Award, Boys' Clubs of America, 1963, for *Stars, Mosquitos and Crocodiles: The American Travels of Alexander Von Humboldt;* Eva L. Gordon Award, American Nature Study Society, 1964, for "many contributions to the literature of natural history"; Thomas A. Edison Award for best juvenile science book of the year, 1965, for *Biography of an Atom;* Junior Book Awards certificate, Boys' Clubs of America, 1966-67, for *Benny's Animals and How He Put Them In Order;* Lucky Book Club Four-Leaf Clover Award, 1973, for body of work; Washington Children's Book Guild Nonfiction Award, 1977, for "total body of creative writing"; Garden State Children's Book Award, 1978, for *How Kittens Grow;* nominee for Laura Ingalls Wilder Award, 1980; Garden State Children's Book Award for younger nonfiction, 1981, for *Tyrannosaurus Rex.*

WRITINGS:

Egg to Chick, illustrated by Frances Wells, International Publishers, 1946, revised edition illustrated by Barbara Wolff, Harper, 1970.

Hidden Animals, illustrated by David Shapiro, International Publishers, 1947, revised edition, Harper, 1969.

Play with Plants, illustrated by James MacDonald, Morrow, 1949, revised edition illustrated by Jerome Wexler, 1978.

Play with Trees, illustrated by Fred F. Scherer, Morrow, 1950.
Play with Vines (also see below), illustrated by Scherer, Morrow, 1951.
Play with Leaves and Flowers (also see below), illustrated by Scherer, Morrow, 1952.
All about Eggs, and How They Change into Animals, illustrated by Helen Ludwig, W. R. Scott, 1952, revised edition, Addison-Wesley, 1980.
Microbes at Work, illustrated by Ludwig, Morrow, 1953.
All Kinds of Babies and How They Grow, illustrated by Ludwig, W. R. Scott, 1953, revised edition published as *All Kinds of Babies,* illustrated by Symeon Shimin, Four Winds, 1967.
A Time for Sleep: How the Animals Rest, illustrated by Ludwig, W. R. Scott, 1953, revised edition published as *How Animals Sleep: A Time for Sleep,* illustrated by Ezra Jack Keats, Scholastic, 1969.
How the Animals Eat, illustrated by Ludwig, W. R. Scott, 1955.
The Plants We Eat, illustrated by Ludwig, Morrow, 1955, revised edition, 1981.
(With Betty Morrow) *See through the Sea,* illustrated by Winnifred Lubell, Harper, 1955.
See through the Forest, illustrated by Lubell, Harper, 1956.
Exploring the Animal Kingdom, illustrated by Leo Ames, Doubleday, 1957.
Play with Seeds, illustrated by Ludwig, Morrow, 1957.
See through the Jungle, illustrated by Lubell, Harper, 1957.
See through the Lake, illustrated by Lubell, Harper, 1958.
Nature Detective, illustrated by Theresa Sherman, W. R. Scott, 1958, revised edition published as *How to Be a Nature Detective,* illustrated by Keats, Harper, 1966.
Plants That Heal, illustrated by Kathleen Elgin, Morrow, 1959.
Seeds and More Seeds, illustrated by Tomi Ungerer, Harper, 1959.
(Editor) Charles Darwin, *The Voyage of the Beagle,* Harper, 1959.
Birth of an Island, illustrated by Lubell, Harper, 1959.
Around the World with Darwin, illustrated by Anthony Ravielli, Harper, 1960.
How to Grow House Plants, illustrated by Elgin, Morrow, 1960.
Plenty of Fish, illustrated by Erik Blegvad, Harper, 1960.
Tony's Birds, illustrated by Kert Werth, Harper, 1961.
See along the Shore, illustrated by Leonard Weisgard, Harper, 1961.
Underwater Zoos, illustrated by Elgin, Morrow, 1961.
The Language of Animals, illustrated by Elgin, Morrow, 1962.
(Editor) *Stars, Mosquitos and Crocodiles: The American Travels of Alexander Von Humboldt,* Harper, 1962.
Terry and the Caterpillars, illustrated by Arnold Lobel, Harper, 1962.
The Quest of Captain Cook, illustrated by Ames, Doubleday, 1962.
Plants that Move (contains *Play with Vines,* and *Play with Leaves and Flowers*), Morrow, 1962.
How Animals Live Together, illustrated by Elgin, Morrow, 1963, revised edition, 1979.
Greg's Microscope, illustrated by Lobel, Harper, 1963.
You and the World around You, illustrated by Greta Elgaard, Doubleday, 1963.
The Doubleday First Guide to Wildflowers, illustrated by Wolff, Doubleday, 1964.
The Courtship of Animals, illustrated by John Kaufman, Morrow, 1964.
Birth of a Forest, illustrated by Wolff, Harper, 1964.
Let's Get Turtles, illustrated by Lobel, Harper, 1965.
(With Jacob Bronowski) *Biography of an Atom,* revised edition illustrated by Weimer Pursell, Harper, 1965.
Animals as Parents, illustrated by Kaufman, Morrow, 1965.
Benny's Animals and How He Put Them in Order, illustrated by Lobel, Harper, 1966.
When an Animal Grows, illustrated by Kaufman, Harper, 1966.
The Bug that Laid the Golden Eggs, photographs by Harold Kreiger, illustrated by Kaufman, Harper, 1967.
Questions and Answers about Ants, illustrated by Arabelle Wheatley, Four Winds, 1967.
How Animals Tell Time, illustrated by Kaufman, Morrow, 1967.
Milkweed, photographs by Jerome Wexler, Morrow, 1967.
Maple Tree, photographs by Wexler, Morrow, 1968.
(With George B. Schaller) *The Tiger: Its Life in the Wild,* Harper, 1969.
Peanut, photographs by Wexler, Morrow, 1969.
The Tomato and Other Fruit Vegetables, photographs by Wexler, Morrow, 1970.
How Puppies Grow, Scholastic, 1971, revised edition, photographs by Esther Bubley, Four Winds, 1972.
Is This a Baby Dinosaur? And Other Science Picture Puzzles, Scholastic, 1971.
The Carrot and Other Root Vegetables, photographs by Wexler, Morrow, 1971.
Vegetables from Stems and Leaves, photographs by Wexler, Morrow, 1972.
More Potatoes!, illustrated by Ben Shecter, Harper, 1972.
The Apple and Other Fruits, photographs by Wexler, Morrow, 1973.
Questions and Answers about Horses, illustrated by Robert J. Lee, Four Winds, 1973.
Bulbs, Corms and Such, illustrated by Wexler, Morrow, 1974.
How Kittens Grow, illustrated by Bubley, Four Winds, 1975.
The Harlequin Moth: Its Life Story, illustrated by Wexler, Morrow, 1975.
Animals of the Sea, illustrated by John Hamberger, Scholastic Inc., 1975.
Popcorn, illustrated by Wexler, Morrow, 1976.
Sea Monsters of Long Ago, Scholastic Inc., 1977.
The Amazing Dandelion, photographs by Wexler, Morrow, 1977.

(With Kenneth Dewey) *Up Down and Around: The Force of Gravity,* Doubleday, 1977.
(With Deborah Peterson) *Don't Throw It Grow It Book of Houseplants,* Random House, 1977.
(And illustrator with Les Line), *Land of the Giant Tortoise: The Story of the Galapagos,* Scholastic Inc., 1977.
Sea Monsters of Long Ago, illustrated by Hamberger, Four Winds, 1978.
Mimosa: The Sensitive Plant, illustrated by Wexler, Morrow, 1978.
Tyrannosaurus Rex, Harper, 1978.
Eat the Fruit, Plant the Seed, photographs by Wexler, Morrow, 1980.
Night Animals, Scholastic Inc., 1980.

Also editor of "How Did We Find Out" series by Isaac Asimov, twenty books, Walker, c. 1972; co-editor with Joyce Hunt of "First Look" Series (juvenile science books), Walker, 1972—.

SIDELIGHTS: Millicent Selsam published her first book, *Egg to Chick,* in 1946, and since that time she has become the award-winning author of countless books for children that communicate her excitement over the process of scientific discovery. "I have certain childlike qualities," she once said in Lee Bennett Hopkins' *Books Are By People.* "I love to investigate everything and get great pleasure from growing plants indoors and out. I have always loved to know the *why* of everything. Science is dynamic and exciting, and it has changed the world."

Selsam grew up in New York City, an unusual place in which to develop an interest in nature. Field trips taken in high school inspired her to explore the fields of botany and biology through college study, and eventually led her to obtain advanced degrees in science from Columbia University. She taught high school science got tired of teaching but still enjoyed the idea of communicating with young people regarding science," she wrote. Looking for another avenue in which to use classes in New York City until the birth of her son. "I her science background, Selsam decided to try her hand at writing science books for children.

"To write about science for children an author needs to know science, to know children, and to know how to write—particularly to understand how to communicate with children on their level. Good science books should communicate some of the excitement of discovery—and the triumph that goes with the solution of scientific problems." In an article for *Children's Literature in Education,* Selsam expanded on the important role which science should play in the education of young people: "When children are taught the elements of the scientific method, they will have a healthy skepticism with regard to prevailing superstitions and exaggerated advertising. They will know that thirteen or any other number is neither unlucky or lucky. If somebody tells them that toads cause warts, or that laetrile cures cancer, they will ask for evidence. And when the radio or television blares out that this product is this or that percentage purer, better, or richer than that of some competitor, the child who has some idea of the scientific method will have his doubts."

WORKS CITED:

Hopkins, Lee Bennett, *Books Are By People,* Citation Press, 1969.
Selsam, Millicent E., "Science Books: Reflections of a Science Writer," *Children's Literature in Education,* summer, 1980, pp. 82-84.

FOR MORE INFORMATION SEE:

BOOKS

Arbuthnot, May Hill, and Zena Sutherland, *Children and Books,* 4th edition, Scott, Foresman, 1972.
Children's Literature Review, Volume 1, Gale, 1976.

From *Let's Get Turtles,* by Millicent Selsam. Illustrated by Arnold Lobel.

Fenwick, Sara Innis, editor, *A Critical Approach to Children's Literature,* University of Chicago Press, 1967.

PERIODICALS

Book Week, November 1, 1964; May 16, 1965; May 7, 1967.
Bulletin of the Center for Children's Books, February, 1974, p. 100; April, 1986, p. 157.
Christian Science Monitor, May 9, 1963; November 14, 1963; November 5, 1964, p. 108; December 21, 1967.
Fire Island News, May 28, 1966.
Horn Book, October, 1962; June, 1963; August, 1964, p. 391; June, 1965; June, 1977; August, 1977; June, 1978; October, 1978; February, 1979; October, 1980, p. 540.
Natural History, December, 1963; November, 1967.
New York Times Book Review, May 12, 1963; November 10, 1963; July 5, 1964; May 9, 1965; November 7, 1965; May 8, 1966; November 5, 1967, p. 52; April 20, 1969; November 9, 1969; May 9, 1970.
Saturday Review, January 19, 1963; April 22, 1967; November 9, 1968.
School Library Journal, November, 1973.
Times Literary Supplement, June 26, 1969.
Young Reader's Review, October, 1966; May, 1967.

* * *

SENDAK, Maurice (Bernard) 1928-

PERSONAL: Born June 10, 1928, in Brooklyn, NY; son of Philip (a dressmaker) and Sarah (Schindler) Sendak. *Education:* Attended Art Students' League, New York, NY, 1949-51.

ADDRESSES: Home—200 Chestnut Hill Rd., Ridgefield, CT 06877.

CAREER: Writer and illustrator of children's books, 1951—. Worked for comic book syndicate All American Comics part time during high school, adapting newspaper strips for comic books; Timely Service (window display house), New York City, window display artist, 1946; F.A.O. Schwartz, New York City, display artist, 1948-51. Co-founder and artistic director of national children's theater, The Night Kitchen, 1990—. Parsons School of Design, Yale University, former instructor. Set and costume designer for numerous of opera productions in the United States and Great Britain, including Mozart's "The Magic Flute," for Houston Grand Opera, 1980; Leos Janacek's "The Cunning Little Vixen," for New York City Opera, 1981; Serge Prokofiev's "Love for Three Oranges," for Glyndebourne Opera, 1982; Mozart's "The Goose of Cairo," for New York City Opera, c. 1984, and "Idomeneo," for the Los Angeles Opera, 1988; and Maurice Ravel's "L'Enfant et les Sortileges" and "L'Heure Espagnol," both for New York City Opera, both 1989; also designer for the film *The Nutcracker: The Motion Picture,* 1986. Has appeared in the films *The Lively Art of Picture Books,* c. 1965, and *Maurice Sendak,* Weston Woods, 1986; appeared in "Mon Cher Papa" episode of *American Master Series,* PBS-TV, 1987. *Exhibitions:* Sendak's illustrations have been displayed in one-man shows at the School of Visual Arts, New York City, 1964, Rosenbach Foundation, Philadelphia, PA, 1970 and 1975, Trinity College, 1972, Galerie Daniel Keel, Zurich, Switzerland, 1974, Ashmolean Museum, Oxford University, 1975, American Cultural Center, Paris, France, 1978, and Pierpont Morgan Library, New York City, 1981.

MEMBER: Authors Guild, Authors League of America.

AWARDS, HONORS: New York Times Best Illustrated Book award, 1952, for *A Hole Is to Dig,* 1954, for *I'll Be You and You Be Me,* 1956, for *I Want to Paint My Bathroom Blue,* 1957, for *The Birthday Party,* 1958, for *What Do You Say, Dear?,* 1959, for *Father Bear Comes Home,* 1960, for *Open House for Butterflies,* 1962, for *The Singing Hill,* 1963, for *Where the Wild Things Are,* 1964, for *The Bat-Poet,* 1965, for *The Animal Family,* 1966, for *Zlateh the Goat and Other Stories,* 1968, for *A Kiss for Little Bear,* 1969, for *The Light Princess,* 1970, for *In the Night Kitchen,* 1973, for *The Juniper Tree and Other Tales from Grimm* and *King Grisly-Beard,* 1976, for *Fly by Night,* 1981, for *Outside Over There,* and 1984, for *The Nutcracker;* Caldecott Medal runner-up, American Library Association, 1954, for *A Very Special House,* 1959, for *What Do You Say, Dear?,* 1960, for *The Moon Jumpers,* 1962, for *Little Bear's Visit,* 1963, for *Mr. Rabbit and the Lovely Present,* 1971, for *In the Night Kitchen,* and 1982, for *Outside Over There;* Spring Book Festival honor book, 1956, for *Kenny's Window;* Caldecott Medal, 1964, Lewis Carol Shelf award, 1964, International Board on Books for Young People award, 1966, Art Books for Children award, 1973, 1974, 1975, Best Young Picture Books Paperback Award from *Redbook,* 1984, and Children's Choice award, 1985, all for *Where the Wild Things Are;* Chandler Book Talk Reward of Merit, 1967; Hans Christian Andersen International Medal (first American to receive this award), 1970, for body of his illustration work; Art Books for Children award, 1973, 1974, 1975, and *Redbook* award, 1985, for *In the Night Kitchen;* American Book Award nomination, 1980, for *Higglety Pigglety Pop!; or, There Must Be More to Life; Boston Globe/Horn Book* award, 1981, *New York Times* Outstanding Book, 1981, and American Book Award, 1982, all for *Outside Over There;* Laura Ingalls Wilder Award, Association for Library Service to Children, 1983, for "a substantial and lasting contribution to children's literature." L.H.D., Boston University, 1977; honorary degrees from University of Southern Mississippi, 1981, and Keene State College, 1986.

Maurice Sendak

WRITINGS:

FOR CHILDREN; SELF-ILLUSTRATED

Kenny's Window, Harper, 1956.
Very Far Away, Harper, 1957.
The Acrobat, privately printed, 1959.
The Sign on Rosie's Door, Harper, 1960.
Nutshell Library (verse; contains *Chicken Soup with Rice: A Book of Months, One Was Johnny: A Counting Book, Alligators All Around: An Alphabet,* and *Pierre: A Cautionary Tale*), Harper, 1962.
Where the Wild Things Are, Harper, 1963, 25th anniversary edition, 1988.
Hector Protector and As I Went Over the Water: Two Nursery Rhymes, Harper, 1965.
Higglety Pigglety Pop!; or, There Must Be More to Life, Harper, 1967.
In the Night Kitchen, Harper, 1970.
Ten Little Rabbits: A Counting Book with Mino the Magician, Philip H. Rosenbach, 1970.
Pictures by Maurice Sendak, Harper, 1971.
Maurice Sendak's Really Rosie (based on the television program of the same title; also see below), Harper, 1975.
(With Matthew Margolis) *Some Swell Pup; or, Are You Sure You Want a Dog?,* Farrar, Straus, 1976.
Seven Little Monsters (verse), Harper, 1977.
Outside Over There, Harper, 1981.

ILLUSTRATOR

M. L. Eidinoff and Hyman Ruchlis, *Atomics for the Millions* (for adults), McGraw, 1947.
Robert Garvey, *Good Shabbos, Everybody!,* United Synagogue Commission on Jewish Education, 1951.
Marcel Ayme, *The Wonderful Farm,* Harper, 1951.
Ruth Krauss, *A Hole Is to Dig: A First Book of Definitions,* Harper, 1952.
Ruth Sawyer, *Maggie Rose: Her Birthday Christmas,* Harper, 1952.
Beatrice S. de Regniers, *The Giant Story,* Harper, 1953.
Meindert De Jong, *Hurry Home, Candy,* Harper, 1953.
De Jong, *Shadrach,* Harper, 1953.
Krauss, *A Very Special House,* Harper, 1953.
Hyman Chanover, *Happy Hanukkah, Everybody,* United Synagogue Commission on Jewish Education, 1954.
Krauss, *I'll Be You and You Be Me,* Harper, 1954.
Edward Tripp, *The Tin Fiddle,* Oxford University Press, 1954.
Ayme, *Magic Pictures,* Harper, 1954.
Betty MacDonald, *Mrs. Piggle-Wiggle's Farm,* Lippincott, 1954.
De Jong, *The Wheel on the School,* Harper, 1954.
Krauss, *Charlotte and the White Horse,* Harper, 1955.
De Jong, *The Little Cow and the Turtle,* Harper, 1955.
Jean Ritchie, *Singing Family of the Cumberlands,* Oxford University Press, 1955.

de Regniers, *What Can You Do with a Shoe?,* Harper, 1955.
Jack Sendak (brother), *Happy Rain,* Harper, 1956.
De Jong, *The House of Sixty Fathers,* Harper, 1956.
Krauss, *I Want to Paint My Bathroom Blue,* Harper, 1956.
Krauss, *Birthday Party,* Harper, 1957.
J. Sendak, *Circus Girl,* Harper, 1957.
Ogden Nash, *You Can't Get There from Here,* Little, Brown, 1957.
Else Minarik, *Little Bear,* Harper, 1957.
De Jong, *Along Came a Dog,* Harper, 1958.
Minarik, *No Fighting, No Biting!,* Harper, 1958.
Krauss, *Somebody Else's Nut Tree,* Harper, 1958.
Sesyle Joslyn, *What Do You Say, Dear?: A Book of Manners for All Occasions,* W. R. Scott, 1958.
Minarik, *Father Bear Comes Home,* Harper, 1959.
Janice Udry, *The Moon Jumpers,* Harper, 1959.
Hans Christian Andersen, *Seven Tales,* Harper, 1959.
Wilhelm Hauff, *Dwarf Long-Nose,* Random House, 1960.
Minarik, *Little Bear's Friend,* Harper, 1960.
Krauss, *Open House for Butterflies,* Harper, 1960.
Udry, *Let's Be Enemies,* Harper, 1961.
Clemens Brentano, *The Tale of Gockel, Hinkel & Gackeliah,* Random House, 1961.
Minarik, *Little Bear's Visit,* Harper, 1961.
Joslyn, *What Do You Do, Dear?,* Young Scott Books, 1961.
Brentano, *Schoolmaster Whackwell's Wonderful Sons,* Random House, 1962.
Charlotte Zolotow, *Mr. Rabbit and the Lovely Present,* Harper, 1962.
De Jong, *The Singing Hill,* Harper, 1962.
Leo Tolstoy, *Nikolenka's Childhood,* Harper, 1963.
Robert Keeshan, *She Loves Me, She Loves Me Not,* Harper, 1963.
Randall Jarrell, *The Bat-Poet,* Collier, 1964.
Amos Vogel, *How Little Lori Visited Times Square,* Harper, 1964.
Jan Wahl, *Pleasant Fieldmouse,* Harper, 1964.
William Engvick, editor, *Lullabies and Night Songs,* Pantheon, 1965.
Jarrell, *The Animal Family,* Pantheon, 1965.
Isaac Bashevis Singer, *Zlateh the Goat and Other Stories,* Harper, 1966.
George Macdonald, *The Golden Key,* Harper, 1967, 2nd edition, Farrar, Straus, 1984.
William Blake, *Poems from William Blake's Songs of Innocence,* Bodley Head, 1967.
Robert Graves, *The Big Green Book,* Crowell, 1968.
Frank Stockton, *Griffin and the Minor Canon,* Collins, 1968.
Minarik, *A Kiss for Little Bear,* Harper, 1968.
Macdonald, *The Light Princess,* Bodley Head, 1969, revised edition, Farrar, Straus, 1969.
Stockton, *The Bee-Man of Orn,* Holt, 1971.
Doris Orgel, *Sarah's Room,* Bodley Head, 1971.
Jakob Grimm and Wilhelm Grimm, *The Juniper Tree, and Other Tales from Grimm,* Farrar, Straus, 1973.
Marie Catherine Jumelle de Berneville Aulnoy, *Fortunia: A Tale by Mme. D'Aulnoy,* translated by Richard Schaubeck, Frank Hallman, 1974.
Jarrell, *Fly by Night,* Farrar, Straus, 1976.
J. Grimm and W. Grimm, *King Grisly-Beard: A Tale from the Brothers Grimm,* Harper, 1978.
E. T. A. Hoffman, *The Nutcracker,* translated by Ralph Manheim, Crown, 1984.
Philip Sendak (father), *In Grandpa's House,* translated and adapted by Seymour Barofsky, Harper, 1985.
Dear Mili: An Old Tale by Wilhelm Grimm, based on a letter by Wilhelm Grimm translated by Manheim, Michael Di Capua Books/Farrar, Straus, 1988.
(With Garth Williams) Jerome Griswold, *The Children's Books of Randall Jarrell,* University of Georgia Press, 1988.
Iona Opie, *I Saw Esau,* Candlewick Press, 1992.

Also illustrator of *Little Stories* by Gladys B. Bond, Anti-Defamation League of B'nai B'rith.

OTHER

Fantasy Sketches (published in conjunction with one-man show at Rosenbach Foundation), Philip H. Rosenbach, 1970.
(Editor and author of introduction) *Maxfield Parrish Poster Book,* Crown, 1974.
(Author of appreciation) *The Publishing Archive of Lothar Meggendorfer,* Schiller, 1975.
(And director and lyricist) *Really Rosie, Starring the Nutshell Kids* (thirty minute animated television special; based on characters from *The Nutshell Library* and *The Sign on Rosie's Door;* broadcast on Columbia Broadcasting System, 1975; also see below), music composed and performed by Carol King, Harper, 1975.
(Editor) *The Disney Poster Book,* illustrated by Walt Disney Studios, Harper, 1977.
(Lyricist and set designer) *Really Rosie* (musical play; revised from the television special of the same title), music by King, first produced in London and Washington, DC, 1978, produced Off-Broadway, October, 1980.
(Lyricist and set and costume designer) *Where the Wild Things Are* (opera; based on his book of the same title), music by Oliver Knussen, first produced at the Opera Nationale in Belgium, November, 1980, produced at New York City Opera in double-bill with Mozart's *The Goose from Cairo,* 1984.
(Author of introduction) Jean de Brunhoff, *Babar's Anniversary Album,* Random House, 1981.
Collection of Books, Posters and Original Drawings, Schiller, 1984.
(With Frank Corsaro) *The Love for Three Oranges: The Glyndebourne Version* (dialogue), Farrar, Straus, 1984.
(Librettist and set and costume designer) *Higglety, Pigglety, Pop!* (opera), first produced by the Glyndebourne Opera in England, October, 1984.
(Author of commentary) Jonathan Cott, editor, *Masterworks of Children's Literature,* Volume 7, Chelsea House, 1984.
(Photographer) Rudolf Tesnohlidek, *The Cunning Little Vixen,* Farrar, Straus, 1985.
(Author of introduction) Cott, *Victorian Color Picture Books,* Stonehill Publishing/Chelsea House, 1985.

Posters, Harmony Books, 1986.

(Author of foreword) John Canemaker, *Winsor McCay: His Life and Art,* Abbeville Press, 1987.

Caldecott & Co.: Notes on Books & Pictures, Michael Di Capua Books/Farrar, Straus, 1988.

(Author of introduction) *Mickey Mouse Movie Stories,* Abrams, 1988.

Maurice Sendak Book and Poster Package: Wild Things, Harper, 1991.

Also contributor of illustrations to *McCall's* and *Ladies' Home Journal,* 1964. Many of Sendak's books have been translated into foreign languages; *Where the Wild Things Are* has been translated into sixteen languages. Collections of Sendak's manuscripts are kept at the Museum of the Philip H. and A. S. W. Rosenbach Foundation in Philadelphia, PA, and in the Kerlan Collection at the University of Minnesota, Minneapolis.

ADAPTATIONS: Film strips with cassettes have been produced by Weston Woods of *Where the Wild Things Are,* 1968, *Pierre, Chicken Soup with Rice, Alligators All Around,* and *One Was Johnny,* all 1976; *Where the Wild Things Are* has also been made into a cassette by Caedmon, 1988; a film of *In the Night Kitchen* has also been produced by Weston Woods, 1988; *Higglety Pigglety Pop!* has been adapted as a Braille book and a record by Caedmon Records; a talking book version of *In the Night Kitchen* is available; toy "Wild Thing" dolls have been created by Harper.

WORK IN PROGRESS: Working on set and costume designs for stage adaptations of "Peter Pan" and "Hansel and Gretel" for his Night Kitchen children's theater.

SIDELIGHTS: The first American to win a Hans Christian Andersen International Medal, Maurice Sendak has been a major figure in the evolution of children's literature since the 1960s. With books like his Caldecott-winning *Where the Wild Things Are,* Sendak has led the way in trying to create more realistic child characters who are not the nostalgic models of innocence and sweetness that many authors portrayed in books before the 1960s. By creating drawings inspired by everything from nineteenth-century illustrators to twentieth-century cartoon artists, Sendak has also demonstrated an artistic adaptability that is nonconventional. Because of these deviations from what was once considered acceptable forms of writing and illustrating for children, Sendak has been the object of much controversy. But Jill P. May observes in the *Journal of Popular Culture* that "although Sendak's works seem disgusting to some U.S. educators, librarians, and parents, his books are found in most public libraries and elementary school libraries." And authorities such as writer and critic John Rowe Townsend, author of *Written for Children: An Outline of English Language Children's Literature,* consider Sendak "the greatest creator of picture books in the hundred-odd years' history of the form."

Critics of Sendak's work often argue that youngsters are not ready for the themes and images he presents. "Sendak has forthrightly confronted such sensitive subject matters as childhood anger, sexuality, or the occasionally murderous impulses of raw sibling rivalry," writes Selma G. Lanes in her *The Art of Maurice Sendak.* This "honesty has troubled or frightened many who would wish to sentimentalize childhood—to shelter children from their own psychological complexity or to deny that this complexity exists," comments *Dictionary of Literary Biography* contributor John Cotham. For the artist this exploration of children's feelings has been more of a personal quest than a desire to break new ground in juvenile literature. Many of his books refer—to a greater or lesser degree—to his own past experiences. "Primarily," Sendak reveals in Steven Heller's *Innovators of American Illustration,* "my work was an act of exorcism, an act of finding solutions so that I could have peace of mind and be an artist and function in the world as a human being and a man. My mind doesn't stray beyond my own need to survive."

The son of Jewish immigrants from Poland, Sendak grew up in a poor Brooklyn neighborhood with his older brother, Jack, and sister, Natalie. A number of factors in the artist's early life prevented him from having a normal, stable childhood. One problem was that his family never stayed in one neighborhood for very long, moving from apartment to apartment every time their landlords painted because Sendak's mother could not stand the smell of fresh paint. Sendak had a hard time making friends not only because of this, but also because he was very sickly—he suffered from measles, double pneumonia, and scarlet fever between the ages of two and four. His parents were very reluctant to let their son go outside and play for fear he would become sick and die. So the young Sendak spent much of his time in bed, looking out his bedroom window at the other children playing and becoming obsessed with the idea that he might not have long to live. "I was a miserable kid," he confesses to Lanes.

But Sendak found some escape through drawing, books, movies, music, and his own imagination. Contrary to what one might think a future writer and artist would read as a child, Sendak mostly read comic books—especially those featuring Mickey Mouse and other Disney characters—and some of his later illustrations clearly reflect this early influence. He also loved to go to the local theater and watch musicals and comedies like the Stan Laurel and Oliver Hardy films. One area where Sendak did deviate in his tastes for popular American culture was in his love of classical music, especially the music of Mozart. He often listened to classical music on the radio, and he would have taken piano lessons except that his parents could only afford lessons for his older brother Jack.

Sendak found a cheaper way to express his creativity by drawing and writing stories. During his many long days spent sick in bed, the young artist would sketch the people and houses in his neighborhood, dreaming up fantasies for them to be in. "There is not a book I have

From *Where the Wild Things Are,* written and illustrated by Maurice Sendak.

written or picture I have drawn that does not, in some way, owe [those neighborhood children] its existence," the artist reveals in Lanes's *Down the Rabbit Hole: Adventures and Misadventures in the Realm of Children's Literature.* He learned to make up stories from his father, who would amuse his children with fantastic tales that he would improvise. "Sendak feels that his father's stories were the first important source from which his work developed," according to Cotham. When he was about seven years old, Sendak and his brother, Jack, started writing down stories on cardboard discarded from shirt wrappings. Later, Jack also became a children's author, and two of his books have been illustrated by Sendak.

Sendak's first step toward becoming a professional illustrator came in high school when he worked on backgrounds for the comic strips "Mutt and Jeff," "Tippy," and "Captain Stubbs"; he also wrote his own comic strip for his school newspaper and illustrated a physics book, *Atomics for the Millions,* for one of his teachers. After he graduated, Sendak did not go to college as his father wished because he hated school and was eager to leave the strictures of the classroom as soon as possible. Instead, he worked for about two years in a warehouse in Manhattan. Leaving that job in 1948, Sendak designed mechanical wooden toys with Jack, and they tried to sell them to the famous New York toy company, F.A.O. Schwartz. Their plan did not succeed, but Sendak was hired to work on the store's window displays. One of his displays was seen by noted illustrator Leonard Weisgard, who offered Sendak a commission to illustrate *Good Shabbos, Everybody.*

At the same time Sendak was working for Schwartz he attended the Art Student's League, where he received encouragement from one of his instructors, John Groth, who told him that his time would be better spent if he left school and actively practiced his art in the real world. This idea appealed to Sendak. He left the art school and tried submitting his drawings to publishing houses. He was rejected many times, though, by editors who felt his work was old-fashioned. Indeed, Sendak had been influenced very early by such nineteenth-century illustrators as George Cruikshank, John Tenniel, Wilhelm Busch, and Louis Maurice Boutet de Monvel, whose intricate, cross-hatching style was nothing like the simpler style preferred by book editors in the 1940s and 1950s.

Then F.A.O. Schwartz's children's book department head Frances Christie introduced Sendak to Harper and Brothers editor Ursula Nordstrom. It was Nordstrom who gave Sendak his education in the business of book publishing, and she also carefully selected books for the artist to illustrate that would help him develop his craft and reputation. "I loved her on first meeting," Sendak remembers in *The Art of Maurice Sendak.* "My happiest memories, in fact, are of my earliest career, when Ursula was my confidante and best friend. She really became my home and the person I trusted most." Nordstrom arranged for Sendak to be the illustrator for Ruth Krauss's *A Hole Is to Dig,* the book that first established Sendak as an important illustrator. *A Hole Is to Dig* was such a popular and critical success that Sendak was able to quit his job at F.A.O. Schwartz and work as a freelancer.

During the 1950s Sendak learned how to be flexible and adapt his drawings to the texts they accompanied. Many illustrators of that time period were not able to do so, the artist tells Heller: "That's what doomed a lot of the illustrators working then. And that was the one thing Ursula was absolutely not going to let happen to me.... I was going to learn how to draw in a variety of styles. I think my books are identifiable, but they all look different because illustrators are secondary to the text. If you insist on being primary to the text, then you're a bad illustrator." Sendak's illustrations have thus varied from the line drawings of *Kenny's Window* and *Where the Wild Things Are* to the cartoonish style of *In the Night Kitchen* to the highly-detailed, cross-hatching style found in *Outside Over There* and his drawings for the books by the Brothers Grimm.

To make ends meet, the artist illustrated as many books as he could, so at first he did not have much time to do any of his own writing. Nordstrom, who had done so much for his illustrating, also later encouraged Sendak to write his own children's books. His first two efforts, *Kenny's Window* and *Very Far Away,* did not satisfy the artist completely. He calls *Kenny's Window* "overwritten" and "not well illustrated"; and although Sendak liked the story in *Very Far Away,* he has considered reillustrating the book. With *The Sign on Rosie's Door,* however, the artist created his first memorable character. Rosie is based on a real girl that Sendak remembers from his Brooklyn childhood. The book draws from the sketches he once made of Rosie and her friends in 1948 and 1949, and the story line uses some actual events and quotes the real Rosie directly in some cases. The fictional Rosie became the model for the typical Sendak character: strong-willed, honest, and—above all—imaginative.

"Rosie personifies Sendak's ability to empathize with the triumphs and terrors of childhood," observes John Lahr in the *New York Times. The Sign on Rosie's Door* is a simple story about a group of children with nothing to do on a long summer day in the city. Rosie, a somewhat bossy, but friendly and highly imaginative ten-year-old girl, shows her friends how to use fantasy to chase away their boredom. Later, Rosie became a television star when Sendak wrote, directed, and composed lyrics for a half-hour animated special that aired in 1975; and this led in turn to the artist's first venture into live theater when he designed the sets and wrote lyrics for a stage version produced in 1980.

Sendak's next work, *The Nutshell Library,* also features some of the characters from *The Sign on Rosie's Door.* Comprised of an alphabet book, a counting book, a book about the seasons, and a cautionary tale—all measuring only two-and-one-half by four inches—*The Nutshell Library* books have been highly praised for Sendak's skill "at integrating text, design, and illustrations," according to Cotham. Today, they are still considered by many critics to form one of the artist's most successful efforts.

After illustrating several picture books for other authors, Sendak decided to write some picture books himself as a way of controlling the wordiness he felt prevented him from expressing what he wanted to say in his illustrated books. "I finally came to grips with what my theme was and found the form most suitable to me as a writer and illustrator," he says in Heller's book. Picture books differ from illustrated books in that they consist mostly of illustrations accompanied by only short passages of text, while illustrated books are mostly text with only a few illustrations. During the following years, Sendak composed three picture books that he considers to form a loose trilogy: *Where the Wild Things Are, In the Night Kitchen,* and *Outside Over There.* Although the three stories seem unrelated, the artist says in *The Art of Maurice Sendak* that they "are all variations on the same theme: how children master various feelings—anger, boredom, fear, frustration, jealousy—and manage to come to grips with the realities of their lives."

One common aspect of these books is that they all involve the main character's voyaging into some type of fantasy world. In *Where the Wild Things Are* Max has an argument with his mother and is sent to his room without supper. He deals with his anger by imagining himself sailing to an island ruled by enormous, frightening monsters and becoming their king. However, Max soon becomes lonesome for his family and decides to return home. The fantasy world of *In the Night Kitchen* is a place that looks like a New York City skyline except that the buildings are made up of 1930s-era food boxes, bottles, and kitchen utensils. Here, bakers who all resemble the comedian Oliver Hardy work all night making goodies. When Mickey—who is named after Mickey Mouse—finds himself in the Night Kitchen he saves the day by finding milk for the bakers' cake. *Outside Over There,* which was marketed as both a children's and adult book, has a much more serious tone than *In the Night Kitchen.* It tells how Ida, who is very jealous of her baby brother, neglects him, until one day goblins kidnap the baby and take him to another world "outside over there." By traveling to this other world Ida reaffirms her love for her brother and manages to rescue him from the goblins.

Just as Sendak's characters resolve any crises they might have by traveling to a world of imagination, Sendak himself uses his imagination in some of these books as a means of releasing some of his own private conflicts. Depending on the book, this is true to a greater or lesser extent. For example, the monsters in *Where the Wild Things Are* were inspired by the artist's hated Brooklyn relatives. "I wanted the wild things to be frightening," Sendak remarks in *The Art of Maurice Sendak.* "But why? It was probably at this point that I remembered how I detested my Brooklyn relatives as a small child.... [T]hey'd lean way over with their bad teeth and hairy noses, and say something threatening like 'You're so cute I could eat you up.' And I knew if my mother didn't hurry up with the cooking, they probably would."

The events that preceded the writing of *In the Night Kitchen* had an even greater role in the creation of that book. In 1967 Sendak suffered a heart attack, lost his mother and beloved Sealyham terrier, Jennie, to cancer, and, two years later, his father also died. After these tragic events, the artist left New York City and moved to Connecticut. *In the Night Kitchen* was a way for Sendak "to do a book that would say goodbye to New York," he tells Martha Shirk in a *Chicago Tribune* article, "... and say goodbye to my parents, and tell a little bit about the narrow squeak I had just been through." In the story, Mickey's brush with death when he is nearly baked in a cake symbolizes Sendak's own close call. *In the Night Kitchen,* the artist concludes in a *New York Times* article by Lisa Hammel, is about his "victory over death."

Although *In the Night Kitchen* is an important book to Sendak, he has called *Outside Over There* his most personal work. "The book is obviously related to my own babyhood when my sister, Natalie, Ida's age, took care of me," he reveals to Jean F. Mercier in *Publishers Weekly.* The tale has its roots in the real-life story of the kidnapping of famous American pilot Charles Lindbergh's baby in 1932. Sendak recalls in his *New York Times Book Review* article how at the time he was "4 years old, sick in bed and somehow confusing myself with this baby. I had the superstitious feeling that if he came back I'd be O.K., too. Sadly, we all know the baby didn't come back. It left a peculiar mark in my mind." *Outside Over There* "is really a homage to my sister, who is Ida," the artist later adds. Sendak has never directly revealed the deep personal turmoils that his books at times express, but whatever they are *Outside Over There* has been the most therapeutic work for him. "I think it's the best thing I've done in my life," he says to *Contemporary Authors* interviewer Jean W. Ross. "It's the book I've searched for and scratched for.... What I got was as close to the realization of vision as I've ever experienced in my creative life.... It's a personal salvation and recovery of vision," he later adds.

Because of the personal value of *Outside Over There* to Sendak the relatively smaller sales of the book have not been a great concern to him. The problems that some of his other books have caused him have been much more troubling. Sendak first became a controversial figure with the publication of *Where the Wild Things Are.* Many critics and educators complained that the monsters were too frightening for small children. Critics like Bruno Bettelheim even felt that the book could cause psychological damage to sensitive children. In the *Ladies' Home Journal* he writes that Sendak "failed to understand ... the incredible fear it evokes in the child to be sent to bed without supper, and this by the first and foremost giver of food and security—his mother." Sendak responds to this criticism in Mark I. West's *Trust Your Children: Writers against Censorship in Children's Literature* by pointing out that Bettelheim had not even read the book. "He simply based his judgment on someone else's summary of it. Because of his article, all sorts of people said that the book was psychologically harmful to children. This hurt the book, and it hurt me. Since then Bettelheim has come full circle, but the damage had already been done."

A number of other books by Sendak have been criticized and even censored for various reasons. *In the Night Kitchen* was attacked by some reviewers because of its use of cartoon-style illustrations. Some people "dismiss comic books as vulgar trash," observes Sendak. But most of the objections have been aimed at the illustration in the book that shows Mickey completely nude from the front. Many librarians defaced the book by drawing diapers or underwear on Mickey to hide his genitals. "It's as if my book contains secret information that kids would be better off not knowing. This whole idea, of course, is ridiculous," says Sendak, pointing out that children are naturally open about their bodies until adults teach them to be ashamed of them. Another more recently-censored book by Sendak is *Some Swell Pup; or, Are You Sure You Want a Dog?,* a realistic guide to taking care of puppies, which was censored because of an illustration showing a dog defecating. According to Sendak in a *New York Times* article by Bernard Holland, censoring books that portray some of the facts of life to children is more for the benefit of the adult than the child: "Children are willing to expose themselves to experiences. We aren't. Grown-ups always say they protect their children, but they're really protecting themselves. Besides, you can't protect children. They know everything."

After moving to Connecticut, Sendak found peace and quiet by living in virtual isolation during much of the 1970s. Here, in a ten-room stone and clapboard house a few miles outside of Ridgefield, he worked ten to eleven hours a day in a room he converted into a studio. Many of the books he worked on at this time were picture books for other authors, as well as his own *Outside Over There.* Sendak felt that with this book he had gone about as far as he could go with picture books and he needed to move on to something else. In 1980, after "years spent on picture books, Sendak was ready to get out of his 'solitary confinement' and do his first opera project," writes *Theatre Crafts* contributor Ellen Levene.

Designing the sets and costumes for Mozart's *The Magic Flute,* Sendak later worked on the designs for such operas as *The Cunning Little Vixen* and *The Love of Three Oranges* and the stage and film versions of *The Nutcracker.* He also wrote the lyrics and did designs for his own *Where the Wild Things Are* and wrote a libretto for *Higglety, Pigglety, Pop!* Since becoming a classical music fan as a boy, Sendak had always wanted to get closer to the works of the masters, especially Mozart. Often, while writing and illustrating his books he would listen to Mozart for inspiration, and he has consequently memorized many of Mozart's compositions. The image of Mozart has even entered into some of Sendak's illustrations, but this was never enough for the artist. "That is why the operas are so important," Sendak tells Ross, "because by costuming and setting them I have come as close to the music as I ever have in my life. I'm now literally on the stage, and I'm coloring Mozart, illustrating him in the way I used to illustrate people's stories."

But Sendak wanted to do more with his work in the opera than repeat what others had done before him. Discussing his stage version of *Where the Wild Things Are* with *Horn Book* interviewer David E. White, the artist observes: "There are too many operas called children's operas. Most of them suffer for this very reason. They are written down to children, as though children could not appreciate the full weight of good musical quality. So I want *Wild Things* to be an opera which is comical and quite serious, a work that will satisfy adults as well as children." The same is true of the previously-produced operas and ballet with which Sendak has been involved. For example, when Sendak was asked to help with a new production of *The Nutcracker* he refused because he did not like the almost plotless story that had been used in earlier performances. However, he accepted the job when his own version of the stage drama was accepted. It was truer to the original book by E. T. A. Hoffman, which centers on the sexual and emotional coming-of-age of a young girl.

In order to have more freedom in the type of work he wanted to do for the theater, Sendak co-founded—with fellow writer Arthur Yorinks—a national theater for children in 1990 that he named The Night Kitchen. As the artistic director of the theater, he now hopes to produce new versions of such plays as *Peter Pan* and *Hansel and Gretel* that will not talk down to children. "Our work is very peculiar, idiosyncratic . . . ," Sendak tells *New York Times* contributor Eleanor Blau. "I don't believe in things literally *for* children. That's a reduction." Believing that children and adults should be treated with equal respect, he later adds: "Children are more open in their hearts and head[s] for what you're doing. . . . They're the best audience in town."

Sendak has never had children of his own or been married, but he tells White that having contact with children is not necessary for him to write tales that young audiences can appreciate. What is important is what he calls the "peculiar relationship with myself that allows me to dip endlessly into feelings which are not available to most people." By maintaining contact with the child within him, Sendak can easily relate to children while also touching on subjects and feelings that can stir recognition in adults. "We've all passed the same places," says the artist. "Only I remember the geography, and most people forget it."

The connection with the imagination and fantasy of childhood has always been Sendak's primary motivation in all that he has done. "The writing and the picture-making are merely a means to an end," he says in *Down the Rabbit Hole.* He then remarks, "It has never been for me a graphic matter—or even, for that matter, a word matter! To discuss a children's book in terms of its pictorial beauty—or prose style—is not to the point. It is the particular nugget of magic it achieves—if it achieves. It has always only been a means—a handle with which I can swing myself into—somewhere or other—the place I'd rather be."

WORKS CITED:

Bettelheim, Bruno, "The Care and Feeding of Monsters," *Ladies' Home Journal,* March, 1969, p. 48.

Blau, Eleanor, "Sendak Is Forming Company for National Children's Theater," *New York Times,* October 25, 1990.

Contemporary Authors New Revision Series, Volume 11, Gale, 1984, pp. 457-465.

Cotham, John, "Maurice Sendak," *Dictionary of Literary Biography,* Volume 61: *American Writers for Children since 1960: Poets, Illustrators, and Nonfiction Authors,* Gale, 1987, pp. 258-272.

Hammel, Lisa, "Maurice Sendak: Thriving on Quiet," *New York Times,* January 5, 1973.

Heller, Steven, editor, *Innovators of American Illustration,* Van Nostrand, 1986, pp. 70-81.

Holland, Bernard, "The Paternal Pride of Maurice Sendak," *New York Times,* November 8, 1987.

Lahr, John, "The Playful Art of Maurice Sendak," *New York Times,* October 12, 1980.

Lanes, Selma G., *Down the Rabbit Hole: Adventures and Misadventures in the Realm of Children's Literature,* Atheneum, 1971, pp. 67-78.

Lanes, Selma G., *The Art of Maurice Sendak,* Abrams, 1980.

Levene, Ellen, "Illustrators Edward Gorey and Maurice Sendak Have New Careers as Scenic Artists," *Theatre Crafts,* April, 1984, pp. 43-45, 75-78.

May, Jill P., "Sendak's American Hero," *Journal of Popular Culture,* summer, 1978, pp. 30-35.

Mercier, Jean F., "Sendak on Sendak," *Publishers Weekly,* April 10, 1981, pp. 45-46.

Sendak, Maurice, "Where the Wild Things Began," *New York Times Book Review,* May 17, 1987.

Shirk, Martha, "Relatively Monstrous: Maurice Sendak Says Nightmarish Kin Inspired His Famous 'Wild Things,'" *Chicago Tribune,* January 29, 1990.

Townsend, John Rowe, *Written for Children: An Outline of English Language Children's Literature,* revised edition, Lippincott, 1974, p. 310.

West, Mark I., *Trust Your Children: Writers against Censorship in Children's Literature,* Neal-Schuman, 1988, pp. 87-91.

White, David E., "A Conversation with Maurice Sendak," *Horn Book,* April, 1980, pp. 145-155.

FOR MORE INFORMATION SEE:

BOOKS

Arbuthnot, May Hill, and Zena Sutherland, *Children and Books,* 4th edition, Scott, Foresman, 1972.

Bader, Barbara, *American Picturebooks from Noah's Ark to the Beast Within,* Macmillan, 1976, pp. 495-524.

Children's Literature Review, Gale, Volume 1, 1976, Volume 17, 1989.

Dooley, Patricia, editor, *The First Steps: Best of the Early "ChLA Quarterly,"* ChLA Publications, 1984, pp. 135-139.

Georgiou, Constantine, *Children and Their Literature,* Prentice-Hall, 1969.

Hopkins, Lee Bennett, *Books Are by People,* Citation Press, 1969.

Kingman, Lee, editor, *Newbery and Caldecott Medal Books: 1956-1965,* Horn Book, 1965.

Lacy, Lyn Ellen, *Art and Design in Children's Picture Books: An Analysis of Caldecott Award-Winning Illustrations,* American Library Association, 1986, pp. 104-143.

Smith, Jeffrey Jon, *A Conversation with Maurice Sendak,* Smith (Illinois), 1974.

PERIODICALS

Appraisal: Science Books for Young People, spring-summer, 1984, pp. 4-9.
Books and Bookmen, June, 1969; December, 1974, pp. 74-75.
Chicago Tribune, July 17, 1980.
Chicago Tribune Book World, May 3, 1981.
Children's Book Review, June, 1971, p. 84.
Children's Literature: Annual of the Modern Language Association Seminar on Children's Literature and the Children's Literature Association, Volume 6, 1977, pp. 130-140; Volume 10, 1982, pp. 178-182; Volume 12, 1984, pp. 3-24; Volume 13, 1985, pp. 139-153.
Children's Literature Association Quarterly, fall, 1985, pp. 122-127.
Children's Literature in Education, November, 1971, p. 48; spring, 1982, pp. 38-43; summer, 1988, pp. 86-93.
Elementary English, February, 1971, pp. 262-263; November, 1971, pp. 825-832, 856-864.
Horn Book, December, 1970, pp. 642-646; October, 1976, p. 495; June, 1977, p. 303; August, 1983, pp. 474-477; May/June, 1986, pp. 305-313; May/June, 1987.
Junior Bookshelf, April, 1966, pp. 103-111; February, 1968, p. 30; August, 1970, pp. 205-206; June, 1971, pp. 165-166.
Los Angeles Times, February 6, 1981; December 10, 1982.
National Observer, November 27, 1967.
Newsweek, May 18, 1981.
New Yorker, January 22, 1966.
New York Review of Books, December 17, 1970.
New York Times, November 1, 1967; December 9, 1970; October 15, 1980; April 11, 1981; June 1, 1981; November 30, 1981; October 24, 1985.
New York Times Book Review, October 16, 1960, p. 40; October 22, 1967; November 1, 1970; February 29, 1976, p. 26; April 29, 1979; April 26, 1981, pp. 49, 64-65; October 9, 1983.
New York Times Magazine, June 7, 1970.
Parabola, fall, 1981, pp. 88-91.
People, December 2, 1985, pp. 215-216.
Quarterly Journal of the Library of Congress, Volume 28, number 4, 1971.
Rolling Stone, December 30, 1976.
Saturday Review, December 14, 1963.
School Library Journal, December, 1970; May, 1976, p. 54.
Signal, September, 1986, pp. 172-187.
Time, July 6, 1981; July 28, 1986, p. 50.
Times Literary Supplement, July 2, 1971; March 27, 1981.
Top of the News, June, 1970, pp. 366-369.
TV Guide, November 11, 1978.
Washington Post, November 1, 1978; November 20, 1981.
Washington Post Book World, May 10, 1981, pp. 1-2.

SEREDY, Kate 1899-1975

PERSONAL: Surname pronounced "*Sher*-edy"; born November 10, 1899, in Budapest, Hungary; immigrated to the United States, 1922; died March 7, 1975, in Middletown, NY; daughter of Louis Peter (a teacher) and Anna (Irany) Seredy. *Education:* Academy of Arts, Budapest, art teacher's diploma; took summer courses in Paris, Rome, and Berlin, 1918-22.

ADDRESSES: Home—Weaver Street, Montgomery, NY.

CAREER: Artist until 1935; author and illustrator of children's books, 1935-1975.

AWARDS, HONORS: John Newbery Medal, 1938, for *The White Stag.*

WRITINGS:

SELF-ILLUSTRATED

The Good Master, Viking, 1935.
Listening, Viking, 1936.
The White Stag, Viking, 1937.
The Singing Tree, Viking, 1939.
A Tree for Peter, Viking, 1940.
The Open Gate, Viking, 1943.
The Chestry Oak, Viking, 1948.
Gypsy, Viking, 1952.

Kate Seredy

From *Christmas Anna Angel,* by Ruth Sawyer. Illustrated by Kate Seredy.

Philomena, Viking, 1955.
The Tenement Tree, Viking, 1959.
A Brand New Uncle, Viking, 1960.
Lazy Tinka, Viking, 1962.

ILLUSTRATOR

Andre Norton, *Prince Commands,* Appleton-Century, 1934.
Sonia Daugherty, *Broken Song,* Nelson, 1934.
Elizabeth J. Gray, *Young Walter Scott,* Viking, 1935.
Wilhelmina Harper, editor, *Selfish Giant: And Other Stories,* McKay, 1935.
Blanche J. Thompson, *With Harp and Lute,* Macmillan, 1935.
Carol R. Brink, *Caddie Woodlawn,* Macmillan, 1935.
Brink, *Mademoiselle Misfortune,* Macmillan, 1936.
Harper, editor, *Gunniwolf: and Other Merry Tales,* McKay, 1936.
Margery Bianco, *Winterbound,* Viking, 1936.
Miriam E. Mason, *Smiling Hill Farm,* Ginn, 1937.
Thompson, editor, *Bible Children: Stories from the Bible,* Dodd, 1937.
Eva R. Gaggin, *An Ear for Uncle Emil,* Viking, 1939.
Mabel L. Hunt, *Michael's Island,* Stokes, 1940.
Thompson, *The Oldest Story: The Story of the Bible for Young People,* Bruce, 1943.
Prudence Cutwright, W. W. Charters, and Mae K. Clark, *Living Together at Home and School,* Macmillan, 1944.
Ruth Sawyer, *Christmas Anna Angel,* Viking, 1944.
Thompson, *A Candle Burns for France,* Bruce, 1946.
Bernice O. Frissell and Mary L. Friebele, *Fun at the Playground,* Macmillan, 1946.
Mabel S. G. LaRue, *Hoot-Owl,* Macmillan, 1946.
Nancy Barnes (pseudonym of Helen S. Adams), *Wonderful Year,* Messner, 1946.
Helen F. Daringer, *Adopted Jane,* Harcourt, 1947.
Daringer, *Mary Montgomery: Rebel,* Harcourt, 1948.
Daringer, *Pilgrim Kate,* Harcourt, 1949.
Miriam E. Mason, *A House for Ten,* Ginn, 1949.
Doris Gates, *Little Vic,* Viking, 1951.
Carolyn S. Bailey, *Finnegan II: His Nine Lives,* Viking, 1953.
Clyde R. Bulla, *A Dog Named Penny,* Crowell, 1955.

TRANSLATOR

Leopold Gedoe, *Who Is Johnny?,* illustrated by Gedoe, Viking, 1939.

OTHER

Also contributor to periodicals, including *Horn Book* and *Elementary English Review.* The original artwork for all the books that Seredy wrote, as well as several books by other authors that she illustrated, are kept at the May Massee Collection at the William Allen White Library, Emporia State University, Emporia, KS.

SIDELIGHTS: Kate Seredy's best-known books are about Hungary, where she grew up in the days before World War I. *The White Stag,* a 1938 Newbery Prize winner, recounts the legend of the country's formation and of the conqueror Attila the Hun. *The Good Master* and *The Singing Tree* describe life in the Hungarian countryside. Seredy's writing is respected not only for its portrayal of the culture she grew up in but also for the positive values it conveys to readers, such as sensitivity to people of other cultures, respect for work, and a love of peace. Seredy's illustrations appear in all of her books and in more than twenty-five books by other authors.

Seredy was born in Hungary on November 10, 1899. Her father was a teacher, and Seredy, an only child, grew up in a home filled with good books, good music, and intelligent adult conversation. She attended the Academy of Art in Budapest, where she learned the skills that made her a successful illustrator of her own books and those of other writers. During World War I, Seredy served for two years as a nurse in front-line hospitals, an experience that brought on a long illness and confirmed her pacifist views.

In 1922 Seredy came to the United States for a visit and decided to stay. Before she left Hungary she had illustrated two books there, and she wanted to do the same work in this country but needed first to learn English so that she could read the books she would illustrate. While she studied the language, she supported herself by doing art work on greeting cards, lamp shades, and book covers. In 1933 she opened a children's bookstore, which failed financially after a year but gave her experience in what children like in books.

By 1934 Seredy had found work illustrating children's books, but not enough to support herself adequately. Early in 1935 she met with May Massee, an editor of children's books at Viking Press, and asked for more work as an illustrator. Massee had nothing to offer in this line, but she took Seredy to lunch and, charmed by the tales Seredy told of her childhood in Hungary, suggested that she write a book of her own, which Massee promised she would publish in time for Christmas. Seredy was skeptical about both her own ability to carry out this suggestion and the possibility of such a book's being published, but she went home and began work on the story that became *The Good Master.* It was indeed published, launching the author's career and beginning her long relationship with Viking, which published all the books she wrote.

Seredy's father was the model for Marton Nagy, the "good master" in her first book, according to Althea K. Helbig in *Writers for Children,* and for Prince Alexander in *The Chestry Oak* and Mr. Smith in *A Brand-New Uncle,* Seredy's next-to-last book. It was her father's telling of the legendary founding of Hungary that inspired *The White Stag.* Seredy's antiwar views are strongly evident in *The Singing Tree,* a sequel to *The Good Master,* and again in *The Chestry Oak,* which is set in Hungary during World War II. Ann Bartholomew, writing in *Twentieth Century Children's Writers,* noted that Seredy was "one of the first children's writers to have dealt with the problems of the alien," citing as examples the Russian prisoners in Hungary in *The Singing Tree* and the homeless Hungarian boy sent to America during World War II in *The Chestry Oak.* As for her illustrations, Seredy's love of horses inspired what became some of the notable elements in her drawings. She also loved cats, which are the subject of *Gypsy,* a book that Kathy Piehl described in the *Dictionary of Literary Biography* as "the closest of all Seredy's works to a genuine picture book."

For many years Seredy lived in a Dutch colonial farmhouse in the Ramapo Mountains of New Jersey. This was the inspiration for the house in *Listening.* In 1936 she moved to a hundred-acre property in Montgomery, New York, which she farmed—with the help of a tractor she called Attila and a disc-harrow named Ferdinand—before she gave up that burdensome job and devoted all her time to writing and illustrating.

Seredy said in *Newbery Medal Books: 1922-1955* that her books came "out of nowhere" and always filled her with awe when she saw them in print, bearing her name. James E. Higgins, an admirer who knew Seredy and wrote about her in *Horn Book* in 1968, said that however varied her books are, they all have one thing in common: "each vividly reflects the person who is the author. She writes not only out of her own experience but out of her own feeling for life." Piehl concluded that "all Seredy's work exudes a fundamental optimism about the future. Even when her stories concern times of upheaval and despair, such as war, she depicts enclaves of human beings that remain loving, strong, and confident."

WORKS CITED:

Bartholomew, Ann, in *Twentieth-Century Children's Writers,* 3rd edition, edited by Tracy Chevalier, St. James Press, 1989, pp. 870-871.

Helbig, Althea K., in *Writers for Children,* edited by Jane M. Bingham, Scribner, 1988, pp. 519-524.

Higgins, James E., "Kate Seredy: Storyteller," *Horn Book,* April, 1986, pp. 162-168.

Piehl, Kathy, "Kate Seredy," *Dictionary of Literary Biography,* Volume 22: *American Writers for Children, 1900-1960,* Gale, 1983, pp. 299-306.

Seredy, Kate, "Concerning Myself," *Newbery Medal Books: 1922-1955,* edited by Bertha Mahony Miller and Elinor Whitney Field, Horn Book, 1955.

FOR MORE INFORMATION SEE:

BOOKS

Children's Literature Review, Volume 10, Gale, 1986, pp. 162-182.

Ferris, Helen, editor, *Writing Books for Boys and Girls,* Doubleday, 1952.

* * *

SERRAILLIER, Ian (Lucien) 1912-

PERSONAL: Born September 24, 1912, in London, England; son of Lucien and Mary (Rodger) Serraillier; married Anne Margaret Rogers, 1944; children: Helen, Jane, Christine Anne, Andrew. *Education:* St. Edmund Hall, Oxford, M.A., 1935. *Hobbies and other interests:* Mountain walking, skiing, swimming.

ADDRESSES: Home—Singleton, Chichester, Sussex PO18 0HA, England.

Ian Serraillier

From *The Silver Sword*, by Ian Serraillier. Illustrated by C. Walter Hodges.

CAREER: Wycliffe College, Stonehouse, Gloucestershire, England, schoolmaster, 1936-39; Dudley Grammar School, Dudley, Worcestershire, England, teacher, 1939-46; Midhurst Grammar School, Midhurst, Sussex, England, teacher, 1946-61; writer.

AWARDS, HONORS: New York Times Best Illustrated Book citation, 1953, for *Florina and the Wild Bird;* Carnegie Medal commendation, 1956, Spring Book Festival Award, 1959, and Boys' Clubs of America Junior Book Award, 1960, all for *The Silver Sword.*

WRITINGS:

(Contributor) *Three New Poets: Roy McFadden, Alex Comfort, Ian Serraillier,* Grey Walls Press, 1942.
(Self-illustrated) *The Weaver Birds* (poems), Macmillan, 1944.
Thomas and the Sparrow (poems), illustrated by Mark Severin, Oxford University Press, 1946.
They Raced for Treasure, illustrated by C. Walter Hodges, J. Cape, 1946, simplified educational edition published as *Treasure Ahead,* Heinemann, 1954.
Flight to Adventure, illustrated by Hodges, J. Cape, 1947, simplified educational edition published as *Mountain Rescue,* Heinemann, 1955.
Captain Bounsaboard and the Pirates, illustrated by Michael Bartlett and Arline Braybrooke, J. Cape, 1949.
The Monster Horse (poems), illustrated by Severin, Oxford University Press, 1950.
There's No Escape, illustrated by Hodges, J. Cape, 1950, educational edition, Heinemann, 1952, Scholastic, 1973.
The Ballad of Kon-Tiki and Other Verses, illustrated by Severin, Oxford University Press, 1952.
Belinda and the Swans, illustrated by Pat Marriott, J. Cape, 1952.
(Translator with wife, Anne Serraillier) Selina Choenz, *Florina and the Wild Bird,* illustrated by Alois Carigiet, Oxford University Press, 1952.
(Editor with Ronald Ridout) *Wide Horizon Reading Scheme,* four volumes, Heinemann, 1953-55.
Jungle Adventure (based on a story by R. M. Ballantyne), illustrated by Vera Jarman, Heinemann, 1953.
(Translator) *Beowulf the Warrior,* illustrated by Severin, Oxford University Press, 1954, Walck, 1961.
The Adventures of Dick Varley (based on a story by Ballantyne), illustrated by Jarman, Heinemann, 1954.
Everest Climbed (poem), illustrated by Leonard Rosoman, Oxford University Press, 1955.
Making Good, illustrated by Jarman, Heinemann, 1955.
The Silver Sword, illustrated by Hodges, J. Cape, 1956, educational edition, Heinemann, 1957, Criterion, 1958, published as *Escape from Warsaw,* Scholastic, 1963.
Guns in the Wild (based on a story by Ballantyne), illustrated by Shirley Hughes, Heinemann, 1956.
Katy at Home (based on a story by Susan Coolidge), illustrated by Hughes, Heinemann, 1957.
Poems and Pictures, Heinemann, 1958.
(Contributor) Eleanor Graham, editor, *A Puffin Quartet of Poets: Eleanor Farjeon, James Reeves, E. V. Rieu, Ian Serraillier,* illustrated by Diana Bloomfield, Penguin, 1958, revised edition, 1964.
Katy at School (based on a story by Susan Coolidge), illustrated by Hughes, Heinemann, 1959.
The Ivory Horn (adaptation of *The Song of Roland,* an early 12th century *chanson de geste* sometimes attributed to Turoldus), illustrated by William Stobbs, Oxford University Press, 1960, educational edition, Heinemann, 1962.
The Gorgon's Head: The Story of Perseus, illustrated by Stobbs, Oxford University Press, 1961, Walck, 1962.
The Way of Danger: The Story of Theseus, illustrated by Stobbs, Oxford University Press, 1962, Walck, 1963.
The Windmill Book of Ballads, illustrated by Severin and Rosoman, Heinemann, 1962.
Happily Ever After, illustrated by Brian Wildsmith, Oxford University Press, 1963.

The Clashing Rocks: The Story of Jason, illustrated by Stobbs, Oxford University Press, 1963, Walck, 1964.

The Midnight Thief: A Musical Story, music by Richard Rodney Bennett, illustrated by Tellosa, BBC Publications, 1963.

The Enchanted Island: Stories from Shakespeare, illustrated by Peter Farmer, Walck, 1964, educational edition published as *Murder at Dunsinane,* Scholastic, 1967.

The Cave of Death, illustrated by Stuart Tresilian, Heinemann, 1965.

Fight for Freedom, illustrated by John S. Goodall, Heinemann, 1965.

Ahmet the Woodseller: A Musical Story, music by Gordon Crosse, illustrated by John Griffiths, Oxford University Press, 1965.

The Way of Danger [and] *The Gorgon's Head,* educational edition, Heinemann, 1965.

A Fall from the Sky: The Story of Daedalus, illustrated by Stobbs, Nelson, 1966, Walck, 1966.

The Challenge of the Green Knight, illustrated by Victor Ambrus, Oxford University Press, 1966, Walck, 1967.

Robin in the Greenwood, illustrated by Ambrus, Oxford University Press, 1967, Walck, 1968.

Chaucer and His World (nonfiction), Lutterworth, 1967, Walck, 1968.

The Turtle Drum (musical story), music by Malcolm Arnold, illustrated by Charles Pickard, BBC Publications, 1967, Oxford University Press, 1968.

Havelok the Dane, illustrated by Elaine Raphael, Walck, 1967 (published in England as *Havelok the Warrior,* Hamish Hamilton, 1968).

Robin and His Merry Men, illustrated by Ambrus, Oxford University Press, 1969, Walck, 1970.

The Tale of Three Landlubbers, illustrated by Raymond Briggs, Hamish Hamilton, 1970, Coward McCann, 1971.

Heracles the Strong, illustrated by Rocco Negri, Walck, 1970, illustrated by Graham Humphreys, Oxford University Press, 1971.

The Ballad of St. Simeon, illustrated by Simon Stern, F. Watts, 1970, Kaye and Ward, 1970.

A Pride of Lions (musical story; produced in Nottingham, England, 1970), music by Phyllis Tate, Oxford University Press, 1971.

The Bishop and the Devil, illustrated by Stern, Kaye and Ward, 1971, F. Watts, 1971.

Have You Got Your Ticket?, illustrated by Douglas Hall, Longman, 1972.

Marko's Wedding, illustrated by Ambrus, Deutsch, 1972.

The Franklin's Tale, Retold, illustrated by Philip Gough, Warne, 1972.

I'll Tell You a Tale: A Collection of Poems and Ballads, illustrated by Charles Keeping and Renate Meyer, Longman, 1973, revised edition, Kestrel Books, 1976.

Pop Festival (reader), illustrated by Hall, Longman, 1973.

Suppose You Met a Witch, illustrated by Ed Emberley, Little, Brown, 1973.

The Robin and the Wren, illustrated by Fritz Wegner, Longman, 1974.

How Happily She Laughs and Other Poems, Longman, 1976.

The Sun Goes Free (reader), Longman, 1977.

The Road to Canterbury, illustrated by John Lawrence, Kestrel Books, 1979.

All Change at Singleton: For Charlton, Goodwood, East and West Dean (local history), Phillimore, 1979.

(With Richard Pailthorpe) *Goodwood Country in Old Photographs,* Sutton, 1987.

Founder and editor with Anne Serraillier, New Windmill series of contemporary literature, published by Heinemann Educational Books.

ADAPTATIONS: The Silver Sword inspired a BBC-TV television series, 1957, and was dramatized as *The Play of the Silver Sword* by Stuart Henson, published by Heinemann Educational Books, 1982, and produced in Oldham, England, 1983.

SIDELIGHTS: Ian Serraillier has tackled the ambitious task of interpreting some of world literature's classic stories for young audiences. Himself a poet, Serraillier also draws upon his knowledge of ancient Greek, Latin, and other archaic tongues to produce readable—and poetic—versions of old myths and ballads. Through Serraillier's efforts, the tales of Sir Gawain, Jason, Heracles, and Beowulf have become accessible to children who might otherwise never approach the original works.

A *Times Literary Supplement* reviewer notes that in his translations for children, Serraillier "has very skilfully succeeded in preserving colour, rhythm and phrase while presenting a more immediately comprehensible language." A *Junior Bookshelf* contributor likewise calls Serraillier "our finest poet writing for the young."

The author has also earned praise for his original writings, many of which draw upon his own experiences as a mountain climber in the Swiss Alps. The best known of Serraillier's novels for children is *The Silver Sword,* a World War II adventure that pits several intrepid children against the rigors of nature and the violence of the German army. In his book *The Nesbit Tradition: The Children's Novel in England 1945-1970,* Marcus Crouch describes *The Silver Sword* as "a book which one cannot read without profound emotional response and personal involvement."

"I cannot remember a time when I did not want to become a writer," the author notes in *Something about the Author Autobiography Series* (*SAAS*). "I was always practising, even while I was still at school, where we were brought up on Latin and Greek and hardly any English—a dry and rather indigestible mixture it might seem today." The oldest of four children, Serraillier was born in London in 1912. His father died when the author was only seven, and his mother's own frail health often kept her in Switzerland where the mountain air helped to abate her asthma. From an early age Serraillier and his brother went to Brighton College, a boarding prep school in Sussex.

Serraillier's best memories of childhood center around his vacation-time visits to Switzerland. There he developed a passion for mountain climbing, going on an expedition to the Matterhorn when he was only sixteen. He also became an experienced downhill skier, and he explored the mountains in all sorts of weather—fair and foul.

Serraillier won a scholarship to St. Edmund Hall, Oxford University, where he studied classics and English literature. After graduating from college with a Master's degree in 1935, he became a schoolmaster. "For many years teaching was my livelihood, and most of my writing was done in school vacations," he remembered in the *Third Book of Junior Authors.* "Much as I enjoyed teaching, I had always wanted to be a writer, and I was glad when I was able to make it a full-time occupation."

As a teacher and a poet, Serraillier discovered that the best stories were those that had stood the test of time—Greek legends, folk tales, fairy tales, and ballads. He told the *Third Book of Junior Authors* that often these works "need reinterpreting for each generation, and I enjoy re-telling them whether in prose or in verse." Along with his volumes of original poetry, Serraillier began to produce books for children based on ancient English and Greek folklore. He also wrote a children's book about some of Shakespeare's plays.

"No one does retellings of ancient tales better than Mr. Serraillier," writes another *Junior Bookshelf* correspondent. "His versions have a quiet, timeless dignity, and he makes sense of ... complicated narrative." The *Times Literary Supplement* reviewer contends that the works could only have been accomplished "by someone who loves the whole body of early ballad, carol and lay and knows it intimately."

Serraillier won multiple awards, however, for an original novel he wrote, *The Silver Sword.* The work follows the fortunes of a group of Polish children who trek across the face of Europe in search of their parents. Based on a true story, *The Silver Sword* reveals the dangers and despair of war—and the violence—in a realistic fashion. Crouch states that the tale "was written without heroics, but the heroism and endurance of the children shone brightly in Serraillier's unobtrusively lovely prose." In *Written for Children: An Outline of English-Language Children's Literature,* John Rowe Townsend calls *The Silver Sword* "the one undeniably first-rate war book for children by a British author."

Today Serraillier lives and works in Sussex, England. "I no longer climb the Matterhorn, but am content with the view from lesser hills nearer to home," he remarked in *SAAS.* The author enjoys getting letters from his readers, among whom he can include his own children and grandchildren. Serraillier added in his autobiographical essay that when he is writing, he sometimes strikes "a really impossible patch" where his ideas seem to dry up altogether. If that happens, he said, "I give up for an hour or two and go for a walk or do a bit of cooking or spend time with family and friends. A phrase I had been trying too hard to find when sitting at my typewriter may well pop into my head as I am making a caramel custard or mowing the lawn or sunbathing."

WORKS CITED:

Crouch, Marcus, *The Nesbit Tradition: The Children's Novel in England 1945-1970,* Ernest Benn, 1972, pp. 28-29.
Junior Bookshelf, December, 1967, p. 382.
Junior Bookshelf, August, 1971, p. 258.
Serraillier, Ian, essay in *Something about the Author Autobiography Series,* Volume 3, Gale, 1987.
Third Book of Junior Authors, H. W. Wilson, 1972, pp. 257-258.
Times Literary Supplement, November 30, 1967, p. 1139.
Townsend, John Rowe, *Written for Children: An Outline of English-Language Children's Literature,* Lippincott, 1974, p. 210.

FOR MORE INFORMATION SEE:

BOOKS

Children's Literature Review, Volume 2, Gale, 1976.

PERIODICALS

Kirkus Reviews, May 15, 1970.
New York Times Book Review, September 20, 1964; December 10, 1967.
Times Literary Supplement, November 19, 1954; November 28, 1963; November 24, 1966; July 2, 1971.

* * *

SEWALL, Marcia 1935-

PERSONAL: Born November 5, 1935, in Providence, RI; daughter of Edgar Knight and Hilda (Osgood) Sewall. *Education:* Pembroke College, B.A., 1957; Tufts University, M.Ed., 1958; studied art at Rhode Island School of Design and Boston Museum School. *Religion:* Unitarian Universalist.

ADDRESSES: Home—Boston, Massachusetts.

CAREER: Writer and illustrator of children's books. Children's Museum, Boston, MA, staff artist, 1961-63; teacher of art in Winchester, MA, 1967-75. Participant in Boston Adult literacy program and School Volunteers of Boston.

AWARDS, HONORS: Come Again in the Spring was named one of the outstanding books of the year, *New York Times,* 1976, and was selected for exhibition by American Institute of Graphic Arts, 1985; notable book citation, American Library Association, 1978, for *Little Things,* and 1981, for *The Song of the Horse;* best picture book of the year designation, *New York Times,* 1978, for *The Nutcrackers and the Sugar-Tongs; The Leprechaun's Story* was selected for exhibition by the

Marcia Sewall

American Institute of Graphic Arts, 1979; Parent's Choice Award for illustration, 1980, for *Crazy in Love;* outstanding book of the year designation, *New York Times,* 1980, for *Stone Fox; The Story of Old Mrs. Brubeck and How She Looked for Trouble and Where She Found Him* was named one of best picture books of the year, and *The Marzipan Moon* named one of outstanding books of the year, *New York Times,* both 1981; selection for exhibition at Bratislava International Biennale, 1983, for *The Song of the Horse,* and 1985, for *Finzel the Far-sighted; Boston Globe/Horn Book* Award for nonfiction, 1987, for *The Pilgrims of Plimoth.*

WRITINGS:

SELF-ILLUSTRATED

(Reteller) *The Little Wee Tyke,* Atheneum, 1979.
(Reteller) *The Wee, Wee Mannie and the Big, Big Coo* (Scottish folk-tale), Little, Brown, 1979.
(Reteller) *The Cobbler's Song,* Dutton, 1982.
Ridin' That Strawberry Roan, Viking, 1985.
(Reteller) *The World Turned Upside Down: An Old Penny Rhyme,* Atlantic Monthly, 1986.
The Pilgrims of Plimoth, Atheneum, 1986.
Animal Song, Joy Street Books, 1988.
People of the Breaking Day, Atheneum, 1990.

ILLUSTRATOR; TEXT BY RICHARD KENNEDY

The Parrot and the Thief, Little, Brown, 1974.
Come Again in the Spring (also see below), Harper, 1976.
The Porcelain Man (also see below), Little, Brown, 1976.
The Rise and Fall of Ben Gizzard, Little, Brown, 1978.
The Leprechaun's Story, Dutton, 1979.
Crazy in Love, Dutton, 1980.
The Song of the Horse, Dutton, 1981.
Richard Kennedy: Collected Stories (includes *Inside My Feet, The Porcelain Man,* and *Come Again in the Spring*), Harper, 1987.

ILLUSTRATOR

Joseph Jacobs, adapter, *Master of All Masters: An English Folktale,* Little, Brown, 1972.
P. C. Asbjoornsen and J. E. Moe, *The Squire's Bride: A Norwegian Folk Tale,* Atheneum, 1975.
Jacobs, *Coo-My-Dove, My Dear,* Atheneum, 1976.
Drew Stevenson, *The Ballad of Penelope Lou and Me,* Crossing Press, 1978.
Anne Eliot Crompton, *The Lifting Stone,* Holiday House, 1978.
Anne Laurin, *Little Things,* Atheneum, 1978.
Edward Lear, *The Nutcrackers and the Sugar-Tongs,* Little, Brown, 1978.
Paul Fleischman, *The Birthday Tree,* Harper, 1979.
Phyllis Krasilovsky, *The Man Who Tried to Save Time,* Doubleday, 1979.
John Reynolds Gardiner, *Stone Fox,* Crowell, 1980.
Nancy Willard, *The Marzipan Moon,* Harcourt, 1981.
Lore Segal, *The Story of Old Mrs. Brubeck and How She Looked for Trouble and Where She Found Him,* Pantheon, 1981.
Clyde Robert Bulla, *Poor Boy, Rich Boy,* Harper, 1982.
Lynn Hoopes, *When I Was Little,* Dutton, 1983.
Fleischman, *Finzel the Far-sighted,* Dutton, 1984.
Walter Wangerin, *Thistle,* Harper, 1984.
Jane Resh Thomas, *Say Goodbye to Grandma,* Clarion, 1988.
Roni Schotter, *Captain Snap and the Children of Vinegar Lane,* Orchard, 1989.
Patricia Foley, *John and the Fiddler,* Harper, 1990.
Ruth Young, *Daisy's Taxi,* Orchard, 1991.

OTHER

Contributor to periodicals, including *Horn Book.*

ADAPTATIONS: The Pilgrims of Plimoth was adapted for inclusion in a Read-Along Cassette series, Weston Woods, 1988.

SIDELIGHTS: Author and illustrator Marcia Sewall was raised in the coastal town of Providence, Rhode Island, entering Pembroke College at Brown University in 1953. Now living and working in Boston, Massachusetts, a city steeped in colonial American history, she is much more influenced by traditions from the past than by the modern city visible from her studio window. Sewall's love for the history and landscape of her New England heritage is embodied within her work, adding a unique vitality to the books she writes and illustrates for children.

Although never formally trained as an illustrator of children's books, Sewall demonstrated an early interest in both drawing and painting. She majored in art while in college and at one point after graduation spent a summer at the prestigious Rhode Island School of

From *The World Turned Upside Down,* retold and illustrated by Marcia Sewall.

Design in an accelerated art program. As she once told *Something about the Author,* "I never worked so hard in my life, and I learned a tremendous sense of discipline there. It was the first extremely structured art training I'd had. I needed it, and loved it." Before becoming a illustrator, Sewall taught art to high school students and was employed as a staff artist at the Children's Museum in Boston. Her desire to become a working illustrator motivated her to show her portfolio to several publishers. There was enthusiasm for her artistic style, and she launched a successful career in book illustration.

The first volume published with Sewall's illustrations was *Master of All Masters: An English Folktale.* As with all the books she has chosen to illustrate, she was immediately drawn to the humor and eccentricity of the characters within its pages. She once told *SATA,* "I don't think you can force a book. If a manuscript seems natural and comfortable and appealing, I accept it readily. You work so hard for three or four months on the material that you must be comfortable with it. I love the wisdom, the character, and the tradition in folk people, so I often choose books with that sort of quality.

"When I first receive a manuscript," explained Sewall, "I walk through the story and divide it into pictures. If it's to be a thirty-two page book then I am limited to about thirteen double-page spreads. I begin to immediately struggle with the sense of character, the movement of character, and then on to the transformation of that flat surface into a believable space. An author gives me clues as to person and place and then it's a matter of sorting them out. The illustrator often makes decisions about the period and costuming. I next try to capture the rhythm and movement of the story in the dummy."

Sewall has illustrated seven books for author Richard Kennedy, including his anthology, *Richard Kennedy: Collected Stories.* "Sometimes I know immediately how a book must look," she commented. "As I read the manuscript for [Kennedy's] *The Song of the Horse,* I visualized the story in scratchboard. Scratchboard is a black ink surface over a white gessoed board. Instead of putting a black line down on white paper you scratch a white line away from a black surface. It is sort of electrical, magnetic. It has a vibrancy that seemed appropriate for that particular story.

"Although I may not immediately 'see' a character, I have to believe that it's within me to see him or her. On reading and rereading a manuscript, a sense of person begins to emerge and it is that which I try to capture in my initial sketches. It took a stack of paper and lots of drawing of *Old Mrs. Brubeck* before she would materialize for me. At first I had difficulty with her as a personality. She worried too much. Then I thought, 'My gosh, she's me and she's everybody I know!' I began to feel that there was humor about her, and then she just took shape. I thought if I gave her wooden shoes we would not only see but could hear her move about the house in her search for 'Trouble' and, as a final statement, I distilled her anxious movements in silhouettes against the endpapers."

The Cobbler's Song, published in 1982, was Sewall's first full-color book. "What an absolute joy it was to sit down and paint, and use colors that seemed to express the changing moods of the story. I used gouache which is an opaque watercolor paint not unlike poster paint. The story is a variation of the old 'rich man, poor man' theme. It deals with feelings, so it made sense to use full-color and to put paint on expressively."

Periodically, Sewall has taken a break from illustrating books by other authors to illustrate some of her own texts. Sometimes she has adapted ethnic folk-tales to a picture-book format and in other instances has written original stories, all characteristically embroidered with Sewall's love of traditional folklore and history. *Ridin' That Strawberry Roan* is based on a traditional ballad from the American west and tells the story of the taming of an outlaw horse. Written in jaunty rhyming couplets, the book is illustrated throughout with bright watercolor paintings reflecting the story's humorous theme. *The Pilgrims of Plimoth* (1987), although based on actual diary entries made by William Bradford and other passengers of the *Mayflower,* was retold by Sewall as an original prose-poem and has been commended—along with its companion volume, *People of the Breaking Day*—for its "scholarship and sensitivity," by a critic in *School Library Journal.*

Taken together, these two books give a sensitive account of the day-to-day experiences of the early settlers of Plimoth Plantation and the Wampanoag Indians, a tribe then making their home in southeastern Massachusetts. Throughout both books, Sewall focuses on the strong fibers of family ritual and community support that unite these two very different groups of people in their struggle to survive the harshness of their common surroundings. Whether it be a young English lad standing on the deck of the *Mayflower* as the ship makes its way along the coast of Cape Cod towards a land full of mystery, or a young Indian girl collecting firewood within a dark, wintery forest, each contributes to the family, thereby playing an integral role in the survival of the entire community. Although somewhat critical of Sewall's attempt at recreating Native American speech patterns as being "overly mystical," a reviewer for *Horn Book* praised *People of the Breaking Day* as "a fine resource that is resonant with integrity, intelligence, and eloquence." The vibrant and impressionistic illustrations accompanying both books draw the reader deeply into that harshly beautiful New England Wilderness, which faced the first settlers upon their landing at Plymouth rock.

Sewall's success as an author has not diminished her desire to continue working as an illustrator. With an artist's eye for culling details from everyday life, she is continuously inspired by her surroundings. As she explained, "I have always enjoyed the sensation of movement ... and that has really helped me with moving figures about a page. My characters are not based on real people, though I notice when I illustrate a book that sometimes people I know will appear. Months later, it will occur to me that I have illustrated the boy in the corner market, or I discover that one of my figures sits like someone I know. I think an artist is constantly taking in visual impressions, but not always consciously. And you don't deliberately pull them out. They come."

WORKS CITED:

Bulletin of the Center for Children's Books, December, 1985.
Horn Book, January, 1991, p. 88.
New York Times Book Review, September 17, 1989.
School Library Journal, January, 1991, p. 106-107.
Something about the Author, Volume 37, Gale, 1985, pp. 170-174.

FOR MORE INFORMATION SEE:

BOOKS

Holmes Holtze, Sally, editor, *Fifth Book of Junior Authors and Illustrators,* H. W. Wilson, 1983, pp. 280-81.
Kingman, Lee, and others, compilers, *Illustrators of Children's Books: 1967-1976,* Horn Book, 1978.

PERIODICALS

Booklist, October 1, 1985, p. 269; September 15, 1986, p. 134; October 1, 1990, p. 329.
Graphis, Number 200, 1979.
Horn Book, December, 1979, p. 657; February, 1983, p. 40; January, 1988, pp. 32-34; July 1990, p. 153; January, 1991, p. 88.
New York Times Book Review, November 23, 1986, p. 32.
Publishers Weekly, January 24, 1977, p. 333; November 5, 1982, p. 71; November 2, 1990, p. 73-74.
School Library Journal, April, 1977, p. 57; December, 1979, p. 77; May, 1986, p. 85.

* * *

SEWELL, Anna 1820-1878

PERSONAL: Born March 30, 1820, in Yarmouth, England; died April 25, 1878, in Old Catton, England; buried near Boston, England; daughter of Isaac (a bank manager) and Mary (a writer; maiden name, Wright) Sewell. *Education:* Educated at home. *Religion:* Quaker. *Hobbies and other interests:* Horses, painting.

CAREER: Author and teacher. Assisted her mother in writing ballads.

Anna Sewell

WRITINGS:

Black Beauty: The Autobiography of a Horse, Jarrold, 1877, published in United States as *Black Beauty: His Grooms and Companions,* Murphy, 1891.

ADAPTATIONS: Many movie versions of *Black Beauty* have been made, the first an adaptation called *Your Obedient Servant,* Thomas A. Edison, 1917. Other adaptations of the story followed in 1921 by Vitagraph, in 1933 by Monogram Pictures and in 1946 by Twentieth-Century Fox. In 1957 a motion picture entitled *Courage of Black Beauty* was made by Alco Pictures. The latest of such movies was produced in 1971 by Tigon British Film Productions Ltd. and Chilton Film and Television Enterprises Ltd. A single filmstrip entitled *Black Beauty* appeared in 1971 from Universal Education and Visual Arts. There is also an audio version of *Black Beauty* which was recorded in 1989.

SIDELIGHTS: In her lifetime Anna Sewell wrote only one book, but *Black Beauty,* written when she was sixty years old and published shortly before she died, has made her name known worldwide. According to *The Junior Book of Authors,* this tale has been called "perhaps the most successful and beloved animal story ever written." It goes on to say that "more copies of the book have been distributed than of perhaps any other book except the Bible," yet Sewell received only twenty English pounds for her work.

This gentle Quaker lady, with her love for horses, helped make life for these animals much easier; the British Society for the Prevention of Cruelty to Animals and its American counterpart adopted the book and used it to educate people on the proper treatment of horses. For this reason the book has been called "the 'Uncle Tom's Cabin' of the Horse."

Sewell was born in Yarmouth, England in 1820, at about the time her father's business was failing. As a consequence the family moved to Dalton, where they lived for ten years. In 1834, when Sewell was fourteen, she fell and sprained her ankle while running down a steep carriage road, and was never able to walk upright again. She could still drive the horses she loved, ride horseback, and walk a little, though. She would drive her father the ten miles to work in a chaise pulled by a pony, a two hour trip during which she could study the pony and make him a companion. A friend who rode with her related that Sewell would guide the animal with words rather than with the reins, and he seemed to understand what she wanted him to do.

Following her accident, Sewell was sent on a long holiday to Yarmouth to recuperate. While there she developed a love for painting, and from that time on was constantly looking for subjects to use for her pictures. In 1846, Sewell spent some time for therapy at a spa in Marienbad, Germany. Her condition improved enough that when she returned to England she could take long walks with her mother, and was even able to make a trip to Spain to visit her brother Philip and his wife. Unfortunately, the improvement was temporary, and for the last eight years of her life she was bedridden.

Her mother was a writer of ballads and verses for young people, and around 1858 Sewell became her editor and critic, making suggestions and corrections. She also took over the housekeeping chores and the care of the garden. In the next year she and her mother established a "Working Man's Evening Institute," at which the two ladies taught local miners and laborers three evenings a week.

By 1871 Sewell was confined to her home by her disability, and was under the constant care of her mother. Some time before this she had been impressed by Horace Bushnell's book, *Essay on Animals,* which a friend had given her. Bushnell's ideas, together with her sympathy for horses, convinced her that "it was worth a great effort to *try* at least to bring the thoughts of men more in harmony with the purposes of God on this subject," as she wrote in a note quoted in *The Junior Book of Authors.*

While her health was failing Sewell started to write with a pencil her only book, *Black Beauty,* with her mother beside her to recopy it. Sewell had for some time thought of writing a book which she hoped would be able "to induce kindness, sympathy, and an understanding treatment of horses." At that time many drivers used a "check rein," which held the horse's head in an unnatural raised position; it was supposed to make the animal look elegant, but was extremely uncomfortable for the horse.

Sewell wrote off and on, when she was able, for six years, and in 1877 *Black Beauty* was finally published. In this story a well-bred horse talks, telling of his life's experiences as he goes from a loving master to a cruel one, until, after being used as a cart horse in unpleasant circumstances, he finally finds another kind owner. Frances Clarke Sayers, in an excerpt from her *Summoned by Books,* quoted a young student as saying, "The fact remains that when you read *Black Beauty* you feel like a horse."

Sewell did not live long after her one book was published. She died in Old Catton, near Norwich in 1878 at the age of fifty-eight, and was buried near Boston, England, in the quiet cemetery owned by the Society of Friends. At the funeral Sewell's mother noticed that the horses there had check reins and, knowing how much Anna had disliked this, ordered them removed.

WORKS CITED:

Kunitz, Stanley J., and Howard Haycraft, editors, *The Junior Book of Authors,* 1st edition, H. W. Wilson, 1934.

Sayers, Frances Clarke, "Books That Enchant: What Makes a Classic?," *Summoned by Books,* edited by Marjeanne Jensen Blinn, Viking, 1965, pp. 152-61.

From *Black Beauty,* by Anna Sewell. Illustrated by Fritz Eichenberg.

FOR MORE INFORMATION SEE:

BOOKS

Children's Literature Review, Volume 17, Gale, 1989.

Twentieth Century Children's Writers, 3rd edition, St. James Press, 1989.

* * *

SEWELL, Helen (Moore) 1896-1957

PERSONAL: Born June 27, 1896, in Mare Island, CA; died February 24, 1957, in New York, NY; daughter of William E. Sewell (a U.S. Navy commander). *Education:* Attended Pratt Institute; later studied painting with the artist Archipenko.

ADDRESSES: Home—New York, NY.

CAREER: Author and illustrator. Also worked as a greeting card designer.

AWARDS, HONORS: A Round of Carols was selected as one of the American Institute of Graphic Art's "Fifty Books of the Year," 1935; Newbery Award Honor Books, 1938, for *On the Banks of Plum Creek,* 1940, for *By the Shores of Silver Lake,* 1941, for *The Long Winter,* 1942, for *Little Town on the Prairie,* 1944, for *These Happy Golden Years,* and 1953, for *The Bears on Hemlock Mountain;* Young Reader's Choice, 1942, for *By the Shores of Silver Lake; New York Herald Tribune*'s Spring Book Festival Award middle honor, 1943, for *These Happy Golden Years; New York Times* best illustrated children's book of the year citation, 1955, for *The Three Kings of Saba;* Caldecott Medal honor book, 1955, for *The Thanksgiving Story; The Bears on Hemlock Mountain, The Thanksgiving Story,* and *The Three Kings of Saba* all received American Library Association notable book citations.

WRITINGS:

SELF-ILLUSTRATED CHILDREN'S BOOKS

ABC for Everyday, Macmillan, 1930.

(Compiler) *A Head for Happy,* Macmillan, 1931.

(Editor) *Words to the Wise: A Book of Proverbs,* Dodd, 1932.

Blue Barns: The Story of Two Big Geese and Seven Little Ducks, Macmillan, 1933.

Ming and Mehitable, Macmillan, 1936.

Peggy and the Pony, Oxford University Press, 1936.

Jimmy and Jemima, Macmillan, 1940.

Peggy and the Pup, Oxford University Press, 1941.

Birthdays for Robin, Macmillan, 1943.

Belinda the Mouse, Oxford University Press, 1944.

(With Elena Eleska) *Three Tall Tales,* Macmillan, 1947.

The Golden Christmas Manger (cut-out book), Simon & Schuster, 1948.

ILLUSTRATOR

Susanne K. Langer, *The Cruise of the Little Dipper and Other Fairy Tales,* Norcross, 1924.

Mary Britton Miller, *Menagerie,* Macmillan, 1928.

Helen Sewell

Miriam S. Potter, *Sally Gabble and the Fairies,* Macmillan, 1929.
Mimpsy Rhys, *Mr. Hermit Crab: A Tale for Children by a Child,* Macmillan, 1929.
Marjorie Cautley, *Building a House in Sweden* (adult), Macmillan, 1931.
Susan Smith, *The Christmas Tree in the Woods,* Minton, 1932.
Laura Ingalls Wilder, *Little House in the Big Woods,* Harper, 1932.
Langston Hughes, *The Dream Keeper and Other Poems* (young adult), Knopf, 1932, 9th edition, 1954.
Wilder, *Farmer Boy,* Harper, 1933.
Johan Falkberget, *Broomstick and Snowflake,* Macmillan, 1933.
Eliza Orne White, *Where Is Adelaide?,* Houghton, 1933.
Jean West Maury, compiler, *A First Bible,* Oxford University Press, 1934, 5th edition, 1955.
Elizabeth Coatsworth, *Away Goes Sally,* Macmillan, 1934.
Frances Clarke Sayers, *Bluebonnets for Lucinda,* Viking, 1934.
Cinderella, Macmillan, 1934.
Thomas Noble, compiler, *A Round of Carols,* Oxford University Press, 1935, new edition, Walck, 1964.
Wilder, *Little House on the Prairie,* Harper, 1935.
White, *Anne Frances,* Houghton, 1935.
Viola May Jones, *Peter and Gretchen of Old Nuremberg,* Albert Whitman, 1935, revised edition, c. 1940.
Carlo Collodi (pseudonym of Carlo Lorenzini), *Pinocchio,* Appleton-Century, 1935.
Mairin Cregan, *Old John,* Macmillan, 1936.
Eleanor Farjeon, *Ten Saints* (Protestant and Catholic editions), Oxford University Press, 1936.
Carol Ryrie Brink, *Baby Island,* Macmillan, 1937.
(With Mildred Boyle) Wilder, *On the Banks of Plum Creek,* Harper, 1937.
A. A. Milne, *The Magic Hill and Other Stories,* Grosset & Dunlap, 1937.
Milne, *The Princess and the Apple Tree and Other Stories,* Grosset & Dunlap, 1937.
Charlotte Bronte, *Jane Eyre,* Oxford University Press, 1938.
Mary Louise Jarden, *The Young Brontes* (young adult), Viking, 1938.
(With Boyle) Wilder, *By the Shores of Silver Lake,* Harper, 1939, special edition, E. M. Hale, 1956.
Coatsworth, *Five Bushel Farm,* Macmillan, 1939.
(With Boyle), Wilder, *The Long Winter,* Harper, 1940.
Coatsworth, *The Fair American,* Macmillan, 1940.
Jane Austen, *Pride and Prejudice,* preface by Frank Swinnerton, Limited Editions, 1940.
(With Boyle), Wilder, *Little Town on the Prairie,* Harper, 1941.
Sayers, *Tag-Along Tooloo,* Viking, 1941.
Coatsworth, *The White Horse,* Macmillan, 1942.
Ferenc Molnar, *The Blue-Eyed Lady,* Viking, 1942.
Thomas Bulfinch, *A Book of Myths: Selections from Bulfinch's Age of Fable,* Macmillan, 1942.
(With Boyle), Wilder, *These Happy Golden Years,* Harper, 1943.
James S. Tippett, *Christmas Magic,* Grosset & Dunlap, 1944.
Coatsworth, *Big Green Umbrella,* Grosset & Dunlap, 1944.
Marion Boss Ward, *Boat Children of Canton,* McKay, 1944.
Coatsworth, *The Wonderful Day,* Macmillan, 1946.
Dorothy Kunhardt, *Once There Was a Little Boy,* Viking, 1946.
Louise H. Seaman, *The Brave Bantam,* Macmillan, 1946.
Maude Crowley, *Azor,* Oxford University Press, 1948.
Crowley, *Azor and the Haddock,* Oxford University Press, 1949.
Crowley, *Azor and the Blue-Eyed Cow: A Christmas Story,* Oxford University Press, 1951.
Irmengarde Eberle, *Secrets and Surprises,* Heath, 1951.
(With Madeleine Gekiere) Mary Chase, *Mrs. McThing,* Oxford University Press, 1952.
Alice Dalgliesh, *The Bears on Hemlock Mountain,* Scribner, 1952.
Emily Dickinson, *Poems,* selected and edited with a commentary by Louis Untermeyer, Limited Editions, 1952.
Alf Evers, *The Colonel's Squad,* Macmillan, 1952.
Dalgliesh, *The Thanksgiving Story,* Scribner, 1954.
Evers, *In the Beginning,* Macmillan, 1954.
(With Gekiere) Brothers Grimm, *Grimm's Tales,* Oxford University Press, 1954.
Evers, *The Three Kings of Saba,* Lippincott, 1955.
Austin, *Sense and Sensibility,* Limited Editions, 1957.

OTHER

Contributor of drawings to the *New Yorker.* Sewell's manuscripts are housed in the May Massee Collection at Emporia State University.

SIDELIGHTS: Helen Sewell authored several self-illustrated books for children during the 1930s and 1940s, including *Blue Barns: The Story of Two Big Geese and Seven Little Ducks, Ming and Mehitable,* and *Peggy and the Pony.* She was much better known, however, for the illustrations she made for the works of other authors, such as Laura Ingalls Wilder and Alice Dalgliesh. Sewell served as an illustrator from the late 1920s until just before her death in 1957, and her artistic contributions garnered several awards, including the prestigious Newbery and Caldecott honors.

Sewell was born June 27, 1896, on Mare Island in California. Her mother died early in her childhood, and she and her sister traveled a great deal with their father, who was a naval commander. She had gone around the world before she was seven, and spent much of her early life on the island of Guam. But when Sewell was almost eight, her father died as well, and she and her sister went to live with an aunt, uncle, and several cousins in Brooklyn, New York. It was in this new city that Sewell decided to become an art student. By the time she was twelve years old she had been admitted to art classes at the Pratt institute, becoming the youngest student ever to attend; she enrolled there full-time when she turned sixteen. Sewell then furthered her education by studying painting with the Russian artist Archipenko.

As an adult, Sewell began supporting herself by designing greeting cards. Eventually, she got work illustrating children's books by other authors; her first published effort was Susanne Langer's *The Cruise of the Little Dipper and Other Fairy Tales* in 1924. This book was seen and admired by editor Louise Seaman Bechtel, who asked Sewell to illustrate Mary B. Miller's collection of poems, *Menagerie.* Two years following *Menagerie*'s publication, Sewell published her own self-illustrated book for children—*ABC for Everyday.*

Sewell's next effort as a children's author, 1931's *A Head for Happy,* the story of three sisters who make a doll and then search the world for the right head to fit it, meant a great deal to her. She explained to Bechtel in an interview for *Horn Book:* "Some of my early books remind me too much of my Christmas card style. They look old-fashioned, as perhaps they should, for their stories. But *Happy* was more my kind of thing. It was really a step toward what I [was] trying to do in the fifties."

In 1932 Sewell was asked to illustrate Laura Ingalls Wilder's first book, *Little House in the Big Woods.* Wilder's books were extremely successful, and at the same time Sewell's career as an author and illustrator began to take off. By the time Wilder published *On the Banks of Plum Creek* in 1937, Sewell had so many other contracts to write and/or illustrate books that another illustrator, Mildred Boyle, was brought in to collaborate with Sewell on the Wilder books. *On the Banks of Plum Creek* was the first of these Wilder-Sewell-Boyle collaborations to be named a Newbery Honor book; others that received this distinction were *By the Shores of Silver Lake, The Long Winter, Little Town on the Prairie,* and *These Happy Golden Years.*

Sewell's own projects during this period included *Ming and Mehitable,* a story inspired by a dog she had during her childhood, and *Peggy and the Pony,* which she derived from a trip to Europe with her sister and niece. Sewell not only created stories from her memories, but used them as the basis of her illustrations as well. Sometimes, however, she drew from life and had local children—she continued to live in New York City—in to model for her. She was open to their ideas and enthusiasms, and learned much about comic strips from them. She recalled in an essay for *Horn Book* that the children enjoyed sharing the genre with her: "The unaccustomed sight of one of their elders who actually wished to be instructed, awakened a missionary zeal in all my young friends. They became voluble and garrulous as they warmed to the task and they went to work with delight and industry. what they taught me was exactly what I wanted to know. It was a way of separating some of the slang and vulgarity abounding in the funnies from the important elements of their form. This standard pattern, which is like a new and antic sort of etiquette, is not only accepted but demanded by the children.... A few minor samples of the things I learned are these: if a person falls into the water he should say, 'Gurgle, blub, blub,' among other things. Exclamation points, curlicues, crisscrosses and question marks were carefully drawn out for me and they went rather neatly into the picture, though I cannot say I mastered entirely their esoteric meanings." This explo-

From *The Thanksgiving Story,* by Alice Dalgliesh. Illustrated by Helen Sewell.

ration led Sewell to collaborate with author Elena Eleska on a children's book done in comic strip style, *Three Tall Tales.* She related in *Horn Book:* "In making ... *Three Tall Tales,* the idea was to transform, if possible, the comics layout into a design, retaining at the same time all the fun in the original stories."

In her later career, Sewell illustrated two books for author Alice Dalgliesh, 1952's *The Bears on Hemlock Mountain* and 1954's *The Thanksgiving Story.* The first won Newbery honors, the second a Caldecott Medal. Sewell also illustrated the works of classic authors; she did pictures for a Limited Editions Club version of Emily Dickinson's *Poems,* and one of her last efforts was to illustrate Jane Austen's *Sense and Sensibility.* Sewell died after a long illness in 1957.

WORKS CITED:

Bechtel, Louise Seaman, "Helen Sewell, 1896-1956: The Development of a Great Illustrator," *Horn Book,* October, 1957.

Sewell, Helen, "Illustrator Meets the Comics," *Horn Book,* March, 1948.

FOR MORE INFORMATION SEE:

BOOKS

Chevalier, Tracy, editor, *Twentieth-Century Children's Writers,* 3rd edition, St. James Press, 1989.

* * *

SHARMAT, Marjorie Weinman 1928- (Wendy Andrews)

Marjorie Weinman Sharmat

PERSONAL: Born November 12, 1928, in Portland, ME; daughter of Nathan (a wholesaler and manufacturer of dry goods and men's furnishings) and Anna (Richardson) Weinman; married Mitchell Brenner Sharmat (an author and investor), February 24, 1957; children: Craig Lynden, Andrew Richard. *Education:* Attended Lasell Junior College, 1946-47; graduate of Westbrook Junior College, 1948. *Politics:* "Keep changing." *Religion:* Jewish. *Hobbies and other interests:* Desperately seeking spare time and marveling at its elusiveness.

ADDRESSES: Home—Arizona. *Office*—c/o Dell Publishing Co., 666 Fifth Ave, New York, NY 10103. *Agent*—Harold Ober Associates.

CAREER: Writer. Yale University, New Haven, CT, circulation staff member of university library, 1951-54, circulation staff member of law library, 1954-55; author of books for children and young adults, 1967—. Writer of greeting card verse and advertising copy; contributor to trade and textbook anthologies; writer of TV and movie novelizations.

AWARDS, HONORS: Book of the Year citations, Library of Congress, 1967, for *Rex,* 1976, for *Mooch the Messy,* 1979, for *Griselda's New Year,* and from the Child Study Association, 1971, 1973-76, 1978, 1979, 1980, 1982, and 1988, and from *Saturday Review, Newsweek, Ladies Home Journal,* and *Ms.;* Best Book of the Season citations from the *Today Show,* 1972, for *Nate the Great,* 1975, for *Maggie Marmelstein for President,* and from *House and Garden;* Classroom Choices citations, International Reading Association and Childrens' Book Council, 1976-88; Tower Award, Westbrook College, 1975; Arizona Young Readers' Award first runner-up, 1978-79; Parents' Choice Award, 1980, for *Taking Care of Melvin;* Irma Simonton Black Honor Book Award, 1981, for *Gila Monsters Meet You at the Airport;* Garden State Children's Book Awards, 1984, for *Nate the Great and the Missing Key,* and 1985, for *Nate the Great and the Snowy Trail;* Alabama Young Readers' Choice Award, 1988, for *My Mother Never Listens to Me;* Notable Trade Book in the Field of Social Studies citations, National Council for the Social Studies, 1977, for *Edgemont* and *Frizzy the Fearful;* numerous other awards and award nominations, including the Los Angeles International Children's Film Festival Award for the adaptation of *Nate the Great Goes Undercover.*

WRITINGS:

JUVENILES

Rex, illustrations by Emily McCully, Harper, 1967.

Goodnight, Andrew, Goodnight, Craig, illustrations by Mary Chalmers, Harper, 1969.

Gladys Told Me to Meet Her Here, illustrations by Edward Frascino, Harper, 1970.

A Hot Thirsty Day, illustrations by Rosemary Wells, Macmillan, 1971.

51 Sycamore Lane, illustrations by Lisl Weil, Macmillan, 1971, published as *The Spy in the Neighborhood,* Collier, 1974.

Getting Something on Maggie Marmelstein, illustrations by Ben Shecter, Harper, 1971.

A Visit with Rosalind, illustrations by Weil, Macmillan, 1972.
Sophie and Gussie, illustrations by Lillian Hoban, Macmillan, 1973.
Morris Brookside, a Dog (Junior Literary Guild selection), illustrations by Ronald Himler, Holiday House, 1973.
Morris Brookside Is Missing, illustrations by Himler, Holiday House, 1974.
I Want Mama, illustrations by McCully, Harper, 1974.
I'm Not Oscar's Friend Anymore (Junior Literary Guild selection), illustrations by Tony DeLuna, Dutton, 1975.
Walter the Wolf, illustrations by Kelly Oechsli, Holiday House, 1975.
Burton and Dudley (Junior Literary Guild selection), illustrations by Barbara Cooney, Holiday House, 1975.
Maggie Marmelstein for President, illustrations by Shecter, Harper, 1975.
The Lancelot Closes at Five, illustrations by Weil, Macmillan, 1976.
The Trip, and Other Sophie and Gussie Stories, illustrations by Hoban, Macmillan, 1976.
Mooch the Messy, illustrations by Shecter, Harper, 1976.
Edgemont, illustrations by Cyndy Szekeres, Coward, 1977.
I'm Terrific (Junior Literary Guild selection), illustrations by Kay Chorao, Holiday House, 1977.
I Don't Care (Junior Literary Guild selection), illustrations by Hoban, Macmillan, 1977.
A Big Fat Enormous Lie, illustrations by David McPhail, Dutton, 1978.
Thornton the Worrier, illustrations by Chorao, Holiday House, 1978.
Mitchell Is Moving (Junior Literary Guild selection), illustrations by Jose Aruego and Ariane Dewey, Macmillan, 1978.
Mooch the Messy Meets Prudence the Neat, illustrations by Shecter, Coward, 1979.
Scarlet Monster Lives Here, illustrations by Dennis Kendrick, Harper, 1979.
Mr. Jameson and Mr. Phillips, illustrations by Bruce Degen, Harper, 1979.
The 329th Friend, illustrations by C. Szekeres, Four Winds, 1979.
(With husband, Mitchell Sharmat) *I Am Not a Pest,* illustrations by Diane Dawson, Dutton, 1979.
Uncle Boris and Maude, illustrations by Sammis McLean, Doubleday, 1979.
Octavia Told Me a Secret, illustrations by Roseanne Litzinger, Four Winds, 1979.
Say Hello, Vanessa, illustrations by Hoban, Holiday House, 1979.
Griselda's New Year (Junior Literary Guild selection), illustrations by Norman Chartier, Macmillan, 1979.
The Trolls of 12th Street, illustrations by Shecter, Coward, 1979.
Little Devil Gets Sick, illustrations by Marilyn Hafner, Doubleday, 1980.
What Are We Going to Do about Andrew?, illustrations by Ray Cruz, Macmillan, 1980.
Taking Care of Melvin, illustrations by Victoria Chess, Holiday House, 1980.
Sometimes Mama and Papa Fight, illustrations by Chorao, Harper, 1980.
(With M. Sharmat) *The Day I Was Born,* illustrations by Dawson, Dutton, 1980.
Grumley the Grouch, illustrations by Chorao, Holiday House, 1980.
Gila Monsters Meet You at the Airport (Junior Literary Guild selection), illustrations by Byron Barton, Macmillan, 1980.
Twitchell the Wishful, illustrations by Janet Stevens, Holiday House, 1981.
Chasing After Annie, illustrations by Simont, Harper, 1981.
Rollo and Juliet, Forever!, illustrations by Hafner, Doubleday, 1981.
The Sign, illustrations by Pat Wong, Houghton, 1981.
Lucretia the Unbearable (Junior Literary Guild selection), illustrations by Janet Stevens, Holiday House, 1981.
The Best Valentine in the World (Junior Literary Guild selection), illustrations by Lillian Obligado, Holiday House, 1982.
Two Ghosts on a Bench, illustrations by Nola Langner, Harper, 1982.
Mysteriously Yours, Maggie Marmelstein, illustrations by Shecter, Harper, 1982.
Frizzy the Fearful, illustrations by John Wallner, Holiday House, 1983.
Rich Mitch, illustrations by Loretta Lustig, Morrow, 1983.
The Story of Bentley Beaver, illustrations by Hoban, Harper, 1984.
Bartholomew the Bossy, illustrations by Normand Chartier, Macmillan, 1984.
Sasha the Silly, illustrations by Stevens, Holiday House, 1984.
My Mother Never Listens to Me, illustrations by Lynn Munsinger, A. Whitman, 1984.
Attila the Angry, illustrations by Hoban, Holiday House, 1985.
Get Rich Mitch!, illustrations by Loretta Lustig, Morrow, 1985.
The Son of the Slime Who Ate Cleveland, illustrations by Rodney Pate, Dell, 1985.
One Terrific Thanksgiving, illustrations by Obligado, Holiday House, 1985.
Who's Afraid of Ernestine? (Junior Literary Guild selection), illustrations by Chambliss, Putnam, 1986.
Hooray for Mother's Day!, illustrations by Wallner, Holiday House, 1986.
Helga High-Up, illustrations by David Neuhaus, Scholastic, 1987.
Hooray for Father's Day!, illustrations by Wallner, Holiday House, 1987.
Go to Sleep, Nicholas Joe, illustrations by Himmelman, Harper, 1988.
What Are We Going to Do about Andrew?, illustrations by Ray Cruz, Macmillan Children's Book Group, 1988.
(With M. Sharmat) *Surprises* (reader), Holt, 1989.
(With M. Sharmat) *Treasures* (reader), Holt, 1989.

(With M. Sharmat) *Kingdoms* (reader), Holt, 1989.
Griselda's New Year, illustrations by Normand Chartier, Macmillan Children's Book Group, 1989.
I'm Santa Claus and I'm Famous, Holiday House, 1990.
I'm the Best! Holiday House, 1991.

"NATE THE GREAT" SERIES; ILLUSTRATIONS BY MARC SIMONT

Nate the Great, Coward, 1972.
Nate Goes Undercover (Junior Literary Guild selection), Coward, 1974.
Nate and the Lost List, Coward, 1975.
Nate and the Phony Clue, Coward, 1977.
Nate and the Sticky Case, Coward, 1978.
Nate and the Missing Key (Junior Literary Guild selection), Coward, 1981.
Nate and the Snowy Trail (Junior Literary Guild selection), Coward, 1982.
Nate and the Fishy Prize (Junior Literary Guild selection), Coward, 1985.
Nate Stalks Stupidweed (Junior Literary Guild selection), Coward, 1986.
Nate and the Boring Beach Bag (Junior Literary Guild selection), Coward, 1987.
Nate Goes Down in the Dumps (Junior Literary Guild selection), Coward, 1989.
Nate and the Halloween Hunt (Junior Literary Guild selection), Coward, 1989.
(With son, Craig Sharmat) *Nate and the Musical Note* (Junior Literary Guild selection), Coward, 1990.
Nate and the Stolen Base, Coward, 1992.

"OLIVIA SHARP, AGENT FOR SECRETS" SERIES; WITH HUSBAND, MITCHELL SHARMAT

The Pizza Monster, illustrations by Denise Brunkus, Delacorte, 1989.
The Princess of the Fillmore Street School, Delacorte, 1989.
The Sly Spy, Delacorte, 1990.
The Green Toenails Gang, Delacorte, 1991.

"THE KIDS ON THE BUS" SERIES; WITH SON, ANDREW SHARMAT

School Bus Cat, HarperCollins, 1990.
The Cooking Class, HarperCollins, 1990.
The Haunted Bus, HarperCollins, 1991.
Bully on the Bus, HarperCollins, 1991.
The Secret Notebook, HarperCollins, 1991.
The Field Day Mix-up, HarperCollins, 1991.

YOUNG ADULT

Square Pegs (novelization of television program), Dell, 1982.
I Saw Him First, Dell, 1983.
How to Meet a Gorgeous Guy, Dell, 1983.
How to Meet a Gorgeous Girl, Dell, 1984.
He Noticed I'm Alive ... and Other Hopeful Signs, Delacorte, 1984.
Two Guys Noticed Me ... and Other Miracles, Delacorte, 1985.
How to Have a Gorgeous Wedding, Dell, 1985.

YOUNG ADULT; UNDER PSEUDONYM WENDY ANDREWS

Vacation Fever! (also see below), Putnam, 1984.
The Supergirl Storybook (novelization of motion picture), Putnam, 1984.
Are We There Yet? (also see below), Putnam, 1985.
(Under name Marjorie Weinman Sharmat) *Vacation Fever!* [and] *Are We There Yet?* Dell, 1990.

"SORORITY SISTERS" SERIES

For Members Only, Dell, 1986.
Snobs, Beware, Dell, 1986.
I Think I'm Falling in Love, Dell, 1986.
Fighting Over Me, Dell, 1986.
Nobody Knows How Scared I Am, Dell, 1987.
Here Comes Mr. Right, Dell, 1987.
Getting Closer, Dell, 1987.
I'm Going to Get Your Boyfriend, Dell, 1987.

OTHER

Contributor to *Just for Fun,* edited by Ann Durell, Dutton, 1977; *Sixteen,* edited by Donald Gallo, Dell, 1984; *Visions,* Delacorte, 1987; and *Funny You Should Ask,* Delacorte, 1992. Also contributor to magazines, newspapers, and textbooks. Sharmat's books have been published in England, Japan, Israel, Canada, the Netherlands, Spain, China, Australia, New Zealand, Denmark, France, Germany, and Sweden. Some of her manuscripts are kept in the Maine Women's Writers Collection, Westbrook College, Portland, ME, and the de Grummond Collection, University of Southern Mississippi, Hattiesburg.

ADAPTATIONS: I'm Not Oscar's Friend Any More was made into a television film and presented as part of the CBS-TV Library Special, *The Wrong Way Kid. Gila Monsters Meet You at the Airport* was made into the pilot film for the PBS-TV *Reading Rainbow* series. *Nate the Great Goes Undercover* and *Nate the Great and the Sticky Case* were made into films. Work has been made into videocassettes and numerous recordings. An excerpt from *Nate the Great* was adapted and is on permanent display in an exhibit on the brain and learning at the Museum of Science and Industry, Chicago, IL. Dramatization of *Scarlet Monster Lives Here* performed April 1990 at White House Easter Egg Roll for 30,000 guests. *The Adventures of Nate the Great* stage production premiered July 1990.

WORK IN PROGRESS: Nate the Great and the Pillowcase, with sister Rosalind Weinman.

SIDELIGHTS: In a *Cricket* article, American children's author Marjorie Weinman Sharmat wrote about her writing process, "I suppose that very few, if any, writers would care to have their brains even remotely compared to litter baskets, but stories do represent the coming together of the diverse and often disparate experiences, emotions, and people that are part of the life of the writer. The writer sorts them out and gives them shape and substance and meaning. Most writers have an almost relentless desire to communicate. It is, perhaps like a sore tooth or a nagging headache, conspicuously

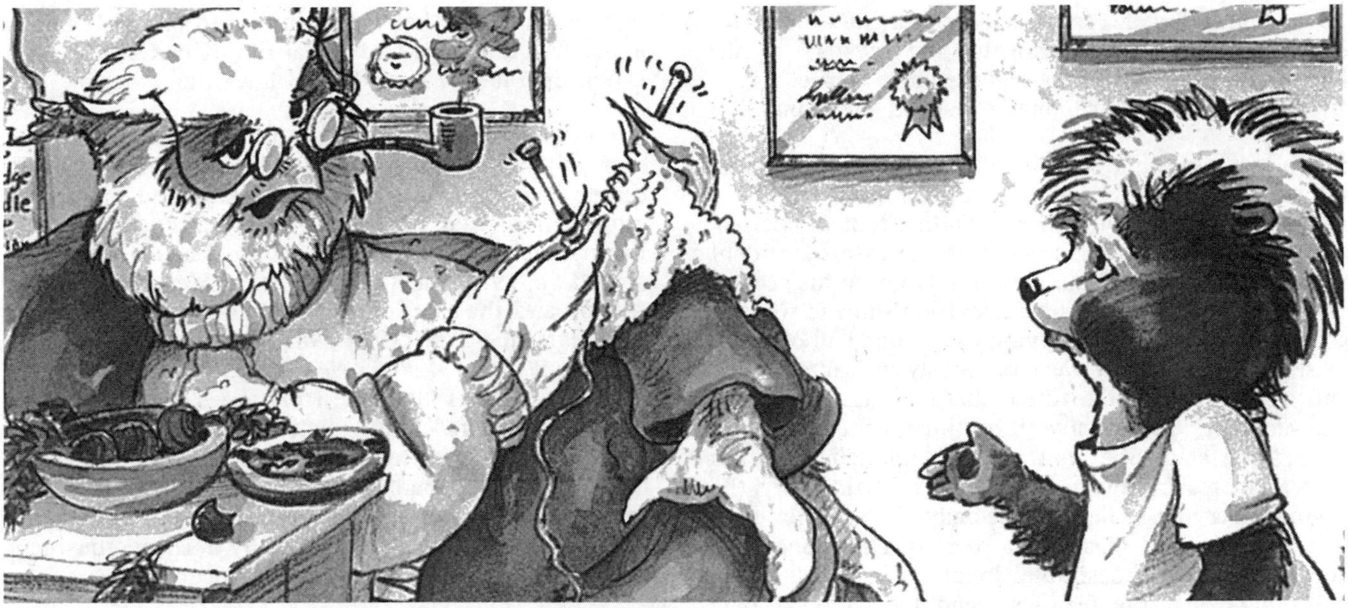

From *Bartholomew the Bossy,* by Marjorie Weinman Sharmat. Illustrated by Normand Chartier.

unremittingly *there.* I have felt this compulsion ever since I can remember.... The down side of having 110 published books is that I can no longer handle the thousands of letters that the books generate. Regretfully I have stopped responding."

Sharmat was born to Anna and Nathan Weinman in Portland, Maine. She recalls she was a shy, introspective child who enjoyed nongroup activities such as piano playing, reading, and drawing. "My earliest ambition was to become a writer or a detective or a lion tamer," she commented. "I began writing when I was eight. A friend and I 'published' a newspaper called *The Snooper's Gazette,* which we filled with news we obtained by spying on grown-ups for our detective agency. It achieved a circulation of about four—her parents and mine. At that time I also wrote my first poem. It was about a neighborhood dog, and I still have the memory of my mother supplying the last line when I was stuck.... [This] poem appeared years and years later in my book *The Lancelot Closes at Five.*"

She continued to write—"diaries, music, more poems, stories, and one chapter of a mystery novel"—and to draw, sometimes adding illustrations to her writing. Eventually she wrote for school magazines and newspapers. Her parents encouraged her to keep writing, and even after having many stories rejected by publishers during her high school years, she continued to send stories out to editors. "I couldn't break the habit of unreasonable optimism," she explained.

In college she studied marketing because she thought it was practical. After graduating, her first job was in a department store. Later she worked at Yale University Library. "My first commercially published 'work' was a national advertising slogan for the W. T. Grant Company for their spring promotion. It consisted of four words. I used to enjoy walking into Grant stores and reading my four words. Eventually I had my first story—a short story for adults—published while I was working at the Yale Library. This unfortunately caused me to break out in hives. I have since regarded a collection of red spots on the skin as a hallmark of literary achievement, and never the result of eating too much chocolate. My second published story, an article about Yale, became a part of the Yale Memorabilia Collection. (More hives.)"

During the 1960s and '70s, Sharmat wrote only for children, producing many picture books, readers, and novels. Her own children often provided her with inspiration. Her first published book, the story of a runaway boy who pretends to be an elderly neighbor's dog, came out of the two facts that her son Craig often visited older neighbors and her son Andrew pretended to be a dog. "*Goodnight Andrew, Goodnight Craig* came about when my two boys were going to sleep, and Craig wished Andrew 'Pleasant nightmares'," she explained.

The hero of her mysteries for young children, Nate, is named after the author's father Nathan Weinman. The small detective solves cases as much by perseverance as by deductive reasoning, but never without a plate of pancakes to get him started. Ideas for some of the mysteries also come from her children's experiences. She wrote, for example, that "*Nate the Great Goes Undercover* had its beginnings when my son, Craig, thought I was the ideal person to effect the rescue of a skunk that he saw in a sewer down the street. I made several phone calls, but I found there was a dearth of people and agencies willing to attempt the removal of a skunk from a sewer. The trail finally led to the game warden whose wife complained (understandably) that she was always being called about such matters, but could offer only advice, not action. Meanwhile, in a related or unrelated incident (never quite determined), garbage cans had been knocked over in my neighborhood. And so the idea for *Nate the Great Goes Undercover* took hold. Nate investigates the mystery of the knocked-over garbage cans and the chief suspect is.... By the way, the police finally rescued the skunk."

Sharmat's topic in a number of books is the emotional life of her characters and her readers. *I'm Terrific* looks at Jason Bear's growing understanding that the perfection he believes he represents is not necessarily evident to the people around him, particularly not to his peers. *I Don't Care* was inspired by a television show in which a group of characters were trying to persuade an old man to stop crying. "They were obviously well-intentioned and it did not occur to them that the man should be allowed to cry. I found myself rooting for the man: 'Cry! Cry!'," she said. She continued, "Although there has been an increasing awareness that it's all right to cry, the stigma of crying remains, especially, I think, for men and boys. A child senses that keeping a stiff upper lip and being cool are desirable. Jonathan in *I Don't Care* holds back his true feelings when his balloon floats away. 'I don't care,' he tells himself and his parents and his friend. But he does care. And finally he lets go and cries. And he cries until he is cried out and satisfied."

In 1975, the Sharmat family moved across the country from New York City to Arizona. For the author, this relocation was an imaginative as well as a physical challenge. Comments by children from the east and west about what they thought might be waiting for them on the other side of the country helped her to write *Gila Monsters Meet You at the Airport.* After moving west, Sharmat has found that both sides of the country have much in common. The book tries to express both the anxieties about moving and the comforts of finding that life is not so different in faraway places.

When stuck for a particular plot solution or phrase, Sharmat has often found her husband Mitchell has the exactly right words. Eventually, she encouraged him to begin writing his own children's books, and he has become the second published children's and young adults' writer in the family with numerous titles including the classic, *Gregory, the Terrible Eater.* Together the Sharmats have produced the series "Olivia Sharp, Agent for Secrets" and several other books. Sharmat has also collaborated with her son Andrew on a number of books called "The Kids on the Bus" series, and with son Craig on the book *Nate the Great and the Musical Note.*

In 1982, Sharmat started writing novels for young adults. Her romances are "intelligent and witty," according Diane Roback in *Publishers Weekly,* and *School Library Journal* critic Kathy Fritts calls them "far more literate and graceful than the usual." In *How to Meet a Gorgeous Girl,* a teen just about ruins his chances for a good relationship with the girl of his dreams by trying to follow the advice in a "How To" book on dating. Two girls make a similar mistake in *How to Meet a Gorgeous Guy* by making a cute guy the subject of an article on dating. Her teens learn about the value of direct and honest communication and develop self-confidence. The author's "flair for dialogue and realistic characterization" enhances her entertaining and plausible books about teen romance and social life, Kim Carter Sands claims in the *Voice of Youth Advocates.*

Critics and readers of all ages have enjoyed Sharmat's books for many years. Their ability to entertain while developing the reader's thinking skills and emotional growth has been rewarded with many awards and honors, including the Irma Simonton Black Honor Book Award in 1981 for *Gila Monsters Meet You at the Airport* and the Garden State Children's Book Award two years in a row (1984-1985) for "Nate the Great" titles. A *Books of Wonder News* reviewer calls the "Nate the Great" books "the finest mysteries we know of for beginning readers," adding that they are also suitable for reading aloud to children as young as three years old. Sharmat believes the humor in her books is an essential ingredient. She wrote, "I like to write funny books because I think that life is basically a serious business and needs a humorous counterbalance."

WORKS CITED:

Books of Wonder News, March, 1988, p. 1.

Bulletin of the Center for Children's Books, November, 1984.

Fifth Book of Junior Authors and Illustrators, H. W. Wilson, 1987, pp. 282-283.

Fritts, Kathy, "Paperback Romance Series Roundup," *School Library Journal,* October 1987, p. 149.

Roback, Diane, "Forecasts: Children's Books," *Publishers Weekly,* June 27, 1986, p. 94.

Sands, Kim Carter, "Sorority Sisters," *Voice of Youth Advocates,* April 1988, p. 35.

Sharmat, Marjorie W., "Meet Your Author," *Cricket,* October, 1975.

Twentieth Century Children's Writers, St. Martin's, 1989, pp. 881-882.

FOR MORE INFORMATION SEE:

BOOKS

For Love of Reading, Consumer Reports, Consumer Union, 1988.

Larrick, Nancy, *A Parents' Guide to Children's Reading,* 4th edition, Doubleday, 1982.

The New York Times Parents' Guide to the Best Books for Children, Times Books, 1988.

Raphael, Frederick, and Kenneth McLeish, *The List of Books,* Harmony Books, 1981.

Sutherland, Zena, editor, *The Best in Children's Books, 1966-1972, University of Chicago Guide to Children's Literature,* University of Chicago Press, 1973, p. 6.

* * *

SHARP, Margery 1905-1991

PERSONAL: Born in 1905; died March 14, 1991, in London, England; daughter of J. H. Sharp; married Geoffrey Lloyd Castle (a major in the Royal Army), 1938 (died, 1990). *Education:* Bedford College, University of London, B.A. (with honors). *Hobbies and other interests:* Embroidering own designs in gros point, gardening, painting, swimming, sailing.

ADDRESSES: Agent—c/o William Heinemann Ltd., Michelin House, 81 Fulham Road, London SW3 6RB, England.

CAREER: Full-time professional writer. Worked for the Armed Forces Education Program during World War II.

AWARDS, HONORS: American Library Association notable book citation, 1959, for *The Rescuers; Horn Book* honor list, 1960, for *Something Light.*

Margery Sharp

WRITINGS:

"MISS BIANCA" SERIES

The Rescuers, illustrated by Judith Brook, Collins, 1959, illustrated by Garth Williams, Little, Brown, 1959.
Miss Bianca, illustrated by Williams, Little, Brown, 1962.
The Turret, illustrated by Williams, Little, Brown, 1963.
Miss Bianca in the Salt Mines, illustrated by Williams, Little, Brown, 1966.
Miss Bianca in the Orient, illustrated by Erik Blegvad, Little, Brown, 1970.
Miss Bianca in the Antarctic, illustrated by Blegvad, Little, Brown, 1971.
Miss Bianca and the Bridesmaid, illustrated by Blegvad, Little, Brown, 1972.
Bernard the Brave: A Miss Bianca Story, illustrated by Faith Jaques, Heinemann, 1976, illustrated by Leslie Morrill, Little, Brown, 1977.
Bernard into Battle: A Miss Bianca Story, illustrated by Morrill, Little, Brown, 1979.

JUVENILE FICTION

Melisande, illustrated by Roy McKie, Little, Brown, 1960.
Something Light, Collins, 1960, Little, Brown, 1961.
Lost at the Fair, illustrated by Rosalind Fry, Little, Brown, 1965.
The Children Next Door, illustrated by Hilary Abrahams, Heinemann, 1974.
The Magical Cockatoo, illustrated by Faith Jaques, Heinemann, 1974.

NOVELS

Rhododendron Pie, Appleton, 1930.
Fanfare for Tin Trumpets, Barker, 1932, Putnam, 1933.
The Nymph and the Nobleman (also see below), Barker, 1932.
The Flowering Thorn, Barker, 1933, Putnam, 1934.
Sophie Cassmajor (also see below), Putnam, 1934.
Four Gardens, Putnam, 1935.
The Nutmeg Tree (also see below), Little, Brown, 1937.
Harlequin House, Little, Brown, 1939.
The Stone of Chastity, Little, Brown, 1940.
Three Companion Pieces (contains *The Nymph and the Nobleman, Sophie Cassmajor,* and *The Tigress on the Hearth;* also see below), Little, Brown, 1941.
Cluny Brown (serialized in *Ladies' Home Journal*), Little, Brown, 1944.
Britannia Mews, Little, Brown, 1946.
The Foolish Gentlewoman, Little, Brown, 1948.
Lise Lillywhite, Little, Brown, 1951.
The Gipsy in the Parlour, Little, Brown, 1954.
The Tigress on the Hearth, Collins, 1955.
The Eye of Love, Little, Brown, 1957, published as *Martha and the Eye of Love,* New English Library, 1969.
Martha in Paris, Collins, 1962, Little, Brown, 1963.
Martha, Eric and George, Little, Brown, 1964.
The Sun in Scorpio, Little, Brown, 1965.
In Pious Memory, Little, Brown, 1967.
Rosa, Heinemann, 1969, Little, Brown, 1970.
The Innocents, Heinemann, 1971, Little, Brown, 1972.
The Faithful Servants, Little, Brown, 1975.
Summer Visits, Heinemann, 1977, Little, Brown, 1978.

PLAYS

Meeting at Night, produced in London, 1934.
Lady in Waiting (based on her novel *The Nutmeg Tree;* produced in New York City, 1940), Samuel French, 1941.
The Foolish Gentlewoman (produced in London, 1949), Samuel French, 1950.

OTHER

The Last Chapel Picnic and Other Stories (short stories), Heinemann, Little Brown, 1973.

From *The Rescuers,* by Margery Sharp. Illustrated by Garth Williams.

Also author of the television play *The Birdcage Room,* 1954. Contributor of articles to *Encyclopaedia Britannica* and to magazines in England and the United States, including *Woman's Home Companion, Ladies' Home Journal, Harper's Bazaar, Saturday Evening Post, Strand, Fiction Parade, Punch,* and *Collier's.* A collection of Sharp's works is housed at the Houghton Library, Harvard University.

ADAPTATIONS: Cluny Brown was adapted for film by Twentieth Century-Fox, 1946; *The Nutmeg Tree* was adapted for film by Metro-Goldwyn-Mayer as *Julia Misbehaves,* 1948; *Britannia Mews* was adapted for film by Twentieth Century-Fox as *The Forbidden Street,* 1949; "The Tenant," a short story, was adapted for film by Columbia as *The Notorious Landlady,* 1962; *The Rescuers* and *Miss Bianca* were adapted for film by Walt Disney Productions as *The Rescuers,* Buena Vista, 1977; Walt Disney Productions and Buena Vista released *The Rescuers Down Under,* featuring characters inspired by the "Miss Bianca" series, 1991.

SIDELIGHTS: Margery Sharp was probably best known for several of her children's books which have been adapted into animated movies by Walt Disney Productions over the past several years, *The Rescuers* and *The Rescuers Down Under.* Her writing has been enjoyed by readers of all ages, and her "Miss Bianca" series of books has been referred to as a refined fantasy for adults as well as for children. The appeal of Sharp's writing is in its language and rhythm and the contrast between the elegance and sophistication of one character and the ordinary manner and simple tastes of another.

Sharp was born in 1905 on the island of Malta to British parents. As a child, she liked to paint and write. She once said that her need to earn a living probably turned her into a writer rather than a painter. Before graduating from Streatham Hill High School in England, Sharp began writing poetry and submitting it to magazines. She was successful at this because the magazine articles seldom ended exactly at the bottom of a page; therefore, the publishers were always willing to buy short poems as fillers. Of this writing experience, she once commented, "I was paid ten and sixpence, half a guinea, for each. For a high school student this is a very rewarding sum, at least it was when I was doing it."

Sharp earned her Bachelor of Arts degree (with honors) in French from London University, where most of her time was spent writing and participating in campus activities. However, she found time to join the British University Women's Debating Team, and in 1929 made her first visit to the United States as a member of this team.

In 1930 Sharp officially began her writing career, writing primarily adult fiction, a trend which she continued for the next thirty years. These novels featured unconventional but charming heroines who brought humor to commonplace situations. One of these characters, Cluny Brown, was a parlor maid whose hobby was plumbing. Through the interaction of the characters in Sharp's novels, a great deal about the inner workings of British society can be learned. Several of her novels were serialized in magazines, and some of her more popular novels were adapted as screenplays for movies. In 1938 Sharp married Geoffrey Lloyd Castle, a major in the British Army, and during World War II she worked in England for the division of Armed Forces Education Program.

Although her adult fiction is very popular, Sharp was probably best known for her books featuring Miss Bianca, Bernard, and the Rescue Aid Society, an animal organization that helps people in distress. In 1959, the first book of the "Miss Bianca" series was published, and in 1977 the first two books of the series (*The Rescuers* and *Miss Bianca*) were adapted for release as the animated movie *The Rescuers.* And in 1991 Walt Disney Productions released *The Rescuers Down Under,* which again featured characters from Sharp's "Miss Bianca" series. The books in this series tell of the Rescue Aid Society and their adventures while attempting to cheer and rescue children who have been wrongly imprisoned. (Mice are typically the prisoner's friends.) Sharp once said that she enjoyed writing children's books because "they are a complete release of the imagination."

Something Light, which was published in 1960 and was named to the *Horn Book* honor list, is a work of adult fiction. The book features one of Sharp's unusual but more appealing heroines, Louisa Mary Datchett, a girl who was indiscriminately fond of men. Louisa kept falling for the wrong men and she spent a lot of time mending, washing, and cooking for them, but at the age of thirty she decided she had more noble plans for her future—she decided to go hunting for a wealthy husband. Her delightful and amusing search is detailed in *Something Light,* a search that becomes complicated by the "aid" of her friend Enid Anstruther and Louisa's deepening feelings for the steadfast Jimmy Brown.

When asked what advice she would give to aspiring writers, Sharp said they should learn to write rather than simply try to be writers. "Write as well as you can. Don't think of what is wanted, what is popular, what will sell. Write what you want, and write as well as you can." She also advised beginning writers against leaving home to start their writing careers without the benefit of actual life experiences. She said that the variety of experiences and jobs a person has had will give him something about which to write and will make his writing more appealing to a wider audience. She believed that the most important quality of a book is that it should be interesting, and readable. Sharp's books have been translated into Spanish, German and Italian.

WORKS CITED:

De Montreville, Doris, and Donna Hill, editors, *Third Book of Junior Authors,* H. W. Wilson, 1972.

FOR MORE INFORMATION SEE:

BOOKS

Chevalier, Tracy, editor, *Twentieth-Century Children's Writers,* 3rd edition, St. James Press, 1989.
Newquist, Roy, *Counterpoint,* Rand McNally, 1964.

PERIODICALS

New Yorker, June 22, 1967; March 6, 1978.
New York Times, July 7, 1977.
Times Literary Supplement, November 3, 1972; September 5, 1975.

* * *

SHEPARD, Ernest Howard 1879-1976

PERSONAL: Born December 10, 1879, in St. John's Wood, London, England; died March 24, 1976, in Lodsworth, England; son of Henry Dunkin (an architect) and Harriet Jessie (Lee) Shepard; married Florence Eleanor Chaplin, September 28, 1904 (died, 1927); married Norah Radcliffe Mary Carroll, 1944; children: (first marriage) Mary Eleanor (Mrs. E. G. V. Knox), Graham Howard (deceased). *Education:* Attended St. Paul's School, London, 1892-94, Heatherleys Art School, 1896, and Royal Academy Schools, 1897-1902.

CAREER: Began drawing for *Punch* magazine, 1907, joined the round table, 1921, senior staff editor, 1929-45, political cartoonist, 1940-45 and afterwards until his retirement in 1953. *Exhibitions:* Exhibited his work in numerous galleries, beginning 1901. *Military service:* Royal Artillery, 1915-19; became major; awarded military cross.

MEMBER: Art Worker's Guild, National Art Collections Fund, Artists General Benevolent Institution, Savage Club.

AWARDS, HONORS: Landseer Scholarship from the Royal Academy of Schools, 1898; British Institution Prize, 1900; Ohioana Award, 1952, for illustrations in *Enter David Garrick;* Spring Book Festival Award, 1955, for illustrations in *Crystal Mountain;* Lewis Carroll Shelf Award, 1958, for *The Wind in the Willows* and *The World of Pooh,* 1962, for *The World of Christopher Robin,* and 1963, for *The Reluctant Dragon;* University of Southern Mississippi Medallion, 1970; Order of the British Empire, 1972.

WRITINGS:

SELF-ILLUSTRATED

Fun and Fantasy (drawings), Methuen (London), 1927.

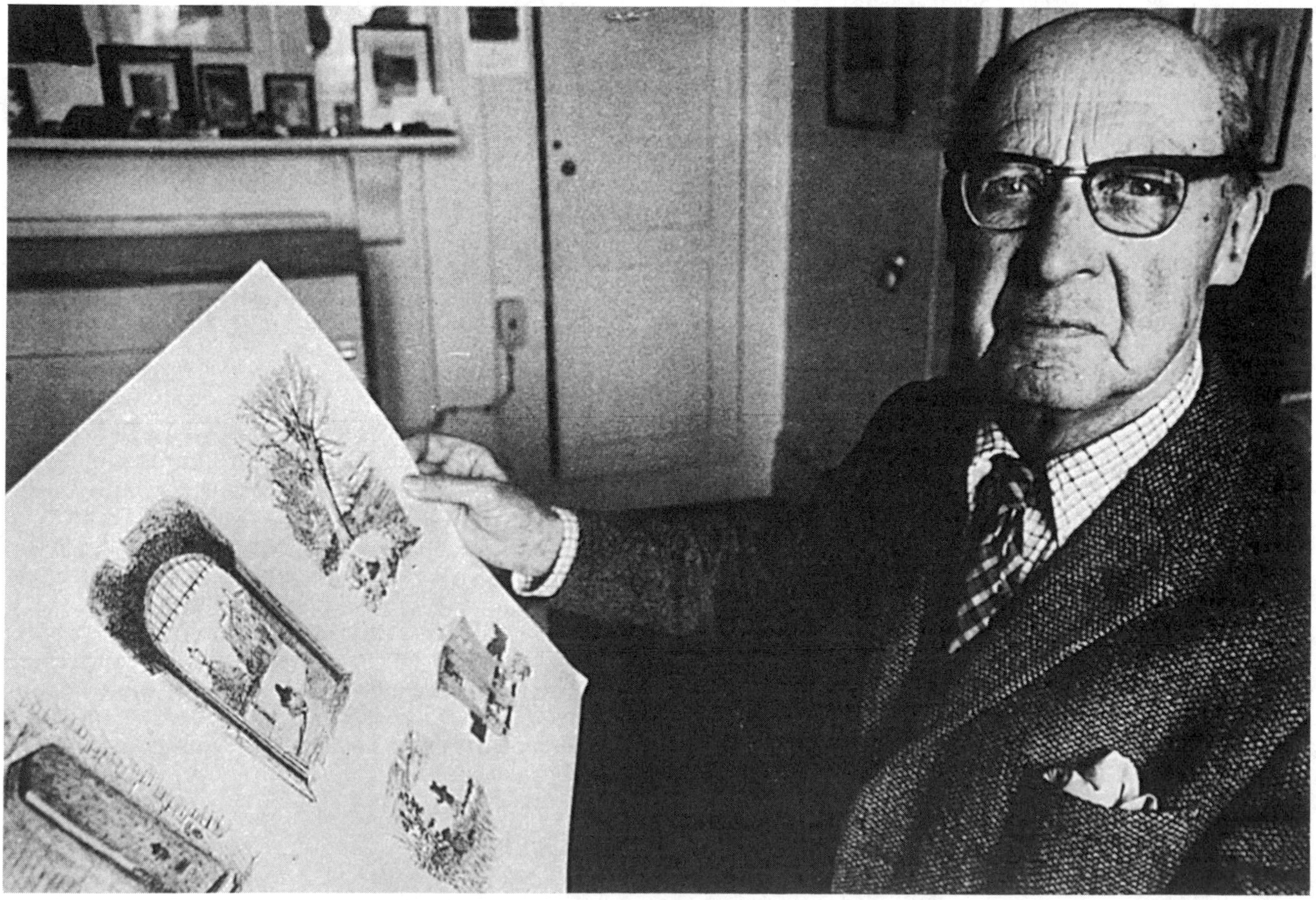

Ernest H. Shepard

(Compiler) Edward V. Lucas, *As the Bee Sucks* (verses), Methuen, 1937.

Drawn from Memory (autobiography; also see below), Lippincott,1957.

Drawn from Life (autobiography; also see below), Methuen, 1961, Dutton, 1962.

Pooh, His Art Gallery: Prints from the World of Pooh and the World of Christopher Robin (drawings), Dutton, 1962.

Ben and Brock (juvenile), Methuen, 1965, Doubleday, 1966.

Betsy and Joe (juvenile), Methuen, 1966, Dutton, 1967.

Drawn from Memory: Drawn from Life: The Autobiography of Ernest H. Shepard, Methuen, 1986.

ILLUSTRATOR; ALL BY A. A. MILNE

When We Were Very Young (poems; also see below), Dutton, 1924.

The King's Breakfast (also see below), Dutton, 1925.

Fourteen Songs from "When We Were Very Young" (also see below), Dutton, 1925.

Teddy Bear, and Other Songs from "When We Were Very Young," music by H. Fraser Simson, Dutton, 1926.

Winnie-the-Pooh (also see below), Dutton, 1926, full color edition, Methuen, 1973, Dutton, 1974.

Now We Are Six (poems; also see below), Dutton, 1927.

The House at Pooh Corner (also see below), Dutton, 1928, full color edition, Methuen, 1974.

The Christopher Robin Story Book (selections from *When We Were Very Young, Now We Are Six, Winnie-the-Pooh,* and *The House at Pooh Corner;* also see below), Dutton, 1929.

The Very Young Calendar, 1930 (verses), Dutton, 1929.

The Christopher Robin Calendar, Methuen, 1929.

When I Was Very Young, Fountain Press, 1930.

Tales of Pooh (selections from *Winnie-the-Pooh* and *The House at Pooh Corner*), Methuen, 1930.

The Christopher Robin Birthday Book, Methuen, 1930, Dutton, 1931.

The Christopher Robin Verses (contains *When We Were Very Young* and *Now We Are Six* with new color illustrations), Dutton, 1932, published as *The Christopher Robin Book of Verse,* 1967.

Songs from "Now We Are Six," Dutton, c. 1935.

More "Very Young" Songs, Dutton, 1937.

The Hums of Pooh (also see below), Dutton, 1937.

Sneezles, and Other Selections, Dutton, 1947.

Old Sailor, and Other Selections, Dutton, 1947.

Introducing Winnie-the-Pooh, and Other Selections, Dutton, 1947.

Year In, Year Out, Dutton, 1952.

The World of Pooh (includes *Winnie-the-Pooh* and *The House at Pooh Corner;* with new illustrations in full color), Dutton, 1957.

The World of Christopher Robin (includes *When We Were Very Young* and *Now We Are Six;* with new illustrations in full color), Dutton, 1958.

Pooh's Library (contains *Now We Are Six, Winnie-the-Pooh, When We Were Very Young,* and *The House at Pooh Corner*), four volumes, Dutton, 1961.

The Pooh Song Book (includes *The Hums of Pooh, The King's Breakfast,* and *Fourteen Songs from "When We Were Very Young"*), Dutton, 1961.

Pooh's Birthday Book, Dutton, 1963.

The Pooh Story Book (with decorations and illustrations in full color), Dutton, 1965.

The Christopher Robin Story Book, Dutton, 1966.

The Christopher Robin Book of Verse (selections from *When We Were Very Young* and *Now We Are Six,* with decorations and illustrations in full color), Dutton, 1967, published in England as *The Christopher Robin Verse Book,* Methuen, 1969.

Pooh's Pot O' Honey (contains stories originally published in *Winnie-the-Pooh*), four volumes, Dutton, 1968.

The Hums of Pooh: Lyrics by Pooh, Methuen, 1972.

Pooh's Alphabet Book, Elsevier/Dutton, 1975.

Eeyore Has a Birthday, Methuen, 1975.

An Expotition to the North Pole, Methuen, 1975.

Kanga and Baby Roo Come to the Forest, Methuen, 1975.

Piglet Meets a Heffalump, Methuen, 1975.

Pooh Goes Visiting and Pooh and Piglet Nearly Catch a Woozle, Methuen, 1975.

Winnie-the-Pooh and Some Bees, Methuen, 1975.

Christopher Robin Gives a Pooh Party (from *Winnie-the-Pooh*), Methuen, 1975.

A House Is Built at Pooh Corner for Eeyore (from *The House at Pooh Corner*), Methuen Children's, 1976.

Piglet Is Entirely Surrounded by Water (from *Winnie-the-Pooh*), Methuen, 1976.

Pooh Invents a New Game (from *The House at Pooh Corner*), Methuen Children's, 1976.

Tigger Comes to the Forest and Has Breakfast (from *The House at Pooh Corner*), Methuen, 1976.

Tigger Is Unbounced (from *The House at Pooh Corner*), Methuen Children's, 1976.

Pooh's Quiz Book, Elsevier/Dutton, 1977.

Eeyore Finds the Wolery (from *The House at Pooh Corner*), Methuen Children's, 1977.

Piglet Does a Very Grand Thing (from *The House at Pooh Corner*), Methuen, 1977.

Tiggers Don't Climb Trees (from *The House at Pooh Corner*), Methuen Children's, 1977.

Pooh's Bedtime Book (collection of stories and poems), Elsevier/Dutton, 1980.

Pooh's Counting Book, Dutton, 1982.

Where Is Eeyore's Tail?, Methuen, 1983.

Who Are Pooh's Friends?, Methuen, 1983.

Pooh's Rainy Day, Methuen, 1983.

Pooh and Piglet Build a House, Methuen, 1983.

What Does Tigger Like?, Methuen, 1984.

The King's Breakfast: A Selection of Verse from "When We Were Very Young," Methuen Children's, 1984.

Winnie-Ille-Pu: A Latin Version of A. A. Milne's "Winnie-the-Pooh," translated by Alexander Lenard, Dutton, 1985.

Winnie-the-Pooh's Calendar Book, 1986, Dutton, 1985.

Brian Sibley, compiler, *The Pooh Book of Quotations: In Which Will Be Found Some Useful Information and Sustaining Thoughts by Winnie-the-Pooh and His Friends,* Methuen, 1986.

The Winnie-the-Pooh Journal, Dutton, 1986.

Shepard's illustrations also appear in *Winnie-the-Pooh's Calendar Book, 1977* and annual revisions, published by Dutton.

ILLUSTRATOR; ALL BY LAURENCE HOUSMAN

Victoria Regina: A Dramatic Biography, J. Cape, 1934, Scribner, 1935.
Golden Sovereign (play), Scribner, 1937.
We Are Not Amused [and] *Happy and Glorious* (play), J. Cape, 1939.
Bedchamber Plot (play), J. Cape, 1939.
Suitable Suitors (play), J. Cape, 1939.
Stable Government (play), J. Cape, 1939.
Promotion Cometh (play), J. Cape, 1939.
Primrose Way (play), J. Cape, 1939.
Great Relief (play), J. Cape, 1939.
Go-Between (play), J. Cape, 1939.
Firelighters (play), J. Cape, 1939.
Enter Prince (play), J. Cape, 1939.
Comforter (play), J. Cape, 1939.
Gracious Majesty (scenes from the life of Queen Victoria), J. Cape, 1941, Scribner, 1942.

ILLUSTRATOR; ALL BY KENNETH GRAHAME

The Golden Age (limited autographed edition), John Lane, 1928, Dodd, 1929, with new illustrations, 1954.
Dream Days (also see below), new edition, John Lane, 1930, Dodd, 1931, with new illustrations, Dodd, 1954.
The Wind in the Willows (first edition published in 1908 without Shepard illustrations), Methuen, 1931, Scribner, 1933, with new color plates, Methuen, 1959.
The Reluctant Dragon (previously published as a chapter in *Dream Days*), Holiday House, 1938.
Bertie's Escapade (first published in *First Whisper of the Wind in the Willows*), Lippincott, 1949.
Toad's Tale, Methuen, c. 1982.

ILLUSTRATOR; ALL BY MALCOLM SAVILLE

Susan, Bill and the Wolf-Dog, Ted Nelson, 1954.
Susan, Bill and the Ivy-clad Oak, Ted Nelson, 1954.
Susan, Bill and the Vanishing Boy, Ted Nelson, 1955.
Susan, Bill and the Golden Clock, Ted Nelson, 1955.
Susan, Bill and the "Saucy Kate," Ted Nelson, 1956.
Susan, Bill and the Dark Stranger, Ted Nelson, 1956.

ILLUSTRATOR

Thomas Hughes, *Tom Brown's Schooldays,* c. 1904, new edition, Ginn, 1956.
Hugh Walpole, *Jeremy,* Cassell, 1919.
A. C. Benson and Sir Lawrence Weaver, editors, *Everybody's Book of the Queen's Doll House,* Methuen, 1924.
Edward Verrall Lucas, *Playtime and Company,* Doubleday, Doran, 1925, published as *A Book of Children's Verse,* 1925.
Samuel Pepys, *Everybody's Pepys,* abridged and edited by F. V. Morshead, G. Bell, 1926, Harcourt, 1931.
Charles Dickens, *The Holly-tree, and Other Christmas Stories,* Scribner, 1926.
Eva Violet Isaacs (Marchioness of Reading), *The Little One's Log,* Partridge (London), 1927.
Georgette Agnew, *Let's Pretend* (poems), Putnam, 1927.
Edward Verrall Lucas, *Mr. Punch's County Songs,* Methuen, 1928.
Anthony Armstrong (pseudonym of Anthony Armstrong Willis), *Livestock in Barracks,* Methuen, 1929.
James Boswell, *Everybody's Boswell,* abridged and edited by F. V. Morley, Harcourt, 1930, Bell & Hyman, 1980, new edition published as *The Life of Samuel Johnson and The Journal of a Tour to the Hebrides with Samuel Johnson,* Harper, 1966.
John Drinkwater, *Christmas Poems,* Sidgwick & Jackson, 1931.
Jan Struther (pseudonym of Joyce Maxtone Graham), *Sycamore Square* (verse), Methuen, 1932.
Richard Jeffries, *Bevis: The Story of a Boy,* new edition, P. Smith, 1932.
Boswell, *The Great Cham (Dr. Johnson),* G. Bell, 1933.
Everybody's Lamb, abridged and edited by A. C. Ward, G. Bell, 1933, with new title page by Shepard, 1950.
Patrick R. Chalmers, *The Cricket in the Cage* (verse), Macmillan, 1933.
Lady Winifred Fortescue, *Perfume from Provence,* Blackwood, 1935.
Euphan (pseudonym of Barbara Euphan Todd), *The Seventh Daughter,* Burn Oats, 1935.
Jan Struther (pseudonym of Joyce Maxtone Graham), *The Modern Struwelpeter,* Methuen, 1936.
John Collings Squire, editor, *Cheddar Gorge,* Collins, 1937, Macmillan, 1938.
(Frontispiece) Fortescue, *Sunset House,* Blackwood, 1937, published as *Sunset House: More Perfume from Provence,* Chivers, 1974.
Roland Pertwee, *The Islanders,* Oxford University Press, 1950.
Anna B. Stewart, *Enter David Garrick,* Lippincott, 1951.
Eleanor Farjeon, *The Silver Curlew,* Oxford University Press, 1953, Viking, 1954.
Juliana Ewing, *The Brownies, and Other Stories,* Dutton, 1954.
Mary Louisa Molesworth, *The Cuckoo Clock,* Dutton, 1954.
Eleanor and Herbert Farjeon, *Glass Slipper,* Oxford University Press, 1955, Viking, 1956.
Pertwee, *Operation Wild Goose,* Oxford University Press, 1955.
Susan Colling, *Frogmorton,* Collins, 1955, Knopf, 1956.
Roger L. Green, editor, *Modern Fairy Stories,* Dutton, 1955.
George MacDonald, *At the Back of the North Wind,* Dutton, 1956.
B. D. Rugh, *The Crystal Mountain,* Riverside Press, 1956.
Frances Hodgson Burnett, *The Secret Garden,* Heinemann, 1956.
Shirley Goulden, *Royal Reflections,* Methuen, 1956.
J. Fassett, editor, *The Pancake,* Ginn, 1957.
Green, editor, *Old Greek Fairy Tales,* Bell & Hyman, 1958.
Fassett, editor, *Briar Rose,* Ginn, 1958.

From *Winnie-the-Pooh,* by A. A. Milne. Illustrated by Ernest H. Shepard.

Hans Christian Andersen, *Fairy Tales,* translated by L. W. Kingsland, Oxford University Press, 1961, Walck, 1962.

J. Compton, editor, *A Noble Company,* Ginn, 1961.

Emile Victor Rieu, *The Flattered Flying Fish, and Other Poems,* Dutton, 1962.

Virginia H. Ellison, *The Pooh Cook Book,* Dutton, 1969.

Ellison, *The Pooh Party Book,* Dutton, 1971.

Katie Stewart, *The Pooh Cook Book: Inspired by "Winnie-the-Pooh" and "The House at Pooh Corner" by A. A. Milne,* Methuen Children's, 1971.

Patsy Kumm, *The Pooh Party Book: Inspired by "Winnie-the Pooh" and "The House at Pooh Corner" by A. A. Milne,* Methuen, 1975.

Ellison, *The Pooh Get-Well Book: Recipes and Activities to Help You Recover from Wheezles and Sneezles,* Dell, 1975.

Rawle Knox, editor, *The Work of E. H. Shepard,* Methuen, 1979, Schocken, 1980.

Benjamin Hoff, *The Tao of Pooh,* Methuen, 1982.

Brian Sibley, editor, *The Pooh Sketch Book,* Methuen, 1982, Dutton, 1984.

Lady Arabella Boxer, *The Wind in the Willows Country Cook Book: Inspired by "The Wind in the Willows" by Kenneth Grahame,* Scribner, 1983.

Ethan Mordden, *Pooh's Workout Book,* Dutton, c. 1984.

Katie Stewart, *Pooh's Fireside Recipes: Inspired by "Winnie-the-Pooh" and "The House at Pooh Corner" by A. A. Milne,* Methuen Children's, 1985.

Stewart, *Pooh's Picnic Recipes,* Methuen Children's, 1985.

Also illustrator of *Toby* by Grace Allingham; *David Copperfield* by Charles Dickens; *Aesop's Fables,* adapted by Rev. G. Henslow; *Henry Esmond* by W. M. Thackeray; *Play the Game!* by Harold Avery; *Money or Wife* by Effie Adelaide Rowlands; and *Smouldering Fires* by Evelyn Everett Green; all published between 1900 and 1914. Contributor of drawings to *Punch* and other illustrated magazines.

SIDELIGHTS: Ernest Howard Shepard illustrated more than 150 books in his distinguished career, but he is best known for his drawings for A. A. Milne's ever-popular *Winnie-the-Pooh* books and Kenneth Grahame's *The Wind in the Willows.*

Shepard was born on December 10, 1879, in London, England. His first drawings were illustrations for his sister's stories. His father, an architect, showed the boy's work to friends and "quite decided that I should be an artist when I grew up," Shepard reported in his autobiography *Drawn from Life.* His mother, the granddaughter of watercolor painter William Lee, also encouraged him; and he acknowledged in *Drawn from Life* that, though he considered an artist's life "to be a dull one," after his mother's death he "determined to justify her faith" and take his talent seriously.

Shepard began to work at his art systematically in a studio rented by his father and began studying it more seriously at St. Paul's school in 1892. At the age of sixteen he went to Heatherleys Art School, and in 1897 he started training at the Royal Academy Schools, where he won a scholarship. At the Royal Academy he met Florence Chaplin, also a painter, and they became engaged.

Shepard exhibited his first painting, a portrait of his sister, at the Royal Academy in 1902; two years later he sold a painting from that exhibition. Around the same time, Chaplin received a commission to paint a mural at a nurses' home, so the two pooled their funds and were married in September, 1904. The couple had two children: Graham Howard, who was killed in World War II, and Mary Eleanor, who illustrated the *Mary Poppins* books. Florence Shepard died in 1927 and Shepard remarried in 1944.

Between 1900 and 1914 Shepard illustrated *David Copperfield, Aesop's Fables,* and other books. He also managed, after several tries, to get his drawings in *Punch,* and by the outbreak of World War I in 1914 he had become a regular contributor to that magazine. After the war, during which he served in combat in France and Italy, Shepard resumed his work as an illustrator and in 1921 became a regular staffer at *Punch. Punch* historian R. G. G. Price credited him in *A History of Punch* with bringing such artistic freshness to the magazine that "the rest of it began to look static."

In 1924 Shepard was commissioned to illustrated Milne's *When We Were Very Young.* The combination of Milne's verse and Shepard's line drawings in book form, after their initial publication in *Punch,* sold out in a day and led to commissions that ensured Shepard's lasting success as an illustrator.

When he was asked to illustrate *Winnie-the-Pooh,* the artist visited Milne's home, where he sketched scenes from the surrounding area and made studies and photographs of the writer's son Christopher and his stuffed toys, all of which had provided inspiration for the book. These served, too, as models for Shepard's illustrations for *Winnie-the-Pooh.* Later Shepard did the illustrations for *Now We Are Six* and *The House at Pooh Corner,* and many offshoots of the original books are illustrated with his work. According to *Publishers Weekly* contributor Kimberly Olson Fakih, Dutton sold 150,000 copies of *Winnie-the-Pooh* in 1926, the year it was published. Sixty years later, a publicity director for Dutton reported yearly sales of 150,000 to 200,000 Pooh-related items, including a children's calendar that she described as "the longest running children's calendar ever." In 1987 *School Library Journal* reported that the original stuffed animals that belonged to Christopher Milne were donated to the Central Children's Room at the Donnell Library Center of the New York Public Library.

The Wind in the Willows, Shepard said in *Horn Book Reflections on Children's Books and Reading,* was a book he felt "should never be illustrated.... Perhaps if it had not already been done, I should not have given way to the desire to do it myself, but it so happened that when the opportunity was offered me, I seized upon it gladly." As he had done for *Winnie-the-Pooh,* for Grahame's *The Wind in the Willows* Shepard visited the author and roamed the territory that had inspired the fictional setting, making sketches and imagining the book's characters going about their activities there. At the edge of the river where Rat's boat house would be and where Mole had crossed the water to join him, "I could," recalled Shepard, "almost fancy that I could see a tiny boat pulled up among the reeds." Burton Lindheim reported in the *New York Times* that Shepard had asked for one-third of the royalties on the book, which provided the basis of his income. Lindheim also said that, though three earlier editions of the book had been done, Shepard was the first illustrator who pleased its author.

In his eighties, Shepard wrote his two autobiographies, and when he was nearly ninety he wrote and illustrated two children's books, *Ben and Brock* and *Betsy and Joe.* At ninety he added color to original drawings for *Winnie-the-Pooh* and *The House at Pooh Corner* for new editions of those books. In 1972 he was awarded the Order of the British Empire for his life's work. When he died in 1976, at the age of ninety-six, preparations were under way for a fiftieth anniversary celebration for *Winnie-the-Pooh.*

WORKS CITED:

Fakih, Kimberly Olson, "Beyond the House at Pooh Corner: Winnie-the-Pooh at 60," *Publishers Weekly,* October 31, 1986, p. 28.

Lindheim, Burton, *New York Times,* March 27, 1976.

Price, R. G. G., *A History of Punch,* Collins, 1957.

Shepard, Ernest H., *Drawn from Life,* Methuen, 1961.

Shepard, Ernest H., "Illustrating *The Wind in the Willows,*" *Horn Book Reflections on Children's Books and Reading,* edited by Eleanor Whitney Field, Horn Book, 1969.

"Winnie the Pooh to Reside at NYPL," *School Library Journal,* October 1987, p. 14.

FOR MORE INFORMATION SEE:

BOOKS

Rawle, Knox, editor, *The Work of E. H. Shepard,* Schocken, 1980.

Shepard, Ernest Howard, *Drawn from Memory,* Lippincott, 1957.

Sibley, Brian, editor, *The Pooh Sketch Book,* Dutton, 1984.

PERIODICALS

Publishers Weekly, October 31, 1986.

* * *

SHEPARD, Mary

See KNOX, (Mary) Eleanor Jessie

SHERBURNE, Zoa (Morin) 1912-

PERSONAL: Born September 30, 1912, in Seattle, WA; daughter of Thomas Joseph and Zoa (Webber) Morin; married Herbert Newton Sherburne, June 5, 1935 (deceased); children: Mrs. Marie Brumble, Mrs. Norene Purdue, Mrs. Zoey Holte, Herbert Jr., Thomas, Philip, Anne, Robert. *Education:* Attended parochial schools in Seattle, WA. *Hobbies and other interests:* Bowling, dancing, civic activities.

ADDRESSES: Home—2401 North East Blakeley, Seattle, WA 98105. *Agent*—Ann Elmo Agency Inc., 52 Vanderbilt Ave., New York, NY 10017.

CAREER: Writer. Cornish School of Allied Arts, Seattle, WA, teacher of short story writing, 1957; lecturer on writing.

MEMBER: National League of American Penwomen (second vice-president, Seattle national branch), Seattle Freelance Writers (president, 1954), Phi Delta Nu (president, 1950).

AWARDS, HONORS: Woman of Achievement award, Theta Sigma Phi Matrix, 1950; Woman of the Year, Phi Delta Nu, 1951; Best Book for Young People award, Child Study Association, 1959, for *Jennifer;* Henry Broderick Award, 1960; Governor's Writers' Day Award, 1967.

WRITINGS:

Shadow of a Star, Hurst & Blacklett, 1959.
Journey out of Darkness, Hurst & Blacklett, 1961.

FOR YOUNG ADULTS

Almost April, Morrow, 1956.
The High White Wall, Morrow, 1957.
Princess in Denim, Morrow, 1958.
Jennifer, Morrow, 1959.
Evening Star, Morrow, 1960.
Ballerina on Skates, Morrow, 1961.
Girl in the Shadows, Morrow, 1963.
Stranger in the House, Morrow, 1963.
River at Her Feet, Morrow, 1965.
Girl in the Mirror, Morrow, 1966.
Too Bad about the Haines Girl, Morrow, 1967.
The Girl Who Knew Tomorrow, Morrow, 1970.
Leslie, Morrow, 1972.
Why Have the Birds Stopped Singing?, Morrow, 1974.

OTHER

Also contributor of over three hundred short stories and articles, and numerous verses, to periodicals.

ADAPTATIONS: Stranger in the House was adapted for television as the film *Memories Never Die,* starring Lindsey Wagner, and first broadcast by Columbia Broadcast Service, Inc. (CBS-TV) in December, 1982.

SIDELIGHTS: Zoa Sherburne began her career as a young adult novelist after she had been married for several years and had three children at home, but her enthusiasm for writing has been with her since childhood. She grew up in Seattle, Washington, and was one of four daughters. Searching for a means to establish an individual identity among all the girls in her family, she decided to become a writer.

Zoa Sherburne

Sherburne's first success at authorship occurred when she was about ten years old. She composed a Mother's Day poem that she read aloud and which, as she remembers, brought tears to her mother's eyes. Several years later, while in the sixth grade, she wrote her first play, which was produced by her schoolmates. The positive feedback she received for her efforts inspired her return to writing several years later after a chance occurrence. While listening to the radio one afternoon, she heard the announcement of a national poetry contest and decided to compose a poem of the required twenty-five lines. Sherburne sent in her entry and was rewarded for her efforts by winning a cash prize. She used the prize money to enroll in a local writing school. "My husband thought it was a great idea and even consented to baby-sit while I attended an evening class in commercial writing," she recalled in *Something about the Author* (*SATA*). "This led to a brief but rewarding career in short story [publication] ... I found that I really loved to write and I met many editors who were happy to encourage me." The advent of television led to a drop-off in the periodical market demand for short stories, so Sherburne tried her hand at novel writing and found that she enjoyed it equally as much.

Throughout her career as a young adult novelist, Sherburne has dealt with many subjects of a timely nature.

The young protagonists within her books have had to deal with such things as alcoholic parents, mental illness, racial prejudice, and compulsive eating disorders. In *The Girl Who Knew Tomorrow,* the main character, Angie, is created with the capacity for "second sight," and the book's story line involves the problems that her uniqueness cause both Angie and her family. Throughout her work, Sherburne shows herself consistently able to handle even the most difficult of topics with sensitivity and realism. For example, in the book *Too Bad about the Haines Girl* she tackles the problem of teenage pregnancy. Melinda Haines is a high school student who discovers that she is pregnant in her senior year. The plot revolves around the choices Melinda faces while coping with her situation, and the consequences she must bear in choosing to keep her child, necessitating a confrontation with both her boyfriend and her family. A critic in *Saturday Review* noted that while the book's plot was not unique, from the available "[books] for teenage girls that [focus] on the problem of the young unwed mother, this is one of the best to date"; and Irene Hunt of the *New York Times Book Review* commented: "Mrs. Sherburne hews to the line with the integrity of a skilled writer."

Although not noted for highly imaginative subplots, Sherburne's books have had great appeal among their teenage audience, which can identify with the element of strong family support that she interjects throughout her stories. While grounding her fiction in optimistic realism, Sherburne flavors some of her novels with historical or Gothic elements. *Why Have the Birds Stopped Singing?* is not only a story of a young girl coping with complications that epilepsy brings to her life, but also "an entertaining time travel adventure," according to a *Booklist* reviewer, who commended the book for its "well-drawn historical setting and unbroken line of tension."

Sherburne has continued to write almost exclusively for teenage girls of junior high school age. "I wrote problem stories because I felt that there were too many boy-next-door books for young girls, and the young girls I knew had more serious things to cope with," she once commented in *SATA.* "They had brothers and sisters who had problems, they fell in and out of love with the wrong boys, they were gay and sad and sometimes tragic and more often very funny. They rebelled, and they made mistakes, and sometimes they were sorry and sometimes not. In short, they were the girls who eventually became the characters in my books and I felt that I knew them as well as I know the palm of my hand."

WORKS CITED:

Booklist, July 1, 1974, p. 1202.

Hunt, Irene, "Girls in Trouble," *New York Times Book Review,* March 5, 1967, p. 30.

Saturday Review, March 18, 1967, p. 36.

Something about the Author, Volume 3, Gale, 1972, pp. 194-95.

FOR MORE INFORMATION SEE:

PERIODICALS

Christian Science Monitor, May 4, 1967.

Library Journal, December 15, 1970, p. 4368; January 15, 1973, p. 270; May 15, 1974, p. 1488.

New York Times Book Review, November 6, 1966, p. 20.

Young Readers' Review, May, 1967.

* * *

SHIMIN, Symeon 1902-

PERSONAL: Born November 1, 1902, in Astrakhan, Russia; immigrated to the United States, 1912; naturalized U.S. citizen, 1927; son of a cabinet maker and antique dealer; separated; children: Tonia, Toby. *Education:* Studied with George Luks, 1920-22, and at Cooper Union Art School.

ADDRESSES: Home—New York City.

CAREER: Illustrator and painter; Work Projects Administration, artist, 1947. Writer. *Exhibitions:* Art Institute of Chicago, Chicago, IL, 1940; Corcoran Gallery of Art, Washington DC, 1940; National Museum of Ottawa, Canada, 1940; Whitney Museum of American Art, New York City, 1940, 1941; U.S. Exhibition, Guatemala, 1941; Portland Museum, Portland, OR, drawings from *Paint Box Sea* and *The Pair of Shoes,* c. 1972. Permanent installations at United States Post Office building, Tonawanda, NY, and U.S. Department of Justice building, Washington DC (see below). Painting in permanent collection of Walter Chrysler Art Museum, Provincetown, MA.

MEMBER: Artists League of America.

AWARDS, HONORS: Received award, 1939, for mural commissioned for U.S. Department of Justice Building, Washington, DC; certificate of excellence, American Institute of Graphic Arts, 1955 and 1957; second purchase award, First Provincetown Arts Festival, 1958; Lewis Carroll Shelf award, and Newbery Award, both 1960, both for *Onion John;* citation of merit, Society of Illustrators, 1964; Nancy Bloch award, 1967, for *Zeely;* special citation, Child Study, 1971, for *Two Pair of Shoes;* New Jersey Institute of Technology award, 1972-73, for *Grandpa and Me;* commendation, Art Books for Children, 1973, for *Santiago;* Christopher Award, 1974, for *Gorilla, Gorilla*; commendation, Art Books for Children, 1978, for *Send Wendell;* book citation, Brooklyn Museum/New York Public Library; citation, U.S. Treasury Department, for war poster.

WRITINGS:

SELF-ILLUSTRATED

I Wish There Were Two of Me, Warne, 1976.

A Special Birthday, McGraw, 1976.

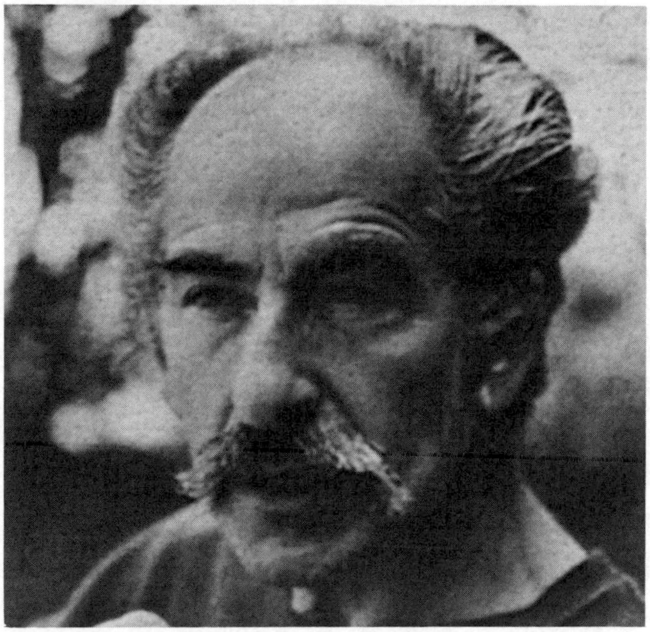

Symeon Shimin

ILLUSTRATOR:

Herman Schneider and Nina Schneider, *How Big is Big?,* revised edition, W. R. Scott, 1950.
H. Schneider and N. Schneider, *You, Among the Stars,* W. R. Scott, 1951.
Miriam Schlein, *Go with the Sun,* W. R. Scott, 1952.
Margaret Wise Brown, *Young Kangaroo,* W. R. Scott, 1953.
Millicent E. Selsam, *All Kinds of Babies and How They Grow,* W. R. Scott, 1953.
Schlein, *Elephant Herd,* W. R. Scott, 1954.
Joseph Krumbold, *Onion John,* Crowell, 1959.
R. Wilson, *Outdoor Wonderland,* Lothrop, 1961.
Aileen Fisher, *Listen, Rabbit,* Crowell, 1964.
Byrd B. Schweitzer, *One Small Blue Bead,* Macmillan, 1965.
Norma Simon, *Passover,* Crowell, 1965.
G. Cretan, *All Except Sammy* (Junior Literary Guild selection), Little, Brown, 1966.
Helen Hoover, *Animals at My Doorstep,* Parents' Magazine Press, 1966.
Mary K. Phelan, *Fourth of July,* Crowell, 1966.
Simon, *Hanukkah,* Crowell, 1966.
Virginia Hamilton, *Zeely,* Dial, 1967.
Claudia Lewis, *Poems of Earth and Stars,* Dutton, 1967.
Joan M. Lexau, *Kite over Tenth Avenue,* Doubleday, 1967.
Selsam, *All Kinds of Babies,* Scholastic Inc., 1967.
Ann Herbert Scott, *Sam,* McGraw, 1967.
Elizabeth Coatsworth, *Lighthouse Island,* Norton, 1968.
Molly Cone, *House in the Tree: A Story of Israel,* Crowell, 1968.
Schweitzer, *The Man Who Talked to a Tree,* Dutton, 1968.
Pura Belpre, *Santiago* (Spanish edition), Warne, 1969.
Fisher, *Sing, Little Mouse,* Crowell, 1969.
Patricia L. Gauch, *Grandpa and Me,* Coward, 1969.
Madeleine L'Engle, *Dance in the Desert,* Farrar, Straus, 1969.
Julian May, *Before the Indians,* Holiday House, 1969.
Alvin Silverstein and Virginia Silverstein, *Star in the Sea,* Warne, 1969.
Aline Glasgow, *The Pair of Shoes,* Dial, 1970.
Sidonie M. Gruenberg, *The Wonderful Story of How You Were Made,* Doubleday, 1970.
Hoover, *Animals Near and Far,* Parents' Magazine Press, 1970.
Bill Martin, Jr., *I Am Freedom's Child,* Bowmar, 1970.
Watty Piper, *All about Story Book,* Platt, 1970.
Isaac Bashevis Singer, *Joseph and Koza,* Farrar, Straus, 1970.
Isaac Asimov, *Best New Thing,* Collins & World, 1971.
May, *Why People Are Different Colors,* Holiday House, 1971.
Byrd Baylor, *Coyote Cry,* Lothrop, 1972.
Florence P. Heide, *My Castle,* McGraw, 1972.
Helen Kay, *A Bridge for a Baby Gibbon,* Abelard, 1972.
Doris H. Lund, *The Paint Box Sea,* McGraw, 1972.
Tobi Tobias, *Marian Anderson,* Crowell, 1972.
Mary Jarrell, *The Knee-Baby,* Farrar, Straus, 1973.
Carol Fenner, *Gorilla, Gorilla,* Random, 1973.
Erma Brenner, *A New Baby—A New Life,* McGraw, 1973.
Genevieve Gray, *Send Wendell,* McGraw, 1974.
Fisher, *Now That Spring is Here,* Bowmar, 1977.
George, *Wentletrap Trap,* Dutton, 1977.
Tobias, *Petey,* Putnam, 1978.
Muriel Rukeyser, *More Night,* Harper, 1981.
Brenner, *When Baby Comes Home,* Janus, 1984.

SIDELIGHTS: Symeon Shimin's renown as an illustrator of children's books has come after many years of hard work in perfecting his unique style as a commercial artist. Self-taught in the skills necessary to pursue his goal of becoming a painter, Shimin's career as a children's book illustrator began in 1950 when friends Nina and Herman Schneider approached him about designing new artwork for a revised edition of their book *How Big is Big?.* Shimin accepted, and since that time has illustrated over fifty books for young children.

"I always wanted to be a musician," Symeon Shimin once told *Contemporary Authors.* "I never drew as a child. I never thought about drawing. I didn't know what a 'painter' meant nor what 'painting' meant. Then one day—the next day or the next week of my childhood, it seems—I drew. And I have never stopped drawing!" As one of six children in a family newly immigrated to the United States from Russia, economics necessitated that Shimin channel his interest in art in a direction whereby he could assist in his family's financial support. Therefore, at the age of sixteen he apprenticed himself to a commercial artist in New York City while attending night classes at Cooper Union Art School. Two years later Shimin began free-lance work as a commercial artist in his own right. Possessing a strong interest in exploring new uses for various painting mediums, he also found time to study in the studio of the artist George Luks for about six months. In 1929 Shimin toured the galleries of France and Spain, gaining insight and inspiration through viewing the works of such masters as El Greco and Francisco Goya, as well as studying the composition and technique of contemporary artists. A year later he returned to New York City to continue with his painting, eventually being given the opportunity to work on such large-scale projects as the mural now housed in the Department of Justice Building in Washington DC, for which he won an award in 1938.

In addition to illustrating the works of many juvenile authors, Shimin has managed to find the time to write and illustrate two of his own books for children. Of these, the first, *I Wish There Were Two of Me,* was inspired by his daughter Toby's child-view of the world: "With two bodies I can stay up as long as I want and you can go to bed when you're told." Although the prose was described by *School Library Journal* reviewer Marjorie Lewis as "terribly sweet, terribly self-conscious," Shimin's illustrations were commended for their delicate beauty.

Working in the mediums of either watercolor or acrylic for his book illustration, the artist explained how he organized his work. "I don't work steadily at book illustration," he once said. "I illustrate for a time and then stop to devote myself to painting." Shimin uses live models from which he compose the subjects for his drawings, and can take up to six weeks to complete the art-work for each book he is commissioned to illustrate. "I do dozens of drawings from each sketch, working and re-working until I am satisfied," he explained, "until I feel the illustrations are perfect." Symeon Shimin expressed some thoughts on his chosen vocation, saying, "Art means everything to me. It is my life. It *is* me.... I like all kinds of art if it is done with conviction."

From *Zeely,* by Virginia Hamilton. Illustrated by Symeon Shimin.

WORKS CITED:

Contemporary Authors, Volume 81-84, Gale, 1979.
de Montreville, Doris and Donna Hill, editors, *Third Book of Junior Authors,* H. W. Wilson, 1972.
Lewis, Marjorie, *School Library Journal,* September, 1976, p. 105.

FOR MORE INFORMATION SEE:

BOOKS

Hopkins, Lee B., *Books Are by People,* Citation Press, 1969.
Kingman, Lee, and others, compilers, *Illustrators of Children's Books: 1957-1976,* Horn Book, 1978.
Viguers, Ruth H., and others, compilers, *Illustrators of Children's Books: 1946-56,* Horn Book, 1958.
Ward and Marquardt, *Illustrators for Young People,* Scarecrow, 1970.

PERIODICALS

Bulletin for the Center for Children's Books, December 1976, p. 66; March, 1977, p. 114.
Publishers Weekly, June 7, 1976, p. 74.
School Library Journal, February, 1977, p. 58.

* * *

SHOWERS, Paul C. 1910-

PERSONAL: Born April 12, 1910, in Sunnyside, WA; son of Frank L. (a music teacher) and M. Ethelyn (a singer; maiden name, Walker) Showers; married Kay M. Sperry (a psychologist), August 5, 1946 (divorced, 1973); children: Paul Walker, Kate Barger (twins). *Education:* University of Michigan, A.B., 1931; New York University, post-graduate study, 1952-53. *Hobbies and other interests:* Music, social history.

ADDRESSES: Home—525 Homer Ave, Palo Alto, CA 94301.

CAREER: Detroit Free Press, Detroit, MI, copyreader, 1937-40; *New York Herald Tribune,* New York City, copy desk staffmember, 1940-41; *New York Times Sunday Mirror,* New York City, writer, copy editor, 1946; *New York Times* New York City, member of Sunday department, 1946-76, assistant travel editor, 1949-61, copy editor of Sunday magazine, 1961-76; free-lance writer, 1976—. *Military service:* U.S. Army, 1942-45; served on staff of *Yank* (army weekly), edited Okinawa edition; became staff sergeant.

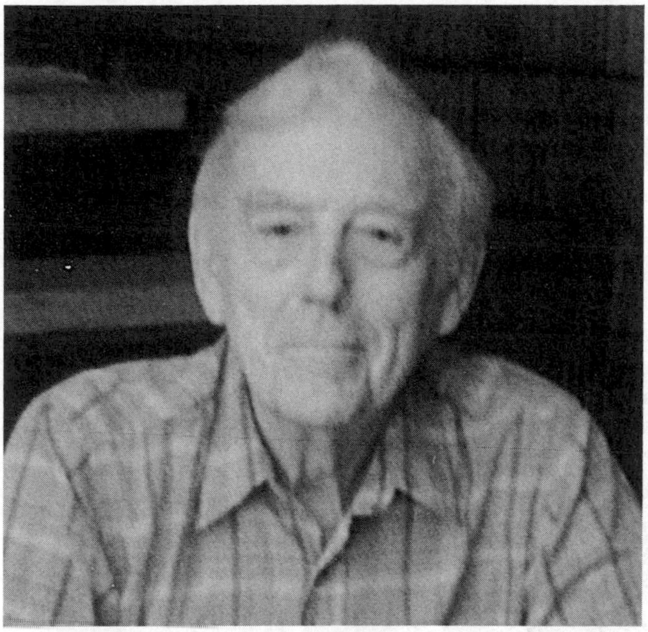

Paul C. Showers

AWARDS, HONORS: Science award, New Jersey Institute of Technology, 1961, for *Find Out by Touching, The Listening Walk* and *In the Night,* 1967, for *How You Talk,* 1968, for *A Drop of Blood, Before You Were a Baby,* and *Hear Your Heart.*

WRITINGS:

"LET'S READ AND FIND OUT SCIENCE BOOK" SERIES; FOR CHILDREN

Find Out By Touching, illustrated by Robert Galster, Trophy, 1961.
In the Night, illustrated by Ezra Jack Keats, Trophy, 1961.
The Listening Walk, illustrated by Aliki, Trophy, 1961.
How Many Teeth?, illustrated by Paul Galdone, Trophy, 1962, revised edition illustrated by True Kelley, 1991.
Look at Your Eyes, illustrated by Galdone, Trophy, 1962.
Follow Your Nose, illustrated by Galdone, Trophy, 1963.
Your Skin and Mine, illustrated by Galdone, Trophy, 1965, revised edition illustrated by Kathleen Kuchera, 1991.
A Drop of Blood, illustrated by Don Madden, Trophy, 1967, revised edition, 1989.
How You Talk, illustrated by Galster, Trophy, 1967, revised edition illustrated by Megan Lloyd, 1990.
(With wife, Kay S. Showers) *Before You Were a Baby,* illustrated by Ingrid Fetz, Trophy, 1968.
Hear Your Heart, illustrated by Joseph Low, Trophy, 1968.
A Baby Starts to Grow, illustrated by Rosalind Fry, Trophy, 1969.
What Happens to a Hamburger?, illustrated by Anne Rockwell, Trophy, 1970, revised edition, 1985.
Use Your Brain, illustrated by Fry, Trophy, 1971.
Sleep Is for Everyone, illustrated by Wendy Watson, Trophy, 1974.
Where Does the Garbage Go?, illustrated by Loretta Lustig, Trophy, 1974.
Me and My Family Tree, illustrated by Madden, Trophy, 1978.
No Measles, No Mumps for Me, illustrated by Harriet Barton, Trophy, 1980.
You Can't Make a Move without Your Muscles, illustrated by Barton, Trophy, 1982.
Ears Are for Hearing, illustrated by Holly Keller, Trophy, 1990.

FOR CHILDREN

Columbus Day, illustrated by Ed Emberly, Crowell, 1965.
Indian Festivals, illustrated by Lorence Bjorklund, Crowell, 1969.
The Bird and the Stars, illustrated by Mila Lazarevich, Doubleday, 1975.
The Moon Walker, illustrated by Susan Perl, Doubleday, 1975.
A Book of Scary Things, illustrated by Perl, Doubleday, 1977.

OTHER

Fortune Telling for Fun and Popularity, New Home Library, 1942, published as *Fortune Telling for Fun,* Newcastle, 1971, and *Fortune Telling for Fun and Profit,* Bell, 1985.

Also contributor of articles and book reviews to *New York Times Book Review;* contributor of humorous verse and short articles to *Life, Judge,* and *Ballyhoo* (national humor magazines). Showers's manuscripts are included in the Kerlan Collection, University of Minnesota.

ADAPTATIONS: All published by Crowell as filmstrip with record and film with cassette: "Look at Your Eyes," 1962, "How Many Teeth," 1962, "Follow Your Nose," 1963, "Your Skin and Mine," 1965, "Drop of Blood," 1967, "How You Talk," 1967, "Hear Your Heart," 1968, "A Baby Starts to Grow," 1969, "What Happens to a Hamburger?" 1970, "Use Your Brain," 1971.

SIDELIGHTS: Showers is a retired newspaperman whose writing for children has always been a part-time occupation. His career in journalism spanned thirty-nine years and found him working for major newspapers in Detroit, Michigan, and New York City. It was while he was a member of the *New York Times* Sunday staff that he was invited by Dr. Franklyn Branley to try his hand at writing a book for children. Dr. Branley, then educational director of the American Museum of Natural History, was preparing to launch the "Let's Read and Find Out" series of nonfiction books, designed for the early grades and originally published by the Thomas Y. Crowell Company. Showers' initial attempt, a book about the sense of touch, was one of the first titles in the new series, and its success encouraged him to continue with more books, work that has since brought him

From *A Baby Starts to Grow,* by Paul C. Showers. Illustrated by Rosalind Fry.

recognition as a noteworthy author in the field of juvenile nonfiction. While the "Let's Read and Find Out" series was taken over by Harper & Row and subsequently by HarperCollins, Showers has continued to author numerous books on science-related topics in the direct and informal style with which he has been able to engage the curiosity of young readers since the 1960s.

Showers graduated from the University of Michigan in 1931 with the desire to become an actor and playwright. He worked sporadically, accepting bit parts and working "summer stock" theater, but never landed significant roles or had success in finding a producer for plays he wrote. 1934 found Showers at the Chicago World's Fair performing in vignettes from Shakespearean plays on the stage of a replica of England's famous Globe Theater specially constructed for the exhibition. During his years as an actor, he supplemented his meager earnings by doing free-lance writing for several national humor magazines, one of which was *Life.* In 1932, *Life* magazine decided to expand its circulation by creating a novelty crossword feature, a gigantic "cockeyed" puzzle which would cover a two-page spread. Showers recalled his involvement in this new project in his autobiographical sketch for *Something about the Author Autobiogra-*

phy Series (*SAAS*). "*Life* called its puzzle 'cockeyed' because the definitions were to be outrageously misleading and, whenever possible, to be funny.... All words had to be in the average reader's vocabulary; none could be used that required a hunt through the dictionary. This rule was thrown in for the benefit of Westchester commuters, who presumably might buy the magazine at Grand Central [Station] and want to work the puzzle while going home on the train, with no dictionary handy.

"I had just sold a standard-size puzzle to *Life* when the decision was made to give the readers the biggest puzzle then on the market, and I was offered the job at fifty dollars a puzzle. At a time when T-bone steak was selling for twenty-eight cents a pound, an income of fifty dollars a month held definite potential, and I accepted. From that moment on, regardless of what else I might be doing, I made crossword puzzles. Filling in the diagram wasn't difficult. In a way it was fun. Thinking up the definitions was the dismaying part. Each month I had to rack my brains for suitably cock-eyed definitions for a list of between 250 and 300 words. The only one I can now recall was for a four-letter word meaning 'A bender you can take the children on.' The answer was KNEE."

Showers's career as a maker of cross-word puzzles ended in 1936 when *Life* was bought up by *Time* Magazine. Casting about for a job in publishing, Showers learned of an opening at the *Detroit Free Press* where he took a job on the copy desk, learning the business of editing reporters' written copy and composing headlines. Three years later, he left the Midwest for New York City and a job with the *New York Herald-Tribune.* Showers served three years in the Army during World War II and then returned to New York City. He married and began raising his twin children Paul and Kate, working as an editor for the *New York Times.* He finally submitted his resignation on July 4, 1976. Showers recalled, "It was a once-in-a-lifetime opportunity to make my personal declaration of independence from the newspaper business to work at my own pace as a free-lance writer. That night the occasion was celebrated with a spectacular fireworks display over the Statue of Liberty in New York Harbor!"

The first book that Showers wrote for the "Let's-Read-and-Find-Out" series was *Find Out by Touching.* Book topics relate exclusively to science and are suggested by the series' editorial staff, but Showers has the freedom to compose his texts in an original manner. "I am less interested in writing about science than in putting together books that will appeal to kids who are still learning to read a new language (as kids in kindergarten and the first three grades are doing)," he once told *Something About the Author.* After extensive research on his subject, Showers organizes the material in a way that, although elementary in the use of vocabulary and grammar, presents the subject matter with some degree of complexity. Although a child might read at a beginning level, Showers believes that his audience of four-to-eight-year-olds is capable of understanding more advanced concepts than their limited reading vocabulary can express. He finds the task of bridging this gap between language and concept while maintaining interesting and enlightening texts to be the greatest challenge in writing juvenile nonfiction.

Showers believes that conversations among children are an excellent method in which to gauge the readability of his books in terms of how well they will be comprehended. "I wanted to combine a simple vocabulary with recognizable speech patterns, the language ability the beginning reader had already acquired through daily speech," Showers explained in *SAAS.* "We lived in the suburbs and had a house and a garden with a swing in it. The swing was a magnet for the kindergarten set in our neighborhood, and when I was preparing to write a book, I would spend time on weekends working the garden and eavesdropping on the swing crowd.... Later, when I sat at my typewriter, I would test each sentence I wrote against my recollection of those conversations. Is this how the kids would have phrased it? If I were talking to them instead of writing it down, is this the way I would say it?

"Repetition and simple sentences may be fine for a beginning reader, but for the writer providing those sentences, they can be a frustrating bore. To relieve the monotony of the endless simplicities, I try mixing in jingles and phonic devices of one sort or another and whenever possible attempt to make a little joke." Showers's sense of humor has not been lost on his young audience. Whether his subject has been heredity, sleep, digestion, hearing, preventative medicine, sight, or blood and its function, his texts have remained popular through several editions, some books selling upwards of eight hundred thousand copies. Reviewer Denise Moll in *School Library Journal* commended Showers's book *Ears are for Hearing,* calling it, "A delightful book that genuinely succeeds in being informative without being boring." The ability to communicate his affection for his young audience while answering basic questions about science makes Showers's books notable in their field. Sparking the enthusiasm of young children to find out more about the world around them continues to be a fulfilling pastime for this retired newspaperman.

WORKS CITED:

Moll, Denise L., *School Library Journal,* August, 1990, p. 143.

Something about the Author, Volume 21, Gale, 1980, pp. 152-154.

Showers, Paul, *Something about the Author Autobiography Series,* Volume 7, Gale, 1989, pp. 285-298.

FOR MORE INFORMATION SEE:

BOOKS

Children's Literature Review, Volume 6, Gale, 1984, pp. 241-249.

PERIODICALS

Booklist, April 15, 1980, p. 1210; March 15, 1990, p. 1459; May 1, 1991, p. 1723.

Horn Book, April, 1969; April, 1975; February, 1983, p. 83; September, 1990, p. 631.
New York Times Book Review, November 7, 1965, p. 56.
Redbook, August, 1974.
School Library Journal, August, 1985, p. 57; February, 1990, p. 85.
Wilson Library Bulletin, October, 1975.

* * *

SHREVE, Susan Richards 1939-

PERSONAL: Born May 2, 1939, in Toledo, OH; daughter of Robert Kenneth (a broadcaster and writer) and Helen Elizabeth (Greene) Richards; married Porter Gaylord Shreve (a family therapist), May 26, 1962 (divorced); married Timothy Seldes (an agent), February 2, 1987; children: Porter Gaylord, Elizabeth Steward, Caleb Richards, Katharine Taylor. *Education:* University of Pennsylvania, B.A. (magna cum laude), 1961; University of Virginia, M.A., 1969.

ADDRESSES: Home—3319 Newark St. N.W., Washington, DC 20008. *Office*—Department of English, George Mason University, Fairfax, VA 22030. *Agent*—Timothy Seldes, Russell & Volkening, Inc., 50 West 29th St., New York, NY 10001.

CAREER: Teacher of English in private schools in Cheshire, England, 1962-63, Rosemont, PA, 1963-66, Washington, DC, 1967-68, and Philadelphia, PA, 1970-72; Community Learning Center (alternative school), Philadelphia, co-founder, 1972-75; George Mason University, Fairfax, VA, associate professor, 1976-80, professor of literature, 1980—, Jerry McKean Moore chair of writing, 1978—. Columbia University, visiting professor, 1982—; Princeton University, visiting professor, 1991-92.

MEMBER: PEN/Faulkner Foundation (president), Authors Guild, Authors League of America, Washington Independent Writers, Children's Book Guild, Phi Beta Kappa.

AWARDS, HONORS: Jenny Moore Award, George Washington University, 1978; Notable Book citation, American Library Association (ALA), 1979, for *Family Secrets: Five Very Important Stories;* Best Book for Young Adults citation, ALA, 1980, for *The Masquerade;* Notable Children's Trade Book in the field of social studies citation, National Council for Social Studies and the Children's Book Council joint committee, 1980, for *Family Secrets: Five Very Important Stories;* Guggenheim award in fiction, 1980; National Endowment for the Arts fiction award, 1982; Edgar Allan Poe Award, Mystery Writers of America, 1988, for *Lucy Forever and Miss Rosetree, Shrinks.*

WRITINGS:

FOR CHILDREN

The Bad Dreams of a Good Girl, illustrations by Diane De Groat, Knopf, 1982.

Susan Richards Shreve

How I Saved the World on Purpose, illustrations by Suzanne Richardson, Holt, 1985.
Lucy Forever and Miss Rosetree, Shrinks, Holt, 1986.
Lily and the Runaway Baby, illustrations by Sue Truesdell, Random House, 1987.

FOR YOUNG ADULTS

The Nightmares of Geranium Street, Knopf, 1977.
Loveletters, Knopf, 1978.
Family Secrets: Five Very Important Stories, illustrations by Richard Cuffari, Knopf, 1979.
The Masquerade, Knopf, 1980.
The Revolution of Mary Leary, Knopf, 1982.
The Flunking of Joshua T. Bates (Junior Literary Guild selection), illustrations by De Groat, Knopf, 1984.
The Gift of the Girl Who Couldn't Hear, Morrow, 1991.
Joshua T. Bates in Charge, Knopf, 1992.
Wait for Me, Morrow, 1992.

ADULT NOVELS

A Fortunate Madness, Houghton, 1974.
A Woman Like That, Atheneum, 1977.
Children of Power, Macmillan, 1979.
Miracle Play, Morrow, 1981.
Dreaming of Heroes, Morrow, 1984.
Queen of Hearts, Linden Press, 1986.
A Country of Strangers, Simon & Schuster, 1989.

Daughters of the New World: A Novel, N. A. Talese/Doubleday, 1992.

SIDELIGHTS: American novelist and children's author Susan Richards Shreve, who once said that she writes "stories of magical realism," grew up in a family fond of storytelling. "There has not been a moment in my life when there was not a drama going on in my mind," Shreve told Megan Rosenfeld of the *Washington Post.* Shreve suffered polio and two other major illnesses before attending kindergarten and entertained herself while bedridden by imagining dramatic stories involving her dolls. Shreve herself was often the center of dramatic situations while trying to lead a life of achievement despite her illnesses and subsequent frailty. For example, she surprised many people when she tried out for her high school cheerleading squad. Shreve lets polio survivor Natty Taylor, a character in *Children of Power,* explain that when a child's health suffers early in life, others feel that "anything she does is astonishing." Natty resists being defined by her limitations in a campaign not unlike Shreve's own childhood ambition to lead a life without restrictions, the author told Rosenfeld.

Living in Washington, D.C., where her father, a crime reporter, headed the wartime radio censorship office, made Shreve's early life interesting. The family moved from Toledo, Ohio, to Washington, D.C., when Shreve was three. "The house was always full of soldiers," she told *Publishers Weekly* interviewer Elizabeth Gleick, "especially war correspondents, who had wonderful stories to tell." Deeply impressed by the excitement of these experiences, Shreve kept an active fantasy life going on in her head. Later in life she realized this was an excellent background for a writer.

After World War II Shreve's parents bought a farm in Vienna, Virginia. With the farm the family inherited "three tenant farmers with piles of children, crops, and animals tended by the black families who had lived there for generations, under owner protection, barely paid—a not uncommon post-slavery arrangement," Shreve wrote in the *Contemporary Authors Autobiography Series.* "My father set about treating those tenant farmers decently, to show the other white Southerners in nearby farms what democracy was all about," Shreve said. Yet her father's influence did not reach as far as the tenant farmers' wives and children. After a Fourth of July dinner one year, Shreve and her family heard gunfire. "Shortly afterwards, the women and children from the houses on the farm streamed into our kitchen, full of bruises, spilling blood on the floor," Shreve said. They told the family that the men were drunk and had beaten them and that they feared for their lives. At first, Shreve's father tried to protect them, holding the men at bay with an unloaded rifle (he had used the last of his ammunition earlier). He realized his attempt to help would be futile when the police refused to intervene and told him to release the women and children. "They won't be killed," one officer said, "but you ought to know it's not your business anyway." The incident became the basis for *A Country of Strangers.*

Shreve said her mother told her that her father "was a fine nonfiction writer, but not much good at fiction." While he had always wanted to write fiction, he never had the opportunity. Having grown up during the end of the Depression, he was unable to choose a career that was not sure to provide a steady income. "It was possible for me to be a fiction writer in a way that was not possible for my father in 1931," Shreve said. She related how her fiction writing began: "I didn't write fiction while my father was alive. Perhaps it is true that I was only free to write after he died. It is also true that in the manner of families, my parents set me up in this business: I have inherited my father's shop, passed from father to child, with the responsibility for maintaining its essential character in changing times."

After graduating from the University of Pennsylvania, she married her high school sweetheart and started her dual careers as mother and writer. While raising four children and working as a schoolteacher, she awoke before dawn to write at the dining room table. Shreve believes having children around is a good thing for a writer, because they keep the author in touch with the real world. Shreve told Gleick, "The world of complications hasn't reached children yet; they see things in a way adults can't. They have an eye on the world that is infinitely less damaged than mine, and they're more truthful. So I think I used them for that kind of truth and for humor."

Children and young adults play significant roles in all of Shreve's fiction. Her books for young adults are prized for their memorable characters who achieve understanding against the backdrop of a changing society. Like the author, the teens in Shreve's books manage not only to survive against the odds—sometimes after making trouble for themselves—but also discover their power to affect the lives of people around them and the importance of learning to handle it responsibly.

In *Children of Power,* a group of Washington, D.C., teens bands together against a man who has compassionately befriended the deposed senator Joseph McCarthy. Natty, Shreve's teen protagonist, learns about abuses of power while watching her friends commit the same sins against McCarthy that they have judged in him as terribly wrong. Their arrogant belief that they are doing something good for their country keeps them from seeing their own errors. *Lucy Forever and Miss Rosetree, Shrinks* shows the harm produced by amateur psychiatrists. Amused by one of their father's mute psychiatric patients, two eleven-year-old girls try to get her to speak. Soon they realize they have put her well-being and their own at risk.

The Bad Dreams of a Good Girl presents nine-year-old Lotty, youngest sibling of three ill-behaved brothers, who feels that her parents expect her "to be a paragon of virtue," Merri Rosenberg wrote in the *New York Times Book Review.* Her mostly virtuous responses to their antagonisms provide the framework for lengthy descriptions of her dreams, in which she pays them back without inhibition or remorse. "Shreve sensitively ex-

From *Family Secrets: Five Very Important Stories,* by Susan Shreve. Illustrated by Richard Cuffari.

plores Lotty's emotional conflict that results from trying to live up to her parents' expectations, even as her 'bad' feelings surface in her dreams," Rosenberg noted.

Even in her novels for adults, teenagers play a significant role. In *A Country of Strangers,* a young woman teaches the adults an important lesson. After the white owner of Elm Grove, a former plantation near Washington, D.C., suddenly disappears, Moses Bellows, a descendant of slaves, moves in. Moses develops a violent jealousy thinking that his wife and the farm's former owner were lovers; Charley, a white journalist who buys the estate and tries to befriend Moses, is also taken by jealous rage when his Danish movie star wife flirts with his new friend. Thus he is unable to erase the past which haunts Moses, despite his efforts to combat the racism that surrounds them all. Though Prudential, named after the insurance company and pregnant at thirteen, was sent to the farm to be 'tamed' by her aunt Miracle and uncle Moses, "it is Prudential who tames everyone else," Jay Parini wrote in the *Times Literary Supplement.* In light of the birth of her son, conflicts subside and a dream of brotherhood is recalled. Citing Shreve's description of the national longing for brotherhood, Malone commented, "Our unending wish to recreate the warm, kind, communal refuge of the first dream of America comes out of our 'inevitable birthright in a country of strangers, of loneliness and isolation and a longing to walk in the company of friends.'"

Rosenberg and other reviewers have criticized Shreve for wrapping up her novels with happy endings. The author's aversion to tragedy has been with her since childhood, when she replaced tragic endings in an opera book with the words "AND THEY ALL LIVED HAPPILY EVER AFTER." She said in *Something about the Author,* "I do not believe in false promises but I do believe that in life as well as in books, we owe our children as well as ourselves the promise of a future." In a *Tribune Books* review, Wanda Urbanska commented that "Shreve certainly adds fireworks" to a kind of literature that usually presents unimportant characters and events, and lacks creativity. As a versatile and insightful novelist who has accomplished far more than her childhood ambition to be "normal," Shreve is now recognized by Jonathan Yardley of the *Washington Post Book World* and other critics as an "exceptionally gifted writer."

WORKS CITED:

Contemporary Authors Autobiography Series, Volume 5, Gale, 1987, pp. 225-241.

Malone, Michael, "Keeping the Home Fires Burning," *Washington Post Book World,* January 8, 1989, p. 1.

Parini, Jay, "Into the Nether Regions," *Times Literary Supplement,* November 24, 1989, p. 1313.

Rosenberg, Merri, review of *The Bad Dreams of a Good Girl, New York Times Book Review,* May 16, 1982, p. 29.

Shreve, Susan Richards, in an interview with Elizabeth Gleick, *Publishers Weekly,* December 19, 1986, pp. 35-36.

Shreve, Susan Richards, in an interview with Megan Rosenfeld, "The Washington Novelist, Breaking Her Boundaries," *Washington Post,* February 2, 1987.

Shreve, Susan Richards, *Children of Power,* Macmillan, 1979.

Something about the Author, Volume 46, Gale, 1987, pp. 197-199.

Urbanska, Wanda, "An Explosive Book Full of Lovingly Portrayed People," *Tribune Books* (Chicago), January 8, 1989, p. 6.

Yardley, Jonathan, "The Secret Lives of Ordinary People," *Washington Post Book World,* December 14, 1986, p. 3.

FOR MORE INFORMATION SEE:

BOOKS

Contemporary Literary Criticism, Volume 23, Gale, 1983, pp. 402-405.

PERIODICALS

Best Sellers, August 1, 1974, p. 212; December, 1977; June, 1980, p. 119.

Books of the Times, July, 1979, p. 326.

Bulletin of the Center for Children's Books, July, 1985; June, 1987, p. 196; January, 1988, p. 100.

Chicago Tribune Book World, October 18, 1981, section 7, p. 4.

Detroit News, February 8, 1987.

Los Angeles Times Book Review, August 11, 1985, p. 6; March 5, 1989, p. 7.

Maclean's, July 30, 1979, p. 45.

Ms., April, 1984, p. 30.

Newsweek, December 18, 1978, p. 102.

New York Times Book Review, August 4, 1974, p. 27; July 10, 1977, p. 28; June 10, 1979, p. 51; July 1, 1979, p. 12; August 16, 1981, pp. 8, 23; November 14, 1982, p. 63; April 1, 1984, p. 8.

People, March 16, 1987, pp. 13-14.

Saturday Review, May 12, 1979, p. 47.

Times (London), March 19, 1987; July 13, 1989.

Times Literary Supplement, September 22, 1978, p. 1056; April 24, 1987, p. 434.

Tribune Books (Chicago), January 4, 1987, p. 7.

Washington Post Book World, December 11, 1977; April 1, 1979, p. E3; May 11, 1980; July 26, 1981, pp. 5, 7; April 11, 1982, p. 11; October 10, 1982, p. 7; March 25, 1984, p. 11; January 8, 1989, p. 1.

Wilson Library Bulletin, February, 1983.

* * *

SHULEVITZ, Uri 1935-

PERSONAL: Given name pronounced *oo*-ree; born February 27, 1935, in Warsaw, Poland; came to United States in 1959; naturalized during the 1960s; son of Abraham and Szandla (Hermanstat) Shulevitz; married Helene Weiss (an artist), June 11, 1961 (divorced). *Education:* Teacher's College, Israel, teacher's degree, 1956; studied painting privately with Ezekiel Streichman, 1950-52; attended Tel-Aviv Art Institute, evenings, 1953-55, and Brooklyn Museum Art School,

1959-61; studied painting at Provincetown workshop with Leo Manso and Victor Candell, summer 1965; studied the painting techniques of the High Renaissance with Peter Hopkins, 1977-83. *Religion:* Jewish. *Hobbies and other interests:* Art, music, travel, old tales and parables of Eastern traditions, movies, theatre, New York City, yoga, and tai-chi-chuan.

ADDRESSES: Agent—c/o Farrar, Straus & Giroux, Inc., 19 Union Sq. W., New York, NY 10003.

CAREER: Kibbutz Ein-Geddi (collective farm), Israel, member, 1957-58; art director of youth magazine in Israel, 1958-59; illustrator of children's books, 1961—; author of children's books, 1962—; School of Visual Arts, New York City, instructor in art, 1967-68; Pratt Institute, Brooklyn, NY, instructor in art, 1970-71; New School for Social Research, New York City, instructor of writing and illustrating of children's books, 1970-86; Hartwick College, Oneonta, NY, director of summer workshop, 1974, in writing and illustrating children's books. *Military service:* Israeli Army, 1956-59.

MEMBER: American Society of Contemporary Artists, Authors Guild, Authors League of America (member of children's books committee), New York Artists Equity Association.

AWARDS, HONORS: Children's Book Awards, American Institute of Graphic Arts, 1963-64, for *Charley Sang a Song,* 1965-66, for *The Second Witch,* 1967-68, for *One Monday Morning,* and Certificates of Excellence, 1973-74, for *The Magician* and *The Fools of Chelm and Their History,* and 1979, for *The Treasure*; American Institute of Graphic Arts Children's Books (AIGACB) citation, 1967-68, for *One Monday Morning;* Notable Book citations, American Library Association (ALA), 1967, for *One Monday Morning,* 1968, for *The Fool of the World and The Flying Ship,* 1969, for *Rain Rain Rivers,* 1974, for *Dawn,* and 1982, for *The Golem; Horn Book* honor list citations, 1967, for *One Monday Morning,* 1969, for *Rain Rain Rivers,* and 1979, for *The Treasure;* AIGACB Show exhibitions, 1973-74, included *The Fools of Chelm and Their History* and *The Magician,* and 1980, included *The Treasure;* Certificate of Merit, Society of Illustrators (New York), 1965, for *Charley Sang a Song;* books displayed at Children's Book Exhibition, New York Public Library, 1967, 1968, 1969, 1972, 1973, and 1974, and at International Biennale of Illustrations (Bratislava, Czechoslovakia), 1969; Caldecott Medal, ALA, 1969, for *The Fool of the World and the Flying Ship; The Fool of the World and the Flying Ship* was included in American Booksellers 1969 Gift to the Nation for the Library of the White House; Child Study Association of America's Children's Books of the Year citations, 1969, for *Rain Rain Rivers,* 1972, for *Soldier and Tsar in the Forest: A Russian Tale,* 1974, for *Dawn,* 1976, for *The Touchstone.*

Bronze Medal, Leipzig International Book Exhibition, 1970, for *Rain Rain Rivers; Book World*'s Children's Spring Book Festival Picture Book honor, 1972, for *Soldier and Tsar in the Forest: A Russian Tale; Book World*'s Children's Spring Book Festival Award for Younger Children, *New York Times* Outstanding Books of the Year, both 1973, and Children's Book Showcase of the Children's Book Council honor, 1974, all for *The Magician; New York Times* Outstanding Books of the Year, 1974, Christopher Award, and Children's Book Showcase of the Children's Book Council, both 1975, International Board of Books for Young People honor list citation, 1976, and Brooklyn Art Books for Children citations, 1976, 1977, and 1978, all for *Dawn; New York Times* Best Illustrated Books of the Year citations, 1978, for *Hanukah Money,* and 1979, for *The Treasure;* Caldecott Honor Book citation, 1980, for *The Treasure; New York Times* Outstanding Books of the Year citation, and *School Library Journal*'s Best Children's Books citation, both 1982, and Parents' Choice Award for Literature, Parents' Choice Foundation, 1983, all for *The Golem.*

Uri Shulevitz

WRITINGS:

SELF-ILLUSTRATED

The Moon in My Room, Harper, 1963.
One Monday Morning (also see below), Scribner, 1967.
Rain Rain Rivers, Farrar, Straus, 1969.
(Adapter) *Oh What a Noise!* (text based on "A Big Noise" by William Brighty Rands), Macmillan, 1971.
(Adapter from the Yiddish by I. L. Peretz) *The Magician,* Macmillan, 1973.

Dawn (also see below), Farrar, Straus, 1974.
The Treasure, Farrar, Straus, 1979.
Writing with Pictures: How to Write and Illustrate Children's Books, Watson-Guptill, 1985.
The Strange and Exciting Adventures of Jeremiah Hush, Farrar, Straus, 1986.
Toddlecreek Post Office, Farrar, Straus, 1990.

FILMS

One Monday Morning (filmstrip), Weston Woods, 1972.
(Filmmaker with Tom Spain) *One Monday Morning,* Weston Woods, 1972.

ILLUSTRATOR

Charlotte Zolotow, *A Rose, a Bridge, and a Wild Black Horse,* Harper, 1964.
Mary Stolz, *The Mystery of the Woods,* Harper, 1964.
H. R. Hays and Daniel Hays, *Charley Sang a Song,* Harper, 1964.
Sulamith Ish-Kishor, *The Carpet of Solomon,* Pantheon, 1964.
Jack Sendak, *The Second Witch,* Harper, 1965.
Molly Cone, *Who Knows Ten? Children's Tales of the Ten Commandments,* Union of American Hebrew Congregations, 1965.
Jacob Grimm and Wilhelm Grimm, *The Twelve Dancing Princesses,* translated by Elizabeth Shub, Scribner, 1966.
Stolz, *Maximilian's World,* Harper, 1966.
Jean Russell Larson, *The Silkspinners,* Scribner, 1967.
Dorothy Nathan, *The Month Brothers,* Dutton, 1967.
John Smith, editor, *My Kind of Verse,* Macmillan, 1968.
Jan Wahl, *Runaway Jonah and Other Tales,* Macmillan, 1968.
Arthur Ransome, adapter, *The Fool of the World and the Flying Ship: A Russian Tale,* Farrar, Straus, 1968.
Wahl, *The Wonderful Kite,* Delacorte, 1971.
Yehoash Biber, *Treasure of the Turkish Pasha,* translation from Hebrew by Baruch Hochman, Blue Star Book Club, 1971.
Alexander Afanasyev, *Soldier and Tsar in the Forest: A Russian Tale,* translation by Richard Lourie, Farrar, Straus, 1972.
Isaac Bashevis Singer, *The Fools of Chelm and Their History,* Farrar, Straus, 1973.
Robert Louis Stevenson, *The Touchstone,* Greenwillow, 1976.
Sholem Aleichem, *Hanukah Money,* translated and adapted by Shulevitz and Shub, Greenwillow, 1978.
Richard Kennedy, *The Lost Kingdom of Karnica,* Sierra Club Books, 1979.
Singer, *The Golem,* Farrar, Strauss, 1982.
Howard Schwartz, *Lilith's Cave: Jewish Tales of the Supernatural,* Harper & Row, 1988.
Schwartz and Barbara Rush, *The Diamond Tree: Jewish Tales from Around the World,* HarperCollins, 1991.
Ransome, *Tontimundo y el barco volador,* Farrar, Straus, 1991.

OTHER

Contributor to *Horn Book.* Art director of a magazine for teens in Israel during the late 1950s.

ADAPTATIONS: Dawn and *The Treasure* were made into a filmstrip with cassette by Weston Woods, 1980.

WORK IN PROGRESS: A picture book, tentatively titled "The King and the Man from the Desert."

SIDELIGHTS: "Drawing has always been with me," said artist Uri Shulevitz, who began drawing before he was three years old. "The encouragement of my parents, who were both artistically talented, probably contributed to my early interest in drawing," he told Lee Bennett Hopkins in *Books Are By People.*

Shulevitz was four years old when bombs fell on Warsaw, Poland, driving his family out of the city where he was born. As exiles, they wandered for eight years before settling in Paris, France, in 1947. There he browsed in book stalls along the Seine. Shulevitz began drawing his own comic books for which a friend wrote the stories. In a district-wide elementary-school drawing contest, he won first prize at the age of twelve.

After two years in Paris, the young artist's family moved to Israel. There, at fifteen, he became the youngest artist to have his drawings on exhibition at the Tel Aviv Museum. He attended high school in the evenings and worked various jobs during the day, among them as apprentice to a rubber stamp maker. At the dog-licensing desk in Tel Aviv City Hall, he filled in slow times with reading and creative writing. Between 1952 and 1956 he studied literature and natural sciences at the Teachers' Institute and, evenings, art at the Art Institute of Tel Aviv. He also continued private lessons with the painter Ezekiel Streichman.

In 1958 Shulevitz went from basic training in the Israeli Army to Ein Geddi Kibbutz, a cooperative farm settlement formed by his friends and located near the Dead Sea. The next year he left for New York City and studied painting at Brooklyn Museum Art School. His first work as an illustrator was for a publisher of Hebrew children's books. He tried to publish several picture books without success until Harper & Brothers accepted *The Moon in My Room* in 1963.

Experiences in Poland, France, Israel, and New York City have given Shulevitz much material to work from when his topic is travel. Yet he has said that anyone with an imagination can be a traveler, like the little boy in *The Moon in My Room* who explores the world without leaving his room.

Shulevitz became a United States citizen in the 1960s, but his interests continue to encompass many cultures. He has studied Chinese picture-writing and practices tai-chi-chuan, a regimen of Chinese exercises that are thought to bring health to the body's internal organs. The interest in Oriental art has influenced his early work. He explained in *Something about the Author,* "Realizing the excess of words in our culture, I [follow] an Oriental tradition, trying to say more with fewer words. *The Moon in My Room* contains very brief text and suggestive rather than descriptive illustrations, that have the purpose of awakening the child's imagination." Viewing such books, children are encouraged to picture in their own minds some of the events and characters described only by the text.

While some artists rely on a single style or technique, Shulevitz uses a variety of materials and artistic styles in his illustrations. The content or implied philosophy of any story suggests its own best method or style of illustration, he believes. "This is the way I approach it," he told *SATA*. "Therefore the variety of methods I have used in different books. I am also constantly searching for a new way of illustrating. I use a lot of pen and ink and watercolor. I have used colored inks and tempera in full color illustrations. In some black and white ones, I have also scratched with a razor blade the pen and ink line and then reworked for a long time to achieve a certain effect as in an etching (*The Carpet of Solomon, The Month Brothers, Runaway Jonah,* and *Rain Rain Rivers*). I have used a Japanese reed pen (*Maximilian's World*) and a Chinese brush (*The Silkspinners*)."

In his book *Writing with Pictures,* Shulevitz describes the time he realized the difference between that which is of primary importance ("*what* I had to say") as opposed to that which is of secondary importance ("*how* to say

From *The Treasure,* written and illustrated by Uri Shulevitz.

it"). "Once I understood that *what* I had to say was of primary importance, I began to concentrate on what would happen in my story. First I visualized the action, and then I thought of how to say it in words. I realized that all I had to do was communicate the action as simply as possible. The few words necessary to communicate the story fell into place on their own. It was all so simple and natural."

With this visual approach, Shulevitz discovered he could not only write books that "unfolded in [his] head like a movie," but teach others to write as well. Whether he is illustrating the works of others, adapting fables, or writing his own stories, Shulevitz's books are a model of book design growing out of the story itself with, as he urges his students, "all the parts of the book coordinated into a coherent whole."

WORKS CITED:

De Montreville, Doris and Donna Hill, ed., *Third Book of Junior Authors,* Wilson, 1972.

Hopkins, Lee Bennett, *Books Are By People: Interviews with 104 Authors and Illustrators of Books for Young Children,* Citation Press, 1969.

Shulevitz, Uri, *Writing with Pictures: How to Write and Illustrate Children's Books,* Watson-Guptil, 1985.

Something about the Author, Volume 3, Gale, 1972, revised entry, Volume 50, 1988.

FOR MORE INFORMATION SEE:

BOOKS

Children's Literature Review, Volume 5, Gale, 1983.

Contemporary Authors, Volumes 11-12R, Gale, 1974.

Contemporary Authors New Revision, Volume 3, Gale, 1981.

Dictionary of Literary Biography, Volume 61: *American Writers for Children since 1960: Poets, Illustrators, and Nonfiction Authors,* Gale, 1987.

Lanes, Selma G., *Down the Rabbit Hole,* Atheneum, 1971.

MacCann, Donnarae and Olga Richard, *The Child's First Books,* Wilson, 1973.

Kingman, Lee, ed., *The Illustrator's Notebook,* Horn Book, 1978.

* * *

SILLY, E. S.
See KRAUS, (Herman) Robert

SILVERBERG, Robert 1935-
(T. D. Bethlen, Walker Chapman, Dirk Clinton, Roy Cook, Walter Drummond, Dan Eliot, Don Elliott, Franklin Hamilton, Paul Hollander, Ivar Jorgenson, Calvin M. Knox, Dan Malcolm, Webber Martin, Alex Merriman, David Osborne, George Osborne, Lloyd Robinson, Eric Rodman, Lee Sebastian, Hall Thornton, Richard F. Watson; Gordon Aghill, Ralph Burke, Robert Randall, Ellis Robertson, joint pseudonyms; Robert Arnette, Alexander Blade, Richard Greer, E. K. Jarvis, Warren Kastel, Clyde Mitchell, Leonard G. Spencer, S. M. Tenneshaw, Gerald Vance, house pseudonyms)

PERSONAL: Born January 15, 1935, in New York, N.Y.; son of Michael (an accountant) and Helen (a teacher; maiden name, Baim) Silverberg; married Barbara H. Brown (an engineer), August 26, 1956 (separated, 1976; divorced, 1986); married Karen Haber (a writer), February 14, 1987. *Education:* Columbia University, B.A., 1956.

ADDRESSES: P.O. Box 13160, Station E, Oakland, Calif. 94661. *Agent*—Ralph Vicinanza, Ltd., 432 Park Ave. S., Suite 1509, New York, N.Y. 10016.

CAREER: Writer, 1956—; president, Agberg Ltd., 1981—.

MEMBER: Science Fiction Writers of America (president, 1967-68), Hydra Club (chairman, 1958-61).

AWARDS, HONORS: Hugo Award, World Science Fiction Convention, 1956, for best new author, 1969, for novella "Nightwings," and 1987, for novella "Gilganish in the Outback"; *Lost Race of Mars* was chosen by the *New York Times* as one of the best hundred children's books of 1960; Spring Book Festival Award, *New York Herald Tribune,* 1962, for *Lost Cities and Vanished Civilizations,* and 1967, for *The Auk, the Dodo, and the Oryx: Vanished and Vanishing Creatures;* National Association of Independent Schools award, 1966, for *The Old Ones: Indians of the American Southwest;* Guest of Honor, World Science Fiction Convention, 1970; Nebula Award, Science Fiction Writers of America, 1970, for story "Passengers," 1972, for story "Good News from the Vatican," 1972, for novel *A Time of Changes,* 1975, for novella "Born with the Dead," and 1986, for novella *Sailing to Byzantium;* John W. Campbell Memorial Award, 1973, for excellence in writing; Jupiter Award, 1973, for novella "The Feast of St. Dionysus"; Prix Apollo, 1976, for novel *Nightwings;* Milford Award, 1981, for editing; Locus Award, 1982, for fantasy novel *Lord Valentine's Castle,*

Robert Silverberg

WRITINGS:

SCIENCE FICTION

Master of Life and Death (also see below), Ace Books, 1957, reprinted, Tor Books, 1986.
The Thirteenth Immortal (bound with *This Fortress World* by J. E. Gunn), Ace Books, 1957.
Invaders from Earth (also see below; bound with *Across Time* by D. Grinnell), Ace Books, 1958, published separately, Avon, 1968, published as *We, the Marauders* (bound with *Giants in the Earth* by James Blish) under joint title *A Pair in Space*, Belmont, 1965.
Stepsons of Terra (bound with *A Man Called Destiny* by L. Wright), Ace Books, 1958, published separately, 1977.
The Planet Killers (bound with *We Claim These Stars!* by Poul Anderson), Ace Books, 1959.
Collision Course, Avalon, 1961, reprinted, Ace Books, 1982.
Next Stop the Stars (story collection; bound with *The Seed of Earth* [novel] by Silverberg), Ace Books, 1962, each published separately, 1977.
Recalled to Life, Lancer Books, 1962, reprinted, Ace Books, 1977.
The Silent Invaders (bound with *Battle on Venus* by William F. Temple), Ace Books, 1963, published separately, 1973.
Godling, Go Home! (story collection), Belmont, 1964.
Conquerors from the Darkness, Holt, 1965, reprinted, Tor Books, 1986.
To Worlds Beyond: Stories of Science Fiction, Chilton, 1965.
Needle in a Timestack (story collection), Ballantine, 1966, revised edition, Ace Books, 1985.
Planet of Death, Holt, 1967.
Thorns, Ballantine, 1967.
Those Who Watch, New American Library, 1967.
The Time-Hoppers (also see below), Doubleday, 1967.
To Open the Sky (story collection), Ballantine, 1967.
Hawksbill Station, Doubleday, 1968 (published in England as *The Anvil of Time*, Sidgwick & Jackson, 1968).
The Masks of Time (also see below), Ballantine, 1968 (published in England as *Vornan-19*, Sidgwick & Jackson, 1970).
Dimension Thirteen (story collection), Ballantine, 1969.
The Man in the Maze (also see below), Avon, 1969.
Nightwings (also see below), Avon, 1969.
(Contributor) *Three for Tomorrow: Three Original Novellas of Science Fiction*, Meredith Press, 1969.
Three Survived, Holt, 1969.
To Live Again, Doubleday, 1969.
Up the Line, Ballantine, 1969, revised edition, 1978.
The Cube Root of Uncertainty (story collection), Macmillan, 1970.
Downward to the Earth (also see below), Doubleday, 1970.
Parsecs and Parables: Ten Science Fiction Stories, Doubleday, 1970.
A Robert Silverberg Omnibus (contains *Master of Life and Death, Invaders from Earth,* and *The Time-Hoppers*), Sidgwick & Jackson, 1970.
Tower of Glass, Scribner, 1970.
Moonferns and Starsongs (story collection), Ballantine, 1971.
Son of Man, Ballantine, 1971.
A Time of Changes, New American Library, 1971.
The World Inside, Doubleday, 1971.
The Book of Skulls, Scribner, 1972.
Dying Inside (also see below), Scribner, 1972.
The Reality Trip and Other Implausibilities (story collection), Ballantine, 1972.
The Second Trip, Doubleday, 1972.
(Contributor) *The Day the Sun Stood Still*, Thomas Nelson, 1972.
Earth's Other Shadow: Nine Science Fiction Stories, New American Library, 1973.
(Contributor) *An Exaltation of Stars: Transcendental Adventures in Science Fiction*, Simon & Schuster, 1973.
(Contributor) *No Mind of Man: Three Original Novellas of Science Fiction*, Hawthorn, 1973.
Unfamiliar Territory (story collection), Scribner, 1973.
Valley beyond Time (story collection), Dell, 1973.
Born with the Dead: Three Novellas about the Spirit of Man (also see below), Random House, 1974.
Sundance and Other Science Fiction Stories, Thomas Nelson, 1974.
The Feast of St. Dionysus: Five Science Fiction Stories, Scribner, 1975.

The Stochastic Man, Harper, 1975.
The Best of Robert Silverberg, Volume 1, Pocket Books, 1976, Volume 2, Gregg, 1978.
Capricorn Games (story collection), Random House, 1976.
Shadrach in the Furnace, Bobbs-Merrill, 1976.
The Shores of Tomorrow (story collection), Thomas Nelson, 1976.
The Songs of Summer and Other Stories, Gollancz, 1979.
Lord Valentine's Castle, Harper, 1980.
The Desert of Stolen Dreams, Underwood-Miller, 1981.
A Robert Silverberg Omnibus (contains *Downward to the Earth, The Man in the Maze,* and *Nightwings*), Harper, 1981.
Majipoor Chronicles, Arbor House, 1982.
World of a Thousand Colors (story collection), Arbor House, 1982.
Valentine Pontifex, Arbor House, 1983.
The Conglomeroid Cocktail Party (story collection), Arbor House, 1984.
Sailing to Byzantium, Underwood-Miller, 1985.
Tom O'Bedlam, Donald I. Fine, 1985.
Beyond the Safe Zone: Collected Short Stories of Robert Silverberg, Donald I. Fine, 1986.
Star of Gypsies, Donald I. Fine, 1986.
Robert Silverberg's Worlds of Wonder, Warner, 1987.
At Winter's End, Warner, 1988.
Born with the Dead (bound with *The Saliva Tree* by Brian W. Aldiss), Tor Books, 1988.
The Masks of Time, Born with the Dead, Dying Inside, Bantam, 1988.
The Time of the Great Freeze, Tor Books, 1988.
To the Land of the Living, Gollancz, 1989.
(With Karen Haber) *The Mutant Season,* Foundation/Doubleday, 1989.
Worlds Imagined: Fifteen Short Stories, Crown, 1989.
The New Springtime, Warner, 1990.

JUVENILE FICTION

Revolt on Alpha C, Crowell, 1955.
Starman's Quest, Gnome Press, 1959.
Lost Race of Mars, Winston, 1960.
Regan's Planet, Pyramid Books, 1964, revised edition published as *World's Fair, 1992,* Follett, 1970.
Time of the Great Freeze, Holt, 1964.
The Mask of Akhnaten, Macmillan, 1965.
The Gate of Worlds, Holt, 1967, reprinted, Tor Books, 1984.
The Calibrated Alligator and Other Science Fiction Stories, Holt, 1969.
Across a Billion Years, Dial, 1969.
Sunrise on Mercury and Other Science Fiction Stories, Thomas Nelson, 1975.
(Editor with Charles G. Waugh and Martin H. Greenberg) *The Science Fictional Dinosaur,* Avon, 1982.

NONFICTION

First American into Space, Monarch Books, 1961.
Lost Cities and Vanished Civilizations, Chilton, 1962.
Empires in the Dust: Ancient Civilizations Brought to Light, Chilton, 1963.
The Fabulous Rockefellers: A Compelling, Personalized Account of One of America's First Families, Monarch Books, 1963.
Akhnaten: The Rebel Pharaoh, Chilton, 1964.
(Editor) *Great Adventures in Archaeology,* Dial, 1964.
Man before Adam: The Story of Man in Search of His Origins, Macrae Smith, 1964.
The Great Wall of China, Chilton, 1965, published as *The Long Rampart: The Story of the Great Wall of China,* 1966.
Scientists and Scoundrels: A Book of Hoaxes, Crowell, 1965.
Bridges, Macrae Smith, 1966.
Frontiers in Archaeology, Chilton, 1966.
The Auk, the Dodo, and the Oryx: Vanished and Vanishing Creatures, Crowell, 1967.
Light for the World: Edison and the Power Industry, Van Nostrand, 1967.
Men against Time: Salvage Archaeology in the United States, Macmillan, 1967.
Mound Builders of Ancient America: The Archaeology of a Myth, New York Graphic Society, 1968.
The Challenge of Climate: Man and His Environment, Meredith Press, 1969.
The World of Space, Meredith Press, 1969.
If I Forget Thee, O Jerusalem: American Jews and the State of Israel, Morrow, 1970.
The Pueblo Revolt, Weybright & Talley, 1970.
Before the Sphinx: Early Egypt, Thomas Nelson, 1971.
Clocks for the Ages: How Scientists Date the Past, Macmillan, 1971.
To the Western Shore: Growth of the United States, 1776-1853, Doubleday, 1971.
The Longest Voyage: Circumnavigators in the Age of Discovery, Bobbs-Merrill, 1972.
The Realm of Prester John, Doubleday, 1972.
(Contributor) *Those Who Can,* New American Library, 1973.
Drug Themes in Science Fiction, National Institute on Drug Abuse, 1974.
(Contributor) *Hell's Cartographers: Some Personal Histories of Science Fiction Writers,* Harper, 1975.

JUVENILE NONFICTION

Treasures beneath the Sea, Whitman Publishing, 1960.
Fifteen Battles That Changed the World, Putnam, 1963.
Home of the Red Man: Indian North America before Columbus, New York Graphic Society, 1963.
Sunken History: The Story of Underwater Archaeology, Chilton, 1963.
The Great Doctors, Putnam, 1964.
The Man Who Found Nineveh: The Story of Austen Henry Layard, Holt, 1964.
Men Who Mastered the Atom, Putnam, 1965.
Niels Bohr: The Man Who Mapped the Atom, Macrae Smith, 1965.
The Old Ones: Indians of the American Southwest, New York Graphic Society, 1965.
Socrates, Putnam, 1965.
The World of Coral, Duell, 1965.
Forgotten by Time: A Book of Living Fossils, Crowell, 1966.

To the Rock of Darius: The Story of Henry Rawlinson, Holt, 1966.
The Adventures of Nat Palmer: Antarctic Explorer and Clipper Ship Pioneer, McGraw, 1967.
The Dawn of Medicine, Putnam, 1967.
The Morning of Mankind: Prehistoric Man in Europe, New York Graphic Society, 1967.
The World of the Rain Forest, Meredith Press, 1967.
Four Men Who Changed the Universe, Putnam, 1968.
Ghost Towns of the American West, Crowell, 1968.
Stormy Voyager: The Story of Charles Wilkes, Lippincott, 1968.
The World of the Ocean Depths, Meredith Press, 1968.
Bruce of the Blue Nile, Holt, 1969.
Vanishing Giants: The Story of the Sequoias, Simon & Schuster, 1969.
Wonders of Ancient Chinese Science, Hawthorn, 1969.
Mammoths, Mastodons, and Man, McGraw, 1970.
The Seven Wonders of the Ancient World, Crowell-Collier, 1970.
(With Arthur C. Clarke) *Into Space: A Young Person's Guide to Space,* Harper, revised edition (Silverberg not associated with earlier edition), 1971.
John Muir: Prophet among the Glaciers, Putnam, 1972.
The World within the Ocean Wave, Weybright & Talley, 1972.
The World within the Tide Pool, Weybright & Talley, 1972.
Project Pendulum, Walker & Co., 1987.

EDITOR

Earthmen and Strangers: Nine Stories of Science Fiction, Duell, 1966.
Voyagers in Time: Twelve Stories of Science Fiction, Meredith Press, 1967.
Men and Machines: Ten Stories of Science Fiction, Meredith Press, 1968.
Dark Stars, Ballantine, 1969.
Tomorrow's Worlds: Ten Stories of Science Fiction, Meredith Press, 1969.
The Ends of Time: Eight Stories of Science Fiction, Hawthorn, 1970.
Great Short Novels of Science Fiction, Ballantine, 1970.
The Mirror of Infinity: A Critics' Anthology of Science Fiction, Harper, 1970.
The Science Fiction Hall of Fame, Doubleday, Volume 1, 1970 (published in England as *Science Fiction Hall of Fame,* Volumes 1 and 2, Sphere, 1972).
Worlds of Maybe: Seven Stories of Science Fiction, Thomas Nelson, 1970.
Four Futures, Hawthorn, 1971.
Mind to Mind: Nine Stories of Science Fiction, Thomas Nelson, 1971.
The Science Fiction Bestiary: Nine Stories of Science Fiction, Thomas Nelson, 1971.
To the Stars: Eight Stories of Science Fiction, Hawthorn, 1971.
Beyond Control: Seven Stories of Science Fiction, Thomas Nelson, 1972.
Invaders from Space: Ten Stories of Science Fiction, Hawthorn, 1972.
Chains of the Sea: Three Original Novellas of Science Fiction, Thomas Nelson, 1973.
Deep Space: Eight Stories of Science Fiction, Thomas Nelson, 1973.
Other Dimensions: Ten Stories of Science Fiction, Hawthorn, 1973.
Three Trips in Time and Space, Hawthorn, 1973.
Infinite Jests: The Lighter Side of Science Fiction, Chilton, 1974.
Mutants: Eleven Stories of Science Fiction, Thomas Nelson, 1974.
Threads of Time: Three Original Novellas of Science Fiction, Thomas Nelson, 1974.
Windows into Tomorrow: Nine Stories of Science Fiction, Hawthorn, 1974.
(With Roger Elwood) *Epoch,* Berkley Publishing, 1975.
Explorers of Space: Eight Stories of Science Fiction, Thomas Nelson, 1975.
The New Atlantis and Other Novellas of Science Fiction, Warner Books, 1975.
Strange Gifts: Eight Stories of Science Fiction, Thomas Nelson, 1975.
The Aliens: Seven Stories of Science Fiction, Thomas Nelson, 1976.
The Crystal Ship: Three Original Novellas of Science Fiction, Thomas Nelson, 1976.
Earth Is the Strangest Planet: Ten Stories of Science Fiction, Thomas Nelson, 1977.
Galactic Dreamers: Science Fiction as Visionary Literature, Random House, 1977.
The Infinite Web: Eight Stories of Science Fiction, Dial, 1977.
Triax: Three Original Novellas, Pinnacle Books, 1977.
Trips in Time: Nine Stories of Science Fiction, Thomas Nelson, 1977.
Lost Worlds, Unknown Horizons: Nine Stories of Science Fiction, Thomas Nelson, 1978.
The Androids Are Coming: Seven Stories of Science Fiction, Elsevier-Nelson, 1979.
(With Greenberg and Joseph D. Olander) *Car Sinister,* Avon, 1979.
(With Greenberg and Olander) *Dawn of Time: Prehistory through Science Fiction,* Elsevier-Nelson, 1979.
The Edge of Space: Three Original Novellas of Science Fiction, Elsevier-Nelson, 1979.
(With Greenberg) *The Arbor House Treasury of Great Science Fiction Short Novels,* Arbor House, 1980.
(With Greenberg) *The Arbor House Treasury of Modern Science Fiction,* Arbor House, 1980.
The Best of Randall Garrett, Pocket Books, 1982.
The Nebula Awards, Arbor House, 1983.
(With Greenberg) *The Arbor House Treasury of Science Fiction Masterpieces,* Arbor House, 1983.
(With Greenberg) *The Fantasy Hall of Fame,* Arbor House, 1983.
(With Greenberg) *The Time Travelers: A Science Fiction Quartet,* Donald I. Fine, 1985.
(With Greenberg) *Neanderthals,* New American Library, 1987.
(With Greenberg) *The Mammoth Book of Fantasy All-Time Greats,* Robinson, 1988.
(With Karen Haber) *Universe 1,* Foundation/ Doubleday, 1990.

EDITOR; "ALPHA" SERIES

Alpha, Volumes 1-6, Ballantine, 1970-76.
Alpha, Volumes 7-9, Berkley Publishing, 1977-78.

EDITOR; "NEW DIMENSIONS" SERIES

New Dimensions, Volumes 1-5, Doubleday, 1971-75.
New Dimensions, Volumes 6-10, Harper, 1976-80.
The Best of New Dimensions, Pocket Books, 1979.
(With Marta Randall) *New Dimensions,* Volumes 11-12, Pocket Books, 1980-81.

UNDER PSEUDONYM WALKER CHAPMAN

The Loneliest Continent: The Story of Antarctic Discovery, New York Graphic Society, 1964.
(Editor) *Antarctic Conquest: The Great Explorers in Their Own Words,* Bobbs-Merrill, 1966.
Kublai Khan: Lord of Xanadu, Bobbs-Merrill, 1966.
The Golden Dream: Seekers of El Dorado, Bobbs-Merrill 1967, published as *The Search for El Dorado,* 1967.

UNDER PSEUDONYM DON ELLIOTT

Flesh Peddlers, Nightstand, 1960.
Passion Trap, Nightstand, 1960.
Backstage Sinner, Nightstand, 1961.
Lust Goddess, Nightstand, 1961.
Sin Cruise, Nightstand, 1961.
Kept Man, Midnight, 1962.
Shame House, Midnight, 1962.
Sin Hellion, Ember, 1963.
Sin Servant, Nightstand, 1963.
Beatnik Wanton, Evening, 1964.
Flesh Bride, Evening, 1964.
Flesh Prize, Leisure, 1964.
Flesh Taker, Ember, 1964.
Sin Warped, Leisure, 1964.
Switch Trap, Evening, 1964.
Nudie Packet, Idle Hour, 1965.
The Young Wanton, Sundown, 1965.
Depravity Town, Reed, 1973.
Jungle Street, Reed, 1973.
Summertime Affair, Reed, 1973.

Also author of eighty other novels, 1959-65, under pseudonyms Dan Eliot and Don Elliott.

OTHER

(With Randall Garrett, under joint pseudonym Robert Randall) *The Shrouded Planet,* Gnome Press, 1957, published under names Robert Silverberg and Randall Garrett, Donning, 1980.
(Under pseudonym Calvin M. Knox) *Lest We Forget Thee, Earth,* Ace Books, 1958.
(Under pseudonym David Osborne) *Aliens from Space,* Avalon, 1958.
(Under pseudonym Ivar Jorgenson) *Starhaven,* Avalon, 1958.
(Under pseudonym David Osborne) *Invisible Barriers,* Avalon, 1958.
(With Randall Garrett, under joint pseudonym Robert Randall) *The Dawning Light,* Gnome Press, 1959, published under names Robert Silverberg and Randall Garrett, Donning, 1981.

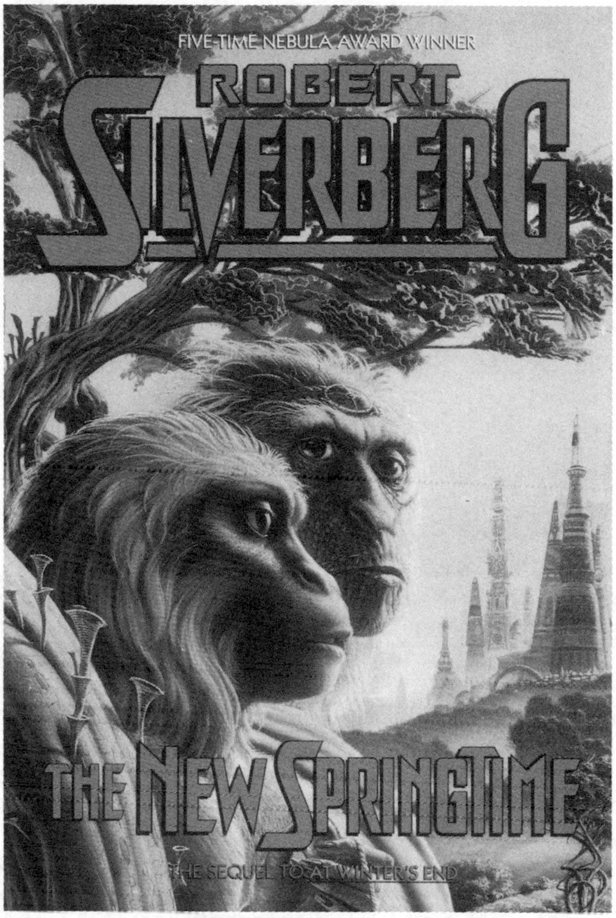

Cover of *The New Springtime,* by Robert Silverberg.

(Under pseudonym Calvin M. Knox) *The Plot against Earth,* Ace Books, 1959.
(Under pseudonym Walter Drummond) *Philosopher of Evil,* Regency Books, 1962.
(Under pseudonym Walter Drummond) *How to Spend Money,* Regency Books, 1963.
(Under pseudonym Franklin Hamilton) *1066,* Dial, 1963.
(Under pseudonym Calvin M. Knox) *One of Our Asteroids Is Missing,* Ace Books, 1964.
(Under pseudonym Paul Hollander) *The Labors of Hercules,* Putnam, 1965.
(Under pseudonym Franklin Hamilton) *The Crusades,* Dial, 1965.
(Under pseudonym Lloyd Robinson) *The Hopefuls: Ten Presidential Candidates,* Doubleday, 1966.
(Under pseudonym Roy Cook) *Leaders of Labor,* Lippincott, 1966.
(Under pseudonym Lee Sebastian) *Rivers,* Holt, 1966.
(Under pseudonym Franklin Hamilton) *Challenge for a Throne: The Wars of the Roses,* Dial, 1967.
(Under pseudonym Lloyd Robinson) *The Stolen Election: Hayes versus Tilden,* Doubleday, 1968.
(Under pseudonym Ivar Jorgenson) *Whom the Gods Would Slay,* Belmont, 1968.
(Under pseudonym Paul Hollander) *Sam Houston,* Putnam, 1968.

(Under pseudonym Lee Sebastian) *The South Pole,* Holt, 1968.

(Under pseudonym Ivar Jorgenson) *The Deadly Sky,* Pinnacle Books, 1971.

"Dying Inside" (recording), Caedmon, 1979.

"Robert Silverberg Reads 'To See the Invisible Man' and 'Passengers'" (recording), Pelican Records, 1979.

Lord of Darkness (fiction), Arbor House, 1983.

Gilgamesh the King (fiction), Arbor House, 1984.

(With Isaac Asimov) *Nightfall,* Doubleday, 1992.

Contributor, sometimes under pseudonyms, to *Omni, Playboy, Amazing Stories Science Fiction, Fantastic Stories Science Fiction, Magazine of Fantasy and Science Fiction,* and other publications.

ADAPTATIONS:

Recordings of Silverberg's work include "Dying Inside," Caedmon, 1979; and "Robert Silverberg Reads 'To See the Invisible Man' and 'Passengers,'" Pelican Records, 1979. Film rights for *The Book of Skulls* have been sold.

SIDELIGHTS: Robert Silverberg is one of the best known of contemporary science fiction writers. He has won the field's Nebula and Hugo Awards and has received more award nominations for his work than any other science fiction writer. He is also, according to Brian M. Stableford in *Masters of Science Fiction,* "the most prolific science fiction writer of the past two decades." But despite his prominence in the field, Silverberg's science fiction work makes up, "at the most, fifteen percent of his output," Barry M. Malzberg writes in the *Magazine of Fantasy and Science Fiction.* Indeed, Silverberg has even left the field entirely on two separate occasions. Most of his work has been nonfiction on such varied topics as archaeology, conservation, history, and the natural sciences. He has received awards for several of these nonfiction books, while his *Mound Builders of Ancient America: The Archaeology of a Myth* is considered one of the standard works on the subject. Still, this considerable success in the nonfiction field is overshadowed by his continuing popularity in science fiction. As George R. R. Martin, writing in the *Washington Post Book World,* admits, Silverberg "is best known and best regarded for his work within science fiction."

Silverberg began his writing career while still a student at Columbia University in the 1950s. He had decided to become a science fiction writer because of his own reaction to the genre as a boy. As he tells Jeffrey M. Elliot in *Science Fiction Voices #2:* "When I was a boy, I read science fiction and it did wonderful things for me. It opened the universe to me. I feel a sense of obligation to science fiction to replace what I had taken from it, to add to the shelf, to put something there for someone else that would do for them what other writers had done for me." Silverberg's first sales were to the science fiction magazines of the 1950s, and his first book was a juvenile science fiction novel. Upon graduation from Columbia in 1956, he became a full-time free-lance writer. His work was already so popular that the World Science Fiction Convention, a gathering of the genre's devotees, voted him the Hugo Award as the best new writer of the year.

During the 1950s Silverberg produced hundreds of stories for the science fiction magazines. His production was so high that he was obliged to publish much of this work under a host of pseudonyms. Silverberg recalls that time to Charles Platt in *Dream Makers: The Uncommon People Who Write Science Fiction,* "I was courted by editors considerably back then, because I was so dependable; if they said, 'Give me a story by next Thursday,' I would." These early stories, George W. Tuma writes in the *Dictionary of Literary Biography,* "conform closely to the conventions of science fiction: alien beings, technological gadgetry, standard plot devices, confrontations between [Earthlings] and extraterrestrial beings, and so forth." In 1959 a downturn in sales forced many science fiction magazines out of business. Silverberg was no longer able to support himself by writing for the genre. He turned to writing articles for the popular magazines instead, maintaining his high level of production by turning out two pieces every working day.

In the early 1960s Silverberg moved from writing magazine articles to writing nonfiction books, a change he remembers with some relief in his *Contemporary Authors Autobiography Series* (*CAAS*) essay. "I severed my connections with my sleazy magazine outlets and ascended into this new, astoundingly respectable and rewarding career," he recalls. In a few years he had established himself as one of the most successful nonfiction writers in the country, publishing books about Antarctica, ancient Egypt, the American space program, medical history, and a host of other topics. "I was considered one of the most skilled popularizers of the sciences in the United States," Silverberg remembers.

During these early years Silverberg maintained a prolific writing pace, publishing nearly two million words per year. He tells Elliot that he managed to write so much due to intense concentration. "I concentrated on a point source and the words just came out right," Silverberg recalls. Malzberg allows that "the man is prolific. Indeed, the man may be, in terms of accumulation of work per working year, the most prolific writer who ever lived."

But the years of prolific writing finally ended in the middle 1960s. Silverberg has cited two factors for the slowdown in his production at that time. The first was a hyperactive thyroid gland, brought on by prolonged overwork, which forced him in 1966 to slow his working pace considerably. The second factor was a fire in early 1968 at Silverberg's New York City home. This fire, he writes in the *CAAS,* "drained from me, evidently forever, much of the bizarre energy that had allowed me to write a dozen or more significant books in a single year."

It was also in the middle 1960s that Silverberg returned to the science fiction field after an absence of several years. It is the work from this period that most observers credit as the beginning of Silverberg's serious fiction in the genre. Thomas D. Clareson, although noting in his book *Robert Silverberg* that "from the beginning, he was a skilled storyteller," nonetheless marks 1969 to 1976 as the period when Silverberg "conducted his most deliberate experiments and attained the most consistent command of his material." Malzberg claims that "in or around 1965 Silverberg put his toys away and began to write literature."

Silverberg began to experiment with technique and style, producing the award-winning novels *A Time of Changes* and *Nightwings,* several award-winning stories and novellas, and other novels nominated for major awards. Speaking of several books from this period in an article for the *New York Times Book Review,* Theodore Sturgeon finds that Silverberg "changed into something quite new and different—his own man, saying his own things his own way, and doing it with richness and diversity." Tuma also sees a transformation in Silverberg's work, stating that he "found his unique approach to science fiction, in terms of both content and writing style."

Through his experiments with style and narrative structure Silverberg sought to extend the range of science fiction. "Having already proved that he could write every kind of s.f. story at least as well as anyone else," Gerald Jones comments in the *New York Times Book Review,* "Silverberg set out . . . to stretch both the genre and himself." In *Son of Man,* for example, called by Stableford a "surreal novel," the story is told as a series of bizarre adventure sequences set on "not the physical planet Earth but the Earth of human perception—the model world of the mind," as Stableford relates.

This new approach in his work put Silverberg in the forefront of the science fiction field. "By the 1970s Silverberg was writing science fiction much as such of his contemporaries as Barth, Reed, Bartheleme, and Coover were presenting their renditions of everyday American life," Clareson writes in *Voices for the Future: Essays on Major Science Fiction Writers.* But Silverberg was dissatisfied with the response to his work. His books won awards, but their sales were poor and they often met with uninformed critical comments from science fiction purists. "I was at first bewildered by the response I was getting from the audience," Silverberg tells Platt. "There are passages in *Dying Inside* or in *Nightwings* which I think are sheer ecstatic song, but people would come up to me and say, Why do you write such depressing books? Something was wrong." By 1975 all of Silverberg's more serious books, upon which he had placed such importance, were out of print. At that point he announced his retirement from science fiction.

For the next four years Silverberg wrote no new science fiction. He devoted his time to the garden of his California home. "I had had my career," Silverberg writes in his *CA Autobiography Series* article. "Now I had my garden." But in 1978, he was pushed back into the field. Silverberg needed to buy a house for his wife, from whom he was separated. To raise the necessary money, he decided to write one last book. The result was *Lord Valentine's Castle,* a massive novel that set a record when it was offered to publishers at auction. Harper & Row paid the largest sum ever given for a science fiction novel—$127,500—and Silverberg was a writer again.

In *Lord Valentine's Castle* Silverberg mixes elements from science fiction and heroic fantasy. The science fiction elements include a far future setting, the imaginary planet of Majipoor, and a host of exotic alien life forms. But the plot, a quest by a disinherited prince to regain his throne, is common to the fantasy genre. The clever combination of genre elements was praised by Jack Sullivan in the *New York Times Book Review.* Sullivan calls *Lord Valentine's Castle* "an imaginative fusion of action, sorcery and science fiction, with visionary adventure scenes undergirded by scientific explanations." In his book *Robert Silverberg,* Clareson states that "whatever else it does, *Lord Valentine's Castle* demands that its readers re-examine the relationship between science fiction and fantasy, for in this narrative Silverberg has fused the two together."

The success of *Lord Valentine's Castle* drew Silverberg back into the writing life again. He began to write stories for *Omni* magazine, where several old friends were working, and in 1982 he published *Majipoor Chronicles,* a novel fashioned from several short stories set on the planet introduced in *Lord Valentine's Castle.* Each story is an episode from Majipoor's history which has been stored on an experience-record. By using a futuristic reading-machine, a young boy is able to "relive" these historical events.

With *Valentine Pontifex,* Silverberg did what he had once vowed he would never do: write a sequel to *Lord Valentine's Castle.* In the sequel, Lord Valentine, now restored to his position as ruler of Majipoor, faces opposition from the Piurivars, an aboriginal race dispossessed years before by Earthling colonists. The Piurivars release plagues and deadly bio-engineered creatures upon the humans. A reviewer for the *Voice Literary Supplement* finds that "the lazy pace through time and space" found in *Lord Valentine's Castle* gives way in this novel "to a dance of conflicting emotions and political intrigue." And, seeing *Lord Valentine's Castle, Majipoor Chronicles,* and *Valentine Pontifex* as related works forming a loose trilogy, the reviewer goes on to state that "the trilogy becomes a whole in a way that the form rarely achieves."

Over a professional writing career spanning three decades, Silverberg has produced an immense body of work in several genres. Commenting on this diversity, Martin writes that "few writers, past or present, have had careers quite as varied, dramatic, and contradictory as that of Robert Silverberg." As a writer of nonfiction, Silverberg has enjoyed particular success. But as a writer of science fiction, he is among a handful of writers who have helped to shape the field into what it is today. He is, Elliot declares, "a titan in the science fiction field."

"Few science fiction readers," Elliot goes on, "have not been enriched and inspired by his contributions to the genre, contributions which reflect his love of the field and his deep respect for its readers." Silverberg's contributions to the field, Clareson writes in the *Magazine of Fantasy and Science Fiction,* are of predictably high quality: "He will tell a good story, he will fuse together content and form, and he will add to our perception of the human condition." In his introduction to *Galactic Dreamers: Science Fiction as Visionary Literature,* Silverberg explains what he has been striving to attain in his work: "To show the reader something he has never been able to see with his own eyes, something strange and unique, beautiful and troubling, which draws him for a moment out of himself, places him in contact with the vastness of the universe, gives him for a sizzling moment a communion with the fabric of space and time, and leaves him forever transformed, forever enlarged."

WORKS CITED:

Clareson, Thomas D., editor, *Voices for the Future: Essays on Major Science Fiction Writers,* Volume 2, Bowling Green State University Popular Press, 1979.
Clareson, Thomas D., *Robert Silverberg,* Starmont House, 1983.
Contemporary Authors Autobiography Series, Volume 3, Gale, 1986.
Dictionary of Literary Biography, Volume 8: *Twentieth-Century American Science-Fiction Writers,* Gale, 1981.
Elliot, Jeffrey M., *Science Fiction Voices #2,* Borgo Press, 1979.
Magazine of Fantasy and Science Fiction, April, 1971, April, 1974.
New York Times Book Review, May 9, 1965, November 3, 1968, March 5, 1972, August 24, 1975, August 3, 1980, August 4, 1985, November 23, 1986.
Platt, Charles, *Dream Makers: The Uncommon People Who Write Science Fiction,* Berkley Publishing, 1980.
Silverberg, Robert, editor, *Galactic Dreamers: Science Fiction as Visionary Literature,* Random House, 1977.
Stableford, Brian M., *Masters of Science Fiction,* Borgo Press, 1981.
Voice Literary Supplement, December, 1983.
Washington Post Book World, February 28, 1982, May 8, 1983.

FOR MORE INFORMATION SEE:

BOOKS

Aldiss, Brian and Harry Harrison, editors, *Hell's Cartographers: Some Personal Histories of Science Fiction Writers,* Harper, 1975.
Clareson, Thomas D., *Robert Silverberg: A Primary and Secondary Bibliography,* G. K. Hall, 1983.
Contemporary Literary Criticism, Volume 7, Gale, 1977.
Magill, Frank N., editor, *Survey of Science Fiction,* Salem Press, 1979.
Rabkin, Eric S. and others, editors, *No Place Else,* Southern Illinois University Press, 1983.
Schweitzer, Darrell, editor, *Exploring Fantasy Worlds: Essays on Fantastic Literature,* Borgo Press, 1985.
Staircar, Tom, editor, *Critical Encounters II,* Ungar, 1982.
Walker, Paul, *Speaking of Science Fiction: The Paul Walker Interviews,* Luna Press, 1978.

PERIODICALS

Analog, November, 1979.
Atlantic, April, 1972.
Essays in Arts and Sciences, August, 1980.
Extrapolation, summer, 1979, winter, 1980, winter, 1982.
Fantasy Newsletter, June-July, 1983.
Los Angeles Times Book Review, May 18, 1980, April 18, 1986.
Megavore, March, 1981.
National Review, November 3, 1970.
New Statesman, June 18, 1976.
Science Fiction: A Review of Speculative Literature, September, 1983.
Science Fiction Chronicle, January, 1985, May, 1985.
Starship, November, 1982.
Times Literary Supplement, June 12, 1969, March 15, 1974, November 7, 1980, August 3, 1984.
Writer, November, 1977.

* * *

SILVERSTEIN, Alvin 1933-
(Ralph Buxton, Richard Rhine, Dr. A, joint pseudonyms)

PERSONAL: Born December 30, 1933, in New York, NY; son of Edward (a carpenter) and Fannie (Wittlin) Silverstein; married Virginia B. Opshelor (a writer and translator), August 29, 1958; children: Robert Alan, Glenn Evan, Carrie Lee, Sharon Leslie, Laura Donna, Kevin Andrew. *Education:* Brooklyn College (now Brooklyn College of the City University of New York), B.A., 1955; University of Pennsylvania, M.S., 1959; New York University, Ph.D., 1962. *Hobbies and other interests:* Vegetable gardening, sports, drawing and painting.

ADDRESSES: Home—3 Burlinghoff Lane, P.O. Box 537, Lebanon, NJ 08833. *Office*—Department of Biology, College of Staten Island of the City University of New York, 715 Ocean Ter., Staten Island, NY 10301.

CAREER: Junior High School No. 60, New York City, science teacher, 1959; College of Staten Island of the City University of New York, instructor, 1959-63, assistant professor, 1963-66, associate professor, 1966-70, professor of biology, 1970—; chair of biology department, 1978-79; writer.

MEMBER: Authors Guild, American Association for the Advancement of Science, American Chemical Society, American Institute of Biological Sciences, National

Alvin and Virginia Silverstein

Collegiate Association for the Conquest of Cancer (national chairperson, 1968-70).

AWARDS, HONORS: All with wife, Virginia B. Silverstein: Children's Book of the Year citations, Child Study Association of America, 1969, for *A World in a Drop of Water,* and 1972, for *The Code of Life, Nature's Defenses,* and *Nature's Pincushion; A World in a Drop of Water* was named an Outstanding Children's Book of 1969, *World Book Yearbook,* 1970; *Circulatory Systems* was named a Science Educators' Book Society Selection; awards from New Jersey Institute of Technology, 1972, for *Guinea Pigs: All about Them,* 1980, for *Aging,* and 1983, for *The Robots Are Here* and *The Story of Your Mouth;* Outstanding Science Books for Children citations, National Science Teachers Association and Children's Book Council, 1972, for *The Long Voyage, The Muscular System, The Skeletal System, Cancer, Nature's Pincushion,* and *Life in a Bucket of Soil,* 1973, for *Rabbits: All about Them,* 1974, for *Animal Invaders* and *Hamsters: All about Them,* 1976, for *Potatoes: All about Them* and *Gerbils: All about Them,* 1983, for *Heartbeats,* 1987, for *The Story of Your Foot,* 1988, for *Wonders of Speech* and *Nature's Living Lights,* and 1990, for *Overcoming Acne.*

Alcoholism was selected among the Notable Trade Books in the Field of Social Studies, National Council for the Social Studies and Children's Book Council, 1975; Older Honor citation, New York Academy of Sciences, 1977, for *Potatoes: All about Them;* Junior Literary Guild selection, and Children's Book of the Year citation, Bank Street College, 1977, both for *The Left-Hander's World;* Books for the Teen Age selections, New York Public Library, 1978, for *Heart Disease,* and 1987, for *AIDS: Deadly Threat;* special certificate of commendation, John Burroughs List of Nature Books for Young Readers, 1988, for *Nature's Living Lights.*

WRITINGS:

The Biological Sciences (college textbook), Holt, 1974.

Conquest of Death, Macmillan, 1979.

Human Anatomy and Physiology (college textbook), Wiley, 1980, 2nd edition, 1983.

NONFICTION CHILDREN'S BOOKS; WITH WIFE, VIRGINIA B. SILVERSTEIN

Life in the Universe, illustrated by L. Ames, Van Nostrand, 1967.

Unusual Partners, illustrated by Mel Hunter, McGraw, 1968.

Rats and Mice: Friends and Foes of Mankind, illustrated by Joseph Cellini, Lothrop, 1968.

The Origin of Life, illustrated by L. Ames, Van Nostrand, 1968.

The Respiratory System: How Living Creatures Breathe, illustrated by George Bakacs, Prentice-Hall, 1969.

A Star in the Sea, illustrated by Simeon Shimin, Warne, 1969.

A World in a Drop of Water, Atheneum, 1969.

Carl Linnaeus, illustrated by L. Ames, John Day, 1969.

Frederick Sanger, illustrated by L. Ames, John Day, 1969.

Cells: Building Blocks of Life, illustrated by G. Bakacs, Prentice-Hall, 1969.

Germfree Life: A New Field in Biological Research, Lothrop, 1970.

Living Lights: The Mystery of Bioluminescence, Golden Gate, 1970.

Circulatory Systems: The Rivers Within, illustrated by G. Bakacs, Prentice-Hall, 1970.

The Digestive System: How Living Creatures Use Food, illustrated by G. Bakacs, Prentice-Hall, 1970.

Bionics: Man Copies Nature's Machines, McCall Publishing, 1970.

Harold Urey: The Man Who Explored from Earth to Moon, illustrated by L. Ames, John Day, 1971.

The Nervous System: The Inner Networks, illustrated by Mel Erikson, Prentice-Hall, 1971.

Mammals of the Sea, illustrated by Bernard Garbutt, Golden Gate, 1971.

Metamorphosis: The Magic Change, Atheneum, 1971.

The Sense Organs: Our Link with the World, illustrated by M. Erikson, Prentice-Hall, 1971.

The Endocrine System, illustrated by L. Ames, Prentice-Hall, 1971.

The Reproductive System: How Living Creatures Multiply, illustrated by L. Ames, Prentice-Hall, 1971.

The Code of Life, Atheneum, 1971.

Guinea Pigs: All about Them, photographs by Roger Kerkham, Lothrop, 1972.

The Long Voyage: The Life Cycle of a Green Turtle, illustrated by Allan Eitzen, Warne, 1972.
(Under joint pseudonym Ralph Buxton) *Nature's Defenses,* illustrated by Angus M. Babcock, Golden Gate, 1972.
The Muscular System: How Living Creatures Move, illustrated by L. Ames, Prentice-Hall, 1972.
The Skeletal System, illustrated by L. Ames, Prentice-Hall, 1972.
Cancer, John Day, 1972, first revised edition, illustrated by Andrew Antal, 1977, second revised edition published as *Cancer: Can It Be Stopped?,* Lippincott, 1987.
The Skin, illustrated by L. Ames, Prentice-Hall, 1972.
(Under joint pseudonym Ralph Buxton) *Nature's Pincushion,* illustrated by A. M. Babcock, Golden Gate, 1972.
The Excretory System, illustrated by L. Ames, Prentice-Hall, 1972.
(Under joint pseudonym Richard Rhine) *Life in a Bucket of Soil,* illustrated by Elsie Wrigley, Lothrop, 1972.
Exploring the Brain, illustrated by Patricia De Veau, Prentice-Hall, 1973.
The Chemicals We Eat and Drink, Follett, 1973.
Rabbits: All about Them, photographs by R. Kerkham, Lothrop, 1973.
Sleep and Dreams, Lippincott, 1974.
(Under joint pseudonym Ralph Buxton) *Nature's Water Clown,* illustrated by A. M. Babcock, Golden Gate, 1974.
Animal Invaders: The Story of Imported Animal Life, Atheneum, 1974.
Hamsters: All about Them, photographs by Frederick Breda, Lothrop, 1974.
Epilepsy, Lippincott, 1975.
Oranges: All about Them, illustrated by Shirley Chan, Prentice-Hall, 1975.
Beans: All about Them, illustrated by S. Chan, Prentice-Hall, 1975.
Alcoholism, introduction by Gail Gleason Milgrom, Lippincott, 1975.
(Under joint pseudonym Ralph Buxton) *Nature's Glider,* illustrated by A. M. Babcock, Golden Gate, 1975.
Apples: All about Them, illustrated by S. Chan, Prentice-Hall, 1976.
Potatoes: All about Them, illustrated by S. Chan, Prentice-Hall, 1976.
Gerbils: All about Them, photographs by F. Breda, Lippincott, 1976.
Heart Disease, Follett, 1976.
The Left-Hander's World, Follett, 1977.
Allergies, introduction by Sheldon Cohen, Lippincott, 1977.
Itch, Sniffle and Sneeze: All about Asthma, Hay Fever and Other Allergies, illustrated by Roy Doty, Four Winds, 1978.
Cats: All about Them, photographs by F. Breda, Lothrop, 1978.
So You're Getting Braces: A Guide to Orthodontics, illustrated by Barbara Remington, with photographs by Virginia B. and Alvin Silverstein, Lippincott, 1978.
(With son Glenn Silverstein) *Aging,* F. Watts, 1979.
World of Bionics, Methuen, 1979.
The Sugar Disease: Diabetes, introduction by consulting editor Charles Nechemias, Lippincott, 1980.
The Genetics Explosion, Four Winds, 1980.
Mice: All about Them, photographs by son Robert A. Silverstein, Lippincott, 1980.
Nature's Champions: The Biggest, the Fastest, the Best, illustrated by Jean Zallinger, Random House, 1980.
The Story of Your Ear, illustrated by Susan Gaber, Coward, McCann & Geoghegan, 1981.
Runaway Sugar: All about Diabetes, illustrated by Harriett Barton, Lippincott, 1981.
Futurelife: The Biotechnology Revolution, illustrated by Marjorie Thier, Prentice-Hall, 1982.
Heartbeats: Your Body, Your Heart, illustrated by Stella Ormai, Lippincott, 1983.
The Story of Your Mouth, illustrated by Greg Wenzel, Coward-McCann, 1984.
The Robots Are Here, Prentice-Hall, 1984.
Headaches: All about Them, Lippincott, 1984.
Heart Disease: America's Number One Killer, Lippincott, 1985.
The Story of Your Hand, illustrated by G. Wenzel, Putnam, 1985.

Cover of *The Robots Are Here,* by Alvin and Virginia Silverstein.

Dogs: All about Them, introduction by John C. McLoughlin, Lothrop, 1986.

World of the Brain, illustrated by Warren Budd, Morrow, 1986.

AIDS: Deadly Threat, foreword by Paul Volberding, Enslow Publishers, 1986, revised and enlarged edition, 1991.

The Story of Your Foot, illustrated by G. Wenzel, Putnam, 1987.

Mystery of Sleep, illustrated by Nelle Davis, Little, Brown, 1987.

Wonders of Speech, illustrated by Gordon Tomei, Morrow, 1988.

Nature's Living Lights: Fireflies and Other Bioluminescent Creatures, illustrated by Pamela and Walter Carroll, Little, Brown, 1988.

Learning about AIDS, foreword by James Oleske, Enslow Publishers, 1989.

Glasses and Contact Lenses: Your Guide to Eyes, Eyewear, and Eye Care, Harper, 1989.

Genes, Medicine, and You: Genetic Counseling and Gene Therapy, Enslow Publishers, 1989.

(With R. A. Silverstein) *Overcoming Acne: The How and Why of Healthy Skin Care,* preface by Christopher M. Papa, illustrated by Frank Schwarz, Morrow, 1990.

Life in a Tidal Pool, illustrated by P. and W. Carroll, Little, Brown, 1990.

(With R. A. Silverstein) *Lyme Disease, the Great Imitator: How to Prevent and Cure It,* preface by Leonard H. Sigal, AVSTAR, 1990.

(With R. A. Silverstein) *So You Think You're Fat: Obesity, Anorexia Nervosa, Bulimia, and Other Eating Disorders,* Harper, 1991.

(With R. A. Silverstein) *Addictions Handbook,* Enslow Publishers, 1991.

(With R. A. Silverstein) *Steroids: Big Muscles, Big Problems,* Enslow Publishers, in press.

(With R. A. Silverstein) *Smell, the Subtle Sense,* Morrow, in press.

(With R. A. Silverstein) *Recycling: Meeting the Challenge of the Trash Crisis,* Putnam, in press.

(With R. A. Silverstein) *Food Power! Proteins,* Millbrook, in press.

(With R. A. Silverstein) *Food Power! Fats,* Millbrook, in press.

(With R. A. Silverstein) *Food Power! Carbohydrates,* Millbrook, in press.

(With R. A. Silverstein) *Food Power! Vitamins and Minerals,* Millbrook, in press.

Also author with wife, Virginia B. Silverstein, under joint pseudonym Dr. A, of syndicated juvenile fiction column, "Tales from Dr. A," which appeared in about 250 American and Canadian newspapers, 1972-74.

"FAMOUS NAME" SERIES; WITH VIRGINIA B. SILVERSTEIN

(With family members Robert A., Linda, Laura, and Kevin Silverstein) *John, Your Name Is Famous: Highlights, Anecdotes, and Trivia about the Name John and the People Who Made It Great,* AVSTAR, 1989.

(With R. A. Silverstein) *John: Fun and Facts about a Popular Name and the People Who Made It Great,* AVSTAR, 1990.

(With R. A. Silverstein) *Michael: Fun and Facts about a Popular Name and the People Who Made It Great,* AVSTAR, 1990.

SIDELIGHTS: Husband-and-wife team Alvin and Virginia B. Silverstein have formed a successful writing partnership, producing almost one hundred scientific information books for young people. Their works cover a wide spectrum, from contemporary issues like bionics, recycling, robotics, and genetics to detailed studies of various animals, foods, body systems, and diseases. Both authors bring an extensive knowledge of science to their collaborations—Virginia is a former chemist and Alvin is a biology professor—and they deal with complex issues in a comprehensible manner. Their books are accessible to young audiences and are often praised as straightforward, detailed, and authoritative. Their "work is carefully organized and written in a clear, direct style, and is dependably accurate," according to Zena Sutherland and May Hill Arbuthnot in *Children and Books.* "The more complicated subjects are not always covered in depth, but they are given balanced treatment, and the Silversteins' writing usually shows their attention to current research and always maintains a scientific attitude."

Both Alvin and Virginia enjoyed similar interests throughout their childhoods. Alvin grew up an avid reader, sometimes even reading the encyclopedia for fun, and found he was particularly fond of scientific literature. "I began a lifelong hobby of 'science watching' practically as soon as I learned to read," he revealed in *Fifth Book of Junior Authors and Illustrators.* "My first love was astronomy, but I also was crazy about animals." Virginia, too, remembers herself as an enthusiastic reader, who especially loved books about animals. "When I was seven or eight," she recalled in *Fifth Book of Junior Authors and Illustrators,* "I used to total up my money saved in terms of how many Thornton Burgess [a prolific animal writer] ... books it would buy." In time she discovered an aptitude for chemistry and languages and was attracted to both fields. Ultimately, though, she decided to study chemistry, as did Alvin. The couple met at the University of Pennsylvania during the late 1950s—in a chemistry lab.

Nearly ten years after their marriage in 1958, Alvin and Virginia collaborated on their first children's book, *Life in the Universe.* "That book was quickly signed up," Virginia related in *Fifth Book of Junior Authors and Illustrators,* "and we plunged happily into children's science writing. Then followed twenty-three straight rejections. We would probably have given up if we hadn't already had a manuscript accepted." The duo persisted, however, and went on to complete more than ninety books, many of which have been named outstanding science books for children, awarded children's book of the year citations, and recognized by the New Jersey Institute of Technology and the New York Academy of Sciences. Among these are works like

Gerbils, which includes a history of the animals as well as information about their intelligence and behavior, and *Aging,* which encompasses such areas as senility, retirement, and the role of the elderly in families. Other Silverstein books examine topics of high interest to many adolescents, such as eating disorders, braces, acne, or glasses, while still others delve into subjects like dreams, chemicals, allergies, or cancer.

Both Silversteins are content with their working relationship. Virginia once told *Something about the Author (SATA)* that she and Alvin "have an almost perfect meshing of minds." Alvin agrees that he and his wife work well together. "I was fortunate to find a marriage that has been both emotionally satisfying and a successful professional partnership," he told *SATA* in 1976. That partnership was expanded in 1988, when the Silversteins' eldest son, Robert, joined the writing team full time.

"Since Bob joined us, it seems as though our ideas have grown exponentially," Alvin recently told *Major Authors and Illustrators for Children and Young Adults.* "We even tried a brief venture into the publishing end and loved the experience of having complete control of a book project from its conception to the finished product. We're proud of the results, and the books were very well reviewed, but we discovered that the profits weren't good enough to compensate for the time and headaches involved in production, promotion, and marketing. Now we're back to just writing, but Bob and I are seriously exploring the possibilities of doing some of the illustrations for new Silverstein books." Virginia adds, "We'd also like to expand the scope of our books, doing more for younger children, books with a lighter touch, and perhaps some imaginative fiction. We get the feeling sometimes that our editors have us a bit too stereotyped."

WORKS CITED:

Silverstein, Alvin, and Virginia B. Silverstein, *Fifth Book of Junior Authors and Illustrators,* edited by Sally Holmes Holtze, H. W. Wilson, 1983, pp. 289-291.

Something about the Author, Volume 8, Gale, 1976, pp. 188-190.

Sutherland, Zena, and May Hill Arbuthnot, "Informational Books," *Children and Books,* fifth edition, Scott, Foresman, 1977, pp. 444-505.

FOR MORE INFORMATION SEE:

BOOKS

Contemporary Literary Criticism, Volume 17, Gale, 1981.

PERIODICALS

Appraisal, fall, 1974; spring, 1975; fall, 1975; spring, 1976; fall, 1976; spring, 1977; spring, 1978; fall, 1978; winter, 1981; spring/summer, 1982; fall, 1983; spring, 1985; winter, 1987.

Booklist, October 1, 1989; May 15, 1990.

Bulletin of the Center for Children's Books, December, 1973; February, 1977; February, 1980; May, 1981; December, 1986; January, 1988.

Horn Book, June, 1981; June, 1983; January/February, 1987; March/April, 1988.

Junior Bookshelf, June, 1972.

Junior Literary Guild, September, 1977.

Kirkus Reviews, March 15, 1972.

School Library Journal, March, 1981; February, 1982; March, 1983; November, 1984; March, 1985; September, 1986; December, 1986; October, 1987; December, 1987; June/July, 1988; September, 1988; May, 1989; September, 1989; June, 1990.

Science Books, May, 1970.

Science Books and Films, January/February, 1985; November/December, 1988; May/June, 1989; September/October, 1989; November/December, 1990.

Wilson Library Bulletin, October, 1986.

* * *

SILVERSTEIN, Shel(by) 1932- (Uncle Shelby)

PERSONAL: Born in 1932, in Chicago, IL; divorced; children: one daughter.

ADDRESSES: *Home*—Greenwich Village, NY; Key West, FL; Sausalito, CA. *Office*—c/o Grapefruit Productions, 106 Montague St., Brooklyn, NY 11201.

CAREER: Cartoonist, composer, lyricist, folksinger, and writer. *Playboy,* Chicago, IL, writer and cartoonist, 1956—. Appeared in film, *Who Is Harry Kellerman and Why Is He Saying Those Terrible Things About Me?,* 1971. *Military service:* Served with U.S. forces in Japan and Korea during 1950s; cartoonist for Pacific *Stars and Stripes.*

AWARDS, HONORS: *New York Times* Outstanding Book award, 1974, Michigan Young Readers' Award, 1981, and George G. Stone award, 1984, all for *Where the Sidewalk Ends; School Library Journal* Best Books award, 1981, Buckeye awards, 1983 and 1985, George G. Stone award, 1984, and William Allen White award, 1984, all for *A Light In the Attic;* International Reading Association's Children's Choice award, 1982, for *The Missing Piece Meets the Big O.*

WRITINGS:

SELF-ILLUSTRATED

Now Here's My Plan: A Book of Futilities, foreword by Jean Shepherd, Simon & Schuster, 1960.

Uncle Shelby's ABZ Book: A Primer for Tender Minds, Simon & Schuster, 1961.

A Playboy's Teevee Jeebies, Playboy Press, 1963.

Uncle Shelby's Story of Lafcadio, the Lion Who Shot Back (juvenile), Harper, 1963.

The Giving Tree (juvenile), Harper, 1964.

Uncle Shelby's a Giraffe and a Half (juvenile), Harper, 1964.

Uncle Shelby's Zoo: Don't Bump the Glump, Simon & Schuster, 1964.

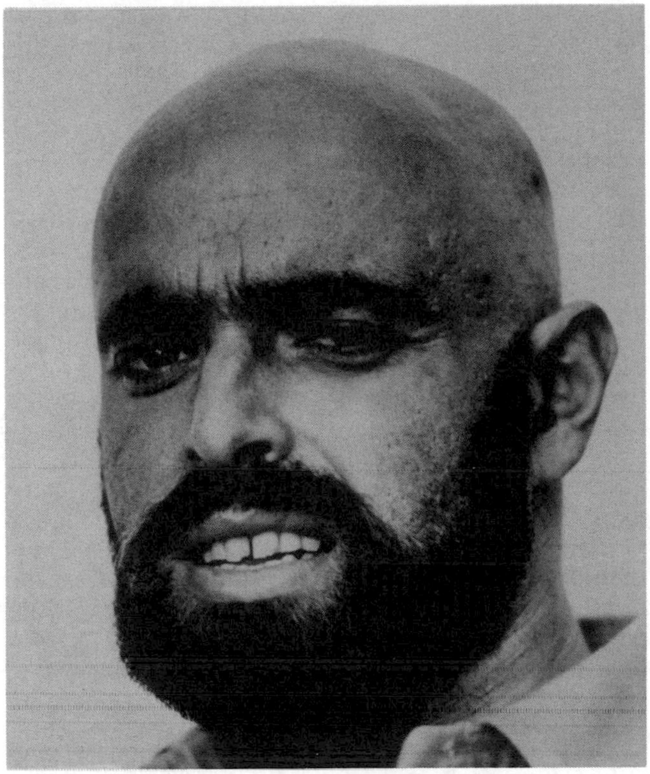

Shel Silverstein

(Under pseudonym Uncle Shelby) *Who Wants a Cheap Rhinoceros?* Macmillan, 1964.
More Playboy's Teevee Jeebies: Do-It-Yourself Dialogue for the Late Late Show, Playboy Press, 1965.
Where the Sidewalk Ends: The Poems and Drawings of Shel Silverstein (juvenile), Harper, 1974.
The Missing Piece (juvenile), Harper, 1976.
Different Dances (drawings), Harper, 1979.
The Missing Piece Meets the Big O (juvenile), Harper, 1981.
A Light in the Attic (poems; juvenile), Harper, 1981.

PLAYS

The Lady or the Tiger (one-act play, starring Richard Dreyfuss), first produced in New York City at Ensemble Studio Theatre, May, 1981.
Gorilla, first produced in Chicago, 1983.
Wild Life (includes "I'm Good to My Doggies," "Chicken Suit Optional," and "The Lady or the Tiger Show"), first produced in New York City, 1983.
Remember Crazy Zelda?, first produced in New York City, 1984.
The Happy Hour, first produced in New York City, 1985.
The Crate, first produced in New York City, 1985.
One Tennis Shoe, first produced in New York City, 1985.
Wash and Dry, first produced in New York City, 1986.
Little Feet, first produced in New York City, 1986.
(With David Mamet) *Things Change* (screenplay), Grove Press, 1988.

OTHER

Composer and lyricist of songs, including "A Boy Named Sue," "One's on the Way," "The Unicorn," "Boa Constrictor," "So Good to So Bad," "The Great Conch Train Robbery," and "Yes, Mr. Rogers." Albums of Silverstein's songs recorded by others include *Freakin' at the Freakers Ball,* Columbia, 1972, *Sloppy Seconds,* Columbia, 1972, *Dr. Hook,* Columbia, 1972, and *Bobby Bare Sings Lullabys, Legends, and Lies: The Songs of Shel Silverstein,* RCA Victor, 1973. Albums of original motion picture scores include *Ned Kelly,* United Artists, 1970, *Who Is Harry Kellerman and Why Is He Saying Those Terrible Things About Me?* Columbia, 1971. Other recordings include *Drain My Brain,* Cadet, *Dirty Feet,* Hollis Music, 1968, *Shel Silverstein: Songs and Stories,* Casablanca, 1978, and *The Great Conch Train Robbery,* 1980.

SIDELIGHTS: Shel Silverstein is responsible for many beloved, if some controversial, children's books. He is perhaps best known for his collections of children's poetry, *Where the Sidewalk Ends* and *A Light in the Attic,* books which have the distinction of incredibly long stays on the *New York Times* bestseller list. Silverstein also penned the children's classic *The Giving Tree,* which has provoked responses ranging from a ministers' praise for its example of Christian altruism to a feminists' complaints that it glorifies the exploitation of women. In addition to his work for children, Silverstein has served as a longtime *Playboy* cartoonist, has written several plays for adults, and has penned and recorded country and novelty songs.

As Edwin McDowell reported in the *New York Times Book Review,* Silverstein "for several years now ... has refused interviews and publicity tours, and he even asked his publisher not to give out any biographical information about him." What is known about Silverstein, however, is that he was born in Chicago in 1932, is divorced, and has one daughter. Most of what is known about his views and opinions, aside from what may be interpreted from his works, comes from a 1975 *Publishers Weekly* interview with Jean F. Mercier. Silverstein discussed the roots of his career in his childhood with Mercier: "When I was a kid—12, 14, around there—I would much rather have been a good baseball player or a hit with the girls. But I couldn't play ball, I couldn't dance.... So, I started to draw and to write. I was ... lucky that I didn't have anyone to copy, be impressed by. I had developed my own style, I was creating before I knew there was a Thurber, a Benchley, a Price and a Steinberg. I never saw their work till I was around 30."

Silverstein's talents were already well-developed by the time he served in the U.S. armed forces during the 1950s. He was stationed in Japan and Korea, and while in the military, he was a cartoonist for the Pacific edition of the military newspaper, *Stars and Stripes.* After his stint in the military, Silverstein became a cartoonist for *Playboy* in 1956. His work for that magazine has resulted in some published collections, such as *A Playboy's Teevee Jeebies* and *More Playboy's*

Teevee Jeebies: Do-It-Yourself Dialogue for the Late Late Show.

Silverstein did not begin writing for children until he penned *Uncle Shelby's Story of Lafcadio, the Lion Who Shot Back,* published in 1963. He confided to Mercier: "I never planned to write or draw for kids. It was Tomi Ungerer, a friend of mine, who insisted ... practically dragged me, kicking and screaming, into (editor) Ursula Nordstrom's office. And she convinced me that Tomi was right, I could do children's books." *Lafcadio, the Lion Who Shot Back* is the story of a lion who obtains a hunter's gun and practices until he becomes a good enough marksman to join a circus. A *Publishers Weekly* reviewer called the book "a wild, free-wheeling, slangy tale that most children and many parents will enjoy immensely," and it met with moderate success, as did Silverstein's *Uncle Shelby's a Giraffe and a Half.*

But Silverstein achieved fame as a children's writer after the publication of *The Giving Tree* in 1964. The story of a tree that gives its shade, fruit, branches, and finally its trunk to make a little boy happy, *The Giving Tree* had slow sales at first, but its audience steadily grew. As Richard R. Lingeman reported in the *New York Times Book Review,* "Many readers saw a religious symbolism in the altruistic tree; ministers preached sermons on *The Giving Tree;* it was discussed in Sunday schools." But feminist critics later saw something else in Silverstein's tale; as Barbara A. Schram noted in *Interracial Books for Children:* "By choosing the female pronoun for the all-giving tree and the male pronoun for the all-taking boy, it is clear that the author did indeed have a prototypical master/slave relationship in mind ... How frightening that little boys and girls who read *The Giving Tree* will encounter this glorification of female selflessness and male selfishness." Nevertheless, the book remains popular with both children and adults.

In 1974 Silverstein published a collection of poems for children called *Where the Sidewalk Ends.* Bringing him comparisons to the likes of Dr. Seuss and Edward Lear, *Where the Sidewalk Ends* contained humorous efforts such as "Sarah Cynthia Sylvia Stout/Would Not Take the Garbage Out," "Dreadful," and "Band-Aids." Kay Winters lauded the author's achievement in *The Reading Teacher:* "With creatures from the never-heard, Ickle Me Pickle Me, Tickle Me too, the Mustn'ts, Hector the Collector and Sarah Cynthia Sylvia Stout (who would not take the garbage out), Silverstein's funny bone seems to function wherever he goes." She further noted that *Where the Sidewalk Ends* "is an ideal book for teachers to have handy." *Where the Sidewalk Ends* has proved popular with child readers as well; it continues to sell many copies, as does Silverstein's 1981 follow-up collection of poems, *The Light in the Attic. Publishers Weekly* called the latter book "a big, fat treasure for Silverstein devotees, with trenchant verses expressing high-flown, exhilarating nonsense as well as thoughts unexpectedly sober and even sad."

Silverstein's 1976 picture book, *The Missing Piece,* like *The Giving Tree,* was subject to varying interpretations. It chronicles the adventures of a circle with a wedge of itself missing, who goes along singing and searching for that missing part. But after the circle finds the right wedge, he decides he was happier on the search—without the missing piece—than he is with it. As Anne Roiphe explained in the *New York Times Book Review, The Missing Piece* can be read in the same way as "the fellow at the singles bar explaining why life is better if you don't commit yourself to anyone for too long—the line goes that too much togetherness turns people into bores—that creativity is preserved by freedom to explore from one relationship to another.... This fable can also be interpreted to mean that no one should try to find all the answers, no one should hope to fill all the holes in themselves, achieve total transcendental harmony or psychic order because a person without a search, loose ends, internal conflicts and external goals becomes too smooth to enjoy or know what's going on. Too much satisfaction blocks exchange with the outside." Silverstein published a sequel, *The Missing Piece Meets the Big O,* in 1981. The latter book is told from the missing piece's point of view; as in the original, the book's protagonist discovers the value of self-sufficiency.

Since 1981, Silverstein has concentrated on writing plays for adults. One of his best known, *The Lady or the Tiger Show,* about a television producer who goes to unbelievable lengths to get his ratings up, has been performed on its own and in a group of one-acts entitled *Wild Life.* Silverstein has also collaborated on the screenplay *Things Change* with playwright David Mamet.

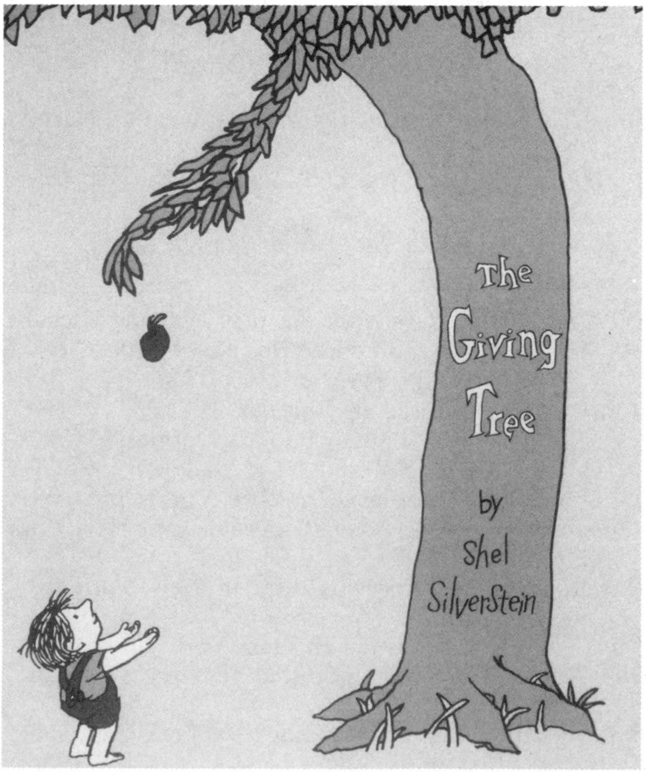

Cover of *The Giving Tree,* by Shel Silverstein.

WORKS CITED:

Lingeman, Richard R., "The Third Mr. Silverstein," *New York Times Book Review,* April 30, 1978.

McDowell, Edwin, "Shel Silverstein," *New York Times Book Review,* November 8, 1981.

Publisher's Weekly, October 28, 1963, September 18, 1981.

Roiphe, Anne, *New York Times Book Review,* May 2, 1976.

Schram, Barbara A., "Misgivings about *The Giving Tree,*" *Interracial Books for Children,* Volume 5, number 5, 1974.

Silverstein, Shel, interview with Jean F. Mercier in *Publishers Weekly,* February 24, 1975.

FOR MORE INFORMATION SEE:

BOOKS

Children's Literature Review, Volume 5, Gale, 1983, pp. 208-213.

Twentieth-Century Children's Writers, 3rd edition, St. James Press, 1989, pp. 886-887.

PERIODICALS

New York Times Book Review, March 9, 1986, pp. 36-37.

* * *

SILVERSTEIN, Virginia B(arbara Opshelor) 1937- (Ralph Buxton, Richard Rhine, Dr. A, joint pseudonyms)

PERSONAL: Born April 3, 1937, in Philadelphia, PA; daughter of Samuel W. (an insurance agent) and Gertrude (Bresch) Opshelor; married Alvin Silverstein (a professor of biology and writer), August 29, 1958; children: Robert Alan, Glenn Evan, Carrie Lee, Sharon Leslie, Laura Donna, Kevin Andrew. *Education:* Attended McGill University, summer, 1955; University of Pennsylvania, A.B., 1958. *Hobbies and other interests:* Reading, listening to classical music, working on various handcrafts, grandchildren (Emily, Shara, and Bobby Lee).

ADDRESSES: Home—3 Burlinghoff Lane, P.O. Box 537, Lebanon, NJ 08833.

CAREER: American Sugar Company, Brooklyn, NY, analytical chemist, 1958-59; free-lance translator of Russian scientific literature, 1960—; writer.

MEMBER: Authors Guild, American Translators Association.

AWARDS, HONORS: All with husband, Alvin Silverstein: Children's Book of the Year citations, Child Study Association of America, 1969, for *A World in a Drop of Water,* and 1972, for *The Code of Life, Nature's Defenses,* and *Nature's Pincushion; A World in a Drop of Water* was named an Outstanding Children's Book of 1969, *World Book Yearbook,* 1970; *Circulatory Systems* was named a Science Educators' Book Society Selection; awards from New Jersey Institute of Technology, 1972, for *Guinea Pigs: All about Them,* 1980, for *Aging,* and 1983, for *The Robots Are Here* and *The Story of Your Mouth;* Outstanding Science Books for Children citations, National Science Teachers Association and Children's Book Council, 1972, for *The Long Voyage, The Muscular System, The Skeletal System, Cancer, Nature's Pincushion,* and *Life in a Bucket of Soil,* 1973, for *Rabbits: All about Them,* 1974, for *Animal Invaders* and *Hamsters: All about Them,* 1976, for *Potatoes: All about Them* and *Gerbils: All about Them,* 1983, for *Heartbeats,* 1987, for *The Story of Your Foot,* 1988, for *Wonders of Speech* and *Nature's Living Lights,* and 1990, for *Overcoming Acne.*

Alcoholism was selected among the Notable Trade Books in the Field of Social Studies, National Council for the Social Studies and Children's Book Council, 1975; Older Honor citation, New York Academy of Sciences, 1977, for *Potatoes: All about Them;* Junior Literary Guild selection, and Children's Book of the Year citation, Bank Street College, 1977, both for *The Left-Hander's World;* Books for the Teen Age selections, New York Public Library, 1978, for *Heart Disease,* and 1987, for *AIDS: Deadly Threat;* special certificate of commendation, John Burroughs List of Nature Books for Young Readers, 1988, for *Nature's Living Lights.*

WRITINGS:

NONFICTION CHILDREN'S BOOKS; WITH HUSBAND, ALVIN SILVERSTEIN

Life in the Universe, illustrated by L. Ames, Van Nostrand, 1967.

Unusual Partners, illustrated by Mel Hunter, McGraw, 1968.

Rats and Mice: Friends and Foes of Mankind, illustrated by Joseph Cellini, Lothrop, 1968.

The Origin of Life, illustrated by L. Ames, Van Nostrand, 1968.

The Respiratory System: How Living Creatures Breathe, illustrated by George Bakacs, Prentice-Hall, 1969.

A Star in the Sea, illustrated by Simeon Shimin, Warne, 1969.

A World in a Drop of Water, Atheneum, 1969.

Carl Linnaeus, illustrated by L. Ames, John Day, 1969.

Frederick Sanger, illustrated by L. Ames, John Day, 1969.

Cells: Building Blocks of Life, illustrated by G. Bakacs, Prentice-Hall, 1969.

Germfree Life: A New Field in Biological Research, Lothrop, 1970.

Living Lights: The Mystery of Bioluminescence, Golden Gate, 1970.

Circulatory Systems: The Rivers Within, illustrated by G. Bakacs, Prentice-Hall, 1970.

The Digestive System: How Living Creatures Use Food, illustrated by G. Bakacs, Prentice-Hall, 1970.

Bionics: Man Copies Nature's Machines, McCall Publishing, 1970.

Harold Urey: The Man Who Explored from Earth to Moon, illustrated by L. Ames, John Day, 1971.

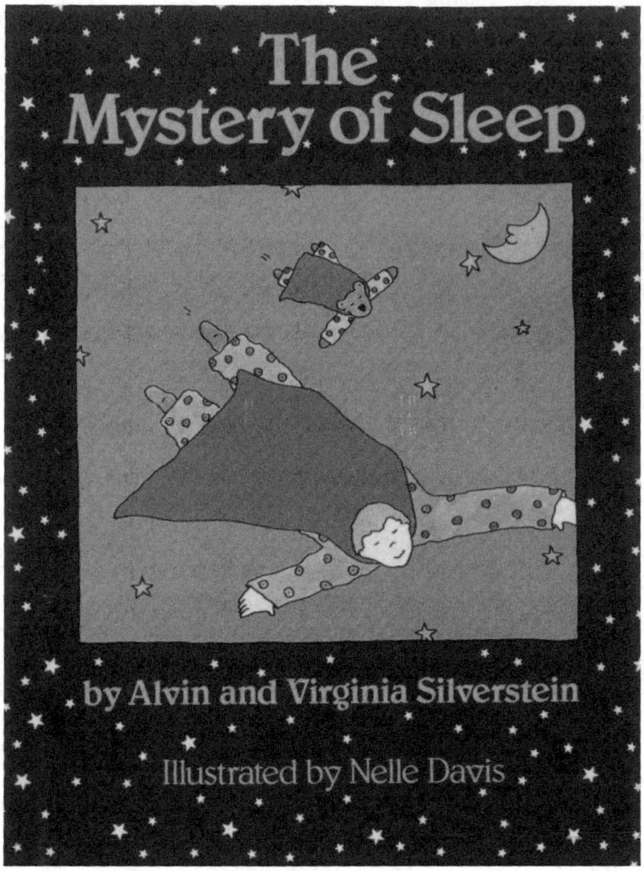

Cover of *The Mystery of Sleep,* by Virginia and Alvin Silverstein.

The Nervous System: The Inner Networks, illustrated by Mel Erikson, Prentice-Hall, 1971.
Mammals of the Sea, illustrated by Bernard Garbutt, Golden Gate, 1971.
Metamorphosis: The Magic Change, Atheneum, 1971.
The Sense Organs: Our Link with the World, illustrated by M. Erikson, Prentice-Hall, 1971.
The Endocrine System, illustrated by L. Ames, Prentice-Hall, 1971.
The Reproductive System: How Living Creatures Multiply, illustrated by L. Ames, Prentice-Hall, 1971.
The Code of Life, Atheneum, 1971.
Guinea Pigs: All about Them, photographs by Roger Kerkham, Lothrop, 1972.
The Long Voyage: The Life Cycle of a Green Turtle, illustrated by Allan Eitzen, Warne, 1972.
(Under joint pseudonym Ralph Buxton) *Nature's Defenses,* illustrated by Angus M. Babcock, Golden Gate, 1972.
The Muscular System: How Living Creatures Move, illustrated by L. Ames, Prentice-Hall, 1972.
The Skeletal System, illustrated by L. Ames, Prentice-Hall, 1972.
Cancer, John Day, 1972, first revised edition, illustrated by Andrew Antal, 1977, second revised edition published as *Cancer: Can It Be Stopped?,* Lippincott, 1987.
The Skin, illustrated by L. Ames, Prentice-Hall, 1972.
(Under joint pseudonym Ralph Buxton) *Nature's Pincushion,* illustrated by A. M. Babcock, Golden Gate, 1972.
The Excretory System, illustrated by L. Ames, Prentice-Hall, 1972.
(Under joint pseudonym Richard Rhine) *Life in a Bucket of Soil,* illustrated by Elsie Wrigley, Lothrop, 1972.
Exploring the Brain, illustrated by Patricia De Veau, Prentice-Hall, 1973.
The Chemicals We Eat and Drink, Follett, 1973.
Rabbits: All about Them, photographs by R. Kerkham, Lothrop, 1973.
Sleep and Dreams, Lippincott, 1974.
(Under joint pseudonym Ralph Buxton) *Nature's Water Clown,* illustrated by A. M. Babcock, Golden Gate, 1974.
Animal Invaders: The Story of Imported Animal Life, Atheneum, 1974.
Hamsters: All about Them, photographs by Frederick Breda, Lothrop, 1974.
Epilepsy, Lippincott, 1975.
Oranges: All about Them, illustrated by Shirley Chan, Prentice-Hall, 1975.
Beans: All about Them, illustrated by S. Chan, Prentice-Hall, 1975.
Alcoholism, introduction by Gail Gleason Milgrom, Lippincott, 1975.
(Under joint pseudonym Ralph Buxton) *Nature's Glider,* illustrated by A. M. Babcock, Golden Gate, 1975.
Apples: All about Them, illustrated by S. Chan, Prentice-Hall, 1976.
Potatoes: All about Them, illustrated by S. Chan, Prentice-Hall, 1976.
Gerbils: All about Them, photographs by F. Breda, Lippincott, 1976.
Heart Disease, Follett, 1976.
The Left-Hander's World, Follett, 1977.
Allergies, introduction by Sheldon Cohen, Lippincott, 1977.
Itch, Sniffle and Sneeze: All about Asthma, Hay Fever and Other Allergies, illustrated by Roy Doty, Four Winds, 1978.
Cats: All about Them, photographs by F. Breda, Lothrop, 1978.
So You're Getting Braces: A Guide to Orthodontics, illustrated by Barbara Remington, with photographs by Virginia B. and Alvin Silverstein, Lippincott, 1978.
(With son Glenn Silverstein) *Aging,* F. Watts, 1979.
World of Bionics, Methuen, 1979.
The Sugar Disease: Diabetes, introduction by consulting editor Charles Nechemias, Lippincott, 1980.
The Genetics Explosion, Four Winds, 1980.
Mice: All about Them, photographs by son Robert A. Silverstein, Lippincott, 1980.
Nature's Champions: The Biggest, the Fastest, the Best, illustrated by Jean Zallinger, Random House, 1980.
The Story of Your Ear, illustrated by Susan Gaber, Coward, McCann & Geoghegan, 1981.
Runaway Sugar: All about Diabetes, illustrated by Harriett Barton, Lippincott, 1981.

Futurelife: The Biotechnology Revolution, illustrated by Marjorie Thier, Prentice-Hall, 1982.
Heartbeats: Your Body, Your Heart, illustrated by Stella Ormai, Lippincott, 1983.
The Story of Your Mouth, illustrated by Greg Wenzel, Coward-McCann, 1984.
The Robots Are Here, Prentice-Hall, 1984.
Headaches: All about Them, Lippincott, 1984.
Heart Disease: America's Number One Killer, Lippincott, 1985.
The Story of Your Hand, illustrated by G. Wenzel, Putnam, 1985.
Dogs: All about Them, introduction by John C. McLoughlin, Lothrop, 1986.
World of the Brain, illustrated by Warren Budd, Morrow, 1986.
AIDS: Deadly Threat, foreword by Paul Volberding, Enslow Publishers, 1986, revised and enlarged edition, 1991.
The Story of Your Foot, illustrated by G. Wenzel, Putnam, 1987.
Mystery of Sleep, illustrated by Nelle Davis, Little, Brown, 1987.
Wonders of Speech, illustrated by Gordon Tomei, Morrow, 1988.
Nature's Living Lights: Fireflies and Other Bioluminescent Creatures, illustrated by Pamela and Walter Carroll, Little, Brown, 1988.
Learning about AIDS, foreword by James Oleske, Enslow Publishers, 1989.
Glasses and Contact Lenses: Your Guide to Eyes, Eyewear, and Eye Care, Harper, 1989.
Genes, Medicine, and You: Genetic Counseling and Gene Therapy, Enslow Publishers, 1989.
(With R. A. Silverstein) *Overcoming Acne: The How and Why of Healthy Skin Care,* preface by Christopher M. Papa, illustrated by Frank Schwarz, Morrow, 1990.
Life in a Tidal Pool, illustrated by P. and W. Carroll, Little, Brown, 1990.
(With R. A. Silverstein) *Lyme Disease, the Great Imitator: How to Prevent and Cure It,* preface by Leonard H. Sigal, AVSTAR, 1990.
(With R. A. Silverstein) *So You Think You're Fat: Obesity, Anorexia Nervosa, Bulimia, and Other Eating Disorders,* Harper, 1991.
(With R. A. Silverstein) *Addictions Handbook,* Enslow Publishers, 1991.
(With R. A. Silverstein) *Steroids: Big Muscles, Big Problems,* Enslow Publishers, in press.
(With R. A. Silverstein) *Smell, the Subtle Sense,* Morrow, in press.
(With R. A. Silverstein) *Recycling: Meeting the Challenge of the Trash Crisis,* Putnam, in press.
(With R. A. Silverstein) *Food Power! Proteins,* Millbrook, in press.
(With R. A. Silverstein) *Food Power! Fats,* Millbrook, in press.
(With R. A. Silverstein) *Food Power! Carbohydrates,* Millbrook, in press.
(With R. A. Silverstein) *Food Power! Vitamins and Minerals,* Millbrook, in press.

Also author with husband, Alvin Silverstein, under joint pseudonym Dr. A, of syndicated juvenile fiction column, "Tales from Dr. A," which appeared in about 250 American and Canadian newspapers, 1972-74.

"FAMOUS NAME" SERIES; WITH ALVIN SILVERSTEIN

(With family members Robert A., Linda, Laura, and Kevin Silverstein) *John, Your Name Is Famous: Highlights, Anecdotes, and Trivia about the Name John and the People Who Made It Great,* AVSTAR, 1989.
(With R. A. Silverstein) *John: Fun and Facts about a Popular Name and the People Who Made It Great,* AVSTAR, 1990.
(With R. A. Silverstein) *Michael: Fun and Facts about a Popular Name and the People Who Made It Great,* AVSTAR, 1990.

TRANSLATOR FROM RUSSIAN

V. N. Kondratev, *Kinetics of Chemical Gas Reactions,* Atomic Energy Commission, 1960.
M. A. Elyashevich, *Spectra of the Rare Earths,* Atomic Energy Commission, 1960.
L. K. Blinov, *Hydrochemistry of the Aral Sea,* Office of Technical Services, 1961.
R. A. Belyaev, *Beryllium Oxide,* Atomic Energy Commission, 1963.
G. V. Samsonov, *High-Temperature Compounds of Rare Earth Metals with Nonmetals,* Plenum, 1965.
M. B. Neiman, *Aging and Stabilization of Polymers,* Plenum, 1965.

Contributor of translations to about twenty scientific journals; translator of monthly journals *Biokhimiya* and *Molekulyarnaya Genetika, Mikrobiologiya, i Virusologiya.*

SIDELIGHTS: Virginia B. Silverstein and her husband, Alvin Silverstein, have combined their writing talents and mutual love of science to become successful authors of more than ninety scientific books for young readers. Please refer to Alvin Silverstein's sketch in this volume for their Sidelights essay.

* * *

SIMON, Norma (Feldstein) 1927-

PERSONAL: Born December 24, 1927, in New York, NY; daughter of Nathan Philip (a restaurant owner) and Winnie Bertha (Lepselter) Feldstein; married Edward Simon (in advertising and consumer research), June 7, 1951; children: Stephanie, Wendy (died, 1979), Jonathan. *Education:* Brooklyn College (now Brooklyn College of the City University of New York), B.A., 1947; Bank Street College of Education, certification in the education of young children, 1948, M.A., 1968; New School for Social Research, graduate study, 1948-50.

ADDRESSES: Home—P.O. Box 428, South Wellfleet, MA 02663.

CAREER: Frances I. duPont & Co. (brokerage), New York City, clerical worker, 1943-46; teacher at Vassar

Norma Simon

Summer Institute, Poughkeepsie, NY, and for Department of Welfare, Brooklyn, NY, 1948-49, at Downtown Community School, New York City, 1949-52, and at Thomas School, Rowayton, CT, 1952-53; Norwalk Community Cooperative Nursery School, Rowayton, founder, director, and teacher, 1953-54; Norwalk Public Schools, teacher, 1962-63; Greater Bridgeport Child Guidance Center, Bridgeport, CT, group therapist, 1965-67; Mid-Fairfield Child Guidance center, Fairfield, CT, special teacher, 1967-69. Consultant, Stamford Pre-School Program, Stamford, CT, 1965-69; consultant to School Division, Macmillan Publishing Co., Inc., New York City, 1968-70; consultant, Davidson Films, Inc., 1969-74, and Aesop Films, 1975; consultant in children's advertising, Dancer-Fitzgerald-Sample, Inc., New York City, 1969-79. Bank Street College of Education, consultant to Publications Division, 1967-74, and to Follow-Through Program, 1971-72.

MEMBER: Authors Guild, Bank Street College Alumni Association, Friends of Wellfleet Library, Delta Kappa Gamma (honorary member).

WRITINGS:

The Wet World, illustrated by Jane Miller, Lippincott, 1954.
Baby House, Lippincott, 1955.
A Tree for Me, Lippincott, 1956.
Up and over the Hill, Lippincott, 1957.
My Beach House, Lippincott, 1958.
The Daddy Days, illustrated by Abner Graboff, Abelard, 1958.
A Day at the County Fair, Lippincott, 1959.
Happy Purim Night, illustrated by Ayala Gordon, United Synagogue of America, 1959.
The Purim Party, illustrated by A. Gordon, United Synagogue of America, 1959.
Rosh Hashanah, illustrated by A. Gordon, United Synagogue of America, 1959.
Yom Kippur, illustrated by A. Gordon, United Synagogue of America, 1959.
Our First Sukkah, illustrated by A. Gordon, United Synagogue of America, 1959.
My Simchat Torah Flag, illustrated by A. Gordon, United Synagogue of America, 1959.
Happy Hanukkah, United Synagogue of America, 1959.
Every Friday Night, illustrated by Harvey Weiss, United Synagogue of America, 1962.
My Family Seder, illustrated by H. Weiss, United Synagogue of America, 1962.
Tu Bishvat, illustrated by H. Weiss, United Synagogue of America, 1962.
Elly the Elephant, illustrated by Stanley Bleifeld, St. Martin's, 1962.
Passover, illustrated by Symeon Shimin, Crowell, 1965.
Benjy's Bird, A. Whitman, 1965.
Hanukkah, illustrated by S. Shimin, Crowell, 1966.
What Do I Say?, illustrated by Joe Lasker, A. Whitman, 1967.
Ruthie, Meredith Corp., 1968.
See the First Star, A. Whitman, 1968.
What Do I Do?, illustrated by J. Lasker, A. Whitman, 1969.
How Do I Feel?, illustrated by J. Lasker, A. Whitman, 1970.
I Know What I Like, illustrated by Dora Leder, A. Whitman, 1971.
I Was So Mad!, illustrated by D. Leder, A. Whitman, 1974.
All Kinds of Families, illustrated by J. Lasker, A. Whitman, 1976.
Why Am I Different?, illustrated by D. Leder, A. Whitman, 1976.
We Remember Philip, illustrated by Ruth Sanderson, A. Whitman, 1978.
I'm Busy, Too, illustrated by D. Leder, A. Whitman, 1980.
Go Away, Warts!, illustrated by Susan Lexa, A. Whitman, 1980.
Nobody's Perfect, Not Even My Mother, illustrated by D. Leder, A. Whitman, 1981.
Where Does My Cat Sleep?, illustrated by D. Leder, A. Whitman, 1982.
I Wish I Had My Father, A. Whitman, 1983.
Oh, That Cat!, illustrated by D. Leder, A. Whitman, 1986.
The Saddest Time, A. Whitman, 1986.
Cats Do, Dogs Don't, A. Whitman, 1986.
Children Do, Grownups Don't, illustrated by Helen Cogancherry, A. Whitman, 1987.

Wedding Days, illustrated by Christa Kieffer, A. Whitman, 1988.
I Am Not a Crybaby, illustrated by H. Cogancherry, A. Whitman, 1989.
Mama Cat's Year, illustrated by D. Leder, A. Whitman, 1991.

Contributor to *Dimensions of Language Experience,* edited by Charlotte Winsor, Agathon Press, 1975. Materials development and skills editor, Bank Street-Macmillan Early Childhood Discovery Materials, 1968; associate skills editor, "Discoveries," Houghton, 1972.

WORK IN PROGRESS: "Another Mama Cat book, a folk tale, two concept books, plus several other ideas I am developing for young children."

SIDELIGHTS: Since the 1950s Norma Simon has been writing children's books that help young readers understand the world around them. Her books explore a range of sensitive topics, including parental separation in *I Wish I Had My Father,* developmental differences in *Why Am I Different?,* crying and its various causes in *I Am Not a Crybaby,* self-esteem in *Nobody's Perfect, Not Even My Mother,* and death in *We Remember Philip* and *The Saddest Time.* Simon has also written about the history and traditions surrounding various Jewish holidays in books such as *Passover, Hanukkah, Rosh Hashanah, Yom Kippur, Our First Sukkah,* and *Every Friday Night.*

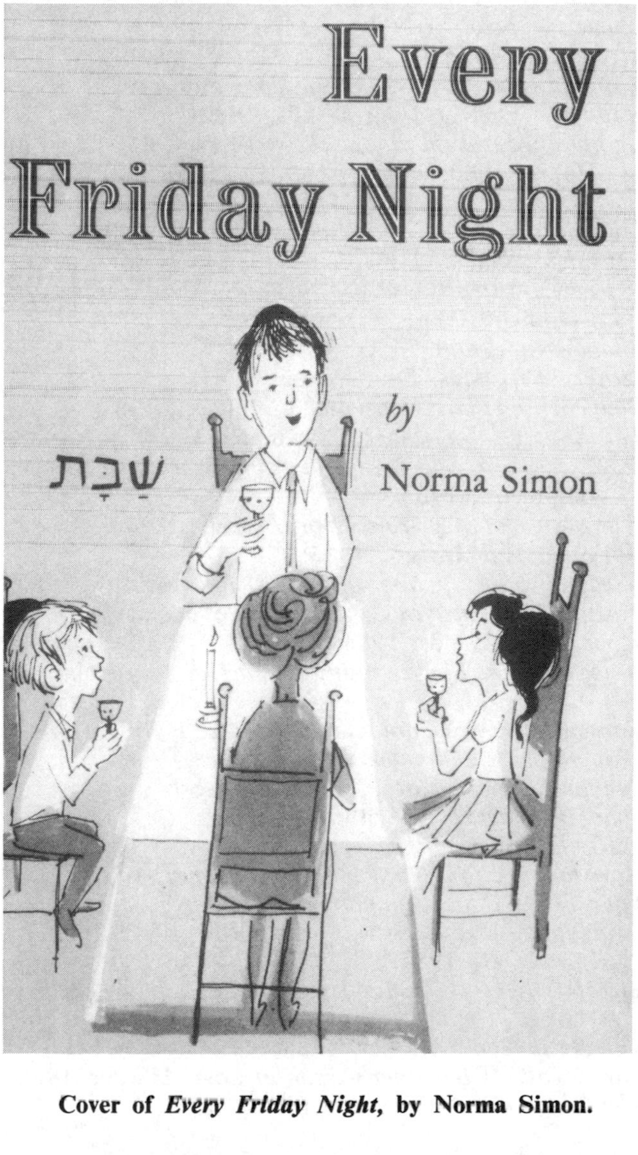

Cover of *Every Friday Night,* by Norma Simon.

Simon commented: "I have thought of children as my life's work more than writing. Writing books for children is one of the ways in which I can touch the lives of children I will never see. Children themselves have provided the material and inspiration for most of my books, and children reading my books often nod their heads in agreement as they recognize my mirror for their very own feelings, experiences and expressions. I have tried to anchor for young children some of the certainties, joys and experiences they know and recognize in spite of the unstable, complex and confusing times of our lives.

"I love to read to children and watch their faces as they move into the feelings expressed in the story. As they are reminded of their own stories and discoveries, they are eager to share their memories with others, and to use language for communication, and this is what books are all about. I begin and end with children, and that explains most of my life."

* * *

SIMON, Seymour 1931-

PERSONAL: Born August 9, 1931, in New York, NY; son of David and Clara (Liftin) Simon; married Joyce Shanock (a travel agent), December 25, 1953; children: Robert Paul, Michael Alan. *Education:* City College (now City College of the City University of New York), B.A., 1953, graduate study, 1955-60. *Hobbies and other interests:* Reading history and poetry, collecting books and art, playing chess and tennis, traveling, listening to music, computers.

ADDRESSES: Home—4 Sheffield Rd., Great Neck, NY 11021.

CAREER: Writer. New York City public schools, science and creative writing teacher, 1955-79. *Military service:* U.S. Army, 1953-55.

MEMBER: Authors Guild, Authors League of America.

AWARDS, HONORS: Children's Book Showcase Award, Children's Book Council, 1972, for *The Paper Airplane Book;* National Science Teachers Association and Children's Book Council awards, 1972-88, for outstanding science books for children; Best Children's Science Book of the Year Award, New York Academy of Sciences, 1988, for *Icebergs and Glaciers;* Eva L. Gordon Award, American Nature Society, for contributions to children's science literature.

Seymour Simon

WRITINGS:

FOR CHILDREN

Animals in Field and Laboratory: Projects in Animal Behavior, McGraw, 1968.
The Look-It-Up Book of the Earth, Random House, 1968.
Motion, Coward, 1968.
Soap Bubbles, Hawthorn, 1969.
Weather and Climate, Random House, 1969.
Exploring with a Microscope, Random House, 1969.
Handful of Soil, Hawthorn, 1970.
Science in a Vacant Lot, Viking, 1970.
Science at Work: Easy Models You Can Make, F. Watts, 1971.
Chemistry in the Kitchen, Viking, 1971.
The Paper Airplane Book, Viking, 1971.
Science at Work: Projects in Space Science, F. Watts, 1971.
Science Projects in Ecology, Holiday House, 1972.
Science Projects in Pollution, Holiday House, 1972.
Science at Work: Projects in Oceanography, F. Watts, 1972.
From Shore to Ocean Floor: How Life Survives in the Sea, F. Watts, 1973.
The Rock Hound's Book, Viking, 1973.
A Tree on Your Street, Holiday House, 1973.
A Building on Your Street, Holiday House, 1973.
Projects with Plants, F. Watts, 1973.
Birds on Your Street, Holiday House, 1974.
Life in the Dark: How Animals Survive at Night, F. Watts, 1974.
Projects with Air, F. Watts, 1975.
Pets in a Jar: Collecting and Caring for Small Wild Animals, Viking, 1975.
Everything Moves, Walker & Co., 1976.
The Optical Illusion Book, Four Winds, 1976.
Life on Ice, F. Watts, 1976.
Ghosts, Lippincott, 1976.
Life and Death in Nature, McGraw, 1976.
Animals in Your Neighborhood, Walker & Co., 1976.
The Saltwater Tropical Aquarium Book: How to Set Them up and Keep Them Going, Viking, 1976.
What Do You Want to Know about Guppies?, Four Winds, 1977.
Beneath Your Feet, Walker & Co., 1977.
Space Monsters, Lippincott, 1977.
Look to the Night Sky, Viking, 1977.
Exploring Fields and Lots, Garrard, 1978.
Killer Whales, Lippincott, 1978.
About Your Lungs, McGraw, 1978.
Animal Fact/Animal Fable, Crown, 1979.
Danger from Below, Four Winds, 1979.
The Secret Clocks, Viking, 1979.
Meet the Giant Snakes, Walker & Co., 1979.
Creatures from Lost Worlds, Lippincott, 1979.
The Long View into Space, Crown, 1979.
Deadly Ants, Four Winds, 1979.
About the Foods You Eat, McGraw, 1979.
Meet Baby Animals, Random House, 1980.
Animals Nobody Loves, Random House, 1980.
Strange Mysteries, Four Winds, 1980.
Goony Birds, Bush Babies, and Devil Rays, Random House, 1980.
Mirror Magic, Lothrop, 1980.
Silly Animal Jokes and Riddles, McGraw, 1980.
Poisonous Snakes, Four Winds, 1981.
Mad Scientists, Weird Doctors, and Time Travelers, Lippincott, 1981.
About Your Brain, McGraw, 1981.
Strange Creatures, Four Winds, 1981.
Body Sense, Body Nonsense, Lippincott, 1981.
The Smallest Dinosaurs, Crown, 1982.
How to Be a Space Scientist in Your Own Home, Lippincott, 1982.
The Long Journey from Space, Crown, 1982.
Little Giants, Morrow, 1983.
Hidden Worlds: Pictures of the Invisible, Morrow, 1983.
Earth: Our Planet in Space, Four Winds, 1984.
Moon, Four Winds, 1984.
Dinosaur Is the Biggest Animal That Ever Lived, Harper, 1984.
Computer Sense, Computer Nonsense, Harper, 1984.
Chip Rogers, Computer Whiz, Morrow, 1984.
Shadow-Magic, Lothrop, 1985.
Soap Bubble Magic, Lothrop, 1985.
Meet the Computer, Harper, 1985.
How to Talk to Your Computer, Harper, 1985.
Your First Home Computer, Crown, 1985.
101 Questions and Answers about Dangerous Animals, Macmillan, 1985.
Bit and Bytes: A Computer Dictionary for Beginners, Harper, 1985.
The Basic Book, Harper, 1985.
Turtle Talk: A Beginner's Book of Logo, Harper, 1986.
The Largest Dinosaurs, Macmillan, 1986.

How to Be an Ocean Scientist in Your Own Home, Harper, 1988.
Whales, Harper, 1989.
Big Cats, Harper, 1991.
Space Words: A Dictionary, Harper, 1991.
Snakes, Harper, 1992.

"DISCOVERING" SERIES

Discovering What Earthworms Do, McGraw, 1969.
Discovering What Frogs Do, McGraw, 1969.
Discovering What Goldfish Do, McGraw, 1970.
Discovering What Gerbils Do, McGraw, 1971.
Discovering What Crickets Do, McGraw, 1973.
Discovering What Garter Snakes Do, McGraw, 1975.
Discovering What Puppies Do, McGraw, 1977.

"LET'S TRY IT OUT" SERIES

Let's Try It Out: Wet and Dry, McGraw, 1969.
Let's Try It Out: Light and Dark, McGraw, 1970.
Let's Try It Out: Finding out with Your Senses, McGraw, 1971.
Let's Try It Out: Hot and Cold, McGraw, 1972.
Let's Try It Out: About Your Heart, McGraw, 1974.

"EINSTEIN ANDERSON" SERIES

Einstein Anderson, Science Sleuth, Viking, 1980.
Einstein Anderson Shocks His Friends, Viking, 1980.
Einstein Anderson Makes up for Lost Time, Viking, 1981.
Einstein Anderson Tells a Comet's Tale, Viking, 1981.
Einstein Anderson Goes to Bat, Viking, 1982.
Einstein Anderson Lights up the Sky, Viking, 1982.
Einstein Anderson Sees through the Invisible Man, Viking, 1983.

"SPACE PHOTOS" SERIES

Jupiter, Morrow, 1985.
Saturn, Morrow, 1985.
The Sun, Morrow, 1986.
The Stars, Morrow, 1986.
Icebergs and Glaciers, Morrow, 1987.
Mars, Morrow, 1987.
Uranus, Morrow, 1987.
Galaxies, Morrow, 1988.
Volcanoes, Morrow, 1988.
Oceans, Morrow, 1990.
Neptune, Morrow, 1991.
Mercury, Morrow, 1992.
Venus, Morrow, 1992.

SIDELIGHTS: Seymour Simon has been publishing science books for young readers since the late 1960s. In addition to many nonfiction titles on such diverse subjects as animal behavior and astronomy, he has also written fictional works that introduce children to sci-

From *Oceans,* by Seymour Simon. Illustrated with photographs by Chuck Place.

ence and computer principles, such as his "Einstein Anderson" and "Chip Rogers" books. Simon explained his motivation in an interview with Geraldine De Luca and Roni Natov for the *Lion and the Unicorn,* "It's very important to get kids to read science books from a very young age. If they're not reading books about science by the time they're twelve, you've probably lost them. When they grow up, they will view science with a great deal of fear and misinformation. Thus, if we want a literate citizenry, we have to start children on science books when they're young. They have no fear at a young age, and they will stay familiar with science all of their lives."

Simon was born August 9, 1931, in New York City. He recalled for De Luca and Natov: "I've always written—even while I was a high school student." He was also very interested in scientific topics while growing up. He attended the Bronx High School of Science, and became president of the Junior Astronomy Club at the American Museum of Natural History—projects he did in this capacity included grinding his own telescope lenses. Simon also enjoyed reading science fiction, which fueled his scientific interests.

After obtaining his bachelor's degree, Simon continued his education by doing graduate study at City College (now City College of the City University of New York). Between his undergraduate and graduate years, Simon served in the U.S. Army and married Joyce Shanock, a travel agent, on Christmas Day of 1953. His graduate work centered on animal behavior, and he later used the study and experience in many of his works for children about animals. After finishing his schooling, Simon became a teacher in the New York City public schools. He commented to De Luca and Natov: "After I began to teach, I decided to try to write while I was teaching. I sent some articles to *Scholastic* magazines and although they didn't accept the articles, the editor of one of the magazines asked me to come in and he gave me an assignment, which happened to be for an article about the moon. The editors were very interested that I taught science because they were having a very difficult time finding anyone who could write who also knew something about science."

Simon continued writing articles for *Scholastic* for a few years, then decided to write an entire book. He explained to De Luca and Natov: "Since my field in graduate school was mostly animal behavior, the first book that I wrote was called *Animals in Field and Laboratory: Science Projects in Animal Behavior.* I was teaching ninth grade then and a lot of kids in my classes were doing projects. I would tend to influence them to do work on animal behavior."

Since *Animals in Field and Laboratory* was published in 1968, Simon has written several books containing simple science experiments that younger readers can do themselves with minimal help from teachers or parents. Though many of his works focus on animals, others focus more on physics or chemistry principals. Several encourage children to explore their own immediate environments to learn about science, such as *Science in a Vacant Lot* and *Chemistry in the Kitchen.* One of Simon's most acclaimed works is 1971's *The Paper Airplane Book,* in which he uses the examples of different paper airplanes to explain the principles of aerodynamics that make real airplanes work. Critic Zena Sutherland, writing in the *Bulletin of the Center for Children's Books,* called *The Paper Airplane Book* "an exemplary home demonstration book," noting that "the author uses the process approach, suggesting variations on the airplane and asking the reader to consider *why* a certain effect is obtained, or which change is most effective for a desired result." This approach is typical of Simon's books; he once explained: "It's questions like these that occur to me and that have been asked of me by children (both my own and in my science classes) that make me want to write science books. The books I write are full of such questions. Sometimes I'll provide an answer, but more often I'll suggest an activity or an experiment that will let a child answer a question by trying it out."

Simon retired from teaching to write full time in 1979. He told De Luca and Natov: "When I stopped teaching, I had published about forty or fifty books. But I found that I wanted to spend more time in selecting the types of books that I would do. I had been doing books that were very curriculum-oriented. They were not textbooks by any means, but they were books that were tied in with class work. What I really wanted was to write the kind of books that a kid might pick up in a library or in a bookstore, and I found that I needed more time to do that kind of book. My newer books are different from the earlier ones."

Some of Simon's later books are completely different from his earlier ones in that they are fiction. Always looking for ways to interest children in science, Simon uses an appealing character who adores bad puns and solves mysteries through his knowledge of science in his "Einstein Anderson" books. The series has been widely compared with the "Encyclopedia Brown" books of Donald Sobol. Similarly, in *Chip Rogers, Computer Whiz,* Simon has his protagonist solve mysteries with his computer, exposing his young readers to actual BASIC programming in the process. As he concluded in his interview with De Luca and Natov: "I'm going to continue to write imaginative books about science, and continue to present them in ways that I think are interesting or novel."

WORKS CITED:

Simon, Seymour, in an interview with Geraldine De Luca and Roni Natov, "Who's Afraid of Science Books? An Interview with Seymour Simon," *Lion and the Unicorn,* Volume 6, 1982, pp. 10-27.

Sutherland, Zena, review of *The Paper Airplane Book, Bulletin of the Center for Children's Books,* May, 1972, p. 146.

FOR MORE INFORMATION SEE:

BOOKS

Children's Literature Review, Volume 9, Gale, 1985.

* * *

SIMONT, Marc 1915-

PERSONAL: Born November 23, 1915, in Paris, France; first came to United States, 1927, but later went back to Europe with parents, returning to America, 1935; naturalized citizen, 1936; son of Josep (an illustrator on staff of *L'Illustration*) and Dolors (Baste) Simont; married Sara Dalton (a teacher), April 7, 1945; children: Marc Dalton. *Education:* Studied art in Paris at Academie Ranson, Academie Julien, and Andre Lhote School, 1932-35, and in New York City at National Academy of Design, 1935-37. *Politics:* Democrat. *Hobbies and other interests:* "Seasonal sports, music (except atonal), improving my Catalan, a good table with friends and Cuban cigars."

ADDRESSES: Home—336 Town St., West Cornwall, CT 06796.

CAREER: Artist and illustrator; since 1939 has worked in portraits, murals, sculpture, prints, and magazine and book illustration; translator and writer of children's books, 1939—. Advocate of community soccer in West Cornwall, CT. *Military service:* U.S. Army, 1943-46; produced visual aids; became sergeant.

Marc Simont

MEMBER: American Veterans Committee, Authors League of America, Authors Guild, American Civil Liberties Union.

AWARDS, HONORS: Tiffany fellow, 1937; Caldecott honor book citation, 1950, for *The Happy Day; Book World* Spring Book Festival Award, and Child Study Association Book Award, both 1952, both for *Jareb;* Caldecott Medal, 1957, for *A Tree Is Nice;* Steck-Vaughn Award, 1957, for *The Trail Driving Rooster;* citation of merit, Society of Illustrators, 1965; Best Book of the Season citation from the *Today Show,* 1972, for *Nate the Great;* National Book Award finalist, 1976, for *The Star in the Pail;* New York Academy of Sciences Children's Younger Book Award, 1980, for *A Space Story;* New Jersey Institute of Technology Award, 1981, for *Ten Copycats in a Boat and Other Riddles; New York Times* Outstanding Books citation, 1982, for *The Philharmonic Gets Dressed;* Garden State Children's Book Awards, 1984, for *Nate the Great and the Missing Key,* and 1985, for *Nate the Great and the Snowy Trail;* American Institute of Graphic Arts certificate of excellence; Jefferson Cup, 1985, for *In the Year of the Boar and Jackie Robinson;* Parents' Choice award, 1986, for *The Dallas Titans Get Ready for Bed.*

WRITINGS:

SELF-ILLUSTRATED

Opera Souffle: 60 Pictures in Bravura, Schuman, 1950.
Polly's Oats, Harper, 1951.
(With Red Smith) *How to Get to First Base: A Picture Book of Baseball,* Schuman, 1952.
The Lovely Summer, Harper, 1952, Bantam, Doubleday, Dell, 1992.
Mimi, Harper, 1954.
The Plumber Out of the Sea, Harper, 1955.
The Contest at Paca, Harper, 1959.
How Come Elephants?, Harper, 1965.
Afternoon in Spain, Morrow, 1965.
(With members of staff of Boston Children's Medical Center) *A Child's Eye View of the World,* Delacorte, 1972.

TRANSLATOR

(And illustrator) Federico Garcia Lorca, *The Lieutenant Colonel and the Gypsy,* Doubleday, 1971.
Francesc Sales, *Ibrahim,* illustrations by Eulalia Sariola, Lippincott, 1989.

ILLUSTRATOR

Emma G. Sterne, *The Pirate of Chatham Square: A Story of Old New York,* Dodd, 1939.
Ruth Bryan Owens, *The Castle in the Silver Woods,* Dodd, 1939.
Albert Carr, *Men of Power,* Viking, 1940.
Mildred Cross, *Isabella, Young Queen of Spain,* Dodd, 1941.
Charlotte Jackson, *Sarah Deborah's Day,* Dodd, 1941.

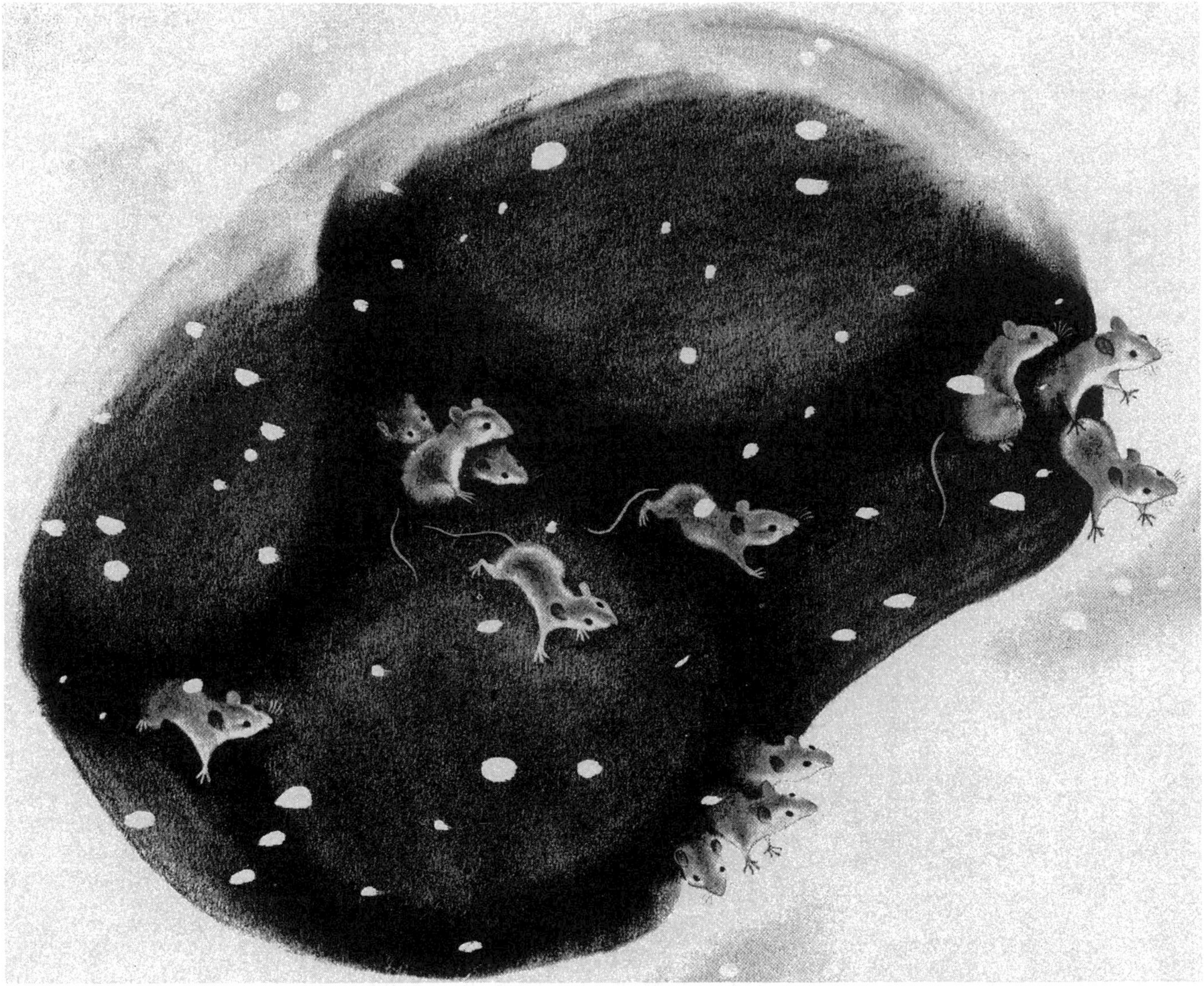

From *The Happy Day,* by Ruth Krauss. Illustrated by Marc Simont.

Richard Hatch, *All Aboard the Whale,* Dodd, 1942.
Dougal's Wish, Harper, 1942.
Meindert DeJong, *Billy and the Unhappy Bull,* Harper, 1946.
Margaret Wise Brown, *The First Story,* Harper, 1947.
Iris Vinton, *Flying Ebony,* Dodd, 1947.
Robbie Trent, *The First Christmas,* Harper, 1948, new edition, 1990.
Andrew Lang, editor, *The Red Fairy Book,* new edition, Longmans, Green, 1948.
Ruth Krauss, *The Happy Day,* Harper, 1949.
R. Krauss, *The Big World and the Little House,* Schuman, 1949.
Red Smith, *Views of Sport,* Knopf, 1949.
M. DeJong, *Good Luck Duck,* Harper, 1950.
R. Krauss, *The Backward Day,* Harper, 1950.
James Thurber, *The Thirteen Clocks,* Simon & Schuster, 1951.
Marjorie B. Paradis, *Timmy and the Tiger,* Harper, 1952.
Alistair Cooke, *Christmas Eve,* Knopf, 1952.
Miriam Powell, *Jareb,* Crowell, 1952.
The American Riddle Book, Schuman, 1954.
Elizabeth H. Lansing, *Deer Mountain Hideaway,* Crowell, 1954.
Jean Fritz, *Fish Head,* Coward, 1954.
E. H. Lansing, *Deer River Raft,* Crowell, 1955.
Fred Gipson, *The Trail-Driving Rooster,* Harper, 1955.
Julius Schwartz, *Now I Know,* Whittlesey House, 1955.
Janice May Udry, *A Tree Is Nice,* Harper, 1955.
P.G. Wodehouse, *America I Like You,* Simon & Schuster, 1956.
J. Schwartz, *I Know a Magic House,* Whittlesey House, 1956.
Thomas Liggett, *Pigeon Fly Home,* Holiday House, 1956.
Chad Walsh, *Nellie and Her Flying Crocodile,* Harper, 1956.
J. Thurber, *The Wonderful "O",* Simon & Schuster, 1957.
Maria Leach, *The Rainbow Book of American Folk Tales and Legends,* World, 1958.
Alexis Ladas, *The Seal That Couldn't Swim,* Little, Brown, 1959.

James A. Kjelgaard, *The Duckfooted Hound,* Crowell, 1960.
R. Krauss, *A Good Man and His Wife,* Harper, 1962.
J. Schwartz, *The Earth Is Your Spaceship,* Whitlesey House, 1963.
David McCord, *Every Time I Climb a Tree,* Little Brown, 1967.
What To Do When There's Nothing To Do, Dell, 1967.
Charlton Ogburn, Jr., *Down, Boy, Down, Blast You!,* Morrow, 1967.
Janet Chenery, *Wolfie,* Harper, 1969.
J. M. Udry, *Glenda,* Harper, 1969.
Edward Fales, Jr., *Belts On, Buttons Down,* Dell, 1971.
D. McCord, *The Star in the Pail,* Little, Brown, 1975.
Beverly Keller, *The Beetle Bush,* Coward, 1976.
Karla Kuskin, *A Space Story,* Harper, 1978.
Faith McNulty, *Mouse and Time,* Harper, 1978.
F. McNulty, *How to Dig a Hole to the Other Side of the World,* Harper, 1979.
Alvin Schwartz, editor, *Ten Copycats in a Boat, and Other Riddles,* Harper, 1979.
F. McNulty, *The Elephant Who Couldn't Forget,* Harper, 1979.
Mitchell Sharmat, *Reddy Rattler and Easy Eagle,* Doubleday, 1979.
D. McCord, *Speak Up: More Rhymes of the Never Was and Always Is,* Little, Brown, 1980.
Marjorie Weinman Sharmat, *Chasing After Annie,* Harper, 1981.
Charlotte Zolotow, *If You Listen,* Harper, 1980.
Peggy Parish, *No More Monsters For Me!,* Harper, 1981.
K. Kuskin, *The Philharmonic,* Harper, 1982.
Julie Delton, *My Uncle Nikos,* Crowell, 1983.
Mollie Hunter, *The Knight of the Golden Plain,* Harper, 1983.
Edward Davis, *Bruno the Pretzel Man,* Harper, 1984.
Bette Bao Lord, *The Year of the Boar and Jackie Robinson,* Harper, 1984.
Joan W. Blos, *Martin's Hats,* Morrow, 1984.
John Reynolds Gardiner, *Top Secret,* Little, Brown, 1984.
Franklyn Mansfield Branley, *Volcanoes,* Crowell, 1985.
M. Hunter, *The Three Day Enchantment,* Harper, 1985.
K. Kuskin, *The Dallas Titans Get Ready for Bed,* Harper, 1986.
F. M. Branley, *Journey into a Black Hole,* Crowell, 1986.
Wendell V. Tangborn, *Glaciers,* Crowell, 1988, revised edition, Harper, 1988.
Sing a Song of Popcorn, Scholastic, 1988.
C. Zolotow, *The Quiet Mother and the Noisy Little Boy,* Harper, 1989.
F. M. Branley, *What Happened to the Dinosaurs?,* Harper, 1989.
J. Thurber, *Many Moons,* Harcourt, 1990.

ILLUSTRATOR; "NATE THE GREAT" SERIES BY MARJORIE WEINMAN SHARMAT

Nate the Great, Coward, 1972.
Nate the Great Goes Undercover, Coward, 1974.
Nate the Great and the Lost List, Coward, 1975.
Nate the Great and the Phony Clue, Coward, 1977.
Nate the Great and the Sticky Case, Coward, 1978.
Nate the Great and the Missing Key, Coward, 1981.
Nate the Great and the Snowy Trail, Coward, 1982.
Nate the Great and the Fishy Prize, Coward, 1985.
Nate the Great and the Boring Beach Bag, Coward, 1987.
Nate the Great Stalks Stupidweed, Coward, 1987.
Nate the Great Goes Down in the Dumps, Coward, 1989.
Nate the Great and the Halloween Hunt, Coward, 1989.
(With Craig Sharmat) *Nate the Great and the Musical Note,* Coward, 1990.
Nate the Great and the Stolen Base, Coward, 1992.

ADAPTATIONS: Nate the Great Goes Undercover and *Nate the Great and the Sticky Case* were made into films. The *Nate the Great* books were once optioned for a television series. An excerpt from *Nate the Great* was adapted and is on permanent display at the Museum of Science and Industry, Chicago, Illinois.

SIDELIGHTS: Marc Simont was born in 1915 in Paris, France, to parents from the Catalonian region of northern Spain. He attended schools in Paris, Barcelona, Spain, and New York City because his parents kept traveling. Simont's father went to the United States after World War I and decided to become an American citizen. Because that process took five years, Simont lived with his grandfather in Barcelona. During this time he sketched soccer players and bullfighters, and while sick in bed with the grippe he learned to write by tracing the text of a picture book called *El Ginesello.*

This repeated relocation affected his performance as a student. "I was always more concerned with what a teacher looked like than what he said, which didn't do my algebra any good," the illustrator explained in *More Junior Authors.* He didn't graduate from high school, although he became fluent in French, English, Spanish, and Catalonian. On the other hand, the traveling sharpened his skills as an observer—skills important for an artist. He studied art at the Academie Julian and the Academie Ranson in Paris and in New York City at National Academy of Design. He also studied art with Andre Lohte, but he said his most important art teacher was his father, an illustrator for *L'Illustration* magazine. With a sister and two uncles also making a living as artists, he considers art the family trade.

When he returned to the United States in 1935, Simont worked odd jobs, painted portraits, and drew illustrations for pulp magazines. Eventually he became an illustrator of books for children. Books by many notable children's writers, including James Thurber, David McCord, P.G. Wodehouse, Alistair Cooke, Ruth Krauss, Charlotte Zolotow and Marjorie Weinman Sharmat, have been published with his illustrations. Simont illustrated Sharmat's book *Nate the Great,* featuring the boy detective who solves neighborhood mysteries, and has won several awards for books in the *Nate the Great* series. Three of them were Junior Literary Guild selections, two were made into films, and the entire series was once optioned for a television series. His illustrations for Janice May Udry's *A Tree Is Nice* won the Caldecott Award in 1957.

Critics have pointed out that Simont's illustrations are perfectly suited to the text in books by a variety of children's authors. George A. Woods comments in the *New York Times Book Review* about Karla Kuskin's *The Philharmonic Gets Dressed:* "Simont has not missed a beat. His musicians are a varied band in terms of age, race and physique. He conveys the awkward stance as well as the graceful pose, the little scenes and moments that are all around us—the hole in the sock, the graffiti inside the subway car as well as the advertising posters." Kenneth Marantz, writing about the same book in *School Library Journal,* notes that Simont's "ability to invest such convincing feelings of life using an almost cartoon-like simplicity is remarkable." *New York Times Book Review* contributor Nora Magid observes that Simont's illustrations in *How to Dig a Hole to the Other Side of the World* have terrific emotional power: "Simont's pictures break the heart. The child voyager is at once intrepid and vulnerable" as he takes an imaginary journey through the earth's crust to China. Other features of Simont's artistic style are a method of composition that gives continuity to the pictures in sequence, and humor that is inviting to readers of all ages.

"I believe that if I like the drawings I do, children will like them also," Simont told Lee Bennett Hopkins for *Books Are By People: Interviews with 104 Authors and Illustrators of Books for Young Children.* He continued, "The child in me must make contact with other children. I may miss it by ten miles, but if I am going to hit, it is because of the child in me."

WORKS CITED:

Hopkins, Lee Bennett, *Books Are By People: Interviews with 104 Authors and Illustrators of Books for Young Children,* Citation Press, 1969, pp. 267-269.

Magid, Nora, review of *How to Dig a Hole to the Other Side of the World, New York Times Book Review,* November 18, 1979, p. 320.

Marantz, Kenneth, review of *The Philharmonic Gets Dressed, School Library Journal,* August, 1982, p. 99.

Simont, Marc, in *More Junior Authors,* H. W. Wilson, 1963, pp. 186-187.

Woods, George A., review of *The Philharmonic Gets Dressed, New York Times Book Review,* October 17, 1982, p. 37.

FOR MORE INFORMATION SEE:

BOOKS

Caldecott Medal Books: 1938-1957, Horn Book, 1957.

Kingman, Lee, editor, *Newbery and Caldecott Medal Books: 1956-1965,* Horn Book, 1965.

Klemin, Diana, *The Art of Art for Children's Books,* Clarkson Potter, 1966.

PERIODICALS

Book World, November 5, 1972, p. 4.

Christian Science Monitor, November 11, 1971.

Horn Book, February, 1980, p. 140; April, 1983, p. 158; February, 1984, p. 54; June, 1984, p. 318; May/June, 1985, p. 326; November/December, 1986, p. 737; November/December, 1989, p. 788.

New York Times Book Review, October 31, 1965, p. 56; November 6, 1983, p. 43; May 20, 1984, p. 28; November 9, 1986, p. 40.

School Library Journal, August, 1984, p. 56; October, 1989, p. 100.

Science Books and Films, November/December, 1988, p. 95.

Time, December 4, 1978, p. 100; December 20, 1982, p. 79.

* * *

SINGER, Isaac
See SINGER, Isaac Bashevis

* * *

SINGER, Isaac Bashevis 1904-1991
(Isaac Bashevis, Isaac Singer; pseudonym: Isaac Warshofsky)

PERSONAL: Born July 14, 1904, in Radzymin, Poland; immigrated to United States, 1935, naturalized citizen, 1943; died after several strokes, July 24, 1991, in Surfside, FL; son of Pinchos Menachem (a rabbi and author) and Bathsheba (Zylberman) Singer; married first wife, Rachel (divorced); married Alma Haimann, February 14, 1940; children: (first marriage) Israel. *Education:* Attended Tachkemoni Rabbinical Seminary, 1920-27. *Religion:* Jewish.

ADDRESSES: Home—209 West 86th St., New York, NY 10024, and 9511 Collins Ave. 703, Surfside, FL 33154. *Office—Jewish Daily Forward,* 175 East Broadway, New York, NY 10002.

CAREER: Novelist, short story writer, children's author, and translator. *Literarishe Bletter,* Warsaw, Poland, proofreader and translator, 1923-33; *Globus,* Warsaw, associate editor, 1933-35; *Jewish Daily Forward,* New York City, member of staff, 1935-91. Founder of the literary magazine *Svivah.* Appeared in *Isaac in America* and *The Cafeteria* (based on one of his short stories), both Direct Cinema Limited Associates, both 1986.

MEMBER: Jewish Academy of Arts and Sciences (fellow), National Institute of Arts and Letters (fellow), Polish Institute of Arts and Sciences in America (fellow), American Academy of Arts and Sciences, PEN.

AWARDS, HONORS: Louis Lamed Prize, 1950, for *The Family Moskat,* and 1956, for *Satan in Goray;* National Institute of Arts and Letters and American Academy award in literature, 1959; Harry and Ethel Daroff Memorial Fiction Award, Jewish Book Council of America, 1963, for *The Slave;* D.H.L., Hebrew Union College, 1963; Foreign Book prize (France), 1965; National Council on the Arts grant, 1966; *New York Times* best illustrated book citation, 1966, Newbery Honor Book Award, 1967, International Board on Books for Young People honor list, 1982, *Horn Book*

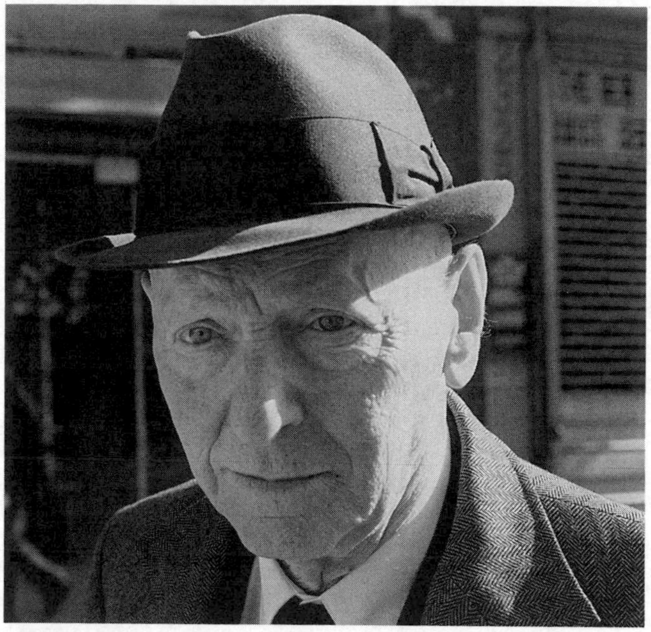

Isaac Bashevis Singer

"Fanfare" citation, and American Library Association (ALA) notable book citation, all for *Zlateh the Goat and Other Stories;* National Endowment for the Arts grant, 1967; *Playboy* magazine award for best fiction, 1967; Newbery Honor Book Award, 1968, for *The Fearsome Inn;* Bancarella Prize, 1968, for Italian translation of *The Family Moskat;* Newbery Honor Book Award, 1969, ALA notable book citation, and *Horn Book* honor list citation, all for *When Schlemiel Went to Warsaw and Other Stories;* Brandeis University Creative Arts Medal for Poetry-Fiction, 1970; National Book Award for children's literature, 1970, and ALA notable book citation, both for *A Day of Pleasure;* Sydney Taylor Award, Association of Jewish Libraries, 1971; Children's Book Showcase Award, Children's Book Council, 1972, for *Alone in the Wild Forest;* D.Litt., Texas Christian University, 1972, Colgate University, 1972, Bard College, 1974, and Long Island University, 1979; Ph.D., Hebrew University, Jerusalem, 1973; National Book Award for fiction, 1974, for *A Crown of Feathers and Other Stories;* Agnon Gold Medal, 1975; ALA notable book citation, 1976, for *Naftali the Storyteller and His Horse, Sus, and Other Stories;* Nobel Prize for Literature, 1978; Kenneth B. Smilen/*Present Tense* Literary Award, *Present Tense* magazine, 1980, for *The Power of Light; Los Angeles Times* fiction prize nomination, 1982, for *The Collected Stories of Isaac Bashevis Singer; New York Times* outstanding book citation, and *Horn Book* honor list citation, both 1982, Parents' Choice Award, Parents' Choice Foundation, 1983, and ALA notable book citation, all for *The Golem; New York Times* notable book citation, and ALA notable book citation, both 1984, both for *Stories for Children;* Handel Medallion, 1986; PEN/Faulkner Award nomination, 1989, for *The Death of Methuselah and Other Stories;* Gold Medal for Fiction, American Academy and Institute of Arts and Letters, 1989; *Mazel and Shlimazel; or, The Milk of a Lioness* and *The Wicked City* received ALA notable book citations.

WRITINGS:

JUVENILE; ORIGINALLY IN YIDDISH; TRANSLATION BY SINGER AND ELIZABETH SHUB

Mazel and Shlimazel; or, The Milk of a Lioness, illustrated by Margot Zemach, Harper, 1966.

Zlateh the Goat and Other Stories, illustrated by Maurice Sendak, Harper, 1966.

The Fearsome Inn, illustrated by Nonny Hogrogian, Scribner, 1967.

When Schlemiel Went to Warsaw and Other Stories (also see below), illustrated by Zemach, Farrar, Straus, 1968.

Elijah the Slave: A Hebrew Legend Retold, illustrated by Antonio Frasconi, Farrar, Straus, 1970.

Joseph and Koza; or, The Sacrifice to the Vistula, illustrated by Symeon Shimin, Farrar, Straus, 1970.

Alone in the Wild Forest, illustrated by Zemach, Farrar, Straus, 1971.

The Topsy-Turvy Emperor of China, illustrated by William Pene du Bois, Harper, 1971.

The Wicked City, illustrated by Leonard Everett Fisher, Farrar, Straus, 1972.

The Fools of Chelm and Their History, illustrated by Uri Shulevitz, Farrar, Straus, 1973.

Why Noah Chose the Dove, illustrated by Eric Carle, Farrar, Straus, 1974.

A Tale of Three Wishes, illustrated by Irene Lieblich, Farrar, Straus, 1975.

Naftali the Storyteller and His Horse, Sus, and Other Stories (also see below), illustrated by Zemach, Farrar, Straus, 1976.

The Power of Light: Eight Stories for Hanukkah (also see below), illustrated by Lieblich, Farrar, Straus, 1980.

The Golem, limited edition, illustrated by Shulevitz, Farrar, Straus, 1982.

Stories for Children (includes stories from *Naftali the Storyteller and His Horse, Sus, and Other Stories, When Schlemiel Went to Warsaw and Other Stories,* and *The Power of Light*), Farrar, Straus, 1984.

NOVELS; ORIGINALLY IN YIDDISH

Der Satan in Gorey, [Warsaw], 1935, translation by Jacob Sloan published as *Satan in Goray,* Noonday, 1955.

(Under name Isaac Bashevis) *Di Familie Mushkat,* two volumes, [New York], 1950, translation by A. H. Gross published under name Isaac Bashevis Singer as *The Family Moskat,* Knopf, 1950.

The Magician of Lublin, translation by Elaine Gottlieb and Joseph Singer, Noonday, 1960.

The Slave (also see below), translation by author and Cecil Hemley, Farrar, Straus, 1962.

The Manor, translation by Gottlieb and J. Singer, Farrar, Straus, 1967.

The Estate, translation by Gottlieb, J. Singer, and Elizabeth Shub, Farrar, Straus, 1969.

Enemies: A Love Story (first published in *Jewish Daily Forward* under title "Sonim, di Geshichte fun a

Liebe," 1966; also see below), translation by Aliza Shevrin and Shub, Farrar, Straus, 1972.

Shosha (also see below), Farrar, Straus, 1978.

Reaches of Heaven: A Story of the Baal Shem Tov, Farrar, Straus, 1980.

Isaac Bashevis Singer, Three Complete Novels (includes *The Slave, Enemies: A Love Story,* and *Shosha*), Avenel Books, 1982.

The Penitent, Farrar, Straus, 1983.

The King of the Fields, limited edition, Farrar, Straus, 1988.

Scum, translation by Rosaline D. Schwartz, Farrar, Straus, 1991.

SHORT STORY COLLECTIONS; ORIGINALLY IN YIDDISH

Gimpel the Fool and Other Stories, translation by Saul Bellow and others, Noonday, 1957.

The Spinoza of Market Street and Other Stories, translation by Gottlieb and others, Farrar, Straus, 1961.

Short Friday and Other Stories, translation by Ruth Whitman and others, Farrar, Straus, 1964.

Selected Short Stories, edited by Irving Howe, Modern Library, 1966.

The Seance and Other Stories, translation by Whitman, Roger H. Klein, and others, Farrar, Straus, 1968.

A Friend of Kafka and Other Stories, translation by the author and others, Farrar, Straus, 1970.

An Isaac Bashevis Singer Reader, Farrar, Straus, 1971.

A Crown of Feathers and Other Stories, translation by the author and others, Farrar, Straus, 1973.

Passions and Other Stories, Farrar, Straus, 1975.

Old Love and Other Stories, Farrar, Straus, 1979.

The Collected Stories of Isaac Bashevis Singer, Farrar, Straus, 1982.

The Image and Other Stories, Farrar, Straus, 1985.

Gifts, Jewish Publication Society of America, 1985.

The Death of Methuselah and Other Stories, Farrar, Straus, 1988.

AUTOBIOGRAPHY; ORIGINALLY IN YIDDISH; UNDER PSEUDONYM ISAAC WARSHOFSKY

Mayn Tatn's Bes-din Shtub, [New York], 1956, translation by Channah Kleinerman-Goldstein published under name Isaac Bashevis Singer as *In My Father's Court,* Farrar, Straus, 1966.

A Day of Pleasure: Stories of a Boy Growing Up in Warsaw (juvenile), translation by author and Shub, photographs by Roman Vishniac, Farrar, Straus, 1969.

A Little Boy in Search of God: Mysticism in a Personal Light (also see below), illustrated by Ira Moskowitz, Doubleday, 1976.

A Young Man in Search of Love (also see below), translation by J. Singer, Doubleday, 1978.

Lost in America (also see below), translation by J. Singer, paintings and drawings by Raphael Soyer, Doubleday, 1981.

Love and Exile: The Early Years: A Memoir (includes *A Little Boy in Search of God: Mysticism in a Personal Light, A Young Man in Search of Love,* and *Lost in America*), Doubleday, 1984.

PLAYS; ORIGINALLY IN YIDDISH

The Mirror (also see below), produced in New Haven, CT, 1973.

(With Leah Napolin) *Yentl, the Yeshiva Boy* (adaptation of a story by Singer; produced on Broadway, 1974), Samuel French, 1978.

Schlemiel the First, produced in New Haven, 1974.

(With Eve Friedman) *Teibele and Her Demon* (produced in Minneapolis at Guthrie Theatre, 1978, produced on Broadway, 1979), Samuel French, 1984.

A Play for the Devil (based on his short story "The Unseen"), produced in New York City at the Folksbiene Theatre, 1984.

TRANSLATOR INTO YIDDISH

Knut Hamsun, *Pan,* Wilno (Warsaw), 1928.

Hamsun, *Di Vogler* (title means "The Vagabonds"), Wilno, 1928.

Gabriele D'Annunzio, *In Opgrunt Fun Tayve* (title means "In Passion's Abyss"), Goldfarb (Warsaw), 1929.

Karin Michaelis, *Mete Trap,* Goldfarb, 1929.

Stefan Zweig, *Roman Rolan* (title means "Romain Rolland"), Bikher (Warsaw), 1929.

Hamsun, *Viktorya* (title means "Victoria"), Wilno, 1929.

Erich Maria Remarque, *Oyfn Mayrev-Front Keyn Nayes* (title means "All Quiet on the Western Front"), Wilno, 1930.

Thomas Mann, *Der Tsoyberbarg* (title means "The Magic Mountain"), four volumes, Wilno, 1930.

Remarque, *Der Veg oyf Tsurik* (title means "The Road Back"), Wilno, 1930.

Moshe Smilansky, *Araber: Folkstimlekhe Geshikhtn* (title means "Arabs: Stories of the People"), Farn Folk (Warsaw), 1932.

Leon S. Glaser, *Fun Moskve biz Yerusholayim* (title means "From Moscow to Jerusalem"), Jankowitz, 1938.

OTHER

(Editor with Elaine Gottlieb) *Prism 2,* Twayne, 1965.

Visit to the Rabbinical Seminary in Cincinnati, [New York], 1965.

(With Ira Moscowitz) *The Hasidim: Paintings, Drawings, and Etchings,* Crown, 1973.

Nobel Lecture, Farrar, Straus, 1979.

The Gentleman from Cracow; The Mirror, illustrated with water colors by Raphael Soyer, introduction by Harry I. Moore, Limited Editions Club, 1979.

Isaac Bashevis Singer on Literature and Life, University of Arizona Press, 1979.

The Meaning of Freedom, United States Military Academy, 1981.

My Personal Conception of Religion, University of Southwestern Louisiana Press, 1982.

One Day of Happiness, Red Ozier Press, 1982.

Remembrances of a Rabbi's Son, translated by Rena Borrow, United Jewish Appeal-Federation Campaign, 1984.

(With Richard Burgin) *Conversations with Isaac Bashevis Singer,* Farrar, Straus, 1986.

The Safe Deposit and Other Stories about Grandparents, Old Lovers and Crazy Old Men ("Masterworks of Modern Jewish Writing" series), edited by Kerry M. Orlitzky, Wiener, Markus, 1989.

Also author under name Isaac Singer. Author of the introduction for Knut Hamsun's *Hunger,* Farrar, Straus, 1967, of the preface for Ruth Whitman's *An Anthology of Modern Yiddish Poetry,* Workmen's Circle, Education Department, 1979, and of the introduction and commentary for Richard Nagler's *My Love Affair with Miami Beach,* Simon & Schuster, 1991. Contributor to books, including *Tully Filmus,* edited by Anatol Filmus, Jewish Publication Society of America, 1971; and *Miami Beach,* by Gary Monroe, Forest & Trees, 1989. Also contributor of stories and articles to periodicals in the United States and Poland, including *Die Yiddische Welt, Commentary, Esquire, New Yorker, Globus, Literarishe Bletter, Harper's,* and *Partisan Review.* Made sound recordings entitled *Isaac Bashevis Singer Reading His Stories* (contains *Gimpel the Fool* and *The Man Who Came Back*), and *Isaac Bashevis Singer Reading His Stories in Yiddish* (contains *Big and Little, Shiddah and Kuziba,* and *The Man Who Came Back*), both Caedmon Records, both 1967. Singer's works are housed in the Elman Collection, Arents Research Library, Syracuse University, and at the Butler Library, Columbia University.

ADAPTATIONS: Filmstrips based on Singer's short stories include: *Isaac Singer and Mrs. Pupko's Bread,* New Yorker, 1973, *Rabbi Leib and the Witch Cunnegunde,* Miller-Brody Productions, 1976, and *Shrewd Todie and Lyzer the Miser,* Miller-Brody Productions, 1976; *Zlateh the Goat and Other Stories* was adapted into a film by Weston Woods, 1973, and broadcast on the National Broadcasting Company (NBC-TV), 1973; works adapted into recordings read by Eli Wallach include: *When Schlemiel Went to Warsaw and Other Stories,* Newbery Awards Records, 1974, *Zlateh the Goat and Other Stories,* Newbery Award Records, 1974, *Eli Wallach Reads Isaac Bashevis Singer* (contains *Zlateh the Goat and Other Stories* and *When Schlemiel Went to Warsaw and Other Stories*), Miller-Brody

From *Mazel and Shlimazel,* by Isaac Bashevis Singer. Illustrated by Margot Zemach.

Productions, 1976, and *Isaac Bashevis Singer* (contains *The Seance* and *The Lecture*), Spoken Arts, 1979; works adapted into filmstrips by Miller-Brody Productions include: *Zlateh the Goat and Other Stories, When Schlemiel Went to Warsaw,* and *Why Noah Chose the Dove,* all 1975, and *Mazel and Shlimazel,* 1976; *The Magician of Lublin* was adapted into a film starring Alan Arkin, produced by Menahem Golan, 1978; *Gimpel the Fool* was adapted for the stage by David Schechter and produced by the Bakery Theater Cooperative of New York, 1982; *Yentl, the Yeshiva Boy* was adapted into the movie *Yentl,* starring Barbara Streisand, Metro-Goldwyn-Mayer/United Artists, 1983; *Enemies: A Love Story* was adapted into a film by Paul Mazursky and Roger L. Simon and released by Twentieth Century-Fox, 1989; *The Family Moskat, The Slave, Satan in Goray, Passions and Other Stories,* and *In My Father's Court* were adapted into audio cassettes; twenty of Singer's works have been adapted into Braille editions; twelve of Singer's works have been adapted into talking books.

SIDELIGHTS: Widely proclaimed to be one of the foremost writers of Yiddish literature, Isaac Bashevis Singer stood clearly outside the mainstream and basic traditions of both Yiddish and American literature. Singer's writing proved difficult to categorize, with critics attaching to him various and sometimes contradictory labels in an attempt to define his work. He was called a modernist, although he personally disliked most contemporary fiction, and he was also accused of being captivated by the past, of writing in a dying language despite his English fluency, of setting his fiction in a world that no longer exists, the *shtetls* (Jewish ghettos) of Eastern Europe which were destroyed by Hitler's campaign against the Jews. And despite the attention called to the mysticism, the prolific presence of the supernatural, and the profoundly religious nature of his writing, Singer was called both a realist and a pessimist. Undeniably a difficult author to place in critical perspective, Singer addressed himself to the problems of labeling his work in an interview with Cyrene N. Pondrom for *Contemporary Literature:* "People always need a name for things, so whatever you will write or whatever you will do, they like to put you into a certain category. Even if you would be new, they would like to feel that a name is already prepared for you in advance . . . . I hope that one day somebody will find a new name for me, not use the old ones."

More than with most writers, the key to Singer's work lies in his background, in his roots in the Polish Yiddish-speaking Jewish ghettos. "I was born with the feeling that I am part of an unlikely adventure, something that couldn't have happened, but happened just the same," Singer once remarked to a *Book Week* interviewer. Born in a small Polish town, his father was a Hassidic rabbi and both his grandfathers were also rabbis. Visiting his maternal grandfather in Bilgoray as a young boy, Singer learned of life in the *shtetl,* which would become the setting of much of his later work. The young Singer received a basic Jewish education preparing him to follow his father and grandfathers' steps into the rabbinical vocation; he studied the Torah, the Talmud, the Cabala, and other sacred Jewish books. An even stronger influence than his education and his parents' orthodoxy was his older brother, the novelist I. J. Singer, who broke with the family's orthodoxy and began to write secular stories. Attempting to overcome the influence of his brother's rationalism and to strengthen the cause of religion, his parents told him stories of *dybbuks* (wandering souls in Jewish folklore believed to enter a human body and control its actions, possessions, and other spiritual mysteries). Singer once commented that he was equally fascinated by both his parents' mysticism and his brother's rationalism. Although he was eventually to break from both traditions, this dualism characterizes his writing.

Singer's desire to become a secular writer caused a painful conflict within himself and with his family; it represented a break from traditional ways. Eventually, Singer rejected his parents' orthodoxy, although not their faith in God. He joined his brother in Warsaw and began working for the Hebrew and Yiddish press and also began to publish stories. At first he wrote in Hebrew but switched to Yiddish because he felt that Hebrew was a dead language (this was before its revival as the national language of Israel). Feeling that the Nazis would certainly invade Poland, Singer followed his brother to the United States where he began to write for the *Jewish Daily Forward.* Here he wrote fiction under the name Isaac Bashevis and nonfiction under the pseudonym Isaac Warshofsky. Most of Singer's stories appeared first in the *Jewish Daily Forward* in their original Yiddish; the novels appeared in serialized form.

Singer continued to do all of his writing in Yiddish up to his death, and much of his large body of writing remains untranslated. Before he felt sufficiently fluent in English, Singer had to rely on other people to do the translations; his nephew Joseph Singer was responsible for much of it. Toward the end of his career though, Singer usually did a rough translation into English himself and then had someone help him polish the English version and work on the idioms. The English translations were often a "second original," according to Singer, differing structurally from the Yiddish. "I used to play with the idea [of writing in English]," Singer admitted in an interview with Joel Blocker and Richard Elman for *Commentary,* "but never seriously. Never. I always knew that a writer has to write in his own language or not at all."

Singer described Yiddish in his *Nobel Lecture* as "a language of exile, without a land, without frontiers, not supported by any government, a language which possesses no words for weapons, ammunition, military exercises, war tactics; a language that was despised by both gentiles and emancipated Jews . . . . Yiddish has not yet said its last word. It contains treasures that have not been revealed to the eyes of the world. It was the tongue of martyrs and saints, of dreamers and cabalists—rich in humor and in memories that mankind may never forget. In a figurative way, Yiddish is the wise and humble language of us all, the idiom of the frightened and hopeful humanity."

Aside from believing that he must write in his native tongue, Singer also believed that the function of his fiction should be entertainment. "I never thought that my fiction—my kind of writing—had any other purpose than to be read and enjoyed by the reader," he commented to Sanford Pinsker in *The Schlemiel as Metaphor: Studies in the Yiddish and American Jewish Novel.* "I never sit down to write a novel to make a better world or to create good feelings towards the Jews or for any other purpose," he continued. "I knew this from the very beginning, that writing fiction has no other purpose than to give enjoyment to a reader.... I consider myself an entertainer.... I mean an entertainer of good people, of intellectual people who cannot be entertained by cheap stuff. And I think this is true about fiction in all times."

Over the course of his career, Singer established himself as a renowned storyteller. Considered to be a master of the short story, it was his most effective and favorite genre because, as he once explained, it was more possible to be perfect in the short story than in a longer work. Also Singer did not think that the supernatural, which was his main element, lent itself well to longer, novelistic writing. Singer's style in the short story was simple, spare, and in the tradition of the spoken tale. In his *Commentary* interview, Singer remarked: "When I tell a story, I tell a story. I don't try to discuss, criticize, or analyze my characters." For Singer, his special stories, the ones that belonged to him, were placed for the most part in the nineteenth-and early twentieth-century *shtetl.* He was criticized for his overuse of this setting, with some critics suggesting that he was not effective in any other surrounding. In an interview for the *Atlantic* Singer told Lance Morrow: "I prefer to write about the world which I knew, which I know, best. This is Bilgoray, Lublin, the Jews of Kreshev. This is enough for me. I can get from these people art. I don't need to go to the North Pole and write a novel about the Eskimos who live in that neighborhood. I write about the things where I grew up, and where I feel completely at home."

Even Singer's children's stories are placed in the setting of his childhood home. And although he did not start writing for children until 1966, Singer claimed in *Top of the News:* "Children are the best readers of genuine literature. Grownups are hypnotized by big names, exaggerated quotes, and high pressure advertising. Critics who are more concerned with sociology than with literature have persuaded millions of readers that if a novel doesn't try to bring about a social revolution, it is of no value," he continued. "But children do not succumb to this kind of belief.... In our epoch, when storytelling has become a forgotten art and has been replaced by amateurish sociology and hackneyed psychology, the child is still the independent reader who relies on nothing but his own taste. Names and authorities mean nothing to him. Long after literature for adults will have gone to pieces, books for children will constitute that last vestige of storytelling, logic, faith in the family, in God and in real humanism."

Most of Singer's children's books are collections of short stories in which "religion and custom dominate life and a rich folktale tradition abounds," described Sylvia W. Iskander in the *Dictionary of Literary Biography.* A number of his stories are set in the humorous Polish city of Chelm—a town that Yiddish people view as a place of fools. And they also include *schlemiel* (eternal loser) characters, who naturally reside in the city of Chelm. They are essentially fools, but are portrayed as being charming and engaging, as is the city itself. Aside from these humorous and silly tales, Singer also wrote about animals and such supernatural beings as witches, goblins, devils, and demons. "Certainly the union of stories by a Nobel laureate storyteller with illustrations by some of the finest artists in the field of children's literature has produced outstanding books," concluded Iskander. "But it is the content of the stories—the combination of folklore, fairy tale, religion, and imagination—that makes Singer's books unique and inimitable."

WORKS CITED:

Iskander, Sylvia W., essay in *Dictionary of Literary Biography,* Volume 52: *American Writers for Children since 1960: Fiction,* Gale, 1986, pp. 334-52.

Pinsker, Sanford, *The Schlemiel as Metaphor: Studies in the Yiddish and American Jewish Novel,* Southern Illinois University Press, 1971.

Singer, Isaac Bashevis, in an interview for *Book Week,* July 4, 1965.

Singer, in an interview for *Top of the News,* November, 1972.

Singer, in an interview with Cyrene N. Pondrom, "Isaac Bashevis Singer: An Interview and Biographical Sketch, Part I," *Contemporary Literature,* winter, 1969, pp. 1-38; Part II, summer, 1969, pp. 332-51.

Singer, in an interview with Joel Blocker and Richard Elman, "An Interview with Isaac Bashevis Singer," *Commentary,* November, 1963, pp. 364-72.

Singer, in an interview with Lance Morrow, "The Spirited World of I. B. Singer," *Atlantic,* January, 1979, pp. 39-43.

Singer, *Nobel Lecture,* Farrar, Straus, 1979.

FOR MORE INFORMATION SEE:

BOOKS

Allentuck, Marcia, editor, *The Achievement of Isaac Bashevis Singer,* Southern Illinois University Press, 1967.

Authors in the News, Gale, Volume 1, 1976, Volume 2, 1976.

Buchen, Irving H., *Isaac Bashevis Singer and the Eternal Past,* New York University Press, 1968.

Children's Literature Review, Volume 1, Gale, 1976.

Concise Dictionary of American Literary Biography: The New Consciousness, 1941-1968, Gale, 1987.

Contemporary Literary Criticism, Gale, Volume 1, 1973, Volume 3, 1975, Volume 6, 1976, Volume 9,

1978, Volume 11, 1979, Volume 15, 1980, Volume 23, 1983, Volume 38, 1986.
Dictionary of Literary Biography, Gale, Volume 6: *American Novelists since World War II,* 1980, Volume 28: *Twentieth-Century American-Jewish Fiction Writers,* 1984.
Kazin, Alfred, *Bright Book of Life: American Novelists and Storytellers from Hemingway to Mailer,* Atlantic Monthly Press, 1973.
Kresh, Paul, *Isaac Bashevis Singer: The Magician of West 86th Street,* Dial, 1979.
Madison, Charles A., *Yiddish Literature: Its Scope and Major Writers,* Ungar, 1968.
Malin, Irving, editor, *Critical Views of Isaac Bashevis Singer,* New York University Press, 1969.
Malin, *Isaac Bashevis Singer,* Ungar, 1972.

PERIODICALS

Atlantic, August, 1962; January, 1965; July, 1970.
Best Sellers, October 1, 1970.
Books and Bookmen, October, 1973; December, 1974.
Book World, October 29, 1967; March 3, 1968; September 1, 1968; November 25, 1979.
Chicago Review, spring, 1980.
Chicago Tribune, October 25, 1980; June 23, 1987.
Chicago Tribune Book World, July 12, 1981; March 21, 1982; November 6, 1983; July 21, 1985.
Christian Science Monitor, October 28, 1967; September 5, 1978; September 18, 1978.
Commentary, November, 1958; October, 1960; February, 1965; February, 1979.
Critical Quarterly, spring, 1976.
Criticism, fall, 1963.
Critique, Volume 11, number 2, 1969; Volume 14, number 2, 1972.
Globe & Mail (Toronto), May 3, 1980; November 23, 1985; June 13, 1988.
Harper's, October, 1965; September, 1978.
Hudson Review, winter, 1966-67; spring, 1974.
Jewish Currents, November, 1962.
Jewish Quarterly, winter, 1966-67; autumn, 1972.
Judaism, fall, 1962; winter, 1974; spring, 1977; winter, 1979.
Kenyon Review, spring, 1964.
Los Angeles Times, November 8, 1978; December 28, 1981; November 18, 1983; March, 18, 1984; December 4, 1986; December 12, 1989.
Los Angeles Times Book Review, November 16, 1980; August 16, 1981; May 2, 1982; February 6, 1983; December 9, 1984; August 25, 1985; May 1, 1988.
Nation, November 19, 1983.
New Republic, November 24, 1958; January 2, 1961; November 13, 1961; June 18, 1962; November 3, 1973; October 25, 1975; September 16, 1978; October 21, 1978.
New Review, June, 1976.
Newsweek, June 26, 1972; November 12, 1973; April 12, 1982; September 26, 1983.
New York, December 31, 1979.
New Yorker, August 17, 1981.
New York Review of Books, April 22, 1965; February 7, 1974; December 7, 1978.
New York Times, October 30, 1966; January 29, 1967; July 10, 1978; July 22, 1978; December 9, 1978; October 17, 1979; December 5, 1979; December 16, 1979; December 17, 1979; April 19, 1980; June 15, 1982; November 30, 1982; September 22, 1983; October 7, 1984; November 7, 1984; October 30, 1985; November 17, 1985; June 24, 1986; September 28, 1986; November 8, 1986; July 6, 1987; April 12, 1988; May 18, 1989; July 30, 1989; December 10, 1989; December 13, 1989.
New York Times Book Review, December 29, 1957; June 26, 1960; October 22, 1961; June 17, 1962; November 15, 1964; October 8, 1967; June 25, 1972; November 4, 1973; November 2, 1975; April 30, 1978; July 23, 1978; October 28, 1979; January 18, 1981; June 21, 1981; January 31, 1982; March 21, 1982; November 14, 1982; September 25, 1983; November 11, 1984; June 30, 1985; October 27, 1985; October 16, 1988.
Paris Review, fall, 1968.
Publishers Weekly, February 18, 1983 (interview).
Saturday Review, January 25, 1958; November 25, 1961; June 16, 1962; November 21, 1964; September 19, 1970; July 22, 1972; July 8, 1978.
Sewanee Review, fall, 1974.
Southern Review, spring, 1972; spring, 1973.
Spectator, October 17, 1958; September 15, 1961; May 11, 1962; June 10, 1966.
Studies in Short Fiction, summer, 1974; fall, 1976.
Time, October 20, 1967; September 21, 1970; October 27, 1975; November 3, 1975; June 15, 1981; April 5, 1982; October 17, 1983; October 28, 1984; July 15, 1985.
Times (London), April 10, 1980; March 8, 1984.
Times Literary Supplement, January 2, 1959; May 4, 1962; April 11, 1980; July 16, 1982; July 22, 1983; March 23, 1984; October 19, 1984; May 3, 1985; April 4, 1986; May 1, 1987; October 21, 1988; September 1, 1989.
Tribune Books (Chicago), April 10, 1988; November 6, 1988.
Washington Post, October 6, 1978; October 16, 1979; October 26, 1979; November 4, 1981; September 17, 1984.
Washington Post Book World, November 30, 1980; June 28, 1981; March 28, 1982 (interview); November 7, 1982; July 7, 1985; September 21, 1986; October 23, 1988.

OTHER

Meet the Newbery Author: Isaac Bashevis Singer (filmstrip with cassette), Miller-Brody Productions, 1976.
Isaac Bashevis Singer (cassette), Tapes for Readers, 1978.

OBITUARIES:

PERIODICALS

Chicago Tribune, July 25, 1991, section 1, p. 11.
Detroit Free Press, July 25, 1991, p. 4A.
Horn Book, September/October, 1991, p. 654.
New York Times, July 26, 1991, p. B5.

School Library Journal, September, 1991, p. 173.
Time, August 5, 1991, p. 61.
Washington Post, July 26, 1991, p. C4.

* * *

SINGER, Marilyn 1948-

PERSONAL: Born October 3, 1948, in Manhattan, NY; daughter of Abraham (a photoengraver) and Shirley (Lax) Singer; married Steven Aronson (a financial manager), July 31, 1971. *Education:* Attended University of Reading, 1967-68; Queens College of the City University of New York, B.A. (cum laude), 1969; New York University, M.A., 1979. *Hobbies and other interests:* Studying Taoist meditation and exercise (Chi Kung, T'ai Chi), Hatha yoga, classical Chinese herbology, avant-garde and independent film, bird watching and caring for animals, tap dancing, singing, baseball, Japanese flower arranging.

ADDRESSES: Home and office—42 Berkeley Pl., Brooklyn, NY 11217.

CAREER: Daniel S. Mead Literary Agency, New York City, editor, 1967; *Where* (magazine), New York City, assistant editor, 1969; New York City Public High Schools, teacher of English and speech, 1969-74; writer, 1974—.

MEMBER: Society of Children's Book Writers, Author's Guild, PEN American Center, Nature Conservancy, Greenpeace, Phi Beta Kappa.

AWARDS, HONORS: Children's Choice Award, International Reading Association, 1977, for *The Dog Who Insisted He Wasn't,* 1979, for *It Can't Hurt Forever,* and 1988, for *Ghost Host;* Maud Hart Lovelace Award, Friends of the Minnesota Valley Regional Library (Mankato), 1983, for *It Can't Hurt Forever;* American Library Association (ALA) best book for young adults citation, 1983, for *The Course of True Love Never Did Run Smooth;* Parents' Choice Award, Parents' Choice Foundation, 1983, for *The Fido Frame-Up;* ALA best book for young adults nomination, 1988, for *Several Kinds of Silence; New York Times* best illustrated children's book citation, *Time* best children's book citation, both 1989, National Council of Teachers of English notable trade book in the language arts, 1990, and Texas Bluebonnet Award nomination, 1992, all for *Turtle in July.*

WRITINGS:

PICTURE BOOKS

The Dog Who Insisted He Wasn't, illustrated by Kelly Oechsli, Dutton, 1976.
The Pickle Plan, illustrated by Steven Kellogg, Dutton, 1978.
Will You Take Me to Town on Strawberry Day?, illustrated by Trinka Hakes Noble, Harper, 1981.
Archer Armadillo's Secret Room (Junior Literary Guild selection), illustrated by Beth Lee Weiner, Macmillan, 1985.

Marilyn Singer

Minnie's Yom Kippur Birthday, illustrated by Ruth Rosner, Harper, 1989.
Turtle in July, illustrated by Jerry Pinkney, Macmillan, 1989.
Nine O'Clock Lullaby, illustrated by Frane Lessac, HarperCollins, 1991.
The Golden Heart of Winter, illustrated by Robert Rayevsky, Morrow, 1991.
Out-of-Work Dog, illustrated by Cat Bowman Smith, Holt, 1992.
In My Tent, illustrated by Emily Arnold McCully, Macmillan, 1992.

CHILDREN'S FICTION

It Can't Hurt Forever, illustrated by Leigh Grant, Harper, 1978.
Tarantulas on the Brain (also see below), illustrated by Grant, Harper, 1982.
Lizzie Silver of Sherwood Forest (sequel to *Tarantulas on the Brain;* Junior Literary Guild selection), illustrated by Miriam Nerlove, Harper, 1986.
The Lightey Club, illustrated by Kathryn Brown, Four Winds, 1987.
Mitzi Meyer, Fearless Warrior Queen, Scholastic, 1987.
Charmed (fantasy), Atheneum, 1990.
Twenty Ways to Lose Your Best Friend, illustrated by Jeffrey Lindberg, Harper, 1990.
California Demon, Hyperion, 1992.

"SAM AND DAVE" MYSTERY SERIES

Leroy Is Missing, illustrated by Judy Glasser, Harper, 1984.
The Case of the Sabotaged School Play, illustrated by Glasser, Harper, 1984.
A Clue in Code, illustrated by Glasser, Harper, 1985.
The Case of the Cackling Car, illustrated by Glasser, Harper, 1985.

From *The Golden Heart of Winter,* by Marilyn Singer. Illustrated by Robert Rayevsky.

The Case of the Fixed Election, illustrated by Richard Williams, Harper, 1989.
The Hoax on You, illustrated by Williams, Harper, 1989.

"SAMANTHA SPAYED" MYSTERY SERIES

The Fido Frame-Up, illustrated by Andrew Glass, Warne, 1983.
A Nose for Trouble, illustrated by Glass, Holt, 1985.
Where There's a Will, There's a Wag, illustrated by Glass, Holt, 1986.

YOUNG ADULT FICTION

No Applause, Please, Dutton, 1977.
The First Few Friends, Harper, 1981.
The Course of True Love Never Did Run Smooth, Harper, 1983.
Horsemaster (fantasy), Atheneum, 1985.
Ghost Host, Harper, 1987.
Several Kinds of Silence, Harper, 1988.
Storm Rising, Scholastic, 1989.

NONFICTION

(Editor and author of introduction) *A History of Avant-Garde Cinema,* American Federation of Arts, 1976.
(Editor and contributor) *New American Filmmakers,* American Federation of Arts, 1976.
The Fanatic's Ecstatic, Aromatic Guide to Onions, Garlic, Shallots and Leeks, illustrated by Marian Perry, Prentice-Hall, 1981.
Exotic Birds (juvenile), illustrated by James Needham, Doubleday, 1990.

OTHER

Also author of several teacher's guides, catalogs, and program notes on films and filmstrips, including Jacob Bronowski's *The Ascent of Man* and David Attenborough's *The Tribal Eye.* Past curator of *SuperFilmShow!,* a series of avant-garde films selected for children. Writer of scripts for the children's television show *The Electric Company.* Contributor of short stories to books, including *Rooms of Our Own,* Holt, 1992; also contributor of poetry to periodicals, including *Yes, Archer, Encore, Corduroy, Tamesis,* and *Gyre.*

WORK IN PROGRESS: Maiden on the Moor, a picture book fairy tale; *In the Palace of the Ocean King,* a picture book fairy tale; *The Painted Fan,* a picture book fairy tale; *Read a Map with a Beagle on Your Lap,* a collection of poetry; *Sky Words,* a collection of poetry; *Dogs,* nonfiction; and *Big Wheel,* a children's novel.

SIDELIGHTS: Marilyn Singer's writings encompass a variety of genres, including picture books, juvenile mysteries, and young adult fantasies. Among her many characters are a dog who insists he isn't a dog, an armadillo, a young heart surgery patient, obsessive Lizzie Silver, Stryker the mischievous ghost, twin detectives named Sam and Dave—even a dog detective! "People often ask me why I write so many different kinds of things," remarks Singer in an essay for *Something about the Author Autobiography Series* (*SAAS*). "I tell them it's because I have so many different parts to my personality, and each part has a different way of expressing itself. I tell them too that I like to challenge myself so that I'll never be bored."

Singer was born in Manhattan in 1948, the result of a bet between her parents. Because her first child had been stillborn, Singer's mother was afraid to try again. Her father was anxious for a child, though, so he dared his wife to pick the winning team for the 1948 Rose Bowl. She lost the bet, and Singer was born nine months later. Singer spent the first five years of her life in the Bronx, living with her parents in her grandmother's apartment. She shared the same bed with her grandmother in the living room at this time, and continued to share a room with her until she was twelve. "I don't think I ever would have become a writer if it hadn't been for Grandma Frieda," claims Singer in her autobiographical essay. "Every night before I went to sleep, she would tell me a marvelous tale.... My grandmother made me feel that the world is magical, beautiful, always interesting, always unique."

Singer's sister was born in 1953 and the family moved to North Massapequa, Long Island. Singer had mixed feelings about the new addition to the family and the move, especially after her father began commuting to the city and had less time to spend with her. There were many good things about the new neighborhood, however, including a larger house, a backyard, and actual woods down the street. It was at this time that Singer began writing. Poems were and still are her favorite form, but she also experimented with plays, this early love of the theater eventually carrying over into many of her books. "It seemed in those years that my childhood would remain pretty carefree," comments Singer in her *SAAS* essay.

In 1956, though, Singer had to undergo heart surgery, and the fact that her parents and doctor kept the truth of her illness from her was more traumatic than the actual surgery. Years later, Singer dealt with her emotional wounds in her 1978 novel *It Can't Hurt Forever.* In this fictionalized version of her experience, Singer presents Ellie Simon, who is to enter the hospital for the same corrective heart surgery Singer had. Unlike Singer, however, Ellie is told what is going to happen to her, with the exception of the catheterization she must undergo. When she learns of it, she tells off the doctors and her parents, just as Singer wished she had done. Singer "provides an honest and thorough look at pre- and post-operative care and at the concerns of a girl facing a major trauma," points out Karen Harris in *School Library Journal.* And a *Kirkus Reviews* contributor concludes that *It Can't Hurt Forever* is "sharp, fast, funny, genuinely serious, and helpfully informative."

The year following her operation, Singer encountered a different kind of trauma—she became unpopular at school. "Throughout junior high and high school, my popularity remained in total decline," recalls Singer in her autobiographical essay. "I took solace in books. I discovered William Shakespeare, who, to this day, remains my favorite author. I kept writing poetry. I told myself that if I couldn't be popular, then at least I'd be cultured." When it came time for college, Singer wanted to go away to school, but her parents saw no reason for this when there was a perfectly good and inexpensive one nearby. In 1965, she began attending Queens College, a branch of the City University of New York, as an education student.

Nobody at Queens College knew about Singer's unpopular high school years, so she was able to start over. Michal, a "smaller, younger and even smarter" girl than Singer, soon became her most important friend at college. "She would be the ringleader of our gang of New York crazies and introduce me to many memorable people, places, and things," reveals Singer in her *SAAS* essay. Although Singer enjoyed her classes at Queens College, she soon grew tired of living at home. When the college sponsored a Junior Year Abroad program to England for the first time, Singer jumped at the chance. She was eventually selected as one of five students to go; and after a summer of working to raise the money, Singer boarded the ocean liner for the ten day voyage. Upon arriving in England, Singer and her new friend Eileen quickly grew weary of the regimented tours and went out on their own for some sightseeing, especially enjoying the British nightlife. They soon discovered that Reading University was only thirty miles away, so they decided early on to commute to London for the weekends.

While in England, Singer made a large number of friends and was invited to stay with people throughout Great Britain, enabling her to see many parts of the country. School was equally exciting and stimulating. "There were always discussions going on, often till the wee hours of the morning," explains Singer in her autobiographical essay. "We talked about art and poetry and truth and beauty and life and death and sex and anything else we could think of. My room became the hub of much group philosophizing. My popularity, which had been so low in high school, reached a zenith here." This, along with her new-found freedom, made it difficult for Singer to go home to the States. Returning to Queens College, Singer finished her last year there and then moved to an apartment in New York City. She began teaching and became very committed to her job. "I wanted to inspire my students, to make literature come alive for them, to make school a pleasure and not a chore," remembers Singer in her *SAAS* essay.

Singer's teaching career continued, and in 1970 she met her future husband, Steve Aronson. He had come to New York from Wisconsin to become an actor, and she met him in the record store at which he worked. A year and a half later, they were visiting some of Singer's friends in England when they decided to get married. "Marrying Steve was one of the best decisions I ever made," maintains Singer in her autobiographical essay. "For the twenty-two years we have been together, Steve has been my best friend—and my toughest, though kindest, critic. Without his support and encouragement I very much doubt that I would have had the nerve to quit teaching in June 1973 and become a writer."

Singer began her writing career doing teaching guides on film and filmstrips, and, although she enjoyed the work for a while, she was not entirely satisfied. She also began looking into magazine writing. Her article proposals were not very successful, but she did manage to have some of her poetry published. The following year, however, brought a major turning point in Singer's life. She was sitting in the Brooklyn Botanic Garden with a pad of paper and a pen in case she wanted to write a new poem, when she suddenly found herself writing a story instead. Upon seeing this first story, her husband encouraged her to write more, so Singer wrote a number of children's stories featuring animals and mailed them off to publishers. In the meantime, she joined a workshop for unpublished children's authors and continued writing. Then one day she received a letter from Dutton, telling her that they wanted to publish one of her books—*The Dog Who Insisted He Wasn't.* "I barely got through reading the letter before I let out a scream," relates Singer in her *SAAS* essay. "A book! A published book! I was about to become an author! A children's author! How extraordinary! How fine! I had a new career. One that might make me if not rich, at least a little bit wealthier, if not famous, at least a little better known. It was perfect. It was right."

In *The Dog Who Insisted He Wasn't* Singer tells the story of Konrad the dog, who is absolutely positive that he is not a dog, but a person instead. He is lucky enough to find Abigail, who convinces her family to go along with Konrad and treat him as a human. Konrad sits at the table to eat, takes baths, and even goes to school. When the other dogs in the neighborhood decide that they too want to be treated like people, all chaos breaks loose. They are eventually convinced to go back to their carefree lives as dogs, and Konrad compromises by agreeing to pretend he's a dog. Although animals pretending to be human has been done before, writes Carol Chatfield in *School Library Journal,* "Konrad is a canine with a winning personality, and Singer's text has enough vitality and action to make it a good choice for reading aloud to one or two children."

The writings Singer has published since *The Dog Who Insisted He Wasn't* cover a wide range of topics and are directed toward various age groups. Among her works for middle grade children are two novels about the obsessions of a young girl named Lizzie Silver. *Tarantulas on the Brain* has ten-year-old Lizzie doing everything she can to earn enough money to buy a pet tarantula. She tries having a junk sale and even works as a magician's assistant to get the necessary money, lying to her mother about what she's doing. In the end, her secret desire and activities are discovered and everyone is much more sympathetic than Lizzie imagined they would be. "The pace" of *Tarantulas on the Brain* "is fast and exciting; the characters are sufficiently quirky to keep the readers engrossed and narrator Lizzie Silver, 10, wins their affections," asserts a *Publishers Weekly* reviewer. In the sequel to *Tarantulas on the Brain, Lizzie Silver of Sherwood Forest,* Lizzie's new preoccupations include her desires to be one of Robin Hood's merry followers and to learn how to play the harp so she can attend the same music school as her best friend. *Lizzie Silver of Sherwood Forest* is a "funny, touching sequel," states a *Publishers Weekly* contributor, adding: "This is an adroitly balanced and enjoyable tale about a naive and eager girl."

Mysteries and young adult fantasy novels are also among Singer's writings. The "Sam and Dave" mystery series stars two young twins who are able to solve the little mysteries that crop up in their everyday lives. *A Clue in Code* has the detectives in search of the thief who stole the class trip money. There is an obvious suspect who insists he's innocent, so Sam and Dave embark on an investigation. "Singer's ability to subtly incorporate the necessary facts of the case into the narrative demonstrates her respect for young readers eager for satisfying mysteries they can solve on their own," points out a *Booklist* reviewer. Elements of the supernatural are introduced into Singer's young adult novel *Ghost Host.* Bart Hawkins seems to have an ideal life—he is the quarterback of the high school football team and dates Lisa, the captain of the cheerleading squad. He secretly loves to read, though, and fears that if this gets out he'll be labelled a nerd. When he discovers that his new house is haunted by Stryker, an nasty poltergeist, his life is thrown into chaos and he must enlist the help of a friendly ghost and the class brain to pacify Stryker. "*Ghost Host* is above all else fun to read," maintains Randy Brough in *Voice of Youth Advocates.* "Singer's deft introduction of the supernatural into the world of a high school junior, his family, and friends creates headaches for everyone, ghosts included."

In her autobiographical essay, Singer mentions that people often ask her why she writes books for children and young adults instead of for a more mature audience. "I've given them a lot of answers such as 1) Kids are interesting to write about and for; 2) If you understand the child in yourself, you can understand the grown-up better. I want to understand myself better; 3) There's nothing else I know how to do. All of these answers are basically true. But now I think the truest, most honest answer I can give is that I write books for children and young adults because I like to."

WORKS CITED:

Brough, Randy, review of *Ghost Host, Voice of Youth Advocates,* June, 1987, p. 83.

Chatfield, Carol, review of *The Dog Who Insisted He Wasn't, School Library Journal,* February, 1977, p. 58.

Review of *A Clue in Code, Booklist,* September 15, 1985, p. 140.

Harris, Karen, review of *It Can't Hurt Forever, School Library Journal,* September, 1978, p. 149.

Review of *It Can't Hurt Forever, Kirkus Reviews,* October 15, 1978, p. 1140.

Review of *Lizzie Silver of Sherwood Forest, Publishers Weekly,* June 27, 1986, pp. 91-92.

Singer, Marilyn, essay in *Something about the Author Autobiography Series,* Volume 13, Gale, 1992, pp. 181-99.

Review of *Tarantulas on the Brain, Publishers Weekly,* July 9, 1982, p. 49.

FOR MORE INFORMATION SEE:

PERIODICALS

Horn Book, July-August, 1989, p. 478; January, 1990.

Publishers Weekly, June 1, 1984, p. 65; February 22, 1985, p. 158; April 24, 1987, p. 71; May 12, 1989, p. 291; April 13, 1990, p. 64.

Science Fiction Review, May, 1985, p. 34.

School Library Journal, December, 1982, pp. 68-69; May, 1984, p. 102; May, 1985, p. 110; September, 1985, p. 149; December, 1985, pp. 82-83; October, 1986, p. 83; May, 1987, p. 104; September, 1987, pp. 182-83; August, 1989, p. 132; November, 1989, p. 99; June, 1990, p. 126; December, 1990, pp. 111-12.

Voice of Youth Advocates, August, 1985, p. 164; June, 1986, p. 83; December, 1990, p. 302.

* * *

SLEATOR, William (Warner III) 1945-

PERSONAL: Surname is pronounced "*slay*-tir"; born February 13, 1945, in Havre de Grace, MD; son of William Warner, Jr. (a professor) and Esther (a physician; maiden name, Kaplan) Sleator. *Education:* Harvard University, B.A., 1967; studied musical composition in London, England, 1967-68. *Politics:* Independent.

ADDRESSES: Home—77 Worcester St., Boston, MA 02118. *Agent*—Sheldon Fogelman, 10 East Fortieth St., New York, NY 10016.

CAREER: Royal Ballet School, London, England, accompanist, 1967-68; Rambert School, London, accompanist, 1967-68; Boston Ballet Company, Boston, MA, rehearsal pianist, 1974-83; writer.

AWARDS, HONORS: Bread Loaf Writers' Conference fellowship, 1969; Caldecott Medal Honor Book, American Library Association, and *Boston Globe-Horn Book* Award, both 1971, American Book Award for Best Paperback Picture Book, 1981, American Library Association (ALA) Notable Book citation, and *Horn Book* Honor List citation, all for *The Angry Moon;* Children's Book of the Year Award, Child Study Association of America, 1972, and ALA Notable Book citation, both for *Blackbriar;* Best Books for Young Adults citations, American Library Association, 1974, for *House of Stairs,* 1984, for *Interstellar Pig,* 1985, for *Singularity,* and 1987, for *The Boy Who Reversed Himself;* Best of the Best for Young Adults citation, ALA Notable Book citation, *Horn Book* Honor List citation, and Junior Literary Guild selection, all for *Interstellar Pig;* Children's Choice Award, International Reading Association and Children's Book Council, and Junior Literary Guild selection, both for *Into the Dream;* Best Book of

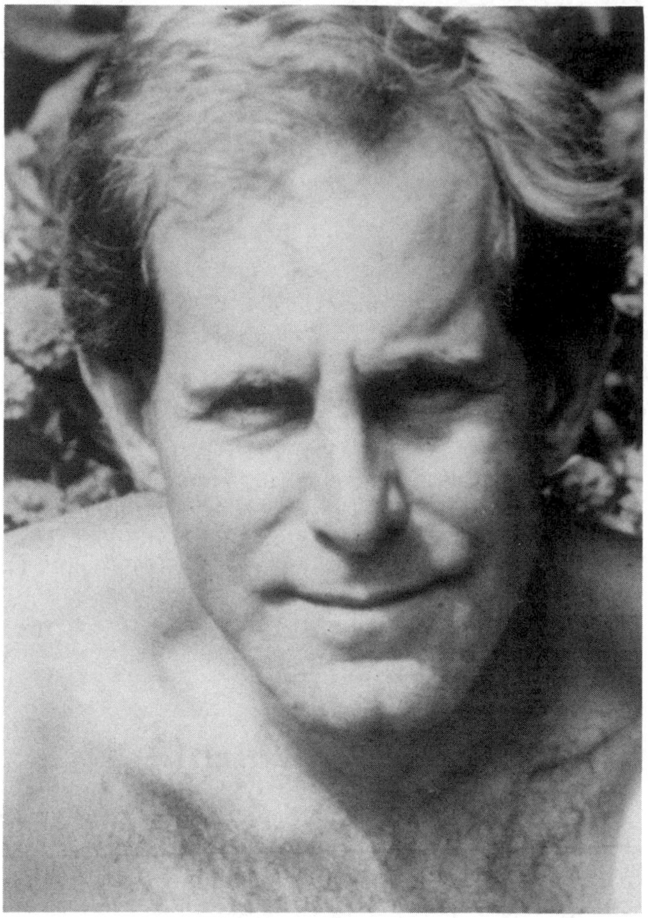

William Sleator

the Year awards, *School Library Journal,* 1981, for *The Green Futures of Tycho,* 1983, for *Fingers,* and 1984, for *Interstellar Pig;* Junior Literary Guild selection, for *Singularity;* Golden Pen Award, Spokane Washington Public Library, 1984 and 1985, both for "the author who gives the most reading pleasure."

WRITINGS:

The Angry Moon (picture book; retelling of a Tlingit Indian tale), illustrated by Blair Lent, Little, Brown, 1970.
Blackbriar (juvenile), illustrated by Lent, Dutton, 1972.
Run (mystery), Dutton, 1973.
House of Stairs (juvenile), Dutton, 1974.
Among the Dolls, illustrated by Trina Schart Hyman, Dutton, 1975.
(With William H. Redd) *Take Charge: A Personal Guide to Behavior Modification* (adult), Random House, 1977.
Into the Dream, illustrated by Ruth Sanderson, Dutton, 1979.
Once, Said Darlene, illustrated by Steven Kellogg, Dutton, 1979.
The Green Futures of Tycho (young adult), Dutton, 1981.
That's Silly (easy reader), illustrated by Lawrence Di-Fiori, Dutton, 1981.
Fingers (young adult), Dutton, 1983.
Interstellar Pig (young adult), Dutton, 1984.
Singularity (young adult), Dutton, 1985.
The Boy Who Reversed Himself (young adult), Dutton, 1986.
The Duplicate (young adult), Dutton, 1988.
Strange Attractors (young adult), Dutton, 1990.
The Spirit House, Dutton, 1991.

Also composer, with Blair Lent, of musical score for animated film *Why the Sun and Moon Live in the Sky,* 1972; composer of scores for professional ballets and amateur films and plays.

ADAPTATIONS: The Angry Moon is available on audiocassette, distributed by Read-Along-House; *Interstellar Pig* is available on audiocassette, distributed by Listening Library, 1987.

WORK IN PROGRESS: Oddballs, stories about growing up; *Others See Us.*

SIDELIGHTS: Recipient of numerous "best book" awards, William Sleator is a popular science fiction writer for both children and young adults. Blending fantasy with reality, his stories depict ordinary teenagers going about their daily lives—gardening, for example, or vacationing at the beach. However, fantastic incidents involving aliens or clones, to name just a few, suddenly disrupt these familiar routines, and the characters are forced into action. "I prefer science fiction that has some basis in reality," Sleator told *Authors and Artists for Young Adults* (*AAYA*), "psychological stories, time-travel stories, but especially stories about people."

Born in Maryland in 1945, Sleator had an early interest in science. "Everybody in my family is a scientist except me," he revealed in *AAYA.* "I always liked science but was never good enough to be a real scientist." He also discovered that he enjoyed playing the piano, reading, and writing—hobbies that allowed him to express his love of the supernatural and bizarre. "Everything I did," he remembered in *AAYA,* "the stories I wrote, the music I played, had an element of weirdness to it. I suppose it came from the kind of stories, mostly science fiction, I read as a kid."

For many years Sleator wavered between a writing career and a musical career. He entered Harvard University in 1963, for example, intent on pursuing a degree in music; however, he later changed his mind and graduated with his bachelor's in English. He then moved to London, England, where he resumed his study of musical composition and also worked as a pianist in ballet schools. He was drawn back into writing, though, after he helped a coworker restore a run-down cottage and became curious about the building's bizarre history. "The place was interesting," he recalled in *AAYA,* "way out in the middle of the woods, and eerie with graffiti from 1756 on the walls. There were burial mounds nearby where druids [members of an ancient priesthood] were buried and festivals were held. The whole thing was like a Gothic novel. So there was my first [novel], *Blackbriar,* handed right to me." By 1974

Sleator had returned to the United States and joined the Boston Ballet Company as an accompanist. But after spending the next nine years juggling rehearsals, ballet tours, and writing, he finally quit the company to become a full-time author.

Among Sleator's more than fifteen books for children and young adults are *House of Stairs* and *Into the Dream,* two stories that focus on the human mind. The former tells of five young orphans who find themselves imprisoned in an area with no walls, ceiling, or floors—only row upon row of stairs. Realizing they are subjects in a bizarre psychological experiment, they struggle to prevent a large food-dispensing machine from completely controlling their responses. In the latter story, *Into the Dream,* two classmates possess extrasensory perception, which includes the ability to see into the future. Foretelling danger, they work together to locate and warn the intended victim of a kidnapping, a young boy who has the extraordinary power to move objects without touching them. *Into the Dream* is "a thriller of top-notch quality," wrote a reviewer for *Booklist.*

In *The Green Futures of Tycho* and *Interstellar Pig,* Sleator turned to the subjects of time travel and extraterrestrials. In the first story, a boy discovers a strange, egg-shaped object buried in his garden. Realizing it allows him to travel through time, he makes frequent trips to the future, where he meets his adult self. However, with each venture forward in time, he sees this adult self becoming more evil and distorted. Finally he realizes he must travel into the past to return the object to its original place. In *Interstellar Pig,* sixteen-year-old Barney is on vacation at the beach when three neighbors move into a nearby cottage. Invited to join their game called "Interstellar Pig," Barney readily accepts; however, he soon finds out that his neighbors are really aliens in disguise who plan to kill him. As Rosalie Byard concluded in the *New York Times Book Review:* "Eery menace penetrates the humdrum normality of the summer holiday scene in a convincing evolution from unsettling situation to waking nightmare."

In his book *Singularity,* Sleator explores the existence of other universes. Sixteen-year-old twins Barry and Harry discover that a playhouse on their uncle's property is built over a singularity—a hole that connects two separate galaxies. Strange cosmic debris keeps appearing through the hole, and the twins find out that their uncle feared the arrival of a dangerous, intergalactic monster. Yet only Harry possesses the courage to venture inside and stand guard. "The details of Harry's year in the playhouse are fascinating," judged Anne A. Flowers in *Horn Book,* who also declared the book "an unusual, suspenseful yarn told by a master storyteller."

Sleator still harbors an interest in music and would one day like to compose scores for films. But he continues to write books and considers his role as a science fiction author for young people to be of utmost importance. "My goal is to entertain my audience and to get them to read," he told *AAYA.* "I want kids to find out that reading is the best entertainment there is. If, at the same time, I'm also imparting some scientific knowledge, then that's good, too. I'd like kids to see that science is not just boring formulas. Some of the facts to be learned about the universe are very weird."

Sleator told *Major Authors and Illustrators for Children and Young Adults:* "I now divide my time between Boston, Massachusetts, and Bangkok, Thailand. I feel more at home in Thailand than in practically any other place I can think of. Partly this is because Thailand is so exotic that it feels almost like being on another planet. (Don't ask me why THAT should make me feel at home.) I also like Thai people because they turn almost any situation into an occasion to have fun; and because they are so pleasant and polite that you never know what is *really* going on in their minds, so they are a mysterious puzzle to try to figure out. It's also a lot of fun to be learning how to speak Thai, which is about as different a language from English as you could imagine. Try pronouncing a word that begins with the sound *ng,* and you'll begin to get an idea of how challenging it is."

Cover of *Fingers,* by William Sleator.

WORKS CITED:

Byard, Rosalie, review of *Interstellar Pig, New York Times Book Review,* September 23, 1984, p. 47.
Flowers, Ann A., review of *Singularity, Horn Book,* May, 1985, pp. 320-321.
Review of *Into the Dream, Booklist,* February 15, 1979, p. 936.
"William Sleator," *Authors and Artists for Young Adults,* Volume 5, Gale, 1991, pp. 207-215.

FOR MORE INFORMATION SEE:

BOOKS

Davis, James and Hazel, *Presenting William Sleator,* Macmillan, 1992.
Roginski, Jim, *Behind the Covers: Interviews with Authors and Illustrators of Books for Children and Young Adults,* Libraries Unlimited, 1985.

PERIODICALS

Booklist, April 1, 1981; January 15, 1990.
Bulletin of the Center for Children's Books, June, 1985; January, 1987; April, 1988; November, 1989.
Fantasy Review, December, 1986.
Horn Book, January, 1987; May, 1988.
Publishers Weekly, July 17, 1972.
School Library Journal, October, 1983; September, 1984; August, 1985; April, 1988; December, 1989.
Voice of Youth Advocates, April, 1985; October, 1985.

* * *

SLEPIAN, Jan(ice B.) 1921-

PERSONAL: Surname is pronounced "*slep*-ee-an"; born January 2, 1921, in New York, NY; daughter of Louis (an engineer) and Florence (a housewife; maiden name, Ellinger) Berek; married Urey Krasnopolsky, October, 1945 (divorced, 1948); married David Slepian (a mathematician), April 18, 1950; children: Steven, Don, Anne. *Education:* Brooklyn College, B.A., 1942; University of Washington, M.A. (clinical psychology), 1947; New York University, M.A. (speech pathology), 1964; attended University of California—Berkeley, 1979. *Hobbies and other interests:* Mycology, reading, music, swimming.

ADDRESSES: Home and office—212 Summit Ave., Summit, NJ 07901. *Agent*—Sheldon Fogelman, 10 East 40th St., New York, NY 10016.

CAREER: Massachusetts General Hospital, Boston, MA, language therapist, 1947-49; private speech thera-

Jan Slepian

pist, 1952-58; Red Seal Clinic, Newton, NJ, speech therapist, 1953-55; Matheny School for Cerebral Palsy, Farhills, NJ, speech therapist, 1955-57; writer.

MEMBER: Society of Children's Book Writers, Authors Guild.

AWARDS, HONORS: The Alfred Summer was named one of the best books of the year by *School Library Journal,* 1980, and was named a notable book by the American Library Association; American Book Award finalist in children's fiction, and *Boston Globe-Horn Book* Honor for fiction, both 1981, for *The Alfred Summer;* Author's awards, New Jersey Institute of Technology, 1981, for *The Alfred Summer,* and 1983, for *The Night of the Bozos; Lester's Turn* was named one of the best books for children by the *New York Times,* and a notable children's book for older readers by *School Library Journal,* both 1981, a notable children's trade book in social studies by *Social Education,* and one of New York Public Library's books for the teen age, both 1982, and a notable book by the American Library Association; *The Night of the Bozos* was named one of the best books for young adults by the American Library Association, one of the children's books of the year by the Child Study Association of America, and one of the books of the year by the Library of Congress, all 1983; *Something beyond Paradise* was named one of the ten great books of the year for teens by *Redbook,* 1987; *The Broccoli Tapes* was named a notable book by the American Library Association, 1989; *Booklist* Editor's Choice, 1989, for *The Broccoli Tapes,* and 1990, for *Risk n' Roses; Risk n' Roses* was named one of New York Public Library's best books, 1990.

WRITINGS:

"LISTEN-HEAR" PICTURE BOOK SERIES; ALL WITH ANN SEIDLER; ALL ILLUSTRATED BY RICHARD E. MARTIN

Alphie and the Dream Machine, Follett, 1964.
The Cock Who Couldn't Crow, Follett, 1964.
Lester and the Sea Monster, Follett, 1964.
Magic Arthur and the Giant, Follett, 1964
Mister Sipple and the Naughty Princess, Follett, 1964.
The Roaring Dragon of Redrose, Follett, 1964.

"JUNIOR LISTEN-HEAR" PICTURE BOOK SERIES; ALL WITH SEIDLER; ALL ILLUSTRATED BY MARTIN

Bendemolena, Follett, 1967, published as *The Cat Who Wore a Pot on Her Head,* Scholastic Inc., 1981.
Ding-Dong, Bing-Bong, Follett, 1967.
An Ear Is to Hear, Follett, 1967.
The Hungry Thing, Follett, 1967.
The Silly Listening Book, Follett, 1967.

FOR CHILDREN; WITH SEIDLER

The Best Invention of All, illustrated by Joseph Veno, Crowell-Collier, 1967.
The Hungry Thing Returns, illustrated by Martin, Scholastic Inc., 1990.

NOVELS FOR YOUNG ADULTS

The Alfred Summer, Macmillan, 1980.

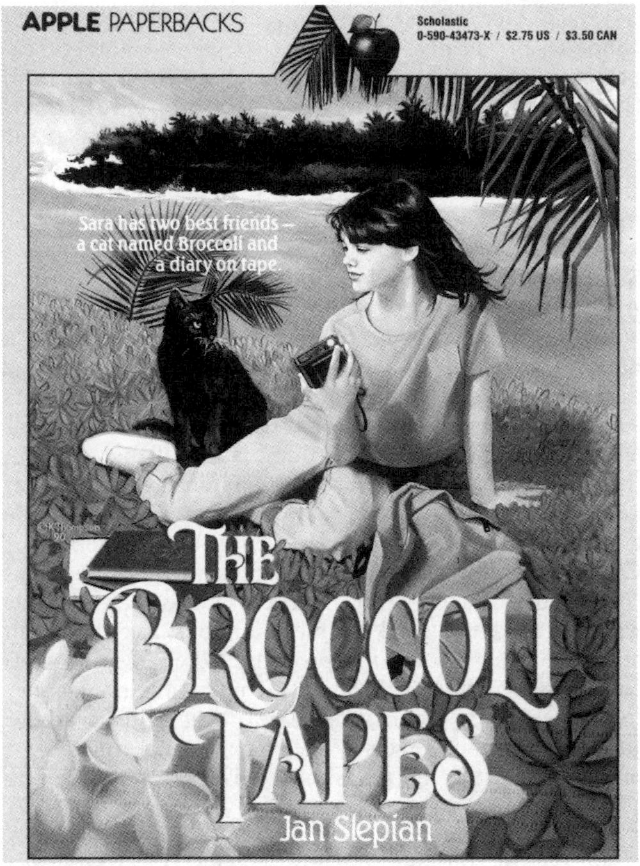

Cover of *The Broccoli Tapes,* by Jan Slepian.

Lester's Turn (sequel to *The Alfred Summer*), Macmillan, 1981.
The Night of the Bozos, Dutton, 1983.
Getting On with It (Junior Literary Guild selection), Four Winds, 1985.
Something beyond Paradise (Junior Literary Guild selection), Philomel, 1987.
The Broccoli Tapes, Putnam, 1989.
Risk n' Roses, Philomel, 1990.
Back to Before, Philomel, in press.

OTHER

Building Foundations for Better Speech and Reading (teachers' training series and cassette tape program; with twelve tapes and discussion guide), Instructional Dynamics Inc., 1974.

Contributor of advice on speech problems, with Ann Seidler, to newspaper column "Parents Ask."

Slepian's works are included in the Kerlan Collection at the University of Minnesota.

WORK IN PROGRESS: The Christmas Moose and *Emily Just in Time,* both picture books, for Philomel; *The Hungry Thing Goes to a Restaurant,* a picture book, for Scholastic Inc.

SIDELIGHTS: Jan Slepian has earned praise for her work on young adult novels that champion society's outcasts. Her characters, many of whom are handicapped—physically, mentally, socially—undergo experiences that cause them to learn about themselves and the world around them while they cope with their afflictions. By beginning her career as a novelist at the relatively late age of 57, Slepian benefited from a wide range of exposure to different experiences and environments which she has often incorporated in her stories.

Slepian had no immediate desire to become a writer. After raising a family with her husband David, she worked with fellow speech therapist Ann Seidler on a handful of articles that discussed children's language difficulties. They submitted these articles to "Parents Ask," a newspaper column that dealt with child psychology. Excited by the ensuing publication of their advice, they collaborated on two series of picture books that dealt with various speech-related topics. Over a decade later, Slepian took an English class at the University of California—Berkeley and was exposed to the genre of young adult novels. Her instructor, who was familiar with her student's work on picture books, asked Slepian about her current writing projects. When Slepian conceded that she was through with writing books, her teacher chided: "Oh no, you're not. You're just ready to go on to something else." This experience played an important part in her decision to write novels for young adults.

Upon completing her first novel, *The Alfred Summer,* Slepian was overcome with joy. She revealed in an autobiographical sketch for the *Something about the Author Autobiography Series:* "I've had many golden moments in my life, but this was something quite different. More than anything in the world I had wanted to write a decent book, and that night I knew that I had. I said to myself, 'You are fifty-seven years old and this is one of the most happy moments of your life.' It seemed to me remarkable that I could say that at my age." Her story details the experiences of four outcast children, including Lester, who is afflicted by cerebral palsy, and Alfred, who is mentally retarded. Together the kids work to construct a small boat, which they call the Getaway. "It is a name they all understand, each in his own terms," assessed Natalie Babbitt of the *New York Times Book Review,* "for they are all prisoners of one kind or another." The inspiration for the title character was provided by Slepian's mentally retarded brother. The real-life Alfred was a source of both joy and anguish for Slepian and her family as the author was growing up in the Brighton Beach section of Brooklyn, New York. "Only aware that Alfred was the cause of fights between my parents, I hated him. People acted funny around him, and he made my mother cry and my father angry," Slepian revealed in her autobiographical sketch. "Yet at the same time I was attached. He was sweet and laughed at my jokes and he was my brother. I learned early that you can hold within yourself contradictory feelings."

The initial story line of *The Alfred Summer* is rooted in an experience that Slepian recalled from her childhood. Her mother had tried to find a friend for Alfred by asking the mother of a child with cerebral palsy if the two boys could play together. The second woman refused to let her Lester associate with the mentally retarded Alfred, "saying that she wanted her son to play only with normal kids. When I remembered that," the author recounted in her autobiography, "I realized I had a what-if story. What if Lester and Alfred had become friends?" After its publication, *The Alfred Summer* received several distinctions. It was named a *Boston Globe-Horn Book* Award Honor Book and was cited as one of the best books of the year by *School Library Journal.* The critical acclaim that *The Alfred Summer* received caused Slepian to reevaluate her brother's impact on other people. "My mother and father thought his life was blasted, wasted," she explained in her autobiographical sketch. "In a sense it was, of course. He still sits in a hospital like a bundle from the lost and found. But in another sense his life wasn't a waste. Because of this book, that's all turned around. He has reached and affected many, many people, more than most of us 'normals' have. Such is the power of words."

The Alfred Summer spawned a sequel that won further praise for its author. *Lester's Turn* begins after Alfred's mother dies. The mentally retarded child is subsequently placed under the guardianship of a hospital. Distraught over the effect of institutionalization on his friend, Lester tries to kidnap Alfred but fails. The hospital eventually allows him to take Alfred out of the building on a trial basis. Alfred becomes ill, however, and is hurried back to the hospital where he dies of a burst appendix. Lester then realizes that his efforts to attend to his friend's needs merely helped him to avoid facing his own problems while Alfred was alive. Impressed by the two novels, Babbitt of the *New York Times Book Review* noted that "Slepian's use of the language is rich, often funny, always fresh, and both stories are worth telling, a condition that has become increasingly rare in novels for young readers."

Just as Slepian used Lester as a model for one of her characters, she has often drawn upon characteristics of her own life and the places that she has visited to flesh out her stories. Her first two novels were both set in Slepian's home community of Brighton Beach. Her character Claire, who appears in both *The Alfred Summer* and *Lester's Turn,* inherited Slepian's methods for overcoming the timidity that the author felt as a child. In her autobiography, Slepian admitted to being a "morbidly shy" first grader—she even ran home from school one day and hid in a clothes hamper until her mother found her. As an adolescent, she began to get over her shyness. "Somehow I got the idea that if I could act as if I were confident and easy, people wouldn't know how I felt inside," she recounted in her autobiography. "I found out that when you pretend something long enough, you wind up believing it yourself. As time went by, the act became real. It was less of an act and more the true me.... I gave this early discovery of mine to Claire.... She needed it. She called it her Aziff (as if) theory, and I let her have it with my blessing."

Slepian set her third novel, *The Night of the Bozos,* around a lake in upstate New York where she spent

Christmas vacations as a teenager. In her autobiography Slepian explained that "[the] book is a good example of how I put together people, or parts of people, I have known from different eras of my life." Slepian drew inspiration from her own son, Don, when creating the character of George Weiss, a reclusive adolescent musician with an obsession for sound in all of its forms. George lives with his mother and his Uncle Hibbie, a character based on a stuttering patient whom Slepian encountered while she was a speech therapist at Massachusetts General Hospital in the late 1940s. Because of his speech problem, Hibbie forms bonds with very few people other than his nephew. The two outcasts are befriended by Lolly, a teenager (modeled on one of Don's girlfriends) who escorts them to a carnival where her family works. There Hibbie gets a job as a "Bozo," a clown who sits above a tank of water and jeers at the crowd. His duty is to coax customers into paying to throw balls at a target that, when hit, will dunk him. Only as the Bozo can Hibbie overcome his stuttering problem, admitting that the urge to tease and joke with people has always been a part of him. With his identity protected by clown makeup, he is able to display the extroverted side of himself.

In her later novels Slepian continued her practice of using settings familiar to her as backdrops to her stories. Both *The Broccoli Tapes* and *Something beyond Paradise* take place in Hawaii, where Slepian and her family spent their summers from 1967 to the early 1980s. Her novel *Risk n' Roses* returns to the author's home state of New York and tells about two sisters whose relationship deteriorates when their family moves to a new neighborhood in the Bronx. Older sister Angela, who is mentally handicapped, becomes friends with Kaminsky, a man who lives across the street and cultivates roses. Younger sister Skip, who has always felt obligated to care for her older sister, falls under the influence of Jean Persico, a young girl who encourages Skip to join her and her clique of friends in wanton wrongdoing. When Jean tricks Angela into clipping the buds from Kaminsky's roses, Skip does not immediately protest: As Slepian writes in the book, "Her sister was nothing to her and Jean was everything." Skip does eventually stop Angela from causing further damage to Kaminsky's garden and comes to understand the sacrifices that must be made in choosing to be loyal to either friends or family.

In her novels Slepian has celebrated the lives of a number of young adult characters who learn to cope with problems caused by their own handicaps, exposure to new environments, and shifting relationships. Concerning her decision to write for young adults, Slepian admitted in her autobiography: "Sometimes, when the writing is going well, when a character has come alive on the page, or I have found the right 'taste,' the right sentence or even the right word, then, I can tell you that there is nothing in the world to match it. I'm like a bystander watching a miracle. I count myself blessed that I'm a writer and think that that is the best possible thing to be."

WORKS CITED:

Babbitt, Natalie, review of *The Alfred Summer, New York Times Book Review,* April 27, 1980, p. 52.

Babbitt, review of *Lester's Turn, New York Times Book Review,* May 27, 1981, p. 38.

Slepian, Janice B., *Something about the Author Autobiography Series,* Volume 8, Gale, 1989.

FOR MORE INFORMATION SEE:

PERIODICALS

Los Angeles Times Book Review, April 23, 1989, p. 10.

* * *

SLOBODKIN, Louis 1903-1975

PERSONAL: Born February 19, 1903, in Albany, NY; died May 8, 1975, in Bar Harbor Islands, Miami Beach, FL; son of Nathan (an inventor) and Dora (Lubin) Slobodkin; married Florence Gersh (an author), September 27, 1927; children: Laurence B., Michael E. *Education:* Beaux Arts Institute of Design, New York, NY, student, 1918-22. *Politics:* Democrat. *Religion:* Jewish. *Hobbies and other interests:* Cooking, traveling and people.

ADDRESSES: *Home*—209 West 86th St., New York, NY 10024.

CAREER: Sculptor, designer, illustrator, and author of children's books. Sculptor in studios in France and the United States, 1931-35; Master Institute of United Arts

Louis Slobodkin

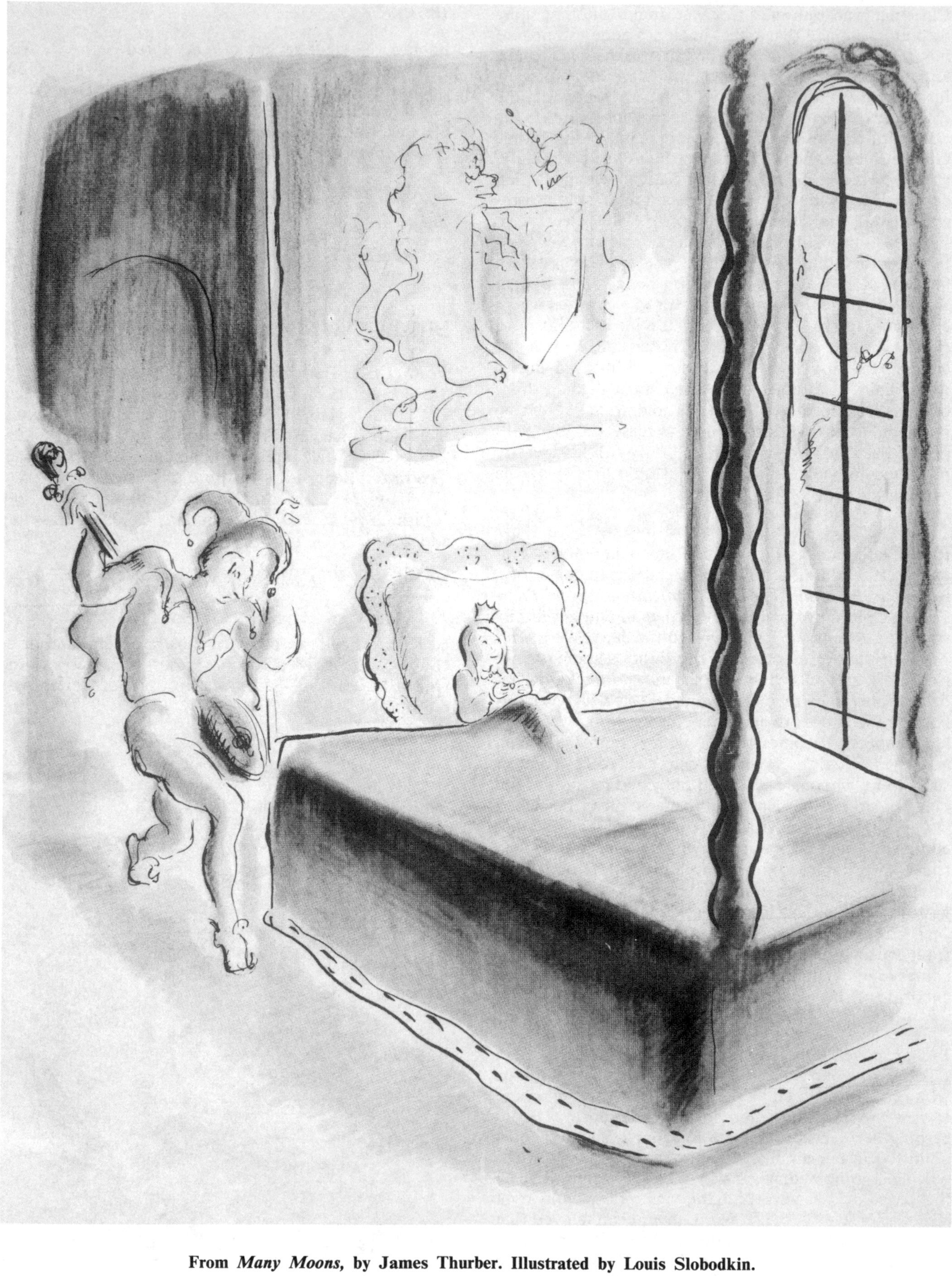

From *Many Moons,* by James Thurber. Illustrated by Louis Slobodkin.

at the Roerich Museum, New York City, head of sculpture department, 1934-37; School Art League, New York City, sculpting instructor, 1935-36; New York City Art Project, head of sculpture division, 1941-42; designer of statues, reliefs and panels for government buildings in Washington, DC, New York, and other cities, including "Young Abe Lincoln" for U.S. Department of the Interior Building in the capital. Exhibitor and lecturer at museums.

MEMBER: Sculptors Guild (board of directors, 1939-41), National Sculpture Society, American Group (president, 1940-42), American Institute of Graphic Arts (chairman of Artists Committee, 1946), Authors Guild of Authors League of America.

AWARDS, HONORS: Winner of various sculpture competitions; Caldecott Medal nomination, 1943, for *Many Moons.*

WRITINGS:

SELF-ILLUSTRATED

Magic Michael, Macmillan, 1944.
Friendly Animals, Vanguard, 1944.
Clear the Track, Macmillan, 1945.
Fo'castle Waltz, Vanguard, 1945.
The Adventures of Arab, Macmillan, 1946.
Seaweed Hat, Macmillan, 1947.
Hustle and Bustle, Macmillan, 1948.
Bixby and the Secret Message, Macmillan, 1948.
Sculpture: Principles and Practice, World Publishing, 1949.
Mr. Mushroom, Macmillan, 1950.
Dinny and Danny, Macmillan, 1951.
Our Friendly Friends, Vanguard, 1951.
The Space Ship under the Apple Tree, Macmillan, 1952.
Circus April 1st, Macmillan, 1953.
Mr. Petersham's Cats, Macmillan, 1954.
The Horse with the High-Heeled Shoes, Vanguard, 1954.
The Amiable Giant, Macmillan, 1955.
Millions and Millions, Vanguard, 1955.
The Mermaid Who Could Not Sing, Macmillan, 1956.
One Is Good but Two Are Better, Vanguard, 1956.
Melvin, the Moose Child, Macmillan, 1957.
Thank You, You're Welcome, Vanguard, 1957.
The Space Ship Returns To the Apple Tree, Macmillan, 1958.
The Little Owl Who Could Not Sleep, Macmillan, 1958.
The First Book of Drawing, F. Watts, 1958.
Trick or Treat, Macmillan, 1959.
Excuse Me, Certainly, Vanguard, 1959.
Up High and Down Low, Macmillan, 1960.
Gogo the French Sea Gull, Macmillan, 1960.
Nomi and the Beautiful Animals, Vanguard, 1960.
A Good Place to Hide, Macmillan, 1961.
Picco, Vanguard, 1961.
The Three-Seated Space Ship, Macmillan, 1962.
The Late Cuckoo, Vanguard, 1962.
Luigi and the Long-Nosed Soldier, Macmillan, 1963.
Moon Blossom and the Golden Penny, Vanguard, 1963.
The Polka-Dot Goat, Macmillan, 1964.
Yasu and the Strangers, Macmillan, 1965.
Colette and the Princess, Dutton, 1965.
Read about the Policeman, F. Watts, 1966.
Read about the Postman, F. Watts, 1966.
Read about the Fireman, F. Watts, 1967.
Read about the Busman, F. Watts, 1967.
Round-Trip Space Ship, Macmillan, 1968.
The Spaceship in the Park, Macmillan, 1972.
Wilbur the Warrior, Vanguard, 1972.

ILLUSTRATOR

Eleanor Estes, *The Moffats,* Harcourt, 1941.
E. Estes, *The Sun and the Wind and Mr. Todd,* Harcourt, 1942.
E. Estes, *The Middle Moffat,* Harcourt, 1942.
James Thurber, *Many Moons,* Harcourt, 1943.
E. Estes, *Rufus M.,* Harcourt, 1943.
Nina Brown Baker, *Peter the Great,* Vanguard, 1943.
E. Estes, *The Hundred Dresses,* Harcourt, 1944.
N. Brown Baker, *Garibaldi,* Vanguard, 1944.
Mabel Leigh Hunt, *Young Man of the House,* Lippincott, 1944.
N. Brown Baker, *Lenin,* Vanguard, 1945.
Mark Twain, *Tom Sawyer,* World Publishing, 1946.
Jacob Blanck, *Jonathan and the Rainbow,* Houghton, 1948.
J. Blanck, *The King and the Noble Blacksmith,* Houghton, 1950.
E. Estes, *Ginger Pye,* Harcourt, 1951.
Edgar Eager, *Red Head,* Houghton, 1951.
Margarite Glendenning, *Gertie the Horse,* McGraw, 1951.
Washington Irving, *The Alhambra,* Macmillan, 1953.
Charles Dickens, *The Magic Fishbone,* Vanguard, 1953.
Edith Unnerstad, *The Saucepan Journey,* Macmillan, 1955.
Irmegarde Eberle, *Evie and the Wonderful Kangaroo,* Knopf, 1955.
E. Unnerstad, *Pysen,* Macmillan, 1955.
Helen F. Bill, *The King's Shoes,* F. Watts, 1956.
Sara Kasden, *Love and Knishes,* Vanguard, 1956.
I. Eberle, *Evie and Cooky,* Knopf, 1957.
E. Unnerstad, *Little O,* Macmillan, 1957.
Robert Murphy, *The Warm-Hearted Polar Bear,* Little, Brown, 1957.
F. Slobodkin, *Too Many Mittens,* Vanguard, 1958.
F. Amerson Andrews, *Upside-Down Town,* Little, Brown, 1958.
Reda Davis, *Martin's Dinosaur,* Crowell, 1959.
Priscilla and Otto Frederich, *Clean Clarence,* Lothrop, 1960.
P. and O. Frederich, *Marshmallow Ghost,* Lothrop, 1960.
F. Slobodkin, *The Cowboy Twins,* Vanguard, 1960.
Andrew Packard, *Mr. Spindles and the Spiders,* Macmillan, 1961.
F. Slobodkin, *Io Sono,* Vanguard, 1962.
Margaret Uppington, *The Lovely Culpeppers,* F. Watts, 1963.
F. Slobodkin, *Mr. Papadilly and Willy,* Vanguard, 1964.
S. Kasden, *Mazel Tov Y'all,* Vanguard, 1968.
F. Slobodkin, *Sarah Somebody,* Vanguard, 1969.

ADAPTATIONS: Magic Michael was adapted as both a movie and filmstrip by Weston Woods, 1960; *Dinny and Danny* was adapted as a filmstrip with teacher's guide and record by Association-Sterling Films, 1975.

SIDELIGHTS: Louis Slobodkin was an author and illustrator of children's books, as well as an artist and sculptor. Among his works are tales of space adventures and aliens, books on behavior, and stories about various professions. In an essay for *Books Are by People,* Slobodkin described part of his inspiration: "My stories are usually inspired by children.... I found out long ago that it's difficult to get children to give you an honest opinion of work in progress. They are so sympathetic and kind that they will say a work is *bad* if that's what you want them to say or *good* if they feel that is the response you want."

Slobodkin loved kindergarten, but the only thing he liked about grade school was the opportunity to decorate the blackboards with chalk drawings at holiday times. When Slobodkin was about ten, his brother gave him a ball of modeling clay; as soon as he began to work with the clay, Slobodkin decided to be a sculptor. His first project was to shape the heads of both an Indian and George Washington, although George "became Benjamin Franklin when I squeezed some spectacles over G. W.'s difficult eyes" the artist wrote in an essay for the *Junior Book of Authors.*

At the age of fifteen Slobodkin decided to quit school and study art. He described the experience in *Fo'Castle Waltz:* "I forced my parents' permission by instigating the first one-man sitdown strike I'd ever heard of." He attended class, but refused to do any work, until "after enough zeroes piled up I was allowed to leave school." He enrolled at the Beaux Arts Institute of Design in New York City, working nights as an elevator operator to earn money. Slobodkin spent nine to twelve hours a day in classes; during what time was left, he studied ancient sculptures at the Metropolitan Museum.

After graduation Slobodkin worked for a commercial architectural modeling studio, turning out cheap imitations of popular art subjects. He left this job after six months and, in the summer of 1923, shipped out as a deck hand on a steamer bound for South America. He made drawings and water colors of the men at work on the ship, later using the pictures as inspiration for his sculptures. Slobodkin also spent several years in Paris studying art and sculpture; when he returned to New York City, he opened his own studio. In 1927 he married Florance Gersh, who was a poet and writer of books for children.

In 1941 Slobodkin's friend Eleanor Estes asked him to illustrate one of her books, *The Moffats.* Over time, the artist was inspired to begin work on his own books. "I began to write my own stories a few years later because I wanted to draw pictures for them," he wrote in his essay. During the three decades that followed Slobodkin turned out forty-six self-illustrated books for children and adults, with topics ranging from *The First Book of Drawing* (1958) to *The Sapceship in the Park* (1972). In *Scupture: Principle and Practice,* Slobodkin summed up his feelings about art and writing by remarking that "an artist's personal style develops when he realizes that there are certain art facets he sees and feels clearer than all others.... A mature artist spends his life struggling to realize and develop this differentiation. His is a continuous battle to preserve and give out through his individuality those aesthetic truths srtongly felt."

WORKS CITED:

Slobodkin, Louis, *Fo'Castle Waltz,* Vanguard, 1945.

Slobodkin, Louis, *Sculpture: Principle and Practice,* World Publishing, 1949.

Slobodkin, Louis, essay in *Junior Book of Authors,* edited by Stanley J. Kunitz and Howard Haycraft, H. W. Wilson, 1951.

Slobodkin, Louis, essay in *Books Are by People,* edited by Lee Bennett Hopkins, Citation Press, 1969.

FOR MORE INFORMATION SEE:

PERIODICALS

Horn Book, July-August, 1944.

* * *

SLOTE, Alfred 1926- (A. H. Garnet)

PERSONAL: Born September 11, 1926, in New York, NY; son of Oscar (an insurance broker) and Sallie (an interior decorator; maiden name, Persky) Slote; married

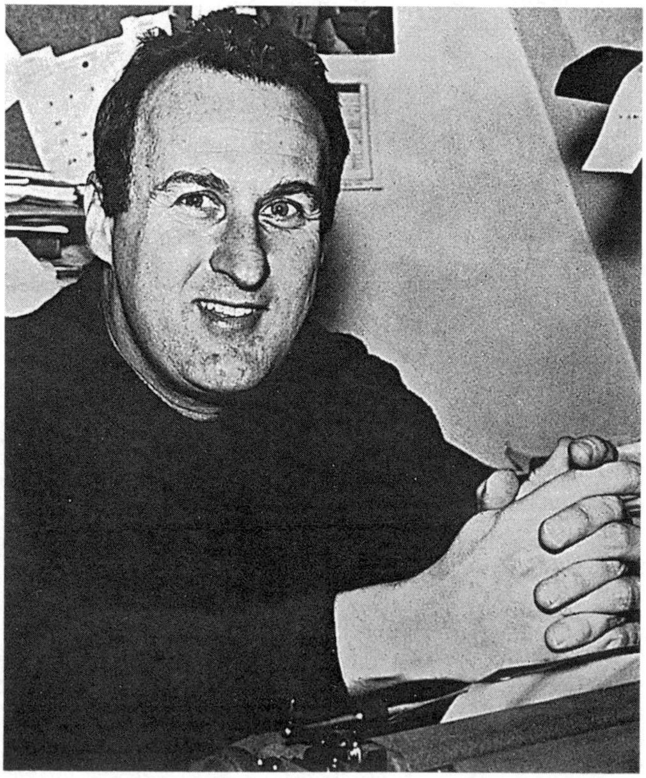

Alfred Slote

Henrietta Howell (retired assistant to the Dean of the University of Michigan Law School), August 23, 1951; children: John, Elizabeth, Ben. *Education:* University of Michigan, B.A., 1949, M.A., 1950; attended University of Grenoble, 1950. *Hobbies and other interests:* Sports.

ADDRESSES: Home—Ann Arbor, MI.

CAREER: Williams College, Williamstown, MA, instructor in English, 1953-56; University of Michigan Television Center, Ann Arbor, 1956-82, began as producer and writer, became associate director, 1968-73, executive producer, 1973-82; writer. Lecturer on children's literature at University of Michigan and University of California, Davis. *Military service:* U.S. Navy, 1944-46.

MEMBER: Authors Guild of America, Phi Beta Kappa.

AWARDS, HONORS: Avery and Jules Hopwood Award in creative writing, University of Michigan, 1949; Fulbright scholar, 1950; Friends of American Writers Award, 1971, for *Jake;* Nene Award, Hawaii Library Association and Hawaii Association of School Librarians, 1981, for *My Robot Buddy;* Edgar Allan Poe runnerup, 1983, for *Clone Catcher.*

WRITINGS:

FOR CHILDREN

The Princess Who Wouldn't Talk, illustrated by Ursula Arndt, Bobbs-Merrill, 1964.
The Moon in Fact and Fancy, World Publishing, 1967, revised edition, 1971.
Air in Fact and Fancy, World Publishing, 1968.
Stranger on the Ball Club, Lippincott, 1970.
Jake, Lippincott, 1971.
The Biggest Victory, Lippincott, 1972.
My Father, the Coach, Lippincott, 1972.
Hang Tough, Paul Mather, Lippincott, 1973.
Tony and Me, Lippincott, 1974.
Matt Gargan's Boy, Lippincott, 1975.
My Robot Buddy, illustrated by Joel Schick, Lippincott, 1975.
The Hot Shot, photographs by William LaCrosse, Watts, 1977.
My Trip to Alpha I, illustrated by Harold Berson, Lippincott, 1978.
Love and Tennis, Macmillan, 1979.
The Devil Rides with Me and Other Fantastic Stories, Methuen, 1980.
C.O.L.A.R.: A Tale of Outer Space, illustrated by Anthony Kramer, Lippincott, 1981.
Clone Catcher, illustrated by Elizabeth Slote, Lippincott, 1982.
Rabbit Ears, Lippincott, 1982.
Omega Station, illustrated by Anthony Kramer, Lippincott, 1983.
The Trouble on Janus, Lippincott, 1985.
Moving In, Lippincott, 1988.
A Friend Like That, Lippincott, 1988.
Make-Believe Ballplayer, illustrated by Tom Newsom, Lippincott, 1989.
The Trading Game, HarperCollins, 1990.
Finding Buck McHenry, HarperCollins, 1991.

Also author of a series of children's television programs titled *The Art of Storytelling.*

FOR ADULTS

Denham Proper (novel), Putnam, 1953.
Lazarus in Vienna (novel), McGraw Hill, 1956.
Strangers and Comrades (novel), Simon & Schuster, 1964.
(With Woodrow W. Hunter) *Preparation for Retirement* (stories), University of Michigan Press, 1968.
Termination: The Closing at Baker Plant (nonfiction), Bobbs-Merrill, 1969.
(Under pseudonym A. H. Garnet; with Garnet Garrison) *The Santa Claus Killer,* Ticknor & Fields, 1981.
(Under pseudonym A. H. Garnet; with Garrison) *Maze,* Ticknor & Fields, 1982.

Also author of television programs including *Science: Quest and Conquest* and *The Progress of Man.*

ADAPTATIONS: Jake was adapted as an "ABC Afterschool Special" titled *The Rag Tag Champs.*

SIDELIGHTS: Alfred Slote has distinguished himself as a knowledgeable writer of both sports- and science-fiction books. A sports enthusiast—with a particular interest in baseball—since childhood, the author later became involved with his sons' little league teams. It was his son John who first suggested that Slote, then an author of novels for adults, write about children's sports. Though his response at the time, according to *Junior Literary Guild,* was "I play ball, John—I don't write about it," he eventually took his son's advice, and became known for his novels about little league baseball players. The author sets most of his works in his own Ann Arbor, Michigan neighborhood, referring to the town as "Arborville." While the protagonists in Slote's books take baseball seriously and tend to be very involved with their teams, the novels are ultimately more concerned with the characters' relationships at home and at school and their growth as people. The novelist once commented, "I don't think of my books as baseball books specifically. Of course, they have a baseball background, but I think of them as books about young people and what happens to them."

Among Slote's better-known works is his 1973 novel, *Hang Tough, Paul Mather.* This story, which concerns a twelve-year-old little league pitcher battling leukemia, focuses on the main character's courage and determination. A *Kirkus Reviews* contributor noted that Slote "handles a sticky subject with finesse." Paul's family moves from California to Arborville so that he can be treated by a specialist there. Although forbidden to play baseball—the thing he loves most in the world—Paul forges his father's signature on a permission slip so that he can pitch in an important game against their rivals, the Ace Appliances. His expert pitching nearly brings the team victory, but Paul injures himself and requires hospitalization. There he meets his new doctor, Tom Kinsella, who—unlike Paul's previous doctors—understands him and treats him like a friend. Tom also lifts Paul's spirits by giving him a tape recorder to document his baseball triumphs. Paul dreams of winning the rematch with the Ace Appliances and convinces his parents and his doctor to let him watch from the sidelines. Although he cannot play, Paul finds a way to help his team win. Recalling that the opposing team's pitcher has trouble shutting out the usual taunting and jeering, Paul calls out a few phrases at opportune moments, causing the pitcher to lose his concentration and his sense of timing. His team's unexpected victory strengthens Paul's resolve to live. Zena Sutherland, writing in *Bulletin of the Center for Children's Books,* praised the novel's "depth and integrity."

Slote further explores the concept of a pitcher whose sensitivity impedes his pitching in his 1982 novel *Rabbit Ears.* Fifteen-year-old Tip O'Hara has a good arm and a sharp ear for music—as well as shouts from the opposing bench. When the other team teases him, he becomes distraught and has difficulty pitching and fielding. Soon the entire league knows of his weakness, and Tip becomes a complete failure on the mound. Tip's coach tries to help him overcome the problem, but finally, despite his talent and love for baseball, Tip quits the team. His bright eleven-year-old brother, Roland, then recruits Tip to play in his rock band. Roland has written a humorous song requiring audience participation. The audience supplies a word and the band integrates it into the song, adding extra syllables so that the word sounds like gibberish. When they perform the song in a contest, the band wins first prize. Roland suggests that Tip apply a similar strategy to his pitching, supplying nonsense responses to the opposing team's comments. Tip rejoins the team and finds this solution effective. He is able to laugh at the situation, regaining his confidence and emerging as his team's hero.

Although Slote integrates realistic game segments into his plots, his philosophy is similar to that of the main character's father in the author's book *Stranger on the Ball Club,* who tells his son that "baseball is fun, but there's more to life." Rather than focusing directly on the sport, Slote often uses the main character's little league experience as a secondary storyline which enriches both the character and the plot. As in *Hang Tough, Paul Mather,* many of the protagonists' more serious difficulties are unrelated to the game. In the author's 1971 work, *Jake,* the eleven-year-old title character lives with his twenty-four-year-old uncle Lenny, whose career as a musician in the city leaves him little time for his nephew. Jake's lack of supervision causes him to arrive late to school and fall asleep in class, until the school principal threatens to send him to a foster home. While Jake worries about being separated from his uncle, he also has a responsibility to his baseball team. The first-place team has lost its coach and has been unable to find a replacement. Tough and determined, Jake acts as temporary coach until the league prohibits this setup. In a desperate attempt to solve their problem, Jake's teammates look for a nearby

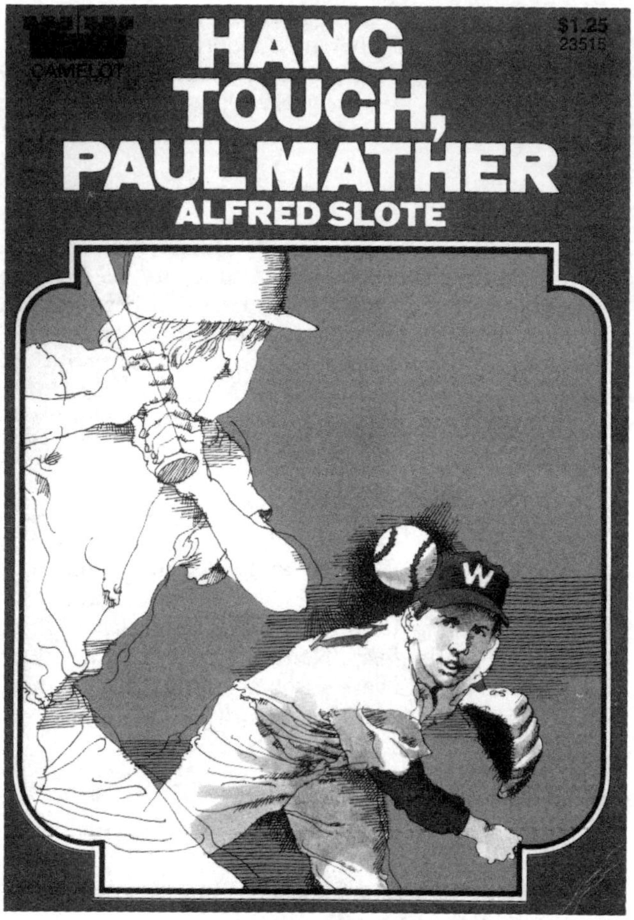

Cover of *Hang Tough, Paul Mather,* by Alfred Slote.

practice space for Lenny. When Jake impresses the rival coach with his determination to win, the coach rewards Jake with the use of his warehouse. Lenny agrees to practice there so that he can coach the team and spend more time with Jake.

Although the majority of Slote's sports fiction novels revolve around baseball, he has also written works about young hockey, tennis, and soccer players. *Moving In* incorporates a soccer team into its complex plot, yet the team plays a minor role. Eleven-year-old Robby Miller and his sister Peggy have moved to Arborville with their father following the death of their mother. Their father joins the computer company his friend Ruth Lowenfeld won from her husband in their recent divorce settlement. Robby and Peggy resent both the move and Mrs. Lowenfeld, whom they are convinced is determined to marry their father. Robby finds, however, that he has some interests in common with Mrs. Lowenfeld's daughter Beth, who plays soccer on a team coached by her father. With Beth's help, Robby and Peggy try to prevent the marriage. While Peggy tries to get their father interested in their student housekeeper, Robby becomes involved in a more daring scheme. He copies a valuable computer program written by his father and gives the disk to Mrs. Lowenfeld's ex-husband, hoping to ruin his father's business and end his partnership with Mrs. Lowenfeld. But Mr. Lowenfeld refuses to accept the disk. Eventually, Mrs. Lowenfeld reveals her predetermined plan to marry her boss.

Like many of his sports fiction books, Slote's series of science fiction novels, which follow the adventures of the futuristic Jameson family, also explores relationships. In his 1975 novel *My Robot Buddy,* ten-year-old Jack, a lonely country boy, convinces his parents to have a robot built according to his specifications. Jack's parents agree to buy him the pricey gift, commissioning the scientist Dr. Atkins to build it. Named Danny One, the robot looks very similar to Jack, but is so perfect that the two have little in common. The family has difficulty getting used to the new member of the family, but they eventually grow attached to him. When robot-nappers mistakenly steal Jack, the real robot must come to Jack's rescue. In the 1978 sequel *My Trip to Alpha I,* Jack, wishing to help his aunt prepare to move to Earth, travels to her planet by means of "VOYA-CODE." His body remains behind, but his mind travels by computer to receive a temporary body on Alpha I. When Jack arrives, his wealthy aunt announces her decision to remain on the planet and give her property to two servants. Jack discovers that his aunt is actually in VOYA-CODE and suspects the two servants of foul play.

The Jamesons continue their adventures in *C.O.L.A.R.: A Tale of Outer Space.* While they are traveling, their spaceship runs out of fuel, leaving them stranded on an asteroid which the Colony of Lost Atkins Robots (C.O.L.A.R.) is using as a hideout. The robots hold the family prisoner, but because Jack and his robot are nearly identical, they manage to escape and eventually make peace between the robots and Dr. Atkins, their inventor. In Slote's 1983 book *Omega Station,* the last work of the series, Dr. Atkins informs Danny and Jack that the evil Otto Drago is robot-napping. To figure out why, Jack poses as Danny and is stolen and taken to Omega Station. Here Drago, hoping to create an all-robot world, reprograms robots to make weapons that will destroy the human race. Drago threatens to kill Jack, but Danny and the other robots come to his rescue, destroying Drago and converting Omega Station into a health resort.

Slote returned to his baseball themes in *The Trading Game* and *Finding Buck McHenry,* both of which focus on baseball cards and the history of the game. *The Trading Game,* Slote's 1990 novel, centers on ten-year-old Andy Harris. An avid baseball card collector, Andy desperately wants his friend Tubby's card featuring Andy's grandfather, a former major league player whom Andy idolizes. Tubby offers it to him in exchange for Andy's 1952 Mickey Mantle card, which is worth $2500. While Andy considers this proposition, his grandfather arrives in town and—though ailing—coaches Andy's little league team. When the two quarrel over a rule, Andy learns of his grandfather's competitive streak, which jeopardizes their relationship. Slote's 1991 book, *Finding Buck McHenry,* concerns Jason, an eleven-year-old who cares more about collecting baseball cards than practicing the game, and has been cut from his little league team. He finds a baseball card displaying a 1930s Negro league star pitcher named Buck McHenry and becomes convinced the player is Mack Henry, a local school custodian. After some hesitation, Mr. Henry confirms Jason's suspicion, but asks him to keep it a secret. Jason asks Mr. Henry to coach a new team that is being formed. Mr. Henry agrees, but then is the subject of a television program about sports which puts the team, Mr. Henry, and Jason in jeopardy.

WORKS CITED:

Junior Literary Guild, March, 1975, p. 32.
Slote, Alfred, *Stranger on the Ball Club,* Lippincott, 1970.
Sutherland, Zena, "New Titles for Children and Young People: 'Hang Tough, Paul Mather,'" *Bulletin of the Center for Children's Books,* June, 1973, p. 162.
"Younger Fiction: 'Hang Tough, Paul Mather'," *Kirkus Reviews,* February 1, 1973, pp. 116-17.

FOR MORE INFORMATION SEE:

BOOKS

Children's Literature Review, Volume 4, Gale, 1982, pp. 198-204.
Something about the Author, Volume 8, Gale, 1976, pp. 192-93.
Twentieth-Century Children's Writers, Third edition, St. James, 1989, pp. 893-94.

* * *

SMALL, Ernest
See LENT, Blair

* * *

SMITH, Dodie
See SMITH, Dorothy Gladys

* * *

SMITH, Doris Buchanan 1934-

PERSONAL: Born June 1, 1934 in Washington, DC; daughter of Charles A. (a business executive) and Flora (Robinson) Buchanan (an executive secretary); married R. Carroll Smith (a building contractor), December 18, 1954, (divorced, 1977); married Bill Curtis, c. 1988; children: (first marriage) Robb, Willie, Randy, Susan, Matthew. *Education:* Attended South Georgia College. *Religion:* None. *Hobbies and other interests:* Travel, biking, reading, walking, canoeing, pottery, ceramic sculpture, music, and stargazing.

ADDRESSES: Home—P.O. Box 266, Canton, MO 63435. *Agent*—John Hawkins & Associates, formerly Paul R. Reynolds, Inc. *Office*—c/o Viking Penguin Inc.

CAREER: Writer, 1971—.

AWARDS, HONORS: American Library Association Notable Book Award and Child Study Association Book of the Year Award, both 1973, Georgia Children's Book Author of the Year and Georgia General Author of the Year Award, both from Dixie Council of Authors and Journalists, 1974, Georgia Children's Book Award, 1975, and Sue Hafner Award and Kinderbook Award, both 1977, all for *A Taste of Blackberries;* Georgia Children's Book Author of the Year Award from Dixie Council of Authors and Journalists and Notable Children's Book Award from National Council for Social Studies, both 1975, for *Kelly's Creek;* Breadloaf fellowship, 1975; Georgia Children's Book Author of the Year Award from Dixie Council of Authors and Journalists and Best Book of the Year Award from *School Library Journal,* both 1982, for *Last Was Lloyd;* Parents' Choice Literature Award, 1986, for *Return to Bitter Creek.*

WRITINGS:

FOR YOUNG ADULTS

A Taste of Blackberries, illustrated by Charles Robinson, Crowell, 1973.
Kick a Stone Home, Crowell, 1974.
Tough Chauncey, illustrated by Michael Eagle, Morrow, 1974.

Doris Buchanan Smith

Kelly's Creek, illustrated by Alan Tiegreen, Crowell, 1975.
Up and Over, Morrow, 1976.
Dreams and Drummers, Crowell, 1978.
Salted Lemons, Four Winds, 1980.
Last Was Lloyd, Viking Kestrel, 1981.
Moonshadow of Cherry Mountain, Four Winds, 1982.
The First Hard Times, Viking Kestrel, 1983.
Laura Upside-Down, Viking Kestrel, 1984.
Return to Bitter Creek, Viking Kestrel, 1986.
Karate Dancer, Putnam, 1987.
Voyages, Viking Kestrel, 1989.
The Pennywhistle Tree, Putnam, 1991.
Best Girl, Viking, 1993.

Also author of an unpublished adventure novel.

SIDELIGHTS: Doris Buchanan Smith has written over fifteen young adult books that deal with important modern-day issues. Praised for their realism and relevance, these books focus on topics including death, divorce, obesity, juvenile delinquency, unwed mothers, dyslexia, and child abuse. However, she stays away from making these issues the focus of her books and concentrates instead on realistic, likable characters who grow, change, and cope as a result of their difficulties.

In looking back on her reasons for becoming a writer, Smith mused in *Something about the Author Autobiography Series* (*SAAS*): "I truly don't know when I became a storyteller, or why. I did not grow up in a storytelling tradition with people sitting around on porches, or in front of fireplaces, telling stories. But my mother read to me and read to me, and those nursery rhymes and stories must have infused me and compelled me to spin my own." Smith remembered knowing all her nursery rhymes by heart at the age of two.

Smith would also create stories with which to entertain others. "From the time I was small," she recalled in *SAAS,* "I sat with two even smaller cousins in their sandbox and regaled them with stories, sculpting the geography of the story in the sand." When asked by adults what kind of stories she was telling, she was embarrassed to admit that she made them up. Her need to tell stories was so great that at the age of eight it got her into some trouble. She had asked for permission to go to her cousins' house on her own for the first time and was refused. Sneaking out, she biked the two miles to their house and began telling her stories. She was soon found out, severely reprimanded, and returned home.

In 1943, the family moved to Atlanta, Georgia. Smith found herself feeling lonely and isolated when other children called her a yankee. She later expressed these feelings in her book *Salted Lemons.* After several more moves within the city, the outgoing Smith became shy and reclusive. However, a kind sixth grade teacher made an impact on Smith's world. Noticing that Smith had talent in writing, she asked her if she wanted to be a writer one day.

Smith was hit with this question like a ton of bricks. "Be a writer? I didn't even know it was something you could be . . . ," she related in *SAAS.* "I'm not sure I ever gave her an audible answer but inside me were flashing lights and eureka bells and a huge 'Yeahhhh!' that has never left me." Still shy, Smith became a closet writer, working privately in her room. She showed an eighth grade teacher a story and was mortified when the teacher read it aloud to each of her classes. Joining the school newspaper, she submitted articles secretly to the editor, but never came forward to reveal her identity. She kept her desired vocation so secret that many years later, when she told her father about her ambitions, he was surprised because he had never heard it mentioned before.

Smith married in 1954 and settled down to raise four children of her own, one adopted child, and scores of foster children. While she was satisfied with motherhood, there was something nagging inside her to continue writing. Never very disciplined at her art, she began to carve out times in the day when she could be alone to write. Attending workshops also helped her to focus. At first, she was disappointed in the seemingly endless rejections she received. One summer, threatened by the loss of serenity from her children being home, Smith decided to write an adventure novel with them as the characters. While this book was never published, she decided to write another children's book while she was waiting to hear from publishers.

This other book was to be her first published novel, *A Taste of Blackberries,* which was released in 1973. It focuses on the guilt and sorrow felt by the narrator when his best friend dies from an allergic reaction to a bee sting. Up until this work, no other modern children's book had tackled this tough topic—the death of a child's playmate. Setting was an important element of this book, too, since it really did not gel in the author's mind until she put it in a familiar Maryland suburb.

Dealing with her own parents' divorce when she was a child provided Smith with some material for writing her second novel, *Kick a Stone Home.* This story tells of a young girl who feels alienated after her parents' divorce. Smith probed juvenile delinquency in *Tough Chauncey,* showing in the end that the protagonist had a better chance dealing with life in a foster home rather than with his own abusive and neglectful family. Both novels show how the characters learn to cope with their lives rather than present an unlikely, storybook ending.

In 1977, Smith herself was divorced. However, this did not keep her from her work. She maintained a home in Georgia and found a writer's getaway in a primitive summer cabin in the woods of North Carolina. Even though she was still in the beginnings of her career, she did not feel the drive to be better than other writers. "My only competition is myself, to do my own best at what I do best and to do a number of other things with a marvelously mad mediocrity," she once remarked.

From *A Taste of Blackberries,* by Doris Buchanan Smith. Illustrated by Charles Robinson.

More novels soon followed. In *Kelly's Creek,* a young boy confronts his dyslexia and learns how to best use his talents; *Up and Over* looks at the crazy days of the early 1970s, when streaking, racial tension, and teenage pregnancy were the issues of the day. In a departure from her usual themes, *Dreams and Drummers* looks at a ninth grade girl who has no problems except that she is more mature than others her age, and this causes her to feel isolated.

In other books, Smith has written about obesity, religion, and sexual awakenings. In a unique novel called *Voyages,* Smith tells the story of a young girl who is kidnapped at a shopping mall. Her captor pushes her from a speeding car, and she is seriously injured. Resentful while recuperating in the hospital, she finds solace in learning about Norse mythology and goes on a fantasy journey amongst the gods. There she learns about fate, the power of the individual, and the strength to face adversity. The novel was praised for its imaginative approach to a serious topic.

Smith ventures onto ground where some novelists fear to tread. Although her works discuss serious issues that are pervasive today, she keeps from being solely an "issues author" by focusing on the characters' growth and development. The author feels strongly about her vocation and stresses discipline as one of the reasons for her success. However, she enjoys this line of work greatly, commenting that the "most wonderful thing in the world to me is doing what I love to do and earning my living at it."

WORKS CITED:

Smith, Doris Buchanan, essay in *Something about the Author Autobiography Series,* Volume 10, Gale, pp. 305-318.

FOR MORE INFORMATION SEE:

BOOKS

Dictionary of Literary Biography, Volume 52: *American Writers for Children since 1960: Fiction,* Gale, 1986.

Twentieth-Century Children's Writers, 3rd edition, St. James Press, 1989.

PERIODICALS

New York Times Book Review, March 11, 1990.

* * *

SMITH, Dorothy Gladys 1896-1990 (Dodie Smith; pseudonyms: C. L. Anthony, Charles Henry Percy)

PERSONAL: Born May 3, 1896, in Whitefield, Lancashire, England; died November 24, 1990; daughter of Ernest Walter and Ella (Furber) Smith; married Alec Macbeth Beesley, 1939 (died, 1987). *Education:* Attended Manchester School and St. Paul's Girls' School, London; studied for the stage at Royal Academy of Dramatic Art, London. *Hobbies and other interests:* Reading, music, dogs, donkeys.

ADDRESSES: Home—The Barretts, Finchingfield, Essex, England.

CAREER: Actress, 1915-22; Heal & Son (furnishing company), London, England, buyer, 1923-32; full-time writer, 1932-90.

WRITINGS:

PLAYS; UNDER PSEUDONYM C. L. ANTHONY

British Talent, first produced in London at Three Arts Club, 1924.

Autumn Crocus (three-act comedy; first produced in London at Lyric Theatre, April 6, 1931; produced on Broadway at Morosco Theatre, November, 1932; also see below), Samuel French, 1931.

Service (three-act comedy; first produced in London at Wyndham's Theatre, October 12, 1932; also see below), Gollancz, 1932, acting edition, Samuel French, 1937.

Touch Wood (three-act comedy; first produced in London at Theatre Royal, Haymarket, May 16, 1934; also see below), Samuel French, 1934.

PLAYS; UNDER NAME DODIE SMITH

Call It a Day (three-act comedy; first produced in London at Globe Theatre, October 30, 1935; produced at Morosco Theatre, 1936), Samuel French, 1936, acting edition, 1937.

Bonnet over the Windmill (three-act comedy; first produced in London at New Theatre, September 8, 1937), Heinemann, 1937.

(And co-director) *Dear Octopus* (three-act comedy; first produced in London at Queen's Theatre, September 14, 1938; produced on Broadway at Broadhurst Theatre, 1939; revived at Theatre Royal, Haymarket, 1967), Heinemann, 1938, acting edition, Samuel French, 1939.

Autumn Crocus, Service, and Touch Wood: Three Plays, Heinemann, 1939.

Lovers and Friends (three-act comedy; first produced on Broadway at Plymouth Theatre, November 29, 1943), Samuel French, 1944.

Letter from Paris (three-act comedy adapted from Henry James's novel, *The Reverberator;* first produced in London at Aldwych Theatre, October 10, 1952), Heinemann, 1954.

I Capture the Castle (two-act romantic comedy adapted by the author from her novel of the same title; first produced at Aldwych Theatre, March 4, 1954; also see below), Samuel French, 1952.

These People, Those Books (three-act comedy), first produced in Leeds at Grand Theatre, 1958.

Amateur Means Lover (three-act comedy; first produced in Liverpool at Liverpool Playhouse, 1961), Samuel French, 1962.

NOVELS; UNDER NAME DODIE SMITH

I Capture the Castle, Atlantic/Little, Brown, 1948.

The New Moon with the Old, Atlantic/Little, Brown, 1963.

The Town in Bloom, Atlantic/Little, Brown, 1965.

It Ends with Revelations, Atlantic/Little, Brown, 1967.

A Tale of Two Families, Walker, 1970.

The Girl from the Candle-lit Bath, W. H. Allen, 1978.

FOR CHILDREN; UNDER NAME DODIE SMITH

The Hundred and One Dalmatians, illustrations by Janet Grahame-Johnstone and Anne Grahame-Johnstone, Heinemann, 1956, Viking, 1957, reprinted with illustrations by Michael Dooling, Viking/Puffin Books, 1989.

The Starlight Barking: More about the Hundred and One Dalmatians, illustrations by J. Grahame-Johnstone and A. Grahame-Johnstone, Heinemann, 1967, Simon & Schuster, 1968.

The Midnight Kittens, illustrations by J. Grahame-Johnstone and A. Grahame-Johnstone, W. H. Allen, 1978.

AUTOBIOGRAPHIES; UNDER NAME DODIE SMITH

Look Back with Love: A Manchester Childhood, Heinemann, 1974.

Look Back with Mixed Feelings, W. H. Allen, 1978.

Look Back with Astonishment, W. H. Allen, 1979.

Look Back with Gratitude, Muller Blond and White, 1985.

SCREENPLAYS

(With Frank Partos) *The Uninvited* (adapted from the novel by Dorothy Macardle), Paramount, 1944.

(With Lesser Samuels) *Darling, How Could You!* (adapted from *Alice-Sit-by-the-Fire* by James M. Barrie), Paramount, 1951.

Also author of screenplay "Schoolgirl Rebels" (under pseudonym Charles Henry Percy), 1915.

ADAPTATIONS: Autumn Crocus was filmed in England, 1934; *Call It a Day* was made into a movie by Warner Brothers, 1937; *Service* was filmed by Metro-Goldwyn-Mayer in 1944 as *Looking Forward; Dear Octopus* was also filmed in England, 1945; *The Hundred and One Dalmatians* was filmed by Walt Disney Productions as *One Hundred and One Dalmatians,* 1961.

SIDELIGHTS: Often remembered as the author of *The Hundred and One Dalmatians,* the children's story that Walt Disney Studios filmed as the animated *One Hundred and One Dalmatians,* Dorothy Gladys Smith was primarily an author of works for adults, including plays, novels, and several autobiographical works. Smith, better known by the name Dodie Smith, first gained recognition as a playwright, going by the name of C. L. Anthony until 1935, when she began to write under her own name. Her plays are generally light comedies about middle-class life that earned enough popular and critical praise in their time for *Dictionary of Literary Biography* contributor Martha Hadsel to deem Smith "one of the few successful women dramatists in England and American during the first half of the twentieth century."

Smith credited her early family life as the greatest factor in determining her future career. "When I was eighteen months old," Smith once said in *Contemporary Authors* (*CA*), "my father died, and after that my mother and I lived with her family—my grandparents, three uncles and two aunts—in an old house with a garden sloping towards the Manchester Ship Canal. It was a stimulating household. Both my mother and grandmother wrote and composed. Almost everyone sang and played some musical instrument (we owned three pianos, a violin, a mandolin, a guitar and a banjo) and one uncle, an admirable amateur actor, was often to be heard rehearsing, preferably with me on hand to give him his cues. Although I had been taken to theatres long before I could read, it was this hearing of my uncle's parts which really aroused my interest in acting and in playwriting; the cues I gave got longer and longer and, by the age of nine, I had written a forty-page play. When I read this aloud to my mother she fell asleep—to awake and say apologetically, 'But darling, it was so dull.'"

Her mother's reaction did not discourage Smith in any way. Nevertheless, her original plan was to become an actress and not a playwright. After studying at the Royal Academy of Art, she performed professionally with some of her fellow students before becoming a member of the Portsmouth Repertory Theatre. During World War I, Smith went to France to help entertain the soldiers there, and she also played a role in a Zurich performance of John Galsworthy's *Pigeon.* But in 1923 the young actress decided to leave the theater and work as a buyer for Heal and Son, a furniture company where she was employed for the next eight years.

Then, in 1931, Smith sold her play *Autumn Crocus* to one of her former stage directors. Although she had written a screenplay and a stage play before, *Autumn Crocus* was the work that turned her career around. The "romantic comedy brought Smith immediate success because of its winning combination of an Alpine setting, humor, music, and a love story," according to Hadsel. The next two plays that Smith published under the C. L. Anthony pseudonym, *Service* and *Touch Wood,* were also critically acclaimed, and Hadsel notes that some reviewers even compared *Touch Wood* to the work of the famous nineteenth-century Norwegian dramatist, Henrik Ibsen.

Call It a Day was the first play Smith wrote under her own name, as well as her most financially rewarding work. It ran for almost two hundred performances in New York City and had over five hundred performances in London. "By this time," related Hadsel, "she had purchased The Barretts, a cottage near the village of Finchingfield, Essex, and had made writing her full-time occupation." Traveling to the United States in 1938 to help with a New York City production of her *Dear Octopus,* Smith decided to remain in America, where she married her business manager, Alec Macbeth Beesley. During the next fifteen years she lived mostly in California and did some writing for Paramount Studios. It was while she was living in Pennsylvania, however, that she published her first—and most popular—novel, *I Capture the Castle.*

After returning to England, Smith continued to write plays and novels, but she also began writing stories for children, including *The Hundred and One Dalmatians* and its sequel, *The Starlight Barking: More about the Hundred and One Dalmatians.* The owner of a number of pet dalmatians herself, it is not surprising that Smith chose to make her main characters—Pongo, Missis Pongo, and their myriad puppies—dalmatians, and the adventures they have while foiling the plans of the evil furrier's wife, Cruella de Vil, have entertained many young readers. The last years of Smith's life were spent working on her autobiography, the four volumes of which, entitled *Look Back with Love: A Manchester Childhood, Look Back with Mixed Feelings, Look Back with Astonishment,* and *Look Back with Gratitude,* relate her experiences from childhood to the years she spent in the United States.

Although some critics have at times complained about what they considered Smith's "superficiality" in her work, Hadsel noted that her characters have appealed to audiences because they are "close enough to reality that . . . [people] feel comfortably at home with them, yet they are imaginative enough that her audience could find refreshment." Having made a successful career for herself as a writer in several genres, Smith nevertheless once revealed to *CA:* "I consider myself a lightweight author, but God knows I approach my work with as much seriousness as if it were Holy Writ."

WORKS CITED:

Contemporary Authors, Volumes 33-36, Gale, 1978, pp. 722-723.

Hadsel, Martha, "Dodie Smith," *Dictionary of Literary Biography,* Volume 10: *Modern British Dramatists, 1900-1945,* Gale, 1982, pp. 158-162.

OBITUARIES:

PERIODICALS

Times (London), November 27, 1990.

* * *

SMITH, Jessie Willcox 1863-1935

PERSONAL: Born September, 1863, in Philadelphia, PA; died May 3, 1935, in Philadelphia, PA; buried in Woodland Cemetery, Philadelphia, PA; daughter of Charles Henry (an investment broker) and Katherine DeWitt (Willcox) Smith. *Education:* Attended the Philadelphia School of Design for Women, 1885, and the Pennsylvania Academy of the Fine Arts, 1885-88; studied art under Howard Pyle at Drexel Institute, beginning in 1894.

ADDRESSES: Home—Cogshill, Chestnut Hill, Philadelphia, PA.

CAREER: Artist; designer of advertisement illustrations; illustrator of books for children. Kindergarten teacher's apprentice, c. 1879.

MEMBER: Society of Illustrators, American Federation of Arts, New York Water Color Club, Pennsylvania Academy of the Fine Arts, Philadelphia Art Alliance, Philadelphia Water Color Club, Plastic Club of Philadelphia.

AWARDS, HONORS: Bronze medal, Charleston Exposition, 1902; Mary Smith Prize of the Pennsylvania Academy of the Fine Arts, 1903; silver medal, St. Louis Exposition, 1904; Beck Prize of the Philadelphia Water Color Club, 1911; silver medal for watercolors, San Francisco Panama-Pacific Exposition, 1915.

ILLUSTRATOR:

(With Violet Oakley) Henry Wadsworth Longfellow, *Evangeline,* Houghton, 1897.

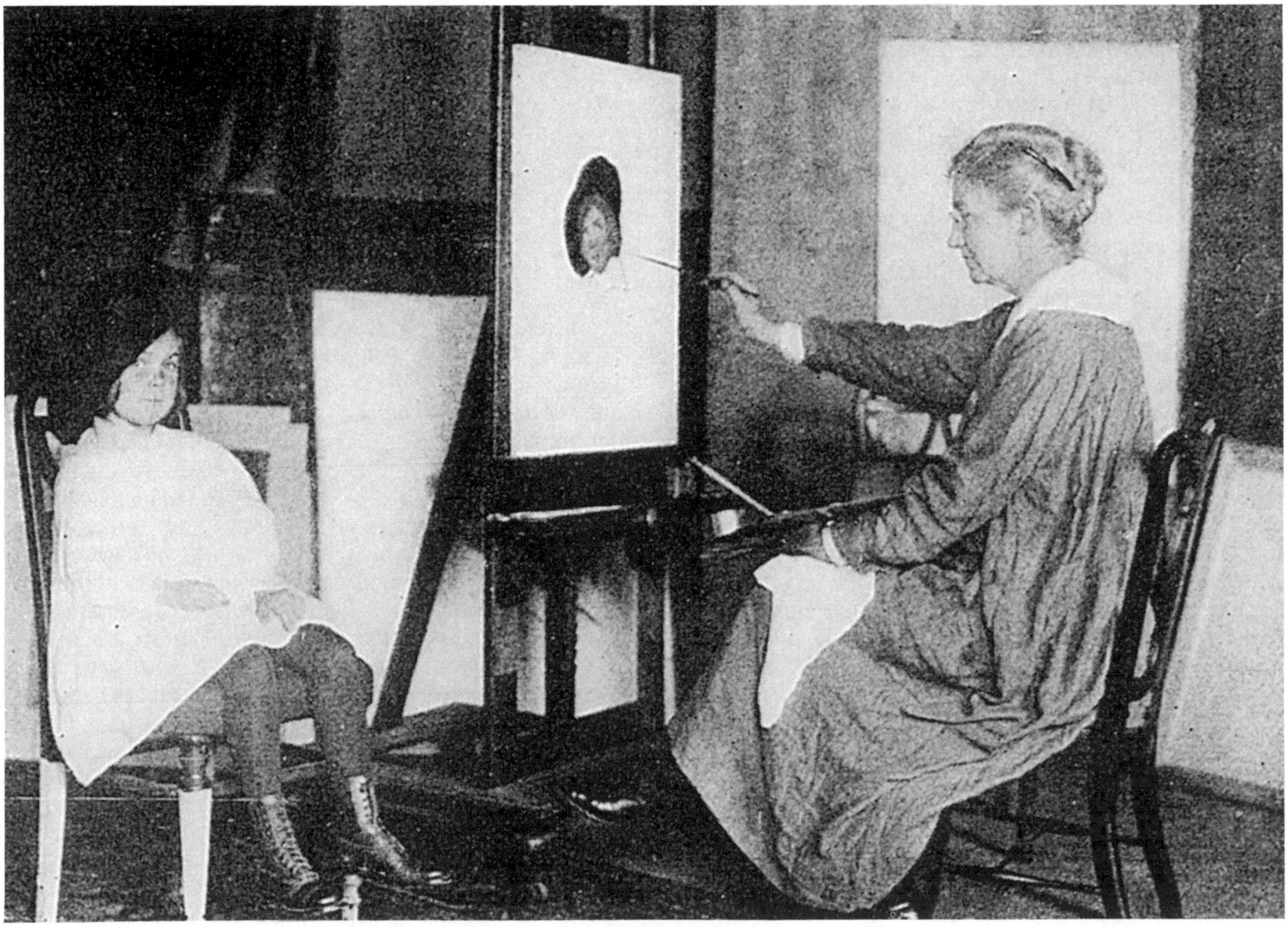

Jessie Willcox Smith

Mary P. Smith, *Young Puritans in Captivity,* Little, Brown, 1899.
Louisa May Alcott, *An Old-Fashioned Girl,* Little, Brown, 1902.
(With Elizabeth Shippen Green) Mabel Humphrey, *The Book of the Child,* F. A. Stokes, 1903.
Frances H. Burnett, *In the Closed Room,* McClure, Phillips, 1904.
Robert Louis Stevenson, *A Child's Garden of Verses,* Scribner, 1905.
Helen Whitney, *The Bed-Time Book,* Duffield, 1907.
Aileen Cleveland Higgins, *Dream Blocks,* Duffield, 1908.
Carolyn Wells, *The Seven Ages of Childhood,* Moffat, Yard, 1909.
(And compiler) *A Child's Book of Old Verses,* Duffield, 1910.
Betty Sage, *Rhymes of Real Children,* Duffield, 1910.
Penrhyn Coussens, compiler, *A Child's Book of Stories,* Duffield, 1911.
Angela M. Keyes, *The Five Senses,* Moffat, Yard, 1911.
Dickens's Children: Ten Drawings by Jessie Willcox Smith, Scribner, 1912.
Clement C. Moore, *'Twas the Night before Christmas,* Houghton, 1912.
The Jessie Willcox Smith Mother Goose: A Careful and Full Selection of the Rhymes, Dodd, 1914.
Louisa May Alcott, *Little Women,* Little, Brown, 1915.
Priscilla Underwood, *When Christmas Comes Around,* Duffield, 1915.
Charles Kingsley, *The Water-Babies,* Dodd, 1916.
Mary Stewart, *The Way to Wonderland,* Dodd, 1917.
The Little Mother Goose, Dodd, 1918.
George MacDonald, *At the Back of the North Wind,* McKay, 1919.
Ada M. Skinner and Eleanor L. Skinner, compilers, *A Child's Book of Modern Stories,* Duffield, 1920.
George MacDonald, *The Princess and the Goblin,* McKay, 1920.
Johanna Spyri, *Heidi,* McKay, 1922.
Ada M. Skinner and Eleanor L. Skinner, compilers, *A Little Child's Book of Stories,* Duffield, 1922.
Nora A. Smith, *Boys and Girls of Bookland,* Cosmopolitan, 1923.
Ada M. Skinner and Eleanor L. Skinner, compilers, *A Very Little Child's Book of Stories,* Duffield, 1923.
Samuel Crothers, *The Children of Dickens,* Scribner, 1925.
Ada M. Skinner and Eleanor L. Skinner, compilers, *A Child's Book of Country Stories,* Duffield, 1925.
Pamela Prince, *Once upon a Time: Twenty Bedtime Stories and Poems* (designed by Christina Donna), Harmony Books, 1988.
The Jessie Willcox Smith Poster Book, Crown, 1988.
Ready-to-Frame Storybook Illustrations, Dover, 1989.

Also illustrator of other books, including *A Child's Book of Stories from Many Lands,* compiled by Ada M. Skinner and Eleanor L. Skinner; *A Portfolio of Real Children;* and *An Old-Fashioned ABC Book.* Illustrator, with Elizabeth Shippen Green, of a 1903 calendar titled "The Child." Designer of advertisements for a variety of companies and products, including Ivory Soap, Cuticura Soap, Kodak, Campbell's Soup, Fleischmann's Yeast, and Cream of Wheat. Contributor of illustrations to periodicals, including *St. Nicholas, Ladies' Home Journal, Collier's, Scribner's,* and *Harper's;* cover illustrator for *Good Housekeeping.*

From *Little Women,* by Louisa May Alcott. Illustrated by Jessie Willcox Smith.

SIDELIGHTS: Award-winning American artist Jessie Willcox Smith was famous for her delicate pencil sketches and watercolor paintings. In a career that spanned five decades, she designed illustrations for advertisements, magazine covers, and children's books. Smith also painted portraits and earned a lasting reputation for her classic watercolor depictions of mothers and children.

Smith's career as an illustrator began by chance. As a child, she never tried her hand at drawing or painting, so her artistic skills went unnoticed for years. Her love of children led her to pursue employment as a kindergarten teacher. But an unusual turn of events occurred when she was seventeen. A friend who had agreed to give drawing lessons to a young man asked Smith to accompany them during the sessions. Smith obliged and, at her friend's request, even participated in the lessons, sketching a remarkably realistic likeness of a simple desk lamp. "That lamp was the turning point in my life," wrote Smith in an autobiographical entry for *Contempo-*

rary Illustrators of Children's Books. She abandoned her teaching plans to work at refining her newly discovered artistic abilities.

Smith began a brief but ultimately unsuccessful stint as a sculptor before determining that her true talent lay in painting. She enrolled in the Philadelphia School of Design for Women in 1885 and transferred to the Pennsylvania Academy of the Fine Arts later that year. But Smith was apparently uninspired by the stark and brooding atmosphere that pervaded the Academy. According to an essay in *American Women Artists,* the students and instructors there felt that "a mood of neurotic gloom was ... a necessary part of the life of a great artist."

Smith completed her instruction at the Academy in 1888. That May, her first illustration was published in *St. Nicholas,* a children's periodical, and for the next five years, she illustrated magazine advertisements. In 1894, Smith decided to continue her formal study of art. She enrolled in an illustration class at Drexel Institute, where she studied under art teacher and illustrator Howard Pyle. In sharp contrast to the rigorous educational philosophy fostered at the Pennsylvania Academy, Pyle approached the teaching of art from a freer perspective. "He made the field of illustration seem delightful and easy," noted the *American Women Artists* contributor. "He taught his students to imagine vividly the scenes they were going to illustrate, after which, he said, the drawings would naturally follow."

It was during her study with Pyle that Smith secured her first book illustration contracts. Pyle's longstanding relationship with various New York publishers enabled him to obtain illustration commissions for some of his exceptional students. Impressed with the quality of Smith's work, Pyle recommended her for the job of illustrating two books on American Indians. She had trouble drawing Indians but eventually completed the task to the publisher's satisfaction. She declined work on a third book about Indians but offered instead to do children's illustrations. The publisher agreed and helped to launch her into the field of professional book illustration.

Smith established a close friendship with two of her fellow students at Drexel Institute, Violet Oakley and Elizabeth Shippen Green. (Along with a fourth friend, the women lived and worked with one another for years.) Smith and Oakley worked together on illustrations for the acclaimed 1897 edition of Henry Wadsworth Longfellow's *Evangeline.* Smith preferred book illustration to advertisement work and went on to illustrate such classics as Robert Louis Stevenson's *Child's Garden of Verses* and Louisa May Alcott's *Little Women.*

In 1917, Smith's first *Good Housekeeping* cover was published. Over the next decade, she provided the magazine with illustrations for more than two hundred of its covers. In addition to her distinction as a book and magazine illustrator, Smith was well known for her children's portraits. Favoring natural subjects over posed models, she frequently painted children at play in outdoor settings and often told them fairy tales to capture their attention and evoke emotional responses. Smith continued her work well into her later years, but by 1933, she had grown weak and debilitated. She died two years later in her native Pennsylvania. In the *Contemporary Illustrators of Children's Books* essay, the artist described her career as "always thrilling and absorbing, with something ahead that one was sure one could do better."

More than half a century after her death, Smith remains a timeless figure in the field of children's art and literature. In the late 1980s, nearly a dozen classic works, including *A Child's Garden of Verses* and *Little Women,* were reprinted with her original illustrations.

WORKS CITED:

American Women Artists, Avon, 1982, p. 161.

Smith, Jessie Willcox, autobiographical essay included in *Contemporary Illustrators of Children's Books,* reprinted, Gale, 1978, pp. 68-69.

FOR MORE INFORMATION SEE:

BOOKS

The Illustrator in America, 1880-1980, Reinhold, 1966.

James, Edward T., editor, *Notable American Women, 1607-1950,* Harvard University Press, 1971.

Mitchell, Gene, *The Subject Was Children: The Art of Jessie Willcox Smith,* Dutton, 1979.

Schnessel, S. Michael, *Jessie Willcox Smith,* Crowell, 1977.

PERIODICALS

American Magazine of Art, July, 1925.

Philadelphia Ledger, July 16, 1922.

* * *

SMITH, William Jay 1918-

PERSONAL: Born April 22, 1918, in Winnfield, LA; son of Jay (a soldier) and Georgia Ella (Campster) Smith; married Barbara Howes (a poet), October 1, 1947 (divorced, June, 1964); married Sonja Haussmann (1966); children: (first marriage) David Emerson, Gregory Jay. *Education:* Washington University, St. Louis, MO, B.A., 1939, M.A. in French, 1941; Institut de Touraine, Universite de Poitiers, diplome d'etudes francaises; graduate study at Columbia University, 1946-47, at Oxford University as a Rhodes Scholar, 1947-48, and at University of Florence, 1948-50. *Politics:* Democrat. *Religion:* Protestant. *Hobbies and other interests:* Painting and travel.

ADDRESSES: Home—R.R. 1, Box 151, Cummington, MA 01026. *Agent*—Harriet Wasserman, 137 East 36th St., No. 19D, New York, NY 10016.

CAREER: Columbia University, New York City, instructor in English and French, 1946-47, visiting professor of writing and acting chairman of writing division,

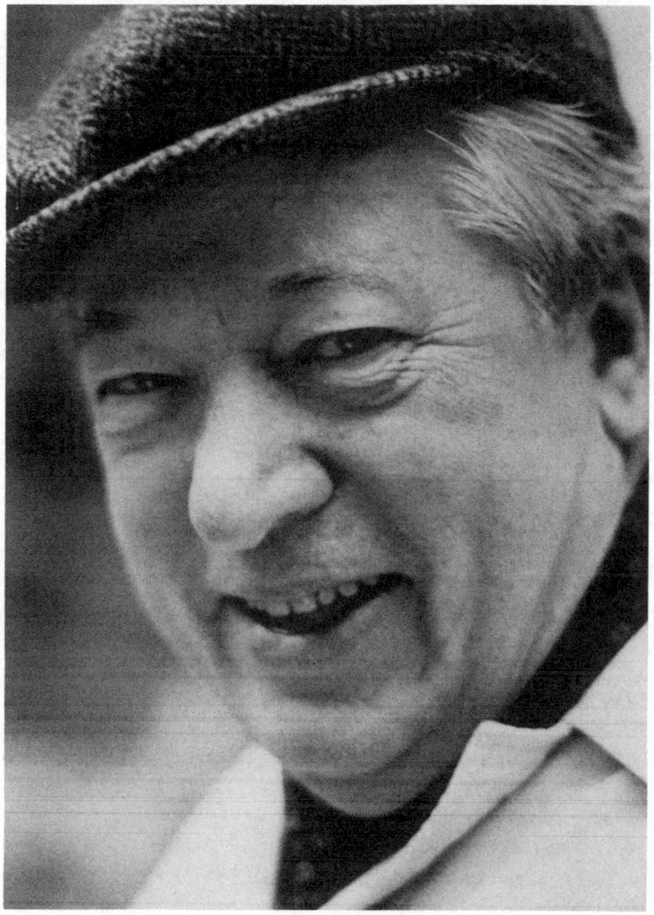

William Jay Smith

1973, 1974-75; Williams College, Williamstown, MA, lecturer in English, 1951, then poet in residence and lecturer in English, 1959-64, 1966-67; free-lance writer in Pownal, VT, 1951-59; Arena Stage, Washington, DC, writer in residence, 1964-65; Hollins College, Hollins College, VA, writer in residence, 1965-66, professor of English, 1967-68, 1970-80, professor emeritus, 1980—. Vermont House of Representatives, Democratic member, 1960-62; Library of Congress, Washington, DC, consultant in poetry, 1968-70, honorary consultant, 1970-76. Staff member, University of Connecticut Writers Conference, 1951, Suffield Writer-Reader Conference, 1959-62, University of Indiana Writers Conference, 1961. Lecturer at Salzburg Seminar in American Studies, 1974; Fulbright Lecturer, Moscow State University, 1981; poet in residence, Cathedral of St. John the Divine, New York City, 1985-88. Has lectured at colleges, clubs, writers' conferences, and book fairs, and has presented television programs on poetry for children. Chairman of board of directors, Translation Center, Columbia University. *Military service:* U.S. Naval Reserve, 1941-45; became lieutenant, awarded commendation by French Admiralty.

MEMBER: American Academy and Institute of Arts and Letters (vice president for literature, 1986-89), Association of American Rhodes Scholars, Authors League of America, Authors Guild (member of council), PEN, Century Association.

AWARDS, HONORS: Young Poets prize, *Poetry,* 1945; alumni citation, Washington University, 1963; Ford fellowship for drama, 1964; Union League Civic and Arts Foundation prize, *Poetry,* 1964; Henry Bellamann Major award, 1970; Loines award, 1972; National Endowment for the Arts grant, 1972; D.Litt, New England College, 1973; National Endowment for the Humanities grant, 1975 and 1989; Gold Medal of Labor (Hungary), 1978; New England Poetry Club Golden Rose, 1980; Ingram Merrill Foundation grant, 1982; California Children's Book and Video Awards recognition for excellence (preschool and toddlers category), 1990, for *Ho for a Hat!;* medal (medaille de vermeil) for service to the French language, French Academy, 1991.

WRITINGS:

POETRY FOR CHILDREN

Laughing Time, illustrated by Juliet Kepes, Little, Brown, 1955.
Boy Blue's Book of Beasts, illustrated by J. Kepes, Little, Brown, 1957.
Puptents and Pebbles: A Nonsense ABC, illustrated by J. Kepes, Little, Brown, 1959.
(And illustrator) *Typewriter Town,* Dutton, 1960.
What Did I See?, illustrated by Don Almquist, Crowell-Collier, 1962.
My Little Book of Big and Little, (Little Dimity, Big Gumbo, Big and Little), three volumes, illustrated by Don Bolognese, Macmillan, 1963.
Ho for a Hat!, illustrated by Ivan Chermayeff, Little, Brown, 1964, revised edition published with illustrations by Lynn Munsinger, Joy Street Books, 1989.
If I Had a Boat, illustrated by D. Bolognese, Macmillan, 1966.
Mr. Smith and Other Nonsense, illustrated by D. Bolognese, Delacorte, 1968.
Around My Room and Other Poems, illustrated by D. Madden, Lancelot, 1969.
Grandmother Ostrich and Other Poems, illustrated by D. Madden, Lancelot, 1969.
Laughing Time and Other Poems, illustrated by Don Madden, Lancelot, 1969.
The Key, Children's Book Council, 1982.
Laughing Time: Nonsense Poems, illustrated by Fernando Krahn, Delacorte, 1980.
Birds and Beasts, illustrations by Jacques Hnizdovsky, Godine, 1990.
Laughing Time: Collected Nonsense, Farrar, Straus, 1990.

Poetry is represented in numerous children's anthologies.

POETRY

Poems, Banyan Press, 1947.
Celebration at Dark, Farrar, Straus, 1950.
Snow, Schlosser Paper Corp., 1953.

The Stork: A Poem Announcing the Safe Arrival of Gregory Smith, Caliban Press, 1954.
Typewriter Birds, Caliban Press, 1954.
The Bead Curtain: Calligrams, privately printed, 1957.
The Old Man on the Isthmus, privately printed, 1957.
Poems, 1947-1957, Little, Brown, 1957.
Two Poems, Mason Hill Press (Pownal, VT), 1959.
A Minor Ode to the Morgan Horse, privately printed, 1963.
Prince Souvanna Phouma: An Exchange between Richard Wilbur and William Jay Smith, Chapel Press (Williamstown, MA), 1963.
Morels, privately printed, 1964.
Quail in Autumn, privately printed, 1965.
The Tin Can and Other Poems, Delacorte, 1966, title poem republished as *The Tin Can,* Stone House Press (Roslyn, NY), 1988.
A Clutch of Clerihews, privately printed, 1966.
Winter Morning, privately printed, 1967.
Imaginary Dialogue, privately printed, 1968.
Hull Boy, St. Thomas, privately printed, 1970.
New and Selected Poems, Delacorte, 1970.
A Rose for Katherine Anne Porter, Albondocani Press, 1970.
At Delphi: For Allen·Tate on His Seventy-fifth Birthday, 19 November 1974, Chapel Press, 1974.
Venice in the Fog, Unicorn Press (Greensboro, NC), 1975.
Song for a Country Wedding, privately printed, 1976.
(With Richard Wilbur) *Verses on the Times,* Gutenberg Press, 1978.
Journey to the Dead Sea, illustrated by David Newbert, Abattoir (Omaha, NE), 1979.
The Tall Poets, Palaemon Press (Winston-Salem, NC), 1979.
Mr. Smith, Delacorte, 1980.
The Traveler's Tree: New and Selected Poems, illustrated by Jacques Hnizdovsky, Persea Books, 1980.
Oxford Doggerel, privately printed, 1983.
Plain Talk: Epigrams, Epitaphs, Satires, Nonsense, Occasional, Concrete and Quotidian Poems, Center for Book Arts, 1988.
Journey to the Interior (broadside), Stone House Press, 1988.
Collected Poems, 1939-1989, Macmillan, 1990.

Also author, with Barbara Howes, of privately printed Christmas card poems, including *Lachrymae Christi and In the Old Country,* 1948; *Poems: The Homecoming and The Piazza,* 1949; and *Two French Poems: The Roses of Saadi and Five Minute Watercolor,* 1950. Poetry is represented in numerous anthologies and textbooks, including *The War Poets,* Day, 1945; *Oxford Poetry,* Basil Blackwell, 1948; *Poetry Awards,* University of Pennsylvania Press, 1952; *The New Poets of England and America,* Meridian, 1957; *Modern Verse in English, 1900-1950,* Macmillan, 1958; *Poems for Seasons and Celebrations,* World Publishing, 1961; *Poet's Choice,* Dial, 1962; *The Modern Poets: An American-British Anthology,* McGraw, 1962; *Modern American Poetry,* edited by Louis Untermeyer, Harcourt, 1962; and *Contemporary American Poets: American Poetry since 1940,* Meridian, 1969.

EDITOR

(And translator) *Selected Writings of Jules Laforgue,* Grove, 1956.
Herrick (criticism), Dell, 1962.
(With Louise Bogan) *The Golden Journey: Poems for Young People* (anthology), illustrated by Fritz Kredel, Reilly & Lee, 1965, revised by Smith as *The Golden Journey: Two Hundred Twenty-five Poems for Young People,* Contemporary Books, 1989.
Poems from France (for children), illustrated by Roger Duvoisin, Crowell, 1967.
Poems from Italy (for children), drawings by Elaine Raphael, calligraphy by Don Bolognese, Crowell, 1972.
Witter Bynner, *Light Verse and Satires,* Farrar Straus, 1978.
A Green Place: Modern Poems, illustrated by Jacques Hnizdovsky, Delacorte, 1982.
(With Emanuel Brasil) *Brazilian Poetry 1950-1980,* Wesleyan University Press, 1983.
(With James S. Holmes) *Dutch Interior: Post-War Poetry of the Netherlands and Flanders,* Columbia University Press, 1984.
(With Dana Gioia) *Poems from Italy,* New Rivers Press, 1985.
(With F. D. Reeve, and author of introduction) Andrei Voznesensky, *An Arrow in the Wall; Selected Poetry and Prose,* Holt, 1987.
(And author of introduction) Nina Cassian, *Life Sentence: Selected Poems,* Norton, 1990.

TRANSLATOR

Romualdo Romano, *Scirroco,* Farrar Straus, 1951.
Valery Larbaud, *Poems of a Multimillionaire,* Bonacio and Saul/Grove, 1955.
Elsa Beskow, *Children of the Forest* (for children), illustrated by E. Beskow, Delacorte, 1969.
Two Plays by Charles Bertin: Christopher Columbus and Don Juan, University of Minnesota Press, 1970.
Lennart Hellsing, *The Pirate Book* (for children), illustrated by Poul Stroeyer, Delacorte, 1972.
Szabolcs Varady, *Chairs above the Danube,* privately printed, 1976.
(With Max Hayward) Kornei Chukovsky, *The Telephone* (for children), illustrated by Blair Lent, Delacorte, 1977.
Andrei Voznesensky, *Saga,* privately printed, 1977.
(With Leif Sjoeberg) Artur Lundkvist, *Agadir,* International Poetry Forum, 1979.
(With Ingvar Schousboe) Thorkild Bjoernvig, *The Pact: My Friendship with Isak Dinesen,* Louisiana State University Press, 1983.
Jules Laforgue, *Moral Tales,* New Directions, 1985.
(With L. Sjoeberg) Henry Martinson, *Wild Bouquet: Nature Poems,* Bookmark Press, 1985.
Collected Translations: Italian, French, Spanish, Portuguese (poetry), New Rivers Press, 1985.
(With Edwin Morgan and others) Sandor Weoeres, *Eternal Moment: Selected Poems,* New Rivers Press, 1988.
(With wife, Sonja Haussmann Smith) Tchicaya U Tam'Si, *The Madman and the Medusa,* edited by A.

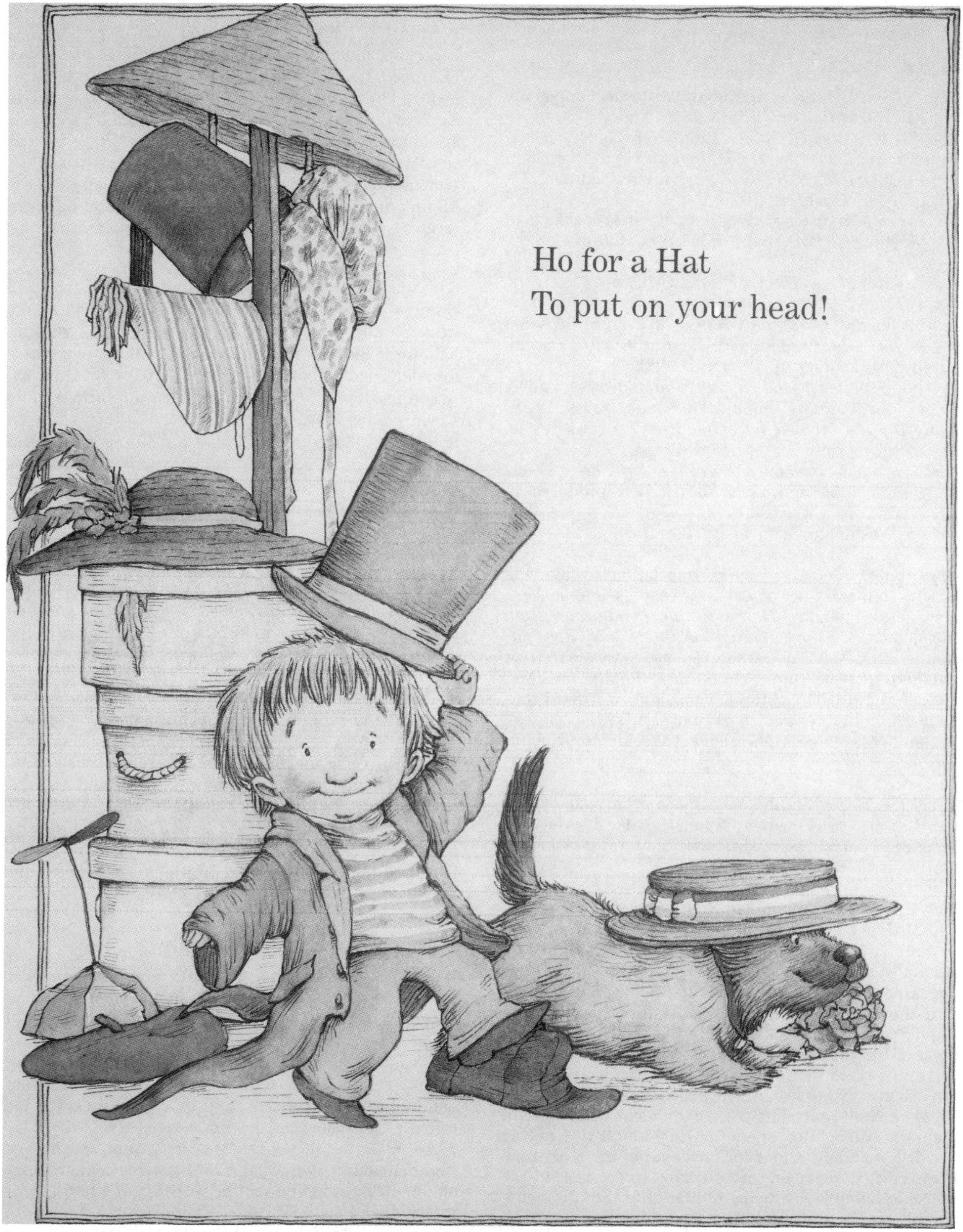
Ho for a Hat
To put on your head!

From *Ho for a Hat!*, by William Jay Smith. Illustrated by Lynn Munsinger.

James Arnold and Kandioura Drame, University Press of Virginia, 1989.

OTHER

The Spectra Hoax (criticism), Wesleyan University Press, 1961.
The Skies of Venice, Andre Emmerich Gallery, 1961.
(With Virginia Haviland) *Children and Poetry: A Selective, Annotated Bibliography,* revised edition, Library of Congress, 1979.
The Straw Market (comedy), first read at Arena Stage in Washington, DC, and produced at Hollins College, 1965.
The Streaks of the Tulip: Selected Criticism, Delacorte, 1972.
Louise Bogan: A Woman's Words; A Lecture Delivered at the Library of Congress, May 4, 1970 (monograph), Library of Congress, 1972.
(Author of preface) *Modern Hungarian Poetry,* edited by Miklos Vajda, Columbia University Press, 1977.
Army Brat: A Memoir (also see below), Persea Books, 1980, reprinted, Story Line Press, 1991.
Army Brat: A Dramatic Narrative for Three Voices (based upon Smith's memoir), first produced in New York City, 1980.
Green, Washington University Libraries, 1980.

Contributor of poetry, reviews, translations, essays, and articles to literary periodicals, newspapers, and national magazines, including *Harper's, Harper's Bazaar, Horn Book, Ladies' Home Journal, Nation, New Republic, New Yorker, New York Times, Poetry, Sewanee Review, Southern Review,* and *Yale Review.* Poetry reviewer, *Harper's,* 1961-64; editorial consultant, Grove Press, 1968-70; editor, *Translations* (journal), 1973—. A collection of his manuscripts is held at Washington University.

ADAPTATIONS: Smith's poetry has been recorded for the Library of Congress, Spoken Arts Treasury of Modern Poetry, Yale University, and for Harvard University libraries.

SIDELIGHTS: William Jay Smith has enjoyed a long and distinguished career as a poet and translator. Fluent in French and Italian, Smith also reads Spanish and Russian; his translations of the French, which have appeared in several periodicals and books, have earned him the French Academy's medal for service to the French language. Born in Louisiana in 1918, he spent most of his youth at Jefferson Barracks, near St. Louis, Missouri, since his father was an enlisted man in the U.S. Army; and in his critically acclaimed *Army Brat: A Memoir,* Smith recounts these early years. Calling it "a memoir unlike any other," Artur Lundkvist of the Swedish Academy added for the cover of the Story Line Press edition that "one would have to go back to the books of Kipling portraying military life seen through a child's eyes in order to find any thing comparable." According to a *Virginia Quarterly Review* contributor's discussion of Smith's memoir, few poets' backgrounds "have ever been so unpromising." Under the guidance of one of his high school teachers, however, Smith developed a love for language, and scholarships to Washington University permitted him to earn both a bachelor's and master's degree. He continued his studies in France, Italy, and in England as a Rhodes scholar to Oxford University. A liaison officer for the U.S. Naval Reserve during World War II, Smith began his career as an educator at Columbia University in 1946. He has since taught at numerous colleges and universities in the United States, and was consultant in poetry to the Library of Congress in Washington, D.C., and has even served a term as a Vermont state representative.

Smith has written many books of poetry for adults and children alike, in addition to editing or translating the work of others. Noted for the diversity of his work in both form and content, Smith writes mainly lyric poetry for adults and whimsical or nonsense verse for children. According to Bob Group in an essay in *Dictionary of Literary Biography: American Poets since World War II,* Smith has a "personal style that transforms his subject matter into a memorable reading experience through a lively wit and a writer's eye perceptive enough to make the reader see more than he thought his vision could accommodate."

According to Patrick Groff in *Twentieth-Century Children's Writers,* "Smith's books of poetry for children offer many cleverly written bits of infectious nonsense on a wide range of topics." Believing that his poems for children "reflect the technical soundness of good adult poetry," Groff calls them "playfully graphic, full of imagery, and song-like." Commenting on *Puptents and Pebbles: A Nonsense ABC,* one of Smith's collections of whimsical verse for children, a *Saturday Review* critic drolly recommended that "only sophisticated readers, like children and grownups, should be allowed such fun and wisdom." And in a *New York Times Book Review* assessment of *Mr. Smith and Other Nonsense,* May Sarton similarly remarks that Smith "remains one of the best of nonsense poets, as well as one of the best of serious poets."

In an autobiographical comment for *Contemporary Poets,* Smith says, "I have always used a great variety of verse forms, especially in my poetry for children. I believe that poetry begins in childhood and that a poet who can remember his own childhood exactly can, and should, communicate to children." Smith believes that children are often gratifyingly quick to recognize the essential idea developed by a verse. In an article for *Horn Book,* Smith writes: "As any parent, teacher, or librarian knows, there is no richer experience than to see children's faces light up at the suspense of a new tale or the surprise of a new poem. The uninhibited joy with which they listen is surely akin to that of adult audiences of old around campfire and hearth. I have felt at times with groups of children that I was really being what every poet would like to be—a bard in the old sense."

WORKS CITED:

Group, Bob, *Dictionary of Literary Biography,* Volume 5: *American Poets since World War II,* Gale, 1980, pp. 262-66.
Review of *Army Brat: A Memoir, Virginia Quarterly Review,* spring, 1981, pp. 48-49.
Review of *Puptents and Pebbles: A Nonsense ABC, Saturday Review,* November 7, 1959, p. 54.
Sarton, May, Review of *Mr. Smith and Other Nonsense, New York Times Book Review,* September 29, 1968, p. 38.
Smith, William Jay, *Contemporary Poets,* 4th edition, edited by James Vinson and D. L. Kirkpatrick, St. Martin's Press, 1985, pp. 802-04.
Smith, William Jay, "Rhythm of the Night," *Horn Book,* December, 1960, pp. 495-500.

FOR MORE INFORMATION SEE:

BOOKS

Arbuthnot, May Hill, Zena Sutherland, and Dianne L. Monson, *Children and Books,* 6th edition, Scott, Foresman, 1981.
Children's Literature in the Elementary School, 3rd edition, edited by Charlotte S. Huck and Doris A. Young, Holt, 1976.
Dickey, James, *Babel to Byzantium: Poets and Poetry Now,* Farrar, Straus, 1968.
Hollins Poets, edited by Louis D. Rubin, University Press of Virginia, 1967.
Modern American Poetry, edited by Louis Untermeyer, Harcourt, 1962.
Modern Verse in English, 1900-1950, edited by David Cecil and Allen Tate, Macmillan, 1958.
Poets On Poetry, edited by Howard Nemerov, Basic Books, 1966.

PERIODICALS

Georgia Review, summer, 1991.
Hollins Critic, February, 1975.
Library Journal, April 15, 1964.
Michigan Quarterly Review, fall, 1991.
New York Times Book Review, May 10, 1964.
Partisan Review, winter, 1967.
Poetry, December, 1966.
Sewanee Review, winter, 1973.
Southern Humanities Review, summer, 1968; winter, 1968.
Voyages, winter, 1970.
Washington Post, March 9, 1969.

* * *

SMUCKER, Barbara (Claassen) 1915-

PERSONAL: Born September 1, 1915, in Newton, KS; daughter of Cornelius W. (a banker) and Addie (Lander) Claassen; married Donovan E. Smucker (a minister and professor of sociology and religion), January 21, 1939; children: Timothy Lester, Thomas Cornelius, Rebecca Mary. *Education:* Kansas State University, B.S., 1936; attended Rosary College, 1963-65, and University of Waterloo, 1975-77. *Politics:* Democrat. *Religion:* Mennonite.

Barbara Claassen Smucker

ADDRESSES: Agent—c/o Penguin Books Canada, #10 Alcorn Ave., Suite 300, Toronto, Ontario, Canada M4V 3B2.

CAREER: Public high school teacher of English and journalism in Harper, KS, 1937-38; *Evening Kansas Republican,* Newton, KS, reporter, 1939-41; Ferry Hall School, Lake Forest, IL, teacher, 1960-63; Lake Forest Bookstore, Lake Forest, bookseller, 1963-67; Kitchener Public Library, Kitchener, Ontario, children's librarian, 1969-77; Renison College, Waterloo, Ontario, head librarian, 1977-82. Has also worked as an interviewer for Gallup Poll.

MEMBER: Children's Reading Roundtable of Chicago, American Association of University Women, Canadian Association of University Women, Canadian Society of Children's Authors, Illustrators and Performers, Canadian Writers Union.

AWARDS, HONORS: Named one of the fifty best books of all time in Canada, Children's Book Center, 1978, Canadian Library Association award runner-up, 1979, Brotherhood Award, National Conference of Christians and Jews, 1980, and top honors from All-Japan Library

Committee and from Catholic Teachers Association of West Germany, all for *Underground to Canada;* children's literary award, Canada Council, and Ruth Schwartz Foundation Award, both 1980, both for *Days of Terror;* distinguished service award for children's literature, Kansas State University, 1980; senior honorary fellow, Renison College, 1982; Dr.Litt., honoris causa, University of Waterloo, 1986. Doctor of Humane Letters, Bluffton College, Bluffton, Ohio, 1989, Municipal Chapter of Toronto IODE Book Award for *Incredible Jumbo,* 1991.

WRITINGS:

CHILDREN'S BOOKS

Henry's Red Sea, illustrated by Allan Eitzen, Herald Press, 1955.
Cherokee Run, illustrated by Eitzen, Herald Press, 1957.
Wigwam in the City, illustrated by Gil Miret, Dutton, 1966, published as *Susan,* Scholastic Book Services, 1978.
Underground to Canada, illustrated by Tom McNeely, Clarke, Irwin, 1977, published as *Runaway to Freedom: A Story of the Underground Railway,* Harper, 1978.
Days of Terror, illustrated by Kim La Fave, Clarke, Irwin, 1979.
Amish Adventure, Clarke, Irwin, 1983.
White Mist, Clarke, Irwin, 1985.
Jacob's Little Giant, Viking, 1987.
Incredible Jumbo, Viking, 1989.
Garth and the Mermaid, Viking, 1992.

OTHER

Also author of oratorio *The Abiding Place,* music by Ester Wiebe, produced in Strasbourg, France, 1984. Contributor of articles to *American Educator Encyclopedia.* Smucker's manuscript collection is housed in the Kerlan Collection at the University of Minnesota and in the Doris Lewis Rare Book Room, University of Waterloo Library, Ontario. Her books have been published in sixteen countries and translated into French, German, Japanese, Swedish, Spanish, Dutch, and Danish.

SIDELIGHTS: Canadian author Barbara Smucker is best known for her well-researched historical fiction for young adults. She often writes about important events that have been overlooked by other authors, such as the underground railroad that led slaves to freedom in Canada in *Underground to Canada,* and the vast immigration of Russian Mennonites to the United States and Canada in *Days of Terror.* Many of her books have some kind of personal significance; for example, her grandfather was involved in the evacuation of Mennonites and she was very involved in the civil rights movement. With her careful research and strong character development, Smucker has been able to bring new dimensions of history alive, while showing that it is the strength of her characters' convictions that bring them through difficult times.

Smucker was born in Kansas in 1915, the granddaughter of a Mennonite family who had come to America from

Cover of *Days of Terror,* by Barbara Claassen Smucker.

East Prussia. She grew up reading and loving books, including *Alice in Wonderland* and *Anne of Green Gables,* while hanging out at her local library. "I would never have dreamed that someday I would write children's books, live in Canada, and speak to schoolchildren in the Anne of Green Gables School on Prince Edward Island," Smucker related in *Something about the Author Autobiography Series* (*SAAS*).

Because her mother was having difficulty keeping up with four young children, the family hired Ella Underwood, a widowed black woman, to take care of them. Smucker would listen to the entrancing stories Underwood told her, many of them about the days of slavery. These tales were to prove important to Smucker in her career: "Years later, when I wrote my book *Underground to Canada,*" she commented in *SAAS,* "I could hear [Ella's] voice and the way she pronounced words."

In the sixth grade, Smucker decided she wanted to be a writer. This happened when her teacher gave the class an assignment to write an original fairy tale. Smucker's was considered to be one of the best. "From then on, I was hooked on writing," Smucker remarked in *SAAS*. The next year, Smucker's life was greatly changed when she became ill with rheumatic fever. After weeks of illness, her fever broke, but she was left with an enlarged heart and a heart murmur. An expert was called in to provide a cure and he suggested that Smucker be put to bed for a year. While this might have been a great tragedy for other children, Smucker used the time to read the classics—from Dickens to Charlotte Bronte.

After finishing high school, Smucker attended the local Bethel College for a year, then went to Kansas State University to study journalism. A year after graduation, she obtained a job at the Newton *Evening Kansas Republican*. She was thrilled to actually have a position as a "real writer." Excitement came when she was granted interviews with movie stars who happened to be travelling by rail from coast to coast. One time, she interviewed a young man named Donovan Smucker, a Mennonite who had come to Kansas to work at Bethel College. Smitten with him, Smucker travelled on a university summer course to Russia, where he was one of the guides. The two were married in 1939.

The next few years of the young couple's life were busy—they moved many times and had three children. They ended up living semi-permanently near Chicago in an interracial cooperative community. While there, a neighbor told Smucker an incredible story about how a thousand Mennonite refugees had escaped from Russia to Paraguay after World War II. The story was so entrancing that Smucker's three small children didn't stir during the two-hour narrative. Realizing that this story should be captured for children, Smucker created a fictionalized account of it in her first book, *Henry's Red Sea*.

In 1967, Smucker's husband was asked to become president of an all-black Presbyterian college in Mississippi, while she was offered a position as the first white teacher in a nearby all-black high school. The couple decided to take on this challenge, despite the threat of racial unrest. Smucker learned a great deal from the students there, especially from one girl who told her that they could never understand each other because Smucker felt with a "white" heart. "I was to use this material many years later when I wrote my book, *Underground to Canada*," Smucker pointed out in *SAAS*. The Smuckers left after tension increased following the assassination of Martin Luther King.

In 1969, Smucker's husband accepted an offer to teach at Conrad Grebel College, a Mennonite school in Ontario, Canada. The couple was thrilled to be involved in a Mennonite community and to be living in a new country. Smucker took a job in a local public library and, disappointed with the lack of children's literature with Canadian content, as well as any literature on the Canadian cause in fighting slavery, Smucker wrote *Underground to Canada*. This work recounts the story of Julilly, Liza, and Lester, three slaves who run away from their cruel master to find freedom in Canada. One of Smucker's most popular books, it has been translated into many languages, including French, German and Japanese. It was also the subject of an essay contest for Japanese junior high school age students.

"At that time," Smucker wrote in *SAAS*, "my mind became filled with historical stories clamoring to be unearthed and turned into fiction." The next book she researched hit close to home—it was about the exodus of 20,000 Mennonites from Russia in the late 1900s and their subsequent lives in the United States and Canada. Smucker had vivid memories of her grandfather wanting to help these people. *Days of Terror* describes the tragedies suffered by the Mennonites in their homeland and their eventual journey to freedom. Cory Bieman Davies says in *Canadian Children's Literature* that the book represents "Smucker's attempt to keep strong within the larger Canadian community her own Mennonite heritage and faith, and to contribute strengthening Mennonite strands to multicultural Canadian peoplehood."

After this book, Smucker took a look at life on an Amish farm in *Amish Adventure*, probed the story of Indians removed from their land in *White Mist*, chronicled the life of a boy who raises the endangered Giant Canada Geese in *Jacob's Little Giant*, and provided a fictionalized account of P. T. Barnum's famous elephant who was killed in a Canadian railway accident in *Incredible Jumbo*.

"I write for young people because I like their fresh response, buoyant enthusiasm, and honest frankness," Smucker wrote in *Twentieth Century Children's Writers*. With her ability to bring historical events to life through fictional, but believable characters, Smucker has become a well-known name in her field. She adds modestly in *SAAS* that "hopefully my books will add positively to [a child's] act of growing."

WORKS CITED:

Davies, Cory Bieman, "Remembrance and Celebration: Barbara Smucker's Days of Terror," *Canadian Children's Literature*, Number 25, 1982, pp. 18-25.

Smucker, Barbara Claassen, essay in *Something about the Author Autobiography Series*, Volume 11, Gale, 1991, pp. 321-335.

Twentieth-Century Children's Writers, 3rd edition, St. James Press, 1989, pp. 902-903.

FOR MORE INFORMATION SEE:

BOOKS

Children's Literature Review, Volume 10, Gale, 1986.

Egoff, Sheila, and Judith Saltman, *New Republic of Childhood: A Critical Guide to Canadian Children's Literature in English*, Oxford University Press, 1990.

Michele Landsberg's Guide to Children's Books, Penguin Books, 1986.

PERIODICALS

Canadian Children's Literature, Number 22, 1981.

Globe and Mail (Toronto), November 30, 1985.

In Review, fall, 1977.
Mennonite Quarterly Review, January, 1981.
Saturday Night, November, 1979.

* * *

SNODGRASS, Quentin Curtius
See CLEMENS, Samuel Langhorne

See CLEMENS, Samuel Langhorne

* * *

SNODGRASS, Thomas Jefferson

See CLEMENS, Samuel Langhorne

* * *

SNYDER, Zilpha Keatley 1927-

PERSONAL: Born May 11, 1927, in Lemoore, CA; daughter of William Solon (a rancher and driller) and Dessa J. (Jepson) Keatley; married Larry Allan Snyder, June 18, 1950; children: Susan Melissa, Douglas; foster children: Ben. *Education:* Whittier College, B.A., 1948; additional study at University of California, Berkeley, 1958-60. *Politics:* Democrat. *Religion:* Episcopalian. *Hobbies and other interests:* "My hobbies seem to change from time to time, but reading and travel remain among the top favorites. And of course writing which, besides being my occupation, is still and always will be my all-time favorite hobby."

ADDRESSES: Home—52 Miller Ave., Mill Valley, CA 94941.

Zilpha Keatley Snyder

CAREER: Writer. Public school teacher at Washington School, Berkeley, CA, and in New York, Washington, and Alaska, 1948-62; University of California, Berkeley, master teacher and demonstrator for education classes, 1959-61; lecturer.

AWARDS, HONORS: George G. Stone Recognition of Merit from Claremont Graduate School, Lewis Carroll Shelf award, Spring Book Festival first prize, all 1967, and Newbery honor book, 1968, all for *The Egypt Game;* Christopher Medal, 1970, for *The Changeling;* William Allen White Award, Newbery honor book, Christopher Medal, all 1972, and Hans Christian Andersen International honor list of the International Board on Books for Young People, 1974, all for *The Headless Cupid; New York Times* Outstanding Book, 1972, National Book Award finalist and Newbery honor book, both 1973, all for *The Witches of Worm; New York Times* Outstanding Book, 1981, for *A Fabulous Creature;* PEN Literary Award, 1983, and Parent's Choice Award, both for *The Birds of Summer;* Bay Area Book Reviewers Award, 1988, William Allen White Master Reading List, 1989-90, and Georgia Children's Book Award Master List, 1990-91, all for *And Condors Danced;* New Mexico State Award, 1989-90, and on the Notable Trade Books in the Language Arts list of the National Council of Teachers of English, both for *The Changing Maze; Season of Ponies, The Egypt Game, The Headless Cupid, The Witches of Worm,* and *A Fabulous Creature* were all named American Library Association Notable Books; *The Velvet Room* and *The Egypt Game* were named on the *Horn Book* honor list; *The Velvet Room, The Changeling, The Headless Cupid, Below the Root, Until the Celebration,* and *Blair's Nightmare* were all Junior Literary Guild selections; *Blair's Nightmare* was included on state awards master lists in Missouri, Texas, Nebraska, Pacific Northwest, and New Mexico; *Libby on Wednesday* was on the Virginia state award master list.

WRITINGS:

FOR CHILDREN

Season of Ponies, illustrated by Alton Raible, Atheneum, 1964.
The Velvet Room, illustrated by Raible, Atheneum, 1965.
Black and Blue Magic, illustrated by Gene Holtan, Atheneum, 1966.
The Egypt Game, illustrated by Raible, Atheneum, 1967.
Eyes in the Fishbowl, illustrated by Raible, Atheneum, 1968.
Today Is Saturday (poetry), photographs by John Arms, Atheneum, 1969.
The Changeling, illustrated by Raible, Atheneum, 1970.
The Headless Cupid, illustrated by Raible, Atheneum, 1971.
The Witches of Worm, illustrated by Raible, Atheneum, 1972.
The Princess and the Giants (picture book), illustrated by Beatrice Darwin, Atheneum, 1973.

The Truth about Stone Hollow, illustrated by Raible, Atheneum, 1974, published in England as *The Ghosts of Stone Hollow,* Lutterworth, 1978.
Below the Root (first volume in the "Green-sky" trilogy), illustrated by Raible, Atheneum, 1975.
And All Between (second volume in the "Green-sky" trilogy), illustrated by Raible, Atheneum, 1976.
Until the Celebration (third volume in the "Green-sky" trilogy), illustrated by Raible, Atheneum, 1977.
The Famous Stanley Kidnapping Case, illustrated by Raible, Atheneum, 1979.
Come On, Patsy (picture book), illustrated by Margot Zemach, Atheneum, 1982.
Blair's Nightmare, Atheneum, 1984.
The Changing Maze (picture book), illustrated by Charles Mikolaycak, Macmillan, 1985.
The Three Men, Harper, 1986.
And Condors Danced, Delacorte, 1987.
Squeak Saves the Day and Other Tooley Tales, illustrated by Leslie Morrill, Delacorte, 1988.
Janie's Private Eyes, Delacorte, 1989.
Libby on Wednesday, Delacorte, 1990.
Song of the Gargoyle, Delacorte, 1991.

YOUNG ADULT NOVELS

A Fabulous Creature, Atheneum, 1981.
The Birds of Summer, Atheneum, 1983.

ADULT NOVELS

Heirs of Darkness, Atheneum, 1978.

OTHER

Snyder's manuscript collection is kept in the Kerlan Collection, University of Minnesota, Minneapolis.

ADAPTATIONS:

Black and Blue Magic (filmstrip with tape), Pied Piper, 1975.
The Egypt Game (recording and cassette), Miller-Brody, 1975.
The Headless Cupid (from *Newbery Award Cassette* stories; recording and cassette), Miller-Brody, 1976, (filmstrip with tape) Pied Piper, 1980.
The Witches of Worm (recording), Miller-Brody, 1978.
Below the Root (computer game), Spinnaker Software's Windham Classics, 1985.

The Egypt Game was produced as a filmstrip and tape by Piped Piper.

SIDELIGHTS: "I was eight years old when I decided I was a writer," Zilpha Keatley Snyder recalls in Lee Bennett Hopkins's *More Books by More People,* "and in spite of many detours, I never entirely gave up the idea." It was not until after she had become a mother of two and spent nine years working as an elementary school teacher that the author finally found time to write. Inspired by childhood memories and her experiences with children, Snyder decided to write stories that combined typical themes about the problems that children face with an element of fantasy. Snyder's stories, writes Jean Fritz in the *New York Times Book Review,* "suggest that magic lies within the power of imagination itself."

From *Egypt Game,* by Zilpha Keatley Snyder. Illustrated by Alton Raible.

As a child growing up in California, Snyder's imagination was very active. According to her, this was a matter of necessity. "We lived in the country during the Depression and World War II," she says in Hopkins's book. "Due to shortages of such things as gasoline and money, I didn't get around much or do many exciting things. In fact, my world might have been quite narrow and uninteresting if it had not been for two magical ingredients—animals and books." As for animals, the author's family lived in a country house and raised everything from cats, dogs, and rabbits to cows, goats, and horses, so there were plenty of four-legged friends to keep her happy. A nearby library supplied the young Snyder with her other magical ingredient. Having learned to read at the very early age of four years, she borrowed many books from the library, reading about one per day during her first years in school.

When she entered the seventh grade, as she recounts in the *Something about the Author Autobiography Series* (*SAAS*), she felt she "was suddenly a terrible misfit" because she had been allowed to skip one grade and was younger than the other children. "So I retreated further into books and daydreams," she later remarked. Snyder began to feel less shy by the time she entered high school. "I became a little less afraid of my peers. I had some good teachers and made some exciting new friends, such as Shakespeare and Emily Dickinson." The author continued to grow as a student at Whittier College, where she also met her husband Larry, who was a music major at the time.

Snyder had romantic dreams of becoming a struggling writer in New York City, but after graduating from Whittier she found that she did not have the money for a ticket to get there, let alone try to live in the city with no dependable income. She took a teaching job instead; and not only did she enjoy teaching elementary school children, but she was so talented at it that she eventually became a master teacher at the University of California at Berkeley. Snyder held several teaching jobs around the United States because her husband transferred to different graduate schools, and also because he was assigned to several bases while he served in the Air Force during the Korean War. They finally ended up in Berkeley, California, where Larry finished his degree. After moving fifteen times and having two children, the Snyders were finally ready to settle down. "I was still teaching but there seemed to be a bit more time and I caught my breath and thought about writing."

For Snyder the appeal of writing lies in the author's power to create an entire world and populate it with people who have never existed before, so she was naturally drawn toward writing stories that dealt with imagination and fantasy. A large source of her inspiration, especially in her earlier books, has been her childhood memories. "Remembering a dream I'd had when I was twelve years old about some strange and wonderful horses," Snyder says, she sat down to write her first book, *Season of Ponies,* and submitted it to Atheneum for publication. Although the editor there, Jean Karl, did not immediately accept the author's manuscript, she encouraged Snyder to revise the book and, after the author rewrote the story twice, it was accepted.

Other early works like *The Velvet Room* and *The Egypt Game* also originated from Snyder's childhood. *The Velvet Room* echoes experiences Snyder had as a child growing up during the Depression. The story itself is based on one that Snyder wrote when she was only nineteen years old about a migratory worker and his family. Despite the realistic subject, magic enters the tale as it is told through a child's imaginative eyes. The inspiration for *The Egypt Game* came from what Snyder calls the "Egyptian period" of her childhood, a year during which she became completely absorbed in anything having to do with ancient Egypt. "However, the actual setting and all six of the main characters came from my years as a teacher in Berkeley," the author related.

"*The Egypt Game* is probably one of this author's most popular novels, and one of her best," claims *Twentieth Century Children's Writers* contributor Kay E. Vandergrift. "The Egypt game is an elaborate game played in a secret 'temple' and filled with ritualistic gestures. Through his observations of the game, an old professor takes a new interest in life and ultimately saves the children from unexpected danger. Although there is no special note taken of the fact, the players are a mixed group racially and ethnically which was at the time of publication (1967) still somewhat rare in American books for children."

The Egypt Game was published one year after the Snyders adopted their son Ben, a native of Kowloon, China. A few years later, in 1970, the Snyders left their home near Berkeley to tour Europe. When they returned they settled into a century-old farmhouse near Santa Rosa, California. It was here that Snyder wrote many of her books, including the science fiction "Green-sky" trilogy. Mystery and magic continue to be important elements in books like *The Changeling, The Witches of Worm,* and *The Truth about Stone Hollow.* The reappearance of paranormal subjects in these books led a *Dell Carousel* interviewer to ask Snyder whether she was interested in the occult. Snyder responds that she was, "but only because I'm interested in everything that suggests a wider reach to knowledge and experience than what is readily available to the five senses." In Hopkins's book she notes: "A long time ago I accepted the fact that I'm probably incurably superstitious.... I've also known for some time that it's not too wise to admit that I still believe in fairy godmothers and some kinds of ghosts and all kinds of magical omens."

Snyder's imagination switched from stories about ghosts and witches to science fiction in the "Green-sky Trilogy," which includes *Below the Root, And All Between,* and *Until the Celebration.* "Like so many of my books," Snyder comments in *SAAS,* "the trilogy's deepest root goes back to my early childhood when I played a game that involved crossing a grove of oak trees by climbing from tree to tree, because something incredibly dangerous lived 'below the root.'" The game is first mentioned in *The Changeling,* in which two of the characters play in the trees much as Snyder did, but it is given life in the trilogy. The people of Green-sky, known as the Kindar, are settlers from another planet who live peacefully in the treetops. The only thing they fear are the Erdlings, an evil race who live beneath the trees and capture and enslave Kindar children. The Green-sky books focus on the adventures of three children and is told from the viewpoints of both the Kindar and the Erdlings in an attempt to deliver a message about peace and brotherhood.

Snyder did not at first plan to write a trilogy, but she enjoyed writing *Below the Root* so much that she returned to the world of Green-sky twice more. The same thing happened with Snyder's books about the Stanley family, which include *The Headless Cupid, The Famous Stanley Kidnapping Case, Blair's Nightmare,* and *Janie's Private Eyes.* The five Stanley children—David, Blair, Esther, Janie, and Amanda—are "favorites of mine," Snyder says in a *Junior Literary Guild* article. "Every so often I get an irresistible urge to find out what they're up to now, and the result is another book."

As to what Snyder is up to, in 1985 she finally fulfilled a childhood dream and traveled to Egypt. She also lived for a time in Italy before returning to the United States and settling in Mill Valley near San Francisco, where she continues to write and occasionally gives talks to adults and school children about her work. Her writing has become increasingly diverse, as her more recent books testify. Since returning to California she has written a historical novel, *And Condors Danced,* a fanciful collection of stories about tiny people called "Tiddlers" in *Squeak Saves the Day and Other Tooley Tales,* a mainstream children's book, *Libby on Wednesday,* and a fantasy novel, *Song of the Gargoyle.*

During one of her lectures a member of the audience asked Snyder why she became an author. Recalling the incident in her *SAAS* entry, Snyder responds that "the maximum reward is simply—joy; the storyteller's joy in creating a story and sharing it with an audience. So I write for joy, my own and my imagined audience's—but why for children? Unlike many writers who say that they are not aware of a particular audience as they write, I know that I am very conscious of mine." She later concludes, "I enjoy writing for an audience that shares my optimism, curiosity and freewheeling imagination."

WORKS CITED:

Dell Carousel, fall/winter, 1985-1986.

Fritz, Jean, "For Young Readers: 'The Witches of Worm,'" *New York Times Book Review,* December 10, 1972, pp. 8, 10.

Hopkins, Lee Bennett, *More Books by More People,* Citation, 1974, pp. 318-322.

Junior Literary Guild, March, 1984.

Snyder, Zilpha Keatley, *Something about the Author Autobiography Series,* Volume 2, Gale, 1986, pp. 215-226.

Vandergrift, Kay E., "Zilpha Keatley Snyder," *Twentieth Century Children's Writers,* 3rd edition, edited by Tracy Chevalier, St. Martin's, 1989, pp. 903-905.

FOR MORE INFORMATION SEE:

BOOKS

Contemporary Literary Criticism, Volume 17, Gale, 1981, pp. 469-475.

PERIODICALS

Booktalker, September, 1989, p. 9.

Book World, December 3, 1967.

Bulletin of the Center for Children's Books, June, 1974; December, 1979, p. 82; March, 1982; January, 1983; April, 1984; November, 1985; November, 1987; May, 1988.

Catholic Literary World, October, 1976, p. 138.

Children's Book Review, October, 1973, p. 146.

Christian Science Monitor, February 29, 1968.

Commonweal, November 19, 1971, pp. 179-182.

Growing Point, September, 1976, p. 2939.

Horn Book, June, 1964, p. 284; April, 1965, p. 173; April, 1967, pp. 209-210; April, 1968, pp. 182-183; October, 1970, p. 479; October, 1971; December, 1972; October, 1973, p. 459; August, 1974, p. 380.

Junior Bookshelf, December, 1978, p. 324.

Junior Literary Guild, March, 1975; November 15, 1985, p. 57.

Kirkus Reviews, March 1, 1974, p. 245; March 1, 1975, p. 239; February 1, 1977, p. 95; September 1, 1978, p. 973.

New York Times Book Review, May 9, 1965; July 24, 1966, p. 22; July 23, 1967; May 26, 1968; November 7, 1971, pp. 42-44; May 4, 1975, pp. 32, 34; May 23, 1976, p. 16; May 8, 1977, p. 41; July 8, 1984; December 27, 1987.

Publishers Weekly, February 7, 1972; February 27, 1977; February 1, 1991, p. 81.

Saturday Review, May 13, 1967, pp. 55-56.

School Library Journal, April, 1990, p. 124.

The World of Children's Books, fall, 1977, pp. 33-35.

Young Readers Review, May, 1966; May, 1967; May, 1968; October, 1969.

* * *

SOBOL, Donald J. 1924-

PERSONAL: Born October 4, 1924, in New York, NY; son of Ira J. and Ida (Gelula) Sobol; married Rose Tiplitz, 1955; children: Diane, Glenn (deceased), Eric, John. *Education:* Oberlin College, B.A., 1948; attended New School for Social Research, 1949-51. *Hobbies and other interests:* Travel, restoring antique cars, boating, fishing, scuba diving, gardening, tennis.

Donald J. Sobol

ADDRESSES: Home—Miami, FL. *Agent*—McIntosh & Otis, 310 Madison Ave., New York, NY 10017.

CAREER: Author of fiction and nonfiction for children. *New York Sun,* New York City, reporter, 1946-47; *Long Island Daily Press,* New York City, reporter, 1947-52; R. H. Macy, New York City, buyer, 1953-55; free-lance writer, 1954—. *Military service:* U.S. Army, Corps of Engineers, 1943-46; served in Pacific Theater.

MEMBER: Authors Guild, Authors League of America.

AWARDS, HONORS: Young Readers Choice Award, Pacific Northwest Library Association, 1972, for *Encyclopedia Brown Keeps the Peace;* Edgar Allan Poe Award, Mystery Writers of America, 1975, for entire body of work; Garden State Children's Book Award, 1977, for *Encyclopedia Brown Lends a Hand;* Aiken County Children's Book Award, 1977, for *Encyclopedia Brown Takes the Case;* Buckeye honor citation (grades 4-8 category), 1982, for *Encyclopedia Brown and the Case of the Midnight Visitor.*

WRITINGS:

FOR YOUNG ADULTS

The Double Quest, illustrated by Lili Rethi, Watts, 1957.

The Lost Dispatch, illustrated by Anthony Palombo, Watts, 1958.

First Book of Medieval Man (nonfiction), illustrated by Rethi, Watts, 1959, revised edition published in England as *The First Book of Medieval Britain,* Mayflower, 1960.

Two Flags Flying (biographies of Civil War leaders), illustrated by Jerry Robinson, Platt, 1960.

A Civil War Sampler, illustrated by Henry S. Gilette, Watts, 1961.

The Wright Brothers at Kitty Hawk (nonfiction), illustrated by Stuart Mackenzie, T. Nelson, 1961.

(Editor) *The First Book of the Barbarian Invaders, A.D. 375-511* (nonfiction), illustrated by W. Kirtman Plummer, Watts, 1962.

(With wife, Rose Sobol) *The First Book of Stocks and Bonds* (nonfiction), Watts, 1963.

(Editor) *An American Revolutionary War Reader,* Watts, 1964.

Lock, Stock, and Barrel (biographies of American Revolutionary War leaders), illustrated by Edward J. Smith, Westminster, 1965.

Secret Agents Four, illustrated by Leonard Shortall, Four Winds, 1967.

(Editor) *The Strongest Man in the World,* illustrated by Cliff Schule, Westminster, 1967.

Two-Minute Mysteries, Dutton, 1967.

Greta the Strong, illustrated by Trina Schart Hyman, Follett, 1970.

Milton, the Model A, illustrated by J. Drescher, Harvey House, 1970.

More Two-Minute Mysteries, Dutton, 1971.

The Amazons of Greek Mythology, A. S. Barnes, 1972.

Great Sea Stories, Dutton, 1975.

Still More Two-Minute Mysteries, Dutton, 1975.

True Sea Adventures, T. Nelson, 1975.

(Editor) *The Best Animal Stories of Science Fiction and Fantasy,* Warne, 1979.

Disasters, Archway, 1979.

Angie's First Case, illustrated by Gail Owens, Four Winds, 1981.

The Amazing Power of Ashur Fine: A Fine Mystery, Macmillan Children's Book Group, 1986.

"ENCYCLOPEDIA BROWN" SERIES

Encyclopedia Brown: Boy Detective (also see below), illustrated by Leonard Shortall, T. Nelson, 1963.

Encyclopedia Brown and the Case of the Secret Pitch, illustrated by Shortall, T. Nelson, 1965.

Encyclopedia Brown Finds the Clues, illustrated by Shortall, T. Nelson, 1966.

Encyclopedia Brown Gets His Man, illustrated by Shortall, T. Nelson, 1967.

Encyclopedia Brown Solves Them All, illustrated by Shortall, T. Nelson, 1968.

Encyclopedia Brown Keeps the Peace, illustrated by Shortall, T. Nelson, 1969.

Encyclopedia Brown Saves the Day, illustrated by Shortall, T. Nelson, 1970.

Encyclopedia Brown Tracks Them Down, illustrated by Shortall, T. Nelson, 1971.

From *Encyclopedia Brown, Boy Detective,* by Donald J. Sobol. Illustrated by Leonard Shortall.

Encyclopedia Brown Shows the Way, illustrated by Shortall, T. Nelson, 1972.

Encyclopedia Brown Takes the Case, illustrated by Shortall, T. Nelson, 1973.

Encyclopedia Brown Lends a Hand, illustrated by Shortall, T. Nelson, 1974.

Encyclopedia Brown and the Case of the Dead Eagles, illustrated by Shortall, T. Nelson, 1975.

Encyclopedia Brown and the Eleven: Case of the Exploding Plumbing and Other Mysteries, illustrated by Shortall, Dutton, 1976.

Encyclopedia Brown and the Case of the Midnight Visitor, illustrated by Lillian Brandi, T. Nelson, 1977, Bantam, 1982.

Encyclopedia Brown's Record Book of Weird and Wonderful Facts, illustrated by Sal Murdocca, Delacorte, 1979, illustrated by Bruce Degen, Dell, 1981.

Encyclopedia Brown Carries On, illustrated by Ib Ohlsson, Four Winds, 1980.

Encyclopedia Brown Sets the Pace, illustrated by Ohlsson, Dutton, 1981.

Encyclopedia Brown's Second Record Book of Weird and Wonderful Facts, illustrated by Degen, Delacorte, 1981.

Encyclopedia Brown's Third Record Book of Weird and Wonderful Facts, illustrated by Murdocca, Delacorte, 1981.

Encyclopedia Brown's Book of Wacky Crimes, illustrated by Shortall, Dutton, 1982.

Encyclopedia Brown (omnibus), illustrated by Shortall, Angus & Robertson, 1983.

Encyclopedia Brown's Book of Wacky Spies, illustrated by Ted Enik, Morrow, 1984.

Encyclopedia Brown's Book of Wacky Sports, illustrated by Enik, Morrow, 1984.

(With Glenn Andrews) *Encyclopedia Brown Takes the Cake!: A Cook and Case Book,* illustrated by Ohlsson, Scholastic, 1984.

Encyclopedia Brown and the Case of the Mysterious Handprints, illustrated by Owens, Morrow, 1985.

Encyclopedia Brown's Book of Wacky Animals, illustrated by Enik, Morrow, 1985.

Encyclopedia Brown's Book of the Wacky Outdoors, illustrated by Enik, Morrow, 1987.

Encyclopedia Brown's Book of Wacky Cars, illustrated by Enik, Morrow, 1987.

Encyclopedia Brown and the Case of the Treasure Hunt, illustrated by Owens, Morrow, 1988.

Encyclopedia Brown and the Case of the Disgusting Sneakers, illustrated by Owens, Morrow, 1990.

The Best of Encyclopedia Brown, illustrated by Ohlsson, Scholastic, in press.

Books from the "Encyclopedia Brown" series have been translated into thirteen languages and Braille.

OTHER

Author of syndicated column, "Two Minute Mysteries," 1959-68. Contributor of more than one hundred stories and articles to national magazines under a variety of pen names. Sobol's manuscripts are kept in the Kerlan Collection, University of Minnesota, Minneapolis, MN.

ADAPTATIONS: Filmstrip: *The Best of Encyclopedia Brown* (includes "The Case of the Natty Nut," "The Case of the Scattered Cards," "The Case of the Hungry Hitchhiker," and "The Case of the Whistling Ghost"), with cassette, Miller-Brody, 1977. Esquire Film Productions purchased the television and motion picture rights to the series. These rights were transferred to Howard David Deutsch Productions and Warner Brothers in 1979. *Encyclopedia Brown: Boy Detective* was filmed for Home Box Office in March, 1990. Books from the "Encyclopedia Brown" series have also been made into comic strips.

SIDELIGHTS: American children's mystery author Donald J. Sobol has kept schoolchildren on their toes since 1963 with the publication of the original Encyclopedia Brown book. *Encyclopedia Brown: Boy Detective* began the popular series, which has continued for over three decades. Over the years, Leroy "Encyclopedia" Brown, Sobol's young sleuth, has faced intriguing cases involving everything from dead eagles to disgusting sneakers. Solutions to each case are printed in the back of the book, but children are encouraged to try to solve the cases themselves.

The *Encyclopedia Brown* books each contain ten mysteries presented in readable sentences and enhanced with witty puns and other verbal jokes. It takes careful reading and a variety of methods—deductive reasoning, psychology, and careful observation of physical evidence—to solve the mysteries. "Complexity in writing style is not Sobol's intent, nor is it required for the success of these books," says Christine McDonnell in *Twentieth Century Children's Writers.* "Although the stories are simply written, they are clever and fresh, and seldom obvious or easy to solve."

Ten-year-old Leroy Brown is called "Encyclopedia" because he is so smart that it seems he must have an entire set of encyclopedias crammed into his head. He is so adept at finding clues that he helps his father, the Chief of Police, solve criminal cases. "Readers constantly ask me if Encyclopedia Brown is a real boy. The answer is no," Sobol told *Something about the Author* (*SATA*). "He is, perhaps, the boy I wanted to be—doing the things I wanted to read about but could not find in any book when I was ten."

Sobol was born in 1924 in New York City, where he attended the Ethical Cultural Schools. During World War II, he served with the engineer corps in the Pacific, and after his discharge he earned a B.A. degree from Oberlin College. It wasn't until he took a short-story writing course in college that Sobol thought of becoming a writer, and even then he waited several years before making writing his profession. Sobol's first job was as a copyboy for the *New York Sun.* Later he became a journalist for the *Sun* and for the *Long Island Daily News.* "At the age of thirty I quit job-holding for good, married Rose Tiplitz, an engineer, and began to write full time," Sobol told *SATA,* adding that he has written more than sixty books since then.

For many years, Sobol has received letters from stumped young readers complaining that his mysteries have no proper explanation. These letters are often written by readers who have missed some significant detail. But in 1990, students in a Philadelphia school detected an actual error in the first *Encyclopedia Brown* book. The story about a trickster who bilks his classmates in an egg-spinning contest fails to explain how the cheater managed to get a boiled egg into the dozen before the contestants bought it at the grocery store. After the students wrote to Sobol asking for the explanation, he re-read the story for the first time in nearly thirty years. He admitted the solution should be more fully explained. "This is the first time in a couple of decades where it is really my fault," Sobol told Martha Woodall of the *Detroit Free Press.* "They are really smart kids." The teacher of the first- and second-graders who spotted the error said it has taught the students the importance of questioning the accuracy of what they read. She said they also learned that when something that is incorrect appears in print, there is something they can do about it. New editions including "The Case of the Champion Egg-Spinner" will contain the revised version.

In addition to the boy detective series, Sobol has written many nonfiction books that required him to do extensive research on topics as varied as King Arthur's England (*Greta the Strong*) and Ancient Greece (*The Amazons of Greek Mythology*). His other nonfiction works include biographies of American military leaders of the Revolutionary and Civil Wars, in *Lock, Stock and Barrel* and *Two Flags Flying.* Sobol has also written an internationally syndicated newspaper feature, "Two-Minute Mystery Series," hundreds of articles and stories for adult magazines, historical books, and biographies. He is the editor of two history collections, *A Civil War Sampler* and *An American Revolutionary War Reader,* and the author of a book on stocks and bonds.

Sobol told *Pacific Northwest Library Association Quarterly,* "Outwitting you, the reader, is hard, but harder still is making you laugh. I try above all else to entertain . . . . I hope to be making children laugh for decades to come."

WORKS CITED:

Pacific Northwest Library Association Quarterly, winter, 1973, pp. 18-20.
Something about the Author, Volume 31, Gale, 1983.
Twentieth Century Children's Writers, St. Martin's Press, 1989, pp. 905-906.
Woodall, Martha, "Youngsters Outsmart Encyclopedia Brown," *Detroit Free Press,* February 12, 1991.

FOR MORE INFORMATION SEE:

BOOKS

Children's Literature Review, Volume 4, Gale, 1982, pp. 205-212.
Fourth Book of Junior Authors, H. W. Wilson, 1978, pp. 318-319.

PERIODICALS

Booklist, February 1, 1983, p. 27; May 1, 1984, p. 1254; March 1, 1991, p. 1382.
Christian Century, December 13, 1967, p. 1602.
Christian Science Monitor, October 5, 1967, p. 10; April 6, 1984, p. B7.
Fantasy Review, May, 1987, p. 795.
Horn Book Guide, July, 1990, p. 79.
New York Times Book Review, November 11, 1979, pp. 56, 69; November 5, 1967, p. 44.
People, March 12, 1990, pp. 17-18.
School Library Journal, February, 1982, p. 81; August, 1982, p. 107; April, 1984, p. 119; April, 1985, p. 93; December, 1984, p. 103; December, 1985, p. 95; November, 1986, p. 94; April, 1987, p. 104; January, 1988, p. 83; January, 1991, p. 97.
Science Fiction Chronicle, August, 1987, p. 53.
Young Readers' Review, November, 1967; November, 1968.

* * *

SORENSEN, Virginia 1912-1991

PERSONAL: Born February 17, 1912, in Provo, UT; died December 24, 1991, in Hendersonville, NC; daughter of Claud and Helen El Deva (Blackett) Eggertsen; married Frederick Sorensen (an English professor), August 16, 1933 (divorced); married Alec Waugh (a writer), July 15, 1969 (died September 3, 1981); children: Elizabeth, Frederick Walter. *Education:* Brigham Young University, B.S., 1934; graduate study at Stanford University. *Politics:* "I choose candidates, but mostly Democrats." *Religion:* Church of Jesus Christ of Latter-Day Saints.

ADDRESSES: *Home*—Hendersonville, N.C. *Agent*—Curtis Brown, 10 Astor Place, New York, N.Y. 10003.

Virginia Sorensen

CAREER: Writer. Part-time teacher of creative writing.

MEMBER: International PEN, Authors League of America, Delta Kappa Gamma (honorary member).

AWARDS, HONORS: Guggenheim fellowship to Mexico, 1946-1947, and to Denmark, 1954-1955; Children's Book Award, Child Study Association of America, 1955, for *Plain Girl;* Newbery Medal, American Library Association, 1957, for *Miracles on Maple Hill.*

WRITINGS:

A Little Lower Than the Angels, Knopf, 1942.
On This Star, Reynal & Hitchcock, 1946.
The Neighbors, Reynal & Hitchcock, 1947.
The Evening and the Morning, Harcourt, 1949.
The Proper Gods, Harcourt, 1951.
Curious Missie, Harcourt, 1953.
The House Next Door, Scribners, 1954.
Many Heavens, Harcourt, 1954.
Plain Girl, Harcourt, 1955.
Miracles on Maple Hill, Harcourt, 1957.
Kingdom Come, Harcourt, 1960.
Where Nothing Is Long Ago, Harcourt, 1963.
Lotte's Locket, Harcourt, 1964.
Around the Corner, Harcourt, 1971.
The Man with the Key, Harcourt, 1974.
Friends of the Road, Atheneum, 1978.

Sorensen's papers are housed in the Special Collection, Boston University; and in the Kerlan Collection, University of Minnesota.

SIDELIGHTS: History, family, and community are thematic concerns in most of Virginia Sorensen's novels for adults and children. Born into a Danish-American family of Mormon pioneers, Sorensen wrote many historical novels about early Mormon settlers in the American West. The author had first-hand knowledge of the period, especially the Mormon trek from Illinois to Utah in 1846. She told *Publishers Weekly:* "In my childhood, I actually heard stories of the long trek and of the settlement of our town from people who had experienced it all."

Sorensen was raised in Monti, a small town in Utah's Sanpete Valley (an area settled by Danish-Americans). The inhabitants of "little Denmark," as the Sanpete Valley was called, formed a close-knit community. "The whole town helped with parades and programs and fireworks, and I've never seen them surpassed anywhere," Sorensen noted in an essay for *More Junior Authors.*

Sorensen realized her literary ambitions early when her fifth-grade teacher praised one of her poems. Later, a poem published in a Salt Lake City magazine fixed Sorensen's course. "When I saw [the poem] in print, my fate seemed sealed," she noted in her essay, "I would be a writer and nothing else." Over the next few years, Sorensen sharpened her writing skills by working on the high school newspaper and yearbook staffs.

From *Miracles on Maple Hill,* by Virginia Sorensen. Illustrated by Beth and Joe Krush.

Near the end of her studies at Brigham Young University, Sorensen got married; she and her new husband later moved to Palo Alto, California, where Frederick Sorensen studied for his Ph.D. in English literature. Sorensen's diploma from Brigham Young was mailed to her the same week the couple's first child was born (a son followed two years later). The Sorensens shared a love of travel and moved often, teaching and writing in various states across the country.

Sorensen's first novel, *A Little Lower Than the Angels,* was published in 1942. The book tells the story of a Mormon family in Illinois prior to the migration west. Reviewers praised Sorensen's insights into the minds of Mormon women and the issues raised by the practice of plural marriage. Clifton Fadiman, writing in the *New Yorker,* noted that he had "read a number of Mormon novels, but none that more convincingly explores the minds of the Mormon women confronted with the tragic, comic, and grotesque problems of plural marriage."

Two Guggenheim Fellowships allowed Sorensen to travel abroad, to Mexico in 1946-1947 and to Denmark in 1954-1955. In Mexico Sorensen studied an Indian tribe; this research later helped form the basis of her

1951 novel *The Proper Gods.* In Denmark Sorensen traced the genealogies of some of the Danish settlers of the Sanpete Valley and gathered background material for two novels set in Danish locales, *Kingdom Come* and *Lotte's Locket.*

Sorensen published her first novel for children in 1953. *Curious Missie* tells the story of a young girl's hunger for knowledge, a hunger eventually satisfied and encouraged by the arrival of a bookmobile. "This book," M. R. Brown of the *Saturday Review* commented, "captures the essence of a small child's feelings and thirst for knowledge." And L. S. Bechtel, writing in the *New York Herald Tribune Book Review,* recommended the novel because "Sorensen writes so well, her Missie is real, and the book, though full of humor, often catches the heart."

Sorensen's next two children's novels, *Plain Girl* and *Miracles on Maple Hill,* were both award winners. *Plain Girl* tells the story of an Amish girl forced to attend public school against her parents' wishes. Critics praised the author's perceptive treatment of issues in Amish life, as well as her style and characterization. *Miracles on Maple Hill* concerns a Pittsburgh family learning to adjust after moving to the country. S. C. Gross, reviewing the novel in the *New York Times,* remarked on its "substance and spiritual worth."

Sorensen's first marriage ended in divorce. With her second husband, Alex Waugh, Sorensen continued to visit countries around the world. Eventually, the couple settled in North Carolina, where the author tended to the health of both her spouse and daughter. In summing up Sorensen's career, Joan McGrath of *Twentieth Century Children's Writers* noted that "Sorensen's books are filled with a wholesome philosophy of love and caring. They are mild ... but it will be a sad world when there is no place left in it for gentle kindness."

WORKS CITED:

Bechtel, L. S., review of *Curious Missie, New York Herald Tribune Book Review,* November 15, 1953.

Brown, M. R., review of *Curious Missie, Saturday Review,* November 14, 1953.

Fadiman, Clifton, review of *A Little Lower Than the Angels, New Yorker,* May 16, 1942.

Gross, S. C., review of *Miracles on Maple Hill, New York Times,* August 26, 1956.

McGrath, Joan, essay in *Twentieth-Century Children's Writers,* edited by Tracy Chevalier, St. James, 1989, pp. 907-908.

Sorensen, Virginia, essay in *More Junior Authors,* edited by Muriel Fuller, H. W. Wilson, 1963, pp. 188-189.

Sorensen, Virginia, interview in *Publishers Weekly,* March 11, 1957.

FOR MORE INFORMATION SEE:

BOOKS

Lee, L. L., and Sylvia B., *Virginia Sorensen,* Boise State University, 1978.

PERIODICALS

Booklist, May 1, 1978.

Christian Science Monitor, May 12, 1949; September 19, 1963.

Horn Book, August, 1957.

* * *

SOUTHALL, Ivan (Francis) 1921-

PERSONAL: Born June 8, 1921, in Canterbury, Victoria, Australia; son of Francis Gordon (in insurance) and Rachel Elizabeth (Voutier) Southall; married Joyce Blackburn, September 8, 1945 (divorced); married Susan Stanton, 1976; children: (first marriage) Andrew John, Roberta Joy, Elizabeth Rose, Melissa Frances. *Education:* Attended Melbourne Technical College, 1937-41. *Politics:* Independent. *Religion:* Methodist.

ADDRESSES: P.O. Box 25, Healesville, Victoria 3777, Australia.

CAREER: Herald and Weekly Times, Melbourne, Victoria, Australia, process engraver, 1936-41 and 1947; free-lance writer, 1948—. Library of Congress, Whittall Lecturer, 1973; American Library Association, Arbuthnot Honor Lecturer, 1974. MacQuarie University, writer-in-residence, 1978. Community Youth Organization (Victoria), past president; Knoxbrooke Training Centre for the Intellectually Handicapped (Victoria), founda-

Ivan Southall

tion president. *Military service:* Australian Army, 1941; Royal Australian Air Force, 1942-46, pilot, 1942-44, war historian, 1945-46; became flight lieutenant; received Distinguished Flying Cross.

MEMBER: Australian Society of Authors.

AWARDS, HONORS: Australian children's book of the year award, 1966, for *Ash Road,* 1968, for *To the Wild Sky,* 1971, for *Bread and Honey,* and 1976, for *Fly West;* Australian picture book of the year award, 1969, for *Sly Old Wardrobe;* Japanese Government's Children's Welfare and Culture Encouragement Award, 1969, for *Ash Road;* Carnegie Medal, Library Association (England), 1972, for *Josh;* Zilver Griffel (Netherlands), 1972, for *To the Wild Sky;* named member of Order of Australia, 1981; National Children's Book Award (Australia), 1986, for *The Long Night Watch.*

WRITINGS:

"SIMON BLACK" SERIES FOR CHILDREN; PUBLISHED BY ANGUS & ROBERTSON, EXCEPT AS INDICATED

Meet Simon Black, illustrated by Frank Norton, 1950.
Simon Black in Peril, 1951.
Simon Black in Space, 1952, Anglobooks, 1953.
Simon Black in Coastal Command, Anglobooks, 1953.
Simon Black in China, 1954.
Simon Black and the Spacemen, 1955.
Simon Black in the Antarctic, 1956.
Simon Black Takes Over: The Strange Tale of Operation Greenleaf, 1959.
Simon Black at Sea: The Fateful Maiden Voyage of A.P.M.I. Arion, 1961.

FICTION, FOR CHILDREN

Hills End, illustrated by Jim Phillips, Angus & Robertson, 1962, St. Martin's, 1963.
Ash Road, illustrated by Clem Seale, Angus & Robertson, 1965, St. Martin's, 1966.
To the Wild Sky, illustrated by Jennifer Tuckwell, St. Martin's, 1967.
The Fox Hole (also see below), illustrated by Ian Ribbons, St. Martin's, 1967.
Let the Balloon Go (also see below), illustrated by Ribbons, St. Martin's, 1968.
Sly Old Wardrobe (picture book), illustrated by Ted Greenwood, F. W. Cheshire, 1968, St. Martin's, 1970.
Finn's Folly, St. Martin's, 1969.
Chinaman's Reef Is Ours, St. Martin's, 1970.
Bread and Honey, Angus & Robertson, 1970, also published as *Walk a Mile and Get Nowhere,* Bradbury, 1970.
Josh, Angus & Robertson, 1971, Macmillan, 1972.
Over the Top (also see below), illustrated by Ribbons, Methuen, 1972, also published as *Benson Boy,* illustrated by Ingrid Fetz, Macmillan, 1972.
Head in the Clouds, illustrated by Richard Kennedy, Angus & Robertson, 1972, Macmillan, 1973.
Matt and Jo, Macmillan, 1973.
Three Novels (contains *The Fox Hole, Let the Balloon Go,* and *Over the Top*) Methuen, 1975.
What about Tomorrow?, Macmillan, 1977.
King of the Sticks, Greenwillow, 1979.
The Golden Goose, Greenwillow, 1981.
The Long Night Watch, Methuen, 1983, Farrar, Straus, 1984.
A City out of Sight, Angus & Robertson, 1984.
Christmas in the Tree, Hodder & Stoughton, 1985.
Rachel, Farrar, Straus, 1986.
Blackbird, Farrar, Straus, 1988.
The Mysterious World of Marcus Leadbeater, Farrar, Straus, 1990.

NONFICTION, FOR CHILDREN

Journey into Mystery: A Story of the Explorers Burke and Willis, illustrated by Robin Goodall, Lansdowne, 1961.
Lawrence Hargrave (biography), Oxford University Press, 1964.
Rockets in the Desert: The Story of Woomera, Angus & Robertson, 1964.
Indonesian Journey (travel), Lansdowne, 1965, Ginn, 1966.
Bushfire!, illustrated by Julie Mattox, Angus & Robertson, 1968.
Seventeen Seconds (children's adaptation of *Softly Tread the Brave;* also see below), Macmillan, 1973.
Fly West, Angus & Robertson, 1974, Macmillan, 1975.

OTHER, FOR CHILDREN

The Sword of Esau: Bible Stories Retold, illustrated by Joan Kiddell-Monroe, Angus & Robertson, 1967, St. Martin's, 1968.
The Curse of Cain: Bible Stories Retold, illustrated by Kiddell-Monroe, St. Martin's, 1968.

Also author, with others, of a screenplay titled *Let the Balloon Go,* 1976.

FICTION, FOR ADULTS

Out of the Dawn: Three Short Stories, privately printed, 1942.
Third Pilot, Horwitz, 1959.
Flight to Gibraltar, Horwitz, 1959.
Mediterranean Black, Horwitz, 1959.
Sortie in Cyrenaica, Horwitz, 1959
Mission to Greece, Horwitz, 1960.
Atlantic Pursuit, Horwitz, 1960.

NONFICTION, FOR ADULTS

The Weaver from Meltham (biography), illustrated by George Colville, Whitcombe & Tombs, 1950.
The Story of The Hermitage: The First Fifty Years of the Geelong Church of England Girls' Grammar School, F. W. Cheshire, 1956.
They Shall Not Pass Unseen, Angus & Robertson, 1956.
A Tale of Box Hill: Day of the Forest, Box Hill City Council, 1957.
Bluey Truscott: Squadron Leader Keith William Truscott, R.A.A.F., D.F.C. and Bar, Angus & Robertson, 1958.
Softly Tread the Brave: A Triumph over Terror, Devilry, and Death by Mine Disposal Officers John Stuart

Mould and Hugh Randall Syme, Angus & Robertson, 1960.
Parson on the Track: Bush Brothers in the Australian Outback, Lansdowne, 1962.
Woomera, Angus & Robertson, 1962.
Indonesia Face to Face (travel), Lansdowne, 1964.
A Journey of Discovery: On Writing for Children (lectures), Kestrel, 1975, Macmillan, 1976.
(Editor) *The Challenge: Is the Church Obsolete?—An Australian Response to the Challenge of Modern Society* (essays), Lansdowne, 1966.

SIDELIGHTS: Ivan Southall is an award-winning Australian author best known for his fictional works for children and young adults. Southall offers realistic portrayals of ordinary children coping with dramatic situations, usually without the guidance of adults. While his characters are in these "severely demanding circumstances ... learning, growth and change take place," according to Geoffrey Fox in an article for *Children's Literature in Education.* Southall has been criticized by some who claim that his subjects are too mature—and potentially frightening—for his readership. Other critics have suggested that the challenging vocabulary and various sophisticated literary devices evident in the author's works—such as steam-of consciousness writing, flashbacks, and a roving point of view—are geared to an adult rather than a juvenile audience. However Southall continues to employ these techniques because he believes in treating his readers as intellectual equals, regardless of their age.

Through his fiction, Southall attempts to identify with the experiences young people have during their lives. In an essay for *Something about the Author Autobiography Series* (*SAAS*) the author remarked, "Life is everyone's undiscovered land coming little by little into view. The excitement of it all is why I've spent the last twenty-five years putting words around it. I've seen this kind of writing as a worthy pursuit and an accomplishment worth the striving. It's why I've gone on largely resisting the urge to write of wider adult experiences. One of my objectives as a writer primarily for the young has been to 'protect' the great moments of live, not to spoil them or 'give them away.' It's why so many of my ending are open and why I've brought the reader to bridges over which imagination has to cross."

Southall draws upon his memories of people, events, and experiences in his own life to use as material for his works. The author was born in 1921 in the Southeast Australian city of Melbourne, Victoria. Relatives from both sides of Southall's family had been lured to the area because of the gold rush that began in 1851. However, while a few fortunate families enjoyed wealth from gold strikes, the majority of newcomers—including Southall's ancestors—faced financial hardship. Southall's maternal grandfather became a manager at a mine, but the hard life of a settler took its toll on the family; his wife died and left three small children, the eldest being the author's mother. As a child, Southall's father was forced to wander the streets selling yeast for making bread to help support his family, half of which was later killed by a diphtheria epidemic. Hard times continued when the author's parents were married and began to raise their family, but Southall attributes part of the financial strain to the practice of giving money to the local church.

Southall revealed in *SAAS* that "a conservative Methodist viewpoint was what we had at home .... Church was our way of life, religiously, intellectually, socially, and recreationally. It was the only way I knew." The author realizes that some consider the upbringing associated with a religious life as too strict and rigid, but he disagrees. "I remember the church with gratitude," he insisted. "Over many years I listened to marvelous stories and received instruction from scholars and orators, some of the best of their day .... If I'm to claim any serious literary foundation, it has to be the influence of the King James Bible, absorbed (at times restlessly) during after-dinner readings at the kitchen table or in the sharp physical discomfort of the church during boyhood and adolescence."

It was during adolescence that Southall was first inspired to write fiction. He discovered that a local paper sponsored a short story competition in which the winning entry was published and the author was awarded prize money. Propelled by the thought of monetary

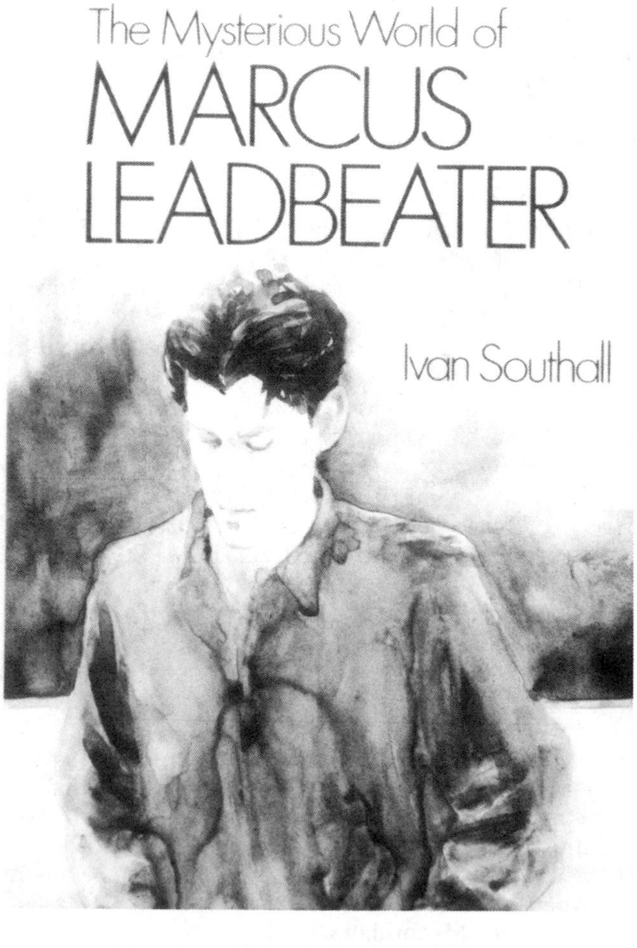

Cover of *The Mysterious World of Marcus Leadbeater,* by Ivan Southall.

reward, the twelve-year-old Southall began a life-long practice of writing. He won the contest—to the astonishment of his school teachers from whom he had previously received only average scores on compositions—the first week he entered, with a story titled "The Black Panther." Over the next three years he wrote a story each week and won the contest five more times, fueling his dream of becoming a famous author.

When he wrote stories at home, Southall would rely on his mother for help with spelling. Even though she had only a sixth grade education, the author recalled that his mother never gave him an incorrect spelling. Southall's father supported his son's decision to become a writer and agreed that after completing eighth grade the boy should continue his education at a Methodist college. However, Southall had earned only a partial scholarship and the cost of tuition placed further economic strain on the family. Later that year when the author's father became sick with tuberculosis and died, Southall—as the oldest child—was forced to abandon his studies and work to support the family.

The author's first job involved cleaning glass equipment for a laboratory. Later, when Southall was sixteen, he began a job as a temporary copyboy for the Melbourne *Herald*—the same paper that had sponsored the children's fiction competition and had published his short stories several years earlier. The author hoped this experience would lead to a position as a reporter, but his supervisor repeatedly reminded him that journalists needed more than a ninth-grade education. After his stint as a copyboy was complete, Southall's boss offered him another job with the paper as an engraver which the author held until World War II began.

Feeling obligated to defend his country, Southall joined the Royal Australian Air Force in 1941, but his first assignment was with an army artillery crew to defend a portion of the nation's coastline. During the early part of the war, several Australian cities had been bombed by Japanese forces. After the 1941 Japanese attack of a U.S. naval base at Pearl Harbor, Australian fears of a Japanese invasion of their own country increased. Southall's artillery crew was assigned to live in a cave on a coastal cliff and watch for and shoot at any approaching Japanese ships. However the invasion never took place. The author kept a diary during his time on the cliff and used it as the basis for his book *The Long Night Watch.*

In June of 1942, Southall finally realized his dream of being in the air force as he joined twenty-nine other young men for flight training. As an incentive, the young man who graduated at the top of the class was able to choose his assignment while the others were assigned duties. Despite his relative lack of education, the author, whose childhood hero had been a pilot, earned the best test scores and was able to become an aviator. Southall was stationed in Great Britain, where he and his ten flight crew members escorted ships, searched for survivors of plane crashes and ship wrecks, and patrolled waters for German submarines. Again, while the author was enlisted in the air force, he kept a journal. Southall remarked in *SAAS* that "more of my writing over forty years—fact, fiction and history—has grown from the air force diary than from any other primary source except feeling and intuition."

In addition to successfully completing fifty-seven missions and earning a Distinguished Flying Cross while serving in England, Southall also met and married Joy Blackburn. The couple returned to Australia in 1946, and when Southall finished his apprenticeship at the Melbourne *Herald,* he decided to leave the paper to write full-time at home. The author and his wife built several homes, the most significant was named Blackwood Farm where three of the couple's four children were born. Southall spent fourteen years completing the house and, at the same time, wrote twenty-five books. However, financial hardship forced the family to leave Blackwood Farm in 1963. Two years later Southall's book *Hill's End,* which he wrote at the farm, became a world-wide success. The author remarked in *SAAS* that *Hill's End* "opened doors within me, began a different life for me, and eventually [inspired] a commitment to serious writing for children."

With this new found commitment, Southall produced works that proved popular, and received critical acclaim. Four times, he won Australian children's book of the year award. *Ash Road,* received the honor in 1966. In this novel, a fire burns out of control in the dry and windy Australian foothills and is rapidly approaching a house full of children. Southall offers an hour-by-hour account that increases in tension as the focus shifts from the boy who started the fire to the children in its path and also to their worried parents. A sudden storm stops the fire before it reaches the house.

Southall again received Australia's children's book of the year award in 1968 for *To the Wild Sky.* In this work, six children are flying across Australia in a private plan in order to attend a birthday party. Midway through the flight, the pilot of the aircraft collapses and although one of the children who has some knowledge of planes is able to safely land, the group is stranded on a deserted island. Southall provides hints that the children can survive, but he ends the novel without revealing the fate of the isolated group. However, eighteen years after *To the Wild Sky* was written, Southall provided the answers about what happened to the characters in his sequel *A City out of Sight.*

In 1972 Southall won England's Carnegie Medal—annually given in recognition of an outstanding book for children—for *Josh.* The story concerns a fourteen-year-old boy who visits his aunt who lives in a country town. Josh is a sensitive boy who writes poetry. During his five-day stay, Josh tries to get along with his somewhat strange aunt and the young people of Ryan Creek whose attitudes and behavior are foreign to him. The town kids bully him and throw him into the water even though he can't swim. Although he is rescued, Josh realizes that he will never adapt to life in this environment and consequently returns home. In his *SAAS* essay, the author remarked, "The half-jesting, half-despairing inner dialogue of *Josh* comes directly out of my own teens."

Southall has continued his success with his more recent books. *Rachel,* published in 1986, is based on the childhood of the author's mother and is set in a gold mining town in the late 1800s. A review for *Horn Book Magazine,* remarked that "emotional intensity, irony, and a fine sense of comedy are brilliantly intermingled" in *Rachel.* Alan Brownjohn, writing in the *Times Literary Supplement,* remarked that Southall "has produced an unusual, oddly memorable tale."

Southall is known for his story-telling ability, his sympathy for his young characters, and his habit of leaving the conclusions of his works ambiguous so the reader must imagine an ending. His label as one of Australia's most popular children's writers indicates that Southall was able to realize his dreams of becoming a famous author even though others thought he would be limited by his lack of education. Summing up the author's positive contribution to children's literature, Fox concluded, "Ivan Southall's ability is evident not merely in his technique, but also in the directness and sensitivity with which he handles areas children want to read about, and even 'should' read about."

WORKS CITED:

Fox, Geoffrey, "Growth and Masquerade: A Theme in the Novels of Ivan Southall," *Children's Literature in Education,* November, 1971, pp. 50, 52.

Review of *Rachel, Horn Book,* January/February, 1987, p. 62.

Southall, Ivan, *Something about the Author Autobiography Series,* Volume 3, Gale, 1987, pp. 268, 270, 275, 277.

FOR MORE INFORMATION SEE:

BOOKS

Children's Literature Review, Volume 2, Gale, 1976.

PERIODICALS

Children's Book Review, December, 1971.

Times Literary Supplement, May 25, 1967; October 3, 1968; February 24, 1984; December 12, 1986.

Voice of Youth Advocates, April, 1987.

* * *

SPANFELLER, James J(ohn) 1930- (Jim Spanfeller)

James J. Spanfeller

PERSONAL: Born October 27, 1930, in Philadelphia, PA; married Patricia Durkin, May 2, 1953; children: James, Jr. *Education:* Studied at the Philadelphia Museum School of Art and the Pennsylvania Academy of Fine Arts.

ADDRESSES: Home—Katonah, New York.

CAREER: Free-lance illustrator, 1957—. Held a one-man show, 1965, at the Society of Illustrators. *Military service:* United States Army, two years.

AWARDS, HONORS: Named Artist of the Year by the Artists Guild of New York, 1964; Carnegie commendation, 1962, for *The Summer Birds;* Spring Book Festival award, 1965, Southern California Council on Literature for Children and Young People Notable Book award, 1966, and Lewis Carroll Shelf award, 1972, all for *Dorp Dead;* National Book Award finalist, 1970, for *Where the Lillies Bloom;* Southern California Council on Literature for Children and Young People Notable Book award, 1973, for *The Malibu and Other Poems.*

ILLUSTRATOR:

Robert Paul Smith, *Where Did You Go? Out. What Did You Do? Nothing,* Norton, 1958.

Penelope Farmer, *Summer Birds,* Harcourt, 1962.

Clyde R. Bulla, *Indian Hill,* Crowell, 1963.

May Sarton, *Joanna and Ulysses,* Norton, 1963.

Jack Kerouac, *Visions of Gerard,* Farrar, Straus, 1963.

Henry Morgan, *O-Sono and the Magician's Nephew and the Elephant,* Vanguard, 1964.

Richard Parker, *The Boy Who Wasn't Lonely,* Bobbs-Merrill, 1964.

Julia Cunningham, *Dorp Dead,* Pantheon, 1965.

Mary F. Shura, *Run Away Home,* Knopf, 1965.

Stephen Vincent Benet, *Thirteen O'Clock,* Franklin Library, 1965.

Flora M. Hood, *Pink Puppy,* Putnam, 1966.

P. Farmer, *Emma in Winter,* Harcourt, 1966.

M. Sarton, *Miss Pickthorn and Mr. Hare,* Norton, 1966.

Catherine Marshall, *God Loves You: Our Family's Favorite Stories and Prayers,* McGraw, 1967.

Myra C. Livingston, editor, *A Tune Beyond Us: A Collection of Poetry,* Harcourt, 1968.
Robert Lamb, *The Plug at the Bottom of the Sea,* Bobbs-Merrill, 1968.
M. C. Livingston, *A Crazy Flight, and Other Poems,* Harcourt, 1969.
Andrew Lang, editor, *The Blue Fairy Book,* Junior Deluxe Editions, 1969.
Vera and Bill Cleaver, *Where the Lilies Bloom,* Lippincott, 1969.
William I. Martin, *"Tricks or Treats?,"* Holt, 1970.
Craig Claiborne, *The New York Times International Cookbook,* Harper, 1971.
M. C. Livingston, *The Malibu, and Other Poems,* Atheneum, 1972.
John Ehle, *The Cheese and Wines of England and France,* Harper, 1972.
M. C. Livingston, *4-Way Stop, and Other Poems,* Atheneum, 1976.
William H. Hooks, *Doug Meets the Nutcracker,* Warne, 1977.
Barbara Brenner, *Beware! These Animals Are Poison,* Coward, 1979.
Gabriel Garcia Marquez, *One Hundred Years of Solitude,* Franklin Library, 1981.
Felice Holman, *The Song in My Head,* Scribner, 1985.
Vit Horejs, *Twelve Iron Sandals, and Other Czechoslovak Tales,* Prentice-Hall, 1985.
Saki, *The Best of Saki,* Franklin Library, 1985.
Walker Percy, *The Thanatos Syndrome,* Franklin Library, 1987.
Rex Stout, *Fer-De-Lance,* Franklin Library, 1988.

Also provided illustrations for many magazines, including *Seventeen* and *Esquire.*

SIDELIGHTS: Jim Spanfeller has been illustrating books for children and adults for over three decades. He has provided pictures for projects as varied as Julia Cunningham's *Dorp Dead* and editions of the works of Stephen Vincent Benet and famed short story author Saki. Spanfeller has also illustrated many magazines, including *Esquire* and *Seventeen.* The artist has won many awards for his work; he was particularly gratified—according to his essay in *Something about the Author Autobiography Series* (*SAAS*)—to receive the Artist of the Year Award from the Artists Guild of New York in 1964.

Spanfeller was born October 27, 1930, in Philadelphia, Pennsylvania. Unbeknownst to him, his mother died three months after giving birth to him—Spanfeller thought until he reached adulthood that his stepmother (who was also his natural mother's sister) was his real mother. Aside from that, Spanfeller recalled of his childhood in *SAAS* that "drawing pictures was for me as natural a thing to do as eating and sleeping," and that he would insist that his stepmother "read to me the words which accompanied the newspaper comic strips," because he was "determined to get the full meaning out of each and every panel, so that I could learn to draw comic strips for myself."

From *The Song in My Head,* by Felice Holman. Illustrated by Jim Spanfeller.

As an adolescent, Spanfeller attended a Catholic high school, where he had no encouragement whatsoever for his artistic ambitions. In his autobiographical essay, he noted: "My guidance counselor ... said that he had never received a request regarding art-school information until mine. The consensus advice from the school principal as well as the other teachers was that since I had done so well scholastically, I did not have to waste my life on a career that would be probably pointless and, perhaps even worse, degenerate." Nevertheless, Spanfeller persisted, and was eventually referred to the Philadelphia Museum School of Art, at which he enrolled after his graduation from high school.

"I subscribe to the idea that art school is the lesser of two evils," Spanfeller opined in *SAAS.* He went on to explain that "on your own, which is the alternative, [it] could take as long as ten years to acquire those same skills (learned in art school) along with a focused direction.... With some luck, at a good art school you may have teachers who do not force their ideas on you as you learn to express yourself." The Philadelphia Museum School of Art apparently met Spanfeller's requirements, though he had some problems. He was told upon admission that it was not his submitted art work but rather his previous academic record that had won him a place at the school, and so he at first received the impression that his original drawings did not suit the school's standards. He took courses in graphic design, because he was advised "that program made you think," as he put it in his autobiographical essay. Spanfeller explained further: "I found the problem-solving approach and the discipline of meeting the deadlines very intellectually stimulating. There was some frustration for me in hardly ever being able to answer the problems with a drawing or painting." Eventually one of Spanfeller's instructors asked to see his private sketchbook, to see which of the many approaches he took to his graphic design work best represented him as an artist. As the illustrator reported in *SAAS:* "After a lengthy viewing this teacher was delighted with the drawings and perplexed that they did not reflect my work in school. From that point on art school was a new experience. I felt right at home.... The amazing conclusion to this was the realization that what art school wanted from me ... was *me.*"

Yet when Spanfeller left the Philadelphia Museum School, he was unsure how he would make his living. The problem was temporarily solved for him when he was drafted by the U.S. Army. Spanfeller entered the service in 1952. For a time he was in danger of being sent to the fighting in Korea; after it became certain that he would remain stationed at Fort Leonard Wood, Missouri, Spanfeller married his childhood sweetheart, Patricia Durkin.

After he was discharged from the army, Spanfeller and his wife returned to Philadelphia. He enrolled for a time at the Pennsylvania Academy of Fine Arts, while his wife worked to support them. Spanfeller eventually began to get illustration assignments; though the first book he illustrated, *Where Did You Go? Out! What Did You Do? Nothing,* was a big success and stayed on the best-seller lists for over a year, he only received a flat fee of five hundred dollars for his work. He also began doing illustrations for *Seventeen* magazine, and his career began looking up. Spanfeller spent the late 1950s and early 1960s "working for a good number of national magazines," as he put it in *SAAS,* and completing "a variety of children's books and a limited number of advertising assignments." His wife continued to work, eventually becoming involved in real estate investments. By 1968, the Spanfellers moved to a house in Katonah, New York—the illustrator was doing well enough that they lived, in his words, "a very comfortable life-style with home and studio surrounded by a hilly, wooded area with many deer, raccoons, and possums."

In 1956 Spanfeller and his wife had a son, Jim, Jr. After his son overcame a problem with dyslexia, he became a writer, and Spanfeller has illustrated many of his son's magazine stories.

While Spanfeller was teaching illustration and drawing, primarily at the Parsons School of Design in New York City, he had talked numerous times with his students about the possibility of artists, writers, and designers forming small groups with a printing press availability, which could create and then control their own artistic products. In an effort to do just that, he and his wife, Patricia, bought a small printing business in Brewster, New York—Spanfeller Graphics Group, Inc.—and in addition to the existing business, they hope to design, print, and market small edition books, posters, and other special projects.

WORKS CITED:

Spanfeller, Jim, essay in *Something about the Author Autobiography Series,* Volume 8, Gale, 1989, pp. 299-315.

FOR MORE INFORMATION SEE:

BOOKS

Something about the Author, Volume 19, Gale, 1980, pp. 230-32.

PERIODICALS

Meglin, Nick, *American Artist,* March, 1977.

* * *

SPANFELLER, Jim
See SPANFELLER, James J(ohn)

* * *

SPEARE, Elizabeth George 1908-

PERSONAL: Born November 21, 1908, in Melrose, MA; daughter of Harry Allan (an engineer) and Demetria (Simmons) George; married Alden Speare (an industrial engineer), September 26, 1936; children: Alden, Jr., Mary Elizabeth. *Education:* Attended Smith College, 1926-27; Boston University, A.B., 1930, M.A., 1932.

Elizabeth George Speare

ADDRESSES: Home—48 Bibbins Rd., Easton, CT, 06612.

CAREER: Writer, 1955—. Rockland High School, Rockland, MA, teacher of English, 1932-35; Auburn High School, Auburn, MA, teacher of English, 1935-36.

MEMBER: Authors Guild, Authors League of America.

AWARDS, HONORS: Society of Colonial Wars Award from the State of New York, and Newbery Medal from the American Library Association, both 1959, International Board on Books for Young People (IBBY) Honor List, and selected one of American Institute of Graphic Arts Children's Books, both 1960, and New England Round Table Children's Librarians Award, 1976, all for *The Witch of Blackbird Pond;* Newbery Medal, 1962, and IBBY Honor List, 1964, both for *The Bronze Bow;* one of American Library Association's Best Young Adult Books, Teachers' Choice from the National Council of Teachers of English, one of Child Study Association of America's Children's Book of the Year, one of *School Library Journal*'s Best Books of the Year, a *Booklist* Children's Reviewers Choice, and one of *New York Times* Outstanding Books, all 1983, and Newbery Medal Honor Book, Scott O'Dell Award for Historical Fiction, and Christopher Award, all 1984, all for *The Sign of the Beaver;* Laura Ingalls Wilder Award, 1989, for a distinguished and enduring contribution to children's literature.

WRITINGS:

HISTORICAL FICTION FOR YOUNG ADULTS

Calico Captive, (ALA Notable Book), illustrated by W. T. Mars, Houghton, 1957.

The Witch of Blackbird Pond, (ALA Notable Book), illustrated by Nicholas Angelo, Houghton, 1958.

The Bronze Bow, (ALA Notable Book; *Horn Book* honor list), Houghton, 1961.

The Sign of the Beaver (ALA Notable Book; *Horn Book* honor list), illustrated by Robert Andrew Parker, Houghton, 1983.

OTHER

Child Life in New England, 1790-1840, Old Sturbridge Village (MA), 1961.

Life in Colonial America (nonfiction), Random House, 1963.

The Prospering (adult novel), Houghton, 1967.

Contributor of articles to periodicals, including *Better Homes and Gardens, Woman's Day, Parents, American Heritage, Today's Health,* and *Horn Book.* Speare's manuscript collection is at the Mugar Memorial Library at Boston University.

ADAPTATIONS: Abby, Julia and the Cows (television play; based on an article for *American Heritage*), Southern New England Telephone Company, January 7, 1958; *The Bronze Bow* (record, cassette, filmstrip with cassette), Random House; *The Witch of Blackbird Pond* (cassette), Random House; *The Sign of the Beaver* (cassette, filmstrip with cassette), Random House.

SIDELIGHTS: Elizabeth George Speare has won some of the most prestigious awards in young adult literature for her historical fiction novels, including two coveted Newbery Awards. She is known for creating believable characters who rely on their inner strength to cope with the challenges they face. Speare's favorite time period to write about is pre-Revolutionary America, although one of her most acclaimed books was set during Christ's lifetime in Galilee. She has been especially praised for her ability to merge historical fact with the fiction of her storylines—a skill which comes from hours of meticulous research.

Speare's childhood was spent in Massachusetts, and she has lived in New England her entire life. In her later writing, Speare reflected that it was easy for her to revisit Colonial times, since many areas of New England look the same now as they did then. About her childhood, Speare commented in *Current Biography:* "I had an exceptionally happy home. My mother was a very wonderful woman of great understanding." Her family

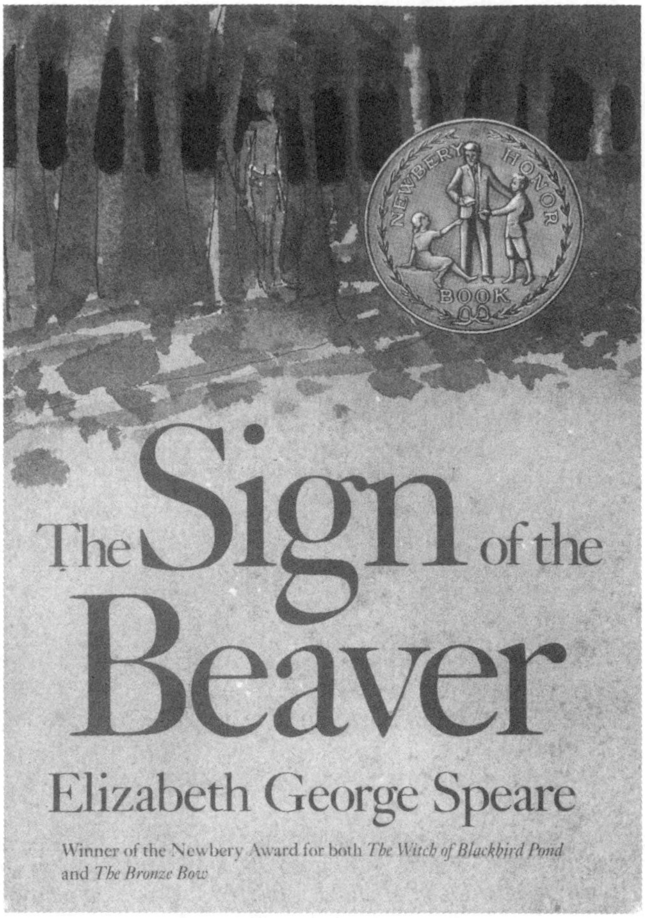

Cover of *The Sign of the Beaver,* by Elizabeth George Speare.

would take her and her only brother on hikes and picnics in the woods, or to Boston for theater or concerts. In the summer, they retreated to the shore, where she and her brother often would be the only children around. "I had endless golden days to read and think and dream," Speare wrote in *More Junior Authors.* "It was then that I discovered the absorbing occupation of writing stories."

Speare wrote a great deal as a child, filling scores of notebooks with stories and poems. Speare had a large extended family that would meet often for reunions and dinners. At these events, she and a close cousin would greet each other heartily, then sequester themselves in an out-of-the-way place to share the stories each of them had written. Even when adults would shake their heads in dismay over their activity, the girls would not be discouraged. Years later, when the two visited each other at college, they would carry their notebooks with them to share their stories as they had done when they were children.

Speare attended Boston University, receiving her master's degree in 1932. She taught high school for a while and then married Alden Speare in 1936. The couple moved to Connecticut and had two children. Speare settled into family life, finding that she had little time for writing with her many duties and activities. "Once in a while I would catch a story of my own peeking out of a corner of my mind," she related in *More Junior Authors.* "But before I found time to sit down with a pencil and paper it would have scurried back out of sight."

When her children were both in junior high, Speare found more time to write. At first, she worked on feature articles about family events like skiing or wrapping Christmas presents. Soon Speare found her niche when she published an article in *American Heritage* about the Smith sisters of Colonial Glastonbury, who refused to pay taxes and had their land confiscated. This article was adapted into a television program.

After reading a history of Connecticut, Speare found a diary of Susanna Johnson from 1807. The diary told the intriguing story of her family's kidnapping by Indians who eventually traded them to the French. From this tragic tale, Speare crafted a full-length novel entitled *Calico Captive.* Speare was haunted not only by the writer of the diary, but also by her sister, Miriam, whose adventures she made up and recorded. Ultimately, a well-rounded character emerged. Margaret Sherwood Libby in the *New York Herald Tribune Book Review* praised the work, saying: "It is that rarity in historical novels, one that does not seem to be written to provide 'background' but to tell a good story."

For her next book, Speare turned to Wethersfield, Connecticut, the town she and her husband had inhabited for twenty years. It was one of the oldest towns in New England and it had a rich history. Instead of finding a key event to write about, characters began to form in Speare's mind: "Each of these people began to take on sharper outlines, individual dimensions, and they were already moving and talking and reaching out in relationship to each other, long before I had found a place for them to live or a time in which they could be born. Finally I was compelled to find a home for them," Speare related in her Laura Ingalls Wilder Award acceptance speech, published in *Horn Book.* The home she found for them was in her book *The Witch of Blackbird Pond,* published in 1958. This captivating tale focuses on Kit Tyler, a native of Barbados who befriends a Quaker woman and is later accused of being a witch. The book won the Newbery Medal by a unanimous vote of the judges.

Speare stepped out of Connecticut to write her next novel, *The Bronze Bow.* The story centers on the boy Daniel, an Israeli who hates the Romans who have taken over his land. He eventually comes to find peace and acceptance through the teachings of Jesus. Speare wanted to write this novel to show young children that Jesus could be a real, living character, and she won a second Newbery for this ambitious book.

In *The Sign of the Beaver,* Speare returned to Colonial New England to tell a memorable tale about a young boy whose life is saved by an Indian. The boys form a friendship, and Matt tries to teach Attean to read and learn the white man's ways. However, Matt soon feels indoctrinated to the Indian ways and begins to question his own beliefs. Jean Fritz commented in the *New York Times Book Review* that "as usual in Mrs. Speare's novels, each word rings true."

In 1989, Speare received the Laura Ingalls Wilder Award for her contribution to children's literature. She established her reputation through only a few books, but each one is noted for its quality. In an acceptance speech for one of her Newbery Medals, published in *Horn Book,* Speare asserted her feelings about writing: "I believe that all of us who are concerned with children are committed to the salvaging of Love and Honor and Duty ... [children] look urgently to the adult world for evidence that we have proved our values to be enduring." She challenged other authors and herself by concluding that "Those of us who have found Love and Honor and Duty to be a sure foundation must somehow find words which have the ring of truth."

WORKS CITED:

Current Biography 1959, H. W. Wilson, 1960.
Fritz, Jean, review of *The Sign of the Beaver, New York Times Book Review,* May 8, 1983, p. 37.
Fuller, Muriel, editor, *More Junior Authors,* H. W. Wilson, 1963, pp. 189-190.
Libby, Margaret Sherwood, review of *Calico Captive, New York Herald Tribune Book Review,* November 17, 1957, p. 32.
Speare, E. G., "Report of a Journey: Newbery Award Acceptance," *Horn Book,* August, 1962.
Speare, E. G., "Laura Ingalls Wilder Award Acceptance," *Horn Book,* July/August, 1989.

FOR MORE INFORMATION SEE:

BOOKS

Apseloff, Marilyn Fain, *Elizabeth George Speare,* Twayne, 1991.
Authors of Books for Young People, 2nd edition, Scarecrow, 1971.
Children's Literature Review, Volume 8, Gale, 1985.
Contemporary Authors, Volumes 1-4, first revision, 1967.
More Books by More People, Citation, 1974.
Something about the Author, Volume 62, Gale, 1990.
Twentieth-Century Children's Writers, 3rd edition, St. James Press, 1989.

PERIODICALS

Horn Book, August, 1959; March/April, 1988.
Publishers Weekly, March 23, 1959; March 19, 1962.

* * *

SPENCER, Leonard G.
See SILVERBERG, Robert

Armstrong W. Sperry

SPERRY, Armstrong W. 1897-1976

PERSONAL: Born November 7, 1897, in New Haven, CT; died April 28, 1976, in Hanover, NH; son of Sereno Cark (a business executive) and Nettie (Alling) Sperry; married Margaret Mitchell, June 12, 1930; children: Susan, John Armstrong. *Education:* Attended Stamford Preparatory School, CT; studied at Yale School of Fine Arts, 1918, Art Students League, New York, NY, 1919-21, Academie Colarossis, Paris, France, 1922.

CAREER: Started as an illustrator and advertising artist, turned to writing, and began combining the two as writer-illustrator of children's books, 1932. *Military service:* U.S. Navy, 1917.

AWARDS, HONORS: Newbery Honor Book award, 1936, for *All Sail Set;* Newbery Medal, 1941, for *Call It Courage; New York Herald Tribune* Children's Spring Book Festival award, 1944, for *Storm Canvas,* and 1947, for *The Rain Forest;* Boys' Clubs of America Junior Book Award, 1949, for *The Rain Forest.*

WRITINGS:

FICTION; SELF-ILLUSTRATED

One Day with Manu, Winston, 1933.
One Day with Jambi in Sumatra, Winston, 1934.
One Day with Tuktu, an Eskimo Boy, Winston, 1935.
All Sail Set: A Romance of the "Flying Cloud," Winston, 1936.
Wagons Westward: The Old Trail to Santa Fe, Winston, 1936, Lane, 1948.

Little Eagle, A Navajo Boy, Winston, 1938.

(Compiler and author of introduction) *Story Parade: A Collection of Modern Stories for Boys and Girls,* Winston, 5 vols., 1938-42.

Lost Lagoon: A Pacific Adventure, Doubleday, 1939.

Call It Courage, Macmillan, 1940, published as *The Boy Who Was Afraid,* Lane, 1942.

Coconut, The Wonder Tree, Macmillan, 1942, Lane, 1946.

Bamboo, The Grass Tree, Macmillan, 1942, Lane, 1946.

No Brighter Glory, Macmillan, 1942, Hutchinson, 1944.

Storm Canvas, Winston, 1944.

Hull-Down for Action, Doubleday, 1945, Lane, 1948.

The Rain Forest, Macmillan, 1947, Lane, 1950.

Danger to Windward, Winston, 1947, Lane, 1952.

Black Falcon: A Story of Piracy and Old New Orleans, Winston, 1949.

Thunder Country, Macmillan, 1952, Lane, 1953.

River of the West: The Story of the Boston Men, illustrated by Henry Pitz, Winston, 1953, Lane, 1954.

Frozen Fire, Doubleday, 1956, Lane, 1957.

NONFICTION

The Voyages of Christopher Columbus, Random House, 1950.

John Paul Jones, Fighting Sailor, Random House, 1953.

Pacific Islands Speaking, Macmillan, 1955.

Captain Cook Explores the South Seas, Random House, 1955, revised edition published as *All about Captain Cook,* W. H. Allen, 1960.

All about the Arctic and Antarctic, Random House, 1957.

South of Cape Horn: A Saga of Nat Palmer and Early Antarctic Exploration, Winston, 1958.

All about the Jungle, Random House, 1959, W. H. Allen, 1960.

The Amazon, River Sea of Brazil, Garrard, 1961, Muller, 1962.

Great River, Wide Land: The Rio Grande through History, Macmillan, 1967, Collier Macmillan, 1967.

ILLUSTRATOR

Helen T. Follett, *Stars to Steer By,* Macmillan, 1934.

Agnes D. Hewes, *The Codfish Musket,* Doubleday, 1936.

Florence C. Means, *Shuttered Windows,* Houghton, 1938.

Clara I. Judson, *Boat Builder: The Story of Robert Fulton,* Scribner, 1940.

William S. Stone, *Teri Taro from Bora Bora,* Knopf, 1940.

Rose Brown, *Two Children of Brazil,* Lippincott, 1940.

Frederic Arnold Kummer, *Courage over the Andes,* Winston, 1940.

James Cloyd Bowman, *Winabojo, Master of Life,* Whitman, 1941.

Helen T. Follett, *House Afire!,* Scribner, 1941.

Marion Florence Lansing, *Nicholas Arnold, Toolmaker,* Doubleday, 1941.

Edith Heal, *Dogie Boy,* Whitman, 1943.

Alexander Laing, *Clipper Ship Men,* Duell, 1944.

Howard Pease, *Thunderbolt House,* Doubleday, 1944.

Trevor Lloyd, *Sky Highways: Geography from the Air,* Houghton, 1945.

Howard Pease, *Jungle River,* Doubleday, 1948.

Allen Chaffee, adapter, *The Story of Hiawatha,* Random House, 1951.

ADAPTATIONS: Call It Courage was produced on television for "The Wonderful World of Disney," April, 1973, and also released as a color filmstrip, Miller-Brody Productions.

SIDELIGHTS: Equally gifted as an author and illustrator, Armstrong Sperry combined these talents in his classic South Seas adventure story *Call It Courage,* which won the coveted Newbery Medal in 1941. Sperry created many stirring books for young people that emphasize courage, heroic deeds, and heroic characters. The beauty and strength of his illustrations reveal the depth of understanding Sperry felt for his subjects, as well as for the needs of his young audience. "In each of [my] books I have given to the major character some challenge he must meet, some great obstacle he must overcome, some ideal toward which he must aspire,"

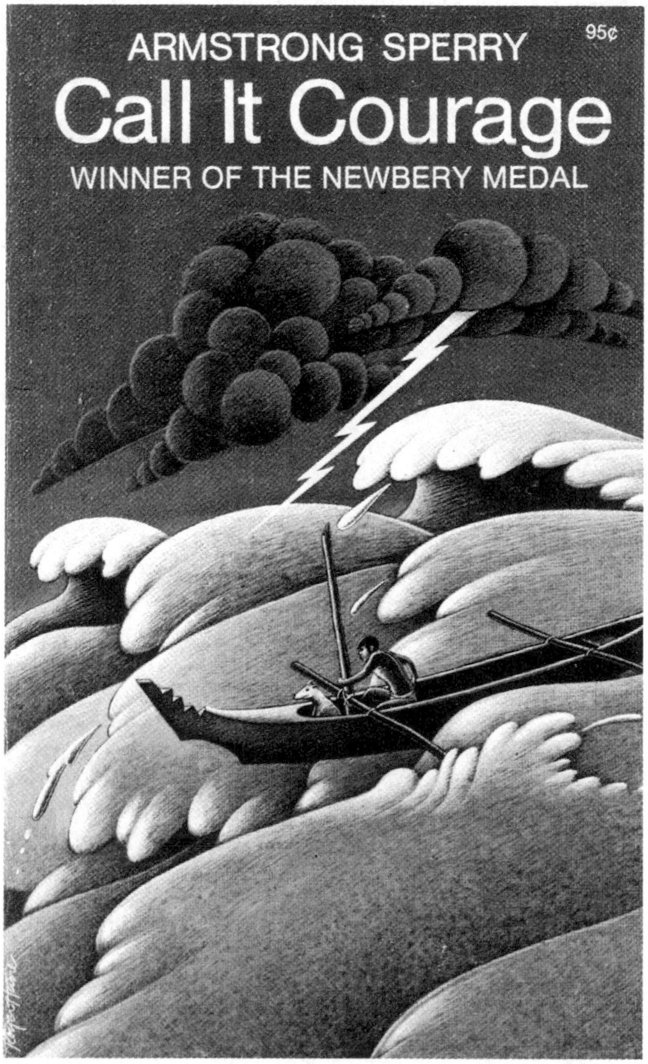

Cover of *Call It Courage,* by Armstrong Sperry.

Sperry noted in his Newbery Medal acceptance speech, published in *Newbery Medal Books: 1922-1955*. "Children identify themselves with the characters they read about, and so it becomes an obligation on the part of the author to create the kind of people with whom we want our children to be identified."

Sperry was born in New Haven, Connecticut, in 1897, where his forebears had settled between 1640 and 1650. On one side of the family the men were mariners, while on the other they became farmers. From childhood Sperry enjoyed reading tales of the sea by Herman Melville, Robert Louis Stevenson, and Jack London. "But my real interest in story telling comes from my great-grandfather," Sperry related in *Junior Book of Authors,* "who had followed the sea all his life, and who used to tell me hair-raising yarns about his adventures in the remotest parts of the world," particularly on the island of Bora Bora, northwest of Tahiti.

Also in childhood Sperry showed a strong interest in drawing, sometimes decorating his schoolbooks rather than studying, to the despair of his mother and teachers. He served in the Navy during World War I, and then received his first formal art training at the Yale School of Fine Arts in 1918. Later Sperry headed to New York City, where he studied at the Art Students League for three years under notable artists such as George Bellows and Luis Mora. Sperry worked as an advertising illustrator in the 1920s, and during this time he also happened upon a book called *White Shadows in the South Seas* by Frederick O'Brien. As Sperry recalled in his Newbery acceptance speech, all his dreams came to life again, for O'Brien had "the power to recreate, through the medium of words, the spell that lies over the South Seas Islands ... the quality of epic which still persists in the handful of natives who are left, and sings through them to this day in their chants and legends."

With these influences working upon him, Sperry moved intuitively toward a career as an author-illustrator of children's books. He based his early works upon loving study of children and their needs, and patiently built a reputation for quality and accuracy in his drawing. One June day in 1925, he finally realized his dream and sailed for Bora Bora, the island that he remembered from his great-grandfather's stories. Sperry described his first sight of the island in his Newbery acceptance speech: "I saw a single great peak that towered two thousand feet, straight up from the plane of the sea. And the peak was buttressed like the walls of an ancient fortress, and it was made of basalt—volcanic rock—which glistened in the sun like amethyst. And there were waterfalls spilling from the clouds, and up in the mountains wild goats were leaping from peak to peak. There was something so fresh about the island that it seemed as if it had just risen up from the floor of the sea that morning. There wasn't a single flaw in the picture. Bora Bora was everything a South Sea island ought to be."

Sperry spent about two years in that archipelago, learning and developing a profound appreciation for the language, legends, heroic sagas, and ancient chants. He was there when vanilla bean trade brought sudden prosperity and "civilization" to the island, and also when a hurricane wiped out much of it. As Sperry noted in his Newbery acceptance speech, "It was an amazing experience to see that beaten little band of people rally, and slowly take up their old life where they had left off ... it called forth all their ingenuity and daring, all the courage with which man from the beginning of time has matched his skill against Nature's might ... a victory not so much over elemental disaster as a personal victory over themselves."

On his return to New York, Sperry began to write a book of his own to capture his South Seas experiences and observations in words and pictures. *One Day with Manu,* set in Bora Bora, appeared in 1933 and is one of the earliest books written for American children to portray a foreign background. Sperry wrote and illustrated two more "One Day with" books, one set in Sumatra, the other an Eskimo story. He researched Native American culture to complete *Little Eagle, A Navajo Boy,* which includes many striking illustrations in shades of yellow, orange, brown, and green—reflecting the brilliance of the desert and mountains where the Navajo lived. A reviewer in *Library Journal* noted that the book was "drenched in sunlight and color."

Sperry's most famous book, with which "he earned a place in the galaxy of notable children's writers," according to Joan McGrath in *Twentieth Century Children's Writers,* was *Call It Courage,* published in 1940. Commended as a study of solitude as well as survival, it is the suspenseful story of an island boy who is afraid of the sea but also determined to prove his courage to his father, the gods, and his tribe. Mafatu, a young Polynesian, makes a lonely voyage to a remote island in a small canoe, testing himself against the terrors of the sea, wild animals, and an unknown warrior tribe who come to the island to perform savage ceremonies. Doris Pattee, quoted in *Current Biography,* explained that in Sperry's "beautiful prose the tale moves smoothly and rapidly like a native chant, and its music rises and falls like the billows of the sea in its setting. Storytellers who have used the story often find children entranced not only by the story itself but by the cadence and rhythm of the language."

Sperry continued to write and illustrate, sometimes two books a year, into his seventies. His later work includes historical fiction and nonfiction—about swashbuckling figures like Jean LaFitte and John Paul Jones, Antarctic explorers, and clipper ship captains. He also illustrated numerous books for other writers, including Howard Pease and Alexander Laing. During World War II, Sperry described the important role of those who write for children in an article for *Horn Book:* "I am aware that, in these days of violent action, it may sound futile to talk about the power of mere words. And yet, surely, words are one of the weapons dictators have feared most of all ... I think it is our great privilege—the privilege of all people who work in any way with children—to help to keep alive that vision of freedom, that these children of today may carry it with them into the world of tomorrow: that imperishable dream of the right to live, to work, and to worship, as free men—in peace."

WORKS CITED:

Review of *Little Eagle, A Navajo Boy, Library Journal,* December 15, 1938.

Pattee, Doris, quoted in *Current Biography,* Wilson, 1941, p. 813.

Sperry, Armstrong, Newbery Acceptance Paper, *Newbery Medal Books: 1922-1955,* edited by Bertha Mahony Miller and Elinor Whitney Field, Horn Book, 1955, pp. 193-207.

Sperry, "A Part of Victory," *Horn Book,* May, 1943, pp. 195-99.

Sperry, essay in *Junior Book of Authors,* Wilson, 1951, pp. 279-80.

McGrath, Joan, *Twentieth Century Children's Writers,* St. James Press, 1989, pp. 912-13.

* * *

SPIER, Peter (Edward) 1927-

PERSONAL: Born June 6, 1927, in Amsterdam, Netherlands; came to the United States, 1951; became U.S. citizen, 1958; son of Joseph E. A. (a journalist and illustrator) and Albertine (van Raalte) Spier; married Kathryn M. Pallister, July 12, 1958; children: Thomas Pallister, Kathryn Elizabeth. *Education:* Attended Royal Academy of Art, Amsterdam, 1945-47; attended Willems Park School, Amsterdams Lyceum. *Religion:* Reformed Church of America. *Hobbies and other interests:* Sailing, history, model ship building.

ADDRESSES: Home—Wardencliff Rd., P.O. Box 210, Shoreham, Long Island, NY, 11786.

Peter Spier

CAREER: Elsevier's Weekblad, Paris, France, junior editor, 1949-51; Elsevier Publishing, Houston, TX, junior editor, 1951-52; author and illustrator, 1952—. *Military service:* Royal Netherlands Navy, 1947-51; became lieutenant.

MEMBER: Netherlands Club (NY).

AWARDS, HONORS: Hans Brinker: or, the Silver Skates was included in the American Institute of Graphic Arts Book Show, 1958-60, *London Bridge Is Falling Down!,* 1967-68, and *Tin Lizzie,* 1976-77; Caldecott Honor Book from the American Library Association, 1962, for *The Fox Went Out on a Chilly Night; Boston Globe-Horn Book* Award for Illustration, 1967, for *London Bridge Is Falling Down!,* Honor Book, 1967, for *To Market! To Market!;* Diploma de Triennale de Milano; *Hurrah, We're Outward Bound!* was chosen one of Child Study Association of America's Children's Books of the Year, 1968, *And So My Garden Grows,* 1969, *The Erie Canal,* 1970, *Crash! Bang! Boom!,* 1972, *Tin Lizzie,* 1975, *The Legend of New Amsterdam,* 1979, and *Dreams,* 1987.

Christopher Award, 1971, for *The Erie Canal; Gobble, Growl, Grunt* was selected as one of the *New York Times* Outstanding Books of the Year, 1971, *The Star-Spangled Banner,* 1973, and *Bored, Nothing to Do,* 1978; New York Academy of Science's Children's Science Book Award, 1972, for *Gobble, Growl, Grunt;* Christopher Award, and chosen one of *New York Times* Best Illustrated Children's Books of the Year, both 1977, Caldecott Medal, and Lewis Carroll Shelf Award, both 1978, International Board on Books for Young People (IBBY) Honor List, 1980, American Book Award finalist for paperback picture book, 1982, all for *Noah's Ark;* Little Archer Award from the University of Wisconsin-Oshkosh, 1978, for *Oh, Were They Ever Happy;* Christopher Award, and American Book Award finalist for children's hardcover nonfiction, both 1980, and Mass Media Award from the Conference of Christians and Jews, all for *People;* University of Southern Mississippi Silver Medallion, 1984, in recognition of his distinguished career as author/illustrator of books for children.

A great many of his books have been designated either as Junior Literary Guild Selections or ALA Notable Books or both.

WRITINGS:

FOR YOUNG ADULTS; SELF-ILLUSTRATED

The Fox Went Out on a Chilly Night: An Old Song, Doubleday, 1961.
Of Dikes and Windmills, Doubleday, 1970.
The Erie Canal, Doubleday, 1970.
Gobble, Growl, Grunt, Doubleday, 1971.
Crash! Bang! Boom!, Doubleday, 1972.
Fast-Slow, High-Low: A Book of Opposites, Doubleday, 1972.
The Star-Spangled Banner, Doubleday, 1973.
Tin Lizzie, Doubleday, 1975.

Noah's Ark, Doubleday, 1977.
Bored—Nothing to Do!, Doubleday, 1978.
Oh, Were They Ever Happy!, Doubleday, 1978.
The Legend of New Amsterdam, Doubleday, 1979.
People, Doubleday, 1980.
The Pet Store, Doubleday, 1981.
My School, Doubleday, 1981.
The Fire House, Doubleday, 1981.
The Food Market, Doubleday, 1981.
The Toy Shop, Doubleday, 1981.
Bill's Service Station, Doubleday, 1981.
Rain, Doubleday, 1982.
Peter Spier's Christmas!, Doubleday, 1983.
Peter Spier's Little Bible Storybooks, Doubleday, 1983.
Peter Spier's Little Cats, Doubleday, 1984.
Peter Spier's Little Dogs, Doubleday, 1984.
Peter Spier's Little Ducks, Doubleday, 1984.
Peter Spier's Little Rabbits, Doubleday, 1984.
(Reteller) *The Book of Jonah,* Doubleday, 1985.
Dreams, Doubleday, 1986.
Peter Spier's Advent Calendar: Silent Night, Holy Night, Doubleday, 1987.
We the People: The Story of the U.S. Constitution, Doubleday, 1987.
Peter Spier's Little Animal Books, Doubleday, 1987.
Pop-Up Peter Spier's Birthday Cake, Doubleday, 1990.
Peter Spier's Circus, Doubleday, 1991.
Father, May I Come?, Lemniscaat (Rotterdam), 1992, Doubleday, 1993.

"MOTHER GOOSE LIBRARY" SERIES

London Bridge Is Falling Down!, Doubleday, 1967.
To Market! To Market!, Doubleday, 1967.
Hurrah, We're Outward Bound!, Doubleday, 1968.
And So My Garden Grows, Doubleday, 1969.

Contributor to *Reader's Digest, National Geographic* magazine, and to Time/Life Books. Spier's manuscript collections are housed at the de Grummond Collection at the University of Southern Mississippi, Kerlan Collection at the University of Minnesota, and Port Washington Public Library in New York. His works have been translated into twenty-four languages, including Japanese and Chinese.

ILLUSTRATOR

Nikolai Gogol, *Mantel,* [Holland], 1946.
P. Baker, *Logboek van de Gratias* (title means "Logbook of the Gratias"), Elsevier, 1948.
E. Elias, *Op Reis Met Prins Bernhard* (title means "On a Journey with Prince Bernhard"), Bezige Bij, 1951.
Steussy, *Straten Schrijven Historie* (title means "Street Names with History"), Schoonderbeek, 1951.
Elmer Reynolds, *Thunder Hill,* Doubleday, 1953.
Louis Untermeyer, *Adventures All,* Golden Press, 1953.
Ruth Langland Holberg, *Tam Morgan, the Liveliest Girl in Salem,* Doubleday, 1953.
Margaret G. Otto, *Cocoa,* Holt, 1953.
H.J. Berkhard, *Wonders of the World,* Simon & Schuster, 1953.
Frieda K. Brown, *Last Hurdle,* Crowell, 1953.
Marjorie Vetter, *Cargo for Jennifer,* Longmans, 1954.
Frances H. Burnett, *Little Lord Fauntleroy,* Doubleday, 1954.
Mark Twain (pseudonym of Samuel L. Clemens), *Prince and the Pauper,* Doubleday, 1954.
(With Emil Lowenstein) Paul Friedlander and Joseph Brooks, *Italy,* Simon & Schuster, 1955.
Michel Rouze, *Mystery of Mont Saint-Michel,* translated by George Libaire, Holt, 1955.
Vera A. Amrein, *Cabin for the Mary Christmas,* Harcourt, 1955.
Science and Living in Today's World series, Volumes 6-8, Doubleday, 1955-56.
Joy Anderson, *Hippolyte: Crab King,* Harcourt, 1956.
Jennie Darlington and Jane McIlvaine, *My Antarctic Honeymoon: A Year at the Bottom of the World,* Doubleday, 1956.
Phyllis Krasilovsky, *The Cow Who Fell in the Canal,* Doubleday, 1957.
Margaret Hubbard, *Boss Chombale,* Crowell, 1957.
England, Ginn, 1957.
Ruth Strang and others, *Teenage Tales,* Volume 4, Heath, 1957.
Margaret B. Boni, *Favorite Christmas Carols: Fifty-nine Yuletide Songs Both Old and New,* arranged by Norman Lloyd, Simon & Schuster, 1957.
Mary Mapes Dodge, *Hans Brinker; or, the Silver Skates,* Scribner, 1958.
Jessica Reynolds, *Jessica's Journal,* Holt, 1958.
Douglas Angus, *Lions Fed the Tigers,* Houghton, 1958.
Kenneth Dodson, *Hector the Stowaway Dog: A True Story,* Little, Brown, 1958.
Elizabeth Fairholme and Pamela Powell, *Esmeralda Ahoy!,* Doubleday, 1959.
Ann Frank, *Works of Ann Frank,* Doubleday, 1959.
Betty Crocker's Guide to Easy Entertaining, Golden Press, 1959.
Richard Watkins, *Mystery of Willet,* T. Nelson, 1959.
Frances Carpenter, *Wonder Tales of Ships and Seas,* Doubleday, 1959.
John L. Strohm, *Golden Garden Guide: A Practical Handbook of Gardening and Outdoor Living,* Golden Press, 1960.
Ardo Flakkeberg, *The Sea Broke Through,* Knopf, 1960.
Elinor Parker, editor, *One Hundred More Story Poems,* Crowell, 1960.
J. L. Strohm, *Golden Guide to Lawns, Shrubs, and Trees,* Golden Press, 1961.
Lavinia Davis, *Island City: Adventures in Old New York,* Doubleday, 1961.
George H. Grant, *Boy Overboard!,* Little, Brown, 1961.
Dola De Jong, *The Level Land,* Scribner, 1961.
J. L. Strohm and others, *Golden Guide to Flowers: Annuals, Perennials, Bulbs, and a Special Section on Roses,* Golden Press, 1962.
Margaretha Shemin, *The Little Riders,* Coward, 1963.
C. W. Ceram (pseudonym of Kurt Marek), *Archaeology,* Odyssey, 1964.
Jan de Hartog, *Sailing Ship,* Odyssey, 1964.
K. Marek, *The History of the Theater,* Odyssey, 1964.
R. Butterfield, *Ancient Rome,* Odyssey, 1964.
M. Valmarana, *Architecture,* Odyssey, 1965.
Anthony West, *Elizabethan England,* Odyssey, 1965.

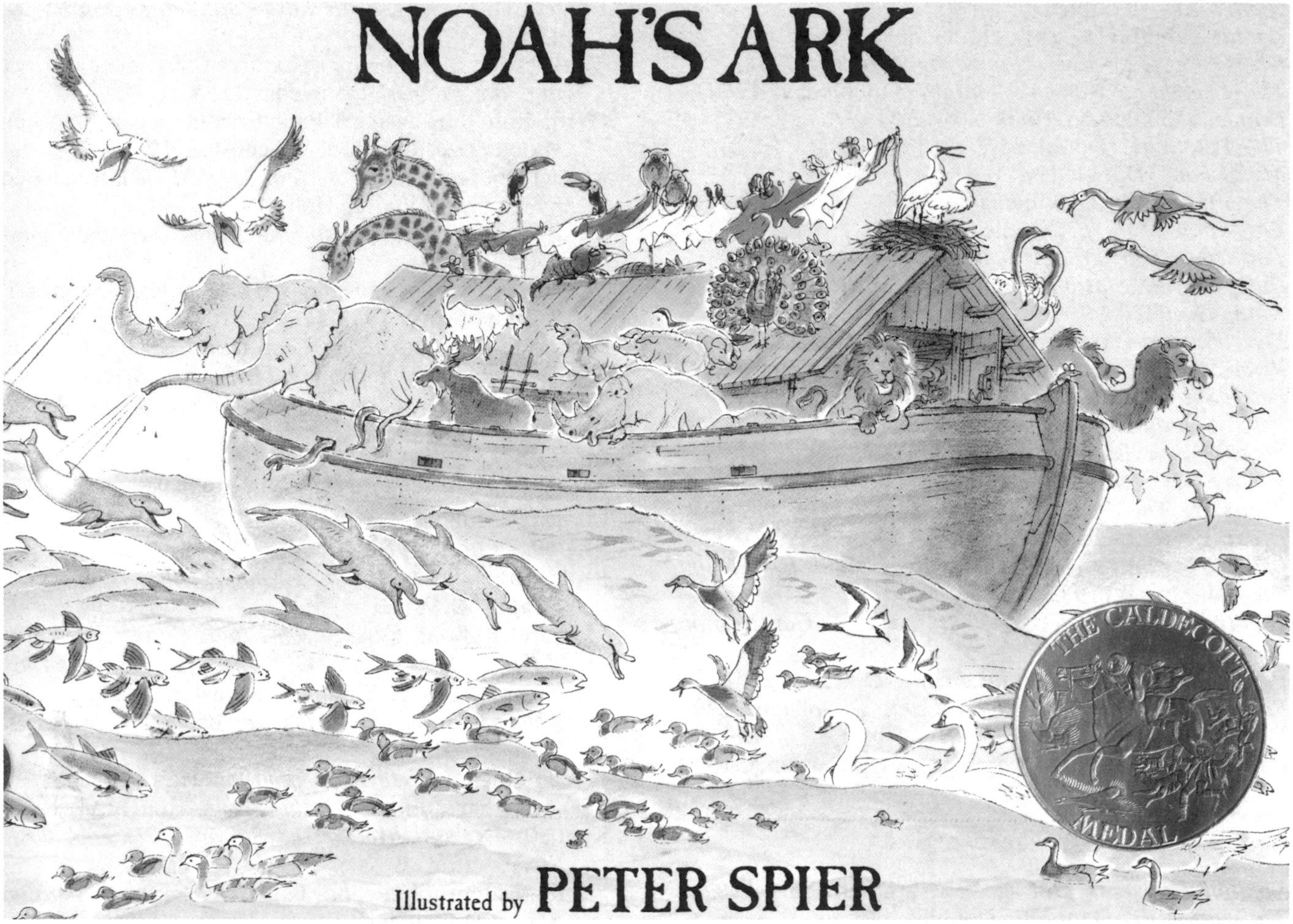

From *Noah's Ark,* translated and illustrated by Peter Spier.

Donald D. MacMillan, *Great Furniture Styles, 1660-1830,* Odyssey, 1965.
World of Michelangelo, Time-Life, 1966.
E. Parker, editor, *Here and There: One Hundred Poems about Places,* Crowell, 1967.
Animals You Will Never Forget, Reader's Digest, 1969.
M. Shemin, *Empty Moat,* Coward, 1969.
T. R. Reese, *Frederica: Colonial Fort and Town,* United States National Park Service, 1969.
Golden Book Encyclopedia, Volume 1, Golden Press, 1970.
Traveler's Tale of Tikal, National Geographic, 1975.
Elmer Bendiner, *Virgin Diplomats,* Knopf, 1975.
Peter Lippman, *Trucks, Trucks, Trucks,* Doubleday, 1984.

Contributor of illustrations to *Ford Almanac,* 1956-72.

ADAPTATIONS:

The Cow Who Fell in the Canal (cassette; sound filmstrip), Weston Woods, 1965, (feature film), 1970.
The Fox Went Out on a Chilly Night (cassette; sound filmstrip), Weston Woods, 1965.
London Bridge Is Falling Down (feature film), Weston Woods, 1969, (cassette, sound filmstrip), 1971.
The Erie Canal (cassette; sound filmstrip), Weston Woods, 1974, (feature film), 1976.
The Star-Spangled Banner (feature film; cassette; filmstrip with cassette), Weston Woods, 1975.
Oh, Were They Ever Happy! (filmstrip with cassette), Random House.
Noah's Ark (cassette; filmstrip with cassette), Weston Woods, (video) "Stories to Remember," Lightyear Entertainment, 1990.

SIDELIGHTS: Peter Spier's numerous illustrated children's books have been lauded for their realistic detail, charming sense of humor, and visual accuracy. Spier began his career illustrating books for other people, but he found a greater sense of satisfaction in working on his own, and he both wrote and illustrated all of his later books. Although Spier was born in Amsterdam, many of his popular books focus on some aspect of his adopted country, the United States, including *The Star-Spangled Banner, The Erie Canal, The Fox Went Out on a Chilly Night,* and *We the People: The Story of the U.S. Constitution.*

Spier was raised in the countryside city of Broek-in-Waterland, the Netherlands. The son of a famous artist and journalist, Spier began to show signs of his artistic talent early. "I cannot remember a time when I did not dabble with clay, draw, or see someone draw," Spier remarked in *The Third Book of Junior Authors.* As a boy, he spent many hours sketching the scenery and animals of his hometown. The Spier household also contributed to his knowledge of history and the world around him: "I grew up in an intellectual milieu. Books were very important, and, needless to say, because of my father's profession, we were very 'up' on current events," Spier commented in an interview for *Something about the Author (SATA).*

However, Spier did not decide on his chosen profession until he was eighteen, when he took art classes at the Royal Academy of Art in Amsterdam. After graduation, he joined the navy and considered making it a career. "I liked the service a lot and almost signed on for a couple of decades. The discipline, the ships, the water, the people—everything about it pleased me ... But my yen for publishing wouldn't let go," Spier related in *SATA.*

Spier left the navy and went to work for a Dutch newspaper. At first he worked in Paris, and a year later he was transferred to Houston, Texas. His father visited the area with him, and they both decided to come to America. Spier eventually decided to move on, and went to New York City to try free-lance work. One of his first meetings was with an editor who asked him if he could draw goats. "Little did I know that all those hours of drawing goats as a kid would pay off!" Spier told *SATA.*

Spier soon was busy illustrating picture books for other authors, as well as contributing drawings to *Collier's, Saturday Evening Post,* and *Look.* In 1958, he married Kathryn Pallister, and the two settled down on Long Island, eventually having two children. After a few years of contributing to books by others, Spier decided to write and illustrate books on his own, thinking he could win more artistic freedom and better economic reward. "To illustrate my own books means that there is no author to tell me that Noah should wear a hat or carry binoculars or that the ark should have portholes; when you come down to it, my own judgement is the only thing that counts," Spier told Janet D. Chenery in *Horn Book.*

The inspiration for his first solo book came when he and his wife were travelling in Vermont. During a picturesque autumn night, his wife began to sing "The Fox Went Out on a Chilly Night." Spier immediately thought that the area was a perfect setting for the folk song. He spent weeks traveling the countryside and making preliminary sketches. After its publication in 1961, *The Fox Went Out on a Chilly Night* was named a Caldecott Honor Book.

Spier went out "on location" to do research for many of his other books. "Whenever possible, I go to the setting of each book to make preliminary pictures," Spier commented in *Publisher's Weekly.* "There is no substitute for an artist seeing and absorbing the feel of a place; you can't just take it easy, stay home, and work from picture postcards." When he began *The Erie Canal,* for example, Spier went into the field and sketched many buildings along the famous waterway.

Another bit of Americana to which Spier brought new life was the national anthem. After some research, Spier concluded that the history of the famous song had not been expressed in a picture book. His *The Star-Spangled Banner* depicts America as hard-working and freedom-loving, and includes both modern and period illustrations. The book is filled with interesting historical facts about the anthem and the American flag. M. Sarah Smedman wrote in *Dictionary of Literary Biography,* "A history of the naval battle which inspired the national anthem, *The Star-Spangled Banner* is also a book about the peace and liberty, courage and determination the artist sees as inspiriting America." Similarly, *We the People* focused on the Constitution and the Bill of Rights from both a past and present perspective. Spier described how the Constitution came into being and also illustrated how people today continue the work of the Constitution.

Perhaps the most notable of Spier's works is the Caldecott Medal-winning *Noah's Ark.* The artist had for a long time wanted to illustrate a book on the topic based on a seventeenth-century Dutch poem by Jacob Revius. Skeptical about whether he would be flooding the market with another version of the tale, he researched all the Noah books in print and found none that were similar to the one he was proposing. "None of them shows Noah shoveling manure or even hinted at the stench and the mess inside," Spier said in his Caldecott acceptance published in *Horn Book.* "It was then that I knew that there was room for one more *Noah's Ark.*" Spier's book won popular and critical praise for its beauty, message, and unique sense of humor. Spier's father was so proud of his crowning achievement that he gave his son his entire collection of Randolph Caldecott's books, which included several first editions.

In some of Spier's other notable books, he has traveled back to his native country to illustrate *Hans Brinker, or, the Silver Skates* and *Of Dykes and Windmills;* made sounds the basis for his books *Crash! Bang! Boom* and *Gobble, Growl, Grunt;* looked at the life of a famous automobile in *Tin Lizzie;* showed facility with another Bible story in *The Book of Jonah;* and made a tribute to multiculturalism in *People.*

Even while illustrating a prodigious body of work which includes over 150 books, Spier still has found time to practice some of his lifelong hobbies, including sailing and model shipbuilding. The artist also has a passion for history and reads historical books avidly. Despite his many achievements, Spier admits that he writes more to please himself than to satisfy the tastes of any audience. Joan Hess Michel concluded in *American Artist,* "Peter Spier sets high standards for himself, demanding his best. He is exact and thorough in his research. His work is careful, detailed, and precise, yet has spontaneity, humor, and charm. His fine illustrations possess a joyous quality; they delight as well as teach."

WORKS CITED:

Chenery, Janet D., "Peter Spier," *Horn Book,* August, 1978, pp. 379-81.

De Montreville, Doris and Donna Hill, editors, *Third Book of Junior Authors,* Wilson, 1972, pp. 274-75.

Michel, Joan Hess, "The Illustrations of Peter Spier," *American Artist,* October, 1969, pp. 49-55, 82-86.

Smedman, M. Sarah, "Peter Spier," *Dictionary of Literary Biography,* Volume 61: *American Writers for Children since 1960: Poets, Illustrators, and Non fiction Authors,* Gale, 1987, pp. 282-296.

Spier, Peter, "The Frog Belongs in the Food Market and Other Perils of an Illustrator," *Publisher's Weekly,* July 25, 1980, pp. 93-4.

Spier, in an interview with Marguerite Feitlowitz for *Something about the Author,* Volume 54, Gale, 1989, pp. 119-134.

FOR MORE INFORMATION SEE:

BOOKS

Books Are by People, Citation, 1969.

Children's Literature Review, Volume 5, Gale, 1983.

Illustrators of Books for Young People, 2nd edition, Scarecrow, 1975.

Illustrator's of Children's Books: 1957-1966. Horn Book, 1968.

Newbery and Caldecott Medal Books: 1976-1985, Horn Book, 1986.

* * *

SPINELLI, Jerry 1941-

PERSONAL: Born February 1, 1941, in Norristown, PA; son of Louis A. (a printer) and Lorna Mae (Bigler) Spinelli; married Eileen Mesi (a writer), May 21, 1977; children: Kevin, Barbara, Jeffrey, Molly, Sean, Ben. *Education:* Gettsysburg College, A.B., 1963; Johns Hopkins University, M.A., 1964; atttended Temple University, 1964. *Hobbies and other interests:* Tennis, country music, travel, pet rats.

ADDRESSES: Home—331 Melvin Rd. Phoenixville, PA 19460. *Agent*—Ms. Ray Lincoln, Ray Lincoln Literary Agency, 7900 Old York Rd., Apt. 107-B, Elkins Park, PA 19117.

CAREER: Chilton Company (magazine publishers), Radnor, PA, editor, 1966-89; writer. *Military service:* U.S. Naval Reserve, 1966-72.

AWARDS, HONORS: Boston Globe/Horn Book Award, 1990, and Newbery Medal, American Library Association, 1991, both for *Maniac Magee;* Carolyn Field Award, 1991.

WRITINGS:

Space Station Seventh Grade, Little, Brown, 1982.

Who Put That Hair in My Toothbrush?, Little, Brown, 1984.

Night of the Whale, Little, Brown, 1985.

Jason and Marceline, Little, Brown, 1986.

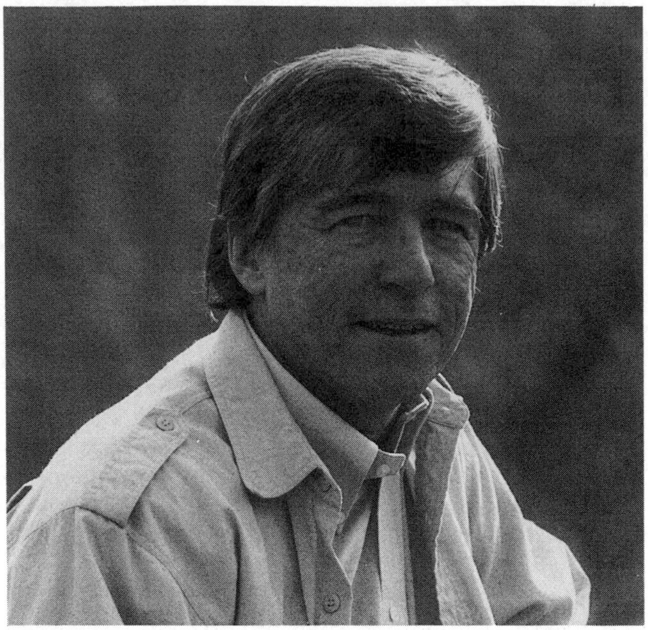

Jerry Spinelli

Dump Days, Little, Brown, 1988.

Maniac Magee, Little, Brown, 1990.

The Bathwater Gang, illustrated by Meredith Johnson, Little, Brown, 1990.

There's a Girl in My Hammerlock, Simon & Schuster, 1991.

Fourth Grade Rats, Scholastic, 1991.

Report to the Principal's Office, Scholastic 1991.

Who Ran My Underwear up the Flagpole?, Scholastic, 1992.

Contributor to books, including *Our Roots Grow Deeper Than We Know: Pennsylvania Writers—Pennsylvania Life,* edited by Lee Gutkind, University of Pittsburgh Press, 1985, and *Noble Pursuits,* edited by Virginia A. Arnold and Carl B. Smith, Macmillan, 1988. Work represented in anthologies, including *Best Sports Stories of 1982,* Dutton.

SIDELIGHTS: Best known for his Newbery-Award-winning book *Maniac Magee,* Jerry Spinelli's entire body of work is distinguished by his accurate and humorous depictions of adolescent life. *Washington Post Book World* contributor Deborah Churchman deemed Spinelli "a master of those embarrassing, gloppy, painful and suddenly wonderful things that happen on the razor's edge between childhood and full-fledged adolescence." While some parents may cringe at his characters' ribald jokes and risque topics of conversation, this approach has earned the author both the respect and loyal following of young readers. Critics maintain that Spinelli is popular because he accepts kids for what they are. The author "neither judges nor berates but shakes everyone up in his own bag of tricks and watches to see what will spill out," according to Ethel R. Twichell in a *Horn Book* review of Spinelli's book *Dump Days.*

Spinelli grew up in Norristown, Pennsylvania, and his first claim to fame was that a local paper published a poem he wrote about a hometown team's football victory. This experience left him eager to continue writing, and the author tried to match this success as an adult. Spinelli thought that because he was older he had to write about issues important to grownups. Publishers, however, were not interested in these topics. Spinelli found his narrative voice after he married. One of his children's feats—eating food that the author had been saving for a snack—inspired him to write, and this incident became part of his first novel, *Space Station Seventh Grade.* Spinelli once remarked in *Contemporary Authors New Revision Series* that when he started writing about youngsters he began "to see that in my own memories and in the kids around me, I had all the material I needed for a schoolbagful of books. I saw that each kid is a population unto him- or herself, and that a child's bedroom is as much a window to the universe as an orbiting telescope or a philosopher's study."

Space Station Seventh Grade recounts the everyday adventures of Jason Herkimer, a junior high school student. With seemingly mundane events—such as masterminding classroom pranks and chasing after girls—the author traces Jason's awkward entrance into adolescence. Although Jason seems impulsive and has a penchant for getting into trouble because he speaks before he thinks, he must also contend with more serious issues, including coping with divorced parents and accepting a stepfather. Some critics disapproved of the crude humor Spinelli's characters sometimes use, but judged that the author accurately represents the adolescent milieu. *Voice of Youth Advocates* contributor James J. McPeak called the story "first-rate," and Twichell, writing in *Horn Book,* deemed *Space Station Seventh Grade* a "truly funny book."

Spinelli followed *Space Station Seventh Grade* with *Who Put That Hair in My Toothbrush?* In this book, the chapters alternate between the first-person narration of Megin and Greg, a sister and brother two years apart with vastly different personalities. Greg is preoccupied with a possible romance, while sports-crazy Megin secretly befriends an elderly woman confined to a nursing home. The pair fight constantly, but when a crisis nearly erupts, they join forces. Critics appreciated Spinelli's humorous depiction of sibling rivalry mixed with his inclusion of weighty themes. In a review for *Horn Book,* Karen Jameyson credited the author with a "sure ear for adolescent dialogue" and called the book "hilarious."

Jason and Marceline, published in 1986, serves as a sequel to *Space Station Seventh Grade.* Now a ninth grader, Jason again copes with the daily trials of adolescence, including attempting romance with Marceline, a trombone player who once beat him up. Marceline initially rejects Jason's advances because he tries to impress her the same bravado and macho behavior that his friends employ in their romantic conquests. When he shows his caring side in a heroic lunchroom incident, however, Marceline forgives Jason's antics and their relationship progresses. With *Jason and Marceline,* Spinelli earned praise for pointing out that respect and friendship are necessary in a loving relationship between people of any age. Writing again in *Horn Book,* Twichell noted that Jason "truly sounds like a teenager."

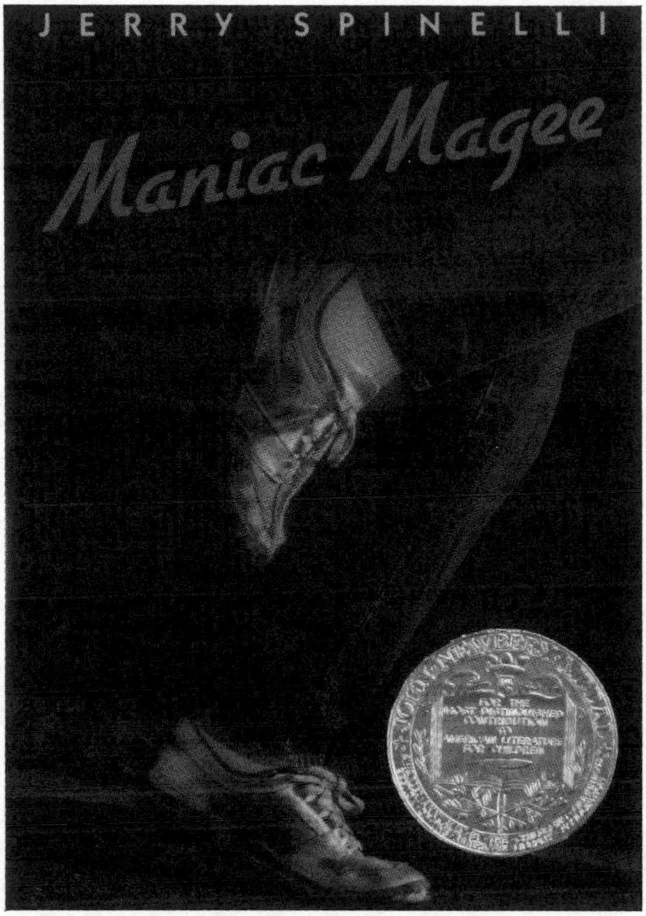

Cover of *Maniac Magee,* by Jerry Spinelli.

Maniac Magee, Spinelli's book that won the prestigious Newbery Medal, is about an athletically gifted boy whose accomplishments ignite legends about him. Jeffrey Magee, a Caucasian boy nicknamed Maniac, is an orphan who has run away from his foster home. His search for a loving household to become a part of is problematic in the racially divided town of Two Mills. Maniac's first stay is with a black family, but after racist graffiti is spray-painted on their house, he leaves. He spends several happy months with an old man in a park equipment room before the man dies. Maniac then moves into a white family's house, filled with roaches, alcohol, and cursing. The sons are gang members and the entire family is racist. Maniac then tries his greatest feat—to initiate better relations between blacks and whites in Two Mills.

Although some critics felt that Spinelli diluted his message about the absurdity of racism by presenting *Maniac Magee* as a fable, others believed the author's focus on such an incident was noteworthy. Alison Teal, in her *New York Times Book Review* appraisal, judged that "Spinelli grapples ... with a racial tension rarely addressed in fiction for children in the middle grades." And *Washington Post Book World* contributor Claudia Logan lauded Spinelli's "colorful writing and originality."

Spinelli produced both *There's a Girl in My Hammerlock* and *Fourth Grade Rats* in 1991. *There's a Girl in My Hammerlock* chronicles the adventures of Maisie Potter, an eighth-grade girl who tries out for her school's wrestling team. The school allows her to participate, but Maisie encounters various roadblocks, including her teammates' jealousy about the media attention she receives. *Fourth Grade Rats* focuses on peer pressure and growing up too fast. The main characters are Suds and Joey, two friends who decide they have to become tough and mean now that they are entering fourth grade. Nice-guy Suds initially balks at the plan, but Joey's relentless needling persuades him to reconsider. The experiment is short-lived, however, as both boys are forced—and relieved—to resume their normal behavior.

Spinelli continues to create witty, refreshing books for young readers and it appears there will be no shortage of ideas for future volumes. In his Newbery Award acceptance speech excerpted in *Horn Book,* the author recounted his conversation with a group of schoolchildren. When they asked him where he gets his ideas, the author replied, "from you." Spinelli continued, "You're the funny ones. You're the fascinating ones. You're the elusive and inspiring and promising and heroic and maddening ones."

WORKS CITED:

Churchman, Deborah, "Tales of the Awkward Age," *Washington Post Book World,* January 13, 1985, p. 8.

Jameyson, Karen, review of *Who Put That Hair in My Toothbrush?, Horn Book,* June, 1984, pp. 343-344.

Logan, Claudia, review of *Fourth Grade Rats, Washington Post Book World,* August 11, 1991, p. 11.

McPeak, James J., review of *Space Station Seventh Grade, Voice of Youth Advocates,* April, 1983, p. 42.

Spinelli, Jerry, "Newbery Medal Acceptance," *Horn Book,* July/August, 1991, pp. 426-432.

Teal, Alison, review of *Maniac Magee, New York Times Book Review,* April 21, 1991, p. 33.

Twichell, Ethel R., review of *Jason and Marceline, Horn Book,* March, 1987, p. 217.

Twichell, Ethel R., review of *Dump Days, Horn Book,* May, 1988, p. 355.

FOR MORE INFORMATION SEE:

PERIODICALS

Alan Review, fall, 1986, pp. 15-18.

Horn Book, July/August 1991, pp. 433-436.

Reading Teacher, November, 1991, pp. 174-176.

School Library Journal, June, 1990, p. 138.

Johanna Spyri

SPYRI, Johanna (Heusser) 1827-1901

PERSONAL: Surname is pronounced "*Spee*-ree"; born July 12, 1827, in Hirzel, Switzerland; died July 7, 1901; daughter of Johann Jakob (a doctor) and Meta (a poet and lyricist; maiden name, Schweizer) Heusser; married Bernhard Spyri (a town clerk), 1852; children: one son. *Education:* Attended the village school in Hirzel, Switzerland.

ADDRESSES: Home—Zurich, Switzerland.

CAREER: Author. Wrote verses and poetry as a small child; began writing career to help the refugees of the Franco-Prussian War, 1870.

WRITINGS:

IN ENGLISH TRANSLATION

Heidi: A Story for Children and Those That Love Children, translation by Louise Brooks, Platt & Peck, 1884, other editions include: illustrations by Gustaf Tenggren, Houghton, 1923; with illustrations from the motion picture starring Shirley Temple, Saalfield, 1937; illustrations by Charles Mozley, F. Watts, 1943; illustrations by Vincent O. Cohen, Dutton, 1952; illustrations by Judith Cheng, Golden Books, 1982 (originally published as *Heidis Lehr und Wanderjahre: Eine Geschichte fuer Kinder und auch fuer solche welche die Kinder lieb haben,* 1880).

Red-Letter Stories, translation by Lucy Wheelock, Lothrop, 1884.

Rico and Wiseli, translation by Louise Brooks, De Wolfe, Fiske, 1885, new edition with translation by M. E. Calthrop published as *All Alone in the World: The Story of Rico and Wiseli's Way,* Dutton, 1959.

Uncle Titus: A Story for Children and for Those Who Love Children, translation by Wheelock, Lothrop, 1886, translation by Clement W. Coumbe published as *Uncle Titus in the Country,* Saalfield, 1926.

Gritli's Children: A Story for Children and for Those Who Love Children, translation by Brooks, Cupples & Hurd, 1887, translation by Elisabeth P. Stork published as *Gritli's Children: A Story of Switzerland,* Lippincott, 1924 (originally published as *Gritlis Kinder,* [Germany]).

Swiss Stories for Children and Those Who Love Children, translation by Wheelock, Lothrop, 1887.

In Safe Keeping, translation by Wheelock, Blackie & Son, 1896.

Dorris and Her Mountain Home, translation by Mary E. Ireland, Presbyterian Committee of Publication, 1902.

Moni the Goat Boy, and Other Stories, translation by Edith F. King, Ginn, 1906 (originally published as *Moni der Geissbub*).

Heimatlos: Two Stories for Children and Those Who Love Children, translation by Emma Stetler Hopkins, illustrations by Frederick Richardson, Ginn 1912.

Chel: A Story of the Swiss Mountains, translation by Helene H. Boll, Eaton & Mains, 1913.

The Rose Child, translation by Helen B. Dole, Crowell, 1916.

What Sami Sings with the Birds, translation by Dole, Crowell, 1917.

Little Miss Grasshopper, translation by Dole, Crowell, 1918.

Little Curly Head: The Pet Lamb, translation by Dole, Crowell, 1919, new edition with translation by M. E. Calthrop and E. M. Popper published as *The Pet Lamb, and Other Swiss Stories,* Dutton, 1956 (originally published as *Beim Weiden-Joseph*).

Cornelli, translation by Stork, illustrations by Maria L. Kirk, Lippincott, 1920, translation by Clement W. Coumbe published as *Cornelli: Her Childhood,* Saalfield, 1926 (originally published as *Cornelli wird erzogen*).

Toni: The Little Wood-Carver, translation by Dole, Crowell, 1920.

Erick and Sally, translation by Boll, Beacon, 1921.

Maezli: A Story of the Swiss Valleys, translation by Stork, illustrations by Kirk, Lippincott, 1921, translation by Coumbe published as *Maxa's Children,* Saalfield, 1926, translation by Dole published as *Castle Wonderful,* Crowell, 1928.

Tiss: A Little Alpine Waif, translation by Dole, illustrations by George Carlson, Crowell, 1921.

Trini: The Little Strawberry Girl, translation by Dole, illustrations by Carlson, Crowell, 1922.

Jo: The Little Machinist, translation by Dole, Crowell, 1923.

Vinzi: A Story of the Swiss Alps, translation by Stork, illustrations by Kirk, Lippincott, 1924.

Joerli: The Story of a Swiss Boy, translation by Frances Treadway Clayton and Olga Wunderli, B. H. Sanborn, 1924, translation by Stork published as *Joerli: The Stauffer Mill,* Lippincott, 1928 (originally published as *Die Stauffermuehle*).

The Little Alpine Musician, translation by Dole, Crowell, 1924, translation by Coumbe published as *A Little Swiss Boy,* Saalfield, 1926.

The New Year's Carol, translation by Alice Howland Goodwin, illustrations by Grace Edwards Wesson, Houghton, 1924.

Veronica and Other Friends, translation by Brooks, Crowell, 1924.

Arthur and Squirrel, translation by Dole, Crowell, 1925.

Children of the Alps, translation by Stork, illustrations by Margaret J. Marshall, Lippincott, 1925.

The Children's Carol, translation by Dole, Crowell, 1925, new edition published as *The Children's Christmas Carol,* edited by Darlene Geis, Prentice-Hall, 1957.

Eveli: The Little Singer, translation by Stork, illustrations by Blanche Greer, Lippincott, 1926.

Eveli and Beni, translation by Dole, Crowell, 1926.

Peppino, translation by Stork, illustrations by Greer, Lippincott, 1926.

In the Swiss Mountains, translation by Dole, Crowell, 1929.

Boys and Girls of the Alps, translation by Dole, Crowell 1929.

Renz and Margritli, translation by Dole, Crowell, 1931.

UNTRANSLATED WORKS

Einer vom Hause Lesa, F. A. Perthes, 1898.

Schloss Wildenstein, F. A. Perthes, 1900.

Was soll denn aus Ihr werden?, F. A. Perthes, c. 1900.

Aus dem Leben, C. E. Mueller, 1902.

ADAPTATIONS:

Heidi (motion picture), starring Shirley Temple and Arthur Treacher, Twentieth Century-Fox, 1937, Teaching Film Custodians, 1947, United Artists, 1953, Warner Brothers/Seven Arts, 1968.

Heidi and Peter (motion picture), United Artists, 1955.

William Friedberg and Neil Simon, *Heidi* (musical play), Samuel French, 1959.

A Gift for Heidi (motion picture), RKO Radio Pictures, 1962.

Beryl Marian Jones, *Heidi* (three-act play), Pitman, 1965.

Heidi (television movies), starring Sir Michael Redgrave, Maximilian Schell, Jennifer Edwards, and Jean Simmons, first broadcast by National Broadcasting Co. (NBC), November 17, 1968.

Favorite Children's Books: Heidi (filmstrip with phonodisc), Coronet Instructional Films, 1969.

Heidi (filmstrip), Universal Education and Visual Arts, 1971.

Highlights from Heidi (filmstrip with phonodisc or phonotape in cassette, each with teacher's guide), Encyclopaedia Britannica Corp., 1973.

Heidi: The Living Legend (motion picture), ACI Films, 1974.

From *Heidi*, by Johanna Spyri. Illustrated by Jessie Willcox Smith.

The New Adventures of Heidi (television movie), starring Burl Ives and Kathy Krutzman, NBC, December, 1978.

Also *Heidi* (six-part "Once Upon a Classic" television series), starring Emma Blake and Dame Flora Robertson, first broadcast by Public Broadcasting Service; a recording entitled *Heidi* has been produced.

SIDELIGHTS: Though little is known about Johanna Spyri's quiet life, her story of the Swiss orphan girl who was sent to live with her grandfather in the Alps has charmed children of every generation since its publication in 1880. *Heidi,* first published anonymously, has enjoyed steady popularity and continues to appear in new editions. Its central character, who restored the humanity of her gloomy grandfather, became a true friend to the poor goatherd Peter, and helped the lame Klara attain health, has lost little if any of the freshness she had for readers of the book's first edition.

Spyri was born in Hirzel, a rural Swiss village near Zurich, on June 12, 1827. Her father, Johann Jakob Heusser, was the village doctor; her mother, Meta Schweizer Heusser, was a locally known poet and songwriter. Spyri had two brothers and three sisters, and the household also included a grandmother, two aunts, and two female cousins, forming a family that was similar to the one in Spyri's book, *Gritli's Children.*

Spyri met her future husband, Bernhard Spyri, through her brother, who was his classmate. By Anna Ulrich's account in *Recollections of Johanna Spyri's Childhood,* theirs was "a childhood love which lasted for life." The couple married in 1852, when Johanna was twenty-five years old, and lived in Zurich, where Bernhard Spyri became the town clerk and where they enjoyed the friendship of such people as the composer Richard Wagner and the poet Conrad Ferdinand Meyer. Their only son, Bernhard Diethelm Spyri, was born in 1855. He died of tuberculosis in 1884, and Johanna Spyri's husband died later the same year.

Spyri had written poems as a child, but she began writing seriously in 1870. The Franco-Prussian War was in progress, and wounded soldiers and war orphans were coming into neutral Switzerland. At the same time, the International Red Cross was founded in Geneva. Spyri's wish was to describe the situation of orphans and to give the needy all of the proceeds from her work. Her first stories, published anonymously (pseudonymously) were successful, and she embarked on the book that became *Heidi.* A second Heidi story, published a year later and subsequently combined with the first, bore Spyri's name as author. It marked the beginning of public recognition for her work. Despite her success, however, she shunned publicity and lived very quietly. By the time of her death in Berlin, on July 7, 1901, she had written more than forty books for children and young adults.

Spyri wrote the story of *Heidi* to amuse her young son; the settings and characters were drawn from the author's childhood. Catherine Eayrs suggested in *Writers for Children* that the village of Jenins, which Spyri visited in her youth, may have inspired the fictional Doerfli. The critic also observed, "The kindly doctor in the story is much like [Spyri's] own father. Klara's grandmamma and Peter's grandmother are storytellers, much as Spyri's own grandmother was."

Many critics have commented on Spyri's empathetic portrayal of children and the emotions they feel—not only in *Heidi* but in all of her work—and on her vivid descriptions of place. May Hill Arbuthnot reflected in *Children and Books* that "no child who has read and loved *Heidi* will ever enter Switzerland without a feeling of coming home.... Nothing about Switzerland will ever seem alien to the child who has read *Heidi.*"

More recently, some critics have objected to *Heidi* because of what they consider its excessive sentimentality, simplicity, and religious nature. The qualities that have given rise to this criticism were not old-fashioned at the time the book was written, however, and they have done little to diminish the book's popularity with readers or its general acceptance among reviewers of children's literature. If *Heidi* was not "an important innovation ... in children's literature," wrote Malcolm Usrey in *Touchstones: Reflections on the Best in Children's Literature,* "for a hundred years, it has been a distinguished and widely read children's book. It is indeed a touchstone."

WORKS CITED:

Arbuthnot, May Hill, *Children and Books,* Scott, Foresman, 1947, pp. 412-414.

Eayrs, Catherine, essay in *Writers for Children,* edited by Jane M. Bingham, Scribner, 1988, pp. 529-533.

Ulrich, Anna, *Recollections of Johanna Spyri's Childhood,* translation by Helen B. Dole, Crowell, 1925.

Usrey, Malcolm, "Johanna Spyri's 'Heidi': The Conversion of a Byronic Hero," in *Touchstones: Reflections on the Best in Children's Literature,* Volume 1, edited by Perry Nodelman, Children's Literature Association, 1985, pp. 232-242.

FOR MORE INFORMATION SEE:

BOOKS

Montgomery, Elizabeth Rider, *The Story behind Great Books,* McBride, 1946.

PERIODICALS

TV Guide, December 9, 1978.

* * *

STARBIRD, Kaye 1916-
(C. S. Jennison)

PERSONAL: Born June 3, 1916, in Fort Sill, OK; daughter of Alfred A. (a general, U.S. Army) and Ethel (Dodd) Starbird; married James Dalton (deceased); married N. E. Jennison (deceased); children: (first marriage) Kit, Beth; (second marriage) Lee. *Education:* Attended University of Vermont, four years.

CAREER: Professional writer.

AWARDS, HONORS: Bread Loaf Writers' Conference fellowship, 1961; MacDowell Colony fellowships, 1966-70, 1972, 1975, 1976, 1979; Helene Wurlitzer Foundation fellowships, 1967-68; Ella Lyman Cabot Trust grant, 1971; Ossabaw Island Project fellowships, 1971-73, 1975, 1977, 1978, 1980, 1981; Virginia Center for Creative Arts fellowships, 1971-73, 1982; Rhode Island Creative Arts Center fellowships, 1980-82.

WRITINGS:

JUVENILE POETRY

Speaking of Cows, Lippincott, 1960.

Don't Ever Cross a Crocodile, and Other Poems, illustrated by daughter, Kit Dalton, Lippincott, 1963.

A Snail's a Failure Socially and Other Poems, Mostly about People, illustrated by Dalton, Lippincott, 1966.

The Pheasant on Route Seven, illustrated by Victoria de Larrea, Lippincott, 1968.

The Covered Bridge House and Other Poems, illustrated by Jim Arnosky, Four Winds, 1979.

Grandmother Goose's Recycled Rhymes, Pratt Publishing, 1988.

Kaye Starbird

ADULT NOVELS

Watch Out for the Mules, Harcourt, 1968.
The Lion in the Lei Shop, Harcourt, 1970.

OTHER

Contributor of poetry to anthologies and periodicals, including *Good Housekeeping, Saturday Evening Post, New York Times, New Yorker,* and *American Mercury.* Also contributor, at times under name C. S. Jennison, of satirical verse, poems, essays, and short stories to magazines, including *Vermont Life, Atlantic, Woman's Day, Reader's Digest, Cosmopolitan, Harper's, Ladies' Home Journal, McCall's,* and *Redbook.*

SIDELIGHTS: Kaye Starbird examines ordinary people and their everyday lives through the light verse which fills her works. Her flowing rhymes present nature in all its glory and introduce a mixture of humorously eccentric characters. "Economically crafted, the poems are appealing not only for their incisive characterization but also for their imaginative wordplay and sense of wonder," remarks Mary M. Burns in *Horn Book.* And *Horn Book* contributor Diane Farrell maintains that Starbird's "shrewd observations give an added dimension to the lives of ordinary people."

Starbird began writing at the age of eight, and sold verse to national magazines such as *Good Housekeeping* and *American Mercury* while in college. Before turning to books in 1960, she also wrote satirical verse and essays for the *Atlantic,* at times under the name C. S. Jennison. *The Pheasant on Route Seven,* Starbird's fourth collection of light verse, introduces the small American town of Pleasantport and its eclectic population. Along with describing the town's surroundings, Starbird also presents a number of humorous characters, including Doctor Ernest Bates, who collects paperweights when he isn't saving lives, and Banjo Scott, the local drunkard. "In this book the village of Pleasantport comes alive," asserts Mary O'Neill in the *New York Times Book Review.* Starbird's "rhymes never falter; her people are real."

The Covered Bridge House and Other Poems, published in 1979, offers a number of poems dealing with nature and a variety of caricatures. Among the characters described are Little Lenore, who wishes for a Coke machine within easy reach, Artie Dole, who has an overactive imagination, and Miss Flynn, who is the proud owner of thirty cats. The poems in *The Covered Bridge House and Other Poems* "are consistently great fun," comments Daisy Kouzel in the *School Library Journal.* "Young readers will be easily captivated by the gentle humor, the easy musicality of the rhymes, and the upbeat windup of each poem."

Starbird's poems are derived "from experience and also from a galloping imagination that I was born with and for which I claim no credit," she once maintained. This imagination is given "free rein" in most of Starbird's books, the form and content of the works being disciplined at the same time. Once she decides on the type of book she wants to do, Starbird once said she writes "eight hours a day until it is completed. Throwing away a lot at the beginning and rewriting until I turn the manuscript in to the publisher. . . . Writing is hard work but I am happier doing it than not doing it. I never Set Out to Be a Writer. I just started writing."

WORKS CITED:

Burns, Mary M., review of *The Covered Bridge House and Other Poems, Horn Book,* February, 1980, p. 70.
Farrell, Diane, review of *The Pheasant on Route Seven, Horn Book,* October, 1968, p. 568.
Kouzel, Daisy, review of *The Covered Bridge House and Other Poems, School Library Journal,* January, 1980, p. 61.
O'Neill, Mary, review of *The Pheasant on Route Seven, New York Times Book Review,* October 27, 1968, p. 42.

FOR MORE INFORMATION SEE:

PERIODICALS

Bulletin of the Center for Children's Books, January, 1980.
Horn Book, October, 1963.
Library Journal, August, 1970, p. 2721; December, 1976, p. 4526.

From *A Snail's a Failure Socially and Other Poems, Mostly about People*, by Kaye Starbird. Illustrated by Kit Dalton.

New York Times Book Review, November 6, 1966, p. 67; October 4, 1970, p. 48; November 11, 1979, p. 53.

Publishers Weekly, November 27, 1967, p. 41.

* * *

STAUNTON, Schuyler
See BAUM, L(yman) Frank

* * *

STEELE, Mary Q(uintard Govan) 1922- (Wilson Gage)

PERSONAL: Born May 8, 1922, in Chattanooga, TN; daughter of Gilbert Eaton (a librarian) and Christine (a writer; maiden name, Noble) Govan; married William O. Steele (a writer), June 1, 1943 (died, 1979); children: Mary Quintard, Jenifer Susan, Allerton William. *Education:* University of Chattanooga, B.S., 1943. *Politics:* Democrat. *Religion:* Episcopalian. *Hobbies and other interests:* Family, poetry, politics.

ADDRESSES: Home—329 Crestway Dr., Chattanooga, TN, 37411.

CAREER: Author of children's books. Tennessee Valley Authority, Chattanooga, TN, map editor, 1943-44.

AWARDS, HONORS: New York Herald Tribune's Children's Spring Book Festival Honor Book, 1960, for *The Secret of Fiery Gorge;* American Library Association's Aurianne Award, 1966, for *Big Blue Island;* Newbery Honor Book, 1970, and Lewis Carroll Shelf Award, 1971, both for *Journey Outside*; *The Eye in the Forest* was named a Notable Children's Trade Book in the Field of Social Studies, 1976, by the joint committee of the National Council for Social Studies and the Children's Book Council; Garden State Children's Book Award for easy-to-read books from the New Jersey State Library Association, 1982, for *Mrs. Gaddy and the Ghost.*

WRITINGS:

Journey Outside, illustrated by Rocco Negri, Viking, 1969.

The Living Year: An Almanac for My Survivors (adult essays), Viking, 1972.

The First of the Penguins, illustrated by Susan Jeffers, Macmillan, 1973.

(With husband, William O. Steele) *The Eye in the Forest,* Dutton, 1975.

Because of the Sand Witches There, illustrated by Paul Galdone, Greenwillow, 1975.

The True Men, Greenwillow, 1976.

The Owl's Kiss: Three Stories, Greenwillow, 1978.

Wish, Come True, illustrated by Muriel Batherman, Greenwillow, 1979.

The Life (and Death) of Sarah Elizabeth Harwood, Greenwillow, 1980.

UNDER PSEUDONYM WILSON GAGE

The Secret of the Indian Mound, illustrated by Mary Stevens, World, 1958.

The Secret of Crossbone Hill, illustrated by Stevens, World, 1959.

The Secret of Fiery Gorge, illustrated by Stevens, World, 1960.

A Wild Goose Tale, illustrated by Glen Rounds, World, 1961.

Dan and the Miranda, illustrated by Rounds, World, 1962.

Miss Osborne-the-Mop, illustrated by Galdone, World, 1963.

Big Blue Island, Illustrated by Rounds, World, 1964.

The Ghost of Five Owl Farm, illustrated by Galdone, World, 1966.

Mike's Toads, illustrated by Rounds, World, 1970.

Squash Pie, illustrated by Rounds, Greenwillow, 1976.

Down in the Boon Docks, illustrated by G. Rounds, Greenwillow, 1977.

Mrs. Gaddy and the Ghost, illustrated by Marylin Hafner, Greenwillow, 1979.

Cully Cully and the Bear, illustrated by James Stevenson, Greenwillow, 1983.

The Crow and Mrs. Gaddy, illustrrated by Hafner, Greenwillow, 1984.

Mrs. Gaddy and the Fast Growing Vine, illustrated by Hafner, Greenwillow, 1985.

VERSE

Anna's Summer Songs, illustrated by Lena Anderson, Greenwillow, 1988.

Anna's Garden Songs, illustrated by L. Anderson, Greenwillow, 1989.

Mary Q. Steele

OTHER

Editor, *The Fifth Day* (poetry anthology), illustrated by Janina Domanska, Greenwillow, 1978.

Steele's works are included in the Kerlan Collection at the University of Minnesota and the de Grummond Collection at the University of Southern Mississippi.

ADAPTATIONS: "Journey Outside" (filmstrip with record); "Living Year" (cassette); "Ghost of Five Owl Farm" (talking book); "Mike's Toads" (talking book).

SIDELIGHTS: Mary Q. Steele is an award-winning author of books for children that focus on the importance of appreciating nature and understanding humanity's place in it. For more than thirty years she has used natural history as the dominant theme in her fiction, with a particular emphasis on birds. Most of Steele's books have been published under the pen name Wilson Gage, which she created as a tribute to American ornithologist Alexander Wilson. A prolific writer, Steele has successfully produced novels on a variety of topics, including magic, witchcraft, and more complex issues like death and suicide.

Steele was born and raised in Chattanooga, Tennessee, where she has spent most of her life. Her parents were literary by profession: her mother was a children's book author, and her father was a bookseller, a librarian, and a book review editor for the Chattanooga *Times.* This meant the family was never short on reading material, as Steele remembered in *Horn Book:* "almost every book published lingered on our desks and tables for a few days, an embarrassment of riches, in the midst of which I could elect to be choosy—and I was."

Despite her love of books, Steele was uncomfortable with formal education and attended school irregularly. She eventually developed an interest in algebra and languages, however, and went on to graduate from the University of Chattanooga with a degree in physics. During this time she became an avid naturalist who considered bird-watching an "important duty," as opposed to a hobby. In 1943 she married William O. Steele, a young World War II serviceman stationed nearby. The couple's oldest daughter was born before the war ended, and a second daughter and a son completed the family several years later.

Following the war, Steele's husband quit his job to become a full-time writer, which motivated Steele to attempt her own children's book once their children reached school-age. In 1958 she published her first book, *The Secret of Indian Mound,* under the pseudonym Wilson Gage. Steele immediately followed this with two more *Secret* books, including the award-winning *Secret of Fiery Gorge* in 1960. Steele explained her affinity for writing in *Something about the Author (SATA):* "I did not become a writer, but was born one, waking up in the morning to sort the day into scenes and characters and descriptions, as presumably an artist sorts the world into lights and shadows and patterns whenever he looks at it."

Steele's longtime appreciation for nature became a dominant theme in her subsequent novels, including: *Mike's Toad,* about creatures who are better off in their natural environments; *Dan and the Miranda,* about the problems a boy scientist encounters with spiders; and even the more serious *The Life (and Death) of Sarah Elizabeth Harwood,* featuring a character who habitually rescues insects. "Natural history is my great passion and I suppose one reason I started writing was in order to be able to talk about geese and spiders and goldfinches just as much as I wanted to," Steele said in *Third Book of Junior Authors.* "I was, of course, surprised to find that the disciplines of writing and the exigencies of fiction made this impossible. But at least no one interrupts."

Steele has received perhaps the greatest critical acclaim for her 1969 Newbery Honor Book, *Journey Outside,* the first to be published under her own name. It tells the story of Dilar, a boy who lives in a community of Raft People, constantly floating down an underground river seeking a better place to live. This short novel, according to Linda S. Levstik in *Twentieth-Century Children's Writers,* is "fascinating on several levels, and could be read as a simple fantasy-adventure story, as well as an allegory" about how people should live their lives.

In 1979 Steele saw the publication of *Mrs. Gaddy and the Ghost*, a book written for six- to eight-year-olds about a woman who has trouble with her house-haunting ghost. Steele used her mother as the inspiration for the amusing Mrs. Gaddy and infused the character with her mother's qualities of strength, courage, and resiliency. Two more *Mrs. Gaddy* books followed and became popular in the mid-1980s: *The Crow and Mrs. Gaddy* and *Mrs. Gaddy and the Fast-Growing Vine.*

Steele also painstakingly focuses on language when writing, and addresses her audiences carefully in this respect. "As a writer I am interested in language and in people and in how the two things go together, for they do bear considerably upon each other," she noted in *Horn Book*. "When I am using for my protagonist a semiliterate ten- or twelve-year-old, I do not think that he should reveal the world in my voice and in my terms, or that he should speak fluently in my vocabulary. I think he should have to struggle with language and find himself ill at ease with it and occasionally get it wrong."

Perhaps the single most important message that Steele has tried to impart to her readers is that it is acceptable—even good—to be different. "What I have tried to say in all my books I do honestly believe: that it is our dissimilarities that give life its astonishing richness and wonder and make life rewarding," she wrote in *Horn Book*. "Concede a spider its inalienable right to eight legs as it has never for a moment doubted your right to two, and you have gone a long way toward being truly human."

WORKS CITED:

Chevalier, Tracy, editor, *Twentieth-Century Children's Writers*, Third Edition, St. James, 1989, pp. 914-915.

From *Mrs. Gaddy and the Ghost*, by Wilson Gage. Illustrated by Marylin Hafner.

De Montreville, Doris, and Donna Hill, editors, *Third Book of Junior Authors*, Wilson, 1972, p. 97.

Something about the Author, Volume 51, Gale, 1988, pp. 159-167.

Steele, Mary Q., "As Far as You Can Bear to See: Excellence in Children's Literature," *Horn Book*, June, 1975.

Steele, "Realism, Truth, and Honesty," *Horn Book*, February, 1971.

FOR MORE INFORMATION SEE:

BOOKS

Authors of Books for Young People, 2nd edition, Scarecrow, 1971.

Children and Literature: Views and Reviews, Lothrop, 1974.

Newbery and Caldecott Medalists and Honor Book Winners, Libraries Unlimited, 1983.

PERIODICALS

Language Arts, January, 1978.

* * *

STEELE, William O(wen) 1917-1979

PERSONAL: Born December 22, 1917, in Franklin, TN; died June 25, 1979, in Chattanooga, TN; son of Core and Sue (Johnston) Steele; married Mary Quintard Govan (a writer), June 1, 1943; children: Mary Quintard, Jenifer Susan, Allerton William. *Education:* Cumberland University, B.A., 1940; University of Chattanooga, graduate study, 1950. *Politics:* Democrat. *Religion:* Protestant. *Hobbies and other interests:* Pioneers of the old Southwest (pre-Revolutionary times), Indians of the Southeast (particularly the Cherokees in historic times), anthropology, American folklore, walking, camping in the mountains, bird watching, nature study, and reading.

CAREER: Author. *Military service:* Army Air Corps, 1940-54.

MEMBER: Authors Guild, Authors League of America, Tennessee Archeological Society, Tennessee Anthropological Association, Archaeological Society of North Carolina, Blue Key National Honor Fraternity, Lambda Chi Alpha.

AWARDS, HONORS: New York Herald Tribune's Spring Book Festival Honor Book, 1954, for *Winter Danger*, 1956, for *Davey Crockett's Earthquake*, 1957, for *Flaming Arrows*, and 1958, for *The Perilous Road;* special citation, Child Study Association of America, 1957, for *The Lone Hunt;* Jane Addams Children's Book Award, 1958, and Newbery Honor Book, 1959, both for *The Perilous Road*, William Allen White Children's Book Award, 1960, for *Flaming Arrows;* Lewis Carroll Shelf Award, 1962, for *Winter Danger;* Thomas Alva Edison Mass Media Award for "special excellence in portraying America's past," 1963, for *Westward Adventure; Year of the Bloody Sevens* was named an American Library Association notable book, 1963; *The Eye in the*

William O. Steele

Forest was named a Notable Children's Trade Book in the Field of Social Studies by the National Council for Social Studies and the Children's Book Council, 1976; *Winter Danger, Flaming Arrows,* and *The Perilous Road* were also all named American Library Association notable books.

WRITINGS:

The Golden Root, illustrated by Fritz Kredel, Aladdin Books, 1951.
The Buffalo Knife, illustrated by Paul Galdone, Harcourt, 1952.
Over-Mountain Boy, illustrated by Kredel, Aladdin Books, 1952.
The Story of Daniel Boone, illustrated by Warren Baumgartner, Grosset, 1953.
Wilderness Journey, illustrated by Galdone, Harcourt, 1953.
John Sevier, Pioneer Boy, illustrated by Sandra James, Bobbs-Merrill, 1953.
The Story of Leif Ericson, illustrated by Pranas Lape, Grosset, 1954.
Winter Danger, illustrated by Galdone, Harcourt, 1954.
Francis Marion, Young Swamp Fox, illustrated by Dick Gringhuis, Bobbs-Merrill, 1954.
Tomahawks and Trouble, illustrated by Galdone, Harcourt, 1955.
We Were There on the Oregon Trail, illustrated by Jo Polseno, Grosset, 1955.
We Were There with the Pony Express, illustrated by Frank Vaughn, Grosset, 1956.
DeSoto: Child of the Sun, illustrated by Lorence Bjorklund, Aladdin Books, 1956.
The Lone Hunt, illustrated by Galdone, Harcourt, 1956.
Davy Crockett's Earthquake, illustrated by Nicolas Mordvinoff, Harcourt, 1956.
Daniel Boone's Echo, illustrated by Mordvinoff, Harcourt, 1957.
Flaming Arrows, illustrated by Galdone, Harcourt, 1957.
The Perilous Road, illustrated by Galdone, Harcourt, 1958.
The Far Frontier, illustrated by Galdone, Harcourt, 1959.
Andy Jackson's Water Well, illustrated by Michael Ramus, Harcourt, 1959.
The Spooky Thing, illustrated by Paul Coker, Harcourt, 1960.
Westward Adventure: The True Stories of Six Pioneers, illustrated with maps by Kathleen Voute, Harcourt, 1962.
The Year of the Bloody Sevens, illustrated by Charles Beck, Harcourt, 1963.
The No-Name Man of the Mountain, illustrated by Jack Davis, Harcourt, 1964.
Wayah of the Real People, illustrated by Isa Barnett, Colonial Williamsburg, 1964.
Trail through Danger, illustrated by Beck, Harcourt, 1965.
Tomahawk Border, illustrated by Vernon Wooten, Colonial Williamsburg, 1966.
The Old Wilderness Road: An American Journey, Harcourt, 1968.
Hound Dog Zip to the Rescue, illustrated by Mimi Korach, Garrard, 1970.
The Wilderness Tattoo: A Narrative of Juan Ortiz, Harcourt, 1972.
Surgeon, Trader, Indian Chief: Henry Woodward of Carolina, illustrated by Hoyt Simmons, Sandlapper Store, 1972.
Triple Trouble for Hound Dog Zip, illustrated by Korach, Garrard, 1972.
(With wife, Mary Q. Steele) *The Eye in the Forest,* Dutton, 1975.
John's Secret Treasure, illustrated by R. Dennis, Macmillan, 1975.
The Man with the Silver Eyes, Harcourt, 1976.
The Cherokee Crown of Tannassy, Blair, 1977.
The War Party, illustrated by Lorinda B. Cauley, Harcourt, 1978.
Talking Bones: Secrets of Indian Burial Mounds, illustrated by Carlos Llerena-Aguirre, Harper, 1978.
The Magic Amulet, Harcourt, 1979.

Book reviewer for the *Chattanooga Times.* Contributor to *World Book Encyclopedia* and *Encyclopedia Americana,* and to magazines. Steele's works are included in the Kerlan Collection at the University of Minnesota

From *The Perilous Road,* by William O. Steele.

and in a special collection at the John Brister Library at Memphis State University.

ADAPTATIONS: A cassette and a filmstrip with record or cassette have been produced by Random House of *The Perilous Road.* The following braille books have been produced: *Far Frontier, Francis Marion, Lone Hunt, Old Wilderness Road, Tomahawk Border, Tomahawks and Trouble,* and *Westward Adventure;* and the talking books *Daniel Boone's Echo, Far Frontier, Flaming Arrows, Lone Hunt, Wilderness Tatoo, Winter Danger,* and *Year of the Bloody Sevens.*

SIDELIGHTS: Writing from his home on Signal Mountain, Tennessee, William O. Steele was the creator of more than thirty works of historical fiction for young adults. These award-winning novels of pioneer life typically feature a boy of ten to twelve years old who rises to face the rigors of wilderness travel and Indian fighting and in the process learns something important about life and himself.

Born and raised in Franklin, Tennessee, Steele early became interested in the history of the region. As a boy he explored old log cabins and hunted for Indian arrowheads in the fields. "I like to tell that I was born in a hollow sycamore tree, deep in the canebrakes of Tennessee with catamounts howling all around," Steele wrote in *More Junior Authors.* "And sometimes I say I was born in a log fort under attack by savages, the stockade fence burned away and flaming arrows everywhere. But it isn't true. I just lie to enjoy myself and the truth is that I was born in the quiet little middle Tennessee town of Franklin."

Steele earned a bachelor's degree from Cumberland University, where he worked for the college newspaper, as well as Franklin's weekly. He spent five years in the army during World War II, marrying writer Mary Govan before serving overseas. Upon his discharge Steele found a clerical job to support his wife, two daughters, and a son. While his wife rocked their oldest daughter, who suffered from allergies, he read aloud to her about the pioneers of the old Southwest. Inspired by this experience and reading Donald Davidson's *The Tennessee: The Old River,* Steele wrote his first book, *The Buffalo Knife. The Golden Root* quickly followed, and soon Steele quit his clerical job to devote his time to writing short and long juvenile fiction based on Tennessee history.

Most of Steele's novels are set in the wilderness of Tennessee and deal with the clash of white and Native American cultures. The author told *Twentieth-Century*

Children's Writers that he tried to make his characters true to the time in which they lived, rather than creating "twentieth-century characters with a fake pioneer dress of split cowhide." To achieve this accuracy, he spent long hours researching background material. "In my books I try to give a true picture of what the unspoiled frontier country was like when it began to be settled, of the dangers and hardships and rewards of settling it," he continued. "Above all I try to convey something of the real essence of the times, something of the restless, tough-bodied, forward-looking pioneer who pushed further and further into the wilderness. And I try to accomplish this in as entertaining a fashion as I can." Steele's novels are particularly noted for their quick pace, wealth of adventure, period detail, and colorful vernacular speech. In his books written during the 1960s—like *Wayah of the Real People* and *The Man with the Silver Eyes*—Steele shifted the point of view of some of his stories from the young white protagonist to the Indian youth involved in the clash of cultures.

Steele also wrote several books of biographies of famous figures, Tennessee folk tales, and nonfictional works, such as *Westward Adventure: The True Stories of Six Pioneers, Andy Jackson's Water Well,* and *The No-Name Man of the Mountain.* Steele won many awards during a career that spanned twenty-seven years; yet he once told *SATA,* "After ... years as a published author I don't find it one bit easier to write a new book than when I first began. Shed no tears for me please, I couldn't or wouldn't be anything else but an author."

WORKS CITED:

Fuller, Muriel, editor, *More Junior Authors,* 2nd edition, H. W. Wilson, 1983, pp. 192-193.

Kirkpatrick, D. L., *Twentieth-Century Children's Writers,* St. Martin's, 1978.

FOR MORE INFORMATION SEE:

BOOKS

American Authors and Books, 1640 to the Present Day, 3rd revised edition, Crown, 1972.

Ward, Martha E., and Dorothy A. Marquardt, *Authors of Books for Young People,* Scarecrow, 1971.

PERIODICALS

Chattanooga Times, December, 1960; April 15, 1962.

Elementary English, December, 1960; December 1961.

Horn Book, February, 1958; October, 1979.

School Library Journal, November, 1979.

* * *

STEIG, William H. 1907-

PERSONAL: Born November 14, 1907, in New York, NY; son of Joseph (a housepainter) and Laura (a seamstress; maiden name, Ebel) Steig; married Elizabeth Mead, January 2, 1936 (divorced); married Kari Homestead, 1950 (divorced, 1963); married Stephanie Healey, December 12, 1964 (divorced, December, 1966); married Jeanne Doron, 1969; children: (first marriage) Lucy, Jeremy; (second marriage) Margit Laura. *Education:* Attended City College (now of the City University of New York), 1923-25; National Academy of Design, New York City, 1925-29.

ADDRESSES: Home—R.F.D. #1, Box 416, Kent, CT 06757.

CAREER: Free-lance cartoonist contributing mainly to the *New Yorker,* 1930—; author and illustrator of children's books, 1968—. Worked for various advertising agencies. Sculptor. *Exhibitions:* Steig's drawings and sculptures were exhibited at Downtown Gallery, New York City, 1939, Smith College, 1940, and have been included in collections at the Rhode Island Museum, Providence, the Smith College Museum, Northampton, MA, and in the Brooklyn Museum, New York City.

AWARDS, HONORS: Children's Book of the Year nomination, Spring Book Festival picture book honor, National Book Award finalist, and *Boston Globe-Horn Book* honor, all 1969, American Library Association (ALA) Notable Book designation and Caldecott Medal, both 1970, and Lewis Carroll Shelf Award, 1978, all for *Sylvester and the Magic Pebble;* National Book Award finalist, *New York Times* Best Illustrated Children's Book of the Year, *New York Times* Outstanding Book, and ALA Notable Book designation, all 1971, and Children's Book Showcase title, 1972, all for *Amos and Boris;* Christopher Award, 1972, National Book Award finalist, 1973, *Boston Globe-Horn Book* honor, ALA Notable Book designation, and William Allen White Children's Book Award, Kansas State College, all 1975,

William Steig

all for *Dominic; New York Times* Outstanding Book of the Year and ALA Notable Book designation, both 1973, for *The Real Thief;* Children's Book of the Year nomination and ALA Notable Book designation, both 1974, for *Farmer Palmer's Wagon Ride; New York Times* Outstanding Book of the Year, 1976, Newbery Honor Book, Children's Book Showcase title, ALA Notable Book designation, Lewis Carroll Shelf Award, and *Boston Globe-Horn Book* honor, all 1977, for *Abel's Island;* Caldecott Honor Book, Children's Book Showcase title, ALA Notable Book designation, and *Boston Globe-Horn Book* honor, all 1977, and Art Books for Children Award, 1978, all for *The Amazing Bone;* Irma Simonton Black Award for best children's book, *New York Times* Best Illustrated Children's Book, *New York Times* Outstanding Book, all 1980, for *Gorky Rises;* nomination, Hans Christian Andersen Medal, 1982, for illustration; *New York Times* Outstanding Book, 1982, American Book Award, Parents' Choice illustration award, *Boston Globe-Horn Book* honor, and Newbery Award, all 1983, and International Board on Books for Young People Honor Book, 1984, all for *Doctor De Soto;* Children's Picture Book Award, *Redbook,* 1984, for *Yellow and Pink;* Children's Picture Book Award, *Redbook,* 1985, for *Solomon the Rusty Nail;* Caldecott Medal, *New York Times* Best Illustrated Book, and Children's Picture Book Award, *Redbook,* all 1986, for *Brave Irene;* nomination, Hans Christian Andersen Medal, 1982, for writing.

WRITINGS:

FOR CHILDREN; SELF-ILLUSTRATED

C D B! (word games), Windmill Books, 1968.
Roland the Minstrel Pig, Windmill Books, 1968.
Sylvester and the Magic Pebble, Windmill Books, 1969.
The Bad Island, Windmill Books, 1969, revised edition published as *Rotten Island,* David Godine, 1984.
An Eye for Elephants (limericks), Windmill Books, 1970.
The Bad Speller (reader), Windmill Books, 1970.
Amos and Boris, Farrar, Straus, 1971.
Dominic, Farrar, Straus, 1972.
The Real Thief, Farrar, Straus, 1973.
Farmer Palmer's Wagon Ride, Farrar, Straus, 1974.
The Amazing Bone, Farrar, Straus, 1976.
Abel's Island, Farrar, Straus, 1976.
Caleb and Kate, Farrar, Straus, 1977.
Tiffky Doofky, Farrar, Straus, 1978.
Gorky Rises, Farrar, Straus, 1980.
Doctor De Soto, Farrar, Straus, 1982.
Yellow and Pink, Farrar, Straus, 1984.
C D C? (word games), Farrar, Straus, 1984.
Solomon the Rusty Nail, Farrar, Straus, 1984.
Brave Irene, Farrar, Straus, 1986.
The Zabajaba Jungle, Farrar, Straus, 1987.
Spinky Sulks, Farrar, Straus, 1988.
Shrek!, Farrar-Straus, 1991.

ILLUSTRATOR

Will Cuppy, *How to Become Extinct,* Garden City Books, 1941.
Eric Hodgins, *Mr. Blandings Builds His Dream House,* Simon & Schuster, 1947.
Wilhelm Reich, *Listen, Little Man!: A Document from the Archives of the Orgone Institute,* translation by Theodore P. Wolfe, Noonday Press, 1948.
Cuppy, *The Decline and Fall of Practically Everybody,* Holt, 1950.
Phyllis R. Fenner, editor, *Giggle Box: Funny Stories for Boys and Girls,* Knopf, 1950.
Steig, Irwin (brother), *Poker for Fun and Profit,* Astor-Honor, 1959.
Jeanne Steig (wife), *Consider the Lemming* (poetry), Farrar, Straus, 1988.
J. Steig, *The Old Testament Made Easy,* Farrar, Straus, 1990.

CARTOONS

Man about Town, Long & Smith, 1932.
About People: A Book of Symbolical Drawings, Random House, 1939.
The Lonely Ones, preface by Wolcott Gibbs, Duel, Sloan, 1942.
All Embarrassed, Duel, Sloan, 1944.
Small Fry (*New Yorker* cartoons), Duell, Sloan, 1944.
Persistent Faces, Duell, Sloan, 1945.
Till Death Do Us Part: Some Ballet Notes on Marriage, Duell, Sloan, 1947.
The Agony in the Kindergarten, Duell, Sloan, 1950.
The Rejected Lovers, Knopf, 1951.
The Steig Album: Seven Complete Books, Duell, Sloan, 1953.
Dreams of Glory, and Other Drawings, Knopf, 1953.
Continuous Performances, Duell, Sloan & Pearce, 1963.
Male/Female, Farrar, Straus, 1971.
William Steig: Drawings (*New Yorker* cartoons), Farrar, Straus, 1979.
Ruminations, Farrar, Straus, 1984.
Our Miserable Life, Farrar, Straus, 1990.

Steig has contributed cartoons to periodicals, including *Collier's, Judge, Life,* and *Vanity Fair.* Steig's manuscripts are included in the Kerlan Collection at the University of Minnesota, Minneapolis.

ADAPTATIONS: Many of Steig's children's books have been adapted for film, including: *Doctor De Soto,* Weston Woods, 1985; *The Amazing Bone,* Weston Woods, 1985; *Abel's Island,* Lucerne Media, 1988; *Brave Irene,* Weston Woods, 1989. Steig's books have also been adapted for film-strip: *Amos and Boris* (narrated by Steig), Miller-Brody, 1975; *Farmer Palmer's Wagon Ride,* Miller-Brody, 1976; *Brave Irene,* Weston Woods, 1988. *Doctor De Soto and Other Stories* was adapted for read-along cassette, Caedmon, 1985.

SIDELIGHTS: William Steig is well known not only as a prolific and talented cartoonist, but also as the author and illustrator of many award-winning books for children. He has found an outlet for his creative talents in two successful careers, embarking on the first at age twenty-three when he submitted his first cartoon to the *New Yorker* and the second thirty-eight years later with the publication of his first book for children. Joshua

Hammer describes Steig in *People* as "an idiosyncratic innocent in a never-never land of his own making, waging a private war against the craziness of modern life with the pen of a master and the eye of a child." Steig's humane and insightful books are very popular with children who immediately respond to the author's vision, which is as enthusiastic and wide-eyed as their own.

Steig was born in Brooklyn, New York, and spent his childhood in the Bronx. His father, an Austrian immigrant, dabbled in painting in his spare time, as did his mother. As a child, Steig was inspired by his creative surroundings with an intense interest in painting and was given his first lessons by his older brother, Irwin, who was also a professional artist. In addition to painting, his childhood imagination was captured by the romance of many other creative works that crossed his path: Grimm's fairy tales, Daniel Defoe's *Robinson Crusoe,* Charlie Chaplin movies, Howard Pyle's *Robin Hood,* the legends of King Arthur and the Knights of the Round Table, Englebert Humperdinck's opera *Hansel and Gretel,* and especially Carlo Collodi's *Pinocchio.*

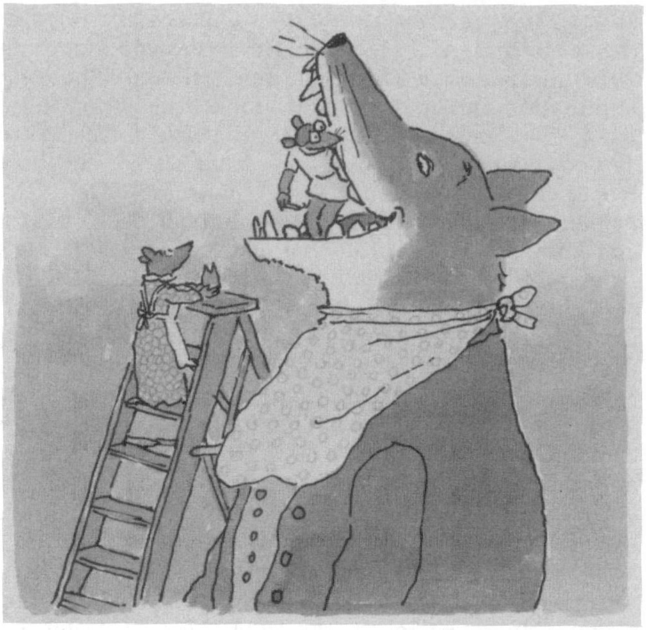

From *Doctor De Soto,* written and illustrated by William Steig.

As a young man, Steig found an outlet for his talent by creating cartoons for the high school newspaper. Throughout his youth he also excelled at athletics, and during college he was a member of the All-American Water Polo Team. After high school graduation, Steig spent two years at City College, three years at the National Academy, and five days at the Yale School of Fine Arts before dropping out. "If I'd had it my way," Steig tells David Allender in *Publishers Weekly,* "I'd have been a professional athlete, a sailor, a beachcomber, or some other form of hobo, a painter, a gardener, a novelist, a banjo-player, a traveler, anything but a rich man. When I was an adolescent, Tahiti was a paradise. I made up my mind to settle there someday. I was going to be a seaman like Melville, but the Great Depression put me to work as a cartoonist to support the family."

"[My] father went broke during the Depression," Steig recalls to Hammer. "My older brothers were married and my younger brother was seventeen, so the old man said to me, 'It's up to you.' The only thing I could do was draw. Within a year I was selling cartoons to the *New Yorker* and supporting a family." His father's strong, independent values greatly influenced Steig: "My father was a socialist—an advanced thinker—and he felt that business was degrading, but he didn't want his children to be laborers. We were all encouraged to go into music or art." Steig has passed his father's ethic on to his own children by encouraging them never to take nine-to-five jobs, and they have taken his advice to heart: son Jeremy is a jazz flautist, daughter Lucy a painter, and Maggie an actress.

Before Steig started writing children's books, he was well established as a noted cartoonist in the *New Yorker.* During his early days as a free-lance artist, he supplemented his income with work in advertising, although he intensely disliked it. During the 1940s, Steig's creativity found a more agreeable outlet when he began carving figurines in wood; his sculptures are on display as part of the collection in the historic home of Franklin D. Roosevelt in Hyde Park, New York, and in several museums in New England. Steig also claims responsibility for originating the idea of the "contemporary" greeting card, telling Alison Wyrley Birch in the *Hartford Courant:* "Greeting cards used to be all sweetness and love. I started doing the complete reverse—almost a hate card—and it caught on."

Writing books for children was a career Steig began relatively late in life and it came about by chance rather than intention. In 1967, Bob Kraus, a fellow cartoonist at the *New Yorker,* was in the process of organizing Windmill Books, an imprint for Harper & Row. Kraus suggested that Steig try writing and illustrating a book for a young audience. The result was Steig's letter-puzzle book entitled *C D B,* published in 1968. *Roland the Minstrel Pig,* published the same year, is the story of a pig who sings and plays the lute for the entertainment of a harmonious assortment of other animals. Roland abandons the security of his community: "He dreamed for days of fame and wealth, and he was no longer satisfied with the life he'd been living." The pig embarks on a romantic quest, discovering loneliness and evil along the road to fame and fortune. He encounters Sebastian the Fox who, true to fox-form, plans to feast on the portly pig. Roland is saved by his own resourcefulness; his singing is heard by the King—a lion—who saves him from the hungry fox and appoints the talented pig court minstrel.

"Like Isaac Bashevis Singer, E. B. White and a select company of others, Steig is a writer of children's books whose work reaches beyond the specific confines of a child audience," writes James E. Higgins in *Children's Literature in Education.* "[He] has the unusual childlike capacity to present incidents of wonder and marvel as if they are but everyday occurrences. He writes not out of a remembrance of childhood, but out of the essence of childhood which no adult can afford to give up or to deny." The power of luck, the capacity of nature for transformation and rebirth, the existence of beneficial magic; all are a part of this "childhood essence" and are ever-present in Steig's books. Wishes, even unspoken ones, are granted in the author's vision of how the world should be. In *The Amazing Bone,* the daydreaming Pearl the Pig dawdles on her walk home from school. "She sat on the ground in the forest . . . , and spring was so bright and beautiful, the warm air touched her so tenderly, she could almost feel herself changing into a flower. Her light dress felt like petals. 'I love everything,' she heard herself say." She discovers a magic bone, lost by a witch who "ate snails cooked in garlic at every meal and was always complaining about her rheumatism and asking nosy questions." That the bone talks is not surprising to our heroine, or even to her parent, and is accepted as a matter of course by the reader.

Positive themes reoccur throughout Steig's works: the abundant world of nature, the security of home and family, the importance of friendship, the strength that comes from self-reliance. Many of the animal characters inhabiting Steig's sunlit world also possess "heroic" qualities; quests, whether in the form of a search for a loved one or for adventure's sake alone, are frequently undertaken. Higgins writes, "In his works for children . . . [Steig] sets his lens to capture that which is good in life. He shares with children what can happen to humans when we are at our best."

Steig populates his stories with animals because they give him more latitude in telling his tales and because it amuses children to see animals behaving like people they know. "I think using animals emphasizes the fact that the story is symbolical—about human behavior," Steig tells Higgins. "And kids get the idea right away that this is not just a story, but that it's saying something about life on earth." Steig avoids interjecting political or social overtones to make his books "mean" anything. Human concerns over existence, self-discovery, and death are dealt with indirectly. "I feel this way: I have a position—a point of view. But I don't have to think about it to express it. I can write about anything and my point of view will come out. So when I am at work my conscious intention is to tell a story to the reader. All this other stuff takes place automatically."

The "other stuff" had occasion to get Steig into trouble in 1970, a time of social unrest marked by protest against the Vietnam War. The International Conference of Police Associations started a campaign against Steig's book *Sylvester and the Magic Pebble,* demanding that it be removed from library shelves because two policemen in the story were depicted as pigs. Steig has always maintained that there was no political reason for this—in fact, pig characters appear quite often in his books. He explains to Hammer that a pig represents "a creature surrounded with filth and danger, a victim of circumstances created by himself, unwilling and unable to do anything about his condition—and even, perhaps, in a way enjoying it." As far as any other significance in using "pig" policemen, Steig is emphatic: "Only an *idiot* would do something like that, bother kids with that kind of stuff," he tells Michael Patrick Hearns in *Washington Post Book World.*

Caleb and Kate was the first of several books where major characters are portrayed in human form. "Caleb the carpenter and Kate the weaver loved each other, but not every single minute," the book begins. It is a story of the separation, loss, search, and joyful reunion of a married couple who love each other deeply despite their human folly. Joy Adamson writes in *Dictionary of Literary Biography:* "Steig is at his best in *Caleb and Kate,* combining what he has learned about prose and using all his artistic gifts; the tongue-in-cheek humor that is never beyond the child, eloquent language as well as inventive play, both in language and illustration."

"Steig's themes are rendered in elegant, sometimes self-consciously literary language," writes Anita Moss in *Twentieth Century Children's Writers.* "The presiding voice in these works is urbane and witty, yet never condescending; rather it invites the young reader to participate in this humorous, sophisticated view of the world." Steig will often pepper his writing with "big words," giving his readers a chance to expand their vocabulary while adding to the verbal patterning of his stories. "And there are the noises!" Steven Kroll of the *New York Times Book Review* comments. "Mr. Steig knows children are just beginning to experience language and love weird sounds. 'Yibbam sibibble!' says the bone in *The Amazing Bone.* 'Jibrakken sibibble digray!' In *Farmer Palmer's Wagon Ride,* the thunder 'dramberamberoomed. It bomBOMBED!' Beyond the noises, there is a rich, wonderfully rhythmic use of language. . . . How clear that is in his very first illustrated story, *Roland the Minstrel Pig,* as Roland and the fox walk along with 'Roland dreaming and the fox scheming.'"

Steig explains to Higgins the process by which he begins his stories: "First of all I decide it's time to write a story. Then I say, 'What shall I draw this time? A pig or a mouse?' Or, 'I did a pig last time; I'll make it a mouse this time.' Then I start drawing. . . . [Usually] I just ramble around and discover for myself what will happen next." Sometimes Steig conjures up a visual image that inspires a story, as with the book *Amos and Boris.* "It was one of the book's last illustrations (the picture of two elephants pushing a whale into the sea) that provided the seed from which the story grew."

Steig does not consider himself a disciplined writer and might work twelve hours at a stretch one day but only two the next. He is a "night person" and usually doesn't enter his studio until evening. However, Steig is not afraid of running out of ideas, telling Birch, "I constantly loosen up new areas in myself. It just flows out. I used to panic that I'd never think of another joke. I've done so much by now I feel I have my whole vocabulary on tap where drawing is concerned. I could work endlessly." "I find it hard, as I've always found it, to do a job on order, even if the order comes from myself," he tells *Publishers Weekly* columnist Sally Lodge. "The more projects and plans I have, the less I produce. I go to my desk without any plans or ideas and wait there for inspiration. Which comes if you get in the right frame of mind. I find I function best when there's nothing that needs to be done. If I have two free hours between chores, I can't use them. There must be a long prospect of peace."

Steig finds writing and illustrating children's books to be much different than drawing cartoons, telling Lodge, "Working for kids is not the same as working for adults. Kids' books take a lot longer. I can do a drawing in 15 minutes. Once my editor, Michael di Capua, approves an idea for a children's book, it takes me about a week to write it and a month to do the illustrations." Steig has always found illustrating to be the most difficult part of his job, confiding to Higgins, "I love to draw, and I love to write—but I hate to illustrate.... When you draw, you draw anything that wants to come out, but when you illustrate you have to draw someone who has on a polka-dot dress. It has to be the same as the previous picture. You have to remember what it says in the story. It's not the way I want to draw at all."

"I carry on a lot of the functions of an adult but I have to force myself. I think I feel a little differently than other people do," Steig tells Hammer. "For some reason I've never felt grown up." The author reflects: "It gets harder and harder to reconstruct my world as a child. But I think it's important to keep those original feelings. It makes you happier if you can feel that way, about how wonderful and mysterious everything is." Through his many books for children, Steig conveys that happiness; to the children discovering his enchanted kingdom, and to the grownups lucky enough to enter that kingdom with them. Kroll writes, "He just tells his stories, and everything he does is magic."

WORKS CITED:

Allender, David, "William Steig at 80," *Publishers Weekly,* July 24, 1987, pp. 116-118.

Anderson, Joy, "William Steig," *Dictionary of Literary Biography,* Volume 61: *American Writers for Children since 1960: Poets, Illustrators and Nonfiction Authors,* Gale, 1987, pp. 297-305.

Birch, Allison Wyrley, "Our Foibles in Simple Lines," *Hartford Courant,* September 8, 1974.

Hammer, Joshua, "William Steig," *People,* December 3, 1984, pp. 87-98.

Hearns, Michael Patrick, "William Steig," *Washington Post Book World,* May 11, 1980.

Higgins, James E., "William Steig: Champion for Romance," *Children's Literature in Education,* spring, 1978, pp. 3-16.

Kroll, Steven, "Steig: Nobody Is Grown-Up," *New York Times Book Review,* June 28, 1987, p. 26.

Lodge, Sally, "PW Interviews: William Steig," *Publishers Weekly,* October 15, 1979, pp. 6-7.

Moss, Anita, "William Steig," *Twentieth Century Children's Writers,* third edition, St. James Press, 1989.

Steig, William, *The Amazing Bone,* Farrar, Straus, 1976.

Steig, William, *Caleb and Kate,* Farrar, Straus, 1977.

Steig, William, *Roland the Minstrel Pig,* Windmill Books, 1968.

FOR MORE INFORMATION SEE:

BOOKS

Children's Literature Review, Volume 15, Gale, 1988.

Contemporary Authors New Revision Series, Volume 21, Gale, 1987, pp. 425-429.

de Montreville, Doris, and Donna Hill, *Third Book of Junior Authors,* H. W. Wilson, 1972.

Fischer, Margery, *Who's Who in Children's Books: A Treasury of the Familiar Characters of Childhood,* Holt, 1975.

Kingman, Lee, editor, *Newbery and Caldecott Medal Books: 1966-1975,* Horn Book, 1975.

Lanes, Selma G., *Down the Rabbit Hole: Adventures and Misadventures in the Realm of Children's Literature,* Athenaeum, 1971.

Townsend, John Rowe, *Written for Children: An Outline of English-Language Children's Literature,* revised edition, Lippincott, 1974.

PERIODICALS

Booklist, January 1, 1975.

Books, January 17, 1943.

Children's Book Review, June, 1973; summer, 1975.

Children's Books, July-August, 1968; December, 1968; November, 1970; April, 1975.

Christian Science Monitor, November 11, 1971.

Horn Book, August, 1968; August, 1970, pp. 359-363; February, 1972; October, 1972; April, 1975; August, 1975; October, 1975; August, 1976; December, 1976; April, 1977; June, 1977.

Junior Bookshelf, February, 1972; February, 1973; April, 1973; August, 1973; June, 1975.

Life, December 17, 1971.

Los Angeles Times Book Review, December 5, 1982.

New Yorker, December 2, 1974.

New York Magazine, December 16, 1974.

New York Times Book Review, April 21, 1968; February 16, 1969; October 19, 1969; October 17, 1971; July 9, 1972; September 2, 1973; November 10, 1974; November 13, 1977; November 25, 1979; December 12, 1982; August 12, 1984; November 9, 1986.

Saturday Review/World, December 4, 1973.

School Library Journal, September, 1968; May, 1969; September, 1972; November, 1973.

Time, December 27, 1971.

Times Literary Supplement, September 12, 1980.

Weekly Book Review, July 23, 1944.

* * *

STEPTOE, John (Lewis) 1950-1989

PERSONAL: Born September 14, 1950, in Brooklyn, NY; died of complications from acquired immune deficiency syndrome (AIDS), August 28, 1989, in New York City; son of John Oliver (a transit worker) and

Eleesteen (Hill) Steptoe; children: Bweela (daughter), Javaka (son). *Education:* Attended New York High School of Art and Design, 1964-67.

ADDRESSES: Home—Brooklyn, NY. *Agent*—Estate of John Steptoe, c/o Ann White, Executrix, Apt. 9-AA, 375 Riverside Dr., New York, NY 10025.

CAREER: Artist; author and illustrator of children's books. Teacher at Brooklyn Music School, 1970.

MEMBER: Amnesty International.

AWARDS, HONORS: Best Book selection, *School Library Journal,* 1969, Gold Medal, Society of Illustrators, 1970, Art Books for Children Citation, Brooklyn Museum and Brooklyn Public Library, 1973, and Lewis Carroll Shelf Award, 1978, all for *Stevie;* Outstanding Book citation, *New York Times,* 1971, for *Train Ride;* Irma Simonton Black Award, Bank Street College of Education, and Honor Book Award (illustration), *Boston Globe-Horn Book,* both 1975, both for *She Come Bringing Me That Little Baby Girl;* Coretta Scott King Award (illustration), 1982, for *Mother Crocodile,* and 1988, for *Mufaro's Beautiful Daughters;* Jane Addams Children's Book Award (Special Recognition), Jane Addams Peace Association, 1983, for *All the Colors of the Race;* Caldecott Honor Book, American Library Association, 1985, for *The Story of Jumping Mouse,* and 1988, for *Mufaro's Beautiful Daughters;* Honor Book Award (illustration), *Boston Globe-Horn Book,* 1987, for *Mufaro's Beautiful Daughters;* Biennale of Illustration, Bratislava Award Honorable Mention in Memoriam, 1989.

John Steptoe

WRITINGS:

SELF-ILLUSTRATED

Stevie, Harper, 1969.
Uptown, Harper, 1970.
Train Ride, Harper, 1971.
Birthday, Holt, 1972.
My Special Best Words, Viking, 1974.
Marcia, Viking, 1976.
Daddy Is a Monster ... Sometimes, Lippincott, 1980.
Jeffrey Bear Cleans Up His Act, Lothrop, 1983.
The Story of Jumping Mouse: A Native American Legend, Lothrop, 1984.
Mufaro's Beautiful Daughters: An African Tale, Lothrop, 1987.
Baby Says, Lothrop, 1988.

ILLUSTRATOR

Lucille B. Clifton, *All Us Come Cross the Water,* Holt, 1972.
Eloise Greenfield, *She Come Bringing Me That Little Baby Girl,* Lippincott, 1974.
Arnold Adoff, *OUTside/INside: Poems,* Lothrop, 1981.
Birago Diop, *Mother Crocodile = Maman-Caiman,* Delacorte, 1981.
A. Adoff, *All the Colors of the Race: Poems,* Lothrop, 1982.
Barbara Cohen, *Roses,* Lothrop, 1984.

ADAPTATIONS: Stevie was adapted as a cassette and released by Live Oak Media, 1987; *Mufaro's Beautiful Daughters* was adapted as both a cassette and 16mm film and released by Weston Woods, 1988; *The Story of Jumping Mouse* was adapted as a filmstrip with cassette and released by Random House.

SIDELIGHTS: John Steptoe was an acclaimed author and illustrator of children's books. Many of his works have been praised for both realistically portraying black life and having universal themes which appeal to children of all races. Steptoe was especially concerned about reaching black children, largely because he felt their literary needs were not being met. He once explained: "One of my great incentives for getting into writing children's books was the great and disastrous need for books that black children could honestly relate to.... I was amazed to find that no one had successfully written a book in the dialogue black children speak."

As a child, Steptoe was considered unusual because he preferred staying home to paint and draw. During his adolescence, Steptoe attended New York's High School of Art and Design; in his senior year he received a grant to attend an eight-week summer program for minority artists at the Vermont Academy. At the Academy, Steptoe helped other students in their quest to better themselves artistically; he also decided that he wanted to write and illustrate books for black children. At the end of the summer program, one of his instructors

From *The Story of Jumping Mouse,* retold and illustrated by John Steptoe.

allowed Steptoe to live over his stables, and there *Stevie* was created.

Stevie was reprinted in *Life* magazine shortly after its first publication, gaining its young author fame at a national level. Critics praised Steptoe's use of black English and accurate portrayal of black people, while noting that its story—that of a black boy's jealousy of a younger boy his mother takes care of—is one that all children can relate to. Steptoe himself, however, had a different objective. He remarked in *Life:* "The story, the language ... is not directed at white children. I wanted it to be something black children could read without translating the language, something real which would relate to what a black child would know."

Steptoe followed the success of *Stevie* with two self-illustrated books, *Uptown* and *Train Ride.* Both describe the adventures of inner-city black children. In *Uptown,* two young boys discuss their future; *Train Ride* concerns a group of boys who, without their parents' permission, ride a subway train from Harlem to Times Square. They experience some culture shock but agree that the adventure they had was worth the punishment meted out when they returned home. In her review of *Train Ride* for *Children's Literature: An Issues Approach,* Masha Kabakow Rudman claimed that the book "again affirms the city and the children's capability of coping with it and enjoying it."

In the 1970s, Steptoe drew inspiration from his own children. Both his son and daughter star in *My Special Best Words* and *Daddy Is a Monster ... Sometimes.* Donna E. Norton, writing in *Through the Eyes of a Child,* praised *Daddy is a Monster ... Sometimes* for "the strong father/child relationship it develops.... The dialect follows the criteria for black literature because it rings true and blends naturally with the story."

Steptoe also dealt with the sexuality of adolescents in his only young adult novel, *Marcia.* While some reviewers were concerned that the author had been too explicit about his subject matter, others, such as Joan Scherer Brewer of *School Library Journal,* praised the author for that very reason. "For urban Black teen-age girls, this book deals frankly with male 'machismo,' responsible sex, and contraception," she concluded.

During his later career, Steptoe wrote many books based on ethnic folk stories, such as *The Story of Jumping Mouse: A Native American Legend* and *Mufaro's Beautiful Daughters: An African Tale.* He also began to experiment with the style of his illustrations. Steptoe explained some of the things that drove him to create in a *Pen Newsletter* article: "In my books and picture books I put all the things I never saw when I was a child, things I'm angry about not having seen, things that make me feel sad, things that have outraged me, and things I long to see happen.... There were so many things that weren't addressed and weren't dealt with for me as a black child in books. And I wanted to see those things. And I want to see them now."

WORKS CITED:

Brewer, Joan Scherer, review of *Marcia, School Library Journal,* May, 1976.

Norton, Donna E., *Through the Eyes of a Child: An Introduction to Children's Literature,* Merrill, 1983, pp. 486-545.

Rudman, Masha Kabakow, *Children's Literature: An Issues Approach,* D. C. Heath & Co., 1977, pp. 185-86.

Steptoe, John, interview in *Life,* August 29, 1969.

Steptoe, J., "Writing for Children: Where Does It Come From and How Is It Different From Writing for Adults?," *Pen Newsletter,* September, 1988.

FOR MORE INFORMATION SEE:

BOOKS

Children's Literature Review, Volume 12, Gale, 1987.

PERIODICALS

New York Times Book Review, October 5, 1969; November 3, 1974; June 28, 1987.

Times Literary Supplement, July 2, 1970.

Washington Post, December 18, 1987; May 13, 1990.

* * *

STERLING, Dorothy 1913-

PERSONAL: Born November 23, 1913, in New York, NY; daughter of Joseph (a lawyer) and Elsie (Darmstadter) Dannenberg; married Philip Sterling (a writer), May 14, 1937; children: Peter, Anne. *Education:* Attended Wellesley College; Barnard College, B.A., 1934. *Politics:* Independent.

ADDRESSES: Home and office—Box 755, South Wellfleet, MA 02667.

CAREER: Art News, New York City, editor and author of weekly column, "Paris Notes," 1935; Federal Writers Project, New York City, writer, 1936; *Architectural Forum,* New York City, secretary, 1936-41; *Life,* New York City, researcher, 1941-49; free-lance writer. Consulting editor, Firebird Books, Scholastic Book Services, New York City; editorial consultant on black history, Beacon Press and Perspective Books, Doubleday.

MEMBER: Authors Guild, Authors League of America, National Association for the Advancement of Colored People (NAACP).

AWARDS, HONORS: Nancy Bloch Memorial Award, 1958, for *Captain of the Planter: The Story of Robert Smalls,* and 1959, for *Mary Jane;* Woodward Park School Annual Book Award, 1960, Community-Woodward Schools Award for promotion of "one-worldness" among children, and Child Study Association of America honorable mention, all for *Mary Jane;* Carter G. Woodson Book Award, National Council for the Social Studies, 1977, for *The Trouble They Seen: Black People Tell the Story of Reconstruction.*

Dorothy Sterling

WRITINGS:

CHILDREN'S FICTION

Sophie and Her Puppies (Junior Literary Guild selection), photographs by Myron Ehrenberg, Doubleday, 1951.
The Cub Scout Mystery, illustrated by Paul Galdone, Doubleday, 1952.
Billy Goes Exploring (Junior Literary Guild selection), photographs by Ehrenberg, Doubleday, 1953.
The Brownie Scout Mystery, illustrated by Reisie Lonette, Doubleday, 1955.
The Silver Spoon Mystery (Junior Literary Guild selection), illustrated by Grace Paull, Doubleday, 1958.
Secret of the Old Post-Box, illustrated by Paull, Doubleday, 1960.
Ellen's Blue Jays, illustrated by Winifred Lubell, Doubleday, 1961.

CHILDREN'S NONFICTION

Trees and Their Story (Junior Literary Guild selection), photographs by Ehrenberg, Doubleday, 1953.
Insects and the Homes They Build, photographs by Ehrenberg, Doubleday, 1954.
(With husband, Philip Sterling) *Polio Pioneers: The Story of the Fight against Polio,* photographs by Ehrenberg, Doubleday, 1955.
The Story of Mosses, Ferns, and Mushrooms, photographs by Ehrenberg, Doubleday, 1955.
Wall Street: The Story of the Stock Exchange, photographs by Ehrenberg, Doubleday, 1955.
The Story of Caves (Junior Literary Guild selection), illustrated by Lubell, Doubleday, 1956.
Creatures of the Night, illustrated by Lubell, Doubleday, 1960.
Caterpillars, illustrated by Lubell, Doubleday, 1961.
Forever Free: The Story of the Emancipation Proclamation, illustrated by Ernest Crichlow, Doubleday, 1963.
Spring Is Here!, illustrated by Lubell, Doubleday, 1964.
Fall Is Here!, illustrated by Lubell, Natural History Press, 1966.
It Started in Montgomery: A Picture of the Civil Rights Movement, Scholastic Book Services, 1972.

YOUNG ADULT NONFICTION

United Nations, N.Y., photographs by Ehrenberg, Doubleday, 1953, revised edition published as *United Nations,* 1961.
Freedom Train: The Story of Harriet Tubman, illustrated by Crichlow, Doubleday, 1954.
Captain of the Planter: The Story of Robert Smalls, illustrated by Crichlow, Doubleday, 1958.
Lucretia Mott: Gentle Warrior, Doubleday, 1964.
(With Benjamin Quarles) *Lift Every Voice: The Lives of Booker T. Washington, W. E. B. Du Bois, Mary Church Terrell, and James Weldon Johnson,* illustrated by Crichlow, Doubleday, 1965.
The Outer Lands: A Natural History Guide to Cape Cod, Martha's Vineyard, Nantucket, Block Island, and Long Island, illustrated by Lubell, Natural History Press, 1967, revised edition, Norton, 1978.
Tear Down the Walls!: A History of the American Civil Rights Movement, Doubleday, 1968.
The Making of an Afro-American: Martin Robinson Delany, 1812-1885, Doubleday, 1971.
Black Foremothers: Three Lives, illustrated by Judith Eloise Hooper, Feminist Press, 1979, 2nd edition, 1988.

EDITOR

I Have Seen War: Twenty-Five Stories from World War II, Hill & Wang, 1960.
Speak out in Thunder Tones: Letters and Other Writings by Black Northerners, 1787-1865, Doubleday, 1973.
The Trouble They Seen: Black People Tell The Story of Reconstruction, Doubleday, 1976.
We Are Your Sisters: Black Women in the Nineteenth Century, Norton, 1984.
Turning the World Upside Down: Proceedings of the Anti-Slavery Convention of American Women Held in the City of New York, May 9-12, 1837, Feminist Press, 1987.

OTHER

(With Donald Gross) *Tender Warriors* (adult nonfiction), photographs by Ehrenberg, Hill & Wang, 1958.
Mary Jane (young adult novel), illustrated by Crichlow, Doubleday, 1959.

Contributor to books, including *Notable American Women,* Harvard University Press, 1980; and *Dictionary of American Negro Biography,* Norton, 1982.

SIDELIGHTS: Dorothy Sterling is considered an intellectual treasure among writers for children, particularly in the fields of nature and African American biography. Over the course of her career, she has established a reputation for literary clarity that makes her work accessible to all ages. And as unrelated as nature science and African American biography may seem, they are both among Sterling's personal passions.

Sterling is the eldest of two daughters born to Joseph and Elsie May Dannenberg, New Yorkers of German Jewish ancestry. Joseph Dannenberg, a lawyer and the first person in his family to attend college, operated a thriving private practice on the west side of the city. Sterling's mother graduated from normal school and taught for a year before getting married. She raised her daughters like princesses in the hope that their ignorance of mundane household responsibilities would somehow lead them to a life of privilege. "Mother was not only pretty and bright, she was an excellent cook, a capable seamstress (she made many of our dresses), and an energetic and efficient housekeeper," Sterling related

From *The Brownie Scout Mystery,* by Dorothy Sterling. Illustrated by Reisie Lonette.

in an essay for *Something about the Author Autobiography Series* (*SAAS*). "But she refrained from passing along these skills to her daughters," continued Sterling. "Even when we were teenagers we neither cooked nor cleaned, sewed nor ironed, nor made our beds.... I concluded that mother, subconsciously at least, had thought that if we didn't know how to do housework, we would never have to do it. How did she think we were to escape the chores which were every woman's fate? One obvious answer was to marry men rich enough to employ servants.... The other was to 'be somebody' ourselves."

Sterling grew up in the section of Manhattan known as Washington Heights, "where the battle of Fort Washington had been fought in 1776," Sterling noted in *SAAS.* She further surmised, "If you had to be a city child, Washington Heights was a good place to start." Sterling recounts with clarity her lack of interest in sports and her fondness for the quieter, more cerebral attractions of nature. "If you're born in New York City and you're no good at sports," she related in the *Third Book of Junior Authors,* "you spend your free time picking violets on Riverside Drive, planting gardens in vacant lots, and feeding ducks in Central Park. At least, that's what I did in those bygone years when urban blight had not yet destroyed the city's wildlife. Summers in camps in Maine where I was conspicuously *not* chosen for the baseball team gave me a further chance to explore the natural world.... Further, no one I knew was interested in nature and I was already marked as a 'nut' because I preferred bugs to baseball."

Sterling was catapulted through elementary school via special programs for intellectually gifted children—Rapid Advance and Special Opportunity; she was sixteen years old when she enrolled at Wellesley College. At the time, Sterling realized that the Depression, though it did not effect her directly, marked an ominous and foreboding time in America's history. "As the only girl in the dorm who subscribed to the *New York Times,* I read of bank failures, farm holidays and thousands, then millions of unemployed," Sterling remarked in *SAAS.* "These events were scarcely noted on Wellesley's serene and beautiful campus. By sophomore year, when there were hunger marchers in Washington and people lining up for handouts at soup kitchens, Wellesley girls began knitting for 'the poor.' With the country tumbling down about our ears, this response did not seem adequate to me."

Sterling also found her efforts to pursue her scientific interests thwarted at Wellesley, discouraged by professors who believed the scientific field had no place for women and advised her against it. "Actually there were a handful of women biologists and geneticists then, but I, a scientific illiterate, had never heard of them and was easily convinced to turn back to liberal arts," Sterling said in *SAAS.* "It was a decision I still regret."

Sterling transferred to Barnard College in New York City to complete the remaining two years of her education. In the city the Depression was very real, there were "unemployed men selling apples at every street corner, people begging for a nickel for subway fare, Hoovervilles—cardboard and tar-paper shacks built by the homeless—on Riverside Drive and in Central Park," Sterling recalled in *SAAS.* But even in the wake of such destitution, Sterling was glad to be back home. "Barnard's tiny urban campus couldn't compare to Wellesley's tree-shaded lawns and lake, but there was an excitement there ... that I had missed," she continued. Sterling graduated from Barnard in 1934 and traveled abroad with her sister Alice, an art history major from Vassar College. In retrospect, Sterling realized how politically charged the atmosphere was worldwide. In addition to touring museums and galleries, Sterling and her sister witnessed Mussolini's militiamen marching through the streets of Rome. They were in Paris when Hitler came to power and the salute of *Heil Hitler* became the order of the day in Germany.

When Sterling returned from Europe she moved from one free-lance job to another, finally landing her first real position as one of three female editors with *Art News,* a weekly magazine. She reviewed minor art exhibits and produced the weekly column "Paris Notes," compiling the information from French newspapers. She enjoyed her position for several months until the magazine was purchased by new owners who replaced the female editors with men.

After a job search that lasted over a year, Sterling became acquainted with the Federal Writers Project. As part of Franklin Delano Roosevelt's "New Deal," funds were channeled into the Works Progress Administration's art program. Projects for musicians, artists, actors, and writers were being financed by the government as one of several attempts to get the nation back on its feet. Sterling regards this job as "one of the major learning experiences" of her life. It was while she was working here that Sterling met her husband, Philip, an associate editor in the Motion Picture Bibliography department. Plans of marriage forced Sterling to seek employment elsewhere as WPA regulations did not allow members of the same household to be on the payroll simultaneously. On November 23, 1936, her twenty-third birthday, Sterling went to work for the *Architectural Forum.* Originally hired as a secretary, Sterling answered to three editors who tended to overlook her deficient secretarial skills, realizing that greater talent lay underneath.

Sterling was married on May 14, 1937, and took residence with her husband in a small apartment in Sunnyside, Queens. Shortly after going to work for the *Forum,* Sterling joined the Time Incorporated unit of the American Newspaper Guild, a newswriter's union. Her life changed radically with the birth of her son, Peter, in June of 1940.

The week of the attack on Pearl Harbor, Sterling was transferred to *Life* magazine as a secretary originally, then as a researcher. The writer-researcher relationship was pivotal to the success of *Life.* The writer usually developed the idea for a story; the researcher investigated it, presented a picture script that was subject to the writer's approval, went on location with the photographer and directed the photo layout. The researcher was also responsible for proofreading the written text and verifying its accuracy.

Even though sex-role stereotyping sometimes provided for a tense atmosphere (*all* writers were male and *all* researchers were female), Sterling was aware that she was gaining precious experience. "The training was valuable," she explained in *SAAS.* "A researcher had to be able to gather information on any conceivable subject quickly.... One day I might have to find out the color of the eyes of the Speaker of the House, on another, the height of the Washington Cathedral. You couldn't say 'I don't know' or 'I can't find out.' You picked up the telephone or searched in the library until you had the answer."

The Sterlings' daughter Anne was born in July of 1944, the same year Sterling was promoted to Assistant Chief of the News Bureau. In addition to the prestige and pay increase the job offered, it provided regular hours and more time for Sterling to spend with her family.

As the war came to an end, women were being replaced in their executive positions by returning soldiers. When Sterling's boss was fired and replaced by a man, she decided that it was time to work independently. Still operating under the assumption that she could not be a writer, Sterling compiled a manuscript of essays, memos, and amusing anecdotes from her years with Time Inc. and contacted a male journalist she knew to write "the book." A year later when he was still too busy to collaborate on the project, he looked at the manuscript of "It's about Time" and assured Sterling that she had indeed already written a book. A literary agent submitted the book for publication. Responses were enthusiastic, but there were no takers. Several years would pass before Sterling realized that she had been blacklisted in the sweep of the McCarthy hysteria because she had signed a nominating petition for a Communist candidate fourteen years earlier.

It was during this time that Sterling, with Myron Ehrenberg, a professional photographer and neighbor, developed her first published work, *Sophie and Her Puppies* (1951), primarily a photo essay. This literary relationship was very compatible and led to several similar photographic stories designed for children: *Billy Goes Exploring* (1953), *Trees and Their Story* (1953), and *Insects and the Homes They Build* (1954).

Oddly enough, even after she had five books published, Sterling still did not consider herself a writer. She thought of her work as research for some mythical writer, gathering information as she had at *Life* magazine. Recognizing this as a weakness, she wanted her next literary project to be something that would empower girls, that would tell them, "You are as strong and capable as boys." On the suggestion of a friend, she researched Harriet Tubman, liberator of over three-hundred slaves and leader of the Underground Railroad.

During the course of her research, Sterling was exposed for the first time to the Schomberg Collection in New York, a major research center for African American history. She was appalled to learn that there was an entire school of biography to which she had not been introduced. Sterling, normally considered a slow writer, recalls writing *Freedom Train: The Story of Harriet Tubman* (1954) "quickly and with confidence." She was passionate about her subject. At forty years of age with five books in print, Sterling finally thought of herself as a writer.

While researching the Harriet Tubman biography, Sterling learned of Sojourner Truth, Frederick Douglass and a host of other abolitionists and freedom fighters. She became interested in Robert Smalls, an ex-slave who became a U.S. Congressman and later the Collector of Customs in Beaufort, South Carolina. Her research took her South, where she and her husband experienced "Jim Crow" segregation first-hand.

While completing *Captain of the Planter: The Story of Robert Smalls* (1958), Sterling watched as a nation struggled with the issue of federal school desegregation. She and her husband went to Tennessee, Kentucky, Virginia, Maryland, and Delaware, interviewing students who were the first blacks to enter "white schools"; walking with them and lending camaraderie and support. *Tender Warriors* (1958) and *Mary Jane* (1959) were published as a result of this experience. Sterling and her husband went on to become active members of the local NAACP Chapter, championing such causes as housing discrimination while continuing to produce important biographical works on African American history.

Having survived the Great Depression, the McCarthy era, and the Civil Rights movement, Sterling brings a personal, historical reality to her writing that is hard to imitate. Her authenticity is further substantiated by her competence in researching her subject thoroughly and her ability to present the information in a straightforward, accessible manner.

WORKS CITED:

Sterling, Dorothy, essay in *Third Book of Junior Authors,* edited by Doris De Montreville and Donna Hill, H.W. Wilson, 1972, pp. 277-79.

Sterling, essay in *Something about the Author Autobiography Series,* Volume 2, Gale, 1986, pp. 227-49.

FOR MORE INFORMATION SEE:

BOOKS

Children's Literature Review, Volume 1, Gale, 1976.

PERIODICALS

Young Wings, May, 1953.

STEVENSON, James

PERSONAL: Born in New York, NY; son of Harvey (an architect) and Winifred (Worcester) Stevenson; married Jane Walker, 1953; children: five sons, four daughters. *Education:* Yale University, B.A., 1951.

ADDRESSES: *Agent*—c/o Greenwillow Books, 1350 Avenue of the Americas, New York, NY 10019.

CAREER: *Life,* New York City, reporter, 1954-56; *New Yorker,* New York City, cartoonist and writer for "Talk of the Town" (comic strip), 1956-1963. Creator of "Capitol Games" (syndicated political comic strip). Writer and illustrator, 1962—. *Military service:* U.S. Marine Corps, 1951-53.

AWARDS, HONORS: *New York Times* Outstanding Children's Book of the Year and *School Library Journal* Best Books for Spring honor, both 1977, for *"Could Be Worse!";* American Library Association (ALA) Notable Book designation, 1978, for *The Sea View Hotel,* 1979, for *Fast Friends: Two Stories,* 1980, for *That Terrible Halloween Night; School Library Journal* Best Books for Spring honor, 1979, for *Monty;* Children's Choice Award, International Reading Association, 1979, for *The Worst Person in the World,* 1980, for *That Terrible Halloween Night,* 1982, for *The Night after Christmas,* 1989, for *The Supreme Souvenir Factory,* and 1990, for *Oh No, It's Waylon's Birthday!;* Best Illustrated Book and Outstanding Book honors, both *New York Times,* 1980, for *Howard; School Library Journal* Best Books of 1981 honor, for *The Wish Card Ran Out!; Boston Globe/Horn Book* honor list, 1981, for *The Night after Christmas;* Christopher Award, 1982, for *We Can't Sleep;* Parents Choice Award, 1982, for *Oliver, Clarence, and Violet; Boston Globe/Horn Book* honor list, ALA Notable Book designation, *School Library Journal* Best

James Stevenson

Books of 1983 honor, all 1983, for *What's under My Bed?;* Garden State Children's Book Award, New Jersey Library Association, 1983, for *Clams Can't Sing;* ALA Notable Book designation, 1986, for *When I Was Nine; Redbook* award, 1987, for *Higher on the Door.*

WRITINGS:

Do Yourself a Favor, Kid (novel), Macmillan, 1962.
The Summer Houses, Macmillan, 1963.
Sorry, Lady, This Beach Is Private! (cartoons), Macmillan, 1963.
Sometimes, But Not Always (autobiographical novel), Little, Brown, 1967.
Something Marvelous Is About to Happen (humor), Harper, 1971.
Cool Jack and the Beanstalk, Penguin, 1976.
Let's Boogie! (cartoons), Dodd, 1978.
Uptown Local, Downtown Express, Viking, 1983.

FOR CHILDREN; SELF-ILLUSTRATED, EXCEPT AS INDICATED

Walker, the Witch, and the Striped Flying Saucer, Little, Brown, 1969.
The Bear Who Had No Place to Go, Harper, 1972.
Here Comes Herb's Hurricane!, Harper, 1973.
"Could be Worse!," Greenwillow, 1977.
Wilfred the Rat, Greenwillow, 1977.
(With daughter, Edwina Stevenson) *"Help!" Yelled Maxwell,* Greenwillow, 1978.
The Sea View Hotel, Greenwillow, 1978.
Winston, Newton, Elton, and Ed, Greenwillow, 1978.
The Worst Person in the World, Greenwillow, 1978.
Fast Friends: Two Stories, Greenwillow, 1979.
Monty, Greenwillow, 1979.
Howard, Greenwillow, 1980.
That Terrible Halloween Night, Greenwillow, 1980.
Clams Can't Sing, Greenwillow, 1980.
The Night after Christmas, Greenwillow, 1981.
The Wish Card Ran Out!, Greenwillow, 1981.
The Whale Tale, Random House, 1981.
Oliver, Clarence, and Violet, Greenwillow, 1982.
We Can't Sleep, Greenwillow, 1982.
What's under My Bed?, Greenwillow, 1983.
The Great Big Especially Beautiful Easter Egg, Greenwillow, 1983.
Barbara's Birthday, Greenwillow, 1983.
Grandpa's Great City Tour: An Alphabet Book, Greenwillow, 1983.
Worse Than Willy!, Greenwillow, 1984.
Yuck!, Greenwillow, 1984.
Emma, Greenwillow, 1985.
Are We Almost There?, Greenwillow, 1985.
That Dreadful Day, Greenwillow, 1985.
Fried Feathers for Thanksgiving, Greenwillow, 1986.
No Friends, Greenwillow, 1986.
There's Nothing To Do!, Greenwillow, 1986.
When I Was Nine (autobiographical), Greenwillow, 1986.
Happy Valentine's Day, Emma!, Greenwillow, 1987.
Higher on the Door (sequel to *When I Was Nine*), Greenwillow, 1987.
No Need for Monty, Greenwillow, 1987.
Will You Please Feed Our Cat?, Greenwillow, 1987.
The Supreme Souvenir Factory, Greenwillow, 1988.
We Hate Rain!, Greenwillow, 1988.
The Worst Person in the World at Crab Beach, Greenwillow, 1988.
Grandpa's Too-Good Garden, Greenwillow, 1989.
Oh No, It's Waylon's Birthday!, Greenwillow, 1989.
Un-Happy New Year, Emma!, Greenwillow, 1989.
Emma at the Beach, Greenwillow, 1990.
July, Greenwillow, 1990.
National Worm Day, Greenwillow, 1990.
Quick! Turn the Page!, Greenwillow, 1990.
The Stowaway, Greenwillow, 1990.
Which One Is Whitney?, Greenwillow, 1990.
Mr. Hacker, illustrated by Frank Modell, Greenwillow, 1990.
Brrr!, Greenwillow, 1991.
That's Exactly the Way It Wasn't, Greenwillow, 1991.
The Worst Person's Christmas, Greenwillow, 1991.
Rolling Rose, Greenwillow, 1991.
Don't You Know There's a War On?, Greenwillow, 1992.
And Then What?, Greenwillow, 1992.
The Flying Acorns, Greenwillow, 1993.

ILLUSTRATOR

William K. Zinsser, *Weekend Guests: From "We're So Glad You Could Come" to "We're So Sorry You Have to Go," and Vice-Versa* (adult), Harper, 1963.
James Walker Stevenson (son), *If I Owned a Candy Factory,* Little, Brown, 1968.
Eric Stevenson, *Tony and the Toll Collector,* Little, Brown, 1969.
Lavinia Ross, *Alec's Sand Castle,* Harper, 1972.
Alan Arkin, *Tony's Hard Work Day,* Harper, 1972.
Sara D. Gilbert, *What's a Father For?: A Father's Guide to the Pleasures and Problems of Parenthood with Advice from the Experts,* Parents Magazine Press, 1975.
John Donovan, *Good Old James,* Harper, 1975.
Janet Schulman, *Jack the Bum and the Halloween Handout,* Greenwillow, 1977.
Schulman, *Jack the Bum and the Haunted House,* Greenwillow, 1977.
Schulman, *Jack the Bum and the UFO,* Greenwillow, 1978.
Charlotte Zolotow, *Say It!* (ALA Notable Book), Greenwillow, 1980.
Jack Prelutsky, *The Baby Uggs Are Hatching* (poetry), Greenwillow, 1982.
Louis Phillips, *How Do You Get a Horse Out of the Bathtub?: Profound Answers to Preposterous Questions,* Viking, 1983.
Wilson Gage (pseudonym of Mary Q. Steele), *Cully Cully and the Bear,* Greenwillow, 1983.
Zolotow, *I Know a Lady,* Greenwillow, 1984.
Prelutsky, *The New Kid on the Block* (poems), Greenwillow, 1984.
John Thorn, editor, *The Armchair Book of Baseball,* Macmillan, 1985.
Franz Brandenberg, *Otto Is Different,* Greenwillow, 1985.
Phillips, *Brain Busters: Just How Smart Are You, Anyway?,* Viking, 1985.

From *Brrr!,* written and illustrated by James Stevenson.

Helen V. Griffith, *Georgia Music,* Greenwillow, 1986.
Cynthia Rylant, *Henry and Mudge,* Bradbury, 1987.
Rylant, *Henry and Mudge in Puddle Trouble,* Bradbury, 1987.
Griffith, *Grandaddy's Place,* Greenwillow, 1987.
Dr. Seuss (pseudonym of Theodor Seuss Geisel), *I Am Not Going to Get up Today!,* Random House, 1987.
Phillips, *How Do You Lift a Walrus with One Hand?: More Profound Answers to Preposterous Questions,* Viking, 1988.
Else Holmelund Minarik, *Percy and the Five Houses,* Greenwillow, 1989.
Prelutsky, *Something Big Has Been Here* (poetry), Greenwillow, 1990.
Rupert Matthews, *Explorer,* Random House, 1991.
Barbara Dugan, *Loop the Loop,* Greenwillow, 1992.
Griffith, *Grandaddy and Janetta,* Greenwillow, 1993.

OTHER

Also author of plays and television sketches. Contributor of articles to *New Yorker.*

ADAPTATIONS: Many of Stevenson's books have been adapted for filmstrip or audio cassette, including: *Fast Friends,* Educational Enrichment Materials, 1981; *"Could Be Worse!"* and *That Terrible Halloween Night,* both Educational Enrichment Materials, 1982; *What's under My Bed?,* Weston Woods, 1984; *We Can't Sleep,* Random House, 1984, re-released on videocassette, 1988. *Howard* was adapted for film as *New Friends,* Made-to-Order Library Products. *"Could Be Worse!"* and *What's under My Bed?* were highlighted on *Reading Rainbow,* PBS-TV.

SIDELIGHTS: James Stevenson, a prolific author and illustrator of books for children, is noted for gently humorous, animated stories that depict the world of childhood with understanding and wit. Stevenson chooses sibling rivalry, nighttime fears, boredom, and other concerns of family life as subjects for his stories, and approaches them from a child's point of view. Incorporating a subtle moral message into his books, Stevenson carries an upbeat view of life throughout his stories and illustrations, always ending on an optimistic note. His sketchy, high-spirited drawings have also illustrated the books of such notable children's authors as Dr. Seuss, Else Holmelund Minarik, Charlotte Zolotow, and Franz Brandenberg.

Stevenson was born in New York City, and was raised in small towns throughout New York state. He credits his public school education with having a great impact on his life: "[One school I went to] had a kind of policy of telling you that everybody could do everything.

Everybody could sing, dance, act, play musical instruments, write stories, make pictures and change the world," he recalled to Kimberly Olson Fakih in *Publishers Weekly.* Stevenson continued his education at Yale University, majoring in English with the intention of becoming a writer. His first success was with art rather than writing, however; he was selling ideas for cartoons to the *New Yorker* magazine while still a student at Yale. After graduating in 1951, Stevenson spent two years in the U.S. Marine Corps Officer Training Program, followed by another two years as a *Life* reporter. In 1956, Stevenson moved to the *New Yorker* art department full-time, developing cartoon ideas for staff artists. During this period he continued to pursue his goal of becoming a writer. In 1960, Stevenson graduated to working as a *New Yorker* reporter while writing a series of three adult novels as well as a book of original cartoons. Stevenson's novels, as well as the many cartoons he has created for the *New Yorker,* are full of social and political satire, poking fun at suburban living, the media, and other aspects of the "establishment."

Gradually Stevenson's focus shifted away from current issues, and he adopted a more nostalgic approach in his art. He became interested in subjects of concern to children and eventually began creating books for a younger audience. His first involvement with picture books was with his eight-year-old son James. Stevenson recalled to Fakih, "[I said to James,] 'Tell me a story and we'll make a book.' He stood at my desk and narrated a story; I wrote it down and then did the pictures. It was a collaboration, and it was published. We split the royalties." The book that resulted was *If I Owned a Candy Factory,* published in 1968.

The first picture book that Stevenson both wrote and illustrated was *Walker, the Witch, and the Striped Flying Saucer,* published the following year. A few years later, *"Could Be Worse!"* firmly established him as a writer of children's books, as well being the first story to introduce the character "Grandpa," Stevenson's "alter-ego." "A more engaging character than Grandpa has not emerged in recent picture books," commented Gertrude Herman in *Horn Book.* A master of the incredibly tall tale, Grandpa responds to grandchildren Mary Ann and Louie's concern that his life is boring by recounting a recent—and totally unbelievable—adventure. In later books, Grandpa helps his grandchildren deal with various problems by concocting suitable tall tales he claims are from his past. Grandpa's whoppers console Mary Ann and Louie when they come home from a terrible first day of school (*That Dreadful Day*), help them deal with the move to a new neighborhood (*No Friends*), and calm their fear of the dark (*What's Under My Bed?*). Stevenson combines verbal nonsense with humorous drawings of Grandpa and his younger brother, Uncle Wainwright, as mustachioed children to appeal directly to children's love of the silly and absurd. Louie and Mary Ann, together with Stevenson's young readers, can count on the fact that, whatever their problem, Grandpa has probably had one like it, but so much worse that theirs don't seem as bad by comparison.

Stevenson has featured Mary Ann, Louie, and Grandpa in several popular books. In *That Terrible Halloween Night,* the two children are busy attempting to frighten Grandpa: "'Something not *too* scary,' said Mary Ann. 'Grandpa's pretty old.'" No matter what they try, Grandpa remains unruffled behind his newspaper, claiming "I don't get very scared anymore—not since that terrible Halloween night." The dapper old gentleman goes on to tell his grandchildren a scary story about what happened to him on a Halloween long ago, complete with pumpkins, a haunted house, spiders, and lots of yucky green stuff. Grandpa's story ends on a typically Stevensonian note, with a quiet chuckle and a warm smile.

Stevenson has expanded his cast of characters throughout his career as a children's author. Several books, including *Emma* and *Un-happy New Year, Emma!,* are about a good-natured young witch/apprentice named Emma who triumphs over the efforts of two older sorceresses, Dolores and Lavinia, to undermine her attempts at magic. Then there are the "worst" books. The worst is a crotchety old gentleman: "The worst person in the world didn't like anything anybody else liked. He didn't like springtime, or music, or dessert, or laughing, or people who were friendly." The worst disguises his need for companionship by grumbling and complaining where the most people will hear him. In *The Worst Person's Christmas,* the old curmudgeon relishes the spirit of the holiday season: "That night the worst put a chair by his front window so that, when the carol singers came, he could tell them to get off his property and go away." As in Stevenson's other "worst" books, *The Worst Person in the World* and *The Worst Person in the World at Crab Beach,* a series of mishaps occur that don't exactly make the worst any nicer, but by story's end he isn't the worst person in the whole *entire* world anymore either.

Stevenson began writing and drawing as a boy and was encouraged by his father who was a watercolorist. He says he was influenced by movies and comics rather than any of the children's books he read as a child. "I think that my experience and creative mind have been formed much more by movies and comic books. I like the idea of a storyboard and I like the idea of a movie and all the different angles from which things can be viewed," he once told an interviewer.

Stevenson's books are often illustrated in comic-book or cartoon style. The intermix of story line with dialogue "balloons" and graffiti adds energy and dimension to his humorously-drawn tales. The use of pencil as an artistic medium in drawing his appealing, scruffy characters brings an air of informality and spontaneity to his stories. Stevenson adds a wash of soft color to his drawings, avoiding the vivid contrasts of the traditional comic book in favor of a more subtle effect.

"I have no ideas until I sit here with the paper in front of me," Stevenson told Fakih from his office at the *New Yorker.* "I never think of cartoon ideas until I'm here. For children's books, it's a different desk. One of the problems of working is that you try to stay fresh. You can't do it unless you just stop and do something else." To his young audience, Stevenson has continued to provide a fresh, lively view of things. As Karla Kuskin wrote in the *New York Times Book Review,* "Whether writing or drawing, Mr. Stevenson understands perfectly the strength of a simple understated line and a quiet laugh."

WORKS CITED:

Fakih, Kimberly Olsen, "James Stevenson," *Publishers Weekly,* February 27, 1987, pp. 148-149.

Herman, Gertrude, "A Picture Is Worth Several Hundred Words," *Horn Book,* September-October, 1985, p. 605.

Kuskin, Karla, "The Art of Picture Books," *New York Times Book Review,* November 15, 1981, p. 57.

Stevenson, James, *That Terrible Halloween Night,* Greenwillow, 1980.

Stevenson, James, *The Worst Person's Christmas,* Greenwillow, 1991.

FOR MORE INFORMATION SEE:

BOOKS

Children's Literature Review, Volume 17, Gale, 1989, pp. 148-168.

Kingman, Lee, and others, compilers, *Illustrators of Children's Books: 1967-1976,* Horn Book, 1978.

Twentieth Century Children's Writers, third edition, St. James Press, 1989, pp. 919-920.

PERIODICALS

Atlantic, July, 1963.

Best Sellers, August 15, 1967.

Books for Your Children, autumn-winter, 1985, p. 25.

Chicago Tribune Book World, October 5, 1980; April 10, 1983.

Christian Science Monitor, November 6, 1969; November 10, 1980.

Commonweal, November 11, 1977.

Horn Book, August, 1977, pp. 432-433.

Junior Bookshelf, December, 1971, p. 367.

Los Angeles Times Book Review, August 14, 1983.

National Observer, July 24, 1967.

Newsweek, April 8, 1963; July 14, 1969; December 29, 1971; December 11, 1978; December 18, 1978; December 7, 1981.

New Yorker, July 20, 1963; August 5, 1967; December 11, 1971; December 2, 1972; December 6, 1982.

New York Times, August 4, 1972.

New York Times Book Review, July 23, 1967; August 7, 1977; November 13, 1977; April 30, 1978; June 17, 1979; October 7, 1979; April 27, 1980; October 26, 1980; April 26, 1981; April 25, 1982; November 14, 1982; March 27, 1983; April 24, 1983; May 20, 1984.

Saturday Review/World, December 4, 1973.

Spectator, November 13, 1971.

Time, August 4, 1967.

Times Educational Supplement, October 21, 1977; December 14, 1979; March 27, 1981; February 18, 1983, p. 30.

Village Voice, December 11, 1978.

Washington Post Book World, October 26, 1969; April 13, 1980; October 12, 1980; December 13, 1981; May 13, 1984.

* * *

STEVENSON, Robert Louis (Balfour) 1850-1894 (Captain George North)

PERSONAL: Born November 13, 1850, in Edinburgh, Scotland; died December 3, 1894, in Apia, Samoa; buried in Samoa; son of Thomas (a civil engineer) and Margaret (Balfour) Stevenson; married Fanny Van de Grift Osbourne, 1880; children: two stepsons, including Lloyd Osbourne. *Education:* Attended Edinburgh University, 1867-72; studied law in the office of Skene Edwards and Gordon, Edinburgh. *Politics:* Near the end of his life, Stevenson immersed himself in Pacific Island politics. Spending his last years in Samoa, Stevenson publicly criticized Western imperialism and advocated self-rule for the local natives. *Religion:* Church of Scotland, Presbyterian, by upbringing. Although extremely pious as a child, Stevenson announced that he was an agnostic when he was twenty-two years old. The prayers he wrote for family use at Vailima, however, clearly attest that in his later years he had reverted back to Christianity.

CAREER: Novelist, poet, essayist, and writer of travel books. Called to the Scottish bar, 1875, but never practiced. Traveled widely in Europe, America, and the South Sea Islands, finally settling in Samoa in 1890.

Robert Louis Stevenson

AWARDS, HONORS: Silver medal, Royal Scottish Society of Arts, 1871, for a scientific essay on lighthouses.

WRITINGS:

NOVELS

Treasure Island (first published serially under the pseudonym Captain George North in *Young Folks,* 1881-82), Cassell, 1883.
Prince Otto: A Romance, Chatto & Windus, 1885, Roberts Brothers, 1886.
The Strange Case of Dr. Jekyll and Mr. Hyde, Scribner, 1886.
Kidnapped (also see below), Scribner, 1886.
The Black Arrow: A Tale of the Two Roses, Scribner, 1888.
The Master of Ballantrae: A Winter's Tale, Scribner, 1889.
(With Lloyd Osbourne) *The Wrong Box,* Scribner, 1889.
(With Osbourne) *The Wrecker,* illustrated by William Hole and W. L. Metcalf, Scribner, 1892.
David Balfour, Scribner, 1893, published in England as *Catriona: A Sequel to Kidnapped,* Cassell, 1893.
(With Osbourne) *The Ebb-Tide: A Trio and a Quartette,* Stone & Kimball, 1894.
Weir of Hermiston: An Unfinished Romance, Scribner, 1896.
St. Ives; Being the Adventures of a French Prisoner in England (completed by Arthur T. Quiller-Couch), Scribner, 1897.

SHORT STORIES

New Arabian Nights, Holt, 1882.
The Story of a Lie, Hayley & Jackson, 1882, published in America as *The Story of a Lie and Other Tales,* Turner, 1904.
(With Fanny Stevenson) *More New Arabian Nights: The Dynamiter,* Holt, 1885.
The Merry Men and Other Tales and Fables, Scribner, 1887.
The Misadventures of John Nicholson: A Christmas Story, Lovell, 1887.
Island Nights' Entertainments: Consisting of The Beach of Falesa, The Bottle Imp, The Isle of Voices, illustrated by Gordon Browne, Scribner, 1893.
The Body-Snatcher, Merriam, 1895.
Fables, Scribner, 1896.
Tales and Fantasies, Chatto & Windus, 1905.
The Waif Woman, Chatto & Windus, 1916.
When the Devil Well, edited by W. P. Trent, Bibliophile Society, 1921.
Two Mediaeval Tales, illustrated by C. B. Falls, Limited Editions Club, 1929.
Tales and Essays, edited by G. B. Stern, Falcon, 1950.
The Complete Short Stories of Robert Louis Stevenson, edited by Charles Neider, Doubleday, 1969.

POETRY

Not I, and Other Poems, self-illustrated, S. L. Osbourne, 1881.
Moral Emblems, self-illustrated, S. L. Osbourne, 1882.
A Child's Garden of Verses, Scribner, 1885.
Underwoods, Scribner, 1887.
Ballads, Scribner, 1890.
Songs of Travel and Other Verses, edited by Sidney Colvin, Chatto & Windus, 1896.
The Poems and Ballads of Robert Louis Stevenson, Scribner, 1896.
R. L. S. Teuila (fugitive lines and verses), privately printed, 1899.
Poetical Fragments, privately printed, 1915.
An Ode of Horace, privately printed, 1916.
Poems Hitherto Unpublished, edited by G. S. Hellman, two volumes, Bibliophile Society, 1916.
New Poems and Variant Readings, Chatto & Windus, 1918.
The Poems of Robert Louis Stevenson (the complete poems), Gordon Press, 1974.

PLAYS

(With William E. Henley) *Deacon Brodie; or, The Double Life* (also see below), privately printed, 1880.
(With Henley) *Beau Austin* (also see below), privately printed, 1884.
(With Henley) *Admiral Guinea* (also see below), privately printed, 1884.
(With Henley) *Macaire,* privately printed, 1885.
(With Henley) *Three Plays: Deacon Brodie, Beau Austin, Admiral Guinea,* Scribner, 1892.
(With Fanny Stevenson) *The Hanging Judge,* edited by Edmund Gosse, privately printed, 1914.
Monmouth: A Tragedy, edited by C. Vale, Rudge, 1928.

TRAVEL BOOKS

An Inland Voyage, Kegan Paul, 1878, Roberts Brothers, 1883.
Edinburgh: Picturesque Notes, with Etchings, Seeley, Jackson & Halliday, 1879, Macmillan, 1889.
Travels with a Donkey in the Cevennes, Roberts Brothers, 1879.
The Silverado Squatters, Chatto & Windus, 1883, Munro, 1884.
Across the Plains, with Other Memories and Essays, Scribner, 1892.
The Amateur Emigrant from the Clyde to Sandy Hook, Stone & Kimball, 1895.
In the South Seas, Scribner, 1896.
A Mountain Town in France: A Fragment, self-illustrated, J. Lane, 1896.
Essays of Travel, Chatto & Windus, 1905.
Silverado Journal, edited by John E. Jordan, Book Club of California, 1954.
From Scotland to Silverado, edited by James D. Hart, Harvard University Press, 1966.
The Amateur Emigrant with Some First Impressions of America, edited by Roger G. Swearingen, two volumes, Osborne, 1976-77.

ESSAYS

The Pentland Rising, privately printed, 1866.
An Appeal to the Clergy, Blackwood, 1875.
Virginibus Puerisque and Other Papers, Collier, 1881.
Familiar Studies of Men and Books, Chatto & Windus, 1882, Dodd, Mead, 1887.

Some College Memories, University Union Committee (Edinburgh), 1886, Mansfield & Wessels, 1899.
Memories and Portraits, Scribner, 1887.
Memoir of Fleeming Jenkin, Longmans, Green, 1887.
Father Damien: An Open Letter to the Reverend Dr. Hyde of Honolulu, Chatto & Windus, 1890, Mosher, 1897.
A Footnote to History: Eight Years of Trouble in Samoa, Scribner, 1892.
War in Samoa, privately printed, 1893.
Essays and Criticisms, Turner, 1903.
Prayers Written at Vailima, with an Introduction by Mrs. Stevenson, Scribner, 1904.
Essays in the Art of Writing, Chatto & Windus, 1905.
Essays, edited by W. L. Phelps, Scribner, 1906.
Lay Morals and Other Papers, Scribner, 1911.
Records of a Family of Engineers, Chatto & Windus, 1912.
Memoirs of Himself, privately printed, 1912.
On the Choice of a Profession, Chatto & Windus, 1916.
Confessions of a Unionist: An Unpublished Talk on Things Current, Written in 1888, edited by F. V. Livingstone, privately printed, 1921.
The Best Thing in Edinburgh: An Address to the Speculative Society of Edinburgh in March 1873, edited by K. D. Osbourne, Howell, 1923.
Selected Essays, edited by H. G. Rawlinson, Oxford University Press, 1923.
The Manuscripts of Robert Louis Stevenson's "Records of a Family of Engineers": The Unfinished Chapters, edited by J. Christian Bay, Hill, 1929.
The Essays of Robert Louis Stevenson, edited by M. Elwin, Macdonald, 1950.

LETTERS AND DIARIES

Vailima Letters: Robert Louis Stevenson to Sidney Colvin, 1890-1894, Stone & Kimball, 1895.
The Letters of Robert Louis Stevenson to His Family and Friends, edited by S. Colvin, Scribner, 1899.
Autograph Letters, Original Mss., Books, Portraits and Curios from the Library of the Late R. L. Stevenson (catalog of the Anderson Galleries sale of Stevenson's literary property), three volumes, Brown, 1914-16.
(With Fanny Stevenson) *Our Samoan Adventure,* edited by Charles Neider, Harper, 1955.
R. L. S.: Stevenson's Letters to Charles Baxter, edited by De Lancey Ferguson and Marshall Waingrow, Yale University Press, 1956.

COLLECTIONS

The Works of R. L. Stevenson, Edinburgh edition, eighteen volumes, edited by S. Colvin, Chatto & Windus, 1894-98; Thistle edition, twenty-six volumes, Scribner, 1902; Biographical edition, thirty-one volumes, Scribner, 1905-39; Pentland edition, twenty volumes, edited by Edmund Gosse, Cassell, 1906-07; Swanston edition, twenty-five volumes, Chatto & Windus, 1911-12; Tusitala edition, thirty-five volumes, Heinemann, 1923-24; South Seas edition, thirty-two volumes, Scribner, 1925.

OTHER

A Stevenson Medley, edited by S. Colvin, Chatto & Windus 1899.
Robert Louis Stevenson: Hitherto Unpublished Prose Writings, edited by H. H. Harper, Bibliophile Society, 1921.
Castaways of Soledad: A Manuscript by Stevenson Hitherto Unpublished, edited by G. S. Hellman, privately printed, 1928.
The Charity Bazaar: An Allegorical Dialogue, Georgian Press, 1929.
Salute to RLS, edited by F. Holland, Cousland, 1950.
A Newly Discovered Long Story "An Old Song" and a Previously Unpublished Short Story "Edifying Letters of the Rutherford Family," edited by Roger G. Swearingen, Archon, 1982.
Robert Louis Stevenson and "The Beach of Falesa": A Study in Victorian Publishing with the Original Text, edited by Barry Menikoff, Stanford University Press, 1984.

Contributor to the *Illustrated London News,* the *Times,* and numerous magazines, including *Academy, Anthenaeum, Black and White, Contemporary Review, Cornhill Magazine, Edinburgh University Magazine, Fortnightly Review, Fraser's Magazine, London, Longman's Magazine, Macmillan's Magazine, Magazine of Art, New Quarterly Magazine, Pall Mall Gazette, Portfolio, Scribner's Magazine, Temple Bar,* and *Young Folks.* Collections of Stevenson's papers are housed at the Beinecke Rare Book and Manuscript Library, Yale University; the Pierpont Morgan Library, New York City; the Henry E. Huntington Library, San Marino, California; the Widener Library, Harvard University; the Edinburgh Public Library; the Silverado Museum, Saint Helena, California; and the Monterey State Historical Monument Stevenson House, Monterey, California.

ADAPTATIONS:

PLAYS

Robert Brome, *Robert Louis Stevenson's "Markheim,"* (one-act), Eldridge Publishing, 1963.
Brome, *Robert Louis Stevenson's "The Suicide Club,"* (one-act), Eldridge Publishing, 1964.

FILMS

The Bottle Imp, Jesse L. Lasky Feature Play Co., starring Sessue Hayakawa, 1917.
Kidnapped, Thomas A. Edison, Inc., 1917; Twentieth Century-Fox, starring Freddie Bartholomew and Warner Baxter, 1938; Teaching Film Custodians, 1947; Monogram Pictures, starring Roddy McDowall and Dan O'Herlihy, 1948; and Walt Disney, starring James MacArthur and Peter Finch, 1950.
Treasure Island, Fox Film Corp., 1917; Famous Players-Lasky Corp., starring Lon Chaney, 1920; Metro-Goldwyn-Mayer, starring Jackie Cooper, Wallace Beery, and Lionel Barrymore, 1934; Teaching Film Custodians, 1945; Walt Disney Productions, starring Bobby Driscoll and Robert Newton, 1950; and Turner Network Television and Agamemnon Films,

starring Charlton Heston, Christian Bale, and Oliver Reed, 1990.

Dr. Jekyll and Mr. Hyde, Pioneer Film Corp., 1920; Famous Players-Lasky Corp., starring John Barrymore and Nita Naldi, 1920; Paramount Publix Corp., starring Fredric March and Miriam Hopkins, 1932; Metro-Goldwyn-Mayer, starring Spencer Tracy and Ingrid Bergman, 1941; and Sterling Educational Films, 1959.

The White Circle (adaptation of "The Pavilion on the Links"), Famous Players-Lasky Corp., starring John Gilbert, 1920.

Ebb Tide, Famous Players-Lasky Corp., starring Milton Sills, 1922; and Paramount Pictures, starring Ray Milland and Barry Fitzgerald, 1937.

Trouble for Two (adaptation of *The Suicide Club*), Metro-Goldwyn-Mayer, starring Robert Montgomery and Rosalind Russell, 1936.

The Body Snatcher, RKO Radio Pictures, starring Boris Karloff and Bela Lugosi, 1945.

Adventure Island (adaptation of *Ebb Tide*), Paramount Pictures, starring Rory Calhoun and Rhonda Fleming, 1947.

Adventures in Silverado (adaptation of *The Silverado Squatters*), Columbia Pictures, starring William Bishop and Forrest Tucker, 1948.

The Black Arrow, Columbia Pictures, starring Louis Hayward and Janet Blair, 1948; and Walt Disney, starring Oliver Reed and Stephan Chase.

Lodging for the Night, Realm Television Productions, 1949.

Lord Maletroit's Door, Realm Television Productions, 1949.

The Secret of St. Ives, Columbia Pictures, starring Richard Ney and Vanessa Brown, 1949.

The Treasure of Franchard, Realm Television Productions, 1949.

The Imp in the Bottle, General Television Enterprises, 1950.

The Strange Door (adaptation of "The Sire de Maletroit's Door"), Universal International Pictures, starring Charles Laughton and Boris Karloff, 1951.

The Treasure of Lost Cannon (adaptation of "The Treasure of Franchard"), Universal International Pictures, starring William Powell, 1951.

The Master of Ballantrae, Warner Brothers, starring Errol Flynn, 1953; and six half-hour episodes by Time Life Television and BBC Enterprises, starring Julian Glover and Brian Cox.

Long John Silver (based on characters from *Treasure Island*), Distributors Corp. of America, starring Robert Newton, 1955.

The Wrong Box, Columbia Pictures, starring John Mills, Peter Sellers, Ralph Richardson, and Michael Caine, 1966.

A Child's Garden of Verses, Sterling Educational Films, 1967; McGraw-Hill, 1968; and University of California Extension Media Center, 1974.

Treasure Island was also adapted into the films *Treasure Island Revisited* and *Treasure Island with Mr. Magoo,* both by Macmillan Films; *Treasure Island with Mr. Magoo* also ran as a thirty minute television series with Robert Newton.

FILMSTRIPS

Kidnapped, Eye Gate House, 1958; Encyclopaedia Britannica Films, 1961; and Carman Educational Associates, 1966.

Treasure Island, Encyclopaedia Britannica Films, 1960; Carman Educational Associates, 1966; Jam Handy School Service, 1968; Dufour Editions, 1969; Walt Disney Educational Materials, 1970; Universal Education and Visual Arts, 1971; Educational Record Sales, 1971; McGraw-Hill, 1972; and Teaching Resources Films, 1974.

The Owl and the Pussy-Cat [and] *My Shadow* (the first poem by Edward Lear, the second by Stevenson), Cooper Films and Records, 1969.

Garden of Verses (transparencies), Creative Visuals, 1970.

Highlights from Treasure Island, Encyclopaedia Britannica Educational Corp., 1973.

RECORDINGS

Treasure Island (record or cassette), read by Ian Richardson, Caedmon; Spoken Arts, 1971.

Treasury of Great Educational Records (includes *Treasure Island;* twelve records), Miller-Brody Productions; also with *Robin Hood,* Columbia Special Products, 1977.

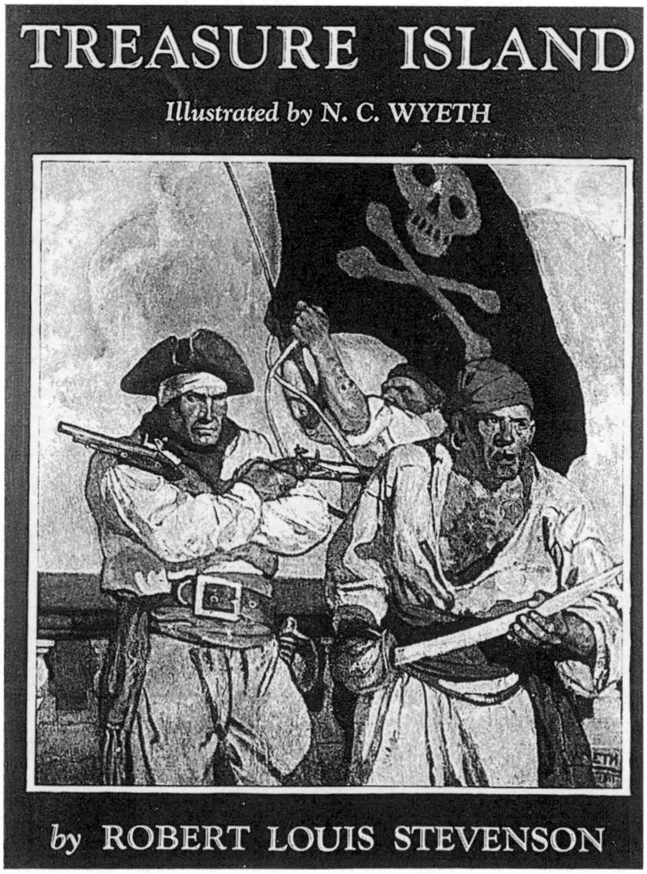

Cover of *Treasure Island,* by Robert Louis Stevenson. Illustrated by N. C. Wyeth.

Adventure Library (includes *Kidnapped* and *Treasure Island;* ten records or sixteen cassettes), Miller-Brody Productions.

Adventure Poets (five cassettes), United Learning.

A Child's Garden of Verses (two records), read by Nancy Wickwire and Basil Langton, Miller-Brody Productions; also read by Dame Judith Anderson, Caedmon.

Dr. Jekyll and Mr. Hyde (three records or cassettes), read by Patrick Horgan, Miller-Brody Productions.

Kidnapped (parts 1 and 2, cassettes only), read by John Franklyn, Alan MacDonald, Pamela Mant, David Thorndike, and Derek Young, Spoken Arts.

Markheim by Robert Louis Stevenson, CMS Records.

Poetry in Song, Crofut Productions.

The Strange Case of Dr. Jekyll and Mr. Hyde, Caedmon; (parts 1 & 2, cassettes only), Spoken Arts.

SIDELIGHTS: Robert Louis Stevenson is best known as the author of the children's classic *Treasure Island,* and the adult horror story, *The Strange Case of Dr. Jekyll and Mr. Hyde.* Both of these novels have curious origins. A map of an imaginary island gave Stevenson the idea for the first story, and a nightmare supplied the premise of the second. In addition to memorable origins, these tales also share Stevenson's key theme: the impossibility of identifying and separating good and evil. *Treasure Island*'s Long John Silver is simultaneously a courageous friend and a treacherous cutthroat, and Dr. Jekyll, who is not wholly good but a mixture of good and evil, is eventually ruled by Hyde because of his own moral weakness. With Silver, Jekyll, and others, Stevenson set standards for complex characterization which were adopted by later writers. His method of rendering ambiguous, enigmatic personalities was one of Stevenson's greatest literary contributions.

Born in Edinburgh, Scotland, on November 13, 1850, Stevenson was the only child of Thomas Stevenson and Margaret Balfour. Inheriting the weak lungs of his mother, he was an invalid from birth. Before he was two years old, a young woman named Alison Cunningham joined the household to act as his nurse. It was to her that Stevenson dedicated *A Child's Garden of Verses* over thirty years later. The sheltered, bedridden nature of his childhood is revealed in this collection through poems like "The Land of Counterpane."

Not all of his childhood was spent in the sickroom, though. During the summer he lived in the country at Colinton Manse where he played outdoors with his many cousins. Most sources say Stevenson was six years old when, competing against his cousins, he won a prize from one of his Balfour uncles for a history of Moses. His next composition was "The Book of Joseph." Stevenson's first published work, *The Pentland Rising,* was also on a religious theme, recounting an unsuccessful rebellion by Covenanters in 1666. Stevenson wrote the account when he was sixteen, and his father had the pamphlet published at his own expense. As these compositions show, young Stevenson was tremendously influenced by the strong religious convictions of his parents. During his college years, however, his beliefs underwent a sharp reversal.

He had attended school since he was seven, but his attendance was irregular because of poor health and because his father doubted the value of formal education. Later, however, Stevenson's father was severely disappointed with his son's performance at the University of Edinburgh. Stevenson entered the university when he was sixteen, planning to become a lighthouse engineer like his father. Instead of applying himself to his studies, he became known for his outrageous dress and behavior. Sporting a wide-brimmed hat and a boy's velveteen coat, Stevenson was called "Velvet Jacket." In the company of his cousin Bob, Stevenson smoked hashish and visited brothels while exploring the seamy side of Edinburgh. At twenty-two, he declared himself an agnostic, crowning his father's disappointment in him.

In order to appease his father, Stevenson studied law. He was called to the bar in 1875, but never practiced. While at the university, Stevenson had trained himself to be a writer by imitating the styles of authors William Hazlitt and Daniel Defoe, among others. Before and after receiving his law degree, Stevenson's essays were published in several periodicals. A constant traveler for most of his adult life, he based his first two books, *An Inland Voyage* (1878) and *Travels with a Donkey in the Cevennes* (1879), on his excursions in France. Many of his journeys were searches for climates which would ease his poor health, but he also had an innate wanderlust. His trip to America in 1879, however, was made to pursue a woman.

Three years earlier, Stevenson had met Fanny Van de Grift Osbourne, an American woman eleven years his senior, at an artist's colony near Paris. At the time she was separated from her husband and living abroad with her two children. Although Stevenson fell in love with her, Fanny returned to her California home and husband in 1878. But in August of the following year, Stevenson received a mysterious cable from her and responded by immediately leaving Scotland for America.

The journey almost killed him. On August 18, 1879, Stevenson landed in New York having traveled steerage across the Atlantic. Already ill, his health became worse as a result of crossing the American plains in an emigrant train. Impoverished, sick, and starving, he lived in Monterey and then San Francisco, nearly dying in both places. His suffering was rewarded, for Fanny obtained a divorce from her husband, and on May 19, 1880, she and Stevenson were married. For the honeymoon, the couple, Fanny's son Lloyd, and the family dog went to Mount Saint Helena and lived in a rundown shack at Silverado. All of Stevenson's American adventures became material for his writing. *Silverado Squatters* (1883) chronicles his honeymoon experiences, while *Across the Plains, with Other Memories and Essays* (1892) and *The Amateur Emigrant from the Clyde to Sandy Hook* (1895) relate his trip to California. Only a year after he had left Scotland to pursue her, Stevenson brought Fanny back to his own country. He, Fanny, and Lloyd eventually settled in a Braemar cottage in the summer of 1881, where Stevenson began writing *Treasure Island.*

Lloyd, Stevenson's twelve-year-old stepson, was confined inside the cottage during a school holiday because of rain, so he amused himself by drawing pictures. Stevenson recalled in his *Essays in the Art of Writing* that he would sometimes "join the artist (so to speak) at the easel, and pass the afternoon with him in a generous emulation, making coloured drawings. On one of these occasions, I made the map of an island; it was elaborately and (I thought) beautifully coloured; the shape of it took my fancy beyond expression; it contained harbours that pleased me like sonnets; and with the unconsciousness of the predestined, I ticketed my performance 'Treasure Island.'"

Filling in the map with names like "Spye-Glass Hill" and marking the location of hidden treasure with crosses, Stevenson conceived the idea of a pirate adventure story to supplement the drawing: "the future characters of the book began to appear there visibly among imaginary woods; and their brown faces and bright weapons peeped out upon me from unexpected quarters, as they passed to and fro, fighting and hunting treasure, on these few square inches of a flat projection. The next thing I knew I had some papers before me and was writing out a list of chapters." He had completed a draft of chapter one by the next morning.

On October 1, 1881, *Young Folks* magazine began publishing the tale serially under the pseudonym of Captain George North. In this medium, the story received little notice. Fanny confessed that she didn't like *Treasure Island* and was against it ever appearing in book form. Nevertheless, it was published as a book late in 1883 and became a best seller. In Stevenson's lifetime the number of copies sold reached the tens of thousands. Reviewers declared that this work of sheer entertainment had single-handedly liberated children's literature from a constraining, didactic rut.

In 1882 Stevenson and Fanny moved to Hyeres in the South of France. There Stevenson suffered a hemorrhage which confined him to bed, prevented him from speaking, and rendered him incapable of writing prose. Simple verse was within his capabilities, so while he recovered he wrote most of *A Child's Garden of Verses* (1885). Stevenson had followed up *Treasure Island* with another boy's adventure story called *The Black Arrow,* which was published serially in *Young Folks* in 1883 and as a book in 1888. Although more popular with the juvenile readers of *Young Folks* than *Treasure Island* had been, *The Black Arrow* is far from being a classic. His next serial was a distinct improvement. *Kidnapped* ran in *Young Folks* in 1886 and was published as a book the same year. Set in the Scottish Highlands in 1751, the story relates the wanderings of young David Balfour in the company of the reckless Alan Breck. *Kidnapped* was an achievement on a level with *Treasure Island,* and its characters are in many ways superior. Jim Hawkins and Long John Silver of the earlier book are charming stereotypes, but Balfour and Breck are personalities with psychological depth. Seven years after *Kidnapped,* Stevenson wrote a sequel called *Catriona,* but it did not measure up to the original work.

Kidnapped was written in Bournemouth, England, which had been the Stevensons' home since 1884. Although the novel earned Stevenson some recognition, it was not his biggest success in 1886, for this year also marked the publication of *The Strange Case of Dr. Jekyll and Mr. Hyde.* This novel was sparked by a dream Stevenson had at Bournemouth in which he visualized a man changing into a monster by means of a concoction made with white powder. Stevenson was screaming in his sleep when Fanny woke him. He scolded her for interrupting the nightmare: "I was dreaming a fine bogey tale," he said. He started writing furiously in bed the next morning. In three days he had a completed draft of almost 40,000 words. He read the story proudly to Fanny and Lloyd, but Fanny's reaction was strangely reserved. Finally she declared that Stevenson should have written an allegory instead of a straight piece of sensationalism. A heated argument arose which drove Lloyd from the room. Even though Fanny's instincts about *Treasure Island* had proven to be completely wrong, this time Stevenson heeded her advice. Throwing the first manuscript into the fire, he rewrote the tale as an allegory in another three days, and then polished it over six weeks. Although he would later claim that it was the worst thing he ever wrote, *Dr. Jekyll and Mr. Hyde* sold forty thousand copies in Britain during the first six months, and brought Stevenson more attention than he had previously ever known.

After living temporarily at Saranac Lake, New York in 1887, Stevenson, Fanny, Lloyd, and Stevenson's widowed mother began touring the South Pacific the following year. Eventually, the clan settled on the island of Upolu in Samoa in 1890. At the foot of Mount Vaea, Stevenson had a house built which was called Vailima. Continuing to write, he also became an advocate for the Samoans who named him "Tusitala," teller of tales. On December 3, 1894, at forty-four years of age, Stevenson died of a cerebral hemorrhage. He left unfinished *Weir of Hermiston,* which promised to be his single greatest work. A path was cleared by nearly sixty Samoan men to the summit of Mount Vaea, where Stevenson was buried.

Immediately after his death, biographers and commentators praised Stevenson lavishly, but this idealized portrait was attacked in the 1920s and 1930s by critics who labeled his prose as imitative and pretentious and who made much of Stevenson's college-day follies. In the 1950s and 1960s, however, his work was reconsidered and finally taken seriously by the academic community. Outside of academia, *Treasure Island* and *Dr. Jekyll and Mr. Hyde* continue to be widely read over a century after they were first published, and show promise of remaining popular for centuries to come.

WORKS CITED:

Stevenson, Robert Louis, "My First Book: 'Treasure Island,'" in his *Essays in the Art of Writing,* Chatto & Windus, 1905, pp. 111-131.

FOR MORE INFORMATION SEE:

BOOKS

Bingham, Jane M., editor, *Writers for Children,* Scribner, 1988.
Chevalier, Tracy, editor, *Twentieth-Century Children's Writers,* St. James Press, 1989.
Daiches, David, *Robert Louis Stevenson and His World,* Thames & Hudson, 1973.
Dictionary of Literary Biography, Gale, Volume 18: *Victorian Novelists after 1885,* 1983, Volume 57: *Victorian Prose Writers after 1867,* 1987.
Hennessy, James Pope, *Robert Louis Stevenson,* Simon and Schuster, 1974.

OTHER

Robert Louis Stevenson (filmstrip and cassette), January Productions, 1985.
Meet the Newbery Author: Robert Louis Stevenson (videocassette and filmstrip), Random House.

* * *

STOCKTON, Francis Richard 1834-1902 (Frank R. Stockton; Paul Fort, John Lewees, pseudonyms)

PERSONAL: Born April 5, 1834, in Blockley, PA; died of a cerebral hemorrhage, April 20, 1902, in Washington, DC; buried in Woodlands Cemetery, PA; son of William Smith (a Methodist minister and writer) and Emily Hepzibeth (a school administrator; maiden name, Drean) Stockton; married Marian Edwards Tuttle (a teacher), 1860. *Education:* Attended public schools in Philadelphia, PA.

ADDRESSES: *Home*—"Claymont," near Charles Town, WV, and New York (winters).

CAREER: Novelist, short-story writer, and editor. Apprenticed as a wood-engraver, 1852, working as an engraver until 1870. Worked as a free-lance writer for several newspapers and periodicals in the late 1860s. *Hearth and Home,* assistant editor, 1868-73; *Scribner's Monthly* (later *Century*), member of editorial staff, beginning in 1872; *St. Nicholas,* assistant editor, 1873-78.

MEMBER: Century Club, Authors Club.

AWARDS, HONORS: Lewis Carroll Shelf Award, 1963, for *The Griffin and the Minor Canon,* and 1969, for *The Storyteller's Pack: A Frank R. Stockton Reader.*

Francis Richard Stockton

WRITINGS:

CHILDREN'S BOOKS UNDER NAME FRANK R. STOCKTON

Ting-a-Ling (fairy tale collection; title story first appeared in *Riverside Magazine for Young People,* 1867; also see below), illustrated by E. B. Bensell, Hurd & Houghton, 1870, published as *Ting-a-Ling Tales,* illustrated by Richard Floethe, Scribner, 1955.
Round-about Rambles in Lands of Fact and Fancy, Scribner, Armstrong, 1872.
What Might Have Been Expected, illustrated by Sol Eytinge and others, Dodd, 1874.
Tales Out of School, Scribner, Armstrong, 1876, new edition, 1903.
A Jolly Fellowship, Scribner, 1880.
The Floating Prince and Other Fairy Tales (also see below), Scribner, 1881.
The Story of Viteau, Scribner, 1884.
The Bee-Man of Orn and Other Fanciful Tales, Scribner, 1887, published as *The Bee-Man of Orn,* illustrated by Maurice Sendak, Holt, 1964.
Personally Conducted (travel book), illustrated by Joseph Pannell and others, Scribner, 1889.
The Clocks of Rondaine and Other Stories, illustrated by E. H. Blashfield and others, Scribner, 1892.
Fanciful Tales, edited by Julia Elizabeth Langworthy, Scribner, 1894.

New Jersey: From the Discovery of the Scheyichbi to Recent Times (history), Appleton Davies, 1896, reissued as *Stories of New Jersey,* American Book Co., 1896.

Captain Chap; or, The Rolling Stones, illustrated by Charles H. Stephens, Lippincott, 1897, published as *The Young Master of Hyson Hall,* illustrated by Virginia Davisson and Stephens, Lippincott, 1900.

A Storyteller's Pack (collection), illustrated by Peter Newell, E. W. Kemble, and others, Scribner, 1897, published as *The Storyteller's Pack: A Frank R. Stockton Reader,* illustrated by Bernarda Bryson, 1968.

Buccaneers and Pirates of Our Coasts (history), illustrated by George Varian and B. West Clinedinst, Macmillan, 1898.

Kate Bonnet: The Romance of a Pirate's Daughter, illustrated by A. J. Keller and H. S. Potter, Appleton Davies, 1902.

The Queen's Museum, and Other Fanciful Tales (also see below), illustrated by Frederick Richardson, Scribner, 1906.

The Poor Count's Christmas, with illustrations from drawings by Bensell, F. A. Stokes, 1927.

The Reformed Pirate: Stories from "The Floating Prince," "Ting-a-Ling," and "The Queen's Museum," illustrated by Reginald Birch, Scribner, 1936.

The Griffin and the Minor Canon (fairy tale), illustrated by Sendak, Holt, 1963.

Old Pipes and the Dryad (fairy tale), illustrated by Catherine Hanley, F. Watts, 1968.

ADULT BOOKS UNDER NAME FRANK R. STOCKTON

(With wife, Marian Stockton) *The Home: Where It Should Be and What To Put in It* (nonfiction), Putnam, 1873.

Rudder Grange (also see below), Scribner, 1879.

The Lady, or the Tiger? and Other Stories (title story first appeared in *Century,* November, 1882), illustrated by Wladyslaw T. Benda, Scribner, 1884.

The Transferred Ghost, Scribner, 1884.

The Casting Away of Mrs. Lecks and Mrs. Aleshine (also see below), illustrated by George Richards, Century, 1886.

Stockton's Stories: The Christmas Wreck and Other Stories, Scribner, 1886.

The Late Mrs. Null, Scribner, 1886.

The Hundredth Man, Century, 1887.

The Dusantes (sequel to *The Casting Away of Mrs. Lecks and Mrs. Aleshine*), Century, 1888, published as *The Casting Away of Mrs. Lecks and Mrs. Aleshine* [and] *The Dusantes,* Appleton-Century, 1933.

Amos Kilbright: His Adscititious Experiences, with Other Stories, Scribner, 1888.

The Stories of the Three Burglars, Dodd, 1889.

The Great War Syndicate, Collier, 1889.

Ardis Claverden, Dodd, 1890.

The Merry Chanter, Century, 1890.

The House of Martha, Houghton, 1891.

The Squirrel Inn, Century, 1891.

The Rudder Grangers Abroad and Other Stories (sequel to *Rudder Grange*), Scribner, 1891.

My Terminal Moraine, Collier, 1892.

The Watchmaker's Wife and Other Stories, Scribner, 1893.

Pomona's Travels (sequel to *Rudder Grange*), Scribner, 1894.

The Adventures of Captain Horn, Scribner, 1895.

A Chosen Few: Short Stories, Scribner, 1895.

Mrs. Cliff's Yacht, Scribner, 1896.

The Girl at Cobhurst, Scribner, 1898.

The Great Stone of Sardis, Harper, 1898.

The Associate Hermits, Harper, 1899.

The Vizier of the Two-Horned Alexander, illustrated by Birch, Century, 1899.

The Novels and Stories of Frank Stockton, twenty-three volumes, Scribner, 1899-1904.

Afield and Afloat, Scribner, 1900.

A Bicycle of Cathay, Harper, 1900.

John Gayther's Garden and the Stories Told Therein, Scribner, 1902.

The Captain's Toll-Gate, Appleton Davies, 1903.

The Magic Egg and Other Stories, Scribner, 1907.

Fable and Fiction: Frank Stockton, selected by J. I. Rodale, Story Classics, 1949.

Best Short Stories, Scribner, 1957.

The Science Fiction of Frank Stockton: An Anthology, Gregg Press, 1976.

OTHER

Contributor to *My Favorite Novelist* (essays), privately printed, 1908. Illustrator of *Poems,* written by brother, Thomas Hewlings Stockton, 1862. Contributor of articles and short stories, under pseudonyms Paul Fort and John Lewees, to *St. Nicholas;* also contributor to additional periodicals, including *Southern Literary Messenger, Lippincott's, Youth's Companion, Round Table, Saturday Press, Vanity Fair,* and others.

ADAPTATIONS:

MOTION PICTURES AND FILMSTRIPS

Fantasy (motion picture; based on "Old Applejoy's Ghost"), Paramount, 1927.

The Lady, or the Tiger? (motion picture), Metro-Goldwyn-Mayer, 1942, Marshall Grant-Realm Television Productions, 1949, Encyclopaedia Britannica Educational Corp., 1969.

The Lady, or the Tiger? (filmstrip with cassette), Listening Library, 1977.

PLAYS

The Lady, or the Tiger? (operetta; libretto by Sydney Rosenfeld), produced in New York at Wallack's Theatre, 1888.

The Apple Tree (three one-act plays, including the one-act play *The Lady, or the Tiger?*), produced on Broadway, 1966.

Eleanor Harder and Ray Harder, *Good Grief, a Griffin* (operetta; based on *The Griffin and the Minor Canon*), Anchorage Press, 1968.

Marathon 81 (four one-act plays, including a one-act play by Shel Silverstein loosely based on *The Lady, or the Tiger?*), first produced at Ensemble Studio Theater, 1981; later produced as *Wild Life,* at the Vandam Theatre, 1983.

From *The Lady, or the Tiger? and Other Stories,* by Francis Richard Stockton. Illustrated by Wladyslaw T. Benda.

Other play adaptations include: Lewy Olfson's *The Lady, or the Tiger?,* published in *Plays,* May, 1962; Adele Thane's *Old Pipes and the Dryad,* published in *Plays,* January, 1964; and Olfson's *The Transferred Ghost,* published in *Classics Adapted for Acting and Reading,* Plays, 1970.

RECORDINGS

The Lady, or the Tiger? [and] *The Dicourager of Hesitancy,* read by Judith Anderson, Caedmon, 1970.

The Lady, or the Tiger?, in *Tales for a Winter's Night,* read by John Carradine, Pelican Records, 1976.

The Casting Away of Mrs. Lecks and Mrs. Aleshine, American Forces Radio and Television Service, 1978.

SIDELIGHTS: During his day Francis Richard Stockton was considered one of the country's leading men of letters; William Dean Howells rated his contribution to American literature second only to Mark Twain. In addition to writing a number of stories for children and young adults, most notably "The Lady, or the Tiger?," Stockton also worked as an editor for several juvenile magazines, including the prestigious *St. Nicholas.* Stockton's "work is never more than charming and enchanting," asserted Michael Patrick Hearn in *Writers for Children.* "And that may be why he is such a superior writer for children."

Stockton was born on April 5, 1834, in Blockley, Pennsylvania, to William Smith Stockton and his second wife, Emily Drean Stockton. The couple had lost their previous two children, and Stockton was himself a slight child. He was born with one leg shorter than the other, but his fragile health did not limit his physical activities—he enjoyed playing outdoors just as much as the town's other boys.

Stockton's family was a literary one. His father, once a prominent organizer in the Methodist church, had turned more to writing after being dismissed as the superintendent of the Philadelphia Alms House for mismanagement of funds. Stockton began his own literary career at a young age: "I was very young when I determined to write some fairy tales because my mind was full of them . . . . These were constructed according to my own ideas," remembered Stockton in *The Storyteller's Pack: A Frank R. Stockton Reader.* "I caused the fanciful creatures who inhabited the world of fairy-land to act, as far as possible for them to do so, as if they were inhabitants of the real world. I did not dispense with monsters and enchanters or talking birds and beasts, but I obliged these creatures to infuse into their extraordinary actions a certain level of common sense." Stockton continued to write stories throughout his school career, and while at Central High School he encountered his first success as a writer, winning a short-story contest sponsored by the *Boys' and Girls' Journal.*

After leaving high school in 1852, Stockton wanted to continue his literary apprenticeship, but he was compelled by his father to pursue a more practical career. He became a wood engraver, but continued over the next five years to meet with his brother and the other members of his "Forensic and Literary Circle." During this time his first stories were published: in 1855 the *American Courier* ran his "The Slight Mistake," and four years later the *Southern Literary Messenger* published "Kate."

In 1860 Stockton married Marian Edwards Tuttle, a South Carolinian who taught at his mother's school. From his wife and his mother, a native Virginian, Stockton gained a certain sympathy for the southern cause, and over the next year he wrote several pieces on secessionist themes: "A Story of Champaigne," which was serialized in the *Southern Literary Messenger,* and *A Northern Voice for the Dissolution of the Union of the United States of America.* The pamphlet, which he had privately printed, was withdrawn after Fort Sumter fell.

As the craft of wood engraving became increasingly obsolete, Stockton turned more to writing as his means of support. He wrote for the *Philadelphia Press* and the *Philadelphia Morning Post* and also published stories in children's magazines and humor magazines such as *Puck.* The 1867 appearance of a fairy story, "Ting-a-

Ling," in *Riverside Magazine* launched his writing career in earnest. The story, which relates the adventures of the elfin title character, is full of bizarre fancy; its book appearance in 1870 earned notice from Mary Mapes Dodge, the children's editor of *Hearth and Home,* who in 1868 asked Stockton to be her assistant. Stockton's chief duty was to provide filler for the children's page of the magazine, which entailed writing on any subject from turtles' eggs to etiquette. He also had the opportunity to write more fairy stories, most of which took the form of the day, sickly sweet and moralistic. When, in 1873, Dodge was asked to edit the new children's magazine *St. Nicholas,* she brought Stockton with her as part of her staff.

Despite an impressive list of contributors, including Lewis Carroll, Louisa May Alcott, and Henry Wadsworth Longfellow, Dodge and Stockton were forced to write much of the early issues of *St. Nicholas* themselves. Stockton signed his pieces with pseudonyms he had contrived from the names of his brothers and sister. By 1876 the stress of working for the magazine had worsened his eyesight, already weakened by his years as an engraver. He took an extended vacation to recover, but the condition persisted. Further tragedy struck when his brother John died in 1877. The next year Stockton resigned his post, but he continued to contribute to the magazine. Although his eyesight improved slightly thereafter, for the rest of his life he had to dictate his stories, first to his wife and later to a secretary.

By the time he left *St. Nicholas* Stockton had already achieved modest success as a writer. *What Might Have Been Expected,* which had been originally serialized in *St. Nicholas,* was published in book form in 1874, and *Tales Out of School,* a mixture of sketches and informational pieces, was published in 1876. In 1879 Stockton achieved his literary breakthrough with *Rudder Grange,* the story of a couple and their servant girl, Pomona. The novel was successful enough to be followed by two sequels.

In 1881 Stockton published *The Floating Prince and Other Tales,* also a collection of his *St. Nicholas* material. Then in 1882 *Century Magazine* published what has remained his most famous work. "The Lady, or the Tiger?" tells the story of a young man who falls in love with a princess. Their romance angers her father the king, who orders that his daughter's suitor be put in a room with two doors: behind one door waits a beautiful woman, the other a tiger. The princess tells her admirer to choose the door on the right—but is she deceiving him? Stockton ends the story without revealing the answer. The impact of "The Lady, or the Tiger?" was enormous. It was made into a play and later a film; Robert Browning even wrote a poem in which he provided a solution, and Hindu scholars probed the problem. Although Stockton was flooded with letters requesting the answer, he never satisfied their curiosity, realizing, probably, that the story's success lay in the ambiguity of its ending.

Other collections and novels published during the 1880s confirmed Stockton's reputation as one of the country's most notable humorists. In 1887 *The Bee-Man of Orn and Other Fanciful Tales,* which included his most significant contributions to children's writing, was published. The reprinting in the 1960s of two of the stories from that volume, *The Bee-Man of Orn* and *The Griffin and the Minor Canon,* with new illustrations by Maurice Sendak, was responsible for a brief revival of interest in Stockton's work.

For the last decade of his life Stockton continued to write stories and novels, but he became rather reclusive. He traveled some, but his increasingly fragile health forced him to remain at his large homes, first in New Jersey and then near Charles Town, West Virginia. The political tensions between the United States and Great Britain over Venezuela in the last years of the nineteenth century moved Stockton to devote much of his literary effort to ridiculing imperialism and war in such collections as *Afield and Afloat* (1900). In 1902 Stockton took a rare trip to New York and Washington, D.C., accepting an invitation to attend a National Academy of Science banquet in the capital. While there he fell ill and died on April 20 of a cerebral hemorrhage.

Toward the end of his life Stockton already had a sense that the literary world was leaving him behind; and in fact after his death he was quickly forgotten by all but his most loyal following. A spurious last addition to his literary works came in 1913, when a woman named Etta De Camp published a collection of stories she claimed Stockton dictated to her from beyond the grave. Since then, however, the once-famous author has stayed securely dead, known only for his famous literary puzzle. His large body of children's stories has not received much attention, and his importance to the genre is now evaluated mainly in terms of his editorship of *St. Nicholas,* establishing a standard of excellence for that magazine and lending prestige to children's writing in general.

WORKS CITED:

Hearn, Michael Patrick, essay in *Writers for Children,* edited by Jane M. Bingham, Scribner, 1988.

Stockton, Frank, *The Storyteller's Pack: A Frank R. Stockton Reader,* Scribner, 1968.

FOR MORE INFORMATION SEE:

BOOKS

Chevalier, Tracy, editor, *Twentieth-Century Children's Writers,* 3rd edition, St. James Press, 1989.

Dictionary of Literary Biography, Gale, Volume 42: *American Writers for Children before 1900,* 1985, and Volume 74: *American Short-Story Writers before 1880,* 1988.

Golemba, Henry, *Frank Stockton,* Twayne, 1981.

Griffin, Martin I. J., *Frank R. Stockton: A Critical Biography,* University of Pennsylvania Press, 1939.

PERIODICALS

Atlantic Monthly, January, 1887; January, 1901.

Book Buyer, February, 1900; June, 1902.
Library Journal, December 15, 1967; February 15, 1969.
Times Literary Supplement, November 30, 1967; April 2, 1976.

* * *

STOCKTON, Frank R.
See STOCKTON, Francis Richard

* * *

STOLZ, Mary (Slattery) 1920-

PERSONAL: Born March 24, 1920, in Boston, MA; daughter of Thomas Francis and Mary Margaret (a nurse; maiden name, Burgey) Slattery; married Stanley Burr Stolz (a civil engineer), January, 1940 (divorced, 1956); married Thomas C. Jaleski (a physician), June, 1965; children: (first marriage) William. *Education:* Attended Birch Wathen School, Columbia University Teacher's College, 1936-38, and Katharine Gibbs School, 1938-39. *Politics:* "Liberal Northern Democrat." *Hobbies and other interests:* Social and environmental issues, ballet, baseball, cats, hard games of Scrabble, bird-watching, reading.

ADDRESSES: Home—P.O. Box 82, Longboat Key, FL 34228. *Agent*—Roslyn Targ Literary Agency, 105 West 13th St., Suite 15E, New York, NY 10011.

CAREER: Writer of books for children and young adults. Worked variously as a bookstore clerk and secretary.

MEMBER: Authors League of America.

AWARDS, HONORS: Notable Book citation, American Library Association (ALA), 1951, for *The Sea Gulls Woke Me;* Children's Book Award, Child Study Children's Book Committee at Bank Street College, 1953, for *In a Mirror;* Spring Book Festival Older Honor Award, *New York Herald Tribune,* 1953, for *Ready or Not,* 1956, for *The Day and the Way We Met,* and 1957, for *Because of Madeline;* ALA Notable Book citation, 1961, for *Belling the Tiger;* Newbery Award Honor Book designation, 1962, for *Belling the Tiger,* and 1966, for *The Noonday Friends;* Junior Book Award, Boys' Club of America, 1964, for *The Bully of Barkham Street;* Honor List citation, *Boston Globe/Horn Book* and National Book Award finalist, Association of American Publishers, both 1975, for *The Edge of Next Year;* Recognition of Merit award, George G. Stone Center for Children's Books, 1982, for entire body of work; ALA Notable Book citation, 1985, for *Quentin Corn;* Children's Science Book Younger Honor Award, New York Academy of Sciences, 1986, for *Night of Ghosts and Hermits: Nocturnal Life on the Seashore;* German Youth Festival Award; ALA Notable Book citation, Notable Children's Trade Books in Social Studies, Children's Book Council, both 1988, and Teacher's Choice citation, International Reading Association, 1989, all for

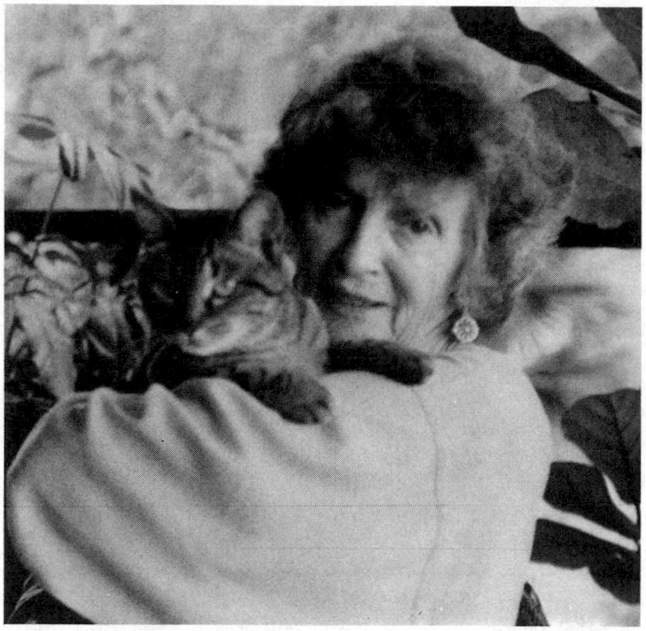

Mary Stolz

Storm in the Night; numerous other ALA Notable Book citations.

WRITINGS:

FOR YOUNG ADULTS

To Tell Your Love, Harper, 1950.
The Organdy Cupcakes, Harper, 1951.
The Sea Gulls Woke Me, Harper, 1951.
In a Mirror, Harper, 1953.
Ready or Not, Harper, 1953.
Pray Love, Remember, Harper, 1954.
Two by Two, Houghton, 1954, revised edition published as *A Love, or a Season,* Harper, 1964.
Rosemary, Harper, 1955.
Hospital Zone, Harper, 1956.
The Day and the Way We Met, Harper, 1956.
Good-by My Shadow, Harper, 1957.
Because of Madeline, Harper, 1957.
And Love Replied, Harper, 1958.
Second Nature, Harper, 1958.
Some Merry-Go-Round Music, Harper, 1959.
The Beautiful Friend and Other Stories, Harper, 1960.
Wait for Me, Michael, Harper, 1961.
Who Wants Music on Monday?, Harper, 1963.
By the Highway Home, Harper, 1971.
Leap before You Look, Harper, 1972.
The Edge of Next Year, Harper, 1974.
Cat in the Mirror, Harper, 1975.
Ferris Wheel, Harper, 1977.
Cider Days, Harper, 1978.
Go and Catch a Flying Fish, Harper, 1979.
What Time of Night Is It?, Harper, 1981.
Ivy Larkin: A Novel, Harcourt, 1986.

FOR CHILDREN

The Leftover Elf, illustrated by Peggy Bacon, Harper, 1952.

Emmett's Pig, illustrated by Garth Williams, Harper, 1959.

A Dog on Barkham Street (also see below), illustrated by Leonard Shortall, Harper, 1960.

Belling the Tiger, illustrated by Beni Montresor, Harper, 1961.

The Great Rebellion (also see below), illustrated by Montresor, Harper, 1961.

Fredou, illustrated by Tomi Ungerer, Harper, 1962.

Pigeon Flight, illustrated by Murray Tinkelman, Harper, 1962.

Siri, the Conquistador (also see below), illustrated by Montresor, Harper, 1963.

The Bully of Barkham Street (also see below), illustrated by Shortall, Harper, 1963.

The Mystery of the Woods, illustrated by Uri Shulevitz, Harper, 1964.

The Noonday Friends, illustrated by Louis S. Glanzman, Harper, 1965.

Maximilian's World (also see below), illustrated by Shulevitz, Harper, 1966.

A Wonderful, Terrible Time, illustrated by Glanzman, Harper, 1967.

Say Something, illustrated by Edward Frascino, Harper, 1968, revised edition illustrated by Alexander Koshkin, 1993.

The Story of a Singular Hen and Her Peculiar Children, illustrated by Frascino, Harper, 1969.

The Dragons of the Queen, illustrated by Frascino, Harper, 1969.

Juan, illustrated by Glanzman, Harper, 1970.

Land's End, illustrated by Dennis Hermanson, Harper, 1973.

Cat Walk, illustrated by Erik Blegvad, Harper, 1983.

Quentin Corn, illustrated by Pamela Johnson, David Godine, 1985.

The Explorer of Barkham Street (also see below), illustrated by Emily Arnold McCully, Harper, 1985.

Night of Ghosts and Hermits: Nocturnal Life on the Seashore (nonfiction), illustrated by Susan Gallagher, Harcourt, 1985.

The Cuckoo Clock, illustrated by Johnson, David Godine, 1986.

The Scarecrows and Their Child, illustrated by Amy Schwartz, Harper, 1987.

Zekmet, the Stone Carver: A Tale of Ancient Egypt, illustrated by Deborah Nourse Lattimore, Harcourt, 1988.

Storm in the Night, illustrated by Pat Cummings, Harper, 1988.

Pangur Ban, illustrated by Johnson, Harper, 1988.

Barkham Street Trilogy (contains *A Dog on Barkham Street, The Bully of Barkham Street,* and *The Explorer of Barkham Street*), Harper, 1989.

Bartholomew Fair, Greenwillow, 1990.

Tales at the Mousehole (contains revised versions of *The Great Rebellion, Maximilian's World,* and *Siri, the Conquistador*), illustrated by Johnson, David Godine, 1990.

Deputy Shep, illustrated by Johnson, HarperCollins, 1991.

King Emmett the Second, illustrated by Williams, Greenwillow, 1991.

Go Fish, illustrated by Cummings, HarperCollins, 1991.

The Weeds and the Weather, Greenwillow, in press.

OTHER

Truth and Consequence (adult novel), Harper, 1953.

Stolz has also contributed short stories to periodicals, including *Cosmopolitan, Cricket, Good Housekeeping, Ladies' Home Journal, McCall's, Redbook, Seventeen, Woman's Day,* and *The Writer.* Her books have been published in over twenty-five languages; several have been made available in Braille editions. Stolz's manuscripts are included in the Kerlan collection at the University of Minnesota, Minneapolis.

ADAPTATIONS: "Baby Blue Expression" (short story; first published in *McCall's*) was adapted for television by Alfred Hitchcock. *The Noonday Friends* was recorded by Miller-Brody, 1976.

WORK IN PROGRESS: Stealing Home, another book about Thomas, the young black protagonist of both *Storm in the Night* and *Go Fish,* to be published by HarperCollins: "There is a good deal about baseball in it, and Thomas's great aunt Linzy moves in on them and just about steals their home"; *Cezanne Pinto, Cowboy,* a book about Thomas's ancestor, a runaway slave who eventually became a cowboy.

SIDELIGHTS: Mary Stolz is the author of numerous novels and short stories for both children and young adults. Noted for her eloquence and sensitivity to the everyday events that shape the lives of her characters, her books for teen-age girls were among the first to be recognized for their accurate representation of the emotional concerns of adolescence. Stolz creates realistic characters to inhabit the vivid settings of her novels and incorporates a boy/girl relationship into many of her plots. She has written on such subjects as divorce, family relationships, social problems, and the growth towards adulthood, all with a characteristic respect for the sensitivity and maturity of her young readers. Stolz's novels are especially noted for their dynamic young female protagonists: intelligent and ambitious young women interested in the arts, curious about the world around them, and desirous of its betterment.

Stolz was born in Boston, Massachusetts, into a family of strong Irish traditions. Together with her sister Eileen and cousin Peg, she moved to New York City where the three girls were raised. Stolz developed a love for books early in her childhood, and was encouraged in her reading by her Uncle Bill. He bought her volumes of literature over the years, including works by such authors as A. A. Milne, Kenneth Grahame, Ernest Thompson Seton, Emily Dickinson, Jane Austen, and John Keats. "They instructed—without scaring me witless—amused, saddened, puzzled, delighted, enriched. Opened worlds, lighted corners. They sustained me," she wrote in *Children's Book Council: 1975.* Her love of reading has oftentimes extended into the lives of her characters and much of her writing is interspersed with literary allusion.

"As a girl I was flighty, flirtatious, impulsive, self-involved and not very thoughtful," Stolz once told *Something about the Author* (*SATA*). "Then I read *Pride and Prejudice* and fell in love with Elizabeth Bennet. To me, she's the loveliest female in fiction, as Rochester is the most captivating male. I used to think they should have married each other. Anyway, I tried to model myself after Elizabeth Bennet, so you can see how much the book affected me. It worked, too. Sort of. My manners improved, even my deportment changed. I think I became more considerate. And *Little Women* ... I don't know if anyone still reads it. I hope so. The book has such warmth and closeness—the closeness of family and friends. The death of Beth March was devastating to me. I used to go back and start over again, actually almost thinking that the next time it would turn out differently. But that book showed how a family faced a loss so great, and survived it, and went on, and even knew happiness again. Quite a lesson to learn from a book."

Stolz's love of reading soon transformed itself into a love of writing, using words to compose the stories of her own imagination. Stolz's prolific outpouring of stories extended into her teenage years, and she wrote constantly while a student at the Birch Wathen School in New York City. The unstructured academic environment of this progressive school allowed her the freedom to both read and write material of her own choosing. Stolz recalled in *Something about the Author Autobiography Series* (*SAAS*), "I always wanted to be a writer, a real, published writer—the way other girls at school wanted to become actresses. A few of them did become actresses, and here am I, a writer."

Stolz went on to study at Columbia University Teacher's College, followed by a year at the Katharine Gibbs School, where she attained typing skills which allowed her to get a secretarial position at Columbia as well as aiding her in her own written effort. When she was eighteen years old, Stolz left her job and married Stanley Burr Stolz. She and her husband had a son, William, who kept her busy and away from writing for several years. However, in 1950, after suffering a great deal of physical pain which necessitated her undergoing an operation, Stolz found herself confined to her home during her recovery. Her physician, Dr. Thomas Jaleski (who later was to become her second husband), encouraged her to occupy herself with something during her recuperation. As she recalled in *SAAS:* "I told him that when I was in school (not so awfully far in the past) I'd liked to write. 'Well, that's excellent,' he said. 'My advice is that you write something that will take you a long time. Write a novel.'" She got a secondhand typewriter, a ream of yellow paper, and started writing. Her efforts paid off when the manuscript was accepted by the first publisher she sent it to. *To Tell Your Love* was published in 1950.

"It is sometimes said that the first novel is written some ten years back in a writer's life. This probably isn't a rule, but I followed it, writing about a fifteen-year-old girl who falls in love and loses her love, which probably should, or anyway does, happen to most fifteen-year-old girls. It had happened to me, and it was easy to recall the disbelief, the *pain* of having to accept that a boy who had seemed to love me, who had *said* he loved me, no longer did. Creating a family, adding some relatives, putting in my cat, July, I simply wrote my own story and sent the book to Harper's."

Stolz developed a strong relationship with her editor at Harper's over the many years since she began her writing career, and told *Major Authors and Illustrators for Children and Young Adults (MAICYA):* "The matchless Ursula Nordstrom supported, inspired, and *put up* with me over many, many years. When she died in 1988, I wrote an essay in her memory, in her honor .... She was the finest children's book editor ever, the trail blazer, and all her artists and writers would say the same. When I finish a book, or when working on one, I actually ache, knowing she will not see it."

Much of Stolz's writing is a patchwork of memories of people, places, and circumstances from her own life. *Ready or Not* is the story of the Connor family, who live in a low-income housing project in New York City and try to get by on a small income. The book centers around the eldest daughter, Morgan Connor, and her efforts to help sustain the family through their rough times with her warmth and mature wisdom. *Ivy Larkin:*

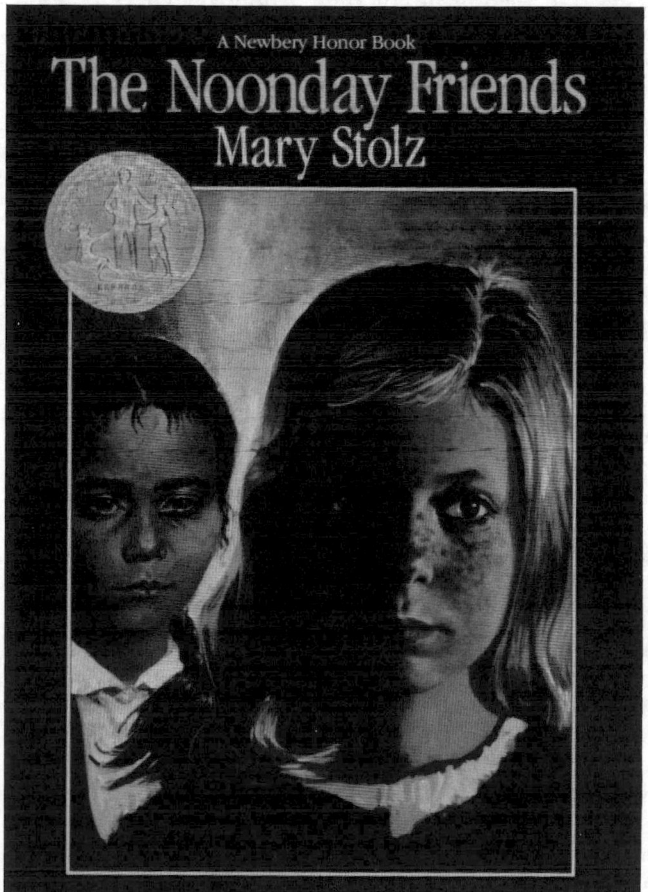

Cover of *The Noonday Friends,* by Mary Stolz.

A Novel, published in 1986, is also set in New York City, and takes place during the Depression era when Stolz herself was a young girl. The protagonist, fourteen-year-old Ivy, faces the isolation of being a scholarship student from a poor family at an exclusive private school catering to the children of wealthy parents. The book tells how Ivy overcomes her fear of being an outsider, her worries when her father loses his job, and her resentments of the snobbishness of the other students.

Although Stolz began her career writing primarily for teenage girls, she soon varied her audience by writing for pre-teens and younger children as well. When her son, Billy, was old enough to be read aloud to, he wanted his mother to write stories that he would enjoy. His insistence inspired her first book for young children, *The Leftover Elf,* which has been followed by many notable children's books, including *Belling the Tiger, The Bully of Barkham Street,* and *Emmett's Pig.* As with her books for teenagers, Stolz's stories for younger readers have emotional depth, as well as being entertaining. *King Emmett the Second,* the sequel to *Emmett's Pig,* deals with the adjustments that young Emmett must make, not only in moving from the city out to a new home in the country, but with the death of his beloved pet pig. Emmett learns to cope with loss and change and by story's end is able to accept a new pet, as well as a new home, into both his life and his heart. *The Noonday Friends,* designated as a Newbery Honor Book in 1966, is written for the junior high school reader. The book tells the story of Franny Davis whose father is an out-of-work artist and whose mother must work to keep the family together. Eleven-year-old Franny develops a close friendship with Simone, a Puerto Rican girl she is only able to meet during school lunch period. The two friends have a great deal in common: they have to give up their social life for the responsibilities of baby-sitting for younger brothers and sisters and keeping house for their working mothers. Franny and Simone feel overwhelmed by their household chores but their friendship helps each girl learn to accept her family situation.

Stolz credits the daily experience of life with providing the inspiration for her writing. Asked where the ideas from her stories come from, she replied to *SATA:* "From living, and looking, and being curious, and eavesdropping, and caring about nearly everything. From reading." Stolz is adamant about the importance of books to the developing writer: "Reading has been my university, my way of living in history, prehistory, the present, the future. I mean that reading has made me know and understand more people than one person ever could know, or possibly understand, in seven lifetimes. I mean that to me, and to most writers, I think, reading has been as necessary as taking nourishment, sleeping, loving. I mean that to me a life without books would not be worth living." She discussed the development of her characters: "Fictional characters are an amalgam of the real, the imagined, the dreamed-of. They are mosaics—bits of a nephew, a stranger, a beloved poet, a character in someone else's fiction (I think that I put a little of Elizabeth Bennet in my heroines). All these, and more, are put together, pulled apart, shuffled, and altered until, on paper, there is someone not to be recognized as that nephew, that woman seen on a subway and never seen again, that reclusive poet, *or* Jane Austen's perfect young lady."

In an article in *The Writer,* Stolz commented: "On the whole, it is my belief—and I have written from that belief—that after infancy there develops between children and adults (especially parents) an uneasiness, a withdrawal, a perplexity, sometimes hostility. In some cases, the feelings persist until the children are adults. Sometimes, between parents and children, it simply never stops. This tension, this loving and hating, this bafflement and struggle to understand is, in my opinion, the underpinning of all I've written."

Stolz's books are highly regarded as quality literature for young adult readers. *New York Times Book Review* critic Ellen Lewis Buell commented on the "wit, originality and a rare maturity," contained within Stolz's books. "Mary Stolz's remarkable empathy with the characters in her books is particularly important in her stories about older boys and girls," Ruth Hill Viguers agreed in *Margin for Surprise: About Books, Children, and Librarians.* "At a time when many teen-age stories are misleading, she always plays fair. The people of her books are alive, their world is the contemporary world, and their stories are told with truth and dignity." Stolz's more recent young-adult novels have been criticized by some as not "relevant" to today's teen-age reader; that her method of dealing with social problems faced by young people has not kept pace with changing times. Stolz agrees that today's high school student is more sophisticated than when she began writing. "I have not dealt with the drug scene. My characters ... are not battered, they are not criminals, they are not homeless on the road," Stolz commented in *The Writer.* "I know that many writers today ... handle all these themes in their books.... But a writer can write only as he can write." Stolz recognizes her limitations in reflecting the issues of modern young people: "I don't understand the drug culture of today," she told Linda Giuca in the *Hartford Courant.* "You can't write about what you don't know." In more recent books, Stolz has shifted her energies to writing for younger children who still seem to grow up in much the same fashion as they did thirty years ago.

Stolz told *SATA*: "Many people who think they want to write want, actually, to have written something. This is not the same as writing, which is very disciplined work, and there are a lot of things to be doing that are simpler and, perhaps, more fun. So—reading, reading, reading ... writing, writing, writing. When I say this sort of thing to groups of children, I can feel them thinking, 'Then what does she *do:* she reads things, and then she goes and writes something.' I had one child tell me right out that it sounded like a funny way to go about it. I tried to explain that, to me, the reading, in addition to everything else it is, is a form of going to school. It's not imitating, it's learning.

"There are books in which you lose yourself and there are books in which you find yourself. There's a place for both. Detective stories, for instance, are fine for getting lost it. But the great books are those in which you find yourself. And a great book needn't be a classic. It just needs to be the right book at the right time for the person who's reading it."

Today, Stolz lives with her second husband, Thomas Jaleski, in Florida. "We live a shell's throw from the Gulf of Mexico, with nothing between us and the ocean but pale sand and sea oats," she told *SAAS.* "Sunrise, sunset, seabirds, shorebirds, and the mockingbird who comes in early spring bringing us the songs of the north. It is not New England, and we shall always miss New England, but in its way this hurricane-threatened island where we live has us in thrall."

Stolz has always been very concerned about the role human beings have played in the custodianship of the earth. Quoting from her acceptance speech for the George C. Stone recognition of merit in *SAAS,* Stolz said: "Perhaps the animals are planning some fine benign surprise for us. Maybe the whales and elephants with their massive brains are conspiring . . . with the eagles . . . and, of course, our pets, to lead us blunderers into respect for this small, shared planet. We seem unlikely to arrive at such an attitude on our own, but without it we won't need to wait for a cosmic finale to the earthly drama. We'll arrange one ourselves." Stolz considers young people best able to look ahead, to change the course of society: "Children do a lot of thinking. They continue to ask the simple-hard questions: What's the world about? Life about? What am I about? Or you? What's worth something? What's worth everything? Who *am* I and who are all these others and what are we going to do about *that?* From my mail, I know that there are many children still looking for answers in books. I used to, as a child. I still think something reassuring is to be found in them. If we read hard enough they can offer us at least part of a perspective . . . Even with that . . . we could, possibly, still save our world. It's a hope." Stolz's faith and optimism in the possibilities of childhood have inspired her as a children's writer. "[Children] are, at present, all we can hope through. Which is why I write for them."

WORKS CITED:

Buell, Ellen Lewis, review of "Ready or Not," *New York Times Book Review,* March 22, 1953, p. 24.

Giuca, Linda, "Add Talent to Volumes of Reading, Writing," *Hartford Courant,* June 2, 1974.

Stolz, Mary, *Something about the Author Autobiography Series,* Volume 3, Gale, 1986, pp. 281-292.

Stolz, Mary, "American Bicentennial Reading," *Children's Book Council: 1975,* 1975.

Stolz, Mary, "Believe What You Write About," *The Writer,* October, 1980, pp. 22-23.

Viguers, Ruth Hill, *Margin for Surprise: About Books, Children, and Librarians,* Little, Brown, 1964, p. 107.

FOR MORE INFORMATION SEE:

BOOKS

Contemporary Literary Criticism, Volume 12, Gale, 1980.

Eakin, Mary K., *Good Books for Children,* third edition, University of Chicago Press, 1966, pp. 318-319.

Fisher, Margerie, *Who's Who in Children's Books,* Holt, 1975.

Fuller, Muriel, editor, *More Junior Authors,* H. W. Wilson, 1963, pp. 195-196.

Hopkins, Lee Bennett, *More Books by More People: Interviews with Sixty-five Authors of Books for Children,* Citation, 1974.

Twentieth Century Children's Writers, third edition, St. James Press, 1989, pp. 921-923.

PERIODICALS

Atlantic Monthly, December, 1953.

Booklist, September 15, 1974; January 1, 1976, p. 628; November 1, 1988.

Bulletin of the Center for Children's Books, November, 1965, pp. 50-51; May, 1969; December, 1969; July, 1979; July, 1981; July, 1983; October, 1985; May, 1988.

Chicago Sunday Tribune, August 23, 1953; November 6, 1960, p. 49.

Christian Science Monitor, November 11, 1971, p. B5.

Cricket, September, 1974.

English Journal, September, 1952; September, 1955; April, 1975; October, 1975.

Horn Book, April, 1957, p. 141; October, 1957, pp. 406-407; October, 1965; October, 1971; October, 1974; December, 1975, p. 598; April, 1981; November, 1985; January, 1986, p. 61; December, 1953, pp. 469-470.

Kirkus Review, October 15, 1974, pp. 111-112.

Los Angeles Times Book Review, July 28, 1985; April 20, 1986; May 3, 1987.

New York Herald Tribune Book Review, October 28, 1951; December 13, 1953; November 14, 1954; November 28, 1954; November 13, 1955; December 30, 1956.

New York Times Book Review, May 13, 1951; August 30, 1953, p. 15; September 26, 1954; April 22, 1956; May 18, 1958; November 13, 1960, p. 28; May 14, 1961; November 12, 1961; October 24, 1971, p. 81; September 3, 1972.

Psychology Today, July, 1975.

Publishers Weekly, July 12, 1985; August 9, 1985; September 20, 1985; September 26, 1986; October 9, 1987; January 15, 1988; February 12, 1988; August 26, 1988; August 31, 1990.

School Library Journal, April, 1964; September, 1985; November, 1985; January, 1986; December, 1986; April, 1987; January, 1988; November, 1990.

Times Literary Supplement, November 26, 1954.

Washington Post Book World, May 10, 1987; February 10, 1991.

Wilson Library Bulletin, September, 1953.

STONE, Rosetta
See GEISEL, Theodor Seuss

* * *

STOWE, Harriet (Elizabeth) Beecher 1811-1896 (Christopher Crowfield)

PERSONAL: Born June 14, 1811, in Litchfield, CT; died July 1, 1896, in Hartford, CT; buried in Andover, MA; daughter of Lyman (a Congregational minister) and Roxana (Foote) Beecher; married Calvin Ellis Stowe (a professor of Biblical literature), January 6, 1836; children: Eliza and Harriet (twins), Henry, Frederick, Georgiana, Samuel, Charles. *Education:* Attended Ma'am Kilbourne's School, Litchfield Academy, and Hartford Female Seminary.

CAREER: Early in her career, assisted sister, Catherine, with teaching at Hartford Female Seminary, Hartford, CT, and taught at Western Female Seminary, Cincinnati, OH; writer, 1834-96.

AWARDS, HONORS: First prize in Litchfield Academy essay contest, c. 1823; first prize in *Western Monthly* magazine contest, 1834, for story "A New England Sketch."

WRITINGS:

Prize Tale: A New England Sketch, Gilman, 1834.

The Mayflower; or, Sketches of Scenes and Characters among the Descendants of the Pilgrims, Harper, 1843, expanded edition published as *The Mayflower and Miscellaneous Writings,* Phillips, Sampson, 1855.

Harriet Beecher Stowe

Uncle Tom's Cabin; or, Life Among the Lowly, two volumes, Jewett, Proctor & Worthington, 1852.

A Key to Uncle Tom's Cabin: Presenting the Original Facts and Documents upon which the Story is Founded, Jewett, Proctor & Worthington, 1853.

Uncle Sam's Emancipation: Earthly Care, a Heavenly Discipline, and Other Sketches, Hazard, 1853.

Sunny Memories of Foreign Lands, two volumes, Phillips, Sampson/Derby, 1854.

The Christian Slave: A Drama Founded on a Portion of Uncle Tom's Cabin, Phillips, Sampson, 1855.

Dred: A Tale of the Great Dismal Swamp, two volumes, Phillips, Sampson, 1856, published as *Nina Gordon: A Tale of the Great Dismal Swamp,* two volumes, Ticknor & Fields, 1866.

Our Charley, and What to Do With Him, Phillips, Sampson, 1858.

The Minister's Wooing, Derby & Jackson, 1859.

The Pearl of Orr's Island: A Story of the Coast of Maine, Ticknor & Fields, 1862.

Agnes of Sorrento, Ticknor & Fields, 1862.

A Reply to "The Affectionate and Christian Address of Many Thousands of Women of Great Britain and Ireland to Their Sisters, the Women of the United States of America," Low, 1863.

Religious Poems, Ticknor & Fields, 1867.

Stories about Our Dogs, Nimmo, 1867.

The Daisy's First Winter, and Other Stories, Fields, Osgood, 1867, revised edition published as *Queer Little Folks,* Nelson, 1886.

Queer Little People, Ticknor & Fields, 1867.

Men of Our Times; or, Leading Patriots of the Day, Hartford Publishing, 1868, published as *The Lives and Deeds of Our Self-made Men,* Worthington, Dustin, 1872.

Oldtown Folks, Fields, Osgood, 1869.

Lady Byron Vindicated: A History of the Byron Controversy, from Its Beginning in 1816 to the Present Time, Fields, Osgood, 1870.

Little Pussy Willow, Fields, Osgood, 1870.

My Wife and I; or, Harry Henderson's History, Ford, 1871.

Pink and White Tyranny: A Society Novel, Roberts, 1871.

Oldtown Fireside Stories, Osgood, 1872, expanded edition published as *Sam Lawson's Oldtown Fireside Stories,* Houghton, Mifflin, 1881.

(With Edward Everett Hale, Lucretia Peabody Hale, and others) *Six of One by Half a Dozen of the Other: An Every Day Novel,* Roberts, 1872.

Palmetto-Leaves, Osgood, 1873.

Woman in Sacred History, Fords, Howard & Hulbert, 1873, published as *Bible Heroines,* 1878.

Betty's Bright Idea: Also Deacon Pitkin's Farm, and The First Christmas of New England, National Temperance Society & Publishing House, 1875.

We and Our Neighbors; or, The Records of an Unfashionable Street, Ford, 1875.

Footsteps of the Master, Ford, 1877.

From *Uncle Tom's Cabin,* by Harriet Beecher Stowe. Illustrated by James Daugherty.

Poganuc People: Their Loves and Lives, Fords, Howard & Hulbert, 1878.

A Dog's Mission; or, The Story of the Old Avery House and Other Stories, Fords, Howard & Hulbert, 1880.

WITH SISTER, CATHERINE BEECHER

Primary Geography for Children on an Improved Plan, Corey, Webster & Fairbank, 1833.

The American Woman's Home, Ford, 1869, revised and enlarged edition published as *The New Housekeeper's Manual,* Ford, 1874.

UNDER PSEUDONYM CHRISTOPHER CROWFIELD

House and Home Papers, Ticknor & Fields, 1865.

Little Foxes, Ticknor & Fields, 1866.

The Chimney Corner, Ticknor & Fields, 1868.

COLLECTIONS

The Writings of Harriet Beecher Stowe, sixteen volumes, Houghton, Mifflin, 1896.

Life of Harriet Beecher Stowe Compiled from Her Letters & Journals, edited by son, Charles Edward Stowe, Houghton, Mifflin, 1897.

Life and Letters of Harriet Beecher Stowe, edited by Annie E. Fields, Houghton, Mifflin, 1897.

Harriet Beecher Stowe (includes *Uncle Tom's Cabin, The Minister's Wooing,* and *Oldtown Folks*), notes and chronology by Kathryn Kish Sklar, Library of America, 1982.

OTHER

Also contributor of short stories and nonfiction to numerous periodicals.

ADAPTATIONS: Uncle Tom's Cabin has been adapted for the stage many times; George Aiken wrote a dramatization that was performed continuously in various theaters in the United States from 1853 to 1934. A musical version was also produced, as well as a 1987 television adaptation by John Day.

SIDELIGHTS: Although Harriet Beecher Stowe was widely renowned as the author of *Uncle Tom's Cabin,* Theodore R. Hovet asserted in the *Dictionary of Literary Biography* that "she not only wrote some of the finest regional novels in American literature but was also a steady contributor of short stories to widely circulated family publications." Still, as Millicent Lenz noted in another *Dictionary of Literary Biography* entry, her significance in literary history is largely founded upon the one novel: "*Uncle Tom's Cabin* is one of the few works by an American woman writer of her time still read today," wrote Lenz. Stowe herself "was one of the most influential women of the Victorian Age." Her strong views against slavery and her success as an author put her much in demand as a respected lecturer both in the United States and abroad.

Stowe was born on June 14, 1811, in the parsonage in Litchfield, Connecticut, the seventh child of the famous preacher, Lyman Beecher, and his first wife, Roxana Foote. Her mother died when Stowe was four years old, but her oldest sister, Catherine, at the age of fifteen took over the care of the younger children. Their father soon remarried, and Stowe had a good relationship with her stepmother, Harriet Porter Beecher, but Catherine still remained the most important person in the young girl's life. When Stowe became depressed after her mother's death she was sent to visit her grandmother and aunt on a farm on the shore of Long Island Sound. While there she learned to read well and for the first time met black people. They were indentured servants; and the fact that they were not treated as equals deeply disturbed the young Stowe.

Back in Litchfield in 1816, Stowe spent five years at "Ma'am" Kilbourne's school, where she was an avid student. Searching for books to read she found a dusty copy of *The Arabian Nights* in her father's attic and read it many times. Eventually her father opened his library to her. One day he read her the "Declaration of Independence." In his *Harriet Beecher Stowe,* Noel Gerson recorded her reaction to this document from her writings: "I was as ready as any of them to pledge my life, fortune and sacred honor for such a cause," Stowe wrote.

At the age of ten Stowe was enrolled in the Litchfield Academy, where she soon became first in her class. Before she was eleven she wrote her first composition, and at twelve she won first prize at the school with her essay, "Can the Immortality of the Soul be Proved by the Light of Nature?" In 1824 Catherine Beecher started a school for teenaged girls in Hartford, Connecticut, and Stowe was one of her first pupils. While there she discovered poetry and began writing an epic poem she called "Cleon," about an early Greek convert to Christianity. However, her sister felt that poetry was rubbish, destroyed her poem, and put Stowe to work teaching a class on Butler's *Analogy* to girls her own age.

In 1832 Dr. Beecher was chosen as president of Lane Theological Seminary in Cincinnati, Ohio, and the family moved into a large house in Walnut Hills. They had many relatives in that city; her uncle, Samuel Foote, took Stowe to the theater to see Shakespeare's plays, which she found enchanting. She also joined a literary society, the "Semi-Colon Club." Fellow members included Salmon P. Chase, who introduced her to the anti-slavery movement. Other acquaintances included Calvin Ellis Stowe, a professor of Biblical literature at Lane Theological Seminary, and his wife, Eliza, with whom Stowe became a close friend.

About the same time, Catherine Beecher started another school she called the "Western Female Institute," where Stowe was a student and later a teacher. The sisters wrote a geography textbook which was used at the school for many years. In 1833 Stowe wrote an article about grammar and punctuation, for which she received fifty dollars. With this sale and the writing of her story, "A New England Tale," Stowe had found her career. In that same year she crossed the Ohio River and saw a southern plantation for the first time, an experience that provided her with the setting for *Uncle Tom's Cabin.*

When her friend, Eliza, died, the author looked after the widower, fixing his meals and mending his clothes; and in January, 1836, they were married. The new Mrs. Stowe kept busy writing short stories, essays, and articles for the *Western Monthly* magazine. In September, 1837, she gave birth to twin daughters and took care of all the household chores and the babies as well, although writing continued to be her most important activity. She used her first earnings to hire a housemaid. By the 1840s she was writing mostly romantic, small town fiction for *Godey's Lady's Book.*

The Fugitive Slave Law of 1850 caused Stowe to begin writing seriously. She read everything available about slavery, but had no idea for a book until, as Gerson related, during a communion service at the college chapel, "a vision suddenly filled her mind. She saw an old slave." Stowe was convinced that God had reached out to her, so she wrote down what she had seen. According to *The Junior Book of Authors,* when she read her account to her children one little boy sobbed, "Oh, Mamma, slavery is the most cruel thing in the world."

The first episode of *Uncle Tom's Cabin* appeared in the *National Era* in March, 1851, and others followed weekly; like Topsy it "just grew" and grew for a year; then it came out in book form. The first printing of five thousand copies sold for fifty-six cents each. Before the Civil War began three million copies were sold. The book was a success all over Europe, too. It was translated into thirty-seven languages and was soon dramatized. The play was among the most successful ever produced in the American theater, and a musical version was also very well received.

To answer attacks on her novel from Southerners, Stowe compiled *A Key to Uncle Tom's Cabin,* which contains case histories to verify the scenes in her book. As a result she was invited by the Glasgow Anti-Slavery Society to make a speaking tour of England and Scotland. With her husband and her brother, Charles Beecher, Stowe sailed for Europe, where she was enthusiastically received, royally entertained, and introduced to many famous authors and admirers. *Sunny Memories of Foreign Lands* is her account of this trip. On a second trip in 1856 she met Queen Victoria. She also became a close friend of Lady Byron, the widow of the famous romantic poet, Lord Byron. Their return to the United States was marred by tragedy, however, when Stowe's son, Henry, drowned in the Connecticut River.

During 1853 and 1854, Stowe wrote an average of one magazine article every two weeks, including stories and articles for *Atlantic Monthly.* The fear of the approaching Civil War did not slow her output of tales about New England life and her childhood. In 1859 the Stowes—this time with several of their children—sailed again for Europe, where they spent the winter in Florence, Italy, hobnobbing with many English and American authors. Stowe referred to this time as the happiest she had ever known.

When Professor Stowe retired from Andover Seminary in 1863, the family moved to Hartford, Connecticut, where they built a large home that they called "Oakholm." It was here during the Civil War that Stowe wrote magazine articles advocating finding jobs for the freed slaves and compassion toward the Confederacy once it had returned to the Union. She received so much mail during this period that she needed the services of two full-time secretaries to handle it.

With the coming of peace Stowe rented a cotton plantation in Florida, installed her son, Fred, as manager, and hired over a hundred former slaves to work for her. The Stowes had planned to spend their winters there, but the project proved to be unsuccessful. Stowe then bought an orange grove in Mandarin, Florida, and founded a school for former slaves. Her contributions to the state earned her the approval of General Robert E. Lee and the acceptance of the Southern people. After the publication of *Palmetto Leaves,* Florida newspapers gave her credit for making the state popular.

By 1871 Stowe was beginning to feel her age, a feeling that worsened with the death of another one of her sons, Frederick, who was lost at sea while crossing the Pacific. Her twin girls never married; they took over the house work and secretarial duties for their mother, who was beginning to need longer periods of rest. The large house was getting to be too much for the family to care for, so they moved to a new home next door to Mark Twain's house in Hartford, Connecticut.

By 1876 Stowe was wealthy, famous, and lonely. Her husband's health was deteriorating, and she felt that her life's work was completed, although there was still a demand for her writings and she received invitations to give lectures. Her seventieth birthday, in 1881, was a national event; newspapers published editorials about her, and the school children in Hartford were given a holiday in her honor. Professor Stowe died in 1886; by 1890 Stowe was bedridden and no longer went out, not even to church. She died in her sleep at eighty-five years of age, on July 1, 1896, and was buried beside her husband in Andover, Massachusetts.

WORKS CITED:

Gerson, Noel B., *Harriet Beecher Stowe,* Praeger, 1976.

Hovet, Theodore R., "Harriet Beecher Stowe," *Dictionary of Literary Biography,* Volume 74: *American Short-Story Writers before 1880,* Gale, 1988, pp. 348-355.

The Junior Book of Authors, H. W. Wilson, 1934.

Lenz, Millicent, "Harriet Beecher Stowe," *Dictionary of Literary Biography,* Volume 42: *American Writers for Children before 1900,* Gale, 1985, pp. 338-350.

FOR MORE INFORMATION SEE:

BOOKS

Dictionary of Literary Biography, Gale, Volume 1: *The American Renaissance in New England,* 1978.

* * *

STRASSER, Todd 1950-
(Morton Rhue)

PERSONAL: Born May 5, 1950, in New York, NY; son of Chester S. (a manufacturer of dresses) and Sheila (a copy editor; maiden name, Reisner) Strasser; married Pamela Older (a businesswoman), July 2, 1981; children: Lia, Geoff. *Education:* Beloit College, B.A., 1974.

ADDRESSES: Agent—Ellen Levine, 432 Park Ave. S., New York, NY 10016.

CAREER: Free-lance writer, 1975—. Beloit College, Beloit, WI, worked in public relations, 1973-74; *Times Herald Record* (newspaper), Middletown, NY, reporter, 1974-76; Compton Advertising, New York, N.Y., copywriter, 1976-77; *Esquire,* New York, NY, researcher, 1977-78; Toggle, Inc., (fortune cookie company), New York City, owner, 1978-89. Speaker at teachers' and librarians' conferences middle schools, and at junior and senior high schools. Lectures and conducts writing workshops for adults and teenagers.

MEMBER: International Reading Association, Writers Guild of America, Authors Guild, Freedom to Read Foundation, PEN.

AWARDS, HONORS: American Library Association's Best Books for Young Adults citations, 1981, for *Friends Till the End,* and 1982, for *Rock 'n' Roll Nights;* New York Public Library's Books for the Teen Age citations, 1981, for *Angel Dust Blues,* 1982, for *The Wave,* 1982, for *Friends Till the End,* 1983, for *Rock 'n' Roll Nights,* and 1984, for *Workin' for Peanuts; Friends Till the End* was chosen a Notable Children's Trade Book in the Field of Social Studies by the National Council for Social Studies and the Children's Book Council, 1982; *Rock 'n' Roll Nights* was chosen for the Acton Public Library's CRABbery Award List, 1983; Young Reader Medal nomination from the California Reading Association, 1983, for *Friends Till the End;* Book Award from the Federation of Children's Books (Great Britain), 1983, for *The Wave,* and 1984, for *Turn It Up!;* Outstanding Book Award from the Iowa Books for Young Adult Program, 1985, for *Turn It Up!;* Colorado Blue Spruce Award nomination, 1987, for *Angel Dust Blues;* Edgar Award nomination from Mystery Writers of America, for *The Accident.*

WRITINGS:

YOUNG ADULT FICTION

Angel Dust Blues, Coward, 1979.

Friends Till the End: A Novel, Delacorte, 1981.

(Under pseudonym Morton Rhue) *The Wave* (novelization based on the television drama of the same title by Johnny Dawkins), Delacorte, 1981.

Rock 'n' Roll Nights: A Novel, Delacorte, 1982.

Workin' for Peanuts, Delacorte, 1983.

Turn It Up! (sequel to *Rock 'n' Roll Nights*), Delacorte, 1984.

A Very Touchy Subject, Delacorte, 1985.

Todd Strasser

Ferris Bueller's Day Off (novelization based on feature film of the same title by John Hughes), New American Library, 1986.
Wildlife (sequel to *Turn It Up!*), Delacorte, 1987.
Rock It to the Top, Delacorte, 1987.
The Accident, Delacorte, 1988.
Cookie (novelization based on feature film of the same title by Nora Ephron), New American Library, 1989.
Moving Target, Fawcett, 1989.
Beyond the Reef, illustrated by Debbie Heller, Delacorte, 1989.
Home Alone (novelization), Scholastic, 1991.
The Diving Bell, illusrated by Debbe Heller, Scholastic, 1992.

OTHER

The Complete Computer Popularity Program, Delacorte, 1984.
The Mall from Outer Space, Scholastic, 1987.
The Family Man (adult novel), St. Martin's, 1988.
Over the Limit (teleplay based on *The Accident*), "ABC Afterschool Special," March 22, 1990.

Teacher's guides are available for *Angel Dust Blues* and *The Wave.* Also contributor to periodicals, including *New Yorker, Esquire, New York Times,* and *Village Voice.*

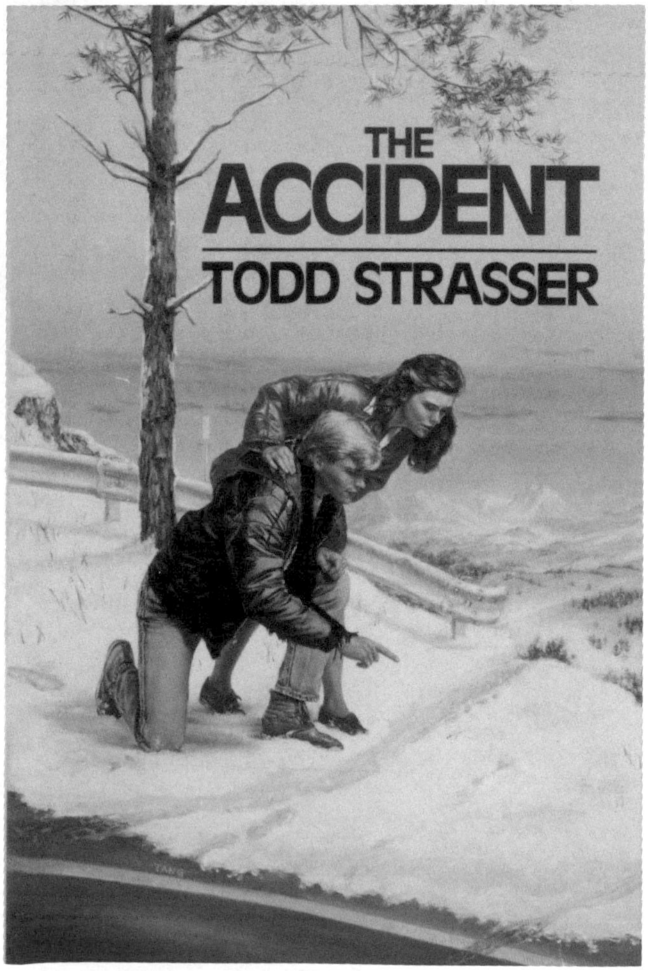

Cover of *The Accident,* by Todd Strasser.

ADAPTATIONS:

Workin' for Peanuts, Home Box Office "Family Showcase," 1985.
Can a Guy Say No? (based on *A Very Touchy Subject*), "ABC Afterschool Special," February, 1986.

WORK IN PROGRESS: Young Adult novels about the importance of the play *Anne Frank: Diary of a Young Girl,* and about a New York teenager's adventure in Alaska; novelizations of screenplays *Honey I Blew Up the Kid* and *Home Alone Again.*

SIDELIGHTS: Todd Strasser writes critically recognized realistic fiction for preteens and teenagers. In works ranging from *Friends Till the End,* the story of a young man stricken with leukemia, to *Wildlife,* a study of the breakup of a successful rock group, Strasser mixes humor and romance with timely subjects to address concerns of teens: drugs, sex, illness, and music. His understanding of the feelings of youth and adolescents has made his works popular with young people.

Strasser was born in New York City, but he grew up on Long Island. "Looking back," he states in *Authors and Artists for Young Adults* (*AAYA*), "I had a fine childhood in a very nice suburban setting. Like any kid I had my insecurities, but I also had a stable family life, attended good public schools and went to summer camp. Scholastically I was an underachiever and had a particularly tough time with reading and spelling. In general I did minimal amounts of homework, but if a subject excited me I would immerse myself in it. Those subjects included dinosaurs, sea shells and James Bond novels.

"Even in the midst of conflict and turmoil, we could usually share a laugh. I think this came from my grandfather, who profited from every loss by turning it into a humorous anecdote. For instance, he used to tell the story of when I was three and he took me clamming near his summer home in Bayville. Leaving me in the boat, he hopped into the shoulder-deep water and began digging the clams with a rake and throwing them into a bushel basket in the boat. As fast as he threw clams in, I dropped them back over the side. He dug in the same spot for almost an hour, amazed at how plentiful the clams were. Of course, when he climbed back into the boat and found an empty basket, he realized what had happened. I guess it's no surprise that my characters sometimes turn to humor in a tough moment. When I think of Tony facing a new school in *The Complete Computer Popularity Program,* and Scott facing new hormones in *A Very Touchy Subject,* I know my grandfather would be proud."

During his teen years Strasser exhibited the "anti-establishment" feelings characteristic of the 1960s. "I grew my hair long, listened to Led Zeppelin and rode my motorcycle to the Woodstock festival," he remembers in *AAYA.* "The Establishment said the war in Viet Nam was good and the counter culture (long hair, rock music,

Day Off (novelization based on feature
e same title by John Hughes), New
Library, 1986.
to *Turn It Up!*), Delacorte, 1987.
Top, Delacorte, 1987.
Delacorte, 1988.
zation based on feature film of the same
Nora Ephron), New American Library,

t, Fawcett, 1989.
eef, illustrated by Debbie Heller, Dela-
89.
(novelization), Scholastic, 1991.
ell, illusrated by Debbe Heller, Scholastic,

e Computer Popularity Program, Delacorte,

rom Outer Space, Scholastic, 1987.
Man (adult novel), St. Martin's, 1988.
mit (teleplay based on *The Accident*), "ABC
hool Special," March 22, 1990.

guides are available for *Angel Dust Blues* and
. Also contributor to periodicals, including

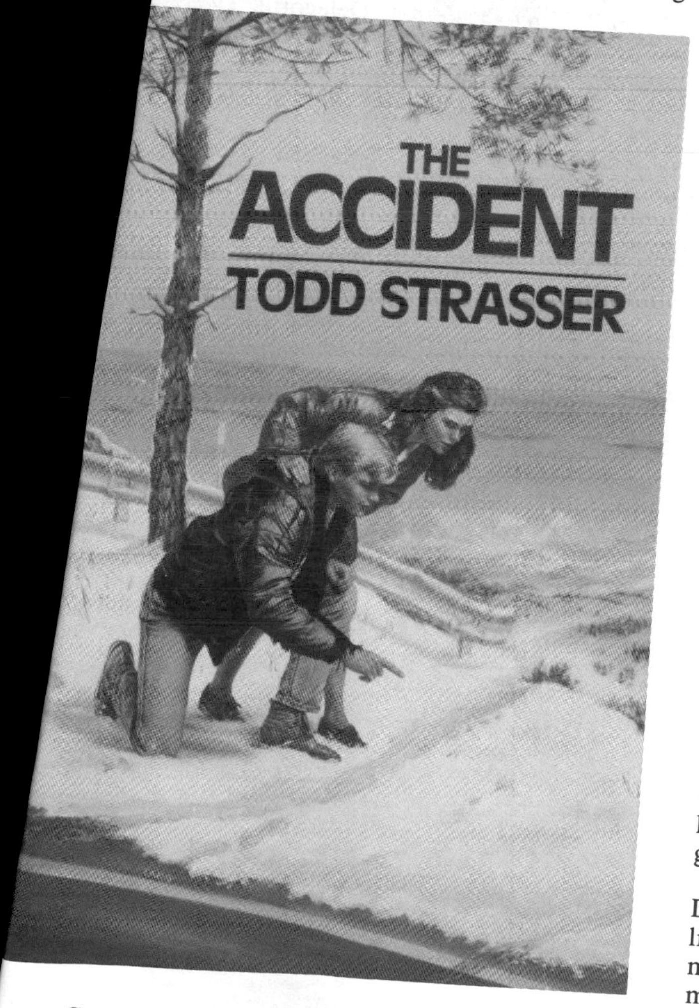

Cover of *The Accident,* by Todd Strasser.

New Yorker, Esquire, New York Times, and *Village Voice.*

ADAPTATIONS:

Workin' for Peanuts, Home Box Office "Family Show-case," 1985.
Can a Guy Say No? (based on *A Very Touchy Subject*), "ABC Afterschool Special," February, 1986.

WORK IN PROGRESS: Young Adult novels about the importance of the play *Anne Frank: Diary of a Young Girl,* and about a New York teenager's adventure in Alaska; novelizations of screenplays *Honey I Blew Up the Kid* and *Home Alone Again.*

SIDELIGHTS: Todd Strasser writes critically recognized realistic fiction for preteens and teenagers. In works ranging from *Friends Till the End,* the story of a young man stricken with leukemia, to *Wildlife,* a study of the breakup of a successful rock group, Strasser mixes humor and romance with timely subjects to address concerns of teens: drugs, sex, illness, and music. His understanding of the feelings of youth and adolescents has made his works popular with young people.

Strasser was born in New York City, but he grew up on Long Island. "Looking back," he states in *Authors and Artists for Young Adults* (*AAYA*), "I had a fine childhood in a very nice suburban setting. Like any kid I had my insecurities, but I also had a stable family life, attended good public schools and went to summer camp. Scholastically I was an underachiever and had a particularly tough time with reading and spelling. In general I did minimal amounts of homework, but if a subject excited me I would immerse myself in it. Those subjects included dinosaurs, sea shells and James Bond novels.

"Even in the midst of conflict and turmoil, we could usually share a laugh. I think this came from my grandfather, who profited from every loss by turning it into a humorous anecdote. For instance, he used to tell the story of when I was three and he took me clamming near his summer home in Bayville. Leaving me in the boat, he hopped into the shoulder-deep water and began digging the clams with a rake and throwing them into a bushel basket in the boat. As fast as he threw clams in, I dropped them back over the side. He dug in the same spot for almost an hour, amazed at how plentiful the clams were. Of course, when he climbed back into the boat and found an empty basket, he realized what had happened. I guess it's no surprise that my characters sometimes turn to humor in a tough moment. When I think of Tony facing a new school in *The Complete Computer Popularity Program,* and Scott facing new hormones in *A Very Touchy Subject,* I know my grandfather would be proud."

During his teen years Strasser exhibited the "anti-establishment" feelings characteristic of the 1960s. "I grew my hair long, listened to Led Zeppelin and rode my motorcycle to the Woodstock festival," he remembers in *AAYA.* "The Establishment said the war in Viet Nam was good and the counter culture (long hair, rock music,

From *Uncle Tom's Cabin,* by Harriet Beecher Stowe. Illustrated by James Daugherty.

Poganuc People: Their Loves and Lives, Fords, Howard & Hulbert, 1878.
A Dog's Mission; or, The Story of the Old Avery House and Other Stories, Fords, Howard & Hulbert, 1880.

WITH SISTER, CATHERINE BEECHER

Primary Geography for Children on an Improved Plan, Corey, Webster & Fairbank, 1833.
The American Woman's Home, Ford, 1869, revised and enlarged edition published as *The New Housekeeper's Manual,* Ford, 1874.

UNDER PSEUDONYM CHRISTOPHER CROWFIELD

House and Home Papers, Ticknor & Fields, 1865.
Little Foxes, Ticknor & Fields, 1866.
The Chimney Corner, Ticknor & Fields, 1868.

COLLECTIONS

The Writings of Harriet Beecher Stowe, sixteen volumes, Houghton, Mifflin, 1896.
Life of Harriet Beecher Stowe Compiled from Her Letters & Journals, edited by son, Charles Edward Stowe, Houghton, Mifflin, 1897.
Life and Letters of Harriet Beecher Stowe, edited by Annie E. Fields, Houghton, Mifflin, 1897.
Harriet Beecher Stowe (includes *Uncle Tom's Cabin, The Minister's Wooing,* and *Oldtown Folks*), notes and chronology by Kathryn Kish Sklar, Library of America, 1982.

OTHER

Also contributor of short stories and nonfiction to numerous periodicals.

ADAPTATIONS: Uncle Tom's Cabin has been adapted for the stage many times; George Aiken wrote a dramatization that was performed continuously in various theaters in the United States from 1853 to 1934. A musical version was also produced, as well as a 1987 television adaptation by John Day.

SIDELIGHTS: Although Harriet Beecher Stowe was widely renowned as the author of *Uncle Tom's Cabin,* Theodore R. Hovet asserted in the *Dictionary of Literary Biography* that "she not only wrote some of the finest regional novels in American literature but was also a steady contributor of short stories to widely circulated family publications." Still, as Millicent Lenz noted in another *Dictionary of Literary Biography* entry, her significance in literary history is largely founded upon the one novel: "*Uncle Tom's Cabin* is one of the few works by an American woman writer of her time still read today," wrote Lenz. Stowe herself "was one of the most influential women of the Victorian Age." Her strong views against slavery and her success as an author put her much in demand as a respected lecturer both in the United States and abroad.

Stowe was born on June 14, 1811, in the parsonage in Litchfield, Connecticut, the seventh child of the famous preacher, Lyman Beecher, and his first wife, Roxana Foote. Her mother died when Stowe was four years old, but her oldest sister, Catherine, at the age of fifteen took over the care of the younger children. Their father soon remarried, and Stowe had a good relationship with her stepmother, Harriet Porter Beecher, but Catherine still remained the most important person in the young girl's life. When Stowe became depressed after her mother's death she was sent to visit her grandmother and aunt on a farm on the shore of Long Island Sound. While there she learned to read well and for the first time met black people. They were indentured servants; and the fact that they were not treated as equals deeply disturbed the young Stowe.

Back in Litchfield in 1816, Stowe spent five years at "Ma'am" Kilbourne's school, where she was an avid student. Searching for books to read she found a dusty copy of *The Arabian Nights* in her father's attic and read it many times. Eventually her father opened his library to her. One day he read her the "Declaration of Independence." In his *Harriet Beecher Stowe,* Noel Gerson recorded her reaction to this document from her writings: "I was as ready as any of them to pledge my life, fortune and sacred honor for such a cause," Stowe wrote.

At the age of ten Stowe was enrolled in the Litchfield Academy, where she soon became first in her class. Before she was eleven she wrote her first composition, and at twelve she won first prize at the school with her essay, "Can the Immortality of the Soul be Proved by the Light of Nature?" In 1824 Catherine Beecher started a school for teenaged girls in Hartford, Connecticut, and Stowe was one of her first pupils. While there she discovered poetry and began writing an epic poem she called "Cleon," about an early Greek convert to Christianity. However, her sister felt that poetry was rubbish, destroyed her poem, and put Stowe to work teaching a class on Butler's *Analogy* to girls her own age.

In 1832 Dr. Beecher was chosen as president of Lane Theological Seminary in Cincinnati, Ohio, and the family moved into a large house in Walnut Hills. They had many relatives in that city; her uncle, Samuel Foote, took Stowe to the theater to see Shakespeare's plays, which she found enchanting. She also joined a literary society, the "Semi-Colon Club." Fellow members included Salmon P. Chase, who introduced her to the anti-slavery movement. Other acquaintances included Calvin Ellis Stowe, a professor of Biblical literature at Lane Theological Seminary, and his wife, Eliza, with whom Stowe became a close friend.

About the same time, Catherine Beecher started another school she called the "Western Female Institute," where Stowe was a student and later a teacher. The sisters wrote a geography textbook which was used at the school for many years. In 1833 Stowe wrote an article about grammar and punctuation, for which she received fifty dollars. With this sale and the writing of her story, "A New England Tale," Stowe had found her career. In that same year she crossed the Ohio River and saw a southern plantation for the first time, an experience that provided her with the setting for *Uncle Tom's Cabin.*

When her friend, Eliza, died, the author looked after the widower, fixing his meals and mending his clothes; and in January, 1836, they were married. The new Mrs. Stowe kept busy writing short stories, essays, and articles for the *Western Monthly* magazine. In September, 1837, she gave birth to twin daughters and took care of all the household chores and the babies as well, although writing continued to be her most important activity. She used her first earnings to hire a housemaid. By the 1840s she was writing mostly romantic, small town fiction for *Godey's Lady's Book.*

The Fugitive Slave Law of 1850 caused Stowe to begin writing seriously. She read everything available about slavery, but had no idea for a book until, as Gerson related, during a communion service at the college chapel, "a vision suddenly filled her mind. She saw an old slave." Stowe was convinced that God had reached out to her, so she wrote down what she had seen. According to *The Junior Book of Authors,* when she read her account to her children one little boy sobbed, "Oh, Mamma, slavery is the most cruel thing in the world."

The first episode of *Uncle Tom's Cabin* appeared in the *National Era* in March, 1851, and others followed weekly; like Topsy it "just grew" and grew for a year; then it came out in book form. The first printing of five thousand copies sold for fifty-six cents each. Before the Civil War began three million copies were sold. The book was a success all over Europe, too. It was translated into thirty-seven languages and was soon dramatized. The play was among the most successful ever produced in the American theater, and a musical version was also very well received.

To answer attacks on her novel from Southerners, Stowe compiled *A Key to Uncle Tom's Cabin,* which contains case histories to verify the scenes in her book. As a result she was invited by the Glasgow Anti-Slavery Society to make a speaking tour of England and Scotland. With her husband and her brother, Charles Beecher, Stowe sailed for Europe, where she was enthusiastically received, royally entertained, and introduced to many famous authors and admirers. *Sunny Memories of Foreign Lands* is her account of this trip. On a second trip in 1856 she met Queen Victoria. She also became a close friend of Lady Byron, the widow of the famous romantic poet, Lord Byron. Their return to the United States was marred by tragedy, however, when Stowe's son, Henry, drowned in the Connecticut River.

During 1853 and 1854, Stowe wrote an average of one magazine article every two weeks, including stories and articles for *Atlantic Monthly.* The fear of the approaching Civil War did not slow her output of tales about New England life and her childhood. In 1859 the Stowes—this time with several of their children—sailed again for Europe, where they spent the winter in Florence, Italy, hobnobbing with many English and American authors. Stowe referred to this time as the happiest she had ever known.

When Professor Stowe retired from Andover Seminary in 1863, the family moved to Hartford, Connecticut, where they built a large home that they called "Oakholm." It was here during the Civil War that Stowe wrote magazine articles advocating finding jobs for the freed slaves and compassion toward the Confederacy once it had returned to the Union. She received so much mail during this period that she needed the services of two full-time secretaries to handle it.

With the coming of peace Stowe rented a cotton plantation in Florida, installed her son, Fred, as manager, and hired over a hundred former slaves to work for her. The Stowes had planned to spend their winters there, but the project proved to be unsuccessful. Stowe then bought an orange grove in Mandarin, Florida, and founded a school for former slaves. Her contributions to the state earned her the approval of General Robert E. Lee and the acceptance of the Southern people. After the publication of *Palmetto Leaves,* Florida newspapers gave her credit for making the state popular.

By 1871 Stowe was beginning to feel her age, a feeling that worsened with the death of another one of her sons, Frederick, who was lost at sea while crossing the Pacific. Her twin girls never married; they took over the house work and secretarial duties for their mother, who was beginning to need longer periods of rest. The large house was getting to be too much for the family to care for, so they moved to a new home next door to Mark Twain's house in Hartford, Connecticut.

By 1876 Stowe was wealthy, famous, and lonely. Her husband's health was deteriorating, and she felt that her life's work was completed, although there was still a demand for her writings and she received invitations to give lectures. Her seventieth birthday, in 1881, was a national event; newspapers published editorials about her, and the school children in Hartford were given a holiday in her honor. Professor Stowe died in 1886; by 1890 Stowe was bedridden and no longer went out, not even to church. She died in her sleep at eighty-five years of age, on July 1, 1896, and was buried beside her husband in Andover, Massachusetts.

WORKS CITED:

Gerson, Noel B., *Harriet Beecher Stowe,* Praeger, 1976.

Hovet, Theodore R., "Harriet Beecher Stowe," *Dictionary of Literary Biography,* Volume 74: *American Short-Story Writers before 1880,* Gale, 1988, pp. 348-355.

The Junior Book of Authors, H. W. Wilson, 1934.

Lenz, Millicent, "Harriet Beecher Stowe," *Dictionary of Literary Biography,* Volume 42: *American Writers for Children before 1900,* Gale, 1985, pp. 338-350.

FOR MORE INFORMATION SEE:

BOOKS

Dictionary of Literary Biography, Gale, Volume 1: *The American Renaissance in New England,* 1978.

* * *

STRASSER, Todd 1950-
(Morton Rhue)

PERSONAL: Born May 5, 1950, in New York, NY; son of Chester S. (a manufacturer of dresses) and Sheila (a copy editor; maiden name, Reisner) Strasser; married Pamela Older (a businesswoman), July 2, 1981; children: Lia, Geoff. *Education:* Beloit College, B.A., 1974.

ADDRESSES: *Agent*—Ellen Levine, 432 Park Ave. S., New York, NY 10016.

CAREER: Free-lance writer, 1975—. Beloit College, Beloit, WI, worked in public relations, 1973-74; *Times Herald Record* (newspaper), Middletown, NY, reporter, 1974-76; Compton Advertising, New York, N.Y., copywriter, 1976-77; *Esquire,* New York, NY, researcher, 1977-78; Toggle, Inc., (fortune cookie company), New York City, owner, 1978-89. Speaker at teachers' and librarians' conferences middle schools, and at junior and senior high schools. Lectures and conducts writing workshops for adults and teenagers.

MEMBER: International Reading Association, Writers Guild of America, Authors Guild, Freedom to Read Foundation, PEN.

AWARDS, HONORS: American Library Association's Best Books for Young Adults citations, 1981, for *Friends Till the End,* and 1982, for *Rock 'n' Roll Nights;* New York Public Library's Books for the Teen Age citations, 1
Wave, 1982,
Roll Nights, a
Till the End
Book in the
Council for S
Council, 1982;
Acton Public L
Young Reader
Reading Associa
Book Award fro
(Great Britain), 1
It Up!; Outstandi
for Young Adult
Colorado Blue Sp
Angel Dust Blues; E
tery Writers of Am

WRITINGS:

YOUNG ADULT FICTIO

Angel Dust Blues, Cow
Friends Till the End: A
(Under pseudonym Mor
tion based on the tel
by Johnny Dawkins)
Rock 'n' Roll Nights: A
Workin' for Peanuts, Del
Turn It Up! (sequel to *Roc*
1984.
A Very Touchy Subject, D

Todd Strasser

Ferris Bueller's
film of th
American
Wildlife (seque
Rock It to the
The Accident,
Cookie (noveli
title by
1989.
Moving Targ
Beyond the
corte, 19
Home Alone
The Diving
1992.

OTHER

The Comple
1984.
The Mall
The Famil
Over the L
Aftersc

Teacher's
The Wav

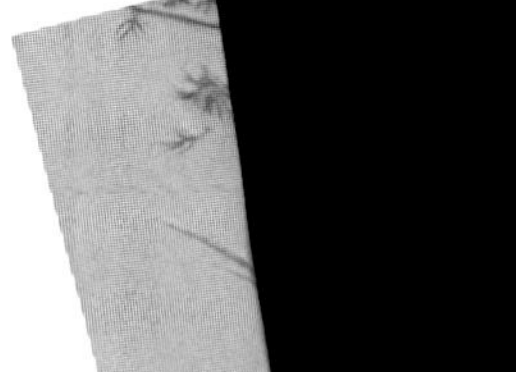

drugs) was bad, and in retrospect they were mostly wrong on the first count and sometimes right (especially concerning drugs) on the second. At the time they appeared to be dead wrong on both counts and I was about as countercultural as they came. Sometimes I think I write YA books because I'm still trying to resolve the conflicts of my own youth. When I say that I hope that each of my books shows an example of a young adult who learns good judgment, I sometimes want to add, 'because I wish I had when I was a teen.'

After high school Strasser enrolled at New York University. He began to write poetry and some short fiction, but regarded it only as a hobby and did not expect to be published. A few years later he dropped out. During the next two years he hitchhiked around most of Europe and the United States, taking odd jobs whenever money ran low. He was a street musician in France and Germany, worked on a ship in Denmark, lived on a commune in Virginia, worked in a health food store in New York and was kidnapped briefly by religious fanatics in South Bend, Indiana.

During these wandering years Strasser continued to write, documenting his travels in journals and letters. "Finally it occurred to me that perhaps I should give writing a try as a student and, possibly, some sort of profession," he recalls in *AAYA*. "I enrolled at Beloit College and began taking literature and writing courses." Strasser told Jim Roginski in *Behind the Covers,* "I guess my becoming a writer was really a process of elimination. I tried a variety of things in college. Medicine, law. Nothing worked. My family felt I had to be a business person, or if I was lucky, a doctor or a lawyer. I never really thought I would be a writer."

After graduation, Strasser worked temporarily for the public relations department at Beloit, wrote for two years for the *Times Herald-Record,* a Middletown, NY, newspaper, and then became an advertising copywriter for Compton Advertising in New York City as well as a researcher for *Esquire* magazine. "When I sold my first novel I quit my advertising job," he told Roginski. "And then I went the route of the poor struggling novelist. I used to do things like cut my own hair." After *Angel Dust Blues,* Strasser's first novel, was accepted for publication, Strasser used the three-thousand dollar advance to start a business of his own. "I . . . realized that [the money] wasn't going to last me very long," he told Roginski. "Since I come from a business family, I had some idea of what to do. I just happened to start with fortune cookies."

Strasser found the cookie business more successful than he expected. "It started as a way to come up with a little extra cash while I did my serious writing," he tells Roy Sorrels in *Writer's Digest.* "In October, 1978, I started with 5,000 cookies hoping to sell them all by Christmas. I sold 100,000!" "To get it going," Strasser continues, "I wore out a pair of shoes hiking from store to store in a seventy-block area of Manhattan. About thirty stores agreed to stock my cookies. They were immediately popular and before long I had sales reps around the city and all over the country." "I recently dropped into one of the shops down the street that sells my fortune cookies," he concludes, "and asked the proprietor how they were moving. He said, 'They're my bestseller!' So I thought—my first bestseller is a one-line manuscript wrapped in cookie dough!" Strasser also found that the business complimented his writing. "It's good to get up from my typewriter and put my real work aside once in a while. And it's a way to supplement my serious writing. I must admit it's fun. When I look around at other friends who are waiting tables or driving cabs, it makes grinding out fortune cookie messages much more palatable. And I'll never be a starving writer. I can always eat my cookies."

Angel Dust Blues appeared in 1979 and won Strasser critical acclaim. The story itself is about, Strasser tells Nina Piwoz in *Media and Methods,* "a group of fairly well-to-do, suburban teenagers who get into trouble with drugs." It was based on actual events Strasser had witnessed when he was growing up. Two years later, he published another young-adult novel, again based on his own experiences. "My second book, *Friends Till the End,* is about a healthy teenager who has a friend who becomes extremely ill with leukemia," he explains to Piwoz. "When I moved to New York, I had a roommate . . . an old friend of mine. Within a few weeks, he became very ill. I spent a year visiting him in the hospital, not knowing whether he was going to live or die." The same year he also married Pamela Older, a production manager of *Esquire* magazine, and did a novelization (using the pseudonym Morton Rhue) of the teleplay *The Wave,* the story of how a teacher's experiment with Nazi-like socialization methods failed disastrously.

Rock 'n' Roll Nights, Strasser's third novel under his own name, was a change of pace from the serious themes of his first two works. "It's about a teenage rock and roll band—something with which I had absolutely no direct experience," he tells Piwoz. "However, I grew up in the 1960s when rock and roll was really our 'national anthem.' I relate much better to rock stars than to politicians. I always wanted to be in a rock band, as did just about everybody I knew." "I think the kind of music teens listen to may change, or what they wear may change," Strasser continues, "but dealing with being popular, friends or the opposite sex, or questions of morality and decency . . . [I don't think] those things really ever change. I hate to say this, but I think authors tell the same stories—just in today's language and in today's settings." Strasser continued the story of the band "Coming Attractions" in two sequels, *Turn It Up!* and *Wildlife.*

In his more recent works, Strasser continues to write hard-hitting, realistic stories about teenagers and their problems. For example, *The Accident,* which Strasser adapted for ABC TV's "Afterschool Special" series under the title *Over the Edge,* deals with a drunken driving incident in which three of four high school swimming stars are killed. The surviving teen commits himself to understanding what actually happened the night of the accident. *Beyond the Reef* has many of the trappings of a traditional boys' adventure story: at first glance, it seems to be about exploration for sunken treasure in the Florida Keys. However, Strasser focusses not so much on the treasure hunting itself as on the father's obsession with it, which threatens to break up the family. *The Complete Computer Popularity Program* deals with questions of the morality of nuclear power; a young boy, whose father is the new security engineer at a local nuclear power plant, must confront the community's hostility with his only friend, a "computer nerd." Strasser has also produced several lighter-hearted books for younger readers: *The Mall from Outer Space,* for instance, is about extraterrestrial aliens who have chosen, for mysterious reasons of their own, to construct shopping centers on Earth.

"Over the years," Strasser writes in *Horn Book,* "I had often complained to my wife that I wished that there were some easier way to do research on teenagers, especially in New York were, except for a few weeks each spring and fall, they seem particularly hard to find. Then . . . we had our first child, a daughter. Shortly after we brought her home from the hospital, my wife turned to me and said, 'Just think, in thirteen years you won't have to leave the house at all to do your research.' Perhaps that's the best solution: grow your own."

WORKS CITED:

Authors and Artists for Young Adults, Volume 2, Gale, 1989, pp. 211-21.

Piwoz, Nina, "The Writers Are Writing: I Was a Teenage Boy—An Interview with Todd Strasser," *Media & Methods,* February, 1983.

Roginski, Jim, *Behind the Covers: Interviews with Authors and Illustrators of Books for Children and Young Adults,* Libraries Unlimited, 1985.

Sorrels, Roy, "The Writing Life: Cookie Funster," *Writer's Digest,* December, 1979.

Strasser, Todd, "Young Adult Books: Stalking the Teen," *Horn Book,* March/April, 1986.

FOR MORE INFORMATION SEE:

BOOKS

Children's Literature Review, Volume 11, Gale, 1986.

Contemporary Authors, Volume 123, Gale, 1988.

Holtze, Sally Holmes, *Sixth Book of Junior Authors and Illustrators,* H. W. Wilson, 1989.

Nilsen, Alleen Pace, and Kenneth L. Donelson, *Literature for Today's Young Adults,* second edition, Scott, Foresman, 1985.

Something about the Author, Volume 45, Gale, 1986.

PERIODICALS

Best Sellers, May, 1983, p. 75; June, 1984, p. 118.

Bulletin of the Center for Children's Books, February, 1980, p. 120.

English Journal, September, 1982, p. 87; January, 1985; December, 1985; December, 1986; November, 1987, p. 93; March, 1988, p. 85.

Horn Book, April, 1980, p. 178; April, 1983, p. 175; May-June, 1985, p. 321; January, 1990, p. 90.

Journal of Youth Services in Libraries, fall, 1988, pp. 64-70.

Library Journal, January, 1988, p. 100.

New Yorker, January 24, 1977, p. 28.

New York Times, January 4, 1976, travel section; October 2, 1983; June 19, 1985.

Publishers Weekly, November 27, 1981, p. 88; April 24, 1987, p. 73; December 4, 1987, p. 63.

School Library Journal, January, 1980, p. 81; March, 1982, p. 160; August, 1983, p. 80; August, 1984, p. 87; April, 1985, p. 100; February, 1988, p. 75; June/July, 1988, p. 59; September, 1989, p. 278.

Variety, March 22, 1990, p. 14.

Voice of Youth Advocates, June, 1981, p. 32; December, 1982, p. 36; October, 1983, p. 209; June, 1984, p. 98; June, 1985, p. 136; December, 1986; December, 1988, p. 242; October, 1989, p. 217.

Wilson Library Bulletin, May, 1981, p. 691; April, 1983, p. 692; March, 1985, p. 485.

* * *

STRATEMEYER, Edward L. 1862-1930 (Manager Henry Abbott, Horatio Alger, Jr., Philip A. Alyer, P. T. Barnum, Jr., Theodore Barnum, Emerson Bell, Captain Ralph Bonehill, Jim Bowie, Jim Daly, Theodore Edison, Albert Lee Ford, Ralph Hamilton, Captain Lew James, Oliver Optic, Peter, Peter Pad, Ned St. Meyer, Roy Rockwood, E. Ward Strayer, Ed Ward, Tom Ward, Arthur M. Winfield, Edna Winfield, Captain Young of Yale, Clarence Young, Zimmy; joint pseudonyms: Louis Charles, Nat Woods; house pseudonyms: Nick Carter, Julia Edwards, Hal Harkaway, Harvey Hicks)

PERSONAL: Born October 4, 1862, in Elizabeth, NJ; died of lobar pneumonia, May 10, 1930, in Newark, NJ; son of Henry Julius (a tobacconist and dry goods dealer) and Anna (Siegal) Stratemeyer; married Magdalene Baker Van Camp, March 25, 1891; children: Harriet Stratemeyer Adams, Edna Camilla Stratemeyer Squier. *Education:* Attended public schools in Elizabeth, NJ.

CAREER: Worked in family's tobacco shop in Elizabeth, NJ, until 1889; briefly owned and managed a stationery store; free-lance writer, 1889-1930. Founder and chief executive of Stratemeyer Literary Syndicate, New York, NY, ca. 1906-30.

WRITINGS:

The Minute Boys of Lexington, Estes & Lauriat, 1898.

(With William Taylor Adams, under pseudonym Oliver Optic) *An Undivided Union,* Lee & Shepard, 1899.

The Minute Boys of Bunker Hill, Estes & Lauriat, 1899.

(Under pseudonym Captain Ralph Bonehill) *Young Hunters in Puerto Rico; or, The Search for a Lost Treasure,* Donohue, 1900.

Between Boer and Briton; or, Two Boys' Adventures in South Africa, Lee & Shepard, 1900, published as

Edward L. Stratemeyer

Volume 13 of "Stratemeyer Popular Series," Lothrop, Lee & Shepard, published as *The Young Ranchman; or, Between Boer and Briton,* Street & Smith, 1920.

(With brother, Louis Stratemeyer, under joint pseudonym Louis Charles) *Fortune Hunters of the Philippines; or, The Treasure of the Burning Mountain,* Mershon, 1900.

(With L. Stratemeyer, under joint pseudonym Louis Charles) *The Land of Fire; or, Adventures in Underground Africa* (originally serialized in *Bright Days,* 1896, under title "The Land of Fire; or, A Long Journey for Fortune"), Mershon, 1900.

American Boys' Life of William McKinley, Lee & Shepard, 1901.

(Under pseudonym Captain Ralph Bonehill) *Three Young Ranchmen; or, Daring Adventures in the Great West* (originally serialized in *Young People of America,* 1895-96, under title "Three Ranch Boys; or, The Great Winthrop Claim" by Edward Stratemeyer), Saalfield, 1901.

(Under pseudonym Arthur M. Winfield) *Larry Barlow's Ambition; or, The Adventures of a Young Fireman* (originally serialized in *Golden Hours,* 1902, under title "Brave Larry Barlow; or, The Fire Fighters of New York" by Roy Rockwood), Saalfield, 1902.

(Under pseudonym Captain Ralph Bonehill) *The Boy Land Boomer; or, Dick Arbuckle's Adventures in Oklahoma,* Saalfield, 1902.

(Under pseudonym Arthur M. Winfield) *Bob the Photographer; or, A Hero in Spite of Himself* (originally serialized in *Good News,* 1893-94, under title "Camera Bob; or, The Thrilling Adventures of a Traveling Photographer" by Edward Stratemeyer), Wessels, 1902.

(Under pseudonym Captain Ralph Bonehill) *The Young Naval Captain; or, The War of All Nations* (originally serialized in *Golden Hours,* 1900-01, under title "Holland, the Destroyer; or, America against the World" by Hal Harkaway), Thompson & Thomas, 1902, published as *Oscar, the Naval Cadet; or, Under the Sea,* Donohue.

(Under pseudonym Arthur M. Winfield) *Mark Dale's Stage Adventure; or, Bound to Be an Actor* (originally serialized in *Good News,* 1895, under title "A Footlight Favorite; or, Born to Be an Actor" by Manager Henry Abbott), McKay, 1902.

(Under pseudonym Captain Ralph Bonehill) *Neka, the Boy Conjurer; or, A Mystery of the Stage* (originally serialized in *Good News,* 1895-96, under title "Neka, King of Fire; or, A Mystery of the Variety Stage" by Manager Henry Abbott), McKay, 1902.

(Under pseudonym Arthur M. Winfield) *The Young Bank Clerk; or, Mark Vincent's Strange Discovery* (originally serialized in *Good News,* 1893-94, under title "Missing Money; or, The Young Bank Messenger's Discovery"), McKay, 1902.

(Under pseudonym Captain Ralph Bonehill) *Lost in the Land of Ice; or, Daring Adventures around the South Pole* (originally serialized in *Golden Hours,* 1900-01, under title *Lost in the Land of Ice; or, Bob Baxter at the South Pole* by Roy Rockwood), Wessels, 1902.

(Under pseudonym Arthur M. Winfield) *The Young Bridge-Tender; or, Ralph Nelson's Upward Struggle* (originally serialized in *Good News,* 1895, under title "By Pluck Alone; or, Ralph Nelson's Upward Struggle" by Harvey Hicks), McKay, 1902.

(Under pseudonym Captain Ralph Bonehill) *The Tour of the Zero Club; or, Adventures amid Ice and Snow* (originally serialized in *Good News,* 1894-95, under title "The Tour of the Zero Club; or, Perils by Ice and Snow" by Harvey Hicks), Street & Smith, 1902.

(Under pseudonym Arthur M. Winfield) *A Young Inventor's Pluck; or, The Mystery of the Wellington Legacy* (originally serialized in *The Holiday,* 1891, under title "Jack the Inventor; or, The Trials and Triumphs of a Young Machinist" by Edward Stratemeyer), Saalfield, 1902.

Two Young Lumbermen; or, From Maine to Oregon for Fortune, Lee & Shepard, 1903, published as Volume 14 of "Stratemeyer Popular Series," Lothrop, Lee & Shepard.

Joe the Surveyor; or, The Value of a Lost Claim (originally serialized in *Good News,* 1894), Lee & Shepard, 1903, published as Volume 11 of "Stratemeyer Popular Series," Lothrop, Lee & Shepard.

Larry the Wanderer; or, The Rise of a Nobody (originally serialized in *Good News,* 1894, under title "Larry the Wanderer; or, The Ups and Downs of a Knockabout"), Lee & Shepard, 1904, published as Volume 12 of "Stratemeyer Popular Series," Lothrop, Lee & Shepard.

(Under pseudonym Captain Ralph Bonehill) *The Island Camp; or, The Young Hunters of Lakeport* (originally serialized in *The Popular Magazine,* 1903-04, under title "Snow Lodge"; also see below), A. S. Barnes, 1904.

American Boys' Life of Theodore Roosevelt, Lee & Shepard, 1904.

(Under pseudonym Captain Ralph Bonehill) *The Winning Run; or, The Baseball Boys of Lakeport* (also see below), A. S. Barnes, 1905.

(Under pseudonym Horatio Alger, Jr.) *Joe the Hotel Boy; or, Winning out by Pluck* (also see below), Cupples & Leon, 1906.

Defending His Flag; or, A Boy in Blue and a Boy in Gray (originally serialized in *The American Boy,* 1906-07, under title "In Defense of His Flag"), Lothrop, Lee & Shepard, 1907.

(Under pseudonym Horatio Alger, Jr.) *Ben Logan's Triumph; or, The Boys of Boxwood Academy* (also see below), Cupples & Leon, 1908.

First at the North Pole; or, Two Boys in the Arctic Circle, Lothrop, Lee & Shepard, 1909, published as Volume 15 of "Stratemeyer Popular Series," published as *The Young Explorers; or, Adventures above the Arctic Circle,* Street & Smith, 1920.

(Under pseudonym E. Ward Strayer) *Making Good with Margaret,* G. Sully, 1918.

"SHIP AND SHORE" SERIES

The Last Cruise of the Spitfire; or, Luke Foster's Strange Voyage (originally serialized in *Argosy,* 1892, under title "Luke Foster's Grit; or, The Last Cruise of the Spitfire"), Merriam, 1894, published as Volume 1 of "Stratemeyer Popular Series," Lothrop, Lee & Shepard.

Reuben Stone's Discovery; or, The Young Miller of Torrent Bend (originally serialized in *Argosy,* 1892), Merriam, 1895, published as Volume 2 of "Stratemeyer Popular Series," Lothrop, Lee & Shepard.

True to Himself; or, Roger Strong's Struggle for Place (originally serialized in *Argosy,* 1891-92), Lee & Shepard, 1900, published as Volume 3 of "Stratemeyer Popular Series," Lothrop, Lee & Shepard.

"BOUND TO SUCCEED" SERIES

Richard Dare's Venture; or, Striking out for Himself (originally serialized in *Argosy,* 1891; also see below), Merriam, 1894, revised edition, Lee & Shepard, 1899.

Oliver Bright's Search; or, The Mystery of a Mine (originally serialized in *Argosy,* 1892-93, under title "One Boy in a Thousand; or, The Mystery of the Aurora Mine" by Arthur M. Winfield; also see below), Merriam, 1895, revised edition, Lee & Shepard, 1899.

To Alaska for Gold; or, The Fortune Hunters of the Yukon, Lee & Shepard, 1899, published as Volume 6 of "Stratemeyer Popular Series," Lothrop, Lee & Shepard.

"BOUND TO WIN" SERIES

Bound to Be an Electrician; or, Franklin Bell's Road to Success (originally serialized in *Bright Days,* 1896, under title "Bound to Be an Electrician; or, A Clear Head and a Stout Heart" by Arthur M. Winfield; also see below), Allison, 1897.

(Under pseudonym Arthur M. Winfield) *The Schooldays of Fred Harley; or, Rivals for All Honors* (originally serialized in *Good News,* 1894; also see below), Allison, 1897.

(Under pseudonym Captain Ralph Bonehill) *Gun and Sled; or, The Young Hunters of Snow-Top Island* (originally serialized in *Young People of America,* 1895-96), Allison, 1897.

Shorthand Tom; or, The Exploits of a Young Reporter (originally serialized in *Good News,* 1894; also see below), Allison, 1897.

(Under pseudonym Arthur M. Winfield) *The Missing Tin Box; or, The Stolen Railroad Bonds* (originally serialized in *Good News,* 1893, under title "The Tin Box Mystery; or, The Stolen Railroad Bonds" by Edward Stratemeyer; also see below), Allison, 1897.

(Under pseudonym Captain Ralph Bonehill) *Young Oarsmen of Lakeview; or, The Mystery of Hermit Island* (originally serialized in *Young People of America,* 1895, under title "Single Shell Jerry; or, The Rival Oarsmen of Lakeview"), Allison, 1897.

The Young Auctioneers; or, The Polishing of a Rolling Stone (originally serialized in *Good News,* 1894-95; also see below), Allison, 1897.

(Under pseudonym Arthur M. Winfield) *Poor but Plucky; or, The Mystery of a Flood* (originally serialized in *Young People of America,* 1895, under pseudonym Albert Lee Ford; also see below), Allison, 1897.

(Under pseudonym Captain Ralph Bonehill) *The Rival Bicyclists; or, Fun and Adventures on the Wheel* (originally serialized in *Young Sports of America,* 1895, under title "Joe Johnson, the Bicycle Wonder; or, Riding for the Championship of the World" by Roy Rockwood), Donohue, 1897, reprinted as part of the "Boys' Liberty" series under title *Rival Cyclists* by Donohue.

Fighting for His Own; or, The Fortunes of a Young Artist (originally serialized in *Argosy,* 1892, under pseudonym Arthur M. Winfield; also see below), Allison, 1897.

(Under pseudonym Arthur M. Winfield) *By Pluck, not Luck; or, Dan Granbury's Struggle to Rise* (originally serialized in *Young Sports of America* [first installment] and *Young People of America* [remaining installments], 1895, under title "Quarterback Dan, the Football Champion; or, Kicking for Fame and Fortune" by Captain Young of Yale [first installment] and Clarence Young [remaining installments]; also see below), Allison, 1897.

(Under pseudonym Captain Ralph Bonehill) *Leo the Circus Boy; or, Life under the Great White Canvas* (originally serialized in *Young Sports of America,* 1895, under title "Limber Leo, Clown and Gymnast; or, With the Greatest Show on Earth" by P. T. Barnum, Jr.; serialized in *Young Sports of America,* 1896, under title "Leo, the Circus Boy; or, Life under the Great White Canvas" by Theodore Barnum), Allison, 1897.

"OLD GLORY" SERIES

Under Dewey at Manila; or, The War Fortunes of a Castaway, Lee & Shepard, 1898.

A Young Volunteer in Cuba; or, Fighting for the Single Star, Lee & Shepard, 1898.
Fighting in Cuban Waters; or, Under Schley on the Brooklyn, Lee & Shepard, 1899.
Under Otis in the Philippines; or, A Young Officer in the Tropics, Lee & Shepard, 1899.
The Campaign of the Jungle; or, Under Lawton through Luzon, Lee & Shepard, 1900.
Under MacArthur in Luzon; or, Last Battles in the Philippines, Lee & Shepard, 1901.

"ROVER BOYS SERIES FOR YOUNG AMERICANS"; UNDER PSEUDONYM ARTHUR M. WINFIELD

The Rover Boys at School; or, The Cadets of Putnam Hall, Mershon, 1899.
The Rover Boys on the Ocean; or, A Chase for Fortune, Mershon, 1899.
The Rover Boys in the Jungle; or, Stirring Adventures in Africa, Mershon, 1899.
The Rover Boys out West; or, The Search for a Lost Mine, Mershon, 1900.
The Rover Boys on the Great Lakes; or, The Secret of the Island Cave, Mershon, 1901.
The Rover Boys in the Mountains; or, A Hunt for Fun and Fortune, Mershon, 1902.
The Rover Boys on Land and Sea; or, The Crusoes of Seven Islands, Mershon, 1903.
The Rover Boys in Camp; or, The Rivals of Pine Island, Mershon, 1904.
The Rover Boys on the River; or, The Search for the Missing Houseboat, Stitt, 1905.
The Rover Boys on the Plains; or, The Mystery of Red Rock, Mershon, 1906.
The Rover Boys in Southern Waters; or, The Deserted Steam Yacht, Mershon, 1907.
The Rover Boys on the Farm; or, Last Days at Putnam Hall, Grosset & Dunlap, 1908.
The Rover Boys on Treasure Isle; or, The Strange Cruise of the Steam Yacht, Grosset & Dunlap, 1909.
The Rover Boys at College; or, The Right Road and the Wrong, Grosset & Dunlap, 1910.
The Rover Boys Down East; or, The Struggle for the Stanhope Fortune, Grosset & Dunlap, 1911.
The Rover Boys in the Air; or, From College Campus to Clouds, Grosset & Dunlap, 1912.
The Rover Boys in New York; or, Saving Their Father's Honor, Grosset & Dunlap, 1913.
The Rover Boys in Alaska; or, Lost in the Fields of Ice, Grosset & Dunlap, 1914.
The Rover Boys in Business; or, The Search for the Missing Bonds, Grosset & Dunlap, 1915.
The Rover Boys on a Tour; or, Last Days at Brill College, Grosset & Dunlap, 1916.

"FLAG OF FREEDOM" SERIES; UNDER PSEUDONYM CAPTAIN RALPH BONEHILL

When Santiago Fell; or, The War Adventures of Two Chums (also see below), Mershon, 1899, published as *For His Country; or, The Adventures of Two Chums* by Edward Stratemeyer, Street & Smith, 1920.
A Sailor Boy with Dewey; or, Afloat in the Philippines (also see below), Mershon, 1899, published as *Comrades in Peril; or, Afloat on a Battleship* by Edward Stratemeyer, Street & Smith, 1920.
Off for Hawaii; or, The Mystery of a Great Volcano (also see below), Mershon, 1899, published as *The Young Pearl Hunters; or, In Hawaiian Waters* by Edward Stratemeyer, Street & Smith, 1920.
The Young Bandmaster; or, Concert, Stage, and Battlefield (originally serialized in *Golden Hours,* 1899, under title "The Young Bandmaster; or, Solving a Mystery of the Past"; also see below), Mershon, 1900.
Boys of the Fort; or, A Young Captain's Pluck (also see below), Mershon, 1901, published as *Boys of the Fort; or, True Courage Wins* by Edward Stratemeyer, Street & Smith, 1920.
With Custer in the Black Hills; or, A Young Scout among the Indians (also see below), Mershon, 1902, published as *On Fortune's Trail; or, The Heroes of the Black Hills* by Edward Stratemeyer, Street & Smith, 1920.

"MEXICAN WAR" SERIES; UNDER PSEUDONYM CAPTAIN RALPH BONEHILL

For the Liberty of Texas, Estes, 1900, reprinted under name Edward Stratemeyer, Lothrop, Lee & Shepard, 1909, reprinted, 1930.
With Taylor on the Rio Grande, Estes, 1901, reprinted under name Edward Stratemeyer, Lothrop, Lee & Shepard, 1909, reprinted, 1930.
Under Scott in Mexico, Estes, 1902, reprinted under name Edward Stratemeyer, Lothrop, Lee & Shepard, 1909, reprinted, 1930.

"SOLDIERS OF FORTUNE" SERIES

On to Peking; or, Old Glory in China, Lee & Shepard, 1900.
Under the Mikado's Flag; or, Young Soldiers of Fortune, Lee & Shepard, 1904.
At the Fall of Port Arthur; or, A Young American in the Japanese Navy, Lothrop, Lee & Shepard, 1905.
Under Togo for Japan; or, Three Young Americans on Land and Sea, Lothrop, Lee & Shepard, 1906.

"RISE IN LIFE" SERIES; UNDER PSEUDONYM HORATIO ALGER, JR.

Out for Business; or, Robert Frost's Strange Career, Mershon, 1900.
Falling in with Fortune; or, The Experiences of a Young Secretary, Mershon, 1900.
Young Captain Jack; or, The Son of a Soldier (originally serialized in *Golden Hours,* 1901), Mershon, 1901.
Nelson the Newsboy; or, Afloat in New York, Mershon, 1901.
Jerry the Backwoods Boy; or, The Parkhurst Treasure, Mershon, 1904.
Lost at Sea; or, Robert Roscoe's Strange Cruise, Mershon, 1904.
From Farm to Fortune; or, Nat Nason's Strange Experience, Stitt, 1905.
The Young Book Agent; or, Frank Hardy's Road to Success, Stitt, 1905.
Randy of the River; or, The Adventures of a Young Deck Hand, Chatterton-Peck, 1906.

Joe, the Hotel Boy; or, Winning out by Pluck, Grosset & Dunlap, 1912.

Ben Logan's Triumph; or, The Boys of Boxwood Academy, Grosset & Dunlap, 1912.

"COLONIAL" SERIES

With Washington in the West; or, A Soldier Boy's Battles in the Wilderness, Lee & Shepard, 1901.

Marching on Niagara; or, The Soldier Boys of the Old Frontier, Lee & Shepard, 1902.

At the Fall of Montreal; or, A Soldier Boy's Final Victory, Lee & Shepard, 1903.

On the Trail of Pontiac; or, The Pioneer Boys of the Ohio, Lee & Shepard, 1904.

The Fort in the Wilderness; or, The Soldier Boys of the Indian Trails, Lee & Shepard, 1905.

Trail and Trading Post; or, The Young Hunters of the Ohio, Lothrop, Lee & Shepard, 1906.

"PUTNAM HALL" SERIES; UNDER PSEUDONYM ARTHUR M. WINFIELD

The Putnam Hall Cadets; or, Good Times in School and Out, Mershon, 1901, reprinted as Volume 5 of series under title *The Cadets of Putnam Hall; or, Good Times in School and Out,* Grosset & Dunlap, 1921.

The Putnam Hall Rivals; or, Fun and Sport Afloat and Ashore, Mershon, 1906, reprinted as Volume 6 of series under title *The Rivals of Putnam Hall; or, Fun and Sport Afloat and Ashore,* Grosset & Dunlap, 1921.

The Putnam Hall Champions; or, Bound to Win Out, Grosset & Dunlap, 1908, reprinted as Volume 4 of series under title *The Champions of Putnam Hall; or, Bound to Win Out,* 1921.

The Putnam Hall Rebellion; or, The Rival Runaways, Grosset & Dunlap, 1909, reprinted as Volume 3 of series under title *The Rebellion at Putnam Hall; or, The Rival Runaways,* 1921.

The Putnam Hall Encampment; or, The Secret of the Old Mill, Grosset & Dunlap, 1910, reprinted as Volume 2 of series under title *Camping Out Days at Putnam Hall; or, The Secret of the Old Mill,* 1921.

The Putnam Hall Mystery; or, The School Chums' Strange Discovery, Grosset & Dunlap, 1911, reprinted as Volume 1 of series under title *The Mystery at Putnam Hall; or, The School Chums' Strange Discovery,* 1921.

"PAN-AMERICAN" SERIES

Lost on the Orinoco; or, American Boys in Venezuela, Lee & Shepard, 1902.

The Young Volcano Explorers; or, American Boys in the West Indies, Lee & Shepard, 1902.

Young Explorers of the Isthmus; or, American Boys in Central America, Lee & Shepard, 1903.

Young Explorers of the Amazon; or, American Boys in Brazil, Lee & Shepard, 1904.

Treasure Seekers of the Andes; or, American Boys in Peru, Lothrop, Lee & Shepard, 1907.

Chased across the Pampas; or, American Boys in Argentina and Homeward Bound, Lothrop, Lee & Shepard, 1911.

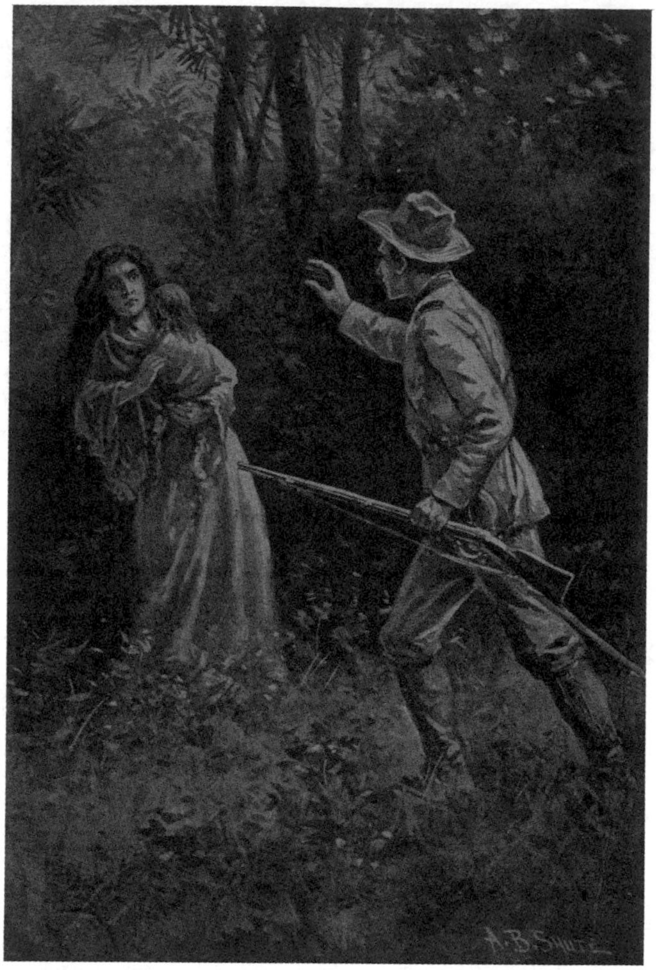

From *Under MacArthur in Luzon,* by Edward Stratemeyer. Illustrated by A. B. Shute.

"WORKING UPWARD" SERIES

The Young Auctioneers; or, The Polishing of a Rolling Stone, Lee & Shepard, 1903, published as Volume 7 of "Stratemeyer Popular Series," Lothrop, Lee & Shepard.

Bound to Be an Electrician; or, Franklin Bell's Road to Success, Lee & Shepard, 1903, published as Volume 8 of "Stratemeyer Popular Series," Lothrop, Lee & Shepard.

Shorthand Tom, the Reporter; or, The Exploits of a Bright Boy (originally published as *Shorthand Tom; or, The Exploits of a Young Reporter*), Lee & Shepard, 1903, published as Volume 9 of "Stratemeyer Popular Series," Lothrop, Lee & Shepard.

Fighting for His Own; or, The Fortunes of a Young Artist, Lee & Shepard, 1903, published as Volume 10 of "Stratemeyer Popular Series," Lothrop, Lee & Shepard.

Oliver Bright's Search; or, The Mystery of a Mine, Lee & Shepard, 1903, published as Volume 5 of "Stratemeyer Popular Series," Lothrop, Lee & Shepard.

Richard Dare's Venture; or, Striking out for Himself, Lee & Shepard, 1903, published as Volume 4 of "Stratemeyer Popular Series," Lothrop, Lee & Shepard.

"FRONTIER" SERIES; UNDER PSEUDONYM CAPTAIN RALPH BONEHILL

With Boone on the Frontier; or, The Pioneer Boys of Old Kentucky (also see below), Mershon, 1903, published as *Boys of the Wilderness; or, Down in Old Kentucky* by Edward Stratemeyer, Street & Smith, 1932.
Pioneer Boys of the Great Northwest; or, With Lewis and Clark across the Rockies (also see below), Mershon, 1904, published as *Boys of the Great Northwest; or, Across the Rockies* by Edward Stratemeyer, Street & Smith, 1932.
Pioneer Boys of the Gold Fields; or, The Nugget Hunters of '49 (also see below), Stitt, 1906, published as *Boys of the Gold Fields; or, The Nugget Hunters* by Edward Stratemeyer, Street & Smith, 1932.

"BRIGHT AND BOLD" SERIES; UNDER PSEUDONYM ARTHUR M. WINFIELD

Poor but Plucky; or, The Mystery of a Flood, Donohue, 1905.
The Schooldays of Fred Harley; or, Rivals for All Honors, Donohue, 1905.
By Pluck, not Luck; or, Dan Granbury's Struggle to Rise, Donohue, 1905.
The Missing Tin Box; or, The Stolen Railroad Bonds, Donohue, 1905.

"DAVE PORTER" SERIES

Dave Porter at Oak Hall; or, The Schooldays of an American Boy, Lee & Shepard, 1905.
Dave Porter in the South Seas; or, The Strange Cruise of the Stormy Petrel, Lothrop, Lee & Shepard, 1906.
Dave Porter's Return to School; or, Winning the Medal of Honor, Lothrop, Lee & Shepard, 1907.
Dave Porter in the Far North; or, The Pluck of an American Schoolboy, Lothrop, Lee & Shepard, 1908.
Dave Porter and His Classmates; or, For the Honor of Oak Hall, Lothrop, Lee & Shepard, 1909.
Dave Porter at Star Ranch; or, The Cowboy's Secret, Lothrop, Lee & Shepard, 1910.
Dave Porter and His Rivals; or, The Chums and Foes of Oak Hall, Lothrop, Lee & Shepard, 1911.
Dave Porter on Cave Island; or, A Schoolboy's Mysterious Mission, Lothrop, Lee & Shepard, 1912.
Dave Porter and the Runaways; or, Last Days at Oak Hall, Lothrop, Lee & Shepard, 1913.
Dave Porter in the Gold Fields; or, The Search for the Landslide Mine, Lothrop, Lee & Shepard, 1914.
Dave Porter at Bear Camp; or, The Wild Man of Mirror Lake, Lothrop, Lee & Shepard, 1915.
Dave Porter and His Double; or, The Disappearance of the Basswood Fortune, Lothrop, Lee & Shepard, 1916.
Dave Porter's Great Search; or, The Perils of a Young Civil Engineer, Lothrop, Lee & Shepard, 1917.
Dave Porter under Fire; or, A Young Army Engineer in France, Lothrop, Lee & Shepard, 1918.
Dave Porter's War Honors; or, At the Front with the Flying Engineers, Lothrop, Lee & Shepard, 1919.

"BOY HUNTERS" SERIES; UNDER PSEUDONYM CAPTAIN RALPH BONEHILL

Four Boy Hunters; or, The Outing of the Gun Club, Cupples & Leon, 1906.
Guns and Snowshoes; or, The Winter Outing of the Young Hunters, Cupples & Leon, 1907.
Young Hunters of the Lake; or, Out with Rod and Gun, Cupples & Leon, 1908.
Out with Gun and Camera; or, The Boy Hunters in the Mountains, Cupples & Leon, 1910.

"LAKEPORT" SERIES

The Gun Club Boys of Lakeport; or, The Island Camp, (originally published as *The Island Camp; or, The Young Hunters of Lakeport* by Captain Ralph Bonehill), Lothrop, Lee & Shepard, 1908.
The Baseball Boys of Lakeport; or, The Winning Run (originally published as *The Winning Run; or, The Baseball Boys of Lakeport* by Captain Ralph Bonehill), Lothrop, Lee & Shepard, 1908.
The Boat Club Boys of Lakeport; or, The Water Champions, Lothrop, Lee & Shepard, 1908.
The Football Boys of Lakeport; or, More Goals Than One, Lothrop, Lee & Shepard, 1909.
The Automobile Boys of Lakeport; or, A Run for Fun and Fame, Lothrop, Lee & Shepard, 1910.
The Aircraft Boys of Lakeport; or, Rivals of the Clouds, Lothrop, Lee & Shepard, 1912.

"FLAG AND FRONTIER" SERIES; UNDER PSEUDONYM CAPTAIN RALPH BONEHILL

With Boone on the Frontier; or, The Pioneer Boys of Old Kentucky, Grosset & Dunlap, 1912.
Pioneer Boys of the Great Northwest; or, With Lewis and Clark across the Rockies, Grosset & Dunlap, 1912.
Pioneer Boys of the Gold Fields; or, The Nugget Hunters of '49, Grosset & Dunlap, 1912.
With Custer in the Black Hills; or, A Young Scout among the Indians, Grosset & Dunlap, 1912.
Boys of the Fort; or, A Young Captain's Pluck, Grosset & Dunlap, 1912.
The Young Bandmaster; or, Concert, Stage, and Battlefield, Grosset & Dunlap, 1912.
Off for Hawaii; or, The Mystery of a Great Volcano, Grosset & Dunlap, 1912.
A Sailor Boy with Dewey; or, Afloat in the Philippines, Grosset & Dunlap, 1912.
When Santiago Fell; or, The War Adventures of Two Chums, Grosset & Dunlap, 1912.

"SECOND ROVER BOYS SERIES FOR YOUNG AMERICANS"; UNDER PSEUDONYM ARTHUR M. WINFIELD

The Rover Boys at Colby Hall; or, The Struggles of the Young Cadets, Grosset & Dunlap, 1917.
The Rover Boys on Snowshoe Island; or, The Old Lumberman's Treasure Box, Grosset & Dunlap, 1918.
The Rover Boys under Canvas; or, The Mystery of the Wrecked Submarine, Grosset & Dunlap, 1919.
The Rover Boys on a Hunt; or, The Mysterious House in the Woods, Grosset & Dunlap, 1920.

The Rover Boys in the Land of Luck; or, Stirring Adventures in the Oilfields, Grosset & Dunlap, 1921.
The Rover Boys at Big Horn Ranch; or, The Cowboys' Double Roundup, Grosset & Dunlap, 1922.
The Rover Boys at Big Bear Lake; or, The Camps of the Rival Cadets, Grosset & Dunlap, 1923.
The Rover Boys Shipwrecked; or, A Thrilling Hunt for Pirates' Gold, Grosset & Dunlap, 1924.
The Rover Boys on Sunset Trail; or, The Old Miner's Mysterious Message, Grosset & Dunlap, 1925.
The Rover Boys Winning a Fortune; or, Strenuous Days Afloat and Ashore, Grosset & Dunlap, 1926.

OTHER

Also author of *Dave Porter on the Atlantic; or, The Castaways of the Menagerie Ship.* Contributor of stories to magazines, including *Golden Days, Argosy, Good News, Boys of America, Bright Days, Young Sports of America,* and *Young People of America,* under a variety of pseudonyms, including Manager Henry Abbott, Horatio Alger, Jr., Philip A. Alyer, P. T. Barnum, Jr., Theodore Barnum, Emerson Bell, Captain Ralph Bonehill, Allen Chapman, Louis Charles, Theodore Edison, Julia Edwards, Albert Lee Ford, Ralph Hamilton, Hal Harkaway, Harvey Hicks, Peter, Roy Rockwood, Ned St. Meyer, Ed Ward, Arthur M. Winfield, Edna Winfield, Captain Young of Yale, and Clarence Young; contributor of stories to dime novel series, under a variety of pseudonyms, including Manager Henry Abbott, Horatio Alger, Jr., Jim Bowie, Nick Carter, Jim Daly, Julia Edwards, Captain Lew James, Peter Pad, Ned St. Meyer, Tom Ward, Edna Winfield, Nat Woods, and Zimmy. Plotter and editor of books for Stratemeyer Literary Syndicate. Editor, *Good News;* founder and editor, *Bright Days.*

SIDELIGHTS: "If anyone ever deserved a bronze statue in Central Park, somewhere between Hans Christian Anderson and Alice in Wonderland," declares Arthur Prager in *Saturday Review,* "it is Edward Stratemeyer, incomparable king of juveniles." Between 1886, when he wrote his first story on wrapping paper in his family's tobacco shop, and his death in 1930, Stratemeyer wrote, outlined, and edited more than 800 books under sixty-five pseudonyms, plus many short stories. His beloved creations include Dick, Tom, and Sam Rover (the Rover Boys), Bert, Nan, Freddie, and Flossie Bobbsey (the Bobbsey Twins), Tom Swift, Frank and Joe Hardy, and Nancy Drew. John T. Dizer, writing in *Tom Swift & Company: "Boys' Books" by Stratemeyer and Others,* calls the literary syndicate that he founded "the most important single influence in American juvenile literature."

"The bulk of Stratemeyer's literary apprenticeship was served in writing and editing for periodicals," explains *Dictionary of Literary Biography* contributor Mary-Agnes Taylor. His initial success—his first story sold to *Golden Days,* a Philadelphia weekly paper for boys, for $75—encouraged the young author. He soon became a regular contributor to *Golden Argosy* and, in 1893, the magazine and dime novel publishers Street & Smith offered him the job of editor of their journal *Good News.* By 1896 he was also editing the Street & Smith periodicals *Young Sports of America* and *Bright Days,* contributing women's serials to the *New York Weekly* and writing dime novels. "Perhaps the greatest advantage of his association with Street and Smith, however," continues Taylor, "was his exposure to the literary idols of his time," including Frederic Van Rensselaer Dey, "creator of dime novel detective hero Nick Carter; Upton Sinclair, who wrote the True Blue series as Ensign Clark Fitch, USN; prolific dime novelist Edward S. Ellis; William Taylor Adams; and Horatio Alger himself." After the deaths of Adams and Alger, Stratemeyer was chosen to complete some of their unfinished manuscripts, using the pseudonyms Oliver Optic and Horatio Alger, Jr.

Stratemeyer's first success as a novelist came in 1898, during the Spanish-American War. "War was glamour in those days. Uniforms were splendid, and battles were glorious," explains Prager. The author had recently submitted a novel about several young men serving on a battleship to a publisher, when news of Admiral Dewey's victory over the Spanish fleet at Manila Bay reached the U.S. The publishers wrote the author, inquiring if he could revise his story to feature Dewey's victory. Stratemeyer did, and *Under Dewey at Manila; or, The War Fortunes of a Castaway,* starring Larry and Ben Russell and their chum Gilbert Pennington, became "the financial hit of the juvenile publishing industry in 1899," according to Prager. Popular demand brought the boys back for many more adventures in the "Old Glory" and the "Soldiers of Fortune" series, and Stratemeyer further exploited the market for war stories with books featuring boys in the French and Indian War, the American Revolution, and the Mexican War. Many were well-received by critics—including parents, teachers, and churchmen—as well as by readers themselves.

"These early books are important in two respects," declares Taylor. "They are crammed with well-researched facts and they make use of some literary techniques that mark virtually all of the author's later works." Stratemeyer directly addressed the reader in the introductions of his books. Frequently the story's action paused near the beginning of the volume to allow the narrator to recap the hero's previous adventures, and each book included an advertisement for the next volume in the series. Stratemeyer's prose was also stiff, reflecting his early association with Alger and Adams at Street & Smith, and he often relied on stereotyped views of ethnic groups. "Except for Alger himself," declares Russel B. Nye in *The Unembarrassed Muse: The Popular Arts in America,* "no writer of juvenile fiction had a more unerring sense of the hackneyed."

Whatever the drawbacks of Stratemeyer's prose, his work became highly popular with young readers. Late in 1899 he introduced the "Rover Boys Series for Young Americans" under the pen name Arthur M. Winfield. These books chronicled the adventures of three brothers—Dick, Tom, and Sam Rover—at Putnam Hall, a military boarding school, and later at midwestern Brill

College, and they captured the imaginations of turn-of-the-century adolescent Americans in a way no previous series heroes had. "Between the publication of the first three volumes late in 1899 and the publication of the last volume in 1926," reports Taylor, "sales ran somewhere between five and six millions of copies." The brothers, described as "lively, wide-awake American boys" by the author, were supported by a memorable cast of characters, including Dora Stanhope, and Grace and Nellie Laning, their sweethearts, their chums John "Songbird" Powell and William Philander Tubbs, and assorted bullies and other villains: Josiah Crabtree, Tad Sobber, Jesse Pelter, and Dan Baxter, among others.

The "Rover Boys" series originally depicted youthful adventures, games and hijinks, but Stratemeyer soon introduced elements of melodrama and detective fiction, claims Carol Billman in *The Secret of the Stratemeyer Syndicate: Nancy Drew, the Hardy Boys, and the Million Dollar Fiction Factory.* Many volumes featured searches for missing people or buried treasure; *The Rover Boys in the Jungle,* for instance, took our heroes to Africa in search of their father. The Rovers and their friends "faced unprecedented dangers," explains the *Literary Digest.* "As the fun-loving Tom expressed it, on the historic occasion when an avalanche was rolling down on them from above, their cabin was in flames, Dan Baxter and his cronies were taking pot-shots at them from across the canyon, Dora Stanhope was clinging to the edge of the cliff, and the battle-ship *Oregon* was still ten miles away, 'Well, we're in a pretty pickle, and no mistake!'" "But always, to our immense surprise," the *Digest* concludes, "they would emerge unscathed, restore the missing fortune, and be rewarded by three rousing cheers and—a sop to the feminine trade—an arch look from Dora and Nellie and Grace; while the discomfited bullies, outwitted again, began plotting at once their future conspiracies, to be related in the next volume of the Rover Boys Series for Young Americans."

The Rovers' success encouraged Stratemeyer to create other series. "Almost as soon as the first sales figures came in," reports Prager in *Saturday Review,* "he was designing a dozen similar series and concocting pseudonyms. He took his basic Rover figures, changed the names, associated them with some kind of speedy vehicle or popular scientific device, and slipped them into his formula." Stratemeyer soon found that his ideas outstripped his writing capacity and began to hire independent writers to fill in his outlines. Working with "Uncle Wiggily" creator Howard R. Garis under the pseudonym Clarence Young, Stratemeyer created the "Motor Boys" series; as Victor Appleton, he devised the adventures of "Tom Swift"; as Franklin W. Dixon, the "Hardy Boys" and "Ted Scott Flying Stories" series, and many others. For girls and younger readers, he introduced the "Outdoor Girls," and the "Bobbsey Twins" series, using the pseudonym Laura Lee Hope; and as Carolyn Keene he invented Nancy Drew.

Stratemeyer engaged in innovative publishing strategies in order to get his many series published. "Using the kind of reasoning that would later make Henry Ford a billionaire," Prager declares in *Saturday Review,* "he talked his publishers into slashing the prices of the 'Rover' and 'Motor Boys' series from a dollar to 50 cents, relying on volume sales to make up and exceed lost profit. The plan was a smashing success. At half a dollar, kids could buy the books without going through the parent-middleman." By around 1906 demand had increased so much that Stratemeyer had to systematize his production by setting up the Stratemeyer Syndicate, "a kind of literary assembly line," according to Prager. Stratemeyer created plot outlines for series titles and sent them to contract writers, who wrote the actual stories. They then returned the manuscript to Stratemeyer, who edited it and had it put on electrotype plates, which were then leased to the publishers. Stratemeyer retained all rights to the stories, paying his contract writers an average of one hundred dollars a book. "The whole process," Prager explains, "took a month to six weeks."

Stratemeyer's success and his factory-like writing process made enemies among those who considered themselves guardians of the juvenile mind. A few years after the Boy Scouts of America were established Franklin K. Mathiews, the Chief Scout Librarian, published an article in *Outlook* magazine savagely denouncing juvenile fiction that did not meet his standards, although he never mentioned the Stratemeyer Syndicate by name. "Mathiews began by noting that in most surveys of children's reading, inferior books, (defined as those not found in libraries), were widely read and probably as influential as the better books," reports Ken Donelson in *Children's Literature.* Mathiews suggested that the lack of moral purpose and uncontrolled excitement of the stories could cripple a young reader's imagination "as though by some material explosion they had lost a hand or foot." "I wish I could label each one of these books: 'Explosives! Guaranteed to Blow Your Boy's Brains Out,'" he declared. The Chief Scout Librarian encouraged other authors to write series fiction, but Stratemeyer's sales remained high. He had, however, learned something from the encounter: future Syndicate series "toned down danger, thrills, and violence in favor of well-researched instruction," says Prager in *Saturday Review.*

One measure of Stratemeyer's success lies in the fact that now, more than half a century after his death, new volumes are added yearly to series he created. The "Bobbsey Twins," "Hardy Boys" and "Nancy Drew" books continue to captivate readers, and sales are as high as ever. Despite critic's misgivings, states Prager in *Rascals at Large,* the books "are well worth a reappraisal in the light of current taste, and like most items handcrafted in those days, they wear like iron and last for years." "Stratemeyer's legacy—respectable or not—is read on," declares Billman, "night after night, reader after reader, generation after generation."

For more information on the Stratemeyer Syndicate and its pseudonyms, see the sketches in *Major Authors and Illustrators for Children and Young Adults* on Harriet S.

Adams, Mildred Benson, Franklin W. Dixon, Carolyn Keene, and Leslie McFarlane.

WORKS CITED:

"Age Does Not Dim the Glory of the Rover Boys," *Literary Digest,* April 21, 1928, p. 38.

Billman, Carol, *The Secret of the Stratemeyer Syndicate: Nancy Drew, the Hardy Boys, and the Million Dollar Fiction Factory,* Ungar, 1986, pp. 17-35, 37-54.

Dizer, John T., Jr., *Tom Swift & Company: "Boys' Books" by Stratemeyer and Others,* McFarland & Co., 1982.

Donelson, Ken, "Nancy, Tom, and Assorted Friends in the Stratemeyer Syndicate Then and Now," *Children's Literature,* Volume 7, 1978, pp. 17-44.

Mathiews, Franklin K., "Blowing Out the Boy's Brains," *Outlook,* November 18, 1914, pp. 652-54.

Nye, Russel B., "For It Was Indeed He: Books for the Young," *The Unembarrassed Muse: The Popular Arts in America,* Dial, 1970, pp. 60-87.

Prager, Arthur, "Edward Stratemeyer and His Book Machine," *Saturday Review,* July 10, 1971, pp. 15-53.

Prager, Arthur, *Rascals at Large; or, The Clue in the Old Nostalgia,* Doubleday, 1971, pp. 7-12, 217-64.

Taylor, Mary-Agnes, "Edward Stratemeyer," *Dictionary of Literary Biography,* Volume 42: *American Writers for Children before 1900,* edited by Glenn E. Estes, Gale, 1985, pp. 351-62.

FOR MORE INFORMATION SEE:

BOOKS

Garis, Roger, *My Father Was Uncle Wiggily,* McGraw-Hill, 1966.

Johnson, Deidre, editor and compiler, *Stratemeyer Pseudonyms and Series Books: An Annotated Checklist of Stratemeyer and Stratemeyer Syndicate Publications,* Greenwood Press, 1982.

McFarlane, Leslie, *Ghost of the Hardy Boys,* Two Continents, 1976.

Reynolds, Quentin, *The Fiction Factory; or, From Pulp Row to Quality Street,* Random House, 1955.

PERIODICALS

American Heritage, December, 1976.

Fortune, April, 1934.

Journal of Popular Culture, spring, 1974.

Midwest Quarterly, October, 1972.

Outlook, November 18, 1914.

Saturday Review, January 25, 1969.

Smithsonian, October, 1991.

OBITUARIES:

PERIODICALS

New York Times, May 13, 1930.

* * *

STRATTON-PORTER, Gene 1863-1924

PERSONAL: Given name, Geneva Grace; born August 17, 1863, in Wabash County, IN; died December 6, 1924, in Los Angeles, CA; daughter of Mark (a farmer) and Mary (Schellenbarger) Stratton; married Charles Darwin Porter (a chemist), April 21, 1886; children: Jeannette. *Education:* Educated privately.

ADDRESSES: Home—Los Angeles, CA.

CAREER: Novelist and naturalist. Worked variously as a photography editor for *Recreation* for two years, as a member of the natural history staff of *Outing* for two years, and as a specialist in natural history photography for *Photographic Times Annual Almanac* for four years. Founded Gene Stratton-Porter Productions film company, 1922.

WRITINGS:

NOVELS

The Song of the Cardinal: A Love Story, Bobbs-Merrill, 1903.

Freckles, illustrated by E. Stetson Crawford, Doubleday, Page, 1904.

At the Foot of the Rainbow, illustrated by Olive Kemp, Outing, 1907.

A Girl of the Limberlost, illustrated by Wladyslaw T. Benda, Doubleday, Page, 1909.

The Harvester, illustrated by W. L. Jacobs, Doubleday, Page, 1911.

Laddie: A True-Blue Story, illustrated by Herman Pfeifer, Doubleday, Page, 1913.

Michael O'Halloran, illustrated by Frances Rogers, Doubleday, Page, 1915.

A Daughter of the Land, Doubleday, Page, 1918.

Her Father's Daughter, Doubleday, Page, 1921.

The White Flag, Doubleday, Page, 1923.

The Keeper of the Bees, illustrated by Gordon Grant, Doubleday, Page, 1925.

The Magic Garden, illustrated by Lee Thayer, Doubleday, Page, 1927.

NONFICTION

What I Have Done with Birds: Character Studies of Native American Birds, Bobbs-Merrill, 1907, revised edition published as *Friends in Feathers,* Doubleday, Page, 1917.

Birds of the Bible, Eaton & Mains, 1909.

Music of the Wild, self-illustrated, Eaton & Mains, 1910.

Moths of the Limberlost, self-illustrated, Doubleday, Page, 1912.

After the Flood, Bobbs-Merrill, 1912.

Birds of the Limberlost, Doubleday, Page, 1914.

Homing with the Birds: The History of a Lifetime of Personal Experiences with the Birds, Doubleday, Page, 1919.

Wings, Doubleday, 1923.

Tales You Won't Believe (natural history), Doubleday, Page, 1925.

Let Us Highly Resolve (essays), Doubleday, Page, 1927.

VERSE

Morning Face, self-illustrated, Doubleday, Page, 1916.

The Fire Bird, illustrated by Gordon Grant, Doubleday, Page, 1922.

Jesus of the Emerald, illustrated by Edward E. Winchell, Doubleday, Page, 1923.

OTHER

Author of a screenplay adaptation of *A Girl of Limberlost,* 1924.

ADAPTATIONS:

MOVIES

Michael O'Halloran, Gene Stratton-Porter Productions, 1923, Republic Pictures, 1937, Windsor Pictures, 1948.
A Girl of the Limberlost, Gene Stratton-Porter Productions, 1924, Monogram Pictures, 1934, Columbia Pictures, 1945.
Keeper of the Bees, Gene Stratton-Porter Productions, 1925, Monogram Pictures, 1935, Columbia Pictures, 1947.
Laddie, Gene Stratton-Porter Productions, 1926, RKO Pictures, 1935, and 1940.
Any Man's Wife (based on *Michael O'Halloran*), Republic Pictures, 1937.
Romance of the Limberlost (based on *A Girl of the Limberlost*), Monogram Pictures, 1938.
Her First Romance, Columbia Pictures, 1951.
Freckles, Twentieth Century-Fox, 1960.

Gene Stratton-Porter

SIDELIGHTS: Gene Stratton-Porter, known primarily for such novels as *Freckles, A Girl of the Limberlost, The Keeper of the Bees,* and *The Harvester,* was one of the best-selling female American writers of her time. Though critics have complained of her unbridled optimism, her stereotypical characters, and her almost steadfast refusal to treat the darker side of life, Stratton-Porter's popularity was undeniable; during the last seventeen years of her life her books sold at the rate of 1,700 copies a day. Stratton-Porter "created a world of good, honest ... people who offered one another whole hearts and an enviable confidence in a wholesome, unspoiled world full of the bounty of nature that was to be theirs and their childrens'," described Joan McGrath in *Twentieth-Century Romance and Historical Writers.*

Stratton-Porter, the last of twelve children in her family, was born on a 240-acre farm in Indiana. Her father provided a model for his children in moral standards and aspirations; Stratton-Porter said in *The Lady of the Limberlost: The Life and Letters of Gene Stratton Porter* that he "believed in God, in courtesy, in honour, in cleanliness, in beauty, in education .... He was constantly reading aloud to us children and to visitors ...." As a child, Stratton-Porter took an active part in all the business of the farm, following her father and brothers and gaining from them some of the excitement about the out-of-doors that provided the impetus for her lifelong nature study and writing.

Accustomed to running at will on the family's farm and pursuing independently whatever interested her, Stratton-Porter was unhappy in a schoolroom. In *Laddie,* a book she acknowledged to be the story of her life, she wrote, "Schoolhouses are made wrong. If they must be, they should be built in a woods pasture beside a stream, where you could wade, swim, and be comfortable in summer, and slide and skate in winter." She read at home at an early age, finding in such classics as *The Vicar of Wakefield* and *The Pilgrim's Progress* affirmation of the ideals she had seen in the lives of her parents and would later portray in her own fictional characters. By the time she was in high school, her writing talent was apparent despite her indifference to the prescribed studies. Later she said in *The Lady of the Limberlost:* "I studied harder after leaving school than ever before, and in a manner that did me real good .... What measure of success I have had comes through preserving my individual point of view, method of expression, and the Spartan regulations of my childhood home."

On April 21, 1886, Stratton-Porter married Charles Darwin Porter, a druggist, and the couple had a daughter—their only child—the following year. That same year, they designed and built a fourteen-room cabin on the edge of the Limberlost Swamp in Northeastern Indiana. From this base Stratton-Porter explored and photographed the swamp and its wildlife, and from this work grew articles that were published in *Recreation* and *Outing.*

Stratton-Porter's first book, *The Song of the Cardinal,* was published in 1903. Its success led her to believe that

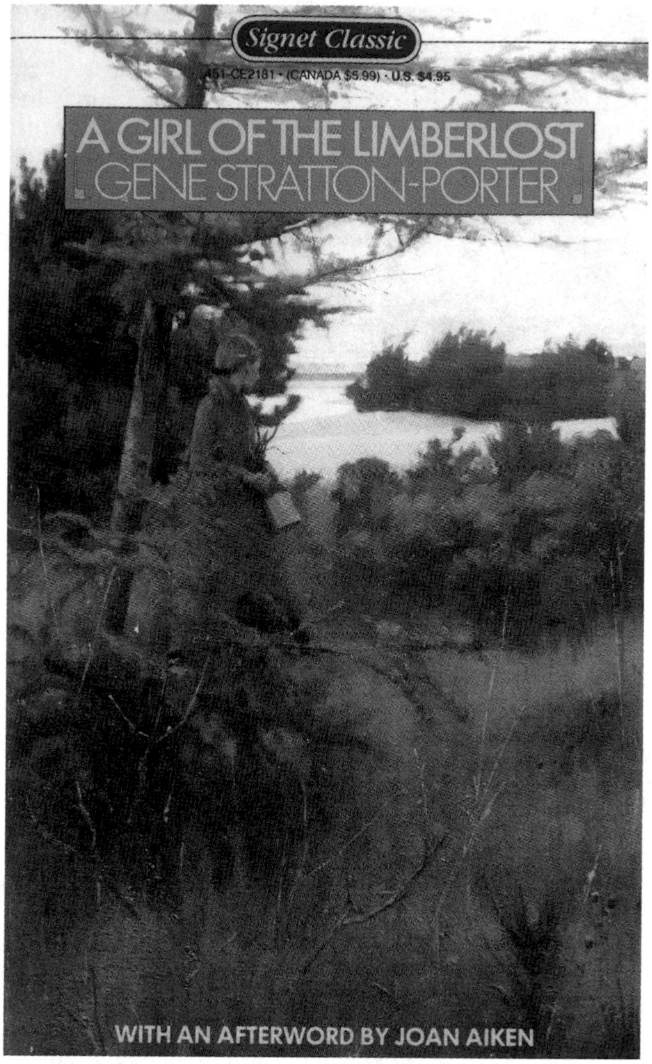

Cover of *A Girl of the Limberlost,* by Gene Stratton-Porter.

all the unpublished writing she had done earlier was amateurish, explained Jeannette Porter Meehan in *The Lady of the Limberlost,* and she accordingly burned three books, a romantic poem, and three short stories, an act she later regretted when she realized they could have been successfully rewritten.

Freckles was published in 1904, and despite Stratton-Porter's refusal to remove the "nature work" from it on the publisher's advice, the book became a bestseller. Its story of the courageous orphan boy who had lost a hand but worked his way to success is what Jane S. Bakerman called in *American Women Writers* "a prime example of the pluck-makes-luck school of American fiction." Its sequel, *A Girl of the Limberlost,* followed in 1909 and portrayed the similar success story of Elnora Comstock, born in the Limberlost but able to work her way out of it and form a close relationship with her estranged mother. Nature played a part in all of Stratton-Porter's fiction, enmeshed with the moral lessons that she always sought to teach her readers.

The Harvester, which sold the most copies of all of Stratton-Porter's books, was published in 1911. In answer to criticism about the purity of its characters and story, Stratton-Porter wrote in *The Lady of the Limberlost,* "To say that this does not reproduce a picture true to life is as great a falsehood as was ever coined.... There is not one tender, loving, thoughtful, chivalrous thing I have described the *Harvester* as saying and doing that I have not seen my father and two of my brothers do constantly for my mother and sisters in my own home."

Though she was popular for her fiction, poetry, and magazine articles, Stratton-Porter thought of herself first and foremost as a naturalist, as Bakerman noted. In some ways her lack of academic training gave her a fresh approach to her work. For example, in *Moths of the Limberlost* she used only pictures of living moths as illustrations rather than using dead and pinned specimens, as scientists often did, despite the moths' sometimes faded condition, unnatural positions, and shriveled bodies.

Stratton-Porter trained herself in photography and developed such fine prints that the Eastman Kodak Company sent an executive to observe her methods. Often, too, she endured discomfort and physical danger to get her photographs. In a *Smithsonian* article she was described walking with heavy photographic equipment through the swamp, sinking into the mire, and being severely bitten by insects every day for three weeks to take pictures of a black vulture nest. She served as photographic editor of *Recreation* for two years and as a specialist in natural history photography for *Photographic Times Annual Almanac* for four.

Stratton-Porter went to Los Angeles, California, in October, 1919, for a six months' rest (though she actually spent most of her time traveling and making personal appearances) and liked it enough to stay there permanently. As the Indiana landscapes of her earlier life had figured in her writing, so did California. She related in *The Lady of the Limberlost* that she found "something in the wonderful air, the gorgeous colour on all hands, and the pronouncedly insistent rhythms of Nature" which enabled her to return to writing poetry. Her first book of poems, *Morning Face,* had been published in 1916. In California she wrote two more: *The Fire Bird* (1922) and *Jesus of the Emerald* (1923).

By this time Stratton-Porter's books were being made into movies. In 1922 she formed her own production company so she could have control over the quality and moral integrity of filmed versions of her stories, and Gene Stratton-Porter Productions made at least four popular movies: *Michael O'Halloran, Keeper of the Bees, A Girl of the Limberlost,* and *Laddie.*

Stratton-Porter died in an automobile accident in Los Angeles on December 6, 1924. Bakerman said of her life and work that though she was "considered somewhat limited in her world view," she was nevertheless "an author of power, invention, and strong narrative ability." McGrath reviewed the negative aspects of Stratton-Porter's work, but concluded that "it is surely to her credit that it is difficult to believe in the existence of a nuclear arms race while in imagination patrolling the Limberlost woodland trail with Freckles, or keeping bees in the beautiful blue garden with Jamie MacFarlane and his little Scout."

WORKS CITED:

Bakerman, Jane S., essay in *American Women Writers,* four volumes, edited by Lina Mainiero, Ungar, 1979-82.

Dahlke-Scott, D., and M. Prewitt, "Writer's Crusade to Portray Spirit of Limberlost," *Smithsonian,* April, 1976.

McGrath, Joan, essay in *Twentieth-Century Romance and Historical Writers,* 2nd edition, edited by Leslie Henderson, St. James Press, 1990, pp. 525-26.

Stratton-Porter, Gene, comments in Jeannette Porter Meehan's *The Lady of the Limberlost: The Life and Letters of Gene Stratton Porter,* Doubleday, Doran, 1928.

Stratton-Porter, *Laddie: A True-Blue Story,* Doubleday, Page, 1913.

FOR MORE INFORMATION SEE:

BOOKS

Finney, Jan Dearmin, *Gene Stratton-Porter, the Natural Wonder: Surviving Photographs of the Great Limberlost Swamp,* Indiana State Museum, 1985.

Hart, James D., *The Oxford Companion to American Literature,* 4th edition, Oxford University Press, 1965.

Richards, Bernard F., *Gene Stratton-Porter,* Twayne, 1980.

* * *

STRAYER, E. Ward
See STRATEMEYER, Edward L.

* * *

STREATFEILD, (Mary) Noel 1897-1986
(Susan Scarlett)

PERSONAL: Born December 24, 1897, in Amberley, near Arundel, Sussex, England; died September 11, 1986; daughter of William Champion (the Bishop of Lewes) and Janet Mary (Venn) Streatfeild. *Education:* Attended Laleham in Eastbourne as well as Hastings and St. Leonards College; studied at the Royal Academy of Dramatic Art, London.

CAREER: Author and editor. Began as an actress with a provincial repertory company in England; later appeared in a variety of theatrical productions in South Africa and Australia; turned to a writing career in 1930; became a book critic for *Elizabethan* magazine; presented book talks for BBC radio.

Noel Streatfeild

AWARDS, HONORS: Carnegie Medal runner-up, 1936, for *Ballet Shoes,* and 1937, for *Tennis Shoes;* Carnegie Medal, 1938, for *The Circus is Coming; Movie Shoes* was chosen for the Spring Book Festival, 1949; *A Young Person's Guide to the Ballet* was chosen as a Children's Book of the Year by the Child Study Association for 1975 and a 1976 Children's Book Showcase Title by the Children's Book Council; Officer, Order of the British Empire, 1983, for body of work for children; *The Growing Summer, Caldicott Place, Thursday's Child,* and *When the Sirens Wailed* were all Junior Literary Guild selections.

WRITINGS:

FICTION

The Whicharts, Heinemann, 1931, Brentano's, 1932.

Parson's Nine, Heinemann, 1932, Doubleday, 1933.

Tops and Bottoms, Doubleday, 1933.

Children's Matinee (plays), illustrated by Ruth Gervis, Heinemann, 1934.

Shepherdess of Sheep, Heinemann, 1934, Reynal & Hitchcock, 1935.

Creeping Jenny, Heinemann, 1936.

It Pays to Be Good, Heinemann, 1936.

Wisdom Teeth (three-act play), Samuel French, 1936.

Caroline England, Heinemann, 1937, Reynal & Hitchcock, 1938.

The Circus Is Coming, illustrated by Steven Spurrier, Dent, 1938, revised edition illustrated by Clarke Hutton, 1960.

Dennis the Dragon, Dent, 1939.

Luke, Heinemann, 1939.

The House in Cornwall, illustrated by D. L. Mays, Dent, 1940.
The Secret of the Lodge, illustrated by Richard Floethe, Random House, 1940.
The Winter Is Past, Collins, 1940.
The Stranger in Primrose Lane, illustrated by Floethe, Random House, 1941, published in England as *Children of Primrose Lane,* illustrated by Marcia Lane Foster, Dent, 1941.
I Ordered a Table for Six, Collins, 1942.
Harlequinade, illustrated by Hutton, Chatto & Windus, 1943.
Myra Carrel, Collins, 1944.
Saplings, Collins, 1945.
Party Frock, illustrated by Anna Zinkeisen, Collins, 1946.
Grass in Piccadilly, Collins, 1947.
Mothering Sunday, Coward-McCann, 1950.
Osbert, illustrated by Susanne Suba, Rand McNally, 1950.
The Theater Cat, illustrated by Suba, Rand McNally, 1951.
Aunt Clara, Collins, 1952.
(With Roland Pertwee) *Many Happy Returns* (two-act play), English Theatre Guild, 1953.
Judith, Collins, 1956.
The Grey Family, illustrated by Pat Marriott, Hamish Hamilton, 1957.
Wintle's Wonders, illustrated by Richard Kennedy, Collins, 1957.
Bertram, illustrated by Margery Gill, Hamish Hamilton, 1959.
Christmas with the Chrystals, Basil Blackwell, 1959.
Look at the Circus, illustrated by Constance Marshall, Hamish Hamilton, 1960.
New Town: A Story about the Bell Family, illustrated by Shirley Hughes, Collins, 1960.
The Silent Speaker, Collins, 1961.
Apple Bough, illustrated by Gill, Collins, 1962.
Lisa Goes to Russia, illustrated by Geraldine Spence, Collins, 1963.
The Children on the Top Floor, illustrated by Jillian Willett, Collins, 1964, Random House, 1965.
Let's Go Coaching, illustrated by Peter Warner, Hamish Hamilton, 1965.
The Growing Summer, illustrated by Edward Ardizzone, Collins, 1966, published as *The Magic Summer,* Random House, 1967.
Caldicott Place, illustrated by Betty Maxey, Collins, 1967, published as *The Family at Caldicott Place,* Random House, 1968.
Gemma, illustrated by Maxey, May Fair Books, 1968.
Gemma and Sisters, illustrated by Maxey, May Fair Books, 1968.
Thursday's Child, illustrated by Peggy Fortnum, Random House, 1970.
When the Sirens Wailed, illustrated by Gill, Collins, 1974, illustrated by Judith Gwyn, Random House, 1976.
Ballet Shoes for Anna, illustrated by Mary Dinsdale, Collins, 1976.
Gran-Nannie, illustrated by Charles Mozley, M. Joseph, 1976.
Far to Go, illustrated by Mozley, Collins, 1977.
Meet the Maitlands, illustrated by Anthony Maitland, W. H. Allen, 1978.
The Maitlands: All Change at Cuckly Place, illustrated by Maitland, W. H. Allen, 1979.

"SHOES" SERIES

Ballet Shoes: A Story of Three Children on the Stage, illustrated by Gervis, Dent, 1936, published as *Ballet Shoes,* illustrated by Floethe, Random House, 1937.
Tennis Shoes, illustrated by Mays, Dent, 1937, illustrated by Floethe, Random House, 1938.
Circus Shoes, illustrated by Floethe, Random House, 1939.
Curtain Up, Dent, 1944, published as *Theater Shoes; or, Other People's Shoes,* illustrated by Floethe, Random House, 1945.
Party Shoes, illustrated by Zinkeisen, Random House, 1947.
Movie Shoes, illustrated by Suba, Random House, 1949, published in England as *Pointed Garden,* Collins, 1949, new edition illustrated by Hughes, Penguin, 1961.
Skating Shoes, illustrated by Floethe, Random House, 1951, published in England as *White Boots,* Collins, 1951, new edition illustrated by Milein Cosman, Penguin, 1976.
Family Shoes, illustrated by Floethe, Random House, 1954, published in England as *The Bell Family,* illustrated by Hughes, Collins, 1954.
Dancing Shoes, illustrated by Floethe, Random House, 1958.
New Shoes, illustrated by Vaike Low, Random House, 1960.
Travelling Shoes, illustrated by Reisie Lonette, Random House, 1962.

Also author of the "Baby Books" series, published by A. Barker, 1959-1986.

NONFICTION

The Picture Story of Britain, edited by Helen Hoke, illustrated by Ursula Koering, Bell Publishing, 1951.
The Fearless Treasure: A Story of England from Then to Now, illustrated by Dorothea Braby, M. Joseph, 1953.
The First Book of the Ballet, illustrated by Moses Soyer, F. Watts, 1953, revised edition, illustrated by Stanley Houghton and Soyer, Edmund Ward, 1963.
The First Book of England, illustrated by Gioia Fiammenghi, F. Watts, 1958.
Magic and the Magician: E. Nesbit and Her Children's Books, Abelard, 1958.
Queen Victoria, illustrated by Robert Frankenberg, Random House, 1958.
The Royal Ballet School, Collins, 1959.
A Vicarage Family: An Autobiographical Story, illustrated by Charles Mozley, F. Watts, 1963, illustrated by Hughes, Penguin, 1968.
The Thames: London's River, illustrated by Kurt Wiese, Garrard, 1964.

Away from the Vicarage (autobiographical), Collins, 1965.
On Tour: An Autobiographical Novel of the 20's, F. Watts, 1965.
The First Book of the Opera, illustrated by Hilary Abrahams, F. Watts, 1966, published in England as *Enjoying Opera,* Dobson, 1966.
Before Confirmation, Heinemann, 1967.
The First Book of Shoes, illustrated by Jacqueline Tomes, F. Watts, 1967.
Beyond the Vicarage (autobiographical), Collins, 1971, F. Watts, 1972.
The Boy Pharaoh: Tutankhamen, M. Joseph, 1972.
A Young Person's Guide to the Ballet, illustrated by Georgette Bordier, Warne, 1975.

NOVELS; UNDER PSEUDONYM SUSAN SCARLETT; PUBLISHED BY HODDER & STOUGHTON

Clothes-Pegs, 1939.
Sally-Ann, 1939.
Peter and Paul, 1940.
Ten Way Street, 1940.
The Man in the Dark, 1941.
Baddacombe's, 1941.
Under the Rainbow, 1942.
Summer Pudding, 1943.
Murder While You Work, 1944.
Poppies for England, 1948.
Pirouette, 1948.
Love in a Mist, 1951.

EDITOR

The Years of Grace, Evans Brothers, 1950, revised edition, 1956.
By Special Request: New Stories for Girls, Collins, 1953.
Growing Up Gracefully, illustrated by John Dugan, A. Barker, 1955.
The Day before Yesterday: Firsthand Stories of Fifty Years Ago, illustrated by Dick Hart, Collins, 1956.
Confirmation and After, Heinemann, 1963.
Merja Otava, *Priska,* translated by Elizabeth Portch, Benn, 1964.
Marlie Brande, *Nicholas,* translated by Elisabeth Boas, Follett, 1968.
Brande, *Sleepy Nicholas,* Follett, 1970.
The Noel Streatfeild Summer Holiday Book, illustrated by Sara Silcock, Dent, 1973.
The Noel Streatfeild Easter Holiday Book, illustrated by Silcock, Dent, 1974.
The Noel Streatfeild Birthday Story Book, Dent, 1977.

Also editor of *Noel Streatfeild's Ballet Annual,* 1959-1986.

OTHER

Them Wings (play), produced in London, 1933.
Children's Matinees (plays), illustrated by Gervis, Heinemann, 1934.
Wisdom Teeth (three-act play), Samuel French, 1936.
(With Jack Whittingham) *Welcome Mr. Washington* (screenplay), 1944.
(With Roland Pertwee) *Many Happy Returns* (two-act play; first produced in Windsor, 1950), English Theatre Guild, 1953.

Author of radio plays based on her "Bell Family" books, 1949-51, and on her "New Town" books, of "Kick Off," 1973, and others.

ADAPTATIONS: Television adaptations have been made of *Thursday's Child,* 1973, and *Ballet Shoes,* 1976; *The Bell Family,* adapted from *New Town: A Story about the Bell Family,* ran as a television serial.

SIDELIGHTS: Chiefly remembered for her novel *Ballet Shoes,* Noel Streatfeild made a lasting place for herself in the literary world with her stories of professional children for middle grade readers. She is credited with creating a new kind of children's book—the career novel—at a time when holiday adventures were popular. Written in a witty and concise style, her stories demonstrate how spirited children who have specialized in various career fields can succeed with hard work.

Streatfeild was born on December 24, 1897, in Amberley, near Arundel, Sussex, England. One of four daughters of William Champion Streatfeild, an Anglican vicar who later became the Bishop of Lewes, Noel keenly felt herself to be the plainest and least accomplished member of her family. As her parents were not interested in the arts and her circle of acquaintances was small, the young girl harbored a sense of dissatisfaction. "I had a narrow childhood," Streatfeild wrote in an article for

From *The First Book of the Ballet,* by Noel Streatfeild. Illustrated by Moses Soyer.

Junior Bookshelf. "We always knew the same sort of people, and never saw anyone outside our own little world. From the time I was a baby I was bored by the *milieu* in which I lived. I was convinced other people's lives were more interesting than my own, a theory which my grown-up experience has found to be perfectly true." While their brother attended a boarding school, the girls went to day school, which Noel intensely disliked because she and her sisters missed the fun activities that took place after they had gone home for the day. However, she was first encouraged to write by a teacher at Laleham School, and she often took part in parish concerts and plays.

After World War I Streatfeild decided to pursue an acting career, so she studied at the Royal Academy of Dramatic Art in London. Upon receiving her credentials, she worked for a short time with the chorus of a musical comedy before signing a two-year contract with a Shakespearean repertory company. She then held various acting jobs, including work with companies that toured South Africa and Australia.

In 1930 Streatfeild turned to writing, drawing on her stage experiences. The following year she published her first novel for adults, *The Whicharts,* about three girls struggling to succeed in show business. Other novels for adults steadily followed and were particularly noted for their vivid portraits of child performers. A new editor at Dent, Mabel Carey, shrewdly approached Streatfeild and suggested that she write about children in the professional theatrical world, then an untouched topic in the juvenile field. Streatfeild was surprised and unenthusiastic, for she had never considered writing for children, but she reluctantly agreed.

She quickly reworked *The Whicharts* into *Ballet Shoes,* the story of three adopted sisters who learn the ropes in the world of the stage. Its immediate bestseller status surprised the author, who at first did not realize its originality. For this work Streatfeild is credited with having created a new genre of children's fiction—the career novel. *Ballet Shoes* remained in print for more than fifty years and in 1976 was made into a movie of the same name.

Ballet Shoes was the first in what was known in North America as Streatfeild's "Shoes" series. Two other works quickly followed: *Tennis Shoes,* about two sisters who want to make it as professional tennis players, and *Circus Shoes,* about two orphaned children, a boy and a girl, who run away to join the circus. These works, along with *Ballet Shoes,* are generally acknowledged to be Streatfeild's best for their convincing characters, lively writing style, humor, and ability to engage the interest of young readers.

During World War II Streatfeild worked with the Women's Volunteer Service in London. Since she was unable to properly research her subjects because of travel restrictions, Streatfeild wrote several wartime adventure stories and *Party Shoes,* which is about a girl in war-torn England who manufactures an event so she can wear the dress she has been sent from America.

At war's end Streatfeild resumed writing full-time, though all her belongings had been destroyed in an air raid. She traveled to the United States, visiting Hollywood to research child actors. *The Painted Garden* was the result. Throughout her career Streatfeild continued to write the "Shoes" books, along with animal tales for younger children.

In the 1950s she wrote radio scripts for "The Bell Family," which were broadcast on the British Broadcasting Corporation's *Children's Hour.* The Bell family was an idealized family of a clergyman in South London; the stories stemmed from the interests and characters of the children. It was one of the most popular children's programs in a time when few people had television sets. The Bell family's exploits later appeared in book form in *Family Shoes* and *New Shoes.*

Critics noted a falling off in quality in Streatfeild's work during the next decade. Angela Bull described her position in *Noel Streatfeild: A Biography:* "Now nearly eighty, Noel saw herself beginning to be patronized as a writer stuck in a groove, outstripped by younger writers with soaring reputations, and blamed for being out of touch with a new generation of readers. She was regarded, she complained, as a 'national monument,' of great age and prestige, but little relevance to modern life—she, who had been considered a daring trend-setter. It was the price she had to pay for living and writing so long." In 1968 the aging author suffered several tragedies: the deaths of her brother-in-law, a close friend and companion, and her beloved dog Pierre. One morning Streatfeild woke up to find herself paralysed on the left side from a rare ailment, but with six month's of therapy she recovered.

In 1970 she published *Thursday's Child,* a bestseller for Christmas that year. It is the story of Margaret Thursday, a foundling left on a church porch in late Victorian England. In 1973 it was shown on television and was reissued with great success in paperback. Library polls of favorite authors throughout the seventies listed Streatfeild as scoring highly with the seven- to eleven-year-olds.

During the final years of her life Streatfeild edited a series of holiday books and wrote some non-fiction works, including the well-received *Boy Pharaoh, Tutankhamen* and *A Young Person's Guide to Ballet.* In her last juvenile stories she introduced the Maitlands in *Meet the Maitlands* and *The Maitlands.* In 1983 she was delighted to accept in person the honor of being named an officer in the Order of the British Empire for the body of her literary work.

Critics have praised Streatfeild's sensitivity to children, citing her accurate observations, direct tone, and ability to create realistic characters. While they note some decline in quality of her later works, they acknowledge her place as a talented author who entertained and inspired young readers for generations. In a *Dell Carousel* article, Richard Peck wrote, "Noel Streatfeild broke new ground for children's books by being who she was: a rebel with goals, a daughter of the vicarage who believed that children with personal discipline could achieve anything, a grande dame who maintained ties with the child within herself." Likewise, Bull said: "Not many people can have lived to her great age, with such a record of successes, and incurred so little resentment and hostility. The memories of her friends were warm and affectionate. That she was occasionally pompous, and sometimes a little vain, were the worst things anyone could find to say about her. She sailed through her adult life, confident that people would like her—and they did."

WORKS CITED:

Bull, Angela, *Noel Streatfeild: A Biography,* Collins, 1984.

Peck, Richard, "Noel Streatfeild," *Dell Carousel,* fall-winter, 1988, pp. 3, 7-8.

Streatfeild, Noel, "Myself and My Books," *Junior Bookshelf,* May, 1939, pp. 121-24.

FOR MORE INFORMATION SEE:

BOOKS

Cadogan, Mary, and Patricia Craig, *You're a Brick, Angela! A New Look at Girls' Fiction from 1839-1975,* Gollancz, 1976, pp. 286-308.

Children's Literature Review, Volume 17, Gale, 1989, pp. 169-200.

Contemporary Literary Criticism, Volume 21, Gale, 1982, pp. 394-417.

Crouch, Marcus, *Treasure Seekers and Borrowers: Children's Books in Britain 1900-1960,* Library Association, 1962, pp. 55-86.

Dixon, Bob, *Catching Them Young: Sex, Race and Class in Children's Fiction,* Volume 1, Pluto Press, 1977, pp. 1-41.

Fisher, Margery, *Intent Upon Reading: A Critical Appraisal of Modern Fiction for Children,* F. Watts, 1962, pp. 187-189.

Wilson, Barbara Ker, *Noel Streatfeild,* Walck, 1964.

PERIODICALS

New York Times Book Review, July 10, 1938; July 30, 1939; August 4, 1940; April 10, 1949; November 25, 1951; November 14, 1954; March 21, 1965; May 14, 1967.

Times Literary Supplement, December 10, 1938; November 13, 1943; November 19, 1954; April 11, 1958; November 23, 1962; October 30, 1970; April 28, 1972; December 8, 1972; December 10, 1976.

* * *

STURE-VASA, Mary
See ALSOP, Mary O'Hara

Yuri Suhl

SUHL, Yuri (Menachem) 1908-1986

PERSONAL: Born July 30, 1908, in Podhajce, Austria-Hungary (now part of Poland); immigrated to the United States, 1923; died of cerebral hemorrhage, November 8, 1986, in Martha's Vineyard, MA; son of Shay and Miriam (Fiksel) Suhl; married Isabelle H. Shugars (a librarian), June 24, 1950. *Education:* Attended Brooklyn College (now Brooklyn College of the City University of New York), 1928-29, and New York University, 1929-30, 1949-53; graduated from Jewish Workers University, 1932. *Religion:* Jewish. *Avocational interests:* Sculpture.

ADDRESSES: Home and office—232 East Sixth St., Apt. 3B, New York, NY 10003. *Agent*—Joan Daves, 59 East 54th St., New York, NY 10022.

CAREER: Writer. During the 1930's worked as an upholsterer, fruit peddler, ditch digger, teacher of Yiddish, and writer on Federal Writers' Project. Teacher of course on Jewish resistance to Nazism at New School for Social Research, beginning 1971; lecturer. Sculpture exhibited in several one-man shows and group exhibitions. *Military service:* U.S. Army, 1942-44.

MEMBER: Authors Guild, Authors League of America.

AWARDS, HONORS: Lewis Carroll Shelf Award, Wisconsin Book Conference, 1972, for *Simon Boom Gives a Wedding;* National Jewish Book Award, Jewish Book Council/Jewish Welfare Board, and Charles and Bertie Schwartz Juvenile Book Award, the Jewish Book Council of America, both 1974, both for *Uncle Misha's Partisans.*

WRITINGS:

JUVENILE FICTION

Der Alter fun Lompaduni un andere meises (title means "The Old Man of Lompaduni and Other Stories"), illustrated by William Gropper, Niedershlesie (Poland), 1948.
Simon Boom Gives a Wedding, illustrated by Margot Zemach, Four Winds, 1972.
Uncle Misha's Partisans, Four Winds, 1973.
The Man Who Made Everyone Late, illustrated by Lawrence di Fiori, Four Winds, 1974.
The Merrymaker, illustrated by Thomas di Grazia, Four Winds, 1975.
On the Other Side of the Gate, F. Watts, 1975.
Simon Boom Gets a Letter, illustrated by Fernando Krahn, Four Winds, 1976.
The Purim Goat, illustrated by Kaethe Zemach, Four Winds, 1980.

JUVENILE NONFICTION

Eloquent Crusader: Ernestine Rose, Messner, 1970.
An Album of Jews in America, F. Watts, 1972.

ADULT FICTION

One Foot in America, Macmillan, 1950.
Cowboy on a Wooden Horse, Macmillan, 1953, published as *You Should Only Be Happy,* Papberback Library, 1969.

ADULT NONFICTION

Ernestine L. Rose and the Battle for Human Rights, Reynal, 1959.
(Editor, translator, and contributor) *They Fought Back: The Story of the Jewish Resistance in Nazi Europe* (documentary anthology), Crown, 1967.

POETRY

Dos Licht oif Mein Gass (title means "The Light on My Street"), illustrated by L. Bunin, Signal, 1935.
Dem Tog Antkegen (title means "Toward the Day"), Signal, 1938.
Yisroel Partisan (title means "Israel the Partisan"), Signal, 1942.
A Vort fun Trayst (title means "A Word of Consolation"), YKUF of Mexico, 1952.

OTHER

(Author of book and lyrics) *Benyomen der Dritter* (choral and dance; title means "Benjamin the Third"), produced in New York City at Carnegie Hall, 1938.
Gedenk, Mein Folk (cantata; title means "Remember, My People"), produced in New York City at Town Hall, 1963.

SIDELIGHTS: Until his death in 1986, Yuri Suhl authored English and Yiddish books for children and adults. Suhl's works include Jewish folk tales, several volumes of poetry, and accounts of the Holocaust endured by the Jews under the Nazi conquest of Europe. Born in 1908, in a section of the old Austro-Hungarian empire that is now part of Poland, Suhl recalled his childhood in an essay for *Something about the Author Autobiography Series* (*SAAS*): "In the summer of 1914, when I was barely six years old, World War I broke out and that part of the southern Ukraine was the first to be occupied by the Russians, an occupation that lasted two years. I have no fond memories of that period. What stands out most vividly in my mind even now is a night of terror when the Cossacks went on a spree of robbing and looting Jewish homes. My parents and grandparents, with whom we then lived, barricaded themselves behind a heap of furniture they had piled up against the door. When the Cossacks approached, shouting commands to open up and pounding on the door, we held our breath in terrified silence until they left."

The author's father was a Talmudic scholar whose temperament was not suited for the business endeavors undertaken to support the family. When Suhl was ten years old, his mother died. "I expressed my grief and sorrow at her loss by fervently saying *Kaddish* (the prayer for the dead) every day for a whole year," said the author. When Suhl was fifteen, he immigrated with his family to Brooklyn, New York. There, he worked during the day and attended high school at night. The author related: "My day began at 6:00 A.M. when I did my homework on the BMT subway during the hour-long ride to my butcher-boy job in Bay Ridge, Brooklyn. Later in the morning when I was out on the bicycle delivering orders, I would compose in my head the writing assignment for my English class that evening. Between deliveries I memorized each sentence and by the end of the day I knew the whole composition by heart and wrote it down from memory." Suhl especially enjoyed writing poetry.

In high school, another student introduced Suhl to Yiddish literature. "He lent me the novel *Noch Alemen* (*When All Was Said and Done*) by the master of Yiddish prose, David Bergelson," the author related. "Though the story had little plot it held my interest throughout by the sheer beauty of the language. I didn't know that Yiddish could be so rich in nuance and imagery. It was like discovering my mother tongue anew. As soon as I finished reading the book, I was overcome by a desire to write a story in Yiddish." Visiting the public library to find other samples of Yiddish literature, Suhl was especially moved by the poetry of Moishe Leib Halperin.

Suhl worked as an upholsterer and a waiter to earn money for college. He enrolled in New York University (NYU) for a year, but the next year saw the onset of the Great Depression. Unable to make his tuition payments, Suhl left NYU and enrolled in Jewish Workers University, a Marxist school from which he graduated in 1932. He then worked as a Yiddish teacher and wrote poetry. "My first collection of Yiddish poems, *Dos Licht oif Mein Gass* (*The Light on My Street*) was published in 1935, the year that Roosevelt initiated the Works Progress Administration (WPA)," Suhl stated. "It was

From *Simon Boom Gives a Wedding,* by Yuri Suhl. Illustrated by Margot Zemach.

followed by a number of projects in the arts, of which the Federal Writers Project was one. After a stint of ditch-digging on the WPA, I was assigned to the Jewish Division of the Federal Writers Project."

In 1948, Suhl returned to Poland for the first time since he left as an immigrant at age fifteen. The author commented: "After attending the unveiling ceremonies of the Warsaw Ghetto Monument I visited the surviving Jewish communities in Lower Silesia and other parts of Poland on a poetry reading tour sponsored by Jewish communal leaders. This experience marked the beginning of my deep interest in the Holocaust theme. When I returned to Poland a second time, in 1959, it was to do research at the Jewish Historical Insitute of Warsaw and interview surviving resistance leaders for *They Fought Back.*"

Now one of Suhl's best-known works, *They Fought Back: The Story of the Jewish Resistance in Nazi Europe* was initially rejected by publishing companies. "The anthology was five years in the making and was turned down by thirteen publishers on the ground that there would not be a market for it ...," the author related. "Six weeks after publication it went into a second printing. Now, eighteen years later and after various editions, both here and abroad, the book is still solidly in print."

Suhl's books about the Holocaust stress the activity of the Jewish resistance movement in Eastern Europe during the Nazi occupation. His accounts are often contrasted to those of some authors who have either downplayed the effectiveness of the resistance or denied its existence entirely. M. E. Marty of *Book Week,* for instance, said that *They Fought Back* is "addressed polemically against [Raul] Hilberg's book *The Destruction of European Jews.*" According to Marty, Suhl makes his point by collecting "dozens of stories that contain hundreds of certifying and certifiable names, locations, dates."

One of Suhl's books for young adults, *Uncle Misha's Partisans,* "evolved from a true story, in my documentary anthology *They Fought Back,* about a twelve-year-old boy who joined the Jewish partisans after his family was killed by the Nazis," the author stated in his *SAAS* essay. Another of Suhl's works for young adults, *On the Other Side of the Gate,* is "a factually accurate, modern story that reads like a folktale, and that turns the sufferings of Polish Jews under Nazism into a parable of hope and survival," according to a writer for *Kirkus Reviews.* In a review for the *Bulletin of the Center for Children's Books,* Zena Sutherland noted that *On the Other Side of the Gate* is based on the true story of a young Jewish couple who successfully smuggled their infant son out of the Warsaw ghetto. Sutherland further stated that the book "shows the range of attitudes among Poles from anti-Semitism to defiant compassion. Suhl creates the atmosphere with caustic conviction and constructs the plot and the characters with solidity."

In addition to documenting the injustices perpetrated against Jews in the past, the author took an active interest in contemporary political injustices. In an obituary appearing in the *New York Times,* Edwin McDowell observed that Suhl "publicly protested the persecution of Jews in Poland and the Soviet Union." Suhl also "became actively involved in the clemency campaign for Ethel and Julius Rosenberg," as he related in his *SAAS* essay. "Like many others in this country and abroad I was disturbed by the cruel and excessive death penalty imposed on two young parents with two small children," the author asserted. Arrested on charges of giving to the Soviet Union classified information regarding nuclear weaponry, the Rosenbergs were executed in 1953. McDowell noted that Suhl became "a trustee of the fund established for the two young sons of Julius and Ethel Rosenberg."

WORKS CITED:

Kirkus Reviews, February 1, 1975.

Marty, M. E., review of *They Fought Back: The Story of the Jewish Resistance in Nazi Europe, Book Week,* May 14, 1967.

Suhl, Yuri, essay in *Something about the Author Autobiography Series,* Volume 1, Gale, 1986, pp. 249-268.

Sutherland, Zena, review of *On the Other Side of the Gate, Bulletin of the Center for Children's Books,* September, 1975.

FOR MORE INFORMATION SEE:

BOOKS

Authors of Books for Young People, supplement to the second edition, Scarecrow, 1979.

Children's Literature Review, Volume 2, Gale, 1976.

Miller, Wayne, *A Gathering of Ghetto Writers,* New York University Press, 1972.

PERIODICALS

Library Journal, December 15, 1966.

New York Times Book Review, June 1, 1967.

Punch, March 20, 1968.

OBITUARIES:

PERIODICALS

International Herald, November 14, 1986.

New York Times, November 13, 1986.

* * *

SUTCLIFF, Rosemary 1920-

PERSONAL: Born December 14, 1920, in East Clanden, Surrey, England; daughter of George Ernest (an officer in the Royal Navy) and Nessie Elizabeth (Lawton) Sutcliff. *Education:* Educated privately and at Bideford School of Art, 1935-39. *Politics:* "Vaguely Conservative." *Religion:* Unorthodox Church of England. *Hobbies and other interests:* Archaeology, anthropology, primitive religion, making collages and costume jewelry.

ADDRESSES: Home—Swallowshaw, Walberton, Arundel, West Sussex BN18 0PQ, England.

CAREER: Writer, 1945—.

MEMBER: PEN, National Book League, Society of Authors, Royal Society of Miniature Painters.

AWARDS, HONORS: Carnegie Medal commendation, 1955, and American Library Association (ALA) Notable Book, both for *The Eagle of the Ninth;* Carnegie Medal commendation, *New York Herald Tribune's* Children's Spring Book Festival honor book, both 1957, and ALA Notable Book, all for *The Shield Ring;* Carnegie Medal commendation, and *New York Herald Tribune*'s Children's Spring Book Festival honor book, both 1958, both for *The Silver Branch;* Carnegie Medal commendation, Hans Christian Andersen Award honor book, both 1959, International Board on Books for Young People honor list, 1960, Highly Commended Author, 1974, and ALA Notable Book, all for *Warrior Scarlet;* Carnegie Medal, 1960, and ALA Notable Book, both for *The Lantern Bearers;* ALA Notable Book, 1960, for *Knight's Fee; New York Herald Tribune*'s Children's Spring Book Festival Award, 1962, ALA Notable Book, and *Horn Book* honor list, all for *Dawn Wind;* ALA Notable Book, and *Horn Book* honor list, both 1962, both for *Beowulf;* ALA Notable Book, and *Horn Book* honor list, both 1963, both for *The Hound of Ulster;* ALA Notable Book, *Horn Book* honor list, both 1965, and Children's Literature Association Phoenix Award, 1985, all for *The Mark of the Horse Lord; Horn Book* honor list, 1967, for *The High Deeds of Finn MacCool;* Lewis Carroll Shelf Award, 1971, ALA Notable Book, and *Horn Book* honor list, all for *The Witch's Brat; Boston Globe-Horn Book* Award for outstanding text, Carnegie Medal runner-up,

Rosemary Sutcliff

both 1972, ALA Notable Book, and *Horn Book* honor list, all for *Tristan and Iseult; Heather, Oak, and Olive: Three Stories* was selected one of Child Study Association's "Children's Books of the Year," 1972, and *The Capricorn Bracelet* was selected, 1973; Officer, Order of the British Empire, 1975; *Boston Globe-Horn Book* honor book for fiction, 1977, and *Horn Book* honor list, both for *Blood Feud; Children's Book Bulletin* Other Award, 1978, for *Song for a Dark Queen; Horn Book* honor list, 1978, for *Sun Horse, Sun Moon;* Children's Rights Workshop Award, 1978; ALA Notable Book, 1982, for *The Road to Camlann: The Death of King Arthur;* Royal Society of Literature fellow, 1982; Commander, Order of the British Empire, 1992.

WRITINGS:

"ROMAN BRITAIN" TRILOGY

The Eagle of the Ninth (also see below), illustrated by C. Walter Hodges, Oxford University Press, 1954, Walck, 1961.
The Silver Branch (also see below), illustrated by Charles Keeping, Oxford University Press, 1957, Walck, 1959.
The Lantern Bearers (also see below), illustrated by Keeping, Walck, 1959, revised edition, Oxford University Press, 1965.
Three Legions: A Trilogy (contains *The Eagle of the Ninth, The Silver Branch,* and *The Lantern Bearers*), Oxford University Press, 1980.

"ARTHURIAN KNIGHTS" TRILOGY

The Light beyond the Forest: The Quest for the Holy Grail, illustrated by Shirley Felts, Bodley Head, 1979, Dutton, 1980.
The Sword and the Circle: King Arthur and the Knights of the Round Table, illustrated by Felts, Dutton, 1981.
The Road to Camlann: The Death of King Arthur, illustrated by Felts, Bodley Head, 1981, Dutton Children's Books, 1982.

CHILDREN'S BOOKS

The Chronicles of Robin Hood, illustrated by C. Walter Hodges, Walck, 1950.
The Queen Elizabeth Story, illustrated by Hodges, Walck, 1950.
The Armourer's House, illustrated by Hodges, Walck, 1951.
Brother Dusty-Feet, illustrated by Hodges, Walck, 1952.
Simon, illustrated by Richard Kennedy, Walck, 1953.
Outcast, illustrated by Kennedy, Walck, 1955.
The Shield Ring, illustrated by Hodges, Walck, 1956.
Warrior Scarlet, illustrated by Charles Keeping, Walck, 1958, 2nd edition, 1966.

The Bridge-Builders, Blackwell, 1959.
Knight's Fee, illustrated by Keeping, Walck, 1960.
Houses and History, illustrated by William Stobbs, Batsford, 1960, Putnam, 1965.
Dawn Wind, illustrated by Keeping, Oxford University Press, 1961, Walck, 1962.
Dragon Slayer, illustrated by Keeping, Bodley Head, 1961, published as *Beowulf,* Dutton, 1962, published as *Dragon Slayer: The Story of Beowulf,* Macmillan, 1980.
The Hound of Ulster, illustrated by Victor Ambrus, Dutton, 1963.
Heroes and History, illustrated by Keeping, Putnam, 1965.
A Saxon Settler, illustrated by John Lawrence, Oxford University Press, 1965.
The Mark of the Horse Lord, illustrated by Keeping, Walck, 1965.
The High Deeds of Finn MacCool, illustrated by Michael Charlton, Dutton, 1967.
The Chief's Daughter (also see below), illustrated by Ambrus, Hamish Hamilton, 1967.
A Circlet of Oak Leaves (also see below), illustrated by Ambrus, Hamish Hamilton, 1968.
The Witch's Brat, illustrated by Richard Lebenson, Walck, 1970, illustrated by Robert Micklewright, Oxford University Press, 1970.
Tristan and Iseult, illustrated by Ambrus, Dutton, 1971.
The Truce of the Games, illustrated by Ambrus, Hamish Hamilton, 1971.
Heather, Oak, and Olive: Three Stories (contains *The Chief's Daughter, A Circlet of Oak Leaves,* and "A Crown of Wild Olive"), illustrated by Ambrus, Dutton, 1972.
The Capricorn Bracelet (based on BBC scripts for a series on Roman Scotland), illustrated by Richard Cuffari, Walck, 1973, illustrated by Keeping, Oxford University Press, 1973.
The Changeling, illustrated by Ambrus, Hamish Hamilton, 1974.
(With Margaret Lyford-Pike) *We Lived in Drumfyvie,* Blackie, 1975.
Blood Feud, illustrated by Keeping, Oxford University Press, 1976, Dutton, 1977.
Shifting Sands, illustrated by Laszlo Acs, Hamish Hamilton, 1977.
Sun Horse, Moon Horse, illustrated by Shirley Felts, Bodley Head, 1977, Dutton, 1978.
(Editor with Monica Dickens) *Is Anyone There?,* Penguin, 1978.
Song for a Dark Queen, Pelham Books, 1978, Crowell, 1979.
Frontier Wolf, Oxford University Press, 1980.
Eagle's Egg, illustrated by Ambrus, Hamish Hamilton, 1981.
Bonnie Dundee, Bodley Head, 1983, Dutton, 1984.
Flame-Coloured Taffeta, Oxford University Press, 1985, published in the United States as *Flame-Colored Taffeta,* Farrar, Straus, 1986.
The Roundabout Horse, illustrated by Alan Marks, Hamilton Children's, 1986.
The Best of Rosemary Sutcliff, Chancellor, 1987, Peter Bedrick, 1989.
Little Hound Found, Hamilton Children's, 1989.
A Little Dog Like You, illustrated by Jane Johnson, Simon & Schuster, 1990.
The Shining Company, Farrar, Straus, 1990.

OTHER

Lady in Waiting (novel), Hodder & Stoughton, 1956, Coward, 1957.
The Rider of the White Horse (novel), Hodder & Stoughton, 1959, abridged edition, Penguin, 1964, published in the United States as *Rider on a White Horse,* Coward, 1960.
Rudyard Kipling, Bodley Head, 1960, Walck, 1961, bound with *Arthur Ransome,* by Hugh Shelley, and *Walter de la Mare,* by Leonard Clark, Bodley Head, 1968.
Sword at Sunset (novel; Literary Guild selection), illustrated by John Vernon Lord, Coward, 1963, abridged edition, Longmans, 1967.
The Flowers of Adonis (novel), Hodder & Stoughton, 1969, Coward, 1970.
Blue Remembered Hills: A Recollection (autobiography), Bodley Head, 1983, Morrow, 1984.
Mary Bedell (play), produced in Chichester, 1986.
Blood and Sand, Hodder & Stoughton, 1987.

Also co-author with Stephen Weeks of a screenplay, *Ghost Story,* 1975, and author of radio scripts for BBC Scotland. *Dragon Slayer, the Story of Beowulf* has been recorded onto audio cassette (read by Sean Barrett), G. K. Hall Audio, 1986. A collection of Sutcliff's manuscripts is housed at the Kerlan Collection, University of Minnesota.

ADAPTATIONS: Song for a Dark Queen was adapted for stage by Nigel Bryant, Heinemann, 1984.

SIDELIGHTS: "For Rosemary Sutcliff the past is not something to be taken down from the shelf and dusted. It comes out of her pages alive and breathing and now," maintains John Rowe Townsend in his *A Sense of Story: Essays on Contemporary Writers.* A Carnegie Medal-winning author, Sutcliff is essentially a storyteller, bringing history to life through her heroes, the atmospheres she creates, and the sense of continuity found in her works. She presents the history of England through the experiences of virtuous young men and women who overcome many difficulties despite their personal and physical limitations. Sutcliff also explores history through her many retellings of old legends or stories, such as those of King Arthur and the Knights of the Round Table and Beowulf. In these works, she presents well-known heroes, often adding a new dimension to their tales. "Most critics," contend May Hill Arbuthnot and Zena Sutherland in their *Children and Books,* "would say that at the present time the greatest writer of historical fiction for children and youth is unquestionably Rosemary Sutcliff."

Although she spends most of her time writing about the history of others, Sutcliff recounts her own history in *Blue Remembered Hills: A Recollection.* She describes her isolated childhood caused by a severe case of rheumatoid arthritis, her father's career as a naval officer, and her mother's obsessive personality. She was constantly moved about, and because her mother was a storyteller, Sutcliff didn't learn to read until she was nine. Unfortunately, Sutcliff's mother was also manic-depressive and became very overprotective during her daughter's illness, refusing any outside help and expecting unlimited love and loyalty in return; she believed Sutcliff should desire no other companions.

When she was eleven years old, Sutcliff's father retired from the navy and the family settled in a somewhat isolated moorland house in north Devon. Despite her illness, Sutcliff was able to attend a normal school for a few years. The onset of World War II had her father returning to the navy, though, leaving mother and daughter alone again. Their isolation was broken when their house became a Home Guard signals post, and Sutcliff's interest in battles and the military can be traced back to this time. Leaving school at the age of fourteen, Sutcliff began training as a miniature painter, a profession that was chosen for her because of her disability. Even though she had no inclination for the work, she made it through three years at Bideford Art School and became a professional.

Realizing that miniature painting was not the career for her, Sutcliff began scribbling stories on pieces of paper she kept under her blotting paper. It was the pain of an early love that drove her to write her first published works, *The Chronicles of Robin Hood* and *The Queen Elizabeth Story,* which she now sees as "too cosy and sweet." These early works were only the beginning —it was not until such later works as *Warrior Scarlet* and *The Lantern Bearers* that Sutcliff found her true voice. Joan Aiken, reviewing *Blue Remembered Hills* in the *Times Educational Supplement,* observes: "Told with robust candour and fond photographic memory for detail, especially for outdoor places and gardens, it is an engrossing record of close family relationships, and also of quite unusually adverse conditions not so much overcome as cheerfully ignored and set on one side."

From *The Witch's Brat,* by Rosemary Sutcliff. Illustrated by Richard Lebenson.

Sutcliff's "Roman Britain" trilogy begins with *The Eagle of the Ninth,* which concerns a young Roman centurion and his first few years spent in second-century Britain. Marcus Aquila is about to begin what he hopes will be a lengthy and magnificent military career and is at the same time resolved to find his father, who mysteriously disappeared on his way to battle with the Ninth Legion ten years earlier. *The Eagle of the Ninth* "is one of the few good stories" covering the period of Roman rule in Britain, maintains Ruth M. McEvoy in *Junior Libraries.* And a *Booklist* contributor concludes that the realistic background and characters make this a novel that "will reward appreciative readers."

The Silver Branch, the second book in the "Roman Britain" trilogy, takes place during the latter part of the third century and tells the story of Justin, a junior surgeon who has just arrived from Albion, and his centurion kinsman Flavius. The two young men are aware of the political turmoil around them, and when the emperor is killed, they are forced into hiding, eventually realizing that the hope of a unified Britain is at risk. "All the characters ... are entirely credible," remarks Lavinia R. Davis in the *New York Times Book Review,* adding that the meticulous details "create a brilliant background for a vigorous and unusually moving narrative." And in a *Horn Book* review, Virginia Haviland recommends the novel for those young people on their way "to becoming discriminating readers of adult historical fiction."

"*The Lantern Bearers* is the most closely-woven novel of the trilogy," claims Margaret Meek in her *Rosemary Sutcliff,* adding that "in it the hero bears within himself the conflict of dark and light, the burden of his time and of himself." In this final book, Sutcliff presents the decline of Roman Britain through the character of Aquila, who deserts in order to remain in Britain when the last of the Romans pull out. "The characterizations are vivid, varied and convincing," maintains Margaret Sherwood Libby in the *New York Herald Tribune Book Review,* and "the plot, both interesting and plausible, has its significance heightened by the recurring symbolism of light in dark days." Meek recognizes this theme of light and dark in all three of the books: "The conflict of the light and dark is the stuff of legend in all ages.... Sutcliff's artistry is a blend of this realization in her own terms and an instructive personal identification with problems which beset the young, problems of identity, of self-realization."

With *Warrior Scarlet* and *Dawn Wind,* Sutcliff continues her tales of the making of Britain through two new young heroes. The story of the Bronze Age in England is told in *Warrior Scarlet* by focusing on a boy and his coming to manhood. In this heroic age, explains Meek, Drem must kill a wolf in single combat in order to hunt with the men, and if he fails, he is an outcast and must keep sheep with the Little Dark People. "Sutcliff has widened her range to cover the hinterland of history and realized," continues Meek, "with the clarity we have come to expect, every aspect of the people of the Bronze Age, from hunting spears and cooking pots to king-making and burial customs, from childhood to old age. The book is coloured throughout with sunset bronze." *Warrior Scarlet,* concludes a *Times Literary Supplement* reviewer, provides a strong "emotional experience" and "is outstanding among children's books of any kind."

Chronologically, *Dawn Wind* follows *The Lantern Bearers,* for it deals with sixth-century Britain at the time of the invasion of the Saxons. The fourteen-year-old British hero, Owain, is the only survivor of a brutal battle with the Saxons that demolished his people. In the destroyed city, the only life Owain finds is Regina, a lost and half-starved girl. The two are bound by misery, then by mutual respect, and when Regina becomes ill Owain takes her to a Saxon settlement. The Saxons take care of Regina but sell Owain into slavery, and eleven years later he comes back for her. "So life is not snuffed out by the night," conclude Arbuthnot and Sutherland. "Sutcliff gives children and youth historical fiction that builds courage and faith that life will go on and is well worth the struggle."

Flame-Coloured Taffeta leaves the battle fields behind, returning to England and the Sussex Downs, between Chichester and the sea. Twelve-year-old Damaris Crocker of Carthagena Farm and Peter Ballard from the vicarage know the woods near their home very well, and it is here that they find Tom, a wounded messenger for the lost cause of the Jacobite court, explains Joanna Motion in the *Times Literary Supplement.* The two children are not concerned with the rights and wrongs of the situation, but feel they must protect and help the wounded man. Many adventures ensue, including a fox hunt, a midnight rescue of Tom, and an exciting escape through the woods. "A beautifully written and intricately woven tale, this novel should appeal to any lover of historical fiction," claims *Voice of Youth Advocates* contributor Ellen Gulick. Motion concludes that *Flame-Coloured Taffeta* "succeeds as an enjoyable, soundly-crafted short novel where no whisker of plot or detail of character is wasted. And the sense of history under the lanes, the past seeped into the landscape, as Damaris looks out to sea from her farm house built of wrecked Armada timbers, will be familiar and satisfying to Sutcliff's many admirers."

Sutcliff's numerous historical adventures have been described by Sheila A. Egoff in her *Thursday's Child: Trends and Patterns in Contemporary Children's Literature* as "a virtually perfect mesh of history and fiction." Sutcliff "seems to work from no recipe for mixing fact and imagination and thus, like fantasy, which it also resembles in its magic qualities, her writing defies neat categorization." Similarly, Neil Philip contends in the *Times Educational Supplement* that "to call the books historical novels is to limit them disgracefully." Sutcliff "does not bring 'history' to the reader," continues Philip, "but involves the reader in the past—not just for the duration of a book, but for ever. She can animate the past, bring it to life inside the reader in a most personal and lasting way." Sutcliff immerses herself and the reader in the time period that she is relating, and "her method of settling on the felt details that remain in the mind, driven along the nerves of the hero, is even more convincing than the historian's account," upholds Meek. "Sutcliff's name," declares Ann Evans in the *Times Literary Supplement,* "will be remembered and revered long after others have been forgotten."

WORKS CITED:

Aiken, Joan, "Rosemary and Time," *Times Educational Supplement,* January 14, 1983, p. 24.

Arbuthnot, May Hill, and Zena Sutherland, *Children and Books,* 4th edition, Scott, Foresman, 1972, pp. 508-09.

Davis, Lavinia R., "Turmoil in Britain," *New York Times Book Review,* June 29, 1958, p. 18.

Review of *The Eagle of the Ninth, Booklist,* February 1, 1955, p. 251.

Egoff, Sheila A., *Thursday's Child: Trends and Patterns in Contemporary Children's Literature,* American Library Association, 1981, pp. 159-92.

Evans, Ann, "The Real Thing," *Times Literary Supplement,* March 27, 1981, p. 341.

Gulick, Ellen, review of *Flame-Colored Taffeta, Voice of Youth Advocates,* February, 1987, p. 287.

Haviland, Virginia, review of *The Silver Branch, Horn Book,* June, 1958, pp. 209-10.

Libby, Margaret Sherwood, review of *The Lantern Bearers, New York Herald Tribune Book World,* February 14, 1960, p. 11.

McEvoy, Ruth M., review of *The Eagle of the Ninth, Junior Libraries,* January, 1955, p. 33.

Meek, Margaret, *Rosemary Sutcliff,* Walck, 1962.

Motion, Joanna, "Helping Out," *Times Literary Supplement,* September 19, 1986, p. 1042.

Philip, Neil, "Romance, Sentiment, Adventure," *Times Educational Supplement,* February 19, 1982, p. 23.

"The Search for Selfhood: The Historical Novels of Rosemary Sutcliff," *Times Literary Supplement,* June 17, 1965.

Townsend, John Rowe, *A Sense of Story: Essays on Contemporary Writers for Children,* Lippincott, 1971, pp. 193-99.

FOR MORE INFORMATION SEE:

BOOKS

Children's Literature Review, Volume 1, Gale, 1976.

Contemporary Literary Criticism, Volume 26, Gale, 1983.

Crouch, Marcus, *Treasure Seekers and Borrowers: Children's Books in Britain 1900-1960,* Library Association, 1962.
Crouch, *The Nesbit Tradition: The Children's Novel in England 1945-1970,* Benn, 1972.
Townsend, John Rowe, *Written for Children: An Outline of English Language Children's Literature,* Lippincott, 1974.

PERIODICALS

Horn Book, June, 1958; February, 1968; April, 1970; December, 1971; August, 1980; February, 1982.
Junior Bookshelf, December, 1981.
New Yorker, October 22, 1984.
New York Times Book Review, October 26, 1952; January 9, 1955; March 17, 1957; January 4, 1959; April 22, 1962; November 11, 1962; May 26, 1963; May 3, 1964; November 7, 1965; January 30, 1966; February 15, 1970; September 30, 1973; April 5, 1987.
Observer, February 6, 1983.
Publishers Weekly, December 1, 1969; November 1, 1971; January 7, 1983; October 6, 1989; June 8, 1990.
School Library Journal, August, 1980; July, 1990.
Times (London), January 26, 1983; June 9, 1990.
Times Educational Supplement, October 23, 1981; January 13, 1984.
Times Literary Supplement, November 27, 1953; November 19, 1954; November 21, 1958; December 4, 1959; November 25, 1960; June 14, 1963; December 9, 1965; May 25, 1967; October 30, 1970; July 2, 1971; September 28, 1973; April 4, 1975; December 10, 1976; July 15, 1977; December 2, 1977; July 7, 1978; November 21, 1980; April 22, 1983; September 30, 1983.
Tribune Books (Chicago), March 8, 1987.
Washington Post Book World, November 5, 1967; September 9, 1990.

* * *

SWINDELLS, Robert (Edward) 1939-

PERSONAL: Born March 20, 1939, in Bradford, England; son of Albert Henry (in sales) and Alice (Lee) Swindells; married, August, 1962; wife's name, Cathy (divorced, c. 1976); married Brenda Marriott, 1982; children: (first marriage) Linda, Jill. *Education:* Huddersfield Polytechnic, teaching certificate, 1972; Bradford University, M.A., 1988. *Politics:* "Ecology." *Hobbies and other interests:* Reading (almost anything), walking, travel, watching films.

ADDRESSES: Home and office—3 Upwood Park, Black Moor Rd., Oxenhope, Keighley, West Yorkshire BD22 9SS, England. *Agent*—Jennifer Luithlen, "The Rowans," 88 Holmfield Rd., Leicester LE2 1SB, England.

CAREER: Telegraph and Argus, Bradford, England, copyholder, 1954-57, advertising clerk, 1960-67; Hepworth & Grandage (turbine manufacturer), Bradford, Yorkshire, engineer, 1967-69; Undercliffe First, Bradford, teacher, 1972-77; Southmere First, Bradford, part-time teacher, 1977-80; full-time writer, 1980—. *Military service:* Royal Air Force, 1957-60.

MEMBER: Society of Authors.

AWARDS, HONORS: Child Study Association of America's Children's Books of the Year, 1975, for *When Darkness Comes;* National Book Award nomination, children's category, Arts Council of Great Britain, 1980, for *The Moonpath and Other Stories;* Other Award, 1984, Children's Book Award, Federation of Children's Book Groups, and Carnegie Medal runner-up, British Library Association, both 1985, all for *Brother in the Land;* Children's Book Award for *Room 13,* 1990.

WRITINGS:

FOR YOUNG ADULTS

When Darkness Comes, illustrated by Charles Keeping, Brockhampton Press, 1973, Morrow, 1975.
A Candle in the Night, David & Charles, 1974.
Voyage to Valhalla, illustrated by Victor Ambrus, Hodder & Stoughton, 1976, Heinemann Educational, 1977.
The Very Special Baby, illustrated by Ambrus, Prentice-Hall, 1977.

Robert Swindells

The Ice-Palace, illustrated by Jane Jackson, Hamish Hamilton, 1977.
Dragons Live Forever, illustrated by Petula Stone, Prentice-Hall, 1978.
The Weather-Clerk, illustrated by Stone, Hodder & Stoughton, 1979.
The Moonpath and Other Stories, Wheaton, 1979, published as *The Moonpath and Other Tales of the Bizarre,* illustrated by Reg Sandland, Carolrhoda Books, 1983.
Norah's Ark, illustrated by Avril Haynes, Wheaton, 1979.
Norah's Shark, illustrated by Haynes, Wheaton, 1979.
Ghost Ship to Ganymede, illustrated by Jeff Burns, Wheaton, 1980.
Norah and the Whale, illustrated by Haynes, Wheaton, 1981.
Norah to the Rescue, illustrated by Haynes, Wheaton, 1981.
World Eater, Hodder & Stoughton, 1981.
The Wheaton Book of Science Fiction Stories, Wheaton, 1982.
Brother in the Land, Oxford University Press, 1984, Holiday House, 1985.
The Thousand Eyes of Night, Hodder & Stoughton, 1985.
The Ghost Messengers, Hodder & Stoughton, 1986.
Staying Up, Oxford University Press, 1986.
Mavis Davis, Oxford University Press, 1988.
The Postbox Mystery, illustrated by Kate Rogers, Hodder & Stoughton, 1988.
A Serpent's Tooth, Hamish Hamilton, 1988, Holiday House, 1989.
Follow a Shadow, Hamish Hamilton, 1989, Holiday House, 1990.
Night School, Paperbird, 1989.
Room 13, Doubleday, 1989.
Daz 4 Zoe, Hamish Hamilton, 1990.
Tim Kipper, Macmillan, 1990.
Dracula's Castle, Doubleday, 1991.
When Darkness Comes, Hodder & Stoughton, in press.
Rolf and Rosie, Andersen Press, 1992.
You Can't Say I'm Crazy, Hamish Hamilton, 1992.

TRANSLATOR; "ALFIE" SERIES

Gunilla Bergstrom, *Alfie and His Secret Friend,* Wheaton, 1979.
Bergstrom, *Who'll Save Alfie Atkins?,* Wheaton, 1979.
Bergstrom, *Alfie and the Monster,* Wheaton, 1979.
Bergstrom, *You're a Sly One, Alfie Atkins,* Wheaton, 1979.

OTHER

Contributor to books, including *The Methuen Book of Strange Tales,* edited by Jean Russell, Methuen, 1980.

SIDELIGHTS: Robert Swindells's best known novel is *Brother in the Land,* the story of a boy's struggle with life after a nuclear holocaust. Many of Swindells's other books have similarly chilling elements, and he is able to demonstrate how the courage of his characters enables them to survive. Without talking down to his younger readers, Swindells offers a variety of imaginative plots and realistic endings in his many novels for young adults. As Myles McDowell noted in *Twentieth Century Children's Writers,* "Swindells offers few cosy endings. He respects the maturity of his young readers and offers them compelling and sometimes profound imaginative experiences in language which is potent and easily accessible."

Swindells was born during World War II, and has memories of being out in a schoolyard when an air raid was being staged. After the war ended, Swindells had more unrest to deal with—his parents were bickering constantly and their tiny house was crowded and noisy with his four other siblings around. Reading became a refuge for him. "My mother had taught me to read before I started school and now, at six, I was an avid reader, but our little home was becoming crowded and it wasn't easy to find a quiet spot to sit with a book," he said in an essay for *Something about the Author Autobiography Series* (*SAAS*). "I learned to sink so deeply into whatever fantasy I was reading about that mayhem might erupt all around and I wouldn't even notice. Books became an escape route for me. A way out of the house. Out of the city. Out of my ordinary life."

At the time in England, all children took a compulsory test at the age of eleven that determined whether they would continue on to a college preparatory "grammar" school, or be routed towards a school where they would leave at age fifteen to work. Swindells's parents didn't have the time or education to adequately prepare him for this task, and his dreams of going to college and being a teacher were crushed when he failed his exam. He was terribly disappointed, and from then on he and his father were at odds with each other.

In school, Swindells was fortunate enough to have an English teacher that inspired him and his classmates to do and be their best. "I don't know to this day why that man was at [the school]," Swindells commented in *SAAS.* "He could have been teaching in a grammar school where the rewards would've been greater, and I would have missed out on a pivotal experience." That teacher encouraged Swindells to enter a country-wide essay contest, which he won over many other students, including those in the grammar schools. Swindells was also quite active in making up stories of his own at that time.

When he was fifteen Swindells graduated and went to work. After a few years, things worsened with his father, and his mother became ill. To get out of the bad family situation, Swindells left home and joined the Royal Air Force for three years, but decided not to re-enlist when his time was over. Instead, he got a job and was married soon after. Two daughters were born in quick succession.

Inspired by an acquaintance, Swindells went back to night school in 1967. Within two years he had passed his exams and applied for a position at a teacher's training college in a nearby town. Swindells was ecstatic at his new-found lease on life: "I'd made it," he wrote in

SAAS. "I was going to be a teacher after all." College years were very happy ones for Swindells, and he discovered a new interest while there. "One of the things we did in college was to read children's novels," Swindells related in *SAAS.* "Lots of them. I loved them. I thought, These are much more fun than most of the stuff I read when I was a kid. These writers don't talk down. It's not about fairies." This convinced him that he wanted to write books for young people.

He proposed to one of his advisors that he write a children's novel instead of an essay to complete his degree work. The idea was approved, and Swindells started the book. He handed in the manuscript and hoped it would allow him to pass and obtain his degree. He was surprised to find out rather quickly that not only did he pass, but the woman who read his manuscript encouraged him to get it published. He sent the manuscript to the first publisher on the list he was given, and within a week he heard it was accepted. The book, *When Darkness Comes,* is about a stone age character and was published in 1973.

Swindells got a full-time job teaching and continued to write on the side. Within a short time, his marriage ended, and he remarried six years later. Then, in 1980, he quit teaching so he could be a full-time writer and make appearances to speak in front of various groups. It was tough going for several years, until he published *Brother in the Land* in 1984. This stirring book about life after a nuclear holocaust was critically acclaimed and won several awards. "A long-time activist with the antinuclear movement, I'd poured my soul into that book, and it was to be my first major success," Swindells confessed in *SAAS.* Soon after that, he received a master's degree from the School of Peace Studies at Bradford University, partly on the strength of this book.

When speculating about the reasons for his success as a writer, Swindells has said that both chance and talent have much to do with it. But he added in *SAAS:* "Mostly though, it's other people. Parents. Teachers .... Some we remember with gratitude and affection." He once expressed that his fondest desire is to "see the day when every child everywhere will enjoy a childhood without hunger, anxiety, war, or any form of deprivation."

WORKS CITED:

Swindells, Robert, essay in *Something about the Author Autobiography Series,* Volume 14, Gale, 1992.

FOR MORE INFORMATION SEE:

BOOKS

Chevalier, Tracy, editor, *Twentieth-Century Children's Writers,* 3rd edition, St. James, 1989.

PERIODICALS

Times Literary Supplement, April 13, 1984; April 12, 1985.

SZEKERES, Cyndy 1933-

PERSONAL: Surname is pronounced "*zeck*-er-es"; born October 31, 1933, in Bridgeport, CT; daughter of Stephen Paul (a toolmaker) and Anna (Ceplousky) Szekeres; married Gennaro Prozzo (an artist), September 20, 1958; children: Marc, Christopher. *Education:* Pratt Institute, certificate, 1954.

ADDRESSES: Home—P.O. Box 280, RFD 3, Putney, VT 05346.

CAREER: Illustrator and writer.

WRITINGS:

FOR CHILDREN; SELF-ILLUSTRATED

Long Ago, McGraw, 1977.
A Child's First Book of Poems, Golden Books, 1981, published as *Cyndy Szekeres' ABC,* Golden Books, 1983.
Puppy Too Small, Golden Books, 1984.
Scaredy Cat!, Golden Books, 1984.
Thumpity Thump Gets Dressed, Golden Books, 1984.
Baby Bear's Surprise, Golden Books, 1984.
Cyndy Szekeres' Counting Book 1 to 10, Golden Books, 1984.
Suppertime for Frieda Fuzzypaws, Golden Books, 1985.
Hide-and-Seek Duck, Golden Books, 1985.
Nothing-to-Do Puppy, Golden Books, 1985.
Good Night, Sammy, Golden Books, 1986.
Puppy Lost, Golden Books, 1986.
Sammy's Special Day, Golden Books, 1986.
Little Bear Counts His Favorite Things, Golden Books, 1986.
Melanie Mouse's Moving Day, Golden Books, 1986.
(Compiler) *Cyndy Szekeres' Book of Poems,* Western Publishing, 1987.
(Compiler) *Cyndy Szekeres' Mother Goose Rhymes,* Golden Books, 1987.
(Compiler) *Cyndy Szekeres' Book of Fairy Tales,* Golden Books, 1988.
Good Night, Sweet Mouse, Golden Books, 1988.
Cyndy Szekeres' Favorite Two-Minute Stories, Golden Books, 1989.
Things Bunny Sees, Western Publishing, 1990.
What Bunny Loves, Western Publishing, 1990.
Cyndy Szekeres' Nice Animals, Western Publishing, 1990.
Cyndy Szekeres' Hugs, Western Publishing, 1990.
Puppy Learns to Share, Western Publishing, 1990.
Ladybug, Where Are You?, Western Publishing, 1991.
(Compiler) *Cyndy Szekeres' Favorite Fairy Tales,* Western Publishing, 1992.
(Compiler) *Cyndy Szekeres' Favorite Mother Goose Rhymes,* Western Publishing, 1992.
Fluffy Duckling, Western Publishing, 1992.
Teeny Mouse Counts Herself, Western Publishing, 1992.
Cyndy Szekeres' Colors, Western Publishing, 1992.
Kisses, Western Publishing, in press.
Puppy Dear, Western Publishing, in press.

Cyndy Szekeres

"TINY PAW LIBRARY" SERIES; SELF-ILLUSTRATED

A Busy Day, Golden Books, 1989.
The New Baby, Golden Books, 1989.
Moving Day, Golden Books, 1989.
A Fine Mouse Band, Golden Books, 1989.
A Mouse Mess, Western Publishing, 1990.

ILLUSTRATOR

Sam Vaughan, *New Shoes,* Doubleday, 1961.
Jean Latham and Bee Lewi, *When Homer Honked,* Macmillan, 1961.
Marjorie Flack, *Walter, the Lazy Mouse,* Doubleday, 1963.
Evelyn Sibley Lampman, *Mrs. Updaisy,* Doubleday, 1963.
Phyllis Krasilovsky, *Girl Who Was a Cowboy,* Doubleday, 1965.
(With others) Alvin Tresselt, editor, *Humpty Dumpty's Storybook,* Parents Magazine Press, 1966.
Edward Ormondroyd, *Michael, the Upstairs Dog,* Dial, 1967.
Nancy Faulkner, *Small Clown and Tiger,* Doubleday, 1968.
Kathleen Lombardo, *Macaroni,* Random House, 1968.
Peggy Parrish, *Jumper Goes to School,* Simon & Schuster, 1969.
Adelaide Holl, *Moon Mouse,* Random House, 1969.
Barbara Robinson, *Fattest Bear in the First Grade,* Random House, 1969.
John Peterson, *Mystery in the Night Woods,* Scholastic Book Services, 1969.
Joy Lonergan, *Brian's Secret Errand,* Doubleday, 1969.
Patsy Scarry, *Little Richard,* McGraw, 1970.
P. Scarry, *Waggy and His Friends,* McGraw, 1970.
Kathryn Hitte, *What Can You Do without a Place to Play?,* Parents Magazine Press, 1971.
Lois Myller, *No! No!,* Simon & Schuster, 1971.
P. Scarry, *Little Richard and Prickles,* McGraw, 1971.
Betty Jean Lifton, *Good Night, Orange Monster,* Atheneum, 1972.
Mary Lystad, *James, the Jaguar,* Putnam, 1972.
Betty Boegehold, *Pippa Mouse,* Knopf, 1973.
A. Holl, *Bedtime for Bears,* Garrard, 1973.
P. Scarry, *More about Waggy,* American Heritage Press, 1973.
Miriam Anne Bourne, *Four-Ring Three,* Coward, 1973.
M. Lystad, *The Halloween Parade,* Putnam, 1973.
Kathy Darling, *Little Bat's Secret,* Garrard, 1974.
Robert Welber, *Goodbye, Hello,* Pantheon, 1974.
Julia Cunningham, *Maybe, a Mole,* Pantheon, 1974.
Albert Bigelow Paine, *Snowed-in Book,* Avon, 1974.

Jan Wahl, *The Muffletumps' Christmas Party,* Follett, 1975.
J. Wahl, *The Muffletumps' Storybook,* Follett, 1975.
Carolyn S. Bailey, *A Christmas Party,* Pantheon, 1975.
B. Boegehold, *Here's Pippa Again!,* Knopf, 1975.
J. Wahl, *The Clumpets Go Sailing,* Parents Magazine Press, 1975.
J. Wahl, *The Muffletumps' Halloween Scare,* Follett, 1977.
J. Wahl, *Doctor Rabbit's Foundling,* Pantheon, 1977.
Tony Johnston, *Night Noises, and Other Mole and Troll Stories,* Putnam, 1977.
Mary D. Kwitz, *Little Chick's Story,* Harper, 1978.
J. Wahl, *Who Will Believe Tim Kitten?,* Pantheon, 1978.
A. Holl, *Small Bear Builds a Playhouse,* Garrard, 1978.
Judy Delton, *Brimhall Comes to Stay,* Lothrop, 1978.
Marjorie W. Sharmat, *The 329th Friend,* Four Winds Press, 1979.
T. Johnston, *Happy Birthday, Mole and Troll,* Putnam, 1979.
Catherine Hiller, *Argentaybee and the Boonie,* Coward, 1979.
J. Wahl, *Doctor Rabbit's Lost Scout,* Pantheon, 1979.
B. Boegehold, *Pippa Pops Out!,* Knopf, 1979.
B. Boegehold, *Hurray for Pippa!,* Knopf, 1980.
P. Scarry, *Patsy Scarry's Big Bedtime Storybook,* Random House, 1980.
Polly B. Berends, *Ladybug and Dog and the Night Walk,* Random House, 1980.
Marci Ridion, *Woodsey Log Library,* four volumes, Random House, 1981.
Margo Hopkins, *Honey Rabbit,* Golden Books, 1982.
Marci McGill, *The Six Little Possums: A Birthday ABC,* Golden Press, 1982.
M. McGill, *The Six Little Possums and the Baby Sitter,* Golden Press, 1982.
M. McGill, *The Six Little Possums at Home,* Golden Press, 1982.
M. McGill, *The Six Little Possums: Pepper's Good and Bad Day,* Golden Press, 1982.
Clement C. Moore, *The Night before Christmas,* Golden Books, 1982.
Selma Lanes, selector, *A Child's First Book of Nursery Tales,* Golden Books, 1983, published as *Cyndy Szekeres' Book of Nursery Tales,* 1987.
T. Johnston, *Five Little Foxes and the Snow,* HarperCollins, 1987.
B. Boegehold, *Here's Pippa!,* Knopf, 1989.
Margaret Wise Brown, *Whispering Rabbit,* Western Publishing, 1992.
Ole Risom, *I Am a Kitten,* Western Publishing, in press.
Beatrix Potter, *Peter Rabbit,* Western Publishing, in press.

Also illustrator of Albert Bigelow Paine's "Hollow Tree" series, three volumes, Avon, 1973.

OTHER

Also creator of calendars, including *Cyndy's Animal Calendar, 1973,* McGraw, 1973, *Cyndy's Animal Calendar, 1975,* McGraw, 1974, and *Long Ago,* McGraw, 1976; and of *My Workbook Diary, 1973,* McGraw, 1972, and *My Workbook Diary, 1975,* McGraw, 1974. Editor of *It's Time to Go to Bed,* by Joyce Segal, Doubleday, 1979.

WORK IN PROGRESS: More books in the "Tiny Paw Library" series.

SIDELIGHTS: Cyndy Szekeres is a well-known illustrator of both her own children's books and those of such writers as Betty Boegehold, Patsy Scarry, and Jan Wahl. Szekeres began drawing at an early age and soon showed promise. As she later recalled in *Something about the Author* (*SATA*): "I can't remember a time when I didn't draw. I was the artist in the family, an aptitude inherited from my father who never had a chance to develop his talent."

A child of the late-Depression era, Szekeres drew on paper bags flattened and trimmed by her father, a toolmaker. Although she continued drawing throughout adolescence and her young adult life, she harbored few illusions about actually working as an artist. "I assumed that I was headed for a job in a factory and probably marriage," she told *SATA.*

Before Szekeres graduated from high school, however, her father learned that advertising might prove a lucrative and fulfilling career for her. Though she did not plan to become a commercial artist, she enrolled at Pratt Institute at her father's urging. "I had no intention of embarking on a career in advertising," she related to *SATA.* "I had my heart set on becoming an illustrator."

Szekeres won admittance to Pratt and studied there until earning her certificate in 1954. But upon leaving the school she discovered that few career opportunities existed for budding illustrators. She eventually obtained commercial work as a designer at display houses serving prominent New York City department stores. "Then I did children's fashion illustration for the Saks Fifth Avenue department store, requiring overly well-groomed, coiffed children wearing perfectly fit clothing," Szekeres told *CA.* "This interrupted the way I usually drew children and I didn't appreciate the influence. It caused me to focus more keenly on anthropomorphic animals and I eventually decided (later on, after several books) to illustrate these animals only."

Marriage to a fellow artist in 1958 changed Szekeres career plans. Writing in *Something about the Author Autobiography Series* (*SAAS*), Szekeres related that her husband "became the occasional boost that I needed, guiding and encouraging me" to become an illustrator. Gradually, Szekeres' luck began to turn for the better. In 1959, the publishing house Doubleday, which had been maintaining a file of Szekeres' department-store works, contacted her with a request that she produce illustrations for Sam Vaughan's *New Shoes,* a book for children. By this time Szekeres was pregnant with her first child, but she nonetheless accepted the Doubleday offer. The results were a success. As Szekeres wrote in *SAAS,* "I became a children's book illustrator and a mother at the same time."